HANDBOOK OF AMERICAN WOMEN'S HISTORY

Garland Reference Library of the Humanities
(Vol. 696)

HANDBOOK OF AMERICAN WOMEN'S HISTORY

Edited by

ANGELA HOWARD ZOPHY

Associate Editor
FRANCES M. KAVENIK

Library of Congress Cataloging-in-Publication Data

Handbook of American women's history / Angela Howard Zophy, editor
Frances M. Kavenik, associate editor.
p. cm. — (Garland Reference library of the humanities ; vol.
696)
ISBN 0-8240-8744-5 (alk. paper)
1. Women—United States—History—Handbooks, manuals, etc.
I. Zophy, Angela Marie Howard, 1945- . II. Kavenik, Frances M., 1944-
III. Series.
HQ1410.H36 1990
305.4'0973—dc20 89-17120

Book and Cover Design by
Renata Gomes

Printed on acid-free, 250-year-life paper
Manufactured in the United States of America

I dedicate this Handbook to those for whom the personal has proven to be professional as well as political, the women and men who have labored to establish and maintain Women's History and Women's Studies, especially Fran and Jonathan.

Contents

Acknowledgments

This *Handbook* is the result of networking among women's history and women's studies colleagues. I owe special gratitude to the Women's Studies Minor Program of the University of Wisconsin-Parkside, chaired by Teresa Peck, professor of education. In a meeting of the women's studies faculty and staff that focused on available resources in women's studies, I boldly asserted the need for such a reference as this *Handbook* in the presence of our guest-presenter, the women's studies librarian for the University of Wisconsin System, Susan E. Searing. Susan passed the suggestion along to Marie Ellen Larcada, reference editor of Garland Publishing Inc., who sent me a request for a proposal for such a reference handbook. My friend and colleague in women's studies, tennis, and life, Frances M. Kavenik, assistant professor of English, taught me enough "remedial" Word Perfect word-processing skills to allow me to produce the requested prospectus, which Marie Ellen found acceptable. My commitment to the need for such a guide, coupled with the support of outstanding women like these, impelled me to accept the challenge of compiling and editing the *Handbook*.

Once I had committed to this insane undertaking for one, I was further encouraged by the unstinting support of the Social Science Divison of the University of Wisconsin-Parkside. For everything from paper clips to staff support, I thank Division Chair Larry Duetsch, professor of economics, and his predecessor, Leon Applebaum, professor of economics, and the division's program assistant, Arlene D. Monson. The generosity and collegial support of the division for its part-time member merits grateful, even extravagant, acknowledgment. Within the Social Science Division office staff, Josephine McCool and Bonnie F. Andrews ably and good-humoredly facilitated the logistical nightmare of recruiting and securing contributors, constantly bailed me out of my circular arguments with my Word Perfect program, and worked closely with my student assistants to get the project off the ground and keep it running smoothly. My student assistants at UW-Parkside were Rose Kolbasnik Callahan, Carol Waterloo, and Marge Reimann. Rose served the longest and, I think, the most difficult tour of duty, for she capably assumed time-consuming clerical tasks with a commitment that was inspiring. Many of my UW-Parkside students in women's history volunteered to contribute entries.

The women's studies liaison librarian, Judith M. Pryor, trained Rose Callahan, Carol Waterloo, and (her greatest challenge) me in the mysteries of the computerized reference and bibliographic search capability of the Wylie Library Learning Center of the University of Wisconsin-Parkside. Robert T. Maleske, academic services consultant for the Computing Support Center, offered his considerable services to assist me in applying the possibilities of the Word Perfect program to the needs of the *Handbook*.

Halfway through the project, Frances M. Kavenik accepted the post of associate editor and thus brought vigor and rigor to the processing of the *Handbook* manuscript. Its form and style benefited greatly from her dedication and professionalism. I just hope Frances recovers her health. She also referred me to Carol Klimick Cyganowski, assistant professor of English at DePaul University, who served as assistant to the editor for entry assignments. It is entirely probable that Carol has not a friend, colleague, associate, or acquaintance remaining who was not drafted into our contributor ranks. For her enthusiasm and perseverance, no less than for her excellent contacts, I thank Carol especially.

As we entered the last few months allocated to completing the *Handbook*, I accepted the position of assistant professor of historical studies at the University of Houston at Clear Lake. Despite this change, the *Handbook* still received crucial support from UW-Parkside: to assist Frances's work on the *Handbook*, the able staff of the Humanities Division took up the daunting task of processing all the original copy of the *Handbook* entries onto floppy diskettes. For this support, Frances and I are inestimably indebted to Humanities Chair Eugene L. Norwood, professor of German, and the division staff: program assistants Marge Rowley, Trudy M. Rivest, Pam LeClaire, and Mildred A. Nutini (who said she thought of all this work for the *Handbook* as job security), and to Marcella Ricciardi, program assistant for the ACCESS Program.

I found commensurate institutional and collegial support upon my arrival at the University of Houston at Clear Lake. Within the School for Human Sciences/Humanities, Dean Wayne Charles Miller, Associate Dean for Faculty Affairs Rita R. Culross, and Associate Dean for Administration Robert Wegmann provided essential assistance. I received a generous grant from the UH-Clear Lake Faculty Research and Support Fund to cover the telephone and mailing costs attendant to completing the *Handbook*. The staff of the Alfred R. Neumann Library at UH-Clear Lake were predictably patient in their assistance with verifying entry references; I am especially indebted to Patricia J. Garrett, Associate Dean for Public Services, and reference librarians Gay E. Carter, Rebecca Christman, and Patricia M. Pate.

Within my faculty suite, our secretary, Tamia L. Leger, picked up the burden of the typing for the editor that had been carried by the staff of the UW-Parkside Social Science Division, and my new colleagues generously shared the limited faculty-suite supplies. Gloria D. Rodrigues, microcomputer specialist for the Computing Services, graciously and patiently instructed and reinstructed me in the wonders of the Word Perfect program. In addition to UH-Clear Lake students who volunteered to assist in the completion of the *Handbook* by writing entries, several undertook the unglamorous work of verifying bibliographic details: Barbara Bradford Novy, Ginger Rae Allee, Cynthia A. Bragg, and Barbara Jean Hayes deserve more than honorable mention for their library research contributions. Another of their number, Jean McGrath Hayes, proofread the first draft of the *Handbook* manuscript. La Donna Williams, as student assistant to the editor, and Merri J. Scheibe, graduate student assistant, worked with dedication as we completed the *Handbook* manuscript at UHCL.

The contributors provided the most essential element of the *Handbook*, the entries. I thank them for their expertise, their professional commitment to a project that offered neither fame nor fortune, and their patience with the editor once their entries were submitted. Especially to those contributors who submitted many entries, and those who accepted "emergency" assignments with very short deadlines, I give my heartfelt gratitude.

My final acknowledgment of gratitude goes to my friend, colleague, and spouse, Jonathan W. Zophy. His reference work *The Holy Roman Empire: A Dictionary Handbook* inspired me to propose such a tool for American women's history. From the inception of this project, he cheerfully and consistently provided consultation, expertise, and advice. As of the fall 1987, he formally accepted the responsibility of serving as an assistant to the editor.

I credit the unbounded support of Jonathan and Frances for having brought me and the *Handbook* this far. If this undertaking were to have had a patron saint, it could have been Blanche Du Bois: I often received the kindest of responses and timely assistance from colleagues whom I had not known before. If this project had a theme song, it must have been "I Get By with a Little Help from My Friends." All those listed above share in whatever praise accrues to the *Handbook*. The editor accepts sole responsibility for its limitations.

Introduction

The *Handbook of American Women's History* was conceived and designed as a reference to assist students, teachers, and librarians who are new to the field of American women's history. It offers introductory and fundamental information necessary for a general understanding of the field through a readily accessible collection of summary definitions with focused bibliography for crucial concepts, events, organizations, and various historical persons. The *Handbook* was not intended to contain references to all of the past or current research in American women's history nor to include an entry for every person, place, event, organization, or concept within this discrete field of historical inquiry. It does, however, attempt to provide entries for those events, organizations, concepts, and individuals that constitute a core of pertinent information regarding the basic materials and sources.

Arranged alphabetically, the entries include both a concise definition that establishes the historical significance of the subject and a basic bibliography to indicate available primary and secondary sources to which the reader may refer for additional, more detailed information. The internal cross references at the end of each entry refer the reader to related entries in the *Handbook*. There is also a comprehensive Index. Notes on the Contributors provides vital information concerning the authors of the entries.

In the past decade, women's history has become established as a recognized field of historical inquiry. Contemporary women's historians have built upon the seminal work of previous generations of scholars and, thus, have produced an expansive body of scholarship that informs the discipline of history regarding women's presence, participation, and contributions. Scholarly debates over discerned trends within women's history have produced contending "schools" of interpretation. Women's history has developed terms and references that have become central to the scholarly vocabulary of historians in the field but are not yet well known in the mainstream of American history. Women's historians now allude to central individuals, groups, events, and to certain primary and secondary sources without including accompanying descriptions or definitions. This development is especially apparent in the concentrated area of American women's history. As a reference work, the *Handbook* utilizes an alphabetical approach to its entries to render accessible introductory information required by nonspecialists as well as to assist those who have considerable exposure to the discipline.

The *Handbook* is encyclopedic in the sense that it includes much that is well known and much that is not. While great effort was made to include entries that cover the fundamental concepts and sources of American women's history, this *Handbook* does not purport to include everything that is significant to the field. Some of its entries reflect the interests and expertise of its editor and of its contributors, and therefore it includes entries on many little-known persons, topics, and events. However, the *Handbook* does not contain all of the entries that every historian of women's history might desire. Only those contemporary persons, events, and issues that the editor deemed crucial to provide critical background for the post-1960 phase of the modern women's movement have been included, since the emphasis of the *Handbook* is history, not current events. The *Handbook* was intended to supplement, not duplicate, existing reference and bibliographic sources; for referral to such sources, readers are encouraged to consult the entry "Archives and Sources."

Readers of the *Handbook* are encouraged to take note of areas that have not yet been well researched. Despite the increased scholarly activity in the field of women's history, clearly there are crucial areas yet to be investigated. Thus, the editor is hopeful that the *Handbook* will provide not only some basic answers to questions but will spark some critical questions that will inspire and direct additional research in this vast and vital field.

The *Handbook* has had the benefit of a superb associate editor, outstanding assistants to the editor who were effective beyond the editor's capability to reward properly their efforts and time given, and fine individual contributors. However, it has limitations and deficiencies, which are the sole responsibility of its editor who has every confidence that both will be duly noted and reported to her for correction by those who use this book.

The Handbook

ABBOTT, EDITH (1876–1957), recognized for her contributions to social work education, lived most of her life in Chicago, teaching, writing, and championing the poor. Born in Nebraska, she earned a doctorate in economics from the University of Chicago (1905), studied at the London School of Economics, and worked for the Women's Trade Union League, the American Economic Association, the Carnegie Institution, Wellesley College, and St. Hilda's Settlement (London) before moving with her sister Grace to Hull House (1908), where she participated in the settlement house movement with Jane Addams, Julia Lathrop, and Florence Kelley. The movement encouraged educated young people to "settle" and work among the urban poor and serve as catalysts for social reform. Abbott joined the Chicago School of Civics and Philanthropy, teaching social research, her hallmark, and by 1919 was helping to organize the first national association of schools of social work. In 1920 she negotiated a merger that resulted in the establishment of the Graduate School of Social Service Administration of the University of Chicago. She advocated "professional education," placing social work under university auspices despite criticism from supporters of the concept of apprenticeship in programs controlled by the charity organizations. By 1924 the University of Chicago had named Abbott a dean, a position she held until her retirement in 1942.

While the casework method became prevalent in eastern schools, Abbott's curriculum emphasized the structures of government, legislation, economics, social research, and the history of social welfare. Her graduates were sought for their expertise in social administration, especially during the post-Depression recovery period. Abbott and her colleague Sophonisba Breckinridge established the *Social Service Review*, which Abbott edited for many years. Her influence on the development of social work education and public policy remains in the more than one hundred books and papers she published.

—*Beverly G. Toomey*

See Also:
Abbott, Grace; Hull House; Social Work; University of Chicago

Reference:
Costin, Lela. *Two Sisters for Social Justice: A Biography of Grace and Edith Abbott.* Urbana: University of Illinois Press, 1983.

ABBOTT, GRACE (1878–1939). Best known for her advocacy of women and children, this outstanding social reformer and public administrator influenced the social welfare policies of five presidential administrations. Trained as a teacher in her native Nebraska, Grace Abbott went to Chicago to study political science at the University of Chicago but was truly educated at Hull House in the social activism of Jane Addams and Julia Lathrop. In 1908 she began serving the immigrant community, and from this experience developed a lifelong commitment to the causes of women and children as well as to world peace, representing Hull House at the International Congress of Women, an antiwar meeting in 1916.

Guided by Lathrop, who became the first director of the U.S. Children's Bureau, Abbott was instrumental in the development of child labor laws, and in 1917 she took her first Washington appointment to administer them. When they were declared unconstitutional, Abbott returned to the Immigrant Protective League in Chicago until President Harding appointed her to head the Children's Bureau in 1921. Under her leadership, the Bureau led the fight for maternal and child health care, child welfare, and child labor laws. Abbott also continued to work for international peace by organizing numerous international conferences on child welfare issues. She left the Bureau in 1934 to join the faculty at the University of Chicago, but remained active as a member of the President's Advisory Council on Economic Security and is credited with having significantly influenced the final passage of the Social Security Act.

Grace Abbott's death from cancer in 1939 left her sister Edith, close compatriot in ideology and activism, in despair. Her legacy lies in the influence she brought to bear on behalf of the needy in America.

—Beverly G. Toomey

See Also:

Abbott, Edith; Hull House; Immigrant Protective League; Protective Legislation; Social Security Act; United States Children's Bureau

References:

Abbott, Edith. "Grace Abbott: A Sister's Memories." *Social Service Review* 4 (September 1939): 351–407.

Abbott, Grace. *The Child and the State.* 2 vols. Chicago: University of Chicago Press, 1945.

———. *From Relief to Social Security.* Chicago: University of Chicago Press, 1941.

Costin, Lela. *Two Sisters for Social Justice: A Biography of Grace and Edith Abbott.* Urbana: University of Illinois Press, 1983.

ABOLITION AND THE ANTISLAVERY MOVEMENT. Thousands of American women in the early nineteenth century braved public disapproval to participate in the antislavery movement. Often veterans of moral reform activities, these women were inspired by a blend of religious principles and republican ideology to call for an immediate end to slavery. Fighting for a place in moral reform activities outside a narrow, domestically defined sphere, the female abolitionist helped set in motion the organized women's rights campaign.

A few women attended the founding convention of the American Anti-Slavery Society (AASS) in 1833, but that organization at first barred female members. Abolitionist women instead formed their own local organizations, which held national conventions in 1837 and 1838. By sponsoring events such as bazaars and picnics, these women's groups soon became invaluable fund-raisers for the abolitionist movement. In the late 1830s female abolitionists entered the political arena by sending large numbers of antislavery petitions to Congress.

The question of the proper role of women in the abolitionist movement surfaced in 1837, when Angelina and Sarah Grimké, expatriate sisters from South Carolina, broke social convention by lecturing to mixed audiences of males and females. When several Massachusetts clergymen condemned the Grimkés, a radical male abolitionist faction led by William Lloyd Garrison championed the right of women to participate in every part of the movement. Many other male abolitionists opposed a public role for female abolitionists—some because of antifeminist principles, and others because they feared a backlash from linking antislavery to an even more unpopular cause. The "woman's issue" became enmeshed with other quarrels among abolitionists regarding tactics in the religious and political spheres. After gaining the right to vote in the AASS's annual meeting in 1839, women provided the Garrisonians with the strength to win control of the society the following year, when their opponents quit to protest the election of a female officer.

Women played key roles in the AASS after 1840. Maria Weston Chapman of Boston served as one of the society's principal propagandists and oversaw the operation of its main office. Lydia Maria Child edited the AASS's official newspaper for almost two years. Abby Kelley, Lucy Stone, Sojourner Truth, Elizabeth Cady Stanton, and dozens of other women braved insults and threats of physical harm to serve as traveling lecturers and organizers. These public figures became important role models for women seeking to overcome other barriers to their sex.

In contrast to the Garrisonians, political and religious abolitionists allowed women little role in their organized activities. The one prominent antislavery woman outside the Garrisonian ranks was Harriet Beecher Stowe, whose novel *Uncle Tom's Cabin* proved the most effective piece of propaganda of the entire abolitionist movement.

The abolitionist ideology of inalienable rights for all gave early feminists powerful arguments with which to challenge the strictures placed upon their sex by institutions such as church and state. Elizabeth Cady Stanton, Susan B. Anthony, Lucy Stone, and hundreds of other female abolitionists also learned valuable organizational and agitational skills that they later brought to the women's rights campaign. Having fought for equal participation in the antislavery movement, these women would continue to struggle to be equal in society.

—*John R. McKivigan*

See Also:

American Antislavery Socities; Garrisonians; Grimké, Angelina; Grimké, Sarah; *Uncle Tom's Cabin*

References:

DuBois, Ellen. "Women Rights and Abolition: The Nature of the Connection." In *Antislavery Reconsidered: New Perspectives on the Abolitionists*, edited by Lewis Perry and Michael Fellman. Baton Rouge: Louisiana University Press, 1979, pp. 238–51.

Friedman, Lawrence J. *Gregarious Saints: Self and Community in American Abolitionism, 1830–1879*. New York: Cambridge University Press, 1982.

Hersh, Blanche Glassman. *The Slavery of Sex: Feminist-Abolitionists in America.* Urbana: University of Illinois Press, 1978.

Hewitt, Nancy A. *Women's Activism and Social Change: Rochester, New York, 1822–1872.* Ithaca, N.Y.: Cornell University Press, 1984.

Melder, Keith E. *Beginnings of Sisterhood: The American Woman's Rights Movement, 1800–1850*. New York: Schocken, 1977.

ABORTION in medical terms is the termination of a pregnancy, whether spontaneous or induced. Reports of the practice of abortion for purposes of selective birth control and maternal health date back to ancient times, and the controversy surrounding this practice also appears to have arisen then. One finds a proscription of the practice in the Hippocratic oath taken by Greek physicians.

In the United States until the latter half of the nineteenth century, physicians regularly performed abortions at the request of pregnant women prior to "quickening." Quickening, the point at which the mother first feels the fetus move, normally occurs between the twelfth and fourteenth weeks. Throughout the eighteenth and early nineteenth centuries, women acknowledged that voluntary abortion was illegal, but generally they did not perceive the practice as a sin. The movement to establish abortion as both criminal and sinful was led by male physicians as part of a crusade from the 1860s to the 1880s to outlaw all forms of contraception. In 1821 Connecticut became the first state to pass legislation restricting abortion, and by 1860 twenty states and territories in the United States had such laws.

By 1965 all fifty states had passed legislation prohibiting abortion during all stages of pregnancy. Generally restricted to life-threatening situations, these laws allowed only therapeutic abortions. Women of means were forced to travel at great expense to procure abortions in other countries. Less fortunate women resorted to dangerous, often fatal, illegal abortions or, worse still, attempts at self-induced abortion. It is important to note that legal prohibition did not have the effect of reducing the incidence of abortion.

In the 1960s, under pressure from the feminist movement, a number of states liberalized their laws to allow abortions for reasons other than the endangerment of a woman's life or physical well-being. The new grounds included rape, incest, and, in several states, fetal deformity. Most feminists saw these changes as welcome but far from ideal. In many states, for example, abortion required the consent of the spouse or parent. Without the availability of abortion-on-demand, the decision of whether to continue a pregnancy remained under the control of the legal and medical communities, not the woman herself.

In the early 1970s legal challenges were increasingly mounted against any prohibition of a woman's ability to obtain an abortion. The resulting Supreme Court decision in *Roe v. Wade* (1973) struck down all state laws prohibiting abortion on any grounds during the first trimester of pregnancy (the first twelve weeks after conception). Further, *Roe v. Wade* allowed state regulation of abortion after the first trimester but before viability (the point at which the fetus can survive outside the womb) only in order to protect the pregnant woman's health and safety. *Roe v. Wade* did not, however, strike down the requirement that a woman obtain spousal or parental consent. Subsequent court action has removed this requirement except in cases of immature, unemancipated minors.

Since *Roe v. Wade,* antiabortion forces have tried in various ways to restrict women's ability to obtain abortions. In 1981 a Human Life Amendment, which declared that human life begins at conception, was introduced in Congress. This proposal, which would have had the effect of giving unicellular conceptuses equal legal status with any United States citizen, failed to make it out of committee. The city of Akron, Ohio, passed legislation that required (l) that physicians inform women seeking abortions of various details of fetal development and of the physical and emotional risks of abortion; (2) that abortions be performed only at hospitals, not clinics (where most early abortions are performed); and (3) that a physician not perform an abortion until at least twenty-four hours after an informed consent form has been signed. This law was subsequently found unconstitutional by the Supreme Court in *City of Akron v. Akron Center for Reproductive Health* (1983). Perhaps the most significant antiabortion legislation since *Roe v. Wade,* however, has been the Hyde Amendment, which restricts federal Medicaid funding for abortion to cases where the mother's life is endangered by continuing the pregnancy or where the pregnancy is the result of rape or incest. The Supreme Court upheld the constitutionality of this legislation in a 1980 decision, *Harris v. McRae.* Although the Court reaffirmed the central holding of *Roe v. Wade* in 1986, a newly constituted Court agreed to hear *Webster v. Reproductive Health Services* in 1989. The Supreme Court decision on the *Webster* case returned to the states the authority to limit a woman's right to a legal abortion.

—*David S. Levin*

See Also:

Right-Wing Political Movements, *Roe v. Wade*

References:

Callahan, Daniel. *Abortion: Law, Choice, and Morality.* New York: Macmillan, 1970.

City of Akron v. Akron Center for Reproductive Health. 462 U.S 416, 76 L. Ed. 2d 687 (1983).

Davis, Nanette J. *From Crime to Choice: The Transformation of Abortion in America.* Westport, Conn.: Greenwood, 1985.

Faux, Marion. *Roe v. Wade: The Untold Story of The Landmark Decision That Made Abortion Legal.* New York: Mentor, 1989.

Gordon, Linda. *Woman's Body, Woman's Right: A Social History of Birth Control in America.* New York: Penguin, 1974, 1976.

Harper, John Paull. "Be Fruitful and Multiply: Origins of Legal Restrictions on Planned Parenthood in Nineteenth Century America." In *Women of America: A History,* edited by Carol Ruth Berkin and MaryBeth Norton. Boston: Houghton Mifflin, 1979, pp. 245–69.

Harris v. McRae, 48 U.S. 917 (1980).

Mohr, James. *Abortion in America: The Origins and Evolutions of National Policy.* New York: Oxford University Press, 1978.

Roe v. Wade, 410 U.S. 113, 35 L. Ed. 2d, 147. 93 S. Ct. 705. (1973).

Webster v. Reproductive Health Services. 851 F. 2d 1074 (8th. Cir. 1988), *probable jurisdiction noted,* 109 S. Ct. 780 (1989).

ABZUG, BELLA SAVITSKY (b. 1920), politician, congressional representative from New York, and a leader of the women's movement of the 1960s and 1970s, is a liberal advocate of the rights of women and other minorities in the United States. In 1947 Abzug graduated from Columbia Law School, where she served as editor of the Columbia *Law Review.* Her sociopolitical activism began during the early years of her legal career, when she began championing causes that were both controversial and unpopular, a tendency that characterized her activities for the next three decades.

In the 1950s Abzug offered legal representation to those involved in the civil rights movement, defended the rights of those indicted during the McCarthy "witch hunts," and worked on the passage of the Civil Rights Act of 1954. In the 1960s Abzug's evolving role as a politician became formalized at the local level. She supported the election of New York mayor John Lindsay and was appointed to his advisory committee. During this period, Abzug traveled to Washington as a lobbyist for the Women's Strike for Peace, actively supported nuclear disarmament, and worked on the passage of the Voting Rights Act of 1965.

Abzug was elected to the U.S. House of Representatives in 1971. Her reaction to the election was vintage Abzug: "I'm no Joanna come lately, believe me, I've been here all along—outside." Outraged by the absence of female representation on congressional committees, Abzug made immediate and futile efforts to penetrate the predominantly male system. As a congresswoman, Abzug increased her efforts on behalf of women, continued to oppose America's involvement in Vietnam, advocated the passage of the Equal Rights Amendment, and was instrumental in securing funding for the 1977 National Women's Conference. After serving three terms in the House of Representatives, Abzug lost her race against Daniel Patrick Moynihan for a seat in the Senate.

Following this defeat, Abzug served briefly as President Jimmy Carter's co-chair of the National Advisory Council on Women. Abzug's "confrontive" style quickly placed her at odds with the Carter staff and led to her dismissal in 1979. Although Abzug remains active in politics and continues to advocate the rights of women, her break with the Carter White House marked a decline in her influence as a national political force.

—Donald R. Martin

See Also:

Democratic Party, Gender Gap, Politics

References:

Abzug, Bella. *Bella!* New York: Saturday Review, 1972.

Mathews, Tom, and Lucy Howard. "Bye, Bye, Bella." *Newsweek* 93 (January 22, 1979): 27–28.

Stineman, Esther. *American Political Women.* Littleton, Colo.: Libraries Unlimited, 1980.

ADAMS, ABIGAIL (1744–1818) was a prodigious letter writer and an astute observer of the revolutionary American political system. As the wife of John Adams, prominent lawyer, legislator, and second president of the United States, she exerted an influence over his political decisions and also had a strong voice in the domestic decisions that affected them both. A champion of the American Revolution, Adams believed in America's right to free itself from Britain's rule. Although she supported America's right to rebel, however, she also held deeply conservative political views regarding the right of others to revolt, especially those who questioned the nature of the newly formed government in America.

Adams held similarly contrasting views about the role of women in society. She believed, for example, that women were the intellectual equals of men and therefore had a right to an equal education. In her philosophy, education symbolized the role of women in the social sphere, and Adams often lamented her own lack of education. Yet she also felt that the proper place for women was in the home, taking care of the children and ensuring a proper environment for the family. Adams thought she herself was unable to manage responsibilities outside the domestic sphere, yet during the extended periods when her husband was in Philadelphia or abroad, she ran the family farm, managed all of the finances, made most of the financial decisions, and raised her children alone.

In her many letters to friends, family, and especially her husband, Adams discussed the role of women in nineteenth-century life. She criticized the legal and social status of women, particularly the lack of available public education. During her husband's absences, she relayed vital political information to him. Abigail Adams enjoyed the excitement of politics and exercised considerable influence over President Adams, who relied heavily on her judgment.

—*Lynn E. Lipor*

See Also:
Revolutionary War

References:

Adams, Abigail. *Familiar Letters of John Adams and His Wife Abigail Adams During the Revolution, with a Memoir of Mrs. Adams.* Edited by Charles Francis Adams. Boston: Houghton Mifflin, 1875; rpt. Freeport, N.Y.: Books for Library Press, 1970.

Withey, Lynn. *Dearest Friend: A Life of Abigail Adams.* New York: Free Press, 1981.

ADDAMS, JANE (1860–1935), pioneer in the settlement house movement, social worker, and peace advocate, was among America's most influential reformers in the late nineteenth and early twentieth centuries. As the founder of Chicago's Hull House settlement—which served the neighborhood poor and served as a center for social reform activities—she rejected women's traditional role in the home for a career in the public sector. Through her speaking and writing, she encouraged other women, particularly those with advanced education, to abandon the domestic sphere for the world of social activism. By the time the settlement was a few years old, it had become a virtual clearinghouse of reform and home to an amazing array of talented women and men. Together they worked to improve the lives of their immigrant neighbors while finding an outlet for their own education, skills, and ambitions.

Addams was born and raised in rural Cedarville, Illinois. Her mother died when she was two years old, and Addams grew up with an unusually strong attachment to her father, a prominent local businessman and politician. In 1877 she enrolled at nearby Rockford Female Seminary. Her father died the summer after her graduation, and Addams plunged into a decade-long period of depression and indecision. She attempted medical school, underwent spinal surgery, and twice journeyed abroad. While in London, she visited Toynbee Hall settlement and determined to launch a similar project upon her return to America.

In September 1889 Addams fulfilled that promise when she and Rockford classmate Ellen Gates Starr moved into the decaying Hull mansion in the heart of Chicago's teeming Nineteenth Ward. By 1893 the settlement housed the regular meetings of over forty different groups that attracted approximately two thousand participants weekly. Moreover, it was a center of scholarly inquiry, as Addams and other practitioners of the new social work methodology attempted to define and describe their environment.

Addams wrote numerous books and articles outlining her experiences at Hull House. In addition, she was a leader in other contemporary reform efforts, including the woman-suffrage and peace movements. Her pacifist opposition to World War I eroded her popularity during the war years, but by the 1930s she had regained prominence. Addams shared the 1931 Nobel Peace Prize, evidence of the recognition she earned by dedicating almost fifty years to social activism and service.

—*Rebecca L. Sherrick*

See Also:
Hull House, Settlement House Movement

References:

Jane Addams Papers. Swarthmore College Peace Collection. Swarthmore, Pa.

Addams, Jane. *The Second Twenty Years at Hull-House.* New York: Macmillan, 1930.

———. *Twenty Years at Hull-House.* New York: Macmillan, 1910.

Davis, Allen F. *American Heroine.* New York: Oxford University Press, 1973.

ADKINS V. CHILDREN'S HOSPITAL was a decision by the conservative majority of the Supreme Court in 1923 that a District of Columbia minimum wage law for women was unconstitutional. The Court ruled that such a federal law deprived a woman of the liberty to bargain, a position endorsed by the National Women's party. The *Adkins* decision struck a blow at Progressive era reform groups because it removed the principal grounds on which they sought legislative assistance. Following the Court's ruling, minimum wage laws for women were struck down in Arizona, Kansas, and Wisconsin, and fell into disuse elsewhere. As labor activist Florence Kelley noted, the Court had in reality affirmed "the inalienable right of women to starve."

—*Jonathan W. Zophy*

See Also:

Kelley, Florence; Progressive Legislation; Protective Legislation

References:

Legislation. Westport, Conn.: Greenwood, 1978.

Chafe, William. *The American Woman: Her Changing Social, Economic, and Political Roles, 1920–1970.* New York: Oxford University Press, 1972.

Daniel, Robert. *American Women in the 20th Century.* New York: Harcourt, Brace, Jovanovich, 1987.

ADVICE TO A DAUGHTER (1688) is an early example of the prescriptive literature for girls that influenced early American women writers of that genre in the nineteenth century. Originally a letter written by the Marquis of Halifax to his daughter, it was one of the first etiquette documents directing a woman of the upper class about what to think and how to act in different situations. The letter begins with an explanation by the Marquis of his reasons for writing it: so his daughter will know what to expect and how to behave in life, and will exemplify "the Picture of a fine Woman." Nine chapters of advice follow, beginning with the most important, Religion, and continuing with Husbands, House and Family and Children, Behavior and Conversation, Friendships, Censure, Vanity, Pride, and, finally, Diversions.

The Marquis's belief in his daughter's intelligence is revealed in his advice. The longest chapter, on husbands, explains how she should deal with men of different temperaments without appearing superior. In the chapter on the management of the house, the father discusses how to balance different areas of expense, such as decoration, menu, clothing, and entertainment. The idea of correct behavior in the company of different people, such as men, friends, servants, and children, is also explained.

While *Advice to a Daughter* considers the proper attitudes necessary for a woman to live comfortably and be well respected by her family and peers, it also acknowledges the difficulties of a woman's life and the intelligence needed to balance her responsibilities, behave correctly, and be happy. Victorian women writers relied heavily upon such seventeenth- and eighteenth-century prescriptive literature in the development of their works that promoted the Cult of True Womanhood.

—*Theresa A. McGeary*

See Also:

Cult of True Womanhood, Prescriptive Literature

Reference:

Marquis of Halifax. *Advice to a Daughter.* London: Matt, Gillyflower, 1688.

AFFIRMATIVE ACTION refers to a series of federal regulations, based upon executive orders and federal statutes, that prohibit employment discrimination by employers who hold contracts with the federal government, and require such employers to make "good faith" efforts to remedy past discrimination by recruiting, hiring, and promoting minority group members. Currently, Affirmative Action regulations apply to businesses and institutions that employ about a third of the U.S. labor force.

Originally promulgated under Executive Order 11246 in 1964, Affirmative Action forbade discrimination only on the basis of race, color, religion, or national origin; sex was added in 1968 through Executive Order 11375. As an executive order, issued by the president, Affirmative Action is not a law, but the courts have ruled that it has the "force and effect of law." It is enforced, however, differently than a law.

The Office of Federal Contract Compliance (OFCC) has been charged with enforcing Affirmative Action regulations, and it, in turn, has delegated the responsibility to fifteen government departments or compliance agencies. Each compliance agency is supposed to conduct periodic reviews of government contractors, and every contractor scheduled to receive $1 million or more in federal funds must pass a compliance review before the money is actually awarded. Each contractor must establish a program of goals for recruitment with a fixed timetable for achievement in the hiring of women and minorities. In addition, individuals and groups may file a discrimination complaint with the OFCC or a compliance agency against a federal contractor. After an investigation in which the employer has been found in violation of Affirmative Action regulations, the OFCC or compliance agency may: (1) withhold funds until compliance is achieved; (2) cancel the federal contract; (3) bar the employer from receiving future federal contracts; or (4) refer the case to the Justice Department or the Equal Employment Opportunity Commission for suit in the federal courts.

Despite these provisions, Affirmative Action has been largely ineffective in preventing and remedying discrimination. One important reason is that the departments and agencies responsible for enforcement are not adequately staffed to carry out effective reviews and investigations. As a result, relatively few employers have actually been sanctioned for violations. In addition, since 1980, the federal government has undertaken to weaken the regulations and to limit their protective applicability. At the same time, the Justice Department has gone to court to oppose the use of numerical goals in Affirmative Action plans and to argue against programs that provide preferential treatment for women and minorities. Such actions signal the dismantling of Affirmative Action, but the congressional override of President Reagan's veto of the Civil Rights Restoration Act in 1988 reestablished the intent of Congress and, therefore, the constitutionality of requiring institution-wide compliance with antidiscrimination laws whenever federal funds are accepted by that institution.

—*Claire M. Renzetti*

See Also:
Equal Employment Opportunity Commission

References:

Babcock, Barbara A., Anne E. Freedman, Eleanor H. Norton, and Susan C. Ross, eds. *Sex Discrimination and the Law.* Boston: Little, Brown, 1975.

Benson, Ronald M. "Searching for the Antecedents of Affirmative Action: The National War Labor Board and the Cleveland Women Conductors in World War I." *Women's Rights Law Reporter* 5 (Summer 1979): 271–82.

Pottinger, J. Stanley. "Race, Sex, and Jobs: The Drive Toward Equality." *Change Magazine* 4 (October 1972): 24, 26–29.

Renzetti, Claire M. "One Step Forward, Two Steps Back: Women, Work, and Employment Legislation." In *Contemporary Issues in Business,* edited by Joseph DesJardins and John McCall. Belmont, Calif.: Wadsworth, 1984, pp. 395–404.

AFRICAN BENEVOLENT SOCIETIES. As far back as the late eighteenth century, black Americans, many of them African-born ex-slaves, joined together in mutual benefit societies. The Free African Societies of Philadelphia and of Newport, Rhode Island, were founded in 1787. Along with the church, these fraternal groups formed the basis for the early institutional organization of the black community in America.

The benevolent societies had both economic and social purposes. Informally, they offered a meeting place where African Americans could gather for friendship, recreation, and a sense of racial solidarity. On a more formal level, they provided economic assistance to members and to the local black community. Dues and other money raised paid for sickness and death benefits to widows and children, and for schools and other community needs.

Perhaps because economic relief for widows and children was an important issue in their lives, black women participated as much as and more than men in the African benevolent societies. The Philadelphia Benevolent Society, established in 1793, was the first African American mutual aid organization of its kind. Male societies like the African Benevolent Society of Newport (1808) stated that they were open "to any person of colour whether male or female," but only men could vote or hold office. As a result, women organized an autonomous group, the African Female Benevolent Society of Newport (1809). The earliest recorded female group was the Female Benevolent Society of St. Thomas, founded in 1793. By 1830 there were more female societies (twenty-seven) in existence than male (sixteen), according to a study done in Philadelphia in that year.

These autonomous female associations successfully raised money for the "mutual relief" of their communities. The Philadelphia study, for instance, showed that the female societies distributed over $3,500 in benefits, compared with just over $2,000 raised by their male counterparts. The largest amount raised that year, over $400, came from the African Female Band Benevolent Society of Bethel, New York. In the case of at least one female organization, however, the African Dorcas Association of New York City (1827), men, predominantly black ministers, supervised meetings and kept financial records, while women mainly sewed the clothes supplied to children attending the African free schools.

The African female benevolent societies can be seen as part of the religious reform movements found in New York State and New England in the early nineteenth century. These charitable and missionary groups were formed primarily by white middle-class women whose goals and priorities revolved around moral guidance and religious conversion. While both types of groups were charitable, there were major differences. Chief among these was the greater emphasis of the African female benevolent societies on real economic assistance to themselves and their communities. Some of the black women's groups were explicitly working-class in nature, like the Daughters of Africa, whose approximately two hundred members joined together to help themselves economically. Other groups directed their aid to the larger black community, like the African Dorcas Association or the Female Benevolent Society of Newport, whose main goal was to raise money for a black school.

By the 1830s these organizations were beginning to take on a more middle-class focus. Instead of "benevolent" or "relief" societies, they began to be known as "mutual improvement" or literary societies. Yet the emphases on economic aid, racial solidarity, and community assistance found in the early African benevolent societies continued to be important throughout the nineteenth century. The early benevolent societies laid the groundwork for late-nineteenth-century black-run banks and insurance companies, as well as many political and community assistance organizations.

—Mary Battenfeld

See Also:

Black Women, Black Women's Clubs

References:

Bracey, John, August Meier, and Elliot Rudwick, eds. *Black Nationalism in America.* New York: Bobbs-Merrill, 1970.

Sterling, Dorothy. *Turning the World Upside Down.* New York: Feminist Press, 1987.

———. *We Are Your Sisters: Black Women in the Nineteenth Century.* New York: Norton, 1984.

AFRO-AMERICAN. The names that persons of African descent in America have used to identify themselves have changed over the years in response to political and social influences. From the colonial and revolutionary era through the early national period, *African* was generally preferred, but was frowned upon after the founding of the American

Colonization Society (1816), an organization whose purpose was to return free persons to Africa and rid the United States of what Henry Clay and others regarded as a social anomaly and political danger. Next the term *colored* was used, but it became unpopular after emancipation because, generally written in the lower-case, it was thought to lack specificity and dignity. By the early twentieth century, *Negro* was considered more proper because it was consistent with the so-called scientific racialism of the times. The term served as a rallying point for international racial solidarity, and a major battle was fought to have it capitalized in written usage. *Negro* fell out of favor in the 1960s, however, when "blackness" became glorified as a positive cultural characteristic, in contrast to its negative connotations in the past. Critics argued, moreover, that the term *Negro* was a racist invention and cultural trap because it suggested neither a geographical or national homeland nor an ethnic identity, and thus seemed to rest primarily on the legacy of slavery. The terms *Afro-American* and *African-American* have been used during both the nineteenth and twentieth centuries, and many believe that they most accurately reflect the ethnic heritage and national identity of persons of African descent in the United States, and that their usage may also help to eliminate our society's preoccupation with skin color.

—*Gwendolyn Keita Robinson*

See Also:
Black Women

AFRO-AMERICAN DOMESTIC WORKERS are women employed in private homes to perform tasks commonly done by the housewife-mother. Afro-American female slaves, like their male counterparts, were always forced to labor outside their homes—in the master's field and house—without compensation. After emancipation, since only sporadic wage-earning opportunities were open to Afro-American men, Afro-American women, most of whom still lived in the South, had to continue working so their families could avoid starvation and homelessness. Southern racial and occupational segregation forced over 80 percent of the employed Afro-American women into just two areas—laundry or domestic service. By 1920 European immigrant and native-born white women servants were replaced by Afro-American servants in households all over the North and West. Thus the entire nation adopted the long-standing racial, gender, and caste system of the South, and Afro-American women's work was synonymous with household work.

It is difficult to investigate Afro-American household workers for the period prior to 1920 because the government excluded servants from its official definition of working women; however, housework would continue to rank first among these women's occupations through the 1940 census. During the Depression of the 1930s, when many white women returned to household employment, Afro-American women faced a deterioration in both working conditions and salaries. During the 1940s, as a result of World War II's expanding employment opportunities, a few Afro-American household workers found higher paying jobs in other areas. By the 1950s, however, household workers still received some of the nation's lowest salaries and benefits.

As recently as 1984 the federal government's efforts at "domestic service" reform were halfhearted and haphazard because federal labor researchers never saw housework as contributing to the national economy. Over the last century, state employment reform laws, originally designed to protect factory workers, have not easily been applied to domestic employees. Even today, few household workers receive federal or state employment benefits, because employers and legislators believe the regulation of household service is a threat to domestic privacy and family autonomy. Without question, the low racial and gender status of Afro-American household workers has prolonged government insensitivity to their requests for employment justice.

—*Elizabeth Clark-Lewis*

See Also:
Black Women, Housework, Slavery

References:

Clark-Lewis, Elizabeth. "This Work Had an End: African-American Domestic Workers in Washington, D.C., 1910–1940." In *To Toil the Livelong Day*, edited by Carol Groneman and Mary Beth Norton. Ithaca, N.Y.: Cornell University Press, 1987, pp. 196–212.

Giddings, Paula. *When and Where I Enter*. New York: Random House, 1984.

Jones, Jacqueline. *Labor of Love, Labor of Sorrow*. New York: Basic Books, 1985.

Katzman, David. *Seven Days A Week*. New York: Oxford University Press, 1978.

AGE OF CONSENT defines the age at which a girl can be assumed to be acting consentually in "carnal relations with the other sex" in the laws concerning fornication, seduction, rape, and prostitution. In the common law that age was ten, but as late as 1895 in Delaware, it was seven.

The leaders of the nineteenth-century social purity movement, spurred by William T. Stead's exposé of child prostitution in England, began to agitate to raise the age of consent as part of the movement's antiprostitution campaign by making seduction of underage girls a criminal offense. Aaron Macy Powell and Emily Blackwell suggested the age-old tactic of a petition campaign, enlisting the help of the Women's Christian Temperance Union and later the Knights of Labor. On the national level, their intent was to force Congress to raise the age of consent in the District of Columbia and the territories as a model for state reform. In 1887 Congress responded, raising the age from ten to sixteen, which disappointed the reformers; their campaign reached its peak of success in 1899, when Congress raised the age to twenty-one.

The major fight was in the state legislatures, none of which was willing to go that far. Legislators worried that a twenty-one-year age of consent would allow nineteen- and twenty-year-old prostitutes to blackmail their clients. The pattern of legislative response was mixed. The general trend was upward, with sixteen being the modal age by the end of the century. In the former slave states, however, the modal age was ten and the mean eleven-and-a-half. Reformers were quick to note that the states with women's suffrage were among those with the highest age of consent. In the twentieth century most states have raised the age to sixteen.

—*William G. Shade*

See Also:
Social Purity Movement

References:

Degler, Carl N. *At Odds: Women and the Family in America from the Revolution to the Present*. New York: Oxford University Press, 1980.

Pivar, David J. *Purity Crusade: Sexual Morality and Social Control, 1868–1900*. Westport, Conn.: Greenwood, 1973.

AGRICULTURE, PREINDUSTRIAL AND NINETEENTH-CENTURY U.S. The role of women in agriculture reflects both the implicit partnership and the inequality of men and women in the agricultural world. The nature of women's participation was altered by the transitions of agriculture on the single-family farm, from colonial- and frontier-era subsistence farming, to semisubsistence farming as settlement progressed, to the raising of commercial crops adapted to the particular region in the nineteenth century. Into the twentieth century there remained strong holdovers of the family economy that required all members of a family to cooperate in producing the means of family survival and, where cash was involved, the family wage. For women this meant participating in the agricultural cycles of planting, cultivating, and harvesting, as well as maintaining the household. Since subsistence was often the key, some women engaged in poultry production and garden work, both to supply family needs and to provide a meager supplemental cash income. Women also contributed the labor for the home manufacturing that coexisted with factory labor through the nineteenth century.

In the primarily agricultural South, planters' wives faced a variation of this reality. Originally the relative scarcity of white women in the South allowed them more autonomy than women elsewhere enjoyed. Competition for women as wives declined by the early eighteenth century, but, although the demographic inequality disappeared, some of its effect continued in the occasional exercise of women's rights under a more traditional system of social inequality. The planter's wife assumed a dual role, serving as mistress of the household and as overseer of the plantation, with authority over the slaves and hired staff who were responsible for crop production. The household was her primary responsibility, but in the absence of the planter-husband, the entire plantation was subject to her direction.

Southern black women faced a more complex agricultural reality. If they were slaves, they were subject to the work and discipline requirements of slavery. While alterations in work assignments because of sex (half tasks, shorter hours, and the like) were possible, female slaves usually assumed workloads identical to those of male slaves. Within their own frequently disrupted families, they played a domestic role as well, responsible for most of the child care and the laundry, cooking, and rudimentary cleaning that were possible in slave quarters. Finally the female slave's situation was often complicated by a sexual liaison with the master.

Frontier women, though seldom credited with occupations within census data, performed the myriad tasks associated with child rearing and household maintenance, and at the same time worked as partners with their husbands in crop production. They were full economic partners in the agricultural world, yet, like other women in agriculture, they lacked social and legal equality.

By the mid-twentieth century the impact of demographic change, technology, and the reform of property rights legislation had improved but not substantially altered the secondary status of women as agricultural workers.

—*Thomas F. Armstrong*

See Also:

Black Women, Migration and Frontier Women, Patrons of Husbandry

References:

Carr, Lois Green, and Lorena S. Walsh. "The Planter's Wife: The Experience of White Women in Seventeenth Century Maryland." *William and Mary Quarterly* 34 (1977): 542–71.

Jansen, Joan M. *Loosening the Bonds: Mid-Atlantic Farm Women, 1750–1850.* New Haven: Yale University Press, 1986.

Jones, Jacqueline. *Labor of Love/Labor of Sorrow.* New York: Basic Books, 1985.

Riley, Glenda. "Not Gainfully Employed: Women on the Iowa Frontier." *Pacific Historical Review* 49 (May 1980): 237–64.

AHERN, MARY EILEEN (1868–1938) was the indefatigable editor of *Public Libraries* from 1896 to 1931. She began her library career as Indiana assistant state librarian in 1889, then became state librarian in 1893. She organized and ran the Indiana Library Association from 1889 to 1896, first as secretary, then as president. After attending library school at Armour Institute in Chicago in 1895, she became editor of a new periodical created to meet the needs of small public libraries recently established throughout the Midwest. *Public Libraries* was intended to rival the older and more genteel New York–based *Library Journal* and emphasized practical information for staff members of small public libraries who could not acquire an apprenticeship or formal library education.

As editor, Ahern was a vocal and articulate critic of professional matters. She regularly battled male leaders of this feminized profession, although usually in private correspondence rather than in the pages of *Public Libraries,* which may have served as a check on their chauvinistic excesses. Ahern was instrumental in wresting the American Library Association headquarters away from New England control and relocating it in Chicago in 1909. She also engaged in a relatively unsuccessful attempt to bring the education and library communities together through her activities as secretary of the library department of the National Education Association.

—*Wayne A. Wiegand*

See Also:
Librarianship

References:

Dale, Doris Cruger. "Ahern, Mary Eileen (1860–1938)." In *Dictionary of American Library Biography*, edited by Bohdan S. Wynar. Littleton, Colo.: Libraries Unlimited, 1978, pp. 5–7.

Wiegand, Wayne A. *Politics of An Emerging Profession: The American Library Association, 1876–1917*. Westport, Conn.: Greenwood, 1986.

AIDS, or Acquired Immune Deficiency Syndrome, is a fatal, sexually transmitted disease, which first appeared in the United States in approximately 1977, primarily among homosexual and bisexual men, intravenous drug users, and hemophiliacs. AIDS is caused by a virus transmitted through the exchange of bodily fluids, primarily blood, semen, and vaginal fluid. The main routes of infection have been from transfusions with infected blood, the sharing of needles, sexual intercourse (homosexual and heterosexual), and from an infected mother during birth.

Political considerations quickly attended the public policy debate over the proper response to what was perceived as an AIDS crisis. Groups that had argued over the political and social consequences of the Sexual Revolution of the 1960s offered predictably conflicting interpretations of the significance of AIDS as they proposed political as well as medical policy to meet the crisis.

People infected with the AIDS virus are often asymptomatic for many years, after which the virus attacks and destroys the helper T-cells, a vital part of the body's immune system. At this point a variety of opportunistic illnesses appear, ranging from relatively minor conditions such as swollen lymph nodes, severe fatigue, and persistent fever to serious infections such as *Pneumocystis carinni* pneumonia, Kaposi's sarcoma, candidiasis, and tuberculosis. In many persons with AIDS, the virus infects the nervous system directly and produces a variety of neurological deficits.

By the spring of 1987, 2,207 women had been diagnosed with AIDS nationwide. This is a misleading figure, however, since the symptoms of AIDS appear so long after infection. As of 1987 only two large population groups of women had been tested for infection: blood donors and armed services applicants. While the blood donors had an extremely low infection rate, the screening, which asks those who even suspect they might be at risk for AIDS not to donate, reduces the significance of that rate. Among armed forces applicants, however, the national rate of infection as of 1987 was .6 per 1,000 women recruits, and in several counties and cities it had reached nearly 1 in 100. Although only approximately 4 percent of the affected population, women are currently the fastest growing category of persons with AIDS, and as of 1986 the number of cases among women acquired through sexual contact with members of high-risk groups began to grow faster than those acquired through shared needles. By January 1989 there were a total of 7,821 cases of women with AIDS nationwide, which included 226 new cases in that month alone.

The U.S. government has been extremely slow in recognizing this risk to women and even slower in recognizing and dealing with this threat as a public-health issue. AIDS was so strongly presented as a plague on gay men and drug addicts that the federal Center for Disease Control established "heterosexual contact" as an official risk category only in 1984, and made the criteria for inclusion in this category so rigid that few cases could unequivocally qualify.

—*Hilary Jo Karp*

See Also:
Sexual Revolution, Venereal Disease

References:

Koop, C. E. *Surgeon General's Report on Acquired Immune Deficiency Syndrome*. Washington, D.C.: U.S. Public Health Service, 1986.

Norwood, Chris. *Advice for Life: A Woman's Guide to AIDS Risks and Prevention.* New York: Pantheon, 1987.
Rieder, Ines, and Patricia Ruppelt. *AIDS: The Women.* San Francisco: Cleis Press, 1988.

ALCOTT, ABBY (MAY) (1800–77), matriarch of the New England transcendentalist family, was a radical thinker, an early feminist, and a prototype of the modern social worker while employed as a missionary to the poor of Boston.

Born into the prominent Quincy and Sewall families, Abigail Alcott grew up amid the reformist fervor of early-nineteenth-century America. Her family and friends supported women's rights, the humane treatment of Native Americans, and abolition. She married Amos Bronson Alcott, the transcendental philosopher and educator, in 1830 and raised four daughters. Bronson Alcott was a genius, but improvident and impractical, thus much of their married life was marred by severe financial problems that necessitated her employment.

Alcott had an unusual ability to empathize with others and to identify with oppressed women, especially slave mothers whose conjugal and maternal rights were unprotected by law. It was this commitment to the oppressed that led her to a career of "servicing the poor." In 1850 she opened an "intelligence service" (employment agency) in Boston. Each month she reported her results in finding jobs for people as well as her views of American society. These reports, reprinted by the press, show the problems of the social welfare movement of the mid-nineteenth century.

Alcott advocated fair and equal wages for immigrant women. She believed that the whole system of servitude in New England was almost as false and dehumanizing as slavery in the South. Alcott walked miles a day, conferring, visiting, preaching, and teaching in the slums of Boston. In the evenings she studied and attended lectures on social conditions. Eventually she established a successful central "relief room" that operated as charity headquarters for Boston.

Along with such practical projects, Alcott also analyzed the fundamental causes of poverty and its effect on urban America. She considered unfair wages the major problem and advocated government programs to relocate immigrants to the western areas of the United States. Alcott eventually turned her attention to the emerging women's rights movement and worked with her good friend Lucretia Mott, the abolitionist and Quaker leader. Alcott organized a petition to the Massachusetts State Constitutional Convention for women to have the right to vote on amendments to the state constitution.

Alcott began as a liberal and became increasingly radical as she aged. Her diaries reflect a commitment to the "new poor." Moreover, as the model for "Marmee," the central character in her daughter Louisa's *Little Women,* she served as an example for late-nineteenth century motherhood. Alcott's life reflected her credo: "Every woman with a feeling heart is answerable to her God, if she does not plead the cause of the oppressed."

—Linda Noer

See Also:
Alcott, Louisa May; *Little Women*

References:

Abigail May Alcott Diary. Houghton Library. Harvard University, Cambridge, Mass.
Bedell, Madelon. *Alcotts: Biography of a Family.* New York: Potter, 1980.

ALCOTT, LOUISA MAY (1832–88) was born into an era of social upheaval that radically transformed Western culture on both sides of the Atlantic. In 1832, the year of Alcott's birth, the British Parliament passed its first Reform Bill. In Massachusetts the recently organized Anti-Slavery Society agitated for emancipation, an activity that would contribute significantly to the eventual outbreak of the Civil War. Reform was thus inescapably a part of Alcott's physical and spiritual environment.

Bronson and Abby (Abigail) Alcott, her parents, enthusiastically supported both the antislavery and the woman's rights movements of the day. During one period of Alcott's life, her mother ran a shelter for lost girls and abused wives. In 1836 Margaret Fuller became a teacher at Bronson Alcott's experimental Temple School in Boston. Fuller, who later wrote the landmark feminist work Woman in the Nineteenth Century (1845), was to become Alcott's lifelong heroine. Through Fuller and her own long-suffering, activist mother, Alcott became particularly sensitive to the apparently insurmountable contradiction in Western culture between femininity—especially in its domestic form—and individuality. That contradiction and the attempt to resolve it supplied the force behind most of Alcott's work.

Besides the celebrated and perennially popular *Little Women* series, Alcott wrote several novels, dozens of "blood-and-thunder" thrillers, numerous short stories, and a diary of her own experiences as a Civil War nurse. Taken as a whole, these works provide a multifaceted reflection of woman's life in nineteenth-century America. Unlike her contemporary Emily Dickinson, who depicted the restrictive life of women in poems elaborated out of imagined experiences, Alcott always actively engaged life. At the age of eighteen, she determined to support herself and her family. From then on Alcott held every type of legitimate job then available to a female: governess, maid, seamstress, teacher, and nurse.

Her experiences with other writers were equally diverse. Dickens, George Eliot, Dante, Shakespeare, and Carlyle all left their marks on her work. Perhaps the most indelible literary brand was left by *The Pilgrim's Progress,* a favorite of her father's and a work that Alcott incorporated into *Little Women.* In many ways, the Pilgrim in the Alcott canon is "woman" seeking salvation in the discovery of her own individuality. Also, despite obvious differences in style, *Little Women* has much in common with the British children's classic *Alice's Adventures in Wonderland.* Like Alice, Jo March breaks through conventional prescriptions for ladylike behavior. Both works lack the preachiness then considered necessary in a children's work, and both challenge the model of the simplemindedly domestic, self-effacing young girl. In fact, the two works aroused similarly critical responses for their revolutionary approaches to budding femininity.

The popularity of the trilogy of *Little Women, Little Men* (1871), and *Jo's Boys* (1886), and the wealth of Alcott's other works that were classified as children's literature, eclipsed the feminist implications of *Little Women* and some of her other novels. *Moods* (1865) explored the myth and realities of love and marriage for nineteenth-century American women; *Old Fashioned Girl* (1870), *Eight Cousins* (1875), and its sequel *Rose in Bloom* (1876) offered incisive social commentary on the lifestyle of Victorian women as well as insights into the social history of the era. Drawn from her own employment experiences, *Work* (1873) presented a devastatingly accurate picture of the conditions of the classic women's employments during the mid-Victorian period.

Louisa May Alcott died in 1888, never having married, on the same day as her father; the two were eulogized at a double funeral ceremony. It seems appropriate that they received a joint tribute, for Bronson Alcott inspired both his daughter's love of literature and her lifelong conflict about the restrictions imposed on the wife in a marriage.

—*Mary Lowe-Evans*

See Also:

Alcott, Abby May; Fuller, Margaret; Little Women; Work: A Story of Experience

References:

Alcott, Louisa May. *Jo's Boys.* 1886; rpt. Boston: Little, Brown, 1930.

———. *Moods.* Boston: Loring, 1865.

———. *Work: A Story of Experience.* 1873; rpt. Introduction by Sarah Elbert. New York: Schocken, 1977.

Bedell, Madelon. *The Alcotts: Biography of a Family.* New York: Clarkson N. Potter, 1980.

Boos, Clair, ed. *Works of Louisa May Alcott.* New York: Avenel, 1982.

Cheney, Ednah Dow. *Louisa May Alcott, Her Life, Letters and Journals.* Boston: Roberts Brothers, 1889.

Elbert, Sarah. *A Hunger for Home.* Philadelphia: Temple University Press, 1984.

———. *So Sweet to Remember, Feminism and Fiction of Louisa May Alcott.* Philadelphia: Temple University Press, 1983.

Payne, Alma J. *Louisa May Alcott: A Reference Guide.* Boston: G. K. Hall, 1980.

Stern, Madeleine. *Behind a Mask: The Unknown Thrillers of Louisa May Alcott.* New York: William Morrow, 1975.

———. *Critical Essays on Louisa May Alcott.* Boston: G. K. Hall, 1984.

———. *Louisa May Alcott.* Norman, Okla.: University of Oklahoma Press, 1971.

AMERICAN ANTISLAVERY SOCIETIES, modeled after organizations in England and spurred by the publication of William Lloyd Garrison's abolitionist paper, the *Liberator* (1831), were begun in the United States in the 1830s. Garrison's New England Anti-Slavery Society, founded early in 1832, was the first such group.

From the beginning, women, particularly free black women, played a large role in the antislavery societies. Just after Garrison's New England Society was formed, a group of black women in Salem, Massachusetts, began the Female Anti-Slavery Society, the first in America (February 1832). Shortly thereafter, Maria Weston Chapman, a member of Boston's aristocracy, organized the Boston Female Anti-Slavery Society as an auxiliary to Garrison's all-male group. Black women worked alongside white women in the Boston group, as well as in the integrated Female Anti-Slavery Societies of Lynn, Massachusetts, and Rochester, New York. In New York City, however, black women were turned away by the existing antislavery societies and formed their own group.

The presence of women in the antislavery societies inevitably raised questions about the position of women in nineteenth-century American society. When the American Anti-Slavery Society held its first convention in Philadelphia in 1833, women were not allowed to join the society or sign the founding statement of purpose. After the meeting, twenty women, including Lucretia Mott, met and formed the Philadelphia Female Anti-Slavery Society. By 1837, when the first National Female Anti-Slavery convention was held in New York, eighty-one delegates from twelve states attended.

Some of the activities of the female antislavery societies were consistent with the nineteenth-century ideology of separate spheres for men and women. These activities included raising money through annual fairs, circulating petitions, and bringing in male speakers for the antislavery cause. But increasingly women themselves began speaking publicly for the cause of abolition: notably, Angelina and Sarah Grimké, and Maria Stewart, a free black woman. Women speakers were attacked both by those opposed to abolition and by antifeminists within the antislavery movement for daring to step outside their "proper sphere."

In 1840 the "woman question" came to a head when the American Anti-Slavery Society split into two separate organizations, ostensibly over the appointment of Abby Kelley to a leadership position within the group. The issue also dominated that year's World Anti-Slavery Convention in London, at which women delegates were required to sit in a screened-off balcony. Present at that meeting were women like Elizabeth Cady Stanton and Lucretia Mott, who would later become leaders of the woman suffrage movement.

The participation of women in the American antislavery societies thus helped pave the way for the suffrage movement by raising the issue of women's access to a broader sphere of activity. Nineteenth-century women gained significant leadership skills and organizational training from their experiences in the antislavery societies and, importantly, developed a consciousness of their own oppression as women.

—*Mary Battenfeld*

See Also:

Abolition and the Antislavery Movement; Foster, Abby Kelley; Public Speakers, Women

References:
Flexner, Eleanor. *Century of Struggle: The Woman's Rights Movement in the United States.* New York: Atheneum, 1974.
Hersh, Blanche Glassman. *The Slavery of Sex: Feminist-Abolitionists in America.* Urbana: University of Illinois Press, 1978.
Lerner, Gerda. "The Political Activities of Antislavery Women." *In The Majority Finds Its Past,* edited by Gerda Lerner. New York: Oxford University Press,1979, pp. 112–28.
Sterling, Dorothy. *We Are Your Sisters: Black Women in the Nineteenth Century.* New York: Norton, 1984.

The **AMERICAN ASSOCIATION OF UNIVERSITY WOMEN (AAUW)** was the first organization of university women in the United States. It was founded in 1882 as the Association of Collegiate Alumnae, and became the American Association of University Women in 1921 after merging with the Southern Association of College Women and the Western Association of Collegiate Alumnae. In 1881 Marion Talbot, Emily Fairbanks Talbot, Alice Hayes, and Ellen Richards organized a meeting for a group of seventeen young women representing eight colleges and universities. These women notified alumnae of their respective institutions, and sixty-five women from Boston University, the universities of Michigan and Wisconsin, Cornell, Oberlin, Smith, Vassar, and Wellesley gathered in Boston on January 14, 1882, for the first organizational meeting of the Association of Collegiate Alumnae.

The Western Association of Collegiate Alumnae (WACA) was organized in December 1883 in Chicago. One of its first actions was to establish a bureau of correspondence to encourage communication between university women in the United States and Europe. Another notable accomplishment of the Western Association was the establishment of a scholarship fund for women. In 1903 the Southern Association of College Women (SACW) was formed with the objective of "devoting their energy to the Southern educational problems at close range." When the regional groups merged in 1921, the name American Association of University Women (AAUW) was adopted.

The AAUW can be credited with leading the movement to improve conditions and facilities for women in many colleges and universities. Early administrators used AAUW institutional admission as leverage to obtain funding for women's dormitories, to improve the salaries of women instructors, and to encourage the hiring of women in positions beyond the instructor level, as well as to promote a cordial attitude for women students. Today the association promotes the advancement of women's education and women in society, and contributes to the betterment of the community. It funds projects of branch and state divisions and individual members through research and projects grants and fellowship programs. The AAUW maintains a comprehensive library and archival collection on women and supports one of the largest lobbying teams on women's issues. In addition to many brochures, research studies, study guides, and booklets, the association publishes "Action Alert" while Congress is in session, "Graduate Woman," and "Leader in Action." There are branches in every state and a membership of nearly two hundred thousand.

—Sandra Fox

See Also:
Association of Collegiate Alumnae, Women in Higher Education

References:
The AAUW Story: Rights, Privileges, and Responsibilities. AAUW Membership Services Pamphlet. Washington, D.C.: I–79.
Talbot, Marion, and Lois Rosenberry. *History of the American Association of University Women, 1881–1931.* Boston: Houghton Mifflin, 1931.

The **AMERICAN BIRTH CONTROL LEAGUE (ABCL)** was a national organization founded in 1921 by Margaret Sanger to promote the founding of birth control clinics and the cause of fertility control. Beginning with a near riot when Sanger's rally at Town Hall in New York

City was prevented by police, the organization attracted public attention to the issue of birth control. Under the auspices of the ABCL, a clinic—the Birth Control Clinical Research Bureau—was established that dispensed spring-type vaginal diaphragms and lactic-acid jelly, soon proving their effectiveness.

The ABCL also identified physicians willing to dispense birth control devices and made their names known to women outside New York. Research on the diaphragms was compiled by the Clinical Research Bureau, under the ABCL's support. Although operating without a dispensary license, the clinics continued, and even considered the possibility of providing abortions. In 1929 a raid on the Clinical Research Bureau ironically aroused private physicians' antagonism to the police. In 1936 a test case on pessaries from Japan induced Judge Augustus Hand to rule that physicians could legally receive contraceptive materials.

Having disseminated information and added greatly to the acceptance of devices, the organization was faced with declining birth rates. Its emphasis shifted, and in 1942 it took on the name Planned Parenthood Federation of America. Research showed that among 35 percent of women the diaphragm had come to replace withdrawal and douching as the commonest birth control method. Sanger influenced the ABCL to become associated with doctors and wealthy women, rather than radical or libertarian proponents. In this way, birth control gradually gained public acceptance.

—*Daryl M. Hafter*

See Also:

Birth Control, Birth Control Clinical Research Bureau; Planned Parenthood Federation of America; Sanger, Margaret

References:

Gordon, Linda. *Woman's Body, Woman's Right: A Social History of Birth Control in America.* New York: Grossman, 1976.

Reed, James. *From Private Vice to Public Virtue: The Birth Control Movement and American Society Since 1830.* New York: Basic Books, 1978.

Sanger, Margaret. *My Fight for Birth Control.* 1931; rpt. Elmsford, N.Y.: Maxwell Reprint Co., 1969.

The **AMERICAN FEDERATION OF LABOR (AFL).** The Federation of Organized Trade and Labor Unions of the United States and Canada was organized in 1881. At its sixth annual session in 1886, the American Federation of Labor was formed, absorbing the original organization. Under the direction of Samuel Gompers, the AFL became the most significant labor organization in the United States, emphasizing labor's immediate concerns: wages, hours, and working conditions. In addition, the AFL stood ready to employ the strike when necessary to achieve its ends. As the name implies, the AFL was a federation of trade unions that rejected the idea of individual membership in one all-inclusive union. Instead, the AFL stressed the organization of skilled workers into separate craft unions, each belonging to the larger federation.

While the name Federation of Organized Trade and Labor Unions implies the inclusion of all laborers, not just males, no women were present at the founding convention in 1881. In 1882 the organization urged the women's labor organizations to join the federation "upon an equal footing . . . with men." The following year Mrs. Charlotte Smith, President of the Women's National Industrial League, was admitted to the AFL convention and was granted a seat at the 1884 convention. At that convention a proposal was drafted entitled "An Address to Worker Girls and Women," which urged women to organize and to support the federation in the premise that "equal amounts of work should bring the same prices whether performed by man or woman." Other than recognizing the problems of women workers, however, the AFL did little by way of concrete action to improve the status or organization of American female laborers. Although the federation's first woman delegate, Mary Burke, introduced a resolution in 1890 to have women appointed to organize women in the trades under AFL jurisdiction, federation action was slow and limited: Mary Kenney was given a fixed, unrenewed five-month appointment in 1892.

Since the AFL concentrated on and consisted primarily of skilled workers, it tended to offer little to workers on the lower rungs of the industrial ladder, where women and blacks were located to a great extent. Typical of the problem facing women interested in participating in the AFL was the stance of the Baker, Carpenter, and Molder Union affiliates of the AFL: each barred women members until well into the twentieth century. Even when women were admitted to a constituent union, the tendency was to establish separate sex-segregated locals for women workers, which proved to be extremely ineffective and therefore languished for members. With the approval of the AFL leadership, the National Women's Trade Union League was organized at the 1903 AFL convention, but this merely reinforced the inadequate representation of women workers in American labor organizations. Until the Great Depression, the NWTUL supported protective legislation that perpetuated wage discrimination and sex segregation of the labor force.

The National Recovery Act (1933) and the National Labor Relations Act (1935) benefited the industrial work force, 20 percent of whom were women. The New Deal labor policies facilitated the revitalization of the International Ladies Garment Workers Union, but the reluctance of the AFL male membership to accept women in union leadership remained and resurfaced after World War II. Women continued to enter the industrial labor force during the 1950s and 1960s, however, which enabled AFL women to assert their presence and demand union attention to their issues. The Coalition of Labor Union Women, organized in 1974, influenced the AFL to reconsider its traditional opposition to the Equal Rights Amendment, which dated from the 1950s and reflected its support of protective legislation for women workers. The AFL merger with the Congress of Industrial Organizations did not increase the union's attention to the needs of women workers. By the mid-1970s, the AFL-CIO had only two women in national leadership posts, an associate director of its civil rights department to service women's activities and the director of the union library.

—Maureen Anna Harp

See Also:

International Ladies Garment Workers Union, National Women's Trade Union League, Protective Legislation, Unions

References:

Kaufman, Stuart. *Samuel Gompers and the Origins of the American Federation of Labor.* Westport, Conn.: Greenwood, 1973.

Kennedy, Susan E. *If All We Did Was to Weep At Home.* Bloomington: Indiana University Press, 1979.

Kessler-Harris, Alice. *Out to Work: A History of Wage-Earning Women in the United States.* New York: Oxford University Press, 1982.

Morris, James. *Conflict Within the AFL.* Ithaca, N.Y.: Cornell University Press, 1958.

Taft, Philip. *The AF of L from the Death of Gompers to the Merger.* New York: Harper, 1959.

———. *The AF of L in the Time of Gompers.* 2 vols. New York: Harper, 1957.

Wertheimer, Barbara. *We Were There.* New York: Pantheon, 1977.

The **AMERICAN FEDERATION OF STATE, COUNTY, AND MUNICIPAL EMPLOYEES (AFSCME).** In 1932 a group of fifty state employees that included professionals, supervisors, and department heads but few rank-and-filers met in the assembly chambers of the Wisconsin State Capitol to organize a union for state employees from the top down. Among the organizers themselves there was controversy over whether to form an independent professional organization or an affiliate of organized labor. Proponents of unionization argued that labor conventions and meetings would publicize state employees' contributions to good government as well as their struggle for reasonable wages, hours, and conditions of employment. Within six months the new union, named the Wisconsin State Employees Association, had won affiliation with the American Federation of Labor.

The unemployed in Wisconsin at the depths of the Depression in 1933 numbered two hundred thousand, which equaled a quarter of the workers in the state. Another one hundred thousand workers had only part-time jobs. Conservative Democrats swept into office by the Roosevelt landslide had campaigned to repeal the civil service law in order to provide jobs for the party faithful. When the Wisconsin legislature convened in 1933, hordes of unemployed people camped in the corridors of the Capitol building in anticipation of appointments to those civil service positions. With the help of the AFL and other citizen groups interested in good government, the new union successfully campaigned to defeat the civil service repeal.

The executive secretary of the union, Arnold Zander, and organizer Roy Kubista drafted a call for a convention in Chicago in December 1935 to form an international union of public employees over the objections of AFL president William Green. Twenty-six delegates attended the first constitutional convention of AFSCME to elect officers, adopt resolutions, and sign an application for an AFL charter that designated Madison, Wisconsin, as AFSCME headquarters.

The new international union doubled its membership between 1937 and 1938. After its first decade, AFSCME had seventy-three thousand members; by the 1955 AFL-CIO merger, its membership topped one hundred thousand, and in 1957 AFSCME transferred its headquarters to Washington, D.C. By the 1980s the AFSCME constituency in the tertiary sector of the economy made it the fastest growing union in the United States with more than a million members in local chapters throughout the states, Puerto Rico, and Panama.

Because AFSCME targeted unionization of clerical occupations in local and state government, it recruited many women members and became a pioneer in the struggle to achieve pay equity for working women. Women constitute over half of the eight hundred thousand members and hold 40 percent of AFSCME leadership positions. AFSCME has confronted the sex discrimination in jobs traditionally held by women who have been underpaid for work that requires skill, effort, and responsibility equal to or exceeding that of male-dominated occupations. AFSCME worked to secure state legislatures' funding of job evaluation studies as well as passage of legislation that committed states to follow the principles of pay equity in their pay scales and employment policies. Through legal action and collective bargaining, AFSCME has won substantial pay increases for its women members in Washington, California, Illinois, and Wisconsin.

—Mary Lou France

See Also:

American Federation of Labor, Sex Equity, Unions

Reference:

Kubista, Roy. Wisconsin State Employees Union. Madison, Wis.: AFSCME, 1982.

The **AMERICAN HOME ECONOMICS ASSOCIATION (AHEA)**, founded in 1909, was one of several organizations that grew out of the home economics or domestic science movement in the late 1800s. During this time, women's seminaries and, later, women's colleges began offering training in home economics; public schools began to offer domestic science; and cooking schools were developed to train teachers of cooking. The AHEA was the culmination of a series of ten conferences, known as the Lake Placid Conferences, that began in 1899. Ellen Richards was instrumental in setting up the conferences; a chemist, she felt that scientific principles should be applied to household work and that homemaking was the most natural and desirable occupation for women. Richards had been working on a new science that she called oekology, the science of right living. Mevil Dewey, president of the New York Efficiency Society, encouraged Richards to organize the new discipline and suggested it be called home economics.

Through the nineteenth century, as home economics was becoming part of American education at all levels, it lacked a body of literature that clarified its philosophy and place in the overall educational system. The Lake Placid Conferences were held to deal with these concerns. During the ten years of its existence, the group attempted to work with other groups such as the National Education Association, resulting in the formation of sections within the NEA on home economics and manual training. The Lake Placid group had less success with the Association of Collegiate Alumnae (later the American Association of University Women), at whose meeting in June 1905 a resolution was passed that home economics had no place in a college course for women. This was a blow for Richards and Marion Talbot, another leader of the Lake Placid Conferences, because they had been co-founders of the Association of Collegiate Alumnae. The home economics movement was embraced by the suffrage movement, however. At the 1897 meeting of the National American Woman Suffrage Association, the keynote address was on the topic of domestic science, which was in keeping with the feeling of many women that they deserved the vote because they were homemakers.

By the time the tenth conference was planned, the leaders decided that an organization was needed to carry on their work. The first official meeting of the American Home Economics Association was held in Washington, and Richards was elected president. There were 143 delegates at this convention, and 700 charter members. The organization had 30,000 members in 1985 and is still active today.

The establishment of the AHEA testified to the success of the domestic science movement and to the influence of the Victorian cult of domesticity on women's education. Courses in home economics at the secondary and postsecondary levels of public education were intended to maintain and enhance the status of homemaking as a respected profession; however, this specialized curriculum served to reinforce the domestic identity of women, regardless of their endeavors in traditional academic fields or their aspirations to careers outside the home.

—*Judith Pryor*

See Also:

Association of Collegiate Alumnae, Home Economics, National Education Association

References:

Baldwin, Keturah E. *The AHEA Saga: A Brief History of the Origin and Development of the American Home Economics Association and a Glimpse at the Grass Roots from which It Grew.* Washington, D.C.: American Home Economics Association, 1949.

Ehrenreich, Barbara, and Deirdre English. *For Her Own Good: 150 Years of the Experts' Advice to Women.* Garden City, N.Y.: Anchor, 1978.

Weigley, Emma Seifrit. "It Might Have Been Euthenics: The Lake Placid Conferences and the Home Economics Movement." *American Quarterly* 26 (March 1974): 79–97.

The **AMERICAN JEWESS** was the first national Jewish women's magazine in the United States. Published in Chicago by Rosa Sonneschein from 1895 to 1899, it encouraged women from German Jewish immigrant stock to continue Jewish life in America. Sonneschein was the upper middle-class wife of a prominent Reform rabbi whom she later divorced. Her twenty-nine thousand readers were also largely upper middle-class Reform Jews.

The magazine promoted domestic feminism and Zionism, and its features included stories for children and columns on scientific housekeeping, medicine, and the social sciences. It also provided reviews of both Jewish and secular literature, music, art, and drama, as well as short stories by popular female authors. Every issue also contained an editorial by Sonneschein, reports of international and national feminist and Jewish activities, and articles by prominent feminists.

Sonneschein hoped that the magazine would become the official publication of the National Council of Jewish Women, but the organization turned down the offer of eight pages per issue in favor of printing its own newsletter. Still, Sonneschein believed that the aims of the NCJW and the American Jewess were identical, so she devoted a major portion of the magazine to reporting NCJW activities, even ignoring the presidential election of 1896 in order to cover the council's first convention. Despite its steady readership, the magazine folded in 1899 when Sonneschein's health failed and no one stepped in to fill her shoes.

—Faith Rogow

See Also:

Domestic Feminism; Jewish Women; Sonneschein, Rosa

Reference:

See ROSA SONNESCHEIN in the Small Collections File, American Jewish Archives, Cincinnati, Ohio.

The **AMERICAN MISSIONARY ASSOCIATION.** Founded in 1846 as a domestic mission for the Congregational Church, the American Missionary Association combined radical abolitionism with Protestant evangelicalism. The AMA sent its missionaries to follow Northern armies in the latter years of the Civil War to convert slaves to the abolitionist as well as the evangelical Protestant cause. From early efforts at Hampton, Virginia, and Port Royal, South Carolina, the American Missionary Association became the most active sponsor of Northern teachers in the immediate postwar period. In Georgia, for example, the AMA funded and sponsored 80 percent of the Northern teacher-missionaries after the war (1865–73).

The narrow focus of this organization had been influenced by the antebellum movement among churchwomen to fund the education, training, and placement of young women missionaries who were to take the gospel to the sequestered women of Asia, Africa, and the Middle East. While the women missionaries were encouraged to wed male missionaries, those who refused were nonetheless supported as independent single missionaries. By the 1850s medical training was added to the program for women missionaries. The placements offered to medically trained graduates of women's nursing and medical institutions provided an outlet for a new professional class of educated women.

The specific thrust of the American Missionary Association was to develop schools and churches. Several hundred primary schools were established in the South, many housed on former plantations in crude buildings built by freedmen. The society was always short of funds, and many of the schools survived on a combination of Northern donations and frugality. The society acknowledged the economic realities of the freedmen's lives by operating the schools when seasonal agricultural work was least demanding. Though many of these primary schools closed their doors after a few years, some survived to bear testimony to AMA efforts; for example, the Dorchester Academy in Liberty County, Georgia, which remained open until the 1930s. A more concentrated educational effort of the AMA led to the founding of several black colleges, including Nashville's Fisk and the Atlanta University complex. These colleges, in turn, trained black ministers to continue the work of the American Missionary Association throughout the South.

The AMA came to mirror mid-nineteenth-century society and challenge it through the roles women played in the organization. Although the bureaucracy of the AMA was fundamentally male, more than 90 percent of the volunteers for Southern service were female and disproportionately single, young, and New England–born. The AMA service experience of these women paralleled that of the next generation in the Settlement House Movement. Expected to demonstrate the modesty and decorum of the Cult of True Womanhood, AMA women missionaries in fact had to join freedmen and freedwomen in the fields, challenge local authorities who often wished to close their schools, and organize the efforts to support their establishments. They demonstrated perseverance and professionalism despite inequities within the AMA that reflected those of the larger society. As the focus of the American Missionary Association shifted to the black colleges by the mid-1870s, the role of women diminished. By the 1890s AMA activity in the South had all but disappeared.

—Thomas F. Armstrong

See Also:
Abolition and the Antislavery Movement

References:
Hill, Patricia. *The World Their Household: American Women's Foreign Mission Movement and Cultural Transformation.* Ann Arbor: University of Michigan Press, 1985.
Jones, Jacqueline. *Soldiers of Light and Love: Northern Teachers and Georgia Blacks, 1865–1873.* Chapel Hill: University of North Carolina Press, 1980.
Rose, Willie Lee. *Rehearsal for Reconstruction: The Port Royal Experiment.* Indianapolis: Bobbs-Merrill, 1964.
Saunders, Frank, and George Rogers. "Eliza Ann Ward: Teacher and Missionary to the Freedman." *In Swampwater and Wiregrass: Historical Sketches of Coastal Georgia,* edited by R. Frank Saunders and George Rogers. Macon, Ga.: Mercer University Press, 1984, pp. 139–50.

The **AMERICAN RED CROSS,** an outgrowth of the International Red Cross, was established in the United States largely through the exertions of Clara Barton. She was made aware of the work of the parent organization, established in Geneva in 1864, by Dr. Louis Appia, whom she met while staying with friends in Geneva in 1869. She was distressed to learn that her own country had declined membership because the government thought it might constitute an "entangling alliance," against which President Washington had warned in his Farewell Address of 1797. Before Barton could return home, she was witness to the Franco-Prussian War, and, while working as a relief organizer under the flag of the Red Cross, provided assistance to civilian women devastated by the war.

Once back in the United States, Barton began a campaign to win American participation in the Red Cross movement, only to meet objections from successive secretaries of state that membership ran counter to historic national policy. Undaunted, she wrote widely in support of American membership, used her numerous high-level contacts inside and outside the government, and set up a Washington, D.C., chapter to keep up pressure on the administration in office. Finally, in March 1884, the U.S. Senate affirmed the Geneva Treaty, and in 1900 Congress gave the American Red Cross a federal charter.

The American branch almost at once undertook to make assistance available to victims of natural as well as man-made disasters. Clara Barton viewed the Red Cross as a standby organization to give aid in the wake of fire, flood, hurricane, or tidal wave. It did an exceptional job of aiding the Cuban wounded in the Spanish-American War.

As the American Red Cross grew, it became increasingly difficult for its president, Clara Barton, to keep a firm hand on its operation. She was not an organization woman, and in 1904 she was succeeded by William Howard Taft, then secretary of war, in a change literally forced on Barton. As it turned out, Taft was but a figurehead. Mabel Boardman was the driving force in reorganizing the American branch, putting its finances in order and enlarging active membership thoroughout the country. In the long view, it was both the inspirational efforts of Clara Barton and the organizational skill of Mabel Boardman that helped to make the Red Cross a permanent and respected institution in American life.

—D. H. Burton

See Also:
Barton, Clara

References:
Barton, Clara. The Red Cross: A History. Washington, D.C.: American Red Cross, 1898.
Bicknell, Ernest P. Pioneering with the Red Cross. New York: Macmillan, 1935.
Dulles, Rhea Foster. The American Red Cross: A History. Westport, Conn.: Greenwood, 1971.

The **AMERICAN WOMAN SUFFRAGE ASSOCIATION (AWSA)** was founded at a convention held in Cleveland, November 24–25, 1869. It was promoted by Lucy Stone and other prominent members of the New England Woman Suffrage Association who disapproved of the program and tactics of the National Woman Suffrage Association started by Elizabeth Cady Stanton, Susan B. Anthony, and their supporters earlier that year. In contrast to NWSA, which was at first loosely structured, largely New York–based, and strongly influenced by Stanton's radical feminist ideas, AWSA took a more moderate stance. AWSA claimed, through its formal delegate system, to represent more accurately the state suffrage associations that were springing up across the nation. In fact, AWSA tended to reflect the views of a core of influential New England members, many of them former abolitionists. Thus the new organization looked to the Republican party as the most likely source of progress on the suffrage issue, supported the Fifteenth Amendment (guaranteeing black male suffrage without reference to women) as the fulfillment of the abolition crusade, and chose to support a separate federal amendment for woman suffrage.

Although individual members favored various reform and philanthropic causes, AWSA officially confined its work to suffrage and avoided taking positions on related but more controversial feminist issues. Men were conspicuous in the AWSA leadership; its first two presidents were Henry Ward Beecher and T. W. Higginson. Beginning in 1874, Julia Ward Howe was president for many years, but Lucy Stone and her husband, Henry B. Blackwell, continued as guiding spirits. Through lecture tours, an ambitious publication program, and the convening of annual conventions in midwestern cities, AWSA attempted to build a national membership. Outside New England, it had considerable success in New Jersey, Ohio, Illinois, Indiana, Maryland, and several other states. But these efforts were soon outstripped by Susan B. Anthony's organizing zeal, and almost from the start NWSA led in both membership and fund raising.

AWSA lobbied steadily for a federal suffrage amendment, but concentrated its energies at the state level, supporting several campaigns for school and municipal suffrage. It gained a wide audience through the Woman's Journal, a Boston weekly. Founded in 1870 and edited from 1872 by Lucy Stone, the Woman's Journal became the most influential and longest-lived of nineteenth-century feminist newspapers.

In response to pressure from younger members, a joint committee met in 1887 to begin negotiating terms under which the two rival wings of the suffrage movement could be reconciled. After long deliberation, agreement was reached, and in 1890 AWSA and NWSA were merged as the National American Woman Suffrage Association.

—*Gail Malmgreen*

See Also:

Abolition and the Antislavery Movement; Anthony, Susan B.; National American Woman Suffrage Association; National Woman Suffrage Association; Stanton, Elizabeth Cady; Stone, Lucy; Woman's Journal

References:

Blackwell, Alice Stone. *Lucy Stone, Pioneer of Woman's Rights.* Boston: Little, Brown, 1930.

Flexner, Eleanor. *Century of Struggle: The Woman's Rights Movement in the United States.* Cambridge: Harvard University Press, 1959.

Hays, Eleanor R. *Morning Star: A Biography of Lucy Stone, 1818–1893.* New York: Harcourt, Brace & World, 1961.

Stanton, Elizabeth Cady, et al., eds. *History of Woman Suffrage.* Vols. 2, 4. Rochester, N.Y.: Privately Printed, 1881, 1902.

The **AMERICAN WOMEN'S EDUCATION ASSOCIATION** was founded in 1852 by noted educator and author Catharine Beecher. The purpose of the organization was to help women secure a liberal education and appropriate employment, which according to the association, was training the mind, taking care of the body, and preserving the family state. In pursuit of these goals, the association provided funding for women's colleges, particularly Milwaukee Female College (later called Milwaukee Normal Institute), which had been started by Beecher. The association supported three other colleges too, but only Milwaukee Normal Institute survived for more than a few years.

Beecher believed that women, especially unmarried women, must be prepared to earn an independent livelihood. But she had the view, conservative even for her time, that women's proper role lay in the traditional domestic areas of housework or working with children. She therefore wanted to head a department of domestic economy at Milwaukee Normal Institute.

For several years the association had provided money for salaries, but its aim had always been to fund the establishment of departments. This it was unable to do, so Beecher went east to raise money for the college, hoping to raise enough to build a home for herself on the Milwaukee campus that would also serve as the domestic economy department. The trustees of the college declined her request for help because they thought it inappropriate to fund a place of residence for Beecher on the campus. Greatly disappointed, Beecher resigned from the association and ended her relationship with the college. In her letter of resignation, she stated that should the association decide to fund a health and domestic department at Milwaukee or anywhere else, she would rejoin. Beecher later rescinded her resignation, but soon thereafter the association lost effectiveness.

The college did later erect a building to be used as a department of domestic education (not funded by the association) and asked Beecher to lead the department, but she declined. By 1862 the association had voted to disband, feeling there was little left that it could accomplish. Beecher ignored this decision and continued its activities alone until her death in 1878.

—Judith Pryor

See Also:

Beecher, Catharine; Normal Schools

References:

Harveson, Mae Elizabeth. *Catharine Esther Beecher.* New York: Arno, 1969.

Sklar, Kathryn Kish. *Catharine Beecher: A Study in American Domesticity.* New Haven: Yale University Press, 1973.

The **AMERICAN WOMEN'S HOSPITALS SERVICE (AWHS)**, established at the second annual meeting of the Medical Women's National Association (American Medical Women's Association [AMWA]), June 5–6, 1917, was the primary organization through which women doctors utilized their professional skills during World War I. Since women physicians were refused entry into the armed forces, AWHS—operating as an AMWA committee—provided an all-female force of doctors, nurses, and ambulance drivers; it organized hospitals in the French war zone, setting up dispensaries to serve the civilian population in the outlying areas. Barely under way when the armistice was signed, AWHS refocused its efforts on reconstruction in Europe and in Serbia (Yugoslavia) beginning in 1918. Reaching its peak in overseas service in 1923, when approximately twelve thousand refugees from Turkey were treated on the offshore Greek island of Macronissi, the organization turned its attention to the Appalachian area of the United States in 1931. Medical service was continued in other parts of the world, however, extending throughout the Near East, Far East, and later into South America, although largely without American women doctors.

Dr. Rosalie Slaughter Morton chaired the AWHS committee the first year, followed by Dr. Mary M. Crawford the second year, then by Dr. Esther Pohl Lovejoy, who retained the position for forty-eight years. AWHS functioned officially under AMWA, but Lovejoy ran the organization independently. In 1959 AWHS separated from AWMA until 1980, when it rejoined the parent organization in its original status as a committee.

The history of AWHS does not bear out the contention that women's rights advance in wartime. In spite of the organization's impressive record overseas during and after World War I, World War II began with the same refusal to accept women physicians into the armed forces. Restrictions barring women doctors from service were lifted in 1943, but were reinstituted at the war's end. It was not until the 1950s that women doctors won rank and commissions in the armed forces permanently.

—*Jayne Crumpler DeFiore*

See Also:

Military Service, Physicians, World War I

References:

Archives and Special Collections on Women in Medicine. Philadelphia: The Medical College of Pennsylvania. (Alumnae Files; American Medical Women's Association Papers; American Women's Hospitals Service Papers.)

Lovejoy, Esther Pohl. *Certain Samaritans.* 2d ed. New York: Macmillan, 1933.

———. *The House of the Good Neighbor.* 2d ed. New York: Macmillan, 1920.

———. *Women Doctors of the World.* New York: Macmillan, 1957.

———. *Women Physicians and Surgeons National and International Organizations.* Livingston, N.Y.: Livingston Press, 1939.

AMES, JESSE DANIEL (1883–1972), suffragist and civil rights activist, led a campaign against lynching in a Ku Klux Klan–dominated era. As founder and director of the Association of Southern Women for the Prevention of Lynching (1930–42), Ames exposed the link between sexual and racial repression that lay at the root of mob violence in the South. She argued that "false chivalry," built upon the myth of the black rapist and the pure white "Southern lady" in need of protection, demeaned white women even as it terrorized blacks. Ames also criticized the double standard that simultaneously condoned white men's lynching of black men and their sexual exploitation of black women.

Ames grew up in Texas, graduating from Southwestern University at Georgetown in 1902. At the age of thirty-one she found herself widowed with three young children to support. The self-confidence and economic independence Ames gained during this period nurtured a growing feminism, and in 1916 she began her public career as a suffragist. Throughout the 1920s Ames mobilized newly enfranchised women behind the social welfare goals of Southern progressivism. But she soon became dissatisfied with the contradiction between social feminism and the exclusion of black women and racial concerns, and turned to the South's chief interracial reform organization, the Commission on International Cooperation (CIC). In 1929 she moved to Georgia as director of the CIC Women's Committee, where she sought to bridge the color line separating black and white middle-class women, calling for female solidarity in the fight against racist stereotypes.

Ames's major contribution came in the 1930s, with the founding of the ASWPL. The association worked through established women's networks to fight mob violence with speeches, writings, investigations, and even intervention. The women combined a nineteenth-century reputation for moral superiority with a twentieth-century potential for political power in their efforts to convince local leaders to denounce lynching. Blending their traditional roles as moral guardians with their resistance to the suppression of women for their own "protection," Ames and her followers made progress in their feminist revolt against chivalry, while still holding to some of the trappings of the traditional "Southern lady."

—*Misti Turbeville*

See Also:

Association of Southern Women for the Prevention of Lynching; Wells-Barnett, Ida B.

References:

ASWPL Papers. Trevor Arnett Library. Atlanta University, Atlanta, Ga.

Jesse Daniel Ames Papers. Southern Historical Collection. University of North Carolina, Chapel Hill, N.C.

Hall, Jacquelyn Dowd. *Revolt Against Chivalry: Jesse Daniel Ames and the Women's Campaign Against Lynching.* New York: Columbia University Press, 1979.

Miller, Kathleen Atkinson. "The Ladies and the Lynchers: A Look at the Association of Southern Women for the Prevention of Lynching." *Southern Studies* 17 (Fall 1978): 221–40.

Scott, Anne Firor. *The Southern Lady: From Pedestal to Politics, 1830–1930.* Chicago: University of Chicago Press, 1970.

ANDROGYNY is the condition of being both male and female, of having both male and female characteristics.

Aristophanes, greatest of the Greek comic playwrights, tells the story of the androgynes in Plato's *Symposium.* When the world was new, Aristophanes explains, Zeus peopled it with complete beings. Each had two faces, four legs, and four arms, and was at once male and female. Very soon, however, these prototypical humans became so powerful that they threatened the gods, and so Zeus sliced them in two. Desperate for their original wholeness, the severed halves clung together, refusing to eat or drink, and soon many of them were dying. Zeus saved the race, and created human beings as we now know them, by making it possible for the halved androgynes to unite sexually and so experience some semblance of their archetypal selves. Romantic lovers, then, are people who have found their other halves.

Within feminism, androgyny has been seen as both a goal and a delusive solution. Virginia Woolf, in *A Room of One's Own,* praises great writers—Shakespeare, Keats, and Coleridge, for instance—for their androgyny: their capacity to write without insistent sexual identification. "[I]t is fatal for anyone who writes to think of their sex," Woolf says, and she looks forward to a time when women and men will be able to accept each other without the sexual resentment she sees pervading early-twentieth-century literature. Adrienne Rich, on the other hand, in *The Dream of a Common Language,* writes:

> There are words I cannot choose again:
> humanism androgyny
>
> Such words have no shame in them, no diffidence before the raging stoic grandmothers . . .
>
> *("Natural Resources" 1977)*

Rich rejects the inadequate goal of androgyny in favor of women's strength, gentleness, and persistence in reconstituting a culture imperiled by competition and male violence.

—Gretchen Mieszkowski

See Also:

European Influences; Rich, Adrienne

References:

Heilbrun, Carolyn G. *Toward a Recognition of Androgyny.* New York: Norton, 1982.

Women's Studies 2 (1974). [Androgyny Issue]

ANGELOU, MAYA (b. 1928), through her autobiographies, poetry, articles, interviews, performances, and presence, has profoundly influenced black American women since the 1960s. Her gentle outspokenness and rich prose inspired novice writers and her reading public of all races and both genders to overcome heartache and hardship through her series of five autobiographical volumes: *I Know Why the Caged Bird Sings* (1970), *Gather Together in My Name* (1974), *Singin' and Swingin' and Gettin' Merry like Christmas* (1977), *The Heart of a Woman* (1981), and *All God's Children Need Traveling Shoes* (1986).

The first volume is the most famous, describing Angelou's childhood during the Depression with her brother, Bailey, and their courageous grandmother, who owned and operated the general store in the poor black community of rural Stamps, Arkansas. When she was eight years old, Angelou's brief reunion with her father and subsequent stay with her mother in East St. Louis resulted in her being raped. When she returned to Stamps, her state of guilt induced a self-imposed silence broken only when her grandmother's friend Mrs. Bertha Flowers insisted that Maya read aloud the great literature of the world. With extaordinary candor and compassion, Angelou presents a textured picture of the kinship and church-centered community of these southern blacks. As a teenager during World War II, she lived with her mother in California, becoming the first black woman fare collector with the San Francisco Streetcar Company. The initial autobiography ends with sixteen-year-old Angelou giving birth to her son, Guy, "the best thing that ever happened to me." Her later books record her development and maturity as an artist and writer during the 1960s and 1970s in New York and Europe. The latest volume relates her travels to Africa, where "she became a hunter for that elusive place and much longed for place the heart could call home."

Singer, dancer, playwright, and political activist, Angelou has accomplished much in diverse areas. During the 1960s she performed in the Obie-award-winning play The Blacks by Jean Genet. Shortly afterward, she served as the northern coordinator for the Reverend Dr. Martin Luther King's Southern Christian Leadership Conference. As a student of the classics, Angelou recalled the experience of being asked by her teacher Mrs. Flowers to memorize and recite poetry: "I have often tried to search behind the sophistication of years for the enchantment I so easily found in those gifts."

—*Janie R. Isakson*

See Also:
Black Women

References:

Angelou, Maya. *All God's Children Need Traveling Shoes.* New York: Random House, 1986.

———. *Gather Together in My Name.* New York: Random House, 1974.

———. *The Heart of a Woman.* New York: Random House, 1981.

———. *I Know Why the Caged Bird Sings.* New York: Random House, 1970.

———. "No Longer Out of Africa." *Ms.* 14 (August 1986): 36–38.

———. *Singin' and Swingin' and Gettin' Merry like Christmas.* New York: Bantam, 1977

Christian, Barbara T. "Maya Angelou's African Sojourn Links Two Worlds." *Chicago Tribune* 6 (March 23, 1987): 37–38.

Gross, Robert A. "Growing Up Black." *Newsweek* 75 (March 2, 1970): 89–90.

ANTENUPTIAL AGREEMENTS, or marriage settlements, were made in early America in an effort to circumvent coverture, the merging of a woman's legal existence with that of her husband at marriage. A contract was signed before marriage, specifying the rights that a wife could continue to hold. Usually it gave a married woman some control over the property she brought to a marriage. Parents used this device to protect a daughter in the event she was widowed. It was more often utilized by a widow to protect her own wealth after remarriage.

A study of eighteenth-century Pennsylvania marriage settlements shows that at first antenuptial agreements were allowable only when placed in trust (supervised by a third party). Increasingly, the Pennsylvania courts recognized simple agreements between engaged couples; settlements made after marriage still required the administration of trustees. An examination of South Carolina marriage settlements indicates they were employed by 1 to 2 percent of all married couples, were largely confined to the upper classes, and involved property in personalty (which was not protected by common law) and slaves, rather than land.

Equity courts enforced marriage settlements, particularly in the late eighteenth and early nineteenth centuries when such settlements became more numerous.

—*Barbara E. Lacey*

See Also:
Coverture, Equity Courts, Marriage, Married Women's Property Acts

References:

Norton, Mary Beth. *Liberty's Daughters: The Revolutionary Experience of American Women, 1750–1800.* Boston: Little, Brown, 1980.

Salmon, Marylynn. "Equality or Submersion? Feme Covert Status in Early Pennsylvania." In *Women of America: A History,* edited by Carol Ruth Berkin and Mary Beth Norton. Boston: Houghton Mifflin, 1979, pp. 92–113.

———. *Women and the Law of Property in Early America.* Chapel Hill: University of North Carolina Press, 1986.

———. "Women and Property in South Carolina: The Evidence from Marriage Settlements, 1730–1830." *William and Mary Quarterly,* 3d ser., 39 (October 1982): 655–85.

ANTHONY, SUSAN B. (1820–1906), suffragist, was the preeminent organizer and strategist of the nineteenth-century agitation for woman's enfranchisement. From 1851, when she met suffragist Elizabeth Cady Stanton, until the end of her life Anthony worked full time to build a political movement among women and direct it toward gaining equal rights. Recognizing Anthony's significance early on, the federal government singled her out for prosecution when she voted in Rochester, New York, in 1872, while it ignored scores of women voting elsewhere. Persistence and intensity made her the symbol of political equality; a popular symbol, she inspired suffragists to coalesce for several decades until a mature political organization could grow.

Born in South Adams, Massachusetts, but associated primarily with her family's later home in Rochester, New York, Anthony received a Quaker education and taught school for a decade before finding her vocation in reform. In the 1850s she threw herself into mobilizing public opinion behind abolition and temperance as well as women's rights. After the Civil War, she singled out woman suffrage as her primary goal. Her personal and political lives were virtually inseparable. Political engagements dictated her yearly schedules, and for months at a time she stayed at hotels or the homes of co-workers, calling no place her home until 1890.

Anthony, along with Stanton, set goals for the National Woman Suffrage Association (NWSA) during postwar Reconstruction. Mindful of how quickly Republicans forgot the cause of women when the war ended, they insisted on an independent movement that would be free to help the party that helped the cause. This stance contributed to the formation of the rival, and soundly Republican, American Woman Suffrage Association in 1869.

The women of NWSA were Republican enough, however, to take the constitutional amendments of Reconstruction as their model of how woman suffrage should be won. A federal amendment offered women the surest protection and most significant recognition of equal rights. To attain a federal amendment, NWSA made Congress its target and met annually in Washington, D.C., where its members became proficient and familiar lobbyists.

In the 1880s Anthony built bridges between suffragists and the mushrooming woman's movement. She courted the Woman's Christian Temperance Union, directed the establishment of the International and National Councils of Women, and saw to it that by 1890 the two major suffrage organizations were united as the National American Woman Suffrage Assocation. Results were mixed. On the one hand, her constituency multiplied, but on the other, it became far more difficult to lead. Lacking the ideal of universal rights that had inspired the pioneers, the later suffrage movement combined various and often rival claims about how women should use the vote.

Eighty years old before she retired from the NAWSA presidency, Anthony kept her sights set on "the right protective of all other rights." She acted defensively to stop efforts to make the suffrage movement an instrument of policy. She appeared tolerant when the demand was to exclude Mormons and intolerant when the demand was to condemn racial discrimination. Nonetheless, she kept alive the dream and the demand for equal rights against half a century of male opposition and female indecisiveness.

—Ann D. Gordon

See Also:

American Woman Suffrage Association; National American Woman Suffrage Association; National Woman Suffrage Association; Stanton, Elizabeth Cady; Suffrage

References:

Anthony, Susan B., and Ida Husted Harper, eds. *History of Woman Suffrage.* Vol. 4. Rochester, 1902; rpt. New York: Arno, 1969.

Barry, Kathleen. *Susan B. Anthony.* New York: New York University Press, 1988.

Gordon, Ann D., and Patricia G. Holland, eds. *The Papers of Elizabeth Cady Stanton and Susan B. Anthony.* Microfilm ed. Wilmington, Del.: Scholarly Resources, forthcoming.

Harper, Ida Husted. *The Life and Work of Susan B. Anthony.* 3 vols. Indianapolis: Bowen-Merrill, 1898–1908; rpt. Salem, N.H.: Ayer, 1983.

Stanton, Elizabeth Cady, Susan B. Anthony, and Matilda Joslyn Gage, eds. *History of Woman Suffrage.* 3 vols. New York: Fowler & Wells, 1881–1887; rpt. New York: Arno, 1969.

ANTIFEMINISM. Twentieth-century women's historians use the term antifeminism to designate opposition to either the assumption or the advocacy of women's equality. An aspect of the political fundamentalism of the 1920s, antifeminism was most apparent in women's participation in the Ku Klux Klan and reflected the Klan's nativist concerns as well as a reaction to the potential freedom for woman inherent in the image of the flapper. After World War II, antifeminism in the late 1940s and 1950s focused upon the definition of the female psychology as quintessentially passive, a definition popularized by the postwar American disciples of Freud. The antifeminism of the 1970s and 1980s, however, criticized feminism and the movement for women's equality as lethal to the divinely ordained domestic role of woman within the patriarchal family unit. Thus, historically, antifeminism has arisen to defend the gender system in response to threats of public acceptance of a feminist definition of womanhood that promotes woman's autonomy at the expense of her duty to the family.

Categorically defining all feminist criticism of the cult of domesticity as neurotic, proponents of this Freudian-based antifeminism argued that they alone understood women's sexuality and therefore had the authority to define women's proper social (and economic) roles. World War II accelerated social and economic changes that presented women, even married ones, with new opportunities in education and employment, which the antifeminists decried as harmful to women and threatening to the survival of the family. Offering little more than a psychobabble version of the tried and true "biology is destiny" argument that relegated women to reproduction as the primary female function, antifeminists such as Helene Deutsch, Marynia Farnham, and Marie Robinson dismissed previous woman's rights advocates and any challenge to the "traditional" role of women as psychologically deviant. Their own interpretation of womanhood used Freudian theory to justify sexual inequality as both natural and biologically unavoidable. There was no scientific evidence to support their definition of women as castrated males, pathetic masochistic narcissists capable of sexual fulfillment only through the (so-called) vaginal orgasm and of personal fulfillment solely through motherhood. The antifeminists of the 1940s and 1950s were thus the primary architects of the new cult of motherhood that became the "feminine mystique."

In response to the resurgence of the women's movement in the 1960s, antifeminism in the 1970s focused its defense of the cult of domesticity on women's inescapable responsibility to fulfill the maternal role if the patriarchal family were to survive as the basic unit of society. There was a strain of political fundamentalism in the view of women's liberation as a threat to traditional sex roles. Antifeminists such as Phyllis Schlafly and Mirabelle Morgan were forced to accommodate their definition of women's role and "total womanhood" to the social and economic changes in American society in the 1970s, changes that brought more and more middle-class women into the labor force, regardless of their marital status or political persuasion. Nevertheless, the antifeminists clung to their emphasis upon the necessity and propriety of women's maternal destiny and subordination within the family. Evoking the twin specters of divorce and the displaced homemaker to politicize a group strongly identified with traditional apolitical domesticity, the antifeminists used a "pro-family" as well as an antiabortion fixation to recruit conservative middle-class housewives to their cause. Thus for the women of the conservative New Right, no less than for the women of the New Left, the personal was political. Moreover, antifeminist leaders ultimately coopted the effective strategies of their feminist opponents, as well as of their political opponents in the antiwar movement, to pursue their goal of preserving woman's traditional role.

By the 1980s, antifeminism represented the concerns of a vocal minority that championed a Protestant fundamentalist interpretation of woman's proper role. After the failure of the effort to ratify the Equal Rights Amendment, the national leadership of antifeminism reflected a shift in focus from the political conservatism of Phyllis Schlafly's Eagle Forum to the religious fundamentalism of Beverly La Haye's Concerned Women for America. Whereas Schlafly had risen to national prominence through her association with the causes of the far-right John Birch Society, La Haye was the wife of the West Coast television evangelist Tim La Haye, and her group wore a militantly "Christian" outlook, rather like the female auxiliary of Jerry Falwell's Moral Majority.

Thus the intensity of antifeminism through the twentieth century has increased proportionally as national economic and political trends have altered the nature and function of the nuclear family and as opportunities for women have increased. While antifeminism has consistently argued that its opinion that women are to be subordinated to men in the patriarchal family represents the concern of the majority, in fact antifeminism has not been a mainstream movement and has not represented the consensus of American public opinion on women's issues.

—Angela Howard Zophy

See Also:

Antisuffragism; Flapper; Freudianism; Modern Woman: The Lost Sex; Right-Wing Political Movements; Schlafly, Phyllis

References:

Conover, Pamela J., and Virginia Gray. *Feminism and the New Right: Conflict Over the American Family.* New York: Praeger, 1983.

Daniel, Robert L. *American Women in the 20th Century: The Festival of Life.* San Diego: Harcourt, Brace, Jovanovich, 1987.

Dexter, Midge. *The New Chastity and Other Arguments Against Women's Liberation.* New York: Coward, McCann and Geoghegan, 1972.

McElroy, Wendy. *Freedom, Feminism, and the State.* Washington, D.C.: CATO Institute, 1982.

Mitchell, Juliet. *Psychoanalysis and Feminism.* New York: Vintage, 1975.

Ryan, Mary P. *Womanhood in America: From Colonial Times to the Present.* 3d ed. New York: New Viewpoints /Franklin Watts, 1984.

Schlafly, Phyllis. *The Power of the Positive Woman.* New York: Jove, 1977.

ANTISUFFRAGISM, a predominantly female movement to oppose the enfranchisement of women, began with state organizations in Massachusetts (1895) and New York (1896) and eventually spread to more than twenty states. In 1911 the National Association Opposed to Woman Suffrage (NAOWS) was formed in New York with Mrs. Josephine Dodge as president. Opposition to woman suffrage was also promoted by separate male organizations, such as the Man-Suffrage Associations in various states and the national American Constitutional League, as well as by conservative ethnic and religious groups and by business and liquor interests.

As a group, antisuffrage leaders were Protestant middle-class, middle-aged women who were less well educated and more religiously conservative than suffragists. In legislative testimony, petitions, and publications such as the *Remonstrance* (1890–1920), the *Anti-Suffragist* (1908–11), and the *Woman's Protest* (1912–18), they rejected suffragists' claims to sex equality. Although they participated in many of the same social welfare activities as suffragists, antisuffragists argued from immutable biological and theological laws that women could best effect reform through their influence within the patriarchal nuclear family, which they claimed to be the basis of social order.

In 1917, for reasons that remain unclear, NAOWS headquarters moved to Washington, D.C., and new leadership emerged that accorded more influence in the organization to men. The *Woman's Protest* was replaced by the *Woman Patriot*, and reasoned arguments about the place of women in society gave way to vituperative accusations linking women's feminist and pacifist activities to radicalism, socialism, and treason. After ratification of the Nineteenth Amendment, antisuffragists, calling themselves the Woman Patriots, continued to oppose federal welfare legislation through the 1920s.

—Joyce Follet

See Also:

Antifeminism, Suffrage

References:

Camhi, Jane Jerome. "Women Against Women: Anti-Suffragism, 1880–1920." Diss. Tufts University, 1973.

Jablonsky, Thomas James. "Duty, Nature and Stability: The Female Anti-Suffragists in the United States, 1894–1920." Diss. University of Southern California, 1978.

Kenneally, James J. "The Opposition to Woman Suffrage in Massachusetts, 1868–1920." Diss. Boston College, 1963.

Kraditor, Aileen S. *The Ideas of the Woman Suffrage Movement, 1890–1920*. New York: Columbia University Press, 1965.

ARBUS, DIANE NEMEROV (1923–71), photographer, has become renowned in the history of American culture for her images of the abnormal, the grotesque, and the eccentric. In her work there seems to be little difference between a suburban couple posed on their lawn and a family of midgets in their New York apartment.

Arbus was born in New York City, one of three children of David and Gertrude Nemerov. Her well-to-do father owned the fashionable women's department store, Russeks Fifth Avenue, and throughout much of her life Arbus rebelled against a background that relied heavily upon the trappings of middle-class success. The Nemerov children were educated at the progressive New York private school Fieldston. Arbus never went to college although she did study fashion design for a short time. At eighteen she married Allan Arbus, a photographer who later became an actor, and the couple had two daughters. The Arbuses worked together as fashion photographers and became prominent in that field. Diane, however, grew to hate fashion work and eventually developed the distinctive artistic vision that made her famous.

Between 1958 and 1960 she studied with the Austrian-born social documentary photographer Lisette Model, and this experience had a major impact on her work. Around this time Arbus turned her attention to subjects considered to be "forbidden"—midgets, giants, transvestites, street people, drug addicts, nudists. During the 1960s she also photographed celebrities. Norman Mailer, Andy Warhol, Susan Sontag, and Mae West were among the many artists, writers, and film stars whom she recorded. Many of these images appeared in major publications such as *Vogue, Harper's Bazaar*, the *New York Times*, and *Esquire*.

In order to supplement her income, Arbus taught photography from 1965 to 1971 at Parson School of Design, Cooper Union, and Hampshire College. She received two Guggenheim fellowships (1963, 1966), and her work was the subject of an exhibition at the Museum of Modern Art in 1967. Arbus gained recognition both within the artistic world and the general public, but despite the acclaim, she committed suicide in 1971. A major retrospective of Diane Arbus photographs opened at the Museum of Modern Art in 1972 and traveled throughout the United States and Europe, attesting to her status as a great force in the world of photography.

—C. Jane Gover

See Also:

Photography

References:

Bosworth, Patricia. *Diane Arbus*. New York: Avon, 1984.

Tucker, Anne, ed. *The Woman's Eye*. New York: Knopf, 1973.

ARCHIVES AND SOURCES. The most renowned repository for primary and secondary works in American women's history is the Arthur and Elizabeth Schlesinger Library at Radcliffe College. Established in 1943, by 1988 the library housed some twenty-five thousand published volumes, hundreds of periodicals, extensive microform holdings, clipping and pamphlet files, and a rich collection of primary documents. Among the latter are personal papers of notable women, archives of organizations, diaries, letters, oral histories, and photographs. The library's collecting policy emphasizes suffrage, feminism, and women's rights; social welfare and reform; women in medicine, politics, government, education, law, and the labor movement; women's organizations; and the history of the family. A special Culinary Collection houses both historic cookbooks and recipes in manuscript. Recently, library staff have made a concerted effort to gather materials reflecting the lives and experiences of "ordinary" women, the progress of the contemporary women's movement, and the academic practice of women's history.

The Sophia Smith Collection at Smith College rivals the Schlesinger. Likewise founded in the forties, the Smith Collection consists of some one hundred thousand books, manuscripts, diaries, letters, and memorabilia; its scope is international. Other library collections specialize in a locale, period, or subject. The Woman's Collection at Texas Woman's University, for example, emphasizes the lives and accomplishments of Texan women; the Cairns Collection of American Women Writers at the University of Wisconsin-Madison documents the writing and publishing activities of women authors, primarily in the nineteenth century; the Medical College of Pennsylvania concentrates on the history of women physicians in its Archives and Special Collections on Women in Medicine.

Many libraries not devoted solely to women's materials hold valuable resources for feminist scholars. The Library of Congress, the nation's largest repository of printed books, retains important manuscript items as well, including the personal papers of prominent suffragists and reformers. Records of the National American Woman Suffrage Association, the National Women's party, and the League of Women Voters have also been deposited at the Library of Congress; and its Prints and Photographs Division is a central source of visual documentation in American women's history. On a smaller scale, many historical agencies and state libraries house manuscripts, organizational and governmental archives, memorabilia, and locally printed materials on women; some, such as the State Historical Society of Wisconsin, have issued comprehensive guides to their collections.

Even with this wealth of resources, the lives of black American women remain inadequately documented. The Bethune Museum-Archives in Washington, D.C., helps to correct this imbalance by making available the nation's largest collection of manuscripts on the contributions of individual black women and black women's associations. The Schlesinger Library has sponsored the Black Woman Oral History Project, recording and transcribing the life stories of numerous influential older black women. And in the 1980s, the Black Women in the Middle West Project began assembling primary materials for the history of black women in Illinois and Indiana.

Lesbians—another underrepresented group—work to recover their heritage through regional, grassroots archives. The Lesbian Herstory Archives in New York City and the West Coast Lesbian Collections in Oakland, California, gather both personal and organizational materials, including rare photographs, and publicize their holdings in irregular newsletters. Activists in many areas of the country have created similar smaller repositories dedicated to preserving local gay history.

Access to archives for women's history is improving. *Women's History Sources* (Bowker, 1978), edited by Andrea Hinding, is a landmark volume, identifying more than eighteen thousand collections of archives and manuscripts in some sixteen hundred libraries and repositories in the United States. Indexed by name and subject, it points to both materials on individual women and records of women's organizations, with brief descriptions of the content and scope of each collection. Another vital finding aid is *Women's*

Periodicals and Newspapers from the 19th Century to 1981 (G. K. Hall, 1982), offering full bibliographic and location data for nearly fifteen hundred periodicals, accompanied by a variety of indexes and chronological charts.

Microfilming offers a solution to the problem of preserving and disseminating unique primary materials. Several important collections are now available in microformat. Foremost among them is the *History of Women*, a set comprising some 8,500 printed books, 2,000 pamphlets, 117 periodicals, 80,000 pages of manuscript materials, and 800 photographs—all relating to American and European women through 1920. The collection draws heavily on holdings of the Schlesinger Library and the Sophia Smith Collection, but also incorporates items from the Jane Addams Hull House Library, the Miriam Y. Holden Collection (now at Princeton), the New York Public Library, the Boston Public Library, the Macpherson Collection at Scripps College, and the libraries of Harvard and Yale. Another valuable microform set is the *Gerritsen Collection of Women's History, 1543–1945*, reproducing an international library first assembled privately in Holland in the late nineteenth century and now housed at the University of Kansas. For the recent history of women's liberation, the *Herstory* microfilms are essential resources. They reproduce women's newsletters, journals, and newspapers from 1956 to 1974; supplemental sets entitled *Women and Law* and *Women and Health/Mental Health* group clippings, articles, pamphlets, and other documents by topic. Other key microform sources include *The Cornell University Collection of Women's Rights Pamphlets, Pamphlets in American History: Women*, and *Periodicals on Women and Women's Rights.*

Automation promises to enhance scholarly access to primary documents. RLIN and OCLC (on-line cataloging networks linking major American libraries) and developing data-bases of archival holdings offer more powerful information retrieval capabilities than comparable printed sources. The National Council for Research on Women, a coalition of women's studies research centers, is also taking steps to develop a national information network for feminist scholars. And the standard two-volume guide to the secondary literature—*Women in American History* (ABC-Clio, 1979, 1985)—draws its abstracts from a computerized bibliographic data-base.

—*Susan E. Searing*

References:

Catalogs of the Sophia Smith Collection, Women's History Archive, Smith College, Northampton, Massachusetts. 7 vols. Boston: G. K. Hall, 1975. *Supplement*, by Mary-Elizabeth Murdock. Northampton, Mass.: Smith College, 1984.

Hildebrand, Suzanne, ed. *Women's Collections: Libraries, Archives, and Consciousness.* New York: Haworth, 1986.

Manuscripts and Pictures of the Arthur and Elizabeth Schlesinger Library. 10 vols. Boston: G. K. Hall, 1983.

King, Patricia Miller. "Fortieth Anniversary Report: The Arthur and Elizabeth Schlesinger Library on the History of Women in America." Cambridge, Mass.: Schlesinger Library, 1983.

Nolen, Anita Lonnes. "The Feminine Presence: Women's Papers in the Manuscript Division." *Quarterly Journal of the Library of Congress* 32 (October 1975): 348–65.

ARENDT, HANNAH (1906–75) was an editor, educator, social worker, political theorist, and philosopher. She was born in Hannover, Germany, and matriculated at Marburg and Freiburg. Arendt completed her Ph.D. at Heidelberg, where she studied under Karl Jaspers. When Hitler and the Nazis took power in 1933, she fled to Paris and did social work for Youth Aliyah, a relief organization placing Jewish orphans. With the fall of France to the Nazis in 1940, Arendt was again forced to flee, this time to the United States.

In the United States Arendt found work as a research director for the Conference on Jewish Relations. She then became head editor for Schocken Books. Between 1949 and 1952 she served as the executive secretary of the Jewish Cultural Reconstruction, a group that collected and relocated Jewish writings dispersed by the Nazis. Then she entered into the academy in America and was the first woman appointed a full professor at Princeton University. Arendt also taught at Brooklyn College, the University of Chicago, the University of California at Berkeley, and finally at the New School for Social Research in New York. Arendt became famous for her controversial writings, in which she argued that revolution and war constitute the central forces of our time. A naturalized citizen since 1950, Arendt was one of the most influential postwar academics.

—*Jonathan W. Zophy*

See Also:
Jewish Women, World War II

References:

Arendt, Hannah. *On Revolution.* New York: Harcourt Brace, 1958.
———. *The Human Condition.* Chicago: University of Chicago Press, 1958.
———. *On Violence.* New York: Faber, 1962.
———. *The Origins of Totalitarianism.* 3 vols. New York: Harcourt Brace, 1951.
Contemporary Authors, Detroit: Gale, 1976.
Young-Bruehl, Elisabeth. *For Love of the World.* New Haven: Yale University Press, 1982.

The **ARMY NURSE CORPS** was created in recognition of the need for military nurses during the Spanish-American War. Some military personnel maintained that untrained corpsmen actually helped to spread disease, so military leaders and the surgeon general started lobbying for the creation of a nurse corps. Dr. Anita Newcomb McGee, a practicing physician, was instrumental in coordinating nursing efforts during the Spanish-American War and in selecting the ANC's first superintendent, Mrs. Dita Kenney, a forty-four-year-old widowed nurse. The Army created the first nurse corps in 1901; the Navy followed suit in 1908. Poor pay, high educational requirements, and inadequate leadership stifled enlistment efforts for the first decade of the corps' existence. By World War I the ANC had been reorganized, nurses' pay was increased, and the Red Cross was designated as the ANC's reserve in case of war.

Nurses had to lobby for years to gain a rank commensurate with their skills and to improve their status. From the beginning, it was assumed that nurses would not be associated with enlisted personnel. But their initial status was similar to that of a cadet. Finally, in 1920 they were granted "relative rank," or approximate rank, which meant that women officers were designated as having the same rank as men officers in the Army and Navy but not the same pay or benefits normally associated with that rank. It was not until 1944 that nurses gained the same rank and status as the men (see WAAC, WAC, WAVES for a different model). Disability benefits were granted ANC members for the first time in 1926.

During World War I, at peak strength, 8,538 nurses served with the American Expeditionary Forces in Europe. At peak strength during World War II, 47,000 nurses served in the Army Nurse Corps. While exact figures are unknown, nurses also served in large numbers during the Korean War and Vietnam War.

In 1955 male nurses were allowed to join the ANC. Until then the men had to serve as corpsmen, without hope of becoming officers. While less than 4 percent of all nurses in the United States are male, 25 percent of today's ANC is male. In part this is a tribute to the excellent benefits and high status that the ANC has been able to achieve as compared with civilian nursing.

Nursing came of age during World War II when the American Nursing Association replaced the American Red Cross as the premier advocate for nurses. Veteran nurses had a rude shock when they returned to America after World War II; they were offered low-paying, low-status positions, whereas in the Army and Navy, because of the shortage of doctors, they had been doing highly responsible work.

—*D'Ann Campbell*

See Also:
Military Service, Nursing

References:

Aynes, Edith A. *From Nightingale to Eagle—An Army Nurse's History.* Englewood Cliffs, N.J.: Prentice-Hall, 1973.

Blanchfield, Florence A., and Mary Standlee. "Organized Nursing and the Army in Three Wars." Unpublished manuscript on file in U.S. Army Medical Department, Historical Unit, Washington, D.C.

Campbell, D'Ann. *Women at War with America: Private Lives in a Patriotic Era.* Cambridge: Harvard University Press, 1984.

Flikke, Julia, Col. A.U.S. (ret.). *Nurse in Action.* Philadelphia: J. B. Lippincott, 1943.

Kalisch, Philip A., and Beatrice Kalisch. *The Advance of American Nursing.* Boston: Little, Brown, 1978.

Maxwell, Pauline. "History of the Army Nurse Corps." Unpublished multivolume history housed at the Center for Military History, Washington D.C. [The ANC has commissioned a history that will draw heavily on Maxwell's materials.]

Redmond, Juanita. *I Served on Bataan.* Philadelphia: J. B. Lippincott, 1943.

Roberts, Mary. *American Nursing: History and Interpretation.* New York: Macmillan, 1954.

Shields, Elizabeth A. "A History of the United States Army Nurse Corps (Female): 1901–1937." Diss. Columbia University Teachers College, 1980.

U.S. Department of the Army. Medical Department. *Highlights on the History of the Army Nurse Corps.* Washington, D.C., 1975.

ART. Women have contributed to every major art movement between America's shores. From the work of the first Native American women who incorporated geometric abstract designs in their weaving, pottery, painted leather, beadwork, and quillwork, to the latest developments in contemporary art, American women have displayed their talents.

Although life for colonial women left little leisure time for art, they channeled their creativity into practical and strikingly beautiful works of stitchery, woven rugs, and quilts. One such woman, Henrietta Deering Johnston, was America's first pastel artist, completing over forty pastel portraits of the leading citizens of Charleston, South Carolina. Considered America's first sculptor, Patience Lovell Wright (1725–86) modeled life-size portraits in wax. Unfortunately, documentation of other women artists during colonial times through the eighteenth century remains scant.

The first artistic field into which a significant number of women entered was miniature painting, a style popular in the late eighteenth and early nineteenth centuries. Miniature painting attracted women artists who lacked access to studio space and materials. Women artists' limited training at this time also led them to concentrate on the face or on bust-length poses. One of the earliest miniaturists, Ann Hall of Pomfret, Connecticut, exhibited in New York City as early as 1817. Hall also had the distinction of being the first woman to become a full member of the National Academy of Design. Other miniaturists included Sarah Goodridge, Anna Claypoole Peale, Mary Ann Hardy, and Lucia Fuller.

By the beginning of the nineteenth century, evidence suggests, the number of women artists substantially increased. At this time nearly all of them were related to male artists—fathers, brothers, and uncles—who practiced art, recognized their talents, and shared studios with them. The best example of an artistically supportive family is the Peale family, in which the daughters of artist James Peale and nieces of artist Charles Willson Peale assisted and learned from their relatives. Without access to studios and built-in family instruction, other American women artists were left on their own to perfect their artistic talents.

Although the Pennsylvania Academy of the Fine Arts allowed women to exhibit in annual shows since its conception in 1805, the first documentation of women students in an American art school is not until 1844. At this time, women's drawing from a live nude model was unthinkable, but the Pennsylvania Academy did permit the women students to draw from nude antique plaster casts for one hour on Monday, Wednesday, and Friday in a segregated class. In 1856 "Ladies Day" was abolished and women drew from the plaster casts of the Apollo Belvedere and Laocoön with the men, but not before the instructor placed a "close-fitting but inconspicuous fig-leaf" on the offending works.

By 1868 the Pennsylvania Academy established the first Ladies Life Class with a live nude female model, a class that Alice Barber Stephens depicted ten years later in her work *Female Life Class.* The academy regularly used nude male models in 1877, but was severely criticized by the public for allowing young ladies to view nude models. Thomas Eakins, who instituted an experimental life drawing class in the 1870s, was dismissed from the academy in 1886 when he removed the loincloth from a male model in an anatomy lecture before a mixed audience.

The conservative National Academy of Design in New York permitted women students to attend its Antique School (drawing from casts) in 1831, but regular enrollment of female students did not occur until 1846. A women's life drawing class opened in 1871, but women could not attend anatomy lectures until 1914. From 1825 to 1953 the National Academy of Design offered membership and associate membership to only seventy-five women of a total of 1,300 members. A more liberal institution in New York, the Art Students League, which opened in 1875, not only included women art students but placed women on its governing board.

Without mastery of anatomy and human proportion, women artists focused primarily on still life and portraiture, which in the hierarchy of the art world were considered far less important than history painting. History painting depicted biblical, mythological, and historical themes in complicated compositions involving many human figures. Once admitted to art institutions and life drawing classes, women had the opportunity to master the human figure for historical painting.

As America expanded westward, new schools such as the Cincinnati Art Academy, St. Louis Art Academy, and Art Institute of Chicago became available to women. Also contributing to the expansion of artistic opportunities was the spread of the women's club movement into the arts. Associations and groups of women artists formed all across the country. The membership of the National Association of Women Painters and Sculptors in America grew large enough to administer its own academy, sponsor exhibits, and fund scholarships. In 1876 a community of women pioneered the Women's Pavilion at the Philadelphia Centennial Exposition. Displayed along with other accomplishments by women, the art dominated the all-female exhibition space. In 1893, at the Women's Building at the Chicago World's Columbian Exposition, major sculpture and painting commissions enabled women like Mary Cassatt and Mary MacMonnies, who painted a monumental mural in the great hall, to produce works of great scale.

In sculpture in the mid-nineteenth century, a maverick group of American women left the United States for Rome to work in the neoclassical style. They chose Rome because it offered an excellent source of marble, readily available trained artisans, and inexpensive living conditions. Harriet Hosmer, for example, arrived in Rome in 1852 and studied with the leading English sculptor John Gibson. Other women artists joined her. Emma Stebbins and Vinnie Ream Hoxie used the skills they mastered in Rome to garner major commissions in the United States. Stebbins's work *Angel of the Water* still remains in New York's Central Park today. These women, along with Edmonia Lewis, Margaret Foley, Louisa Landers, Elizabet Ney, Anne Whitney, and fellow male sculptors helped create the first major school of American neoclassical sculpture.

During the last quarter of the century, another wave of American women participated in the major art movement called impressionism. In Europe, particularly in France, artists moved their canvases outdoors and developed the en plein air technique to capture the effects of natural light. Devoted to light and color, impressionism is characterized by loose brushstrokes, thick application of paint, and interest in everyday subject matter as opposed to the historical subjects of past realism. Among the American women artists who traveled to France to explore the avant-garde technique were Mary Cassatt, Cecilia Beaux, Lilla Cabot Perry, and Elizabeth Nourse.

By the close of the nineteenth century, women's position within the artistic community had clearly changed. Educational opportunities had opened up and, increasingly, women entered art institutions, traveled abroad, and received awards and commissions for their work. The year 1895 also saw the first woman professor of art, Cecilia Beaux, at the Pennsylvania Academy of the Fine Arts.

Twentieth-century America dramatically altered, and art reflected those changes. Neither past realism nor avant-garde impressionism could adequately express the pace and clamor of industrial society. Skyscrapers, speedy trains, bright city lights, photography, factories and their poor working conditions, waves of homeless immigrants, and the insights of Einstein, Freud, and Marx—all affected America and its art scene as well. Like changing seasonal fashions, art movements matched the fast pace. The first of the shocking new art waves was the Ash Can School of 1908. Ash Can artists portrayed street life and the slums of New York realistically, departing from the color and light of the impressionists in their severe examination of the dirty urbanization of America.

A prominent Ash Can sculptor, Mary Abastenia St. Leger Eberle (1878-1942) moved to New York from Ohio to study at the Art Students League, sharing a studio with another sculptor, Anna Hyatt Huntington. Eberle furthered her studies in Europe and returned to take trips into Manhattan's Lower East Side, which inspired her compassionate and lively works. Eberle's sculptures, small-scale bronzes, evoke motion—a child roller skating or an immigrant woman sweeping. Other women painters and illustrators in the Ash Can School included May Wilson Preston, Florence Shinn, Marjorie Organ, and Marianna Sloan.

The 1913 Armory Show in New York City brought radical American and European styles such as cubism and fauvism to the American public. More than forty American women participated in the Armory Show, including Marguerite Thompson Zorach.

The development of new exhibition spaces, as well as exposure to the modernists, helped foster a more egalitarian environment for women artists. The authority of the traditional art institutions was challenged by such galleries as Alfred Stieglitz's "291." The first nonphotographic art exhibited, in January 1907, was that of artist Pamela Coleman Smith. "291" also showed the work of photographers Gertrude Kasebier and Alice Boughton. Painters such as Marion H. Beckett, Katherine N. Rhodes, and Georgia O'Keeffe gained valuable exposure from such galleries, and other women found encouragement in the liberal environment of the New York School of Art (later the Art Students League) studying with Henri and William Merritt Chase.

The woman suffrage movement during the early 1900s, together with the rise of labor unions and women's clubs, contributed to women's self-awareness and feelings of independence. Katherine Dreier, a modernist-cubist painter, opened the Société Anonyme with Marcel Duchamp in 1920. It was the first gallery devoted entirely to modern art. Dreier's collection now forms the core of Yale University's modern art.

Promoter, patron, and sculptor, Gertrude Vanderbilt Whitney founded the Whitney Studio Club in New York. Here artists met, shared creative talents, and displayed their works. In 1931 she opened the Whitney Museum of American Art, devoted to America's avant-garde. As a sculptor, Whitney produced many works herself and won the *Titanic Memorial* commission in 1931 in Washington, D.C.

As American art expanded, women continued as forerunners in major movements. New materials and techniques opened new avenues for artistic expression. Canvases expanded, and color, line, and form dominated compositions.

In 1952 Helen Frankenthaler took an unprimed canvas and poured paint on it. Without the gesso, the paint soaked into the surface, staining the canvas. This piece, *Mountains and Sea*, began a whole new art movement called color-field or stain painting. Modern landscapes continued to be a theme for Frankenthaler as she allowed the pigments to flow and create their own shapes and forms. Frankenthaler's technique inspired others, namely, Morris Louis and Kenneth Noland.

Surrealists Kay Sage and Dorothea Tanning contributed to America's interest in this mysterious movement. Lee Krasner and Joni Mitchell both practiced abstract expressionism, while Alma Thomas experimented with blocks of color, allowing a bit of the canvas to show through. America's renewed interest in the figure is partly due to the work of artists Elaine de Kooning, Marcia Marcus, and Grace Hartigan.

In sculpture, Louise Nevelson used scraps of wood to create unique environmental works. Lee Bontcou, Anna Hyatt Huntington, Marisol, and Anne Truitt all employed a variety of materials in their sculptures.

American women continue to make history with their artistic endeavors. The opening of the National Museum of Women in the Arts in 1987 with over eighty thousand members both celebrates women artists and encourages scholarship on the subject. Only through increased research, exhibitions, and continued integration into art history will the full impact of women artists on art in America be realized.

—Cynthia Lynn Gould

See Also:

Beaux, Cecilia; Cassatt, Mary; Dreier, Katherine; Hosmer, Harriet; Hoxie, Vinnie Ream; Johnston, Henrietta Deering; Kasebier, Gertrude; O'Keeffe, Georgia; Lewis, Edmonia; National Museum of Women in the Arts; Peale Family; World's Columbian Exhibition; Zorach, Marguerite Thompson

References:

Gerdts, William H. *Women Artists of America, 1707–1964*. Newark, N.J.: The Newark Museum, 1965.

Greer, Germaine. *The Fortunes of Women Painters and Their Work*. London: Farrar, Straus, & Giroux, 1979.

Harris, Ann Sutherland, and Linda Nochlin. *Women Artists: 1550–1950*. New York: Knopf, 1976.

Parker, Rozsica, and Griselda Pollack. *Old Mistresses: Women, Art, and Ideology*. New York: Pantheon, 1981.

Rubenstein, Charlotte Streifer. *American Women Artists from Early Indian Times to the Present*. Boston: G. K. Hall, 1982.

Tufts, Eleanor. *American Women Artists, 1830–1930*. Washington, D.C.: National Museum of Women in the Arts, 1987.

ARZNER, DOROTHY (1900–79), along with Lois Weber and Ida Lupino, was one of the few women to direct more than a single major film between 1925 and 1960. Many of her films addressed women's issues of the period when she was most active (1927–42) and have been at the heart of the recent reexamination of the Hollywood feature film by feminist critics.

After a childhood on the fringes of the developing California film colony, Arzner left the study of medicine at the University of California shortly after World War I to enter the film industry. She worked her way up through the already rigidly defined segregated crafts system; patterns of promotion for women were circumscribed, but nonetheless offered more genuine opportunity than was possible in the post-sound film era. Arzner began as a script typist, and moved on to become a manuscript reader, script girl, cutter, and finally editor in chief and scenario writer. Her work on such films as James Cruze's *The Covered Wagon* (1923) gained her a directing opportunity at Paramount Studios.

When her first film, *Fashions for Women* (1927), was a success, Arzner was typed as a "women's film" specialist—which suited her. "The greater part of the motion picture audience is feminine," she said in a 1936 interview. "Box office appeal is thought of largely in terms of the women lined up at the ticket window. If there are no women directors, there ought to be." In silent films with Esther Ralston and Clara Bow, Arzner became a key figure in dramatizing "the new attention to sexuality [that] colored a whole range of related behavior" (Fass 279).

Arzner's career from 1930 to 1943 was spent free-lancing at different studios. Her work with Joan Crawford, Rosalind Russell, Katharine Hepburn, and others during this period includes direct and often lyrical examinations of the many paradoxes 1920s feminism had brought to light. Films such as *Merrily We Go to Hell* (1932), *Craig's Wife* (1936), and *Christopher Strong* (1933) display her ability to rechannel the currents of the melodramatic "woman's film" away from sexist ideological obstacles into the realm of ambiguity, even outright feminist posturing.

Cast by the popular media as an "exotic" in the Hollywood community, Arzner seems to have viewed her career with almost clinical detachment. Her greatest work, *Dance, Girl, Dance* (1940), reflects this objectivity; it is a near-Brechtian analysis of the nature of celebrity and the power and manipulative potential of sexual representation—all set in a Brooklyn vaudeville house.

Saying she had "had enough" of the film industry, Arzner finished her career by directing WAC training shorts during World War II. In the years to follow, she directed television commercials and set up filmmaking programs at UCLA and the Pasadena Playhouse.

Dance, Girl, Dance was a crucial text in the renaissance of interest in mainstream women's filmmaking that developed in the early 1970s. Tributes to her work (by the Directors Guild and many film festivals, including the Créteil International Film Festival in 1986) continue, and Arzner lived long enough to see her films accorded the status of legitimate feminist artworks.

—*Kevin Jack Hagopian*

See Also:

Hepburn, Katharine; Lupino, Ida; Weber, Lois; Woman's Film

References:

"Distaff Side Director." *The New York Times Magazine* (September 27, 1936) X4: 4.

Fass, Paula. *The Damned and the Beautiful: American Youth in the 1920's*. Oxford: Oxford University Press, 1977.

"Hommage à Dorothy Arzner." In *Films de Femmes: Festival International de Créteil 8°, 1986*. Créteil, France: International Women's Film Festival, 1986, pp. 39–45.

Johnston, Claire, ed. *Notes on Women's Cinema*. London: Society for Education in Film and Television, n.d.

ASHBRIDGE, ELIZABETH SAMPSON (1713-1755), Quaker preacher and American autobiographer, wrote a personal narrative of her early years and her conversion to the Quaker faith, *Some Account of the Fore-Part of the Life of Elizabeth Ashbridge*, that serves as the main source of information about her life. Numerous editions of this narrrative were printed throughout the nineteenth and early twentieth centuries, with some minor variations in the title, and it is important for the challenges it poses to traditional understandings of early British North America, shaped largely from primary documents written by male members of the dominant Puritan culture. Ashbridge's narrative documents a life lived outside the dominant culture and provides the perspective of someone marginalized by her religious beliefs as well as by her gender.

Born in England the only child of Thomas and Mary Sampson, Ashbridge eloped at age fourteen against her parents' wishes and was thereby estranged from her father. Widowed only a few months after her marriage, she was unable to return to her childhood home and went instead to live with relatives in Ireland. In 1732 she emigrated to New York as an indentured servant and began a period of servitude to a master who treated her cruelly. Owing to her skill at needlework, she earned enough money to pay off the last year of her indentureship, and a few months after gaining her freedom she married a man named Sullivan, who was attracted to her because of her ability to dance.

Throughout her marriage to Sullivan,

Ashbridge, dissatisfied with her Anglican heritage, explored a variety of religions. Her search ended during a visit to relatives in Pennsylvania, where she encountered Quaker teachings. Her conversion to the Quaker faith and the accompanying changes in her life-style occasioned abusive behavior by her husband, and her life became a series of daily trials during which her faith grew.

In 1746, after Sullivan's death in Cuba where he refused to engage in combat even though he had enlisted in the British army, Ashbridge married her third husband. Aaron Ashbridge, a Quaker, shared her religious convictions and supported her work as an itinerant preacher. Her preaching took her to Ireland in 1753, where she remained until her death.

—*Cristine M. Levenduski*

See Also:
Society of Friends

References:

Ashbridge, Elizabeth. *Some Account of the Fore-Part of the Life of Elizabeth Ashbridge.* Nantwich, England: J. Bromley, 1774.

Shea, Daniel B. *Spiritual Autobiography in Early America.* Princeton, N.J.: Princeton University Press, 1968.

ASIAN AMERICAN WOMEN include women whose ancestral background links them to China, Japan, Korea, the Philippines, India, Pakistan, Bangladesh, Thailand, Vietnam, Laos, Kampuchea, and a dozen other Asian countries. Although ethnically diverse, Asian American women share a common history as women of color in the United States that makes them a distinct racial and political entity among Americans.

The Chinese were the first Asians to emigrate to the United States. Driven overseas by war and poverty in China during the time of the California gold rush, early Chinese sojourners, who intended to strike it rich and return home, did not bring their families with them. Cultural restrictions at home, lack of traveling funds, and anti-Chinese violence in the West further discouraged the early immigration of women. Only the merchant class, which made up less than 1 percent of the immigrant population, could afford to bring their wives, children, and domestic servants to America. In 1860 there were only 1,784 Chinese women among 33,149 Chinese men.

This sexual imbalance, combined with antimiscegenation attitudes and laws that discouraged Asian men from marrying white women, created a demand for prostitution. Most white prostitutes were independent professionals or worked in brothels for wages, but Chinese prostitutes, who formed an estimated 85 percent of the Chinese female population in San Francisco in 1860 and 71 percent in 1870, were almost always indentured servants who had been kidnapped, lured, or purchased from poor parents in China and resold in America for high profits. Treated as chattel and subjected to physical and mental abuse, the average prostitute did not outlive her contract term of four to five years. Some were redeemed by wealthy clients; others sought refuge at Protestant mission homes and were later married to Chinese Christians. By 1900 organized prostitution had declined due to antiprostitution laws, the Chinese Exclusion Act of 1882, which barred the further entry of Chinese laborers and their families, and successful rescue raids by Protestant missionaries.

Although a few women other than prostitutes did emigrate alone, most of the remaining Chinese women were wives who lived in urban Chinatowns or in remote rural areas where their husbands could find work. Following Chinese decorum, Chinatown wives seldom left their homes, where, in addition to housework and caring for their children, they often worked for low wages—sewing, washing, rolling cigars, and making slippers and brooms. In rural areas, Chinese wives also tended livestock and vegetable gardens, hauled in the catch and dried seafood for export, or took in boarders to help with the family income. Regardless of their residence or their husbands' social status, Chinese immigrant wives led hard-working lives and remained subordinate to their husbands and confined to the domestic sphere.

The second Asian group to emigrate to the United States in large numbers was the Japanese, followed by the Koreans and Filipinos. Just as there were few Chinese women in the United States at first, few Japanese women emigrated before 1900, when the ratio of Japanese men to women was twenty-four to one. Among the early Japanese immigrant women there were prostitutes who worked in Hawaii, California, the Pacific Northwest, and the Rocky Mountain states, but the combined efforts of Japanese government officials and community leaders who were anxious to promote a positive image of Japan in America, as well as the institution of "picture brides," soon put an end to Japanese prostitution.

Like the Chinese Exclusion Act of 1882, the Gentleman's Agreement of 1907–08 between Japan and the United States barred the further entry of Japanese, and later Korean, laborers. Unlike the Chinese, however, Japanese and Korean men in Hawaii and on the mainland were allowed to send for picture brides between 1907 and 1921. Matched through photographs according to the *omaiai-kekkon* or arranged marriage custom, more than forty-one thousand Japanese and Korean women arrived in America this way, often misled by visions of wealth and photographs of younger versions of their new husbands. Their willingness to assume the double burden of housewife and laborer allowed for the establishment of families and enabled their husbands to leave plantation and migrant farm work and move into family-operated farms growing rice, vegetables, and grapes, or into family enterprises such as laundries, bathhouses, restaurants, grocery stores, and boarding houses. Life for these picture brides was marked by toil—working alongside their husbands in the fields or in their small businesses, or as domestic servants, seamstresses, or cannery workers—while assuming the responsibilities of homemaker and mother, often under primitive living conditions.

Filipino wives also emigrated to Hawaii, California, and Washington between 1907 and 1945. Having lived under Spanish and American colonialism, they were usually different from other Asian women in being educated, Catholics, and highly Americanized. But, subjected to the same discrimination as other Asian immigrants, they also led dual lives, working in the fields, doing domestic chores, or managing restaurants, pool halls, and stores, as well as taking care of their own homes. By 1930 there were 2,500 Filipino women among a total population of 45,200 Filipinos in America; some of them were teachers, nurses, and pharmacists—occupations denied their men, who were still relegated to culinary and custodial jobs regardless of their educational background.

Despite their hard-working lives, the Chinese, Japanese, Korean, and Filipino immigrant women did not forget their obligations to their children, home country, or new communities in America. They ensured that cultural traditions and language were maintained among the second generation, and contributions were made to overseas independence movements—the Chinese revolution of 1911, the Sino-Japanese war relief program during the 1930s, and Korean independence from Japanese domination. At the same time, they worked to improve their communities by participating in church activities and women's clubs organized to promote education and charitable work. Women were also visibly active in labor protests such as the 1920 strike by plantation workers in Hawaii and the 1938 strike by garment workers in San Francisco.

World War II heralded profound changes in the lives of Asian American women. After Japan bombed Pearl Harbor, 120,000 Japanese Americans were deprived of their civil rights and life-long investments and possessions, uprooted from their homes on the West Coast, and incarcerated in concentration camps in desolate desert areas. Family life was rudely disrupted by the makeshift conditions of camp life. Fathers lost their means of livelihood and status as head of the household, while sons were forced to choose between enlistment or imprisonment at Tule Lake, a camp set up for dissidents. While women also suffered, at least camp life provided mothers with time for educational and social activities and daughters with accelerated acculturation through peer group influence within the camps and educational and employment opportunities outside the camps.

While Japan was seen as the enemy during World War II, China and the Philippines were considered allies, which helped to improve conditions for Chinese and Filipino women working in the war factories and filling jobs in the private sector once closed to them. After the war, legislation was passed allowing Asian Americans to send for war brides, wives, and families previously barred from immigrating. Women and children could now come from China, Japan, Korea, the Philippines, and India as nonquota immigrants. Often the differences in age and educational background between war brides and their husbands made these marriages difficult. Then, because of their husbands' meager incomes, the women found they had to work, usually at low-paying jobs as garment, restaurant, cannery, or farm workers, as domestic servants, or in small businesses catering to an ethnic community. Like the picture brides before them, war brides and reunited wives and families infused the Asian American communities with a new vitality.

Thousands of Japanese, Filipino, and Korean women also came as wives of non-Asian U.S. servicemen after World War II and the Korean conflict. Although many of these marriages proved to be happy and stable, others were troubled by serious problems: language and cultural adjustment difficulties, wife abuse, and alienation caused by racial isolation on scattered military bases or ostracism from ethnic communities.

Beginning in the nineteenth century, each successive wave of immigrant women from Asia was followed by the birth of a second generation and the establishment of family life in America. Like other children of immigrant parents, American-born Asian daughters experienced cultural conflicts and identity crises in attempting to follow Asian traditions and at the same time adjust to American society. In addition, their sex and race often proved to be liabilities, both within and outside their ethnic communities. Despite their ability to speak English, their high educational attainment, and their Western outlook, Chinese and Japanese American women of the 1920s and 1930s had difficulty finding gainful employment in their chosen fields as well as acceptance in the larger American society.

Assimilation became easier for Asian Americans after World War II, as educational and employment opportunities opened up and laws limiting their civil rights and social interactions were repealed. Increased numbers of Asian American women began leaving domestic and clerical work and entering technical, sales, and professional fields, but their earning power was often not commensurate with their level of education. At the same time, stereotypes of Asian American women as passive, exotic China dolls impeded their advancement up the managerial ladder. Subtle discrimination barred Asian American women from living in the most desirable neighborhoods and joining the most prestigious social groups. Yet, if one uses outmarriage rates to indicate assimilation, one-fourth of all Asian American women were marrying outside their race according to the 1970 U.S. Census.

The Naturalization Act of 1965, which established an annual quota of twenty thousand immigrants from each country under a preference system favoring family reunification, skilled and professional labor, and refugee resettlement, resulted in increased immigration and a more diversified population of Chinese, Koreans, Filipinos, and South Asians (Indians, Pakistanis, and Bangladeshis) in America. Refugees from China and Southeast Asia (Vietnam, Laos, and Kampuchea) were admitted under special refugee acts. Over half of these newcomers have been women, some separated from their husbands for as long as ten to thirty years due to immigration restrictions. Many others have been highly educated, urban women from China, Korea, the Philippines, and South Asia—doctors, nurses, teachers, dentists, and lawyers—who have come for economic opportunities but often found themselves locked out of professional jobs because of language barriers and discriminatory licensing examinations.

Women from Southeast Asia face unique problems due to the aftereffects of war in their homeland. Like other immigrant women, they confront the difficulties of language and cultural adjustment and economic survival in America. As refugees from Southeast Asia, they also carry deep psychological scars from the traumatic experiences of war, dispossession, family separation, harsh treatment under the new government, rape and pillage at sea, and the ordeal of resettlement. While those with education and entrepreneurial skills have found paraprofessional or high-technology jobs or have established small family businesses, women from preindustrial, rural societies in Laos and Kampuchea have been concentrated in truck farming or fruit growing, or have required intensive education and employment training to survive in urban America.

According to the 1980 U.S. Census, there are approximately 1.9 million Asian American women, comprising 51 percent of the total Asian American population. Sixty percent of Asian American women are married. Their nativity and socioeconomic backgrounds vary among the ethnic groups. The Hawaiians and Japanese are 70–90 percent native-born, while the majority of the Chinese, Filipinos, Koreans, and Vietnamese are foreign-born. As a group, 71 percent of all Asian American women have a high school education, and 20 percent have college degrees, but within specific groups, one-fourth of Chinese and about one-fifth of Korean and Filipino women completed only eight years of education. Fifty-seven percent of Asian American women are in the labor force (higher than any other group of women), earning a median annual income of $6,685 (slightly higher than the median income for the U.S. female population but lower than for any group of males). Of these, two-fifths are in technical, clerical, and sales positions; one-fourth are in managerial and professional jobs; and the remaining one-fifth hold service, low-skilled, and semiskilled jobs. Within these occupations, the tendency is for Asian American women to earn less than their male counterparts. Economic survival and parity remain a major concern of Asian American women in the 1980s and 1990s.

In addition to economic concerns, Asian American women today are committed, like their predecessors, to their families, communities, and cultures. As wage earners, wives, and mothers, they have been able to keep a tenuous balance between these roles, a balance easily upset if husbands choose not to cooperate or if social changes gained through the civil rights and women's liberation movements are reversed. As individuals concerned about their communities, they have been active in educational, religious, ethnic, women's, political, and mainstream organizations, often assuming leadership to bring about improvements. They also continue to work toward assimilation into American society while maintaining a strong sense of their Asian cultural heritage and ethnic identity.

—Judy Yung

See Also:

Kingston, Maxine Hong

References:

Chai, Alice. "Korean Women in Hawaii, 1903–1945." In *Women in New Worlds*, edited by Hilah Thomas and Rosemary Keller. Nashville: Abington Press, 1981, pp. 328–44.

Fujitomi, Irene, and Diane Wong. "The New Asian-American Woman." In *Asian Americans: Psychological Perspectives*, edited by Stanley Sue and Nathaniel Wagner. Palo Alto, Calif.: Science and Behavior Books, 1973, pp. 252–63.

Gee, Emma. "Issei: The First Women." In *Asian Women*. Berkeley: University of California, 1971, pp. 8–15.

Glenn, Evelyn Nakano. *Issei, Nisei, War Bride: Three Generations of Japanese American Women in Domestic Service*. Philadelphia: Temple University Press, 1986.

Hirata, Lucie Cheng. "Chinese Immigrant Women in Nineteenth-Century California." In *Asian and Pacific American Experiences: Women's Perspectives*, edited by Nobuya Tsuchida. Minneapolis: Asian/Pacific American Learning Resource Center, 1982, pp. 38–55.

———. "Free, Indentured, Enslaved: Chinese Prostitutes in Nineteenth Century America." *Signs: A Journal of Women in Culture and Society* 5 (1979): 3–29.

Ichioka, Yuji. "Amerika Nadeshiko: Japanese Immigrant Women in the United States, 1900–1924." *Pacific Historical Review* 69 (May 1980): 339–57.

Kim, Elaine. "Asian Women in America." In *With Silk Wings: Asian American Women at Work.* Oakland, Calif.: Asian Women United of California, 1983, pp. 120–35.

Kumagai, Gloria. "The Asian Woman in America." *Explorations in Ethnic Studies* 1 (July 1978): 27–39.

Lott, Juanita Tamayo. "Asian and Pacific American Women as Vital Forces Across the Nation." Washington, D.C.: Organization of Pan Asian American Women, 1984, pp. 1–14.

Navarro, Jovina. "Immigration of Filipino Women to America." In *Asian American Women.* Stanford, Calif.: Stanford University Press, 1976, pp. 18–22.

Wong, Diane, ed. *Making Waves: Writings About Asian American Women.* Boston: Beacon, 1989.

Yang, Eun Sik. "Korean Women of America: From Subordination to Partnership, 1903–1930." *Amerasia Journal* 11 (Fall/Winter 1984): 1–28.

Yu, Eui-Yang, and Earl H. Phillips. *Korean Women in Transition: At Home and Abroad.* Los Angles: Center for Korean-American and Korean Studies, 1987.

Yung, Judy. *Chinese Women of America: A Pictorial History.* Seattle: University of Washington Press, 1986.

The **ASSOCIATION OF COLLEGIATE ALUMNAE.** In 1882 Marion Talbot, Alice Freeman (Palmer), Alice Hayes, Ellen Swallow Richards, and thirteen other women met in Boston to establish the Association of Collegiate Alumnae, uniting college graduates for "practical educational work." Members of the first generation of college-educated women, they had struggled for an education only to find that society had no place for them and no interest in utilizing their abilities. Through the new organization (ACA), they hoped to promote and raise standards for women's higher education. To distinguish themselves from normal-school and academy graduates, they limited membership to alumnae of specified, carefully selected four-year colleges and universities. Additionally, they expected the ACA to help end the social isolation often faced by women college graduates when they returned home. Women in other regions responded enthusiastically and set up ACA branches across the country. Founded in 1901, the Southern Association of College Women served a similar community. In 1921 the ACA and the SACW merged, forming the American Association of University Women. Although the ACA, the SACW, and later the AAUW were committed to equal access to education, they avoided identification as explicitly feminist organizations. Until the 1970s, AAUW leaders rejected controversial and potentially divisive issues like woman suffrage and the Equal Rights Amendment.

During its first fifty years, the ACA studied a variety of issues related to women's education. In the 1880s it sponsored and published research refuting Dr. Edward Clarke's dictum that females ruined their health when they attended college. ACA members promoted the scientific study of child development and euthenics, believing that as mothers and teachers, college women were uniquely qualified to pave the way for more enlightened methods of child rearing, and thus for a more efficient society. They addressed the status of women within the academy by lobbying for women to serve as college trustees, fought discrimination on coeducational campuses, and argued for inclusion in the curriculum of home economics courses designed to make homemaking more professional and scientific. Additionally, the ACA provided fellowships for undergraduate, graduate, and postdoctoral study, and encouraged women's careers, particularly in the social sciences. Activities of regional branches and local groups of the ACA varied a good deal. Particularly during the Progressive era, some ACA members formed industrial committees and engaged in reform work; others, more concerned with self-improvement, practiced French conversation.

World War I temporarily disrupted the customary work of the ACA, as members directed their energies toward educating the public on the need for U.S. intervention. The internationalism of the war years carried over into the 1920s, when the AAUW joined similar organizations from eight other countries to promote women's education around the world and to create an international community of college women through the International Federation of College Women.

—*Catherine E. Kelly*

See Also:

American Association of University Women, Women in Higher Education

References:

ACA *Publications* (1888–1911).

The Graduate Woman (1978).

Journal of the American Association of University Women (1912–1978).

Papers of the American Association of University Women. Washington, D.C.: AAUW Archives. (Also available on microfilm.) [Records of regional ACA/AAUW groups are often available in local archives.]

Talbot, Marion, and Lois Kimball Mathews Rosenberry. *The History of the American Association of University Women, 1881–1931*. Boston: Houghton Mifflin, 1931.

The **ASSOCIATION OF SOUTHERN WOMEN FOR THE PREVENTION OF LYNCHING** (1930–42) was founded and directed by feminist reformer Jesse Daniel Ames. Recognizing a link between racial and sexual repression, Ames challenged the justification commonly given for lynching: that it was necessary for the defense of white Southern womanhood. Through the ASWPL she hoped to use the moral and social leverage of enfranchised white women to prevent mob violence in the rural South.

The ASWPL was sponsored and financed primarily by the Commission on Interracial Cooperation, the South's major interracial reform organization. For years black women had pressed the issue within the CIC Women's Committee. "When Southern white women get ready to stop lynching, it will be stopped, and not before," they said. In the ASWPL, Southern white women accepted this challenge, working through missionary societies to denounce the claim that lynchers acted in the defense of womanhood. With pledges and press statements, informal talks and public speeches, investigations and local intervention, ASWPL members hammered home their argument that black men did not provoke lynching by raping white women and that the "false chivalry" of lynching demeaned white women even as it terrorized blacks.

Just as the temperance movement had earlier channeled women into the political arena, the ASWPL linked mob violence to the special concerns of women and brought them to the forefront of the antilynching campaign. Ames made ingenious use of Southern institutions and the modes of influence available to middle-class women, drawing eclectically on nineteenth-century feminist ideals of sisterhood, moral superiority, and a separate public sphere for women. At the same time, she presented an implicitly feminist antiracism and led ASWPL members toward an understanding of lynching's deepest roots.

—*Misti Tuberville*

See Also:

Ames, Jesse Daniel

References:

ASWPL Papers. Trevor Arnett Library. Atlanta University, Atlanta, Ga.

Jesse Daniel Ames Papers. Southern Historical Collection. University of North Carolina, Chapel Hill, N.C.

Hall, Jacquelyn Dowd. *Revolt Against Chivalry: Jesse Daniel Ames and the Women's Campaign Against Lynching*. New York: Columbia University Press, 1979.

Miller, Kathleen Atkinson. "The Ladies and the Lynchers: A Look at the Association of Southern Women for the Prevention of Lynching." *Southern Studies* 17 (Fall 1978): 221–40.

ATHERTON, GERTRUDE FRANKLIN HORN (1857-1948) was the author of forty novels, an autobiography, and numerous short stories and prose essays. Though she was descended from Northern businessmen (including Benjamin Franklin) and Southern landowners, and was the widow of a wealthy Californian, Atherton, due to family estrangement and financial disaster, earned her living entirely from writing.

She criticized the "thin, anemic" Realistic presentation of the dull lives of the bourgeoisie epitomized by W. D. Howells and countered with her own Romantic Realism, influenced in part by Taine and Saint-Beuve, in which the conflict of character with the forces of heredity and environment create a highly dramatic course of cause and effect. She was especially interested in characters who transcended limitations, forged new personalities, and sought new life adventures. Most of her novels focus on women characters. A few, such as *Julia France and Her Times*, dealt directly with the women's rights movement. In fact she believed that the real birth of democracy lay in the awakening of women to the pursuit of their own happiness.

Atherton was known for her attention to historical detail both as an observer of her own time and as a student of the past. She wrote three very successful historical novels about antiquity, inaugurated the form of the biographical novel, and fictionalized well-researched contemporary issues, personalities, and scenes. Though she was often associated with California as a regional writer or viewed mainly as an interesting personality, Atherton may more appropriately be seen as a gifted literary observer of American culture.

—*Anne Dzamba Sessa*

References:

Atherton, Gertrude. *Adventures of a Novelist.* New York: Liveright, 1932.

McClure, Charlotte S. *Gertrude Atherton.* Boston: G. K. Hall, 1979.

ATHLETICS/SPORTS. Despite the fact that traditionally women have been encouraged less than men to develop athletic ability, they have always been active in sports. In the nineteenth century, some upper- and middle-class women engaged in physical exercises and recreational sports although lower-class women were generally unable to find time for any sport activity. Toward the end of the century, some women were able to participate in a limited number of intercollegiate games and occasional private tournaments. In the 1870s socialite Mary Ewing Outerbridge helped popularize lawn tennis in the United States, and by 1887 interest in women's tennis had grown so much that the first national competition for women in the sport was held at the Philadelphia Cricket Club.

Fears that women would lose "femininity" by ruining their complexions and would injure themselves in strenuous physical activity, as well as Victorian notions about propriety, all worked to retard women's sports development well into the twentieth century. Despite these and other obstacles, such as limited access to athletic facilities and coaching and lack of societal support for women athletes, interest in women's athletics continued to grow, as evidenced by a White House conference on the subject in 1923.

The growth of interest in women's sports is also reflected in the participation by women in the modern Olympic Games. When the first modern games were held in Athens, Greece, no female athletes were allowed to compete. Four years later in the next round of the Olympics, eleven women took part, and that number has steadily increased. The 1984 Olympics in Los Angeles saw 1,620 women competing in seventy-three events. A number of American women have achieved international renown as Olympic athletes, including "Babe" Didrikson Zaharias in the 1932 games; sprinter Wilma Rudolph in the 1960 games; and gymnast Mary Lou Retton, sprinters Evelyn Ashford and Valerie Briscoe-Hooks, marathon runner Joan Benoite, volleyball star Flo Hyman, and basketball star Cheryl Miller in the 1984 games. Women stars of the 1988 Seoul Olympics included sprinter Florence Griffith Joyner, swimmer Janet Evans, and decathelete Jackie Joyner Kersee.

Olympian "Babe" Zaharias was one of the first women to gain international recognition as an athlete. Not only did she win gold medals in the javelin throw and the hurdles as well as a silver medal in the high jump in the 1932 Los Angeles Olympics, but she also had a glittering career in basketball and softball. One of the finest all-round athletes in the history of sport, Zaharias also gave tennis demonstrations and in her later years achieved fame as a golfer.

Golf and tennis have become the first women's sports to achieve lasting financial success as professional sports. The Ladies Professional Golf Association was formed in 1949 and has become a commercial success, annually awarding millions of dollars in prize money and making celebrities of performers such as Patty Berg, Joanne Carner, Nancy Lopez, Jan Stephenson, and others.

Professional women's tennis has also become established as a viable spectator sport and achieved commercial success. Athletes such as Billie Jean King, Chris Evert, and Martina Navratilova have made great fortunes and their names have become household words. King in particular has been an active feminist and has publicly linked the women's movement to women's sports. In 1957 Althea Gibson became the first black player to win a championship at Wimbledon, England, the most prestigious tennis tournament in the world. The talented Gibson had been restricted to blacks-only competitions for many years before her triumph at Wimbledon.

Other women's sports have not enjoyed the same commercial success as tennis and golf. For example, a professional women's basketball league proved short-lived in the late 1970s. Nevertheless, women's participation in athletics continues to grow dramatically. Between 1970 and 1984, the number of women in varsity high school sports rose by 600 percent; at the college level, by 900 percent.

The increase in women's participation in sports can be explained by a number of factors. Among them are the success of the women's movement in providing role models, concern for good health and physical fitness, the success of women in Olympic and professional competitions as well as subsequent publicity and recognition, and the implementation of Title IX of the Education Amendments of 1972. Title IX prohibited exclusion from participation in educational activities on the basis of sex at institutions receiving federal financial. The fear of losing federal revenues caused many colleges and universities to expand opportunities for women's athletics. During the Reagan years the implementation of Title IX lacked the vigor of previous years, but it still serves to assure women access to scholarships, facilities, and coaching in most colleges and universities.

Ironically, while opportunities for women athletes have increased, the number of female college coaches has decreased in recent years. One reason for this was the demise of the Association for Intercollegiate Athletics for Women (AIAW) in 1983, as women's college sports came under the authority of the male-dominated National Collegiate Athletic Association. Also, as separate women's and men's athletic departments have merged, women have tended to lose athletic directorships and coaching positions. Despite these limitations, women's sport continues to be an important part of North American culture and society.

—Jonathan W. Zophy

See Also:

Gibson, Althea; King, Billie Jean; Zaharias, "Babe" Didrikson

References:

Baker, W. J. *Sports in the Western World.* Totowa, N.J.: Rowman and Littlefield, 1982.

Boutilier, Mary, and Lucinda San Giovanni, eds. *The Sporting Women.* Champaign, Ill.: Human Kinetics, 1983.

Coakley, Jay. *Sport in Society.* 3d ed. St. Louis: Times Mirror/Mosby, 1986.

Noverr, D. A., and Lawrence Ziewacz. *The Games They Played: Sports in American History.* Chicago: Nelson Hall, 1983.

AUSTEN, ALICE (1866–1952) was a dedicated amateur photographer whose images of genteel middle-class society on Staten Island,

New York, at the turn of the century have become a rich source of social history.

Born into a middle-class family, Austen spent most of her life living in the family home, Clear Comfort, on Staten Island. Austen's father deserted the family before she was born, and she was raised by her mother and other close family members. She attended a fashionable girls' school near her home. As a young girl, Austen was introduced to the camera by her uncles, who taught her the technical side of photography and built a darkroom for the aspiring young photographer. By the time she was eighteen, Austen emerged as a dedicated photographer with professional standards.

Like many educated women of the late nineteenth century, Austen never married. She lived and traveled for over fifty years with her close and constant companion, Gertrude Tate, with whom she shared domestic responsibilities and emotional and financial resources.

Austen recorded diverse aspects of her world. She depicted her many friends and family playing tennis, riding bicycles, horseback riding, swimming, bowling. They are seen at teas, musicales, dances, or strumming a banjo on a shaded piazza. Austen was particularly fond of recording the richness of Victorian interiors. Her photographs also provide insights into the private experiences of young women during the late nineteenth century. Images of her women friends at slumber parties, secretly smoking cigarettes, dressing up in men's clothes, or cavorting playfully on a lawn offer rare glimpses into the intimacy of woman's sphere.

Alice Austen is representative of the thousands of amateur women photographers who, at the turn of the century, appropriated the camera to take tentative steps beyond the restrictions of Victorian society.

—C. Jane Gover

See Also:

Photography

References:

Gover, C. Jane. *The Positive Image: Women Photographers in Turn of the Century America.* New York: State University of New York Press, 1987.

Novotny, Ann. *Alice's World.* Old Greenwich, Conn.: Chatham, 1976.

AVIATION. Almost from the beginning of manned flight, women have participated in aviation. In 1784, only months after the first free manned balloon flight was made, Madame Elisabeth Thible became the first woman to ascend into the air, as a passenger in a Montgolfier balloon over Lyons, France. There is evidence that the first U.S. citizen to make a solo flight in this country was an exhibition balloonist who flew under the name of Madame Johnson in New York in 1825.

In the early 1900s interest shifted from balloons to airplanes. In 1910 Blanche Stuart Scott became the first American woman to solo in an airplane. The following year, Harriet Quimby became the first American woman to receive a pilot's license. By World War I eleven women in the United States had earned their pilots' licenses, and many others were flying without them.

During the 1920s, the era of barnstorming and stunt flying, women performed daredevil aerial feats along with men. One, Mabel Cody, ran her own "flying circus." In 1929 women competed in their first national aviation event—the Women's Air Derby. Although the prize money was good, the real incentive was for women to prove that they were competent professional pilots. The race was won by Louise Thaden, who in 1936 also became the first woman to win the prestigious cross-country Bendix Trophy Race.

The 1920s and 1930s were also the years of famous long-distance flights. Until 1928 no woman had flown across the Atlantic Ocean. That year, Amelia Earhart flew from Newfoundland to Ireland. Although she was only a passenger on that flight, it launched her career, and in 1932 she became the first woman to fly solo across the Atlantic. Three years later she became the first pilot, male or female, to fly solo from Hawaii to the U.S. mainland.

In 1943 the United States took the important step of initiating a program for women pilots. The Women's Airforce Service Pilots (WASPs) was established under the leadership of Jacqueline Cochran. The WASPs did almost all the domestic flying for the United States during World War II, including ferrying all types of aircraft, from fighters to heavy bombers, from factories to the coast for shipment overseas.

Today there are many women flying for the airlines and for the military, serving as corporate pilots, and running their own aviation-related businesses and flight training centers. Women such as Olive Ann Beech, who headed Beech Aircraft for many years, are also prominent in the aviation industry at management levels.

—*Claudia M. Oakes*

See Also:

Earhart, Amelia; Quimby, Harriet; Women's Airforce Service Pilots (WASPs)

References:

Brooks-Pazmany, Kathleen. *United States Women in Aviation 1919–1929.* Washington, D.C.: Smithsonian Institution, 1983.

Dwiggins, Don. *They Flew the Bendix Race.* New York: Lippincott, 1965.

Keil, Sally V. *Those Wonderful Women in Their Flying Machines.* New York: Rawson, Wade, 1978.

Oakes, Claudia M. *United States Women in Aviation 1930–1939.* Washington, D.C.: Smithsonian Institution, 1985.

———. *United States Women in Aviation through World War I.* Washington, D.C.: Smithsonian Institution, 1978.

THE AWAKENING (1899) is a novel by Kate Chopin that tells the story of a woman who wakens to her identity and to the conflicts initiated within her by that realization. Set in the Creole society of New Orleans, the novel shows not only the struggle between male and female but also the struggle between self and society. The protagonist, Edna Pontellier, must confront both her husband's expectations of her as a wife and society's expectation that she will conform to its conception of a woman, wife, and mother.

Edna is initially awakened to sexuality by falling in love with a young Creole, but also experiences other awakenings as she moves toward life as an independent woman.

A friend's torturous childbirth makes clear that, even if Edna struggles against society's demands, she cannot escape the biological realities that are part of being a woman. That episode, in conjunction with her lover's desertion, makes Edna believe the only way to avoid surrender is suicide, and she drowns herself.

The novel was thoroughly castigated by contemporary critics. Although some recognized its artistic merit, all were outraged by Edna's actions and shocked that she was not condemned by the author. Chopin did not stop writing after its publication, but she published only three more stories before her death in 1904.

The very strength of the critics' hostility—the book was called "moral poison" and was banned in St. Louis, Chopin's home—attested to the power of *The Awakening* when it appeared. Since the 1960s, Chopin's work has become associated with issues related to the women's movement, primarily because of *The Awakening,* and today the novel is called a masterpiece.

Born in St. Louis, Missouri, in 1851 into a French Creole and Irish family, she married Oscar Chopin in 1870 and lived with him in New Orleans. Business failure caused them to leave the city to live on Chopin's property in the country, and in 1879 they settled in the Cane River area of Louisiana, Natchitoches Parish, the site of most of her fiction. In 1884, two years after her husband's death, Chopin and her six children returned to St. Louis, where she began her writing career.

She was first known as a short-story writer. A number of her early works display the same themes as *The Awakening*—women's independence, women's sexuality, and the biological determination of women's experience—but her early works were praised despite, not because of, these qualities. Appreciation of *The Awakening* has brought attention and audiences to Chopin's other, long-neglected works, and now she can be characterized as a writer who portrayed women through a woman's perspective, with a vision far ahead of her time.

—*Mabel Benson DuPriest*

References:

Chopin, Kate. *The Awakening: An Authoritative Text, Contexts, Criticism.* Edited by Margaret Culley. New York: Norton, 1976.

———. *The Complete Works of Kate Chopin.* Edited, with an introduction by Per Seyersted; forword by Edmund Wilson. Baton Rouge: Louisiana State University Press, 1970.

Rankin, Daniel S. *Kate Chopin and Her Creole Stories.* Philadelphia: University of Pennsylvania Press, 1932.

Seyersted, Per. *Kate Chopin: A Critical Biography.* Baton Rouge: Louisiana State University Press, 1969.

BABCOCK, CAROLINE LEXOW (1882–1980), suffragist, pacifist, and feminist, was born in New York City, the eldest daughter of New York State Senator Clarence Lexow (1894–98) and women's rights advocate Katharine Morrow Ferris. Although she lived most of her life in Nyack, New York, Babcock attended Barnard College from 1900 to 1904 and there met suffrage leader Harriot Stanton Blatch. In 1904 Babcock helped organize and became president of the Collegiate Equal Suffrage League of New York State. In 1908 she served as executive secretary of the National College Equal Suffrage League, and in 1910 as executive secretary and then field secretary for Blatch's Women's Political Union.

She married Philip Westerly Babcock in 1915, and they had three children by 1919. Although a member of the Woman's Peace party during World War I, Babcock did not actively work for peace until 1919, when she became an executive board member of the Women's Peace Society and an organizer of the Women's Peace Union, an interwar pacifist organization that tried to outlaw war through a constitutional amendment. Due to the Depression, in 1935 Babcock took a paying position with the Women's International League for Peace and Freedom. This was followed by a nine-month term with the Campaign for World Government and then a longer position as executive secretary for the National Woman's party from 1938 to 1946. After leaving the NWP because of internal conflicts, Babcock retired at age sixty-four to her farm in Blairstown, New Jersey.

—*Harriet Hyman Alonso*

See Also:

National Woman's Party, Women's International League for Peace and Freedom, Women's Peace Union

References:

Babcock, Caroline Lexow, and Olive E. Hurlburt Papers. The Arthur and Elizabeth Schlesinger Library on the History of Women in America. Radcliffe College, Cambridge, Mass.

Women's Peace Union Papers. Swarthmore College Peace Collection, Swarthmore, Pa., and New York Public Library.

Alonso, Harriet Hyman. *The Women's Peace Union and the Outlawry of War, 1921–1942.* Knoxville: University of Tennessee Press, 1989.

Savell, Isabelle K. *Ladies' Lib: How Rockland Women Got the Vote.* New City, N.Y.: The Historical Society of Rockland County, 1979.

"BABY BOOM" refers to the explosion of births in America—approximately 76,441,000—between 1946 and 1964. Although both Europe and America experienced a rapid rise in birthrates immediately following World War II as servicemen and their wives made up for lost time, the European boomlet faded quickly, while America's boom continued, peaking in 1957 with a record 4.3 million births.

America's baby boom was accompanied and made possible by a great marriage boom, as average age at marriage dropped from 24.3 to 22.6 for men and from 21.5 to 20.4 for women by 1951, and the marriage rate soared. The economic prosperity of the postwar era enabled men, especially those in the upper middle class, to provide for large families of four or more children, while an ideology that stressed "traditional" sex roles deemed child-bearing and motherhood woman's highest callings. Finally, having many children made sense in the atmosphere of confidence and the strong, if sometimes confused, faith in the future that characterized postwar America.

The baby boom generation or "cohort" is often inelegantly referred to as the "pig in the python" because of the disconcerting bulge it makes in the population curve as baby boomers pass through the stages of life. Through sheer weight of numbers, this group has had and will continue to have a profound impact on American social and economic policy and on the shape of American culture. The women within the baby boom and their mothers played a significant role in the resurgence of the women's rights movement in the 1960s.

—*Beth L. Bailey*

See Also:
Demography

Reference:

Jones, Landon Y. *Great Expectations: America and the Baby Boom Generation.* New York: Coward, McCann & Geoghegan, 1980.

BAEZ, JOAN C. (b. 1941), musician and social activist, is an advocate of nonviolence in the modern American movement for peace and justice. Having received national attention at the Newport Folk Festival in 1959, Baez began a musical career that has been combined with a life of political action through the use of her music, writing, and speaking as a form of protest against violence and oppression.

While she has had no formal music training, Baez's entrancing voice has allowed her to explore many forms of music, but her singing career began in the rediscovery of folk music that flowered in the 1960s. Her early albums were comprised primarily of traditional songs, but as her career developed, her albums became more political, for example, *Carry It On, Where Are You Now, My Son?,* and *Come from the Shadows.* Her later albums have become increasingly dependent on more contemporary music, some written by Baez herself and combining both traditional roots with country, rock, and pop. Baez's departure from pure folk music and reluctance to research the folk music she performs have been criticized by purists, but both critics and audiences applaud her performance of both traditional and contemporary songs.

While incorporating protest into her music, Baez did not limit her social activism to performance. During the 1960s and early 1970s, Baez participated in both the civil rights and anti–Vietnam War movements. In protest against the war, Baez refused payment of war taxes, blocked induction centers, toured North Vietnam, and spoke in favor of draft resistance. During much of this period, she was married to David Harris, imprisoned for his draft resistance. The marriage ended after the war. In the mid-1970s, Baez subordinated her musical career to her social activism, protesting in Belfast and meeting with dissidents in the USSR. She supported the oppressed in America and throughout the world. Her condemnation of the government of the Socialist Republic of Vietnam was criticized by her political allies on the Left. Despite this criticism, Baez spoke out against oppression wherever it existed, serving as founder of Humanitas International Human Rights Committee and as a member of the National Advisory Board of Amnesty International.

In the 1980s Baez continued her musical career, recording new albums and touring; but, still a socially conscious artist, she also appeared at many benefit concerts for organizations such as Amnesty International, Bread and Roses, and We Are the World.

—*Avery Preston Lane*

See Also:
Pacifism and the Peace Movement, Popular Vocalists

References:

Baez, Joan C. *And a Voice to Sing With.* New York: Summit Books, 1987.
———. *And Then I Wrote . . .* New York: Big 3 Music Corp., 1979.
———. *Daybreak.* New York: Dial, 1968.
Playboy Interview: Joan Baez. Chicago: Playboy Press, 1971.

BAGLEY, SARAH G. (fl. 1835–47), the first notable woman trade unionist in the United States, was born in Meredith, New Hampshire, and received a typical New England common school education. She obtained employment as a weaver in the Hamilton Manufacturing Company, a cotton mill in Lowell, Massachusetts, in 1836. Working under the adverse conditions of a badly ventilated building, poor lighting, and a twelve-hour day stimulated her to join and become a leader in the labor battles for women mill workers during the 1840s.

In 1840 Bagley was contributing innocuous articles to the apolitical magazine written by the mill girls, the *Lowell Offering*; but as wages declined and working conditions deteriorated between 1844 and 1847 she voiced the workers' discontent in her speeches and writings. As the founder and first president of the Lowell Female Labor Reform Association in 1845, she argued for the ten-hour day in the New England Workingman's Association periodical the *Voice of Industry*. She became editor after its purchase by the Lowell Female Labor Reform Association (LFLRA). With the aid of the LFLRA, she obtained two thousand signatures on petitions to the Massachusetts state legislature for a ten-hour day. Bagley and other female operatives testified in February 1845 at a public hearing, but without result; the legislature declined to interfere in the business of the mills.

Shortly thereafter, Bagley left her mill position and devoted herself to full-time labor activities through her organization of branches of the LFLRA in other mill towns, her speaking engagements for the New England Workingman's Association, her work as their corresponding secretary, and also her founding of the Lowell Industrial Reform Lyceum, which was a platform for speakers such as William Lloyd Garrison, George Ripley, and Horace Greeley.

When an article by Sarah Bagley was published in 1845 in the first of the *Factory Tracts* issued by the LFLRA, she seemed a militant radical, stating "we will show those drivelling cotton lords . . . that our rights cannot be trampled upon with impunity." Bagley's courageous and innovative acts stood out as a beacon and unifying force for the early female factory operatives. Her health declined, and in February 1846 another mill girl replaced her as president of the LFLRA. But Sarah Bagley was not through—she blazed another trail as the first woman telegrapher in this country by accepting the position of superintendent of the Lowell Telegraph Office.

—*Virginia Beattie Mattes*

See Also:

Lowell Female Industrial Reform and Mutual Aid Society, Lowell Mill Girls, *Voice of Industry*

References:

Flexner, Eleanor. *Century of Struggle: The Woman's Rights Movement in the United States.* New York: Atheneum, 1959.

Josephson, Hannah. *The Golden Threads, New England's Mill Girls and Magnates.* New York: Russell and Russell, 1967.

Stern, Madeline B. *We the Women: Career Firsts of Nineteenth Century America.* New York: Schulte, 1963.

BAKER, JOSEPHINE (1906–75), singer, dancer, and comedienne, was born in St. Louis and rose from an impoverished background to international acclaim as an entertainer. By the age of thirteen, Baker had begun to appear at the Booker T. Washington Club in St. Louis and soon afterward joined the Dixie Steppers and traveled on the Theatre Owner's Booking Association (TOBA) circuit through the South. TOBA was the booking agency for black entertainers in southern black theaters and a few northern theaters which sustained those entertainers in a segregated market. In 1921 she joined the Broadway company of the Eubie Blake and Noble Sissle musical *Shuffle Along* after originally being turned down for the road company production for being "too black." She became the hit of the show as a comedy chorus-girl. In 1925 she starred in another Blake and Sissle musical, *Chocolate Dandies.*

Baker journeyed to Paris to be part of a black vaudeville show called "La Revue

Nègre" in October 1925. Her "Dance of the Savages" was soon the toast of Paris, and Baker became the quintessential "garçonne," the French version of the flapper. She later opened at the Folies-Bergère, where she appeared onstage wearing only a girdle of rhinestone-studded bananas, a costume that became her trademark.

In 1926 Baker opened up her own club in Paris called Chez Joséphine, which became a commercial and financial success. She returned to the United States to appear in the Ziegfield Follies in 1936. The show was a critical and box office flop, and Baker returned to France. During World War II Baker became a member of the Free French Forces, acting as a spy and entertaining troops in North Africa, where she was in exile. After the war she received the Legion of Honor, the Rosette of the Resistance, and the Medallion of the City of Paris.

Radicalized by her wartime experiences, Baker returned to the United States in 1951. She lectured on racial equality and performed before mixed audiences. She received the NAACP's Most Outstanding Woman of the Year Award for 1951. Between 1954 and 1965, Baker and her husband, Jo Bouillon, adopted twelve children of various races and nationalities. She came out of retirement for a triumphant seventeen-city tour of the United States in 1973. She returned to Paris and debuted a new stage show on April 8, 1975. Five days later she died of a cerebral hemorrhage.

—Rose Kolbasnik Callahan

See Also:

Black Women, Popular Vocalists

References:

Baker, Josephine, and Jo Bouillon. *Josephine,* translated by Mariana Fitzpatrick. New York: Harper & Row, 1977.

Haney, Lynn. *Naked at the Feast: A Biography of Josephine Baker.* New York: Dodd, Mead, 1981.

Papich, Stephen. *Remembering Josephine.* Indianapolis: Bobbs-Merrill, 1976.

BALCH, EMILY GREENE (1867–1961), peace advocate, social reformer, and economist, was born near Boston and educated at Bryn Mawr, where she earned her A.B. in 1889. She then went on to additional study at the Harvard Annex (later Radcliffe College), the University of Chicago, and the University of Berlin. Balch began her teaching career at Wellesley College in 1896 and remained there until dismissed in 1918 for her outspoken pacificism. From 1919 to 1922 she served as the international secretary-treasurer of the Women's International League for Peace and Freedom and continued to work for that organization for the rest of her life in a variety of capacities. A prolific writer, Balch also promoted the cause of peace and social justice through numerous books and articles. In 1946 she was awarded the Nobel Peace Prize.

—Jonathan W. Zophy

See Also:

Addams, Jane; Hamilton, Alice; Pacifism and the Peace Movement

References:

Balch, Emily Greene. *Occupied Haiti.* New York: Garland, 1972.

———. *Our Slavic Fellow Citizens.* New York: Arno, 1969.

Randall, Mercedes. *Improper Bostonian: Emily Greene Balch.* New York: Twayne, 1964.

Solomon, Barbara. *Ancestors and Immigrants, a Changing New England.* Cambridge: Harvard University Press, 1956.

BALDWIN, MARIA LOUISE (1856–1922) was an educator, clubwoman, and community worker in Boston. The eldest of three children born to Baltimore native Mary Blake and Haitian emigrant Peter Baldwin, Maria Baldwin was born and educated in Cambridge, Massachusetts. After graduating from the town's Teachers' Training School, she taught in Maryland before returning to Cambridge to teach in the Agassiz School, which many of the children of Harvard professors attended. Her expertise and integrity led to her assumption of higher positions, first as principal and later as master of Agassiz School. This position made her one of two women and the only black to hold such an important position in Cambridge. She served as a positive role model to young blacks and opened opportunities for black women in education throughout New England.

Baldwin carried her role as educator into the community: holding reading classes for black students attending Harvard University; teaching black children at the Robert Gould Shaw settlement house; lecturing to audiences throughout the United States on topics such as woman suffrage, poetry, history, and racial justice; and discussing issues of social concern in the many clubs and literary societies to which she belonged. She served on the Urban League of Greater Boston and in the local branch of the NAACP. In 1879 she became the first woman to deliver the annual George Washington Birthday Memorial Address at the Brooklyn Institute. Educators and intellectuals in the Boston community held Baldwin in such high regard that after her death from a heart attack in 1922, the auditorium at Agassiz School was renamed Baldwin Hall, a scholarship was established, and a memorial library was dedicated in her honor. In 1950 a women's dormitory at Howard University was named Maria Baldwin Hall.

—Dorothy C. Salem

See Also:
Black Women

References:

Daniels, John. *In Freedom's Birthplace: A Study of Boston Negroes.* Boston: Houghton-Mifflin, 1914.

Dannett, Sylvia, ed. *Profiles of Negro Womanhood.* Chicago: Education Heritage, 1964.

Du Bois, W. E. B. "Maria Baldwin." *The Crisis* 22 (January 1922): 248–49.

Washington, Margaret Murray. "Club Work Among Negro Women." In *Progress of a Race,* edited by John William Gibson. Naperville, Ill.: J. L. Nichols, 1920, pp. 186–89.

BARNARD, KATE (1875–1930) was the first woman to be elected to a major state office, serving as Commissioner of Charities and Corrections for Oklahoma from 1907 to 1914. A professional politician and a social justice progressive, she fought for the rights of children, workers, convicts, the insane, and the handicapped.

In many respects Barnard's prepolitical life typified the lives of women in Oklahoma in the late nineteenth century. She helped her father homestead a claim, spent several years as a rural schoolteacher, then became a stenographer in Oklahoma City. However, she began to depart from the traditional role for single women when she became a labor organizer in Oklahoma City. Attracting statewide attention as a champion of laborers and children, she influenced the Oklahoma Constitutional Convention (1906–07) to adopt planks providing for compulsory education and protection for laboring children. In Oklahoma's first election in 1907, and again in 1910, Barnard received more votes than any other candidate, a remarkable accomplishment considering that Oklahoma had not granted women suffrage at the time.

During her tenure in office Barnard pushed through the state legislature measures implementing the constitutional provisions compelling the education of children and limiting their work outside the home. Owing to her persistent pressure, legislators also created a juvenile court system and a program of mothers' pensions. Her sensational investigations of asylum and penitentiary conditions resulted in reforms in the institutional care of the insane and convicts. As a labor advocate, Barnard was instrumental in persuading the legislature to establish a free state employment bureau and to pass laws concerning employer liability, mining safety, and factory inspection.

Barnard not only figured prominently in Oklahoma reform politics but also rose to national prominence through her work with the National Child Labor Committee, the National Conference of Charities and Corrections, the International Prison Commission, and the Lake Mohonk Conference on Indian rights.

Evidence of widespread fraud committed against Indian orphans prompted Barnard to undertake a crusade on their behalf in 1910. Barnard publicized the legal chicanery used to loot the orphans' estates. While Barnard's previous reform efforts had attracted substantial support, advocacy of Indian orphan rights, and attacks by the Oklahoma legislature as well as her own ill health contributed to her political demise in 1914. Sixteen years later she died alone and obscure in an Oklahoma City hotel.

–*Suzanne Jones Crawford and Lynn Musslewhite*

See Also:
Politics, Prison Reform

References:

Charities and Corrections Collection. State Archives of Oklahoma, Oklahoma City.
Bryant, Keith L., Jr. "The Juvenile Court Movement: Oklahoma as a Case Study." *Social Science Quarterly* 49 (September 1968): 368–76.
———. "Kate Barnard, Organized Labor and Social Justice in Oklahoma during the Progressive Era." *Journal of Southern History* 35 (1969): 145–64.
Houghen, H. R. "Kate Barnard and the Kansas Penitentiary Scandal." *Journal of the West* 17 (January 1978): 9–18.

BARNARD COLLEGE. In the late nineteenth century, increasing pressure was brought to bear on men's universities to admit women as students. By 1879 Columbia College in New York City had allowed females to attend selected classes, but when in 1882 appeals were made to the Columbia College by certain prominent New Yorkers urging the admittance of women as degree candidates, the proposal was overwhelmingly rejected by the board of trustees. Consequently, in 1883 "The Collegiate Course" was established, based on the Harvard precedent, whereby women could earn certificates of completion from Columbia College provided they passed the requisite examinations. Preparatory instruction for these examinations, however, was not provided.

In 1889 Barnard College was established, providing instruction and absorbing the work of "The Collegiate Course." Barnard College was completely independent of Columbia College in nonacademic matters, but it did utilize Columbia College instructors and professors, library facilities, course standards, and examinations. As Columbia College professors became less available, Barnard College began to hire its own instructors. Early enrollments were low, with only nine graduates in the first class and only thirty-five graduates five years later.

Although the Barnard College curriculum was on a par with that of Columbia College, a chronic problem at Barnard (as well as at other female colleges) was the paucity of academically prepared women able to meet the rigors of legitimate university study. This was due primarily to the often inferior secondary preparation of the young women, particularly in the sciences, classics, and mathematics, which carried over into the university setting, where women were often discouraged from excelling in these typically "male" domains. Nonetheless, in 1900 Barnard College was incorporated into the Columbia University system, where it remains an integral part of the university to this day.

—*Maureen Anna Harp*

See Also:
"Seven Sisters," Women in Higher Education

References:

"A History of Barnard College." [Published in honor of the Seventy-fifth Anniversary of the College, 1964.] New York: Columbia University Press, 1964.
Meyer, Annie Nathan. *Barnard Beginnings*. New York: Houghton Mifflin, 1935.
Miller, Alice Duer, and Susan Meyers. *Barnard College, The First Fifty Years*. New York: Columbia University Press, 1939.
White, Marian Churchill. *A History of Barnard College*. New York: Columbia University Press, 1954.

BARRY, MOTHER GERALD (1881–1961) was prioress general of the Dominican Sisters of Adrian, Michigan (Congregation of the Most

Holy Rosary), from 1933 to 1961. Born Bridget Catherine Barry in West Clare, Ireland, one of eighteen children of prosperous farmers, Michael and Catherine (Dixon) Barry, she was educated at Inagh National School in County Clare and emigrated to Chicago in 1896, where she studied business at Powers Business College. After teaching for four years, she worked as a secretary to her brother in a law firm at Nogales, Arizona. In 1912 she entered the Sisters of St. Dominic, Adrian, Michigan, and received the religious name "Mary Gerald." From 1914 to 1933 she served in various teaching and administrative positions in the community until she was elected prioress general of the congregation.

She served as leader of her community for over twenty-eight years and guided it through one of its most dynamic periods of growth and expansion. Not only did the numbers of Adrian Dominicans increase (930 to 2,480), but Mother Gerald pressed for expansion of the elementary, secondary, and higher education ministries of the order. Under her direction the Adrian Dominicans accepted the staffing of seventy new parochial schools, established four high schools for girls, founded two colleges (Barry College, Florida, and Aquinas Teachers College, Nassau, Bahamas), and expanded the order's Siena Heights College in Adrian. Moreover, a number of missions in the Caribbean and Peru were accepted as well.

Mother Gerald was a firm advocate of higher education for nuns. To effect this she not only established a house of studies in Washington, D.C., for her sisters studying at the Catholic University of America, but also sent them to prestigious secular universities. She also recognized the great potential for uniting and coordinating the efforts of American women religious. In 1952 the Sacred Congregation for Religious called on her to act as executive chairperson of the National Committee for Sisters, a subgroup of the National Congress of Religious that met at the University of Notre Dame that year. Four years later, Rome appointed her to chair a meeting of Mothers General in the United States. Out of this grew the Conference of Major Superiors of Women Religious, now known as the Leadership Conference of Women Religious. She received honorary degrees from the University of Santo Domingo, Dominican Republic (Ph.D., 1949); University of Notre Dame (J.D., 1952); and Loyola University of Chicago (J.D., 1960). She died at the motherhouse of the Adrian Dominicans in 1961.

—Steven M. Avella

See Also:
Christianity

References:

Barry, M. Gerald. *The Charity of Christ Presses Us: Letters to Her Community.* Edited by M. Philip Ryan. Milwaukee: Bruce, 1962.

McKeough, M. Paul. "Mother Mary Gerald, O.P." *Dominican Educational Bulletin* 3 (Winter 1962): 17–23.

BARTON, CLARA (1821–1912) was the founder of the American branch of the International Red Cross, but came to that enterprise in an indirect and far from predictable way. Born Clarissa Harlowe Barton, she was the fifth and last child of a family well established in the town of Oxford, Massachusetts. Somewhat spoiled by her older brothers and sister, she grew up a willful child and became a self-willed adult. Working under others was never easy for her, often impossible, and this personality trait contributed to her successes and failures.

As a schoolteacher, Barton established the first free school in New Jersey in 1852; as an employee of the Patent Office in Washington in 1854, she made $1,400 a year. She then became a semirecluse—fits of physical lassitude and emotional deflation were common throughout her lifetime—until the Civil War provided the opportunity for her to fulfill what she saw as her great purpose in life, service to others. Her genius in wartime was not nursing as such but the gathering and distribution of supplies to supplement the work of the Union Army and, where needed, the efforts of the U.S. Sanitary Commission. For these efforts, she was celebrated as "the American Nightingale" and the "Angel of the Battlefield" for the rest of her life.

While visiting Europe in 1869, Barton first became aware of the relatively new organization, the International Red Cross, begun in 1864. She was taken with the Red Cross ideal: to succor all military and civilian casualties of war. Ready to return home to preach the idea in America, which had not joined the International Red Cross, Barton became involved in the Franco-Prussian War. Under the flag of the Red Cross, she worked to relieve the misery of the populations of Strasbourg, Metz, and Paris.

After a long, uphill fight on her part, the U.S. government finally joined the International Red Cross by signing the 1864 Geneva Convention in March 1882. Meanwhile Barton saw the Red Cross as a standby organization, ready to offer aid in the wake of all manner of natural and man-made disasters. The organization was widely accepted in the United States and received a federal charter in 1900. But Clara Barton's egocentric leadership style fitted poorly into the formal structure of organizational charity, and she was forced to resign the presidency in 1904.

—*D. H. Burton*

See Also:

American Red Cross, Nursing, U.S. Sanitary Commission

References:

Barton, Clara. *The Story of My Childhood.* New York: Baker & Taylor, 1907.

Ross, Ishbel. *Angel of the Battlefield.* New York: Harper, 1956.

Williams, Blanche C. *Clara Barton, Daughter of Destiny.* Philadelphia: Lippincott, 1941.

BAXTER, ANNIE (1864–1944), the first female county clerk in the United States and first elected female official in Missouri, assumed her duties as Jasper County clerk in January 1891 at Carthage, Missouri. Her career provided an example of women's entry into local politics and government in the late nineteenth century, before women were federally enfranchised by the ratification of the Nineteenth Amendment. Baxter was nominated by the Democratic County Convention after years of service as deputy county clerk. Her subsequent election was challenged by one of her opponents, Julius Fischer. When the Green County Circuit Court upheld her election in January 1892, Baxter had already served one year in her position.

Born Anna White in Pittsburgh, Pennsylvania, she moved with her family to Carthage in 1877, graduated from high school in 1882, then joined the staff of the county clerk. In 1888 she married Charles W. Baxter, whom she employed as an assistant clerk in her office. It is unknown how active Baxter was in Carthage's newly formed prohibition or suffrage organizations or the town's active women's club movement.

Baxter lost her bid for reelection with the Republican landslide in 1894. After a short period in St. Louis, she resumed her career and moved to Jefferson City, Missouri, to work for the secretary of state. When the office was reorganized in 1913, Baxter became land registrar and held that position until 1921. In 1922 she became financial secretary to the Missouri Constitutional Commission and was the commission's only female staff member.

After serving briefly in a position at the University of Missouri, Baxter returned to Jefferson City, where she continued to be active in Missouri Democratic circles. However, her landmark 1890 election was not included in *Missouri Democracy,* her party's 1935 history. Included among Jasper County's "distinguished Democrats and Partyworkers" were thirteen other women, including Emily Newell Blair, vice chairman of the National Democratic Committee in 1924.

Annie Baxter died on June 23, 1944. She is memorialized with a street named in her honor in Joplin, Missouri, and with a stone embedded at the east steps of the Jasper County Courthouse (1895), authorized and started during her term as county clerk. Despite the memorial's claim, Baxter was not the first female elected to public office. In the neighboring state of Kansas, Susanna Maldora Salter had been elected mayor of Argonia in 1887, preceded in elective office by several female school superintendents.

Nonetheless, Annie Baxter's election and public service was a milestone in the region and served as a source of inspiration to many Carthage women who pursued interests and careers long closed to them. Among these women were Sara Frank, first woman to run for Jasper County school superintendent, 1894; Ella Harrison, president of the Missouri State Suffrage Association, 1896; the Reverend Lucy B. Lindsey, first ordained woman of the Christian denomination in Missouri, 1895; and Emma Knell, one of the first female morticians in Missouri in the late 1890s and first Republican woman elected to the Missouri House of Representatives, 1925.

—Michele Newton

See Also:
Democratic Party, Politics

References:

Annie Baxter Research Files of the Powers Museum, Carthage, Mo. Including: Michelle Cheney. "Annie White Baxter: A Silent Movement for the Rights of the Individual Woman." Unpub. manuscript, 1987.

Logan, Mrs. John A. *The Part Taken by Women in American History.* Wilmington, Del.: Perry-Nalle, 1912.

Willard, Frances, and Mary A. Livermore. *American Women.* New York: Mast, Crowell & Kirkpatrick, 1893.

BEACH, AMY MARCY CHENEY (MRS. H. H. A.) (1867–1944) was a composer and pianist. She began as a pianist-prodigy and had her first public appearance in 1883 at age sixteen. In 1885 she married Henry Harris Aubrey Beach, a distinguished surgeon, who encouraged her musicianship. Between 1885 and 1910, she concentrated on composition and then resumed her concert tours both in Europe and the United States. She settled in New York and often spent summers at the MacDowell Colony, a retreat for creative artists.

Her *Gaelic Symphony,* completed in 1896, was the first symphony composed by an American woman. She composed other large works, including an opera, *Cabildo* op. 149, Piano Concerto in C Sharp op. 45, Mass in E Flat op. 5, and Sonata in A Minor for violin and piano op. 34. In addition, she wrote many small works, including over 150 songs by which she became known to the general public. Beach was considered a leading representative of the late-nineteenth-century romantic style, with its emphasis on broad lines of melody and complex harmonies. Having little formal instruction in music theory, she taught herself orchestration and composition. Her works and performances received critical acclaim in her lifetime.

—Anne Dzamba Sessa

See Also:
Music

References:

Ammer, Christine. *Unsung: A History of Women in American Music.* Westport, Conn.: Greenwood, 1979.

Block, Adrienne Fried and Carol Neuls-Bates, eds. and comps. *Women in American Music.* Westport, Conn.: Greenwood, 1979.

BEALS, JESSIE TARBOX (1870–1942), considered by many to be the first female photojournalist, is also recognized as a portraitist and as an architectural photographer. Born in Canada of New England–born parents, Beals moved to Williamsburg, Massachusetts, at age eighteen to become an elementary school teacher. In the 1880s teaching was considered an acceptable profession for young middle-class women, and Beals taught for over ten years. However, the spirited Beals found teaching tedious. After winning a tin box-camera in a magazine contest, she became devoted to photography and left the classroom for the new medium.

She married Alfred Beals in 1897, and the two eventually set up a photography studio in which she took over as photographer and business manager while he set up the darkroom. She consistently dominated the business relationship, and in 1917 she left the marriage permanently.

Throughout her career, Beals was known for her energy, enthusiasm, and her "ability to hustle." She contributed photographs to many newspaper magazines and newspapers, including the *Ladies Home Journal, Vogue, Town and Country*, the *New York Herald Tribute*, and the *Buffalo Courier*. As a photojournalist, she photographed the Louisiana Purchase Exposition in St. Louis in 1904.

In 1905 Beals went to New York City to realize her dream of establishing a studio there. As a portraitist, she photographed celebrities from the worlds of art, business, government, and entertainment. Beals is also important for being part of a great tradition of urban photography that emerged between 1880 and 1920. She used her camera to photograph what she called the "soul of New York," recording Greenwich Village, Chinatown, the Lower East Side, Central Park, and many examples of city architecture. Known to go anywhere and to any lengths to take a desired photograph, she also traveled to Florida, Texas, Chicago, and California. After 1920 Beals concentrated more on photographing the homes and gardens of well-to-do clients.

Jessie Tarbox Beals's life illuminates the positive nature of women's experience in photography. With over thirty-five hundred women working as professional photographers in 1900, Beals was not an isolated individual but was connected to other women who in the early twentieth century entered photography and a variety of other professions.

—*C. Jane Gover*

See Also:

Journalism, Photography

References:

Jessie Tarbox Beals Collection. Arthur and Elizabeth Schlesinger Library. Radcliffe College, Cambridge, Mass.

Alland, Alexander, Sr. *Jessie Tarbox Beals: First Woman News Photographer*. New York: Camera/Graphic Press, 1978.

BEARD, MARY (RITTER) (1876–1958), historian, writer, and activist, established her reputation by her books on women in history, by her pioneering work in women's studies, and by her active participation in the suffragist movement. She was born into a middle-class suburban Indianapolis family. A graduate of DePauw University in 1897, she also studied at the Columbia University Graduate School, but abandoned graduate work as being far too theoretical to offer solutions to pressing social problems. She preferred active politics to academic speculation. Her work for women's suffrage was tied directly to a belief that government should act to improve the lives of all people in society who were disadvantaged, not only women. She considered suffrage one means to that end but refused to support the Equal Rights Amendment of the 1920s as too narrow in its focus.

After the Nineteenth Amendment was passed, Beard focused on scholarship in women's history as a discrete field. By that time, the mid-1920s, she was already well known as the co-author (with her husband) of an important textbook on American history, but she wanted to strike out on her own. In 1931 she made a major statement in *On Understanding Women*. In her judgment women had been central to history: "women, assuming chief responsibility for the continuance and care of life [are] a force so vital and so powerful that anthropologists can devise no meter to register it." She elaborated this basic theme in two later books, *Women as a Force in History* (1946) and *The Force of Women in Japanese History* (1953).

In addition, Beard organized the short-lived Center for Women's Archives in New York City and actively promoted women's studies at Radcliffe, Smith, Barnard, Vassar, and at Syracuse University. Despite the fact that she was something of a "loner" in the women's movement and did not seek to organize a following, Mary Beard was a pioneer for women's rights and women's history in the twentieth century.

—*D. H. Burton*

See Also:

Suffrage, Women in Higher Education

References:

Beard, Mary R. *On Understanding Women.* New York: Grosset & Dunlap, 1931.

———. *Women as a Force in History: A Study in Traditions and Realities.* New York: Collier, 1946.

———. *The Force of Women in Japanese History.* Washington, D.C.: Public Affairs Press, 1953.

Lane, Ann J., ed. *Mary Ritter Beard: A Sourcebook.* New York: Schoken, 1977.

BEAUTY INDUSTRY. The twentieth-century beauty industry both shaped and responded to the changing role of women in American society. Previously, puritanical strictures had largely confined acceptable cosmetic practices to medicinal and hygienic contexts, but in the twentieth century beauty was more openly pursued for its own sake. These changes were wrought in part by the new cosmopolitanism of the World War I era, the expansion of consumerism, urbanization, progress on the suffrage issue, and the enhanced economic role of women.

The mode of operation and social impact of the beauty industry diverged significantly for Afro-American and white women. In the former case, the beauty industry was not only in the vanguard of Afro-American business activity, but it helped to give women a sense of femininity and self-esteem that slavery had denied them, while also creating new avenues for capital formation, entrepreneurship, and dignified alternatives to menial labor. As a result, industry pioneers such as Annie M. Turnbo Malone and Madam C. J. Walker were among the wealthiest self-made women of their day. While the Afro-American beauty industry concentrated on mass-based direct sales distribution, white cosmetic firms, such as those of Helena Rubinstein (1870–1965) and Elizabeth Arden (1878–1966), manufactured expensive products that were mainly distributed through exclusive salons and retail establishments. Eventually, however, advertising, especially the Sears catalog or "wish book," along with the image-making power of the movie industry, conspired to shape popular tastes and concepts of beauty for women generally. This standardization process was compounded by the "trickle-down" effect of French haute couture with its "models" of beauty that critics argued made the "average" woman hopelessly unperfectible and therefore a "slave" to the vicissitudes of fashion.

Today the beauty business is a largely male-dominated multibillion dollar worldwide enterprise that is closely linked with the pharmaceutical industry. The cosmetic industry continues to be highly profitable for women, however, as demonstrated by Mary Kay's corporate sales projections of $400 million for 1988.

—*Gwendolyn Keita Robinson*

See Also:

Malone, Annie Turnbo; Walker, Madame C. J. (Sara Breedlove)

References:

Banner, Lois. *American Beauty.* New York: Knopf, 1983.

Gunn, Fenja. *The Artifical Face: A History of Cosmetics.* New York: Hippocrene, 1983.

Lauder, Estée. *Estée: A Success Story.* New York: Random House, 1985.

Robinson, Gwendolyn Keita. *Crowning Glory: An Historical Analysis of the Afro-American Beauty Industry and Tradition.* Urbana, Ill.: University of Illinois Press, forthcoming.

Rubinstein, Helena. *My Life for Beauty.* New York: Simon & Schuster, 1964.

Sims, Naomi. *All About Health and Beauty for the Black Woman.* Garden City, N.Y.: Doubleday, 1976.

BEAUTY PAGEANTS. Beauty contests were not American in origin. From feudal times, Austria, France, and Great Britain celebrated folk festivals, various holidays, and observances for which a beautiful female was crowned queen. May Day celebrations were the first competitions in the United States for a beauty queen; however, the Puritans of the Massachusetts Bay colonies replaced the May Day observance and all other English holidays with Thanksgiving. Nevertheless, May Day celebrations survived and expanded to include many other events.

By the middle of the nineteenth century, these festivals were popular in the West. They reached their height in the Pasadena Tournament of Roses, 1889, and in the Rose Festival of Portland, Oregon, 1909. Festivals also became popular in cities in the heartland of America. Surprisingly, the Victorians rarely protested the selection of queens for various festivals, in spite of their dislike of women displayed in public. As early as 1699, Mardi Gras, the common ancestor for all American festivals, legitimized queens and kings, using a selection process based on fate, luck, and a democratic process. The selection of queens demonstrated the social mobility of American society. For all festivals, queens were considered crucial, since women were the guardians of morality and a symbol of community values. The selection of festival queens was not always based on physical beauty. Early queens were selected for their civic leadership, community popularity, or in honor of a male relative. Nevertheless, May Day and other festival queens reinforced the importance of physical beauty as a matter of competition and elitism.

P. T. Barnum introduced photographic beauty contests, which became popular in the late 1800s and early 1900s. City newspapers spread this idea. Contests occurred in many cities and were popular because the women did not have to display themselves before the public or the judges. About the same time, the carnival that had won acceptance among the middle class began to promote local civic and business ventures. The main feature of this event was the selection of a queen based on physical beauty. The emergence of modeling as a respectable career for women in the twentieth century helped to popularize beauty contests. The fusion of the features of the lower-class carnivals with the upper-class festivals, however, would not occur in a natural and national setting until the Miss America Pageant in 1921.

Miss America, while not the only beauty pageant, is the only pageant that provides $3 million in scholarships for participants. The other two major pageants, Miss Universe and Miss USA, are strictly beauty contests. Pacific Knitting Mills created the Miss Universe Pageant as a protest when the Miss America Pageant refused to provide photographs of the contestants wearing Catalina swimsuits made by Pacific. A vehicle for advertising, the contest was first held in Long Beach, California, in 1951. The next year, it was moved to Miami, Florida, to accommodate its sole sponsor, Procter and Gamble. In 1981 Paramount Pictures took over the Miss Universe Pageant. The contestants for these pageants are differentiated on the state level—for instance, Miss Texas-USA. In 1984 Miss America was paid $25,000, while Miss Universe was paid $175,000; Miss Universe also receives as much as $2,500 for personal appearances, twice as much as Miss America receives. These pageants are held close together: Miss USA in April, Miss Universe in July, and Miss America in September. Prizes continue to reflect the assumption that women desire jewels and furs. The co-host of the Miss USA and Miss Universe Pageant for twenty-one years, Bob Barker in 1988 resigned his six-figure salary because furs were given as prizes. An advocate for animals, Barker felt his credibility would be damaged if he continued to host the show.

The Miss Universe organization includes the Miss Teen-USA pageant. Other teenage pageants—such as America's Junior Miss, Miss Teenage America, and Miss United Teenager—include talent competitions, recognize high school academic standing and activities, and give scholarships. Special pageants include the Mrs. America Pageant in Palisades Park, New Jersey, and the local pageants for the very young, such as Our Little Miss. Competitions for men include Mr. America, Mr. Universe, and Mr. Olympia. These, however, are bodybuilding contests, and little emphasis is placed on the interview or formal evening wear.

Other countries have beauty contests and pageants such as the Miss World Pageant in London, England. The U.S. contestant in this pageant is called Miss World-USA. The newest additions to the beauty pageant scene are Miss and Mr. Canton from the People's Republic of China. These contestants are judged on talent, physical appearance, nationalism, culture, and history. The latest addition to the pageant scene in the United States is the Mother-Daughter Pageant in which both compete as a team in swimsuits and evening gowns.

—Judith B. Lucas

See Also:
Miss America Pageant

References:

Banner, Lois W. *American Beauty*. New York: Knopf, 1983.
Kindel, Stephen, ed. "Beauty You Can Take to the Bank." *Forbes* 133 (June 18, 1984): 136–39.
Martin, Nancie S. *Miss America Through the Looking Glass*. New York: Messner, 1985.
Meckel, Rob. "Barker Resigns over Fur Flap." *The Houston Post* (January 13, 1988), A 2.

BEAUX, CECILIA (1855–1942) was a painter of the early-twentieth-century elite. Raised in Philadelphia in a genteel tradition where appreciation for the arts was emphasized, she received early encouragement and support from relatives who recognized her talents.

After Beaux's first major composition, *Les Derniers Jours d'Enfance* ("The Last Days of Childhood"), was accepted by the Paris Salon in 1887, her career was launched and she became a well-established Philadelphia portraitist. In 1888 Beaux traveled for the first time to Europe. She entered classes in Paris at the Académie Julian, where she received criticism from painters William Bouguereau and Tony Robert-Fleury. She also studied the paintings of the Old Masters that she saw in the museums, particularly those by Titian, Rembrandt, and Rubens. Though aware of the impressionist movement, Beaux resisted any overpowering influences, determined to select from the diverse trends around her only those qualities that seemed appropriate to her emerging style.

In the 1890s a surge of commissions caused Beaux to move to New York. She started a series of "white" paintings, followed by a series of impressive double portraits. Her portrait *Mother and Daughter* (1898) won four gold medals. Earlier, in 1887, she had received wide acclaim for her first painting in white tones, *A Little Girl* (Fanny Travis Cochran).

By 1900 Beaux was established as a leading portrait painter in New York. Her commissions came from prominent figures in the arts, finance, and government, among them Mrs. Theodore Roosevelt and Mrs. Andrew Carnegie. Her more academic portraits, such as those of Georges Clemenceau, Sir David Beatty, and Cardinal Mercier, were commissioned by the U.S. government. For the first Portrait Gallery (now the National Portrait Gallery), the artist successfully produced dignified portrayals of each sitter's office and position. Between 1897 and 1933 Beaux had fourteen one-woman shows, and her work was exhibited at the Pennsylvania Academy of Fine Arts, several New York galleries, and the Paris Salon. She received numerous prizes and awards.

Beaux's best work reveals simple forms and innovative figure placement, as well as an original compositional style. She was acclaimed for her psychological insight, rich brushwork, and subtle color. Her principal concerns, she claimed, were "imaginative insight and design." Beaux painted continuously until 1924, when she started her autobiography, *Background with Figures* (1930).

One of Beaux's greatest distinctions is that she was the first woman to be engaged as a full-time member of the Pennsylvania Academy of the Fine Arts faculty, thereby influencing the careers of countless women. In addition, the superior skills of Cecelia Beaux kept portraiture alive at a time when photography was rapidly replacing it in popularity.

—Florence Davis

See Also:
Art

References:

Harris, Ann Sutherland, and Ruth Nochlin. *Women Artists, 1550–1950*. New York: Knopf, 1981.

Rubinstein, Charlotte Streifer. *American Women Artists: From Early Indian Times to the Present.* Boston: G. K. Hall, 1982.
Tufts, Eleanor. *American Women Artists 1830–1930.* Washington, D.C.: The National Museum of Women in the Arts, 1987.

BEECHER, CATHARINE (1800–78), a nineteenth-century writer and advocate of female educational reform, was the eldest of Lyman and Roxana Foote Beecher's seven children. When her mother died in 1816, Catharine took over many of the domestic duties for the family. Lyman Beecher married Harriet Porter in 1817, and the family grew to include eleven children. Catharine had a very central role in this remarkable family. Her seven brothers became ministers, the most famous being Henry Ward Beecher; her sister Harriet Beecher Stowe shared her vocation as a writer and educator; and her sister Isabella Beecher Hooker was a major advocate of women's rights.

Beecher's writings and career as an educator were dedicated to her vision of woman's particular domestic responsibility. Her ideas about home design and landscaping advanced the ideal of the "suburban" setting for the home. She wrote about women's life-style and fashion and championed the reform of female education, insisting on physical exercise and specialized studies in home economy to equip women for their special role as wives, mothers, and teachers of their children. Concerned that women should exercise their role properly, she disagreed with the manner in which Sarah and Angelina Grimké spoke out publicly regarding abolition, and claimed that the influence of women was best confined to the domestic sphere.

Beecher's contributions to advancement of women's education placed her among the mid-Victorian proponents of domestic feminism. She addressed the lack of education and instruction in moral/religious values available to children in the West with a plan to establish seminaries for young women who would be trained in both teaching and the inculcation of religious and moral values, and who in turn would train other potential teachers for the West. Beecher initiated the establishment of the Central Committee for Promoting National Education in 1840. Later named the Board of National Popular Education, with the former governor of Vermont, William Slade, as its director, Beecher's organization trained teachers in four-week sessions at Hartford, Connecticut, in preparation for sending them on to schools in Ohio, Illinois, Iowa, and Wisconsin.

The initial funding for this plan was through private sources, but Beecher hoped to enlist enough public awareness to enable these seminaries to receive "legislative and national aid." Beecher believed strongly that Christian women should assume the role of teaching the young and that the teaching profession should be regarded as a noble calling. In 1846 her *Address on the Evils Suffered by American Women and American Children* sought to awaken the public to the plight of uneducated women and children.

Beecher and Slade ended their collaboration in 1848 after a major dispute, and he continued the work of the committee, changing its name to the Board of National Popular Education. During the Beecher-Slade years, 481 women were trained and sent westward. Before it declined in the late 1850s, the Board of National Popular Education was responsible for sending several thousand young women teachers westward.

All of the Beecher children departed to some degree from the Orthodox Calvinism of their father's generation, but Catharine's reaction against this conservative religious tradition in New England occurred as a response to an early tragedy in her life. Shortly after her engagement to Alexander Metcalf Fisher, a young and enthusiastic teacher of mathematics, he died in a boating accident. Though he had not as yet had the "experience of grace," which would count him among the "elect" (those certain to go to heaven), Beecher was unwilling to believe that her fiancé was damned to hell. She consoled herself with the belief that the mercy of God could not so harshly judge this young man. Later in her life she wrote two theological essays on the question of religion, *Letters on the Difficulties of*

Religion (1836) and *Common Sense Applied to Religion* (1857). Though Beecher never married, her concern as a writer and reformer lay with improving the lives of women who did.

—*Maria Erling and Jean Nettles*

See Also:

Coeducation; Domestic Feminism; Education; Stowe, Harriet Beecher

References:

Beecher, Catharine. *The Domestic Receipt Book.* New York: Harper, 1846.

———. *The Evils Suffered by American Women and American Children: The Causes and the Remedy.* New York: Harper and Bros., 1846.

———. *Treatise on Domestic Economy for the Use of Young Ladies at Home and at School.* Boston: T. H. Webb, 1843.

———. *The True Remedies for the Wrongs of Women.* Boston: Phillips, Sampson, 1851.

———, and Harriet Beecher Stowe. *The American Women's Home.* New York: Ford, 1869.

Boydston, Jeanne, Mary Kelley, and Anne Margolis. *The Limits of Sisterhood: The Beecher Sisters on Women's Rights and Woman's Sphere.* Chapel Hill: University of North Carolina Press, 1989.

Hoffman, Nancy. *Woman's "True" Profession.* New York: Feminist Press, 1981.

Riley, Glenda. *Inventing the American Woman.* Arlington Heights, Ill.: Harlan Davidson, 1986.

Rugoff, Milton. *The Beechers: An American Family in the 19th Century.* New York: Harper & Row, 1981.

Sklar, Kathryn Kish. *Catharine Beecher: A Study in American Domesticity.* New Haven: Yale University Press, 1973.

BENEDICT, RUTH FULTON (1887–1948) was one of the first women in the United States to become a professional anthropologist. At the time of her appointment as assistant professor in the Department of Anthropology of Columbia University in 1930, she was the first and only woman on the anthropology faculty. In 1936 her status was elevated to that of associate professor, and in 1948, just three months before her untimely death of coronary thrombosis at the age of sixty-one, she was made a full professor.

She studied as an undergraduate with Elsie Clews Parsons, who later helped to fund her research, and then as a graduate student with Franz Boas, one of the founders of anthropology in the United States. Benedict went on, with Margaret Mead and Edward Sapir, to help found "culture and personality" studies, which attempt to link the personalities of particular individuals to the cultural forms of the society in which they live. Benedict believed that certain characteristic patterns of personalities could be found within each culture and that these overall patterns could be described in psychological terms. Her two most famous books, *Patterns of Culture* (1934) and *The Chrysanthemum and the Sword* (1946), helped to establish the legitimacy of anthropology in the minds of the American public. *Patterns of Culture* was written about three different cultures—the Zuni, the Dobu, and the Kwakiutl—which she believed represented different cultural psychological "types," Apollonian and Dionysian. *The Chrysanthemum and the Sword* was written during World War II about the Japanese in order to help Americans understand the psychological makeup of an enemy culture.

One of the goals behind her studies of the patterns that define a culture was an understanding of the mechanisms behind these patterns so that one day human beings could actively take control of the way their societies are patterned. She wanted human beings to be able to organize and shape their own cultures "with intelligence." She believed that complex behavior was learned, that biology did not determine cultural forms, and that all human "races" were equal. During World War II she wrote *Race, Science, and Politics* (1940), in which she argued that differences between groups of people could only be explained effectively in terms of the different cultures from which they come rather than innate biological differences. The intent of the book was political; her aim was to show the fallacies upon which Nazism and all other racist philosophies rest.

Because of a childhood illness, Benedict lost most of her hearing at a young age. Combined with her own shyness, her deafness made fieldwork an unpleasant chore for her. Nevertheless, she went out to the American Southwest and worked among the Serrano (summer 1922), the Zuni (1924, 1925, and 1927), the Pima (1927), the Apache (summer 1930), and the Blackfoot (summer 1938).

—*Steven Mandeville-Gamble*

See Also:

Mead, Margaret; Women in Higher Education

References:

Benedict, Ruth. *The Chrysanthemum and the Sword.* Boston: Houghton Mifflin, 1946.

———. *Patterns of Culture.* Boston: Houghton Mifflin, 1934.

———. *Race, Science and Politics.* New York: Viking, 1940.

Mead, Margaret. "Ruth Fulton Benedict, 1887–1948." *American Anthropologist* 51 (1949): 457–68.

Wenner-Gren Foundation for Anthropological Research. *Ruth Fulton Benedict: A Memorial.* New York: Viking Fund, 1949.

BENEVOLENCE refers to the charity and missionary activities of antebellum women, adapting the noblesse oblige of the European nobility to the rising middle class in the United States. From the colonial and revolutionary periods, benevolence was integrated into the prescribed activities for middle-class women, first as part of the late-eighteenth-century concept of Republican Motherhood which defined women's role in the new nation, and then during the nineteenth century as an aspect of Woman's Sphere and of its attendant concepts of Woman's Influence and Woman's Proper Role. In addition to their educational, religious, and missionary efforts at home and abroad, middle-class women dispensed their aid and comfort to the deserving poor and needy of early industrial America through their voluntary associations.

Charity activities fell within the historic, preindustrial sexual division of labor, and therefore within the limits of the Woman's Sphere, which was defined as the private, domestic sphere, although these sanctioned benevolence efforts required women to enter the Public Sphere and to undertake organizational and fund-raising enterprises that demanded both political and financial acumen. Through an astute application of Piety, one of the traits of True Womanhood, True Women parlayed women's imperative to benevolence to support women's venture into the public and political arenas without challenging the legitimacy of the gender limitations imposed by Woman's Sphere. Thus, conservative spokeswomen and women's magazines could be and were enlisted to employ their unimpeachable respectability and their considerable influence to promote women's charity activities that established self-help agencies, educational institutions, and even small businesses to provide job training and employment for women and girls. Benevolence work provided a classic model of the dynamic of domestic feminism that expanded Woman's Sphere into the public arena without challenging its assumption that women belonged in the private sphere.

Benevolence efforts paved the way for women's entry into many Victorian reform movements. The earliest benevolent groups were sponsored by ministers, but it was the women in their congregations who provided the working membership. Eventually women established separate voluntary associations such as the Boston Female Society for Missionary Purposes, founded in 1800, which financially supported educating ministers and sending male missionaries to serve the Native American tribes of the West in addition to providing material and spiritual assistance to the poor of Boston. By the 1820s more secular women's benevolent groups were established that went beyond the traditional "Lady Bountiful" distribution of food and clothes to the deserving poor. For example, Boston women organized the Seaman's Aid Society to provide assistance for the widows and orphans of American sailors through establishing a sewing workshop to employ these women and their daughters. After the Civil War, such efforts focused women's energies on various causes and issues associated with social welfare and community improvement.

During the nineteenth century, women sponsored craft fairs and used the sale of their donated handcrafted items to raise the funds necessary to support their charity services and agencies. Ironically, the actual handling of the money required the presence and participation of male trustees since antebellum women lacked the legal identity required to manage their own or public funds. By the end of the nineteenth century, legal incorporation of women's benevolent institutions required that male boards of trustees replace the female volunteers who had established and capably managed thriving institutions.

The experience and success of women's benevolence activities before the Civil War made possible and respectable women's participation in latter-nineteenth-century civic politics. Ultimately, the development of social work as a woman's profession and many of the accomplishments of the Progressive era can be traced to the humble amateur efforts of women's benevolence that began in the early nineteenth century. The rise and increase of governmentally supported social welfare programs before and after World War II depended upon the participation of civic and religious women's groups to provide the volunteer work force of such services to the community. By the 1980s the increased participation of married women in the paid labor force drained the reservoir of volunteer middle-class matrons who historically had been crucial to the survival of such community service organizations as Meals on Wheels and the Girl and Boy Scouts.

—Angela Howard Zophy

See Also:

Black Women's Clubs, Cult of True Womanhood, Voluntarism

References:

Clinton, Catherine. *The Other Civil War: American Women in the Nineteenth Century.* New York: Hill and Wang, 1984.

Lerner, Gerda. *The Female Experience: An American Documentary.* Indianapolis: Bobbs-Merrill, 1977.

Scott, Anne Fior. "Women's Voluntary Associations in the Forming of American Society." In *Making the Invisible Woman Visible,* edited by Anne Fior Scott. Urbana: University of Illinois Press, 1984, pp. 274–94.

Welter, Barbara. *Dimity Conditions: The American Woman of the Nineteenth Century.* Athens: Ohio University Press, 1976.

Zophy, Angela Howard. "'For the Improvement of My Sex': Sarah Josepha Hale's Editorship of *Godey's Lady's Book,* 1837-1877." Diss. The Ohio State University, 1978.

BERDACHE. Many Native American cultures accepted people who took on the gender roles associated with the biologically opposite sex. The controversial French/North African term *berdache* refers to these individuals. Historically, such women, or, more commonly, men were accorded positions of high prestige as people possessing great spiritual power.

Commonly, women who became berdaches found out their male identity in their dreams through the intercession of supernatural powers. Alternately, girl children who played with male-identified toys were allowed to take up male gender identities. From that time forward, they would live their lives as men, go on hunting parties, fight in battles, and take wives. Interestingly enough, their wives are rarely portrayed in ethnographic accounts as being different from other women. The cultures that accepted female homosexuality include Chiricahua, Creek, Crow, Hopi, Mandan, Maricopa, Menomini, Natchez, Navaho, Ojibwa, Omaha, Oto, Papago, Ponca, Quinault, Seminole, Tabatulabal, Yuma, Yurok, and Zuni.

—Steven Mandeville-Gamble

See Also:

Lesbianism, Native American Women

References:

Denig, Edwin Thompson. *Five Indian Tribes of the Upper Missouri: Sioux, Arickaras, Assiniboines, Crees [and] Crows.* Edited by John C.

Ewers. Norman: University of Oklahoma Press, 1961.
Ford, Clennan S., and Frank A. Beach. "Homosexual Behavior." In *Patterns of Sexual Behavior.* New York: Harper and Row, 1951, pp. 136–40.
Greenberg, David F. "Why Was the Berdache Ridiculed?" In *The Many Faces of Homosexuality,* edited by Evelyn Blackwood. New York: Herrington, 1986, pp. 179–89.
Katz, Jonathon. *Gay American History.* New York: Harper, 1976.
Williams, Walter L. *The Spirit and the Flesh: Sexual Diversity in American Indian Culture.* Boston: Beacon, 1986.

BETHUNE, MARY MCLEOD (1875–1955), school founder, civic leader, club woman, and government appointee, was the fifteenth child born to slave parents in Mayesville, South Carolina. Encouraged to pursue further education by mission-school teacher Emma Wilson, Bethune received a scholarship to attend Scotia Seminary in Concord, North Carolina, to complete her secondary education. Since she wanted to become a missionary in Africa, Bethune went on to Moody Bible School in Chicago to prepare for the field. No positions were available when she graduated in 1895, so she returned to the South to teach.

At Lucy Laney's Haines Institute in Augusta, Georgia, Bethune learned directly and through Laney's example that black women had a "mission" to educate and uplift the race. In 1897 Mary married a fellow teacher, Albertus Bethune. She had one son, Albert, whom she took with her on her educational expeditions. She helped to reorganize a mission school in Palatka, Florida, and soon moved on to Daytona Beach, where the problems of black railroad workers led her to found the Daytona Normal and Industrial School for Negro Girls in 1904. Within two years, the school expanded to include her son and other boys, and the school and services continued to expand to meet changing needs. When blacks were refused service at white hospitals, Bethune organized a hospital that trained black nurses and employed black and white doctors. She described herself as a "good beggar" in her efforts to raise money from churches, lodges, clubs, and philanthropists, and she developed a school choir, which raised money through concert tours. Combining academic, manual, and moral training, the school merged with a men's college in 1925 to become Bethune-Cookman College.

Education was only one of the fields in which Bethune excelled. Within the black club movement, Bethune was a leader in the National Association of Colored Women and a founder of the National Council of Negro Women; the latter was intended to serve as an umbrella organization to unite the variety of black women's groups that had developed by 1935. She served on several committees for both the National Association for the Advancement of Colored People (NAACP) and the National Urban League. While both a college president and club leader, Bethune became a life member and president of the Association for the Study of Negro Life and History. This prominence led to her appointment as the director of minority affairs in the New Deal's National Youth Administration from 1936 to 1943. She became a close friend of Eleanor Roosevelt, who helped Bethune raise awareness about discrimination and conditions for blacks.

She received many honorary doctorates and honors, including the NAACP's Spingarn Medal, the Medal of Honor from Haiti, the Star of Africa from Liberia, and the Thomas Jefferson Award. In 1974 the first statue to honor any black woman leader in a public park was erected in her honor in Lincoln Park, Washington, D.C. Through works and example, Bethune dedicated her life to the development of racial pride and heritage to help America realize its democratic ideals.

—*Dorothy C. Salem*

See Also:

Black Women, Democratic Party, Higher Education for Southern Women, National Association for the Advancement of Colored People, National Association of Colored Women, National Council of Negro Women, New Deal

References:

Brewer, William. "Mary McLeod Bethune." *Journal of Negro History* 40 (1955): 393–94.

Dannett, Sylvia. *Profiles of Negro Womanhood.* Chicago: Education Heritage Press, 1964.

Holt, Rackham. *Mary McLeod Bethune: A Biography.* Garden City, N.Y.: Doubleday, 1964.

Peane, C. O. *Mary McLeod Bethune.* New York: Vanguard, 1951.

Ross, B. Joyce. "Mary McLeod Bethune and the National Youth Administration." *Journal of Negro History* 60 (January 1975): 1–28.

BIRTH CONTROL has become a synonym for contraception, but in fact the phrase originally had broader meanings. Coined by Margaret Sanger during a campaign for the legalization of contraception that began about 1914, the phrase *birth control* has since gained a generic meaning—referring to any method of controlling reproduction, including abstinence and abortion. In this sense, birth control is as old as civilization: few ancient societies were without some attempts to control reproduction. Traditional birth control reflected both women's desire for control over reproduction and community interests in controlling population size.

The first political campaign for birth control was not directly connected with women's rights agitation. Rather it developed, in early-nineteenth-century England, out of the neo-Malthusians' attempt to reduce birthrates among the poor in order to improve their standard of living and to reduce their social radicalism. Soon afterward, in the United States in the mid-nineteenth century, feminists began a birth control campaign associated with the slogan Voluntary Motherhood, which expressed women's longings to control their reproduction and their sexual activity. For these feminists, the recommended birth control method was abstinence.

Contraception, by contrast, refers to methods that allow sexual intercourse without pregnancy. Mechanical contraceptive techniques are of ancient origin and operate on the simple principle of blocking the cervical opening. Homemade pessaries were often combined with homemade spermicides and were somewhat effective. In the late nineteenth century, however, commercially produced thin rubber allowed the manufacture of modern vaginal diaphragms. In the first decades of the twentieth century, U.S. socialist feminists became aware of the availability of these devices in Europe and began a civil disobedience campaign for the legalization of contraception. They were gradually victorious, and in the 1920s most states legalized contraception by physicians' prescription.

The feminists' victories of the World War I period in making contraception respectable created both gains and losses for women. Contraceptives were increasingly available, but promoters of birth control increasingly separated themselves from a women's rights perspective. Contraception became a commercial commodity, and access to its more effective forms (such as vaginal diaphragms, hormones, and IUDs) was controlled by physicians rather than by women. Contraception helped women limit family size and permitted some women more sexual leeway, but it did not produce the increase in women's freedom and power that the original birth control campaigners had wanted. Only with the second wave of feminism in the late 1960s and 1970s was birth control reclaimed by feminists in a renewed campaign for women's reproductive self-control, largely focused on the right to legal abortion.

—Linda Gordon

See Also:

Abortion; Sanger, Margaret; Socialist Feminism; "Voluntary Motherhood"

References:

Gordon, Linda. "Margaret Sanger: From Voluntary Motherhood to Planned Parenthood." In *Margaret Sanger: From Voluntary Motherhood to Planned Parenthood,* edited by Dorothy Green and Mary-Elizabeth Murdock. Northampton, Mass.: Sophia Smith Collection, 1982, pp. 32–43, 61–66.

———. "The Struggle for Reproductive Freedom: Three Stages of Feminism." In *Capitalist Patriarchy and the Case for Socialist Feminism,* edited by Zillah Eisenstein. New York: Monthly Review, 1978, pp. 104–32.

———. *Woman's Body, Woman's Right: A Social History of Birth Control in America*. New York: Viking/Penguin, 1976.

Petchesky, Rosalind. *Abortion and Woman's Choice*. New York: Longman, 1984.

Reed, James. *From Private Vice to Public Virtue: The Birth Control Movement and American Society Since 1830*. New York: Basic, 1978.

The **BIRTH CONTROL CLINICAL RESEARCH BUREAU** was located across the hall from the office of the American Birth Control League, founded in 1921 by Margaret Sanger. In this office, doctors cooperating with Sanger's organization examined the women who came for contraceptive advice. There, doctors fitted the clients with spring-form diaphragms, taught them how to use spermicidal jelly, and gave medical counseling. The bureau was crucially important in Sanger's campaign to promote the diaphragm as the optimum birth control device. Over the years, doctors kept records that validated the effectiveness and safety of the diaphragm. As her recommended method of birth control gained doctors' confidence, Sanger's influence over the birth control movement was reinforced.

The Birth Control Clinical Research Bureau also served as a training station, instructing hundreds of doctors in the methods of contraception and promoting the safety and medical appropriateness of birth control for the wider public. It was Margaret Sanger's insistence on having doctors fit the women with the medical devices that was the justification for establishing this office. Her approach paid off in the general acceptance of birth control within the medical profession.

—Daryl M. Hafter

See Also:

American Birth Control League; Birth Control; Sanger, Margaret

References:

Gordon, Linda. *Woman's Body, Woman's Right: A Social History of Birth Control in America*. New York: Grossman, 1976.

Reed, James. *From Private Vice to Public Virtue: The Birth Control Movement and American Society Since 1830*. New York: Basic Books, 1978.

BLACHÉ, ALICE GUY (1875–1968) was a producer, director, inventor, writer, the first woman filmmaker, and perhaps, along with the Lumiére brothers in France and the Edison group in the United States, one of the originators of film narrative itself. Yet not until her death in 1968 did the full range of her contributions to film even begin to be appreciated.

A well-educated, middle-class Parisian, Blaché was working as industrialist Leon Gaumont's secretary in 1895 when she became interested in the brand new cinematographic apparatus that Louis Lumiére was then perfecting. She shot her first film, a fantasy called *La Fee aux Choux*, at Gaumont's home early in 1896—surely one of the earliest narrative films ever made. Thereafter she made dozens of films for Gaumont, and helped in developing the cameras, processing equipment, and projectors used, with an eye toward standardization and greater exhibition in front of larger, even worldwide audiences.

Between 1896 and 1901 she was responsible for *all* of Gaumont's filmmaking projects. She laid the foundation for what would be one of France's largest media empires by hiring for Gaumont assistants such as Louis Feuillade, Ferdinand Zecca, and Victorin Jasset. Each would achieve international renown on his own. It seemed, according to one writer, that by surrounding herself with such remarkable subordinates, "with one mighty stroke, she had created the entire early French film industry" (Slide, 15).

She directed hundreds of short films during this time, and produced two of the earliest feature films: *Passion* (1902), which was unusually long for its time, and *Life of Christ* (1906). In 1906 she began to experiment with synchronized sound, producing some one hundred films in the Chronophone system.

In 1907 she married Herbert Blaché and settled in the United States, where her husband was to act as Gaumont's major U.S. distributor. Bored with domestic life, Blaché returned to directing at a small studio in Flushing, New York. Releasing under the name the Solax Company, she gained a reputation for quality and innovation with a series of thrillers, romances, and even a Western shot in New Jersey. She personally planned the company's new, state-of-the-art studio facility in Fort Lee, New Jersey. There, filmmaking and processing were under her total control; Solax produced longer films, and the studio's output became eagerly sought after by exhibitors. By 1915 a trade publication could say that "to her, credit is due for many of the best-known features produced in the early days of feature productions." World War I brought great changes to the American film industry, and independent operations like Blaché's were soon swallowed up by large combines. She directed her last film, *Tarnished Reputations,* in 1920. In 1922 her marriage dissolved, leaving her disconsolate. Like many other women directors, Blaché argued tirelessly for programs in film education, believing that this would open channels of activity and promotion in the industry previously closed to women.

Although she was recognized as a Knight of the Legion of Honor in a ceremony at France's Cinémathèque Française in 1953, she died in comparative obscurity in the United States at the age of ninety-five.

—*Kevin Jack Hagopian*

See Also:
The Woman's Film

References:

Blaché, Alice Guy. *The Memoirs of Alice Guy Blaché.* Edited by Anthony Slide, translated by Roberta and Simone Blaché. Metuchen, N.J.: Scarecrow, 1986.

Heck-Rabi, Louise. "Alice Guy Blaché: Photoplay Pioneer." In *Women Filmmakers: A Critical Reception.* Metuchen, N.J.: Scarecrow, 1984, pp. 1–25.

Lacassin, Francis. "Out of Oblivion: Alice Guy Blaché." *Sight and Sound* 40 (Summer 1971): 150–55.

Peary, Gerald. "Alice Guy Blaché: Czarina of the Silver Screen." In *Women and the Cinema,* edited by Karyn Kay and Gerald Peary. New York: E. P. Dutton, 1977, pp. 139–45.

Slide, Anthony. *Early Women Directors.* New York: A. S. Barnes, 1977.

BLACK WOMEN. The African women who were captured, enslaved, and transported by ship to North America from the seventeenth through the nineteenth centuries were usually taken from the Bantu linguistic groups of West Africa that lived in the areas watered by the Gambia and Niger rivers. West African women were generally agriculturalists, an occupation that provided them with skills that would be exploited by their captors. Although slavery and warfare were common on the African continent, nothing like the Atlantic slave trade, with its alarming death toll, or North American chattel slavery were a part of the African woman's experience.

African women were first brought to Jamestown, Virginia, in 1619 to work as indentured servants, but within a generation some had become slaves in various parts of the American colonies. Brought to the plantations of the southern United States and the small land-holdings of the North, black women were expected to work as hard as their male counterparts and were given little consideration during and after pregnancy. Those women who did not labor in the fields worked as maids, nannies, cooks, personal servants, seamstresses, and laundresses within their owners' households. Although work indoors was often less grueling than that in the fields, the proximity of the enslaved women to the owners' families often resulted in injustice, cruelty, jealousy, and sexual oppression. No slave woman, whether in the house, field, or slave quarters, was safe either from the advances of her master or the corrective influence of the lash.

Within the confines of slavery, black women attempted to create as stable a family life as possible. Although black female slaves did not become runaways as frequently as males, they did run away, often in pursuit of husbands, children, or other family members. When slave families were divided, black women were sold with impunity on the auction blocks, sometimes with their breasts bared. To protest their lot or the destruction of their families, black women sometimes feigned illness or ineptitude, sabotaged their work, pilfered food and supplies, or resorted to violent acts such as infanticide, homicide, and suicide.

Although the institution of slavery continued to expand until it was destroyed by the Civil War and the passage of the Thirteenth Amendment, some owners had been freeing African women held in bondage from the seventeenth century on, so that a small class of free black women arose. Domestic work, akin to that performed by slave women, was generally the only work open to them. By the end of the eighteenth century, all of the northern states had outlawed slavery. Before the Civil War, some free black women joined the crusade for the abolition of slavery.

Freedom afforded black women the opportunity for individual creativity and group organization. They were founders and leaders in churches, schools, literary societies, and mutual aid organizations. Some free black women joined colonists moving to Haiti, Liberia, Canada, and the midwestern United States during the nineteenth century. After the Civil War, emancipated black women generally remained in the rural areas of the South, working along with their families as sharecroppers or tenant farmers. Attempting to annul the political gains made by blacks during Reconstruction, white terrorist groups such as the Ku Klux Klan victimized black families and even lynched some black women who refused to abide by discriminatory laws and social codes. Despite oppression, by the turn of the twentieth century most black women were literate and increasingly anxious to improve their political and social status.

The need for laborers during the two world wars drew many black women workers to the urban centers of the North. Although some black women were able to obtain factory jobs, the majority become household workers for white families. Generally the only type of employment open to black professional women in rural or urban areas was teaching in segregated schools. By the middle of the twentieth century, black women were moving from domestic work in private households to service work in public buildings, cafeterias, and hotels. Growing numbers of black women were engaged as clerical workers in public and private industries.

At the approach of the twenty-first century, about 25 percent of all black women were engaged in skilled or professional occupations and had distinguished themselves as politicians, managers, congresswomen, performing artists, writers, academicians, and religious leaders.

—*Debra Lynn Newman*

See Also:

Afro-American Domestic Workers, Slavery

References:

Harley, Sharon, and Rosalyn Terborg-Penn. *Afro-American Women: Struggles and Images.* New York: Kennikat, 1978.

Jones, Jacquelyn. *Labor of Love, Labor of Sorrow.* New York: Vintage, 1985.

Lerner, Gerda, ed. *Black Women in White America: A Documentary History.* New York: Random House, 1972.

Sterling, Dorothy. *We Are Your Sisters: Black Women in the Nineteenth Century.* New York: Norton, 1984.

White, Deborah Gray. *Ar'n't I a Woman?* New York: Norton, 1985.

BLACK WOMEN'S CLUBS were organized in the late nineteenth century after the rise of a small, but vocal, black middle class. The national organization for the black women's club movement, the National Association of Colored Women, was formed in 1896. Club work was midway between the work of personal charity and professional institutions and as such, influenced the direction of social welfare work during the Progressive era. For Afro-Americans, club work provided services denied to them because of segregation and discrimination. For black women, the club movement was a way of elevating the status of black womanhood.

Black club women believed that community improvement would uplift their race and that efforts on behalf of working women and girls would uplift their sex. Club women established day nurseries and kindergartens in response to the needs of working mothers. They opened working girls' homes to assist young, black migrants from rural areas with housing, employment information, job training, and moral instruction. Club women also provided important support to institutions in their cities, such as hospitals and nurses' training schools. The middle-class women overcame the social and economic barriers between their own more prosperous life-style and that of the women who were served by their philanthropic and welfare club activities. These club activities laid the groundwork for the work of such organizations as the National Urban League, and for the profession of social work. Self-respect, public respect, and self-sufficiency were the goals club women set for themselves and for the women and girls they aided.

—*Susan Lynn Smith*

See Also:

Black Women, National Association of Colored Women

References:

Davis, Elizabeth Lindsay. *Lifting as They Climb.* n.p.: National Association of Colored Women, 1933.

Giddings, Paula. *When and Where I Enter: The Impact of Black Women on Race and Sex in America.* New York: William Morrow, 1984.

Lerner, Gerda, ed. *Black Women in White America.* New York: Random House, 1972.

———. *The Majority Finds Its Past.* New York: Oxford University Press, 1979.

Smith, Susan Lynn. "The Black Women's Club Movement: Self-Improvement and Sisterhood, 1890–1915." Master's thesis. University of Wisconsin-Madison, 1986.

BLACKWELL, ALICE STONE (1857–1950), daughter of nineteenth-century feminists Lucy Stone and Henry Brown Blackwell, was involved throughout her life with the cause of feminism. For years she edited the *Woman's Journal*, founded in 1870 by her mother. A brilliant theorist, writer, scholar, translator, and reformer, Blackwell was also responsible for editing and distributing the "Woman's Column," an early publicity release distributed nationwide for inclusion in the editorial columns and on the opinion pages of the nation's newspapers. She was instrumental in effecting the reunion in 1890 of the two wings of the woman suffrage movement, and later it was she who prepared the notes used in 1916 by Woodrow Wilson in his historic speech declaring his support for woman suffrage.

In the decades leading to passage of the woman suffrage amendment, millions of flyers and leaflets were prepared and distributed nationwide, most of them signed by Alice Stone Blackwell. Her prose was forthright; her writing style a model of concise persuasion. In addition to the tracts, Alice translated Russian, Armenian, and Spanish poetry, and her biography of her mother, published in 1930, is still useful to scholars. Although she made many public speeches, extreme shyness kept Blackwell from attracting the widespread public and press attention her mother had enjoyed. As a consequence, the value of her contribution to theoretical and political feminism is underrated.

Blackwell was also directly involved in a number of other twentieth-century reform movements. She was a partisan of the Russian Revolution, a friend and publicist for the Russian noblewoman-turned-socialist Marie Breshkovsky, an outspoken opponent of the 1915 slaughter of the Armenians, and a leader in the fight to vindicate Sacco and Vanzetti. Nevertheless, her major efforts throughout her lifetime were on behalf of women. Old, impoverished, and nearly blind, Blackwell maintained her interest in woman's rights up until her death in 1950.

—*Andrea Moore Kerr*

See Also:

Stone, Lucy; Suffrage; *Woman's Journal*

References:
Catt, Carrie Chapman. *The Ballot and the Bullet.* Philadelphia: A. J. Ferris, 1897.
Hays, Elinor Rice. *Those Extraordinary Blackwells.* New York: Harcourt, Brace & World, 1967.
Shaw, Anna Howard. *The Yellow Ribbon Speaker.* New York: C. T. Dillingham, 1891.

BLACKWELL, ANTOINETTE (BROWN) (1825–1921), pioneer woman's rights reformer, theologian, and social scientist, is generally credited with having been the first ordained woman minister in the United States. Blackwell worked as a teacher until she could afford to attend Oberlin College, where she studied theology from 1846 to 1850.

At Oberlin, Blackwell befriended Lucy Stone, the fiery woman's rights activist and Garrisonian abolitionist. In 1850 Stone persuaded Blackwell to speak at the first National Woman's Rights Convention in Worcester, Massachusetts, and her speech repudiating the biblical argument that women should not speak in public established her as a premier feminist theorist. In 1853 she was invited to become pastor of the Congregational Church in South Butler, New York. There, on September 15, 1853, she was ordained a Congregational minister—an American first.

In January 1856 she married Samuel Chase Blackwell—brother of Dr. Elizabeth Blackwell, the first American female physician, and brother-in-law of Lucy Stone—who helped care for their five children, cooked meals, and aided his wife's career. In 1869 Blackwell published *Studies in General Science,* an attempt to integrate the growing body of scientific knowledge with her belief in woman's equality, a theme she later elaborated in *The Sexes Throughout Nature* (1875).

An active advocate of woman suffrage, Blackwell spoke frequently at woman's rights conventions. In 1881 she was elected to membership in the American Association for the Advancement of Science, one of few women in that august body. She remained active into her old age in woman's rights and general social reform causes. *The Philosophy of Individuality,* published in 1893, was followed by *The Making of the Universe* (1914). At age ninety, Blackwell produced her last book, *The Social Side of Mind and Action.* She alone of the pioneer woman suffragists lived to see the long-awaited suffrage legislation passed. On November 2, 1920, accompanied by her daughter, Blackwell rode to the local schoolhouse near Elizabeth, New Jersey, and cast her ballot.

—*Andrea Moore Kerr*

See Also:
Christianity; Stone, Lucy; Suffrage

References:
Cazden, Elizabeth. *Antoinette Brown Blackwell: A Biography.* Old Westbury, N.Y.: Feminist Press, 1983.
Flexner, Eleanor. *A Century of Struggle: The Woman's Rights Movement in the United States.* New York: Atheneum, 1974.

BLACKWELL, ELIZABETH (1821–1910) was the first American female physician and, in 1859, became the first woman to be placed on the British Medical Register. Blackwell was born in Bristol, England, and in 1831 her family emigrated to the United States after losing their fortune in the sugar business. Blackwell's father, Samuel, encouraged her education and was an active abolitionist. William Lloyd Garrison was a frequent visitor in the family home, and Blackwell joined the Anti-Slavery Society at an early age.

After her father's death, Blackwell became a teacher in Henderson, Kentucky, in 1844, but disgusted by the abusive treatment slaves received in the area, she soon quit her post. She began to think of the possibility of becoming a doctor after a terminally ill female companion complained to her about the indignity of being examined and treated by men.

In 1847, at the age of twenty-six, Blackwell was finally accepted at Geneva College in upstate New York after being rejected by twenty-nine other American medical colleges. At first subjected to some harassment by male students and a failed attempt by a professor to keep her out of lectures dealing with the reproductive organs, Blackwell managed to prove herself a capable student. She passed her exams and graduated from Geneva on January 23, 1849. Blackwell served her residency at La Maternité Hospital in Paris and at St. Bartholemew's in London. After the initial publicity, much of it negative, surrounding Blackwell's degree, women's medical colleges were founded in Philadelphia and Boston. Blackwell returned to the United States to help with the effort. In 1851, with the aid of Horace Greeley, who agreed to run an ad for her in his newspaper, the *New York Tribune*, Blackwell set up a private practice in New York City. She was deluged with obscene letters and was subjected to epithets like "abortionist" and "harlot" on the streets. At first business was poor, but it improved greatly when Blackwell moved her office into the Eleventh Ward, a city slum.

Blackwell spent the later part of her life lecturing and writing on subjects like hygiene and preventive medicine. In these areas she proved to be ahead of her time. Late in her life, Blackwell lectured against prostitution and social disease and urged other physicians to be active in the campaign against vice, which she thought victimized women and children. Blackwell's pioneering effort to become a physician eased the way for other women to enter the profession in the late nineteenth century.

—*Rose Kolbasnik Callahan*

See Also:

Abolition and the Antislavery Movement, Physicians

References:

Ross, Ishbell. *Child of Destiny*. New York: Harper and Bros., 1949.

Wilson, Dorothy Clarke. *Lone Woman*. Boston: Little, Brown, 1970.

BLAIR, EMILY NEWELL (1877–1952), writer, suffragist, and political figure, led a campaign for the Missouri Equal Suffrage Association in 1914 and served as first editor of *Missouri Woman*, a suffrage magazine endorsed by the Missouri Parent-Teachers Association and the Federation of Women's Clubs. Blair saw the results of her labor in 1919, when the Missouri legislature ratified the Nineteenth Amendment, granting woman suffrage. She helped organize the League of Women Voters, believing that women could gain political power by holding office and taking part in political organizations.

A native of Joplin, Missouri, Blair graduated from Carthage High School in 1894 and attended Goucher College in Baltimore, Maryland, and the University of Missouri. In 1900 she married Harry W. Blair, a Carthage lawyer, and wrote about her life in "Letters of a Contented Wife," published in *Cosmopolitan* in 1910. She also wrote articles for *Lippincott's*, *Harper's*, *Outlook*, and *Woman's Home Companion*.

During World War I Blair worked in Washington, D.C., for the U.S. Council of National Defense, and in 1920 she wrote the official history of the council's work. That same year, she was elected to the National Democratic Committee and became the first woman to serve as the committee vice chairman (1922–28). In this position, she organized women voters, formed Democratic women's clubs, and directed their party activities, traveling and speaking throughout the country. She helped organize the Woman's National Democratic Club, serving as secretary from 1922 to 1926 and president in 1928.

Blair continued her writing interests, serving as associate editor of *Good Housekeeping* from 1925 to 1933, and publishing *Creation of a Home* (1930) and *A Woman of Courage* (1931). Appointed to the consumer division of the National Industrial Recovery Act in the 1930s, she served as chairman in 1935. During World War II she became public relations director for the women's interest section of the War Department.

Blair was one of twenty-six Missouri women to have her name inscribed on a bronze tablet in Washington, D.C., in 1924, honoring Missouri pioneers in the woman suffrage movement. Later she became disillusioned with women's political accomplishments. Instead of working with men in existing parties, she began to urge women to band together, run for office, and support women candidates regardless of party affiliation.

—*Mary K. Dains*

See Also:

Democratic Party, League of Women Voters, Magazines, Suffrage

References:

"Mrs. Emily Blair Dies." [obit.] *Carthage Evening Press* 67 (August 3, 1951): 1.

"Missouri Women in History." *Missouri Historical Review* 63 (October 1968) [inside back cover].

BLATCH, HARRIET STANTON (1856–1940), political organizer and woman's rights activist, was the sixth of seven children born to Henry and suffragist Elizabeth Cady Stanton. After graduating from Vassar College in 1878, she traveled in Europe. Returning, she assisted her mother with the preparation of Volume 2 of the *History of Woman Suffrage*, for which she wrote the chapter on the American Woman Suffrage Association. In 1882 she married Englishman William Henry Blatch and returned with him to Basingstoke, England, where she spent the next twenty years.

In England she worked for woman suffrage, becoming one of its most effective speakers. A Fabian, she won the friendship and admiration of Beatrice and Sidney Webb and George Bernard Shaw. In 1892, while in England, she completed the degree requirements for an M.A. from Vassar, writing about English working-class women. Returning to America in 1902, Blatch became active in the National American Woman Suffrage Association and in the Woman's Trade Union League. In 1907 she was instrumental in organizing a coalition of industrial, business, and professional women that became the Equality League of Self-Supporting Women, later known as the Women's Political Union, which later still merged with the National Woman's party.

In 1913 and 1914 Blatch edited a suffrage newspaper, *Women's Political World*. A tireless political organizer, she recalled a stormy evening in which she spoke at two separate trade union meetings as well as at a woman's industrial school, where an audience of more than a thousand women had gathered to hear her speak. In 1917 Blatch helped organize the group of one thousand women who picketed the White House to demand woman suffrage. During World War I Blatch headed the Speakers Bureau of the Food Administration, serving simultaneously as director of the Woman's Land Army. In 1918, hoping to draw attention to women's contribution to the war effort, Blatch wrote *Mobilizing Woman Power*, with a foreword by Theodore Roosevelt.

Following passage of the suffrage amendment, Blatch worked for international peace, traveling and speaking throughout Europe, and in 1920 published *A Woman's Point of View, Some Roads to Peace*. She continued her political work through the 1920s and 1930s, channeling her efforts through the Progressive and Socialist parties.

Shortly after the publication in 1940 of her memoirs, *Challenging Years*, Harriet Blatch died of a stroke in Greenwich, Connecticut. Blatch's memoirs concluded: "The world is calling for women of vision and courage." Harriet Stanton Blatch may justifiably have numbered herself among such women.

—*Andrea Moore Kerr*

See Also:

History of Woman Suffrage; Stanton, Elizabeth Cady; Suffrage

References:

Blatch, Harriet Stanton. *Challenging Years*. New York: G. P. Putnam & Sons, 1940.

———. *Mobilizing Woman Power*. New York: The Woman's Press, 1918.

———. *A Woman's Point of View*. New York: The Woman's Press, 1920.

———, and Theodore Stanton, eds. *Elizabeth Cady Stanton as Revealed in Her Letters*. New York: Harper & Bros., 1922.

Flexner, Eleanor. *Century of Struggle*. Cambridge, Mass.: Belknap, 1976.

BLOOMER, AMELIA JENKS (1818–94), advocate for dress reform and women's rights, was born in Homer, New York, on May 27, 1818. She married Quaker reformer and editor Dexter C. Bloomer in 1840 and moved to Seneca Falls, New York. She was active in the temperance movement and was a frequent contributor to the temperance newspaper the *Waterbucket*, writing under the pseudonym "Gloriana."

Temperance was an issue raised at the Women's Rights Convention held at Seneca Falls in 1848. As a result, the Ladies' Temperance Society was organized by Lucretia Mott and Elizabeth Cady Stanton, and Bloomer was appointed an officer. On January l, 1849, the feminist and temperance newspaper the *Lily* was launched, with Bloomer as editor and publisher. The editorial policy of the newspaper focused on temperance, dress reform, suffrage, women's rights, and repeal of unjust marriage and inheritance laws. The masthead included the words, "Devoted to the Emancipation of Woman from Intemperance, Injustice, Prejudice, and Bigotry." Bloomer merged her advocacy for temperance and women's rights during her lecture tour of Rochester and New York City, as well as the state capitals of the Midwest in 1852 and 1853.

In the mid-nineteenth century feminine attire consisted of restrictive corsets, layers of heavy petticoats, and a dress made up of at least twenty yards of fabric. Many early feminists urged dress reform, and the costume designed by Elizabeth Smith Miller was adapted and worn by Elizabeth Stanton, Lucretia Mott, Susan B. Anthony, Sarah and Angelina Grimké, and Amelia Bloomer. Bloomer publicized the costume in the *Lily*. The costume consisted of a relatively short skirt reaching five inches below the knee and Turkish pants gathered at the ankles. Corsets and petticoats were discarded. The outfit was ridiculed in the press and denounced from the pulpit. Many goals of the women's movement had been advanced by the publicity lavished on the "Bloomer costume"; however, many feminists felt that the notoriety of the costume drew attention away from the more important issues of the movement. Stanton was the first to abandon the outfit, and the other women followed suit.

Bloomer's move to the Midwest in 1853 did not interrupt her activism for temperance and women's rights. She continued to edit the *Lily*, now a nationally circulated magazine with six thousand subscribers, from her home in Ohio and then in Iowa. However, by 1856 the difficulties of its national distribution from the Midwest compelled her to sell it. With the outbreak of the Civil War, Bloomer organized the Soldiers Aid Society of Council Bluffs, Iowa, in 1861; by 1865 she was involved in coordinating the statewide contributions of Iowa women to the U.S. Sanitary Commission. Her postwar activities focused upon the issues of woman suffrage and the revision of married women's property rights in Iowa.

Amelia Bloomer died in Council Bluffs on December 30, 1894. She was a prime force for women's suffrage in Iowa, an active feminist, lecturer, author, and editor, but generally her name continued to be associated with the costume that bore her name.

—*Therese M. Graziano*

See Also:

Nineteenth-Century Dress Reform, Suffrage, Temperance Movement

References:

Bloomer, Dexter C. *Life and Times of Amelia Bloomer*. Boston: Arena, 1895.

Gattey, Charles Neilson. *The Bloomer Girls*. New York: Coward-McCann, 1968.

Gurko, Miriam. *The Ladies of Seneca Falls: The Birth of the Women's Rights Movement*. New York: Macmillan, 1974.

Russell, Frances F. "A Brief Summary of the American Dress Reform Movement of the Past with Views of Representative Women." *The Arena* 6 (August 6, 1892): 325–39.

BLOW, SUSAN ELIZABETH (1843–1916), pioneer in the American kindergarten movement, advocated the plan of Friedrich Froebel, a German educator, for qualitative child nurture through the systematic training of women for their "divinely ordained mission"

as nurturers. With the support of William Harris, superintendent of schools in St. Louis, socialite Blow organized and administered the first public school kindergarten in the United States there in 1873. Having successfully demonstrated the viability of Froebel's system of child nurture, in 1874 Blow established a training school geared to nurture the nurturers.

Working from an elevated sense of woman's status implicit in Froebel's assumption of the importance of the maternal sphere, Blow claimed the right to an appropriate education for those who nurtured others. Within the woman's world of Blow's kindergarten enterprise, apprenticing students were steeped in Froebelian principles and methods in order to learn the nature, means, and implications of their particular function. She augmented kindergarten training with an advanced course of study that stressed self-making through self-culture in literature, philosophy, religion, art, history, and education.

For a decade Blow held a position of leadership in the movement. Her work in St. Louis was the subject of growing public attention. Then in 1884 ill-health necessitated her withdrawal from kindergartening. By the time Blow recovered from her illness ten years later, the focus of the kindergarten movement had shifted from demonstrating the inherent validity of Froebel's ideas about the value and values of the domestic sphere to an emphasis on the utility of a modified kindergarten as an advocacy agency for the children of the immigrant poor.

Through lectures and writing, Blow attempted to reassert Froebelian ideology as the reason for the kindergarten, to urge that women hold fast to his ideal of nurture, and to argue that any change in the Froebelian system be held in abeyance until his mission for women was understood and accepted. Despite the fact that Susan Blow was accorded much respect by her colleagues, the course of the kindergarten movement had undergone too fundamental a change for even a woman of her reputation to reverse. As kindergartens were increasingly assimilated within the schools, Blow's vision of the Froebelian ideal of nurture as the instrument of choice for empowering the woman's sphere within the culture was eclipsed by a new concentration on the kindergarten as a preparation for first grade.

—Catherine Cosgrove

See Also:

Education, International Kindergarten Union, Teaching as an Occupation for Women

References:

Blow, Susan. "The History of the Kindergarten in the United States." *Outlook* 55 (April 1897): 932–38.

———. "The Ideal of Nurture." *Kindergarten Magazine* 14 (June 1902): 586–98.

———. "Kindergarten Ideal." *Outlook* 56 (August 1897): 890–94.

———. *Letters to a Mother on the Philosophy of Froebel.* New York: D. Appleton, 1896.

"BLY, NELLIE" (1865–1922), journalist, wrote social commentary urging reform of the conditions poor women faced in their workplaces and in charitable institutions. She made the working woman's plight visible to the general public and demonstrated that an American girl could take care of herself anywhere without an escort. Although not the first woman to be a serious reporter, she became one of the best known.

Her real name was Elizabeth Cochrane Seaman, but using her pen name "Nellie Bly," she began writing as a teenager for the *Pittsburgh Dispatch*, where she faced stiff competition from other women journalists. In 1886 she traveled to Mexico. Her articles from this trip were widely reprinted, and from them she wrote her first book *Six Months in Mexico.* In 1887 she left Pittsburgh for New York to become a stunt writer for the *New York World.* For her first articles, she pretended insanity to get inside Blackwell's Island, a women's insane asylum, and expose the conditions there. These articles were revised and published as her second book *Ten Days in a Madhouse.* The articles caused an investigation, resulting in increased funding and improved conditions for the insane. Nellie Bly continued to use undercover investigation to expose women's conditions in various factories, shops, and prisons. Her articles, sensationalized but factual, were tempered with just enough lighthearted humor to keep her popular.

She is best remembered for her attempt in 1889 to match the feat of Phineas Fogg, the fictional hero of Jules Verne's *Around the World in 80 Days*. Traveling alone, she cabled home articles of social commentary and amusing travelogue that made her famous, and wrote her third book *Nellie Bly's Book: Around the World in 72 Days,* from them. This trip by steamship, railroad, rickshaw, and sampan was important because it showed Americans that travel abroad was safe and fun even for a woman and that the age of lightning-fast travel had arrived. It was also one of the first times a celebrity was used to advertise everything from soaps to dolls.

On her return, Nellie Bly continued to write, exposing poor social conditions around the country until she married millionaire Robert Seaman in 1895. When he died in 1904, Nellie Bly took over his business but was unsuccessful. In 1919 she went back to writing for the *New York Journal*. She died relatively unknown and alone in 1922.

—*Terri Dennison*

See Also:
Journalism

References:

Baker, Nina Brown. *Nellie Bly*. New York: Henry Holt, 1956.

Beasley, Maurine, and Sheila Gibbons. "Nellie Bly: Stunt Reporting." In *Women in Media: A Documentary Source Book*. Washington, D.C.: Women's Institute for Freedom of the Press, 1977, pp. 47–53.

Belford, Barbara. *Brilliant Bylines*. New York: Columbia University Press, 1986.

New York World. October 1887–April 1895

Pittsburgh Dispatch. October 1885–March 1887

Rittenhouse, Mignon. *The Amazing Nellie Bly*. New York: Dutton, 1956.

The **BOARDING/HOUSEKEEPING SYSTEM** was one of the most common forms of work for women, especially immigrant women, during the nineteenth and early twentieth centuries. Taking in boarders was an acceptable job for women and often an attractive choice in areas where positions in light industry and opportunities for homework were scarce.

Women provided lodging, food, and personal services such as cleaning and laundering for the boarder, usually an unmarried, foreign-born male who paid about \$3–\$4 per month at the turn of the century. Both parties benefited from this arrangement. The boarder could save money to send home to his family. Because he generally chose to live with fellow immigrants who were also in his age group, his adjustment to a new land and culture was eased. He could continue to eat familiar foods and speak his own language, although often the family with whom he boarded attempted to impose certain communally accepted norms of behavior on him. On the other hand, the woman was adding substantially to the family income. The boarder's rent money was used for family living expenses, for a down payment on a house, for the education of children, or for paying off the mortgage. Such income often meant the difference between deprivation and starvation.

Boarding houses provided lodging on a larger scale than merely letting a room or a bed within a family's household to a nonfamily member; as small-scale enterprises, such establishments supplied housing to single men and women as well as to married couples who were "boarding out." Respectable widows or married women with houses could offer rooms and board to accommodate people in need of housing, both as a means of livelihood and as a way of maintaining their home and middle-class life-style.

Recent immigrant families, families where the husband was the sole wage earner, and those whose heads had laboring positions were more likely to have a higher proportion of boarders than other families. Thus, the number of boarders who lived with a family varied with its income, the life cycles of the family members, and its other circumstances. All ethnic groups, including native-born whites, and all economic classes were likely to take in boarders at one time or another. For example, women of middle- and upper-class families often boarded their husbands' clerks or apprentices during the nineteenth century. By the end of the century, however, keeping boarders had become a common economic strategy mostly among working-class women, especially those in tenements.

The percentage of families housing boarders varied from 20 percent to 50 percent from the mid-nineteenth through the early twentieth centuries. Most scholars agree that boarding was not common after 1930. The U.S. Bureau of Labor reported in that year that only 11 percent of American families took in boarders. By the 1970s that figure had fallen to less than 5 percent.

—*Mary Jane Capozzoli*

See Also:

Housework

References:

Bodnar, John, Roger Simon, and Michael P. Weber. *Lives of Their Own: Blacks, Italians, and Poles in Pittsburgh, 1900–1960.* Urbana: University of Illinois Press, 1982.

Modell, John, and Tamara K. Hareven. "Urbanization and the Malleable Household: An Examination of Boarding and Lodging in American Families." *Journal of Marriage and the Family* 35 (August 1973): 467–79.

Strasser, Susan. *Never Done: A History of American Housework.* New York: Pantheon, 1982.

BONNIN, GERTRUDE SIMMONS [ZITKALA SA OR REDBIRD] (1876–1938) was a Dakota Sioux author and political activist. After spending her first eight years on the Yankton Reservation in South Dakota, she attended White's Manual Institute in Wabash, Indiana, and later Earlham College in Richmond, Indiana, where she gained honors as an orator and poet. Both a musician and teacher, Simmons taught at Carlisle Indian School from 1898 to 1899. In 1902 she married Raymond T. Bonnin. She was an early contributor to *The Atlantic Monthly, Harper's Monthly,* and *American Indian Magazine,* as well as author of two collections: *Old Indian Legends* and *American Indian Stories.* Bonnin was a member of the Women's National Foundation, the League of American Pen-Women, and the Washington Salon, and was active in the Society of American Indians organized at Ohio State University in 1911.

In 1916 Bonnin was elected secretary of the society and moved to Washington, D.C. She was acting editor of the society's publication *The American Indian Magazine* from 1918 to 1919. She lectured and campaigned for American Indian citizenship (finally granted in 1924) and worked for the employment of Indians in the Bureau of Indian Affairs as well as for settlement of land claims. Until her death in 1938, Bonnin served as the president of the National Congress of American Indians, which she founded in 1926. She was instrumental in interesting the General Federation of Women's Clubs in issues concerning American Indians, persuading them to join with the Indian Rights Association to sponsor investigations of the government's relationship with tribes. Bonnin moved easily between the worlds of her tribe and the Eastern establishment; both groups, however, found it difficult to reconcile her formal education with her tribal loyalty.

—*Gretchen M. Bataille*

See Also:

Native American Women

References:

Bonnin, Gertrude S. *American Indian Stories.* Washington, D.C.: Hayworth, 1921; rpt. Lincoln: University of Nebraska Press, 1985.

———. *Old Indian Legends.* Boston: Ginn, 1901; rpt. Lincoln: University of Nebraska Press, 1985.

Fisher, Dexter. "Zitkala Sa: The Evolution of a Writer." *American Indian Quarterly* 5 (August 1979): 229–38.

BOSONE, REVA BECK (1895–1978), a Congresswoman and judge, was born in American Fork, Utah. She was the third child and only daughter born to Christian Mateus Beck—who operated a hotel and livery stable, managed a telephone company, and represented Standard Oil—and Zilpha Ann (Chipman) Beck. Both her parents were descendants of Mormon polygamist families that had migrated to Utah as converts to the Church of Jesus Christ of Latter-Day Saints. However, her parents had disavowed their membership in the Mormon church in a controversy over the practice of plural marriage; thus, Bosone and her brothers grew up attending Presbyterian church with their mother.

Because of a heart problem, Bosone did not enter public school until she was eight years old. After graduation from the two-year Westminster College in Salt Lake City, Bosone attended the University of California at Berkeley, graduating with teaching credentials in 1919. For the next eight years, she taught in high schools in Utah, spending the summer of 1926 touring Europe.

At age thirty-one, Bosone followed her mother's advice to "go where the laws are made" if she wanted to benefit mankind, and like her brothers, she chose the law as her profession. In 1927 she enrolled in the College of Law at the University of Utah, where she met an Italian Catholic law student, Joseph P. Bosone, whom she married in 1929. (It was her second marriage; seven years earlier she had married Harold G. Cutler, the youngest son of the second governor of the state of Utah, but within a year she had divorced him.) After law school and the birth of their daughter, Zilpha Teresa, the Bosones opened a law office in his hometown of Helper, a small coal-mining town in central Utah populated predominately by Italian and Greek coal miners. Bosone was sensitive to the poor working conditions of the miners and their dependence on the company store. As a lawyer, she represented miners, gave legal advice to prostitutes, and gained notoriety for her defense of two young men charged with attempted rape.

Inspired by Theodore Roosevelt and Robert LaFollette, Bosone broke with the family Republican tradition and joined the Democratic party. In 1932 she ran for the Utah state legislature, and along with the other Democratic candidates was swept into office. During her two terms in the legislature, she sponsored minimum-wage and maximum-hour laws for women and children that resulted in the establishment of the Women's Division of the Utah State Industrial Commission. This legislation placed Utah in the forefront of social welfare legislation and won the state the praise of President Franklin D. Roosevelt and his secretary of labor, Frances Perkins.

In 1936 Bosone was elected to a city judgeship, becoming Utah's first woman judge. In her effort to decrease traffic fatalities, she increased fees for traffic violations and established a traffic school in Salt Lake City. Arguing that many defendants were sick people rather than criminals, she often ordered psychiatric and medical examinations for sex offenders and alcoholics. During her campaign in 1940, she divorced the husband whose unfaithfulness she could not endure, although she still loved him; despite the divorce, she was elected to a second term on the bench.

A lifelong defender of women's rights, Bosone contributed to a number of events concerning women. During World War II, she worked to counter the slander campaign against the Women's Army Corps. When the United Nations was created in 1945, she was on hand to help formulate the charter's equality clause for women.

In 1948 Reva Bosone was elected to the U.S. House of Representatives from Utah in the Democratic victory that kept Harry Truman in the White House. She got herself appointed to the Interior Committee and the Subcommittee for Indian Affairs. She put forth bills to control the nation's natural resources, to provide a federal health insurance plan, to initiate programs to help juveniles, to promote international peace, to study alcoholism, to institute price controls, and to remove Indians from federal wardship by dissolving the Bureau of Indian Affairs. In 1950 she successfully campaigned for a second congressional term against the Republican candidate Ivy Baker Priest, who would later be appointed treasurer of the United States. Two years later, however, Bosone lost to Republican William A. Dawson in her bid for reelection. During the campaign, Dawson accused Bosone of being "soft on Communism," behaving in an "unladylike manner" in Congress, and violating the Corrupt Practices Act. (The last was a reference to Bosone's admission that she had accepted a $400 and a $250 donation for her reelection from two of her employees.) After a number of years serving as legal counsel and running unsuccessfully for reelection to Congress, Bosone was appointed by President John F. Kennedy to serve as the nation's first woman judicial officer and chairman of the Contract Board of Appeals for the U.S. Post Office Department. Having served seven years in this capacity, she retired in 1968.

—Beverly Beeton

See Also:

Democratic Party, Politics, Women's Army Corps

References:

Bosone, Reva Beck. Special Collections Division, Marriott Library. University of Utah. Salt Lake City.

Congressional Record, Eighty-first and Eighty-second Congress. Washington, D.C.

Walton, Juanita Irva Heath. "Reva Beck Bosone: Legislator, Judge, Congresswoman." M.A. thesis. University of Utah, 1974.

BOSTON MARRIAGES, a term from the late nineteenth century, refers to intense relationships between two unrelated women, relationships that usually endured throughout the life cycles of the pair whether they lived apart or in cohabitation. Some of these relationships included sexual intimacy but others did not. The term was often applied to a cohabitational intimate relationship between the women who for economic or affectional purposes combined their resources to create a "home." Boston Marriages also reflected the influences of the rigid sex segregation of male and female spheres that encouraged intense relationships between women. An almost separate culture for women in late-Victorian society limited their casual interaction with the opposite sex while it facilitated intense female bonding in women's domestic circles, institutions of education, professions, and civic and political activities. For professional women at the turn of the century, living with another single woman would not entail the loss of their job as marriage would, since married women were not employable in teaching and other fields. Although their individual earnings were insufficient to support a separate household, independent single women required a more autonomous situation than one in which they would live as dependents with their families. Boston Marriages provided them a reasonable alternative to remaining at home as well as a long-term relationship with a peer.

—Angela Howard Zophy

See Also:

Women's Friendships

References:

Faderman, Lillian. *Surpassing the Love of Men: Love Between Women from the Renaissance to the Present.* New York: Morrow, 1981.

James, Henry. *The Bostonians.* London: Macmillan, 1886; rpt. [Introduction by Irving Howe.] New York: Modern Library, 1956.

BOURKE-WHITE, MARGARET (1906–71), one of the world's foremost photojournalists, was one of the first and perhaps the most notable woman to work in that field. As a member of the original staff of *Life* magazine, she helped to bring a new kind of visual communication, the photographic essay, into being. She used the camera not just to record an event but to say something about it, to place the subject in a social context in order to make a statement about the world and our place in it.

Bourke-White's rise to prominence in a male-dominated profession came from her singular devotion to her craft and her ideas, without any consideration to what was "woman's work" and what was not. She not only worked in a man's world, but chose subjects—war and industry, to name two—that were "masculine." Bourke-White's work also took her to dangerous locations where few men, and almost certainly no women, dared to venture.

Bourke-White first gained recognition for her photographs of steel mills that captured the beauty and drama of industry, a subject she considered to be the vital force of her age. This work attracted the attention of Henry Luce, who wanted her to be a photographer for his new publication about business, *Fortune*. She traveled to Germany to photograph the steel industry, and to Russia to document the birth of industrialism. In 1936 she began her work at *Life* magazine with the magazine's first cover photo and a photo essay. Throughout the 1930s, 1940s, and 1950s, Bourke-White traveled widely and photographed the events and leaders that shaped world history. In 1942 she became the first woman to be fitted with a war correspondent's uniform, as an official photographer for the U.S. Air Force. She photographed the American forces in North Africa, Patton's entrance into Germany, the human devastation of the concentration camps at Buchenwald, and the effects of the guerrilla-style civil war in Korea. She captured Churchill, Ghandi, Haile Selassie, and other famous figures with her lens.

Bourke-White was also a writer, and collaborated with her husband, Erskine Caldwell, on a number of books, including *You Have Seen Their Faces*, a social documentary about poverty in the rural South. As a world-renowned photojournalist and artist who often worked in spheres that had included only men, Bourke-White made a place for her own abilities, and certainly for the women who follow her.

—Carol Ann Sadtler

See Also:
Journalism, Photography

References:

Bourke-White, Margaret. *Portrait of Myself*. New York: Simon & Schuster, 1963.

Goldberg, Vicki. *Margaret Bourke-White: A Biography*. New York: Harper & Row, 1986.

Silverman, Jonathan. *For the World to See: The Life of Margaret Bourke-White*. New York: Viking, 1983.

BOYD, LOUISE A. (1877–1972), an expert photographer, led seven expeditions to Greenland between 1926 and 1941, and in 1955 was the first woman to fly over and around the North Pole. Her first expedition, from Norway to Franz Josef Land, was organized primarily to hunt and photograph landscape and wildlife. She canceled the second, scheduled for 1928, to help search for the missing Norwegian explorer Roald Amundsen. On subsequent trips she combined her interest in photography with gathering geographic and scientific data. Although the press persisted in describing Boyd as a debutante and an "eccentric American millionairess," her work was taken seriously by those nations engaging in Arctic research and exploration.

Boyd's expeditions to Greenland in the 1930s resulted in the publication by the American Geographical Society of two major works, *The Fiord Region of East Greenland* (1935) and *The Coast Region of Northeast Greenland*, withheld from publication until 1948 because of the strategic importance of the information. The Swedish government awarded Boyd the Order of Saint Olaf for her courageous Arctic voyages, the only foreign woman to receive that honor, and in 1938, she received the Cullum Medal from the American Geographical Society, one of the only two women awarded a medal by that organization. Boyd continued her association with the AGS, attending the International Geophysical Congress at Warsaw in 1934, conducting investigations of magnetic radio phenomena in Greenland in 1941, and in 1960 serving as the Society's first woman councillor. When queried about problems maintaining her "femininity" in such arduous conditions, Louise Boyd would answer that her primary concern was not the smoothness of her hands but avoiding frostbite.

—Nancy Fogelson

See Also:
Photography

Reference:
Wright, John Kirtland. *Geography in the Making.* New York: American Geographical Society, 1952.

BRADSTREET, ANNE (DUDLEY) (1612?–72) is best known as the author of *The Tenth Muse Lately Sprung Up in America* (London: Stephen Bowtell, 1650), the first book of poetry written in America. She received a classical education under the supervision of her English father, Thomas Dudley, steward to the Earl of Lincolnshire, and in 1628 she married Simon Bradstreet, a Cambridge graduate and assistant to her father. In 1630 she emigrated to America, where both her father and husband became governors of the Massachusetts Bay Colony.

Anne Bradstreet's colonial experience was shaped by her duties as wife of an important government official and as mother of eight children. Her first book, *The Tenth Muse,* was published in London by her brother-in-law, Reverend John Woodbridge, without her knowledge or approval, and was revised for posthumous publication as *Several Poems* (Boston: John Foster, 1678). The subjects of Bradstreet's early poems are largely secular, and they reflect a desire for literary recognition, a modest self-appraisal, and a sense of indebtedness to such poets as Sir Philip Sidney and Guillaume Du Bartas. Her later lyric poetry deals more directly with the experiences of motherhood and conjugal love. Bradstreet also experimented with short prose pieces, which she wrote especially for the instruction of her children (*Meditations Divine and Morale,* 1664). Underlying all of Bradstreet's work is a strong belief in God, though not to the exclusion of honest religious doubt.

Bradstreet's considerable volume of writing, produced in spite of the hardships of colonial life, attests to her extraordinary vitality and intellectual vigor.

—*Marilyn Demarest Button*

References:
Bradstreet, Anne. *The Complete Works of Anne Bradstreet.* Edited by Joseph R. McElrath, Jr., and Allan P. Robb. Boston: Twayne, 1981.
Piercy, Josephine K. *Anne Bradstreet.* New York: Twayne, 1965.
Stanford, Ann. *Anne Bradstreet: The Worldly Puritan.* New York: Burt Franklin, 1975.
White, Elizabeth Wade. *Anne Bradstreet: The Tenth Muse.* New York: Oxford University Press, 1967.

BRESETTE, LINNA ELEANOR (?–1960) was a Catholic social activist and field secretary of the Social Action Department of the National Catholic Welfare Conference and of the Catholic Conference on Industrial Problems, 1921–31. Born in Rossville, Kansas, she attended the Kansas State Normal School and worked for a time as a teacher in the Topeka public schools. She lobbied the Kansas state legislature for minimum-wage and maximum-hour laws for women, and in 1913 was appointed the first female factory inspector for the state. In 1915 she was chosen the secretary of the Kansas Industrial Welfare Commission. Later she became chairperson of the women's division of the state industrial court and industrial mediation board. From this position she helped write the minimum wage laws for women and the child labor laws for the state of Kansas. She also served as an inspector of mines, and her inspections became synonymous with improved working conditions.

After World War I the reforming impulse in Kansas politics fell away, and Bresette was asked to resign. She was then employed by the Social Action Department of the National Catholic Welfare Conference, where her social vision and organizational skills were put to work in behalf of American Catholicism's progressive social agenda. She organized conferences on blacks and Mexicans in industry and the first Catholic summer schools for women, and was the driving force behind traveling schools of social thought known as the Catholic Conference on Industrial Problems. Guided by the teachings of the social encyclicals, Bresette became one of the most influential Catholic social activists of her generation. She received honorary degrees from Conception College, Missouri, and

Rosary College, Illinois. She retired from her position in 1951 and died in 1960.

—*Steven M. Avella*

See Also:

Christianity, Minimum-Wage Laws

References:

Bresette, Linna Elizabeth. "Campaigning for Economic Justice." *Catholic Action* 19 (May 1937): 19.

———. "Negro in Industry Conference: New York City, September 1932." *Interracial Review* 5 (October 1932): 190–94.

———. "1941 Women's Industrial Institute." *Catholic Action* 23 (August 1941): 15.

BROOKS, GWENDOLYN (b. 1917), poet, writer, and editor, Poet Laureate of the State of Illinois (1968–), the first black to win the Pulitzer Prize (1950, for the volume *Annie Allen*), and the first black to be poetry consultant for the Library of Congress, became the premiere black woman poet of her generation. Her extensive publications in both poetry and prose have established Brooks as a major writer of the twentieth century. Recipient of multiple national honors, she has continuously served as an agent for culture and an advocate of empowerment through writing and giving voice to the voiceless. Especially concerned with the development of young people as writers, she, for example, directs and funds yearly Poet Laureate Awards for Illinois high school students. Brooks's continual availability to her community, state, and nation has marked her as a public poet and personage to an extent unprecedented in America.

Beyond her historic multiple firsts as a black poet, Brooks is outstanding among American poets for her formal adeptness and versatility, her invention of the sonnet ballad and of verse journalism, and her celebration of subjects and characters in the everyday life of the black community. Writing of the neighbors and community of the black South Side of Chicago, Brooks brought both a distinctive and accomplished poetic voice and a new sympathy and subject matter to American poetry.

Though born in Topeka, Kansas, Brooks moved to Chicago in the same year, was educated in the Chicago public schools, and has always considered herself a Chicagoan, placing her texts and her activities in the black community of that city. Brooks married Henry Blakely in 1939; her son, Henry, Jr., was born in 1940; her daughter, Nora, in 1950.

Her first collection of poems, *A Street in Bronzeville* (1945), celebrated a multiplicity of city voices in masterly use of traditional poetic forms, especially sonnets and ballads. Her clear woman's perspective came through in lines like: "Abortion will not let you forget. / You remember the children you got that you did not get." In both *Bronzeville* and her next collection, the Pulitzer Prize winner *Annie Allen* (1949), Brooks's audience heard iambic pentameter and the rocking rhythms of the contemporary street. In *Annie Allen* Brooks invented the form of the sonnet ballad. Within the complex rhyme schemes and formal adeptness, however, Brooks brought to life the children of the poor.

A semiautobiographical novel, *Maud Martha* (1953), and another collection, *The Bean Eaters* (1960), with many woman-centered poems, increased Brooks's audience and established her as a major voice in the black community and the nation. Brooks's *Selected Poems* (1963), drawn from her previously published work, is generally classed as one of the best twentieth-century poetry collections.

In 1967, at age fifty, Brooks radically reordered her life and work, as she discovered the black consciousness and black arts movement. She now often describes her life in terms of pre-1967 and post-1967. Her mind- and life-changing experience began at the 1967 Fisk University Black Writers' Conference, where Brooks came to read and was transformed by the life and spirit and engagement of black pride. She joined with the new generation of young black poets like LeRoi Jones (Imamu Amiri Baraka) and Don L. Lee, who were celebrating black power and taking their poetry to the people. Knowing that her audiences had always been predominantly from the white, establishment culture, Brooks awakened to a whole new perspective on poetry as a focus of black culture. Though never imitating the young black poets she admired and advanced, Brooks changed her purpose and voice to address "all black people."

Her next new collections, *In the Mecca* (1968), *Riot* (1969), *Family Pictures* (1970), and *Beckonings* (1975), show a more spare and direct prosody directed to wide black audiences. As sign of her identification with black artists and audiences, after *In the Mecca,* Brooks switched from her longtime publisher, Harper & Row, to a new black publishing firm, Broadside Press. Harper & Row's last Brooks publication, *The World of Gwendolyn Brooks* (1971), reprinted in one volume Brooks's first five books.

The Broadside publications in 1969 and 1970 are more forceful and more oral than Brooks's previous work—grounded in the movement and the celebration of black empowerment and black culture. Brooks's increasing involvement in the black power movement led to her separation from her husband in 1969, a separation that lasted until 1974. She edited *A Broadside Treasury, 1965–70* and also edited *Jump Bad: A New Chicago Anthology* (1971), which collected the works of the young black Chicago poets. For a time, Brooks conducted poetry workshops for members of the Blackstone Rangers, a Chicago street gang.

In the late 1960s and early 1970s, Brooks became the focus of tribute by young black artists. In 1972 she published an autobiography, *Report from Part One,* a compendium of reprints of earlier essays, transcripts of interviews, and a collage of personal notes and criticism. While she wrote of her pleasure in a continuous series of major awards—from the Midwestern Writers' Conference poetry awards in the 1940s through the Pulitzer and more than a dozen honorary doctorates—Brooks claimed that a late-1969 tribute at Chicago's Afro-Arts Theater was "the most stirring tribute of my life, the most significant" (1972). In 1970 the Black Cultural Center at Western Illinois University was named for Gwendolyn Brooks.

Her work in the 1980s included *To Disembark* (1981), *Primer for Blacks* (1981), *Mayor Harold Washington and Chicago, the "I Will" City* (1983), and *Very Young Poets* (1983), the last being advice to young poets with examples of Brooks's own writing.

—*Carol Klimick Cyganowski*

See Also:

Black Women

References:

Brooks, Gwendolyn. *Maud Martha: A Novel.* New York: Harper, 1953.

———. *Report from Part One.* Prefaces by Don L. Lee and George Kent. Detroit: Broadside, 1972.

———. *Selected Poems.* New York: Harper & Row, 1963.

———. *The World of Gwendolyn Brooks.* New York: Harper & Row, 1971.

Melhem, D. H. *Gwendolyn Brooks, Poetry and the Heroic Voice.* Lexington: University Press of Kentucky, 1987.

Moore, Maxine Funderburk. *Gwendolyn Brooks: A Reference Guide.* New York: Garland, 1987.

Mootry, Maria K., and Gary Smith, eds. *A Life Distilled: Gwendolyn Brooks, Her Poetry and Fiction.* Urbana: University of Illinois Press, 1987.

Shaw, Harry B. *Gwendolyn Brooks.* Boston: Twayne, 1980.

BROOKS, ROMAINE (GODDARD) (1874–1970), an American artist who painted the Parisian elite between the two world wars, created such penetrating and provocative portraits that she became known as the "thief of souls." Her sitters included such vanguard personalities as dancer Ida Rubenstein, poet Jean Cocteau, and longtime friend Natalie Barney, whose weekly literary salon was second in popularity only to that of Gertrude Stein. This dynamic, eccentric group made perfect subjects for Brooks's rather unorthodox portraits.

Brooks's own eccentric sense of independence dated back to her troubled childhood, during which she grew up alone with an irrational mother and a mentally ill brother. In her unpublished memoirs, "No Pleasant Memories," she described her childhood as an irrational circus of demons, apparitions, and fear. Out of this childhood came her highly acclaimed drawings, in which these unconscious fears take linear form. Perhaps most symbolic is her own artistic signature: a chained wing.

The melancholy of her life and drawings is also the core of her painting. On the advice of Charles Freer, a prominent art dealer whom she met while working in the artistic community of Capri, Brooks studied the work of James McNeill Whistler. His mastery of subtle gray tones fascinated her, and she learned to perfect her own shades of gray, incorporating them so well into her paintings that the critics pronounced her work bitterly beautiful, revealing as much about her own passionately despairing life as about the lives of her sitters.

The public agreed with this assessment; between 1910 and 1935, the work of Romaine Brooks was exhibited in Paris, London, and New York, and she was awarded the Cross of the French Legion of Honor in 1920. Although her ability to capture the soul of a personality was in great demand, Brooks was free, due to a family inheritance, to choose to paint only those individuals who intrigued her. In fact, she herself kept most of her paintings, preferring to remain out of the public eye.

The 1935 exhibition of her drawings in Chicago was her last; she then turned her attention away from art and spent the years after the war alone, composing her memoirs. Finally, in 1971, just a few months after her death, the National Collection of Fine Arts in Washington, D.C. (now the National Museum of American Art) organized her first exhibition since 1935. Reviews of this exhibition led modern critics to proclaim her (along with Mary Cassatt and Cecilia Beaux) one of the most important women artists in the history of America.

—Karen P. Mattox

See Also:

Art; Beaux, Cecilia; Cassatt, Mary Stevenson

References:

Breeskin, Adelyn D. "The Rare, Subtle Talent of Romaine Brooks." *Art News* 79 (October 1980): 156–59.

———. *Romaine Brooks: Thief of Souls.* Washington, D.C.: Smithsonian Institution, 1971.

Brooks, Romaine. "No Pleasant Memories." Unpublished manuscript. Washington, D.C.: National Museum of American Art, n.d.

Secrest, Meryle. *Between Me and Life: A Biography of Romaine Brooks.* Garden City, N.Y.: Doubleday, 1974.

BROWN, ALICE M. (1857–1948) was one of the most prolific writers in the local-color school of realistic fiction between the Civil War and the 1920s. Born on a small Hampton Falls, New Hampshire, farm in 1857, Brown was educated at the female academy in nearby Exeter. After a short career as a teacher, Brown migrated to Boston, where she began her writing career on the staff of the Unitarian-Universalist church publications office. She began to write and publish short stories in the early 1880s, and in 1884 her first novel, *Stratford by the Sea*, appeared. Her first short-story collection to catch the notice of the critics and earn her recognition as one of the leading local colorists was *Meadow-Grass*, published in 1895.

Brown also began to take an increasingly active role in the life of literary Boston beginning in the 1890s; she became a member of the Boston Athenaeum and bought a town house on Beacon Hill. Brown and the poetess Louise Imogen Guiney—a lifelong friend—took many trips to explore literary England on foot, founding the Women's Rest Tour Association, which later became a part of the Women's Educational and Industrial Union in Boston. Elected president of the Boston Author's Club, Brown turned to writing poetry, novels, and one-act plays in the early years of the twentieth century. One of her plays, *Children of the Earth*, won a prize for the best new play of 1914, and several other plays were performed around the East and Midwest in small playhouses of the day. Although her novels reflected much that made her New England stories strong—the local-color realism of the post–Civil War era—none of her novels received major critical acclaim. She wrote prolifically and published more than one book a year until she was dropped by Houghton Mifflin and Macmillan during the early years of the Depression. She is remembered as a local colorist, and as a woman writer who made a handsome living (she had a mountain farm in Hill, New Hampshire, and a home in Newburyport, Massachusetts, besides her residence on Beacon Hill). Brown also collaborated on a jointly written novel, *The Whole Family*, with a group of authors including Henry James and Henry Van Dyke.

Brown died at age ninety-two in Boston. A proponent of peace, she had been greatly embittered after her struggles with the Creel Committee on Public Information in 1917, which defended U.S. entry into the "War to End All Wars," and further disheartened by the advent of World War II.

—*Ellen D. Langill*

References:

Alice Brown Letters. Holy Cross, Worcester, Mass.; Yale University, New Haven; The Library of Congress, Washington, D.C.; The Huntington Library, San Marino, Calif.

Langill, Ellen D. "Alice Brown: A Critical Study." Diss. University of Wisconsin, 1975.

Overton, Grant M. *The Women Who Make Our Novels.* New York: Dodd, Mead, 1918.

BROWN, OLYMPIA (1835–1926), feminist, orator, minister, and lifetime activist for women's suffrage, was born in rural Michigan. She entered Antioch College because its president, Horace Mann, admitted and encouraged education for women (though discouraging their entering the professions). After graduation in 1860, Brown entered the St. Lawrence University theological school in Canton, New York. In 1863 she became a Universalist minister, the first woman to be ordained by full denominational authority. (Antoinette Brown Blackwell's Congregationalist ordination preceded hers, but was performed by a local congregation without ecclesiastical jurisdiction.)

During those years when women fought for the right to speak in public, Brown was one of the very few who trained professionally as a public speaker. Determined to improve her somewhat high and shrill voice, she worked both in Boston and later in Racine, Wisconsin, at schools of gymnastics and voice culture, doing light gymnastics, studying elocution, breathing, and voice projection, and working with Indian clubs to strengthen her shoulder and arm muscles and improve her gestures.

Brown met woman's rights activists Susan B. Anthony, Lucy Stone, and Elizabeth Cady Stanton in 1866. Recognizing her intensity, her practical, political nature, and her speaking talents, they invited her to campaign in Kansas in 1867 for the first referendum on woman suffrage. The Kansas campaign was poorly planned, and Brown faced difficult conditions, including sabotage from within the ranks of the Republican party. Yet she made almost three hundred speeches within four months.

Returning to parish work, Brown married John H. Willis in 1873 (though continuing to be known throughout her professional life as the Reverend Olympia Brown), had two children, and moved to Racine, Wisconsin, in 1878 to accept the pastorate of a Universalist church. There she was elected president of the state Woman Suffrage Association, a position she maintained for twenty-eight years, and she worked ceaselessly on legislative reform and suffrage issues, eventually resigning from the church in 1887 to concentrate on politics. Surviving many factional splits within the movement, Brown continued to be an indefatigable activist for women's suffrage. She was the only one of the original suffrage workers to live to see the passage of the Nineteenth Amendment—for which she had worked for more than fifty-five years.

—*Nan Nowik*

See Also:

Blackwell, Antoinette Brown; Public Speakers, Women; Suffrage

References:

Brown, Olympia. *Acquaintances, Old and New, Among Reformers.* Privately printed, 1911.

Greene, Dana, ed. *Suffrage and Religious Principle: Speeches and Writings of Olympia Brown.* Metuchen, N.J.: Scarecrow, 1983.

Neu, Charles E. "Olympia Brown and the Woman Suffrage Movement." *Wisconsin Magazine of History* 43 (Summer 1960): 277–87.

BROWN, RITA MAE (b. 1944), writer and political activist, was born in Hanover, Pennsylvania, but was adopted and transplanted to Florida during childhood. As an adolescent, she chose a lesbian life-style; she received a scholarship to the University of Florida, but was ejected for civil rights activities in 1965—the dawn of her lifelong commitment to political struggle. She traveled penniless to New York City, lived on the street for a time, and eventually attended New York University, where she majored in English and classics and helped form the first Student Homophile League in 1967. She did graduate work in comparative literature, studied cinematography, holds a Ph.D. in political science, and was once a fellow of the Institute for Policy Studies, Washington, D.C.

Meanwhile, Brown briefly pursued her political goals as a member of the New York chapter of the National Organization for Women (1968) and marshalled the first post-suffrage White House picket in 1969, but was rejected by mainstream feminists in NOW for her outspoken lesbian views and aggressive tactics. Brown moved similarly into and out of the feminist consciousness-raising Redstockings in 1969. She then worked with Radicalesbians, the collective that shifted the New Left newspaper *Rat* to a radical feminist and lesbian forum and produced the landmark essay "The Woman-Identified Woman" in 1970. Brown participated in the "Lavender Menace" lesbian takeover of the Second Congress to Unite Women (May 1970). Living as a lesbian separatist—one favoring the creation of an exclusively female culture—she next helped form the Furies collective, which published a Washington, D.C., newspaper espousing separatist ideology from January 1972 to June 1973. Ousted again, Brown finally set herself to writing full time. She had published two volumes of poetry—*The Hand That Cradles the Rock* and *Songs to a Handsome Woman*—when her fabled first novel, *Rubyfruit Jungle*, came out in 1973. At that point, this founding mother of the women's movements of the sixties became a preeminent feminist novelist, and Brown has enjoyed success as a screen writer as well.

Rubyfruit Jungle has remained perennially popular, cementing Brown's literary reputation. The semiautobiographical work illuminates the social movements of the 1960s that created its audience. No previous popular book detailed a lesbian life in realistic or positive terms: this novel's main character, Molly Bolt, chose, accepted, and preferred life as a lesbian, with no pornographic or Puritanical overtones. *Rubyfruit* liberated fictional lesbianism, providing an affirmative text for newly raised consciousnesses.

Readers recognize in Molly a quintessential lesbian "type," faced with a variety of presumed handicaps: her poor white southern background, her adoption, her sex, her father's death when she was sixteen, her achievement of college matriculation followed by her expulsion for lesbian activities, her struggle alone in New York City. But Molly overcomes all obstacles, always relying on her intelligence, fortitude, and acid wit. Molly also travels a remarkable sexual odyssey, beginning with easygoing cousin LeRoy and ending with Professor Polina's daughter Alice, with a football hero and a cheerleader thrown in for good measure. Molly is achingly normal. The novel does suffer, however, from an episodic story line and from a slight lack of depth in its minor characterizations; Brown favors verbal richness over visual detail, but even that storytelling effect mirrors reality, and the novel succeeds admirably, as it surveys lesbian culture of the last several decades.

Molly, the smart-alecky tomboy, is a lesbian Huck Finn, and perhaps the most appealing facet of *Rubyfruit* is Brown's talent for comedy, especially in dialogue. The novel stands as the first and foremost example of a "new" literary subgenre, the lesbian/comic novel. Subsequent authors, like Noretta Koertge, have followed Brown's lead, furthering a revised lesbian image: the tough but funny, smart and seductive, tomboyish yet entirely womanly dyke. Molly is always assertive, out of the closet, "liberated," and through her, Brown provides lesbians and all women with a powerful role-model that dispels negative stereotypes. *Rubyfruit* remains, perhaps, the most significant lesbian novel ever written, for its readability, psychological honesty, and historicity.

After the success of *Rubyfruit,* Brown published *In Her Day,* a candid lesbian novel concerning the movement, and a collection of her political essays, *A Plain Brown Rapper,* before Bantam republished *Rubyfruit* and Harper & Row published *Six of One,* perhaps her finest lesbian-content novel, in 1978. This book was Brown's first to focus on her beloved South, and it recaptures the hilarious touch of her early novels as it bounces through 110 years of U.S. history, showcasing the lives of several unique women. In 1982 Brown published *Southern Discomfort,* another tragicomic southern tale centered on two inimitable whores and an interracial love affair. In it, Brown hones her ability to sustain emotion and narrative. Her snapshot of lesbian love on the women's pro tennis circuit, *Sudden Death* (1983), is perhaps her weakest effort. But *High Hearts* (1986), consistent and powerful, affirms Brown's literary skill with its well-researched portrayal of Civil War–era women (and men) of the South. In *Bingo* (1988), Brown extends the saga of Runnymede, Maryland, begun in *Six of One,* with some surprising twists.

Rita Mae Brown participated in the significant feminist and lesbian political actions of the 1960s and early 1970s, becoming a strong though controversial figure with extremely radical views on the liberation of poor people, lesbians, and women, a figure who once advocated revolt over revisionism. Brown's commitment to social change has continued into the 1980s, expressed literarily rather than polemically.

—Penelope J. Engelbrecht

See Also:

Lesbian Separatism, Lesbianism, Radicalesbians

References:

Alexander, Dolores. "Rita Mae Brown: 'The Issue for the Future Is Power.'" *Ms.* 3 (September 1974): 110–13.

Brown, Rita Mae. *Bingo.* New York: Bantam, 1988.

———. *The Hand That Cradles the Rock.* New York: New York University Press, 1971.

———. *High Hearts.* New York: Harper & Row, 1986.

———. *In Her Day.* Plainfield, Vt.: Daughters, 1976.

———. *Poems.* Freedom, Calif.: Crossing, 1987.

———. *A Plain Brown Rapper.* Oakland, Calif.: Diana, 1977

———. *Rubyfruit Jungle.* New York: Daughters, 1973.

———. *Six of One.* New York: Harper & Row, 1978.

———. *Songs to a Handsome Woman.* Oakland, Calif.: Diana, 1973.

———. *Starting From Scratch: A Different Kind of Writer's Manual.* New York: Bantam, 1988.

———. *Southern Discomfort.* New York: Harper & Row, 1982.

———. *Sudden Death.* New York: Bantam, 1983.

Faderman, Lillian. *Surpassing the Love of Men: Romantic Friendship and Love Between Women from the Renaissance to the Present.* New York: Quill/William Morrow, 1981.

Koertge, Noretta. *Who Was That Masked Woman?* New York: St. Martin's, 1981.

Radicalesbians. "The Woman Identified Woman." 1970; rpt. in *Radical Feminism,* edited by Anne Koedt, Ellen Levine, and Anita Rapone. New York: Quandrangle, 1973, pp. 240–45.

"Redstockings Manifesto." In *Masculine/Feminine: Readings in Sexual Mythology and the Liberation of Women,* edited by Betty and Theodore Roszak. New York: Harper Colophon, 1969, pp. 272–74.

In ***BROWN V. BOARD OF EDUCATION OF TOPEKA,*** 347 U.S. 483 (1954), the Supreme Court established the fundamental legal principle that "racial discrimination in public education is unconstitutional." The Court held that the "separate but equal" formula in public education is inherently unequal because it creates and perpetuates feelings of inferiority in members of minority groups. This decision rejected the legal assumption present in the United States from 1896 to 1954 that in areas of racial segregation "separate" can be equal.

The Fourteenth Amendment (1868) declares that "No state . . . shall deny any person within its jurisdiction the equal protection of the laws." *Brown* and some companion cases [i.e. *Bolling v. Sharpe*, 347 U.S. 497 (1954)] extended this protection to the area of racial discrimination in public education. While the Court established this fundamental principle in the 1954 *Brown* decision, it postponed a decision on the application of this principle, inviting all interested parties to present their positions in the Court's next term. It was in *Brown v. Board of Education II*, 349 U.S. 294 (1955) that the original cases were remanded to the courts from which they originated to fashion decrees of enforcement on equitable principles and with regard to the "varied local school problems."

—*Sue E. Strickler*

See Also:
Civil Rights, Fourteenth Amendment

References:

Bolling v. Sharpe, 347 U.S. 497; 74 S. Ct. 693; 98 L. Ed. 884 (1954).
Brown v. Board of Education of Topeka, 347 U.S. 483; 74 S. Ct. 686; 98 L. Ed. 873 (1954).
Brown v. Board of Education of Topeka, 349 U.S. 294; 75 S. Ct. 753; 99 L. Ed. 1083 (1955).
Goldstein, Leslie Friedman. *The Constitutional Rights of Women*. New York: Longman, 1987.
Rossum, Ralph A., and G. Alan Tarr. *American Constitutional Law*. 2d ed. New York: St. Martin's, 1987.

BRYANT, LOUISE (1887–1936), journalist, author, and suffragette, was best known as the wife and widow of John Reed, the American communist and author of *Ten Days That Shook the World*. Though Bryant was married three times, it was her life with Reed that brought her to Greenwich Village and a circle of friends that included poetess Edna St. Vincent Millay, birth control pioneer Margaret Sanger, anarchist Emma Goldman, and playwright Eugene O'Neill, who became her lover. With Reed's help she became an effective advocate of labor unions, equality of the sexes, communism, and pacifism. Bryant's articles and poems were published in, among others, *The Masses, Poetry, Dial*, and *Current Opinion*. She wrote several plays that were produced by the Provincetown Players, of which she, Reed, and O'Neill were founding members.

During World War I, Bryant traveled to Europe as a correspondent for the Bell News Syndicate. Upon her return to the United States in the late summer of 1917, Reed proposed a joint trip to witness and report the great events happening in Russia. They were in Petrograd (now Leningrad) during the Bolshevik Revolution, witnessed the storming of the Winter Palace, listened to Trotsky at the Petrograd Soviet, and interviewed revolutionary leaders. Bryant also interviewed heroines of the revolution such as Marie Spirodonova, leader of the Peasant Soviet; Alexandra Kollontai, welfare minister; and Katherine Breshko-Breshkovskaia, known as the "Babushka" (grandmother) of the Russian Revolution, who had survived half a century of Siberian exile. Bryant's best writing was done during these hectic months filled with the hardship and danger that both she and Reed seemed to relish. Her dispatches were compiled and published in 1918 as *Six Red Months in Russia*. On a lecture tour of major American cities in 1919, Bryant spoke glowingly of Soviet Russia and pleaded against American intervention in Russia's civil war.

Suffering the abuse of the Red Scare of 1919 in America, Bryant had joined Reed in 1920 during his second stay in Russia despite the revocation of her passport, and therefore she was with him when he died of typhus that year. In the years after Reed's death, Bryant reported for the Hearst press from Turkey and Russia. She wrote her second book, *Mirrors of Moscow* (published in 1923), during this period. Between 1923 and 1930 she was married to William C. Bullitt and gave birth to her only child, Anne. Following a divorce and the loss of Anne's custody, Bryant, now addicted to alcohol and drugs, spent her last years in Paris in poverty. She died of a cerebral hemorrhage at the age of forty-nine, on January 6, 1936, in Sèvres, France.

—*Tamerin Mitchell Hayward*

See Also:

Journalism

References:

Bryant, Louise. *Six Red Months in Russia.* New York: George H. Doran, 1918.

Gelb, Barbara. *So Short a Time: A Biography of John Reed and Louise Bryant.* New York: Norton, 1973.

Rosenstone, Robert A. *Romantic Revolutionary: A Biography of John Reed.* New York: Knopf, 1975.

Schneir, M. "Meet the Real Louise Bryant." *Ms.* 10 (April 1982): 43, 45–6, 92–3.

The **BRYN MAWR SUMMER SCHOOL FOR WOMEN WORKERS**, 1921–38, with Brookwood Labor College, which also opened in 1921, launched the American workers' education movement. Brookwood, sponsored by unionists and socialists, evolved into the leading year-round coeducational program for the training of labor activists. Bryn Mawr's rapidly became the flagship humanistic program for women workers. Its residential, collegiate program ran for seventeen summers and served both a national and international constituency of organized and unorganized blue-collar women. The workers' or labor education movement, which was loosely organized and dedicated to broadening the consciousness of workers and empowering them, experienced its heyday in labor's years of struggle in the 1920s and 1930s.

The Bryn Mawr Summer School built on a fusion of the best impulses from progressive social and educational reform as well as women's higher education, suffragism, and feminism. The innovative institution drew its primary inspiration from organizations with similar goals: the National Women's Trade Union League, the National Consumers' League, and the Young Women's Christian Association. All were mixed-class undertakings engaged in promoting evolutionary change. While the school was a product of its time, it required the bold initiative of Bryn Mawr president M. Carey Thomas to authorize a workers' school within her elite domain. Thomas provided the vision and imprimatur appointing her then-dean, Hilda Worthington Smith, as director.

The Bryn Mawr Summer School for Women Workers forever changed not only the lives of many of its students, but also its faculty, who were politicized by the experience. Rita Heller's unique follow-up study of 3 percent of the students and twenty-eight teachers, conducted forty to sixty years after the experience, documented the school's long-term effects. An overwhelming proportion of the workers said the school had had a considerable impact on their lives, self-image, and skill development. Many moved into union leadership, with Carmen Lucia and Elizabeth Nord becoming vice presidents of national unions. Many teachers turned to federal government and other public service. Among the most renowned in academic and government service in labor and economics were Alice Hanson Cook, Broadus Mitchell, Esther Peterson, Caroline Ware, and Colston Warne. Rita Heller co-produced a National Endowment for the Humanities documentary film on the Bryn Mawr Summer School for Women Workers, entitled *The Women of Summer* (1985).

The Bryn Mawr Summer School linked the progressivism of Jane Addams to the emerging liberalism of the remarkable women's network that surrounded Eleanor Roosevelt. In connecting the educated elite with the workers, introducing Progressive Era leaders to newly militant unionists and fusing an ebbing suffragism to a dynamic New Deal, the school constituted a powerful force for change in the inter–World War decades.

—*Rita Rubinstein Heller*

See Also:

National Women's Trade Union League, New Deal, Unions, Workers' Education for Women

References:

Several archival collections on the Bryn Mawr Summer School are extant in the following locations: American Labor Education Service

Papers, School of Industrial and Labor Relations, Cornell University, Ithaca, N.Y.; American Labor Education Service Papers, Wisconsin State Historical Society, Madison, Wis.; Bryn Mawr Summer School Papers, Bryn Mawr College Archives, Bryn Mawr, Pa.; Bryn Mawr Summer School Papers, Institute of Management and Labor Relations Library, Rutgers University, New Brunswick, N.J.; Eleanor Coit Papers, Sophia Smith Collections, Smith College, Northampton,Mass.; Hilda Worthington Smith Papers, Schlesinger Library, Radcliffe College, Cambridge, Mass.

Heller, Rita R. "Blue Collars and Blue Stockings: The Bryn Mawr Summer School for Women Workers." In *Sisterhood and Solidarity: Workers Education for Women, 1918–1984,* edited by Joyce Kornbluh and Mary Frederickson. Philadelphia: Temple University Press, 1984.

———. "The Bryn Mawr Worker's Summer School, 1921–1938: A Surprising Alliance." *History of Higher Education Annual, 1981,* pp. 110–13.

———. "The Women of Summer: The Bryn Mawr Summer School for Women Workers, 1921–1938." Diss. Rutgers University, 1986.

———, co-producer. *The Women of Summer: The Bryn Mawr Summer School for Women Workers, 1921–1938.* A National Endowment for the Humanities Film, 1985.

Hill, Helen. *The Effect of the Bryn Mawr Summer School as Measured in the Activities of its Students.* New York: Affiliated Summer Schools for Women Workers in Industry and American Association for Adult Education, 1929.

Schneider, Florence Hemley. *Patterns of Workers' Education: The Story of the Bryn Mawr Summer School.* Washington, D.C.: American Council on Public Affairs, 1941.

Smith, Hilda Worthington. *Opening Vistas in Workers' Education: An Autobiography of Hilda Worthington Smith.* Washington, D.C.: by the author, 1978.

———. *Women Workers at the Bryn Mawr Summer School.* New York: Affiliated Summer School for Women Workers in Industry and American Association for Adult Education, 1929.

BUSINESS. Women have been actively involved in the business life of the United States since its inception. A female print shop owner, Mary Katherine Goddard (1738–1816), was the official printer of the Declaration of Independence. During the New Nation period enterprising women such as Abigail Adams (1744–1818) and Eliza Pinckney (1722–93) managed their family businesses and property so well that their husbands, John and Charles, were able to devote themselves almost full time to public service. America's first great fortune, that of John Jacob Astor in the fur trade, was helped greatly by the business skills of Astor's wife, Sarah Todd Astor (1762–1832). However, most of these women in business were unique cases to some extent as business was still predominantly a man's world in the early years of the United States.

The Industrial Revolution transformed the American economic landscape and increased nonagricultural and domestic-service employment opportunities for women. Iron magnate Rebecca Pennock Lukens (1794–1854) of Pennsylvania was one of those rare female entrepreneurs involved in the rise of early industrialism at the managerial level. Ellen Curtis Demorest (1824–98) and Margaret Getchell La Forge (1824–98) were on the cutting edge of the nineteenth-century fashion industry and were among the first to utilize the growing women's market.

Women capitalists in a few cases began to make large fortunes in business during the nineteenth and early twentieth centuries, although most of the great American fortunes were still controlled by men and most women were still expected to remain in their domestic sphere. Breakthrough women included Margaret Haughery (1813–82), who made a fortune in the bakery business in New Orleans, and Susan King (1818–80), who prospered with her Woman's Tea Company. Hetty Green (1834–1916) made $100 million speculating in the money market and became known as the "witch of Wall Street." Black entrepreneur and inventor Madame C. J. Walker (1867–1919) became wealthy in the cosmetics industry. On the American frontier, Henrietta Chamberlain King (1832–1925) successfully managed the huge King Ranch in Texas for many years.

Despite the few women who made large fortunes, most women in business did not, and few women obtained management positions even by the late nineteenth century. Women still held only 5 percent of the white-collar office jobs—as clerks, copyists, bookkeepers, stenographers, and typists. The business office from top to bottom was still predominantly a masculine environment. Mary Seymour Foot (1846–93) was one of those who was determined to change all that. She set up a successful business school to train women in the new office skills, while also launching *Business Woman's Journal* in 1889. Foot's work was further extended by Katherine Gibbs (1865–1934), who developed a chain of business schools for women. The "Pink Collar Ghetto" was on its way.

As business became more sophisticated and complex in the twentieth century, businesspeople began to turn to the new social science disciplines for guidance and ideas. Mary Parker Follett (1868–1933) was an influential pioneer in the new field of management theory. Her 1924 book *Creative Experience* was widely respected in business circles for its advice about decision making and the handling of labor problems. In the modern world, financial writer Sylvia Porter (b. 1913) is only one of a number of widely respected female business and financial advisers.

Women have also become increasingly influential in the fashion world, especially after World War I. Ida Rosenthal (1889–1973) was the founder of Maidenform, Inc., the first manufacturer of brassieres. Rosenthal was also instrumental in developing the mass-production, "ready to wear" industry. Nell Quinlan Donnelly (b. 1889) was also instrumental in transforming the garment industry.

While the contributions of Rosie the Riveter and her sisters to industrial production during the Second World War have not gone unrecognized, businesswomen also contributed to the war effort. Olive Ann Beech (b. 1903) converted a small commercial airplane operation into a major defense contractor that supplied 90 percent of the planes on which American bombardiers and navigators were trained. During the war Tillie Lewis (b. 1901) introduced the Italian tomato industry to California. After the war she developed the first artificially sweetened canned fruit and became the first woman director of the billion-dollar Ogden Corporation.

In recent decades there has been a dramatic expansion of the role of women in business. Women are finding their way into the management structure of most large corporations at all levels. High-profile women such as advertising executive Mary Wells Lawrence (b. 1928) and *Washington Post* publisher Katharine Meyer Graham (b. 1917) are no longer the rare exceptions that they would have been in the business world of previous eras. The beauty industry—with moguls such as Elizabeth Arden (1878–1966), Mary Kay Ash, and Helena Rubinstein (1870–1965)—is now only one of many industries in which women are in real positions of power. And women are an increasingly active force in businesses ranging from professional sports franchises to computing firms.

—*Jonathan W. Zophy*

See Also:

Adams, Abigail; Beauty Industry; Industrial Revolution; Kreps, Juanita; Pinckney, Eliza; Walker, Madame C. J. (Sarah Breedlove)

References:

Bird, Caroline. *Enterprising Women.* New York: Norton, 1976.

Coffee, Robert, and Richard Scace. *Women in Charge: The Experience of Female Entrepreneurs.* Boston: Unwin, 1985.

Kanter, Rosabeth. *Men and Women of the Corporation.* New York: Basic, 1977.

Leavitt, Judith. *Women in Management: An Annotated Bibliography and Sourcelist.* Phoenix, Ariz.: Oryx, 1987.

Matthaei, Julie A. *An Economic History of Women in America.* New York: Schocken, 1982.

CABRINI, FRANCES XAVIER (1850–1917) was the first citizen of the United States to be declared a saint by the Roman Catholic church. Frail but strong-willed, this "Italian Immigrant of the Century" founded a worldwide religious community of missionary women.

Cabrini was born on July 15, 1850, at Sant'Angelo, near Lodi, in Lombardy, Italy. Her parents, Agostino and Stella, supported their thirteen children by farming. She attended private school in nearby Arluno, earned a teacher's certificate, and then taught for two years at the public school in Vidardo. In 1874 she went to Codogno to work at the House of Providence Orphanage and joined the Sisters of Providence, taking vows in 1877. When the House of Providence was dissolved in 1880, Cabrini, with seven young nuns, started her own community, called the Missionary Sisters of the Sacred Heart. As the number of sisters increased, new foundations were opened in Italy.

Though originally interested in missionary work in China, she was persuaded by Bishop Giovanni Battista Scalabrini of Piacenza and Pope Leo XIII to go to the United States and work among the Italian immigrants there. With a small group of nuns, Cabrini left for the United States in 1889. In New York City she opened an orphanage, a school, and a hospital, the sisters depending on gifts and begging to support their work. In the next fifteen years, she established similar institutions in New Orleans, Chicago, Scranton, Denver, Seattle, Los Angeles, and elsewhere. Cabrini also established predominantly educational foundations in Europe and Latin America. By 1905 Cabrini's community had spread into eight countries, the number of houses had grown to fifty, and the number of sisters totaled almost one thousand.

The community received papal approval in 1907. Two years later, Cabrini became a naturalized American citizen. She died of malaria in Chicago on December 22, 1917, and in 1946 she was canonized by the Roman Catholic church.

—*Edward C. Stibili*

See Also:
Christianity

References:

Borden, Lucille P. *Francesca Cabrini: Without Staff or Scrip.* New York: Macmillan, 1945.

Dall'Ongaro, Giuseppe. *Francesca Cabrini, La Suora che Conquistò l'America.* Milan: Rusconi, 1983.

DeMaria, Saverio. *Mother Frances Xavier Cabrini.* Translated and edited by Rose Basile Green. Chicago: Missionary Sisters of the Sacred Heart of Jesus, 1984.

Maynard, Theodore. *Too Small A World: The Life of Francesca Cabrini.* Milwaukee: Bruce, 1945.

Sullivan, Mary L. "Mother Cabrini: Italian Immigrant of the Century." Diss. Bryn Mawr College, 1984.

CARSON, RACHEL (1885–1964), environmental writer and scientist, was born in Springdale, Pennsylvania. She earned her B.A. in science at the Pennsylvania College for Women in Pittsburgh and her M.A. in biology from the Johns Hopkins University. Carson was affiliated with the zoology staff at the University of Maryland and did postgraduate work at the Marine Biological Laboratory in Woods Hole, Massachusetts.

In 1936 she joined the U.S. Fish and Wildlife Service as an aquatic biologist. She remained with the service until 1952, writing and editing many of their publications. Her own essays and books, beginning with *Under the Sea Wind* (1941) with its beautifully vivid descriptions of sea life, made her internationally famous. *The Sea Around Us* (1951) and *The Silent Spring* (1962) became best-sellers. *The Silent Spring* touched off an international controversy over the effects of pesticides on the environment. Her writings and concern for nature helped to stimulate the larger movement to help save the environment from the depredations of modern industrialism.

—Jonathan W. Zophy

See Also:
Science

References:

Brooks, Paul. *The House of Life: Rachel Carson at Work.* Boston: Houghton Mifflin, 1972.

Carson, Rachel. *The Sea Around Us.* Boston: Houghton Mifflin, 1951.

———.*Silent Spring.* Boston: Houghton Mifflin, 1962.

———. *Under the Sea Wind.* Boston: Houghton Mifflin, 1941.

CASSATT, MARY STEVENSON (1844–1926), a major American artist and the only American to win acceptance as a respected colleague of the French impressionists, was born in Allegheny City (now Pittsburgh), Pennsylvania. The daughter of the president of the Pennsylvania Railroad, she moved to Europe and lived in Germany and France with her family for nearly five years. While in Paris, she developed a fascination with that city that would last a lifetime. She worked there most of her adult life although she always considered herself to be an American.

Over strong objections from her family, Cassatt began her art education at the Pennsylvania Academy of the Fine Arts at the age of seventeen. When she first announced her intention to become an artist, her father exclaimed, "I'd rather have you dead!" After four years of study in the United States, Cassatt prevailed upon her family to permit her to go abroad, with a "proper chaperone," to study the Old Masters. She traveled to Spain and Italy first, then settled in Paris. In 1868 her first painting was accepted at the Paris Salon, and she continued sending works there until 1877, when Edgar Degas saw her work and invited her to join the impressionist group. Along with Japanese prints and photography, Degas profoundly influenced her later work.

Cassatt approached her subject matter—generally young women and children, many of them relatives who came to visit—with unsentimental, vigorous craftsmanship. Her keen interest in line and form, carefully modeled to exhibit her deep concern for fine drafting, resulted in a more realistic rendering than that of most of the impressionists. Working in both oils and pastels, Cassatt enjoyed highly successful one-woman shows. During the 1880s she reached artistic maturity in both fine and graphic arts. Her other greatest contribution to the art world was her encouragement of American tourists abroad to purchase contemporary art and have it exhibited in the United States, as in the Havermeyer collection at the Metropolitan Museum of Art.

In 1904 Cassatt was made a Chevalier of the French Legion of Honor. By 1918 she had become blind from cataracts. At the time of her death in 1926, Mary Cassatt, because of her achievements, had raised the position of women artists to a higher level than anyone had previously considered possible.

—Janet G. Baldinger

See Also:
Art

References:

Boyle, Richard J. *American Impressionists.* Boston: New York Graphic Society, 1971.

Breeskin, Adelyn D. *Mary Cassatt, Catalogue Raisonné of the Oils, Pastels, Watercolors and Drawings.* Washington, D.C.: Smithsonian Institution, 1970.

Bullard, E. John. *Mary Cassatt Oils and Pastels.* New York: Watson-Guptill, 1972.

Haruki, Yorgashi, and Takeshi Kashiwa. *Cassatt.* Tokyo: Japan Art Center, 1978.

Love, Richard. *Cassatt: The Independent.* Chicago: Milton H. Kreines, 1980.

Roudebush, Jay. *Mary Cassatt.* New York: Crown, 1979.

CATHER, WILLA (1873–1947), author, was born Wilella Cather in Back Creek, Virginia, the oldest of seven children. When she was nine, the family moved to Red Cloud, Nebraska, where Cather encountered immigrants who later found their way into her fiction. Her childhood dream was to become a medical doctor. She attended the University of Nebraska in Lincoln, where she studied Greek and Latin and wrote for several college papers. She also began to write for several Lincoln papers, and by the time she graduated, she had written over three hundred columns.

In 1895 Cather moved to Pittsburgh to edit the *Home Monthly* for a year and to work on the *Pittsburgh Daily Leader*. In 1903 she wrote *April Twilights*, a book of verse, and in 1905 *The Troll Garden*, a collection of short stories. Cather moved to New York City the following year to become managing editor of *McClure's Magazine*. Her first novel, *Alexander's Bridge* (1912), was serialized in *McClure's*, after which Cather left the magazine to devote herself to writing. In 1913 she began a relationship with Edith Lewis that lasted until Cather's death.

With her next novel, *O Pioneers* (1913), Cather introduced one of the subjects to which she would return again and again in her fiction, the old American frontier experience and the heroism of those who lived there contrasted with twentieth-century America and the changes that were occurring in the new machine age. *The Song of the Lark* (1915), her next novel, introduced the second of Cather's favorite subjects, the artist's struggle to adjust to society. *My Antonia* (1918) celebrates the courage of an immigrant pioneer woman. *Youth and the Bright Medusa* (1922) is a short-story collection centered around the lives of artists.

Although her nostalgia for the past brought her criticism from liberals who accused her of ignoring the present in her fiction, Cather was still considered one of the best regional writers in the country during the 1920s. Her later books are *A Lost Lady* (1923), *The Professor's House* (1925), *My Mortal Enemy* (1926), *Death Comes for the Archbishop* (1927), *Shadows on the Rock* (1931), *Obscure Destinies* (1932), *Lucy Gayheart* (1935), and *Sapphira and the Slave Girl* (1940). Her novel *One of Ours* (1922) won the Pulitzer Prize in 1923, making Cather only the second woman writer to have done so. *Not Under Forty* (1936) is a collection of essays that includes pieces on various writers who influenced Cather, most notably Henry James, and presents her theory of fiction.

—*Victoria L. Shannon*

References:

Cather, Willa. *The Kingdom of Art: Willa Cather's First Principles and Critical Statements, 1893–1896*. Edited by Bernice Slote. Lincoln: University of Nebraska Press, 1966.

———. *The Novels and Stories of Willa Cather*. 13 vols. Boston: Houghton Mifflin, 1937–41.

———. *The Old Beauty and Others*. New York: Knopf, 1948.

———. *On Writing*. New York: Knopf, 1949.

O'Brien, Sharon. *Willa Cather: The Emerging Voice*. New York: Oxford University Press, 1987.

CATT, CARRIE CHAPMAN (LANE) (1859–1947) challenged social thinking in the late nineteenth and early twentieth centuries as a teacher, school administrator, suffragist, and peace advocate. After graduating from Iowa State College in 1880, she studied law for a while, but chose to become principal of the Mason City (Iowa) High School in 1881, and in 1883 became one of the first women superintendents of schools. Between 1887 and 1890 she established suffrage clubs in the state and eventually organized the Iowa Woman Suffrage Association. Recognizing her abilities, the National American Woman Suffrage Association (NAWSA) elected her in 1900 to succeed Susan B. Anthony as president, a post she held until 1904.

The next phase of Catt's career focused on international and New York suffrage. She founded the International Woman Suffrage Alliance and remained active in it until World War I intervened. While working on the international scene, she organized the New York woman suffrage movement and masterminded its unsuccessful campaign in 1915. These activities reveal her talents for leadership, organization, imaginativeness, and determination. With war hindering her participation in world suffrage, she thus became a viable candidate again for the national leadership of NAWSA.

Elected in 1915 to succeed Anna H. Shaw as president, Catt immediately set the national organization on course to win enfranchisement. Her insight suggested a shift from educational propaganda to political action, while her strategy included the development of a master plan for action. This represented a "turning of the corner" in the drive for the Nineteenth Amendment. She did not openly support either Woodrow Wilson or his Republican rival, Charles Evans Hughes, in the 1916 election, and this foresight probably helped her to be able to call on Wilson for his support during the final drive for woman suffrage. Catt also had the political savvy to understand that women needed to support the war effort in order to gain the political favor needed to pass the woman suffrage amendment.

With successful ratification of woman suffrage in August 1920, Catt only slightly altered her course. She assisted in creating the League of Women Voters to continue the struggle to insure full suffrage, remove legal discrimination, and democratize political structures. Also, during the 1920s she urged women to support the League of Nations. Her later years were devoted to peace and disarmament through the National Committee on the Cause and Cure of War. She also sponsored the Woman's Peace party.

—Ted C. Harris

See Also:

League of Women Voters, National American Woman Suffrage Association, Suffrage, Woman's Peace Party

References:

Blatch, Harriott Stanton, and Alma Lutz. *Challenging Years: The Memoirs of Harriott Stanton Blatch.* New York: Putnam, 1940.

Catt, Carrie C., and Nettie R. Shuler. *Women Suffrage and Politics: The Inner Story of the Suffrage Movement.* New York: Scribner, 1923.

Flexner, Eleanor. *Century of Struggle: The Women's Rights Movement in the United States.* Rev. ed. Cambridge, Mass.: Belknap, 1975.

Fowler, Robert B. *Carrie Catt: Feminist Politician.* Boston: Northeastern University Press, 1986.

Peck, Mary Gray. *Carrie Chapman Catt, A Biography.* New York: Wilson, 1944.

Van Voris, Jacqueline. *Carrie Chapman Catt, A Public Life.* New York: Feminist Press, 1987.

The **CENTER FOR WOMEN AND RELIGION**, an example of the impact of the modern women's movement of the 1960s upon the role of women in religion, is located in Berkeley, California, and serves the San Francisco Bay Area with an ecumenical, international membership. A result of consciousness-raising among women in the religious community, this oldest center for women in theological education in the United States was founded in 1970 and is sponsored by ten theological institutions, all of which are related to the Graduate Theological Union.

Reflecting the pattern of contemporary self-help groups begun by femininists, the center began with a small group of students and women from throughout the Bay Area who were committed to searching for an end to sexism while promoting issues of justice through religion and religious beliefs. Fostered by the theological community, the center's primary intention has been to transform theological education by offering curriculums that utilize feminist structure and process; its secondary goals focus on members' participation in and sponsorship of ecumenical and denominational events and meetings, conferences, and forums, as well as various publications.

The center has provided moral support and a facility, a place of their own, to further a sense of community among women faculty of the Graduate Theological Union. Its house provides meeting space to host theology students and a variety of programs to encourage a spirited recognition of the struggles, suffering, and searching that challenges women in religion as they pursue or prepare for a life in the ministry or theological studies.

—Joanne S. Richmond

See Also:

Christianity, Consciousness-Raising, Theologians

References:

"Center for Women and Religion." Berkeley, Calif.: Center for Women and Religion. [pamphlet]

Juhnke, Chris, and Karen Ludwig, eds. *Membership Newsletter.* Berkeley, Calif: Center for Women and Religion, 1988.

Moody, Linda, ed. *The Journal of Women and Religion* 5 (Summer 1986).

CHARLOTTE TEMPLE, A TALE OF TRUTH (1791), by Susanna Haswell Rowson, was intended, as the author mentions on the third page of the text, to be a guide "for the perusal of the young and thoughtless of the fair sex." While providing the story of the title character, Rowson hoped the book would enlighten those young women who had no friends to help them cope with life's evils. As a prototype of nineteenth-century prescriptive fiction for women, the book became more than a mere guidebook; by the early 1800s this classic among the didactic literature that utilized the seduction theme had sold more copies than any other book in the history of either Britain or the United States.

The implicit moral enforced by the "seduced and abandoned" plot of *Charlotte Temple* entertained while instructing its readers that the unavoidable fate of a woman's fall from grace and respectability was the ruin of her character and her social status. Charlotte and an instructor at her private school, Mademoiselle LaRue, walk beyond the school grounds and are noticed by a man named Montraville and his friend Belcour. Charlotte and Montraville, LaRue and Belcour form couples and continue to arrange assignations that result in an impulsive elopement to America by both couples. On board the ship, LaRue leaves Belcour for another gentleman, Colonel Clayton, but Charlotte remains enraptured with Montraville, who marries her although he repents his infatuation. In America the faithless Montraville leaves his hapless and now pregnant bride but plans to provide financial support for her through the even more faithless Belcour, who purloins the money for himself without contacting Charlotte. Destitute and desperate, Charlotte seeks out the respectably married LaRue, who callously refuses to acknowledge or aid her former pupil. Although LaRue's servants save Charlotte from the streets, help her through labor, and provide her and the baby with a few necessities, Charlotte dies of heartache before her grandfather arrives in America to rescue her. He returns to Britain with the baby.

Revealing Charlotte's death as a traumatic but inevitable incident, this popular cautionary tale for young women was far-reaching in its influence on the development of the genre of the domestic novel in the nineteenth century.

—James A. Howley

See Also:

Domestic Literature in the United States, Prescriptive Literature

Reference:

Rowson, Susanna Haswell. *Charlotte: A Tale of Truth.* London: William Lane, 1791; Philadelphia: Mathew Carey, 1794.

CHESNUT, MARY BOYKIN (MILLER) (1823–86), Confederate diarist, was born into a socially and politically prominent South Carolina family and married James Chesnut, Jr., also of an important South Carolina family. Her upbringing included education in Charleston, wide reading in literature, life on plantations in South Carolina and Mississippi, and intense interest in Southern politics. Her husband's political career in federal and state government enlarged her social universe, including a brief stay in Washington, D.C. (1859-60), during which she became friends with such Southern families as the Jefferson Davises. Secession brought the Chesnuts back to the South and gave Mary Chesnut an excellent vantage point to observe the social and political world of the Confederacy.

Accompanying her husband to Montgomery, Alabama, to Richmond, Virginia, to Columbia, South Carolina, and to their plantation home, Mulberry, near Camden, South Carolina, Chesnut lived intimately with the problems of nation-building, war, and human relations within the Confederacy. Fiercely loyal to the Southern cause, she became intimate with the Davises and, while in Richmond, maintained a salon of sorts that wielded considerable influence.

During the war, Chesnut wrote a secret diary that formed the basis of her later writings. Her wartime diaries recorded penetrating sketches of numerous Confederate personalities, reactions to Southern fortunes in war, and Chesnut's hatred of slavery and the oppression of women that slavery encouraged. Her account is one of the most important primary sources on Confederate leaders and Southern society during the Civil War.

After the war, the Chesnuts lost most of their lands and political influence, but Mary Chesnut, who lived most of the postwar years in straitened circumstances in Camden, continued to write. She drafted three novels (never published), several stories, and a biography of her husband, and sought the proper genre to express her wartime experiences. She transcribed the diaries, adding material from memory to create narrative flow and fill in gaps in the original record, and revised and polished them over several years. By the 1880s she had produced a massive manuscript. In adopting the diary form as the genre to give her experiences full literary expression, she blended autobiography, memoir, letters, history, and fiction to create what is now generally regarded as the best single literary contribution from the Civil War.

She never published her book. Two editions of it appeared that established Chesnut's reputation. In 1905 her friend Isabella Martin helped bring out an edition, entitled *A Diary from Dixie*, comprising less than half the original manuscript and cleansed of "offensive" material. Critics regarded the book as a classic example of Southern "Lost Cause" literature. In 1949 novelist Ben Ames Williams edited an even shorter version in which he altered Chesnut's original meaning in several ways. In 1981 historian C. Vann Woodward published the complete, unexpurgated 1880s manuscript under the title *Mary Chesnut's Civil War*. Chesnut's surviving Civil War diaries for 1861 and 1865 were published in 1984 as *The Private Mary Chesnut*.

Chesnut's book reveals an uncommon intellect. Her condemnations of slavery and women's plight in a slave society, even as she enjoyed the amenities of the "peculiar institution" and the indulgences of her class, have been cited repeatedly by historians as evidence of Southern guilt over slavery and an emerging feminine consciousness among privileged Southern white women. Chesnut's brilliant journal, with its full cast of characters embracing all strata of Southern society, captures the spirit of Southern resistance so well that it has become the metaphor for the historic crisis of her age.

—*Randall M. Miller*

See Also:
Civil War, Slavery, Southern Lady

References:

Chesnut, Mary Boykin. *Mary Chesnut's Civil War*. Edited by C. Vann Woodward. New Haven: Yale University Press, 1981.

———. *The Private Mary Chesnut: The Unpublished Civil War Diaries*. Edited by C. Vann Woodward and Elisabeth Muhlenfeld. New York: Oxford University Press, 1984.

Muhlenfeld, Elisabeth. *Mary Boykin Chesnut: A Biography*. Baton Rouge: Louisiana State University Press, 1981.

CHICAGO, JUDY (b. 1939), a feminist artist, was born Judy Cohen in Chicago, Illinois, and studied at UCLA, receiving her B.A. in 1962 and M.A. in 1964. She became a successful West Coast minimal sculptor in the late 1960s. A veteran founder and co-founder of the first feminist art programs of Womanhouse, Woman's Building, and the Feminist Studio Workshop, she also taught at California State University at Fresno and California Institute of Arts. Although primarily a sculptor and painter, her media have included ceramics, needlework, plastics, environments, and china-painting.

In 1973 she started work on her famous project *The Dinner Party*. Chicago worked on the project alone for three years, then decided to seek the help of several administrative assistants, artists (numerous professional embroiderers), and researchers, approximately four hundred people altogether. One of the rich legacies of the feminist movement of the 1970s, *The Dinner Party* celebrates the history and achievement of Western women through the media of women's traditional crafts: china painting, embroidery, and weaving.

Six large woven banners introduce *The Dinner Party* and spell out its themes: its centerpiece, however, is a 48' x 48' x 48' triangular banquet table set with thirty-nine painted ceramic plates on richly embroidered place mats. Each plate evokes the accomplishments of an outstanding woman, from the Primordial Goddess and Ishtar to Sojourner Truth, Susan B. Anthony, Virginia Woolf, and Georgia O'Keeffe. The place mats are made with materials and techniques of embroidery appropriate for each subject, and they develop the themes of the plates in more explicit imagery. An egg, crescent, breastplate, and double axe, for instance, appear on the Amazon's place mat. Mary Wollstonecraft's, on the other hand, is decorated with pictures of her life embroidered in stumpwork, a style of raised needlework popular in England in the seventeenth century.

The triangle, a sign of the goddess, appears repeatedly throughout *The Dinner Party*. The huge triangular banquet table stands on a "Heritage Floor" formed from triangular opalescent porcelain tiles. Each tile is inscribed with a woman's name, 999 in all. As light plays on the titles, the names appear and disappear, symbolizing both Western woman's tenuous hold on her place in history and the rootedness of the thirty-nine honored guests in the lives and accomplishments of other women.

The Dinner Party made women's history at the same time that it honored the achievements of women of the past. Judy Chicago oversaw the production of every element of the work, but an army of volunteers wove the tapestries, embroidered the place mats, amassed the 999 names, and painted the floor tiles—and most of those volunteers were women. Producing *The Dinner Party* yielded a new feminist approach to art in which mutually supportive women worked together to replace the isolated individual creator of traditional art.

Two series of photo-documentary panels accompany the exhibition. One provides histories of the thirty-nine *Dinner Party* guests; the second documents the five-year process of creating the work.

Although record-breaking crowds of more than one hundred thousand people stood in line two to three hours to see *The Dinner Party* when it first opened at the San Francisco Museum of Modern Art in 1979, few museums were willing to show it. Its second opening was at a university, the University of Houston-Clear Lake, after the Houston museums had refused it. In Chicago, a women's collective spent two years raising the money to bring *The Dinner Party* to a converted warehouse. Why were the major museums of the United States unwilling to exhibit this work? Was it the expense of shipping such a large show that held them back, or the status of needlework and china painting as crafts? Many suspected that the real reason for the official neglect of *The Dinner Party* was its polemical feminist themes. Whatever the cause, *The Dinner Party* remains a major achievement of feminist art.

In 1980 Chicago began an extension of *The Dinner Party*, entitled *The Birth Project*. This project expresses the universal experience of childbirth, celebrates the mythical and the painful through creation and goddess images, images of women giving birth, of the birth trinity, birth tear, and many other births.

Chicago explained the technicalities in, history behind, and people involved with the projects in *The Dinner Party: A Symbol of Our Heritage, Embroidering Our Heritage: Dinner Party Needlework*, and *The Birth Project*. She also wrote *Through the Flower: My Struggle as a Woman Artist* and made two films, *Womanhouse* and *Right Out of History: The Making of "The Dinner Party."*

—*Ginger Costello and Gretchen Mieszkowski*

See Also:

Anthony, Susan B.; Art; O'Keeffe, Georgia; Truth, Sojourner

References:

Chicago, Judy. *The Birth Project.* Garden City, N.Y.: Doubleday, 1985.

———. *The Dinner Party: A Symbol of Our Heritage.* Garden City, N.Y.: Anchor, 1979.

———. *Embroidering Our Heritage: The Dinner Party Needlework.* Garden City, N.Y.: Doubleday, 1980.

———. *Thru the Flower: My Struggle as a Woman Artist.* Introduction by Anaïs Nin. Garden City, N.Y.: Doubleday, 1975, 1977.

Lippard, Lucy. "Judy Chicago's Dinner Party." *Art in America* 68 (1980): 115–26.

CHICANA, the feminine form of *Chicano*, has become the preferred term to refer to women of Mexican ancestry in the United States. *Chicano* became the popularly shortened version of *Mexicanos* to connote the dignity and pride of Mexican-Americans working to achieve political, economic, and social equality. The term *Mexican-American* became tainted with efforts toward mainstream assimilation and accommodation in the 1960s; *Hispano* and *Latino* were deemed euphemistic and too imprecise to distinguish *Chicanos* from other Spanish-speaking peoples, and seemed to attempt to identify a person as European and Caucasian as a means of class distinction.

Chicanas have significant diversity in their ethnic identity, primary language, education, occupations, and economic status, as well as within generations; this often produces contrast between first-generation *hermanas* and subsequent generations. Common characteristics of *Chicanas* as resident members of a colonized minority within the United States include being of Mexican descent and yet of a unique culture with both Mexican and American influences. The important *Chicano* cultural concepts of *Hembraismo* and *Machismo* were appropriated by the mainstream of Anglo culture as terms that oversimplify the gender patterns within the *Chicano* family; however, *Hembraismo* actually designates the time-honored role of competent and enduring woman in the home, rather than woman as only docile, weak, and submissive. Likewise, *Machismo* encompasses the traditional patriarchal male role of protector and provider, not merely the male traits of power, assertion, and domination.

Chicanas inherited the disenfranchisement and displacement of those Mexican people who were summarily absorbed by the United States after the Treaty of Guadalupe-Hidalgo in 1848, which ended the Mexican-American War; as the victims of internal colonialism, *Chicanas* have sustained the added disability of their sex as well as their race.

—*Angela Howard Zophy*

See Also:

Mexican War, Triple Jeopardy

References:

Melville, Margarita, ed. *Twice a Minority.* London: C. V. Mosby, 1980.

Mirande, Alfredo, and Evangelina Enriquez. *La Chicana: The Mexican-American Woman.* Chicago: University of Chicago Press, 1979.

Zavella, Patricia. *Women's Work and Chicano Families: Cannery Workers of the Santa Clara Valley.* Ithaca: Cornell University Press, 1989.

CHILD, LYDIA MARIA FRANCIS (1802–80), author and abolitionist, was born in Medford, Massachusetts, the youngest child of a prosperous baker, David Francis, who believed in education for his children. After her mother died, she lived with a sister in Nurridgewock, Maine; when her brother Convers married and settled in Watertown, near Boston, she joined his family. Among his friends were Emerson, Whittier, and other informed men whose conversation interested the young Maria Francis; both her antislavery attitudes and her desire to write grew in this congenial atmosphere.

Her first book, *Hobomok* (1824), was a romance based on the Abenaki Indian lore she had learned as a young girl in Norridgewock. Although she signed the book "An American," her name was soon known, and fame and attention followed. She wrote *The Rebels* (1825), a novel based on Revolutionary War history, and edited the *Juvenile Miscellany*, the first American magazine for children. These were followed by other novels and by collections of verse and prose. In October 1828, against all the advice and wishes of her family, she married the charming, idealistic, and totally improvident David Lee Child, a lawyer who shared her strong abolitionist sentiments. The establishment of their small household on her income led to *The Frugal Housewife* (1830), a very popular compendium of advice for the economic managing of a home.

An early example of Victorian efforts to standardize and prescribe the household arts, this book reflected two major aspects of domestic feminism in its author's attempt to establish housewifery as a respected profession and to foster proper esteem for woman's role. She examined the practical details of running a household, and she instructed the aspiring young matron in proper social behavior. *The Frugal Housewife* described the problems of running a house, and therefore presents a detailed portrayal of the lives of white middle-class women in antebellum America. Because of its popularity, this publication inaugurated the genre of the domestic manual in America, which proved useful and lucrative for the proponents of domestic feminism, such as Sarah Josepha Hale and Catharine Beecher. Moreover, *The Frugal Housewife* ultimately contributed to the rise of the home economics movement, which institutionalized the professional training of housewives.

At their small house in Roxbury, the Childs enjoyed entertaining their friends, chief among whom were abolitionist writers Theodore Parker, William Ellery Channing, and John Greenleaf Whittier. Her antislavery commitment strengthened, and in 1833 she severely damaged her popularity with *An Appeal in Favor of That Class of Americans Called Africans*. This reasoned appeal for just treatment and an end to slavery, based on history, ethics, and religious thought, was too far ahead of its time to win popular approval. The book lost her editors and friends and ruined the *Juvenile Miscellany*, but she never regretted it, for it had a strong influence on Channing, other abolitionist leaders such as Thomas Wentworth Higginson, and, most important, Wendell Phillips.

David Child had become interested in growing sugar beets to replace imported sugar; much of his life was dedicated to that cause although financial returns from his agricultural experiments were slight. Maria wrote *The History of the Condition of Women* (1835) and *Philothea, A Story of Ancient Greece* (1836), a luxurious novel set in the days of Pericles, that won back some of her lost popularity. In 1839 David Francis bought a farm in Northampton, Massachusetts, where he hoped his daughter could live in comfort while his worthless son-in-law grew sugar beets. Mr. Francis lived with them there and, caught between her father and her husband, Maria felt trapped and exiled. She cherished the occasional drives with the Reverend John Sullivan Dwight to Boston, where she could visit friends, go to libraries or transcendentalist meetings, and attend the "conversations" run by her close friend Margaret Fuller.

When David Child refused the editorship of the New York *Anti-Slavery Standard* in 1841, Maria took the job instead, moving to New York and lodging with a Quaker family whose house was a station on the Underground Railroad, a secret network that helped slaves escape to the North and Canada. From New York she wrote newsletters for the *Boston Courier*, which were eventually published as *Letters from New York* (1843; second series 1845). These widely read newsletter reestablished Child as a major literary figure. In 1843 she resigned, and David came to New York to replace her. They remained in New York until 1849; during the period Maria wrote innumerable stories and articles for newspapers, magazines, and annuals, as well as her newsletters, and a great deal for children.

They returned to live with her father in Wayland, Massachusetts. Francis died in 1856, leaving the farm to his daughter but carefully arranging matters through the use of a trusted third person so that control of money and property was kept from his son-in-law. A major work, *The Progress of Religious Ideas* (1855), a study of comparative religion, displayed her wide knowledge and intellect; it was admired by theologians and scholars, although it had no popular audience. She kept a steady income, however, with books for children and with anthologies.

Child's abolitionism and the fugitive slave controversy inspired her to write pamphlets and articles. *The Correspondence Between Lydia Maria Child, Governor Wise, and Mrs. Mason* (1860), published by the Anti-Slavery Society, recorded her attempt to help John Brown in prison and its aftereffects. It contained letters from Governor Wise of Virginia and an attack from Mrs. Mason, whose husband had written the Fugitive Slave Act; Mason accused Child of being unchristian and not knowing her Bible; Child's response was informed, thorough, and scorching. She edited and wrote the introduction for *Incidents in the Life of a Slave Girl* by Harriet Brent Jacobs ("Linda Brent"), and in 1865, concerned for the newly freed slaves, wrote *The Freedmen's Book*, a combination of inspiration and advice. But most of her writing at this time was short and aimed at periodicals.

After David Child died in 1874, she wrote very little. In the last years of her life, she visited friends and relatives and lived with a companion; she gradually failed, and died in October 1880.

—Shirley Marchalonis and Theresa A. McGeary

See Also:

Abolition and the Antislavery Movement; Beecher, Catharine; Domestic Feminism; Domestic Literature; Home Economics; Housework

References:

Baer, Helene G. *The Heart Is Like Heaven.* Philadelphia: University of Pennsylvania Press, 1964.

Child, Lydia Maria. *The Freedmen's Book.* Boston: J. Allen, 1835.

———. *The Frugal Housewife: Dedicated to Those Who Are Not Ashamed of Economy.* London: T. T. & J. Tegg, 1832.

———. *The History of the Condition of Women in Various Ages and Nations.* Boston: Ticknor & Fields, 1865.

———. *The Mother's Book.* Boston: Carter & Hendee, 1831.

———. *Selected Letters, 1817–1880.* Edited by Milton Meltzer and Patricia G. Holland. Amherst: University of Massachusetts Press, 1982.

Osborne, William S. *Lydia Maria Child.* Boston: Twayne, 1980.

CHILD REARING. The primary occupation of most women at some point in their lives, child rearing is both a source of emotional satisfaction and a stressful job that can tie women to the home. Between 1800 and 1900 the number of living children born to married white women dropped from 7.04 to 3.56. This reduction in family size, along with a decline in infant mortality and the leisure afforded to middle-class women by the removal of industrial production from the home, changed the focus of child care from physical health to psychological development.

Colonial women typically spent most of their lives raising children, but household and farm chores left little time for child care per se. Mothers breast-fed infants, but shared responsibility for child rearing with fathers, older children, and neighbors. Children as young as six years old might be apprenticed outside the family.

The nineteenth and twentieth centuries saw the flowering of an ideology that placed children at the center of family life, glorified the mother-child relation, and stressed women's responsibility for the physical and psychological well-being of their offspring. Although most middle-class women embraced the "professionalization" of motherhood by 1900, many working-class women, immigrants, and women of color continued to follow traditional child-rearing practices. At the turn of the twentieth century, experts taught mothers to raise children to succeed in an industrial world by adhering to strict schedules, beginning toilet training early, and bottle-feeding by the clock. In the 1920s psychologists warned that excessive mother love obstructed children's personality development. By the 1950s warnings against mothers' tendency to spoil children coexisted with a renewed idealization of the mother-child bond. Benjamin Spock's influential *Baby and Child Care* (1946) maintained that the mother's loving attention was essential to her child's emotional health and security. Breast-feeding on demand returned to vogue, and women structured household routines and careers around their children.

Despite the existence of these experts, most women had neither the time nor financial resources to follow child rearing advice. With the exception of blacks, few mothers worked outside the home until World War II, yet housework and poverty took time away from child care. Despite efforts to socialize child rearing or to provide government allowances for child care at home, child rearing is still done without pay by women in private households.

—*Molly Ladd-Taylor*

See Also:
Housework, Scientific Motherhood

References:

Beekman, Daniel. *The Mechanical Baby: A Popular History of the Theory and Practice of Child Raising.* Westport, Conn.: Lawrence Hill, 1977.

Hardyment, Christina. *Dream Babies.* New York: Harper & Row, 1983.

Ladd-Taylor, Molly. *Raising a Baby the Government Way: Mothers' Letters to the Children's Bureau, 1915–1932.* New Brunswick, N.J.: Rutgers University Press, 1986.

CHILDBIRTH, or parturition, is the act of giving birth. Early American women spent the majority of their married life either pregnant or nursing an infant. Childbirth was the culmination of nine months of preparation, pregnancy, as well as the precipitating event of usually thirteen months of breast-feeding an infant. Such childbirth matters occupied about sixteen years of a seventeenth-century woman's married life, during which she gave birth about ten times. By the last half of the nineteenth century, a woman gave birth closer to four times; a century later, typically a woman will give birth twice or less.

In early America, childbirth was a women's rite. A woman recognized the signs of her own impending birth; she knew when to call "her women," when to send her husband for the midwife, and what to expect in the hours ahead. In a room or area set apart from the activity of the household, the women would gather. Soothing teas would ease the expectant mother through the dilation stage of her labor. When she felt ready to deliver, she might do so on a birthing stool the midwife had brought, or she might choose another comfortable position. The midwife was in charge, but comments and suggestions from all would be heard. The midwife was well equipped to handle difficulties such as excessive pain, slow progress, and a poorly positioned foetus, but most labors were normal, and the women were used to waiting.

When physicians moved into the birthing chamber in the second half of the eighteenth century, they were less willing to wait. They brought instruments—forceps in particular—to hurry along the delivery, and bloodletting and such other measures as tobacco enemas and later ergot (an oxytocic drug derived from a rye grain fungus) to speed up labor or opium to slow it down. By the mid-nineteenth century, doctors were using ether and chloroform to dull or erase childbirth pain.

With doctors' increasing role, childbirth was becoming a singular event to be managed medically rather than one part of the sequence from pregnancy through the nursing period that fit into the rhythms and rituals of everyday life. Women were still present at birth through the nineteenth century, but they were rarely in charge and were less often the only ones present. Attention at childbirth increasingly focused on medical aspects of the labor and delivery, on managing the woman's experience.

The twentieth century saw birth moved out of the home and into the hospital, where management could be controlled even more effectively. A variety of drugs and other interventions were introduced during the century as childbirth became thoroughly medicalized. But since the 1960s, a movement to reinstate "natural childbirth" has endeavored to return childbirth to its nonmedical state. The home-birth and midwifery movements are working to return birth to the realm of women's experience in the family, to have it perceived as an essentially normal process that sometimes requires medical backup but is not pathological and does not necessarily call for a medical response.

—*Janet Carlisle Bogdan*

See Also:

"Granny" Midwifery, Immigrant Midwifery, Midwifery

References:

Arms, Suzanne. *Immaculate Deception*. Boston: Houghton Mifflin, 1975.

Eakins, Pamela S., ed. *The American Way of Birth*. Philadelphia: Temple University Press, 1986.

Leavitt, Judith Waltzer. *Brought to Bed*. New York: Oxford University Press, 1986.

Rothman, Barbara K. *In Labor: Women and Power in the Birthplace*. London: Junction, 1982.

The **CHILDREN'S LIBRARY MOVEMENT** (1876–1910). The increasing presence of women on the staff of American public libraries from the mid-1870s brought with it the development of public library services to children. This development drew on several movements and attitudes common to the period. For example, the tendency of professional women to innovate new areas distinct from established male specialties is evident in the growth of children's services. The growing interest in the child during this period, as exemplified by the influential work of Evelyn Key, *The Century of the Child* (1909), which popularized modern child development principles, and the ongoing tradition that women had a special gift for working with children both contributed to the service. Finally the middle-class women who promoted this service among poor immigrant children in the large industrial cities of the Northeast and Midwest remembered their own cultured upbringing and sought to re-create it for their charges. The growth of services to children in the public libraries brought those institutions into closer collaboration with schools, settlement houses, and hospitals caring for children, where many like-minded women were also building careers. Not surprisingly, considering the identification with women, the growth of services to children in public libraries is one of the most poorly researched areas in library history.

Minerva Saunders, librarian of the Pawtucket (R.I.) Public Library, is generally credited with being the first, beginning in 1877, to end age restrictions on access to the collection, provide suitable books for children, and provide suitable furniture in one corner of the reading room to be used by the children. The two major missing ingredients of modern children's services were soon added in 1894, when the Denver Public Library set aside a separate room, formerly a ladies' reading room, for children, and in 1898, when Anne Carroll Moore began giving courses in work with children at the Pratt Institute in Brooklyn. The first comprehensive children's department was opened in the Carnegie Library of Pittsburgh by Frances Jenkins Olcott in 1898. In 1910 this library issued a classic document authored by Olcott, entitled *Rational Library Work with Children and the Preparation for It*, which summarizes the role of the children's library and librarians. The library, it said, should "take the place of a child's private library," giving the child a chance to browse among books of all kinds in a "beautifully proportioned and decorated room," assisted by a "genial and sympathetic woman" with a genuine interest in the child's personality.

—*Suzanne Hildenbrand*

See Also:
Librarianship

References:

Long, Harriet G. *Public Library Service to Children: Foundation and Development.* Metuchen, N.J.: Scarecrow, 1969.

McNamara, Shelley G. "Early Public Library Work With Children." *Top of the News* 43 (Fall 1986): 59–71.

Thomas, Fannette Henrietta. "The Genesis of Children's Services in the American Public Library: 1875–1906." Diss. University of Wisconsin-Madison, 1982.

CHISHOLM, SHIRLEY (ST. HILL) (b. 1924) became in 1968 the first black woman elected to the U.S. House of Representatives. From 1968 to 1982 she served in Congress as a Democrat representing the Twelfth district of Brooklyn, New York. She is currently Purrington Professor of Political Science at Mount Holyoke College in South Hadley, Massachusetts. She is the author of *Unbought and Unbossed* (1970) and *The Good Fight* (1973).

Chisholm was born in New York but went to live with her grandparents on their farm in Barbados at age four, living there and attending British schools until the age of ten, when she returned to her parents' home. She attended schools in Brooklyn and graduated from Brooklyn College in 1946, later receiving an M.A. in elementary education from Columbia University. After leaving school, she worked as a teacher, and as assistant director of a nursery school in Harlem, director of a small private school, and director of the Hamilton-Madison Day Care Center in Manhattan.

Simultaneously, Chisholm became more involved in the politics of the Bedford-Stuyvesant area of New York. Capitalizing on her political tutelage in Democratic political clubs, she secured a vacant seat in the state assembly in 1964, and was reelected in 1965 and 1966. Race was less of an issue in the Twelfth congressional district in Brooklyn than sex or other topical issues. There were thirteen thousand more women than men in the district, and more than three times as many black women as black men were registered to vote. Chisholm mobilized this potential constituency and defeated James Farmer.

In 1972 Chisholm made history again by announcing her candidacy for the Democratic presidential nomination. Responding to the rising consciousness of women of all races and their increased interest and participation in politics, she and her running mate, Cissy Farenthal of Texas, introduced the major women's rights issues into the presidential primaries debate. The congresswoman emerged from the unsuccessful campaign a national spokesperson for women and the black community. Her dynamic speeches and adamant support of women's rights established her presence and prominence in the history of the modern women's movement.

—*Susan Kinnell*

See Also:
Black Women, Democratic Party, Politics

References:

Brownmiller, Susan. *Shirley Chisholm, A Biography.* Garden City, N.Y.: Doubleday, 1971.

Haskins, James. *Fighting Shirley Chisholm.* New York: Dial, 1975.

Hicks, Nancy. *The Honorable Shirley Chisholm: Congresswoman from Brooklyn.* New York: Lion Books, 1971.

CHRISTIANITY. Women have been involved with Christianity from its beginnings, although generally in a subordinate role. In colonial times, Anne Hutchinson (1591–1643) became the leader of the opposition party in the antiauthority crisis in seventeenth-century Massachusetts. She believed that individuals regardless of their sex could communicate with the spirit of Christ and interpret biblical teachings and sermons on their own. Other colonial women such as Mary Dyer and Ann Easton also resisted the subordinate role that most religious communities assigned women. Only a minority sect, the Society of Friends, or Quakers, extended to colonial women full participation in the ministry.

In the nineteenth century, women participated fully in the second Great Awakening. Women fostered and organized revivals and directed a militant piety against unchurched men. By the mid-1800s women comprised the majority of active church membership, and were active in the Sunday schools that were beginning to appear in many churches. Religious women participated in many of the reform movements of the 1830s and 1840s, including the abolition and antislavery movement and the various American missionary movements. Whether in religious orders or as lay women, Roman Catholic women were active in educational and reform endeavors. Piety was one of the primary values of the Victorian Cult of True Womanhood, facilitating the religious activism of mainstream women beyond the confines of their individual congregation or parish.

Because women were denied admission to the ministry and priesthood in most Christian denominations, they were unable to reduce significantly the patriarchial nature of Christianity until the latter half of the twentieth century, although occasionally a woman evangelist such as Aimee Semple McPherson (1890–1944) or a female religious such as Sister Frances Xavier Cabrini (1850–1917) would achieve widespread recognition. The leadership roles in most Christian communities continued to be a male monopoly until the 1970s, when women were admitted to the ministry among evangelical Lutherans, Methodists, and Presbyterians. Episcopalians in the United States also began to ordain women priests. However, the largest Protestant group in the nation, the Baptists, refused to admit women into their ministry, and the Roman Catholic priesthood remained open to men only. Most fundamentalist groups continued to hold women in a subordinate position and became a vocal part of the backlash against the modern women's movement.

Although there is an enormous variety in belief and practice within Christianity, there are some issues that recur frequently in the literature on women and Christianity: scriptural interpretation, use of language and image, church leadership, and social issues. The Bible is fundamental to the Christian faith; however, many of the texts in the Christian scriptures from the account of Creation in Genesis 2 to the admonishment to silence for women in 1 Timothy bear reflections of the patriarchal societies in which they were written. A major influence on the reappraisal of the proper role and place of women in Christianity has been the recovery of women's history in the Old Testament, in the life of Jesus, and in early Christianity, as well as the use of modern approaches to scriptural interpretation and reconstruction.

Much of the language that Christian churches use in their worship is not inclusive. Likewise, many of the masculine terms for God (*Father, King, Lord*) have cast man but not woman in God's image. While women make up the majority of church members, many denominations still exclude women from the leadership positions of pastor, deacon, or service on the governing bodies.

—Sandra E. Roberts and
Jonathan W. Zophy

See Also:

American Missionary Association; Cabrini, Frances X.; Center for Women and Religion; Coughlin, Mother Mary Samuel; Lentfoehr, Sister Mary Therese; McPherson, Aimee Semple; Methodist Women in the Nineteenth Century; Presbyterian Women's Groups; Shakers; Society of Friends; Southern Baptist Woman's Missionary Society; Southern Christian Leadership Conference; Theologians; Women's Missionary Societies

References:

Fiorenza, Elizabeth Schussler. *In Memory of Her: A Feminist Reconstruction of Christian Origins.* New York: Crossroad, 1983.

Fischer, Clare B., Betsy Brenneman, and Anne M. Bennett, eds. *Women in a Strange Land: Search for a New Image.* Philadelphia: Fortress, 1975.

Jewett, Paul K. *The Ordination of Women: An Essay on the Office of Christian Ministry.* Grand Rapids, Mich.: Eerdmans, 1980.

Mollenkott, Virginia. *The Divine Feminine: The Biblical Imagery of God as Female.* New York: Crossroad, 1983.

Ramshaw-Schmidt, Gail. *Christ in Sacred Speech: The Meaning of Liturgical Language.* Philadelphia: Fortress, 1986.
Ruether, Rosemary. *Sexism and God-Talk: Toward a Feminist Theology.* Boston: Beacon, 1983.
Scanzoni, Letha, and Nancy Gardesty. *All We're Meant to Be: A Biblical Approach to Women's Liberation.* Waco, Tex.: Word Books, 1975.
Wahlberg, Rachel Conrad. *Jesus and the Freed Woman.* New York: Paulist, 1978.

CIGAR MAKERS/TOBACCO WORKERS. Women's role in the tobacco, cigar, and cigarette industries has ranged from highly prized positions as hand rollers of fine cigars to lowly jobs in the stemming rooms. Skilled Bohemian and Cuban women cigar makers arrived in the United States beginning in the late nineteenth century, and manufacturers soon took advantage of their abilities. At the same time, unskilled immigrant and native-born black women stripped leaves from stems, earning low wages and suffering from the heat and humidity necessary to maintain quality tobacco. Women only came to dominate the labor force in these industries when automation increased demands for less skilled workers.

Male cigar makers forged the powerful Cigar Makers International Union in the 1880s, but they generally excluded women from their ranks. The radical, Havana-based union, *La Resistencia*, which was active in Florida, was one of the few where skilled and unskilled women and men were organized together. In most areas of the country, women's massive entry into the cigar industry rested on the union-busting tactics of the larger cigar manufacturers as well as on expanded production of cheaper cigars and automation. By 1919 these conditions prevailed, and women formed 58 percent of the total cigar factory labor force; by 1940 they comprised 81.3 percent. Lower production figures and lower-priced cigars combined in the 1930s to reduce both work force and wages, reductions only temporarily halted by World War II.

The cigarette industry was established in Virginia and North Carolina in the 1880s but expanded most rapidly in the early 1900s with the amalgamation of the tobacco trusts, which led to more centralized control of the market, and the full automation of production. Though men served as machine operators and foremen, women early formed a significant portion of the cigarette labor force. Both black and white women from rural areas, equally unskilled, were drawn into the industry out of economic necessity. Yet white women soon dominated the more skilled positions, while black women were relegated to the stemmeries. Attempts to organize the cigarette industry, which peaked in the 1930s, were inhibited by the racial and sexual division of labor. In cities such as Durham, North Carolina, unionization reinforced racial tensions by protecting white but not black women's jobs. In the same period, more progressive organizers from the Congress of Industrial Organizations aided in organizing black stemmery workers in Richmond, Virginia, and Winston-Salem, North Carolina.

The tobacco, cigar, and cigarette industries were critical sources of employment for immigrant women in northern cities and in Florida and for black and white women in the Carolinas and Virginia. Though the sexual division of labor circumscribed women's opportunities in these industries, variations in skill, in levels of automation, and in the extent of unionization, in addition to racial tensions, placed women in competition with each other. In general, as women came to dominate the labor force manufacturing tobacco products, wages and working conditions deteriorated.

—*Nancy A. Hewitt*

See Also:

Congress of Industrial Organizations, Industrial Revolution, Unions

References:

Cooper, Patricia. *Once a Cigar Maker: Men, Women and Work Culture in American Cigar Factories, 1900–1919.* Urbana: University of Illinois Press, 1987.
Hewitt, Nancy A. "Women in Ybor City: An Interview with a Woman Cigar Maker." *Tampa Bay History* 7 (Fall/Winter 1985): 161–65.

Janiewski, Dolores. *Sisterhood Denied: Race, Gender, and Class in a New South Community.* Philadelphia: Temple University Press, 1985.

The **CIVIL LIBERTIES MOVEMENT DURING WORLD WAR I.** The United States declared war on Germany on April 6, 1917. One week later, New York City members of the Woman's Peace party (WPP/NYC) initiated the establishment of the New York Bureau of Legal First Aid (later renamed and hereafter referred to as the New York Bureau of Legal Advice, or BLA), the first organization of the World War I era to offer free legal aid and counsel to draft-age men and conscientious objectors to military service. The executive secretary and directing force of the BLA was Frances Witherspoon, who, like many of her female comrades of the young peace movement generation, was a feminist, a pacifist, and a socialist. She enlisted the assistance of both women and men in civil liberties work, but capable women like birth-control advocate and lawyer Jessie Ashley and socialist labor organizer Ella Reeve Bloor provided the backbone of her organization.

At the same time that the Woman's Peace party was helping to launch the BLA, several members of the American Union Against Militarism (AUAM), notably Crystal Eastman, a feminist socialist labor lawyer and the head of the WPP/NYC, and Roger Baldwin, a social worker and the associate director of the AUAM, were establishing a legal aid committee within the AUAM that by fall 1917 had become autonomous, the National Civil Liberties Bureau (NCLB). Despite the involvement of a few women like Eastman on the initial directing committee, the NCLB, unlike Witherspoon's group, quickly became a predominantly male organization.

In 1917 and 1918 the BLA (for New York City) and the NCLB (for the rest of the country) provided legal assistance not only to draft-age men and conscientious objectors, but also to labor leaders and rank-and-file members of "radical" labor groups like the Industrial Workers of the World (IWW) and to political radicals (and liberals) arrested for alleged violations of wartime sedition laws. Both groups helped to influence the federal government to eliminate one of the cruelest punishments of military prison : manacling of prisoners to cell bars for nine hours per day for up to fourteen days was halted in late 1918. The BLA and NCLB, in concert with other associations, also lobbied, in this case unsuccessfully, for immediate amnesty for conscientious objectors and political prisoners after an armistice was declared on November 11, 1918. The BLA enjoyed a special triumph when in 1919 it was able to quash deportation proceedings for a number of IWW members with alien status.

The BLA and the NCLB shared leadership of the World War I civil liberties movement. But other organizations arose as well, sometimes as affiliates of the NCLB, but often as autonomous groups that were nonetheless linked to the larger organizations by personal ties and common goals. Women were important in such associations; for example, Emma Goldman of the No-Conscription League, Eleanor Fitzgerald of the League for the Amnesty of Political Prisoners, and Lola Maverick Lloyd and Lenetta Cooper of the American Liberty Defense Union.

None of the wartime civil liberties groups in which women were so prominent existed beyond 1919 although the male-led and male-dominated NCLB survived, becoming the American Civil Liberties Union after the war. The reasons for the fading of women's involvement in civil liberties work are complex, but contributing factors include "burnout" of leaders like Witherspoon, who needed time to recover from the demands of wartime activism; the reactionary antifeminist political climate of the 1920s, which demoralized many women activists; and factionalism in the feminist movement after 1920. Then, too, although women and men had worked shoulder-to-shoulder during the war and immediately thereafter in civil liberties work, a number of men, especially the "big guns," according to Witherspoon, were "antifeminist." This attitude influenced postwar developments and women found themselves, to a degree, edged out of the civil liberties field, particularly at the leadership level.

—*Frances H. Early*

See Also:

Goldman, Emma; Industrial Workers of the World; Witherspoon, Frances; Woman's Peace Party

References:

[Ed. Note: There are no secondary sources for this topic, but the author is currently preparing a manuscript for publication. Key primary sources include the records of the New York Bureau of Legal First Aid at the Tamiment Institute of Labor History at New York University and the records of the New York Bureau of Legal Advice, the American Union Against Militarism, and the Woman's Peace party at the Swarthmore College Peace Collection, Swarthmore, Pa.]

CIVIL RIGHTS refers to the governmental means used to ensure the equality of rights for persons regardless of their race, gender, or ethnic background. The Declaration of Independence states that "all men are created equal." This declaration did not embrace slaves and women. Thus, the history of the United States is a process of slow democratization of the basic liberties guaranteed in the guiding principles and the Constitution. Virtually all minority groups have suffered discrimination. The civil rights movement and the feminist movement are the struggles that are being fought to destroy those legal, social, and economic barriers that deny women and other minorities the ability to participate equally and fully in all phases of American society.

The women's movement pressured the government over the years to remedy the inequalities of opportunity for women. In the area of employment, the Equal Pay Act of 1963 mandates equal pay for equal work, and the Civil Rights Act of 1964 forbids discrimination on the basis of gender as well as race at the points of hiring, promoting, and firing. The Education Amendments of 1972 disallow discrimination on the basis of gender in schools and colleges that receive federal aid. In order to promote equal credit opportunities, the Equal Credit Opportunity Act of 1974 forbids discrimination on the basis of gender or marital status in credit transactions.

The courts have also provided an avenue for women seeking equal treatment, although women were not successful in that avenue immediately. The courts initially upheld laws that discriminated against women and also upheld "protective" laws for women during the Progressive era. It was not until the decisions of the U.S. Supreme Court under Chief Justice Warren C. Burger in the early 1970s that this pattern was reversed. The courts have been a relatively successful, albeit slow, means for women to address discriminatory barriers to their full use and full guarantee of the basic civil liberties and civil rights as outlined in the Constitution and the Bill of Rights.

—*Sue E. Strickler*

See Also:

Affirmative Action, *Brown v. Board of Education*, Civil Rights Act of 1964, Equal Pay Act of 1963

References:

Deckard, Barbara Sinclair. *The Women's Movement*. 2d ed. New York: Harper & Row, 1979.

DeCrow, Karen. *Sexist Justice*. New York: Vintage, 1975.

Morris, Aldon D. *The Origins of the Civil Rights Movement: Black Communities Organizing for Change*. New York: Macmillan, 1985.

The **CIVIL RIGHTS ACT OF 1964** was a comprehensive law empowering the federal government to move against discrimination on a variety of fronts. Promoted by the civil rights movement and its supporters, the bill initially focused on racial discrimination. But Title VII of the act, which prohibited discrimination by employers and labor unions and created an Equal Employment Opportunity Commission (EEOC) to enforce the measure, included a ban on sex discrimination as well.

The amendment to insert "sex" into Title VII was introduced by a Virginia representative who supported legal equality for women but opposed civil rights legislation. Although liberals and civil rights supporters sought defeat of the amendment that they felt would jeopardize passage of the entire section, the amendment passed and was subsequently accepted by the Senate. While there was no mass women's movement demanding an attack on sex discrimination, a handful of congresswomen fought for the "sex" clause, and a small group of women lobbyists exerted pressure from the outside.

Once enacted, the ban on sex discrimination spurred women's activism and helped launch a new surge of feminism. Women began to complain that the EEOC did not take seriously the ban on sex discrimination, and frustration with lack of enforcement of Title VII was an important catalyst for the founding of the National Organization for Women (NOW), the first national feminist organization. In addition, Title VII caused federal courts to strike down protective labor laws that applied only to women, and thus eliminated a major source of opposition to an Equal Rights Amendment.

By the early 1970s more than thirty thousand charges of sex discrimination had been filed with the EEOC. In 1972 Title VII was amended to bring educational institutions and state and local governments under the law, and to empower the EEOC with the right to take cases to court on its own initiative. In addition to suits brought by feminist organizations and labor unions, the EEOC filed class-action suits against a number of large corporations. Although overall occupational segregation by sex persisted and a large pay gap between men and women continued, Title VII diminished discrimination against women workers. Through out-of-court settlements or consent decrees, thousands of women won back-pay and affirmative action remedies amounting to millions of dollars.

—Susan M. Hartmann

See Also:

Affirmative Action, Equal Employment Opportunity Commission, National Organization for Women, Sex Discrimination

References:

Braver, Carl M. "Women Activists, Southern Conservatives, and the Prohibition of Sex Discrimination in Title VII of the 1964 Civil Rights Act." *Journal of Southern History* 49 (1983): 37–57.

Harrison, Cynthia. *On Account of Sex: The Politics of Women's Issues, 1945–1968.* Berkeley: University of California Press, 1988.

Robinson, Donald A. "Two Movements in Pursuit of Equal Employment Opportunity." *Signs: Journal of Women in Culture and Society* 4 (Spring 1979): 413–33.

Wallace, Phyllis A. "Impact of Equal Employment Opportunity Laws." In *Women and the American Economy*, edited by Juanita M. Kreps. Englewood Cliffs, N.J.: Prentice-Hall, 1976, pp. 123–45.

CIVIL WAR (1861–65). The outbreak of the U.S. Civil War mobilized thousands of women as well as men. Over seven thousand local societies in the North banded together to form the U.S. Sanitary Commission, collecting and distributing supplies, training nurses, and equipping hospitals. Bazaars and fairs raised millions for relief, aiding widows, orphans, and disabled soldiers. Dorothea Dix (superintendent of nurses for the Union Army), Mary Ann ("Mother") Bickerdyke, and Clara Barton were heroines for their medical prowess in the North, while Sally Tompkins (awarded the rank of captain by Confederate president Jefferson Davis) won similar acclaim in the South running a Richmond infirmary.

Women not only performed their traditional roles as nurses and organizers of voluntary associations, but some served as agents for their respective governments: Rose O'Neal Greenhow died a martyr's death smuggling gold for the Confederacy, Charlotte Cushman (a spy for the Union) narrowly escaped imprisonment for passing information, and Belle Boyd was a celebrated Confederate daredevil in the Shenandoah Valley. Over four hundred women were discovered posing as soldiers, many of whom had accompanied husbands and sweethearts into battle.

The majority of American women served their respective causes by holding together families and households during times of loss, stress, and disruption. Women in the border states were especially vulnerable to shortages in food and clothing and other hardships of occupation. By the winter of 1864, many women left to manage farms in the South were facing impending starvation. Brides were widowed, children were orphaned, and the death of six hundred thousand men left a generation bereft.

On the other hand, there were meaningful gains made by slave women, whose emancipation led to unprecedented freedoms. Women in Washington, D.C., were able to make significant inroads while men went off to war; five hundred women clerks were in federal employ, with over one hundred in Frances Spinner's Office of the Treasury alone. These "government girls" were the victims of a backlash at war's end, but many gained confidence and experience through their wartime tenures. Despite the horrors and hardship of war, a generation of women gained greater insight into the dimensions of their struggles for autonomy, and the postwar era witnessed the growth of feminist agitation.

—Catherine Clinton

See Also:

Barton, Clara; Dix, Dorothea; U.S. Sanitary Commission

References:

Bennett, Nina. "The Women Who Went to War: The Union Army Nurse in the Civil War." Diss. Northwestern University, 1981.

Clinton, Catherine. *The Other Civil War.* New York: Hill and Wang, 1984.

Massey, Mary Elizabeth. *Bonnet Brigades.* New York: Knopf, 1966.

Wiley, Bell Irwin. *Confederate Women.* Westport, Conn.: Greenwood, 1975.

Woodward, C. Vann. *Mary Chesnut's Civil War.* New Haven: Yale University Press, 1981.

CLITORIDECTOMY is an operation in which the clitoris is excised. In many societies, female circumcision has been part of puberty rites, although some such rituals attempted to increase the size and heighten the sensitivity of the clitoris and the labia.

The emerging practice of gynecology in Victorian America looked upon the latter as primitive and the former as civilized. Passionate women were defined as abnormal and looked upon as a danger to society. Female masturbation drew universal condemnation as the product of a diseased sexual appetite. Clitoridectomy was one of several cures proposed for "nymphomania," as it was termed in the nineteenth century, and the process involved cauterization of the clitoris with a white-hot iron or "circumcision," which involved cutting away the hood of the clitoris. Drawing on the work of a British gynecologist, American doctors following the Civil War performed the operation to cure female masturbation and to alleviate "unnatural" desires. The easy prescription of such radical surgery was the most extreme result of Victorian sexual ideology.

—William G. Shade

References:

Barker-Benfield, Graham John. *The Horrors of the Half-Known Life.* New York: Harper & Row, 1972.

Duffy, John. "Masturbation and Clitoridectomy: A Nineteenth Century View." *Journal of the American Medical Association* 186 (October 1963): 246–48.

COCHRAN, JACQUELINE (?–1980) was the first woman to fly faster than the speed of sound. At the time of her death in 1980, she held more speed, altitude, and distance records than any other pilot in aviation history.

Cochran began flying to help promote her fledgling cosmetics business, receiving her pilot's license in 1932. She began almost immediately entering major air races open to both male and female pilots. She strove for absolute records rather than women's records, because she believed that women's records would be broken by men. In 1938 she won the prestigious Bendix Trophy Race from Burbank to Cleveland against all male competition. Her record setting and air racing continued until World War II, when she went to England with a group of twenty-five other American women pilots to serve with the

British Air Transport Auxiliary. In 1943 Cochran returned to the United States to head the Women's Airforce Service Pilots (WASPs), who did the majority of domestic flying during the war.

After the war, she returned to setting records, and on May 18, 1953, she became the first woman to fly faster than the speed of sound. Well into her sixties, she was setting speed records in aircraft capable of twice the speed of sound, flying over twelve hundred miles per hour. During her forty-year flying career, Cochran received many awards, including the French Legion of Honor, the U.S. Air Force Distinguished Flying Cross, and the Harmon Trophy for outstanding female pilot of the year, the latter awarded to her fourteen times.

—Claudia M. Oakes

See Also:

Aviation, Women's Airforce Service Pilots (WASPs)

References:

Cochran, Jacqueline. *The Stars at Noon.* Boston: Little, Brown, 1954.

———, and Maryann Bucknum Brinley. *Jackie Cochran: An Autobiography.* New York: Bantam, 1987.

COEDUCATION, the practice of educating women and men together, has been an important theme in American history. While the earliest schools in English-speaking North America appear to have been for males alone, there is evidence that, by the mid-eighteenth century, many schools in New England enrolled both girls and boys. This was probably associated with the growing incidence of female church membership in this period and the need for women to be literate in order to read and understand the Bible and other religious writings. As common schools were established in Massachusetts and other states in the years following the American Revolution, coeducation appears to have become quite ordinary. It was considerably cheaper, after all, to educate girls and boys together than to conduct separate schools for each, especially in rural areas where school budgets (and the numbers of children) were meager. By the mid-nineteenth century, most schoolchildren in the United States probably attended coeducational schools.

Coeducation became a matter of controversy when women began to attend high schools and colleges in larger numbers after 1870. Some male scientists and educators argued that extended study threatened the health of young women, who were believed to be quite frail. A vigorous debate among educators on this issue continued into the opening decades of the twentieth century. Women continued to enroll in high schools and colleges, however, despite dire warnings from critics of coeducation. By 1900 more than three-quarters of all women enrolled in such institutions attended coeducational schools. After World War I there appears to have been little debate about whether or not boys and girls should attend school together, though the development of home economics and other gender-specific courses in high schools and colleges may have diminished the extent to which they actually sat in the same classrooms. By the third decade of the twentieth century, in any case, coeducation had become a firmly established feature of American education.

—John L. Rury

See Also:

Education, *Sex in Education, or a Fair Chance for the Girls,* Women in Higher Education

References:

Hansot, Elisabeth, and David Tyack. "Gender in Public Schools: Thinking Institutionally." *Signs: Journal of Women in Society and Culture,* 13 (Fall 1988): 741–60.

Rothman, Sheila M. *Woman's Proper Place: A History of Changing Ideals and Practices, 1870 to the Present.* New York: Basic, 1978.

Rury, John L., and Glenn Harper. "The Trouble with Coeducation: Mann and Women at Antioch, 1853–1860." *History of Education Quarterly* 26 (Winter 1986): 481–503.

COLCORD, JOANNA CARVER (1883–1960), author and social welfare administrator, was born at sea aboard her father's sailing ship and spent her childhood on ships. Reflections of these years appear in her works *Sea Language Comes Ashore* (1945) and *Songs of American Sailormen* (1938).

Colcord received a B.S. from the University of Maine in 1906 and an M.S. there in 1909. In 1911 she received a certificate from the New York School of Philanthropy, which would later become the Graduate School of Social Work at Columbia University. She was assistant district secretary of the New York Charity Organization Society from 1914 to 1925. Under a leave of absence from that organization, she served with the Home Service Bureau of the American Red Cross, Virgin Islands, during 1920 and 1921. From 1925 to 1929 she was general secretary of the Family Welfare Association of Minneapolis and lecturer at the University of Minnesota.

Recognized as an outstanding practitioner of social research and community organization, Colcord succeeded Mary Richmond as director of the Charity Organization Department of the Russell Sage Foundation from 1929 to 1944. The Great Depression and World War II focused her work in resource mobilization, studies of social security, and public welfare administration.

Among her numerous publications are *Community Planning in Unemployment Emergencies* (1930), *Community Programs for Subsistence Gardens* (1933), *Richmond, Mary Ellen, 1861–1928—The Long View* (1930), *Cash Relief* (1936), *Your Community* (1939), and "Desertion and Non-Support in Family Case Work," in *The Annals of the Academy of Political and Social Science* (May 1918).

Her work *Emergency Work Relief* (1932) describes community models of administration in work relief programs. *Broken Homes* (1919, preface by Mary Richmond) was written in response to treatment needs in "social maladjustments." Colcord is credited with breaking new ground in applying social services to individuals.

Colcord was a member of Phi Kappa Phi, the American Association of University Women, and the Congregationalist church. In 1950 she married Frank Bruno, an authority on social welfare and the director of what was to become the George Warren Brown School of Social Work at Washington University, St. Louis. She was widowed five years prior to her death.

—Karen V. Harper

See Also:

Social Work

References:

Colcord, Joanna Carver. *Broken Homes: A Study of Family Desertion and Its Social Treatment.* New York: Russell Sage Foundation, 1919.

Glenn, John M., Lilian Brandt, and F. Emerson Andrews. *Russell Sage Foundation.* Vols. I–2. New York: Russell Sage Foundation, 1947.

Young, Whitney M., Jr., and Frankie V. Adams. *Some Pioneers in Social Work.* Atlanta: University of Atlanta Press, 1957.

COLEMAN, BESSIE (1896–1926) was the first licensed black pilot in the world. In the early years of aviation, women, especially black women, had difficulty finding flying schools that would admit them for training. Determined to learn to fly, however, Coleman went to France, and in June 1921 earned her pilot's license. After her return to the United States, she began a career as a barnstormer, or stunt pilot. Her goal was to earn enough money to open a flying school so that other blacks would not have to face the obstacles she did. However, on April 30, 1926, she was killed while practicing for an air meet in Orlando, Florida. Three years later, a group of black aviation enthusiasts in Los Angeles organized the Bessie Coleman Aero Clubs to promote aviation among blacks. Later the Bessie Coleman School was established, and many young blacks learned to fly there.

—Claudia M. Oakes

See Also:

Aviation, Black Women

References:

Brooks-Pazmany, Kathleen. *United States Women in Aviation 1919–1929.* Washington, D.C.: Smithsonian Institution, 1983.

Hardesty, Von, and Dominick Pisano. *Black Wings: The American Black in Aviation.* Washington, D.C.: National Air and Space Museum, 1984.

COLLEGE SETTLEMENT (New York), which opened on the Lower East Side on September 1, 1889, was the second settlement house in the United States and the first to be established by women. The settlement was the first project of the College Settlements Association, which grew out of a Smith College reunion in 1887 and expanded to include graduates from other eastern women's colleges such as Wellesley, Vassar, and Bryn Mawr. In 1892 the group began sponsoring Denison House in Boston and College Settlement in Philadelphia, and added College Settlement in Baltimore in 1910. Of these, College Settlement in New York was most influential in popularizing among women the concept of college graduates' taking up residence in a settlement house in the slums and, as neighbors of the poor, providing a variety of educational and recreational services while also advocating social reform.

Although never generously funded, College Settlement attracted a number of influential women and provided a base for their social service activities. Lillian Wald lived at College Settlement while looking for a location for Henry Street Settlement, and Mary Kingsbury briefly headed College Settlement prior to marrying Vladimir Simkhovitch and founding Greenwich House. Florence Kelley used her College Settlement contacts to battle child labor. Frances Kellor, another resident, agitated to improve employment bureaus. The women of College Settlement also participated in a variety of civic improvement campaigns. College Settlement head residents included first Jean Fine, then Fannie W. McLean, Jane Robbins, Mary Kingsbury (Simkhovitch), and finally Elizabeth Williams.

By 1929 a number of College Settlement's services, such as its public library, playground, music lessons, and bathhouse, had been supplanted by other agencies, including additional settlement houses on the Lower East Side. Consequently, College Settlement decided to leave the neighborhood, cut its ties to the settlement house movement, and drop all activities other than creative arts for working-class women. In 1929 it reorganized as the Art Workshop. Although established and run entirely by women, College Settlement had served neighbors of both sexes.

—*Judith Ann Trolander*

See Also:

Henry Street Settlement; Kelley, Florence; Settlement House Movement; Wald, Lillian

References:

Davis, Allen F. *Spearheads for Reform: The Social Settlements and the Progressive Movement, 1890–1914.* New York: Oxford University Press, 1967.

McFarland, Marjorie. "A Quarter Century of the College Settlements." *Survey* 33 (November 14, 1919): 170.

———. "Settlement for Sale." *Survey* 63 (March 15, 1930): 707, 733.

Scudder, Vida. *On Journey.* New York: Dutton, 1937.

The **COLONY CLUB** was formed at the beginning of the twentieth century as New York's first social club for women, and its first members were from some of the most exclusive families in New York. Having such a club for women was considered a daring innovation at the time. Florence Harriman, one of the founders and the first president of the club, felt that women would find the union in social life that men had discovered in business and working life.

The club set up a group to investigate working conditions in factories and stores. In 1909 Alva Belmont, a member of the club, enlisted the financial aid of the club in support of striking waist-makers. These workers, mostly single women under the age of twenty-five, had been striking for several months for better pay and working conditions. Belmont convinced the Colony Club to produce a fund raiser for the strikers. Several waist-makers presented their stories to the members, and $1,000 was contributed to the striking women.

—Judith Pryor

See Also:

National Women's Trade Union League, Shirtwaist Makers Strike of 1909, Social Feminism

References:

Flexner, Eleanor. *Century of Struggle: The Woman's Rights Movement in the United States.* Cambridge, Mass.: Belknap, 1959, 1979.

O'Neill, William L. *Everyone Was Brave: A History of Feminism in America.* New York: Quadrangle, 1971..

Woloch, Nancy. *Women and the American Experience.* New York: Knopf, 1984.

The COLORED WOMAN'S LEAGUE. Black activist Hallie Q. Brown traveled from Wilberforce, Ohio, to Washington, D.C., several times in the early 1890s to meet with local black women and organize a group devoted to publicizing the accomplishments of Afro-Americans. When planning began for the World's Columbian Exposition at Chicago in 1893, a Women's Board of Managers was established. Believing that blacks' contributions had been neither recognized nor compensated, Brown went to the chairperson and asked to be put on the board to represent the interests of black women. Told that members were selected as representatives of groups and not as individuals, Brown returned to Washington and held a rally at a Presbyterian church that resulted in the formation of the Colored Woman's League. However, Helen A. Cook was elected president and served as the group's representative to the World's Columbian Exposition.

Brown's desire to organize black women reflected a growing sentiment in favor of self-help. Local groups were springing up everywhere, and several sought to establish a national federation of these groups. Finally, in 1896 members of the Colored Woman's League joined with the women of the National Federation of Afro-American Women to form the National Association of Colored Women (NACW), which became a permanent and effective vehicle for self-help.

With the motto "Lifting As We Climb," the association was a confederation of local and state groups; it held biennial conventions and published *National Notes* and a literary organ, the *Woman's Era*. The organization provided black women with a forum to express their concerns and a means of sharing ideas for the improvement of local conditions. Some of the group's activities included the organization of a "big sisters" movement to provide young girls with positive role models, the compilation of information to aid women going into business for themselves, and a campaign to improve traveling conditions on the railroads for blacks.

Reflecting the self-help mood of blacks at the turn of the century, the NACW tapped the resource of increasing numbers of well-educated black women to improve the conditions of the masses. It provided the impetus for the establishment of numerous local groups and in 1910 gained membership in the National Council of Women. Most of its leaders were busy professional women who found time to "lift others as they climbed."

—Linda O. McMurry

See Also:

National Association of Colored Women, National Federation of Afro-American Women, World's Columbian Exposition

Reference:

Davis, Elizabeth Linsay. *Lifting As They Climb.* Washington, D.C.: National Association of Colored Women, 1933.

COMMON LAW is the English system of judge-made law based on decrees and precedents that formed the basis for the American legal system in every state except Louisiana. Although not as oppressive to single women as Continental civil law, the common law placed severe restrictions on the legal status of married women. Under the doctrine of coverture, married women were legally merged with their husbands. As *feme covert,* meaning literally covered by her husband, a married woman could not own personal property nor keep any of her own wages or earnings. She could not make a contract nor draft a will, nor could she sue or be sued without being joined by her husband.

Real estate that a wife brought into the marriage could be used, mortgaged, or rented by her husband, but could not be sold without her consent. Early American courts tried to make provisions for private hearings to determine if a wife's decision to sell had been made under duress, but these procedures were not always adequate for the protection of the few rights married women had under common law. Under the concept of dower rights, a wife was entitled to one-third of her husband's estate if there were children and one-half if there were none. This rule applied if the husband died without making a will or if he attempted to give less than her dower rights in his will. This portion might well be insufficient, especially if the wife had minor children to support from a previous marriage. Finally, if a tort, or legal wrong, was committed by the wife in the husband's presence, under common law only the husband was liable.

William Blackstone's widely read *Commentaries on the Laws of England,* first published in 1765, defended these restrictions as examples of the beneficial paternalism of English law for women. The popularity of Blackstone's interpretation of coverture later earned for his work the opprobrium of the early feminists.

Unlike their married sisters, single women under common law, known as *feme sol,* could sue and be sued, sign contracts, and consequently could carry on their own businesses. Realizing that certain categories of married women had to carry on their own businesses in the absence of their husbands, colonial legislatures passed laws also granting the status of *feme sol* to women married to seamen or women whose husbands had deserted them. The legal basis for these laws and similar court decisions was the existence of customary trading regulations in many English towns that permitted married women to engage in business independent of their husbands. These regulations benefitted creditors as much as the women and their families, and also reduced the need for public poor relief.

So limited were the rights of married women under the common law that another sort of legal remedy was needed, as for example to protect wealthy families from the spendthrift ways of sons-in-law. In England this was provided by the system of equity jurisprudence, which was handled outside the common law in chancery proceedings. This system allowed married women and their families to protect their property through the legal concept of a separate equitable estate. A married woman could protect her property through the appointment of a trustee, whose role was to look after her interests. Under this arrangement, a wife could protect her property from a previous marriage, her family's property, or a husband could protect his wife's property in case his own estate was threatened by creditors.

While equity procedures were widely used in early American law, many states never had chancery courts, and judges often limited the rights of married women under the principles of equity. Furthermore, many women lacked the knowledge or the money to protect their property in this way. While common law could be modified, elements of coverture remained, despite the work of feminists and legal reforms, until the second half of the twentieth century.

—*Neil W. Hogan*

See Also:

Coverture, Dower, Equity Courts, *Feme Covert, Feme Sol*

References:

Blackstone, William. *Commentaries on the Laws of England.* Vol. I. 1765; rpt. Chicago: University of Chicago Press, 1979.

Holdsworth, Sir William. *A History of English Law.* Vol. 3. 5th ed. London: Methuen, Sweet and Maxwell, 1942.

Kannowitz, Leo. *Sex Roles in Law and Society.* Albuquerque: University of New Mexico Press, 1973.

Kerber, Linda K. *Women of the Republic.* Chapel Hill: University of North Carolina Press, 1980.
Rabken, Peggy. *The Legal Foundations of Female Emancipation.* Westport, Conn.: Greenwood, 1980.
Salmon, Marylynn. *Women and the Law of Property in Early America.* Chapel Hill: University of North Carolina Press, 1986.
Wortman, Marlene Stein. *Women in American Law.* Vol. 1 New York: Holmes and Meir, 1985.

COMMUNIST PARTY. The first Marxist organization in the United States was founded by German immigrant Joseph Weydemeyer, who had participated in the Revolution of 1848 in Germany as an artillery officer and colleague of Karl Marx and Frederick Engels. According to Angela Davis, a noted scholar on women in the Communist party, "No women appear to have been associated with the Proletarian League when it was established by Weydemeyer in 1852." Other Marxist organizations, including the Communist Club and Workingmen's National Association, were also dominated by men.

However, the beginning of the twentieth century introduced a period of change to the socialist movement. As the broad plea for women's equality grew, women's interest in the Marxist Left also increased. The Socialist party soon became an active advocate for women's equality. With the assistance of dedicated Socialist women such as Pauline Newman and Rose Schneiderman, a working-class suffrage movement was further advanced. The year 1908 introduced a national women's commission that had been established by the Socialist party. Mass demonstrations in support of women's equality incited women nationwide to participate in the equal suffrage movement.

Many of the former Socialist party women soon became leaders and activists of the Communist party after its founding in 1919. According to Davis, "Ella Reeve Bloor, Anita Whitney, Margaret Prevey, Kate Sadler Greenhalgh, Rose Pastor Stokes, and Jeanette Pearl were all Communists who had been associated with the left wing of the Socialist party."

Previously, in 1905, the Industrial Workers of the World (IWW) was founded. Although the IWW was an industrial union and not a political party, its main goal was socialism as a means to curb a growing class struggle. Women such as Mary Jones and Lucy Parsons were also active in this organization. In fact, the IWW encouraged women to become not only members of the group but also active leaders. Additionally, only the IWW endorsed a policy of struggle against racism. The Socialist party chose not to focus upon the plight of black people. Davis notes the battle of black Socialist Helen Holman in her fight against the social dilemma of her race and gender: "As a black woman, Helen Holman was a rarity within the ranks of the Socialist party. The Socialists' posture of negligence vis-à-vis black women was one of the unfortunate legacies the Communist party would have to overcome." However, the following decade brought a positive change in the black racial stance held by the Communist party.

Other active participants in the Communist movement in the United States included Lucy Parsons, Elizabeth Gurley Flynn, and Claudia Jones. The endeavors of these women to achieve equality for both women and minorities greatly contributed to the growth of the Communist party in spite of widespread antagonism against it.

—*Amy Yeary*

See Also:

Davis, Angela; Flynn, Elizabeth Gurley; Industrial Workers of the World (IWW); Jones, "Mother"; Schneiderman, Rose; Socialism

References:

Dancis, Bruce. "Socialism and Women in the United States, 1900–1912." *Socialist Revolution* 6 (1976): 76–88.
Davis, Angela. "Communist Women." In *Women, Race and Class.* New York: Random House, 1981, pp. 149–71.
Foster, William. *History of the Communist Party of the United States.* New York: International Publishers, 1952.

COMPLEX MARRIAGE was a form of group marriage practiced between 1846 and 1879 in communities founded by John Humphrey Noyes in Putney, Vermont; Oneida, New York; and Wallingford, Connecticut. At Oneida after 1848, approximately two hundred adults, equally balanced between the sexes, considered themselves married not as couples but to the entire group. Women and men frequently exchanged sexual partners; all exclusive interpersonal attachments, defined as "special love," were broken up because they were viewed as posing a threat to group stability. Central to the Oneida Community's functioning was loyalty to Noyes and his perfectionist religious principles: "male continence,"a means of birth control by *coitus reservatus*; "mutual criticism," a system of group criticism; and "ascending and descending fellowship," the group's informal hierarchy. After 1868 a "stirpiculture" or eugenics experiment was also instituted among some members.

At Oneida, sex roles were perhaps more radically revised than in any similar American group for which extensive documentation exists. Both sexes worked alongside each other in many jobs; women served in some positions of authority over men, and there were no areas in which women were prohibited from working. Communal child rearing, involving both women and men, freed women to become a full part of community life. Women cut their hair short and wore an unusual outfit comprised of a mid-length skirt over pants, similar to the attire popularized by Amelia Bloomer.

Noyes, however, was no feminist. Although he favored doing away with any distinctions between the sexes that were not intrinsic, he considered men to be ultimately superior to women, and he criticized the antebellum women's movement for helping to polarize relations between the sexes, thereby risking social chaos. His solution was to use complex marriage and other community practices to meet what he considered to be the true needs of both men and women. When internal and external pressures eventually convinced Noyes that his sexual system was no longer working, he recommended its abandonment in 1879. In 1881 the group also gave up its communistic form of economic organization, reorganized as a joint-stock corporation, and went on to become one of the most successful small businesses in the United States, best known for its silverware. Although the Oneida Community neither sought nor achieved full equality between the sexes, its experiment with complex marriage continues to raise many issues of importance for feminists today.

–Lawrence Foster

See Also:

Marriage, Oneida Community, Utopian Communities

References:

Carden, Maren Lockwood. *Oneida: Utopian Community to Modern Corporation.* Baltimore: Johns Hopkins University Press, 1969.

Foster, Lawrence. "Free Love and Feminism: John Humphrey Noyes and the Oneida Community." *Journal of the Early Republic* I (Summer 1981): 165–83.

———. *Religion and Sexuality: The Shakers, the Mormons, and the Oneida Community.* Urbana: University of Illinois Press, 1984, pp. 72–122, 226–47.

Kern, Louis J. *An Ordered Love: Sex Roles and Sexuality in Victorian Utopias—The Shakers, the Mormons, and the Oneida Community.* Chapel Hill: University of North Carolina Press, 1981, pp. 207–279.

Parker, Robert Allerton. *A Yankee Saint: John Humphrey Noyes and the Oneida Community.* New York: Putnam, 1935.

Robertson, Constance Noyes. *Oneida Community: The Breakup, 1876–1881.* Syracuse: Syracuse University Press, 1972.

Wayland-Smith, Ellen. "The Status and Self-Perception of Women in the Oneida Community." *Communal Societies* 8 (1988): 18–53.

COMSTOCK LAW. A new era of repression of birth control material began with the passage of the Comstock Law. In 1873 the moral crusader Anthony Comstock (1844–1915) induced Congress to pass a bill strengthening the law (passed a year earlier) that forbade using the mails to circulate obscene materials. The 1873 law specified that birth-control information was considered obscene. This definition ended the widespread appearance of advertisements in American newspapers for birth-control devices, which had demonstrated the frank interest of Americans in obtaining means of controlling fertility. The anti-birth-control faction headed by Comstock, however, lumped together all such devices as inducements to debauchery. State laws that followed were modeled on the congressional statute banning birth-control materials in the mails.

Subsequently appointed a special postal agent, Comstock set himself to enforce the law. He resorted to entrapment, writing under an assumed name to request articles advertised and then pouncing on the evidence that they were being sold for birth control. His actions also put a damper on the public discussion of birth control. Among the individuals accused of obscenity was the highly respected writer Edward Bliss Foote, as well as his son and his daughter-in-law, who were both doctors.

Birth control advocate Margaret Sanger ran afoul of the law in 1912. In a satirical response, the newspaper *Call* printed the title of Sanger's series of articles, "What Every Girl Should Know," and underneath it on an otherwise blank page, the legend: "Nothing, by order of the Post Office." Despite considered criticism of the law and opposition by the U.S. Army, which wanted to circulate information to protect against venereal disease, the Comstock Law was not rewritten to remove prohibitions against birth control material until 1971.

—*Daryl M. Hafter*

See Also:

Birth Control; Obscenity; Pornography; Sanger, Margaret

References:

Gordon, Linda. *Woman's Body, Woman's Right: A Social History of Birth Control in America.* New York: Grossman, 1976.

Reed, James. *From Private Vice to Public Virtue: The Birth Control Movement and American Society Since 1830.* New York: Basic, 1978.

Sanger, Margaret. *My Fight for Birth Control.* 1931; rpt. Elmsford, N.Y.: Maxwell, 1969.

The CONGRESS OF INDUSTRIAL ORGANIZATIONS (CIO). Throughout the 1930s, the concept of industrial unionism had gained enough ground to prove a challenge to the traditional craft-union approach to labor organization upon which the American Federation of Labor (AFL), founded in 1886, was based. Industrial unionism advocated the inclusion in one union of all workers in a particular industry, regardless of skill or job, thereby increasing the potential power of the industry's workers in securing their demands and safeguarding their interests. As this ran contrary to the approach of the AFL, that organization vigorously opposed this development in unionization. Nonetheless, on November 9, 1935, eight union affiliates of the AFL, led by John L. Lewis, head of the United Mine Workers, met and formed the Committee for Industrial Unionism. At its first convention (November 14–18, 1938) in Pittsburgh, the committee adopted a constitution and officially became the Congress of Industrial Organizations (CIO). As such, it was regarded as an autonomous body and a direct rival to the AFL.

The CIO was supported primarily by workers in mass-production industries, especially the automobile, steel, electrical appliance, and textile industries, the latter encompassing a high percentage of women workers. Women constituted approximately 40 percent of the textile industry's work force, and in this industry the CIO made significant gains, winning over mill workers from the AFL's United Textile Workers, which refused to represent unskilled women textile workers. During the decade of the 1930s, hundreds of thousands of textile workers joined the CIO's Textile Workers Union of America. The TWUA, however, failed to win over the southern textile industry, where by 1939 less than 10 percent of textile workers, most of whom were women, remained unorganized.

It was precisely because American working women were located primarily in mass-production industries that the CIO became extremely valuable to them. This does not mean the CIO was an avid supporter of feminist demands. Simply put, the CIO needed to win the support of women workers in order to attain a majority membership within a given industry. As in previous unions, very few women rose to any position of leadership in the CIO, and therefore women had little control over CIO policy at any level of operation. On December 5, 1955, the AFL and the CIO formally merged to become the AFL-CIO, with little change in the status of women within the organization.

—*Maureen Anna Harp*

See Also:

American Federation of Labor; Textile Industries, Northern and Southern; Unions

References:

The AFL-CIO American Federationist. Washington, D.C.: AFL-CIO, 1955–.

Foner, Philip S. *Women and the American Labor Movement: From World War I to the Present.* New York: Free Press, 1980.

Galenson, Walter. *The CIO Challenge to the AFL: A History of the American Labor Movement, 1935–1941.* Cambridge: Harvard University Press, 1960.

Mason, Lucy Randolph. *To Win These Rights: A Personal History of the CIO in the South.* New York: Harper, 1952.

Preis, Art. *Labor's Giant Step: Twenty Years of the CIO.* New York: Pioneer, 1964; rpt. New York: Pathfinder, 1972.

CONSCIOUSNESS-RAISING (C-R) is a term used to describe an intellectual process of self-realization and radicalization adapted by the women's liberation movement of the late 1960s as a tool of political organization. Practiced in small groups, C-R promoted women's awareness of the societal origins of "personal" problems that had influenced or limited their lives, and encouraged collective action to seek positive changes for all women.

Many members of the women's liberation movement participated in the civil rights and New Left movements of the early and mid-1960s. Therefore, besides their experience in political organizing, these young women brought to their movement the egalitarian democratic ideologies and strategies that stressed a leaderless, participatory democratic approach to group action. It was as co-workers within the Students Non-Violent Coordinating Committee (SNCC) and Students for a Democratic Society (SDS) that these women first recognized and confronted the sexist discrimination inherent in women's being treated as secondary and ancillary support workers regardless of the work they actually performed within those movements.

Derived from the earliest SNCC "rap groups" (which fostered uncensored candor among members), the SDS "Guatemala Guerrilla" group approach to organizing (which stressed an introspective, personalized sharing of individual experience), and the ruthless confrontational tactic of the "Speaking Truth" practiced by the Chinese revolutionaries, the feminist C-R group provided its members with a controlled and confidential environment for openly discussing and analyzing their past in a feminist perspective. This structured format fostered a sense of commonality that would impel not only personal but collective political action. Thus, "The Personal Is Political" became the slogan summarizing the C-R process that facilitated the women's liberation movement's development of theory and strategies for recruiting and organizing its members. In their structureless, supportive C-R groups, women became feminists as they explored the practical meaning in their lives of absolute equality of the sexes.

As the radical and leftist orientation of women's liberation gave way to a more mainstream emphasis in the 1970s, the National Organization for Women (NOW) utilized the C-R group to strengthen its members' stands on the more difficult feminist issues of abortion and lesbian rights. The C-R process fostered in group members a willingness to question authority as well as a sense of autonomy and a disposition to explore all their choices. NOW's formalization of the C-R process supplied the means to initiate its new members into the issues, theories, and strategies on the basis of The Personal Is Political.

The process of consciousness-raising not only empowered individuals to change their lives but also comforted and politicized self-help groups. The members of these self-help groups were organized around a shared problem, experience, or situation; within such groups, the members could confront the personal consequences of their common cause and shape an agenda of action to address that issue. Through self-help groups, consciousness-raising as a feminist process was mainstreamed and utilized around a single issue such as sexual assault, single parents' special circumstances, or legal action against drunk drivers.

—*Angela Howard Zophy*

See Also:

National Organization for Women, New Left, Women's Liberation Movement

References:

Daniel, Robert L. *American Women in the Twentieth Century: The Festival of Life.* San Diego: Harcourt Brace Jovanovich, 1987.

Evans, Sara. *Personal Politics: The Roots of Women's Liberation in the Civil Rights Movement and the New Left.* New York: Random House, 1979.

NOW Guidelines for Feminist Consciousness-Raising. Rev. ed. Washington, D.C.: National Organization for Women, 1983.

CONSUMERISM is a basic principle of capitalism: economic growth and vitality depend upon individuals purchasing (consuming) a never-ending quantity of goods and services. The society that develops within a consumerist economic system is democratic: patterns of consumption are not regulated, and the only constraint on an individual's purchases is personal disposable wealth. Social status is, therefore, generally equal to economic status, and not determined by birth, intelligence, or nonmaterial factors.

Consumerism changed the lives of American women in the nineteenth and twentieth centuries. As the capitalist economy matured under the Industrial Revolution in the late nineteenth century, women were freed from producing goods needed by their families, such as food, thread, yarn, fabric, clothing, and household furnishings, and were able to buy them already manufactured. Between 1880 and 1930, a variety of new goods appeared that transformed women's work in the home: electricity and electric appliances such as refrigerators, irons, vacuum cleaners, washing machines; indoor plumbing with running cold and hot water; the telephone, automobile, and radio; and movies.

With much of the drudgery of housework removed, women redefined their roles. Most middle-class women became purchasing agents for their families. While their husbands supported the family with their income, the women managed the family budget. They assessed their family's needs, then purchased the goods required. In some cases, discretionary income might be spent on material goods that could immediately enhance a family's social standing; in others, social mobility might be deferred for the next generation as parents saved money for their children's education. In either case, the woman's financial competence and personal taste affected the whole family's social standing.

After World War I, the service sector of the economy expanded dramatically, and many women, married and unmarried, moved into the newly created jobs. This movement into the labor force enhanced women's role as consumers; they had more money to spend and, because they were away from the home for extended periods, were obligated to purchase many of the goods they had earlier made at home.

Consumerism in the industrial age transformed American culture. The relentless search for novelty, fashion, and new technology accelerated changes in society. Companies developed products that anticipated or created what women and their families might want or need, then devised elaborate advertising campaigns to promote such products. Although women have played a critical role in maintaining the consumerist economy of the United States throughout the twentieth century, not until the 1970s did advertisers perceive and woo women as rational and practical adult consumers, rather than as the easily manipulated "Mrs. Middle Majority" of the 1950s and 1960s.

—*Jane Crisler*

See Also:
Housework, Industrial Revolution

Reference:
Matthaei, Julie A. *An Economic History of Women in America: Women's Work, the Sexual Division of Labor, and the Development of Capitalism.* New York: Schocken, 1982.

CONSUMPTION is a term that was used to describe tuberculosis between the eighteenth and mid-twentieth centuries. It generally referred to the pulmonary tuberculosis that tended to affect young adults, and described the wasting of the flesh caused by accelerated metabolism and the deterioration of the lungs themselves. Though tuberculosis had been known in the Western world since ancient times, it acquired a particular cultural significance during the romantic age (late eighteenth to mid-nineteenth centuries), when major literary figures, such as Rousseau, Musset, Keats, Shelley, the Brontë sisters, Thoreau, and Edgar Allen Poe suffered from the disease and wrote about it in vivid terms.

The symptoms of "consumption"—thinness, pale skin, languor, and occasional physical and psychological excitation (especially when feverish)—were considered aesthetically attractive by the Romantics, signs of a refined, vulnerable sensibility. These characteristics, combined with the fact that tuberculosis has always been a disease that affects young people—children and young adults between twenty and thirty years old—provided the material for many tragic novels, plays, and poems, especially in nineteenth-century women's literature. Though drugs were developed between 1944 and 1952 that could cure and prevent tuberculosis, the aesthetic created by the disease—that thin, pale young adults are attractive—persists, though it is applied primarily to young women.

The social consequences of tuberculosis were dramatic at the beginning of the twentieth century; in 1900 it was the leading cause of death. As industrial growth attracted people into crowded urban centers, children and their young parents suffered in conditions that were far from romantic. Their desperate plight was a major impetus for the health and welfare reforms of the twentieth century. As reformers studied the course of tuberculosis, they realized that the entire family—father, mother, and children—had to be treated simultaneously. The resulting programs enhanced the civil rights of women and children and fostered many other social programs that promoted their welfare.

—*Jane Crisler*

See Also:
"The Vapors"

References:
Dowling, Harry F. *Fighting Infection: Conquests of the Twentieth Century.* Cambridge: Harvard University Press, 1977.
Sontag, Susan. *Illness as Metaphor.* New York: Vintage, 1977.

COOKBOOKS. It is significant that, until the 1960s, the vast majority of cookbooks in America were written by women. The publishing of cookbooks was one of the few areas of literary endeavor in which women were taken seriously. Consequently, women expressed their lives and times, not just recipes, in their cookbooks.

Until 1796, cookbooks in America were reprints of European books, even if they were published under American imprints. Then Amelia Simmons wrote *American Cookery,* in which she left out those dishes whose ingredients could not be obtained in America and established national dishes including Indian pudding, flapjacks, and johnnycake. This book was so successful that Lucy Emerson plagiarized it in its entirety in *New England Cookery* in 1808.

Largely due to the influence of cookbook authors, measurements, cooking methods, and serving practices became more consistent throughout the country, making cooking easier. In the late 1820s cooking practices began to be codified by Lydia Maria Child, Eliza Leslie, Sarah Hale, Esther Howland, and Mary Randolph. Catharine Esther Beecher extended the idea of a code to household arts in *A Treatise on Domestic Economy for the Use of Young Ladies at Home and at School* published in 1841. This included instructions for setting a table; suggestions for serving special luncheons, teas, and large dinners; guidance for behavior at table; and even recommendations on how to dress. This information was included because, with the onset of the industrial age, cooking and housekeeping were learned less from mother to daughter and more from books.

An interesting side-note about Catharine Beecher is that she became a militant feminist and argued in her cookbooks that women's supremacy is clearly shown in the kitchen. To her, kitchen work was not demeaning, but in reality gave women much control over other areas of the family and society.

The advent of ladies' cooking classes in the 1870s led to cooking's becoming an even more exact science. The most influential of these were offered at the Boston Cooking School, whose most famous principal, Fannie Merritt Farmer, known as the "mother of level measurement," in 1896 wrote the *Boston Cooking School Cook Book*, establishing the most exact possible standards for cooking. This book, *The Betty Crocker Cookbook*, and *The Good Housekeeping Cookbook*, both revised and reprinted on numerous occasions in the twentieth century, have become the standard cookbooks found in most American kitchens.

Two developments in American society in the past two decades have led to a sharp increase in the number of cookbooks published annually. The first is that the intense interest in the feminist movement has also opened up new opportunities for men. With the realization that women were much more than domestic servants, it became fashionable for men to do their share of the cooking. This led to an increase of cookbooks written by and for men. The second is a general increase in the public's interest in physical health and nutritious foods. Dozens of cookbooks have been written as companions to specific fad diets and exercise programs. Thousands of church, school, and neighborhood groups have compiled their own suggestions for healthful eating, and each state or general area of the country seems to have its list of favorites. Cooking has become very specialized according to preference for certain ingredients and cooking methods, and there are sure to be several books available for each possible variable.

—*Mari Lynn Kortier*

See Also:

Beecher, Catharine; Child, Lydia Maria; *A Treatise on Domestic Economy*

References:

The American Heritage Cookbook and Illustrated History of American Eating and Drinking. New York: American Heritage, 1964.

Harrison, Molly. *The Kitchen in History*. New York: Charles Scribner's Sons, 1972.

Lincoln, Waldo. *American Cookery Books 1742–1860*. Worcester, Mass.: American Antiquarian Society, 1954.

Root, Waverly, and Richard de Rochemont. *Eating in America: A History*. New York: Morrow, 1976.

Shapiro, Laura. *Perfection Salad: Women and Cooking at the Turn of the Century*. New York: Farrar, Straus, & Giroux, 1986.

Simmons, Amelia. *American Cookery*. 1796; rpt. Grand Rapids, Mich.: Eerdmans, 1965.

Tannahill, Reay. *Food In History*. New York: Stein and Day, 1973.

The **CORSET**, as a device for moulding the thorax and particularly waist (primarily female) for aesthetic, sexual, and status-expressive purposes (rather than orthopedic or protective purposes, not here considered) may be said to have originated in Minoan Crete, but disappears thereafter until the fourteenth century. A rigid and compressive garment, usually called stays until the nineteenth century, the corset became customary in the sixteenth century, and was periodically subject to medical and clerical opposition, often in disapproval of décolletage. (The brassiere as a separate breast-supporting device did not arrive until the twentieth century.)

The hostility to a device deemed both unhealthy and provocative climaxed in the eighteenth century, when the corset was blamed for just about every disease under the sun, gynecological and otherwise. In the nineteenth century the abuse metastasized, on a popular level, in countless magazine articles, reaching vitriolic form by the 1870s and after. By this time the opponents of the corset as such, and especially its extreme form known as tight-lacing, began for the first time to reveal fully their misogynistic, antifeminist bias. While the relation of fashion and fashion-reform campaigns to late-nineteenth-century feminism remains problematical, it is clear that the criticism of tight-lacing (a minority habit, not a fashion) was used to castigate women generically as irrational, slavish, and deliberately and literally homicidal—of their God-given procreativity, which the corset seemed to jeopardize. Evidence of the use of the corset as an abortifacient added fuel to the fires of conservative male moral outrage. Tight-lacing became a symbol of the new woman's resistance to an age-old maternal stereotype and, insofar as it exposed and sexualized the body, a harbinger of a sexual revolution. Yet, at the same time, the corset preserved an illusion of bodily captivity deeply satisfying to male supremacist fantasies. The paradox is profound and subversive of the simplistic and traditional view, still upheld by feminists today, of the corset as a prime symbol and instrument of female slavery.

In fact, conspicuous tight-lacing, always adduced by fashion and social history as a "fashion" of the dominant social classes, proves to have been the practice of a relatively few lower-class younger women (girls), who strove for what was deemed an upper-class appearance, and were willing to risk social opprobrium in order to attract attention in a narcissistic and exhibitionistic way. Their sexual motivation, cruelly lambasted by the male moralists, was vaunted by the women themselves in pro-corset, "fetishist" correspondence in popular magazines, starting with the progressive but mainstream *English Woman's Domestic Magazine* in the 1860s.

After 1900, when fashion moved to looser and unencumbered styles (including shorter skirts), the waist-compressive corset became functionally superfluous and incompatible with the rhetoric of female liberation. By the end of World War I it was virtually dead, surviving in vestigial forms that were further attenuated as a result of World War II. The "soft" revival in the 1950s, manipulated by male-dominated corporate and consumerist interests, presents other problems.

—*David Kunzle*

See Also:

Nineteenth-Century Dress Reform

Reference:

Kunzle, David. *Fashion and Fetishism: A Social History of the Corset and Other Forms of Body Sculpture.* Totowa, N.J.: Rowman and Littlefield, 1982.

COUGHLIN, MOTHER MARY SAMUEL (1868–1959) was prioress general of the Dominican Sisters of Sinsinawa, Wisconsin (Congregation of the Most Holy Rosary) from 1909 to 1949 and a strong supporter of higher education for women. She was born Ellen Coughlin in Fairbault, Minnesota, the third child of Irish immigrant parents Daniel and Ellen (O'Mahoney) Coughlin, and graduated from Bethlehem Academy, Fairbault. She entered the teaching community of Dominican Sisters in 1886, at St. Clara's Convent, Sinsinawa, receiving the name "Mary Samuel." She served in mission grade schools of the congregation until 1901, when she was appointed bursar general. In 1904 she was appointed prioress of the motherhouse community at St. Clara's Convent. Upon the death of Mother Emily Power in 1909, Sister Mary Samuel assumed leadership of the Sinsinawa Dominicans and guided the community through an era of significant growth and development. Over fourteen hundred sisters entered the Dominicans under her administration, and sixty-three new foundations were made in various regions of the country.

Mother Samuel's greatest achievements lay in the field of higher education for women. She was responsible for the relocation of St. Clara's College, Sinsinawa, to River Forest, Illinois, where it was renamed Rosary College in 1922. She enhanced Rosary's program by founding two centers for European study: Villa de Fougères in Fribourg, Switzerland (1924), which she had acquired in 1917, and the Pius XII Institute (1948), a Florentine estate donated to the Holy See by Myron Taylor. Mother Samuel also established Edgewood College (1927) at Madison, Wisconsin, to prepare religious and lay women for teaching careers. In 1932 she was awarded an honorary degree by Loyola University of Chicago.

Mother Samuel welcomed black women to the Dominican community and was an early advocate of liturgical participation by the Catholic faithful. She was a shrewd and astute manager, and the affairs of the congregation prospered under her guidance and assumed a more American character. Mother Mary Samuel's spiritual life was the mainspring of her activity. She cherished the communal prayer life of her Dominican community. At the community's centenary in 1949, she relinquished her duties as prioress general. She lived ten more years at St. Clara's Convent until her death on October 17, 1959, at the age of ninety-one.

—Steven M. Avella

See Also:
Christianity, Women in Higher Education

References:

McCarty, Sister Mary Eva. *The Sinsinawa Dominicans: Outlines of Twentieth Century Development, 1901–1949*. Dubuque, Iowa: Hoermann, 1952.

O'Rourke, Sister Alice. *Let Us Set Out: Sinsinawa Dominicans 1949–1985*. Dubuque, Iowa: Union-Hoermann, 1986.

COUNTRYMAN, GRATIA ALTA (1866–1953) was an early leader in public library development who set professional standards for innovation and energy as director of the Minneapolis Public Library from 1904 to 1936. Born in Hastings, Minnesota, she accepted a job at the Minneapolis Public Library in 1889. She became assistant librarian in 1892, then librarian in 1904, but only after a successful letter-writing campaign from friends and peers who had to convince the board of trustees it was acceptable to hire a woman as director. Still, Countryman was paid one-third less than her predecessor; the board also eliminated the position she had just vacated.

Countryman was a tough manager with a vision for library service. During her tenure she tried to deemphasize fiction, extend library services, and enhance the library's role in Americanizing recent immigrants. Like most librarians of her time, she accepted the "uplift" theory, which called for developing a collection endorsed by cultural, literary, and intellectual canons; she differed from her peers, however, in the energy she applied to her work and her intense pursuit of nonlibrary users. During her tenure, the Minneapolis Public Library system expanded by scores of branches and library stations. Countryman was also very active in community affairs. She was first president of the Minneapolis Women's Welfare League, first president of the Business Women's Club, and founding organizer of the Woman's Club of Minneapolis.

—Wayne A. Wiegand

See Also:
Librarianship

References:

Benidt, Bruce Weir. *The Library Book: Centennial History of the Minneapolis Public Library*. Minneapolis: Minneapolis Public Library and Information Center, 1984.

Dyste, Mena C. "Gratia Alta Countryman, Librarian." Master's thesis. University of Minnesota, 1965.

Rohda, Nancy Freeman. "Countryman, Gratia Alta (1866–1953)." *Dictionary of American Library Biography*, edited by Bohdan S. Wynar. Colorado: Libraries Unlimited, 1978, pp. 98–100.

COVERTURE. Under English common law, which prevailed in the American colonies, married women were limited in their freedom by the concept of coverture. While a single woman (*feme sol*) had property rights but no political rights, a married woman (*feme covert*) had her legal existence merged with that of her husband. Her property, inheritance, and any wages she earned legally became her husband's. She could not sign contracts nor sue in court, and the children of the marriage were under the custody of the father. Divorce was rarely possible in cases of unhappy marriage, because it was believed that human law should not dissolve marriage performed in accordance with God's law. The concept of coverture continued in the early years of the Republic, bolstered by the publication and dissemination in America of William Blackstone's concise, readable *Commentaries on the Laws of England* (1765). Typically, coverture was a permanent condition for women since most married early and stayed married until they or their spouses died. Divorce statutes varied by colony but were all based on the submersion of the wife's separate legal identity.

A married woman did have some protection under coverture. She had a right to a dower, or a life interest in one-third of the family property at the husband's death. However, this right eroded in the years after the Revolution. She also had the right, in a private examination with a judge, to give or withhold consent to any sale of the family real estate. Yet, since she would have to face her husband afterward, a woman might have felt pressured to agree to the proposed sale. Some married women gained rights during the Revolution when their husbands were away; they petitioned their legislatures for designation as *feme sol* traders, enabling them to engage in business and be self-supporting. In New York and Virginia, some married women acted as agents for their husbands and managed businesses without bothering to have themselves declared *feme sol* traders.

The major recourse from coverture for married women in the colonial period was in courts of equity that recognized prenuptial agreements. By the mid-nineteenth century, the passage of married women's property acts replaced equity jurisdiction in safeguarding women's control of property.

—*Barbara E. Lacey*

See Also:

Common Law, Divorce, Dower, Equity Courts, *Feme Covert*, *Feme Sol*, Married Women's Property Acts

References:

Kerber, Linda K. *Women of the Republic: Intellect and Ideology in Revolutionary America.* Chapel Hill: University of North Carolina Press, 1980.

Norton, Mary Beth. *Liberty's Daughters: The Revolutionary Experience of American Women, 1750–1800.* Boston: Little, Brown, 1980.

COYLE, GRACE LONGWELL (1892–1962) was an educator and author who had a significant impact on the twentieth-century-social-group-work movement as it evolved its purposes, methods, roles, and identity. Born in North Adams, Massachusetts, Coyle earned her A.B. from Wellesley College in 1914 and a year later completed a certificate from the New York School of Philanthropy (subsequently the Graduate School of Social Work of Columbia University). She became involved in social reform through settlement-house work and other group work organizations, including the Industrial Women's Department of the YWCA, where she focused on adult education and recreation. She completed graduate study at Columbia with an M.A. in economics (1928) and a doctorate in sociology (1931).

As a result of her experiences with women in industry and children in groups, she began to appreciate the regularities that characterize the functioning of small groups. In 1930 she authored *Social Process in Organized Groups*, an insightful analysis of the universal processes that occur in small groups. This conceptual formulation was an important landmark that gave direction to subsequent research and knowledge about group behavior.

Coyle joined the faculty of the School of Applied Social Sciences at Western Reserve University of Cleveland (1934–62). She was a prolific author and researcher on small groups, and her work shows the influence of John Dewey and the progressive education movement, with its emphasis on democratic ideals and learning by doing. She advocated for the small group as an effective vehicle for the attainment of educational and recreational goals, for promoting civic and social responsibility, and for its potential to enhance the social functioning of individual members (*Group Experience and Democratic Values* and *Group Work with American Youth*).

During the 1930s and 1940s, interest in small-group behavior grew rapidly, attracting professionals from diverse fields, including education, recreation, mental hygiene, and social work. They formed the American Association for the Study of Group Work in 1936 to provide a forum for professional exchange, but they continued to feel ambivalent about group work's lack of alignment with an established field. It was Coyle who in 1946 articulated the persuasive rationale for association with the field of social work. Coyle was credited with stimulating the transition that resulted in group work becoming identified as one of the basic social work methods.

Coyle's numerous leadership roles included those as president of the National Conference of Social Work (1940), the American Association of Social Workers (1942–44), and the Council on Social Work Education (1958–60).

—*Marie Taris*

See Also:

Social Work

References:

Alissi, Albert S., ed. *Perspectives on Social Group Work Practice.* New York: Free Press, 1980.

Coyle, Grace L. *Group Experience and Democratic Values.* New York: Woman's Press, 1947.

———. *Group Work and American Youth: A Guide to the Practice of Leadership.* New York: Harper, 1948.

———. "On Becoming Professional." In *Toward Professional Standards.* New York: Association Press, 1947, p.1.

———. *Social Process in Organized Groups.* New York: Smith, 1930.

Konopke, Gisela. *Social Group Work.* 3d ed. Englewood Cliffs, N.J.: Prentice-Hall, 1983.

Reid, Kenneth E. *From Character Building to Social Treatment.* Westport, Conn.: Greenwood, 1981.

Trecker, Harleigh B., ed. *Group Work Foundations and Frontiers.* New York: Whiteside and Morrow, 1955.

CRANDALL, PRUDENCE (1804–89), teacher and abolitionist, was originally a Quaker from Rhode Island. In 1831 she founded a school for girls in Canterbury, Connecticut. Three years later, Crandall's school had gained a statewide reputation for excellence. Inspired by a copy of William Lloyd Garrison's the *Liberator*, Crandall admitted the first black girl to the school in 1833.

Immediately, white parents began withdrawing their children from the school. Crandall, ignoring community hostility, boldly announced that henceforth she would teach blacks exclusively. The residents of Canterbury reacted quickly. A town meeting was held, which Crandall could not attend because she was female. Crandall was accused of promoting racial amalgamation, and resolutions were passed to get rid of the school. Shopkeepers refused to supply the school, and vandalism to the property occurred. Students were pelted with manure, dead cats, and chicken heads when they attempted to exercise in the yard. Despite these brutal and inhumane acts, Crandall refused to close the school.

On May 24, 1833, the Connecticut state legislature passed the infamous "Black Law," making it illegal to set up a school for blacks not from Connecticut (many of Crandall's pupils were from out of state) or to set up a boarding school for blacks in a town where they were not residents, without prior written consent of the majority of the town's civil authority and selectmen. On June 27 Crandall was arrested for violating the "Black Law." Although she was convicted in 1834, the Court of Errors later reversed the decision. Crandall returned to Canterbury and reopened her school.

This time, harassment from local residents became more violent. Arson was attempted, and finally on September 9, 1834, the school was rendered uninhabitable by men armed with iron bars and clubs. The school was closed and put up for sale on September 11, 1834.

Crandall lived to see many of her former black pupils become teachers themselves. In 1886 Crandall was granted an annuity of $400 from the state legislature of Connecticut at the urging of Mark Twain.

—*Rose Kolbasnik Callahan*

See Also:

Abolition and the Antislavery Movement, Black Women, Education

References:

Foner, Phillip S., and Josephine F. Pacheco. *Three Who Dared: Prudence Crandall, Margaret Douglass, Myrtilla Miner—Champions of Antebellum Black Education.* Westport, Conn.: Greenwood, 1984.

Fuller, Edmund. *Prudence Crandall: An Incident of Racism in Nineteenth Century Connecticut.* Middletown, Conn.: Wesleyan University Press, 1971.

CRIMINALS. While reliable criminal data exist only since the 1930s, broad historical patterns of female offenses are discernible. Since colonial New England, with its excessive concern with the individual's private behavior, status offenses such as truancy and promiscuity have predominated among women. Most of the colonial women punished by the criminal justice system were public order offenders. This concern with proper and accepted behavior remained strong through the eighteenth and nineteenth centuries, although property crimes, mostly theft, became more common. Crimes of violence remained rare.

In the 1870s criminologists began predicting that the growing involvement of women outside the home would lead to an increase in crime among them. Common perceptions of female offenders shifted in the late 1800s from the idea of a sinister individual, a "Dark Lady," to that of a childlike individual, a fallen woman. The emphasis on status offenses intensified with the social purity reformers of the 1890s who focused on venereal disease, white slavery, and prostitution. These reformers launched an influential national campaign to eradicate what they identified as serious female offenses. Society needed to be protected from those women who, as one reformer put it, "scatter disease through every community."

Similar concerns emerged in the 1930s and again during the Second World War, with the widespread campaigns against venereal disease. Since the 1960s the number of women involved in crime, especially serious crime, has increased as their position in society has changed. Recently, scholars have studied women's offenses more intensely, often focusing on the role of women in contemporary society, and how these forces have affected their involvement in crime. During the 1960s and 1970s, for example, the number of serious property offenses committed by women more than doubled, and criminologists maintain that, with more women working outside the home and with greater opportunities to commit crimes, the rate will continue to increase. In the same period, the proportion of females arrested for violent crimes has hardly changed. Women continued to be prosecuted most often for property and status offenses.

—*Robert G. Waite*

See Also:

Law Enforcement, Prison Reform, Prostitution, Women's Prisons

References:

Freedman, Estelle. *Their Sisters' Keepers: Women's Prison Reform in America, 1830–1930.* Ann Arbor: University of Michigan Press, 1981.

Hull, N. E. H. *Female Felons: Women and Serious Crime in Colonial Massachusetts.* Champaign: University of Illinois Press, 1987.

Pollak, Otto. *The Criminality of Women.* Philadelphia: University of Pennsylvania Press, 1950.

Rosen, Ruth. *The Lost Sisterhood: Prostitution in America, 1900–1918.* Baltimore: Johns Hopkins University Press, 1982.

Simon, Rita James. *The Contemporary Woman and Crime*. Rockville, Md.: National Institute of Mental Health, 1975.

CROWELL, FRANCES ELISABETH (1875–1950) was a leader in the international public health movement. Crowell was at the forefront of nursing from the beginning of her career: she was a member of the first class to graduate from St. Joseph's Hospital School of Nursing in Chicago, in 1895. The following year she made a drastic change in her working environment, moving from a large city hospital to the Pensacola Infirmary, a small facility that served seamen on the Florida coast and treated a wide range of medical problems, including venereal disease, epidemics of yellow fever and other tropical diseases, and industrial accidents. In 1900 the infirmary moved to larger quarters, changed its name to St. Anthony's Hospital, and became a chartered corporation.

Crowell's role in the expanded enterprise was prominent and unusual for an unmarried woman: she was a major stockholder. In 1898 she had purchased a half-interest in the infirmary, an investment that appreciated as the medical establishment grew. Her concern for the financial security of unmarried working women, especially nurses, was a lifelong preoccupation and the topic of a number of her publications in nursing journals.

As a stockholder and nursing superintendent of St. Anthony's Hospital in Pensacola, Crowell grappled with the problems of providing nursing services to the indigent. In 1905 she moved to New York City to study social work for a year at the New York School of Philanthropy (subsequently the Graduate School of Social Work of Columbia University). After graduation she went to work as a special investigator for the Association of Neighborhood Workers in the city and four years later became executive secretary of the Association of Tuberculosis Clinics in New York City, a post she held until 1917.

The education of health personnel was a continuing concern for Crowell. In Pensacola she established her own nurses' training program to provide qualified nurses for St. Anthony's. While an administrator with the Association of Tuberculosis Clinics, she wrote a series of educational materials on tuberculosis and its control.

Her career as a leader of the international public health movement began when the Rockefeller Foundation appointed her to the commission it sent to France in 1917 to combat tuberculosis. She demonstrated her considerable skill as a diplomat and administrator in setting up schools to train French nursing personnel. She singlehandedly established the public health nurse as the cornerstone of the antituberculosis programs in France. In recognition of her contribution, the French awarded her the Legion of Honor.

In 1922, when her work in France was completed, Crowell embarked upon a new assignment for the Rockefeller Foundation: assessing nurse training programs in Europe and advising political and health leaders on quality education. Her assignment took her all over Europe, from Turkey to Spain, with frequent trips to England and the United States. She was an effective emissary who communicated equally well with physicians, nursing professionals, political leaders, and the board of the Rockefeller Foundation. She retired in 1941 to live in Italy, where she was an adviser to the Red Cross in the early days of World War II, but spent most of the war years as a refugee confined to a convent. She died in 1950 of a stroke.

—*Jane Crisler*

See Also:

Nursing

References:

Rockefeller Foundation Archives: RG 12.I, F. Elisabeth Crowell Diaries, 1926–1931.

Vickers, Elizabeth D. "F. Elisabeth Crowell: Pensacola's Pioneer Nurse." *Journal of the Florida Medical Association* 70 (1978): 642–46.

The **CULT OF TRUE WOMANHOOD**. In her seminal article published in 1966, historian Barbara Welter analyzed the prescribed role of Victorian American women as the role was depicted in women's magazines, gift annuals, and religious literature of the nineteenth century. Enshrining the sexual division of labor that relegated women to the home, this prescriptive literature presented Purity, Piety, Domesticity, and Submission as the essential dogmas of the Cult of True Womanhood. As the hostage in the home and the moral guardian of an increasingly materialistic and secular national culture, the middle-class True Woman was to preserve the values of the family and the Republic, while the middle-class True Man forged an economic empire for himself and his family within the Public Sphere. As the "lady of leisure" displaced from the economic production of the rural woman, the matron of the rising urban middle-class family required a means of maintaining and enhancing her social esteem and status, one that would acknowledge the value of woman's unpaid labor in the home. The ideology of femininity presented within the Cult of True Womanhood ennobled woman's reproductive function while obscuring the sexual connotation inherent in motherhood.

The Cult of True Womanhood spawned a constellation of concepts to explain and enhance this essentially restricted role for woman in the nineteenth century. Marriage was deemed the only acceptable career for woman. Denied any political or economic participation in her own right, woman was to use her Woman's Influence (moral suasion exerted on men) to preserve the religious and social values of early America. Woman was to limit herself to the domestic concerns of family and home, Woman's Sphere. As the Mother of the Race, woman was to teach America's daughters to be dutiful helpmeets to her patriotic and achieving sons. Woman was to perform the household and child-care chores of the home, Woman's Work. Woman was to be satisfied with her domestic role, Woman's Proper Place.

As a form of social control of women in Victorian America, the Cult of True Womanhood emphasized the restrictions upon respectable women's lives and choices. But the domestic feminists turned the prison of Woman's Sphere into a fortress, from which the True Woman could sally forth to do her duty even when that duty took her into the Public Sphere. Economic and social circumstances allowed—and sometimes required—the True Woman to seek paid employment to support herself and her family. The Mother of the Race became the Teacher of the Race, as women acquired education adequate to train them to "feminize" not only the profession of teaching, but nursing and the female-centered medical practices. Domestic feminists ruthlessly appropriated industrial and technological occupations that could be defined as extensions of Woman's Work in the preindustrial home. The Piety of the True Woman impelled her participation in the moral reform movements of the nineteenth century. The values of Domesticity as well as of the True Woman's Purity drove her to confront social and political graft, vice, and corruption in the Public Sphere because these contagions threatened the sanctity of the domestic sphere.

Thus the domestic feminist throughout the nineteenth century utilized the socially acceptable Cult of True Womanhood to advance women's opportunities in education and employment as prerequisites to women's performance of their womanly duties rather than as challenges to the status quo. The development of the Cult of True Womanhood reflected the social and economic changes during the antebellum period; the refinement of its concepts after the Civil War provided a means of simultaneously accommodating Victorian America's emotional ties to the past and its contemporary economic and social needs. The seemingly stagnant Cult of True Womanhood actually provided a dynamic access tool for the domestic feminists such as Catharine Beecher, Sarah Josepha Hale, and Harriet Beecher Stowe to utilize as they sought to assure due social regard for Woman's Place and Woman's Role.

—*Angela Howard Zophy*

See Also:

Beecher, Catharine; Domestic Feminism; Education; Hale, Sarah J.; Stowe, Harriet Beecher; Women's Work—Nineteenth Century

References:

Clinton, Catherine. *The Other Civil War: American Women in the Nineteenth Century.* New York: Hill and Wang, 1984.

Cott, Nancy. *The Bonds of Womanhood: "Woman's Sphere" in New England, 1780–1835.* New Haven: Yale University Press, 1977.

Douglas, Ann. *The Feminization of American Culture.* New York: Knopf, 1977.

Sklar, Katharyn Kish. *Catharine Beecher: A Study in American Domesticity.* New Haven: Yale University Press, 1973.

Welter, Barbara. "The Cult of True Womanhood: 1820–1860." *American Quarterly* 18 (Summer 1966): 151–74.

Zophy, Angela Howard. "'For the Improvement of My Sex': Sarah Josepha Hale's Editorship of *Godey's Lady's Book,* 1837–1877." Diss. The Ohio State University, 1978.

CURTIS, EMMA GHENT (1860–1918), novelist, poet, editor, and suffragist, was born in Frankfort, Indiana, to Ira and Mary (Palmer) Ghent. She graduated from Frankfort High School, moved to Canon City, Colorado, and married James Curtis, a rancher, in 1882. The couple had two children, Benjamin and Mary.

Curtis wrote several sentimental didactic novels including *The Administratrix* (1889) and *Fate of a Fool* (1890), and her poetry and short stories were printed in various Populist and suffrage newspapers. She was active in both Populist party and woman suffrage campaigns in 1893 in southern Colorado, where the constituency was composed primarily of coal miners, many of whom did not speak English. In addition, she edited the *Royal Gorge,* a Populist newspaper.

In 1891 Curtis attended a convention of farm, labor, and reform organizations in Cincinnati to assist in the planning of the first Populist party convention. To this end, Curtis worked on both the national organizing committee and the committee on resolutions. The following year, Curtis was a delegate to the National Conference of Industrial Associations of America, where the newly formed Populist party organized the presidential nominating convention to be held several months later. In opposition to WCTU president Frances Willard, who was also a delegate, Curtis supported separate planks for suffrage and temperance and offered a substitute to Willard's prohibition resolution. Curtis's action was approved by convention delegates. In 1894, following the election of Populist Davis Waite as governor of Colorado, Curtis was rewarded for her campaign efforts and appointed a commissioner on the Board of Control of the Colorado State Industrial School for Boys.

—*MaryJo Wagner*

See Also:

Politics, Populist Party, Suffrage in the American West

References:

Blocker, Jack S. "The Politics of Reform: Populism, Prohibition, and Woman Suffrage, 1891–1892." *Historian* 34 (1972): 628.

Brown, Joseph G. *The History of Equal Suffrage in Colorado. 1868–1898.* Denver: News Job Printing, 1898.

Curtis, Emma G. *The Administratrix.* New York: John B. Alden, 1889.

Diggs, Annie. "The Women in the Alliance Movement." *Arena* 6 (July, 1892): 161–79.

DALL, CAROLINE WELLS (HEALEY) (1822–1912), feminist author, researched and wrote about women's economic, legal, and educational plight. The daughter of a wealthy businessman, she grew up in Boston, where she became a follower of Margaret Fuller, later publishing a book recounting her conversations with the famous transcendentalist. She was forced to find a job teaching school after her father experienced financial reverses. Her marriage to Charles Dall, a Unitarian clergyman, produced several children but eventually disintegrated. He left the United States to become a missionary in India, and Dall's experiences as a single parent sensitized her to the plight of women workers.

Dall lectured widely and wrote extensively, publishing *Women's Right to Labor* (1860), *Woman's Rights Under the Law* (1862), and, perhaps her best-known book, *The College, the Market, and the Court: or, Woman's Relation to Education, Politics, and Law* (1867). In these and other works she argued that the relegation of women to only a few types of jobs led to competition and low pay. The end result was that many turned to prostitution. Critical of middle-class women whose lives were dominated by fashion and frivolity, Dall insisted that education and job could provide more women with financial and intellectual independence. Because of her tendency toward dogmatism and her emphasis on economics rather than suffrage, Dall was not closely allied with other late-nineteenth-century feminists.

—*Wendy F. Hamand*

See Also:

Fuller, Margaret

References:

Riegel, Robert E. *American Feminists.* Lawrence: University of Kansas Press, 1963.

Stanton, Elizabeth C., Susan B. Anthony, and Matilda J. Gage. *History of Woman Suffrage.* 6 vols. Rochester, N.Y.: Charles Mann, 1886.

Welter, Barbara. "The Merchant's Daughter: A Tale from Life." *New England Quarterly* 42 (March 1969): 3–22.

DALY, MARY (b. 1928), a renowned radical feminist and theologian, was born October 16, 1928, in Schenectady, New York. She received her B.A. at the College of St. Rose in nearby Albany in 1950. Shortly after acquiring her M.A. at the Catholic University of America in 1952, she became a visiting lecturer in English at St. Mary's College in Notre Dame, Indiana, and started work on a Ph.D. In 1954 she completed her degree, then taught philosophy and theology, first at Cardinal Cushing College in Brookline, Massachusetts (1954–59), then at the University of Fribourg in Switzerland (1959–66). After returning to the United States, Daly began teaching at Boston College, a Catholic school, in 1966. Her first controversial book, *The Church and the Second Sex* (1968), exposed church policies that deny women full participation in the affairs of society, and almost cost her her tenure. Much of the same anger and hope of her first book appeared in its sequel, *Beyond God the Father* (1974), but the focus changed and the perception was deeper and wider.

Gyn/Ecology (1978), the first book in Daly's trilogy, focuses on a radical feminist voyage undertaken by a woman struggling to become herself. The book emphasizes women's need to rid themselves of patriarchy at its roots in everything from language, consciousness, myths, and institutions to ways of seeing, being, and doing. The second book in the trilogy, *Pure Lust* (1984), continues the journey and summons women to break through patriarchal barriers and live the feminist philosophy that reunites women with themselves and nature. Written in the powerful language that marks Daly's finest works, *Pure Lust,* in exploring the demands of the voyage, creates a shock of awakening for those strong enough to understand and accept new perceptions. The third volume of the trilogy, *Outer Course,* written with Jane Caputi, was begun in 1987, and Daly's *Websters' First New Intergalactic Wickedary of the English Language* was completed in 1987.

Daly has described the 1980s as an urgent time because of the increasing fear for the planet's continued existence. She considers the work of radical feminism to be central to all causes and has stressed the importance of seeing the connections. Through her challenges to religion and patriarchy, as well as her exposure of the historic persecution of women, Daly has established her place among contemporary radical feminist theorists.

—*Ginger Costello*

See Also:

Feminism, Radical Feminism, Theologians

References:

Daly, Mary. *Beyond God the Father.* Boston: Beacon, 1974.

———. *Gyn/Ecology.* Boston: Beacon, 1978.

———. *Pure Lust.* Boston: Beacon, 1984.

———. *Websters' First New Intergalactic Wickedary of the English Language.* Boston: Beacon, 1977.

Mainiero, Lina, ed. *American Women Writers.* New York: Ungar, 1979.

Nasso, Christine, ed. *Contemporary Authors.* Rev. ed. Vol. 25–28. Detroit: Gale, 1977.

Stuttaford, Genevieve. "Publisher's Weekly Forecasts." *Publisher's Weekly* 46 (November 1978): 1281.

Uglow, Jennifer S., and Frances Hinton, eds. *International Dictionary of Women's Biography.* New York: Continuum, 1982.

DATING emerged in the early twentieth century as a new and peculiarly American form of courtship. It gradually replaced the nineteenth-century practice of "calling"—a system involving varying degrees of formality, but which basically entailed a man's paying a call upon a woman in her family's home. A date, in contrast, was an occasion on which a man invited a woman to "go out" with him to a public place and paid for her entertainment.

Though the rise of the dating system is traditionally traced to the automobile and the increased mobility it offered middle-class youth, the origins of dating actually lie with the urban lower classes. The term *date* first appears in lower-class slang in the 1880s. Pushed out of crowded apartments that lacked parlors for receiving callers, subject to decreasing parental authority, and enticed by the excitements of the city, young people took their courtships into the streets and to public places of amusement. Upper- and middle-class youth were also attracted by the freedoms offered by dating, and the term and the practice had achieved solid middle-class respectability by the 1920s.

By shifting the acts of courtship away from the watchful eyes of family and local community, dating lessened parental control over courtship. But dating also shifted the balance of power between men and women in courtship. According to the rules governing the calling system, the woman asked the man to call, and he was a guest in her home. In the dating system, the woman became the man's guest in the public sphere, he paid for her entertainment, and thus she lost the power of initiative. Women did not ask men out on dates.

Between 1920 and the mid-1960s, dating was governed by a detailed set of rules that prescribed the appropriate behavior for each sex. The dating system yielded a mammoth body of advice literature and magazines primarily aimed at women and devoted to spelling out the arcane and changing rules of courtship. The dating system has gone through three major phases. From 1920 through World War II, men and women tried to demonstrate popularity by dating many different people. During the postwar era, "going steady" was the ideal. And from the mid-1960s on, the dating system has become more flexible, gradually incorporating the Sexual Revolution and making some accommodation to women's equality.

—Beth L. Bailey

See Also:

Sex Role Socialization, Sexual Revolution

Reference:

Bailey, Beth L. *From Front Porch to Back Seat: Courtship in 20th Century America*. Baltimore: Johns Hopkins University Press, 1988.

The **DAUGHTERS OF BILITIS (DOB)**, a social and civil rights group for lesbians, was founded in 1955 by eight women in San Francisco. The name, taken from an erotic poem, "Songs of Bilitis," was intended to hold meaning for lesbians while protecting the anonymity of members by sounding like a traditional women's club.

By 1960 DOB had a membership of 110 women, a bimonthly newsletter called the *Ladder*, and chapters in New York City, Los Angeles, Chicago, and Rhode Island. The focus of the group was lesbian rights and culture. Education was seen as the most important avenue for achieving civil rights and higher status for lesbians. Like the primarily male Mattachine Society, with which DOB worked closely, DOB attempted to dispel myths and prejudice about homosexuality. To do this, DOB provided speakers for television and radio shows, colleges, and high schools. The organization also assisted in research projects and maintained a library for research and recreational reading.

In the late 1960s the growing Women's Movement brought a more explicitly lesbian-feminist orientation to DOB. This new radicalism also caused conflicts in DOB, and in 1970 the national organization was dissolved. Nonetheless, DOB's commitment to obtaining basic civil rights for lesbians made it an important and early forerunner of both the feminist and gay rights movements.

—Mary Battenfeld

See Also:

Lesbian Rights, Lesbianism

References:

Damon, Gene. "The Least of These: The Minority Whose Screams Haven't Yet Been Heard." In *Sisterhood Is Powerful*, edited by Robin Morgan. New York: Vintage, 1970, pp. 333–43.

D'Emilio, John. *Sexual Politics, Sexual Communities: The Making of a Homosexual Minority in the U.S., 1940–1970*. Chicago: University of Chicago Press, 1983.

The **DAUGHTERS OF TEMPERANCE** was founded in the 1840s as an auxiliary to the Sons of Temperance, a fraternal temperance organization begun in New York in 1842. The middle-class members of the Daughters helped the men by making meals for temperance meetings and collecting signatures on anti-liquor petitions. In 1852 Susan B. Anthony, Mary C. Vaughn, and others attended a convention of the Sons as representatives of the Daughters group. The women's credentials were accepted, but they were not allowed to speak since the men felt that the women were there to listen and learn. A group of women left and organized their own group. Vaughn was elected president and spoke out strongly against the conventional image of women's role of meekness and submissiveness. She encouraged women to put that image aside in order to play a more active role in the reform movement. The Daughters of Temperance, with thirty thousand members, became the largest female organization of its kind and of its day; it sought passage of local and state ordinances to outlaw the sale of liquor. Anthony was appointed to prepare for a Women's State Temperance Convention in New York. This convention was held in April 1852 and led to the formation of the Woman's State Temperance Society.

—Judith Pryor

See Also:

Anthony, Susan B.; Temperance Movement

References:

Levine, Harry Gene. "Temperance and Women in Nineteenth-Century United States." In *Research Advances in Alcohol and Drug*

Problems. Vol. 5: *Alcohol and Drug Problems in Women*, edited by Oriana Josseau Kalant. New York: Plenum, 1980, pp. 25–67.

Stanton, Elizabeth Cady, Susan B. Anthony, and Matilda Joslyn Gage, eds. *History of Woman Suffrage*. Vol. I. 1881; rpt. New York: Arno, 1969.

Tyrnell, Ian R. "Women and Temperance in Antebellum America, 1830–1860." *Civil War History* 28 (June 1982): 128–52.

The **DAUGHTERS OF THE AMERICAN REVOLUTION (DAR)** was founded in 1890. The founders, who included Eugenia Washington, Helen H. Walworth, Mary Desha, and Mary S. Lockwood, were encouraged to begin the society by the existing Sons of the American Revolution. The Sons excluded women from belonging to their organization although they considered some women to be auxiliary members. After the annual convention of the Sons in 1890, when they flatly denied full membership to women descendants of revolutionary ancestors, these women, spurred on by a letter from Lockwood to the editor of the *Washington Post* concerning the convention's decision, founded their own group.

Although not one of the women active in founding the Daughters, Caroline Scott Harrison, wife of President Benjamin Harrison, was elected its first president-general. According to the constitution adopted at the first meeting, the purposes of the society are to perpetuate the memory and spirit of the men and women who achieved American independence, to promote education that would develop in the population the capacity for becoming good citizens, and to foster true patriotism and love of country. To be eligible for membership in the DAR, a woman must be eighteen years or older and be descended from a man or woman who served in the cause of independence during the Revolutionary War, or was a recognized patriot, or gave material aid to the cause. In addition, the applicant must be personally acceptable to the society. The DAR has a special group for young women and also sponsors a National Society of the Children of the American Revolution, which is coeducational.

Both the membership and the activities of the society reflected the patriotism, nativism, and domestic feminism of the middle and upper classes in the late Victorian era in reaction to the influx of immigrants in the 1880s who were less well educated and tended to stay within their ethnic groups more than earlier groups. The DAR expressed concern for the cultural assimilation and political indoctrination of these new immigrants and prepared educational materials and inaugurated programs to help immigrant women. At the same time, the society made clear its support for restrictive immigration laws in the 1920s, in particular the law passed in 1924, which the members of the society saw as needed to protect the character of the country as they thought it should be.

Generally the DAR did not get involved in the suffrage movement or on behalf of social issues. President-General Hazel Scott attempted to foster a social conscience in the society, but after her tenure, from 1909 to 1913, the society was more conservative in its involvement with social issues. It did not, however, completely abandon interest in national problems. For example, in 1919 the DAR joined with almost every other women's organization in supporting the League of Nations. Between the wars, the society hosted ceremonial social events for national governmental officials and their wives in Washington, D.C.

A controversial chapter in the society's history stemmed from the DAR's refusal to allow black opera star Marion Anderson to perform in its Constitution Hall in 1939. The official reason for the denial was that the hall had been booked for another event, but later it was admitted that there was a general practice in the Washington area restricting the use of public facilities to white artists. Eleanor Roosevelt resigned from the society in protest, and there was a great deal of support for Anderson from other quarters. Finally, an outdoor concert was arranged at the Lincoln Memorial. In January 1943 Anderson did finally perform at Constitution Hall, but only after the DAR agreed to abandon its segregated seating arrangement for the concert.

The society has made fewer headlines since the 1940s. The only exception to the lower profile that the society seems to have assumed after World War II came in 1967 when Joan Baez was denied permission to give a concert in Constitution Hall because she had refused to pay a part of her federal income taxes as a protest against the Vietnam War. Baez later gave an outdoor concert near the Washington Monument, despite the DAR protest of this use of federal property to Interior Secretary Stewart L. Udall. The Daughters of the American Revolution continued to be identified with conservative patriotism and a primary concern for preserving genealogies and local history focused on the American Revolution.

—*Judith Pryor*

See Also:

Baez, Joan; Domestic Feminism; General Federation of Women's Clubs

References:

Gibbs, Margaret. *The DAR.* New York: Holt, 1969.

Somerville, Mollie. "A DAR Legacy: The Beginning." *Daughters of the American Revolution Magazine* 116 (1982): 568–73.

Strayer, Martha. *The D.A.R: An Informal History.* Washington, D.C.: Public Affairs Press, 1958.

DAVEY V. TURNER (1764) was a colonial Pennsylvania Supreme Court decision that affirmed the joint deed system of conveyance, the legal procedure for the sale or transfer of property, in regard to married women's property rights in colonial America. The joint deed system required that the *feme covert,* or married woman, formally consent to the sale or transfer of property to protect the property that the woman brought into the marriage as well as to prove her relinquishment of her dower rights to the sold or transferred property. The formal consent was established by an oral examination of the wife by a justice of the peace.

—*Angela Howard Zophy*

See Also:

Coverture, Dower, Marriage, Married Women's Property Acts

Reference:

Salmon, Marylynn. "Equality or Submersion? Feme Covert Status in Early Pennsylvania." In *Women of America: A History,* edited by Carol Ruth Berkin and Mary Beth Norton. Boston: Houghton Mifflin, 1979, pp. 92–113.

DAVIS, ANGELA (b. 1944), black scholar and social activist, was born in Birmingham, Alabama, and grew up in a segregated, middle-class neighborhood, the daughter of two schoolteachers. Her father, B. Frank Davis, left teaching to operate a service station; her mother, Sallye Davis, taught primary school in Birmingham while working on an M.A. from New York University during the summers. Encouraged by her parents, Davis left home during high school to attend the progressive Elisabeth Irwin School in New York City and later went on to graduate with honors from Brandeis University.

As a major in French literature, Davis spent her junior year at the Sorbonne in Paris. During her senior year at Brandeis, she was tutored in philosophy by the legendary Marxist philosopher Herbert Marcuse, who regarded her as his best student in over thirty years of teaching. She went on to study philosophy at Goethe University in Frankfurt, West Germany, but felt compelled to return to the United States to participate in the civil rights movement in this country. In September 1963 racist terrorists had blown up the Sixteenth Street Baptist Church in Birmingham, killing four young girls well known to the Davis family.

Following her return to the United States, Davis pursued graduate work in philosophy with Herbert Marcuse and others at the University of California at San Diego and also continued her career as a social activist. She was involved both with the Student Non-Violent Coordinating Committee (SNCC) and the Black Panthers. On June 22, 1968, Davis joined the Communist party.

In the fall of 1969, Davis joined the philosophy faculty at the University of California at Los Angeles. An FBI informer wrote a letter to the UCLA student newspaper charging that an unnamed Communist had been hired to teach in the philosophy department contrary to the new state law that prohibited California universities from employing known Communists. (That law had been strongly supported by California's conservative governor, Ronald Reagan.) Although Davis had not been aware of the law at the time of her initial hiring, she was fired by the university system's board of regents under obvious political pressure on September 19, 1969. Quickly reinstated by the courts, she continued to teach with distinction until dismissed for making "inflammatory speeches" in defense of the "Soledad brothers," three black convicts accused of killing a white prison guard the previous January. Davis had long been a defender of the three and had become especially close to one of them, George Jackson, mostly through correspondence.

On August 7, 1970, George Jackson's teenage brother Jonathan walked armed into a courtroom in San Rafael, California, where a case was being heard involving other black prisoners. He apparently wanted to make a political statement about the need to free his brother and other "black political prisoners." Instead he ended up taking the presiding judge, the district attorney prosecuting the case, and several jurors hostage, leading them to a van parked in a lot outside the courthouse. A guard from San Quentin prison fired on the van, which set off a barrage of shots. Jonathan Jackson ended up dead, as did Judge James Haley and two of the black prisoners. District Attorney Garry Thomas and a woman juror were wounded. The carbine used by seventeen-year-old Jonathan Jackson had allegedly been purchased by Angela Davis, who was in the Bay Area doing research on her doctoral dissertation.

Fearing that as a known Communist who had been active in the black prisoners' rights movement she would not receive a fair trial, Davis fled from California and "went underground." She soon found herself on the FBI's "ten most wanted" fugitive list and achieved additional media recognition as a "black, Communist revolutionary—brilliant and beautiful and highly dangerous." Nearly two months later, on October 13, 1970, she was arrested in New York. Davis was held in jail for almost two months and had to endure the ordeal of a trial that lasted for nearly twenty months and attracted international attention. When it was finally over in June 1972, she was declared innocent of all charges.

Appealing to the coalition of minorities and sympathetic whites who had come together in her defense, Davis became a cause célèbre. In 1974 she published her autobiography in the hope that it might make "more people understand why so many of us have no alternative but to offer our lives—our bodies, our knowledge, our will—to the cause of our oppressed people." Angela Davis has also resumed her academic career, teaching courses in black philosophy and aesthetics and women's studies at San Francisco State University. In 1981 she published a major scholarly work, *Women, Race and Class.*

—Jonathan W. Zophy

See Also:

Communist Party, New Left

References:

Davis, Angela. *Angela Davis: An Autobiography.* New York: Random House, 1974.

———. *Women, Race and Class.* New York: Random House, 1981.

Major, Reginald. *Justice in the Round: The Trial of Angela Davis.* New York: Third Press, 1973.

Nadelson, Regina. *Who is Angela Davis? The Biography of a Revolutionary.* New York: Wyden, 1972.

Noble, Jeanne. *Beautiful, Also, Are the Souls of My Black Sisters: A History of the Black Women in America.* Englewood Cliffs, N.J.: Prentice-Hall, 1978.

Parker, J. A. *Angela Davis: The Making of a Revolutionary.* New York: Arlington House, 1973.

DAVIS, BETTE (1908-89), American film actor, was born Ruth Elizabeth Davis in Lowell, Massachusetts. She was descended from two lines of old New England stock, the Davises through her father, Harlow Morrell Davis, and the Keyeses through her mother, Ruth Favor. Her parents separated when she was ten, and she, her mother, and sister Bobby lived a peripatetic existence for many years. She attended Crestalban School in the Berkshires and Cushing Academy in Massachusetts, where she met her first husband-to-be, Harmon O. Nelson. It was during these school days that Davis began to envision herself an actress, and her mother worked hard to pay her daughter's tuition at the John Murray Anderson-Robert Milton Dramatic School in New York City, where she learned her trade with personages like George Arliss and Martha Graham.

In 1928, at the age of twenty, Davis left school for a summer stock theater in Rochester, New York, operated by George Cukor, and within a year had made her Broadway debut. A year after that, she and her mother left for Hollywood with a Universal contract in hand; Davis thus became part of the vast army of stage-trained actors who were to revolutionize the new "talkies." After a series of inauspicious roles at Universal, Davis moved to Warner Bros., the working [wo]man's studio, and found herself in a number of tight-budget, fast-talking films like *Cabin in the Cotton* (1932) and *20,000 Years in Sing Sing* (1933). Her first demand of Warner's—to be released to play Mildred in *Of Human Bondage* (1934) at RKO—was granted reluctantly, but despite her Academy Award–nominated performance, the film failed at the box office. She returned to Warner's and another series of "bad girl" roles, with a change of pace in *The Petrified Forest* (1936). Right afterward came her first suspension—after her refusal to make a picture called *The Man with the Black Hat* (later retitled *Satan Met a Lady*); it lasted only a few days, but the lines of battle between Davis and Jack Warner were drawn. Her demands for a better contract, more vacation time, and one picture a year at another studio were met with intransigence; and in a fit of pique, she accepted an offer to make two films in England. Warner's successfully sued for breach of contract, and in November 1936 Davis returned to Hollywood, bloody but unbowed.

Her most productive period followed, but it was also the most emotionally disruptive period in her life. Over the next decade, Davis turned out films noteworthy for her astonishing performances, among them *Marked Woman* (1937), *Jezebel* (1938), *Dark Victory* (1939), *The Letter* (1940), *The Little Foxes* (1941), *Now, Voyager* (1942), *The Corn Is Green* (1945), and *A Stolen Life* (1946). During that same decade or so, she was twice divorced, once widowed, became a mother, and was terminated by Warner's after more than fifteen years of servitude.

The 1950s began auspiciously, with what some believe to be her greatest film, *All About Eve* (1950), a new marriage to her co-star in that film, Gary Merrill, and the adoption of two more children. But a series of poor vehicles, including the play *Two's Company*, Davis's own health problems, and those of adopted daughter Margot began to take their toll. Merrill's career went into a sharp decline, and the marriage began to break down a few years after it began, although they were not divorced until 1960. In 1955 Davis made *The Virgin Queen* for Fox, intended to be her comeback film, but it lost money. The following year she made *Storm Center* and *The Catered Affair*, and in 1957 began working in television. The next few years saw lesser parts in films, television work, and a stage tour of *The World of Carl Sandburg* with Merrill, followed by their divorce.

In 1961 she made *A Pocketful of Miracles* with Frank Capra, and began working on her autobiography, *The Lonely Life*, with ghostwriter Sandford Dody; she also acted in Tennessee Williams's play, *Night of the Iguana*. In 1962 she made *Whatever Happened to Baby Jane* with Joan Crawford, followed by other similar genre films, the best of which were *Hush . . . Hush, Sweet Charlotte* (1964) and *The Nanny* (1965). During the late 1960s she did various television shows. In early 1970 she produced a "running commentary" to Whitney Stine's biography *Mother Goddam*; throughout the 1970s and into the 1980s, she continued to do personal appearances and television shows. In 1987, at the age of seventy-nine, she appeared in her one hundredth film, *The Whales of August,* along with Lillian Gish, Vincent Price, and Ann Southern.

Outstanding among the many awards she has won over the years are Best Actress Academy Awards for *Dangerous* (1935) and *Jezebel* (1938), and the New York Film Critics' Best Actress award for *All About Eve* (1950). In 1977 she became the fifth person, and the first woman, to receive the American Film Institute's Life Achievement Award.

Davis's life and career in many ways epitomize the Hollywood studio system at its best and worst. Taken under contract by Warner Bros. at the start of her career, she soon achieved stardom and developed her talent with an array of directors and a variety of films. She stayed at the top of her profession for nearly twenty years and remained a name to be reckoned with even after her popularity waned. Yet the cost of that career has been equally great. She arrived in Hollywood youthful but determined, and her refusal to accept meekly what studio bosses demanded taxed her mental and physical strength. Growing up in an era with firm notions about women's role, she was deeply ambivalent about her own identity. In *The Lonely Life,* she speaks obliquely of her failed marriages: "A woman has to fly high and fight to reach the top. She tires and needs a resting place. She should travel light—unburdened—but I've always done things the hard way." Later, she speaks frankly of the hard lessons she has learned: "It has been my experience that one cannot, in any shape or form, depend on human relationships for lasting reward. It is only work that truly satisfies." In most of her relationships with men or women, Davis was the stronger partner, and that dominance made her uncomfortable. But it was that strength that she put into her best roles, creating unforgettable portraits and models of extraordinary women for her own and future generations of film audiences to marvel at and perhaps learn from.

—*Frances M. Kavenik*

See Also:

Movie Stars, The Woman's Film

References:

Davis, Bette. *The Lonely Life: An Autobiography.* New York: Putnam, 1962.

Higham, Charles. *Bette: The Life of Bette Davis.* New York: Macmillan, 1981.

Ringgold, Gene. *The Films of Bette Davis.* Secaucus, N.J.: Citadel, 1966.

Stine, Whitney, with Bette Davis. *Mother Goddam: The Story of the Career of Bette Davis.* New York: Hawthorn, 1974.

DAVIS, PAULINA KELLOGG WRIGHT (1813–76), author and editor of the woman's suffrage paper the *Una* from 1853 to 1855, played a prominent role in organizing the woman's rights movement in New England. She presided over the National Woman's Rights Convention in Worcester in 1850, helped found the New England Woman Suffrage Association in 1868, and was president of the Rhode Island Suffrage Association until 1869.

Davis's writings represented nineteenth-century feminist perspectives. She supported equality within marriage, health reform, and professions for women. She spoke out against contemporary mainstream magazines for "ladies" such as *Godey's Lady's Book,* and consequently established the *Una,* attempting to provide "stronger nourishment" for the fight for equality between the sexes.

Raised in New York by her aunt, a strict orthodox Presbyterian, Davis chose to marry Francis Wright, a New York merchant, instead of serving as a missionary. During their marriage, the Wrights became involved in temperance, abolition, and woman's rights issues. Davis supported herself after her first husband died by lecturing to women in anatomy and physiology, subjects in which she was self-taught. She was the first woman to use a mannequin in her classes, shocking some of her students but attracting others. Her second marriage to Thomas Davis, a Rhode Island legislator, allowed her to finance such ventures as the *Una* while speaking out on women's issues. Her writing career culminated with articles in *Revolution*, the periodical Elizabeth Cady Stanton and Susan B. Anthony founded when the national suffrage association split, and a pamphlet, *A History of the National Woman's Rights Movement*, in 1871.

—*Karen C. Knowles*

See Also:
Revolution, Suffrage, The *Una*

References:

Stanton, Elizabeth C., Susan B. Anthony, and Matilda J. Gage, eds. *History of Woman Suffrage*. 6 vols. New York: National American Woman Suffrage Association, 1888–1922.

The *Una*. Vols. 1–3. Boston: Sayles, Miller & Simons, 1853–55.

DAY, DOROTHY (1897–1980), journalist and activist, was born November 8, 1897, in Brooklyn, New York . A convert to Roman Catholicism, she lived to become one of the leading Catholics of her time. While remaining critical of the church, she nonetheless embraced the faith with all the passion peculiar to a convert. Her service in and to the church was hardly conventional. She helped to establish the Catholic Worker party and to edit its journal, the *Catholic Worker*, activities far removed from mainstream Catholicism, and she was a firm pacifist at a time when pacifism was tinged in the public mind with un-Americanism.

From early life, Day was attracted to radical and unpopular causes. Her first job, at the age of nineteen, was with the Socialist *Call*, reporting on strikes, protests, and walkouts. Later she wrote for the *Masses* and the *New Masses*, both radical organs. Her protests, whether as a Socialist or as a Catholic, caused her to run afoul of the law, and she learned what life was like in jail. It is somewhat of an irony that a maverick of her disposition and outlook would find her true home in a relatively authoritarian church; her upbringing had been at best indifferent, and in some ways hostile, to religion. Yet her adherence to the Catholic church from the time of her conversion in 1927 remained firm.

Day liked to describe herself as a "Christian anarchist," which meant that she was often at odds with church officials but always animated by the spirit of love that she found perfectly exemplified in the life of Christ. Unlike others in the Catholic Worker movement, Day had a strong streak of practicality. She supported the reforms of the New Deal, not because she accepted whatever theory might lie behind them, but because they had practical, good results. She refused to retreat to some remote, idealized concept of society derived from the medieval world, and was instead very much a twentieth-century woman.

—*D. H. Burton*

See Also:
Christianity, Journalism, Socialism

References:

Day, Dorothy. *The Long Loneliness*. New York: Harper, 1952.

Ellesberg, Robert, ed. *By Little and By Little: The Selected Writings of Dorothy Day*. New York: Knopf, 1983.

Miller, William. *Dorothy Day: A Biography*. San Francisco: Harper & Row, 1982.

———. *A Harsh and Dreadful Love: Dorothy Day and the Catholic Worker Movement*. Garden City, N.Y.: Doubleday, 1974.

DAY CARE, or day nurseries, became an important factor in mothers' lives with the onset of the Industrial Revolution. Before the mid-nineteenth century, women worked at home, had relatives living in the home providing child care, or were engaged in home-based cottage industry. The goal of the first day nursery that opened in New York City in 1852 was to support the impoverished woman who had to support her family. The need for day nurseries expanded during the Civil War. Federal funds were provided to meet the needs of children of war widows and women working in hospitals or industry. During this period there were no guidelines for nurseries. The situations that surrounded the children varied from sturdy buildings to shabby rooms. Fear was a factor for the mother. If she complained, the child was dropped from the enrollment.

With the peak immigration in the early 1900s, the need for day care shifted from the single mother to working families. The programs began to change at this time from custodial care to child-centered programs with a nursery school as a model. The 1930s and 1940s brought about a greater need for quality child care. The federal government in 1942 established the Lanham Child Care Centers in forty-one states and closed them in 1946. In the 1960s, as more women joined the work force, they became more selective about the center to which they would entrust their children.

Day care workers, as far back as 1892, began to look critically at their industry. In 1892 there were ninety recognized nurseries; by 1921 there were six hundred. In 1924 the Association of Day Nurseries published its annual report, which stated these concerns: nurseries were poorly adapted due to inadequate quarters and personnel; nurseries that had the longest hours had the largest enrollment; 57 percent of the nurseries that belonged to the association had minimum standards. In 1960 Elinor Guggenheimer initiated a major campaign to bring day care needs to the attention of local community groups and organizations. The first federal funds since World War II were approved by Congress and signed into law by President John F. Kennedy in 1962. At that time, $4 million was allocated to be used throughout the country for day care. As a result of this funding many states established day care guidelines. During the 1980s the need for outstanding day care continued to be critical and became an issue during the 1988 presidential campaign.

—Bonnie Lou Rayner

See Also:

Child Rearing, Industrial Revolution

References:

Goldsmith, Cornelia. *Better Day Care for the Young Child.* Washington, D.C.: National Association for the Education of the Young Child, 1972.

Hymes, Jr., James. *Living History Interviews—Book 2.* Carmel, Calif.: Hacienda, 1978.

Maynard, Fredelle. *Child Care Crisis.* Markham, Ontario: Viking, 1985.

New, Caroline, and Miriam David. *For the Children's Sake.* Middlesex, England: Penguin, 1985.

Watkins, Kathleen Pullan, and Lucius Durant, Jr. *Day Care: A Source Book.* New York: Garland, 1988.

DECLARATION OF RIGHTS OF WOMEN: 1876. When America prepared to celebrate its centennial, the National Woman Suffrage Association declared that "the women of the United States, denied for one hundred years the only means of self-government, the ballot," are "political slaves" and "have greater cause for discontent, rebellion and revolution, than the men of 1776." "As Abigail Adams predicted," they continued, "we are determined to foment a rebellion, and will not hold ourselves bound by laws in which we have no voice or representation."

Renting headquarters in Philadelphia, where they held nightly meetings, the radical suffragists decided to "demand justice for the women of this land" by presenting a Declaration of Rights of Women at the official ceremonies on July 4. Matilda Joslyn Gage and Elizabeth Cady Stanton composed the document, and then were denied permission to present it on the grounds that "if granted, it would be the event of the day—the topic of discussion to the exclusion of all others." The women decided to go ahead with their plan, risking the possibility of arrest in order to "place on record for the daughters of 1976, the fact that their mothers of 1876 had thus asserted their equality of rights, and thus impeached the government of today for its injustice towards women."

On July 4, 1876, five women—Matilda Joslyn Gage, Susan B. Anthony, Sara Andrews Spencer, Phoebe Couzins, and Lillie Devereux Blake—took their seats in the press section facing a crowd of 150,000 in Independence Square. They had only a few seconds to make their presentation after the reading of the Declaration of Independence, knowing there was a good chance they would be stopped before they reached the speakers' platform by the guards surrounding it. Anthony went first, followed by Gage, who held concealed the three-foot scroll containing the declaration. They moved rapidly, and as they approached the stand, the foreign guests, military officers, and guards—taken by surprise—all made way. Gage passed the document to Anthony, who placed it in the hand of a startled President *Pro Tempore* of the U.S. Senate Thomas W. Ferry, saying "we present this Declaration of Rights of the women citizens of the United States." With his silent acceptance, the declaration became an official part of the day's proceedings.

The declaration ended with the words: "We ask justice, we ask equality, we ask that all the civil and political rights that belong to citizens of the United States, be guaranteed to us and our daughters forever."

—*Sally Roesch Wagner*

See Also:

National American Woman Suffrage Association, Suffrage

References:

Stanton, Elizabeth C., Susan B. Anthony, and Matilda J. Gage, eds. *History of Woman Suffrage*. Vols. 1–3. New York: Fowler and Wells, 1881–86.

Wagner, Sally Roesch. *A Time of Protest: Suffragists Challenge the Republic, 1870–1887*. Sacramento, Calif.: Spectrum, 1987.

The **DECLARATION OF SENTIMENTS AND RESOLUTIONS** was written at the 1848 Seneca Falls Convention, held July 19–20 in Seneca Falls, New York, by the convention's leaders, Elizabeth Cady Stanton and Lucretia Mott, and the convention's female and male delegates, who numbered between one hundred and three hundred. The Declaration became the first major document to define the issues and goals of the nineteenth-century woman's rights movement. Purposely modeled after the Declaration of Independence to invoke the political heritage of the American Revolution, this document broadly and candidly stated women's demands for legal, economic, social, and political equality and listed the convention's resolutions concerning women's rights.

The Declaration began: "We hold these truths to be self-evident; that all men and women are created equal; that they are endowed by their Creator with certain inalienable rights: that among these are life, liberty, and the pursuit of happiness. . . ." It continued by condemning the unjust practices of men against women: "The history of mankind is a history of repeated injuries and usurpations on the part of man toward woman, having in direct object the establishment of an absolute tyranny over her. To prove this, let facts be submitted to a candid world."

After naming the abuses of women, the Declaration offered eighteen resolutions that showed how society limited women's behavior, education, and opportunities, and thus demonstrated women's need for equality in education, employment, and religious participation as well as for reformed property statutes for married women. Of all the resolutions, only one, pertaining to woman suffrage, received negative response. Eventually, though by a narrow margin, the woman suffrage resolution passed as well.

At the conclusion of the convention, sixty-eight women and thirty-two men signed the Declaration, making it the first formal statement regarding women's rights.

—*Katherine Teschner*

See Also:

Nineteenth-Century Woman's Movement, Seneca Falls Convention, Suffrage

References:

Stanton, Elizabeth C., Susan B. Anthony, and Matilda J. Gage, eds. *History of Woman Suffrage*. 6 vols. New York: National American Woman Suffrage Association, 1888–1922.

Flexner, Eleanor. *A Century of Struggle: The Woman's Rights Movement in the United States*. New York: Atheneum, 1974.

Sochen, June. *Herstory: A Record of the American Woman's Past*. Palo Alto, Calif.: Mayfield, 1982.

DECONSTRUCTION is a concept developed in the mid-twentieth century that has been employed among some Women's Studies scholars as a means of addressing the obstacle of sexism in the English language. In modern American feminist theory as well as in feminist literary criticism, sexist language thwarts the development of a bias-free scholarship, and so the language itself must be "de-constructed" and re-created to produce an essentially gender-neutral terminology that will allow scholars to approach women's topics and issues in terms that do not take their basic definition from the "woman-as-the-other" perspective.

Deconstruction is a poststructuralist twentieth-century conceptual position (equivalent to Heidegger's "destruction" or "dismantling") associated especially with Jacques Derrida and various American disciples in literary and historical theory. In general, it has a dual pedigree: the sort of philosophical "destruction" implied by Nietzsche and Freud; and Saussurean linguistics, which stresses the relational rather than the referential character of language.

The theory and practice of deconstruction cannot be analyzed in the conventional terms of rational, "intentionalist" discourse. Rather, deconstruction offers fundamental critiques of conventional philosophical, linguistic, literary, and political assumptions. Philosophically, it rejects traditional metaphysics and all absolutist ideas in the theory of meaning, including ideas of historical continuity and "humanism." Linguistically, it denies the sovereignty of the self or "authorial will" in writing; assumes that speech is the operation of language, not of the individual; and, in more radically textualist terms, assumes that there is no conceptual ground outside of the text. Politically, deconstruction insists on the correlation between language and power and by indirection seeks to dismantle, or to unmask, the "dominant" (institutional, social, sexual) discourse of conventional views of history and culture in the interests of egalitarian ideals and for the benefit of supposedly "marginal" groups.

The adoption of deconstruction by contemporary scholars and feminists has caused great debate precisely because it tends to examine structures of power in language and knowledge. Instead of investigating women's oppression in the workplace, for example, deconstructionists favor undermining texts and using wordplay. Nor in terms of deconstructive theory do texts ordinarily cited as oppressive to women always directly reveal such oppression. The growth of such scholarship has attracted the charge that it maintains a kind of irrelevant, hyper-sophisticated elitism, whereas scholarship should examine bread-and-butter issues. Issues raised by deconstruction and French feminist theory had an airing at a conference at Barnard College in 1979, and major journals such as *Signs* and *Feminist Studies* are clearly enmeshed in the deconstruction debate.

—*Bonnie G. Smith*

See Also:

Feminist Literary Criticism, Language and Linguistics

References:

Culler, Jonathan. *On Deconstruction*. Ithaca, N.Y.: Cornell University Press, 1984.

Eisenstein, Hester, and Alice Jardine, eds. *The Future of Difference*. New Brunswick, N.J.: Rutgers University Press, 1985.

Jardine, Alice. *Gynesis: Configurations of Women and Modernity*. Ithaca, N.Y.: Cornell University Press, 1985.

The **DEMOCRATIC PARTY** in the United States has been around in one form or another since the origins of the Republic in the eighteenth century. Since women were not eligible to vote until 1920, the Democrats, like the Republicans, were not overly concerned with women's issues. Throughout the early histories of both major political parties in the United States, women have had to exert their influence indirectly and through male politicians. The results have frequently been disappointing.

In the late 1860s Elizabeth Cady Stanton and Susan B. Anthony looked to the Democratic party for help in the struggle for woman suffrage, but the Democrats proved to be as unreliable as the Republicans, and the struggle for suffrage dragged on with little support from either major party. In 1913 Alice Paul and others organized a massive protest against the inauguration of Democratic president Woodrow Wilson, who had consistently failed to support a woman suffrage amendment to the Constitution. In 1914 the Congressional Union, a suffrage organization, actively campaigned against Democratic candidates for office. The union claimed that it had helped to defeat twenty-three of forty-three western Democratic congressional candidates in the 1914 elections. The union was later reorganized as the National Women's party in June 1916.

Partly in response to this kind of pressure, the Democratic platform of 1916 favored "the extension of suffrage to women, state by state, on the same terms as men." However, the Democrats continued to be divided on the issue, especially in the South, where traditional, conservative "Dixiecrats" were adamant in their opposition to votes for women. Nonetheless, conservative opposition to an increased political role for women was sufficiently overcome so that in 1920 the party's National Committee was reconstituted to include one female member from each state.

After women had secured the vote, they slowly but surely become more prominent actors in the politics of the 1920s and 1930s. Women such as Mary Norton began to get elected to Congress in 1924, although the number of women in the U.S. Congress has never been greater than two dozen at any one time. Women were appointed as senators to finish the terms of their husbands, as was Hattie Caraway in 1931. Much the same thing occurred at the state level, where "Ma" Ferguson in Texas and Nellie Ross in Wyoming succeeded their deceased husbands as governors. Not until Democratic candidate Ella Grasso's election as governor of Connecticut in 1974 was a woman elected to a gubernatorial post.

The influence of women behind the scenes of Democratic party life grew apace in the same period. New York social worker Belle Moskowitz became one of the top advisers to Democratic presidential candidate Al Smith in 1928. With the election of Franklin Delano Roosevelt to the White House in 1932, the role of women reached a new zenith. Acting partly under the influence of his talented wife, Eleanor, Roosevelt appointed Frances Perkins as secretary of labor, a post she maintained until 1945. Perkins, a graduate of Mount Holyoke, was the first woman to hold a cabinet position in the history of the United States, and she was one of a host of women who became a major part of Roosevelt's New Deal administration.

It is difficult to overestimate the importance of Eleanor Roosevelt in reshaping the attitudes of the Democratic party and the nation toward political women and women's issues. A highly visible First Lady, Roosevelt published a daily newspaper column—"My Day"—and held weekly press conferences. A former teacher and social worker, she cared deeply about a host of reform issues and was influential in getting her husband's administration to hire women in record numbers. Women in Washington knew they had a friend in the White House in Eleanor Roosevelt.

In addition to Frances Perkins, the Roosevelt era women's network included Molly Dewson, who headed the Women's Division of the Democratic party from 1932 to 1937 and was a member of the Social Security Board from 1937 to 1938. A close friend of the Roosevelts, Dewson spent a lot of time lobbying the president to hire more women and to respond to women's issues. Among the many other women who were active in this period, one can mention Ellen Sullivan Woodward and Mary McLeod Bethune. Woodward helped set up relief programs for women under the auspices of the Federal Emergency Relief Administration and later became head of Women's and Professional Projects for the Works Progress Administration. She also served a six-year term on the Social Security Board. Bethune headed the Office of Minority Affairs from 1936 to 1944.

Ironically, Franklin Roosevelt did not use women, even his wife, as his top advisers, and neither he nor his wife supported the Equal Rights Amendment, which had first been proposed by the National Women's party in 1923. Indeed, the Equal Rights Amendment was not endorsed by the Democratic party until 1944, although the party has remained faithful to it since that time.

Democratic women in Washington further enhanced their women's network by the creation of the Women's National Democratic Club, founded in 1924. Influential women within the Democratic party, such as Emily Newell Blair, Marion Glass Banister, and Daisy Harriman, were important backers of this club, which became a significant meeting place for Democratic women.

The gains women had made in the Democratic party during World War II were not lost in the aftermath of the war. The administration of Harry Truman continued to employ women in high places and low, and in 1948 Truman signed the Women's Armed Forces Integration Act, which gave women the chance for military careers.

In 1960 about six million women worked on the successful presidential campaign of John F. Kennedy, and he responded to his own failure to name a female cabinet-member by accepting Esther Peterson's proposal for a Presidential Commission on the Status of Women. Peterson was the head of the Women's Bureau, and as assistant secretary of labor was the highest woman in the Kennedy administration. Eleanor Roosevelt headed the commission until her death in 1962, when she was succeeded by Peterson. Although a majority of the commission failed to support the ERA movement, it did produce the most comprehensive document about women ever produced by the federal government.

Women continued to be important, if underrepresented, voices into the administration of Lyndon Johnson. Johnson's wife, "Lady Bird," was an extremely active and effective First Lady. The Johnson years also featured the election of Shirley Chisholm to Congress in 1969—its first black female member. In 1972 Chisholm ran for the Democratic presidential nomination for president, while civil rights leader Fannie Lou Hamer fought for increased black representation.

During the presidency of Jimmy Carter (1978–82), women reached their peak of influence in the life of the Democratic party and its administration. Influenced by a strong mother, Lillian, and a talented wife, Rosalynn, Carter had two women in his cabinet, and 12 percent of his presidential appointees in 1978 were women. The Carters were not afraid to let the world know that their marriage was a partnership and that talented people like Patricia Harris could rise to cabinet-level positions regardless of sex or race. By this time, Democratic women were rising to key positions in the party and the nation. For example, Jane Byrne was elected as Chicago's first woman mayor in 1979. Diane Feinstein in 1978 became mayor of San Francisco, Kathy Whitmire was elected mayor of Houston in 1981, and a number of women were elected to a host of local and state offices around the country. In 1984 the Democratic party named Congresswoman Geraldine Ferraro as its vice-presidential nominee.

While women are still underrepresented in public life around the country, they have become a force to be reckoned with by both major political parties. How large the political "gender gap" continues to be remains open to question. Few dispute that it exists and that women will continue to play an increasingly powerful role in the future of the political life of the United States.

—Jonathan W. Zophy

See Also:

Abzug, Bella; Bethune, Mary McLeod; Chisholm, Shirley; Douglas, Helen Gahagan; Ferraro, Geraldine; Gender Gap; New Deal; Perkins, Frances; Roosevelt, Eleanor; Suffrage

References:

Abzug, Bella, with Mim Keller. *Gender Gap: Bella Abzug's Guide to Political Power*. Boston: Houghton Mifflin, 1984.

Flexner, Eleanor. *Century of Struggle: The Women's Rights Movement in the United States*. Cambridge: Harvard University Press, 1975.

Gruberg, Martin. *Women in American Politics: An Assessment and a Sourcebook.* Oshkosh, Wis.: Academia, 1968.
Jones, Jacqueline, ed. *Women in Politics.* New York: Wiley, 1974.
Lash, Joseph. *Eleanor and Franklin.* New York: Norton, 1971.
———. *Eleanor: The Years Alone.* New York: Norton, 1972.
Martin, George. *Madam Secretary: Frances Perkins.* Boston: Houghton Mifflin, 1976.
Ware, Susan. *Beyond Suffrage: Women in the New Deal.* Cambridge: Harvard University Press, 1981.
———. *Holding Their Own.* Boston: Twayne, 1982.

DEMOGRAPHY focuses upon birth, death, marriage, migration, and life-cycle patterns for women in American history within the study of the size, growth, density, distribution, and vital statistics of the national population. Among the significant changes in women's lives since the seventeenth century are the following trends for white women: a doubling of their life expectancy as well as in the rise of female-headed households, reduced childbearing, a relatively stable age of marriage between twenty-one and twenty-three for nine out of ten women, and a proportional divorce-rate increase that parallels improvements in increased life expectancy. Among minority women, these trends are altered by a different, higher mortality. There were gender-specific results from the three great migrations in American history—to the New World in the seventeenth century, Westward in the eighteenth and nineteenth centuries, and the rural/urban migration which began in the nineteenth century. Typically, women lacked authority in the family decision to migrate to the New World and then to the western frontier. They were a numerical minority in numbers in those migrations, and the rural-urban-suburban migration resulted in reduced family sizes that brought changes to women's social and economic lives. The specific pattern of women's migration was characterized in their moving shorter distances than men and by their urban, rather than rural destination to seek employment opportunities in the cities.

—*Angela Howard Zophy*

See Also:

Fertility, Life Cycle—Nineteenth Century, Migration and Frontier Women

References:

Degler, Carl N. *At Odds: Women and the Family in America from the American Revolution to the Present.* New York: Oxford University Press, 1980.
Wells, Robert V. "Women's Lives Transformed: Demographic and Family Patterns in America, 1600–1970." In *Women of America: A History,* edited by Carol Ruth Berkin and Mary B. Norton. Boston: Houghton Mifflin, 1979, pp. 16–33.

DENNETT, MARY COFFIN (WARE) (1872–1947) was a pioneer in the movements for woman suffrage, peace, birth control, and sex education. Married and divorced from architect William Hartley Dennett and the mother of three children, Dennett was trained as an artist and interior designer. Politically active and an ardent supporter of the growing peace movement during World War I, she was also deeply committed to the cause of women's suffrage, serving as secretary of the National American Woman Suffrage Association from 1912. It was her support of women's rights that soon led Dennett to a growing involvement in efforts to legalize birth control.

Opposed to the radical, confrontational tactics of Margaret Sanger, who challenged the laws prohibiting the dissemination of birth control, Dennett focused her efforts on lobbying for legislative reform. In 1915 she founded the first American birth control organization, the National Birth Control League (NBCL), to lobby for a bill that would allow the transmission of contraceptive information. Uncomfortable with the radical overtones associated with Sanger and birth control, Dennett reorganized the NBCL into the Voluntary Parenthood League in 1918 and emerged as Margaret Sanger's rival for leadership of the growing movement.

When Sanger and her American Birth Control League adopted the more conservative strategy of supporting laws that would allow physicians to disseminate birth control, Dennett was vehemently opposed. Promoting "doctors-only" laws, in her view, undermined the right of all citizens to have equal access to contraceptive information. For Dennett, the only solution was to remove all legal restraints on birth control by redefining the obscenity laws. Though Sanger's pragmatic efforts eventually won more adherents than Dennett's legalistic approach, Dennett refused to compromise and instead continued to fight the whole concept of legal obscenity.

Dennett began to openly challenge the obscenity laws in 1922 when the government attempted to suppress a sex education article she had published in 1918. Arguing that access to sex education was an essential prerequisite for a just and enlightened society and any attempts to censor such material violated civil liberties, she defied the ban and continued to circulate the article. Indicted, convicted, and fined in 1929, Dennett was determined to fight the decision. With the aid of counsel provided by the American Civil Liberties Union, an appeal was mounted, and in 1930, the conviction was overturned.

While committed to women's rights, Mary Ware Dennett believed that advancing the position of women in the United States depended upon protecting the First Amendment rights of both women and men to freedom of speech and expression. In her efforts to challenge the definition of legal obscenity, she became one of the nation's most effective defenders of civil liberties.

—*Esther Katz*

See Also:

Birth Control; National American Woman Suffrage Association; Obscenity; Sanger, Margaret; Voluntary Parenthood League

References:

Dennett, Mary Ware. *Birth Control Laws.* New York: F. H. Hitchcock, 1926.

———. *The Prosecution of Mary Ware Dennett for Obscenity.* New York: ACLU, 1929. [pamphlet]

———. *The Sex Education of Children: A Book for Parents.* New York: Vanguard, 1931.

———. *Who's Obscene?* New York.: Vanguard, 1930.

Gordon, Linda. *Woman's Body, Woman's Right: A Social History of Birth Control in America.* New York: Grossman, 1976.

Kennedy, David. *Birth Control in America: The Career of Margaret Sanger.* New Haven: Yale University Press, 1970.

Sanger, Margaret. *An Autobiography.* New York: Norton, 1938.

DENNY, DOROTHY (DETZER) (1893–1981), executive secretary of the U.S. Section of the Women's International League for Peace and Freedom from 1924 to 1946, was an uncompromising pacifist who led the WILPF to national prominence within the interwar peace movement. Highly respected as an astute political lobbyist, she almost singlehandedly initiated the congressional investigation of the munitions industry in the mid-1930s.

Born and raised in Fort Wayne, Indiana, Denny had the middle-class background typical of the woman interwar peace activist. Shocked by the outbreak of World War I though supportive of American involvement, she volunteered with the American Friends Service Committee to alleviate postwar famine in Austria and Russia.

Committed to the WILPF's philosophy that there can be no lasting nor just peace without freedom and no freedom without peace, Denny played a prominent role in the peace movement's effort to avert war between the United States and Central America in the mid-1920s. Denny and the WILPF supported the Kellogg-Briand Pact (1928), which outlawed war, advocated international disarmament and the congressional debates over neutrality legislation in the 1930s, and attempted to prevent American involvement in World War II.

An unswerving proponent of democracy as both means and end, Denny personified the WILPF's belief that war would bring fascism to America. Convinced by the war's end that such fears were justified by events, Denny resigned from the WILPF in 1946; her role as peace activist died when she lost her faith in democracy.

As was true of a growing number of women in the interwar period, Denny, although opposed to the Equal Rights Amendment, was primarily a "career woman"; not until 1954 did she marry her longtime friend, journalist Ludwell Denny. Though no longer a political activist, Denny regained her faith in the United States as a democracy when outraged public opinion brought an end to American involvement in Vietnam and the downfall of Richard Nixon in the Watergate scandal.

—Carrie Foster

See Also:

Pacifism and the Peace Movement, Women's International League for Peace and Freedom

References:

Dorothy Detzer Denny Papers. Women's International League for Peace and Freedom Papers. Swarthmore College Peace Collection, Swarthmore, Pa.

Women's International League for Peace and Freedom Papers. University of Colorado, Boulder, Colo.

Bussey, Gertrude, and Margaret Tims. *Pioneers for Peace. Women's International League for Peace and Freedom, 1915–1965.* London: George Allen & Unwin, 1965; rpt. London: WILPF British Section, 1980.

Detzer, Dorothy. *Appointment on the Hill.* New York: Holt, 1948.

Foster-Hayes, Carrie. "The Women and the Warriors: Dorothy Detzer and the WILPF." Diss. The University of Denver, 1984.

DEUTSCH, HELENE (1884–1982) was born in Przemysl, Galicia (Poland), which at that time belonged to the Austro-Hungarian Empire. Her father, a lawyer, encouraged his daughter's education, and by the time she was an adolescent, she was dedicated to revolutionary ideology, including equal rights for women.

In 1907 she was admitted to the University of Vienna Medical School, an accomplishment almost unheard of in those days. She became interested in the nascent field of psychiatry, but was initially frustrated in her attempts to obtain a clinical position by laws that limited women's participation in medical practice. However, the outbreak of World War I allowed her the opportunity to work as a "civilian war doctor" in a prestigious psychiatric clinic in Vienna. After the war she entered into analysis with Sigmund Freud and became a convert to the psychoanalytic approach and a loyal disciple of Freud. She subsequently devoted her career to the clarification of psychoanalytic concepts and to the rigorous training of psychoanalysts, becoming one of the original founders of the Vienna Psychoanalytic Institute in 1925.

Her dedication to psychoanalytic principles soon prompted Deutsch to attempt to revise the image of women propounded by traditional Freudian thought. She devoted over fifty years of her life to the development of a psychoanalytic explanation of normal and neurotic female behavior. Her first approach to the definition of a female personality concerned the resolution of penis envy. In a discussion paper entitled "The Psychology of Women in Relation to the Functions of Reproduction," written in 1924, she reinforced the supremacy of the penis over the clitoris as an organ of power and pleasure and outlined the theory of women's "masochistic subjugation to the penis" (Fleiss).

Deutsch's analysis of the female psyche was detailed in her now-classic publication, *The Psychology of Women* (1944). In this two-volume text, based upon a series of discussion papers she wrote between 1925 and 1931, Deutsch details the psychological development of women from birth to maturity. Central to this development are themes of passivity, masochism, and narcissism. In keeping with traditional psychoanalytic thinking, Deutsch believed that a child's relationship with her parents, and in particular her resolution of the Oedipal conflict, determined adult personality structure. Following this line of thought, it seemed to Deutsch that woman's personality was strongly affected by her relationship with her mother, to whom she turned after the psychic rejection of the Oedipal conflict. The Oedipal conflict, as identified by Freud, focused on the rivalry of the daughter with the mother for the father's affection. In a conceptualization that anticipated feminist thought by some thirty years, Deutsch maintained that woman's dependency was a direct outgrowth of the overly dependent relationship with her mother that could result at this time. Likewise, woman's dependent relationship with men, in adulthood, stemmed from this learned dependency. Deutsch also explained that this excessive dependency created intense anger, at both the mother and the lover, that the woman strove to contain. As a result of this repressed rage, the woman was constantly in danger of developing neurotic character traits. This line of thought is very similar to that of Nancy Chodorow and other feminist psychologists who are defining a contemporary psychology of women.

Unfortunately, this feminist aspect of Deutsch's work has been overshadowed by other aspects of her depiction of female personality. Her inability to turn away from a Freudian framework for analysis led Deutsch to describe women as passive, masochistic creatures who expected, and indeed derived pleasure from, psychological pain. She cited rape fantasies, the more passive involvement of women in sexual intercourse (by which she meant being the recipient of the male's energy), the loss of self often evident in women's love relationships, and childbirth as clear examples of woman's psychic need for submission and pain. Moreover, she described women as being "narcissistically involved," by which she meant that they were capable of becoming fixated upon their own needs to the extent of selfish self-absorption. This complex and unflattering picture of women's psyche has become accepted in classical psychoanalytic thought.

For most women psychologists and psychiatrists, the work of Helene Deutsch is problematic. Although toward the end of her life she softened her approach to woman's psychic structure and integrated into her therapy with women approaches for overcoming dependency, passivity, and masochism, her ideas about the psychoanalytic development of women have been perceived as perpetuating the androcentric approach toward women that has been prevalent in the human sciences.

Helene Deutsch's autobiography (1973) and a recent feminist reconstruction of her work (Webster, 1985) provide us with insight into how and why her thinking developed as it did. Deutsch was extremely attached to her father and devoted much early energy to catching and keeping his attention. She felt strong rivalry with her brother and two sisters for her father's affection. Her desire to be named as her father's heir, over her brother, illustrates the depth of this feeling. The fact that this desire was realized illustrates Helene's proficiency. This strong, emotionally dependent relationship resurfaced in Deutsch's association with Sigmund Freud. Her unquestioning devotion to Freudian concepts, in the face of mounting experiential evidence of their inappropriateness for women, caused her to devise a theoretical stance toward women that was in direct contradiction to her own life and work. She did not see herself as passive, masochistic, narcissistic, or dependent, yet she allowed herself to describe all other women in those terms. She worked all her life and combined the roles of wife and mother with that of psychiatrist. She dedicated many years to the training of analysts, especially after coming to the United States in 1935 to help found the Boston Psychiatric Institute. She led a long and very productive life, dying at the age of ninety-seven.

In sum, Helene Deutsch is a transitional woman for feminist psychology. By its example, her life shows the way in which women can be strong, productive members of society. But her written work, circumscribed by an outmoded, androcentric philosophy, provides us with a model of women's psychology against which contemporary feminist psychologists rebel.

—Teresa Peck

See Also:

Freudianism, Psychiatry, Psychology

References:

Chodorow, Nancy. *The Reproduction of Mothering.* Berkeley: University of California Press, 1978.

Deutsch, Helene. *Confrontations with Myself.* New York: Norton, 1973.
———. *The Psychology of Women.* New York: Grune & Stratton, 1944.
Fleiss, Robert. *The Psychoanalytic Reader: An Anthology of Essential Papers and Critical Introductions.* New York: International University Press, 1969.
Webster, Brenda. "Helene Deutsch: A New Look." *SIGNS: A Journal of Women in Culture and Society* 10 (1985): 553–71.

DIAZ, ABBY MORTON (1821–1904), social reformer, woman's rights activist, metaphysical healer, and author, was born in Plymouth, Massachusetts. Ichabod Morton, an antislavery, temperance, and educational reformer, bred in his only daughter a commitment to reform that was to last throughout her long and exceptionally active life. Before the age of ten, she had become secretary of the Juvenile Anti-Slavery Society. In 1843 her father, an admirer of abolitionist and transcendentalist Theodore Parker, moved his family for a short time to Brook Farm, a utopian community founded in 1841. The community's precarious finances quickly convinced the thrifty shipbuilder to reverse his decision, but his daughter remained at the farm to teach in its infant school until the community folded in 1847.

While at Brook Farm in 1845, she married Manuel A. Diaz, a Cuban who probably came to the farm for tutoring. The marriage was short-lived but left her with two sons whom she supported by teaching, running a singing school out of her father's home in Plymouth, conducting dance classes, and occasionally hiring herself out as a housekeeper and nurse. She next tried her hand at writing for a juvenile audience, publishing her first short story in 1861. Cheerful and lively in person as well as on paper, she soon attracted a broad readership with tales of youthful adventure and character development, advice on "domestic art" and female self-improvement, and musings on self-culture through "spiritual healing." Her better-known works are *The William Henry Letters* (1870), *Lucy Maria* (1874), *Polly Cologne* (1881), *Domestic Problems* (1884), *Bybury to Beacon Street* (1887), *Only a Flock of Women* (1893), and *The Religious Training of Children* (1895).

Diaz was one of the earliest members of the Bellamy nationalist movement of the late 1880s, which proposed to ameliorate class antagonism through state socialism. She worked on behalf of woman's rights as president of the Belmont (Mass.) Woman's Suffrage League and as a founder and leader of the Woman's Educational and Industrial Union, an organization committed to sisterly self-improvement and economic advancement for women of all classes. She was also a zealous advocate of New Thought, a spiritual heir to Emersonian transcendentalism, and strongly advocated the practice of mental healing.

Abby Morton Diaz spent the last twenty years of her life in Belmont, where she made a home for three of her grandchildren. She died of pneumonia at the age of eighty-two.

—*Catherine Tumber*

See Also:
Socialism, Suffrage, Utopian Communities

References:

Articles by and about Abby Morton Diaz. Sophia Smith Collection. Smith College, Northampton, Mass.
Blackwell, Alice Stone. "The Life Work of Mrs. Abby Morton Diaz." *Woman's Journal* 33 (June 13, 1903): 188–89.
———. "Mrs. Abby Morton Diaz." *Woman's Journal* 34 (April 9, 1904): 113, 116–17.

DICKINSON, EMILY (1830–86) is now acknowledged as a major American poet. Her first poem was published when she was twenty-two years old, with a title she had not chosen herself: "A Valentine." Her second poem was published in 1861, when she was thirty-one, under the title "May Wine," but we know it better by its first line, as is the case with all of her poetry now: "I taste a liquor never brewed." During her lifetime, only five other poems were printed, the last in 1878 in an anthology entitled *A Masque of Poets,* which also included a previously unpublished poem by Henry David Thoreau. Her image as a complete unknown during her lifetime has been encouraged by devotees but does not match the Dickinson of her own correspondence to family and close friends. Her letters reveal earnest efforts to win the favor of the powerful editor of *The Atlantic Monthly*, Thomas Wentworth Higginson. The coyness of tone in the letters to Higginson is deliberate, and must be read against the societal pressures of the times for women to know their place in the literary hierarchy.

She lived her life in her father's house in Amherst, Massachusetts, by choice, restricting the sphere of her physical environment to a smaller and smaller diameter as the range of her poetry expanded. Nature, love, passion, death, and immortality were her themes. Her experimentation with metaphor and imagery is set against the counterpoint of traditional American hymnal meters, creating a tension between visual and sound imagery, stressing that all is more complex beneath the surface of the world.

While biographers and critics continue to debate the enigmatic puzzle pieces of her life—her not-so-secret loves and family disputes—readers have never let the academic wars stand in the way of empathy with her tragic vision, as it has been called by the most reliable editor of her letters and poems, Thomas H. Johnson. Likened by one critic to Shakespeare's timely appearance in a period of historic crisis, her presence is both a product and revelation of a driving force in the American nineteenth century.

Rather than as frail or self-pitying victim, vile dissenter in her household, or passive maid spurned, the strongest and yet perhaps the most controversial view of her is simply as a poet creating her own immortality: her poetry.

—*Carol Lee Saffioti*

References:

Bloom, Harold, ed. *Emily Dickinson*. New York: Chelsea House, 1985.

Dickinson, Emily. *Letters*. Edited by Thomas H. Johnson, associate editor Theodora Ward. 3 vols. Cambridge, Mass.: Belknap, 1958, 1965.

———. *The Manuscript Books*. Edited by R. W. Franklin. 2 vols. Cambridge, Mass.: Belknap, 1981.

———. *Selected Letters*. Edited by Thomas H. Johnson. Cambridge, Mass.: Belknap, 1958, 1985.

Howe, Susan. *My Emily Dickinson*. Berkeley, Calif.: North Atlantic, 1985.

Juhasz, Suzanne. *Feminist Critics Read Emily Dickinson*. Bloomington: Indiana University Press, 1983.

———. *The Undiscovered Continent: Emily Dickinson and the Space of the Mind*. Bloomington: Indiana University Press, 1983.

Martin, Wendy. *An American Triptych: Anne Bradstreet, Emily Dickinson, and Adrienne Rich*. Chapel Hill: University of North Carolina Press, 1984.

Shurr, William. *The Marriage of Emily Dickinson: A Study of the Fascicles*. Lexington: University of Kentucky Press, 1983.

DIGGS, ANNIE LEPORTE (1848–1916), social reformer, journalist, and Populist politician, was born in London, Ontario. She moved to Lawrence, Kansas, in 1873, marrying Alvin S. Diggs a few months later; the couple had three children. Diggs's interest in reform began with her involvement in and writings about woman suffrage and temperance in the 1870s. Diggs and her husband edited the *Kansas Liberal* until she began writing weekly columns for the *Lawrence Journal*. By the late 1880s Diggs had become increasingly concerned with the economic problems of farmers and began supporting the National Farmers' Alliance.

As an associate editor of the *Alliance Advocate*, a Topeka newspaper with wide circulation in the plains states, Diggs gained a reputation as a spokesperson for agricultural reform and was asked in 1890 to campaign for the newly formed Populist party in Kansas. Diggs's influence among Populists increased due to her organizing and lobbying efforts at national conventions of the National Farmers' Alliance and at the nominating convention of the Populist party in 1892. During the presidential campaigns of 1892 and 1896, Diggs toured the country extensively, supporting

James Weaver, the Populist presidential candidate. She moved to Washington, D.C., became the Washington correspondent for the *Alliance Advocate*, and was a frequent congressional lobbyist for woman suffrage, temperance, the Alliance, and the Populist party. In 1896 she served on the Populist National Committee. She also served alternately as vice president and president of the Kansas Equal Suffrage Association.

A pragmatic politician, Diggs supported the Populist party despite its failure on a national level to include woman suffrage or temperance in its platform. As late as 1900 she was still supporting the fusion of the Democratic party and the Populist party rather than an independent Populist party, believing as many Populists did that a fusion party would have a better chance of winning elections. In 1898 she was appointed Kansas State Librarian as a reward for helping elect a Populist-Democratic administration. By 1902 Diggs had become discouraged with fusion politics and began endorsing Eugene Debs and the Socialist party. In 1904 Diggs moved to New York City, worked with a civic reform bureau, and continued writing. Her books include *The Story of Jerry Simpson* (1908) and *Bedrock* (1912). She left New York in 1912 to live with her son in Detroit, where she died in 1916.

—*MaryJo Wagner*

See Also:

Journalism, National Farmers' Alliance, Populist Party, Suffrage in the American West

References:

Barr, Elizabeth N. "The Populist Uprising." In *A Standard History of Kansas and the Kansans*, edited by William Connelley. Vol. 2. Chicago: Lewis Publishing Co., 1918, pp. 1115–95.

Kansas Scrapbooks, Biog. D. Kansas State Historical Society, Topeka, Kansas.

Weddle, Connie Andes. "The Platform and the Pen: The Reform Activities of Annie L. Diggs." M.A. thesis. Wichita State University, 1979.

DILLING, ELIZABETH ELOISE (KIRKPATRICK) (1894–1966), author and lecturer, crusaded against Communism and for conservative causes in the 1930s, 1940s, and 1950s. She published the *Elizabeth Dilling Bulletin* monthly, wrote numerous tracts, and wrote and published four books: *The Red Network: A Who's Who and Handbook of Radicalism for Patriots* (1934), *The Roosevelt Red Record* (1936), *The Octopus* (1940), and *The Plot Against Christianity* (1952). A tireless researcher and an inveterate opponent of President Franklin D. Roosevelt, she was an isolationist and a foe of foreign aid.

Born in Chicago in 1894, she graduated from Starrett High School for Girls there, studied harp at the University of Chicago, and briefly was a concert harpist before marrying Albert Wallwick Dilling, a Chicago attorney and engineer, in 1918. They had a son Kirkpatrick and a daughter Elizabeth Jane.

Dilling's life changed after she visited the Soviet Union with her husband in 1931 and was appalled by conditions there under Communism. When she returned to America, she lectured about Communism and showed home movies she had made in Russia. She studied Communism intensively and collected a large library of books about and against Communism. Her first book *The Red Network* was a collection of summaries of the associations of some thirteen hundred individuals and groups she labeled as pro-Communist.

Dilling opposed American participation in World War II before Pearl Harbor. In 1941 she led a group of mothers to Washington to lobby against the Lend-Lease Bill. She was arrested several times for demonstrating at the Capitol and the Senate Office Building. Her opposition to the foreign policies of the Roosevelt administration led to her indictment for sedition in 1942, 1943, and 1944, along with other isolationists, but the trial ended without a verdict in 1944 when the presiding judge died.

After World War II, Dilling crusaded against the United Nations, the Bricker Amendment (a proposed amendment to limit executive authority in foreign policy), and recognition of Red China. She also opposed racial desegregation and wrote extensively on alleged Jewish support of Communism. Allied with a network of ultra-Right activists, she worked against leftist influence in the Democratic and Republican parties and campaigned for minor party candidates for the presidency and lesser offices.

Dilling divorced Albert Wallwick Dilling in 1943 and in 1948 married Jeremiah Stokes, a Salt Lake City attorney, Mormon elder, and anticommunist crusader. Stokes died in 1954.

Dilling was one of the most prominent anticommunist women in the nation for nearly forty years. Her newsletter had only a few thousand subscribers, but her books were read by millions and utilized as references by some government agencies. A controversial woman, she provoked substantial opposition. She made little money from her crusades and was supported by her husbands and by a modest inheritance. She died in Chicago in 1966.

—*Glen Jeansonne*

See Also:
Right-Wing Political Movements

References:

Dilling, Elizabeth. *The Red Network.* Chicago: published by the author, 1934.
Dilling Newsletter, 1942–1966.

DISPLACED HOMEMAKERS is a term coined in the 1970s to describe women who have been keeping house most of their adult lives, not participating in the paid labor force, suddenly displaced by divorce or the death of a spouse, often without adequate means of support for themselves or their families. Because of the drastic rise in the divorce rate since 1960, these women have become a growing and important group in our society who need education or job training to improve their skills and confidence in their efforts to support themselves. Many programs at both the federal and local level have been established to provide these women with needed services. Money for this purpose became available with the beginning of the Comprehensive Employment and Training Act [CETA] program in 1973 and has continued in various programs from the federal government, which in turn awards grants to local agencies and programs to help the women acquire skills *and* recognize, appreciate, and market those skills they have gained during their years as homemakers.

—*Anne A. Statham*

See Also:
Housework

References:

André, Rae. *Homemakers: The Forgotten Workers.* Chicago: University of Chicago Press, 1981.
U.S. Department of Education. *Services to Displaced Homemakers.* Washington, D.C.: USDE Office of Vocational and Adult Education, 1981.

DIVORCE. In England the ecclesiastical courts had jurisdiction over marriage and applied canon law, which made a valid marriage indissoluble. A true divorce, *divortium a vinculo matrimonii,* which was absolute and allowed remarriage, was never granted unless the marriage was *void ab initio* because of defects such as consanguinity, bigamy, or sexual incapacity. This absolute divorce bastardized the children of the void marriage and ended all support obligations of the husband for the wife. Late in the seventeenth century, the House of Lords began to grant a very limited number of absolute legislative divorces.

Divortium a mensa et thoro, separation from bed and board, could be granted for adultery, desertion, or cruelty. All the legal obligations of the marriage, except cohabitation, continued, and the parties could not remarry. The husband could be ordered to provide support in the form of alimony (payments in cash) to the innocent wife who obtained this decree. The children of the marriage remained legitimate.

In America, the southern colonies followed the English practice, but New England courts and legislatures sometimes granted divorces. The Puritan reformers viewed marriage as a civil contract that could be dissolved if one of the spouses breached the terms of the covenant through adultery, long absence, incest, or irremediable cruelty. That influence was reflected in Connecticut and Massachusetts, the only colonies to enact statutes allowing absolute divorce and to enforce them regularly. The more conservative Pennsylvania statute of 1705 provided for annulments on the grounds of consanguinity and affinity, and permitted separations from bed and board where adultery, bigamy, buggery, or sodomy was shown. In those colonies that had equity courts, as in England, private contracts to live apart and divide property were enforceable if they took the form of a postnuptial trust involving a third party.

After the American Revolution, many states passed divorce laws. By 1800 every New England state had a divorce law, as did New York, New Jersey, and Tennessee. The southern states, however, continued their more conservative policies.

In America absolute divorce usually meant a division of the property, with the woman receiving one-third to one-half of the estate owned during the marriage. In a separation, husbands retained control of the marital property but were obligated to make monetary payments to innocent wives. Pennsylvania, however, was the only state that continued the English practice of disallowing any alimony in cases of absolute divorce. The New England states were more willing to grant absolute divorce, but less willing to enforce women's property rights during marriage through devices such as separate estates. Conversely, states such as New York and South Carolina, which were conservative about granting absolute divorces, strongly enforced private separation agreements according to equitable principles of law.

From 1850 to 1870, although divorce laws varied, many states enacted fairly liberal laws, such as the Connecticut statute that authorized divorce for any misconduct that permanently destroyed the happiness of the petitioner and defeated the purposes of the marriage relation. After 1870, however, moralists such as Horace Greeley, editor of the *New York Tribune*, and Theodore D. Woolsey, president of Yale University and founder of the New England Divorce Reform League, attacked permissive divorce with increasing force. In 1882 Connecticut repealed its permissive statute.

Despite the tightening of the law, the divorce rate continued to rise. Some unhappy spouses took advantage of "divorce colonies" where they could obtain migratory divorces by satisfying short-residency and liberal-grounds requirements. Other states followed Indiana, which before the 1870s was one of the first divorce colonies. A series of Supreme Court decisions delineated the circumstances under which one state had to recognize a migratory divorce obtained in one of its sister states. The Court developed the idea of the "divisible divorce," in which a state may have the power to dissolve the marital union but not to determine other issues such as support.

Until 1966 New York State retained its very conservative statute that permitted divorce only for adultery, thus producing in-state divorce mills that collusively manufactured evidence to satisfy a court. In effect, New Yorkers, if they had the money and the stomach for it, could obtain divorces by mutual consent.

In 1970 California began what has been called "the divorce revolution" by enacting the first completely no-fault divorce law in the Western world. The term *no fault* indicated that no grounds needed to be established to allow legal dissolution of the union. Since then, every state has enacted some form of no-fault divorce, which allows divorce on the unilateral demand of just one party to the marriage. The evidence suggests that unilateral divorce law results in significantly lower alimony and child support payments to women who have lost the bargaining leverage of the power to block or at least to delay the divorce.

Even before the no-fault revolution, only a minority of divorced women received alimony. In recent years the trend is toward division of the marital property at the time of divorce, rather than the award of continuing support payments in the form of alimony.

Custody rights remain the other significant issue in divorce disputes. In England and early America, fathers possessed a paramount claim to the guardianship and custody of their children during marriage and in the event of divorce. In nineteenth-century America, courts modified this doctrine by asserting their right to select a different guardian in the best interests of the child. Using the doctrine of *parens patriae* and the procedure of the writ of habeas corpus, courts claimed the right to make custodial dispensations. Nineteenth-century activists considered maternal custody rights a central issue of the women's rights movement. Around mid-century, state legislatures codified the judicial inroads on paternal power, and the courts thereafter defined the limits of maternal rights.

By 1860 New Jersey codified the "tender years" doctrine, which decreed that infants, children below puberty, and youngsters afflicted with health ailments be placed in a mother's care unless she was unworthy. Rather than formally granting women equal custody and guardianship rights, by 1900 most statutes instead vested judges with the discretion to place children.

Modern statutes typically direct placement based on the sex-neutral standard of the best interests of the child. Although the tender-years maternal preference may retain some customary force, courts have ruled that it constitutes prohibited sex-discrimination. Statutes in a number of states now incorporate a preference for joint custody. Some observers argue that a "primary caretaker" presumption, adopted in West Virginia in 1981, offers the best hope of promoting stability for children and ensuring that a custody challenge will not be used as a bargaining chip to reduce support payments and property settlements.

—*Laura Oren*

See Also:

Equity Courts, Marriage

References:

Blake, Nelson Manfred. *The Road to Reno: A History of Divorce in the United States.* Westport, Conn.: Greenwood, 1962.

Cott, Nancy. "Divorce and the Changing Status of Women in Eighteenth-Century America." *William and Mary Quarterly* 33 (October 1976): 587–614.

Friedman, Lawrence M. *A History of American Law.* New York: Touchstone, 1973.

Grossberg, Michael. "Who Gets the Child? Custody, Guardianship, and the Rise of a Judicial Patriarchy in Nineteenth-Century America." *Feminist Studies* 9 (1983): 235–60.

Howard, George E. *A History of Matrimonial Institutions.* Chicago: University of Chicago Press, 1904.

O'Neill, William L. *Divorce in the Progressive Era.* New Haven: Yale University Press, 1967.

Salmon, Marylynn. *Women and the Law of Property in Early America.* Chapel Hill: University of North Carolina Press, 1986.

Weitzman, Lenore J. *The Divorce Revolution: The Unexpected Social and Economic Consequences for Women and Children in America.* New York: Free Press, 1985.

Wright, Carroll D., ed. *A Report of Marriage and Divorce in the United States, 1867–1886.* Washington, D.C.: U.S. Government Printing Office, 1889.

DIX, DOROTHEA (1802–87), humanitarian and reformer, crusaded for improved treatment of the mentally ill. Born in Hampden on the Maine frontier, she started a dame school for young girls in Boston in 1821 and authored a children's textbook, *Conversations on Common Things,* published in 1824.

How she became interested in the plight of the unbalanced is unclear, although she was aware of the reforms of Philippe Pinel of Paris and Henry Tuke of York, England. In 1841 she surveyed prison and jail conditions throughout Massachusetts, recording her observations of chained inmates living amid squalor. Dix sought the segregation of the insane and the idiotic from criminals. With the aid of Horace Mann and Charles Sumner, in January 1843 she petitioned the state legislature, which then authorized the construction of additional buildings at the state hospital at Worcester. Dix then focused on conditions in other states, including New Jersey and Rhode Island, where she persuaded state legislatures to fund the establishment of mental hospitals.

In June 1848 she petitioned Congress for passage of a land grant bill. The proceeds from the sale of five million acres of public land were to benefit the indigent insane, but Congress deferred the bill and allowed it to die. Dix tried again with a proposal to sell 12.5 million acres of public land, the proceeds from which would go to the indigent insane and the deaf, dumb, and blind. The House and Senate passed a modified version of her proposal, but it was vetoed by President Franklin Pierce in March 1854.

Dix sailed to Liverpool, England, the following September and continued her crusade, securing a royal investigation of asylums in Scotland. In January 1856 she met with Pope Pius IX, who made an unannounced visit to an asylum she had reported to him. Dix then toured hospitals and prisons throughout Europe, from Constantinople to Sweden, and returned to the United States in September 1856.

After serving in the Civil War as superintendent of female nurses, she resumed her investigation of jails, poor houses, and mental institutions throughout the United States in 1867. She spent the next fifteen years surveying hospital conditions and engaging in charitable activities. On her last major tour in 1881, she visited mental hospitals in Virginia, North Carolina, Georgia, and Florida. Dix is buried in Mount Auburn Cemetery near Boston.

—Casey Edward Greene

See Also:

Nursing, Prison Reform

References:

Marshall, Helen E. *Dorothea Dix: Forgotten Samaritan.* Chapel Hill: University of North Carolina Press, 1937; rpt. New York: Russell & Russell, 1967.

Snyder, Charles M. *The Lady and the President: The Letters of Dorothea Dix and Millard Fillmore.* Lexington: University Press of Kentucky, 1975.

DOMESTIC FEMINISM is a term applied by contemporary historians to refer to the conservative philosophy and activities of nineteenth-century middle-class advocates of improving women's education and employment opportunities without challenging the concept of a discreet Woman's Sphere to which women were to be confined. This extension of autonomy for women within the family accompanied the gradual enlargement of the social territory assigned to the domestic sphere. The proponents of domestic feminism accepted patriarchy and its nineteenth-century gender system as natural, God-given, and appropriate, yet worked within Woman's Sphere to expand its limits to include women's conditional entry into the Public Sphere on the basis of necessity and propriety.

Utilizing a dynamic definition of the Cult of True Womanhood to justify improvements in women's social and economic conditions, antebellum domestic feminists urged and supported the creation of institutions of education to insure women's proper preparation for their domestic maternal duty to rear and teach children. Liberally defining Woman's Work enabled the domestic feminists to designate emerging industrial and clerical occupations of the mid-nineteenth century as extensions of Woman's Sphere, thus paving the way for women's entry into paid employments beyond sewing, teaching, and writing as consistent with True Womanhood. Eschewing an emphasis on women's legal and political rights, domestic feminists did support reforms in married women's property rights as appropriate protections of Woman's Sphere.

After the Civil War, domestic feminism continued to expand Woman's Sphere. Consolidating previous gains that now provided basic educational, employment, and civic opportunity for True Women, domestic feminism harnessed the restless energy of a generation of educated young women by focusing their attention on their womanly duty to others. The women's club movement provided a respectable forum for married women to gather, develop their intellectual interests, and address community needs for improvement in late Victorian industrial and urban society. Applying their domestic values of Woman's Sphere, the generation of recently college-graduated women, whose social housekeeping developed into the profession of social work, contributed to the achievements of the Progressive era.

Although frequently the goals of domestic feminists paralleled those of contemporary feminists, they disavowed any support or approval of attempts to achieve equality of the sexes as degrading to woman's spiritual and moral superiority over men. Thus domestic feminism was an expedient for improving women's conditions in a piecemeal fashion only because it denied woman's right to self-definition of herself or of her goals. The legacy of domestic feminism into the twentieth century was not addressed until after World War II. In the 1960s the modern women's movement challenged the gender system that relegated women to "separate but equal" status within the human race.

—*Angela Howard Zophy*

See Also:

Cult of True Womanhood, Married Women's Property Acts

References:

Clinton, Catherine. *The Other Civil War: American Woman in the Nineteenth Century.* New York: Hill and Wang, 1984.

Norton, Mary Beth. "The Paradox of 'Woman's Sphere.'" In *Women of America: A History,* edited by Carol Ruth Berkin and Mary Beth Norton. Dallas, Tex.: Houghton Mifflin, 1979, pp. 139–49.

Riley, Glenda. *Inventing the American Woman: A Perspective on Women's History.* Arlington Heights, Ill.: Harlan Davidson, 1986.

Smith, Daniel Scott. "Family Limitation, Social Control, and Domestic Feminism in Victorian America." In *A Heritage of Her Own: Toward a New Social History of American Women,* edited by Nancy F. Cott and Elizabeth H. Pleck. New York: Touchstone/Simon & Schuster, 1979, pp. 222–45.

DOMESTIC LITERATURE IN THE UNITED STATES (1822–c.1870) was predominantly fiction (but included poetry and the personal essay) that focused on the domestic setting and valorized woman's role in the home and community.

Personal essays on domestic subjects were often the first publications of novice women writers. In a variety of new-writer contests for essays, poems, and stories, regional and national magazines with predominantly women subscribers encouraged contributions focused on domestic life. Publishers promoted women writers in terms of their domestic roles—e.g., Harriet Beecher Stowe's introduction in the role of young wife and mother. Poets, essayists, and novelists published in magazines as well as books, and many magazines' fortunes depended upon the serialization of popular domestic novels.

Domestic literature frequently is equated with the popular domestic novel, a genre dating from the 1820s with Catharine Maria Sedgwick's publication of *A New England Tale* (1822), *Redwood* (1824), and *Hope Leslie* (1827). From Sedgwick's first rocketing sales, domestic novelists individually and collectively were among the best-selling American novelists of their period—dominating popular American fiction in the 1850s and 1860s. The list of domestic novelists and novels is long. Among the most prolific authors and popular works were Augusta Jane Evans, *Beulah* (1859), *St. Elmo* (1867); Mrs. E.D.E.N. Southworth, *Retribution* (1849), *The Hidden Hand* (1859; 1889); Harriet Beecher Stowe, *The Minister's Wooing* (1859), *My Wife and I* (1871); Susan Warner, *The Wide, Wide World* (1851), *Queechy* (1852); and Sara Payson Willis Parton (Fanny Fern), *Ruth Hall* (1855).

Domestic novelists traditionally have been seen as anomalies: public, professional, breadwinning women who wrote of private, domestic, dependent lives. But while dependent domesticity is often the starting point and conclusion of these novels, most plots feature significant episodes of independent and even professional roles. A comfortable home, domestic life based on love between equal partners, happy children, and a stable community of strong Christian values are ultimate goals, but being dependent on others' health, wealth, and good will is shown to be a risky means of gaining or continuing such values.

As many of the authors stepped out of strictly domestic roles and supported themselves and their families, so in the novels the positive values of home and hearth were most often secured by those who deserved them and worked for them. Rather than promoting dependency or self-sacrifice, the novels supported determination, independence, and enlargement of the traditional "domestic sphere."

Though positive valuing of woman's domestic sphere has defined the genre, the plots of domestic novels often featured young women redefining the scope of domesticity. While domestic essays promoted scientific homemaking and domestic economy, the novels associated domestic restrictions and drudgery with bleak, unattractive, or even vile characters—not with the successful protagonists whose strengths were in values and imagination, not housekeeping.

Rather than endorsing limited cultural and domestic roles for women, the novels showed characters overcoming their own socialization and the restrictions of a narrow world view to achieve independence, vision, and accomplishment for themselves—as well as a satisfying domestic life. Feminist scholars' close readings of individual texts catalog rebellion against restriction and authority, self-assertion, independent worth, and professional competence, along with more traditional values of influence from the domestic sphere. While both conformity and rebellion vary between works and throughout the period, most scholars agree that by the late 1860s the genre had run its course and that the later works are more conservative than their predecessors.

Traditional American literary history, which uses a dichotomy between popular and high culture, dismissed domestic authors and texts as simplistic and conformist, mindless upholders of traditional social values, religion, and morality. While this view lost favor in the 1950s, it continues to reappear, most recently in Ann Douglas's *The Feminization of American Culture.* Feminist literary critics and historians, however, have firmly established the richness and conflict in these texts and in their authors' lives—as well as confirming the works' significance as historical sources in American women's history.

—Carol Klimick Cyganowski

See Also:

Domestic Feminism; Feminist Literary Criticism; Stowe, Harriet Beecher

References:

Baym, Nina. *Woman's Fiction: A Guide to Novels by and About Women in America, 1820–1870.* Ithaca, N.Y.: Cornell University Press, 1978.

Douglas, Ann. *The Feminization of American Culture.* New York: Knopf, 1977.

Garrison, Dee. "Immoral Fiction in the Late Victorian Library." *American Quarterly* 28 (Spring 1976): 71–89.

Kelley, Mary. *Private Woman, Public Stage: Literary Domesticity in Nineteenth-Century America.* New York: Oxford University Press, 1984.

Papashvily, Helen Waite. *All the Happy Endings: A Study of the Domestic Novel in America, the Women Who Wrote It, the Women Who Read It, in the Nineteenth Century.* New York: Harper, 1956.

THE DOMESTIC MANNERS OF THE AMERICANS (1832) by Frances Milton Trollope (1779–1863) was a satire of the American people and their institutions based on Trollope's controversial journal from her travels in the United States from 1827 to 1831. Having been faced with her family's bankruptcy, the fifty-three-year-old British author journeyed to America on November 4, 1827, with three of her five children, two domestics, and an artist friend. Hoping for personal enrichment as well as financial gain, she first visited the experimental community of Frances Wright in Nashoba, Tennessee, and then undertook a series of imaginative, though unsuccessful, business ventures in Cincinnati. Before returning to England in July 1831, she toured selected cities of the East Coast, and from notes taken during her stay in America developed the manuscript that launched her literary career.

The Domestic Manners focused on what Mrs. Trollope perceived to be a serious fault of

American society: the inferior social position of American women. Much popular and critical response to this work in America and abroad ensured a wide audience for Mrs. Trollope's subsequent work, which consisted of five more journals describing various European countries, two long narrative poems, several antievangelical verse dramas, and thirty-four novels, four of which use American characters and settings. In most of her work, Frances Trollope championed the strong, independent woman for whom marriage was only one career option, and she also addressed problems of social concern: the British Poor Laws, which regulated welfare and relief; English factory working conditions; the plight of unwed mothers and orphans; and particularly the rights and privileges of women. Her second American novel, *The Life and Adventures of Jonathan Jefferson Whitlaw; or, Scenes on the Mississippi* (1836), denounced the cruelties of the American slave system.

Mrs. Trollope retired in May 1850 to the family villa in Florence, Italy, and published her last novel in 1856. Her amazing productivity as well as her success in two popular Victorian genres, the travel journal and the novel, are generally considered to have inspired the work of her more famous son, Anthony Trollope.

—*Marilyn Demarest Button*

See Also:

Nashoba

References:

Bethke, Frederick John. *Three Victorian Travel Writers: A Bibliography of Criticism*. Boston: G. K. Hall, 1977.

Button, Marilyn D. "American Women in the Works of Frances Milton Trollope and Anthony Trollope." Diss. University of Delaware, 1985.

Heineman, Helen. *Frances Trollope*. Boston: Twayne, 1984.

———. *Mrs. Trollope: The Triumphant Feminine in the Nineteenth Century*. Athens: Ohio University Press, 1979.

Trollope, Frances Milton. *Domestic Manners of the Americans*. London: Whittaker, Treacher, 1932; rpt. Donald A. Smalley, ed. New York: Knopf, 1949.

———. *The Life and Adventures of Jonathan Jefferson Whitlaw; or, Scenes on the Mississippi*. London: Bentley, 1836.

DOMESTIC SERVICE, considered a traditional "woman's job," historically has offered the working class one of the earliest paid employments for women. Though they presented a limited and excessively exploitative situation, domestic service positions for young women were available and required no special training nor job skill. Domestic service in England and Europe has had the status of a hierarchical profession of lifetime service.

In British North America during the colonial period, possibly half of the female colonists were unmarried women between eighteen and twenty-five years old who secured their passage to the New World as indentured servants under a seven-year contract. Especially in the southern colonies, these unmarried women comprised a pool of future wives for the men, who were the majority of colonists, since almost all indentured women married after their contract term expired. In addition to their passage, female indentured servants were to receive a small wage and clothing at the termination of their contract, which was often extended for violations. Chief among the severely punished violations were running away and pregnancy, for indentured women were barred from marriage while under contract. All colonial women performed crucial household chores in addition to the agricultural work required to establish a farm or plantation. As settlement progressed, the labor of indentured women increasingly centered upon the household functions of domestic service. Gradually, as the slavery codes evolved, slave women were denied both the legal protection of the indentured status and its limited term of servitude.

In the United States after the eighteenth century, domestic service attracted women who had become displaced from the domestic sphere due either to industrialization and urbanization or to immigration. Throughout the nineteenth and into the early twentieth century, room and board were included in the domestic service situation; for young single women, being able to live in the homes of their employers was supposed to compensate for the meager wage, interminable hours of drudgery, and absence of privacy that characterized life in domestic service. In the United States, both single and married black and immigrant women had few other employment options during the nineteeth century, while urban middle-class households required and could still afford at least one servant. Black and immigrant Irish women constituted a significant proportion of domestic servants, the number of which doubled between the Civil War and the turn of the century. Despite the romantic myth of the housemaid's social mobility through exposure to the middle-class mores, which would enable her eventually to marry well, domestic service more often brought seduction and abandonment, and a decline into prostitution.

By the twentieth century, the increase in opportunities for women's employment offered positions with more status, mobility, and autonomy for women workers, while the disadvantages of domestic service remained relatively constant. Consequently, the number of willing domestic workers dwindled as advanced technology in household appliances, the smaller urban household, and the more limited middle-class income all combined to render domestic servants, especially those "living in," a luxury for the wealthy. Limited job options persisted for disadvantaged and unskilled black women in the North and South, who continued to supply domestic service for urban and suburban middle-class households from the 1920s through the 1960s. The dramatic increase in married women's participation in the paid labor force in the 1970s and 1980s created among middle-class "working wives" an urgent demand for domestic service, which was increasingly supplied by first- and second-generation immigrants from Mexico and Central America. In the 1970s some women entrepreneurs established professional home-cleaning services, but few of these businesses survived because of the general reluctance to pay women adequately for services in the marketplace that are obligatory but unremunerated for women in their family and households.

Domestic service as a woman's job most clearly represents the origin and the persistence of wage discrimination against women within the gender system, due to its expectation that women will provide lifetime unpaid household service to their families. The wages and the status of domestic service have continued to be low and therefore to attract only unskilled women workers for whom few job alternatives exist.

—Angela Howard Zophy

See Also:

Afro-American Domestic Workers, Housework, Sex-Gender System, Women's Work—Nineteenth Century

References:

Berch, Bettina. *Endless Day: The Political Economy of Women and Work.* New York: Harcourt Brace Jovanovich, 1982.

Carr, Lois Green, and Lorena S. Walsh. "The Planter's Wife: The Experience of White Women in Seventeenth-Century Maryland." In *The Private Side of American History: Readings in Everyday Life,* edited by Gary B. Nash. Vol. I, 3d ed. New York: Harcourt Brace Jovanovich, 1975, 1983, pp. 67–94.

Daniel, Robert L. *American Women in the Twentieth Century: The Festival of Life.* San Diego: Harcourt Brace Jovanovich, 1987.

Hellerstein, Erna Olafson, Leslie Parker Hume, and Karen M. Offen, eds. *Victorian Women: A Documentary Account of Women's Lives in Nineteenth-Century England, France, and the United States.* Stanford, Calif.: Stanford University Press, 1981.

Howe, Louise Kapp. *Pink Collar Workers: Inside the World of Women's Work.* New York: Putnam, 1977.

Lerner, Gerda. *The Female Experience: An American Documentary.* Indianapolis: Bobbs-Merrill, 1977.

Riley, Glenda. *Inventing the American Woman: A Perspective on Women's History.* Arlington Heights, Ill.: Harlan Davidson, 1987.

DOOLITTLE, HILDA (1886–1961), commonly known as H.D., was the catalyst for the Imagist movement in American poetry. Her short, free-verse Imagist poems, first published in *Poetry* in 1916 under the pseudonym "H.D., Imagiste," were modeled on fragments of classical Greek verse and derived their power from a juxtaposition of images rather than from words alone. Concerned mainly with natural images, they embodied the qualities of Imagism that Ezra Pound later identified as direct treatment of the subject, concise diction, and musical rather than strictly metrical rhythms.

H.D.'s artistry and her search for a feminine and artistic identity result from a rich but unconventional life. Especially important to H.D. were the Moravian traditions of her mother's family, inspiring her attraction to images, myth, the occult, numerology, tarot, and psychoanalysis. Other events that figured prominently in her life and work were her temporary engagement but lifelong attachment to Ezra Pound, her brief marriage to the English poet Richard Aldington, her sustained companionship with Winifred Ellerman (commonly known as Bryher), several breakdowns, and psychoanalysis by Sigmund Freud.

While H.D. is primarily known for the short, controlled, and intense Imagistic poems that she wrote at the beginning of her career, critics have rediscovered the long poetic narratives and autobiographical novels she devoted the rest of her life to writing, works informed by her personal experiences. In them H.D. had a dual purpose—to bring meaning to a world torn apart by two world wars and to find her feminine and artistic identity in a masculine culture. She accomplishes this by intertwining layers of historical and personal experience with myths and legends and images of war from Trojan times to the present to create a timeless, spiritual structure that is more manageable and more meaningful to her than the chaotic present. Especially noteworthy among her longer works are the poetic trilogy *The Walls Do Not Fall* (1944), *Tribute to Angels* (1945), and *The Flowering of the Rod* (1946), as well as *Helen in Egypt* (1961) and the prose *HERmione* (1981). Many notes and full-length works remain unpublished.

—*Kenneth E. Gadomski*

References:

DuPlessis, Rachel Blau. *H. D.: The Career of That Struggle*. Brighton, England: Harvester, 1986.

Friedman, Susan Stanford. *Psyche Reborn: The Emergence of H. D.* Bloomington: Indiana University Press, 1981.

King, Michael, ed. *H.D.: Woman and Poet*. Orono, Me.: National Poetry Foundation, 1986.

DOUGLAS, HELEN MARY (GAHAGAN) (1900–80) enjoyed auspicious success in three separate careers during her lifetime. At twenty-two she was a Broadway star. In 1931 she married Melvyn Douglas, her leading man in *Tonight or Never*. Their fifty-year marriage produced two children. She gave up the stage at the height of her success to sing opera, touring successfully in Europe before the anti-Semitism she witnessed in Germany and Austria convinced her to cancel her remaining contracts. When her husband's film career took them to California, both the Douglases became involved in such local issues as the mistreatment of the migrant population and the misuse of California's resources.

In 1940 Douglas became Democratic National Committeewoman, and in 1944 she was elected to Congress from California's fourteenth district. Re-elected in 1946 and 1948, she served ably on the Foreign Affairs Committee and was appointed as alternate to the United Nations General Assembly by President Truman. An advocate of arms control and international control of nuclear energy, she fought any legislation—such as the House Un-American Activities Committee and the McCarran-Woods acts, which sought restrictions on communists and immigrants—that endangered civil liberties. Her liberal ideals brought her the respect and friendship of Eleanor Roosevelt, Walter Reuther, Henry Wallace, and William O. Douglas.

In 1950 Douglas became a candidate for the Senate, campaigning on the same liberal issues she had always espoused. Her Democratic opponent, Manchester Boddy, and later her Republican opponent, Richard Nixon, used smear tactics, equating liberalism with communism. The Nixon forces printed

550,000 "pink sheets" that claimed Douglas' congressional voting record was identical to the Communist party line. The onset of the Korean War probably doomed her campaign, which was already plagued by the opposition of wealthy oil, lumbering, and agricultural groups whose power she sought to limit. The Catholic Church and the major California newspapers also worked to foil her campaign.

After her defeat, Douglas moved back to the East Coast and retired from politics, though she continued to support liberal causes and candidates. She traveled to South America, Russia, and Israel and lectured about the conditions she found there. She maintained a dignified silence regarding the unfounded accusations raised in the 1950 Senate race. Even after the revelations of Watergate, she expressed only sorrow.

Helen Gahagan Douglas died of cancer June 28, 1980, at the age of seventy-nine.

—Tamerin Mitchell Hayward

See Also:

Democratic Party, Politics

References:

Helen Gahagan Douglas Project. [Women in Politics Oral History Project] The Bancroft Library, The University of California-Berkeley, 1981–82.

Douglas, Helen Gahagan. *A Full Life.* Garden City, N.Y.: Doubleday, 1982.

O'Connor, Colleen Marie. "Through the Valley of Darkness: Helen Gahagan Douglas' Congressional Years." Diss. University of California-San Diego, 1982.

Scobie, Ingrid Winther "Helen Gahagan Douglas and her 1950 Senate Race With Richard M. Nixon," *Southern California Historical Quarterly*, LVIII, No. 1 (Spring 1976), pp. 113–26.

DOWER. As in England, common law in America provided that a man had to leave his wife a dower, or a life interest in one-third of his real estate and one-third of his personal property. The purpose of dower was to prevent the widow from becoming a public charge. If the man did not provide for his wife in his will, the widow could contest the will in court. If the man died without leaving a will, the court would see that she received her "thirds." Life interest in part of an estate meant she could not sell it nor significantly change it because it had to be passed on to future heirs, usually her children, at her death. Some wills stipulated that if a woman remarried, she would lose the accommodations her husband had provided for her.

Some colonies were liberal in the provision for dower. A study of seventeenth-century Maryland shows that one-fifth of the men who had children left all their wealth to their wives, trusting the women to see that the children received fair portions. Only a few of the Maryland men indicated that the estates were only for use during their wives' widowhood or until children came of age. When men did not leave a life estate, they often gave land outright, or more than a dower third of their movable property.

After the Revolution, courts and legislatures increasingly encroached on the sacred "widow's thirds." A North Carolina statute included revision of dower rights in the general statute that revised the system of descents. In Pennsylvania dower was not guaranteed to women when husbands died in debt. Eventually, with the passage of married women's property acts in the mid-nineteenth century, women gained significant control of their property, including inheritances.

—Barbara E. Lacey

See Also:

Common Law, Marriage, Married Women's Property Acts

References:

Carr, Lois Green, and Lorena S. Walsh. "The Planter's Wife: The Experience of White Women in Seventeenth-Century Maryland." *William and Mary Quarterly*, 3d ser., 34 (October 1977): 542–71.

Salmon, Marylynn. "Equality or Submersion? Feme Covert Status in Early Pennsylvania." In *Women of America: A History*, edited by Carol Ruth Berkin and Mary Beth Norton. Boston: Houghton Mifflin, 1979, pp. 91–113.

———. "Women and Property in South Carolina: The Evidence from Marriage

Settlements, 1730-1830." *William and Mary Quarterly*, 3d ser., 39 (October 1982): 655–85.

DRAPER, MARGARET GREEN (1727–1807) published the *Massachusetts Gazette and Boston News-Letter* from 1754 to February 1776 and was one of the most successful American female printers in the eighteenth century.

Prior to 1800 American women seldom worked outside the home. Their primary roles were as housewives and mothers. Some women, however, found themselves forced to work in the public arena in order to survive. Women functioned as dressmakers, taverners, and shopkeepers. Several women also published newspapers. In fact, seventeen women printed newspapers in the years prior to the adoption of the Constitution. Several of the women entered the printing field in order to help relatives, but most of them were forced into a new profession because of the death of a husband. Most of them left the business as soon as a son or other male relative became old enough to take charge. Female entrance into the printing fraternity was primarily a matter of necessity, and even the women who succeeded as printers did not remain in the business for more than a year or so.

Draper's publishing career mirrored the general stereotype. The granddaughter of one printer and the wife of another, she spent most of her life in and around the publishing business. Born in 1727, she married Richard Draper in 1750, and following the death of her husband twenty-four years later, she continued to publish the paper with her husband's partner John Boyle. The partnership ended in late 1774, primarily because Boyle supported the American position in the conflict with Great Britain, while Draper was a staunch Loyalist and used her paper to give aid to the British cause. After Boyle's departure, she managed the paper alone for several months. In October 1775 she formed a partnership with John Howe, and they continued to publish until the British evacuated Boston in March 1776. Expecting ill-treatment from the Americans, Draper left with the British army, going first to Halifax, Nova Scotia, and then on to England. The Americans seized her property in Boston in 1783, but the British government rewarded her for her loyalty by granting her a lifetime pension. She died in London early in 1807.

Margaret Draper's strong loyalty to Britain guided her throughout her brief, successful printing career. Her staunch refusal to support the more popular patriot cause in the Revolution, even in the face of severe public ridicule and criticism, indicates her strength of character. Refusing to take the easy route to end her troubles, she took a public stand for what she believed in. She just happened to be on the losing side.

—*Carol Sue Humphrey*

See Also:
Business, Journalism

References:

Brigham, Clarence S. "Women Newspaper Publishers." In *Journals and Journeymen: A Contribution to the History of Early American Newspapers*. Philadelphia: University of Pennsylvania Press, 1950, pp. 71–79.
Kiessel, William C. "The Green Family: A Dynasty of Printers." *New England Genealogical Register* 104 (April 1950): 81–93.
Oldham, Ellen M. "Early Women Printers of America: Margaret Draper, The Loyalist." *The Boston Public Library Quarterly* 10 (July 1958): 141–46.

DREIER, KATHERINE SOPHIE (1877–1952), artist, collector, and founder of the Société Anonyme, devoted herself to the cause of modern art. Born in Brooklyn, New York, the youngest of five children, Dreier had a private art tutor at age twelve. From 1895 to 1897 she studied at the Brooklyn Art School. During these formative years, her German parents also instilled in her a commitment to social reform, as she witnessed them dedicating their lives to the immigrant families of Brooklyn. In 1898, at the age of twenty-one, Dreier became treasurer of the German Home for Recreation for Women and Children founded by her mother. Five years later she served as director for the Manhattan Trade

School for Girls and also established and became president of the Little Italy Neighborhood Association in South Brooklyn.

Dreier and her sisters actively campaigned for women's rights and labor laws protecting women. In 1911 she served as a delegate to the Sixth Convention of the International Woman's Suffrage Alliance in Stockholm and later directed the German American Committee of the Woman Suffrage party in New York City.

While she pursued social reforms, Dreier also continued to study art at the Pratt Institute in 1900. Two years later, she and her sister Dorothea traveled to Europe and studied traditional art. Walter Shirlaw, whose liberal teachings introduced Dreier to the theories of the modernists, took her as a private pupil when she returned to New York. During later trips to study in Europe, Dreier met Ralph Collin in Paris, Gustav Britsch in Munich, and the avant-garde artists at the home of Gertrude and Leo Stein. She held her first exhibition in London at the Doré Galleries, with later exhibitions in Frankfurt, Leipzig, Dresden, and Munich. In 1913 Americans witnessed Dreier's work for the first time at the Armory Show, and solo shows in New York and Boston followed.

Dreier founded the Cooperative Mural Workshops, an art school and workshop devoted to the notion of artistic freedom, and subsequently helped organize the Society of Independent Artists in 1916. Concentrating on modern art, she contacted New York's avant-garde community and met artist Marcel Duchamp. Dreier and Duchamp, along with surrealist artist Man Ray, produced America's first museum of modern art, the Société Anonyme, in 1920. Located in a gallery at 19 East Forty-Seventh Street in New York, the Société Anonyme introduced more than seventy important modern artists, including Kandisky, Klee, and Mondrian, for the first time to the American public. When Duchamp left the United States for France, Dreier took sole responsibility for the Société Anonyme's activities. She lectured, sponsored symposiums, and wrote publications to educate the American public on modern art. Traveling exhibits organized by the Société Anonyme gave those outside the New York community the opportunity to view the new modern art. With the stock market crash of 1929, Dreier could no longer fund the Société, and she moved to Connecticut and began to paint again.

Dreier continued as a nonobjective painter, utilizing organic shapes, geometric forms, and muted colors with a hint of force. The Museum of Modern Art included Dreier's work in its exhibitions "Fantastic Art, Dada, Surrealism" (1936) and "Classic and Romantic Traditions in Abstract Painting" (1939). In 1941 Dreier and Duchamp donated the Société Anonyme's collection of 616 works of art to Yale University. She co-authored the catalog of the collection with Yale professor George Heard Hamilton. Her legacy for modern art continued even after her death in 1952. Katherine Dreier left over two hundred works of art for the public to view, learn from, and enjoy at Yale University, the Museum of Modern Art, the Guggenheim Museum, the Phillips Collection, and the American University.

—Cynthia Lynn Gould

See Also:

Art, Suffrage

References:

Bohan, Ruth L. *The Société Anonyme's Brooklyn Exhibition: Katherine Dreier and Modernism in America.* Ann Arbor, Mich.: UMI Research Press, 1980.

Rubinstein, Charlotte Streifer. *American Women Artists from Early Indian Times to the Present.* Boston, Mass.: G. K. Hall, 1982.

Russell, John. "At Yale, One Publication Inspires Two Fresh Shows." *New York Times* (May 27, 1984): H 27.

The Société Anonyme and the Dreier Bequest at Yale University: A Catalogue Raisonné. New Haven: Yale University Press, 1984.

Tufts, Dr. Eleanor. *American Women Artists 1830–1930.* Washington, D.C.: The National Museum of Women in the Arts, 1987.

DUNCAN, ISADORA (1878–1927), dancer, revolutionist, and defender of the poetic spirit, is considered one of the most important forerunners of modern dance. A free spirit whose legendary exploits have sometimes overshadowed her artistic achievements, Duncan viewed dance as a lever of human emancipation. She was a liberating influence on costume, women's moral standards, and education, invoking a widespread acceptance of the dance as physically healthy and intellectually respectable. An early champion of the struggle for women's rights, she maintained, "If my art is symbolic of any one thing, it is symbolic of the freedom of woman and her emancipation." An enduring influence on twentieth-century culture, she had a natural and expressive approach to the dance, which lifted it from the realm of entertainment to that of art.

Born in San Francisco, Duncan and her siblings were raised in poverty by their mother, who nevertheless instilled in her children a great and abiding love for the arts. In addition to developing a tremendous sensitivity to music, Duncan was profoundly moved by nature. Using nature as her teacher, she approached the dance with a naturalness and freedom of expression characterized by an emotional intensity previously unknown to the world of dance.

Beginning her career first as a showgirl in Chicago then as a salon dancer in New York, Duncan soon left the United States for London, then Paris, where she toured with a dance company organized by Loie Fuller. She was profoundly influenced by Greek civilization and culture, and her costumes, often classical tunics, further reflected the influence this civilization had upon her. For Duncan, the real purpose of dance was to express the deepest concerns of humanity. Having a natural sympathy for those attempting to overthrow established order, she composed dances using political and social themes of the day. The music to one of her most successful dances, *La Marseillaise* (1915), was to become the French national anthem, and her dance *Marche Slave* (1917) symbolized the Russian peasants' struggle for freedom.

Although militantly opposed to schools, systems, and doctrine of any kind, Duncan founded schools of the dance in Germany, France, and Russia. Rather than developing a standardized system of movement, however, she attempted to inspire in her students a receptivity to the natural impulse she herself felt in her dance: an impulse she believed originated in the solar plexus, the soul's habitat. Duncan was interested in discovering a basic dance, biological in origin and spiritual in impulse, one in which she would find the universal impulse toward movement.

Duncan's private life was as unconventional as her professional career. She bore three children out of wedlock—one died shortly after birth and two others drowned in a tragic car accident. Although violently opposed to the institution of marriage, in 1922 she married Russian poet Sergei Essenin, a man twenty years her junior, and became a Soviet citizen. In 1924 her husband committed suicide, and in 1927 she herself was killed in a tragic accident when her scarf became entangled in the rear spokes of an automobile wheel and strangled her.

For Isadora Duncan, dance was synonymous with life: "To dance is to live." Intensely personal in nature, her art reflected passion, integrity, and vision that has been impossible to recapture. She left a legacy of beauty and truth as expressed in her art, and her spirit continues to influence the dance in America today.

—Cecelia A. Albert

References:

Duncan, Isadora. *The Art of the Dance.* 1928; rpt. New York: Theatre Arts Books, 1969.

———. *Isadora Speaks.* Edited, with an introduction by Franklin Rosemont. San Francisco: City Lights Books, 1981.

———. *My Life.* New York: Horace Liveright, 1927.

Macdougall, Allan Ross. *Isadora: A Revolutionary in Art and Love.* Edinburgh: Thomas Nelson and Sons, 1960.

Magriel, Paul, ed. *Isadora Duncan.* New York: Holt, 1947.

Terry, Walter. *Isadora Duncan: Her Life, Her Art, Her Legacy.* New York: Dodd, Mead, 1963, 1984.

DUNIWAY, ABIGAIL JANE SCOTT (1834–1915), a suffrage leader in the Northwest, was born the second daughter in Ann and John Scott's family of nine on a farm outside Groveland, Illinois. Seventeen-year-old Duniway lost her mother to cholera on the trek to Oregon in 1852. After teaching one year near Eola, Oregon, she married Benjamin C. Duniway and returned, as in earlier years, to the extreme drudgery of the farm. In 1857 the Duniways moved to a new farm near Lafayette, but in 1862 they lost this farm because her husband endorsed notes for a friend against Duniway's wishes. Following their move to town, her husband was permanently disabled, and she supported her family by running a boarding school. In 1866 she moved to Albany, where she taught in a private school for a year and operated her own millinery and notions shop for five years. It was during this period that Duniway became aware of the various injustices, facilitated by laws, that all women had to endure. It was her invalid husband who encouraged her to work for suffrage as the best means to change unjust laws.

Thus in 1871 Duniway moved to Portland and, with her five sons and one daughter, established a weekly newspaper, the *New Northwest,* to further the cause of women's rights. Her only experience in publishing prior to this was as the author of the novel, *Captain Gray's Company.* That same year, she managed Susan B. Anthony's speaking tour in the Pacific Northwest and realized her own speaking ability, which she relentlessly pursued to further the suffrage movement. In 1873 Duniway led in founding the Oregon Equal Suffrage Association and was elected its president. During this period she attended Oregon's legislative sessions, presented petitions, lobbied, and at times spoke from the floor. Duniway's tireless work was important in obtaining suffrage rights in Washington Territory in 1883, in Idaho in 1896, and in Oregon in 1912. Although she denounced the policies and methods of the National Woman Suffrage Association as a hindrance, she was its vice president in 1884 and welcomed at its conventions. In recognition of her years of service, she was given major credit for suffrage being achieved in Oregon in 1912. She authored Oregon's suffrage proclamation, signed it along with the governor, and became Oregon's first registered woman voter.

—Dianna Dingess Retzlaff

See Also:

Journalism, Suffrage in the American West

References:

Duniway, Abigail Scott. *Captain Gray's Company.* Portland, Ore.: S. J. McCormick, 1859.

———. *Path Breaking: An Autobiographical History of the Equal Suffrage Movement in Pacific Coast States.* 2d ed. 1914; rpt. New York: Schocken, 1971.

Flexner, Eleanor. *Century of Struggle: The Woman's Rights Movement in the United States.* Cambridge, Mass.: Belknap, 1959, 1975.

DYER, MARY (?–1660), a Quaker martyr, was born in England though no record remains of her early years. With her husband, William Dyer, a milliner and a prominent Puritan, she emigrated to the Massachusetts Bay Colony in 1635, received membership in the Boston church in December of that year, and soon thereafter gained public recognition as a supporter of Anne Hutchinson, leader of the opposition to Puritan orthodoxy. In 1637 Dyer gave birth to a severely malformed stillborn baby, an event that John Winthrop described as divine retribution for her involvement with Hutchinson. Winthrop's chastisement seems to have had little effect on Dyer, however, for when Hutchinson was excommunicated in 1638, Dyer rose and walked out of the church by her side. Later, the Dyers were themselves banished from the Bay Colony and moved to Rhode Island with their five sons.

In 1652 Dyer returned to England, where, during her five-year stay, she became an adherent of the Quaker faith. Returning to the colonies in 1657, she encountered new laws enacted by the Massachusetts General Court against Quakers, and less than two years after her return she became the victim of this legislation. Learning of the imprisonment of two English Friends, William Robinson and Marmaduke Stephenson, Dyer visited the jail and was arrested, banished from the colony, and threatened with death if she returned. One month later, they returned to Massachusetts with several other Quakers to test the law. The group was again imprisoned, and three Friends—Robinson, Stephenson, and Dyer—were selected by the authorities for sentencing. Receiving the death sentence from Governor John Endecott, the three went to the gallows amid a large procession of armed militia. Dyer, arms and legs bound to her body and the noose already around her neck, received a last-minute pardon and was again banished to Rhode Island. In 1660 she returned to Boston, and Endecott again sentenced her to death. This time no pardon was issued, and Mary Dyer was hanged.

The south lawn of the Boston State House is the site of a seven-foot bronze statue of Mary Dyer, sculpted by Sylvia Judson and erected in 1959. The statue depicts a seated woman in seventeenth-century plain-style dress, her head bowed slightly; the inscription reads "Witness for Religious Freedom."

—Cristine M. Levenduski

See Also:

Hutchinson, Anne; Society of Friends

References:

Bacon, Margaret Hope. *Mothers of Feminism: The Story of Quaker Women in America.* San Francisco: Harper & Row, 1986.

Battis, Emery. *Saints and Sectaries: Anne Hutchinson and the Antinomian Controversy in the Massachusetts Bay Colony.* Chapel Hill: University of North Carolina Press, 1962.

Erickson, Kai T. *Wayward Puritans: A Study in the Sociology of Deviance.* New York: Wiley, 1966, pp. 107–36.

EAKINS, SUSAN HANNAH (MACDOWELL) (1851–1938) was a realist painter and photographer whose artistic career was overshadowed by that of her husband, artist Thomas Eakins. Daughter of an engraver, she enrolled in the Pennsylvania Academy of Fine Arts in 1876, where she studied under Thomas Eakins and earned the first Mary Smith Prize for the best picture submitted to the Academy by a woman. She was a strong proponent of study from the nude, a discipline advocated by Thomas Eakins and opened for the first time to women artists in 1877, in large part due to her advocacy.

She was noted for strong draftsmanship and skilled composition and regarded as a skilled artist by a variety of colleagues. Thomas Eakins deemed her the finest female artist of the century, and artist-contemporary William Sartain billed her "an artist of talent." Nonetheless, she virtually abandoned her career in 1884 when she married Thomas Eakins, thereafter dedicating her life to advancing her husband's career. During her married years, she is believed to have maintained a separate studio; however, she rarely did more than sketches, instead serving as agent, hostess, secretary, clerk, and cataloger for her husband. After her husband's death, Eakins was responsible for spearheading a show in Philadelphia on Thomas Eakins and his followers. She also took up painting once again. Nevertheless, little is known today of either the quantity or whereabouts of her works. Experts surmise that many of her works, including many photographs, are erroneously attributed to her husband.

A recently renewed interest in Susan Eakins resulted in the first major exhibition of her work at the Pennsylvania Academy of Fine Arts in 1973, followed four years later by a solo show at North Cross School, Roanoke, Virginia.

—Anne deHayden Neal

See Also:
Art, Photography

References:

Casteras, Susan. "Mr. & Mrs. Eakins: Two Painters, One Reputation." *Harper's Magazine* 255 (October 1977): 69–71.

Rubenstein, Charlotte Streifer. *American Women Artists from Early Indian Times to the Present.* Boston: G. K. Hall, 1982.

Tufts, E. *American Women Artists: 1830–1930.* Washington, D.C.: The National Museum of Women in the Arts, 1987 [exhibition catalog].

EARHART, AMELIA (1897–1937) was an American aviator who, among her many accomplishments, helped establish the need and the justification for commercial transport, as well as women's capability and proficiency as pilots. She could write of her own flight experience in simple, direct terms that, to this day, speak to the lay person and the experienced flier.

Her world records are many. In 1922 she set her first world record—in her own plane, a Kinner Canary—for the highest altitude flown by a woman. However, her most significant achievements were in setting world-class records, such as, in 1935, the first solo flight from Hawaii to the U.S. mainland. Dissatisfied with being only a passenger on her first transatlantic flight in 1928, one year after Lindbergh's historic flight, she flew it alone in 1932. She was also the first woman to fly from the Atlantic to the Pacific and back again, as part of her "vagabond" tour for fun after her first transatlantic trip.

In her varied career, Earhart was aviation editor for *Cosmopolitan* from 1928 to 1930, a post created for her. She was an executive of Ludington Airways from 1930 to 1931, and vice president of National Airways, Inc. Her international acclaim included being made a Chevalier of the French Legion of Honor and receiving a medal from the National Geographic Society in 1932; she served on the Guggenheim Commission on Aeronautical Education, and later as the director of the Institute for Professional Relations for Women at Purdue University. She was a member of the National Aeronautic Association (NAA), the National Woman's party, and the Society of Woman Geographers. In 1932 she was also the first woman to receive the Distinguished Flying Cross.

In her own time she was heralded as the symbol of the "new womanhood"; she supported her fellow fliers, often recognizing achievements that would otherwise have gone unnoticed. She was the first woman elected as an officer in a chapter of NAA, and she was a charter member of the first association of female pilots, the Ninety-Nines, a group in existence to this day.

Born in Kansas at the turn of the century, Earhart took an early interest in mechanical things that led her in a natural progression from cars to planes. She attended Hyde Park High School in Chicago, the Ogontz School for Girls in Rydal, Pennsylvania, and later, Columbia University. While she served in the more traditional duties of volunteer nurse in World War I and settlement house worker at Denison House in Boston, these occupations all seem to fade in the background of her drive and determination to learn to fly, which she did, from an early woman flier, Neta Snook.

She aspired to fly the globe, setting out twice to do so, noting in 1937 that there was "one more flight left in my system." Prophetic or no, the words haunt those who continue to piece together the last years, and the events of those years. In March 1937 she set out with a navigator to attempt the flight westbound, landed in Hawaii, and, due to an accident, was forced to ship the Lockheed Electra back for repairs to the mainland. Her second attempt was eastbound from Florida, passing over Europe, southern Asia, Australia, and the Pacific Islands. She stopped for refueling at Lae, New Guinea, and was lost on July 2, 1937 on her way to the next refueling stop on tiny Howland Island.

A maverick in so many ways, including writing her own marriage ceremony to acknowledge her need to establish her own terms when she married publisher George Putnam, she was determined to make a woman's emerging from the cockpit a regular sight. She leaves us wondering what progress she would have noted for others and what achievements she herself would have made in the fields of civil and commercial aviation by the last quarter of the twentieth century had she lived.

—*Carol Lee Saffioti*

See Also:

Aviation, The Ninety-Nines

References:

Bachus, Jean L. ed. *Letters from Amelia: An Intimate Portrait of Amelia Earhart.* Boston: Beacon, 1982.

Earhart, Amelia. *The Fun of It.* 1932; rpt. Chicago: Academy, 1977.

———. *Twenty Hours Forty Minutes: Our Flight in the Friendship.* New York: Putnam, 1928.

Goerner, Fred. *The Search for Amelia Earhart.* London: Bodley House, 1966.

Hamill, Peter. "The Cult of Leather and Pearls." *Ms. Magazine* 5 (September 1976): 51–54, 86–90.

Putnam, George Palmer. *Soaring Wings.* New York: Harcourt Brace, 1939.

Rich, Doris. *Amelia Earhart: A Biography.* Washington, D.C.: Smithsonian Institution, 1989.

EATING DISORDERS. Three eating disorders reported most frequently in women in the 1980s are anorexia nervosa, bulimia, and obesity. While none of these disorders is new—anorexia was first described a little over a hundred years ago in England and France by Sir William Gull, the outstanding British physician of his time—their rapidly increasing occurrence over the last twenty years has brought them to the attention of doctors, researchers, dieticians, parents, teachers, counselors, and—most important—to the patients themselves. While none of these disorders is communicable, each is fast approaching epidemic levels. In addition, anorexia and bulimia rarely occur in poor families or in underdeveloped countries. In fact, surveys indicate the highest prevalence in daughters of well-to-do, educated, and successful families. Why these disorders are increasing at such an alarming rate and during a time when American women are considered to have more societal options available to them than at any other time in recorded history presents an urgent question to be addressed by women's historians as well as health professionals.

Anorexia nervosa primarily affects young, adolescent, or prepubescent girls; it also occurs in boys but much less frequently. A psycho-sociological disease, it is characterized mainly by severe, self-imposed starvation, resulting in a devastating weight loss. If not properly treated in a timely manner, the effects of acute and/or chronic starvation and its accompanying psychic and biochemical changes may lead to death. Improperly named, "anorexia" means loss of appetite, which anorectics do not experience, although they vehemently deny this. On the contrary, although their food intake is drastically reduced, anorectics are obsessed with the subject of food—its preparation, consumption, et cetera.

Bulimia is characterized by "binge-purge" symptoms of consuming enormous amounts of food followed by "purging" the body through vomiting and/or the use of laxatives. These bouts of overeating—almost always conducted in secret and followed by vomiting—may occur only occasionally or up to several times a day. Approximately 25 percent of anorectics also engage in binging followed by forced vomiting. In addition, both anorectics and bulimics (more so anorectics) become obsessed with exercise, putting themselves through torturous physical regimens at any cost.

Obesity is caused by compulsive overeating and, along with anorexia, is the most conspicuous of the three eating disorders. Unlike anorexia or bulimia, obesity affects all income levels, particularly those in lower economic sectors of society. Obese persons normally do not follow a strict exercise regimen to control their weight, but they share the anorectic's and bulimic's obsession with food, many times eating only in private or with eating friends, hiding or storing food for later consumption.

In all three disorders, food plays an inordinately important role in the lives of the afflicted and is the source of enormous suffering, guilt, self-loathing, disgust, fear, and shame. Food becomes the subject/object around which their entire world revolves. That which these women so long to control—their intake of sustenance—has come to control and rule their every moment, seriously jeopardizing their physical, mental, emotional, and psychic health in the process.

It is important to examine why the occurrence of these disorders has become so prevalent during the last twenty years. Dr. Hilde Bruch (1904–80), author and former psychiatrist and teacher at the Baylor College of Medicine in Houston, Texas, related the disorders, particularly anorexia, to three social factors: (1) the increasing emphasis on slimness as advertised by the fashion industry, magazines, movies, and television; (2) the experience of increased women's liberation as a demand to become or do something outstanding with their lives, to acquiesce to societal pressures to "be and do it all"; and (3) the greater sexual freedom experienced by women today and its accompanying pressures to have heterosexual experiences at a much earlier age.

Likewise Susie Orbach, co-founder of the Women's Therapy Center in London (1976) and the Women's Therapy Center Institute in New York (1981) and a specialist in the treatment of compulsive eating, views eating disorders in women not as a physical illness to be treated with drugs or other traditional types of therapy, but as a direct protest against the inequalities of the sexes. Therefore, Orbach calls for a major reorientation of the medical society, its organization and practice, "based on the demands of the women's health movement."

Clearly, the rapid increase in the phenomenon of eating disorders in women in the wake of the modern women's movement and during an era that supposedly offers greater freedom, economic independence, and choices demands a careful examination of its nonmedical, social aspects. In a society where 80 percent of ten-year-old females have reportedly been on a diet or are now dieting, it becomes imperative to examine the cultural values and principles as well as the contemporary definition of womanhood that direct and form the underlying causes of these diseases, which are fatal, at a conservative estimate, in 2–15 percent of all cases.

—Cecelia A. Albert

References:

Bruch, Hilde. *Eating Disorders: Obesity, Anorexia Nervosa and the Person Within.* New York: Basic, 1973.

Brumberg, Joan. *Fasting Girls: The Emergence of Anoxexia Nervosa as a Modern Disease.* Cambridge: Harvard University Press, 1988.

———. *The Golden Cage: The Enigma of Anorexia Nervosa.* Cambridge: Harvard University Press, 1978.

Chernin, Kim. *The Hungry Self: Women, Eating and Identity.* New York: Harper & Row, 1985.

———. *The Obsession: Reflections on the Tyranny of Slenderness.* New York: Harper & Row, 1981.

Orbach, Susie. *Fat Is a Feminist Issue.* New York: Berkeley, 1979.

———. *Fat Is a Feminist Issue II: A Program to Conquer Compulsive Eating.* New York: Berkeley, 1982.

EDDY, MARY BAKER (1821–1910), the founder of Christian Science, was born in Bow, New Hampshire, the youngest of Mark and Abigail Baker's six children. This remarkably powerful religious leader was frail and sickly as a child and spent a great deal of her youth struggling with chronic back pain and emotional distress. As a result, she attended school irregularly, was tutored by an older brother, and was exceptionally attached to her mother.

Eddy's life can be seen as a continual search for health amid a tumultuous series of relationships. Her first husband, George Washington Glover, died shortly after the couple moved to North Carolina. Eddy was pregnant, emotionally distraught, and penniless. Her parents took care of her during a period of emotional collapse while her son, George, was raised by another woman, never living with his mother. In 1853 Eddy married her second husband, a dentist named Daniel Patterson who traveled extensively, leaving her alone for long stretches. Loneliness and recurrent spinal trouble contributed to hysterical episodes when her husband was around and, as a result of customary medical practice, to a morphine addiction that plagued her all her life.

Eddy intensified her search for health during this period and found some relief in the doctrines of Phineas Parkhurst Quimby, a clock maker who used a form of hypnotism (mesmerism) to heal people. She went to Portland, Maine, after reading about his cures, was touched by him, and was suddenly well, able to walk up the stairs of the town hall. When Quimby died in 1866, she was desolate. Consulting friends, she decided to take up the reins of this movement, and she packed up her things and moved to Lynn, Massachusetts, leaving her husband. When she arrived there, she fell on the ice and, according to her memoirs, almost died. On the third day, reading the gospel story of the raising of Jairus's daughter, she rose from her bed and was healed. This episode marked the beginning of Christian Science, formally chartered in 1879, which gave a religious aspect to the belief that disease was caused and could be cured by one's mental state. In between, she married her third husband, Asa Gilbert Eddy, who was a steadying influence in her life until his death in 1882.

Eddy's strong personality, conviction of the power of the mind over matter, and enormous persuasive power soon drew students (primarily female) to her home in Lynn. From there, the movement grew and moved to Boston in 1881. The first edition of *Science and Health*, explaining these teachings, was published in 1875. This book went through 382 editions, all with revisions by Eddy. She exerted strong control over her church, which continued to grow despite frequent falling outs between her and her followers.

During the final years of her life, Mary Baker Eddy became a recluse and only appeared on selected occasions. Her constant pain, together with her dread of "malicious animal magnetism"—the hostile spiritual energy she felt her enemies had directed at her—contributed to her isolation. She died in her home of pneumonia at the age of eighty-nine.

—Maria E. Erling

References:

Bates, Ernest Sutherland, and John Dittemore. *Mary Baker Eddy: The Truth and the Tradition.* New York: Knopf, 1932.

Corey, Arthur. *Christian Science Class Instruction.* Los Gatos, Calif.: Farallon Foundation, 1950.

Eddy, Mary Baker. *Science and Health.* Boston: Christian Science,1875.

———. *Science and Health; With a Key to the Scriptures.* Boston: First Church of Christ, Scientist, 1875.

Peel, Robert. *Mary Baker Eddy: The Years of Authority.* New York: Holt, Rinehart and Winston, 1977.

———. *Mary Baker Eddy: The Years of Discovery.* New York: Holt, Rinehart and Winston, 1966.

———. *Mary Baker Eddy: The Years of Trial.* New York: Holt, Rinehart and Winston 1971.

Wilbur, Sybil. *The Life of Mary Baker Eddy.* New York: Concord, 1908.

EDUCATION. Women's educational history demonstrates the dual claims of home and school and the tension between the two institutions. In the colonial era, women's lives and their education were defined solely in terms of household needs. The growing importance of schools in the nineteenth and twentieth centuries, and the gradual access women won to primary, secondary, and higher education reflects economic change, women's shifting roles within the home, and consciousness among women themselves that schools provided intellectual stimulation, vocational opportunities, companionship, and perhaps alternatives to domesticity. Yet access to schools did not end the family's influence or claim. Battles over the curriculum—should women study the liberal or the domestic arts? would their health break down if they studied the same subjects as men?—reflected the fears and concerns of many Americans that educated women would subordinate or reject family life. Schooling inevitably raised questions about women's relationship to the family. Should they simply return, minds and spirits enriched, to domestic concerns? Or did formal education mark the beginning of a new life? For women outside the white middle class, access to good schooling remains problematic even into the 1980s, and for all women, the relationship between curriculum and vocation, work and family, is different from what it used to be but equally complex.

Before the American Revolution, education for both sexes took place within the household economy, linked to the future occupations of children. Boys' possibilities varied according to the means and wishes of their fathers and their own abilities and inclinations. Girls, however, had but one destiny: to marry and raise children. Primarily from their mothers, girls of the colonial era learned to cook, weave, sew, clean, and care for children while assisting or directing the household's economic enterprises. Daughters of the urban merchant class or of wealthy planters often had tutors or attended finishing schools, where they studied additional topics and acquired skills appropriate for young women of their social class, e.g., dancing, drawing, music, French, and decorative needlework. Some town dwellers attended the "dame schools" of poor but genteel women who themselves had little or no formal education. The better of these schools offered a curriculum that included learning the alphabet, writing, reading, and arithmetic as well as needlework.

Protestantism provided a spiritual rationale for colonial girls to learn reading and writing: only thus could they study the Scriptures, prepare for conversion, and work for salvation. Girls learned to read from parents or tutors, or possibly at impromptu local "adventure schools" run by older women in the community. However, their exclusion from schools and apprenticeships meant that they had a significantly lower literacy rate than young men.

Some women, born into families of wealth, distinction, or public spirit, read and studied with their brothers' tutors, or craved the opportunity to do so. By the end of the eighteenth century, American writers such as Judith Sargent Murray and Charles Brockden Brown, influenced by the work of British feminist Mary Wollstonecraft, argued that women needed to be educated for self-support and to fulfill their duties as mothers. The American Revolution intensified these concerns: Were women qualified to raise their children with the citizenship ideals suitable for a republic? Early in the nineteenth century, in response to these concerns, academies and primary schools began admitting white girls. The ideology of Republican Motherhood, which stressed domesticity and patriotism, set a pattern for the relationship between women and schooling: access came more easily when proponents argued that female education would enhance performance of domestic roles, whether traditional or newly defined.

In the nineteenth century, industrialization and urbanization eroded, then ended, the household economy. Daughters had less to occupy them and after marriage increasingly found themselves isolated in their homes while men worked for wages elsewhere. No longer household producers, women's chief domestic tasks became housekeeping and mothering. During the antebellum era, religious leaders, novelists, educators, and publicists, male and female, promoted and sentimentalized women's role in the home. This "cult of domesticity," confining though it was, opened new educational opportunities for women. Academies, normal schools, a small number of coeducational public high schools, and even some colleges were established for or admitted females, on the ground that women needed advanced education to perform their duties. Horace Mann, Catharine Beecher, Emma Willard, Mary Lyon, Sarah Josepha Hale, and others argued that women's innately nurturing and spiritual qualities made them the repositories of important social values at a time when men had abandoned religion and culture in pursuit of wealth. Teaching became an unmarried women's profession in the mid-nineteenth century partly because it was viewed as an extension of mothering, and partly because women could be paid less than men. Although the Declaration of Sentiments issued in 1848 by the women's rights convention at Seneca Falls, New York, specifically mentioned lack of schooling as a grievance, women's educators vehemently denied any connections to feminism. They insisted, instead, that women's education led only to happier homes and cultivated motherhood.

Barred by law from formal education before emancipation, black women in the South attended elementary schools established by the Freedmen's Bureau and by various missionary societies after the Civil War. At the turn of the century, the newly reconstituted state governments took over most of these schools, administering them as segregated institutions until the 1960s and beyond. Southern states established some segregated public higher education for blacks, but missionaries and Northern philanthropists made available a higher quality and wider range of institutions. At these institutes, normal schools, and colleges, black women studied the liberal arts, education, nursing, social work, home economics, and agriculture. Through relying too heavily on white faculty, and conservative in their social philosophy, such schools helped to create a black middle class, and ultimately nurtured the modern civil rights movement. With the exception of Spelman College in Atlanta and Bennett College in North Carolina, black schools and colleges were coeducational. In the North, black children had been attending segregated elementary schools since the early nineteenth century, when Northern states freed their slaves. While some whites argued for integrated schooling, attempts to provide even segregated higher education for blacks met with violence. A few black men and women attended such places as Oberlin and Bowdoin Colleges before the Civil War; in the late nineteenth century small numbers of blacks attended Northern universities and colleges.

Between 1860 and 1890, many new state universities and a number of private institutions offered access to women students; at the same time, women's colleges were established, mostly in the East and the South. Although public debate raged throughout this period as to the desirability of a woman's obtaining a "man's" education, parents and daughters looked to the B.A. degree as a means of self-support, of providing entry into a specific occupation, or of satisfying deeply felt needs for self-improvement and intellectual stimulation. Although educators and other writers continued to rationalize women's higher education as enhancing domesticity, a significant number of the first generation of college women never married at all; those who did had small families. Some graduates distinguished themselves in education and literature, while others entered medicine, academics, science, law, and founded the social work profession. Those following more traditional life patterns, marriage and children or staying home to care for parents, often engaged in a wide range of civic, cultural, intellectual, and reform activities. The second generation of college women (1890–1920), educated during an era of reform feminist activity and sociocultural change, seemed eager to follow the example of their predecessors.

At various times in the twentieth century, educators urged a special curriculum for women. During the Progressive era, those fearing the careerism of college women argued for domestic science courses. Some social reformers and feminists felt that the chief task lying ahead for educated women was the rationalization of housekeeping and the reformation of home, family, and community; to these ends they, too, promoted a home economics curriculum. Although women's liberal arts colleges rarely instituted such courses, state and private universities and black colleges frequently did so. It should be noted, however, that home economics majors normally expected their studies to lead to careers in nutrition, chemistry, institutional management, or home economics education; few women students regarded them as preparation for domestic life. Settlement workers in urban areas taught home economics courses to immigrant women, hoping to instill standards of middle-class American housekeeping. As the twentieth century high school became a mass institution, attended by more girls than boys, proponents of vocational and life-adjustment education made sure that public schools offered home economics.

Tension between family and school continued to characterize American women's education in the mid-twentieth century. While women went to elementary and secondary schools in numbers matching or exceeding men, their attendance at college, graduate and professional schools, and entry into prestigious and remunerative careers did not match the achievements nor the promise of the pre-suffrage era. By the 1930s marriage and child-bearing patterns of women college graduates resembled those of noncollege women in the general population. Many factors contributed to the fact that schooling, even advanced education, had little effect on women's social roles. Although women's education had never been explicitly linked to women's rights, the lack of a social-reform or feminist context between the 1920s and the 1960s meant that certain issues were not raised and traditional family values were generally left unquestioned. The national crises of depression and war led to a reaffirmation of domesticity, when Americans turned to home and family as sources of social stability. Jobs and professions continued to bar women from obtaining the necessary training or from advancement. And finally, social research on gender and on sexuality confirmed that the only "normal" women were heterosexual and married—mothers who shopped wisely, helped their husbands' careers, and encouraged their children's social activities.

Since the 1960s, in the context of the modern feminist movement, schooling has become a key factor in determining the course of women's lives. Women outnumber men in undergraduate education and have entered professional and graduate schools in record numbers. Older women, with grown families, have reentered school. Curricular sexism, from elementary school textbooks to scholarly monographs, has come under attack. Women's studies research examines the nature and structure of gender roles. Affirmative Action legislation and judicial decisions have affirmed women's rights to educational access, equal treatment within schools, and freedom from sexual harassment. Yet the classic tension remains. Education continues to raise aspirations that must be realized, for most women, within the context of familial obligations.

—Lynn D. Gordon

See Also:

Coeducation, Female Academies, Higher Education for Southern Women, Home Economics, Women in Higher Education, Women's Studies

References:

Cuthbert, Marion V. *Education and Marginality: The Negro Woman College Graduate.* Diss. Columbia University, 1942. Reprint, New York: Garland, 1987.

Friedan, Betty. *The Feminine Mystique.* New York: Norton, 1963.

Kerber, Linda K. *Women of the Republic.* Chapel Hill: University of North Carolina Press, 1980.

Komarovsky, Mirra. *Women in College.* New York: Basic, 1985.

Newcomer, Mabel. *A Century of Higher Education for American Women.* Washington, D.C.: Zenger, 1959.

Rossiter, Margaret. *Women Scientists in America.* Baltimore: Johns Hopkins University Press, 1982.

Sklar, Kathryn Kish. *Catharine Beecher.* New Haven: Yale University Press, 1973.

Solomon, Barbara Miller. *In the Company of Educated Women.* New Haven: Yale University Press, 1985.

Woody, Thomas. *A History of Women's Education in the U.S.* 2 vols. New York: Science Press, 1929.

The ELIZABETHTON, TENNESSEE, STRIKE of 1929 was a pivotal event in southern women's labor history. It began on March 12 when young women in the inspection department of the German-owned American Glazstoff rayon plant walked off their jobs in protest against low wages. Joined by workers from the nearby American Bemberg plant, they formed a local of the United Textile Workers (UTW-AFL). The conflict engulfed the whole county, as strikers defied injunctions prohibiting picketing near the plants and confronted National Guardsmen sent by the governor to escort strikebreakers into town. These events made national headlines when local businessmen kidnapped a union organizer; the strike also set off a wave of strikes throughout the southern textile industry, signaling the beginning of an era of labor turbulence that peaked in the 1930s but lasted until after World War II.

Women, most of whom were farmers' daughters who commuted to work from their hillside homes, made up approximately 37 percent of the town's thirty-two hundred rayon workers. These women played highly visible roles in the conflict, marching through the streets draped in American flags, blocking mountain roads, and teasing and cursing the guardsmen. When arrested and brought to trial, they neither denied their actions nor curbed their provocations.

Opponents equated women's militancy with sexual misbehavior. But this attempt to discredit the strike with insinuations of promiscuity or prostitution had little effect on the union's rural supporters, who subscribed to a sexual ethic at odds with the values of the companies' backers among the town's middle class. Female strikers adapted rural customs of premarital sex, cohabitation, and early marriage to the new erotic opportunities of working-class life. The townspeople, by contrast, sought to define themselves through privacy, domesticity, and female chastity. Expressing those differences through dress and gesture, the women of Elizabethton devised a highly effective gender- and class-based protest style.

They also symbolized, through their actions, a transitional moment in the history of the southern mountains. On the one hand, their activities harked back to preindustrial rebellions that mobilized heterogeneous coalitions of the poor, relied on crowd action, and provided ample opportunity for female participation. On the other hand, young women were bellwethers of modernity; dressed in the latest store-bought fashions and reveling in new forms of commercialized pleasure, they signaled their identity as "new women" of the 1920s and laid claim to the material promise of post–World War I American life.

Women's activism both drew upon and enhanced community support, but neither militancy nor solidarity could make up for the weakness of the UTW or prevail against the combined power of the corporations and the state. On May 26, six weeks after the first walkout, the union negotiated a settlement that made virtually no concessions to the workers and did nothing to prevent the blacklisting of strike leaders. Yet despite this defeat, the Elizabethton strike did have significant consequences. The parent companies recalled an unpopular manager, installed plant council and welfare systems, and raised wages. Oral history interviews, moreover, reveal that for some participants there were other, less tangible rewards: a feeling of empowerment, a belief that they had made history and that subsequent generations benefited from what they had done.

—Jacquelyn D. Hall

See Also:

American Federation of Labor; New Woman; Textile Industries, Northern and Southern; Unions

References:

Hall, Jacquelyn Dowd. "Disorderly Women: Gender and Labor Militancy in the Appalachian South." *Journal of American History* 73 (September 1986): 354–82.

———, James Leloudis, Robert Korstad, Mary Murphy, Lu Ann Jones, and Christopher B. Daly. *Like a Family: The Making of a Southern Cotton Mill World.* Chapel Hill: University of North Carolina Press, 1987.

Hodges, James. "Challenge to the New South: The Great Strike in Elizabethton, Tennessee, 1929." *Tennessee Historical Quarterly* 23 (December 1964): 343–57.

Holly, John F. "Elizabethton, Tennessee: A Case Study of Industrialization." Diss. Clark University, 1949.

Tippett, Tom. *When Southern Labor Stirs.* New York: Jonathan Cape and Harrison Smith, 1931.

EMERY, SARAH ELIZABETH VAN DE VORT (1838–95) was born in Phelps, New York, and supported third-party politics as a writer, speaker, and campaigner in Michigan, where she had moved in 1866 to teach school. In 1869 she married Wesley Emery, a widower with a three-year-old, who shared her concern for economic and social reform. The Emerys' one daughter, Effie, who died in childhood, was born in 1874.

Emery was a state delegate and speaker to the conventions of the national Greenback party, the Union Labor party, the National Farmers' Alliance, and the Populist party. She was also active in the Knights of Labor and the Women's Christian Temperance Union. She spent fifteen years as the superintendent of the Lansing Universalist Sunday School and worked for woman suffrage. In 1886 she argued for woman suffrage at both the Democratic and Prohibition party state conventions. Five years later she campaigned for municipal suffrage before a state legislative committee.

Emery was best known among her contemporaries by her writing. She edited the *Cornerstone*, a reform newspaper with a focus on woman suffrage, and wrote two popular economic tracts, *Seven Financial Conspiracies Which Have Enslaved the American People* and *Imperialism in America.* Emery was also an associate editor for the *New Forum*, a national Populist party newspaper. Wesley Emery published his wife's newspaper and books. *Seven Financial Conspiracies*, first published in 1887, was reprinted in 1888, revised in 1891 and 1892, and reprinted again in 1894. It sold four hundred thousand copies, was translated into several languages, and was used extensively in Populist congressional and presidential campaigns. The book explained the financial legislation following the Civil War and argued that this legislation had ruined farmers and laborers alike while increasing the wealth of bankers and politicians. Poor health forced Emery to retire from lecturing and writing. She died of cancer at age fifty-seven in 1895.

—MaryJo Wagner

See Also:

National Farmers' Alliance, Populist Party

References:

Adams, Pauline, and Emma S. Thornton. *A Populist Assault: Sarah E. Van De Vort Emery on American Democracy, 1862–1895.* Bowling Green, Ohio: State University Popular Press, 1982.

Bliss, William D. P., ed. *Encyclopedia of Social Reform.* New York: Funk & Wagnalls, 1897.

Diggs, Annie L. "Women in the Alliance Movement." *Arena* 6 (July 1892): 161–79.

The EQUAL EMPLOYMENT OPPORTUNITY COMMISSION (EEOC) enforces Title VII of the Civil Rights Act of 1964, which prohibits discrimination in employment on the basis of race, color, religion, national origin, or sex. Adding *sex* to the bill was actually a ploy by an opponent, Virginia representative Howard W. Smith, who hoped it would help defeat the proposed bill. Michigan representative Martha Griffiths championed the change, however, and it remained in the act when it became law.

The EEOC, composed of five members appointed by the President with Senate approval, at first had only the power to investigate and persuade as it attempted to settle disputes arising from allegations of discrimination. Several minority groups sought to make use of the limited enforcement resources allocated to the EEOC, with the net result that the commission generally ignored the inclusion of the word *sex* in Title VII; the National Organization for Women (NOW) was formed in 1966 partly to pressure the EEOC to pay more attention to women.

In 1967 Executive Order 11375 extended Title VII to prohibit discrimination by holders of federal contracts, who then employed about one-third of the labor force in the United States. And by 1969, Court decisions finding "protective" state laws limiting the hours a woman could work per week or the weight she could lift on the job, to be illegal under Title VII nudged the EEOC in 1969 into declaring all such state legislation invalid. Finally, in 1972 the EEOC acquired some real teeth against discrimination when it was given the option of taking violators to court.

Although the EEOC represents a national endorsement of equal opportunity in both private and public employment, it has been from the beginning short of both funds and staff and only occasionally interested in the plight of women. Some important settlements resulting in substantial gains for women have been pursued; in 1973, for example, an out-of-court settlement between the American Telegraph and Telephone Company and the government resulted in over $38 million in back pay (of an estimated $3.5 billion owed) awarded to women employees who were the victims of job discrimination. And there is little question that the inclusion of *sex* in Title VII has laid the groundwork for what can be profoundly significant changes in the employment structure in favor of women. However, under the Reagan administration, the EEOC's effectiveness was crippled by its drastically cut budget and by the appointment of commissioners who proved hostile to the congressionally defined purpose of the commission.

—J. A. Sandoz

See Also:

Civil Rights Act of 1964, National Organization for Women

References:

Freeman, Jo. *The Politics of Women's Liberation.* New York: David McKay, 1975, pp. 177–90.

———. "Women and Public Policy: An Overview." In *Women, Power and Policy,* edited by Ellen Boneparth. New York: Pergamon, 1982, pp. 47–67.

Kahn, Wendy, and Joy Ann Grune, "Pay Equity: Beyond Equal Pay for Equal Work." In *Women, Power and Policy*, edited by Ellen Boneparth. New York: Pergamon, 1982, pp. 75–89.

Power, Marilyn. "Falling Through the Safety Net: Women, Economic Crisis, and Reaganomics." *Feminist Studies* 10 (1984): 31–58.

The **EQUAL PAY ACT of 1963** was a result of the recommendations of President John F. Kennedy's Commission on the Status of Women. The first national legislation for women's employment since the Progressive era, this law requires employers to pay their male and female employees the same wages when both men and women perform jobs that entail equal skill, effort, and responsibility, and that are carried out under similar working conditions. In addition, it prohibits labor unions from causing or trying to cause an employer to violate this law, and it forbids employers to lower the wages of one sex in order to come into compliance with the law. There are, however, exceptions to the equal pay requirement; that is, employers may justifiably pay their male and female employees different wages if those wages are determined by (1) a seniority system; (2) a merit system; (3) "a system which measures earnings by quantity or quality of production"; or (4) "a differential based on any other factor other than sex."

Because the Equal Pay Act is an amendment to the Fair Labor Standards Act of 1938, the U.S. Labor Department is responsible for its enforcement. Department officials are charged with making routine checks for violations and with investigating individual complaints against specific employers. Although there has been some success under the act in recovering wages for underpaid female employees, several factors have mitigated against its serving as an effective means of closing the male-female wage gap. One problem stems from the wording of the law itself. In providing a limited but complex definition of wage discrimination, the act allows the courts to arrive at varying, and frequently contradictory, assessments of what constitutes equal skill, effort, and responsibility.

In addition, the Equal Pay Act does not directly address the problem of occupational sex segregation in which men and women are concentrated in different jobs typically labeled "men's work" and "women's work." Because traditional female occupations historically have been undervalued in the United States, women who hold such positions are generally paid less than men, even when their jobs require higher qualifications and entail greater responsibilities. In the 1970s women acted to rectify this problem by bringing comparable-worth suits against their employers. Comparable worth, later termed sex equity, extends the principle of "equal pay for equal work" by requiring equal pay for jobs of similar value. In 1985 women workers won comparable-worth suits in six states, indicating the potential of this concept as an important supplement to Equal Pay Act litigation. However, hostility to the concept from the New Right and conservatives generally and from the Reagan administration particularly has obstructed its application at the federal level.

—Claire M. Renzetti

See Also:

President's Commission on the Status of Women, Sex Equity/Comparable Worth, Sexual Division of Labor, Wages, Women's Work—Nineteenth Century

References:

Babcock, Barbara A., Ann E. Freedman, Eleanor H. Norton, and Susan C. Ross, eds. *Sex Discrimination and the Law.* Boston: Little, Brown, 1975.

Blumrosen, Ruth G. "Wage Discrimination, Job Segregation, and Women Workers." *Women's Rights Law Reporter* 6 (Fall/Winter, 1979-80): 19–57.

Harrison, Cynthia. *On Account of Sex: The Politics of Women's Issues, 1945–1968.* Berkeley: University of California Press, 1988.

Renzetti, Claire M. "One Step Forward, Two Steps Back: Women, Work,and Employment Legislation." In *Contemporary Issues in Business*, edited by Joseph DesJardins and John McCall. Belmont, Calif.: Wadsworth, 1984, pp. 395–404.

The **EQUAL RIGHTS AMENDMENT (ERA).** The struggle to assure women's equality under the supreme law of the land through a federal amendment to the U.S. Constitution began soon after the ratification of the Nineteenth Amendment, which gave women the vote. The name Equal Rights Amendment was first used in the 1870s on the first federal woman suffrage bill, which was voted down in 1878. Alice Paul, leader of the National Woman's party, lobbied Congress in 1923 for an Equal Rights Amendment to eradicate discrimination on the basis of sex in existing federal, state, and local laws. Paul's originally proposed amendment read, "Men and women shall have equal rights throughout the United States and every place to its jurisdiction." Nineteen subsequent Congresses failed to grant the approval necessary to send this amendment to the states for ratification.

Initially, former suffragists and social feminists opposed the concept of an Equal Rights Amendment during the 1920s, on the grounds that women's equality under the law would have threatened the pre–World War I special-protection legislation that had been gained for women workers during the Progressive era. Nor did the ERA receive attention or significant support during the New Deal or World War II eras. The undaunted Alice Paul and the National Woman's party persevered. Finally in 1967 the National Organization for Women responded to Paul's persuasion with an endorsement of a federal Equal Rights Amendment, thus initiating a renewed campaign that was invigorated by the support of the modern women's rights movement.

In 1972 the momentum of the civil rights movement no less than the astute politicking of Michigan representative Martha Griffiths and others induced Congress to approve an Equal Rights Amendment, which was then sent to the states with a seven-year deadline for ratification. Also known as the Alice Paul Amendment, the ERA now read, "Equality of Rights shall not be denied or abridged by the United States or any state on account of sex." The economic impact of an increased number of single and married women in the paid labor force made visible the economic discrimination against women, while the issues of equality and justice that had been raised by the political reform movements of the 1960s heightened public awareness to the shameful lack of legal, social, political, and economic rights for American women.

By 1973 thirty of the thirty-eight states needed to ratify this Equal Rights Amendment had done so. However, by the mid-1970s no new states had entered the ratified column, and the opposition to the ERA had organized and gathered strength. The success of the International Women's Year national conference in Houston in 1977 focused mainstream support for a national agenda to address women's issues: Its National Plan of Action included support of ERA ratification.

The ERA, however, still lacked the last three states of the required thirty-eight, and the opposition, though a minority, had been successful in raising doubts as to the legal and social consequences of the ERA. The general support of the ERA influenced Congress to grant an unprecedented extension of the original ratification deadline to June 30, 1982. But by the mid-1980s the instability of the post-Vietnam economy fueled a resurgence of political fundamentalism that was reminiscent of the conservative political backlash of the 1920s. Ultimately, it was a handful of state legislators in only three or four states who, representing a minority opinion within their own states as well as a minority opinion within the nation, thwarted the ratification of the ERA by the June 1982 deadline.

—Angela Howard Zophy

See Also:

Antifeminism; National Woman's Party; Nineteenth-Century Woman's Movement; Paul, Alice; Right-Wing Political Movements; Schlafly, Phyllis; Social Feminism; Twentieth-Century Women's Rights Movement

References:

Becker, Susan D. *The Origins of the Equal Rights Amendment.* Westport, Conn.: Greenwood, 1982.

Eisler, Riane Tennenhaus. *The Equal Rights Handbook: What ERA Means to Your Life, Your*

Rights, and the Future. New York: Avon, 1978.
Gager, Nancy, ed. *Women's Rights Almanac.* New York: Harper Colophon, 1974.
Riley, Glenda. *Inventing the American Woman: A Perspective on Women's History.* Arlington Heights, Ill.: Harlan Davidson, 1987.
Ryan, Mary P. *Womanhood in America: From Colonial Times to the Present.* 3d ed. New York: New Viewpoints/Franklin Watts, 1984.
Whitney, Sharon. *The Equal Rights Amendment: The History and the Movement.* New York: Franklin Watts, 1984.

EQUAL RIGHTS ASSOCIATION. In January 1866 Elizabeth C. Stanton and Susan B. Anthony proposed a union of the American Anti-Slavery Society and their Women's Rights Society under the name Equal Rights Association. The intended objective of the organization was to work for the citizenship of both women and Negro men. Although this union had the approval of a number of influential leaders—including Horace Greeley, Theodore Tilton, Charles Sumner, and Thaddeus Stevens—the president of the Anti-Slavery Society, Wendell Phillips, was cool to the idea, and, as a consequence, the ASS at its May 1866 annual convention did not take action on the resolution.

However, the Women's Rights Society, at its annual convention in May 1866, did unanimously adopt a change in its name to the Equal Rights Association. The organization elected Lucretia Mott as its president and a slate of vice presidents including Stanton, Tilton, Frederick Douglass, and Robert Purvis. Shortly after the convention, Tilton, in association with Phillips, proposed to Stanton that the organization, at least for the moment, drop all plans for woman suffrage and work solely for the Negro. For the next three years, members of the ERA argued bitterly among themselves over their goals and tactics. During this time, certain factions within the ERA assailed Stanton and Anthony for threatening to rob the "Negro of his hour" by their impolitic linking of woman's and Negro rights.

At the third annual convention, in 1869, abolitionist and woman's rights advocate Ernestine Rose stated that one-half of the objective of the ERA had been achieved with the ratification of the Fourteenth Amendment and congressional approval of the Fifteenth Amendment. Therefore, she proposed that the name of the organization be changed to the National Woman Suffrage Association. Other delegates promptly protested that this motion was out of order. Stanton, as presiding officer, agreed that the constitutional bylaws did not allow such a name change without a three-month notice. Immediately following the meeting, however, Stanton and Anthony—feeling that the male leadership in the ERA had betrayed women's interests—organized the National Woman Suffrage Association for women only. Several months later, the more conservative women within the ERA organized the rival American Woman Suffrage Association. Thus the Equal Rights Association served as a transitional organization for the woman's rights movement, as its supporters transferred their focus from the issues of abolition to a primary concern for woman suffrage.

—*Terry D. Bilhartz*

See Also:

American Woman Suffrage Association; Anthony, Susan B.; National Woman Suffrage Association; Stanton, Elizabeth Cady

References:

Du Bois, Ellen. *Feminism and Suffrage: The Emergence of An Independent Women's Movement in America, 1848–1869.* Ithaca, N.Y.: Cornell University Press, 1978.
Flexner, Eleanor. *Century of Struggle.* New York: Atheneum, 1968.
Harper, Ida Husted. *The Life and Work of Susan B. Anthony.* 3 vols. Indianapolis: Bowen-Merrill, 1898–1908; rpt. Salem, N.H.: Ayer,1983.
Stanton, Elizabeth Cady, Susan B. Anthony, and Matilda Joslyn Gage, eds. *The History of Woman Suffrage.* Vol. 2. Rochester: n.p., 1881.

EQUALITY DAY commemorates the date of the ratification of the Nineteenth Amendment on August 26, 1920. Although there is no national holiday to memorialize the passage of woman suffrage, Equality Day has been celebrated informally by various women's groups at the national, state, and local chapter level since the 1920s. After 1972, Equality Day was used by the National Organization for Women, the American Association of University Women, and other national women's organizations as a symbolic occasion around which to rally support for contemporary women's issues, especially the effort to ratify the Equal Rights Amendment, as well as to pay homage to the suffragists whose long struggle won women the vote.

—Angela Howard Zophy

See Also:

Equal Rights Amendment, Nineteenth (Woman Suffrage) Amendment, Suffrage

References:

Eisler, Riane Tennenhaus. *The Equal Rights Handbook.* New York: Avon, 1978.

Whitney, Sharon. *The Equal Rights Amendment: The History and the Movement.* New York: Watts, 1984.

EQUITY COURTS. In early America, legal restrictions on women were often mitigated by equity courts, which used common sense rather than common law in making judgments. Equity jurisprudence recognized and enforced antenuptial agreements, or marriage settlements, which circumvented coverture and preserved for a woman some control over the property she brought to a marriage. It also allowed her to bequeath her property as she wished. However, few women took advantage of marriage settlements, which were seen as a device for the wealthy or as evidence of distrust. The influence of equity courts eroded slowly and sporadically during the early nineteenth century and was superseded after the 1840s by state married women's property acts which codified an expanding definition of married women's legal rights.

—Barbara E. Lacey

See Also:

Antenuptial Agreements, Common Law, Coverture, Married Women's Property Acts

Reference:

Norton, Mary Beth. *Liberty's Daughters: The Revolutionary Experience of American Women, 1750–1800.* Boston: Little, Brown, 1980.

ESSENCE **(1969–)** is a popular monthly magazine for black American women. With a readership of several million, it follows the *Cosmopolitan* and *Vogue* formats, with features on fashion and beauty, love and relationships, contemporary living, business and finance, health, and current affairs. Utilizing the standard women's magazine format, *Essence* regularly publishes poetry by black artists and has followed in the tradition of mass market black magazines such as *Negro Digest* (1942–), now titled *Black World*, and *Ebony* (1945–). The success of *Essence* in the competition for the black woman's market has helped move *Ebony* from its earlier preoccupation with "sex and sensation" to a more positive image of the black woman. While all of these mainstream black magazines are still quite traditional in their depiction of women, they do provide an important outlet for black artists and writers. They also help black businesses reach the black community.

—Patricia Haire

See Also:

Beauty Industry, Black Women, Magazines

References:

Greenburg, Jonathan "It's a Miracle." *Forbes* 130 (December 20, 1982): 104–10.

Rottenberg, Dan. "Atop the *Ebony* Empire." *United Magazine* 30 (January 1985): 39–40, 84.

ETHNICITY AND GENDER ROLES. Historically, the experiences of women have differed dramatically among the many ethnic and racial groups that compose American society. Economic conditions, societal discrimination, and ethnic cultural values have all affected gender roles. The circumstances that led immigrants to leave their native lands for America included poverty, forced removal through enslavement or deportation, political turmoil, and religious intolerance. These circumstances profoundly influenced the conditions under which women adapted to life in the United States and the roles that they would play in American society.

For example, the intense poverty of nineteenth-century Ireland sent many single Irish women off to America in search of employment. Domestic service and factory employment were common occupations of single women in Ireland, and consequently many Irish immigrants pursued such occupations in the United States. Poverty in Ireland had forced both men and women to postpone marriage or not to marry at all, and these patterns persisted in America and encouraged Irish-American girls to pursue careers in fields such as teaching and nursing.

Ethnic and racial discrimination has touched the lives of most immigrant groups in the United States, but no group has suffered more discrimination than black immigrants and their descendants. Brought to this country in slavery, black immigrant women and their children were compelled to assume roles in domestic and agricultural labor. Their legal status under slavery prevented black women from assuming the full responsibilities of marriage and motherhood and kept their daily lives under an owner's control. Discrimination after Emancipation made it necessary for black wives, mothers, and family heads to remain in the labor force when most other American women remained in the home.

For all ethnic groups, distinctive family values have influenced the roles that women as well as men have played within the family and in the large society. Italian and Hispanic immigrants, for example, have cherished the importance of mothers being at home full time. On the other hand, economic necessity often forced these same mothers to earn wages. More than other women, Italian and Hispanic wives chose to earn wages through industrial homework, employment that allowed them to remain at home but forced them to accept the lowest of wages. Similarly, cultural values of ethnic groups encouraged or discouraged the education of women, encouraged women to respect or to challenge authority, discouraged or encouraged family planning, and influenced women in other ways that determined when and whom they would marry and the economic roles that they would assume as daughters, wives, or mothers.

—Julia Kirk Blackwelder

See Also:

Asian American Women, Black Women, *Chicana*, Immigration, Jewish Women

References:

Blackwelder, Julia Kirk. *Women of the Depression: Caste and Culture in San Antonio, 1929–1939.* College Station: Texas A & M University Press, 1984.

Ewen, Elizabeth. *Immigrant Women in the Land of Dollars: Life and Culture on the Lower East Side, 1890–1925.* New York: Monthly Review, 1985.

Kessler-Harris, Alice. *Out to Work: A History of Wage-Earning Women in the United States.* New York: Oxford University Press, 1982.

EUROPEAN INFLUENCES. The development of women's literature and feminism in the United States has been influenced by European sources that date from the seventeenth to the twentieth centuries. The existence of works by Aphra Behn, Fanny Burney, Eliza Carter, Jane Austen, the Brontë sisters, and George Eliot inspired the early generations of American women writers. The women whose writings articulated the development of feminist theory in the United States since the Revolution drew on the works and words of Mary Wollstonecraft, John Stuart Mill, Virginia Woolf, and Simone de Beauvoir, among others.

English and French women authors especially served as role models for the "scribbling women" in early nineteenth-century America. Sarah Josepha Hale and Lydia Maria Child drew inspiration to become writers from Mrs. Ann Radcliffe's eighteenth-century gothic novel *The Mysteries of Udolpho* (1794), and later women authors such as Louisa May Alcott, Kate Chopin, and Charlotte Perkins Gilman reassessed women's role in the tradition of George Sand's *Indiana* (1831). Struggling intellectuals such as Margaret Fuller were encouraged to apply their analytical and scholarly powers by the heroine of Madame de Staël's *Corinne* (1807). American feminists such as Elizabeth Cady Stanton were influenced by Wollstonecraft's arguments in her *Vindication of the Rights of Woman* (1792), as twentieth-century feminists have been called to introspection and action by the powerful and moving image of Shakespeare's sister in Woolf's *A Room of One's Own* (1929) and challenged to reevaluate their female identity as "the other" by de Beauvoir's *The Second Sex* (1949).

Although all the non-American sources that have had an impact on women's literature and feminist theory are too numerous for inclusion within the limited scope of this entry, the works of Wollstonecraft, de Staël, John Stuart Mill, Woolf, and de Beauvoir have become standard references within the literature of American women's history. A brief summary of the content and influence of these particular works, with some background information on their historical contexts and their authors, seemed appropriate and necessary.

As Mrs. Radcliffe's *Mysteries of Udolpho* redefined the gothic novel as one centered upon a heroine who ultimately triumphs over danger and betrayal, Madame de Staël's *Corinne* (1807) created a new kind of heroine, the woman genius, who served as a role model for many antebellum women writers as they established their rightful place among the literati of Victorian America. An often expurgated version of the life and works of the author herself validated the careers of these women writers. The publication of Madame de Staël's letters to her daughters became a part of the European contribution to a body of prescriptive literature often cited by Victorian women and further increased de Staël's reputation among nineteenth-century American women writers.

Of mixed heritage, de Staël's heroine Corinne is a Florentine improvisator who draws adoring crowds to her recitals. Not only is she a brilliant speaker, she possesses abundant wisdom. Yet all of this ultimately fades away when she falls in love with a man who ultimately jilts her. Love topples this genius and in so doing sets up the prototypical plight of the great woman. Indeed, *Corinne* formed feminist ideas about human relationships for decades thereafter; it also provided inspiration for women who aspired to similar genius in the United States. Margaret Fuller, for one, tried to find the Stahlian path, as did Anna Jameson in Great Britain.

De Staël (1766–1817) was the daughter of Jacques Necker, famous banker and minister during the French Revolution, and the former Suzanne Curchod, who conducted a successful literary salon and claimed to have educated her only child, Germaine, "like a boy." Married to Swedish diplomat Staël-Holstein at an early age, de Staël set up her own circle of friends and championed her father's political career. She favored the French revolutionary cause until it grew too radical but remained nonetheless an advocate of reform and liberty. Exiled by Napoleon at the height of his power, she travelled to the German states, to Italy, and through the Hapsburg Empire in search of roots and inspiration. In fact, she found both, though Paris remained her desideratum. Travels inspired her greatest works, *Corinne* and *De l'Allemagne* (1813), which changed the course of European cultural life, while her lucid *Considerations on the French Revolution* (1818) gave one of the first clear accounts of that event.

While de Staël's romantic fiction offered inspiration to individual women in their search for artistic identity, the political and feminist commentary of Wollstonecraft, Mill, Woolf, and de Beauvoir informed and challenged American feminists in their development of feminist theory and feminist literary criticism. In *A Vindication of the Rights of Woman* (1792) Wollstonecraft argued that women's intellectual and moral deficiencies were a result of men's tyranny. If women were educated and acknowledged to have an independent existence as moral beings, Wollstonecraft claimed, they would be capable of attaining the level of virtue requisite for participation in the duties of the state. Most contemporary liberal theorists saw civic virtue as an exclusively male quality; Wollstonecraft, however, envisioned a society in which rational mothers, too, could be admitted to an identity in the eyes of the state.

Although Wollstonecraft's stated goal in *A Vindication* was to help women gain power over themselves, she framed both the content and form of her argument for the educated male reader. She asked men to break women's chains of dependence, promising that as women became more rational and virtuous, they would make better companions as wives, daughters, and mothers

Mary Wollstonecraft (1759–97) applied the Enlightenment tenets of liberal individualism popular among her circle of British and Parisian intellectuals to the problems of middle-class womanhood. Her career as a liberal theorist began in 1790 with *A Vindication of the Rights of Man*, the first published response to Edmund Burke's classic statement of political conservatism, *Reflections on the Revolution in France* (1790). While Wollstonecraft had written *Thoughts on the Education of Daughters* in 1787, her best-known work was *A Vindication of the Rights of Woman*.

Wollstonecraft traveled to revolutionary France in 1792. After being jilted by her American lover, she returned to London with her daughter and began a friendship with philosopher William Godwin, who soon became her lover and critic. They married after discovering Wollstonecraft was pregnant, but maintained separate residences. Wollstonecraft died of childbed fever in 1797 following the birth of their daughter, Mary Godwin. In a fit of impassioned grief, Godwin published all of Wollstonecraft's letters (including those to her first lover) and several unfinished works. The response to these revelations was swift and vicious. In the United States, some reprints of *A Vindication of the Rights of Woman* were prefaced with condemnations of Wollstonecraft's sexual misconduct.

Despite the immediate furor upon its publication *A Vindication* was largely forgotten until rediscovered in the 1840s by the American and European women's movements. Advocates of education and legal rights for women (including Margaret Fuller, Lucretia Mott, and Elizabeth Cady Stanton) who were influenced by Wollstonecraft's equal rights doctrine were careful to dissociate themselves from the sexual radicalism with which her name had become synonymous. Only Frances Wright combined Wollstonecraft's Englightenment egalitarianism with sexual radicalism.

Modern feminists have admired Wollstonecraft for both her personal life and the strong-worded demands of her *Vindication*, but have been less comfortable with the emotional vulnerability revealed in her letters and sentimental novels. The reissue of these other works has rejuvenated scholarship on the woman who, for nearly two hundred years, has been looked upon as a pioneer by liberal feminists in England and the United States.

The Subjection of Women, published in England in 1869, inspired contemporary feminists and suffragists in the United States and thus contributed to the development of the nineteenth-century woman's movement and American feminism. Its author, British philosopher and politician John Stuart Mill (1806–73), withheld the publication of this essay until after his unsuccessful attempt to include woman suffrage in the British Reform Bill of 1867, although it had been written in 1861 following the death of Harriet Taylor (1807–58), his colleague in the cause of human liberty, as well as his wife.

Mill was a feminist particularly active on behalf of the nineteenth-century women's movement. Raised in the utilitarian creed by his father, James Mill, he came to believe, with the founder of utilitarianism, Jeremy Bentham, that the full measure of social happiness would not be realized without the happiness of women. At the age of seventeen, Mill had been detained by the London constabulary for distributing birth-control information. The utilitarian influence ultimately took second place to that of Harriet Taylor, with whom Mill maintained an intimate friendship; they married in 1851 after the death of her first husband. Taylor had published in the

Monthly Repository, and she and Mill wrote essays for one another, particularly on the relationship of women and men. Mill's subsequent essay on "The Enfranchisement of Women" derived largely from her ideas. Mill acknowledged that *The Subjection of Women* was the result of conversations and work with Taylor and her daughter, Helen.

After his wife's death from tuberculosis, the heartbroken Mill worked mightily as a member of Parliament to add woman's suffrage to the Reform Bill of 1867. Despite an enormous display of support through petitions signed by many prominent women, his motion to use "person" in all such bills was defeated. Mill proceeded to support measures giving women control of their property, and he testified for repeal of the Contagious Diseases Acts, which allowed the forcible examination of women for venereal disease.

His most lasting contribution to the cause of women, however, was *The Subjection of Women*, which was translated into many languages and exerted international influence on the intellectual discussion of the Woman Question. In it, Mill showed how regressive the condition of women was, how like it was to slavery, and how cruelly the much-vaunted social unit of the family treated its female members. Unlike his wife, he favored the conventional division of labor on which separate spheres ideology rested. Nonetheless, Mill's rational but convincing arguments against the unequal legal and educational status of women particularly touched the reforming temper of the times and inspired the woman's movement everywhere.

American suffragists of the nineteenth century utilized the arguments of Wollstonecraft and Mill as they pursued the Woman vote, which by the turn of the twentieth century had become the sole feminist goal of their organized movement. Their achievement of the Nineteenth Amendment, however, did not fundamentally address or challenge the legal, economic, or social subordination of women. In the twentieth century, Woolf's *A Room of One's Own* and de Beauvoir's *The Second Sex* emerged as the major European works which assisted American women in their efforts to define the feminist issues of the twentieth century.

A Room of One's Own (1929) was based upon the speeches of English author and critic Virginia Woolf (1882–1941), which had been delivered at two British women's colleges after World War I. As an essay, *A Room of One's Own* rivaled *A Vindication of the Rights of Woman* in its profound contribution to feminist writing and commentary. This particular work by Woolf is consistently included in lists of benchmark works of feminist critical theory, usually in tandem with Woolf's *Three Guineas* (1938). Woolf confronts directly the problems encountered by women artists and writers, arguing that a woman artist lacks not only money and freedom but also the sanction of her society that is so essential to her achievement of success and influence.

Woolf was born Virginia Stephen in London and died by her own hand when, fearing the onset of incurable madness, she drowned herself in the Ouse River, Lewes, Sussex. Until the mid-1970s, she had typically been studied in courses on "Modern British Fiction," where her contributions to Modernism—though sometimes grudgingly acknowledged—earned her the designation "the greatest woman novelist of the twentieth century." Since then, however, the feminist aspects of her writing have come under scrutiny. Not surprisingly, critics have discovered that the various Victorian and "modern" images of women emerge, assert themselves, and challenge one another in her works.

Although Woolf's voluminous and influential writings include critical treatises, autobiographical essays, short stories, novels, and experimental prose fiction, the American public recognizes her most readily, perhaps, as the enigmatic woman in the title of Edward Albee's play, *Who's Afraid of Virginia Woolf?* (1962). Woolf never visited the United States and, in fact, retained a condescending attitude toward Americans all her life; nonetheless, her influence on American as well as British feminist writers has been substantial. American critics Jane Marcus and Elaine Showalter, for example, have added their voices to the debate about Woolf's contribution to the women's movement. Woolf did most of her writing at the height of the early British version of that movement, during the first three decades of the twentieth century.

Woolf was not convinced, as many of her contemporaries were, that political power for women, in and of itself, would guarantee their equality with men. She was most concerned with the psychological and economic underpinnings of masculine "superiority." In particular, she sought in her works to assess the consequences to society of the repressed anger of acquiescence of women in the face of masculine power. Two of her most widely studied novels, *Mrs. Dalloway* (1925) and *To the Lighthouse* (1927), reveal Woolf's concern about the systematic though subtle discounting of women's work (and therefore worth) in a patriarchal society. The psychological consequences—both to the individual woman and to society—of women's maintenance of patriarchal conventions is a theme which surfaces in the works of American writers like poet Adrienne Rich. In the collection *Snapshots of a Daughter-in-Law*, Rich examines the self-disgust and resentment experienced by a woman in a society where she must remain subordinate to men. It is an issue now debated pervasively in American feminist writing, and therefore Woolf's influence significantly transcends the specious bounds of Modern British Fiction which originally restrained it.

The Second Sex (1949) is Simone de Beauvoir's masterful analysis of womanhood. The book begins with the premise that no book about manhood would ever be written because men's experience is taken as so normative or absolute that it hardly needs talking about. By contrast, women appear as different, other, and in constant need of explanation. Each person acquired and created self-definition, *The Second Sex* argued, in terms of engaging and coming to terms with "others" in society. Whereas this confrontation with individual "others" occurred on a personal basis, general categories of otherness, such as blacks, Jews, and women, existed. Oddly enough, while blacks and Jews struggled to escape this otherness, women in fact acquiesced to its terms as they were arranged by male culture. As the "eternal female," women thus surrendered their subjectivity and freedom. Rootedness in nature or "immanence" became women's fate once they made this decision, instead of the quest for "transcendence."

Expanding on this general theme, *The Second Sex* provided a rich panorama of women's lives as viewed by scientists, Freudians, and Marxists, and by poets and artists across the centuries. Further, it examined the world of the daughter, mother, lesbian, and many other experiences of womanhood. Pointing to the difficulties facing the "independent woman," de Beauvoir championed her economic struggle as preliminary to freedom. But the final step involved mentally escaping self-conceptualization as exclusively an "other." Though *The Second Sex* did not present the author's final word on the subject of feminism, it eschewed organizing in favor of individual recognition and action.

Part of existentialist literature of the 1940s and 1950s, *The Second Sex* sold twenty thousand copies almost immediately in France because readers assumed it to be the work of Jean-Paul Sartre, leading existentialist and de Beauvoir's companion. In 1953 H. M. Parshley, professor of zoology at Smith College, translated the work into English and severely expurgated it. Nonetheless, it had an early impact in the United States, and in particular helped inspire Betty Friedan's *Feminine Mystique* (1963). From then on, the new women's movement recognized *The Second Sex* as a classic statement and an innovative analysis of women's cultural and psychological situation.

Its author, Simone de Beauvoir (1908–86), was a French author, philosopher, and activist. Born into a middle-class Parisian family, de Beauvoir thought seriously of a career after her father's financial ruin in World War I. She entered the Sorbonne in the mid-1920s and received her *agrégation* (teaching diploma) in 1927. While there, she met and fell in love with philosopher Jean-Paul Sartre. This began a lifelong companionship that de Beauvoir refused to turn into marriage. Meanwhile, she pursued a teaching career until the mid-1940s, when she turned all her energies to writing. Her first novel, *L'Invitée/She Came to Stay,* appeared in 1943; many more followed. From this time on, de Beauvoir and Sartre were at the center of an important radical circle of intellectuals.

In novels, memoirs, and philosophic writings, de Beauvoir developed the existentialist ideas for which she and Sartre were so well known. Her pathbreaking *Le deuxième sexe/The Second Sex* continued that philosophical line into the study of women and formed the basis for reconstructing feminist ideas and for rebuilding the women's movement of the 1960s and later. Despite her disclaimer at the close of *The Second Sex* that her book made activism unnecessary, de Beauvoir continued her writing as well as her activism. Her special masterpieces included *Les Mandarins* (1954) and several volumes of memoirs.

De Beauvoir's life reflected the feminist axiom, "The personal is political." With the student uprisings of the late 1960s, the Vietnam War, and the rebirth of feminism, de Beauvoir finally realized the need for public political involvement. From then on, often with Sartre, she participated in many demonstrations, petitioning movements, and other radical endeavors. In 1971 she shocked the French public when, along with other prominent women, she signed a declaration that she had had an abortion. Later she co-founded the periodical *Questions feministes/Feminist Questions.* These were but the highlights of a life built of writing and activism. De Beauvoir's death in April 1986 brought international recognition of her seminal role in contemporary feminist philosophy as well as in its organizational successes.

The impact of *The Second Sex* and the introduction of deconstruction as a tool for feminist literary criticism established a significant French influence on American feminist theory since the 1960s. The presence of British influence on that theory continued with Germaine Greer's *The Female Eunuch* (1972) and the feminist literary works of writers such as Doris Lessing.

—Kathleen Mary Brown, Mindy Dunker, Mary Lowe-Evans, Bonnie G. Smith, and Angela Howard Zophy

See Also:

Deconstruction; Feminism; Feminist Literary Criticism; Friedan, Betty; Nineteenth-Century Woman's Movement; Prescriptive Literature; Rationalism; Rich, Adrienne; Suffrage; Twentieth-Century Women's Rights Movement

References:

Ascher, Carol. *Simone de Beauvoir: A Life of Freedom.* New York: Beacon, 1981.

Borghi, Liana. *Dialogue in Utopia: Manners, Purpose and Structure in Three Feminist Works of the 1790s.* Pisa: ETS, 1984.

de Beauvoir, Simone. *The Second Sex.* Translated by H. M. Parshley. New York: Knopf, 1953.

Flexner, Eleanor. *Mary Wollstonecraft: A Biography.* Harmondsworth, England: Penguin, 1973.

Gutwirth, Madelyn. *Madame de Staël, Novelist.* Urbana: University of Illinois Press, 1978.

Mill, John Stuart. *The Subjection of Women.* London: Longmans, 1869.

Moers, Ellen. *Literary Women.* Garden City, N.Y.: Doubleday, 1976.

Showalter, Elaine. *A Literature of Their Own: British Women Novelists from Brontë to Lessing.* Rev. ed. London: Virago, 1982.

Wollstonecraft, Mary. *A Vindication of the Rights of Woman.* London: Scott, 1792; rpt. New York: Dutton, 1929, 1974.

Woolf, Virginia. *A Room of One's Own.* London: Hogarth, 1931.

EXTRAMARITAL SEX, or sex outside of marriage, was once considered a male prerogative, but recent studies indicate a waning of the double standard with estimates that roughly half of both husbands and wives violate the Seventh Commandment.

Historically, the practice existed in colonial America and continued into the modern world. In 1631 Massachusetts enacted the death penalty for adultery, which was defined as sexual relations between a man and a married woman. Most other colonies followed suit in punishing extramarital sex, although enforcement remained minimal in most instances. After 1660, New England courts usually imposed fines upon convicted adulterers, along with public whipping or the wearing of the letters AD on a garment or burned onto the forehead. Over half the seventeenth-century divorce cases in New England cited adultery as a cause.

In the antebellum South, extramarital sexual relations between owners and slaves were common and usually involved white men with black women. Divorce records also indicate that in some cases white women consorted with black men despite enormous social pressures and the possibility of horrible punishments.

Sometimes extramarital sex became an occasion for public scandal. In the middle of the nineteenth century, Kate Chase Sprague, the wife of a senator and daughter of the chief justice after the Civil War, had a scandalous affair. In 1869, to highlight some of the hypocrisy of those who opposed free love, editor Victoria Woodhull exposed in her radical feminist newspaper *Woodhull and Claflin's Weekly* that prominent Brooklyn minister Henry Ward Beecher was having an affair with a married parishioner, Elizabeth Tilden. While the extramarital involvements of President John F. Kennedy were kept out of the public eye, 1988 presidential candidate Gary Hart saw his chances for the White House evaporate on the heels of newspaper reports of alleged sexual indiscretions.

Historically, there has been a high degree of tolerance for most males indulging in extramarital relations if they kept their liaisons quiet. Women have generally been more harshly condemned than men for sex outside of marriage. Alfred Kinsey's research in the 1930s and 40s revealed that half of the males he surveyed had committed adultery while only 25 percent of the women in his sample admitted to sex outside of marriage. Since the 1950s the percentage of women admitting to extramarital sexual relations has increased to a percentage roughly equal to that for men. Both the sexual double standard and the incidence of extramarital sex now appears to be declining.

—William G. Shade and Angela Howard Zophy

See Also:

Marriage; *New Morality*; Woodhull, Victoria

References:

D'Emilio, John, and Estelle Freedman. *Intimate Matters: A History of Sexuality in America.* New York: Harper & Row, 1988.

Gay, Peter. *The Education of the Senses.* New York: Oxford University Press, 1983.

Hunt, Morton. *Sexual Behavior in the 1970s.* New York: Dell, 1974.

Smith, Daniel Scott, and Michael S. Hindus. "Premarital Pregnancy in America, 1640–1971: An Overview and Interpretation." *Journal of Interdisciplinary History* 5 (Spring 1978): 537–70.

The FAIR LABOR STANDARDS ACT, 1938, was the first piece of federal legislation to provide wage and hour protection for both women and men workers in the United States. The act guaranteed to wage workers in industries involved in interstate commerce: a minimum wage of twenty-five cents an hour, rising over seven years to forty cents; no wage differentials on grounds of age or sex; a maximum work week of forty-four hours, reducing to forty over three years; overtime pay for additional hours worked; and an end to child labor (the employment of persons under sixteen). The act was held constitutional by the Supreme Court in *United States v. Darby* (1941).

Frances Perkins, secretary of labor in the Roosevelt administration, was responsible for formulating the law and winning the acquiescence of organized labor. Opposition came from some industrial and employers' organizations and from southern states where labor conditions lagged; it was met by allowing certain exceptions and special terms in the coverage of the act. Passed just a year after its introduction to Congress, the act achieved several goals long associated with women's organizations, but it had mixed results for women workers and significantly changed the nature of sex discrimination within the labor market.

Previous wage and hour restrictions were state controlled, restricted to women, and protected only an estimated 12 percent of adult female workers. The new act covered 57 percent of women workers and 39 percent of men workers. On the other hand, some of the occupations excluded from its coverage were major employers of the poorest women: domestic service, in which 97 percent of the workers were women and 52 percent black; agriculture, which employed many women seasonally in the fields; and many small retail and service employments that were not involved in interstate commerce. Moreover, Perkins's attempt to include in the act a ban on homework, a major mode of exploitation of women, was vetoed by legal advisers who feared it would imperil the entire act in the courts.

Thus, de jure, the act ended the explicit discrimination that had singled women workers out for separate treatment on the invidious argument that they were the weaker sex as well as "the mothers of the race." It therefore opened the way to the reunifying of the women's movement, split for two decades over whether protective laws for women helped by improving their conditions or hindered by contradicting the idea of equality embodied in the proposal for an Equal Rights Amendment. But, de facto, the act introduced a different discrimination by focusing upon the national and industrial economy in which, given the existing sex-segregated labor market, the work force was largely male. Subsequent amendments to the act have helped to rectify this situation, notably by the inclusion in 1973 of domestic labor in its minimum wage clause.

—*Vivien Hart*

See Also:

Perkins, Frances; Wages

Reference:

Frances Perkins Papers. Schlesinger Library. Radcliffe College, Cambridge, Mass.

Steinberg, Ronnie. *Wages and Hours: Labor and Reform in Twentieth-Century America*. New Brunswick, N.J.: Rutgers University Press, 1982.

U.S. Department of Labor, Records, 1933–1945. National Archives, Washington, D.C.

FAMILY LIMITATION (12 editions, 1914–21) is a sixteen-page pamphlet that catapulted its author, Margaret Sanger, to national prominence as leader of the birth control movement. With its clear and frank descriptions of various methods and its graphic illustrations of contraceptive devices, *Family Limitation* was the most useful guide to birth control then available to American women.

Although Sanger addressed *Family Limitation* to working women, who she assumed were the most burdened by the consequences of unplanned pregnancies, she asserted the right of *all* women to own and control their bodies. Emphasizing the importance of recognizing and accepting women's sexual needs, she urged women to arm themselves with a thorough understanding of their bodies and make use of the various contraceptive techniques available to them, including the use, when necessary, of abortion. She then encouraged them to share this knowledge with other women.

Aware that distributing the pamphlet would violate the legal prohibition on the dissemination of birth control material, Sanger was prepared to break the law and use her arrest to generate publicity for the cause. Margaret Sanger, however, was in England when the first copies of *Family Limitation* were circulated. Ironically, it was her husband, William Sanger, who was arrested for possessing a copy of the offending pamphlet. In a nationally publicized trial, William Sanger was found guilty and sentenced to thirty days in jail.

Anxious to keep the public focused on her cause, Margaret Sanger returned to the United States, and in 1916 embarked on a nationwide lecture tour to promote birth control. In the wake of the controversy generated by her speeches and the continued distribution of the now infamous pamphlet, Margaret Sanger soon emerged as the leader of the new birth control movement.

Some ten million copies of the pamphlet were to be distributed in the next two decades, and it was translated into thirteen languages. Although subsequent editions of the pamphlet muted some of the radical tone of the first edition and omitted specific reference to abortion, *Family Limitation* remains one of the most effective statements of the feminist position on the question of birth control. In clearly articulating the importance of recognizing women's sexuality and by insisting on their right to practice birth control, Margaret Sanger had set the parameters for the ongoing debate over reproductive rights.

—*Esther Katz*

See Also:

Birth Control; Sanger, Margaret

References:

Forster, Margaret. *Significant Sisters.* New York: Oxford University Press, 1984, pp. 239–75.

Gordon, Linda. *Woman's Body, Woman's Right: A Social History of Birth Control in America.* New York: Grossman, 1976.

Goulard, Joan M. "Woman Rebel: The Rhetorical Strategies of Margaret Sanger and the American Birth Control Movement, 1912–1938." Diss. Indiana University, 1978.

Jensen, Joan. "The Evolution of Margaret Sanger's 'Family Limitation' Pamphlet, 1914–1921." *Signs* 6 (Spring 1981): 548–67.

Sanger, Margaret. *An Autobiography.* New York: Norton, 1938.

———. *My Fight for Birth Control.* New York: Farrar & Rinehart, 1931.

FAMILY VIOLENCE has a long history, but it has only become a highly visible public issue at specific moments in the past. Victims have fought back in a variety of ways, and often called on kin and neighbors for aid; powerful legal sanctions against such abuse and the intervention of state and private welfare agencies into family disputes are more recent developments. Discussions of family violence have mainly centered on wife beating, physical and sexual abuse of children, and child neglect. However, much controversy over the definitions of family violence has existed over time among those affected, those called upon to intervene, and investigators today. The causes of different abusive relations also remain in dispute. "Moral," social, or environmental factors such as drink and poverty were often featured prominently in explanations of family violence over the last 150 years. In recent decades, many professional family service agencies promoted psychological explanations. These as well as previous causal analyses often led to victim-blaming or mother-blaming. Very recently, feminists have seen both male dominance and the sexual division of labor in parenting as important factors in producing violence.

Family violence and its history need to be understood through shifts in the politics of the family, and in the power struggles between husbands and wives, parents and children, and males and females generally. Where causal analyses have remained too narrow, solutions and aid remained too limited. Thus mothers and children have often commanded few resources that might have enabled them to escape abusive relationships.

Politicization and visibility of different forms of family violence varied, often reflecting heightened cultural anxieties about social disorder. The Puritans of the Massachusetts Bay Colony featured family violence as a public problem when they enacted laws against wife beating and "any unnatural severitie" toward children, beginning in 1641 (Pleck). In the nineteenth century, a diverse range of voices brought public attention to family violence. Temperance activists, divorce law reformers, and a number of woman's rights activists put wife abuse on the public agenda again in the mid-1800s. Sexual cruelty toward wives became a theme among feminist agitators and social purity reformers of the 1870s. Women's activists and law-and-order campaigners continued to organize against "crimes against women" in the last decades of the nineteenth century. Beginning in the 1870s, cruelty to children also rose to prominence as a public issue. Intervention into child abuse and wife abuse was linked in many periods; beaten wives often sought help through child welfare organizations that sprang up all across the United States in this era, such as the Societies for the Prevention of Cruelty to Children.

Early in the twentieth century, child "neglect" received increasing attention, and a number of state welfare initiatives arose around child poverty. Child sexual abuse received sporadic attention from the late nineteenth century onward, but girls were frequently blamed for "provoking" their assailants or were simply disbelieved about attacks. Much alarm about child abuse and particularly wife abuse waned after the first decades of this century. In the 1960s the battered child was "rediscovered," this time by the medical profession. Not until the 1970s did wife beating, marital rape, and sexual abuse of children again receive public attention, largely through the feminist movement.

—Jan Lambertz

See Also:

Marital Rape, Social Purity Movement

References:

Gordon, Linda. *Heroes of Their Own Lives. The Politics and History of Family Violence: Boston, 1880–1960.* New York: Viking, 1988.

Pleck, Elizabeth. *Domestic Tyranny: The Making of Social Policy Against Family Violence from Colonial Times to the Present.* New York: Oxford University Press, 1987.

FARLEY, HARRIET (1813–1907), operative in the Lowell textile mills, teacher, writer, and editor of the *Lowell Offering* (1842–45), was a strong proponent of the intellectual and artistic capabilities of the women mill workers, dedicated to removing the social "stigma" of factory work. The *Offering*, developed out of the publications of church self-improvement societies, brought the writings of young women mill workers to a larger regional and national audience.

The daughter of a New Hampshire clergyman, Farley was primarily self-educated. She worked as a teacher before coming to the mills, married in 1854, and moved to New York City; she had one child. Farley continued to attract attention with published collections of her own writings—*Shells from the Strand of the Sea of Genius* (1847) and *Happy Nights at Hazel Nook* (1852).

Farley's *Offering* focused on mill workers' intellectual and cultural development and on promotion of the dignity and capacities of mill workers. Not only Farley herself but also a number of other contributors and editors went on to publish books, articles, poems, and stories after and outside the *Offering*.

Farley was criticized for keeping the *Offering* out of the fray when the paternalism of the mill communities turned to pressure for increased productivity and lower wages. She ignored the Female Labor Reform Association's organizing in the mills ca. 1842–45. Sarah Bagley, a former *Offering* contributor, attacked Farley in the *Voice of Industry*, a local labor paper—accusing her of using the *Offering* to promote the interests of the mill owners instead of the mill operatives. While changing conditions belied the *Offering*'s image of Lowell operatives' active cultural life and leisure time for intellectual pursuits, Farley staunchly maintained the focus on culture and self-improvement.

—*Carol Klimick Cyganowski*

See Also:

Lowell Mill Girls, *Lowell Offering, Voice of Industry*

References:

Adickes, Sandra. "Mind Among the Spindles: An Examination of Some of the Journals, Newspapers, and Memoirs of the Lowell Female Operatives." *Women's Studies* I (1973): 279–87.

Douglas, Ann. *The Feminization of American Culture*. New York: Knopf, 1977.

Josephson, Hannah. *Golden Threads: New England's Millgirls and Magnates*. New York: Duell, Sloan and Pearce, 1949.

Robinson, Harriet Hanson. *Loom and Spindle, or Life Among the Early Mill Girls. With a Sketch of "The Lowell Offering" and Some of its Contributors*. New York: T. Y. Crowell, 1898; rpt. Kailua, Hawaii: Press Pacifica, 1976.

FARMER, SARAH JANE (1847–1916), a founder of the American Ba'hai movement, was born in Eliot, Maine, the only surviving child of Moses G. Farmer and Hannah Shipleigh Tobey Farmer. Her father, an electrical inventor, is credited with devising the first incandescent light bulb, electric trolley car, and electric fire alarm system—none of which he patented. Her mother was an abolitionist who was active in the Underground Railroad, a secret network that helped slaves escape to the North and Canada, and a feminist who in 1882 opened a home for unwed mothers in Eliot for the Boston City Mission Society.

Inspired by a visit to the World Parliament of Religions in Chicago in 1893, Farmer persuaded her co-partners in the Greenacre summer resort to allow her to turn the enterprise into a summer school devoted to the study of philosophy, religion, art, and contemporary social problems with a strong emphasis on comparative religion. The Greenacre Summer Conferences opened in the summer of 1894. In its first few years, the institute acted as a successor to the Concord School of Philosophy, with Franklin Sanborn, the last of the transcendentalists, and his associate Charles Malloy taking active roles. Until the mid-1900s, the school attracted a large number of literary and reform luminaries, particularly from the Boston area.

In 1900 overwork, financial difficulty, and early signs of mental illness (caused in part by arteriosclerosis) forced Farmer to bring the school's activities to a minimum. To recuperate, she spent the year on a cruise of the Mediterranean; while traveling in Persia, she met Abdu'l-Baha', leader of Ba'hai, who was in prison for his religious and political beliefs. Instantly converted, Sarah believed she had found in Ba'hai a spiritual home for her conviction that the world's great religions shared universal characteristics. Upon her return to Greenacre in 1901, she gave priority to the institute's Monsalvat School of Comparative Religion and personally espoused the "Persian Revelation." These changes caused rifts between the original conferees and the followers of Ba'hai. By 1913 Ba'hais achieved a majority on the board of directors; in 1928 Greenacre formally became an institute of the Ba'hai National Spiritual Assembly, a status it has maintained to the present.

Amid mounting sectarian rivalries, so contrary to her original vision of Greenacre, Farmer's mental health slowly deteriorated until by 1910 she was committed to an insane asylum in nearby Portsmouth, where she died of heart failure in 1916. While it is unclear whether after her conversion she intended Greenacre to become an official center of Ba'hai activity, Ba'hais rightfully claim her as a leading force in the early days of their movement.

—*Catherine Tumber*

References:

Atkinson, Robert. "Ba'hai's American Beginnings in Maine." *East/West* 17 (December 1977): 78–80.

Cameron, Kenneth Walter, ed. *Transcendentalists in Transition*. Hartford, Conn.: Transcendental Books, 1980.

Ingersoll, Anna Josephine. *Greenacre on the Piscataqua*. New York: Alliance, 1900.

Remy, Charles Mason. "Reminiscences of the Summer School, Greenacre, Eliot, Maine." Unpublished manuscript. Remy Family Records. Dartmouth College, Dartmouth, N.H.

FARNHAM, ELIZA WOOD BURHAM (1815–64), antebellum proponent of prison reform and woman's superiority, was born in Rensselaersville, New York, and, after her mother's death, was brought up by a "bad-tempered nagging aunt." While she spent a year at a Quaker school, Eliza was basically self-educated. At twenty she left for Illinois and later wrote a book about her experiences, *Life in Prairie Land* (1846). There she married Thomas Jefferson Farnham.

The couple moved east in 1840, and she wrote an article against political rights for women, whom she believed should elevate society in their domestic role. But Eliza Farnham was hardly the typical wife and mother. In 1844 she was chosen as the matron of the women's prison at Sing Sing. During her four-year tenure, she attempted to reform the system along principles based on phrenology. Believing criminals were not fully responsible for their crimes, she attempted to alter the environment to encourage their best instincts. She introduced education through lectures and reading, allowed the women to speak to each other, and attempted to brighten up the gloomy interior with large lamps, flowerpots, colorful maps, and even music. A series of personal and political conflicts eventually forced her out.

She went to Boston for a short time to aid Samuel Gridley Howe in his work with the blind. Then her husband's death and a desire to civilize the men in the gold rush lured her to California with a small party of unmarried women to create stable communities; this experience resulted in a book, *California: In-Doors and Out* (1856). While in California, she married William Fitzpatrick and taught school. After their only child died, the turbulent marriage ended in divorce. By the mid-1850s she was back in New York, studying medicine and encouraging other women to go to California. Although she moved back and forth, acting in 1861 as a matron at Stockton Insane Asylum and tending wounded at Gettysburg in 1863, somehow she managed to write her slightly fictionalized autobiography, *Eliza Woodson; Or, the Early Days of One of the World's Workers* (1864), and her classic feminist statement, *Woman and Her Era* (1865).

She believed women ranked higher than men on the evolutionary scale, because "woman's organism is more complex and her totality of function larger." Women's sexual nature was more "spiritual or super-sensual" than that of men, who focused exclusively on "corporeal" relations. Women's intellectual powers were more subtle and their maternal nature suited to projects of social reform.

—*William G. Shade*

See Also:

Prison Reform, Women's Prisons

References:

Farnham, Eliza W. *Woman and Her Era*. New York: C. M. Plumb and Co., 1865.

Riegel, Robert E. *American Feminists*. Lawrence: University Press of Kansas, 1963.

FAUSET, JESSIE REDMON (1882–1961), author and literary editor from 1919–26 of *The Crisis: A Record of the Darker Races* published by the National Association for the

Advancement of Colored People, was a major figure during the Harlem Renaissance. Fauset was born in Camden, New Jersey in 1882. Her father, Redmon Fauset, was an African Methodist Episcopal minister. A bright student, Fauset attended Philadelphia's High School for Girls and intended to continue her studies at Bryn Mawr, but was denied admission on the basis of her race. She entered Cornell and graduated Phi Beta Kappa in 1905. She received her M.A. from the University of Pennsylvania.

In addition to her role on *The Crisis,* where she was able to encourage the works of many gifted young writers such as Langston Hughes, Fauset was a major contributor to *Brownies' Book,* a publication for black children. She also wrote essays and poetry. During her life, Fauset published four novels: *There Is Confusion* (1924), *Plum Bun* (1929), *The Chinaberry Tree* (1931), and *Comedy: American Style* (1933). These novels generally dealt with the black middle class, and her protagonists were often mulattoes. Fauset often depicted marriage as a woman's ultimate fulfillment. This posture is understandable in view of the double burden of race and gender black women have traditionally endured. Although Fauset's novels are stylistically flawed, they were well received at the time. Critic Stanley Braithwaite compared her favorably with other major female literary figures.

For unknown reasons, Fauset left *The Crisis* in 1926. She taught high school in New York City from 1927 until 1944. Her works faded into obscurity, and she died in Philadelphia in 1961.

—*Rose Kolbasnik Callahan*

See Also:

Black Women

Reference:

Sylvander, Carolyn Wedin. *Jessie Redmon Fauset: Black American Writer.* Troy, N.Y.: Whitston, 1981.

FEMALE ACADEMIES (also often called "seminaries") were secondary schools for young women that appeared in greatest numbers in the years between 1820 and 1860. This period is sometimes referred to as the "age of the academy" in the history of American education, simply because of the large number of independent secondary schools for students of both sexes established at that time.

The earliest academies were all male, but many—perhaps most—academies in the antebellum period were coeducational, or offered separate courses of study for both boys and girls. The appearance of female academies was a significant development in the history of women's education, however, for it signaled the rise of a new appreciation for women's intellectual powers. The female academies also presented important career alternatives for women interested in a life of intellectual growth and public service; they offered women the opportunity of becoming professional educators and afforded them public visibility as educational reformers. Of course, the female academies represented a valuable resource to thousands of young women whose opportunities for advanced education would have been quite narrow had these schools not existed. The movement of women into higher education in the latter nineteenth century probably would not have been possible without the earlier efforts of educators in female academies to prove that young women were indeed capable of intellectual accomplishment.

Female academies were founded in the eighteenth century as a tangible result of the patriotic post-Revolutionary concept of Republican Motherhood, which refined and adapted the defintion of American womanhood to the needs of the new nation. The Young Ladies Academy of Philadelphia was established by socially prominent and educated men, with a curriculum that paralleled that of a college preparatory school for boys. This academy served as a prototype for the secular girls' schools of the early national period. However, the female academy movement is generally recognized as having started with the establishment of Emma Willard's Troy (N.Y.) Female Seminary in 1821. This school was designed to provide young women with an education generally equivalent to that given boys, at least as regarded standards of intellectual accomplishment. Willard and other women educators were critical of girls' "finishing" schools, which taught little more than embroidery, table manners, music appreciation, and perhaps a smattering of foreign language. Accordingly, the Troy Female Seminary offered courses in history, the sciences, and literature, as well as studies traditionally deemed important for young ladies. Willard and other women educators argued that women needed to study subjects such as these in order to educate their children (and especially their sons) better for the responsibilities of citizenship in the new republican social and political order. Following Willard's lead, dozens of other women dedicated themselves to careers as educators and founded their own academies. Among the most prominent were Zilpah Grant (Ipswich Academy), Catharine Beecher (Hartford Academy), and Mary Lyon (Mount Holyoke Seminary). Although many of these schools closed after a relatively short time (often because a founder moved on to new interests), their very existence was an affirmation of female intellectual accomplishment in an age when female abilities were often subject to denigration.

It is difficult to gauge the overall effect of the female academy movement on the course of women's history in the United States. Historian Anne Firor Scott has argued, for example, that Troy Female Seminary alumnae comprised a national network of early advocates for feminist reform. Although more study is needed, it is likely that other female academies exerted a similar influence. For thousands of women in the early- to mid-nineteenth century, the female academy may have been an enlightening—and in certain ways a liberating—experience, and one which subsequent generations of women could build upon.

—John L. Rury

See Also:

Beecher, Catharine; Education; Mount Holyoke Seminary; Rush, Benjamin; *Thoughts on Female Education*; Troy Female Seminary; Women in Higher Education; The Young Ladies Academy of Philadelphia

References:

Gordon, Ann D. "The Young Ladies Academy of Philadelphia." In *Women of America: A History*, edited by Carol Ruth Berkin and Mary Beth Norton. Boston: Houghton Mifflin, 1979, pp. 69–91.

Scott, Anne Firor. *Making the Invisible Woman Visible*. Urbana: University of Illinois Press, 1981.

Solomon, Barbara. *In the Company of Educated Women: A History of Women and Higher Education in America*. New Haven: Yale University Press, 1986.

Woody, Thomas. *A History of Women's Education in the United States*. Vol. I. New York: Science Press, 1929.

FEMALE-HEADED HOUSEHOLDS. A female family head is a woman who maintains a domicile and who may or may not have dependents. From the colonial period to the present, the majority of American families have been headed by males, but the proportion of households headed by women has increased gradually over time. In the early twentieth century the proportion of households headed by women increased more rapidly than previously. After World War II the rate of growth in female-household headship rose even more sharply. In 1890 approximately fourteen of one hundred American households were headed by women, but by 1970 twenty-one of one hundred households were.

Throughout the eighteenth and nineteenth centuries, widowing was the most common cause of female headship, but in the twentieth century new trends developed as single women began to establish separate households and as divorce rates rose. Rapidly increasing divorce rates in the 1960s and 1970s were the principal cause of the great increase in female headship during those years. By 1980 twenty-six of one hundred American households were headed by women.

The long-term rise in female headship indicates an increase in independence and autonomy among women, but it also reflects the rise in marital instability and the effects of increased life expectancy. Despite the rise in divorce rates, which is the principal cause of family headship among young mothers, the proportion of female household heads over the age of fifty-five has also risen in the twentieth century. Female headship among separated, divorced, and widowed women has always been associated with poverty. As the share of women living alone or heading families has grown, the relative poverty of these women and their children has also increased.

—*Julia Kirk Blackwelder*

See Also:
Divorce

References:

Ross, Heather L., and Isabel Sawhill, with the assistance of Anita R. MacIntosh. *Time of Transition: The Growth of Families Headed by Women.* Washington, D.C.: Urban Institute, 1975.

U.S. Bureau of the Census. *Historical Statistics of the United States, Colonial Times to 1970.* Bicentennial ed., Part 1. Washington, D.C.: U.S. Government Printing Office, 1975, Table A, 320–49, p. 42.

———. *U.S. Census of Population: 1980.* U.S. Summary, Vol. 1. Washington, D.C.: U.S. Government Printing Office, 1981, Table 121, p. 93.

FEMALE SEXUALITY is a subject in which survey research provides only the parameters of behavior. Knowledge of the female life cycle and its historical environment indicates that sexuality is physical while gender is socially defined.

The most traumatic period for women has always been puberty, when their bodies change dramatically and they have to deal with menstruation. Since the seventeenth century, the age of menarche has fallen by about three years, but women's response to it, as well as to childbirth and menopause, continues to be related to social definitions. The decline of death in childbirth has promoted a more positive view of bearing children, and various forms of birth control have separated sexual activity from procreation, thereby freeing women to express and enjoy sexuality as a source of sensual pleasure rather than as an inescapable biological function. Menopause, as the end of fertility, has been looked upon as a mixed blessing in a society that has defined and valued women according to their reproductive capacity. Although historically perceived as the beginning of "old age," menopause only modestly affects women's sexual response. By the mid-twentieth century women's life expectancy was double that of the seventeenth century. Women now outlive men by about a decade and find themselves in a sexually frustrating situation. Society has a prejudice against the "elderly," especially women, having sex in any form.

In general, in the modern era, society and women themselves have begun to acknowledge female sexuality. The social acceptance of female sexuality has increased gradually since the nineteenth century. Whereas the Victorians described women as pure, pious, and passionless, the behavioral studies done in this century indicate that roughly three-fourths of the women questioned admitted that they had masturbated. For women, unlike men, the practice seems to increase with age. Women's sexual activity is not a new phenomenon. In the eighteenth century a third of the brides in New England were pregnant; throughout the nineteenth and twentieth centuries similar indicators continue to show premarital sexual activity. In the late twentieth century, typically, women in their twenties have between four and five lovers before marriage, and the average married woman over thirty has sex twice a week.

Bisexuality is another area of sex in which there are significant differences between women and men. In Victorian America, women were isolated together and told that their sensibilities were of a higher order than men's. Half of the "first generation of college women" had intimate relations with female friends, and 20 percent carried these liaisons to orgasm. The lesbian feminist movement also enlarged choices for women's sexuality.

Psychologist Juanita Williams recently estimated that "one in five single women and one in ten married women" have had homoerotic experiences. In a society in which the sex/gender system is defined by men, women continue to experiment with and be troubled by their sexuality.

—*William G. Shade*

See Also:

Extramarital Sex, Kinsey Report, Lesbianism, Masturbation, Menarche, Menopause

References:

Davis, Katherine B. *Factors in the Sex Life of Twenty-Two Hundred Women.* New York: Harper, 1929.

D'Emilio, John, and Estelle Freedman. *Intimate Matters: A History of Sexuality in America.* New York: Harper, 1988.

Haller, John S., and Robin M. Haller. *The Physician and Sexuality in Victorian America.* Urbana: University of Illinois Press, 1974.

Hite, Shere. *The Hite Report: A Nationwide Study of Female Sexuality.* New York: Dell, 1976.

Hunt, Morton. *Sexual Behavior in the 1970s.* New York: Dell, 1974.

Kinsey, Alfred, et al. *Sexual Behavior in the Human Female.* Philadelphia: Saunders, 1953.

Shaefer, Leah Cahan. *Women and Sex: Sexual Experiences and Reactions of a Group of Thirty Women as Told to a Female Psychotherapist.* New York: Pantheon, 1973.

Smith-Rosenberg, Carroll. *Disorderly Conduct: Visions of Gender in Victorian America.* New York: Oxford University Press, 1985.

Williams, Juanita H. *Psychology of Women: Behavior in a Biosocial Context.* New York: Norton, 1983.

FEME COVERT is a legal term describing a married woman whose rights were restricted in early America by the common law concept of coverture. The woman and her husband became one will at the time of marriage, and the will was that of the husband. Her property, inheritance, and wages belonged to the husband, although the wife was protected in her right to dower and her right to veto any sale of family property. There were regional variations in the legal status of the *feme covert*; for example, married women enjoyed more independence in the Chesapeake colonies than they did in New England, particularly with respect to dower. Equity courts gave women some recourse from the restrictions of coverture.

—*Barbara E. Lacey*

See Also:

Coverture, Common Law, Dower, Equity Courts, *Feme sol*

References:

Kerber, Linda K. *Women of the Republic: Intellect and Ideology in Revolutionary America.* Chapel Hill: University of North Carolina Press, 1980.

Norton, Mary Beth. *Liberty's Daughters: The Revolutionary Experience of American Women, 1750–1800.* Boston: Little, Brown, 1980.

FEME SOL is a legal term describing a single or widowed woman in early America who was legally free from the male control established in marriage under the concept of coverture. A *feme sol* could own property, enter into contracts, bequeath possessions, and serve as a legal guardian or administrator of an estate, although she had few political rights. A married woman could gain *feme sol* trader status upon petition to the legislature if she could show that a husband was away for long periods of time, at sea or at war, and if the husband approved.

Few colonial women chose *feme sol* status deliberately. It was universally expected that a woman would marry, and there was little opportunity for financial support outside of marriage. However, of the tiny percentage of women who experienced personal autonomy, some came to develop conceptions of the self that differed from those of their married contemporaries.

The incremental success of nineteenth-century reform of state statutes that governed married women's property rights gradually rendered less significant the distinction between *feme sol* and *feme covert.* However, even in the late twentieth century, single women retained more legal autonomy than their married counterparts.

—*Barbara E. Lacey*

See Also:

Coverture, *Feme covert*, Married Women's Property Acts

References:

Chambers-Schiller, Lee Virginia. *Liberty, A Better Husband: Single Women in America: The Generations of 1780–1840.* New Haven: Yale University Press, 1984.

Lebsock, Suzanne. *The Free Women of Petersburg: Status and Culture in a Southern Town, 1784–1860.* New York: Norton, 1984.

Norton, Mary Beth. *Liberty's Daughters: The Revolutionary Experience of American Women, 1750–1800.* Boston: Little, Brown, 1980.

FEMINISM is a term used to describe collectively the historical movement for women's equality and (human) liberty within the nineteenth-century woman movement as well as the twentieth-century women's movement in the United States. *Feminism* was originally a French term that referred to the nineteenth-century American woman's movement, but has since proved a useful term to designate the diverse goals and groups that were involved in the pursuit of the advancement of women's position in American society.

The phrase *woman movement* was deemed adequate by nineteenth-century women's rights advocates to encompass the contemporary pluralistic activities of reform-minded women and men who worked for women's advancement, though not necessarily for women's equality. The phrase *woman movement*, however, unlike *feminism*, defies application as an adjective: this explains the popularity of *feminism* as the generic term preferred by twentieth-century women's historians to connote in either century the wide range of strategies and tactics, theories, and goals of efforts to improve conditions for women. Regarding the use of *woman movement* versus *women's movement*, generally women's historians observe the historically contemporary usage of *woman* in the generic sense—as in "the *Woman* Question" and the woman suffrage movement—when referring to the issues, events, and groups that date to the nineteenth century specifically; however, women's historians customarily use the plural form *women's* as indicative of the twentieth-century historical context.

At the turn of the century, the term *feminist* was applied narrowly to those women's rights advocates who espoused women's gender-unique nature and mystical maternal potential, rather than to designate those who emphasized their gender-neutral humanity and their similarity to men. By the latter half of the twentieth century, *feminist* became popular as the appropriate modifier term to connote advocacy of increased women's rights.

As a response to the Victorian emphasis on the nuclear family as a social and psychological unit rather than a functional one, feminism was both a radical and a conservative movement in the nineteenth century. Initially, American feminists challenged all aspects of the Victorian definition of woman that simultaneously degraded and elevated her. Collectively, their efforts focused upon agitation and propaganda on behalf of all the sex, while individually they seized upon new opportunities for women to realize personal advantage.

This pattern impelled feminists' participation in the mainstream reform movements of both the nineteenth and twentieth centuries, whether abolition, temperance, or other moral reform movements of the nineteenth century, or Progressivism, pacifism, or civil rights of the twentieth. As the interest of late Victorian feminists narrowed solely upon the suffrage issue, they pursued a conservative strategy and tactics to induce enfranchised male support for women's enfranchisement as a means of consolidating mainstream middle-class values. Feminism followed the fate of other reform movements during the 1920s; its visibility and impact ebbed until the New Dealers recruited its leaders to assist in the modification of national policies in the wake of the Great Depression. In a restricted fashion, the national emergency of World

War II opened doors for women as patriotic citizens that were closed with the onset of demobilization. However, those temporary opportunities in education and employment, again coupled with significant changes in the national economy, fostered women's resurgence as a presence in the civil rights and New Left movements of the 1950s and 1960s. Again, the women reformers confronted gender discrimination and responded by applying the egalitarian democratic philosophies of those movements to women's education in contemporary society.

Thus, since the 1960s in the wake of the modern women's movement, *feminism* has become the designated term for activities and issues connected with the entire spectrum of the struggle for improvement of women's conditions in society. By the 1980s the term *feminism* was commonly employed generally and imprecisely to designate a variety of doctrines, organized movements, theories, and assertions regarding women as a discrete group with a gender-specific history.

—*Angela Howard Zophy*

See Also:

Deconstruction, Domestic Feminism, Nineteenth-Century Woman's Movement, Patriarchy, Rationalism, Social Feminism, Socialism, Socialist Feminism, Suffrage, Twentieth-Century Women's Rights Movement

References:

Cott, Nancy F. *The Grounding of Modern Feminism.* New Haven: Yale University Press, 1988.

Flexner, Eleanor. *Century of Struggle: The Woman's Rights Movement in the United States.* Rev. ed. Cambridge, Mass.: Belknap, 1975.

Gordon, Linda. *Woman's Body, Woman's Right: A Social History of Birth Control in America.* New York: Penguin, 1977.

Lerner, Gerda. *The Creation of Patriarchy.* New York: Oxford University Press, 1986.

Ryan, Mary P. *Womanhood in America: From Colonial Times to the Present.* Ist ed. New York: New Viewpoints/Franklin Watts, 1975.

Schneir, Miriam. *Feminism: The Essential Historical Writings.* New York: Vintage, 1972.

FEMINIST LITERARY CRITICISM includes gender as a fundamental basis for literary analysis. It developed along with the women's movement in the late 1960s. Feminist literary criticism is unique in that it is atheoretical, employing all major approaches to literary criticism in its analysis of literature. Initially, feminist literary critics examined the traditional male canon of "great literature," exposing the misogynist elements in it. Then a search was begun for women's literature that had been relegated to obscurity by patriarchal decree, and a female literary canon emerged that led to the recognition of a female aesthetic in women's writing. Currently, feminist literary critics are continuing to explore the female aesthetic in women's writing, expose the misogyny in male literature, and search for women's writing with which to round out the female canon.

—*Victoria L. Shannon*

See Also:

Deconstruction, Feminism, Women's Liberation Movement

Reference:

Showalter, Elaine, ed. *Feminist Criticism: Essays on Women, Literature and Theory.* New York: Pantheon, 1985.

FERBER, EDNA (1885–1968) was a prolific journalist, novelist, short-story writer, and playwright whose works portray the American experience and whose fiction often depicts strong women characters.

Daughter of a Hungarian-born small businessman, she often reflected the pattern of her own family life in her literary works. Her father's inability to make a success of any of his various businesses and his eventual blindness led to his wife's taking control of the family finances. This theme of the strong woman who courageously faces adversity and achieves success is seen in a number of Ferber's works, most notably in her Emma McChesney short stories and the novels *So Big* and *Cimarron.*

Emma McChesney, a spunky divorced woman who sells Feather Loom petticoats to support her son, is the character that made Ferber a popular success. More than twenty stories based on this character were published between 1911 and 1915, and when Ferber was covering the 1912 Democratic National Convention, Theodore Roosevelt reportedly asked her when Emma McChesney was going to marry.

Marriage, however, does not appear in Ferber's novels as a deus ex machina for her female protagonists. Rather, in *So Big*, a woman who is widowed receives only a debt-ridden farm as a legacy. However, due to her unceasing effort and strength of mind, she reverses the ineptitude that characterized her husband's management and makes the farm prosper. In *Cimarron*, the wife is the practical, hard-working half of the couple.

Ferber was a great popular success and a prolific writer. She wrote fourteen novels, ten collections of short stories, and nine plays (some in collaboration). *So Big* received a Pulitzer Prize in 1924; many of her works were turned into movies (*Show Boat*, *Cimarron*, *Giant*, for example); some of her plays also enjoyed successful runs on Broadway. Although not generally regarded highly by literary critics, Ferber is an interesting and important writer, especially in her portrayal of women, her sensitivity to the values of the land, and her interest in the social and cultural life of the working classes.

—*Mabel Benson DuPriest*

See Also:
Journalism

References:

Brenni, V. J., and B. L. Spencer. "Edna Ferber: A Selected Bibliography." *Bulletin of Bibliography* 22 (1958): 152–56.

Gilbert, Julie Goldsmith. *Ferber: A Biography*. Garden City, N.Y.: Doubleday, 1978.

FERRARO, GERALDINE (b. 1935) in 1984 became the first woman to be the vice-presidential candidate of a major political party in the United States. Ferraro was born in Newburgh, New York, to Dominick and Antonetta (Corrieri) Ferraro. Her father was a restaurateur and dime-store owner who died when she was only eight years old. Her mother then moved to the Bronx and supported the family in part by crocheting beads on dresses. Partly because of the sacrifices of her mother, and partly due to her own hard work, Ferraro was able to graduate from Marymount College, Tarrytown, New York, in 1956.

She then began a career as a second-grade teacher in the New York City public school system and began attending law school classes at night at Fordham University. In 1960 she married John Zaccaro, a real estate broker, and they eventually raised a family of three children. That same year, she graduated from Fordham's law school. She was admitted to the New York Bar in 1961. Between 1961 and 1974 Ferraro stayed in private practice. In 1974 she became an assistant district attorney for Queens County, New York, handling many child-abuse, domestic-violence, and rape cases. These experiences between 1974 and 1978 turned her from a self-confessed "small-*c* conservative to a liberal."

Active in local Democratic party politics, Ferraro ran successfully for the U.S. House of Representatives in 1978, representing the Ninth District (Queens). One of fewer than two dozen congresswomen, Ferraro was reelected for two additional terms in the House. Respected by her colleagues and the House Democratic leadership, she served on the House's Public Works Committee, the Democratic Steering and Policy Committee, and in 1983, the powerful Budget Committee. Her stature as a politician was further enhanced when she was named secretary of the House Democratic Caucus. Ferraro's voting record was generally mainstream liberal Democratic. This took considerable political courage, for she represented an often conservative, ethnic, blue-collar district. She did placate her more conservative constituents on one occasion by voting against mandatory busing for school integration. Ferraro's support for the right to choice on abortion also took a great deal of courage and soul-searching for a convinced Roman Catholic.

In July 1984 her name became a household word in the United States when Democratic presidential nominee Walter Mondale named her as his vice-presidential running mate. Her nomination sparked widespread jubilation among women and sympathetic men—another barrier had been shattered. As Ferraro noted in her acceptance speech to the Democratic National Convention, "By choosing a woman to run for our nation's second highest office, you send a powerful signal to all Americans. There are no doors we cannot unlock."

Despite the harsh glare of public scrutiny, Ferraro ran a spirited and vigorous campaign. She impressed many people with her command of the issues and her ability as a public speaker. Nevertheless, despite her abilities as a campaigner, there was little that could be done to overcome the incredible popularity of Ronald Reagan. Geraldine Ferraro returned to private life and completed her campaign memoirs in 1985.

—Jonathan W. Zophy

See Also:

Democratic Party, Gender Gap, Politics

References:

Adams, James R. "The Lost Honor of Geraldine Ferraro." *Commentary* 81 (January 1986): 34–38.

Ferraro, Geraldine. *Ferraro: My Story*. New York: Bantam, 1985.

Thomas, Evan. "'Just One of the Guys' and Quite a Bit More." *Time* 124 (July 23, 1984): 18–20, 33.

FERTILITY. With the exception of short-term fluctuations, the birthrate in America has declined consistently from the colonial period to the present. From the seventeenth century until the early nineteenth century, it was very high in comparison with that of other Western societies. For these years, average "completed fertility" was about eight children for every married woman in America. Although demographers variously date the beginning of the modern fertility decline between 1770 and 1830, there is general agreement that the late nineteenth century was a period of sharp decline.

Among women who had completed their childbearing by 1910, the average number of children born to each was 5.4. Since 1910, completed fertility has declined to between two and three children per "ever-married" woman. A noticeable but temporary "boom" in fertility occurred between 1947 and 1964, with the birthrate reaching a twentieth-century high of 25.3 births per 1000 women between the ages of fifteen to forty-five years in 1957. But these rates were still considerably below the estimated 65 to 77 births per 1000 women in the late nineteenth century. Fertility in the United States has declined since 1964.

Important differences in fertility exist between regions and among ethnic or racial groups in the United States. Fertility has consistently been higher in rural than in urban areas, and immigrant women and nonwhite women have generally had higher fertility than native-born white women. During the years of Negro slavery, black women had consistently higher fertility than white women, but black fertility rates declined gradually after emancipation, and during the 1930s, the black fertility rate dropped below that of whites.

—Julia Kirk Blackwelder

See Also:

Demography

References:

Grabill, Wilson H., Clyde V. Kiser, and Pascal K. Whelpton. *The Fertility of American Women.* New York: Wiley, 1958.

Taeuber, Conrad, and Irene Taeuber. *The Changing Population of the United States.* New York: Wiley, 1958.

U.S. Bureau of the Census. *Historical Statistics of the United States, Colonial Times to the Present.* Part 1, Bicentennial ed. Washington, D.C.: U.S. Government Printing Office, 1975.

FITZGERALD, ZELDA (SAYRE) (1900–48) was born in Montgomery, Alabama, the daughter of Judge Anthony D. Sayre and Minnie Machen, but left the South in 1920 when she married writer F. Scott Fitzgerald. Because of the immediate popularity of his writing, which embodied the freewheeling yet restless spirit of the era, and because of the Fitzgeralds' considerable good looks and charm, they captured the imagination of the American public during the 1920s and came to be known as "the couple" of the era.

Newspapers reported on their flamboyant life-styles, on the East Coast and then in Europe, and accounts invariably cast Zelda in a 1920s flapper mold. Scott's writing reinforced this image, as he modeled his free-spirited but spoiled heroines after Zelda. Increasingly, it became difficult for Zelda to separate herself from this fictionalized image and also from her husband's fame. In 1925, shortly after the critically acclaimed publication of Fitzgerald's *Great Gatsby*, the couple joined the American expatriate community in France, where the strain on their marriage due to Scott's success and the accompanying life-style, excessively self-indulgent and extravagant, began to tell. Scott found it difficult to write during the last half of the decade, and Zelda showed signs of extreme introversion.

Although Scott and Zelda had collaborated on the writing of some stories and essays during the early 1920s, Zelda received only slight recognition, and this began to bother her. Having failed to achieve acclaim as a writer, she sought to earn recognition as a dancer. But she began to study ballet too late in life (at the age of twenty-eight), and eventually the strain of her obsessive workouts, complicated by the strains in the Fitzgeralds' marriage, began to take both a physical and psychological toll. Zelda suffered her first mental breakdown in France in 1930, and what her doctors diagnosed as schizophrenia kept her in and out of institutions, in Europe and in America, for the rest of her life. Interned on the top floor of the main building of the Ashville (North Carolina) Highland Mental Hospital, she died in 1948 when the structure caught fire.

Although Zelda was unable to pursue her dancing, she did achieve a degree of success both as a writer and a painter. Her autobiographical novel *Save Me the Waltz*, which was published in 1932 and which received limited recognition, is generally regarded today as a work that shows potential but lacks discipline, its imagery evocative but disjointed and overwrought. Zelda's painting (primarily watercolors that she began to execute after the appearance of her novel) employed wild, grotesque images—flowers and human figures that were almost cartoonlike in their vibrant colors and flat, distorted dimensions. Zelda seemed to derive her greatest artistic rewards from her paintings, which she continued to execute throughout the 1940s until her death. Some of these paintings were exhibited in New York at private galleries and purchased by friends. Zelda's creativity was considerable, but the circumstances of her life made it difficult, if not impossible, for her to find a suitable focus for her genius.

—Linda Patterson Miller

See Also:

Flapper

References:

Bruccoli, Matthew J., and Margaret M. Duggan, eds. *Correspondence of F. Scott Fitzgerald.* New York: Random House, 1980.

Mayfield, Sara. *Exiles from Paradise: Zelda and Scott Fitzgerald.* New York: Delacorte, 1971.

Mellow, James R. *Invented Lives: F. Scott & Zelda Fitzgerald.* Boston: Houghton Mifflin, 1984.

Milford, Nancy. *Zelda.* New York: Harper & Row, 1970.

FLAPPER. The image of the flapper has become inseparable from the popular perception of the 1920s. Originally the British term for pre-debutantes, flapper came to designate those young women who flaunted unconventional behavior and dress during and after World War I. The flapper was immortalized in the contemporary literature and media of an era that was characterized by disillusionment and obsessed with the impact of political fundamentalism. A symbol of the social rebellion of youth in the 1920s, the flapper was glamorized far beyond the actual minority of middle-class educated young women who indulged in the unfettered and scandalously hedonistic life-style that centered on publicly smoking cigarettes and drinking illegal alcohol while frequenting the after-hours speakeasies and jazz clubs. As a version of womanhood, the flapper not only expressed the power struggle between the rising city and waning rural heartland, but also repudiated the duty, dedication, and civic activism of both domestic feminism and social feminism.

The flapper was a commercialized sex object, but she floated between androgyny and child pornography. Physically, she should look like a sexy boy and intellectually and emotionally be a woman of the world. Thus, the fashionable costume of the flapper emphasized her immediate role as a glamorous playmate for idle, over-indulged young men, rather than offering a suitable ensemble for her ultimate role as worker, wife, or mother. The marketable image of the flapper had little relevance to the lives of the majority of women who—either as sex-segregated workers or as homemaker-consumers—became the mainstay of the unstable and overheated economy of the 1920s. Therefore, the flapper vanished quickly from both literature and the media after the Crash of '29 brought the Great Depression and the repeal of prohibition.

—William G. Shade and Angela Howard Zophy

See Also:

Fitzgerald, Zelda; Freudianism; New Woman; Social Feminism

References:

Fass, Paula. *The Beautiful and the Damned: American Youth in the 1920s.* New York: Oxford University Press, 1977.

Ryan, Mary P. *Womanhood in America: From Colonial Times to the Present.* 2d ed. New York: New Viewpoints, 1979.

Yellis, Kenneth. "Prosperity's Child: Some Thoughts on the Flapper." *American Quarterly* 21 (Spring 1969): 44–64.

The **FLINT AUTO WORKERS' STRIKE**, in Flint, Michigan, was the most famous of the "sit-down" strikes introduced by the United Auto Workers union. Lasting forty-four days—from December 30, 1936, to February 11, 1937—the strike was a response to pent-up anger over an intolerable speedup on the assembly line and management's refusal to bargain with the union even though the law required it. Settlement of the strike brought about recognition of the United Auto Workers (UAW) by General Motors and a wage increase from thirty to forty cents an hour to one dollar an hour; the union also grew from thirty thousand to five hundred thousand members because of the success of the strike.

During the strike, sit-downers occupied three Fisher Auto Body Assembly plants, subsidiaries of GM. The sit-down strike was an effective tactic because any assault against the workers inside the plant would endanger the expensive machinery there. Scabs couldn't be used and a solidarity developed among the workers living in the plant. A network of committees helped with legal defense, food, picketing, transportation, publicity, and other needs. Women played a big part in this outside organization. (The union leadership had decided that only men would occupy the plants, to the anger of many women workers.) When the police began to threaten the workers inside the plants, women established a Women's Emergency Brigade with three hundred fifty volunteers who formed a protective picket line between strikers and police. "A new type of woman was born in the strike," one of the women said. "Women who only yesterday were horrified at unionism, who felt inferior to the task of organizing, speaking, leading, have, as if overnight, become the spearhead in the battle of unionism."

On January 21 the police shot fourteen people in a conflict that became known as the Battle of Bulls Run. Mary Heaton Vorse, who wrote about the strike, said it was called that because the "bulls" (the police) ran: "Preparatory to the battle the street had been cleared. The women said, 'Nothing was going to stop us getting food in to our men.' The police were firing point-blank into the crowd that included women. Union sympathizers were retaliating with the only means of defense they had—stones, lumps of coal, steel hinges, milk bottles. That, and their courage, were their only weapons. Yet they held their ground."

In the final crisis of the strike, after the sit-downers occupied the "Chevrolet 4" plant, thousands of workers came into Flint. To avoid the appearance of provocation, organizers declared the mobilization Women's Day, and women's brigades came in from Lansing, Pontiac, Detroit, and Toledo, Ohio. A woman's voice addressed a great picket line from the sound wagon. Mary Heaton Vorse described it: "She told the crowd that the women had gone to union headquarters to wipe their eyes clear from tear gas and would soon be back. 'We don't want any violence; we don't want any trouble.... But we are going to protect our husbands.'"

The Flint Auto Strike proved significant to both labor and women's history. The success of the strike strengthened the UAW and the organized labor movement of the 1930s because the publicity surrounding the strike bolstered public support for unionization as well as spurring the passage of the major piece of New Deal labor legislation, the Wagner Act of 1935. The strike also demonstrated the importance to the achievement of the union victory in 1937 of women's support for and within the local union. The drama of women's participation in the strike was captured in the documentary *With Babies and Banners* [New Day Films].

—*Abby Schmelling*

See Also:

Unions, United Auto Workers

References:

Boyer, Richard, and Herbert Morais. *Labor's Untold Story.* New York: United Electrical, Radio and Machine Workers of America, 1974.

Brecher, Jeremy. *Strike!* Greenwich, Conn.: Fawcett, 1974.

Fine, Sidney. *Sit-Down, The General Motors Strike of 1936–37.* Ann Arbor: University of Michigan Press, 1969.

Vorse, Mary Heaton. *Labor's New Millions.* New York: Modern Age, 1938.

FLYNN, ELIZABETH GURLEY (1890–1964), a political activist for over fifty years, was fondly known as "the Rebel Girl" of the Industrial Workers of the World (IWW). Her mother, Annie Gurley Flynn, was a member of the Knights of Labor and the Irish Feminist Club in New York City; her father, Thomas Flynn, belonged to the Socialist Labor party and the IWW, a revolutionary organization that worked to radicalize the labor movement in the early twentieth century. Flynn made her first political speech at the age of sixteen, addressing the Harlem Socialist Club on the topic "What Socialism Will Do for Women." The following year she joined the IWW.

Flynn cut her political teeth in the free-speech fights of 1909 on behalf of the IWW effort to organize labor in the West and soared to national prominence as one of the fiery speakers at the 1912 textile strike in Lawrence, Massachusetts. In 1908 she met and married IWW organizer Jack Jones and bore two children, a premature baby who died shortly after birth and a son, Fred. The marriage lasted only two years, and in Lawrence she met the anarchist Carlo Tresca, with whom she lived for the next thirteen years.

From 1910 until 1917, Flynn worked ceaselessly to organize workers into the IWW and spoke out forcefully on women's issues. She accepted, however, the IWW philosophy that women's problems could not be separated from the problems of the working class. After 1917 Flynn specialized in labor defense work, supporting the hundreds of radicals arrested and imprisoned during the first Red Scare of 1919. In 1926, exhausted from her efforts on behalf of Sacco and Vanzetti and from her breakup with Tresca, she retired to Portland, Oregon, and spent ten years regaining her physical and emotional health.

Flynn was a founding member of the American Civil Liberties Union in 1920 and served on its board of directors until 1940. In 1937 she joined the Communist party, and three years later the ACLU board voted narrowly to expel her for her defiance of a resolution designed to purge members who belonged to "any political organization which supports totalitarian dictatorship." (The resolution, originally intended to exclude fascists, was mostly used against members of the Communist party.)

Flynn remained in the Communist party, and in 1961 became its first woman chairperson. In 1951 she, along with other party leaders, was prosecuted under the Smith Act, also known as the Alien Registration Act. Convicted in 1953, she served two and a half years in Alderson Prison, Alderson, West Virginia. Elizabeth Gurley Flynn died in Moscow in 1964 on her first visit to the U.S.S.R. In 1978 the ACLU posthumously rescinded her expulsion.

—Mary Murphy

See Also:

Communist Party, Industrial Workers of the World, Lawrence Strike of 1912

References:

Baxandall, Rosalyn Fraad. *Words on Fire: The Life and Writing of Elizabeth Gurley Flynn.* New Brunswick, N.J.: Rutgers University Press, 1987.

Flynn, Elizabeth Gurley. *The Rebel Girl, An Autobiography.* New York: International Publishers, 1973.

FOLKLORE means folk learning, and includes any and all knowledge transmitted by word of mouth. The term *folklore* therefore encompasses all techniques, arts, and crafts learned by imitation rather than formal instruction. The field encompasses studies of arts, crafts, tools, costumes, customs, beliefs, medicine, recipes, dance, games, gestures, speech, and verbal arts such as folktales, legends, myths, proverbs, riddles, poetry, and humor. Folklore functions in society to provide education, transmit social norms, support political relations, and provide psychological releases from cultural and social restrictions and taboos. Women's folklore has been included in studies of fairy tales and folktales, rituals and rites of passage, storytelling, and, in brief, most aspects of folklore and folk arts.

—Mary G. Hodge

See Also:

Native American Women, Native American Women's Literature, Quilts

References:

Dorson, Richard M., ed. *Folklore and Folklife, An Introduction.* Chicago: University of Chicago Press, 1972.

Farrer, Claire R., ed. *Women and Folklore.* Austin: University of Texas Press, 1975.

Harding, M. Esther. *Women's Mysteries, Ancient and Modern.* New York: Rider, 1955.

Lincoln, Bruce. *Emerging from the Chrysalis: Studies in Rituals of Women's Initiation.* Cambridge: Harvard University Press, 1981.

von Franz, Marie Louise. *Problems of the Feminine in Fairytales.* Irving, Tex.: Spring Publications, 1972.

Weigel, Marta. *Spiders and Spinsters: Women and Mythology.* Albuquerque: University of New Mexico Press, 1982.

FONDA, JANE (b. 1937), actress, political activist, and entrepreneur, has matured from a young sex symbol to a socially conscious artist and businesswoman. The daughter of acclaimed actor Henry Fonda, she spent her early years trying to avoid a career in theater. She studied for a short time at Vassar, then left to study art in Paris and piano in New York. In 1958 she entered Lee Strasberg's Actors Studio. Within two years, she began the career that would eventually make her prominent in American film, politics, and business.

While Fonda's earliest success as an actress was onstage, she is primarily a film actress. Early films such as *Barbarella* (1968), directed by her first husband, Roger Vadim, established her as an American sex symbol. But by the early 1970s, Fonda had a political epiphany that changed the direction of her film career.

Her political activism, growing out of a reaction to the civil rights movement and the Vietnam War, was developed in films such as *Coming Home* (1978) and *The China Syndrome* (1979) that promoted her political beliefs. Deeply disturbed by violence and oppression, Fonda became one of America's most vocal critics of American involvement in Southeast Asia. She toured army bases with a show satirizing the war in Vietnam and spoke out against the war in interviews and at colleges across the nation. Her criticism of American foreign policy led to arrests and antipathy from the film industry and much of her audience. She received the Sour Apple Award from the Hollywood Women's Press Club for presenting a sour image of the industry. But Fonda remained undaunted by the criticism and continued her activism energetically. In 1972 she outraged many by touring North Vietnam and posing next to an antiaircraft gun.

Fonda survived the attacks on her beliefs and remained active in politics after the Vietnam War ended. With her second husband, Congressman Tom Hayden, she formed the Campaign for Economic Democracy, an egalitarian grassroots organization designed to create a middle-class revolution for economic opportunity. Working with Hayden in the 1980s, Fonda was a vocal critic of nuclear energy, big business, sexual discrimination, and other social justice issues. She has also mixed politics and performances in the films produced by her company, Indo-China Peace Campaign, to redefine herself as an actress.

In the mid-1970s Fonda's professional life brought her to national attention as a successful businesswoman. Her first business venture was Indo-China Peace Campaign (IPC), a film company established to produce films on contemporary issues. The company has produced such phenomenal successes as *Coming Home, The China Syndrome,* and *Nine to Five* (1980). Fonda's second business venture, Workout, Inc., proved even more successful than IPC, and is revolutionizing both the fitness and video markets. Owned by the Campaign for Economic Democracy, Workout, Inc. operates fitness studios and produces books, records, videotapes, and clothing. Fonda's workout books are best-sellers, and her first *Jane Fonda's Workout* videotape became the top grossing video of all time. All the clothing manufactured under Fonda's name is 100 percent union-made and 100 percent American-made. Fonda supports Affirmative Actions, a Boston organization that invests in ventures that are attractive to liberals, and has used her business ventures to pursue her political and artistic goals.

While many predicted that her political activities would end her career, Jane Fonda has survived criticism to establish herself as one of the most acclaimed public figures in America. Winner of Academy Awards for *Klute* (1971) and *Coming Home,* as well as a New York Film Critics' Award for *They Shoot Horses, Don't They?* (1969), a Golden Globe for *Coming Home,* and an Emmy for *The Dollmaker* (1984), Fonda has proved herself to be one of America's most talented actresses. But public-opinion polls ranking her as the number-one heroine of young Americans (*U.S. News and World Report,* 1985) and as the fourth most admired woman in America (Roper Poll, *Ladies' Home Journal,* 1984) suggest she is respected not only as an artist, but as a political activist and businesswoman. Maturing from sex symbol to a professional woman, Fonda has emerged as a role model for American women.

—*Avery Preston Lane*

See Also:

Movie Stars, Vietnam War

References:

Fonda, Jane. *Jane Fonda's New Workout and Weight-Loss Program.* New York: Simon & Schuster, 1986.

———. *Jane Fonda's Workout Book.* New York: Simon & Schuster, 1981.

——— with Mignon McCarthy. *Women Coming of Age.* New York: Simon & Schuster, 1984.

Guiles, F. L. *Jane Fonda.* New York: Doubleday, 1982.

Vadim, Roger. *Bardot, Deneuve, Fonda.* Translated by Melinda Camber Porter. New York: Simon & Schuster, 1986.

FOOTE, MARY HALLOCK (1847–1918), popular writer and illustrator, published a total of thirteen novels, fourteen short stories and story collections, and innumerable illustrations of life on the western frontier. Born in Milton, New York, to an old agrarian Quaker family and educated at the Cooper Institute for Art, Foote had launched a promising career as an artist when she suddenly gave it up to marry Arthur DeWint Foote, a mining engineer from the West.

After the wedding in 1876, her husband took her away from the genteel, established East to the rough-hewn, developing frontier in Colorado. Over the next thirty years, he moved his family from mining camp to mining camp in Colorado, Mexico, Idaho, and California, wherever he could find work. Because her husband's career was less than successful, Foote was forced to write novels so that the bills could be paid and the children fed.

Set in various mining and irrigation camps, Foote's novels and tales made a significant contribution to nineteenth-century western realism and local color. Her observations of the character of frontier lands and the people who lived there are important because Foote's perspective was unique: she was writing from the point of view of a moderately wealthy Easterner who was suddenly transplanted to the West; and she was writing from the point of view of a woman, a wife, and a mother.

Many of Foote's novels, including *The Led-Horse Claim* (1882), *The Last Assembly Ball* (1886), *The Chosen Valley* (1892), and *Edith Bonham* (1917), were first published serially in *Scribner's Monthly*; the books were all published by Houghton Mifflin, & Co. of Boston. Wallace Stegner's 1971 novel *The Angle of Repose* is based upon the life of Mary Hallock Foote.

—*Deborah Dawson Bonde*

See Also:

Migration and Frontier Women

References:

Johnson, LeeAnn. *Mary Hallock Foote.* Boston: Twayne, 1980.

Maguire, James. *Mary Hallock Foote.* Caldwell, Idaho: Caxton Printers, 1972.

Paul, Rodman, ed. *A Victorian Gentlewoman in the Far West: Reminiscences of Mary Hallock Foote.* San Marino, Calif.: Huntington Library, 1972.

FORSYTH, JESSIE (1847–1937), temperance organizer and editor, was a leading figure in the Good Templar fraternal temperance society and an advocate of total abstinence, prohibition, and saving children from the evils caused by alcohol. She also advocated women's suffrage, racial equality, world peace, and the utopian socialism of Edward Bellamy, and was a devout Anglican.

Her life illustrates the internationalism of the temperance movement and its connections with other reform agitations. She was born in London, England, where she joined the Good Templars in 1872, emigrated to Boston in 1874, and to Australia, where her sister lived, in 1911. When her organization, between 1876 and 1887, became divided over rights for blacks, she emerged as a leader in the faction that advocated full rights for peoples of all races. From 1883 to 1887 she edited the monthly *Temperance Brotherhood.* After the reunion of the Good Templars, she served as International Superintendent of Juvenile Templars, 1893–1908 (in the final year the membership in this children's auxiliary approached 240,000) and edited the monthly *International Good Templar* from 1901 to 1908.

Forsyth also served as state president of the Woman's Christian Temperance Union of Western Australia, 1913–16, and as organizing secretary of the Australian National Prohibition League, 1917–18.

—*David M. Fahey*

See Also:

Good Templars, Suffrage, Temperance Movement

References:

Fahey, David M., ed. *The Collected Writings of Jessie Forsyth, 1847–1937: The Good Templars and Temperance Reform on Three Continents.* Lewiston, N.Y.: Edwin Mellen, 1988.

Forsyth, Jessie. "Thirty Years of Good Templary." *International Good Templar*, 1903–04.

FOSTER, ABBY KELLEY (1811–87) was the unwitting symbol of the women's rights movement of the 1840s. Born in Massachusetts of Irish Quaker parents, Abigail Kelley inherited a strong belief in human and sexual equality, and pacifism. It is no wonder that the antislavery teachings of William Lloyd Garrison became the major influence on her adult life, casting her fully in the role of abolitionist. Her relationship and subsequent marriage to Stephen Foster, an abolitionist and follower of the Quaker-influenced nonviolence called nonresistance, broadened her circle of concern and helped her focus her activities. Together, the Fosters emphasized the importance of individual independent effort, mistrusting all organizations, including the formal church and political groups. Their only child, Alla, provided Foster with the challenge of proving one could be a wife and mother while remaining an active, freethinking woman. She was more closely aligned with modern woman than with her peers.

Foster was the first woman to insist on speaking in the public arena, and the first to insist on speaking to mixed male-female audiences. She steadfastly recognized the urgent need to resolve the antislavery issues and opposed efforts to merge the rights of blacks with the rights of white women and the poor. The validation of Foster's life work was the ratification of the Thirteenth Amendment (1865), which abolished slavery forever in the United States, and ratification of the Fifteenth Amendment (1870), which secured this freedom by giving black men the right to vote. In her zeal to achieve freedom for blacks, Foster furthered the woman's rights movement.

—Beverly Falconer Watkins

See Also:

Abolition and the Antislavery Movement; Public Speakers, Women

References:

Foster Papers. American Antiquarian Society. Worcester, Mass.

Bacon, Margaret Hope. *I Speak for My Slave Sister*. New York: Crowell, 1974.

Pease, Jane. "The Freshness of Fanaticism, Abby Kelley Foster, An Essay in Reform." Diss. University of Rochester, 1969.

The **FOURTEENTH AMENDMENT** to the U.S. Constitution, which enfranchised freedmen, was passed by Congress on June 16, 1866, and ratified by the required three-fourths of the states on July 28, 1868. Proposed by the majority Radical Republicans through their Joint Committee of Fifteen, this amendment followed the Union victory in the Civil War and was proposed as a consequence of the Thirteenth Amendment, which abolished the institution of slavery within the United States. In the Constitution as ratified in 1789, the designation of enfranchisement had been left to the individual states. The Fourteenth Amendment reflected the Unionists' determination to assert the preeminence of federal authority in an area that previously constituted a major "states' right." However, in their concern to ensure the enfranchisement of the freedmen in the recalcitrant Southern states, the abolitionist-minded Radical Republicans allowed the specific introduction of gender into the Constitution through the Fourteenth Amendment.

Section 1 of the Fourteenth Amendment provided a formal definition of national citizenship that included "all persons born or naturalized in the United States . . ." and prohibited a state's right to "abridge the privileges or immunities" of those citizens. Moreover, Section 1 denied to any state the power to "deprive any person of life, liberty, or property, without due process." This passage of the Fourteenth Amendment became known as the "equal protection" clause.

Section 2 prescribed diminished representation in Congress for any state that denied or abridged the right to vote in federal or state elections to "any of the male inhabitants of such state, being twenty-one years of age and citizens of the United States" (except Indians, who were not taxed, and convicts or participants in rebellion). The word *male* in Section 2 introduced the issue of gender into the Constitution.

The next two sections focused on the congressional repudiation of former Confederate officers and officials as well as of the Confederacy's war debt. The last section was the standard enabling clause, authorizing

Congress to pass the legislation necessary to put the ratified amendment into effect.

While the definition of citizenship in Section 1 included women and seemingly ensured their equal protection under the law, the gender-specific definition of the franchise in Section 2 made the task of woman suffrage advocates more difficult. The debate over passage of the Fourteenth Amendment initiated a split within the ranks of woman suffrage supporters because it presented a dilemma for a significant proportion of their number, the female supporters of the abolition and antislavery movement. Capitalizing on the unconditional support for the Thirteenth Amendment, antislavery and abolition men and women of both races established the Equal Rights Association in 1866 to pursue both black and woman suffrage. However, fearing the loss of freedmen's suffrage if that issue were linked with woman suffrage, the Radical Republicans and most of the black political leaders disassociated themselves and black suffrage from their previous equal support of black and women's rights, especially suffrage. The disastrous and divisive "Kansas Campaign" of 1867, in which separate state referenda on black and woman suffrage were defeated, precipitated the schism within the woman suffrage movement that produced first the National Woman Suffrage Association in 1868 and then the American Woman Suffrage Association in 1869.

In 1871 the flamboyant free love advocate Victoria Woodhull appeared before the House Judicial Committee to present a petition on woman suffrage, arguing that the Fourteenth and Fifteenth amendments guaranteed the political rights of all citizens and that suffrage was a right of citizenship. Passed in response to the abortive attempt by the presidentially "reconstructed" states to maintain their pre–Civil War racist system through the infamous "Black Codes," the barely disguised reinstitution of restrictive antebellum slave codes, the Fifteenth Amendment (1870) had established federal authority to guarantee the voting rights of all citizens regardless of "race, color, or previous condition of servitude." Although neither Congress nor the federal courts were convinced, many suffragists, including Susan B. Anthony, asserted their right to the franchise by voting in the 1872 federal elections: Anthony was subsequently convicted of "illegal voting," and an 1884 Supreme Court decision, by affirming a state's right to interpret the rights of citizenship, categorically denied women's claim to equal protection as citizens under the Fourteenth Amendment. The high court's hostile ruling in *Minor v. Happersett* (1875) ended, for the remainder of the nineteenth century, the suffragists' attempts to win the franchise for women through judicial fiat based on the equal-protection clause of the Fourteenth Amendment.

After the ratification of the Nineteenth Amendment (1920) granted women the vote, the potential efficacy of the equal-protection clause of the Fourteenth Amendment was frequently offered by social feminists as well as conservatives and antifeminists to support their argument that the proposed Equal Rights Amendment was unnecessary and a possible threat to protective legislation. However, the equal-protection clause of the Fourteenth Amendment has not been employed effectively as a judicial basis for furthering women's equality under the law in the twentieth century.

—*Angela Howard Zophy*

See Also:

Abolition and the Antislavery Movement; American Woman Suffrage Association; Anthony, Susan B.; *Minor v. Happersett* (1875); National Woman Suffrage Association; Nineteenth Amendment; Woodhull, Victoria

References:

Clinton, Catherine. *The Other Civil War: American Women in the Nineteenth Century.* New York: Hill and Wang, 1984.

Daniel, Robert L. *American Women in the Twentieth Century: The Festival of Life.* New York: Harcourt Brace Jovanovich, 1987.

DuBois, Ellen. *Feminism and Suffrage: The Emergence of An Independent Women's Movement in America, 1848–1869.* Ithaca, N.Y.: Cornell University Press, 1978.

Flexner, Eleanor. *Century of Struggle: The Woman's Rights Movement in the United States.* Rev. ed. Cambridge, Mass.: Belknap, 1959, 1975.
Hofstadter, Richard, ed. *Great Issues in American History: From the Revolution to the Civil War, 1765–1865.* Vol. 2. New York: Vintage, 1958.
Kraditor, Aileen. *The Ideas of the Woman Suffrage Movement, 1890–1920.* Garden City, N.Y.: Anchor/Doubleday, 1971.
Schneir, Miriam. *Feminism: The Essential Historical Writings.* New York: Random House, 1972.
Woloch, Nancy. *Women and the American Experience.* New York: Knopf, 1984.

FREE LOVE is a nineteenth-century term to describe the opposition of some individuals and groups to legal and clerical marriage, which they believed stifled a naturally loving relationship between women and men. Free-love groups were typically small, sectarian, and usually male-dominated, and offered intellectual leadership to the later birth-control and suffrage movements. Free lovers strongly favored motherhood, but they separated a woman's free choice to bear children from the sexual exclusivity required by the legal institution of marriage. Therefore, the free lovers scandalized mainstream American Victorian society and challenged the very core of the "cult of domesticity." Victoria Woodhull and her sister Tennessee Claflin were two of the more notorious nineteenth-century advocates of free love. Woodhull unreservedly supported each woman's right to decide whether, when, and with whom to become sexually active in the sisters' publication of the early 1870s, *Woodhull & Claflin's Weekly.*

Conservative opponents of the nineteenth-century woman's movement raised the free-love issue to impugn the respectability of the advocates of women's rights. This antifeminist, antisuffragist tactic persisted into the twentieth century, as the specter of the wanton free-lover woman was thrust into any and all discussions of women's rights or an expanded role for women. The ever-increasing divorce rate appeared to these critics as proof that women's unfettered sexuality would bring the destruction of the family and the nation.

In the twentieth century the free-love issue resurfaced first after World War I, and then as a result of the cold war and the Vietnam War. The so-called Lost Generation expressed its disillusionment with the results of the "War to End All Wars" and its challenge to the political fundamentalism of the Roaring Twenties by applying popularized Freudianism to justify sensual indulgence and immediate gratification. Affluent and college-educated women described as flappers were believed to engage in sexual activity with abandon, now having general if illicit access to contraception devices such as the diaphram and douching. This provoked a strong reaction in a time when women were defined as subordinate to men in all respects, with motherhood their only avenue to mental health.

As an issue of the so-called new morality of the 1960s, the concept of free love was adopted by the affluent baby-boomer generation; the modern application was facilitated by advances in and an availability of contraception (especially "the pill"), and reflected more the youth movement's search for an identity distinct from their parents than an issue of the nascent modern women's rights movement. Reflecting the male-identified youth movement's challenge to authority, these advocates of total sexual freedom argued that premarital, extramarital, and communal/group variations of sexual activity offered an expanded experience on an "if it feels good, do it" basis, sententiously adding the proviso, "just as long as you don't hurt anybody." According to this hedonistic philosophy, people could indulge and satiate their sensual appatites without personal commitment or lingering obligations.

For women, this concept of free love now required that they acquiesce to sex on male demand or be labeled repressed and bourgeois; moreover, it assumed that women's sexuality, no longer repressed, would result in an insatiable sensuality, thus fulfilling the male fantasy of women as casual sex objects. Rejecting this sexist application of the concept of free love, feminists of the early 1970s reasserted the Woodhull interpretation, which offered the opportunity for women to define their own sexuality as as aspect of women's autonomy, beyond the strictures of marriage and motherhood. Again, conservatives labeled all feminists free-lovers, and thus a threat to decency and national survival.

The excesses of the late 1960s and 1970s ultimately proved unsatisfying for either men or women. The medical concerns over venereal disease, especially herpes and AIDS, discredited this variety of free love by the 1980s, as the uncertain economic situation refocused the priorities of the baby-boomer generation on personal and professional stability.

—Barry Arnold

See Also:

AIDS; Birth Control; Divorce; Female Sexuality; Freudianism; New Morality; Sexual Revolution; Venereal Disease; Woodhull, Victoria

References:

Berman, Marshall. *All That Is Solid Melts into Air, The Experience of Modernity.* New York: Simon & Schuster, 1982.

D'Emilio, John, and Estelle Freedman. *Intimate Matters: A History of Sexuality in America.* New York: Harper & Row, 1988.

Keen, Sam. *Beginnings Without End.* New York: Harper & Row, 1975.

Tipton, Steven. *Getting Saved from the Sixties.* Berkeley: University of California Press, 1982.

The **FREEDMEN'S BUREAU** was the popular name for the Bureau of Refugees, Freedmen, and Abandoned Lands. The Freedmen's Bureau Bill, passed in March 1865, established this agency in response to demands by abolitionists, particularly those of Josephine Griffing, who was also a prominent woman's rights activist. President Abraham Lincoln's endorsement of the Freedmen's Bureau was largely due to the influence of Griffing, who organized and solicited volunteers to work in the newly formed bureau.

The Freedmen's Bureau served as a temporary means of assisting newly freed blacks by providing education, food, and shelter, and by managing the distribution of abandoned and confiscated Confederate estates. It extended the work begun by the freedmen's aid societies that had formed in Boston, New York, and Philadelphia. These societies, composed of missionaries and abolitionists, were concerned with the welfare and educational needs of the former slaves, and they were responsible for sending supplies and funds for the recruiting and maintenance of teachers for newly freed blacks. The Freedmen's Bureau assisted by establishing a system of record-keeping, providing school buildings, and funding the transportation for teachers. At a cost of $3 million, the bureau enabled between 150,000 and 200,000 freedmen to obtain the beginnings of an education.

Women volunteers played a large part in the educational assistance rendered to freed blacks, such that by 1869 one-half of the nine thousand teachers were women. These dedicated teachers endured many hardships and a great deal of intolerance by Southerners, but they persisted in this venture and were later referred to as the "tenth crusade." Some of these women stayed on even after the 1870s to continue providing education for freed blacks. The bureau was terminated in 1869.

—Jean Nettles

See Also:

Griffing, Josephine

References:

Clinton, Catherine. *The Other Civil War.* New York: Hill and Wang, 1984.

McPherson, James M. *The Struggle for Equality.* Princeton: Princeton University Press, 1964.

Sorin, Gerald. *Abolitionism.* New York: Praeger, 1972.

FREEMAN, MARY ELEANOR WILKINS (1852–1930) was one of the foremost authors in the school of regional local colorists who wrote short stories and novels in the realistic style popular during the late nineteenth and early twentieth century. She drew upon the rural New England environment and its strong women, an environment she knew well from her childhood in rural Massachusetts.

Wilkins was educated in the best New England school tradition but found no career plans that suited her. With no "marriage prospects" on the horizon, she created her own avenue for her talents in her writing, as had other well-educated New England women of her day. The publication of her stories in *Harper's Bazaar* in the 1880s brought economic self-sufficiency. *A New England Nun* (1891) described the peculiarities of small-town people and settings as well as the strength of character that upheld many New Englanders, especially women. The author's skill at characterization and the appeal of her strong women figures made her stories popular in her day and have given them a lasting quality. Accepting her "spinsterhood," she enjoyed the fruits of her success by traveling freely and tasting the social life in New York and Boston, which included friendships with many publishers and writers.

Through these contacts, she later met and married Charles M. Freeman in 1902, when she was almost fifty years old. She continued her writing career with *Six Trees* in 1903; the revenues from earlier works such as *Pembroke* (1894, novel) and *A Humble Romance* (1887, story collection) sustained her well financially. Remaining active into the 1920s, Freeman was one of the most successful of the many female regional local colorists. Problems with her marriage before her husband's death in 1923 were offset by the receipt of literary rewards and honors, such as her election to the National Institute of Arts and Letters in New York. Upon her death in 1930 at the age of seventy-eight, Mary E. Wilkins Freeman was one of the few writers of the early local-color realistic movement in fiction whose reputation had outlived both the world war and the changed literary tastes of the 1920s.

—Ellen D. Langill

References:

Foster, Edward. *Mary E. Wilkins Freeman.* New York: Hendricks House, 1956.

Hamblin, Abigail Ann. *The New England Art of Mary E. Wilkins Freeman.* Amherst, Mass.: Green Knight, 1966.

Overton, Grant. *The Women Who Make our Novels.* New York: Dodd, Mead, 1918.

Westbrook, Perry D. *Mary Wilkins Freeman.* New York: Twayne, 1967.

FREUDIANISM refers to the psychoanalytic theories of Viennese physician Sigmund Freud (1856–1939), who developed a picture of the human psyche as a conflicted and divided entity, challenging the then-prevailing belief in the individual as autonomous and harmonious. His theory of unconscious areas of psychic experience and of the power of sexual drives beginning in infancy disputed the century-old faith in human rationality. For Freud the id (sexual force), ego (reality principle), and superego (morality and law) were sections of the psyche competing for energy in a never-ending struggle. Any balance achieved by an individual, moreover, differed according to whether one was male or female.

Since many of Freud's patients were middle-class women, it is hardly surprising that his theories paid them a good deal of attention. For one thing, he totally revised common wisdom that those suffering from hysteria—a psychiatric illness particularly associated with nineteenth-century women—were immoral and of low intelligence. Instead, his *Studies in Hysteria* (1899) maintained that they were usually very intelligent and excessively moral. Indeed, Freudianism blamed many psychological ills on society's extreme repression of women's sexuality. Although this opinion broke with Victorian conventions, other aspects of Freudianism reinforced their assumptions about women. Notably, the Oedipal and Electral moments during which one reached an adult gender identity differed sharply for boys and girls. Boys, recognizing their mother's lack of a penis and their own possession of one, rejected their infantile love for her and identified with their father's power gained from the penis. By contrast, girls did not have to fear castration and so did not have to develop a strong ego to deal with that reality. Instead, they could devote themselves to love of their father rather than repress it and substitute having a baby for a having penis. Freudianism saw feminists as women who failed to accept their castration, but rather suffered from "penis envy." They sought not love and children, but masculine identity.

After World War II, Farnham and Lundbert's *Modern Woman: The Lost Sex* (1946) and other journalistic writings popularized these normative aspects of Freudianism. Neurosis and other disorders, these writings maintained, were a result of women rejecting their femininity. In 1963 Betty Friedan's *Feminine Mystique* took issue with Freudianism, especially the concept of "penis envy" and the attendant stereotyping of sex roles. A culture oriented toward psychological therapy, she argued, was making women who wanted to achieve feel abnormal because of Freud. A decade later, however, Juliet Mitchell's *Psychoanalysis and Feminism* (1974) sought to rehabilitate the doctrine as one that explicitly pointed out the cultural power of the phallus and the resulting power accorded fathers. Other feminist psychologists have attempted to refute even this fundament by postulating breast and womb envy. As of this writing, the jury is still out on Freudianism.

—Bonnie G. Smith

See Also:

Deutsch, Helene; Friedan, Betty; Horney, Karen; Hysteria; *Modern Woman: The Lost Sex*; Psychiatry; Psychology; Sex-Gender System; Sex Role Socialization

References:

Deutsch, Helene. *The Psychology of Women, a Psychoanalytic Interpretation.* 2 vols. New York: Grune & Stratton, 1944/1945.

Mitchell, Juliet. *Psychoanalysis and Feminism.* New York: Vintage, 1974.

FRIEDAN, BETTY (b. 1921), author of *The Feminine Mystique* and a founder of the National Organization for Women (NOW), was born Betty Naomi Goldstein in Peoria, Illinois. Her father was a small businessman, and her mother had been the editor of a local women's page but gave up that job when she married. In high school Friedan founded a literary magazine and was named class valedictorian. Then she traveled east to Smith College, later described by her as "a great marvelous thing." A psychology major, she was editor of the college paper, graduated summa cum laude (1942), and won a research fellowship to Berkeley. A year later, she left Berkeley to work in New York City as a reporter for the labor press. In 1947 she married Carl Friedan.

More radical than many of her contemporaries, she supported Henry Wallace, the Progressive party's presidential candidate, in 1948 and returned to work after the birth of her first child. However, she was fired as the result of her second pregnancy, and throughout the early 1950s led the life of a suburban housewife, first on Long Island and then in an "eleven-room Victorian house in Rockland County." In 1957 Friedan began to research and write what was to become *The Feminine Mystique* as a reaction to questionnaire answers she had gathered from Smith College classmates. Responding to their unhappiness and her own, she described "the problem that has no name" and detailed the ways in which American society forced women into traditional, unfulfilling, subservient roles.

Published in 1963, *The Feminine Mystique* is often viewed as trumpeting the rebirth of American feminism. As futurist Alvin Toffler put it, "*The Feminine Mystique* will be remembered as the book that pulled the trigger of history"; and sociologist Amitai Etzioni described it as "one of those rare books . . . which launches a major social movement." *The Feminine Mystique* has sold three million copies and reached millions more through excerpts in *Ladies' Home Journal, Good Housekeeping, Mademoiselle,* and *McCall's.*

The Feminine Mystique questioned the assumptions underlying the alleged "happiness" of well-educated, middle-class housewives. It was originally written by Friedan as a reaction to findings culled from questionnaires she sent to her former classmates at Smith. The book described the problems of women who identified themselves as wives, mothers, and homemakers, but never as persons. In developing her argument, Friedan indicted women's magazines for dealing with trivial topics. She portrayed the dilemma of college-educated women who, despite their intellectual interests and worldly inclinations, saw nothing but marriage in their future. The book also roundly condemned the social sciences for supporting the status quo of sexual inequality by embracing Freudian and neo-Freudian models of masculine activity and feminine passivity. Friedan demonstrated how functionalist theory is used to justify traditional sex roles.

Friedan concluded her picture of American social and sexual realities by showing how advertisers goad women into becoming housewife consumers and educational institutions strive to produce well-educated but subservient women. To solve the problems created by a society that pushes women into the background of its political, economic, and social life, the book counsels individual women to say no to the "housewife image" and adopt "a new life plan" based on meaningful activity.

After the publication of *The Feminine Mystique*, Friedan became a lecturer for feminist causes. In 1966 she cofounded the National Organization for Women (NOW) and became its president. NOW's stated goal was to enable women to achieve full equality with men in American society. Its first success was the banning of sex distinctions in employment advertising. In 1970 Friedan helped organize the Women's Strike for Equality, a massive nationwide demonstration on the fiftieth anniversary of the suffrage victory. The aims were: free abortion on demand; free twenty-four-hour, community-sponsored child-care centers; and equal opportunity in education and jobs. Seeking to establish mainstream respectability and credibility for NOW, Friedan during this period reflected in her leadership the ambivalence among the organization's professional and middle-class members regarding an open declaration of support for lesbianism and the minority of lesbians within the membership. The ensuing controversy and criticism of her leadership style contributed to her decision to step down as NOW president in 1970. She quickly became involved in organizing such feminist enterprises as the Women's Political Caucus, the National Association to Repeal Abortion Laws, and the First Women's Bank. As a nationally recognized spokeswoman for the modern women's movement, she participated in the cooperative effort of national women's groups to achieve ratification of the Equal Rights Amendment. Entering the academic world, she held appointments at Yale and Temple universities, and at Queens College in New York.

In 1981, responding to criticisms that the feminist movement failed to recognize the importance to most women of family and relationships with men, Friedan published *The Second Stage*, in which she condemned the "feminist mystique" that denied "love, nurturance and home," and she called for women and men to transcend the false polarization between feminism and family. Friedan recommended restructuring the home and workplaces to make them truly humane environments for both sexes. As the grande dame of the modern women's movement, she then focused upon the life issues of older women in American society.

Friedan's writings and activities have led one feminist, Barbara Seaman, to conclude, "Betty Friedan is to women what Martin Luther King was to blacks."

—Barbara McGowan

See Also:

Freudianism, National Organization for Women, Women's Liberation Movement

References:

Friedan, Betty. *The Feminine Mystique*. New York: Norton, 1963.

———. *It Changed My Life*. New York: Random House, 1976.

———. *The Second Stage*. New York: Summit, 1981.

FRY, LAURA ANNE (1857–1943) was an important figure in Cincinnati's "golden age" of art, 1870–90, and played an especially prominent role in the city's emergence as a center of the decorative arts. While still a young girl, Fry made some minor contributions to the "women's wood-carving movement" of the 1870s, a phenomenon nurtured to a large extent by her grandfather Henry L. Fry and her father, William H. Fry, both of whom had regional reputations. During the 1880s she joined the decorating staff at the nationally recognized Rookwood Pottery in Cincinnati and gained a reputation as a leading ceramic artist. Although she maintained constant contact with Cincinnati and would eventually retire there, Fry spent most of the next three decades in West Lafayette, Indiana, as a professor of industrial art at Purdue University.

Fry's career illustrates the degree to which women in the arts had become professionalized by the late nineteenth century. Her identity as an artist was defined by the specific roles (such as student, employee, and teacher) that she performed within a series of hierarchically structured organizations. For example, even though she had learned the basics of wood carving in her family's studio, Fry received formal training in the various decorative arts at the University of Cincinnati's School of Design, and later in painting at the Art Students League in New York. At Rookwood, she was one member of one department in a business enterprise that increasingly encouraged the efficient production, distribution, and inventory of its pottery wares. Fry was the decorator most closely associated with the fine spray application of background colors, a technique that helped standardize Rookwood's designs and make them more commercially dependable.

As a professor at Purdue, she shifted her focus from the making of art to the teaching of it. She was regarded by the surrounding community as an art "expert," and it was in this capacity that she exhibited her work and that of others, spoke on numerous topics, and aided in the establishment of the Lafayette Art Association in 1909. Thus Fry devoted her life not only to the practice of the crafts, but also to the wider responsibilities and the service ethic of the "professional."

—*Bruce R. Kahler*

See Also:
Art

References:
The Ladies, God Bless 'Em: The Women's Art Movement in Cincinnati in the Nineteenth Century. Cincinnati: Cincinnati Art Museum, 1976.

Perry, Mrs. Aaron F. "Decorative Pottery of Cincinnati." *Harper's New Monthly Magazine* 62 (May 1881): 834–45.

Trapp, Kenneth R. "Toward a Correct Taste: Women and the Rise of the Design Reform Movement in Cincinnati, 1875–1880." In *Celebrate Cincinnati Art,* edited by Kenneth R. Trapp. Cincinnati: Cincinnati Art Museum, 1982, pp. 48–70.

Vitz, Robert C. *The Queen and the Arts: Cultural Life in Nineteenth-Century Cincinnati.* Kent, Ohio: Kent State University Press, 1988.

FULLER, MARGARET (1810–50), translator, editor, conversationalist, critic, philosopher, journalist, revolutionary, and feminist, was one of the most important women of her time, influencing not only her own century but also the twentieth. Gravely misunderstood and misinterpreted by her male and many of her female contemporaries, Fuller has only recently begun to be accorded a more appropriate scholarly approach.

The first child of Timothy and Margaret (Crane) Fuller, Sarah Margaret Fuller enjoyed (and suffered under) a typically masculine education, having studied Latin, Greek, French, Italian, and German by the time she was twenty. This lack of a more carefree childhood was at once one of the many denials of her life and the means to her future livelihood. Up to the time of her father's death in 1835, her life was spent mostly in study in Cambridge, Massachusetts. In 1833 in Groton, Fuller took over her siblings' education, denying herself a trip to Europe with friends.

She pursued acquaintanceships with Ralph Waldo Emerson and Harriet Martineau and in 1836 took up a teaching post at Bronson Alcott's experimental Temple School in Boston. Overexertion led her to take a post in Providence, Rhode Island, until 1839, where she began working on translations of Goethe and her critical writings. Returning to Boston in 1839 led to her deeper involvement in transcendentalism and the beginnings of her "conversations." These weekly sessions concentrated on a variety of aesthetic topics and were held in fall and spring from 1839 to 1844 for women subscribers only, with the exception of a brief attempt in 1841 to include men as well. In 1840 she founded, with other transcendentalists, the quarterly *Dial*, which she then edited for two years and which continued until 1844 as the mouthpiece of the New England transcendentalists. She was also involved in plans for the utopian Brook Farm community, although she did not choose to live there.

In 1845, shortly after publication of her first book, *Summer on the Lakes* (1844), Fuller was offered a job on Horace Greeley's *New York Tribune* as a literary critic. She also extended her 1843 essay "The Great Lawsuit: Man *versus* Men. Woman *versus* Women," originally published in *Dial*, into a second book, *Woman in the Nineteenth Century*. Residing in Greeley's New York house, Fuller concentrated on her critical writings over the following fifteen months, publishing over two hundred articles on a variety of aesthetic and social topics. The failure of a love affair and a renewed opportunity for a European tour led Fuller to leave the *Tribune* at the height of her success to become Greeley's foreign correspondent.

In 1846 Fuller traveled to England, then on to France and Italy. She met major writers and politicians at each stop. In Italy in 1847 she became involved in the revolutionary drive to unify Italy and with fellow revolutionary Giovanni Angelo, Marchese d'Ossoli. Fuller's activities during the following years are uncertain, but the period does seem to represent a liberation for her, despite the military setbacks of the Italian cause. Fuller became pregnant, which cut off her contacts with most of the Anglo-American community. Angelo Eugene, the son of Fuller and d'Ossoli, was born in May 1848 outside Rome. Soon after his birth, Fuller returned alone to Rome to continue her work for the revolution, running a hospital and carrying supplies. In the summer of 1849 the Roman Republic was defeated, and Fuller and d'Ossoli fled with their child to Florence. Fuller may have married d'Ossoli in 1849, which made her more welcome in the expatriate community, and she began her work on a revolutionary history. Despite her very deep ties to Rome and premonitions of disaster, Fuller decided to return to the United States with d'Ossoli and her son in 1850. Their ship, the *Elizabeth*, sank off Fire Island, New York; most biographers agree that, of the three, only Fuller's son's body was recovered.

It is safe to say that Sarah Margaret Fuller's life was much too short for her to continue developing her great promise, and this has made the attempts of biographers and literary critics to evaluate her more difficult. We know Fuller today mainly due to *Woman in the Nineteenth Century*, which does little justice to her accomplishments as critic, conversationalist, and translator, and one who contributed a great deal to the advancement of women's liberation.

—*Maureen Ruth Liston*

See Also:

Journalism, Transcendentalism, *Woman in the Nineteenth Century*

References:

Blanchard, Paula. *Margaret Fuller: From Transcendentalism to Revolution*. New York: Dell, 1978.

Chevigny, Bell Gale. *The Woman and the Myth: Margaret Fuller's Life and Writings*. New York: Feminist Press, 1976.

Fuller, Margaret. *The Letters of Margaret Fuller*. Edited by Robert N. Hudspeth. 4 vols. to date. Ithaca, N.Y.: Cornell University Press, 1983–.

———. *Woman in the Nineteenth Century*. 1845; rpt. New York: Norton, 1971.

Liston, Maureen Ruth. "A Cultural History of American Women Expatriates, ca. 1850–1939." Ongoing research project.

Myerson, Joel, ed. *Critical Essays on Margaret Fuller*. Boston: Hall, 1980.

———. *Margaret Fuller: An Annotated Secondary Bibliography*. New York: Burt Franklin, 1977.

GAGE, MATILDA JOSLYN (1826–98), more radical than the other two members of the suffrage "triumvirate" (Susan B. Anthony and Elizabeth Cady Stanton), was regarded as "one of the most logical, fearless, and scientific writers of her day." Stanton lauded her for "bringing more startling facts to light than any woman I ever knew" through a series of pamphlets, including evidence that a woman invented the cotton gin ("Woman as Inventor," 1870) and planned the military strategy that changed the course of the Civil War ("Who Planned the Tennessee Campaign?" 1880).

An excellent speaker and capable organizer on the local, state, and national level, Gage held positions in the National Woman Suffrage Association (NWSA) that were roughly equivalent to those of Anthony. Gage created the NWSA's "Relief from Political Disabilities" campaign in 1878 and ran as an elector-at-large for Belva Lockwood's presidential bid on the Equal Rights party ticket in 1884. When Gage was prosecuted for exercising school board suffrage in New York state, her 1893 court action became the test case for the constitutionality of state school suffrage. Threatened with arrest three times because of her reform work, Gage responded that the "country owes its existence to disobedience to law."

A prolific writer, Gage edited a suffrage paper, the *National Citizen and Ballot Box*, for four years and penned many of the strongest protests, resolutions, and addresses of the NWSA, including her "Woman's Rights Catechism" (1868). With Stanton, she co-authored the Declaration of Rights of Women (1876), which Gage and Anthony—fully expecting to be arrested—illegally presented at the nation's official centennial celebration that year.

Unable to stop the radical NWSA from merging with the conservative American Woman Suffrage Association in 1889, Gage turned to what she believed was her "grandest, most courageous work": to free woman "from the bondage of the church," which was the "chief means of enslaving woman's conscience and reason." She formed the anti-church National Woman's Liberal Union (1890), contributed to the *Woman's Bible* (1898), and published her magnum opus, *Woman, Church and State* (1893), acclaimed as one of the most important theoretical documents produced by the nineteenth-century woman's movement. Gage made a major contribution to American feminist theory in the latter publication, which was a persuasive critique of the role of the church and the state in the historic subordination and subjection of women. Specifically, Gage directly challenged the male-identified image of women that mainstream Christianity had promulgated.

Gage's contributions to nineteenth-century woman's rights and American feminism were eclipsed somewhat by the fame of Anthony and Stanton, both of whom she preceded in death.

—*Sally Roesch Wagner*

See Also:

Anthony, Susan B.; *History of Woman Suffrage*; National Woman Suffrage Association; Stanton, Elizabeth Cady; Suffrage; *Woman's Bible*

References:

Gage Collection. Schlesinger Library. Radcliffe College, Cambridge, Mass.

Gage, Matilda Joslyn. *Woman, Church and State*. Introduction by Sally Roesch Wagner. Watertown, Mass.: Persephone, 1980.

Spender, Dale. *Women of Ideas*. London: Routledge and Kegan Paul, 1982.

The **GARMENT INDUSTRIES** were those American business enterprises, factories, sweatshops, and family sewing operations involved in the mass production of ready-to-wear clothing since the mid-nineteenth century. The large-scale manufacture of clothing was made possible by the invention of the sewing machine in 1846, as well as by the development of the textile industry, which, by the 1820s, had established women's presence as workers in the paid labor force that mass-produced wool and cotton cloth. Replaced by immigrants and men in the New England factories by the 1850s on account of declining wages, these women workers gravitated to the garment industry as a paid employment that paralleled traditional Woman's Work. The percentage of women employed in the clothing industry rose from 45 percent in 1860 to 56 percent in 1890. Throughout the nineteenth and twentieth centuries, the clothing industry has been one of the ten primary areas of employment for women workers in the United States. But, as was the case in other industries, women in this industry remained second-class workers in terms of status, wages, and working conditions.

During the late nineteenth century, the garment industry operated on various levels: manufacturers, sweatshops, contractors, and homeworkers. Manufacturers established factories where cloth was cut from patterns. Most clothing production took place in sweatshops generally run by immigrant contractors. Workers recruited and supervised by the contractor were often foreign-born women and children. The contractor paid them and delivered the completed order to the manufacturer. Homeworkers were women who did work at home for a contractor or factory and were paid at a piece rate.

These transient, unskilled workers, generally Jewish or Italian women, worked ten- to fourteen-hour days, seasonally, under poor sanitary and lighting conditions for low wages (from four to seven dollars for a five-and-a-half- to six-day work week). Women usually rented or bought their sewing machines, needles, and thread; shop owners often charged for the electricity they used. Workers were fined for breaking equipment, being late, and talking. Although unions of garment workers existed before 1900, the Amalgamated Clothing Workers and the International Ladies Garment Workers Union helped effect changes in sweatshop conditions thereafter. The Triangle Shirtwaist fire of 1911, which caused the deaths of 147 workers in New York City, tragically demonstrated the need for better factory conditions, while the Uprising of the Twenty Thousand (1909–10), a walkout of New York City shirtwaist workers from 500 shops, led to the growth of unionization.

New Deal legislation attempted to standardize hours and wages throughout America while supporting unionization. But even before World War I, manufacturers left the mid-Atlantic region for the South in order to utilize nonunion labor. The creation of "runaway" shops continued through the 1950s as black females entered the industry. Sweatshops, often employing illegal aliens and the new immigrants from Latin America and the Far East, still prospered in many parts of America in the 1980s.

—*Mary Jane Capozzoli*

See Also:

Industrial Revolution, International Ladies Garment Workers Union, Triangle Fire

References:

Dye, Nancy Schrom. *As Equals and As Sisters: Feminism, Unionism, and the Women's Trade Union League of New York.* Columbia: University of Missouri Press, 1980.

Kessler-Harris, Alice. *Out to Work: A History of Wage-Earning Women in the United States.* New York: Oxford University Press, 1982.

Tentler, Leslie Woodcock. *Wage-Earning Women: Industrial Work and Family Life in the United States, 1900–1930.* New York: Oxford University Press, 1979.

GARRISONIANS were the followers of William Lloyd Garrison (1805–79), a radical abolitionist. In 1831 he off his earlier support for the colonization of liberated slaves to Africa and established the *Liberator,* a newspaper that pressed the cause of immediate abolition. He was an eccentric individualist who in 1854 publicly burned the Constitution, which he described as a "covenant with death and an agreement with Hell." His uncompromising position on a wide agenda of reforms split the abolition movement. While he supported health reform, the nineteenth-century peace movement, and temperance, Garrison's most divisive positions involved anarchism and women's rights. Late in his life he moderated his position, but in the 1840s he opposed voting even for the abolitionist Liberty party and criticized northern Protestants for hypocrisy in giving even tacit approval to slavery. Based on the twin ideas of perfectionism and nonresistance, Garrison called for universal emancipation of all men the world over. However, he insisted that by "universal emancipation" he meant the redemption of "women as well as men from a servile to an equal condition." Female abolitionists like Abby Kelley Foster and Lydia Maria Child were allied with Garrison. In 1840 at the World Anti-Slavery Convention, when Lucretia Mott, Ann Green Phillips, and Elizabeth Cady Stanton were denied seats on the floor and forced to sit in the gallery, Garrison joined them. Not all women abolitionists were Garrisonians, but he and his followers were more open to feminist activism than the majority of male antislavery leaders.

—*William G. Shade*

See Also:

Abolition and the Antislavery Movement; Child, Lydia Maria; Foster, Abby Kelley; Stanton, Elizabeth Cady

References:

Hersh, Blanch Glassman. *The Slavery of Sex.* Urbana: University of Illinois Press, 1978.

Kraditor, Aileen S. *Means and Ends in American Abolitionism.* New York: Pantheon, 1969.

Thomas, John L. *The Liberator.* Boston: Houghton Mifflin, 1963.

GENDER GAP is a term used to refer to differences in voting patterns between men and women. The first generations of women voters after enfranchisement in 1920 seemed generally to vote along similar lines with their husbands, fathers, and other males. It was hard to see that women as a group cast their votes differently from men. However, given the vagaries of the secret ballot and early election polls, one must be cautious about the existence or nonexistence of the gender gap prior to the 1980s.

With the growth of the modern women's movement in the late '60s and '70s, many politically active women such as Congresswomen Bella Abzug and Shirley Chisholm, as well as feminist Gloria Steinem, predicted that the gender gap would become a potent force to be reckoned with in American politics. Still, the failure of male-dominated legislatures to ratify the Equal Rights Amendment and the popularity of Ronald Reagan, an anti-ERA president, seemed to indicate that women were still not identifying their own interests as a voting group. All this began to change during the 1980s as women in increasing numbers began to realize that on some issues they had a different agenda from many men.

The gender gap became most noticeable during the 1982 elections when, according to historian Robert Daniel, female voters showed "less enthusiasm for conservative candidates than men by a margin of 5 percent." Daniel notes further that exit polls demonstrated that female voters were less supportive of Reagan policies regarding the economy, Social Security, inflation, unemployment, and the military. Former president of the National Organization for Women Ellie Smeal found that on core women's rights issues (ERA, abortion, child care) "women are consistently from 10 to 20 percent more supportive than men."

While American women still do not vote as a bloc, there is no doubt of their potential for power. Women constitute about 53 percent of the voting-age population and are registered in slightly higher numbers than men. As women increase in political self-awareness and power, the gender gap and the need to bridge it will become an even greater reality in American political life.

—*Jonathan W. Zophy*

See Also:
Democratic Party, Republican Party

References:

Abzug, Bella, with Mim Keller. *Gender Gap: Bella Abzug's Guide to Political Power.* Boston: Houghton Mifflin, 1984.

Daniel, Robert L. *American Women in the 20th Century.* New York: Harcourt Brace Jovanovich, 1987.

Smeal, Ellie. *Why and How Women Will Elect the Next President.* New York: Harper and Row, 1984.

GENDER ROLES refer to the set of social expectations pertaining to females and males. Gender roles have been shaped less by the biological and anatomical differences between the sexes than by parental teaching, formal education, religion, and the law, all of which serve to define and reinforce gender roles. From the colonial period to the present day, legal inequalities between the sexes have prevented women from achieving economic and political parity with men. Although America is a pluralistic nation, the teaching of secondary and passive roles for women has characterized religious and secular instruction until very recently. Women's roles have consistently been linked with child care, the nurturing of children and adults, and domestic work, whether or not women's work had been directly connected to home and family.

In the seventeenth century the social and legal inferiority of women followed from religious and scientific precepts that held women to be morally and physically weak and therefore rightly subject to the superior male. In the eighteenth and the nineteenth centuries Enlightenment and Romantic philosophers challenged these views. By the mid-nineteenth century the concept that women were morally inferior had been replaced by the view that women were more capable than men of moral purity, but that women were delicate creatures whose ability to bear children was jeopardized by extended rigorous physical or mental activity. In the late nineteenth century the acceptance of women's moral superiority improved their status within the family, but it also reinforced notions that women's ideal place was in the home while economic trends were drawing increasing numbers of women into paid employment outside the home. The Industrial Revolution created jobs for women. Expanding on traditional notions of women as producers of food and clothing, factories employed women as operatives beginning in the late 1820s. By the time of the Civil War, women had moved into positions as teachers and as office workers as well. Here, too, women's jobs were defined as extensions of women's nurturing instincts and their contentment with simple, repetitive tasks.

The Seneca Falls (N.Y.) Woman's Rights Convention of 1848 initiated a long campaign to redefine women's roles in society and under the law. The ratification of the Nineteenth Amendment, which secured woman suffrage, ended one phase of the broadening of gender roles in America. During this period women gained legal authority over their own children, the right to own property, the right to possess their own wages, and the right to participate in the political process.

Such nineteenth-century political and theoretical challenges wrought slight modifications in the gender role for women. In the twentieth century the dominant definition of women's gender role fixed woman's place within the family and presumed motherhood for all women. However, the post–World War II economic situation has reshaped that gender role as married women increasingly have entered the paid labor force out of inescapable necessity.

—Julia Kirk Blackwelder

See Also:
Sex-Gender System, Sex Role Socialization

References:

Berkin, Carol. *Within the Conjurer's Circle: Women in Colonial America.* Morristown, N.J.: Grossmann, 1974.

Degler, Carl. *At Odds: Women and the Family in America from the Revolution to the Present.* New York: Oxford University Press, 1980.

Demos, John. *A Little Commonwealth: Family Life in the Plymouth Colony*. New York: Oxford University Press, 1970.

Filene, Peter G. *Him/Her/Self: Sex Roles in Modern America*. 2d ed. Baltimore: Johns Hopkins University Press, 1986.

Gordon, M., ed. *The American Family in Social Historical Perspective*. 2d ed. New York: St. Martin's, 1978.

Welter, Barbara. "The Cult of True Womanhood, 1820–1860." *American Quarterly* 18 (Summer 1966): 151–74.

The **GENERAL FEDERATION OF WOMEN'S CLUBS (GFWC)** became the largest national organization of women in the late nineteenth century, providing middle-class women a crucial social nexus between the domestic values of the Cult of True Womanhood and the political activism of the woman suffrage movement. In 1889 journalist Jane Cunningham Croly, who had earlier founded the women's club Sorosis, invited other women's literary clubs to help Sorosis celebrate its twenty-first anniversary. By the next year many of these clubs had joined together to form the federation. Women's literary clubs had flourished in the late 1890s, but Croly believed that these clubs could undertake other activities and apply Woman's Influence through the strength of the federation, especially in such areas of social reform as expansion of public libraries and betterment of conditions in public schools. Though the GFWC worked for the rights of women workers, it was slow to endorse women's suffrage. While most of the leaders did, the federation itself did not endorse the right of women to vote until 1914.

The GFWC had always had pacifist leanings, and during World War I the federation supported the Woman's Peace party. However, when the country joined the war effort, the federation raised money for liberty bonds and supported the Red Cross. After the war, many clubs were disheartened since the problems the war had sought to solve still remained. The federation sought to maintain its commitment to worthwhile projects, supporting Prohibition and joining other women's groups in favoring censorship in the movie industry. The federation was reluctant to support the Equal Rights Amendment. In fact, the GFWC did not support the amendment until 1944, when it sent representatives to the Democratic and Republican national conventions to ask for support for equal rights.

After World War II the federation was less visible nationally, but it continued to grow. In 1953 there were fifteen thousand clubs involved. Currently, there are five hundred thousand members in eleven thousand clubs.

—*Judith Pryor*

See Also:

Black Women's Clubs, Cult of True Womanhood, Equal Rights Amendment, Woman's Peace Party

References:

Blair, Karen J. *The Clubwoman as Feminist: True Womanhood Redefined, 1868–1914*. New York: Holmes & Meier, 1980.

O'Neil, William L. *Everyone Was Brave: The Rise and Fall of Feminism in America*. Chicago: Quadrangle, 1969.

Wells, Mildred White. *Unity in Diversity; The History of the General Federation of Women's Clubs*. Washington, D.C.: General Federation of Women's Clubs, 1953.

Wood, Mary I. *The History of the General Federation of Women's Clubs*. New York: General Federation of Women's Clubs, 1912.

GEOLOGY. In the early years of the nineteenth century, women provided drawings of landscapes and fossils for state geological survey reports. Their early schooling in science and sketching prepared them for this "genteel" work. Among the first such artists was Orra White Hitchcock, whose illustrations appeared in the 1830s and 1840s in publications written by her husband, Edward, the first state geologist of Massachusetts. Later Cecilia Beaux contributed drawings for the four federal surveys, 1867–79. Early writings in geology, few in number, were for the most part textbooks or personal observations. Amateur fossil and mineral collectors contributed to research. One of the first amateur geologists, Erminnie Adelle Platt Smith (1836–96), an ethnologist, classified and labeled specimens for European collections and presented a paper on jade at the 1879 American Association for the Advancement of Science meeting.

In the latter nineteenth century, women had the opportunity to pursue formal education in geology. Florence Bascom (1862–1945) played an important role in developing such training. She had received her doctorate at Johns Hopkins University, the first woman to do so. In the 1880s she introduced the use of microscopic techniques in petrology in the United States. She founded the Department of Geology at Bryn Mawr College, a training ground for most U.S. female geologists well into the 1930s. Among her notable students were Ida Ogilvie (1874–1963), who later established Barnard College's Department of Geology and conducted studies of New York State geology and Alberta glaciology; Anna Isabel Jonas Stose (1881–1974), who worked for the Maryland, Pennsylvania, and Virginia state geological surveys and the U.S. Geological Survey and made an outstanding contribution to the understanding of Appalachian geology; Julia Anna Gardner (1882–1960), who conducted paleontological studies in Texas and southeastern Mexico; and Eleanora Frances Bliss Knopf (1883–1974), whose work at the U.S. Geological Survey led to the reporting of a Pennsylvania deposit of the mineral glaucopane, previously believed to be found only on the Pacific coast.

Early paleontologists associated with museums included Winifred Goldring (1888–1971), whose research at the New York State Museum led to the publication of *The Devonian Crinoids of the State of New York* in 1923. In 1949, she became the first woman president of the Paleontological Society. Billie Untermann (1906–73) assembled dinosaur skeletons at the Utah Field House of Natural History and later became its director. Angelina Messina (1910–68) compiled extensive catalogs of foraminifera and ostracoda at the American Museum of Natural History and co-founded in 1955 the journal *Micropaleontology*. Tilly Edinger (1897–1967), born and educated in Germany, published a monumental work on fossil brains while working as an unpaid curator of the Senckenberg Museum's vertebrate collection. In 1940 she arrived at Harvard University and spent the rest of her life at its Museum of Comparative Zoology.

Those women who elected to work for oil companies in the 1920s encountered some hostility from their male colleagues. At that time, micropaleontology was just receiving recognition. Alva Ellison of Humble Oil and Esther Applin of Rio Bravo were among the first to recognize the importance of using microfossils to date formations and predict the likelihood of petroleum deposits. Carlotta Maury (1876–1938) served from 1910 until her death as a consultant for the Royal Dutch Shell Petroleum Division. Elizabeth Florette Fisher (1873–1941), one of the few women field geologists, made extensive surveys in the Texas oil regions.

Mention should be made of those women, some unheralded, whose contributions to geology may be found in the assistance they gave their husbands or relatives. One such is Lou Henry Hoover (1874–1944), wife of President Herbert Hoover. She studied geology at Stanford (1894–98) and later collaborated with her husband in their 1950 translation of Georgius Agricola's *De Re Metallica* (1556).

—Regina A. Brown

See Also:

Beaux, Cecilia; Science; Women in Higher Education

References:

Aldrich, Michele L. "Women in Paleontology in the United States 1840–1960." *Earth Science History* 1 (1962): 14–22.

Elder, Eleanor S. "Women in Early Geology." *Journal of Geological Education* 30 (November 1982): 287–93.

Ogilvie, Marilyn Bailey. *Women in Science, Antiquity Through the Nineteenth Century, A Biographical Dictionary with Annotated Bibliography*. Cambridge: MIT Press, 1986.

Rossiter, Margaret W. *Women Scientists in America: Struggles and Strategies to 1940.*

Baltimore: Johns Hopkins University Press, 1982.
Siegel, Patricia Joan. *Women in the Scientific Search: An American Bio-Bibliography, 1724–1979*. Metuchen, N.J.: Scarecrow, 1985.

GIBSON, ALTHEA (b. 1927) was the first black invited to play in the American Lawn Tennis Association championships, and in 1957 and 1958 she won both at Wimbledon and at Forest Hills.

Born in Silver, South Carolina, Gibson was raised in Harlem in New York City. It was in Harlem that she began to play "paddle tennis" on the streets. She entered and won the Department of Parks Manhattan Girls' Tennis Championship and in 1942 began to receive professional coaching. She dominated the girls' and women's divisions of the black tennis circuit from 1945 to 1958. She received a Bachelor of Science degree in physical education from Florida Agricultural and Mechanical University in Tallahassee in 1953.

After her successes at Wimbledon and Forest Hills, she was named Woman Athlete of the Year in the Associated Press polls of 1957 and 1958 and was elected to the Lawn Tennis Hall of Fame and Tennis Museum in 1971. She won the world professional tennis championship in 1960 and then joined the women's professional golf tour in 1963. She became the athletic commissioner of New Jersey in 1975 and married Sydney Llewellyn in 1983.

Althea Gibson's contributions to the world of tennis will long stand as a monument to talent and determination. Her rise to the top in a sport dominated by white, affluent, "private club" players is an inspiring success story.

—Susan Kinnell

See Also:
Athletics/Sports

Reference:

Gibson, Althea. *I Always Wanted to Be Somebody*. New York: Harper & Row, 1958.

GILBRETH, LILLIAN EVELYN (MOLLER) (1878–1972) was a pioneer in the field of scientific management and the principles of motion study, which she formulated with her husband, Frank Gilbreth. They established efficient techniques for saving wasted motion in industry so that the workers could maximize production with minimal exertion. The whole idea was to find the "one best way" to do a job.

Believing the home was an important institution, Gilbreth applied the principles of scientific management to achieve efficiency in household tasks. She sought to provide women with shorter, simpler, and easier ways of doing housework to enable them to seek paid employment outside the home.

In 1904 she married efficiency expert Frank Gilbreth, and over a period of seventeen years bore twelve children. Widowed in 1924, she nonetheless managed to rear her family and send her children to college while she continued to develop efficient techniques for industry and the home. Her son and daughter provided a description of this unusual household in the books *Cheaper by the Dozen* (1948) and *Belles on Their Toes* (1950). Ultimately, many of her techniques were used by the defense industry during World War II.

Gilbreth's academic degrees included a bachelor's (1900) and a master's (1902) in literature, both obtained from the University of California at Berkeley, and a doctorate in industrial psychology from Brown University (1915). Among her more important publications are *Psychology of Management* (1914), *The Home-Maker and Her Job* (1927), and *Management in the Home* (1954).

Lillian Gilbreth was atypical of women during her time; the mother of twelve, she nevertheless pursued a successful career and effectively challenged the myth that a woman's place was in the home.

—Michael A. de León

See Also:
Housework, Science

References:

Gilbreth, Lillian M. "Women in Industry." In *American Women: The Changing Image*, edited by Beverly Benner Cassara. Boston: Beacon, 1962, pp. 90–98.

Spriegel, William R., and Clark E. Myers, eds. *The Writings of the Gilbreths*. Homewood, Ill.: Irwin, 1953.

Yost, Edna. *American Women of Science*. Philadelphia: Frederick A. Stokes, 1943.

GILMAN, CHARLOTTE ANNA PERKINS (1860–1935) was recognized as a writer of conscience and as a fighter for women's equality. Gilman's unconventional childhood without a real home after her parents' separation and divorce taught her practical lessons regarding the realities of Victorian womanhood that were at odds with the ideology of the separation of spheres. Her attempts to satisfy the requirements of True Womanhood resulted in a postpartum "nervous prostration" after the birth of her daughter in 1885, an extended separation from her husband, Charles W. Stetson, after a move to California for her health, and an extraordinary amicable divorce in 1894. That same year, she granted custody of her daughter to Stetson and his new wife, Grace Channing, who was also Gilman's lifelong friend. Gilman lived and worked as a writer and speaker on women's issues in California; she published collections of poems, short stories, and essays on social justice as she pursued a life of intellectual integrity and autonomy.

In 1898 she wrote the book that established her as a giant in the woman's movement, *Women and Economics*. Translated into many languages, this book provided an insightful analysis of women's position in society. In it, Gilman concluded that women must challenge the contemporary social norms of sex and domesticity to achieve equality and independence; their role as the submissive sex had been played too long, and only through economic independence could women become self-sufficient, autonomous individuals. *Women and Economics* revealed Gilman to be not only a social feminist and an advocate of the advancement of women but also a practitioner of the new social science approach, which was influenced by the Social Darwinists. She quickly became an internationally recognized speaker and author who worked actively to improve labor conditions and society in general.

In 1909 she created the magazine *The Forerunner*; as its editor and major contributor until 1916, Gilman fostered discussion of social justice as well as feminist issues. Her other books drew upon her personal experience (as in *The Yellow Wallpaper*, 1899), as well as her interest in the new fields of sociology and economics (as in *The Home*, 1903, and *His Religion and Hers*, 1923). All of Gilman's writings reflected her concern and respect for the individual members of a society threatened by the potential dehumanization of industrialism.

Her autobiography, *The Living of Charlotte Perkins Gilman* (1935), was praised by the critics as an outstanding recollection of her life. Intended as a legacy to her daughter, this autobiography demonstrated to the world the struggle of one woman who tried to change how humans thought and behaved toward each other. Finally, it was not the outside forces that overtook this courageous woman; suffering from cancer, she committed suicide in 1935.

—Samuel E. Perez and
Angela Howard Zophy

See Also:

Cult of True Womanhood, *Herland*, *Woman and Economics*, *The Yellow Wallpaper*

References:

The Charlotte Perkins Gilman Papers. Schlesinger Library. Radcliffe College, Cambridge, Mass.

Berkin, Carol Ruth. "Private Woman, Public Woman: The Contradictions of Charlotte Perkins Gilman." In *Women of America: A History*, edited by Carol Ruth Berkin and Mary Beth Norton. Boston: Houghton Mifflin, 1979, pp. 150–76.

Gilman, Charlotte Perkins. *Concerning Children*. Boston: Small, Maynard, 1900.

———, ed. *The Forerunner* (1911–16). Rpt. New York: Greenwood, 1968.

———. *Herland.* New York: Pantheon, 1979.
———. *His Religion and Hers: The Faith of Our Fathers and the Work of Our Mothers.* New York: Appleton-Century, 1923.
———. *The Home: Its Work and Influence.* New York: McClure, Phillips, 1903.
———. *Human Work.* New York: McClure, Phillips, 1904.
———. *In This Our World.* Boston: Small, Maynard, 1898.
———. *The Living of Charlotte Perkins Gilman.* New York: Appleton-Century, 1935.
———. *The Man-Made World.* New York: Charlton, 1911.
———. *What Diantha Did.* New York: Charlton, 1910.
———. *Women and Economics.* Boston: Small, Maynard, 1898.

The **GIRL SCOUTS OF AMERICA** was founded in 1912 by Juliette Gordon Low. An American who spent much of her time in England, Low became acquainted with Sir Robert Baden-Powell, who founded the Boy Scouts, and his sister Agnes Powell, who directed the girls' branch known as the Girl Guides. With the Powells' encouragement, Low started several troops of the Girl Guides, one in Scotland and the rest in London.

On her next trip to the United States, she told an old friend, Nina Pape, that she was going to start a new program for girls all over the world. She enlisted Pape and other friends to start two troops in Savannah, enrolling her niece Daisy Gordon as the first Girl Guide. After the first year, the name was changed to Girl Scouts, partly to match the Boy Scout movement and also because the members thought the name Scouts fit the American pioneer heritage. In 1913 she set up a national headquarters in Washington, D.C., with Edith D. Johnston as the first national secretary. Later the headquarters was moved to New York.

Low was just as successful at recruiting leaders and building a national organization as she was at starting troops. The movement grew rapidly, partly because there was an interest at this time in an organization for girls. Girls were no longer willing to play the role of decorative and proper young ladies; they wanted to engage in spirited and adventurous activities and to become more self-reliant. Having been raised to play only the role of wife, hostess, and mother, Low was in favor of this expanded role for young girls, but she did not see the Girl Scouts as a feminist organization nor herself as a feminist. In fact she was publicly opposed to the suffrage movement, and her handbook for the organization proposed a rather conservative role for girls and advised the members not to try to imitate men. The movement also succeeded because of Low's enthusiasm and ability to recruit family members and friends to be a part of this new organization.

The first national council in 1915 elected Low president. Many of the original leaders were leisured middle-class young women eager to find a meaningful activity to fill their time. By 1919 there were troops in every state except Utah and in the territory of Hawaii as well. Although the founders and original leaders of the organization were middle- and upper-class white women, the Girl Scouts organization reached out to girls of all races and economic backgrounds.

Although the organization owed much to the Boy Scouts, which had been founded in 1909, and despite the similarity of names, the Girl Scouts of America leaders did not want it to be a female version of that organization. The Girl Scouts emphasized outdoor activities, encouraged the traditional interests and skills of homemaking and crafts, and inculcated good citizenship in native-born and immigrant girls. The United States entry into World War I soon after the founding of the GSA spurred the organization to support the war effort by working with the Red Cross, selling war bonds, and conducting other activities. The wartime emphasis on marching and drills was abandoned after 1920.

Despite changes through the years, the GSA purpose remained to emphasize good citizenship, outdoor activities, and the idea that girls should do something for someone else every day. The organization handbook of the late 1970s reflected the change in women's employment patterns by including a section about career selection that encourages girls to think that any career is appropriate for girls. The largest women's volunteer organization in the world, the Girl Scouts of the U.S.A., as the organization is now called, still uses volunteers as leaders: only a small percent of the adults involved are professional workers.

—*Judith Pryor*

See Also:
Low, Juliette

References:

Girl Scouts of America. *How Girls Can Help Their Country.* New York: Girl Scouts of America, 1917.

———. *Worlds to Explore: Handbook for Brownie and Junior Girl Scouts.* New York: Girl Scouts of the U.S.A., 1977.

Schultz, Gladys, and Daisy Gordon Lawrence. *Lady from Savannah: The Life of Juliette Low.* Philadelphia: Lippincott, 1958.

Strickland, Charles E. "Juliette Low, the Girl Scouts, and the Role of American Women." In *Woman's Being, Woman's Place: Female Identity and Vocation in American History,* edited by Mary Kelley. Boston: G. K. Hall, 1977, pp. 252–64.

GODEY'S LADY'S BOOK, *and American Ladies' Magazine* was originally published in Philadelphia by Louis A. Godey. Initiated in 1831, *Godey's Lady's Book* offered lavish embellishments (fashion plates, woodcuts, engraved pictures), but only reprinted poetry and prose that Godey shamelessly "cut and pasted" from contemporary fashionable English women's periodicals to accompany the plates and prints. *Godey's* was a flashy women's magazine with no discernible substance when Godey recruited Sarah Josepha Hale to edit it in 1837. Determined to offer American women a magazine that would both "amuse and instruct," Hale had edited her own *American Ladies' Magazine* in Boston from 1828 to 1836. Godey convinced Mrs. Hale, as she was known to three generations of readers, to merge her magazine with his own, thereby bringing Hale's editorial substance to enrich the lavish but heretofore superficial *Lady's Book.*

Hale brought her established agenda of "improving her sex" to the more prosperous and popular monthly. She introduced original poetry, prose, and nonfiction written by American authors, many of whom became the notable (male and female) literati of Victorian America. Hale's most enduring contribution to women's magazines was the development, indeed the perfection, of the standard content format for that genre of periodical: sentimental poetry and unimpeachably correct fiction (written primarily by women and designed to inculcate the traits of True Womanhood in readers), instructional but noncontroversial nonfiction (which included patriotic and women's history), and the popular fashion plates and other hallmark "embellishments," supplemented by craft and homemaking arts instructions. At the "back of the book" appeared Hale's monthly editorials, "The Editors' Table"; her literary notices, which featured books by and for women; and Godey's own monthly notices to his gentle readers. As a medium of both women's and popular culture, *Godey's* dominated the market during the 1840s and 1850s; however, the Civil War marked the beginning of the magazine's decline until Hale retired in 1877, following Godey's sale of the magazine. As a national institution, *Godey's* survived until the end of the nineteenth century, when its market and its message were supplanted by *The Ladies' Home Journal.*

Hale concurred with her publisher's dictum that all political references be avoided as inappropriate and outside the domestic limits of Woman's Sphere. Although Hale maintained the absolute propriety of *Godey's* contents, she circumspectly used her editorials to expand the limits of Woman's Sphere by supporting and urging increased educational and other opportunities for women. Arguing that True Women required an adequate education to perform their domestic and maternal roles, Hale succeeded in promoting improvements in women's education without challenging the basic concept of a Woman's Sphere with discrete limitations. Likewise, Hale imparted her own respectability to efforts to establish certain professions and employments as merely extensions of Woman's Sphere, and thus assisted women's entry into the nineteenth-century occupations that eventually became established as women's jobs by the turn of the century.

Although *Godey's* is remembered as a quaint publication that catered to the Victorian Lady of Leisure, under Hale's control the magazine advanced women's interests in subtle ways. In her capacity as editor of *Godey's,* Hale served her readers as a combination of Heloise, Emily Post, Betty Crocker, and Dear Abby; thus her support of certain women's issues, though a part of domestic feminism, translated into significant and effective propaganda among the middle class. Whether Hale led or rode the crest of public opinion on the necessity and propriety of expanding Woman's Sphere, her use of Woman's Influence provided a model for consistent if conservative reform that allowed women to breach the Public Sphere without incurring censure for violating their duty or abandoning their own proper sphere.

—Angela Howard Zophy

See Also:

Cult of True Womanhood; Domestic Feminism; Hale, Sarah Josepha; Magazines

References:

Mott, Frank Luther. *A History of American Women's Magazines.* 3 vols. New York: Appleton, 1930.

Woodward, Helen. *The Lady Persuaders.* New York.: Ivan Oblensky, 1960.

Zophy, Angela Howard. "'For the Improvement of My Sex': Sarah Josepha Hale's Editorship of *Godey's Lady's Book,* 1837–1877." Diss. The Ohio State University, 1978.

GOLDMAN, EMMA (1869–1940), anarchist lecturer and author, was possibly the most charismatic speaker among women leftists in American history. She embodied anarchism in the United States and campaigned against government and organized religion and on behalf of individualism, civil liberties, sexual freedom, free speech, feminism, birth control, and modern drama. Through her annual lecture tours, "Red Emma" fascinated an American public unresponsive to her basic message. Harassed by the authorities as much for her feminist message of women's absolute equality as for her avowed anarchism, Goldman staunchly confronted the reality and the implications of the "woman question" for radical reform philosophies. Raising the consciousness of women and men on the actual conditions of women, she decried women's sexual exploitation and declared women's right to both sexual autonomy and reproductive freedom of choice.

Born in Kovno, Russia, to a lower-middle-class Jewish family, Goldman emigrated in 1886, settling in Rochester, New York. While working in sweatshops in various eastern cities, she was radicalized by the executions of four anarchist protesters in the aftermath of the Haymarket Affair in 1886 and briefly became a disciple of the anarchist editor Johann Most. She soon established a lifelong association with anarchist Alexander Berkman; in 1892 she served as an accomplice in his attempted assassination of steel company official Henry Clay Frick after the Homestead Strike, in which ten people were killed in clashes between striking steel workers and armed guards hired by the Carnegie Steel Company in Homestead, Pennsylvania. Thereafter, she opposed such individual acts of violence but was persecuted by police and mobs, blamed for the assassination of President William McKinley by the self-styled anarchist Leon Czolgosz, and occasionally jailed for her public remarks.

Goldman edited the monthly *Mother Earth* from 1906 to 1917, and published *Anarchism and Other Essays,* among various works. As an anarchist influenced by the Russian theorist Peter Kropotkin, she believed that all governments were inherently oppressive, and instead of endorsing political methods of promoting revolution—as did socialists—she favored direct economic action to undermine capitalism. Her goal was individual liberty within a decentralized, collectivist framework of autonomous, loosely organized units.

During World War I Goldman and Berkman organized the No-Conscription League and were convicted in 1917 for conspiring against the draft. Goldman, already denaturalized by the government's stripping of citizenship from Jacob Kersner, her apolitical ex-husband, was deported with other radicals to the Soviet Union during the First Red Scare of 1919. There, she became one of the first revolutionaries to condemn totalitarianism in the new Soviet system after the Russian Revolution, and for the next two decades she wandered as a woman without a country. She died in Toronto, Canada, while raising money for the antifascists in Spain's Civil War.

—*Sally M. Miller*

See Also:

Civil Liberties Movement During World War I, The Woman Question, World War I

References:

Drinnon, Richard. *Rebel in Paradise: A Biography of Emma Goldman.* Boston: Beacon, 1961.

Goldman, Emma. *Living My Life.* New York: Knopf, 1931.

Wexler, Alice. *Emma Goldman: An Intimate Life.* New York: Pantheon, 1984.

GOOD TEMPLARS, a fraternal temperance order founded in New York State in 1851, was superseded by the Independent Order of Good Templars (IGOT), organized in 1852. Hostile to alcoholic drink, the Order demanded total abstinence from its members and worked for prohibition. Weekly lodge meetings provided the mostly youthful membership with fellowship and recreation in a morally uplifting atmosphere. At the end of 1868 the IOGT claimed more than five hundred thousand members in North America. In the 1870s it became a power in Britain and Sweden. By the early 1900s it had few American members, and many of those few were Scandinavian immigrants.

Nearly a generation before the founding of the Woman's Christian Temperance Union (1874), the IOGT offered women the opportunity to work for temperance and other social reforms. Women were admitted to membership in August 1852 and were made eligible for election to all offices in November. Woman's rights and temperance advocate Amelia Bloomer was one of the first woman Good Templars.

Although men dominated the IOGT, women served in the Good Templars as officers, organizers, and speakers. Amanda Way headed the Grand Lodge of Indiana in 1867 and 1868, while Martha McClennan Brown led the Grand Lodge of Ohio in 1872. Martha B. O'Donnell was elected to superintend the international children's auxiliary from 1874 to 1878. Jessie Forsyth held the same international office between 1893 and 1908.

—*David M. Fahey*

See Also:

Bloomer, Amelia; Forsyth, Jessie; Temperance Movement; Woman's Christian Temperance Union

References:

Hill, George W. E. *Brief Biographies of Many of Our Most Eminent Workers: Some Good Templars I Have Known.* Grand Rapids, Mich.: Valley City, 1893.

Larsen-Ledet, Lars. *Good Templary Through One Hundred Years.* Aarhus, Denmark: International Supreme Lodge, 1951.

Pierce, Isaac Newton. *The History of the Independent Order of Good Templars.* Philadelphia: Daughaday and Becker, 1869.

Turnbull, William W. *The Good Templars: A History of the Rise and Progress of the Independent Order of Good Templars: 1851–1901, Jubilee Volume.* Edited by James Yeames. N.P.: IOGT, 1901.

GRAHAM, MARTHA (b. 1894), dancer and choreographer, has left an indelible mark on the dance of the twentieth century. Developer of a unique dance technique based on the principle of contraction and release of the torso, Graham attempted in her work to affirm the universal experiences of humankind, her purpose being "to objectify in physical form my beliefs." Creating over one hundred and fifty dances and twenty-five plays for herself and her company, she defied conventional standards of movement and rhythm in her performances, moving her audience to experience something of the truth of human nature through an enormously personal and passionate means of communication.

Born in Allegheny, Pennsylvania, Graham and her family moved in 1908 to Santa Barbara, California, where she grew up. Receiving her first dance instruction at the Cumnock School in Los Angeles, in 1916 she attended a summer session of the Denishawn School, the original modern dance company in the United States, where she subsequently taught and performed as a member of the company from 1919 to 1923. In 1926 she formed her first independent dance company, consisting of herself and three other dancers, and a year later opened her own studio—the Martha Graham School of Contemporary Dance.

Graham's influence on the dance is matched only by her influence on the artists, musicians, poets, sculptors, and stage designers with whom she collaborated. Persons of note include Aaron Copland, composer of the famous score to *Appalachian Spring*; Louis Horst, considered to be the father of modern choreography and the greatest artistic influence in Graham's life; poet Ben Belit; artist/sculptor Isamu Noguchi; and light designer Jean Rosenthal.

Graham's breadth of vision is evidenced most clearly in the range of works she created, including *Primitive Mysteries* (1931), her first unanimously acclaimed masterpiece; *Letter to the World* (1940), inspired by the poetry of Emily Dickinson and one of the most successful marriages of verse and movement ever achieved; *Appalachian Spring* (1944), an enduring signature work; *Clytemnestra* (1958), Graham's first evening-long work, in which she masterfully resolved the tension between the themes of passion and duty; and *Acts of Light* (1981), a joyous celebration and rebirth out of darkness into the light, considered by some to be the most significant creation of her later, nondancing years.

Graham's technique of movement is the most widely taught system of instruction in colleges and universities today. She has received numerous honors and awards, including the Handel Medallion, New York City's highest award for cultural achievement. In 1964 the Aspen Institute for Humanistic Studies chose her as "the individual anywhere in the world to have made the greatest contribution to the advancement of the humanities." Although retired as a performer, she continues to serve as an active company director, choreographer, and teacher. In the words of Martha Graham, "My dancing . . . is an affirmation of life through movement."

—*Cecelia A. Albert*

See Also:

Duncan, Isadora

References:

Graham, Martha. *The Notebooks of Martha Graham*. Introduction by Nancy Wilson Ross. New York: Harcourt Brace Jovanovich, 1973.

McDonagh, Don. *Martha Graham: A Biography*. New York: Praeger, 1973.

Morgan, Barbara. *Martha Graham*. New York: Duell, Sloan and Pearce, 1941.

Terry, Walter. *Frontiers of the Dance: The Life of Martha Graham*. New York: Crowell, 1975.

GRAHAMISM was a movement initiated by Sylvester Graham (1794–1851), for whom today's cracker is named. The son of a Connecticut clergyman, Graham himself was a Presbyterian minister who began his public career as a temperance lecturer in Philadelphia. During the cholera epidemic of 1832, he broadened his message to emphasize other harmful foods and practices.

During the remainder of his life, he lectured and wrote on diet and hygiene. He opposed the drinking of coffee and tea as well as alcohol, the use of spices, and the eating of meat. The center of his health regimen, laid out in his *Treatise on Bread and Bread Making* (1837), was homemade bread made with coarsely ground flour. He advocated that, aside from changing their diet, people change their life-style by opening their homes to fresh air, wearing less restrictive clothing, and bathing regularly. Much of this advice was directed specifically to women. In his *Lecture to*

Young Men on Chastity (1834), he warned against sexual indulgence as well. He was an early and extreme Victorian who denounced "venereal indulgence" (sex for pleasure) in marriage as well as "solitary vice" (masturbation). A clean mind and a clean body led to salvation.

His ideas were picked up and disseminated by numerous Grahamites with whom he had little personal connection. In 1837 the American Physiological Society was founded in Boston. This organization published *The Graham Journal of Health and Longevity* and held several health conventions in the late 1830s. Oberlin College turned over its refectory to a Grahamite, and boardinghouses such as that run by Mary Gove Nichols in Boston followed Grahamite principles. Stores resembling modern health food co-ops sprang up across the country. Although Graham died in 1851, and the health reform movement became fragmented, his influence was embodied in the religious practices of the Seventh Day Adventists, founded by Ellen White, and in the work of John Harvey Kellogg, an opponent of masturbation and the "inventor" of corn flakes. A wide range of women health reformers from Mary Gove Nichols to Amelia Bloomer and Catharine Beecher echoed many of Graham's ideas.

—William G. Shade

See Also:

Beecher, Catharine; Bloomer, Amelia; Nichols, Mary Gove

Reference:

Nissenbaum, Stephen. *Sex, Diet and Debility in Jacksonian America: Sylvester Graham and Health Reform.* Westport, Conn.: Greenwood, 1980.

"GRANNY" MIDWIFERY. A "granny" midwife is a traditional lay midwife who has received little formal training and who usually serves low-income women. The term is most often associated with black midwives living in the southern region of the United States. However, granny midwives may also be found among whites in Appalachia, Mexican-Americans, Native Americans, the Cajuns of southwestern Louisiana, and other impoverished ethnic and regional communities.

During the early years of the twentieth century, granny midwives attended as many as 90 percent of all black births occurring in the southern states. These women usually received a "calling by the Lord" before beginning a lengthy apprenticeship with an older, senior midwife. The typical "granny" was also a married woman who had borne several children.

In the early twentieth century the black granny midwife subscribed to a noninterventionist approach to childbirth, letting nature take its course. Her chief duty was to comfort the parturient woman during the long and often arduous hours of labor. Basically it was her responsibility to catch the baby, tie the umbilical cord, and, if necessary, fetch the placenta. She probably encouraged the laboring woman to walk around and may also have offered her herbal teas, wine, or perhaps hard liquor to help ease the birthing pains. In order to determine the progress of labor, she sometimes examined the cervix. During complicated cases, she might even have found it necessary to turn the fetus. Although the major function of the granny midwife was to care for the laboring woman, she could also be depended upon to provide information about prenatal care, food preparation, and child-care training. Indeed, the granny midwife was a highly respected member of her community, and many people turned to her for advice on a variety of medical and social problems.

With the passage of the Sheppard-Towner Maternity and Infancy Protection Act of 1921, federal funds were made available to the states to provide for midwife training and regulation. Many southern states used these funds to establish educational and certification programs for their grannies. In recent years health departments across the nation have discontinued issuing certificates to granny midwives. Although a few elderly grannies continue to practice, their ranks are rapidly dwindling, and this last generation of granny midwives will soon die out.

—Judy Barrett Litoff

See Also:
Childbirth, Midwifery, Sheppard-Towner Act

References:

Campbell, Marie. *Folks Do Get Born.* New York: Rinehart, 1946.

Dougherty, Molly C. "Southern Lay Midwives as Ritual Specialists." In *Women in Ritual and Symbolic Roles,* edited by Judith Hoch-Smith and Anita Spring. New York: Plenum, 1978, pp. 151–64.

Holland, Endesha Ida Mae. "Granny Midwives." *Ms.* 15 (June 1987): 48–51, 73–74.

Holmes, Linda. "Alabama Granny Midwife." *The Journal of the Medical Society of New Jersey* 81 (May 1984): 389–91.

Litoff, Judy Barrett. *American Midwives, 1860 to the Present.* Westport, Conn.: Greenwood, 1978.

Mongeau, Beatrice. "The 'Granny' Midwives: A Study of a Folk Institution in the Process of Social Disintegration." Diss. University of North Carolina, 1973.

GRANT, ZILPAH P. (1794–1874) was an important advocate of increased education for girls. Born in South Norfolk, Massachusetts, Grant attended the local school and at the age of fourteen began her career in teaching. Her first position was in the public schools of nearby East Norfolk, where she taught for twelve years.

In 1821 Grant began studying grammar, history, and English literature with Reverend Ralph Emerson, a minister in Norfolk. Emerson's brother had a school for young ladies at Saugus, Massachusetts, and Grant was interested in continuing her studies there. After considerable thought, she took her savings and enrolled in Emerson's school. Here she met Mary Lyons, another reformer, and, with the encouragement of Emerson, took over a select school for young ladies at Winsted in 1821. Her success there led to an invitation to direct Adams Female Academy at Derry, New Hampshire. As was characteristic in administering girls' schools, Grant received the building free of charge, but she was responsible for all other expenses. She managed both the business and educational affairs of the school. With the assistance of Mary Lyon, Grant turned it into an influential girl's school.

But in 1828 Grant became dissatisfied with the trustees and moved to the Ipswich Female Seminary. Many of the pupils followed Grant, and here she achieved her greatest success. At Ipswich, Grant found a school with no provisions for boarders; pupils and teachers were scattered throughout the community. Already in 1834, Grant advocated the construction of a facility to house pupils and teachers. The emphasis of the school program was on individual care of the pupils and close supervision by the teachers. Each teacher was required, as the early regulations noted, "to acquaint herself with the health, habits, intellectual improvement, and moral and religious state of every young lady in her section; to attend to the investigation and recitation of a Bible lesson every week; to be the friend and adviser of each; to interest herself in everything that concerned their general improvement."

At Ipswich, the three-year program of study was rigorous and included a variety of courses, such as a three-year course of English studies and Bible instruction, the main subject. "The primary objective of the school seems to be to provide faithful and enlightened teachers; but the course of instruction is such as to prepare the pupil for any destination in life," wrote an observer in 1833. After 1834 the number of pupils was limited to one hundred, as the program focused on the solid training of girls. The teachers trained at Ipswich went west, into Ohio, Indiana, Illinois, Iowa, and Wisconsin, to offer educational opportunities in an expanding America. The demand for these well-schooled teachers was great. In addition, the seminaries built up by Grant made important contributions to the ideal of higher education for females. In 1839 Grant's ill health forced her to withdraw from the direction of Ipswich Seminary.

—*Robert G. Waite*

See Also:
Education, Female Academies

References:

Barnard, Henry. *Female Education: Memoirs of Founders, Promoters, and Teachers of Institutions for Girls and Young Women.*

American Journal of Education 30 (1880). [Special Issue]
Cowles, John P. "Ipswich Female Seminary." *American Journal of Education* 30 (1880): 593.
———. "Miss Zilpah P. Grant—Mrs. William B. Banister." *American Journal of Education* 30 (1880): 611-19.
"Seminary for Female Teachers, at Ipswich, Mass." and "Motives to Study in the Ipswich Female Seminary." *American Annals of Education* 3 (February 1833): 69–80.

The **GREAT AWAKENING** of the 1740s was the first major religious revival in America. Religious emotionalism spread rapidly under the leadership of ministers Theodore Frelinghuysen, Jonathan Edwards, and George Whitefield, who exhorted their listeners about God's omnipotence, human depravity, and saving grace. Emphasis on the conversion experience as the condition for admission to a church gave a new quest to individuals who felt lost in a communal society undermined by concern for wealth. The frequency of religious conversion among young persons may be seen as an eighteenth-century expression of adolescent crisis, experienced by those coming to adulthood in a new, uncertain world.

While proportionately more men than women joined the church during the revivals, increasing numbers of women joined and continued to form the majority of the membership, a trend known as the "feminization of the church." By the 1760s, 92 percent of the women who became full communicants were single, widowed, or married women unaccompanied by their husbands. Some of these women, diarist Hannah Heaton for example, criticized the established form of religion, while others, such as schoolmistress Sarah Osborn, formed close reciprocal relationships with ministers, establishing a pattern that became more widespread in the nineteenth century.

Study of sermons and the pious poetry of the laity during this period reveals that a definition of the spheres of women and men was beginning to emerge in the mid-eighteenth century. Men were praised for diligence in their vocational calling, while women were lauded for their spiritual gifts. Women attended church regularly, studied Scripture, and testified to extraordinary visions. These accounts were offered by ministers as models of behavior for both sexes. By the nineteenth century, women learned to incorporate their spiritual experiences into secular literature.

—*Barbara E. Lacey*

See Also:
Christianity; Heaton, Hannah

References:

Cowing, Cedric B. "Sex and Preaching in the Great Awakening." *American Quarterly* 20 (Fall 1968): 624–44.
Lacey, Barbara E. "Women and the Great Awakening in Connecticut." Diss. Clark University, 1982.
Shiels, Richard D. "The Feminization of American Congregationalism, 1730–1835." *American Quarterly* 33 (Spring 1981): 46–62.

GREER, GERMAINE (b. 1939) is a feminist theoretician, writer, teacher, scholar, lecturer, television performer, and journalist. A native of Melbourne, Australia, Greer took her B.A. in 1959 from Melbourne University, an M.A. with first-class honors from Sydney University, and a Ph.D. in Renaissance literature from Cambridge University in 1968. A woman of many talents, Greer was teaching at Warwick University while writing for popular magazines and appearing on the British television series *Nice Times*.

While at Warwick, where she taught English literature from 1968 to 1973, she published her international best-seller, *The Female Eunuch* (1970), whose impact on the modern women's movement rivaled that of Betty Friedan's *The Feminine Mystique*. In it, Greer argued that "female sexuality had been masked and deformed" by a sexist society and called for women to "take possession" of their bodies and glory "in their power." Her bold and provocative statement created a great sensation in the United States and throughout the English-speaking world. She became a media celebrity and one of the most visible feminists of the 1970s, in constant demand on the talk-show circuit.

However, despite the pressures of the life of a media celebrity, Greer has never abandoned her academic interests. Indeed, her intellectual horizons have been continually expanding. For example, in 1979 she published a major scholarly work on women painters, *The Obstacle Race*. Between 1979 and 1982 Greer taught for and directed the Center for the Study of Women and Literature at the University of Tulsa. Since then, she has devoted herself to her research and writing projects, which have ranged from *Shakespeare* (1985) to another controversial study entitled *Sex and Destiny: The Politics of Human Fertility* (1984). Although she now resides almost exclusively in Europe, Greer's writings—both her books and her articles for a host of popular journals here and abroad—continue to exert a great influence in the United States.

—Jonathan W. Zophy

See Also:

Women's Liberation Movement

References:

Greer, Germaine. *The Female Eunuch*. 1970; rpt. London: Granada, 1980.

———. *The Obstacle Race: Women Painters and Their Work*. New York: Farrar, Strauss & Giroux, 1979.

———. *Sex and Destiny: The Politics of Human Fertility*. New York: Harper & Row, 1984.

Plante, David. *Difficult Women: A Memoir of Three*. New York: Atheneum, 1983.

GRIFFING, JOSEPHINE (1814–72) was an abolitionist and activist for the early women's movement. A founding member of the Ohio Woman's Rights Association, Griffing was elected its president in 1853. She arrived in Washington, D.C., in 1863 as the general agent for the National Freedmen's Relief Association of the District of Columbia (1863–72). The sight of the miserable condition of freed blacks in that city so moved Griffing that she converted her own home into a settlement house and devoted much of her remaining life to helping the former slaves. She was determined that freed men and women should be self-supporting if they were physically able, but she furnished care and medical help for those who were not. Griffing wanted to keep freedmen from being dependent on charity offered by benevolent organizations, so she established sewing and other vocational schools, and sought employment and housing for families.

When this responsibility became overwhelming for one individual, she convinced President Abraham Lincoln to support the creation of the Bureau of Refugees, Freedmen and Abandoned Lands. In 1865 she became subassistant commissioner of the Freedmen's Bureau in Washington, D.C., and during the period from 1865 to 1867 she was instrumental in locating jobs and housing for seven thousand blacks in the Washington, D.C., area. In late 1865 the Bureau tried to reduce funding, and Griffing spoke out in a series of lectures to gain public support against any such reduction. Griffing constantly lobbied for congressional aid, even attempting to get congressional approval of public works projects to benefit the unemployed.

During the same period she was also active in the woman's movement. She was the first vice-president to the American Equal Rights Association, and a corresponding secretary in the National Woman Suffrage Association. She also founded the Universal Franchise Association of the District of Columbia. Despite opposition and instances of mob violence, Griffing lectured and worked tirelessly in support of both causes.

—Jean Nettles

See Also:

Freedmen's Bureau, National Woman Suffrage Association

References:

McPherson, James M. *The Struggle for Equality*. Princeton: Princeton University Press, 1964.

Riley, Glenda. *Inventing the American Woman*. Arlington Heights, Ill.: Harlan Davidson, 1986.

Sterling, Dorothy, ed. *We Are Your Sisters*. New York: Norton, 1984.

GRIMKÉ, ANGELINA EMILY (1805–79) was a Southern-born woman raised amid wealth on a plantation in Charleston, South Carolina, but she abhorred the institution of slavery and was a firsthand witness to its cruelties. In 1829 she joined her sister Sarah in Philadelphia and became a member of the Quakers. There, Grimké joined the American Anti-Slavery Society, to which she would devote much of her life. After a letter she had written to the *Gazette*, an abolitionist newspaper, was published, she began her career as a speaker for the society.

Public speaking by a woman in front of an assembly of both men and women was unheard of in the years before the Civil War, and Grimké's speeches drew curious onlookers and also fiery criticism from the clergy and much of the public. An eloquent, emotional speaker, she dramatized her speeches with descriptions of events she had witnessed on the plantation. Using this technique, she effectively illustrated the horrors of slavery to an audience that had no direct, personal contact with slavery.

The Grimké sisters drew large audiences in the North made up of abolitionists, sympathizers, and also women working in the factories of New England. Grimké's pamphlet *An Appeal to the Christian Women in the South* detailed the tragedies of life under slavery and asked the women of the South to influence their husbands and sons to put an end to slavery. The pamphlet was burned in the South, and a warrant was issued for her arrest if she ever returned to South Carolina.

In 1838 Grimké married Theodore Weld, a prominent abolitionist. As Mrs. Weld she discontinued her lectures and helped administer a school they established in New Jersey. Angelina Grimké was one of the first woman abolitionists in the country and paved the way for others like her to speak out in public against injustice.

—Lynn E. Lipor

See Also:

Abolition and the Antislavery Movement; Grimké, Sarah; Public Speakers, Women; Society of Friends

References:

Grimké, Angelina Emily. *An Appeal to the Christian Women of the Southern States.* New York: N.N., 1836; rpt. New York: Arno, 1969.

Lerner, Gerda. *The Grimké Sisters from South Carolina: Rebels Against Slavery.* Boston: Houghton Mifflin, 1967.

Weld, Theodore Dwight. *Letters of Theodore Dwight Weld, Angelina Grimké Weld, and Sarah Grimké, 1822–1844.* Edited by Gilbert H. Barnes and Dwight L. Dumond. New York: DeCapo, 1970.

GRIMKÉ, SARAH MOORE (1792–1873) was an abolitionist and also the earliest advocate of women's rights. She began her effort to expose the deficiencies in women's social and legal status soon after joining the abolitionist lecture tour with her sister Angelina.

Grimké moved to Philadelphia from the South and became a Quaker after the death of her father. She spent much of her time studying the Scriptures in preparation for the ministry, an occupation she was subsequently denied by the Quakers. When her sister decided to speak publicly against slavery, Grimké accompanied her as a chaperon, but soon she too was publicly speaking out against slavery and later for women's rights. She traced the connection and developed the common elements that characterized the institution of slavery and the status of women in pre–Civil War society.

Hundreds of women from the factories of the North came to hear both sisters speak. Sarah Grimké questioned a society in which women were not allowed to own property, could be beaten by their husbands, and had no right to an education. Her familiarity with the Bible, acquired during the years with the Quakers, enabled Grimké to repudiate those clergy who used the Bible to support both the institution of slavery and the prevailing economic, legal, and social status of women.

Her pamphlet *Letters on the Equality of the Sexes* examined sexual inequality in the United States and attacked the institutions that supported the existence of a male-dominated society. She drew a parallel between slaves and women, especially the prohibitions against owning property and being able to choose an occupation freely. Her ideas formed the basis of the future women's rights and suffrage movements and greatly influenced many of the future leaders of the movements, such as Susan B. Anthony and Elizabeth Cady Stanton. With intelligence and an analytical perception of American society, Grimké influenced scores of women who sought to rectify the injustices of slavery and the oppression of women. After her sister's marriage to Theodore Weld, she lived with the couple and helped care for their children. The two sisters contributed research and editorial assistance to Weld's monumental antebellum antislavery pamphlet, *American Slavery As It Is* (1839).

—*Lynn E. Lipor*

See Also:

Abolition and the Antislavery Movement; Grimké, Angelina; Public Speakers, Women; Society of Friends

References:

Nies, Judith. "Sarah Moore Grimké." In *Seven Women: Portraits from the American Radical Tradition.* New York Viking, 1977, pp. 1–35.

Grimké, Sarah Moore. *Letters on the Equality of the Sexes and the Condition of Women.* Boston: Knapp, 1838.

Lerner, Gerda. *The Grimké Sisters from South Carolina: Pioneers for Woman's Rights and Abolition.* New York: Schocken, 1967.

In ***GRISWOLD v. CONNECTICUT,*** 381 U.S. 479 (1965), the Supreme Court declared unconstitutional a Connecticut statute that made the use of birth control devices illegal and made it a criminal offense for anyone to give information about them or instruction on their use. This decision gave legal foundation to the right of privacy in matters of marital intimacy. The same statute had previously been unsuccessfully challenged before the Supreme Court in *Tileston v. Ullman* (1943).

Estelle Griswold, executive director of the Planned Parenthood League of Connecticut, and Dr. C. Lee Buxton, its medical director and a professor at the Yale Medical School, were convicted under this statute for dispensing birth control information to married persons and were fined one hundred dollars each. Their conviction was upheld by two different appeals courts within Connecticut before its review by the U.S. Supreme Court.

Writing for the Court, Justice William O. Douglas viewed the enforcement of this law, which entailed police searching the bedrooms of married couples for evidence of contraceptive use, as an idea that is "repulsive to the notion of privacy surrounding the marriage relationship." Justice Douglas found the greatest strength for this decision in the fact that these were the "intimate relation(s) of husband and wife"; the relationship of marriage was the source of privacy—contraceptives were the extension of the relationship. *Griswold's* heavy emphasis on the privacy of the conjugal bed in a marital relationship was surpassed by *Eisenstadt v. Baird* (1972), in which the Court invalidated a Massachusetts law that made it a felony to give any one other than a married person contraceptives; in this court decision, Justice William J. Brennan argued that the right of privacy inheres in the person and is not limited to certain relationships.

—*Sue E. Strickler*

See Also:

Birth Control, Comstock Law, Planned Parenthood Federation of America

References:

Eisenstadt v. Baird, 405 U.S. 438 at 453 (1972).

Goldstein, Leslie Friedman. *The Constitutional Rights of Women.* New York: Longman, 1987.

Griswold v. Connecticut. 381 U.S. 479; 85 S. Ct. 1678; 14 L. Ed. 2d 510 (1965).

Rossum, Ralph A., and G. Alan Tarr. *American Constitutional Law.* New York: St. Martin's, 1987.

GYNECOLOGY is traditionally thought of by its practitioners as the study and treatment of the reproductive organs of women. A physician who is a gynecologist is often (but not always) an obstetrician as well, administering prenatal care to pregnant women and assisting in the birth process. Gynecology, however, was not always a medical specialty. At least up until the mid-nineteenth century, gynecologic disorders were treated by general practitioners or pediatricians, responsible at the time for diseases of women and children.

The progress of gynecology was slowed by the moral atmosphere prevalent in the Victorian era, for apparently the concern for modesty existed as much on the part of the physicians as of the patients. The vaginal speculum, though in use, was regarded in some quarters as an indecent instrument.

It was only in the latter half of the nineteenth century with the development and widespread use of anesthesia and antiseptics that gynecology came into its own as predominantly a surgical specialty. Here, the courage of women patients played as important a role as did the daring and ingenuity of the early doctors. Mrs. Jane Crawford of Danville, Kentucky, for example, journeyed sixty miles on horseback to be examined by Dr. Ephraim McDowell for the possible removal of an ovarian cyst. At the time (1809), these cysts were regarded as incurable, and earlier surgical attempts had proved fatal. Nonetheless, Crawford bravely consented to be operated upon, and the success of this operation marked the beginning of abdominal gynecologic surgery.

Later, Dr. James Marion Sims of Montgomery, Alabama, addressed the challenge of repairing vesico-vaginal fistulas, or tears between the bladder and the vagina that resulted in uncontrollable seepage of urine. Up until 1845 there was no cure for this condition, and those afflicted existed as social pariahs; but in that year, Sims encouraged three slaves—Anarchia, Betsy, and Lucy—to submit to his experimental procedures. After forty attempts, he achieved fistula repair.

Despite the Victorian prudery, the specialization of medicine in the nineteenth century established the dominance of male physicians in the treatment of women. The issue of the propriety of male doctors' attending female patients, however, proved useful in justifying women's entry into the medical profession before the Civil War. Nonetheless, the field of gynecology and its research held a low status within the medical profession as a whole well into the twentieth century, and most women were attended by general practictioners rather than gynecological specialists. The authority of gynecologists, as of most physicians, remained largely unquestioned by their patients until the 1960s: consciousness-raising among women led to their identification of medical issues with feminist implications and enlightened consumerism prompted investigatory news reporting and governmental inquiry into the actual quality of medical treatment women received from gynecologists.

Women today continue to shape the treatment issues in gynecology. Surgery has secured gynecology's place as a distinct specialty, and with the increasing demands and sophistication of women's own awareness of their bodies, gynecology is broadening its emphasis to include care for the whole person, not merely the isolated problem. In addition to its surgical base, gynecology now addresses issues of birth control, fertility, sexual dysfunction, nutrition, cancer prevention and treatment, hormonal changes and imbalances, and problems related to the postmenopausal aging patient. As the patient population changes, so too does this specialty, with increasingly subtle focal points of research and treatment.

—Louise M. Kawada

See Also:

Childbirth, Lying-in, Midwifery, Physicians

References:

Danforth, David N., ed. *Obstetrics and Gynecology.* 4th ed. Philadelphia: Harper & Row, 1982.

Morantz-Sanchez, Regina. *Sympathy and Science: Women Physicans in American Medicine.* New York: Oxford University Press, 1985.

Speert, Harold. *Obstetrics and Gynecology in America: A History.* Baltimore: Waverly, 1980.

HADASSAH, the Women's Zionist Organization of America, is the largest volunteer women's organization in the United States. In the eighty-eight years since its founding, it has operated as Israel's major partner in research and development of educational and social programs. Hadassah chapters with 360,000 members nationwide raise money for work being done in Israel and have enabled hundreds of thousands to migrate to Israel.

Hadassah was founded by Henrietta Szold, a Jewish scholar who, along with twelve other women on February 24, 1912, in New York City, formed the organization to foster Jewish religious and social ideals through education in America and to begin public-health nursing and nurses' training in Palestine. By the time the new organization was a year old, the first Hadassah medical installation in Palestine had begun operation. In 1918 the Henrietta Szold Hadassah School of Nursing opened with thirty students. The Rothschild-Hadassah University Hospital opened in 1939 in partnership with Hebrew University, and in 1949 the Hebrew University-Hadassah Medical School began in Jerusalem. These and other medical facilities serve Moslems, Christians, and Jews.

Youth Aliyah, Hadassah's relief movement for refugee children, was cofounded in 1934 by Recha Freier and others in Germany, and Henrietta Szold, who became its director in Palestine. This branch of Hadassah has relocated successive waves of children, from Germany and Europe in the 1930s to Ethiopia in the 1980s. Currently there are eighteen thousand children age twelve to eighteen in 320 Youth Aliyah installations receiving agricultural and vocational training and secondary education leading to university study.

Education has been a priority with Hadassah since the days of its founders, who stressed a commitment to Jewish values, a basic understanding of Jewish problems, and the creation of a strong bond between the Jewish community here and in Israel. At the national level, the education department produces guides that are adaptable for beginning or advanced students in many areas, including history, literature, Hebrew, and current events. *Hadassah Magazine* is sent monthly to every member, making it the largest-circulation Jewish publication in the United States. Each issue includes articles on Hadassah-related people and projects in Israel and the United States, book reviews, current affairs, and a Hebrew lesson.

—*Abby Schmelling*

See Also:

Jewish Women

References:

Fineman, Irving. *Woman of Valor*. New York: Simon & Schuster, 1961.

Kur, Carol. "Hadassah Way." *Moment Magazine* 3 (March 1978): 19–22.

HALE, SARAH JOSEPHA (BUELL) (1788–1879), author and editor of *Godey's Lady's Book and American Ladies' Magazine* (1837–77), was a conservative advocate of increased education and employment opportunities for women. As editor of the major nineteenth-century women's magazine for forty years, Hale became a nationally influential supporter and purveyor of the contemporary antebellum concepts defining womanhood and woman's role; she urged expanding women's educational facilities and curriculum as well as their entry into professions and employments suitable for "ladies" who supported themselves and their families.

Hale's life and career typified that of popular women writers who promulgated the Cult of True Womanhood in the antebellum United States. Born and reared in New England and self-educated, Hale briefly taught before marrying David Hale in 1813. Hale was widowed at age thirty-five, with five young children whom she supported and educated through her writing and editing of women's magazines. Editing her own *American Ladies' Magazine* (1828–36) established Hale's reputation for producing original and native material before her tenure at *Godey's* assured her prominence as a social and literary critic for her largely female audience. Hale's major works commemorated women's accomplishments, educated children, and instructed her readers in the homemaking arts and patriotic values.

As the unimpeachable authority on Woman's Sphere and a consummate practitioner of Woman's Influence, Hale in her conservative campaigns publicized and made respectable reform movements to improve women through education and employment opportunities, including their entry into medical and teaching professions. Hale opposed the woman's rights movement, but contributed to increasing women's access to education and paid employments outside the home.

—*Angela Howard Zophy*

See Also:

Cult of True Womanhood, *Godey's Lady's Book*

References:

Finley, Ruth. *The Lady of Godey's.* Philadelphia: Lippincott, 1931.

Godey's Lady's Book. Vols. 14–94. Philadelphia: Louis A Godey, 1837–77.

Hale, Sarah Josepha. *Woman's Record.* New York: Harper's, 1853.

Woodward, Helen. *The Lady Persuaders.* New York: Ivan Obolensky, 1960.

Zophy, Angela Howard. "'For the Improvement of My Sex': Sarah Josepha Hale's Editorship of *Godey's Lady's Book,* 1837–1877." Diss. The Ohio State University, 1978.

HALEY, MARGARET A. (1861–1939) was business agent for the Chicago Teachers Federation for over forty-one years and leader of the teachers of Chicago in the most vibrant demonstration of teacher power in the early twentieth century. A schoolteacher for twenty years in Chicago's South Side stockyards district, Haley became interested in the Chicago Teachers Federation when she was thirty-eight and the organization was in its first few years of existence. Concerned over a district announcement that teachers would not receive a pay increase, Haley went to the Cook County tax office to find that five city corporations owed the county over $2 million in back taxes. After three years of legal pursuit, a federal court awarded Cook County its back taxes, but the board of education continued to deny teachers their pay raise. Haley then led the teachers in an unprecedented affiliation with the Chicago Federation of Labor, and the next year the teachers gained their back pay through a scathing decision by a municipal judge.

Her persistence, defiance, and courage earned Margaret Haley the reputation of a woman of leadership in education. In a stunning speech delivered to the National Education Association in 1904, Haley urged teachers to pursue the goal of democracy in education and to resist becoming agents of the materialism and consumerism that she thought were taking over the schools. Finally in 1910 she organized the campaign that made a woman—Ella Flagg Young—the first president of the NEA.

Haley had become so powerful in Chicago politics by 1906 that the new mayor asked her for names to appoint to the city board of education. Haley chose Jane Addams, but the two parted ways on educational policy because Haley's pro-union policies conflicted with Addams's willingness to find compromises, especially at the expense of working teachers. Haley's involvement in local campaigns for a municipal petition process, penny gas, and a municipal ownership gave her a citywide reputation as a power broker. As legislative lobbyist for the Chicago Federation of Labor, Haley remained a close ally and friend of John Fitzpatrick, president of the Chicago Federation of Labor. In 1913, when the governor hesitated to sign the bill for woman's suffrage in the state of Illinois, Haley stood at his desk to make sure he did so.

Haley also gained a national reputation in educational, municipal reform, and suffrage circles in the years between 1903 and 1917. A tireless campaigner, Haley worked actively in the California and Washington suffrage campaigns in 1911 and 1912. In 1915, after an ugly and protracted dispute, Haley's organization was outlawed by a school board ruling that was upheld by the Illinois Supreme Court in 1917. Haley was forced to withdraw her affiliations with trade unions in order to keep her organization going. Unaffiliated and disgraced by a two-year name-calling campaign, the Chicago Teachers Federation and Margaret Haley never recovered from the board attack. When she died on the eve of World War II, thousands of teachers paid their respects to the woman who brought teachers to the trade union movement.

—*Marjorie Murphy*

See Also:

National Education Association; Politics; Progressive Era; Social Feminism; Suffrage; Teaching as an Occupation for Women; Unions; Young, Ella Flagg

References:

Davis, Allen F. *American Heroine: The Life and Legend of Jane Addams.* New York: Oxford University Press, 1973.

Reid, Robert, ed. *Battleground: The Autobiography of Margaret Haley*. Urbana: University of Illinois Press, 1982.

HAMILTON, ALICE (1869–1970), reformer, physician, and toxicologist, was the daughter of Montgomery and Gertrude Pond Hamilton. Though born in New York, she was raised on the family compound in Fort Wayne, Indiana. She had a strong relationship with her mother, who encouraged her four daughters' ambitions. As a child, Hamilton was educated at home with her sisters and cousins, and later followed family custom by attending Miss Porter's School in Farmington, Connecticut. She studied medicine at the University of Michigan, receiving her M.D. in 1893, and held internships at the Northwestern Hospital for Women and Children in Minneapolis and the New England Hospital for Women and Children in Boston. She then did postgraduate work in bacteriology and pathology at the universities of Michigan, Leipzig, and Munich, and the Johns Hopkins Medical School. In the autumn of 1897 she became a professor of pathology at Chicago's Woman's Medical School of Northwestern University.

Shortly after arriving in Chicago, she fulfilled a lifelong dream and moved to Hull House, a settlement house, where educated young people worked among the poor and advocated social reform. She quickly became a member of the settlement's inner circle. It was there that she was introduced to the field of industrial medicine. Her investigation of lead poisoning in the modern factory system was a pioneering study and established Hamilton as one of the nation's leading industrial toxicologists. In time her work in the field earned Hamilton an appointment to Harvard Medical School as assistant professor of industrial medicine, making her the first woman member of the Harvard medical faculty. While teaching, she continued to conduct the field studies that were important to her as a reformer. Her book *Industrial Poisons in the United States* was published in 1925 and quickly established her as one of the world's leading experts in the field. In 1935 she left Harvard and became a consultant in the Department of Labor's Division of Labor Standards. After her professional retirement, Hamilton continued her career as a reformer, heading the National Consumers' League for five years, writing an autobiography, and remaining politically active. The social and political values established in her youth and through her lifelong involvement with Hull House drew her to public service and achievement in the cause of both peace and civil rights. She died in 1970 at the age of 101.

—*Rebecca L. Sherrick*

See Also:

Hull House, Physicians, Science, Social Feminism, Women in Higher Education

References:

Alice Hamilton Papers. Schlesinger Library. Radcliffe College, Cambridge, Mass.

Hamilton, Alice. *Exploring the Dangerous Trades.* Boston: Little, Brown, 1943.

HAMILTON, GORDON (1892–1967), a leader in social work education, nurtured and contributed to the development of casework theory. In 1940 she published her *Theory and Practice of Social Case Work,* used by many schools as a basic text and as a leading proponent of the "diagnostic" school of casework. It was revised in 1951.

A practitioner after graduation from Bryn Mawr, she worked in Denver for the American Red Cross during World War I and worked for the New York City Charity Organization Society as a caseworker and researcher from 1920 to 1923. In 1923 she became associated with the New York School of Social Work, where she taught, wrote, and consulted. While there, she helped establish the doctoral program in social welfare. She was an outstanding teacher and associate dean of the Columbia University School of Social Work, also known as the New York School of Social Work, from 1952 to 1955 and retired in 1957.

In addition to her practice, and her teaching and writing career, Hamilton also served as a consultant to the Social Service Department of Presbyterian Hospital in New York City (1925–32), director of social services in the Temporary Emergency Relief Administration (1935-36), research consultant at the Jewish Board of Guardians of New York (1947–50), and consultant to the committee on social issues of the Group for the Advancement of Psychiatry (1949–53). From 1944 to 1952 she was a consultant and seminar leader for several international social work organizations, including Church World Service and the U.N. Relief and Rehabilitation Administration. In 1962, five years after her retirement from Columbia, Hamilton became the editor in chief of *Social Work,* the professional journal of the National Association of Social Workers.

Gordon Hamilton's career is noteworthy when one considers she was born into an upper-class family that did not consider education and a career suitable goals for a young woman at that time. Many of the positions she held were usually held by men.

—Sarah Ann Foster

See Also:

Social Work, Women in Higher Education

References:

Hamilton, Gordon. *Principles of Social Case Recording.* New York: Columbia University Press, 1946.

———. *Psychotherapy in Child Guidance.* New York: Columbia University Press, 1947.

Longres, John F. "Gordon Hamilton." In *Encyclopedia of Social Work.* 18th ed., 1987, pp. 926–27.

HANSBERRY, LORRAINE (1930–65) was the first black woman to have a play produced on Broadway. This play, her first, *A Raisin in the Sun,* found popular and critical acclaim, winning the prestigious New York Drama Critics' Circle Award as the best play of the 1958–59 season. The Broadway production was also the first for a black director, Lloyd Richards, and marked the beginning of national prominence for players like Sidney Poitier, Diana Sands, and Claudia McNeil. Bringing the black experience and black actors to prominence with mainstream, national audiences, Hansberry's play helped to reshape the response of the theatrical world and the public to black writers and subjects.

Later a film and then adapted as the musical *Raisin,* Hansberry's drama showed a multigeneration black family struggling for opportunity and dignity. Set against Langston Hughes's famous poem, "Montage of a Dream Deferred," *A Raisin* attempted to answer Hughes's question: "What happens to a dream deferred?/Does it dry up/like a raisin in the sun?/Or fester like a sore—/and then run?" Its action generated by the family's receiving the proceeds of a life insurance settlement, the play follows the characters as they work through their competing dreams—for education, for a business, for a home of their own. It concludes with the family's purchase of a house in an all-white neighborhood and with their dignified rejection of the white homeowners' offer to buy them out.

A native Chicagoan, Hansberry lived through a parallel incident herself. The daughter of middle-class blacks who democratically sent their daughter to public schools, but who also dressed her and taught her in ways that set her off from her peers, Hansberry moved at age eight to a middle-class, white neighborhood. Their fair housing suit (*Hansberry v. Lee*), supported by the NAACP, went to the Supreme Court, and Hansberry's memories of their time in the house cemented her dedication to civil rights. After graduation from a Chicago public high school, Hansberry attended the University of Wisconsin, where she discovered modern drama. Residence in New York, marriage to and later divorce from Robert Nemiroff, and a move to the country draw the outlines of Hansberry's life as she struggled to find her voice and struggled against the cancer that killed her.

Hansberry's other writings include *The Drinking Gourd* (1960), a television script on slavery that was never produced despite popular interest in its author. A second play, *The Sign in Sidney Brustein's Window* (1965), was originally planned with a woman as the central character, but, as finished, focused on a male, urban intellectual. Not as critically or popularly well received as *A Raisin*, *Sign* was kept in production by an informal but widespread movement among her associates and supporters until the day after Hansberry died. *Les Blancs* (1970), an aesthetically more ambitious play dealing with an African returning to his community at a time of crisis, remained unfinished at Hansberry's death but was completed by her ex-husband Robert Nemiroff.

More telling than either of these last plays in the popular image and memory of Lorraine Hansberry was the biographical compilation and tribute, *To Be Young, Gifted and Black*, created by Nemiroff and others from Lorraine Hansberry's scattered writing and interviews—especially from a filmed interview, "The Black Experience and the Creation of Drama," in which Hansberry engagingly discusses her life and work and her views of fellow playwrights. (Hansberry explains, for example, the fun she had modeling Beneatha, the young and ambitious daughter of *A Raisin*, on herself.)

What Hansberry saw as a lack of dramatic unity in *A Raisin*, a diffused focus on the family rather than on a strong central character, brought distinctive women's voices to her stage. What Hansberry saw as increasing dramatic unity in her later plays also represented a movement away from these pluralistic women's voices and roles—movement toward a male playwright's tradition and form.

While traditional critics have occasionally faulted Hansberry's work for sentimentality or melodrama, feminist critics have lamented that her drama remained male-centered. Hansberry's sense that the collective voice of *A Raisin* was an artistic weakness seemed to urge her toward finding a more centered vision through a male protagonist, though her notes for both plays after *A Raisin* show her struggling with the possibility of women characters as centers. Well aware of the dramatic tradition, Hansberry wrote of other playwrights, pointing out without hesitation the misogyny in male playwrights such as Strindberg.

—Carol Klimick Cyganowski

See Also:

Black Women, Theater

References:

Cheney, Anne. *Lorraine Hansberry*. Boston: G. K. Hall, 1984.

Hansberry, Lorraine. *The Collected Last Plays*. Edited by Robert Nemiroff. New York: New American Library, 1983.

———. *A Raisin in the Sun*. New York: New American Library, 1961.

———. *To Be Young, Gifted and Black*. Adapted by Robert Nemiroff. New York: New American Library, 1970.

Malpede, Karen. "Lorraine Hansberry: Introduction and Selections." In *Women in Theatre: Compassion and Hope*. New York: Limelight, 1985.

Rich, Adrienne. "The Problem with Lorraine Hansberry." *Freedomways* 19 (Fourth Quarter 1979): 247–55.

HARPER, FRANCES ELLEN WATKINS (1825–1911) was a writer and lecturer on a variety of social reforms during the nineteenth century. She was born in Baltimore, the only child of free black parents, but was raised by an uncle after she became an orphan as a young child. Her uncle, a shoemaker by trade, was very active in the black community; he served as a minister and founded a school. Harper met abolitionists Benjamin Lundy and William Lloyd Garrison through her uncle's antislavery activities. At the age of twenty-five, she left Baltimore to teach for two years at a manual training school for semiskilled laborers near Columbus, Ohio. A second move—to teach in Little York, Pennsylvania—brought her into contact with a lifelong friend and fellow antislavery proponent, William Still. Through her contacts, she became a lecturer for the antislavery societies in New England and a fundraiser for aiding fugitive slaves. Her collection *Poems on Miscellaneous Subjects* (1854) inaugurated her national reputation as an antislavery poet and writer.

She married Fenton Harper in 1860, bore a daughter, Mary, and was widowed within four years. For the remainder of her life, she found fulfillment through writing and lecturing for her several causes. As a writer of moralistic poetry and prose, Harper became the most widely recognized black poet since Phillis Wheatley, her stories appearing in both white and black journals and periodicals. The Civil War heightened her interest in education, women's rights, temperance, and family life for blacks newly freed by the struggle. During and after Reconstruction, Harper's poetry and fiction focused upon the issues of lynching and the economic and social improvement of the black community—*Sketches of Southern Life* (1872); *The Martyr of Alabama and Other Poems* (ca. 1894). Her most widely read work, the novel *Iola Leroy; or, Shadows Uplifted* (1883), charted the experience of a quadroon—a child of a mulatto and a white—through the Civil War to a successful marriage. Despite the continued popularity of *Iola Leroy*, her other fiction and poetry has yet to be made readily accessible through either a new collection of her works or a reissuing of the original volumes.

During her lifelong activism, Harper served as the head of the Colored Department of the National Woman's Christian Temperance Union, a leader in the American Association of Education of Colored Youth and the National Association of Colored Women, and a lecturer for the more conservative American Woman Suffrage Association. Harper worked with both black and white women to achieve the moral and educational uplift of black families. Her activities within white and black groups indicated the respect she received in reform circles. She died at age eighty-five in Philadelphia.

—*Dorothy C. Salem*

See Also:

Abolition and the Antislavery Movement, Black Women, Suffrage

References:

Brown, Hallie Q. *Homespun Heroines.* Xenia, Ohio: Aldine, 1921.

Cleagle, Rosalyn. "The Colored Temperance Movement, 1830–1860." M.A. thesis. Howard University, 1969.

Daniel, Theodora W. "The Poems of Frances E. W. Harper." M.A. thesis. Howard University, 1937.

Loewenberg, Bert, and Ruth Bogin, eds. *Black Women in Nineteenth-Century American Life.* University Park, Pa.: Pennsylvania State University Press, 1976, pp. 243–51.

Stanton, Elizabeth C., Susan B. Anthony, and Matilda J. Gage. *History of Woman Suffrage.* Vol. 2. New York: National American Woman Suffrage Association, 1881, pp. 391–92; rpt. New York: Arno, 1969.

Sterling, Dorothy. *We Are Your Sisters: Black Women in the Nineteenth Century.* New York: Norton, 1984.

HEATON, HANNAH (COOK) (1721–94) wrote one of the few surviving autobiographies by eighteenth-century American women. It records events and reflections from the time of the Great Awakening—an intense and widespread religious revival—to the early years of the Republic.

Born on Long Island, New York, she married Theophilus Heaton, Jr., and, with her husband and their two sons, spent her life on a farm in North Haven, Connecticut. There she described her spiritual reflections, including her conversion experience, and noted her daily prayers, times of despair, books she read, and omens she saw in dreams. She also revealed the social conditions of her time, portraying tempestuous relationships with her husband, children, neighbors, ministers, and magistrates. She gave an account of political events of the Revolutionary period reported in the newspapers she read and the sermons she heard. She recorded revivals that occurred near the end of her life (the beginnings of the Second Great Awakening), which seemed to announce the millennium. While she composed a deeply religious autobiography, her account foreshadows the romantic sensibility that values a life lived with feeling, sensitivity, and suffering.

—Barbara E. Lacey

See Also:
Great Awakening

Reference:

Lacey, Barbara E. "The World of Hannah Heaton: The Autobiography of an Eighteenth-Century Connecticut Farm Woman." *William and Mary Quarterly* 3d Ser., 45 (April 1988): 280–304.

HELLMAN, LILLIAN (1905–84), dramatist, was born in New Orleans, the only child of Julia Newhouse and Max Hellman. When she was five, the family moved to New York, and for several years she lived six months in each of these cities, attending school in both. Her life in the South had a profound influence on her plays, and several people from that time and place found their way into her work.

She attended New York University for two years, following which she was a manuscript reader for a publishing firm, wrote book reviews for the *Herald Tribune*, published a few short stories, and worked as a theatrical agent. It was at this time that she met Arthur Kober, a playwright whom she married and later divorced, and a number of literary and theatrical figures including Dashiell Hammett, the novelist and screenwriter who was to become her literary mentor, confidant, and lover until his death in 1961.

Through Hammett's encouragement, she wrote her first play, *The Children's Hour* (1934). It was enormously successful, partly due to its then-shocking theme of lesbianism, but also due to its sensitive probing of moral issues, an interest that continued to dominate her personal life and her plays. All of her dramas are explorations into the nature of evil, deriving their great power from fine characterizations, economy of language, and carefully structured plots. Her most famous plays are *The Little Foxes* (1939), whose theme of monstrous egotism and ruthless greed within a single southern family had its roots in the history of her mother's family, the Newhouses; and *Watch on the Rhine* (1941), the story of an anti-Nazi German who sacrifices his personal happiness for the cause of freedom.

While Hellman is frequently celebrated as America's finest woman playwright, she was equally well known for her involvement in liberal political causes. She was an early and ardent antifascist in the thirties, a left-wing sympathizer into the forties, and was called before the House Un-American Activities Committee in 1952, where her refusal to implicate others (to "name names") led to her famous statement: "I will not cut my conscience to fit this year's fashions." She and Hammett were blacklisted in Hollywood, losing most of their sources of income, and were forced to sell "Hardscrabble Farm," the home in New York State where they had spent many of their happiest and most productive years.

At the time of her death in 1984, a new storm of controversy surrounded her. Many critics asserted that much of the biographical "fact" in her memoirs was distortion and invention, most notably in the story "Julia" (*Pentimento*, 1973). She began litigation against the writer, Mary McCarthy, who had attacked her as a liar on a national television program, but Hellman died before the case came to trial.

Her memoirs—*An Unfinished Woman* (1969), *Pentimento* (1973), and *Scoundrel Time* (1976)—have achieved nearly as much critical acclaim as her plays. They are filled with rich character studies, serve as a vivid record of an earlier period in our history, and document Hellman's determined battle to win recognition for her art and her principles.

Among the awards Hellman received in her lifetime were the New York Drama Critics' Circle Awards for *Watch on the Rhine* (1941) and *Toys in the Attic* (1960); the National Book Award for *An Unfinished Woman* (1969); and Academy Award nominations for her screenplays of *The Little Foxes* (1939) and *The North Star* (1943). She received honorary degrees at Douglass, Smith, and Wheaton colleges and Tufts, Brandeis, Yale, and New York universities.

—*Bobby Ellen Kimbel*

See Also:

Theater

References:

Adler, Jacob H. *Lillian Hellman.* Austin: University of Texas Press, 1969.

Bryer, Jackson. *Conversations with Lillian Hellman.* Jackson: University of Mississippi Press, 1986.

Falk, Doris V. *Lillian Hellman.* New York: Ungar, 1977.

Hellman, Lillian. *Another Part of the Forest.* New York: Viking, 1947.

———. *The Autumn Garden.* Boston: Little, Brown, 1951.

———. *Candide.* New York: Random House, 1957.

———. *The Children's Hour.* New York: Random House, 1934.

———. *The Little Foxes.* New York: Random House, 1936.

———. *Pentimento: A Book of Portraits.* Boston: Little, Brown, 1973.

———. *Scoundrel Time.* Boston: Little, Brown, 1972.

———. *Toys in the Attic.* New York: Random House, 1960.

———. *An Unfinished Woman.* Boston: Little, Brown, 1969.

———. *Watch on the Rhine.* New York: Random House, 1941.

Wright, William. *Lillian Hellman: The Image, the Woman.* New York: Simon & Schuster, 1986.

HENRY STREET SETTLEMENT, established on the Lower East Side of New York in 1893 by two nurses, Lillian Wald and Mary Brewster, is one of the best-known and most influential settlement houses in the United States. Initially called Nurses' Settlement, it was used by Wald as a base to originate a visiting nurse service designed to provide home nursing care for the poor, who paid whatever they could. Brought into intimate contact with the effects of poverty through home nursing, Wald and others at Henry Street Settlement campaigned for reforms to improve housing and working conditions and to end child labor. Wald was an effective speaker, writer, and lobbyist. Her concerns extended beyond the poverty of her neighborhood to embrace women's suffrage and pacifism. She also attracted to Henry Street other prominent women such as reformer Florence Kelley and Lavinia Lloyd Dock, who was instrumental in improving nursing education.

Besides trying to solve the problems of poverty through social reform, Wald also implemented the settlement house idea through educational, cultural, and recreational programs. Among the volunteers at Henry Street were Rita Wallach Morgenthau and Irene and Alice Lewisohn, who in 1915 established the Neighborhood Playhouse there, a project important to the development of little theater. The settlement also operated one of the first playgrounds in New York and pioneered a vocational counseling service in 1920.

When Wald resigned in 1933 due to ill health, Helen Hall replaced her. Hall was the most prominent among the second generation of settlement workers. The former head of Philadelphia's University Settlement and a president of the National Federation of Settlements, Hall continued Wald's emphasis on social reform. Hall served on the advisory committee that constructed the Social Security Act, frequently testified before congressional committees on consumer and welfare issues, and helped to originate Mobilization for Youth, a program that increased social services on the Lower East Side in the early 1960s and became the prototype for the War on Poverty. In 1967, at the age of seventy-five, Hall resigned as head of Henry Street. Since then, the settlement has had a series of male executive directors and has not been as prominent in social reform.

—Judith Ann Trolander

See Also:

National Federation of Settlements; Nursing; Settlement House Movement; Social Work; Wald, Lillian

References:

Hall, Helen. *Unfinished Business.* New York: Macmillan, 1971.

Trolander, Judith Ann. *Settlement Houses and the Great Depression.* Detroit: Wayne State University Press, 1975.

Wald, Lillian. *The House on Henry Street.* New York: Holt, 1915.

———. *Windows on Henry Street.* Boston: Little, Brown, 1934.

HEPBURN, KATHARINE (b. 1907), stage and film actor, has enthralled successive generations of audiences and maintained her popularity in an industry that has typically discarded female stars within a decade or so. Her indomitable personality and individuality have won her the respect of her colleagues, along with the admiration of a new generation of feminists.

She was born in Hartford, Connecticut, the second of six children, to parents renowned for unconventional thinking and activities. Her father, Norval Thomas Hepburn, was a "radical" surgeon interested in social hygiene; her mother, Katharine Martha Houghton, was an activist in the suffrage and birth control movements and an associate of other activists such as Emmeline Pankhurst, Charlotte Perkins Gilman, and Emma Goldman. Throughout her life, Hepburn remained close to her family, returning to Connecticut at regular intervals to refresh herself, away from the publicity and the tinsel of Hollywood.

She began her lifelong love of acting while attending Bryn Mawr College, her mother's alma mater, and started acting with a Baltimore stock company right after graduation. Her career was rocky at first, fraught with mixed reviews and several dismissals for insubordination, yet she persevered with bit parts on Broadway and in summer stock. In her first starring role, in Julien Thompson's *Warrior's Husband,* she was spotted by Hollywood agent Leland Hayward and persuaded to do a screen test for RKO. Seeing it, George Cukor convinced producer David O. Selznik to offer her a contract. Because she did not want to go to Hollywood yet, Hepburn demanded the staggering sum of $1,500 a week and was chagrined when it was accepted. Her first film, *A Bill of Divorcement* (1932), won her rave reviews and a long-term contract with RKO, and was the first in a long series of creative partnerships with Cukor.

It also launched a Hollywood career that has spanned more than five decades and resulted in four Best Actress Academy Awards (*Morning Glory,* 1933; *Guess Who's Coming to Dinner,* 1967; *The Lion in Winter,* 1968; and *On Golden Pond,* 1981) and eight more nominations (*Alice Adams,* 1935; *The Philadelphia Story,* 1940; *Woman of the Year,* 1942; *The African Queen,* 1951; *Summertime,* 1955; *The Rainmaker,* 1956; *Suddenly Last Summer,* 1959; and *Long Day's Journey Into Night,* 1962). In the course of her career, she has worked with the best actors of several generations, from Cary Grant, Edith Evans, and Laurence Olivier, to Vanessa Redgrave, Peter O'Toole, and Judy Holliday. She has been directed by Hollywood's finest: George Cukor, Dorothy Arzner, George Stevens, John Ford, Howard Hawks, Vincente Minnelli, Elia Kazan, Frank Capra, John Huston, Sidney Lumet, and Stanley Kramer.

Viewed in retrospect, her life seems to be a string of successes, but her career and offscreen life were often less than smooth. From the outset, she did not fit the image of the Hollywood starlet and insisted on keeping her private and professional lives separate. She avoided Hollywood crowds and entertainments, and demanded the respect of studio executives who preferred to dictate to their contract players, especially females. When in the late 1930s the Independent Theatre Owners Association labeled her, along with Joan Crawford, Greta Garbo, and Marlene Dietrich, "box office poison," she left Hollywood, prepared to return only when she could call the shots. The vehicle she chose was Philip Barry's play *The Philadelphia Story*, which made her a Broadway star and for which she had received the film rights in lieu of salary. She sold those rights to MGM and chose both her director (Cukor) and co-stars (Cary Grant, James Stewart). From that point on, Hepburn exerted control over all her films.

Her personal life was no less unusual. Her marriage to Philadelphia stockbroker Ludlow Ogden Smith lasted six years (1928–34), and during the next decade in Hollywood she remained relatively unattached, except for brief interludes with agent Leland Hayward and Howard Hughes. The situation changed radically in 1942 when she met co-star Spencer Tracy on the set of *Woman of the Year*; thus began the relationship that lasted until his death in 1967. They made nine memorable films together, and her offscreen liaison with the still-married Tracy was Hollywood's best-kept secret until Garson Kanin's *Tracy and Hepburn* became a best-seller in 1970. Hepburn's longest period of professional inactivity was the last five years of Tracy's life, when she spent much of her time tending him during his final illness.

In recent years, beset with physical problems herself, she continues to act on stage and television and in films; when asked by Barbara Walters in a televised interview how she has managed to continue, she responded with typical directness: "Just *do* it," she said.

—*Frances M. Kavenik*

See Also:

Movie Stars, Woman's Film

References:

Edwards, Anne. *A Remarkable Woman: A Biography of Katharine Hepburn*. New York: Morrow, 1985.

Higham, Charles. *Kate: The Life of Katharine Hepburn*. New York: Norton, 1975.

Kanin, Garson. *Tracy and Hepburn: An Intimate Memoir*. New York: Viking, 1970.

HERLAND (1915) by Charlotte Perkins Gilman is a story of an all-female utopia that challenges traditional thinking about woman's place in male-dominant society. The women of Herland have been living without men for over two thousand years, until three young American men discover the hidden society. The men expected the women to behave similarly to all women they know. In turn, the Herland women are curious about the men and their civilization.

Each man has a different idea of how a woman should appear and behave. Terry feels a woman should be subordinate to a man and has an extremely difficult time adjusting to the Herland women. Van, a sociologist and the narrator of the story, is interested in the culturally based sex differences. He is intrigued about how the Herland women are similar to and different from American women. Lastly, Jeff is a romantic and views a woman as a precious prize that needs to be protected. Although the Herland women do not need protection, their gentle manner makes him feel perfectly at ease in his assumption.

The women of Herland are strong, intelligent, and kind. In two thousand years they have developed a thriving civilization that is superior to America's. There is no form of money in Herland. Each woman does the work that best suits her, and each is given an equal amount of food, clothing, and shelter. The women of Herland deem it an honor to have a child. The baby does not take on a family name and is raised with all the other children by the women who are best suited for child rearing. The children are allowed to play freely, and all the Herland children's games are designed to teach the children about themselves and their environment. The women consider all the children to be their own and are very concerned with the children's physical and mental development.

As a humanistic and socialist society, Herland demonstrates two common themes of Gilman's writing. The Herland ideology shows how male domination makes American society cruel and complicated. And the society presented offers a series of interesting comparisons between the American concept of women and what a woman's self-concept might be without male influence.

—Susan Deborah Kogen

See Also:
Gilman, Charlotte Perkins

References:

Berkin, Carol. "Private Woman, Public Woman: The Contradictions of Charlotte Perkins Gilman." In *Women in America: A History.* Boston: Houghton Mifflin, 1979, pp. 150–73.
Gilman, Charlotte Perkins. *Herland.* Rpt. New York: Pantheon, 1979.
Pearson, Carol. "Coming Home: Four Feminist Utopias and Patriarchal Experience." In *Future Females: A Critical Anthology,* edited by Marleen S. Barr. Bowling Green, Ohio: Bowling Green State University Popular Press, 1981, pp. 63–70.

HERNÁNDEZ, MARÍA (N.d.) was a recognized activist in the area of education and civil rights. Although she was born in Mexico, her political activity was aimed at civil rights issues in the United States. Beginning in 1924 and continuing through the 1970s, María Hernández remained politically active and became a distinguished orator and author in Texas. Her book *México y Los Cuatro Poderes que Dirigen al Pueblo/Mexico and the Four Powers that Direct the People* was written about Mexico; however, the political message was extended to the Chicano situation in Texas. Her writings advocated political activism at home and in every other aspect of society, particularly the workplace.

In 1929, along with her husband, Hernández organized the mutualist (voluntary association) group Orden Caballeros de America in their struggle for civil rights. In 1934, she worked with Liga de Defensa Escolar in San Antonio to fight segregation and upgrade education in the barrios. In the following decades, she joined labor and civil rights movements in the struggle for justice for Chicanos. Her major involvement in the 1970s was the development of the Raza Unida party in Texas. She was the keynote speaker at the statewide Raza Unida conference in Austin, Texas, July 1970.

Because of her lifelong commitment, she has become an important model and leader in the Chicano movement. Working side by side with her husband, Don Pedro Hernández, she has urged family unity and cooperation between men and women as essential for political struggle.

—Mary Romero

See Also:
Chicana

References:

Cotera, Marta. *Diosa Y Hembra: The History and Heritage of Chicanas in the United States.* Austin, Tex.: Information Systems Development, 1976.
Hernández, María L. *México y Los Cuatro Poderes Que Dirigen al Pueblo.* San Antonio, Tex.: Munguia Printers, 1945.
Herrera, Gloria, and Jeanette Lizcano. *La Mujer Chicana.* Crystal City, Tex.: Crystal City ISD, 1974.

HETERODOXY, a Greenwich Village woman's organization, 1912–42, was named and founded by Marie Jenney Howe to give the new woman of her time a place to voice unorthodox ideas without fear of reprisal. Therefore, no official minutes were recorded, and the club's activities and membership were ascertained only through biographies, personal papers, and scant news clippings.

Through a series of public forums—"Twenty-five Answers to Antis" (1912) and "What is Feminism?" (1914)—Heterodoxy transformed its public image from a suffrage support group to a genuinely feminist organization. Almost all the club's members were involved with the National American Woman Suffrage Association in some capacity at various times. The members were independently so active in various reform movements that only a third of them attended any one luncheon meeting.

Such names as Elizabeth Gurley Flynn, Charlotte Perkins Gilman, and Henrietta Rodman are on the list of the club's 105 documented members. Most members were traveled, educated, and financially independent. They were writers, journalists, theatrical artists, educators, and business professionals such as doctors, lawyers, and stockbrokers. Democrats, Republicans, Prohibitionists, Socialists, anarchists, liberals, and radicals were represented among the membership. The members' marital status also varied: any living arrangement that accommodated the individual involved was acceptable. In its willingness to accept and discuss different points of view, Heterodoxy was the forerunner of what the later modern feminist movement would call consciousness-raising groups.

The one issue that even Heterodites could not discuss intellectually was World War I. Some members left the club following bitter disputes between pacifists and those favoring U.S. involvement. The First Red Scare of 1919 brought persecution to many of the club's members, who were socialists. Some were put under surveillance, and others were jailed for various activities. Its chosen paper, the *Masses*, was closed down. Although the club supported its needy members both financially and emotionally, its cause and membership were old and dying. Once suffrage was achieved, few new members joined. High food prices during World War I caused remaining members to abandon their luncheons. Slowly the club slid into oblivion, holding only memorials for its members. Agnes deMille is listed as Heterodoxy's last surviving member.

—Dianna Dingess Retzlaff

See Also:

Consciousness-Raising, New Woman, Woman Question

References:

Banner, Lois W. *Women in Modern America: A Brief History*. New York: Harcourt Brace Jovanovich, 1974, 1984.

Loeb, Catherine R., Susan E. Searing, and Esther F. Stineman, with the assistance of Meredith J. Ross. *Women's Studies: A Recommended Core Bibliography, 1980–1985*. Littleton, Colo.: Libraries Unlimited, 1987.

Schwarz, Judith. *Radical Feminists of Heterodoxy: Greenwich Village 1912–1940*. Lebanon, N.H.: New Victoria, 1982.

HETEROSEXISM is the assumption that all people are heterosexual and the resulting negation of the needs, desires, and life experiences of gay men and lesbians. Heterosexuality, especially heterosexual intercourse, is sanctioned, indeed almost sanctified, while homosexuality is criminalized and seen as a perversion, sickness, or abnormality. The persecution of lesbian relationships—and the refusal to take the lesbian feminist view seriously—has untold repercussions on society at large as well as on the women directly affected. Lost are role models of viable egalitarian relationships, not based on predetermined sex roles; a deep and abiding valuing of women's concerns; and new perspectives on how societies not based on aggression and competition can be formed.

Lesbian feminist theorists often see other feminist theorists suffering from heterosexism—by assuming that all women are straight, heterosexual feminists focus on economic or biological variables in trying to explain women's oppression. They fail to see women's oppression as a sexual oppression, in which women are tied to their oppressors by affection, marriage, and sexual desire, and thus unable to form bonds with other women that would elucidate their common plight. Lesbian feminists argue that straight women expend much time, as well as emotional and physical energy, in trying to understand, placate, and change their oppressors. Exhausted from "polishing their chains" and blamed for all the emotional ills of men and children if they desist, they have little energy left to create positive social changes for women.

Heterosexism can also be seen as a form of institutionalized homophobia. The unions between gay women are not legally recognized: They are at best ignored and at worst seen as reason enough for a person to lose her job, not have equal access to housing, or be unable to adopt a child. Heterosexism and homophobia are the mortar holding together the bricks of patriarchal structures and, as such, are inherently political rather than sexual ideologies.

—*Susan Weeks*

See Also:
Homophobia, Lesbianism

References:

Cavin, Suzanne. *Lesbian Origins.* San Francisco: Ism Press, 1985.

Cruickshank, Margaret, ed. *The Lesbian Path.* Tallahassee, Fla.: Naiad, 1981.

Dworkin, Andrea. *Our Blood: Prophecies and Discourses on Sexual Politics.* New York: Perigree, 1981.

Wittig, Monique, and Sandra Zeig. *Lesbian Peoples: Material for a Dictionary.* New York: Avon, 1979.

HEWINS, CAROLINE MARIA (1846–1926), librarian, pioneer of library services to children, and librarian of Hartford, Connecticut, for a half century, was one of nine children born to a cultivated middle-class Roxbury, Massachusetts, family. Educated at home or in private schools for the most part, she briefly attended the public Boston Girls' High and Normal School, which brought her into contact with the Boston Athenaeum, a private lending library, and established her lifelong interest in libraries. In 1875 she moved to Hartford, Connecticut, to become librarian of the subscription library at the Young Men's Institute, which became the Hartford Public Library in 1893. Hewins's life and career illustrate the merging of three separate ideas: that books played a major role in the development of the child, that the city or state had a responsibility to provide books for children, and that no child was exempt from the benefits of books and libraries.

Recalling her own childhood, where good books were a part of everyday life, Hewins was shocked at the lack of reading materials for Hartford children. Her efforts to remedy the situation included the publication of lists of recommended titles for the young, distributed to schools and parents; giving papers before child development conferences, book talks, and clubs; and finally in 1904 the opening of the children's room. Her 1882 *Books for the Young: A Guide for Parents and Children* summarizes her views of the place of reading in the development of the child. Hewins targeted the large population of immigrant children as especially in need of library service. Programs and exhibits focused on the holidays and customs of the countries of origin of many of the children as well as on those of their new homeland.

Instrumental in the formation of the Connecticut Public Library Committee in 1893 and its only woman member, Hewins encouraged the development of public libraries throughout the state. She also helped form the Connecticut Library Association in 1891, and she participated in the memorable first meeting of children's librarians at the American Library Association meeting in 1900.

Hewins was active in community affairs, participated in the work of the settlement houses, indeed living at the North Street Settlement for years, and was a supporter of local schools and the museums.

—*Suzanne Hildenbrand*

See Also:
Children's Library Movement, Librarianship

References:

Hewins, Caroline M. *Books for the Young.* New York: Leypoldt, 1882.

———. "A Mid-Century Child and Her Books." In *Caroline M. Hewins: Her Book.* Boston: Horn Book, 1954, pp. 1–76.

Lindquist, Jennie D. "Caroline M. Hewins and Books for Children." In *Caroline M. Hewins: Her Book.* Boston: Horn Book, 1954, pp. 79–107.

Root, Mary E. S. "Caroline Maria Hewins." In *Pioneering Leaders in Librarianship,* edited by Emily Miller Danton. Chicago: American Library Association, 1953, pp. 97–107.

HIGHER EDUCATION FOR SOUTHERN WOMEN in the late nineteenth and early twentieth centuries was shaped by race and gender in ways unique to the region. Segregated by race—and among whites by sex—higher education was nonetheless a central element for women of both races in their movement from the traditional domestic sphere into more public arenas of clubs, social reform, and paid white-collar work.

For white women the entrenched ideal of the Southern Lady affected both the timing and format of the development of higher education. More than twenty years after Vassar College opened in 1865, a handful of southern women's colleges were just beginning to offer a standard liberal arts curriculum; by 1911, only 4 of over 140 women's schools were accredited. While coeducation was the dominant mode nationally (coeducational outnumbered single-sex institutions two to one by 1870), sex segregation continued to be the most common form in the South well into the twentieth century.

Education in the antebellum South was primarily the creation of evangelical denominations, which established a plethora of white women's academies and seminaries, many calling themselves colleges. By 1900, however, most were junior colleges at best and often little more than secondary or even finishing schools dedicated to perpetuating the Southern Lady. Women's colleges continued to be plagued by the postwar poverty of the region and the lingering conviction that higher education was neither necessary nor suitable for ladies. Such attitudes, coupled with a paucity of secondary schools, ensured that women were seldom prepared for college work. Thus, generally underendowed women's colleges had to devote significant portions of their meager resources to preparatory departments at the expense of the facilities and faculty needed to meet national norms. By the 1920s, however, conditions had improved, and many schools were able to drop their preparatory departments and became accredited four-year colleges.

Impelled in part by the desperate need for teachers, southern states began establishing normal colleges for women in the 1890s. While such institutions challenged the concept of the Southern Lady by preparing women for employment, the education they offered remained separate and distinct from that for men. State universities were only gradually opened to women, usually only as graduates and upper-division transfer students; not until the second half of the twentieth century would many southern state universities, pressured by feminists and the federal government, admit women on the same basis as men.

Higher education for black women was shaped by racism as well as sexism. Educated black women were expected to play a crucial role in racial uplift as mothers and teachers, but when W. E. B. DuBois spoke of the "talented tenth" who should be educated as leaders of the race, he meant men.

Unlike white institutions, black colleges were predominantly coeducational—only four out of seventy-five schools established between 1865 and 1933 were exclusively for women—and vocational. Although the denominational sponsors of black schools in the postwar South sought to provide classical or liberal arts education for future black leaders, their attempts foundered on inadequate funding, lack of local support, and unprepared students, the latter caused by the lack of primary and secondary schools. A 1916 study found only one southern black school, Fisk, of true college status, a situation that continued into the thirties. By the turn of the century, a combination of New South conservatives and northern philanthropists controlled many black schools and had shifted the emphasis to vocational and technical education designed to train a labor force that would both fill the needs of southern industry and not threaten the region's racial order. For women, this meant teacher training and domestic skills. The approximately one-half of black college students who were women were heavily concentrated in institutions emphasizing normal rather than liberal arts or agricultural and mechanical curricula.

Little research has been done to determine how black college women's experiences differed from those of either black men or white women or how they responded to or shaped those experiences. What little we know suggests that, like white women, black coeds lived under more strict social controls than men and, compared to whites, were subjected to an even greater emphasis on morality, the latter a response to the slave-owner's fantasy of the lasciviousness of black women. The thrust of their education was to create wives, mothers, and teachers who would promote respectability and responsibility of the race and not challenge racial or gender norms of southern society.

In their postcollege lives, black women, who, unlike their white counterparts, generally worked even after marriage, sought to utilize their training in the great work of racial uplift. As teachers, they played a central role in the development of much needed primary and secondary schools for their race. They also went into nursing and were leaders in civic improvement and social welfare organizations in their communities.

State-supported or privately funded, southern universities and women's colleges remained racially—and to a lesser degree sexually—segregated until the 1960s. They nonetheless provided education that aided women of both races in moving out of the traditional roles of Southern Lady for whites and of domestic or field worker for blacks. However, cultural and economic forces shaped distinct regional patterns that also tended to reduce the challenge to established gender and racial norms implicit in higher education.

—*Pamela Dean*

See Also:

Black Women, Education, Southern Lady, Women in Higher Education

References:

Colton, Elizabeth. "Southern Colleges for Women." *Proceedings of the Seventeenth Annual Meeting of the Association of Colleges and Preparatory Schools of the Southern States.* Nashville: Publishing House of the Methodist Episcopal Church, South, 1911, pp. 48–68.

Corley, Florence. "Higher Education for Southern Women: Four Church-Related Women's Colleges in Georgia." Diss. Georgia State University, 1985.

Guy-Sheftall, Beverly. "Black Women and Higher Education: Spelman and Bennett Colleges Revisited." *Journal of Negro Education* 51 (1982): 278–87.

Neverdon-Morton, Cynthia. *Afro-American Women of the South and the Advancement of the Race,* 1895–1925. Knoxville: University of Tennessee Press, 1989.

Solomon, Barbara Miller. *In the Company of Educated Women.* New Haven: Yale University Press, 1985.

Stringer, Patricia, and Irene Thompson, eds. *Stepping off the Pedestal: Academic Women in the South.* New York: Modern Language Association, 1982.

U.S. Bureau of Education. *Survey of Negro Colleges and Universities.* Bulletin No. 7. Washington, D.C.: U.S. Government Printing Office, 1928.

HIGHGATE, EDMONIA (1844–70) was a teacher, lecturer, and fund-raiser who advocated education for blacks during the latter half of the 1800s. In addition, she lectured on the peculiar institution of slavery, temperance, and the suffragette movement. She traveled extensively throughout Canada and the United States raising money and resources for the post-Civil War Freedmen's Association and the American Missionary Association.

Highgate was born in Albany, New York, in 1844. Her parents, Charles and Hannah Highgate, moved their family to Syracuse, New York, following the denial of the Albany school commissioners to admit the Highgate children to the district school. Highgate graduated from the Syracuse High School with distinction. Her high school senior thesis was a paper on slavery that, when publicly presented, was very well received. She was certified as a teacher. However, she was not able to obtain a position as a teacher of white children because of her color. Her first teaching position was in Binghamton, New York, where she taught in the "colored" school.

Noted abolitionists who admired and encouraged Highgate were Reverend Jermain Loguen, Frederick Douglass, Gerrit Smith, and Samuel J. May. They were impressed with her ability as a lecturer and her unfailing dedication to addressing the educational needs of blacks. She was the first of two women to address the all-male National Convention of Colored Citizens of the United States held in Syracuse in 1864. Her commitment to bring education to former slaves was not without threat to her person and her students. Both were shot at. Highgate taught under deplorable conditions with meager support and resources; one of her schools consisted of a former slave pen. A woman of high ideals, she refused to teach or be a part of a segregated public school system in New Orleans. In protest, as the only woman officer of the Louisiana Education Relief Association, she gave up a highly coveted salary of $1,000 per year rather than be a part of a segregated system. Subsequently, the New Orleans school district adopted and implemented a plan to integrate its schools.

Highgate was plagued with ill health, caused in part by exhaustion from work and the circumstances under which she was forced to live as a black teacher and principal in the South. She died prematurely at the age of twenty-six in Syracuse.

—Constance H. Timberlake

See Also:

Black Women, Education, Teaching

References:

Untitled clippings without page numbers on file at the Onondaga Historical Society, Syracuse, N.Y.: *Albany Press* (Albany, N.Y.). Aug. 31, 1870. *Binghamton Standard* (Binghamton, N.Y.) Sept. 5, 1863. *Syracuse Standard.* Dec. 9, 1858.

The Gerrit Smith Papers. Bird Library. Syracuse University, Syracuse, N.Y. 1869–70.

American Missionary Association Archives. Amistad Research Center, New Orleans, La. 1864–65.

"Coroner's Inquest." *Syracuse Journal* (Oct. 19, 1870). Onondaga Historical Society, Syracuse, N.Y.

Federal Census Bureau. "1850 Census Taken in Albany." The New York State Library, Albany, N.Y. (Aug. 16, 1850)

Sterling, Dorothy, ed. *We Are Your Sisters: Black Women in the Nineteenth Century.* New York: Norton, 1984.

HISTORY OF THE RISE, PROGRESS, AND TERMINATION OF THE AMERICAN REVOLUTION, INTERSPERSED WITH BIOGRAPHICAL AND MORAL OBSERVATIONS (3 vols. 1805), established Mercy Otis Warren as a historian. Previously known for her drama and poetry, she utilized her firsthand knowledge of famous revolutionary figures in her political analysis. Warren staunchly believed in and fought for the political independence of colonial America. Her historical analysis of this period shows her own personal beliefs while delving into the social, economic, and intellectual principles of the American colonies and the American Revolution.

Warren's loyalties and her personalized voice make this treatment of well-known historical figures predictable. British Loyalists fare worse than Americans in Warren's brief biographies. Thomas Hutchinson, for example, is presented as stereotypically British and Machiavellian, while some of her family members win higher acclaim. James Otis, Mercy's older brother, was recognized in the history as "the first champion of the American Freedom" for his representation of the New England merchants in the 1761 Writs of Assistance case, which challenged Britain's authority to issue unspecified general search warrants. Nevertheless, Warren's work transcended mere family bias. Her privileged position in colonial society enabled her to reconstruct an insightful political history of that era. The most substantial contribution of the work, however, is its autobiographical elements.

Although the *History* is an attempt at an all-inclusive historical account of Revolutionary America, Warren devotes considerable attention to biographical descriptions and offers her readers intellectual insights into these historical personages. Warren attempts to draw corollaries between the political and human ideals and those who are professing them. Her desire to link historically social variables with political events of the Revolutionary era grounds her perception of history in human elements.

—Robin S. Taylor

See Also:

Revolutionary War; Warren, Mercy Otis

References:

Anticaglia, Elizabeth. *12 American Women.* Chicago: Nelson-Hall, 1975.

Warren, Mercy Otis. *History of the Rise, Progress, and Termination of the American Revolution.* 1805; rpt. New York: AMS, 1970.

THE HISTORY OF WOMAN SUFFRAGE (1881–1922). When the "triumvirate" of the radical wing of the suffrage movement—Susan B. Anthony, Matilda Joslyn Gage, and Elizabeth Cady Stanton—decided to tell the story of their reform work in 1876, they envisioned writing a short pamphlet in two months. But as the *History* took shape, it grew. Gage and Stanton agreed to "write, collect, select and arrange the material for said history," while the nonwriter Anthony, under the terms of their contract, would arrange for publication. Veteran reform activists from the various states were asked to prepare "a general resume of what has been done, by whom and when," and prominent workers were asked to provide their reminiscences. Much of the submitted material had to be rewritten for clarity; Stanton bemoaned how "dry bones" boring it was.

The project had its share of internal dissent and external criticism. Gage and Stanton disagreed on political interpretation with the more conservative Anthony, and were angry when she didn't provide them with a regular financial accounting. Discontented contributors wanted credit for their writing. Lucy Stone of the American Woman Suffrage Association—more conservative than the National Woman Suffrage Association, which the "triumvirate" supported—refused to submit information, with "ceaseless regrets that any 'wing' of the suffragists should attempt to write the history of the other." One newspaper suggested that writing about a cause that had not been won resembled the celebrated book on "Snakes in Iceland": its subject matter did not exist. Despite the problems, the women proceeded, believing that "those who fight the battle can best give what all readers like to know—the impelling motives to action; the struggle in the face of opposition; the vexation under ridicule; and the despair in success too long deferred." When they finished editing ten years later, the *History* had grown to three volumes, each one thousand pages long, consisting of letters, speeches, petitions, reminiscences, and convention proceedings—all tied together with a brilliant and passionate radical suffragist analysis. As Stanton predicted, these volumes remain the major source for anyone studying "the most momentous reform that has yet been launched on the world—the first organized protest against the injustice which has brooded over the character and destiny of one-half the human race."

Fourteen years later, after Gage had died and Stanton had largely withdrawn from the increasingly conservative suffrage movement, Anthony asked her hand-picked biographer, Ida Husted Harper, to assist in editing the fourth volume of the *History,* picking up where the third volume had left off in 1883. Harper finished the *History* in two more volumes, ending with the passage of the woman suffrage amendment in 1920.

These last three volumes differ fundamentally from the first three. Essentially a bland chronicle of campaign and convention dates from the pen of a professional publicist, Harper's volumes served the needs of a conservative movement denying its radical origins. Her systematic exclusion of references to many important protests, major figures, fundamental theoretical differences, and nonsuffrage feminist organizations create a questionable historical source. Ironically, in her attempt to "clean up" the movement's history and make it respectable, Harper emphasized the work of Anthony and virtually eliminated the contributions of her coeditor Gage and, to a lesser extent, Stanton.

—*Sally Roesch Wagner*

See Also:

Anthony, Susan B.; Gage, Matilda J.; Stanton, Elizabeth Cady; Suffrage

References:

Vols. 1 and 2 of the *History of Woman Suffrage* (ed. Elizabeth C. Stanton, Matilda J. Gage, and

Susan B. Anthony) were published in Rochester, N.Y. in 1881; vol. 3 in 1886. Susan B. Anthony and Ida Husted Harper published vol. 4 in Rochester in 1902; Ida Husted Harper, vols. 5 and 6 in New York in 1922. All six volumes of the *History* were reprinted by Arno and the New York Times Company in 1969.
Harper, Ida Husted. *Life and Work of Susan B. Anthony.* 3 vols. Indianapolis: Bowen-Merrill, 1899, 1908.
Stanton, Theodore, and Harriot Stanton Blatch, eds. *Elizabeth Cady Stanton as Revealed in Her Letters, Diary, and Reminiscences.* 2 vols. New York: Harper, 1922.
Wagner, Sally Roesch, intro. *Woman, Church and State,* by Matilda Joslyn Gage. Chicago: Charles Kerr, 1893; rpt. Watertown, Mass.: Persephone, 1980.

HOFFMAN, MALVINA CORNELL (1887–1966) was one of the foremost American sculptors after World War I. Born in New York City, Hoffman attended the Brearley School for Girls as well as the Women's School of Applied Design before taking up sculpture under the tutelage of Herbert Adams, George Grey Barnard, and Gutzon Borglum. In 1910 she traveled to France with a letter of introduction to Auguste Rodin. When her efforts to meet the great sculptor were rebuffed, Hoffman literally camped outside the famous sculptor's door to obtain his attention and, ultimately, his support. It was, indeed, at Rodin's urging that Hoffman returned to the United States from 1911 to 1913 to undertake anatomy and dissection classes at the Columbia (New York) College of Physicians and Surgeons. Upon her return to Paris, Hoffman enrolled at the Colarossi Academy, a private art school, and began once again to obtain weekly criticism of her work from Rodin.

Hoffman was acutely concerned that her technical training and skills had suffered because she was female. Accordingly, she devoted special attention to the fundamentals of sculptural technique, learning to build tools, chase and finish bronze, and accomplish various castings of her works. Hoffman worked in a variety of media, at first sculpting in plaster, then bronze, and then directly in stone. Hoffman's career in large part capitalized on a contemporary fascination with primitivism and anthropology as well as a growing demand from the newly famous for portrait busts. Hoffman's works include portrait busts of English poet John Keats and Polish pianist and statesman Ignace Paderewski, as well as intimate sculptural portrayals of famous ballet stars such as her close friend Anna Pavlova.

Hoffman is most remembered today for her series of 110 bronzes entitled "The Races of Man," now on display in the Hall of Man, Marshall Field Museum of Natural History, Chicago. Commissioned by the museum to identify and document the major ethnic types throughout the world, Hoffman, along with her husband, traveled the world for two years to locate and model identifiable racial types. In one of her two autobiographies, *Heads and Tales* (1936), Hoffman recounts her colorful experiences.

In 1964 Hoffman received the Gold Medal of Honor from the National Sculpture Society and five honorary degrees. In 1931 she had been made a full member of the National Academy of Design, followed in 1951 by her designation as chevalier of the French Legion of Honor. She also wrote *Yesterday Is Tomorrow: A Personal History* (1965), and a textbook on sculpture entitled *Sculpture Inside and Out* (1939).

—*Anne deHayden Neal*

See Also:
Art

References:

Armstrong, *et al. 200 Years of American Sculpture.* New York: Whitney Museum of American Art, 1976. [exhibition catalog]
Hoffman, M. *Heads and Tales.* New York: Scribner, 1936.
Rubenstein, Charlotte Streifer. *American Women Artists from Early Indian Times to the Present.* Boston: G. K. Hall, 1982.
Tufts, E. *American Women Artists: 1830–1930.* Washington, D.C.: The National Museum of Women in the Arts, 1987 [exhibition catalog].

HOLIDAY, BILLIE (ELEANORA) (1915–59) was one of the greatest female vocalists in the history of jazz. Her particular talent was for finding emotional and melodic beauty in the second-rate material she often had to work with. Holiday helped revolutionize jazz singing by being the first singer to realize the microphone's potential for amplifying many vocal subtleties that had previously been inaudible on recordings or before a large audience. She made more than 350 records in her lifetime. Her supple, elegant voice and emotional reticence were best captured when recorded with a small jazz combo or a piano accompaniment.

Her childhood in Baltimore was difficult and violent. Forced to live for a time with her grandparents, she was physically abused and probably raped. In her early teens she was arrested for prostitution. Holiday had a precocious talent, however, and her singing career advanced quickly.

In 1934 she teamed up with the great saxophonist Lester Young, whose highly original improvisational style influenced her tremendously. Their simultaneous improvising on such songs as "Me, Myself and I" and "A Sailboat in the Moonlight" rate among the finest jazz recordings of the 1930s. Because she refused to alter her unique vocal style, she was allowed to record only second-rate popular and jazz material throughout her early career. Yet she still managed to make brilliant records, especially with Teddy Wilson leading an orchestra composed of some of the leading jazz musicians of the day. In 1937 she performed with the Count Basie band, an all-black group. So as not to appear to be a white singer, Holiday was forced to darken her skin. The following year she toured with the all-white Artie Shaw band, and was forced to use service elevators, stay in dingy hotels, and eat separately from the band. The tensions caused by racism were exacerbated by her tempestuous personality, alcoholism, and drug addiction.

Despite the increasing mental and physical troubles that eventually claimed her life at age forty-four, Holiday continued to make distinguished music throughout her career. In the 1950s she toured Europe and the United States with her own orchestra, and she retained her magnetic powers, if not her magnificent voice. Although she never reached a wide audience, Holiday was and is respected by knowledgeable jazz fans and musicians for her spiritual powers of creativity and expression.

—Richard Prouty

See Also:

Black Women, Jazz, Music, Popular Vocalists

References:

Chilton, John. *Billie's Blues.* New York: Quartet Books, 1973.

Holiday, Billie. *The Lady Sings the Blues.* New York: Sphere Books, 1956.

James, Burnett. *Billie Holiday.* New York: Hippocrene Books, 1984.

HOME ECONOMICS is the name given to an area of academic study that takes the family and problems of domestic life as its subject. Historically, the overwhelming preponderance of students in home economics courses have been women, and home economics has constituted an important aspect of women's education. Home economics educators often trace their lineage to Catharine Beecher, who first advocated making the family and domestic problems a focal point of study in women's education. Beecher's best-selling book *A Treatise on Domestic Economy,* published in 1841, was instrumental in establishing domestic science as a legitimate course of study in girls' schools across the country in the nineteenth century.

Home economics did not gain a distinctive identity as an academic discipline until the early twentieth century, however, when the American Home Economics Association was formed by a group of leading women scientists, scholars, and educators. With the rapid growth of high school enrollments in this period, home economics courses became a standard element of secondary school curricula across the country. At the same time, as larger numbers of women enrolled in colleges and universities, home economics became an important aspect of collegiate curricula as well. By 1919, when home economics was included in the battery of vocational subjects approved for federal support under the Smith-Hughes Act, it had become a central dimension of women's education in the United States, from elementary school through college. Indeed, insofar as there was a gender-related differentiation in the organization of American education, home economics was probably the most distinctively sex-typed subject taught in American schools.

The development of home economics as an established course of study in American schools and colleges was related to a host of developments in social and educational history. The first courses in sewing and cooking appeared in major public school systems as a part of the manual training movement in the latter nineteenth century. They were intended to help girls improve their dexterity, while providing valuable practical lessons in domestic science. In the 1890s an influential group of educators and scientists, most of them women, began to explore the possibility of defining an area of academic study with problems of families and the home as its focal point. Led by Ellen Richards, a chemist and the first female faculty member at the Massachusetts Institute of Technology, this movement took shape in a series of annual conferences in Lake Placid, New York, and led directly to the founding of the American Home Economics Association.

The rise of home economics was related to Progressive era anxieties about the role of the family in the emerging urban-industrial society in turn-of-the-century America. Many educated, middle-class observers of American life felt that family life was threatened by the development of vast urban slums, by new patterns of female labor-force participation, by child labor, by rising rates of divorce, and by other social problems. Educators and social reformers saw home economics as a means of helping young women to develop the skills and scientific knowledge necessary to cope with the complex problems they would face as homemakers in this new social environment. Home economics also provided career opportunities for thousands of women who were interested in studying these issues, particularly as they related to women. In this regard, the home economics movement also functioned as a very early precursor to women's studies, particularly in colleges and universities.

—*John L. Rury*

See Also:

American Home Economics Association; Beecher, Catharine; Smith-Hughes Act; *A Treatise on Domestic Economy*

References:

Rury, John L. "Vocationalism for Home and Work: Women's Education in the United States, 1890–1930." *History of Education Quarterly* 21 (Spring 1984): 21–44.

Solomon, Barbara Miller. *In the Company of Educated Women: A History of Women and Higher Education in America*. New Haven: Yale University Press, 1985.

THE HOME: ITS WORK AND INFLUENCE, a feminist treatise on the domestic economy by Charlotte Perkins Gilman, was first published in 1903. *The Home* discussed further some of the ideas Gilman had expressed in *Women and Economics* (1898).

In *The Home*, Gilman applied Darwin's theory of evolution to domestic America of the early 1900s. She showed that while man evolved from cave dweller to farmer and finally to industrialist, his dwelling remained relatively unchanged. Gilman felt the average single-family American home had been arrested in a state of development more primitive than that of the rest of society. As man progressed through the ages, he had shed unnecessary social conventions, at the same time acquiring new conventions as he needed them. But man's sentimental attachment to his home prevented its changing and evolving to suit his needs better. The result was that the female half of the population was not allowed to evolve because women were required to service this primitive institution, the traditional home.

Gilman insisted that the main purpose of a home should be the care of children. But she contended that children would be better cared for under the guidance of professionals, rather than their overworked mothers, who had outdated notions concerning health, nutrition, and education. She also believed that since such a common institution as the home was slow in evolving, it made all other facets of society cater to its needs, thus inhibiting their growth and slowing the progress of society as a whole.

—*Laura Hynes*

See Also:

Gilman, Charlotte Perkins; *Women and Economics*

Reference:

Gilman, Charlotte Perkins. *The Home: Its Work and Influence*. New York: McClure Phillips, 1903; rpt. Introduction by William L. O'Neill. Urbana: University of Illinois Press, 1972.

HOMEOPATHY was one of the most popular of a profusion of medical sects founded in the mid-nineteenth century that offered an alternative to the "heroic" therapeutics of the so-called regular medical establishment. "Regular" physicians of the time employed purging, leeching, bloodletting, sweating, and surgery to effect dramatic changes in the patient's bodily state. The homeopathic maxim was "the less the better." Heavily diluted drugs, often served in sugar cubes, were prescribed on the principle that their curative power was enhanced by a reduction in quantity.

Women were attracted to many of the "irregular" sects, partly due to the less dangerous methods employed and partly to the more equal roles advocated for women in the healing professions. Homeopathic colleges were more willing to accept women students, and homeopathic hospitals were more willing to admit them to practice than were their orthodox competitors. Homeopathic treatment was especially popular among the middle- and upper-class women who were also the prime customers of "regular" physicians. Thus homeopathy posed a significant threat to orthodox physicians' attempt to regularize and regulate the profession. Nonetheless, most homeopaths were not feminists per se, and leading male practitioners debated the propriety of coeducation and its potential effects on homeopathic medicine's status in the larger society.

Homeopathy, along with many other forms of nineteenth-century therapeutics, declined in the early twentieth century in the face of scientific medicine. In its heyday, however, homeopathy offered some women access to professional careers and offered all women a form of treatment that, if it did little to promote cures, at least did not cause harm.

—*Nancy A. Hewitt*

References:

Barlow, William, and David O. Powell. "Homeopathy and Sexual Equality: The Controversy over Coeducation at Cincinnati's Pulte Medical College, 1873–1879." In *Women and Health in America*, edited by Judith Walzer Leavitt. Madison: University of Wisconsin Press, 1984, pp. 422–28.

Ehrenreich, Barbara, and Deirdre English. *For Her Own Good: 150 Years of Experts' Advice to Women*. Garden City, N.Y.: Anchor, 1978.

HOMOPHOBIA is the irrational fear of homosexuality that results in hatred, fear, and prejudice directed toward lesbians and gay men. Even though since 1973 homosexuality has not been seen as a deviant behavior by the American Psychiatric Association, many otherwise liberal and tolerant people suffer from homophobia, displaying behaviors ranging from open derision toward gays to discomfort at being associated with them. Extreme forms of homophobia are sometimes thought to stem from latent homosexuality in a person who cannot consciously accept being identified with gays. All homophobia is ultimately the fear of loving one's own sex, and hating those who do.

The United States is a very homophobic society. One common but mistaken (and arrogant) assumption is the paranoid belief that all homosexuals want to sleep with heterosexuals in the hope of turning them into homosexuals. Functionally, a person is homophobic if s/he:

Thinks of all touching and affection by a lesbian friend as a sexual advance;

Thinks that a lesbian is just a woman who couldn't find a man;

Feels repulsed by displays of affection between homosexuals that would be endearing in heterosexuals;

Fails to be supportive when a gay friend is upset about a quarrel or breakup.

Homophobia has many negative effects on lesbian women's lives. As marriage between lesbians is not legally recognized, there are no spousal rights for partners in long-term, permanent relationships (i.e., insurance benefits, next-of-kin hospital visits, social security benefits). There is often little recognition by heterosexual friends of the relationship in social situations, such as inquiry about the partner's health or work, or including both women in "couples" functions. Perhaps the most devastating result of homophobia is that the word *lesbian* is often seen as negative and accusatory. It becomes a threat that can be used against someone, a way to divide women, insuring against their independence from men and their solidarity with one another.

—Susan Weeks

See Also:

Heterosexism, Lesbianism

References:

Lorde, Audre. *The Black Unicorn.* New York: Norton, 1978.

Millet, Kate. *Sexual Politics.* New York: Avon, 1971.

Myron, Nancy, and Charlotte Bunch, eds. *Lesbianism and the Women's Movement.* Baltimore: Diana, 1975.

Weinberg, George M. *Society and the Healthy Homosexual.* New York: St. Martin's, 1972.

HOPE, LUGENIA BURNS (1871–1947), community organizer and proponent of racial justice, was born in Mississippi, where her grandparents had moved from Canada. Her parents migrated to the North to seek better employment and educational opportunities. When her father died, the family moved to Chicago, where Hope helped to support her deaf mother and younger siblings.

The Chicago environment was extremely conducive to social reform during the 1880s and 1890s. She became a member of King's Daughters (a black club), became acquainted with intellectuals from the University of Chicago, worked with Jane Addams, and met black intellectuals like Paul Laurence Dunbar. At the Chicago Columbian Exposition in 1893, her beauty led her to be labeled "Genie with the light brown hair." She met John Hope, a student at Brown University, a person with whom she could share similar interests in urban reform. In 1897 they married and moved to Nashville; he taught at Roger Williams University, and they became friends with the families of nationally known black business and education leaders, such as John Napier and W. E. B. DuBois.

His career in education brought the young couple to Atlanta in 1898, where he headed Morehouse College, while she raised their two sons and extended her community concerns by organizing the Atlanta Neighborhood Union in 1908. Under the motto And Thy Neighbor as Thyself, the black women of the community developed lecture courses, fresh-air work, clean-up campaigns, probation and employment services, reading rooms, clubs, instruction, health and recreation campaigns; they also advocated scientific investigations of schools, sanitation, and vice to improve community life and stimulate community responsibility. In cooperation with professionals in the sociology department at Morehouse College, Hope improved the efficiency and efficacy of black social work. The techniques she developed influenced other communities as she shared her experiences as director of neighborhood work in the National Association of Colored Women. As an affiliate of the National Urban League, the Neighborhood Union became the model for urban reform recommended by the league.

Hope did not limit her activities to the Atlanta community. During World War I she served as the director of the YWCA-sponsored Hostess House at Camp Upton in New York. She felt that the efforts of blacks in World War I merited improved conditions in postwar America. When worsening race relations followed the war, Hope was instrumental in organizing black women to pressure the YWCA to become more interracial in its policies and leadership. Hope continued pressing for racial justice after the Neighborhood Union became part of the Community Chest, thereby institutionalizing her programs for future generations.

—*Dorothy C. Salem*

See Also:
Black Women

References:

Chivers, Walter. "Neighborhood Union: An Effort of Community Organization." *Opportunity* 3 (June 1925): 178–79.

Hall, Jacqueline Dowd. "Revolt Against Chivalry: Jessie Daniel Ames and the Women's Campaign Against Lynching." Diss. Columbia University, 1974.

Johnson, Georgia D. "Frederick Douglass and Paul Laurence Dunbar at the World's Fair." *National Notes* 49 (January-February 1947): 10, 29.

Lerner, Gerda. "Early Community Work of Black Club Women." *Journal of Negro History* 59 (April 1974): 158–66.

Torrence, Ridgely. *Story of John Hope*. New York: Macmillan, 1948.

HOPKINS, SARAH WINNEMUCCA [THOCMETONY, TOS-ME-TO-NE, SHELL FLOWER, SONOMETA, SOMITONE, SA-MIT-TAU-NEE, WHITE SHELL] (1844?–1891) was born near Humboldt Sink in Nevada, the daughter of Paiute Chief Winnemucca and the granddaughter of Chief Truckee. In the spring of 1847 she went with her family to California. For three years she attended Catholic convent school in San Jose, where she gained the speaking and writing skills she used as an interpreter at Camp McDermitt in northern Nevada close to the Oregon border and later at the Malheur Agency, headquarters for the Malheur reservation in Oregon. She was also the personal interpreter and guide for General Oliver O. Howard in the battle against the Bannocks in 1878.

Although Hopkins viewed her mission as a lifelong crusade for justice for her people, she was often duped by the very people she beseeched her people to trust. The Nevada Paiutes were sent to the Yakima Reservation in Washington Territory, and Hopkins's autobiography ends with a plea to readers to urge Congress to restore her people to their land. In 1883 she went east and became the protégée of Elizabeth Palmer Peabody and her sister Mary (Mrs. Horace) Mann. Hopkins was controversial because she had friends among the whites and at times appeared to be contradicting the Indians' interests, but she always believed she was doing what was best for her people.

She spoke English, Spanish, and three Indian dialects. Her real history is in the legacy she left the Paiute people. Although she failed to restore rights to her people, she left them with an example of how to fight. Since her time, the Paiutes have augmented their reservation by recovering land lost in the 1860s and have won a court order to preserve Pyramid Lake, Nevada.

–*Gretchen M. Bataille*

See Also:
Native American Women

References:

Brimlow, George. "The Life of Sarah Winnemucca: The Formative Years." *Oregon Historical Quarterly* 53 (June 1952): 103–34.

Gehm, Katherine. *Sarah Winnemucca*. Phoenix: O'Sullivan, Woodside, 1975.

Hopkins, Sarah Winnemucca. *Life Among the Paiutes: Their Wrongs and Claims*. Edited by Mrs. Horace Mann. Boston: Putnam's, 1883.

———. "The Pah-Utes." *The Californian, A Western Monthly Magazine* 6 (1882): 252.

Morrison, Dorothy Nafus. *Chief Sarah: Sarah Winnemucca's Fight for Indian Rights*. New York: Atheneum, 1980.

Richey, Elinor. "Sagebrush Princess with a Cause: Sarah Winnemucca." *American West* 12 (November 1975): 30–33, 57–63.

Stewart, Patricia. "Sarah Winnemucca." *Nevada Historical Society Quarterly* 14 (Winter 1971): 23–38.

HORNEY, KAREN (1885–1952), psychoanalyst and pioneer in the psychology of women, was born in Hamburg, Germany. She completed her M. D. in 1913 at the University of Berlin. From 1914 to 1918 Horney underwent psychoanalytic training at the Berlin Psychoanalytic Institute. She began private practice in 1919 while serving as a faculty member at the Berlin Institute. Horney immigrated to the United States in 1932 as an associate director of the Chicago Institute for Psychoanalysis. Two years later she returned to private practice and took a teaching position at the New York Psychoanalytic Institute, which she found excessively Freudian.

Dr. Horney soon broke with the New York Institute and founded the American Institute of Psychoanalysis, which she headed until her death in 1952. While accepting certain aspects of Freud's teaching, she challenged his bias against women and stressed the social rather than the biological determinants of sex differences and "feminine psychology." She promulgated these viewpoints in a widely read series of books including: *The Neurotic Personality of Our Time* (1937), *New Ways in Psychoanalysis* (1939), and *Our Inner Conflicts: A Constructive Theory of Neurosis* (1945). Horney went beyond Freud in arguing that the neurotic's basic conflicts are neither innate nor inevitable, but arise out of undesirable social situations in childhood and can be prevented.

—Jonathan W. Zophy

See Also:
Freudianism, Psychiatry, Psychology

References:
Horney, Karen. *The Neurotic Personality of Our Time.* New York: Norton, 1937.

———. *New Ways in Psychoanalysis.* New York: Norton, 1939.

———. *Our Inner Conflicts.* New York: Norton, 1945.

Schultz, Duane. *A History of Modern Psychology.* New York: Academic Press, 1975.

HOSMER, HARRIET GOODHUE (1830–1908) was the first internationally renowned American woman sculptor. Born in Watertown, Massachusetts, she was educated by her physician father; the results of this permissive upbringing with its emphasis on an outdoor life were later balanced at Mrs. Charles Sedgwick's school, where she was also encouraged to develop her interests in sculpting and mechanics. Hosmer also became closely acquainted here with Fanny Kemble, an English actress who would foster Hosmer's career. There were few opportunities to study art in the United States during this period, even fewer for women. Hosmer received technical lessons from Paul Stephenson, after Cornelia Crow and her father, Wayman, arranged for Hosmer to study anatomy in St. Louis, Missouri, with Dr. J. N. McDowell. Hosmer defied Victorian expectations for women by traveling first to St. Louis and, after studying there, then down and up the Mississippi, instead of marrying.

In 1852 Hosmer traveled to Rome (at first accompanied by actress Charlotte Cushman, who recognized and encouraged Hosmer's talent, although she would later travel throughout Europe and between continental Europe, England, and the United States frequently unaccompanied) in search of a teacher. John Gibson, the famous English neoclassical sculptor, took her as his student. Unique as an individual and as an artist, Hosmer quickly gained fame as a sculptress and a presence. Her first commissions date back to 1855. By the end of the Civil War, Hosmer had attained international recognition and completed some of her most important works. Neoclassicism was, however, being replaced by realism, and Hosmer's commissions became fewer. While her base moved from Rome to England, she remained in Europe until around 1900, when she returned to Watertown and her scientific experiments.

Harriet Hosmer remains important today as one of the foremost American neoclassical sculptors; she also designed fountains and gates (mainly for English estates), carried out mechanical experiments, and is renowned for her friendships, especially among women. Her most important statues include *Puck* (1856), *Beatrice Cenci* (1857), and *Zenobia in Chains* (1859).

—Maureen Ruth Liston

See Also:

Art; Kemble, Fanny

References:

Gerdts, William H. *The White Marmorean Flock: Nineteenth Century American Women Neoclassical Sculptors.* Poughkeepsie, N.Y.: Vassar College Art Gallery, 1972.

Hosmer, Harriet. *Letters and Memories.* Edited by Cornelia Carr. New York: Moffat, Yard, 1912.

Leach, Joseph. *Bright Particular Star: The Life and Times of Charlotte Cushman.* New Haven: Yale University Press, 1970.

Liston, Maureen Ruth. "A Cultural History of American Women Expatriates, ca. 1850–1939." Ongoing research project.

Thorp, Margaret Farrand. "The White, Marmorean Flock." *The New England Quarterly* 32 (June 1959): 147–69.

HOUSEWORK, women's unpaid service to the family household, represents the fundamental sexual division of labor. The ways in which women cook, clean, launder, and perform a multitude of tasks for their homes sheds light on both the level of technology and the status of women in any culture or era. In the preindustrial period, ending at about the turn of the nineteenth century, housework, although considered "women's work," was done by all household members, including husband and children. Simplicity of life and scarcity of resources made the care of the home only one aspect of a woman's activities; many housework chores, such as the large-scale food preparation of canning or collective spinning and cloth production, were performed by groups of women together. Preindustrial housework was not only arduous but dangerous: for example, to do the laundry, women were exposed to the harmful effects of lye soap and had to lift heavy sodden clothing; many housewives' skirts caught fire as they cooked at the hearth.

With industrialization, housework became the wife's province alone. The husband's duties shifted exclusively to the outside world of work, while children spent longer amounts of time in school, which changed the nature of the home itself. Moreover, women's housework played a hidden role in the economics of industrialization since their unpaid labor subsidized the paid labor of employed men and women. Coupled with urbanization, technological innovations in the form of cast-iron stoves, manufactured cloth, commercially prepared flour, and municipal water altered the housewife's basic tasks, making housework the private enterprise of each woman working alone in her home. As housework became a woman's major responsibility, writers like Catharine Beecher produced a voluminous literature promoting the cult of domesticity not only to help women learn how to do housework but to celebrate the joys of caring for a home, as well as to raise the esteem of woman in her divinely ordained sphere. By the end of the nineteenth century, secondary schools and women's institutions of higher education included home economics in their curricula to train women in standardized housework skills, to establish that housework now constituted a professional vocation even if it continued to be unpaid when performed by women within their families.

By the twentieth century, housework shifted from an emphasis on production to consumption. As the size of the middle-class household and family decreased, the number of mechanical and electric devices for the home—refrigerator, vacuum cleaner, washing machine, dishwasher—compensated for the loss of domestic servants and actually raised the standard of cleanliness. Goods that during the previous century had been made in the home were now mass produced in factories, thus requiring the housewife to assume responsibility for purchasing these goods for the family's consumption. The invention of the automobile and increased suburbanization added the duties of chauffeuring of the children as well as traveling some distances to stores, thereby expanding the physical boundaries within which the housewife performed her increased role. By the 1950s, housework included the social and psychological services required to rear achieving and well-adjusted children as well as to maintain a well-stocked, harmonious, spotless, and comfortable home.

—Hasia R. Diner

See Also:

Consumerism, Home Economics, Industrial Revolution, *Treatise on Domestic Economy*, Women's Work–Nineteenth Century

References:

Cowan, Ruth Schwartz. *More Work for Mother: The Ironies of Household Technology from the Open Hearth to the Microwave.* New York: Basic, 1983.

Oakley, Ann. *Women's Work: The Housewife Past and Present.* New York: Pantheon, 1974.

Sklar, Katharine Kish. *Catharine Beecher: A Study in American Domesticity.* New Haven: Yale University Press, 1973.

Strasser, Susan. *Never Done: A History of American Housework.* New York: Pantheon, 1982.

HOWE, JULIA WARD (1819–1910) was born in New York City to Samuel Ward, a prosperous banker, and Julia Cutler Ward, a poet. Howe's mother died when she was five, and she was raised by governesses and educated in private schools. In 1843 she married Samuel Gridley Howe, a well-known social activist and the founder of the first American school for the blind. Together, the Howes edited the abolitionist newspaper the *Commonwealth.*

Howe began writing unsuccessful plays: *Hippolytus* was never produced, and *The World's Own* (1857) was a dismal failure. She had more success as a poet, producing three volumes of verse: *Passion Flowers* (1854), *Words for the Hour* (1857), and *Later Lyrics* (1865).

In 1861, following the Battle of Bull Run, the Howes accompanied a group to Washington, D.C., to observe conditions and morale among soldiers in the Union army. On November 18 the Howes attended a grand review, which was cut short by attacking Confederate troops. On the way back to their hotel the group, which included Massachusetts governor John Andrew and James Freeman Clarke, began singing "John Brown's Body," and the soldiers along the road joined in. The next morning, inspired by the song's haunting melody, Julia Ward Howe wrote "The Battle Hymn of the Republic." The poem was published in the *Atlantic Monthly* in February 1862, and Howe received five dollars for it. The poem became extremely popular, and people began singing it at public events. As a direct result of "The Battle Hymn of the Republic," Howe became the first woman inducted into the American Academy of Arts and Letters.

After the emancipation of the slaves in 1865, Julia Ward Howe was active in the campaigns for women's rights, prison reform, international relations, and sex education. She supported ratification of the Fourteenth Amendment and co-founded the New England Women's Club in 1868. A leader of the more conservative American Woman Suffrage Association, which she helped found in 1869, Howe approved its merger with the National Woman Suffrage Association in 1890. She died in 1910.

—Rose Kolbasnik Callahan

See Also:

Abolition and the Antislavery Movement, American Woman Suffrage Association, Civil War, General Federation of Women's Clubs, National American Woman Suffrage Association, National Woman Suffrage Association

References:

Clifford, Deborah Pickman. *Mine Eyes Have Seen the Glory.* Boston: Little, Brown, 1978.

Howe, Julia Ward. *Is Society Polite? and Other Essays.* Boston: Lamson, Wolffe, 1895.

HOXIE, VINNIE (REAM) (1847–1914), sculptor, was the first woman artist awarded a U.S. government commission. Born in Madison, Wisconsin, Hoxie thereafter moved to Washington, D.C., with her family, where she commenced work as a U.S. postal clerk. Through the intervention of several government officials who were also family friends, she began to pursue her interest in sculpture and obtained access to President Abraham

Lincoln for daily sittings in 1864–65. Because of these sittings, Hoxie was one of the last persons to see the president alive. After Lincoln's assassination, she was selected from a group of nineteen competitors to create a commemorative statue of the president to stand in the Capitol Rotunda.

Hoxie's struggle to win the Lincoln commission typifies the career difficulties of many women artists in nineteenth-century America. Award of the $10,000 commission to eighteen-year-old Hoxie created a major uproar in the nation's capital. Mary Todd Lincoln publicly disavowed the young sculptor, and abolitionist Charles Sumner strongly criticized Hoxie's selection on the grounds that she was too inexperienced to create a statue suitable for the nation's capitol. Many other contemporaries, both male and female, condemned her selection as masterminded by "feminine wiles." Despite opposition, she completed the greater-than-life-size statue of Lincoln in 1871.

During this same period, Hoxie did a series of portrait busts, as well as a variety of neoclassical pieces, many of which are lost today. Several of these works were exhibited at the Philadelphia Centennial Exposition of 1876. In 1875 Hoxie was awarded a $20,000 commission to prepare a full-size bronze of Admiral David G. Farragut from the bronze propeller retrieved from Farragut's flagship.

In 1878 she married then-Lieutenant Richard Leveridge Hoxie. At the apparent urging of her husband, she virtually abandoned sculpture in favor of charitable work and became a well-known hostess. She lived on K Street, overlooking Farragut Square, within view of her own sculpture. Later in life, however, already stricken by a fatal kidney ailment, Hoxie recommenced sculptural activity, completing a full-size statue of Governor Samuel Kirkwood of Iowa for the Capitol and commencing a statue of Sequoya for the state of Oklahoma.

Hoxie is buried in Arlington Cemetery, Arlington, Virginia, where a bronze replica of her neoclassical sculpture *Sappho* stands over her grave.

—Anne deHayden Neal

See Also:

Art

References:

Becker, Carolyn Berry. "Vinnie Ream: Portrait of a Young Sculptor." *Feminist Art Journal* 5 (Fall 1976): 29–31.

Gerdts, William H., Jr. *The White Marmorean Flock: Nineteenth Century American Women Neoclassical Sculptors.* Poughkeepsie, N.Y.: Vassar College Art Gallery, 1972 [exhibition catalog].

Peterson, Karen, and J. J. Wilson. *Women Artists: Recognition and Reappraisal from the Early Middle Ages to the Twentieth Century.* London: The Women's Press, 1976.

Rubenstein, Charlotte Streifer. *American Women Artists from Early Indian Times to the Present.* Boston: G. K. Hall, 1982.

Tufts, E. *American Women Artists: 1830–1930.* Washington, D.C.: National Museum of Women in the Arts, 1987 [exhibition catalog].

HUERTA, DOLORES (b. 1930), vice president and chief negotiator for the United Farm Workers (UFW), began her political activity in the late 1950s in Stockton, California, when founder Fred Ross recruited her assistance in the Community Service Organization (CSO), a grassroots advocacy group. She began helping Ross and César Chávez while working with the CSO. Huerta was involved in registering *Chicano* voters and organizing against police brutality. In 1960 she assisted Chávez in building twenty-two active CSO chapters in California and Arizona. Huerta demonstrated her leadership skills in 1961 by successfully lobbying a legislative program that extended old-age pensions to first-generation Mexicans regardless of citizenship and included farm workers in disability coverage.

Chávez, and later Huerta, left the CSO when the 1962 convention rejected a rural-oriented organizing program. Huerta joined Chávez in Delano, California, organizing agricultural workers and began the United Farmworkers Union. As the director of picketing in the Delano Strike, she was influential in recruiting women to the picket lines. Her example as a role model has been important in placing women at the forefront of farm labor union activity.

—*Mary Romero*

See Also:
Chicana, United Farm Workers

References:

Huerta, Dolores. "Dolores Huerta Talks About Republicans, César, Children, and Her Home Town." *Regeneración* 2 (1974): 20–24.

London, Joan, and Henry Anderson. *So Shall Ye Reap*. New York: Crowell, 1970.

Rose, Margaret Eleanor. "Women in the United Farm Workers: A study of Chicana and Mexicana Participation in a Labor Union, 1950–1980." Diss. University of Calfornia, Los Angeles 1988.

HUGHAN, JESSIE WALLACE (1875–1955), pacifist proponent of nonviolent resistance, Christian socialist, and feminist, was born in Brooklyn, New York, of parents who were prominent citizens of their community and devoted "single taxers," followers of Edward Bellamy. Hughan attended Northfield Seminary in Northfield, Massachusetts, the school founded by Dwight L. Moody and famous as one of the first girls' boarding schools in the country. She received her B.A. from Barnard College in 1898 and earned an M.A. and Ph.D. at Columbia University.

While researching her dissertation on American socialism (published in 1911 as *American Socialism of the Present Day*), Hughan became a socialist herself. As an active socialist before and during World War I, she was barred from university teaching and became instead a New York public school teacher and administrator. Hughan was an absolute pacifist by 1914. Acting upon her principles, she became a charter member of the Christian pacifist Fellowship of Reconciliation (FOR), served on the executive committee of the New York City branch of the Woman's Peace Party, and organized the Anti-Enlistment League (1915–17) to enroll men pledged against enlistment in any international war. During this period Hughan also worked for woman suffrage under the aegis of the Woman Suffrage Party and ran on the Socialist ticket for the offices of lieutenant governor, congressman, and U.S. senator (New York State).

After the war, with the cooperation of FOR, the Women's Peace Society (in which she was active), and the Women's Peace Union, she founded the War Resisters League (WRL), which had as its object the enrollment of women and men "who for any reason whatsoever are uncompromisingly opposed to all war" and "have determined to give no support to any war." In the twenties Hughan, as executive secretary, worked hard to build up the league and in the thirties contributed significantly to the success of a number of no-more-war parades. During World War II Hughan and the WRL supported all conscientious objectors, including those who accepted alternative civilian service. The WRL helped to ensure that by 1942 men serving in Civilian Public Service Camps were paid a nominal amount for their work and were permitted to choose between service in private, church-administered camps or government camps.

Hughan wrote extensively on pacifism, socialism, and world government, both as a scholar and theorist and as a poet. In addition to her published Ph.D. dissertation, her books and pamphlets include: *The Facts of Socialism* (1913), *A Study of International Government* (1923), *The Challenge of Mars and Other Verse* (1932), *The Beginnings of War Resistance* (1935), and *Pacifism and Invasion* (1941). Her writings on organized war resistance and nonviolent national defense constitute important contributions to pacifist theory.

—*Frances H. Early*

See Also:
Pacifism and the Peace Movement, Socialism, Woman's Peace Party

References:

Gara, Larry. "Hughan, Jessie Wallace." In *Biographical Dictionary of Modern Peace Leaders*, edited by Harold Josephson. Westport, Conn.: Greenwood, 1985, pp. 432–34.

Hughan, Jessie Wallace. *American Socialism of the Present Day*. New York: Lane, 1911.

———. *The Beginnings of War Resistance.* New York: City Resisters League, 1935.
———. *The Challenge of Mars and Other Verse.* New York: Correlated Graphic Industries, 1932.
———. *The Facts of Socialism.* New York: Lane, 1913.
———. *Pacifism and Invasion.* New York: War Resisters League, 1942.
———. *A Study of International Government.* New York: Crowell, 1923.

HULL HOUSE was the third settlement house to be established in America. The original residence, on Halsted Street in Chicago, was constructed in 1856 for Charles J. Hull, a philanthropist and realtor. When first built, it was situated in a rural area. By the time it opened as a settlement house, the city had grown so much that it sat in a poor, multiethnic community on the southwest side of Chicago.

Jane Addams, together with Ellen Gates Starr, created and founded Hull House, which they moved into on September 18, 1889. Although Addams assumed the leadership position, she could not have done her part without support from a cadre of other women who not only influenced Hull House but went on to make their own contributions to society. Among these women were Julia Lathrop, Florence Kelley, Grace and Edith Abbott, Sophonisba Breckinridge, and Alice Hamilton, who contributed to the founding of social work as a profession. Mary Smith was a friend and financial backer. Helen Culver, who was Charles Hull's heir, eventually gave the property to Addams. There were many male residents, visitors, and supporters, including intellectuals such as educational theorist John Dewey, historian Charles Beard, and social behavioral thinker George Mead.

The motivation for establishing Hull House was humanitarian, democratic, and Christian. It was considered beneficial to residents and the community that educated young people "settle" among and associate with the poor. In the early years, Hull House sponsored lectures, art exhibits, and other cultural activities that were open to the neighbors. Before long the settlement house responded to the community needs for day nurseries, sewing classes, a cooperative residence for working women, clubs, citizenship classes, and space in which labor unions could meet. Hull House also became active in working for reforms in child labor, sanitation, and housing conditions.

Hull House lost some of its financial support during World War I because of Jane Addams's unpopular pacifist views and the Red Scare. Following the war, there was a waning of interest in social activism. After Addams's death in 1935 there was a period of leadership confusion and conflict. Consistent leadership was restored from 1943 to 1962. In 1963, however, the Hull House property was taken over by the University of Illinois, which had for years been seeking a site for a Chicago campus. Subsequently, Hull House relocated and adopted decentralized community centers around the city.

—Roberta G. Sands

See Also:

Abbott, Edith; Abbott, Grace; Addams, Jane; Hamilton, Alice; Kelley, Florence; Lathrop, Julia; Settlement House Movement; Social Work

References:

Addams, Jane. *Second Twenty Years at Hull-House.* New York: Macmillan, 1930.
———. *Twenty Years at Hull-House.* 1910; rpt. New York: Signet, 1960.
——— *et al. Philanthropy and Social Progress: Seven Essays.* College Park, Md.: McGrath, 1893.
Davis, Allen F. *American Heroine: The Life and Legend of Jane Addams.* London: Oxford University Press, 1973.
———, and Mary Lynn McCree, eds. *Eighty Years at Hull-House.* Chicago: Quadrangle Books, 1969.

HUNTER COLLEGE OF THE CITY UNIVERSITY OF NEW YORK was the first college in the United States to provide free education for all women and, until 1964, was the largest women's college in the world. Since its opening in 1870, it has expanded from a teacher training school to a large, coeducational liberal arts college.

Established as a free academy known as the Female Normal and High School, it opened on February 14, 1870. Its purpose was to provide free higher education for women so as to afford the city "a constant supply of trained and competent teachers." In keeping with this role, the college adopted the motto *Mihi Cura Futuri* ("Mine Is the Care of the Future"). Two months after the school's inception, its name was changed to the Normal College of the City of New York, although it granted no degrees at that time.

Its principal founder and first president was Irish-born Thomas Hunter, who insisted that the school admit blacks and whites on equal terms, even though New York in that period was still maintaining separate elementary schools. President Hunter also advocated a liberal arts education along with professional training. In 1914, to honor the founder-president, the college was renamed Hunter College of the City of New York.

Its first class consisted of 1,095 young women who were officially called "teacher-pupils." After completing five months of professional teacher training, they took their places as teachers in the city's elementary schools. By 1879 the curriculum was extended to four years, and in 1888 Hunter became the first tuition-free college in the country to grant degrees. At the turn of the century, Hunter was no longer a college serving solely as a professional school for prospective teachers, but had a broad liberal arts curriculum. In 1961 the college, together with City, Brooklyn, and Queens colleges, united to become the City University of New York with the power to grant doctoral degrees. In size the City University is second only to the University of California and is the largest system of municipal education in the United States. After nearly a century of service as an exclusively women's college, Hunter became coeducational in 1964.

Its students have advanced from the rigidly disciplined, very young "ladies" of the early classes to a contemporary group of self-governing young women and men, and its alumni include such notables as Bella Abzug, Bess Meyerson, and Sylvia Porter. Hunter's past two presidents, Jacqueline Grennan Wexler and Donna E. Shalala, have been women.

—Ruth Jacknow Markowitz

See Also:

Education, Women in Higher Education

References:

Hunter College Bulletin.

Hunter College Wisterian.

Patterson, Samuel White. *Hunter College: Eighty-Five Years of Service.* New York: Lantern, 1955.

Shuster, George N. *The Ground I Walked On: Reflections of a College President.* New York: Farrar, Straus & Giroux, 1961.

Stern, Elizabeth Vera Loeb. "1870–1970: A History of Hunter's Splendid Century." *Hunter College Alumni Quarterly* 78 (Winter 1970): 13–21.

HURSTON, ZORA NEALE (1901?–1960) was the author of five novels, numerous short stories, various articles, an autobiography, and a collection of folktales. Aside from her interest in writing, she has been highly regarded for her anthropological studies, focusing primarily on the language and lore of her people: black Americans. A daughter of black culture in the rural South, and a participant in the Harlem Renaissance, she committed herself to the preservation of her heritage. This is evident in her writing.

As a black woman writer during the Harlem Renaissance, Hurston was ahead of her time. Rather than limit herself to the themes and characters of her male counterparts in the literary world, Hurston wrote not only about the freedom of blacks, but also about the specific issues and feelings related to the freedom of black women. The needs, thoughts, and words of black women—never stereotyped—were communicated in a style that established Hurston as the first in a continuing series of black North American women writers to give voice to black women's experiences.

Because she was a social and political nonconformist, Hurston's literary place in history has often been overshadowed by the controversy that surrounded her as a person. She was forceful, defying traditional roles with open rebellion. Personally, she demanded equality; the characters of her novels and stories became an extension of her own private demands. The current interest and respect given to her work provides a belated awareness of the universality of her voice of integrity in the face of oppression.

—*Joanne S. Richmond*

See Also:
Black Women

References:

Brown, Rosellen. "Writers Under a Double Disadvantage." *The New York Times Book Review* 23 (January 23, 1984): 15.
Cannon, Katie Geneva. "Resources for a Constructive Ethic in the Life and Work of Zora Neale Hurston." *Journal of Feminist Studies in Religion* 1 (1975): 37–51.
Evans, Marie. *Black Women Writers (1930–1980).* Garden City, N.Y.: Anchor, 1984.
Hurston, Zora Neale. *Their Eyes Were Watching God.* Foreword by Sherley Anne Williams. Urbana: University of Illinois Press, 1978.

HUTCHINSON, ANNE MARBURY (1591–1643), leader of the opposition party to Puritan orthodoxy in seventeenth-century Massachusetts, was the eldest daughter of Francis Marbury, an Anglican cleric, and his second wife, Bridget Dryden. Owing to her mother's tutelage, Hutchinson became a skilled nurse and midwife, while her father, censured and without clerical responsibilities during her early years in Alfred, Lincolnshire, took charge of her education, providing her with detailed knowledge of doctrinal issues and a willingness to question established authority. In 1612 she married William Hutchinson, a merchant, and began to assume the prominent role that his successful business required.

The Hutchinsons became followers of John Cotton, an Anglican minister with Puritan leanings, who emphasized a "Covenant of Grace" and an inward awareness of one's spiritual salvation, rather than a "Covenant of Works," in which one's ability to lead a sanctified life was seen as a sign of election. When Cotton went to the Massachusetts Bay Colony, the Hutchinsons followed.

Arriving in New England in September 1634 aboard the *Griffin*, Hutchinson found a community alert to any signs of strife or challenges to its orthodoxy, and the twice-weekly meetings that Hutchinson held in her home came to be seen as such a challenge. In the beginning the meetings consisted of Hutchinson's recitations of sermons for those women unable to attend the weekly lecture or worship service, but gradually they moved toward exegesis and commentary on the sermons, and prominent members of the community, men as well as women, began to gather in her home. When Hutchinson denounced all Boston clergymen, with the exception of Cotton and John Wheelwright, her husband's brother-in-law, for preaching a Covenant of Works rather than a Covenant of Grace, the political content of her meetings became clear.

The issue was much more than a point of dogmatic dispute. By challenging clerical authority, she was striking at the primary supports of the entire Puritan system. In November 1637 Anne Hutchinson stood trial, charged with having "troubled the peace of the commonwealth" through actions "not fitting for [her] sex." The magistrates found her guilty and banished her from Massachusetts.

The Hutchinson family moved to Rhode Island. When her husband died in 1642, Hutchinson and those of her fifteen children still at home moved to New Netherlands—a Dutch colonial territory later divided into New York and New Jersey—where she and all but one of her children were killed in 1643 in a war between the Dutch settlers and the Indians.

—*Cristine M. Levenduski*

See Also:
Christianity

References:
Battis, Emery. *Saints and Sectaries: Anne Hutchinson and the Antinomian Controversy in the Massachusetts Bay Colony.* Chapel Hill: University of North Carolina Press, 1962.
Hutchinson, Thomas. *The History of the Colony and Province of Massachusetts Bay.* Edited by Lawrence Shaw Mayo. Cambridge: Harvard University Press, 1936.
Lang, Amy Schranger. *Prophetic Women: Anne Hutchinson and the Problem of Dissent in the Literature of New England.* Berkeley: University of California Press, 1987.
Williams, Selma. *Divine Rebel: The Life of Anne Marbury Hutchinson.* New York: Holt, Rinehart and Winston, 1981.

HYATT, ANNA VAUGHN (HUNTINGTON) (1876–1973), sculptor, gained international recognition for her accurately executed animal sculptures. Hyatt became an expert in animal anatomy and behavior through careful observation of animals, both at zoos and at her family's Maryland farm, where she spent summers as a child. She began sculpting at the age of nineteen after finding she enjoyed assisting her sculptor sister Harriet Hyatt (Mayor). Hyatt studied in Boston and later at the Art Students League in New York, and in 1900 she had her first solo exhibit at the Boston Art Club, where she showed forty animal figures, all portrayed with vigor and power. Her nephew A. Hyatt Mayor remembered that she worked quickly "and from such a precise mental image that she rarely had to revise."

In 1907 Hyatt spent a year at Auvers-sur-Oise, France, where she executed a large jaguar sculpture that was shown at the Paris Salon Exhibition that year. After completing a massive lion statue for Dayton, Ohio, she dropped all commissions to devote her time to an equestrian statue of Joan of Arc. To assure accuracy in the monument, Hyatt brought a horse into her studio and made detailed studies of armor. Her model won honorable mention in the Paris Salon of 1910, and the city of New York commissioned her to execute the monument in bronze. The sculpture now stands on Riverside Drive, and replicas appear in other cities in the United States and France. The government of France made her a Chevalier of the Legion of Honor for this piece.

Among her many other awards were the Saltus Medal from the National Academy of Design in 1922 for *Diana and the Chase*; the Grand Cross of Alfonso XII for *El Cid Campeador*, erected in Seville, Spain, in 1927; and gold medals from the American Academy of Arts and Letters and the National Sculpture Society. Her works are in the collections of over two hundred museums.

At age forty-seven Anna Hyatt married poet and philanthropist Archer M. Huntington. Together they established Brookgreen Gardens near Charleston, South Carolina. This ten-thousand-acre sculpture garden exhibits works by Hyatt and over 150 other artists. Anna Hyatt Huntington completed the last of seven equestrian statues at age ninety and left works in progress when she died at ninety-seven.

—*Anne L. Clare*

See Also:
Art

References:
Brookgreen Journal. (Brookgreen Gardens, S.C.) 15 (1985).
Evans, Cerinda W. *Anna Hyatt Huntington.* Newport News, Va.: Mariners Museum, 1965.
Hill, May Brawley. *The Woman Sculptor: Malvina Hoffman and Her Contemporaries.* New York: Berry-Hill Galleries, 1984 [exhibition catalogue].
McHenry, Robert, ed. *Liberty's Women.* Springfield, Mass.: Merriam, 1980.
Rubinstein, Charlotte Streifer. *American Women Artists: From Early Indian Times to the Present.* Boston: G. K. Hall, 1982.
Tufts, Eleanor. *American Women Artists 1830–1930.* Washington, D.C.: National Museum of Women in the Arts, 1987.

HYSTERIA is a psychiatric illness particularly associated with nineteenth-century women. Common enough even earlier, the disease reached a peak in the half century before

World War I. Hysterics suffered fits, tics, fainting spells, and paralysis of limbs, and often experienced long periods of invalidism. Doctors diagnosed a variety of sometimes mortal illnesses as hysteria, so dominant had it become in the medical literature. Until recently, historians assumed hysteria to be a disease predominantly affecting the middle class, but in fact there were as many and sometimes more victims among working-class women. Treatment involved electrotherapy, hypnosis, and especially the famous rest cure devised by S. Weir Mitchell, whose patients were encouraged to stay in bed for weeks on end and to gain thirty or forty pounds. Since anorexia was another manifestation of hysteria, the cure sometimes worked.

Sigmund Freud revolutionized the understanding of hysteria when he attributed its origins in part to the sexual repression of women and their attendant hypermoralism. Once divorced from physical causes and from explanations grounded in sufferers' inferior intelligence or immorality, the disease received a psychological rather than a medical treatment. Indeed, from being a major malady across North America and Europe, hysteria declined in frequency. Moreover, after World War I it came to afflict those in the countryside who were remote from psychological discourse.

Among famous hysterics or invalids during this period, Alice James, sister of renowned intellectuals Henry and William James, has received careful study, while feminist Charlotte Perkins Gilman has left her account of the rest cure. Some victims of the Salem witch trials centuries before are also believed to have suffered hysterical symptoms.

—Bonnie G. Smith

See Also:

Freudianism; Gilman, Charlotte Perkins; James, Alice; Salem Witch Trials Yellow Wallpaper

References:

Ehrenreich, Barbara, and Dierdre English. *For Her Own Good: 150 Years of Experts' Advice to Women.* New York: Doubleday, 1978.

Mitchell, S. Weir. *Lectures on Diseases of the Nervous System, Especially in Women.* Philadelphia: H. C. Lea's Sons, 1881.

Shorter, Edward. "Paralysis: The Rise and Fall of a 'Hysterical' Symptom." *The Journal of Social History* 19 (Spring 1986): 549–82.

Showalter, Elaine. *The Female Malady.* New York: Pantheon, 1985.

Strouse, Jean. *Alice James: A Biography.* Boston: Houghton Mifflin, 1980.

Wood, Ann Douglas. "The Fashionable Diseases: Women's Complaints and Their Treatment in Nineteenth-Century America." *Journal of Interdisciplinary History* 4 (1973): 25–52.

IMMIGRANT MIDWIFERY. During the latter decades of the nineteenth century, it appeared that American midwifery would soon become obsolete. The growth of medical professionalism and the advancement of obstetrics as a recognized medical specialty seemed to ensure that the midwife would be displaced by the physician. However, the arrival of millions of immigrants from eastern and southern Europe onto American shores between 1880 and 1920 brought a new visibility to the midwife. Midwifery was a long-established and highly respected profession throughout Europe, and most European midwives held distinguished positions within their communities. When immigrant women arrived in America, they continued to employ midwives. In fact, by the early decades of the twentieth century, many cities and towns of the urban northeast and midwest, where immigrants most often settled, had begun to experience an unexpected revival of midwifery.

Most immigrant midwives were mature, married women with children. Some had earned diplomas from European midwifery schools before coming to America, while others were empirically trained. A minority of immigrant midwives received training at one of the few well-recognized midwifery schools established in the United States, such as New York City's Bellevue School for Midwives. Although opponents of midwifery often characterized these women as ignorant, incompetent, and dirty, most immigrant midwives were intelligent, literate women who were concerned with aseptic techniques and whose maternal and infant-mortality rates were equal to or better than those of local physicians.

Recently arrived immigrants sought out midwives for a variety of reasons. Midwives spoke the same language and shared similar traditions and customs with the parturient women whom they served. Immigrant contempt for men in the birthing room also contributed to the popularity of midwives. Furthermore, the midwife generally charged less than the physician, and she also allowed for the informal arrangement of payment in kind. Immigrant midwives rarely joined together to form professional midwifery associations. Because they usually worked independently of each other, they were ill-equipped to help frame training and regulatory legislation or to respond to the charges that they were ignorant and dirty.

The halting of immigration from eastern and southern Europe in the early 1920s, coupled with the enactment of more stringent state regulatory measures, resulted in a significant decline in the number of immigrant midwives. In addition, second- and third-generation immigrant women were beginning to express a preference for the "American way" of physician-managed childbirth. By the 1930s the immigrant midwife, who had been the predominant birth attendant among ethnic communities three decades earlier, was becoming less commonplace and would eventually disappear from the American setting.

—*Judy Barrett Litoff*

See Also:

Childbirth, "Granny" Midwifery, Immigration, Midwifery

References:

Baker, S. Josephine. "Schools for Midwives." *American Journal of Obstetrics and the Diseases of Women and Children* 65 (1912): 256–70.

Declercq, Eugene. "The Nature and Style of Practice of Immigrant Midwives in Early Twentieth Century Massachusetts." *Journal of Social History* 19 (Fall 1985): 113–29.

———, and Richard Lacroix. "The Immigrant Midwives of Lawrence: The Conflict Between Law and Culture in Early Twentieth-Century Massachusetts." *Bulletin of the History of Medicine* 59 (1985): 232–46.

Levy, Julius. "The Maternal and Infant Mortality in Midwifery Practice in Newark, New Jersey." *American Journal of Obstetrics and the Diseases of Women and Children* 77 (1918): 41–53.

Litoff, Judy Barrett. *American Midwives, 1860 to the Present.* Westport, Conn.: Greenwood, 1978.

The **IMMIGRANT PROTECTIVE LEAGUE (IPL)** evolved out of a committee formed by the Women's Trade Union League at its 1908 convention to deal with the peculiar problems faced by immigrant women traveling alone. The committee discovered that each year about 20 percent of such travelers leaving Ellis Island for Chicago failed to arrive at the proper address and that many of them were steered by unscrupulous cabbies, baggage-express men, and policemen to saloons and brothels. It recommended the creation of a permanent agency to register single immigrant women at the port of entry and to assist them in their passage to their ultimate destination. Once formed, the IPL became aware of the multitude of problems that faced immigrants in general and expanded its scope accordingly. The initial impetus for the league's formation was provided by Jane Addams and Sophonisba Breckenridge, with the latter serving as temporary director for several months. The directorship was eventually assumed by Grace Abbott, who served in that capacity for the duration of the league's most active years.

The IPL was funded by private philanthropy and had close ties to Hull House, the Chicago Commons, the Chicago School of Civics and Philanthropy, and the Women's Trade Union League. Besides Addams, Breckenridge, and Abbott, it also numbered in its ranks Julia Lathrop, Mary McDowell, Agnes Nestor, and Margaret Dreier Robbins. Its board of directors included such male luminaries as philanthropist Julius Rosenwald, juvenile court Judge Julian Mack, and legal scholar Ernst Freund. By and large, the IPL was a typical reformist organization of the Progressive era; its members were mostly professionals, businessmen, and civic leaders who were predominantly old-stock, Protestant, well-educated, and affluent. They agreed with the fundamental outlines and tenets of American society and wanted these extended to newcomers. They concentrated upon concrete practical solutions for specific evils and proposed no radical reconstruction of the socioeconomic or political order. Most of the staff were social workers and other professionals who sought to bring the values and methods of their various disciplines to bear upon the problems faced by immigrants. The primary goal was to facilitate the assimilation of immigrants while preserving much of the "gifts" and "contributions" the newcomers added to the American cultural mix. The league aimed to make immigrants self-sustaining in every sense—employed at useful, renumerative labor; exercising their full citizenship rights; gaining access to opportunity; and supporting their children in the educational system. Its members believed that the immigrants' problems were due to their temporarily debased status in American society rather than innate inferiority. The IPL hired only bilingual staff members, challenged the ethnic biases of the Dillingham Immigration Commission, and opposed the literacy test required by immigration restriction laws of the period. Along with most native-born reformers of the era, IPL members believed that assimilation was the end result of the immigrant experience, but that it should come naturally rather than through coercive legislation or administration.

Much of the league's work involved the provision of direct services to immigrants. IPL workers met immigrants at train stations, found lost luggage, arranged accommodations for those who were stranded, delivered others to the correct address, found temporary employment, provided translators, or arranged for continuing passage. They protected the new arrivals from exploitative actions by ticket brokers, steamship and railroad companies, employment agencies, taxi drivers, and baggage express men. In 1913 they persuaded the Chicago and Western Indiana Railroad to donate one of its buildings across from the Dearborn Street station as a refuge. In the first year, it served the needs of over forty thousand people. The IPL also served as an advocate of the newer immigrant groups, representing their interests in court, before government regulatory commissions, and with municipal and state agencies. It lobbied for laws to police private employment offices, to regulate immigrant banks, and to increase state and federal responsibility for the welfare of immigrants. In 1913 the league was largely instrumental in the passage of a federal law requiring that the Immigration and Naturalization Service inspectors be in railroad stations and at ports of entry. Its staff conducted important studies of immigrant employment and of the status of women and children.

In 1918 it convinced the State of Illinois to create an Immigrant's Commission with Abbott as director, thereby virtually subsuming the IPL. The commission produced two important studies on the educational needs of immigrants in Illinois and on the status of immigrant coal miners. The former led to the institution of adult education programs and a significant reduction in immigrant illiteracy. Abbott's work with the IPL largely provided the basis for her influential work *The Immigrant and the Community.*

From 1917 on, the league's direct service work was significantly reduced, as World War I and immigration restriction drastically reduced the number of newcomers. Its work became largely legal and technical rather than social in nature. Abbott became increasingly involved in the work of the League of Nations, serving on commissions to control international white slavery and to provide protection for children and young people. In 1921 Illinois governor Len Small vetoed the commission's appropriation, and the league was reduced to a staff of two people operating out of donated space in Hull House. In 1958 the IPL changed its name to the Immigrants Service League, and in 1967 it became an administrative arm of the Traveler's Aid Society of Metropolitan Chicago.

—John D. Buenker

See Also:

Abbott, Grace; Hull House; National Women's Trade Union League

References:

Buroker, Robert L. "From Voluntary Association to Welfare State: The Illinois Immigrant's Protective League, 1908–1926." *Journal of American History* 58 (December 1971): 643–60.

Costin, Lela. *Two Sisters for Social Justice: A Biography of Grace and Edith Abbott.* Urbana: University of Illinois Press, 1983.

Leonard, Henry B. "The Immigrants Protective League of Chicago, 1908–1921." *Journal of the Illinois State Historical Society* 66 (1973): 271–84.

IMMIGRATION represents a significant, yet largely neglected aspect of women's history in the United States. The migration of the over fifty million people from Europe, Asia, and the Western Hemisphere to America has been analyzed primarily from the point of view of the male experience. Historians who have attempted to analyze the experience of women migrants have tended to create a collective category, "immigrant women," ignoring cultural and social variations.

The processes of female migration, modes and rates of adaptation to life in the United States, and patterns of retention of traditional ways, varied historically from group to group. Particularly noteworthy were the differences in male-female ratio from one immigrant group to the next. Among several of the western European immigrant groups of the mid-nineteenth century, like the Germans and the Scandinavians, men and women migrated in roughly equal number, although single people predominated. Jewish men and women from eastern Europe in the years between 1881 and 1924 came to the United States at the same rate, with married couples being just as numerous as single people of either gender. The Irish, whose migration began in massive numbers in the 1840s and continued through the last decades of the nineteenth century, were the only group in which women outnumbered male migrants. Owing to land-holding patterns in Ireland that prevented most men and women from marrying, and the acute shortage of domestic servants in the United States, Irish women found themselves more "pulled" to America than were their brothers. Among other groups, such as the Italians, the Greeks, and the Chinese, male migrants far outnumbered women. The paucity of female immigrants reflects the relative impermanence of at least the initial migration from these countries, and as more women from Italy, Greece, and China did arrive in the United States, the process of permanent ethnic community building began in earnest.

—Hasia R. Diner

See Also:

Asian American Women, Black Women, *Chicana*, Hull House, Immigrant Protective League, Jewish Women, Settlement House Movement

References:

Bodnar, John E. "Socialization and Adaptation: Immigrant Families in Scranton, 1880–1890." *Pennsylvania History* 43 (1976): 147–62.

Diner, Hasia R. *Erin's Daughters in America: Irish Immigrant Women in the Nineteenth Century*. Baltimore: The Johns Hopkins University Press, 1983.

Seller, Maxine. "Beyond the Stereotype: A New Look at the Immigrant Woman, 1880–1924." *Journal of Ethnic Studies* 3 (1975): 59–70.

Smith, Judith E. *Family Connections: A History of Italian and Jewish Immigrant Lives in Providence, Rhode Island, 1900–1940*. Albany: State University of New York Press, 1985.

Yans-McLaughlin, Virginia. *Family and Community: Italian Immigrants in Buffalo, 1880–1930*. Ithaca: Cornell University Press, 1977.

INCIDENTS IN THE LIFE OF A SLAVE GIRL, 1861, was an autobiography, published under the pseudonym Linda Brent, recording the horrors of life under slavery for Harriet Brent Jacobs. Born into slavery in 1818, Jacobs was bequeathed at age thirteen to a child of five whose father, called Dr. Flint in the book, became her master. Without the protection of her parents, who were deceased, Jacobs faced the sexual advances of Flint and the jealous rage of his wife. Only the fact that she and her younger brother lived in Flint's home town and that the master felt some concern for his local reputation protected Jacobs from violent assault. It did not save her from Flint's domination in other ways, however.

At age twenty-one Jacobs escaped to her grandmother's house a few miles away and hid there for seven years. Finally she made her way to Philadelphia, where she found work as a domestic servant in the Nathaniel P. Willis family and a home in the antislavery cause. Her brother John escaped about the same time, 1841, and became an antislavery lecturer. Harriet joined John in Rochester, New York, in 1849–50 and worked with the Western New York Anti-Slavery Society, whose members included abolitionists Frederick Douglass and Amy Post. Jacobs returned to the Willis family's employ from 1850 to 1861, continuing to confide in Amy Post through letters. A feminist as well as an abolitionist, Post was particularly concerned with the plight of slave women and encouraged Jacobs to write the story of her life.

Often exhausted from household chores, responsible for the care of a son and daughter brought out of slavery, insecure in her literary abilities, and rebuffed by abolitionist writer Harriet Beecher Stowe, Jacobs finally completed her autobiography with the encouragement of Post and abolitionist William C. Nell. In 1861 *Incidents* was finally published with the aid of and an introduction by Lydia Maria Child and an afterword by Post. Its publication, coinciding with the opening campaigns of the Civil War, never aroused the attention of the public as earlier slave histories had done. Long believed to be a fictionalized account penned by a white abolitionist, *Incidents* only recently came to be recognized as an important and authentic source of information about black women's lives under slavery.

—Nancy A. Hewitt

See Also:

Abolition and the Antislavery Movement; Child, Lydia Maria; Slavery

References:

Amy and Isaac Post Family Papers. University of Rochester, Rochester, N.Y.

Sterling, Dorothy. *We Are Your Sisters: Black Women in the Nineteenth Century.* New York: Norton, 1984.

Jacobs, Harriet Brent. *Incidents in the Life of a Slave Girl.* Edited by Jean Fagan Yellin. Cambridge: Harvard University Press, 1986.

INDUSTRIAL REVOLUTION is the term used to describe a society's rapid transformation from an agrarian to industrial base. Specifically, it refers to the period in late-eighteenth-century and early-nineteenth-century England when dramatic social and economic change occurred because of the development of mechanical means of textile production in factories. Because of the accompanying increase in both the number and the size of factories that made large-scale production possible, all segments of the population, workers and consumers alike, were affected. By the mid-eighteenth century, the invention of the flying shuttle and spinning jenny had significantly increased the volume of textiles produced by spinning and weaving. The further development of the mule-jenny, water frame, and eventually the mechanical loom sparked the imagination of would-be entrepreneurs to place these latter machines in factories where steam engines provided a nonhuman source of power. Simultaneously, changes in the production of iron began transforming metallurgy as well. None of these technological innovations would have changed production, however, without a prior agricultural revolution on the land in which many self-sufficient farms succumbed to absorption into large agricultural holdings that functioned as capitalist enterprises. These developments drove people to search for work, thus creating a labor supply. In creating landless day laborers, the agricultural revolution also created a pool of consumers. Finally, an emerging middle class born of cottage industry and growing trade created an entrepreneurial class ripe for industrial adventures.

Samuel Slater set up the first textile mill in the United States in 1791. Like many European industrialists, he hired whole families, who worked as teams, with tasks allocated in accord with traditional divisions of labor. In the 1820s entrepreneurs in Lowell, Massachusetts, developed another model, employing female labor almost exclusively. Underemployed daughters from New England farms moved into Lowell's boardinghouses and from there joined the industrial work force. Initially, such industrial employment provided a happy alternative to other possibilities for work such as domestic service, schoolteaching, and farm work. For one thing, it was "socialized," that is, accomplished with large numbers of people. For another, wages were higher than could be obtained in other forms of employment. These beneficial conditions in fact remained constant, if compared with alternatives.

The next stage in the Industrial Revolution—that occurring in metallurgy and transport—affected women's work much less. In the United States the initial phase of the Industrial Revolution, which was associated with the rise of the textile industry, gave way to the post–Civil War expansion into steel, railways, and chemical production. After the turn of the twentieth century, these industries were superseded by automobile, airplane, and other durable-goods production until the 1950s brought the development of the computer and, in its wake, related so-called hi-tech industries.

Women in the antebellum industrial sector had prevailed in textiles above all else. Moreover, although factory work did employ many females, women in the nineteenth-century paid labor force were more likely to work in domestic service, the "needle trades," and other nonindustrialized sectors. As an aspect of the postindustrial era, the rise of the service or tertiary sector reflected the greatest increase in women's employment. Thus, although the Industrial Revolution changed familial relations, patterns of work, and patterns of opportunity, women's work lives continued to be variegated and not necessarily "industrialized."

—Bonnie G. Smith

See Also:
Lowell Mill Girls; Textile Industries, Northern and Southern; Unions; Urbanization; Women's Work—Nineteenth Century

References:
Dublin, Thomas. *Women at Work: The Transformation of Work and Community in Lowell, Massachusetts, 1826–1860.* New York: Columbia University Press, 1979.
Kennedy, Susan Estabrook. *If All We Did Was to Weep at Home: A History of White Working-Class Women in America.* Bloomington: Indiana University Press, 1979.
Kessler-Harris, Alice. *Out to Work: A History of Wage-Earning Women in the United States.* New York: Oxford University Press, 1982.

The **INDUSTRIAL WORKERS OF THE WORLD (IWW)**, founded on June 27, 1905, advocated the creation of a worker-controlled system of industrial democracy. The Wobblies, as members were known, were most successful in the American West, where they concentrated on organizing the transient male workers of the agriculture, mining, and lumber industries. But they also achieved considerable success in the East, mobilizing textile workers. The famous "Bread and Roses" strike in Lawrence, Massachusetts, in 1912 was organized by the IWW. The Wobblies gave the American labor movement some of its most dramatic characters and martyrs, including Elizabeth Gurley Flynn, Big Bill Haywood, Frank Little, and Joe Hill.

The IWW made several attempts to organize women, employing Matilda Rabinowitz to unionize textile workers in New York and the South, and forming locals of domestic workers in Chicago, Salt Lake City, Denver, and Seattle. More than any other early twentieth-century labor or radical organization, the IWW advocated equality for women. It lowered initiation fees and dues in recognition of that fact that women earned less than men; it demanded equal pay for equal work; and it supported the birth control movement. Yet the IWW was a creature of its times and as such was limited by the sexual ideology of the early twentieth century. Women, in Wobblies' eyes, were chaste, moral, and essentially domestic. While Wobblies recognized the need to organize women who were in the labor force, they strove for a society in which men would earn enough to support a family and allow wives to remain in their rightful place—the home. When IWW representative Jane Street organized domestic workers in Denver, she received little support from male Wobblies, who felt the women's local existed only to provide them with girlfriends. Street discouraged a friend from undertaking a similar effort, warning her that "sex can come rushing into your office like a great hurricane and blow all the papers of industrialism out of the window."

While small numbers of Wobblies continued to agitate in the 1920s, the ranks of the organization were decimated by the savage repression of the Left during and after World War I. Today only a skeleton of the organization remains.

—*Mary Murphy*

See Also:
Flynn, Elizabeth Gurley; Lawrence Strike of 1912; Unions

References:
Bird, Stewart, Dan Georgakas, and Deborah Shaffer. *Solidarity Forever: An Oral History of the I.W.W.* Chicago: Lake View, 1985.
Schofield, Ann. "Rebel Girls and Union Maids: The Woman Question in the Journals of the A.F.L. and I.W.W., 1905–1920." *Feminist Studies* 9 (Summer 1983): 335–58.
Tax, Meredith. *The Rising of the Women: Feminist Solidarity and Class Consciousness, 1880–1917.* New York: Monthly Review, 1980.

The **INSTITUTE FOR COLORED YOUTH** (now Cheyney University, Cheyney, Pennsylvania) in Philadelphia was established in 1837 through a legacy designated for training black youth for the teaching profession. The institute was one of a handful of nineteenth-century schools offering qualified blacks an opportunity for rigorous preparatory, high school, and normal school education from an all-black faculty. Graduates with degrees from the institute were in high demand for teaching and administrative positions in the growing black school systems both in the North and South.

Educated, activist women such as Grace Mapps and her daughter Sarah Mapps Douglass taught at the institute during its formative years. Fanny Jackson Coppin, a former slave, was hired in 1865 to teach Latin, Greek, and higher mathematics and to serve as principal of the girls' department. During her thirty-five-year tenure, which included many years as principal, she introduced innovative pedagogical methods, raised educational standards, and expanded the institute's role in the black community. Her awareness of the need for blacks to have steady employment prompted her to organize an industrial-skills department at the institute in 1882. This nondegree training program eventually offered a wide variety of courses, including carpentry, bricklaying, millinery, tailoring, and dressmaking. Because it was one of Philadelphia's few industrial training schools for blacks, the institute's enrollment swelled to the point that, by the turn of the century, the school's focus had shifted from teacher training to vocational skills education.

Fanny Jackson Coppin viewed the institute as playing an integral role in improving the economic and social conditions in the black community. To this end, the institute offered night classes, sponsored lecture series, opened a dormitory for girls, and had a library. In 1903 the institute held its final classes in Philadelphia, as the move to the new suburban campus in Cheyney, Pennsylvania, had been completed.

—*Cynthia J. Little*

See Also:

Bethune, Mary McLeod; Black Women; Crandall, Prudence; Education

References:

Institute for Colored Youth. Annual Reports, 1837–1912. Historical Society of Pennsylvania.

Perkins, Linda M. *Fanny Jackson Coppin and the Institute for Colored Youth, 1837–1902.* New York: Garland, 1987.

Silcox, Harry. "The Search by Blacks for Employment Opportunity: Industrial Education in Philadelphia." *Pennsylvania Heritage* 4 (December 1977): 38–43.

The **INTERNATIONAL KINDERGARTEN UNION (IKU)**, an association of women organized by Sarah Stewart at Saratoga Springs, New York, in 1892, was intended to showcase the idea of, consolidate the interests in, and build the momentum for establishing kindergarten work as a profession. The charter membership of the IKU consisted of thirty prominent kindergartners whose initial task was to oversee the preparation of an exhibit for the World's Fair in Chicago in 1893. While this presentation was successful from the standpoint of providing publicity, it was also problematic for the would-be profession because it served as a catalyst for the entrenchment of competing conceptions of the purpose and nature of kindergartening. For the next two decades the IKU served as a forum for an ideological battle between conservative and liberal factions, as each group sought control of the theory and the practice that would define the aspiring profession.

The conservatives' platform centered on promoting the validity of the philosophy espoused by Friedrich Froebel, the German educator who founded the kindergarten system—namely, that the understanding and training of the divine maternal instinct was imperative for appropriate child nurture. These kindergartners claimed the right of professional status on the basis of thirty years of success of Froebelian methodology in American kindergartens, the demonstrated need of specialized training for kindergarten work, and an elevated sense of woman's mission.

The liberals' view pivoted on the utility of scientific knowledge as the guarantor of a profession of child nurture. These kindergartners sought to realign the traditional system with the new insights provided by the scientific study of the child. They assumed that by focusing on the extensive knowledge necessary to understand the intricate nature and needs of the child, the kindergarten could logically claim professional status. If they could ally themselves with other progressive reforms that had a scientific base, they felt that kindergartners could build a coalition of public support sufficient to realize their professional goals.

Unable to resolve their ideological differences, the two factions could only agree to disagree. In the vacuum of effective leadership for the would-be profession, the kindergarten became redefined by its existence in the public schools. By the time the IKU merged with the National Council of Primary Education to form the Association of Childhood Education International in 1931, kindergartners had assumed the role of teachers and been absorbed into the grade system of the schools.

—*Catherine Cosgrove*

See Also:

Education, National Education Association, Teaching as an Occupation for Women

References:

Haven, Caroline, Annie Laws, and Bertha Payne. "The International Kindergarten Union." *Kindergarten Review* 18 (June 1908): 634–43.

Hill, Patty Smith. *Kindergarten.* Washington, D.C.: Association for Childhood Education International, 1942.

Vandewalker, Nina. *Kindergarten in American Education.* New York: Macmillan, 1908.

The **INTERNATIONAL LADIES GARMENT WORKERS UNION** was the one union formed with a signficant female membership in the late-nineteenth and early-twentieth centuries. Traditionally this industry had proved extremely difficult to organize, due primarily to the fact that the ladies' garment industry operated largely on a contract basis, with workers scattered in shops throughout urban areas, isolated from each other in a way other industrial workers, concentrated in the large factories and workshops, were not. Through the 1890s, early efforts to organize the garment workers had failed; however, in 1900 the situation changed. In March of that year, the New York local of the United Brotherhood of Cloak Makers in New York called for the formation of a national union to promulgate a national union label and effectively to resist injunctions against striking garment workers. All workers in the manufacturing of ladies' garments were, subsequently, invited to a conference in New York City on June 3, 1900. On that day, delegates from New York, Brooklyn, Philadelphia, Newark, and Baltimore, representing two thousand workers, met, and later that month the American Federation of Labor (AFL) issued a charter to their new union, the International Ladies Garment Workers Union.

The founders of the ILGWU were socialist; however, they discouraged strikes and favored instead the effective use of the boycott and sought to create popular support for the new union label. Unlike other AFL unions, the ILGWU was in no position to overlook women workers since women dominated the ladies' garment industry work force. Nonetheless, men occupied all positions of leadership within the union, feeling, as most labor leaders did, that women were not capable of competent work within the union hierarchy, and that this inability to function on a par with men was only exacerbated by women's preoccupation with marriage. As evidence of the strength of this bias against women, one may note that only one woman during this time, Fannia Cohn, sat on the ILGWU executive board, from 1916 through 1918.

The ILGWU became a union of some significance when, in 1909, the New York City ladies' shirtwaist makers went on strike. This strike of twenty thousand workers, 80 percent of whom were women (75 percent of whom were age twenty-five or younger), is today known as the Great Uprising, and when it ended, more women had been organized than had ever been unionized before in the United States. In New York City shops alone, over thirty thousand women were unionized by the ILGWU.

In 1913 the ILGWU approved the "Protocol in the Dress and Waist Industry," which formalized division of labor and wages by gender within the garment industry. All skilled and higher paying jobs were thus reserved for male workers, so much so that the lowest paid male earned more wages than the highest paid female worker. This occurred despite the fact that women made up half the ILGWU membership, illustrating the poor position to which women were relegated within the union.

By 1930 the ILGWU had lost much of its former status and influence and was on the verge of folding. Within a short span, however, a reversal occurred that placed the ILGWU once again in the ranks of America's more powerful unions. In the mid-1930s the ILGWU staged a series of extremely effective strikes, paving the way for reduced hours and increasing wages by as much as 50 percent in some cases. In addition, ILGWU membership soared once again. By 1940 membership was up 300 percent from a decade before. Of the then eight hundred thousand members, 75 percent were women, including for the first time substantial numbers of black, Hispanic, and Oriental workers. Despite these advances, only one of twenty-four members of the ILGWU executive board was female, and the union continued to sign contracts permitting unequal pay for men and women.

—Maureen Anna Harp

See Also:

American Federation of Labor; Garment Industries; National Consumers' League; Shirtwaist Makers Strike, 1909; Unions

References:

Foner, Philip S. *Women and the American Labor Movement: From Colonial Times to the Eve of World War One.* New York: Free Press, 1979.

———. *Women and the American Labor Movement: From World War One to the Present.* New York: Free Press, 1980.

Levine, Louis. *The Women's Garment Workers.* New York: B. W. Huebsch, 1924.

Willet, Mabel Hured. *The Employment of Women in the Clothing Trade.* New York: Columbia University Press, 1902.

INTERNATIONAL WOMEN'S DAY (March 8) was initially inspired by a New York City demonstration on March 8, 1857, of women garment and textile workers who were protesting low wages, the twelve-hour workday, and uncompensated increased workloads. Although their march was brutally broken up by the police, they repeated their call for improved working conditions and equal pay for all working women as they formed their own union in March 1860. A subsequent demonstration of thousands of women workers in the "needle trades" on March 8, 1908, called for child-labor-protection legislation and woman suffrage in addition to their long-standing demands. Two years later, Clara Zetkin, a German labor leader, proposed that an International Women's Day be established on March 8 to commemorate the historic struggle to improve women's lives. International Women's Day, observed in socialist countries during the following sixty years, began to be celebrated in the United States in 1967 by various women's groups, and as a result of the consciousness-raising of the women's liberation movement, International Women's Day commemorative events occurred in most major American cities after 1970.

In 1977 the schools in Sonoma County, California, designated March as Women's History Month as a means of raising awareness of women's history and encouraging its integration into the public and post-secondary curriculum. The development of the National Women's History Project in Santa Rosa, California, in 1980 provided a national clearinghouse for information on International Women's Day as the focal point for the celebration of Women's History Month. Since 1981 Congress has annually passed a National Women's History Week proclamation for the week surrounding March 8.

—Angela Howard Zophy

See Also:

International Ladies Garment Workers Union, National Women's History Project

References:

Stites, Richard. *The Women's Liberation Movement in Russia: Feminism, Nihilism, and Bolshevism, 1860–1930.* Princeton, N.J.: Princeton University Press, 1978.

Wertheimer, Barbara Mayer. *We Were There: The Story of Working Women in America.* New York: Pantheon, 1977.

Women's History Resources: Resources Catalogue for 1984. Santa Rosa, Calif.: National Women's History Project, 1984.

The **INTERNATIONAL WOMEN'S YEAR (IWY) CONFERENCE OF 1977** was held in Houston, Texas, from November 18 to 21. The conference was attended by two thousand delegates and twenty thousand guests from all over the world. According to feminist Gloria Steinem, Congresswoman Bella Abzug was the "main author of the idea for the conference and the presiding officer of its commissioners."

The delegates heard speeches by many of the superstars of the women's movement and adopted a twenty-six-plank "National Plan of Action," which was presented to President Jimmy Carter on March 22, 1978, as part of the official report of the conference, entitled *The Spirit of Houston.* The plan included specific recommendations for national policies on issues such as child abuse, child care, disabled women, education, employment, the Equal Rights Amendment, health, homemakers, insurance, minority women, older women, rape, reproductive freedom, rural women, and poverty. Its concerns were global in scope and provided a document that could well serve as a blueprint for governmental action, especially since many of its suggested reforms have still not been implemented.

The event drew widespread media attention and in some ways served as a 1970s counterpoint to the 1848 women's rights convention in Seneca Falls, New York. The Houston conference served as a landmark event in the history of the women's movement in the United States if only for the many ways in which it served to inspire several generations of women and supportive men.

—Jonathan W. Zophy

See Also:

Abzug, Bella; Steinem, Gloria

References:

Bird, Caroline, et al. *What Women Want: From the Official Report to the President, the Congress and the People of the United States.* New York: Simon & Schuster, 1979.

Daniel, Robert. *American Women in the 20th Century.* New York: Harcourt Brace Jovanovich, 1987.

Ryan, Mary P. *Womanhood in America from Colonial Times to the Present.* 3d ed. New York: New Viewpoints/Franklin Watts, 1984.

JACKSON, HELEN MARIA (FISKE) HUNT (1830–85), writer and crusader for American Indian rights, was born in Amherst, Massachusetts, in 1830. In 1865, after the deaths of her husband and two of her children, Jackson began a writing career, eventually producing over thirty books and hundreds of articles, including children's stories, poems, essays, and travel sketches. In 1874 Ralph Waldo Emerson called her the "greatest American woman poet."

But it is not for her poetry or children's literature that Jackson is remembered today. In 1879, when Jackson was visiting Boston, she heard the Ponca leader, Standing Bear, make a plea for his tribe. Although never sympathetic to the women's movement or the abolitionist movement, Jackson devoted the remaining six years of her life to the promotion of American Indian rights. In 1884 she published *A Century of Dishonor,* which chronicled the duplicity of U.S. government relations with the Indians. Jackson sent each member of Congress a copy of this work after inscribing the following words by Benjamin Franklin, "Look upon your hands! They are stained with the blood of your relations." Jackson followed up this work with a second exposé entitled *California and the Missions* (1883). However, Jackson's most popular book by far on American Indians was her romantic novel *Ramona* (1884), which tells the story of a young woman, Ramona, who marries an Indian man, Allessandro, against her family's wishes. The novel has inspired three movies and one stage play and undergone three hundred printings.

Once Jackson became convinced of the injustices done to the Indians, she never tired of advocating their cause. Her writing exhibits an uncompromising sense of outrage and indignation. She was not afraid of a fight or of the censure of her friends and neighbors. Like most white writers on the subject of Indians, she endorsed an assimilationist view, although her main focus was to end the exploitation of Indians rather than propose a grand scheme for their assimilation. Despite her acute sense of injustice and her courage, Jackson still clung to a faith in the system and appealed to the good impulses of those powerful people in government who were often the cause of the misery of the Indians. Jackson, naively at times, assumed the whole country would share her outrage when the facts were known. Although her book *A Century of Dishonor* did provoke outrage, very little was done to better the condition of the Indians. Unfortunately, *Ramona* did not inspire reform either. The novel was popular for the wrong reasons. The tragic romance of Allessandro and Ramona overshadowed the theft of Indian lands.

—*John Snider*

See Also:

Native American Women

References:

Banning, Evelyn I. *Helen Hunt Jackson.* New York: Vanguard, 1973.

Jackson, Helen Hunt. *California and the Missions.* 1902; rpt. Boston: Little, Brown, 1916.

———. *A Century of Dishonor.* Edited by Andrew F. Rolle. 1882; rpt. New York: Harper & Row, 1965.

———. *Helen Hunt Jackson's Poems.* Boston: Roberts Bros., 1895.

———. *Ramona.* Introduction by May Lamberton Becker. 1884; rpt. Boston: Little, Brown, 1939.

Odell, Ruth. *Helen Hunt Jackson.* New York: Appleton-Century, 1939.

Snider, John. "Helen Hunt Jackson: The Contradictions of Reform." In "The Treatment of American Indians in Selected American

Literature: A Radical Critique." Diss. University of Illinois, 1983, pp. 129–59.

JAMES, ALICE (1848–92), the sister of the novelist Henry, and the psychologist William, was the last-born of five and the family's only daughter. The diary she wrote during her last three years, her sole bid for literary fame, was published in 1934 and reissued in 1964. In her invalid's life and in the *Diary* and her extant letters, scholars in the 1980s have found important insights into the phenomenon of female invalidism that was so prevalent among certain classes in Victorian America.

James's story reflects the limitations of the patriarchal family as well as the larger limitations of an era that denied range and scope for women's aspirations. Gender, birth order, and general family dynamics provide a partial explanation for Alice's invalidism. All of the James children suffered from ill health, mental and physical, but while William and Henry were able to move beyond their neuroses through redemptive careers, Alice made a career of her health.

Denied education and vocation, treated by her family with condescending affection, Alice reached adolescence with a confused gender identity and a temperament increasingly unable to endure psychic strain. After age nineteen she was often ill, sometimes suicidal, variously diagnosed as hysterical, neurasthenic, melancholic, neuralgic—all labels for chronic female nervousness.

James began the *Diary* when she was forty. Living in England and writing from her invalid's bed, aided by Henry's visits and the care of her longtime companion, Katherine Loring, she offered this evaluation of herself and her life: "A collection simply of fantastic unproductive emotions enclosed within tissue paper walls, rent equally by pleasure as by pain; animated by a never ceasing belief in and longing for action, relentlessly denied . . . ." She was generally free of self-pity and as fiercely interested in life as she was contemptuous of it. When she writes of her elation after a doctor tells her she has breast cancer, the tone is chilling, yet comprehensible from someone who had suffered psychosomatic illnesses for more than thirty years.

—*Nan Nowik*

See Also:

Hysteria

References:

Strouse, Jean. *Alice James: A Biography.* Boston: Houghton Mifflin, 1980.

Strout, Oushing. "Mr. James's Daughter and Shakespeare's Sister: A Review-Essay on Jean Strouse's *Alice James: A Biography." The Henry James Review* 3 (Fall 1981): 59–63.

Yeazell, Ruth. *The Death and Letters of Alice James: Selected Correspondence Edited, with a Biographical Essay.* Berkeley: University of California Press, 1981.

The **JANE CLUB** was founded in 1891 as part of the Hull House settlement endeavor in Chicago's Halsted Street neighborhood. It was conceived as a cooperative housing arrangement for young working women, intended to provide inexpensive living arrangements to protect the women against eviction and homelessness in the event of loss of income resulting from layoffs or strikes. The latter aspect was uppermost in the mind of Mary Kenney, under whose leadership the housing cooperative took shape. Kenney was at the time a twenty-seven-year-old Irish immigrant and labor organizer, and historian Allen F. Davis has referred to her as one of the people whose influence transformed Jane Addams from a Christian philanthropist to a social reformer. Addams initially invited Kenney to visit Hull House after learning of her role in organizing the first bookbinders' union for women in Chicago. Kenney went reluctantly, suspecting that Addams and the other Hull House residents "were all rich and not friends of the workers." She changed her mind upon meeting Addams, who won over the younger woman when she put the facilities of Hull House, in particular its parlor ("different from anything I had ever seen before"), at Kenney's disposal for meetings of union women.

Kenney realized that women workers were in a vulnerable position during labor-organizing efforts and disputes, since their fear of being unable to meet room and board expenses in the event of lost work and wages would often lead them to capitulate to employer demands. It was during the course of a strike meeting at Hull House, according to Jane Addams, that one young woman stated: "Wouldn't it be fine if we had a boarding-club of our own, and then we could stand by each other in a time like this?"

Accordingly, in May 1891 Hull House paid the first month's rent and supplied furnishings for two vacant apartments in a tenement on Ewing Street, near Halsted. Fifteen women, plus a cook and "general worker," moved in. Residents organized themselves as the "Jane Club" and voted to pay three dollars per week to cover room, board, and service. Within three years the club had grown to fifty members, occupying all six apartments in the tenement. Reflecting and accepting the contemporary racism of Progressive America, the club was racially segregated.

As with all Hull House undertakings, a philosophical approach guided the development of the Jane Club. According to Addams, the first little group of members met together, read "Cooperation" and "Diligence" aloud from Beatrice Potter's book, *The Co-Operative Movement in Great Britain*, and "discussed all the difficulties and fascinations of such an undertaking." The Jane Club concept, that of providing inexpensive lodgings to women in order to allow them to be able to save their money, echoes earlier communal undertakings in Europe, such as the *béates* in seventeenth-century France: pious widows or spinsters who ran dormitories for female lacemakers, allowing the young women to pool their earnings for food and materials and thus save money for their dowries. The Jane Club was part and parcel of the interest in communal living arrangements expressed by such turn-of-the-century feminists as Charlotte Perkins Gilman and also finds parallels in the ideas that shaped the formation of women's colleges in the nineteenth century, with attention given to the implications of living as a community of women. In keeping with the spirit of Hull House, however, the Jane Club was democratic in structure. Members elected officers and determined duties and regulations. The club, following the initial contribution from Hull House, was financially self-sustaining.

In 1898 a benefactor donated $15,000 to build a new facility for the Jane Club. The club continued as a residence for working women until 1938 with the arrival, following Addams's death, of a new head resident at Hull House. In that year Charlotte E. Carr came from New York to lead the foundation. During her tempestuous five years as head of Hull House, she was determined to reinvigorate the foundation with the spirit of its first twenty years. Carr complained that Hull House was in danger of becoming a museum, a monument to past achievements rather than an institution facing the challenges of the mid-twentieth century. The Jane Club, in her opinion, belonged to a past era. According to Allen Davis, "Charlotte Carr put carpenters to work inside the ancient buildings of Hull House, and classrooms took shape in such holy relics as the Jane Club. Founded by Miss Addams as a cooperative home for working women who were dispossessed when they went out on strike, the Jane Club had become just a good cheap place to live."

—Laura Gellott

See Also:

Addams, Jane; Hull House; O'Sullivan, Mary Kenney

References:

Addams, Jane. *Twenty Years at Hull-House.* New York: Macmillan, 1910.

Davis, Allen F. *American Heroine: The Life and Legend of Jane Addams.* New York: Oxford University Press, 1973.

———, and Mary Lynn McCree, eds. *Eighty Years at Hull-House.* Chicago: Quadrangle, 1969.

———, and ———. *Hull-House Maps and Papers.* New York: Arno, 1970.

Linn, James Weber. *Jane Addams: A Biography.* 1935; rpt. New York: Greenwood, 1968.

Phipott, Thomas. *The Slum and the Ghetto: Neighborhood Deterioration and Middle Class Reform, Chicago, 1880–1930.* New York: Oxford University Press, 1978.

Webb, Beatrice Potter. *The Co-Operative Movement in Great Britain.* London: F. Sonnenschein & c [sic], 1891.

JAZZ. Aside from the human voice, the piano is the only instrument with which women have made a significant impact upon the music frequently termed America's only native art. In the 1920s Lil Hardin Armstrong, a competent composer as well as pianist, came to the public's attention largely through her association with her far more famous husband, Louis. During the 1930s and 1940s another composer-pianist, Mary Lou Williams, became recognized as a leading exponent of the modern idiom called "bebop." The 1950s saw the emergence of numerous prominent keyboard stylists, two of whom remain powerful forces on the music of the 1980s: British-born Marian McPartland is not only a prodigious player but popular host of a regular jazz program on National Public Radio; Toshiko Akiyoshi, a Japanese expatriate, is pianist, co-leader, and exclusive composer-arranger of the big band many critics acclaim the finest large jazz ensemble of the 1980s, the Akiyoshi-Lew Tabackin Big Band. Among the younger pianist-composers whose music frequently expresses elements of the avant-garde, three deserve special mention: Alice Coltrane, Carla Bley, and JoAnne Brackeen.

While women have had to struggle for acceptance in instrumental jazz by proving they can "sound" like their male counterparts, they are under no such strictures as vocalists; in that area, in fact, they have exerted a greater influence upon the music than have men. Bessie Smith, the "Empress of the Blues," virtually popularized the blues form singlehandedly while achieving fame second only to Louis Armstrong's. During the "Swing Era" that followed, Billie Holiday gained international recognition as the outstanding interpreter of American popular song. Though Holiday's life ended tragically and abruptly, several of her contemporaries have remained active, vital contributors into the late 1980s. Betty Carter and Carmen MacRae are fastidious "keepers of the flame" who have at the same time never ceased to experiment and grow. Of all living jazz singers, none command greater respect and crowds than Sarah Vaughan and Ella Fitzgerald. Both are experts at "scat," a vocal style substituting instrumental sounds for words. Paradoxically then, women have managed to gain mass acceptance as jazz instrumentalists, if only under the guise of being vocalists.

As jazz gives ground to current pop styles, younger jazz vocalists are increasingly rare, though a few, such as Nancy Wilson, have left their mark. Primarily a creative rather than a commercial music, jazz has been a major inspiration for numerous popular stylists, from Diana Ross to Natalie Cole. In the area of vocal music, at least, jazz has provided undeniable opportunities for all women, regardless of race.

—*Samuel L. Chell*

See Also:

Holiday, Billie; Popular Vocalists; Smith, Bessie

References:

Feather, Leonard. *The Book of Jazz.* New York: Dell, 1976.

Placksin, Sally. *American Women in Jazz: 1900 to the Present.* New York: Wideview Books, 1982.

JEWETT, SARAH ORNE (1849–1909) was author of *The Country of the Pointed Firs* and numerous other works that depict rural New England. Although her work transcends the category of local colorist, she writes of her native region with great accuracy and affection and is best known as a chronicler of New England life and character.

Unlike many of her female contemporaries in the literary world, Jewett had the opportunity to write as she wished, without financial constraint. Nor did she consider writing an unsuitable occupation. Due to her admiration of her father, a doctor, she had considered a medical career, but her own poor health made that an impractical choice, and she concluded that writing was the work she ought to do.

Her first major work *Deephaven* (1877) uses a technique she later brought to full artistic achievement in her highly acclaimed *Country of the Pointed Firs* (1896). Both are collections of "sketches," and in both, visitors from outside a New England village come for a summer's trip. These visitors get to know the local inhabitants, and the stories told by the villagers are the sketches. This narrative technique is more fully developed in *The Country of the Pointed Firs,* where one visitor hears the stories from her landlady Mrs. Almiry Todd, the town herbalist. Almiry Todd is perhaps the most memorable character in all Jewett's works, and the relationship between her and the narrator provides a structural counterpoint to the sketches themselves.

Many of Jewett's works portray friendship between women, a relationship she enjoyed with several women throughout her life. Most notable was her friendship with Annie Fields, whose Boston home was a center of literary social life. Jewett also had a significant influence on Willa Cather.

Although Jewett was not a vocal advocate for women's rights, her work often portrayed women in men's roles. The fullest example of this is *The Country Doctor,* in which the protagonist, Nan, chooses to pursue a medical career rather than marry.

Jewett died in 1909, having achieved national fame as a writer.

—*Mabel Benson DuPriest*

See Also:

Women's Friendships

References:

Cary, Richard, ed. *Appreciation of Sarah Orne Jewett: 29 Interpretive Essays.* Waterville, Me.: Colby College Press, 1973.

———. *Sarah Orne Jewett.* New York: Twayne, 1962.

Eicheberger, Clayton. "Sarah Orne Jewett (1849–1909): Critical Bibliography of Secondary Comment." *American Literary Realism, 1897–1910* 2 (1969): 189–262.

Farrant, Margaret. *Sarah Orne Jewett.* Minneapolis: University of Minnesota Press, 1966.

Frost, John Eldridge. "Sarah Orne Jewett Bibliography: 1949–1963." *Colby Library Quarterly* Series 6, 10 (June 1964): 405–17.

Jewett, Sarah Orne. *A Country Doctor.* Boston: Houghton Mifflin, 1884.

———. *The Country of the Pointed Firs.* Boston: Houghton Mifflin, 1896.

———. *Deephaven.* Boston: James R. Osgood, 1877.

Matthieson, F. O. *Sarah Orne Jewett.* Boston: Houghton Mifflin, 1920.

Weber, Clara Carter, and Carl J. *A Bibliography of the Published Writings of Sarah Orne Jewett.* Waterville, Me.: Colby College Press, 1949.

JEWISH WOMEN. Historically, Judaism has been a patriarchy. Halakah (law) continues to define women as "other": outside the main body of laws concerning religious and legal responsibility. Women's role has traditionally been defined within the home, and women have been exempted and/or forbidden from fulfilling religious injunctions, testifying at a *bet din* (court of law), religious study, and full participation in synagogue life.

Beginning in the mid-1800s the Jewish religion split into three main branches: Orthodox, Conservative, and Reform. The response of these three movements to the issue of women in Jewish life and worship varies greatly. The Orthodox movement has remained basically unchanged, relying on legal interpretations dating back to the *Shulhan Arukh* (sixteenth-century code of Jewish law); all modern expressions of Jewish values are considered heretical. The Conservative movement, which arose in America as an attempt to reconcile the vast differences between traditional halakah and modernity, has moved slowly toward granting women some measure of equality. It is primarily the Reform movement that has been instrumental in redefining the role of women in Judaism. In 1922 the Central Conference of American Rabbis resolved that complete equality between men and women, including ordination, be established. It was not until 1972, however, that Sally Preisand became the first woman ordained as an American Reform rabbi.

Not all Jewish women regard their affiliation as essentially religious. Barred from seeking fulfillment in the synagogue or through employment, American Jewish women have focus their energies in volunteer organizations concerned with social reform. Beginning with the development of "sisterhoods," whose main function was to serve the congregation, Jewish women's groups such as the National Council of Jewish Women and Hadassah have provided means of working toward social and political reform. The talent and expertise of women volunteers, however, has not been recognized in the larger (male) Jewish community, and women have frequently been denied key leadership positions in Jewish communal organizations.

Jewish women have exerted a presence in the leadership of the major women's reform movements since the turn of the twentieth century. Their contribution to the efforts for woman suffrage, unionization of women workers, protective legislation, civil rights and civil liberties, and especially in the modern women's movement testified to their commitment and dedication to improving the conditions of the gender and the nation.

The international renown of Golda Meir (1898–1978) offers but one example of the achievement of Jewish women. Meir demonstrated through her life and career the contribution and potential of Jewish and immigrant women. She was the fourth prime minister of Israel and a major force in modern world politics. She was born in Kiev, Russia, migrating to the United States with her family in 1906. Her family settled in Milwaukee, and she attended public schools there except for a brief period in high school when she joined a married sister in Denver. She graduated from North Division High School in Milwaukee and then began attending the Milwaukee Teachers' Training College, from which she graduated in 1917. While in college, Meir worked as a librarian and as a part-time teacher in a Yiddish folk school; she also became immersed in local Zionist politics.

After graduation from college, she became a staff member of a socialist labor Zionist group called Poale Zion. Her involvement in Zionist politics resulted in a chance meeting with David Ben-Gurion, who furthered her resolve to migrate to Palestine. She and her husband, Morris, whom she had married in December 1917, moved to a collective farm ten miles south of Nazareth in 1921. Two years later, the couple moved to Tel Aviv, where Meir took an office job with the Office of Public Works of Histadrut (the Israeli Labor Federation).

Meir worked her way up the ranks in a number of Israeli labor organizations and often represented those organizations at international conferences. She lived in the United States from 1931 to 1934 as secretary of the Pioneer Women's Organization. After World War II she resumed her work for the establishment of a Jewish state in Palestine. In January 1948 she returned to the United States and collected $50 million for Israel. On the eve of Israeli independence, she made a daring visit to Jordan's King Abdullah disguised as an Arab woman in an effort to lessen Arab opposition. She was one of the signers of the May 14, 1948, Proclamation of Independence for Israel and was the only woman in Israel's first legislature. Later that year she was sent to Moscow as Israel's ambassador.

Meir returned to Israel to serve as minister of labor from 1946 to 1956, where she was able to devise a national insurance plan and provide employment and housing for thousands of immigrants. She also frequently led Israel's delegation to the United Nations from 1953 to 1966. From 1956 to 1966 she served as Israel's minister of foreign affairs, and between 1969 and 1974 she served as Israel's prime minister. As prime minister, Meir insisted on "secure, recognized, and agreed upon boundaries" as part of a general peace settlement with the Arab nations. She also worked diligently to strengthen Israel's ties with the United States. Meir continued as a leading voice in Israeli labor politics even after her resignation as prime minister following the Yom Kippur War of 1973. She lived long enough to see Egypt's president Anwar Sadat make the journey to Israel for a peace plan engineered in part by President Jimmy Carter of the United States.

—Mary Lind Temmer and Jonathan W. Zophy

See Also:

Hadassah, Politics, Synagogue Sisterhoods

References:

Baum, Charlotte, Paula Hyman, and Sonya Michel. *The Jewish Women in America*. New York: New American Library, 1975.

Henry, Sondra, and Emily Taitz. *Written Out of History: Our Jewish Foremothers*. 3d ed. Sunnyside, N.Y.: Bilbo Press, 1988.

Marcus, Jacob Radar. *The American Jewish Woman, 1654–1980*. New York: KTAV Publishing, 1981.

Meir, Golda. *My Life*. New York: Putnam, 1975.

Preisand, Sally. *Judaism and the New Woman*. New York: Behrman House, 1975.

Schneider, Susan Weidman. *Jewish and Female*. New York: Simon & Schuster, 1984.

JOHNSTON, FRANCES BENJAMIN (1864–1952) was probably the best-known professional woman photographer in turn-of-the-century America. Throughout a long career, Johnston specialized in photo-stories for popular magazines, architectural photography, and portraiture. Known for her artistry as well as for her energy and enthusiasm, she consistently promoted photography as a viable profession for women.

Many aspects of Johnston's life and career bear similarities to the experiences of other professional women of the late nineteenth century. The women were from the middle class; many never married, and most were educated. The only child of a well-to-do family, Johnston grew up in Washington, D.C., and after graduating from the Notre Dame Convent, she studied painting in Paris. Her parents encouraged and supported her artistic, business, and photographic pursuits.

By the late 1880s Johnston embarked on a serious career as a professional photographer by doing photo assignments for popular magazines such as *Demorest's Family Magazine, Frank Leslie's*, and the *Ladies Home Journal*. She produced photographs and stories on a wide range of subjects —coal miners in Pennsylvania, women factory workers in Massachusetts, cadets at Annapolis, the beauty of Yellowstone Park. In 1895 she opened her own up-to-date public studio built onto the rear of her parents' V Street home. As a well-known Washingtonian, Johnston photographed many among the elite of that city. She wrote about and photographed Presidents Harrison, Cleveland, McKinley, Roosevelt, and Taft, as well as many other government officials and national celebrities. Of particular interest are her photographs of well-known Washington women, including Alice Roosevelt, Ida McKinley, and Lillian Paunceforte. Her series of photographs taken in 1899 and 1900 depicting life at the Hampton Institute—a training school for black youth in Hampton, Virginia—have gained special recognition. First shown at the Paris Exposition of 1900, these evocative photographs were exhibited at the Museum of Modern Art in 1966.

Johnston always demonstrated an interest in women and their lives and was the center of an informal network of female amateur and professional photographers. In the late 1880s women from all over the United States wrote to Johnston asking for her advice and support of their photographic efforts. In addition, Johnston made a unique contribution to the history of photography by organizing an exhibition of the work of twenty-eight American women photographers for the International Photographic Congress of the Paris Exposition in 1900. She herself served as a delegate to that exposition.

—*C. Jane Gover*

See Also:

Photography

References:

Daniel, Pete, and Raymond Smock. *A Talent for Detail*. New York: Harmony Books, 1974.

Glen, Constance W., and Leland Rice. *Frances Benjamin Johnston: Women of Class and Station*. Long Beach: California State University Press, 1979.

Gover, C. Jane. *The Positive Image: Women Photographers in Turn of the Century America*. Albany: State University of New York Press, 1987.

Quitslund, Toby. "Her Feminine Colleagues—Photographs and Letters Collected by Frances Benjamin Johnston in 1900." In *Women Artists in Washington Collections*, edited by Josephine Withers. College Park: University of Maryland Art Gallery and Women's Caucus for the Arts, 1979, pp. 97–109.

JOHNSTON, HENRIETTA (DEERING) (c. 1670–1728/9) was a pioneer both in America and in the field of pastel portraiture. Pastel painting (the use of applying dry pigments onto a ground, using only the binder necessary to hold the pigments in a crayon shape) was approaching its finest development in Europe at the same time Henrietta Johnston was putting the medium to use for the support of her family in the New World. It is thought that she was born in Ireland and married in 1704 or 1705 in Dublin to the Reverend Gideon Johnston, an impecunious minister of the Church of England. He was assigned to the Carolinas and the Bahamas, and they moved to what was to become known as Charleston, South Carolina. Their arrival and tenure in the New World were marked by episodes of bureaucratic misunderstandings relating to his employment, illness, misadventures on the high seas, Indian wars, and other tragedies.

The needs of their extended family and retinue were often met by her efforts at portraiture using pastel crayons, an art she may have learned in Ireland. The economic necessity to exploit her talent and the scarcity of art supplies may have limited her aesthetic exploits in this new medium. Her small portraits are of single figures, simply arranged. They are treasured by their owners, many of whom are descendants of the original subjects, for their charm and historical importance. Johnston is known to have worked in the Carolinas and in New York. After her husband died at sea in 1716, it may be supposed that Johnston lived out her days bartering art for sustenance, for she received no pension.

—Susan K. Portney

See Also:

Art

References:

Rubinstein, Charlotte Streifer. *American Women Artists.* Boston: G. K. Hall, 1982.

Willis, Euola. "The First Woman Painter in America." *Studio* 87 (July 1927): 13–20.

JONES, "MOTHER" (1830–1930), labor organizer and agitator, was a unique figure in the American labor movement. For decades, "Mother" Jones organized miners and was involved in all the famous labor upheavals of her era. A fiery speaker, she used the rhetoric of socialism in pursuit of social justice for workers but was beholden to no ideology or party.

Biographical details of her life, even her year of birth, are obscured by tales of a white-haired, petite woman tramping from one mining camp to another. Born Mary Harris in Cork, Ireland, she emigrated with her family to the United States, taught school, and became a dressmaker. After losing her husband, George Jones of the Iron Molders' Union, and her four young children to yellow fever in 1867 in Memphis, she operated a dressmaking business. When it was destroyed in the Chicago fire of 1871, she was drawn to the Knights of Labor and became a full-time organizer without a permanent home.

She worked for the United Mine Workers and was also a founding member of the Social Democratic party and the Industrial Workers of the World but remained aloof from all party activities. From 1900 to 1920 she organized among bituminous and anthracite miners in West Virginia and Pennsylvania, and among miners in Colorado, Arizona, Michigan, and Minnesota; garment strikers in New York; and steel strikers in Pennsylvania. She was adept at winning media attention for her causes, whether through her arrests or testimony before congressional investigating committees, or through leading marches of strikers' wives or of working children to the Oyster Bay, New York, home of President Theodore Roosevelt.

Sometime friend of Terence Powderly of the Knights of Labor and of John Mitchell and John L. Lewis of the UMW, she was an outspoken individualist who could irritate both labor colleagues and management foes, while her ideological eccentricities annoyed socialists and suffragists alike. Her one-hundredth birthday saw her celebrated by all sides as an American legend.

—*Sally M. Miller*

See Also:

Industrial Workers of the World, Knights of Labor, Unions, United Mine Workers of America

References:

Fetherling, Dale. *Mother Jones: The Miners' Angel*. Carbondale: Southern Illinois University Press, 1974.

Foner, Philip S., ed. *Mother Jones Speaks: Collected Writings and Speeches*. New York: Anchor Foundation, 1983.

Jones, Mary Harris. *The Autobiography of Mother Jones*. Chicago: Charles Kerr, 1925.

JONES, VIRGINIA LACY (1912–84) was a black librarian and library educator whose distinguished career, although it began inauspiciously in the segregated and underfunded libraries of the South, contributed enormously to American librarianship. Jones studied librarianship first at Hampton Institute and later at the University of Illinois and eventually became, in 1945, the second black to receive a doctorate from the Graduate Library School at the University of Chicago. (Dr. Eliza Gleason, 1940, was the first). During her thirty-six years as dean of the Atlanta University School of Library Service, more than fifteen hundred black librarians were educated there, more than at any other school in the country. Jones was an energetic fund-raiser, and numerous conferences and in-service training programs were held in an effort to upgrade library service to black schools, colleges, and communities.

Jones's numerous awards and honors included the presidency of the Association of American Library Schools in 1967, receipt of the Melvil Dewey Award for professional achievement of high order in 1973, and an honorary doctorate from the University of Michigan in 1979.

A prolific writer, her "A Dean's Career" presents an unforgettable picture of black student life at the University of Illinois in the 1930s. She also contributed to the *Proceedings of the Governor's Conference on Georgia Libraries and Information Services* (1976), *Proceedings of Two Symposia Sponsored in Honor of Louis Round Wilson's 100th Birthday* (1976), and *Dictionary of American Library Biography* (1978), among other publications.

—*Suzanne Hildenbrand*

See Also:

Librarianship, Black Women

References:

Jones, Virginia Lacy. "A Dean's Career." In *The Black Librarian in America*, edited by E. J. Josey. Metuchen, N.J.: Scarecrow, 1970.

———. *Reminiscences in Librarianship and Library Education*. Ann Arbor: University of Michigan Press, 1979.

Totten, Herman L. "Southeastern Black Library Educators." In *The Black Librarian in the Southeast: Reminiscences, Activities, Challenges*, edited by Annette L. Phinazee. Durham, N.C.: North Carolina Central University Press, 1980.

JONG, ERICA (MANN) (b. 1942), author and editor, is best known for her bold and controversial novels that explore contemporary American social and sexual relationships. She has also published volumes of poetry and scholarly editions of eighteenth-century English novels.

After receiving a master's degree from Columbia University, teaching English, being honored with poetry awards, and publishing two volumes of poems, Jong soared into the public eye with her 1973 novel, *Fear of Flying*. The novel was published while she was married to Allan Jong, from whom she was divorced in 1975. In 1977 Jong examined her observations of the western United States and the populace's common ricochetting from coast to coast in a prose poem published in *Mademoiselle*, "East-West Blues: A New Yorker Goes West." That same year, she married Jonathan Fast and published another novel, keeping "Jong" as her publishing name. She was divorced from Fast in 1982 and has one daughter.

Jong has been a prolific author and researcher, combining these skills in her 1980 novel, *Fanny, Being the True History of the Adventures of Fanny Hackabout-Jones.* Her poetry volumes span her publishing career and include *Here Comes & Other Poems* (originally published as *Fruits & Vegetables,* 1971, and *Half-Lives,* 1973), 1975; *Loveroot,* 1975; *At the Edge of the Body,* 1979; and *Ordinary Miracles,* 1983. Jong's 1984 novel, *Parachutes & Kisses,* is in many ways a sequel to *Fear of Flying* in the re-creation of the protagonist with a fictional memory, her search for herself and her liberation. Jong's writing mixes sophisticated literary allusions with a popular style, while examining contemporary situations and erotic imaginings. Her honest examinations of individuals within the culture reveal a rich blend of popular and scholarly expression.

—Therese L. Lueck

References:

Jong, Erica. "East-West Blues: A New Yorker Goes West." *Mademoiselle* 83 (April 1977): 201, 228, 230.

———. *Fear of Flying.* New York: Holt, Rinehart and Winston 1973.

———. "Introduction." *Three Eighteenth-Century Novels.* New York: New American Library, 1982, pp. v–xi.

———. *Parachutes and Kisses.* New York: Signet, 1984.

JORDAN, BARBARA (CHARLINE) (b. 1936), attorney, was elected to the House of Representatives from Texas in 1972, the first black congresswoman to come from the Deep South. An assertive member of the Texas state senate since 1966, she was instrumental in the passage of an improved workmen's compensation act and the state's first minimum-wage law.

A member of the House Judiciary Committee, she distinguished herself during the committee's hearings on the so-called Watergate affair, which revealed widespread corruption in the administration of President Richard M. Nixon and led to his resignation in 1974. Although only a freshman legislator at the time, Jordan proved to be one of the most articulate and thoughtful members of the committee. She viewed the whole process surrounding the Watergate affair as a "cleansing experience" for American politics.

Committed to civil rights, the welfare of the underprivileged, and the environment, she sponsored key legislation in these areas during her three terms in Congress, including a bill to extend social security coverage to American women working within the home. A strong opponent of increased military expenditures, Jordan consistently voted to curb the military involvement in Southeast Asia and voted to override President Nixon's veto of the War Powers Bill limiting presidential war-making authority.

Jordan joined the faculty of the Lyndon B. Johnson School of Public Affairs at the University of Texas in Austin in 1979.

—Sue E. Strickler

See Also:

Black Women, Democratic Party, Politics

References:

Christian Science Monitor (March 18, 1974): 6.

Robinson, Louie. "Women Lawmakers on the Move." *Ebony* 27 (October 1972): 48–56.

The Washington Post (October 22, 1972): K 1.

JOURNALISM. Although not always recognized, women have been involved in American journalism from its earliest beginnings. Women have served as printers, publishers, editors, and reporters from the early eighteenth century to the present.

Prior to the adoption of the Constitution in 1787, at least seventeen women served as newspaper printers in America. Generally, they assumed the job when their husbands were unable to continue because of imprisonment, illness, or death. Many women kept the business going until their sons were old enough to assume control. Most of them then returned to the home. Thus, women's involvement in journalism in the eighteenth century came primarily out of necessity and ended when the need no longer existed.

In the nineteenth century, more jobs opened up for women. As a result, more took jobs to supplement the family income. Female editors, publishers, and owners became more common and accepted. Ann Royall (1769–1864) published *The Huntress* in Washington, D.C., from 1836 to 1854, supporting Andrew Jackson, free public education, free speech, and justice for the downtrodden. She reportedly had to sit on the clothes of President John Quincy Adams on a riverbank where he was swimming before he would grant her an interview. Jane Grey Swisshelm, editor of the Pittsburgh antislavery sheet the *Saturday Visiter*, became the first woman to sit in the congressional press gallery in 1850. Women also succeeded as magazine editors, the most famous being Sarah Josepha Hale, editor of *Godey's Lady's Book* from 1836 to 1877. Although the Civil War opened up more opportunities for women in journalism, the Capitol Press Galleries barred them as more women came to Washington as correspondents.

In 1870 only 35 of 5,286 journalists listed in the U.S. Census were women, but by 1900 there were 2,193 women among the 30,098 journalists cited. Increasingly, newspapers and magazines had female columnists who provided the women's perspective on a variety of topics and issues. This change was partially due to newspaper editors' efforts to increase circulation. In the early half of the nineteenth century most women read only books and magazines; however, newspaper editors wanted to attract women readers. Early women journalists such as Jennie June (1829–1901), the first woman to write daily for a newspaper, helped develop women's pages. At first, newspaper women wrote about domestic life, food, and fashion, often from their homes. Gradually, women began working from the newsrooms, covering the same range of topics as the men. Women's pages appeared in the *Philadelphia Ledger* and the *New York Times* in the 1890s.

The antebellum desire for reform sweeping the country brought women into journalism and was fired by women journalists. Women were often editors of abolitionist and suffragist papers, such as the *Revolution.* Editors hired women for stunt writing and often used their sex to sensationalize the dangers of undercover investigation and titillate readers. Competing men, writing in the same highly emotional style, called these women "Sob Sisters." Annie Laurie (1863–1936), who covered the Galveston tidal wave in 1900 and the San Francisco earthquake in 1906 with first-person, tear-jerking accounts, hated this label. She thought of herself simply as a practical, all-around newspaper woman. The last half of the century witnessed several famous female reporters, including Elizabeth Cochrane Seaman ("Nellie Bly") (1865–1922) of the *New York World,* Sally Joy ("Penelope Penfeather") (1852–1910) of the *Boston Herald,* and Ida Tarbell (1857–1944) of *McClure's,* one of the original "muckrakers." From Margaret Fuller (1810–50), who wrote of women's rights and duties and produced caustic literary criticism, to Dorothea Dix (1861–1951) and her widely reprinted advice columns, to Ida Bell Wells-Barnett (1862–1931), who fought for racial pride and against lynchings in her writing, early newspaperwomen opened the way for women reporters and helped open doors for women in ever-expanding job fields.

Slow, steady gains were made in the early twentieth century, with more women working in most areas of journalism. Beginning in the 1930s, women served as foreign correspondents for several American newspapers and news services. Anne O'Hare McCormick (1880–1954) won a Pulitzer Prize in 1937 for her European reporting for the *New York Times* News Service. One of her first stories was a 1921 profile of unknown Benito Mussolini, in which she predicted that he would one day master Italy. During World War II, women served as correspondents in several theaters of war, primarily in Europe. Margaret Bourke-White (1904–71) served in Europe as a photographer for *Time* and *Life.* Leah Burdette (1900–42), correspondent for *PM,* lost her life in Iran. Marguerite Higgins (1920–66) of the *New York Herald Tribune* served in Europe during the 1940s and became Berlin bureau chief after the war ended.

Since World War II, women have become increasingly involved in all areas of American journalism. The women's rights movement of the 1960s and 1970s has helped many women advance into new areas. Women now serve as sports reporters and editorial columnists, as newspaper publishers and White House correspondents, as copy editors and television anchorpersons.

—Terri Dennison and Carol Sue Humphrey

See Also:

Beals, Jessie Tarbox; "Bly, Nellie"; Bourke-White, Margaret; Bryant, Louise; Day, Dorothy; Diggs, Annie LePorte; Dix, Dorothea; Draper, Margaret; Duniway, Abigail; Ferber, Edna; Fuller, Margaret; Hale, Sarah Josepha; O'Hare, Kate Richards; Ramírez, Sara Estella; *Revolution*; Shadd, Mary Ann; Spanish Civil War; Tarbell, Ida; Thompson, Dorothy; Valesh, Eva McDonald; Wells-Barnett, Ida B.

References:

Beasley, Maurine, and Sheila Gibbons. *Women in Media: A Documentary Source Book.* Washington, D.C.: Women's Institute for Freedom of the Press, 1977.

Belford, Barbara. *Brilliant Bylines.* New York: Columbia University Press, 1986.

Emery, Edwin, and Michael Emery. *The Press and America: An Interpretive History of the Mass Media.* 5th ed. Englewood Cliffs, N.J.: Prentice-Hall, 1984.

Mott, Frank Luther. *American Journalism: A History, 1690–1960.* 3d ed. New York: Macmillan, 1962.

KAHN, FLORENCE PRAG (1866–1948) served as Republican representative to Congress from San Francisco's Fourth District from 1925 to 1936. Like many daughters of her generation, Kahn was forced to give up dreams of becoming a lawyer to support her Polish Jewish immigrant parents. After graduating from the University of California at Berkeley in 1887, she taught high school English until 1899, when she married Congressman Julius Kahn. Julius built his political reputation on support for military preparedness. When elected to fill the seat vacated at his death, Florence continued to support that policy.

Unlike many women of her day who "inherited" offices from their husbands, Kahn quickly forged an independent political identity largely based on her quick wit. When asked if she favored birth control, she answered, "I will if you make it retroactive." Kahn rejected the notion of a distinct feminine contribution and did not concentrate on "women's issues." She opposed female politicians who promoted pacifism as the political expression of women's "naturally" superior nurturing capabilities.

While in office, Kahn supported increasing the size of the military, even when such increases were opposed by President Calvin Coolidge, a Republican. She also sponsored a bill to create military pensions for nurses, arguing for it not as a feminist issue, but as practical legislation necessary to attract nurses away from higher paying, less dangerous, private-sector jobs. In April 1929 Kahn was honored by being appointed Speaker of the House to chair a debate on the military budget. One likely reason behind Kahn's pro-military stance was that as an anti-Zionist she saw the United States as the only place in the world where Jews could live safely, and she believed military might was the only means of insuring that security. Kahn also promoted the interests of the Federal Bureau of Investigation so successfully that J. Edgar Hoover dubbed her "the mother of the FBI." In contrast to most feminists of her day, Kahn opposed Prohibition and motion picture censorship, considering the first unenforceable and the second an impediment to the growing movie industry in California.

Before Kahn was defeated by Roosevelt's Democratic landslide in 1936, she managed to attract much federal construction to San Francisco, including the San Francisco-Oakland Bay Bridge. After her defeat, Kahn remained active in the Republican party. She was a member of the American Association of University Women, Temple Emanu-El (San Francisco-Reform), Woman's City Club (San Francisco), and the Congressional Club. She was also a member of Hadassah and the National Council of Jewish Women, but since she opposed much of what these organizations worked for, she probably joined them because it seemed the proper thing to do as an upper-class, prominent Jewish woman.

—Faith Rogow

See Also:

Hadassah, Jewish Women, Politics, Republican Party, Right-Wing Political Movements

References:

Congressional Record. Sixty-ninth to Seventy-fourth Congresses.

"Kahn, Florence Prag." Nearprint Box, Bos 2282. American Jewish Archives, Cincinnati, Ohio.

Keyes, Frances Parkinson. "The Lady From California." *Delineator* 118 (February 1931): 14 ff.

Longworth, Alice Roosevelt. "What Are the Women Up To?" *Ladies' Home Journal* 51 (March 1934): 9, 120, 122.

KÄSEBIER, GERTRUDE STANTON (1852–1934) established an impressive reputation as an art photographer in the late nineteenth century. She was included in Alfred Stieglitz's famed Photo-Secession, founded in 1902 to promote the art of photography, and was well known for her portraiture and her soft-focus, impressionistic images of women and children.

Born in Leadville, Colorado, and brought up in the East, Käsebier attended a girls' seminary in Bethlehem, Pennsylvania. In 1873 she married Edward Käsebier, a German businessman, and then after several years of attending to the traditional roles of wife and mother, she changed the pattern of her life. In 1888, when her children were nearly grown, Käsebier enrolled at Brooklyn's Pratt Institute to study painting. She also spent two summers in France as a student of academic painter Frank Vincent Dumond. During this period Käsebier was discouraged by her art teachers from taking up photography; by 1893, however, she had committed herself to the controversial new medium. She gained practical experience in the field by apprenticing herself to a Brooklyn portrait photographer, Samuel Lifshey.

Close to forty years old, married, and the mother of three teenage children, Käsebier opened a portrait studio in New York City in 1897. Fame and recognition came quickly because of her innovative approach to portraiture, which emphasized simple principles of design, dramatic lighting, and natural settings. She rejected the banal techniques of commercial portraiture that depended upon theatrical props, unimaginative lighting, and stiff, conventional poses.

Most of Käsebier's photographs were done in the pictorial tradition popular among art photographers of the late nineteenth and early twentieth century. Typically, a pictorialist photograph was impressionistic in style—hazy, moody landscapes. In her pictorial work, Käsebier frequently favored the mother and child theme. She remained committed to pictorialism throughout her career. In 1916 Käsebier and photographers Clarence White and Alvin Langdon Coburn organized the Pictorial Photographers of America.

Käsebier's relationship with photographer and art patron Alfred Stieglitz was very significant to her career. Stieglitz published her work in his journal *Camera Notes* (1897–1902) and in 1903 featured Käsebier's images in the renowned journal *Camera Work*. Also, Stieglitz often exhibited Käsebier's photographs at the New York Camera Club and at his "291" gallery.

—*C. Jane Gover*

See Also:

Art, Photography

References:

Gover, C. Jane. *The Positive Image: Women Photographers in Turn of the Century America*. New York: State University of New York Press, 1987.

Homer, William Innes. *A Pictorial Heritage: The Photographs of Gertrude Käsebier*. Wilmington: Delaware Art Museum and the University of Delaware, 1979.

KELLEY, FLORENCE (1859–1932) was a leader in the effort to enact protective labor legislation for American workers. She was born in Philadelphia, the youngest surviving daughter of William and Caroline Bonsall Kelley, and was raised in a family rich with a tradition of public service. Her father, for instance, was a longtime member of the House of Representatives and a Republican organizer. Kelley was especially close to him and wanted to follow his example. With his support, she earned a bachelor's degree in 1882 from Cornell University. She then undertook a tour of Europe before settling in Zurich to study at the University of Zurich, one of the few to accept women. There she met and married a young Russian medical student, a union that lasted seven years and produced three children. In 1891 Kelley and the children went to Illinois, where she obtained a divorce and became a resident of Chicago's Hull House settlement.

From that vantage point, she began her investigation of the factory system. She studied the sweatshops of the garment industry, surveyed city slums, earned a law degree, and served as chief factory inspector for the state of Illinois. Largely as a result of her work, the Illinois General Assembly passed an act limiting women's work hours, banning child labor, and controlling the sweatshops. In 1899 Kelley and her family returned to New York, where she lived at Lillian Wald's Henry Street Settlement and became the executive secretary of the National Consumers' League, a position she held for the remainder of her life. The league attempted to use customer pressure to insure that products be manufactured and marketed under proper conditions.

That was only one of the ways Kelley encouraged industrial reform. She was also an avid speaker on the subject, outlining her objectives in *Some Ethical Gains Through Legislation*, published in 1905. Together with league cohort Josephine Goldmark, Kelley persuaded attorney Louis Brandeis to use medical and sociological data in his Supreme Court defense of an Oregon ten-hour law for woman laborers. The famous "Brandeis brief" of 1914 revolutionized the use of such evidence in the American judicial system. Beyond her work at the league, Kelley championed woman suffrage, opposed World War I, and helped organize the National Association for the Advancement of Colored People. In the final years of her life until her death in 1932, she struggled to preserve earlier legislative gains.

—*Rebecca L. Sherrick*

See Also:

National Consumers' League, Social Feminism, Wages

References:

Blumberg, Dorothy Rose. *Florence Kelley: The Making of a Social Pioneer*. New York: A. M. Kelly, 1966.

Goldmark, Josephine. *Impatient Crusader: Florence Kelley's Life Story*. Urbana: University of Illinois Press, 1953.

O'Neill, William. *Everyone Was Brave: A History of Feminism in America*. New York: Quadrangle, 1971.

KELLIE, LUNA ELIZABETH SANFORD (1857–1940), state secretary of the Nebraska Farmers' Alliance, journalist, and Nebraska pioneer, was born in Pipestone, Minnesota, moving with her family to Madison, Wisconsin, and then to Rockford, Illinois. In 1874 she married James Thompson Kellie. Two years later her father, two brothers, and her husband moved to Adams County, Nebraska, to homestead. Kellie followed a few months later. In addition to homesteading, the Kellies raised eleven children, operated a grocery store for a short time, and participated locally in reform politics. When the first homestead failed, the Kellies took over her father's timber claim and turned it into a successful orchard.

After being active briefly in county politics, Kellie attended the Nebraska state Farmers' Alliance convention in 1894 and was elected as state secretary. Her duties consisted of keeping the records of the alliance, lecturing for the alliance in surrounding counties, and writing for the *Wealthmakers*, a reform newspaper in Lincoln. A year later, having decided that the *Wealthmakers* was not sufficiently radical, she bought a used printing press and began, with the help of her oldest daughter, Jessie, to publish the *Nebraska Farmers' Alliance and Industrial Union*.

As the Nebraska Farmers' Alliance waned and the Populist party lost the 1896 election, Kellie changed the name of the newspaper to the *Prairie Home*, hoping to gain more subscriptions. Still clinging to the hope that the Populists could alleviate the economic crisis of farmers, Kellie and her husband, members of the National Reform Press Association, attended the 1900 National Populist Convention in Cincinnati as delegates. Soon after this convention, Kellie became discouraged with the lack of economic reform, sold the newspaper, and resigned from the alliance. Her husband died in 1918.

Kellie continued managing the orchard and again operated a small grocery store. She also wrote two sets of memoirs. The first detailed her involvement with the Farmers' Alliance, its financial difficulties and the factions within the organization. The second described the Kellies' early homesteading years. During the Depression, Kellie lost the homestead and moved back and forth between Arizona and Nebraska. In the Arizona desert north of Tucson, she attempted homesteading a second time, but failing health prevented her from obtaining a permanent deed to her claim. She died in Phoenix on March 4, 1940.

—*MaryJo Wagner*

See Also:

Journalism, Migration and Frontier Women, National Farmers' Alliance, Populist Party

References:

Baaken, Douglas A. "Luna E. Kellie and the Farmers' Alliance." *Nebraska History* 50 (1969): 185–205.

Kellie, Luna E. "The Farmers' Alliance in Nebraska." Lincoln: Nebraska State Historical Society, 1926.

———. "Memoirs." Lincoln: Nebraska State Historical Society, ca. 1918.

Wagner, MaryJo. "Prairie Populists: Luna Kellie and Mary Elizabeth Lease." In *Northwest Women's Heritage*, edited by Karen Blair. Seattle: Northwest Center for Research on Women, 1984, pp. 200–10.

KEMBLE, FANNY (1809–93) was born in London into one of the great English theatrical families. When she made her own stage debut in 1829, she became an overnight sensation, her success rivaling that of her recently retired aunt, Sarah Siddons.

During an American tour, she fell in love with Philadelphian Pierce Butler. When they married in June 1834, she gave up the stage and settled into his Pennsylvania home. But Butler's vast estates in Georgia and his slaveholding soon became a source of conflict for the couple. Also, although Kemble had abandoned her acting career, she wanted to resume her writing. Her frank and vivid travel account of her American tour had been promised to a publisher before her engagement. Although Butler forbade her to pursue this project, she prepared the manuscript for publication, and when the journal appeared in 1835, it caused further disharmony. After years of marital discord, bitterness, and several separations, the couple divorced in 1849 due to irreconcilable differences. Butler was granted complete custody of their two daughters, while Kemble returned to England to resume her stage career. Although she was unable to regain her former popularity (and to maintain the pace), Kemble gathered a new following through her Shakespearean readings, her occasional benefit performances, and her many publications.

Her *Journal of Residence on a Georgian Plantation*, written in the winter of 1838–39 while living on Butler's Sea Islands estates, was a British best-seller when it appeared in 1863. In addition, Kemble's harsh portrait of slavery served to dampen English enthusiasm for support of the Confederacy. Her volume had considerable impact in its day and remains an important primary source for scholars. Her talent for fiction (she published three plays, three volumes of poetry, and even a novel—at the age of eighty) was surpassed by her talent for living; her witty and engaging memoirs (*Records of Girlhood*, 3 vols.; *Records of Later Life*; and *Further Records*, 2 vols.) display impressive gifts. She lived in Italy for several years, acquainting herself with American artists in exile, including Harriet Hosmer and Henry James. She made annual treks to Switzerland to mountain climb and revisit friends, and wrote a humorous tale, *The Adventures of Mr. John Timothy Homespun in Switzerland* (also published when she was eighty).

She spent her later years in the country of her birth, but her involvement in American abolitionist and literary circles during the middle decades of the nineteenth century places her firmly at the center of New England culture and reform during its antebellum flowering. She was especially fond of her elder daughter's only son Owen Wister, who went on to become a popular novelist, author of *The Virginian*. Kemble's strong will, eccentricity, and generosity were all lauded by those who knew her. And the writing she left behind gives valuable insights into the attitudes and experiences of women during the nineteenth century.

—*Catherine Clinton*

See Also:

Abolition and the Antislavery Movement, Civil War, Theater

References:

Clinton, Catherine. *Fanny Kemble's Journals.* Cambridge: Harvard University Press, forthcoming.
James, Henry. *Essays in London and Elsewhere.* New York: Harper, 1893.
Kemble, Fanny. *Further Records.* New York: Henry Holt, 1890.
———. *Journal.* Philadelphia: Carey, Lea & Blanchard, 1835.
———. *Journal of Residence on a Georgian Plantation.* Edited by John A. Scott. Athens: University of Georgia Press, 1985.
———. *Records of Girlhood.* New York: Henry Holt, 1879.
———. *Records of Later Life.* New York: Henry Holt, 1882.
Marshall, Dorothy. *Fanny Kemble.* London: Weidenfeld & Nicholson, 1977.
Wister, Fanny Kemble. *Fanny: The American Kemble.* Tallahassee, Fla.: South Pass Press, 1972.

KING, BILLIE JEAN (b. 1943), one of the world's greatest and best-known tennis players, played a monumental role in establishing women's tennis as a major sport. King accomplished this not only through her prowess on the court, but with her unflagging efforts as an organizer and promoter of the sport.

In 1961, at the age of eighteen, she became the youngest player to win at Wimbledon (a doubles title). During the next twelve years, she went on to win a record number of Wimbledon titles—twenty in all—in singles, doubles, and mixed doubles. During those years, she also won titles at Forest Hills, the U.S. Open, and the French Open. She captured the Virginia Slims singles title from 1970 to 1977. It was not just her victories that won the world's attention, but the way she played the game. Her quick, aggressive moves on the court drew a large audience to women's tennis, a game that had previously been dismissed as slow and uninteresting.

The fact that women players were grossly underpaid compared to their male counterparts (even though women were beginning to draw large crowds) led King to spearhead the formation of the Women's Tennis Association in 1973. The group was a "union" that gave the women the power to bargain for the same advantages the men enjoyed. She and other women professionals also agreed to appear in the high-paying Virginia Slims tournaments organized by Gladys Heldman, a move that forced increases in prize money for women throughout the sport. In 1973 King increased the stature of women in the sport by thrashing her male challenger, Bobby Riggs, in a much-publicized match.

In the late 1980s King became involved in promoting Team Tennis, which comprises teams of men and women playing singles, doubles, and mixed doubles, and gives exposure to some of the best but lesser-known players in the sport. She is also the author of several books on playing tennis and an autobiography.

King's efforts to create a place for women to compete in sports have not been limited to tennis. In 1974 she and husband Larry King founded *WomenSports,* a magazine now published by the Women's Sports Federation as *Women's Sports and Fitness.* She further expanded the place of women in sports by serving as a broadcaster for ABC from 1975 to 1978. The honors King has gathered attest to her visibility as a great sportswoman and strong example for other women: she was named Sportswoman of the Year by *Sports Illustrated* in 1972, Woman Athlete of the Year by the Associated Press in 1967 and 1973, and Woman of the Year by *Time* in 1976.

In addition to the strides she has made for women's professional tennis, King must be credited with helping to create a place for all women's sports in this century. King's career paralleled the rise of the modern women's movement, of which she was a part: the athlete's publicized experience with the two most controversial issues of the 1970s, abortion and lesbianism, provoked public furor. However, she confronted and survived the adverse publicity and continued to work for the advancement and improvement of women's tennis.

—Carol Ann Sadtler

See Also:

Athletics/Sports; Gibson, Althea

References:

Collins, Bud. "Billie Jean King Evens the Score." *Ms.* 11 (July 1973): 39–43, 101–2.

King, Billie Jean, with Frank Deford. *Billie Jean.* New York: Viking, 1982.

KING, CORETTA SCOTT (b. 1927), civil rights crusader and spokesperson, first came into the public view as the wife of Martin Luther King, Jr., but after his death in 1968 established her own place within the leadership of the civil rights movement.

King was born in Marion, Alabama, on April 27, 1927. She graduated from Antioch College in 1951 and went on to study music and singing at the New England Conservatory of Music in Boston. She received a bachelor's degree in 1954 and a doctorate in music in 1971. She married Martin Luther King, Jr., on June 18, 1953, and they moved to Montgomery, Alabama, the following year. From 1955 to 1963, she became the mother of two daughters and two sons. On December 5, 1956, she gave a concert in New York City to celebrate the first anniversary of the bus boycott initiated by blacks in Montgomery to protest racist policies and treatment. She subsequently gave over thirty concerts in the United States and Europe to benefit the Southern Christian Leadership Conference (SCLC).

In 1968 King was voted Woman of the Year and Most Admired Woman by college students across the country. In March 1969 she become the first woman to speak from the pulpit during a regularly scheduled service at St. Paul's Cathedral in London. She wrote a book entitled *My Life With Martin Luther King, Jr.* in 1969, and has been active in the SCLC. She has organized antinuclear lobbies and anti-Vietnam protests and has maintained an active interest in the Martin Luther King, Jr., Memorial Center in Atlanta.

—Susan Kinnell

See Also:

Civil Rights, Southern Christian Leadership Conference

References:

Patterson, Lillie. *Coretta Scott King.* Champaign, Ill.: Garrard, 1977.

Taylor, Paula. *Coretta King, A Woman of Peace.* Mankato, Minn.: Creative Education, 1974.

Vivian, Octavia. *Coretta: The Story of Mrs. Martin Luther King, Jr.* Philadelphia: Fortress, 1970.

KINGSTON, MAXINE HONG (b. 1940), author of *The Woman Warrior,* an autobiography, explored a new dimension in women's quest for independence. Written from the perspective of a young Chinese-American girl struggling to grow beyond the confining limits of both Old World tradition and modern American hypocrisy, *The Woman Warrior* won the 1976 National Book Critics Circle Award for nonfiction.

Originally published in 1975, the book intermingles childhood flashbacks with mystic images and ironic humor. As Chinese immigrants who run a laundry, Kingston's parents exist in a world that reveres pain and hard work, yet embraces ethereal symbols and legend-myths. As a growing child (both within the book and in reality), Kingston was numbed by these values, finding them exhausting and somehow intangible.

Despite her traditional and almost stereotypical childhood, Kingston fought hard to establish a concrete life void of cloistering myths and superstitions of Chinese culture. She graduated with a bachelor's degree from the University of California at Berkeley and returned one year later to obtain a teaching certificate. Her autobiography is a touchstone for minority women who have had to overcome the constraints of a foreign culture; it is also a sensitive, triumphant contribution to women's writing in general.

—Anne Cooperman

See Also:
Asian American Women

References:

Kingston, Maxine Hong. *Tripmaster Monkey: His Fake Book.* New York: Knopf, 1989.
———. *The Woman Warrior: Memoirs of a Girlhood Among Ghosts.* New York: Knopf, 1976.
Kramer, Jane. Review of *The Woman Warrior. New York Times Book Review.* November 7, 1976, pp. 1, 16.

The **KINSEY REPORT** refers to two studies by Alfred Kinsey, a biologist who sought to apply scientific methodology to the elusive subject of human sexuality. *Sexual Behavior in the Human Female* appeared in 1953 after a similar study of men that was published four years earlier.

Kinsey and his team interviewed a large number of volunteers and then in a rather modest fashion statistically analyzed the results. The publication of two volumes on the subject at the time was more startling than Kinsey's findings, which critics attacked on two fronts. Kinsey had assaulted traditional views on American sexual mores and editorialized on some controversial questions such as oral sex, female orgasm, and homosexuality. On these subjects he took the position that normality should be defined in terms of behavior. He also directly confronted and rejected both religious doctrines and psychoanalytical theories. One critic thought it "characteristically American" in "its impulse toward acceptance and liberation."

The publication of the first of the two studies was such a cultural event that a committee was appointed by the president of the American Statistical Association to analyze Kinsey's methods. After making it clear that Kinsey's was not an ideal sample, they generally gave it very high marks. Meanwhile, humanists like Lionel Trilling would have none of it. They found the very idea that human sexuality could be measured in terms of "contacts" and orgasms demeaning.

Kinsey portrayed Americans as both sexually active and sexually troubled. In his sample nearly all the men and three-fourths of the women had masturbated. Premarital sex was commonplace, and extramarital sex was not uncommon. Although his figures were low, Kinsey documented that a sizable number of Americans were homosexuals and lesbians. He put Americans under a microscope and produced the benchmark study of American sexual behavior.

—*William G. Shade*

See Also:
Female Sexuality

References:

Kinsey, Alfred, et al. *Sexual Behavior in the Human Female.* Philadelphia: Saunders, 1953.
Pomeroy, Wendell B. *Dr. Kinsey and the Institute for Sex Research.* New York: Harper & Row, 1972.
Trilling, Lionel. *The Liberal Imagination.* New York: Doubleday, 1957.

KIRBY, CHARLOTTE IVES COBB GODBE (1836–1908) was a feminist, Mormon, and woman suffragist leader in the nineteenth-century American West. She became associated with the Mormons as a child, when her mother, a member of the prominent Bostonian Adams family, abandoned her husband and five of her children to become Brigham Young's fifth wife. When Augusta Adams Cobb went West to join the Mormon leader, she took six-year-old Charlotte and an infant that later died. Thus Kirby was raised in Utah in Brigham Young's "Lion House" as one of his daughters and was given by him in polygamous marriage as the fourth wife of a prosperous and liberal Mormon.

Many years later, Kirby would attribute her interest in woman suffrage to her mother, who had been an acquaintance of suffragist Lucy Stone in Boston. Kirby attributed the commencement of woman suffrage in Utah to her mother and reported that it had been her mother's deathbed wish that her daughter continue the work she had begun.

For three decades, from 1869, when the discussion of women's rights first began in Territorial Utah, until 1896, when the state of

Utah was created with a clause in its constitution enfranchising women, Kirby was spokesperson for woman suffrage in Utah and at national suffrage meetings. Arguing that one's sex should not "prevent the full and free expression of intelligence," she repeatedly called for women around the world, regardless of religious or political affiliations, to unite to promote the well-being of all women. "The rights of all[,] as women, must be respected," she said; then she went on to urge women "to stand by each other, setting aside trifling differences and all work unitedly for the good of the whole."

Kirby gave speeches promoting woman suffrage and temperance in Boston, Washington, D.C., and Utah, and she was an officer of the earliest suffrage organization in Utah. Remaining a member of the Church of Jesus Christ of Latter-Day Saints, she divorced William S. Godbe, who had been excommunicated from the church for his liberal views. Five years later, in 1884, she married a wealthy, non-Mormon mining man, John Kirby, who was twenty years younger than she was.

—Beverly Beeton

See Also:

Migration and Frontier Women, Mormonism and Women, Suffrage in the American West

References:

Beeton, Beverly. *Women Vote in the West: The Woman Suffrage Movement, 1869–1896.* New York: Garland, 1986.

Cable, Mary. "She Who Shall Be Nameless." *American Heritage* 16 (February 1965): 50–55.

The Noble Order of the **KNIGHTS OF LABOR** was established as a secret society in 1869 by nine Philadelphia garment cutters under the leadership of Uriah S. Stephens. The society's basic premise was that since all workers had common interests, all workers should belong to a common society. Membership was open to all those who "toiled" and excluded only professional gamblers, lawyers, bankers, and liquor dealers. While the founders mentioned the inclusion of women, membership was not initially open to women because of the assumption that they could not keep secrets and thus would be a liability to a secret society. On this basis, women were excluded from the Knights of Labor for over a decade; when secrecy was discouraged, the rationale against women collapsed.

The Knights of Labor was organized on the basis of local assemblies. These assemblies could consist of workers from one particular trade or simply all the workers in a given locality, regardless of occupation. A general assembly presided over the entire organization. At the first national convention (1878), the impact of unskilled female laborers on the wages of men was discussed. In order to safeguard the wages of male workers, the Knights included in their constitution a provision stating that the goal of the organization was to secure "for both sexes equal pay for equal work." Nonetheless, no provision was made at this time for female membership.

In 1881 shoe workers of Local Assembly 64 (Philadelphia) refused a wage cut, and nonunion female workers were brought in to work in their place at a 30–60 percent reduction in wages. Under the leadership of Mary Strikling, the women went on strike and the local Knights' organizer inducted the women into the Knights of Labor, thereby paving the way for the entrance of other female assemblies. By 1886 there were 121 such women's assemblies in the Knights of Labor.

Women were included in both mixed and trade assemblies, and while figures on exact female membership vary considerably, when the Knights' membership was at a high point (1886), women constituted approximately 9 percent of the total membership (approximately fifty thousand). There were assemblies for black female domestic workers in four cities (Washington, D.C.; Wilmington, North Carolina; Norfolk, and Philadelphia). In addition, the Knights became the first American labor organization to establish a Department of Women's Work, which concentrated on the status and needs of female workers.

The Knights of Labor, although initially closed to women, in its time did more to open its doors to women and their labor problems than any previous labor organization had done. In theory, at least, the Knights placed women and men workers on an equal footing; in reality, the Knights did little to give women an equal voice, status, or influence within the organizational structure. It did not alter the condition of the American working woman, but did provide training and experience for women in a labor-organization setting, which would be of value to future movements on behalf of women workers.

By 1890 the Knights of Labor began a decline that was not reversed and so faded from the American labor scene.

—Maureen Anna Harp

See Also:
Unions

References:

Dubofsky, Melvyn. *Industrialism and the American Worker.* Arlington Heights, Ill.: AHM, 1975.

Foner, Philip S. *Women and the American Labor Movement: From Colonial Times to the Eve of World War One.* New York: Free Press, 1979.

Levine, Susan. *Labor's True Woman.* Philadelphia: Temple University Press, 1984.

Montgomery, David. *Beyond Equality.* New York: Knopf, 1975.

———. *Workers' Control in America: Studies in the History of Work, Technology, and Labor Struggles.* Cambridge: Cambridge University Press, 1979.

KOREAN WAR (1950–53). At the conclusion of World War II, Korea was divided at the 38th parallel into two zones, one occupied by the United States and the other by the Soviet Union. The United States informed the Soviets that it wanted the United Nations to make the arrangements for reuniting Korea and securing its independence. The Soviets and their North Korean allies refused to cooperate with the U.N.; instead, in February 1948 they established the Democratic People's Republic of Korea. In July, U.N.-sponsored measures resulted in the creation of the Republic of Korea based in the South. Both governments claimed jurisdiction over all of Korea and announced their intention to achieve unification by force if necessary.

On June 25, 1950, the North Korean army, trained and armed by the Soviets, attacked over the 38th parallel with about one hundred thousand troops. On June 26 President Harry Truman ordered the U.S. Air Force and Navy to support the South Korean forces. The next day the United Nations Security Council called upon the U.N. membership to help the South Koreans "repel the armed attack and to restore international peace and security to the area." The United States was joined by U.N. contingents from fifteen other countries.

The United States eventually put 1.6 million servicemen and women into the undeclared war. While the exact number of women serving in the conflict went undocumented, their presence in Korea was the result of the Women's Armed Forces Integration Act of 1948, which gave women the prospect of a career in the military. Although denied combat status, women served in Korea in nursing, health services, and administrative fields. The use of mobile army hospitals and numerous helicopter evacuations of casualties meant that there were many real-life counterparts to the fictional "Major Margaret Hoolihan" of the motion picture and television series *M*A*S*H.* Furthermore, women served in the U.S. military civilian work force, with the Red Cross and with USO entertainment groups. Marguerite Higgins of the *New York Herald Tribune* covered the war as a combat correspondent almost from the inception of the "police action."

Despite the arrival of regular army units from mainland China to reinforce the North Korean troops, the U.N. forces were able to hold onto the south of Korea. Finally, on July 27, 1953, an armistice was signed. The United States suffered 54,246 deaths and 103,284 wounded, and 4,675 Americans were captured. The Korean War cost the United States a great deal of suffering and around $40 billion. Korea remains a divided country today, and democratic reforms have still not been fully implemented even in South Korea. Women played an even larger role in the next American land war in Asia, the Vietnam War.

—Jonathan W. Zophy

See Also:
Military Service, Vietnam War

References:

Heller, Francis, comp. *The Korean War: A 25 Year Perspective.* Lawrence: Regents Press of Kansas, 1977.

Higgins, Marguerite. *War in Korea; the Report of a Woman Combat Correspondent.* New York: Doubleday, 1951.

Holm, Jean. *Women in the Military: An Unfinished Revolution.* Novato, Calif.: Presidio, 1982.

Rees, David. *Korea: The Unlimited War.* New York: St. Martin's, 1964.

KRAWCZYK, MONICA (1887–1954), teacher, social worker, and author of about thirty short stories, including *If the Branch Blossoms and Other Stories,* a collection of twelve works, was the most important Polish-American woman author during the first half of the twentieth century. Raised in Winona, Minnesota, throughout her life this first-generation American child of Polish immigrants had two specific goals: writing short fiction about her ethnic traditions and disseminating information about the culture of her parents' mother country.

Krawczyk took creative writing courses and worked with Jane Addams at Hull House in Chicago before moving back to Minnesota, where she became one of the first social workers in the Minneapolis public schools, teaching immigrants English, organizing clubs, and helping the needy find employment. One summer she posed as a menial worker in order to expose the unsanitary conditions that newly arrived migrants faced, and was successful in obtaining much-needed reform. In 1915 Krawczyk married a Polish newcomer, one of her night-school students; they had three children, the eldest becoming a doctor and fulfilling the American dream of upward mobility. In spite of home responsibilities, she published articles on innovative teaching techniques for exceptional children, gave lectures, organized a Polish Society at the University of Minnesota, and established the Polanie Club of Minneapolis, still active today.

In addition to promoting Polish pride at the state level, Krawczyk was actively involved in the Kościuszko Foundation, the Polish American Historical Society, and the Polish Museum. These contacts provided material for her realistic depictions of first- and second-generation family life in her thinly disguised narrative sketches. Krawczyk's short stories appeared in *Woman's Day* and *Good Housekeeping* during the second and third decades of the twentieth century. One work, "Luxuries," was given honorable mention recognition by the *Minnesota Quarterly,* and another story, "No Man Alone," was chosen from over five thousand entrants in a contest sponsored by *Country Home* magazine for the best narrative about farm life during the 1930s and awarded $1,000. A third tale, "My Man," was listed in the "Index of Distinctive Short Stories" of E. J. O'Brien's *Best Short Stories for 1934.* Krawczyk's unpublished novel, *Not for Bread Alone,* explored the adjustment techniques of Polish immigrants to the United States.

Critics have labeled Krawczyk's short stories artistically simple but convincingly real—products not only of her imaginative skills in depicting immigrant family life, especially the demanding role of women, but also in re-creating Polish customs and ceremonies that have flowed into the mainstream of American life. These lifelong efforts were recognized by the Polish government when she received the national honor of the Polania Restituta. Ironically, Krawczyk died without traveling beyond the United States, never seeing the Old World country whose traditions she helped preserve by recording with loving skill the transformation of that Polish culture in the New World.

—Edith Blicksilver

See Also:
Hull House, Social Work

References:

Blicksilver, Edith. "Chronicler of Polish-American Life." In *Ethnic Women Writers, I: MELUS, The Journal of the Society for the Study of the Multi-Ethnic Literature of the United States,* edited by Katherine Newman. 7 (Fall 1980): 13–20.

———. "Monica Krawczyk's Polish Pride." In *Turn-of-the-Century Women*, edited by Margaret D. Stetz. 1 (Winter 1984): 42–44.

Krawczyk, Monica. "For Dimes and Quarters." In *The Ethnic American Woman: Problems, Protests, Lifestyle*, edited by Edith Blicksilver. Dubuque, Iowa: Kendall/Hunt, 1978, pp. 118–25.

———. *If the Branch Blossoms and Other Stories*. Minneapolis: Polanie Press, 1950.

KREPS, JUANITA MORRIS (b. 1921), economist, was not only the first female secretary of commerce, but the first woman to serve as a director of the New York Stock Exchange and several major corporate boards. Because she had enhanced her theoretical training with administrative roles and directorships in conjunction with her academic career, President Jimmy Carter became interested in Kreps when he was searching for the best-qualified woman to serve in his administration. When Carter told her about the role he envisioned for the Department of Commerce, which would include a concern for consumer issues, she accepted the position, taking office on January 23, 1977.

Juanita Morris was born in Lynch, Kentucky, a coal-mining community where her father was a mine operator. She attended Berea College, a work-study school that catered to students with limited financial support. Kreps then went on to Duke University, earning her Ph.D. in 1948. Early in her career, she assumed short-term academic positions, and in 1955, when she was ready to enter the work force on a full-time basis, she was able to secure a post only as a part-time visiting lecturer at Duke. The apparently inadequate title did not deter her. She advanced in academic rank, and in 1971 received her greatest academic distinction by being named a James B. Duke Professor.

Her research focused on women's employment within the context of the changing demographics of the work force. Kreps had addressed such issues in *Sex, Age and Work* (1975) as well as in *Sex in the Marketplace: American Women at Work* (1971), where she analyzed the changing composition of the American work force. In 1975 she organized a major conference on "Women and the American Economy" that developed policy regarding young women's knowledge about work in the marketplace and public education for preschoolers. She also encouraged the formation of the President's Interagency Task Force on Women Business Owners in 1977.

Committed to equality, Kreps acted as a role model for her own daughters as well as for all the women who now work at all ages, make greater investments in their human capital, and remain in the work place for greater periods of time regardless of marriage or childbearing.

—Patricia M. Deutsch

See Also:

Democratic Party, Politics

References:

"Her Own Woman." *Time* 109 (January 3, 1977): 44–45.

Lamson, Peggy. *In the Vanguard*. Boston: Houghton Mifflin, 1979.

Langway, Lynn, and Rich Thomas. "The Cabinet: First Lady of Commerce." *Newsweek* 89 (February 7, 1977): 61.

Stineman, Esther. *American Political Women*. Littleton, Colo: Libraries Unlimited, 1980, pp. 95–98.

The **LADIES ASSOCIATION OF PHILADELPHIA**, informally known as George Washington's sewing circle, was an organization engaged in women's relief work during the American Revolution. It was organized in 1780 by Esther De Berdt Reed, a British-born daughter of a colonial merchant, to donate clothing and supplies to colonial patriots as an "offering of the Ladies." A broadside asking women to contribute to the public cause generated such a great response that the idea spread nationally. The membership of the Association included wives of prominent revolutionary politicians and military officers such as Martha Wayles Jefferson and Mrs. Robert Morris. They collected $300,000 in Continental money ($7,500 specie) from Pennsylvania alone, which George Washington requested be used for linen shirts for his soldiers. The ladies delivered 2,005 linen shirts to the soldiers of the Revolution; each shirt bore the name of the lady who made it.

After Reed died in 1780, Sarah Franklin Bache, daughter of Benjamin Franklin, continued the project.

—*Ginger Rae Allee*

See Also:

Revolutionary War

References:

Adelman, Joseph. *Famous Women*. New York: Lonow, 1926, p. 87.

Bruce, H. Addington. *Women in the Making of America*. Rev. ed. Boston: Little, Brown, 1928, pp. 87, 106–08.

Ellet, Elizabeth F. *The Women of the American Revolution*. Vol. 1. New York: Baker & Scribner, 1848; rpt. New York: Arno, 1974, pp. 332–43.

Green, Henry Clinton, and Mary Wolcott Green. *The Pioneer Mothers of America*. Vol. 2. New York: Putnam, 1912, p. 14; Vol. 3. p. 144–52, 179–92, 279–80. [portrait]

Leonard, Eugene Andruss, Sophia Drinker, and Miriam Young Holden. *The American Women in Colonial and Revolutionary Times, 1765–1800*. Philadelphia: University of Pennsylvania Press, 1962, pp. 112, 120–21.

Logan, Mary Simmerson. *The Part Taken by Women in American History*. 1912; rpt. New York: Arno, 1972, pp. 150–52, 202.

Norton, Mary Beth. *Liberty's Daughters*. Boston: Little, Brown, 1980, pp. 178–94.

The ***LADIES MAGAZINE AND REPOSITORY OF ENTERTAINING KNOWLEDGE*** (1792–93) was published biannually by William Gibbons in Philadelphia. It contained reviews of contemporary literature, essays, travelogues, and poetry. This bold experiment marked the debut of women's magazines. Entries that focused on the importance of women's intellectual growth distinguished the provocative and innovative *Ladies Magazine* from contemporaneous popular women's literature, which was primarily either romantic escapist pap or religious prescriptive tracts. The editorial policy of the magazine proposed to "inspire the Female mind with love of religion, of patience, of prudence, and fortitude."

In an attempt to preserve the "fairer sex," general guidelines for appropriate reading material were set by men such as lexicographer Noah Webster and reformer Dr. Benjamin Rush. While their opinions differed as to the appropriate degree of edification, both argued in favor of female learning only insofar as it enabled women to understand and uphold the new Republican ideals. In an attempt to broaden this definition, the *Ladies Magazine* included comprehensive works to elucidate female intellectuality—for example, excerpts from Mary Wollstonecraft's *A Vindication of the Rights of Woman* (1792). More subtle works also conveyed the rights and responsibilities of women as equal to those of men. One essay, "On Love," professed that the institution of marriage was a mutual venture between woman and man. As a contemporary voice, the *Ladies Magazine* elevated women's reading material ideologically and culturally to a position of equality with that of men's.

—*Robin S. Taylor*

See Also:

European Influences; Magazines; Rush, Benjamin

References:

Cott, Nancy F. *The Bonds of Womanhood.* New Haven: Yale University Press, 1977.

Kerber, Linda. "Daughters of Columbia: Educating Women for the Republic, 1787–1805." In *Our American Sisters: Women in American Life and Thought*, edited by Jean E. Friedman and William G. Shade. Lexington, Mass.: Heath, 1982, pp. 137–53.

LANGUAGE AND LINGUISTICS. Although contemporary U.S. feminists since about 1970 have paid close attention to language about the sexes as well as sex differences in the use of language, few attempts have been made to place this inquiry in the context of American women's history. In fact, however, leading nineteenth-century feminists, notably Elizabeth Cady Stanton and Susan B. Anthony, did concern themselves with such linguistic issues as women's authority to speak in public, the married woman's right to her own name, the possibility of feminine imagery for God, and the legal interpretation of *person, man,* and *he*. For example, after the Civil War many suffragists objected strenuously to the wording of the Fourteenth Amendment, which for the first time inserted the word *male* into the Constitution, and they noted the irony of laws that imposed criminal penalties upon women while denying them civil rights. This analysis led to lawsuits such as *United States v. Susan B. Anthony* (1873) and *Minor v. Happersett* (1875), which challenged the courts to establish a consistent interpretation of "generic" legal language. Near the turn of the century, Stanton's *Woman's Bible* incorporated religious and legal linguistic arguments into a radical feminist critique. Not long afterward, Henry James penned a vicious attack on the "degenerate" speech of American women, blaming feminism for the breakdown of linguistic standards of social class. Exactly the opposite view was held by the very influential feminist writer Charlotte Perkins Gilman, who believed that improvements in language would accompany a socialist-feminist transformation of society.

The first decades of the twentieth century saw the establishment of linguistics as a unified discipline. Researchers in the new field observed male and female speech in different cultures and contributed a feminist perspective to lexicography; however, a feminist historiography of linguistics has yet to be written. In 1946 Mary R. Beard devoted an entire chapter of *Woman as Force in History* to documenting the still-troublesome ambiguity of masculine generic usage.

One difficulty of historical research on women in language is that feminist historians and linguists alike have shown little interest in crossing each other's disciplinary boundaries. As a result, there is little direct knowledge of what women in general (and feminists in particular) have been saying about language and the sexes throughout most of American history.

—*Lou Ann Matossian*

See Also:

Anthony, Susan B.; Beard, Mary; Deconstruction; *Minor v. Happersett*; Stanton, Elizabeth Cady

References:

Barron, Dennis. *Grammar and Gender.* New Haven: Yale University Press, 1986.

Beard, Mary R. *Woman as Force in History.* New York: Macmillan, 1946.

James, Henry. "The Speech of American Women." *Harper's Bazar* [sic] 40 (1906): 979–82, 1103–06; 41 (1907): 17–21, 113–17.

Kramarae, Cheris, and Paula A. Treichler. *A Feminist Dictionary*. London: Pandora, 1985.
Matossian, Lou Ann. "A Woman-Made Language: Charlotte Perkins Gilman and *Herland*." *Women and Language*, 10 (Spring 1987): 16–20.
Stannard, Una. *Mrs. Man*. San Francisco: Germainbooks, 1971.
Stanton, Elizabeth C. et al. *The Woman's Bible*. New York: European Publishing Co., 1895, 1898.
Thorne, Barrie, Cheris Kramarae, and Nancy Henley, eds. *Language, Gender, and Society*. Rowley, Mass.: Newbury House, 1983.

The **LANHAM ACT** (1943). The application of this act for the construction of wartime facilities to build day-care centers and to support their operating costs exemplified the ambivalent response of the federal government to married women in the work force and to working mothers' need of child-care services for their young children during World War II. In response to the inability of local governments to provide these facilities for women working in the defense industries, the Lanham Act allocated federal funds through a complicated system that involved seven federal agencies.

Although the U.S. Children's Bureau championed the cause of the working mother's need for adequate child-care services, ultimately control of the development of day-care facilites was achieved by those within the Roosevelt administration who accepted married women into the labor force only as an emergency wartime measure. Thus by 1944 day-care centers serviced a mere l0 percent of the children of working mothers. Without adequate child care, the working mother retained the pre–World War II sense that her primary obligation was to care for her children in her home, while she was barraged with the relentless propaganda of the Office of War Information, which exhorted her to do her patriotic duty in the work force.

—*Angela Howard Zophy*

See Also:

Child Rearing, U.S. Children's Bureau, World War II

References:

Chafe, William H. *The American Woman: Her Changing Social, Economic, and Political Roles, 1920–1970*. New York: Oxford University Press, 1972.
Daniel, Robert L. *American Women in the Twentieth Century: The Festival of Life*. New York: Harcourt Brace Jovanovich, 1987.
Riley, Glenda. *Inventing the American Woman: A Perspective on Women's History*. Arlington Heights, Ill.: Harlan Davidson, 1986.
Rupp, Leila M. *Mobilizing Women for War: German and American Propaganda, 1939–1945*. Princeton: Princeton University Press, 1978.
Woloch, Nancy. *Women and the American Experience*. New York: Knopf, 1984.

LARCOM, LUCY (1824–93), teacher, editor, lecturer, and poet, achieved a national reputation in the late 1850s that lasted to her death and beyond. Most of her poems and articles appeared in newspapers and magazines, and four collections of her poems were published in her lifetime. Though primarily a poet, her best and best-known work is her partial autobiography, *A New England Girlhood* (1889).

She was born in Beverly, Massachusetts, to a large but comfortably situated family; her father's death when she was six sent her mother to Lowell, Massachusetts, as a mill-boardinghouse keeper. From age ten to twenty-one, Larcom worked in the Lowell mills; taking advantage of the opportunities available to the much-publicized mill girls, she developed her passionate desire to read and learn, and she also developed the independence characteristic of the mill girls but unusual in other women of the time. In 1846 she went to the West (then Illinois) to teach in a district school; she was able to get the formal education she longed for in an excellent academy there. She was engaged, but the sight of her brilliant sister's talents lost in the drudgery of a prairie marriage turned her away from that commitment. At Lowell she had been a frequent contributor to the *Lowell Offering*, which published the works of the mill girls; she continued to write for it and its continuation, the *New England Offering*, which expanded its contributors beyond the mill girls. She had also attracted the attention of John Greenleaf Whittier, who published some of her work in the abolitionist paper, the *National Era.*

In 1852 she returned to Massachusetts, and two years later began to teach at Wheaton Female Seminary. Her first book, *Similitudes, from the Ocean and Prairie,* was published in 1853. This collection of moral-religious stories aimed at children was pushed into print by Whittier, who had adopted her as his protégée. During her nine years at Wheaton, she published three similar books and many poems, but she suffered psychosomatic illnesses as a result of conflict between her need for security (which the teaching she disliked gave her) and her desire to be free of restrictions and to write. National fame came suddenly in 1858 with a poem called "Hannah Binding Shoes": it was set to music, inspired paintings, was frequently anthologized, and, ironically, since she did not much like it, followed her all her life. (William Dean Howells felt it was her sure claim to immortality.) In 1861 her "The Rose Enthroned" made the *Atlantic Monthly;* this literary effort to reconcile Christianity and Darwinism and the Civil War brought her into the orbit of the influential publishers Ticknor and Fields.

She left Wheaton in 1863 and the following year became an editor of a new magazine for children, *Our Young Folks.* Her first collection, called *Poems,* was published in 1868; two years before she had done an anthology of inspirational passages called *Breathings from the Better Life.* When the magazine was sold in 1873, she tried teaching again, but hated it and determined to support herself as a free-lance writer and lecturer. She managed to earn enough money to live, in a modest way, the life she wanted. Her publications in the seventies include *An Idyl of Work,* a blank-verse story of the Lowell mill girls; *Childhood Songs,* a collection of her poems for children; and five anthologies. Three of these were collaborations in which she did the work and Whittier took the credit. In the eighties she published *Wild Roses of Cape Ann,* mostly local-color poems, and Houghton Mifflin's Household Edition, *Lucy Larcom's Works* (1884). Her autobiography, *A New England Girlhood* (1889), was a critical success. In the last years of her life, she wrote three religious books that sold well.

Most of Larcom's poems begin with richly textured descriptions of the natural world—she was a painter, too, and had a good eye for visual detail—then move to a moral or religious insight. Much of her work is topical and autobiographical; it reflected her own experience and thinking. None of her poetry is particularly original, but her descriptions of nature still make pleasant reading. A deeply religious woman, she struggled painfully from the Puritanism into which she was born to a kind of Christian transcendentalism that informs much of her work. Although she had been an abolitionist, she avoided the controversial women's rights movement; she agreed with those who glorified woman as the light of the home, although several of her poems indicate that she was aware of women's problems, and certainly her own life choices contradicted her stated position. Both her work and her public behavior stayed safely within the norms of the nineteenth-century American literary establishment.

—*Shirley Marchalonis*

See Also:

Lowell Mill Girls, Transcendentalism

References:

Addison, Daniel Dulany. *The Life, Letters and Diary of Lucy Larcom.* Boston: Houghton Mifflin, 1894. [unreliable biography]

Larcom, Lucy. *A New England Girlhood.* Boston: Houghton Mifflin, 1889; rpt. Boston: Northeastern University Press, 1985.

Marchalonis, Shirley. *The Worlds of Lucy Larcom, 1824–1893.* Athens: University of Georgia Press, 1989.

LATHROP, JULIA CLIFFORD (1858–1932), social reformer, was born in Rockford, Illinois, the eldest of William and Sarah Potter Lathrop's five children. The family had a long tradition of public activism. William was a leader in the Republican party and served first in the state general assembly and later in Congress, while Sarah was an ardent advocate of woman suffrage. Lathrop received her bachelor's degree in 1880 from Vassar College and then returned home to read law in her father's office. In 1890 she moved to Chicago's Hull House, the third "settlement house" established in America in a movement that encouraged educated young people to "settle" and work among the poor. She quickly became a member of the settlement's inner circle. There she launched a reform career that would span over forty years and eventually carry her to a post in Washington.

At Hull House Lathrop worked in a variety of capacities. She volunteered to be a county agent investigating the neighborhood's relief applicants. Next she joined the Illinois Board of Charities, an assignment that she filled by visiting all of the state's county farms and almshouses, institutions that provided minimal shelter for the poor. In subsequent years, she traveled to Europe to explore treatment of the insane, helped found the Chicago School of Civics and Philanthropy, participated in the juvenile court movement, and established the Illinois Immigrants' Protective League.

In 1912 President William Howard Taft appointed Lathrop the first director of the newly established U.S. Children's Bureau. Under her leadership, the agency undertook studies of maternal and infant mortality, nutrition, juvenile delinquency, juvenile courts, illegitimacy, mental defectives, child labor, and mothers' pensions. The bureau also was responsible for enforcement of the nation's first child labor law, passed by Congress in 1916. Lathrop served in Washington until 1921, when she resigned and was replaced by Grace Abbott, another Hull House veteran.

Lathrop returned to Rockford to live with her sister, but even in retirement remained active. She was president of the Illinois League of Women Voters from 1922 to 1924 and served on a presidential commission to study conditions at New York's Ellis Island center for immigration. Lathrop died in Rockford in 1932 following surgery.

—*Rebecca L. Sherrick*

See Also:

Hull House, Immigrant Protective League, U.S. Children's Bureau

References:

Julia Lathrop Papers. Rockford College, Rockford, Ill.

Addams, Jane. *My Friend, Julia Lathrop.* New York: Macmillan, 1935.

LAW ENFORCEMENT. The first efforts to bring women into law enforcement date from the mid-1800s. In 1845 the American Female Reform Society of New York City advocated the employment of matrons in local jails, and matrons were hired to deal with the arrested women and juveniles. Other reform groups, such as the Woman's Christian Temperance Union, also called for matrons, and by 1900 most major cities had adopted their use.

The first woman with police duties was Mrs. Lola Baldwin, appointed to the Portland, Oregon, police department in 1905. She was assigned to "child protection" work during that summer's world's fair. The 1910 appointment of Mrs. Alice Stebbins Wells to the Los Angeles police department marked the beginning of a vigorous and organized movement. She led the campaign to get cities to hire women police, and in 1915 she organized the International Association of Policewomen. The movement gained strength, and over the next fifteen years more than 140 cities hired women police. Their responsibilities, however, remained much the same: dealing with juveniles and females, counseling and protecting them, and serving essentially as social workers. After the mid-1920s, however, few additional cities had added women to their police forces. The crime-prevention model of police work that aided the policewomen's movement was relegated to a position of minor importance, supplanted in the late 1920s and 1930s by the crime-fighter model of policing. But no new concept of women police emerged to fit this emphasis, and the movement stagnated for the next three decades.

In 1968 Indianapolis opened new opportunities with the appointment of two women officers to patrol duty, and in the 1970s the use of women police again expanded and attracted much attention. Since then, women have been involved in a broader range of police work. One indication of the expanding role is that the term *policeman* has given way to *police officer* as women once again enter the law enforcement profession and expand their role in it.

—*Robert G. Waite*

See Also:

Criminals, Women's Prisons

References:

Horne, Peter. *Women in Law Enforcement.* Springfield, Ill.: Charles C. Thomas, 1980.

Owings, Chloe. *Women Police: A Study of the Development and Status of the Women Police Movement.* 1925; rpt. Montclair, N.J.: Patterson Smith, 1969.

Walker, Samuel. *A Critical History of Police Reform.* Lexington, Mass.: Heath, 1977.

The **LAWRENCE STRIKE OF 1912** was the most publicized strike prior to World War I; twenty-three thousand textile workers challenged powerful corporations and won. Foreign-born and unskilled workers, more than half of whom were women and children, the strikers represented twenty-seven different ethnic groups, speaking dozens of different languages.

By 1912 the city of Lawrence, Massachusetts, was a one-industry town, a slum worse than most other industrial cities, with twelve wool and cotton mills supporting thirty-two thousand textile operatives and sixty thousand more dependent on them for their daily bread. Foul tenements, poor diets, and lack of warm clothing created a daily living hell for America's new immigrants. In view of the low wages paid the textile workers, most found it necessary for the entire family to work in the mills. Lodgers and boarders were an economic necessity for the majority of immigrant households, increasing the burden of work for the woman of the house, particularly when she too worked in the mill. Lawrence held the distinction of having one of the highest mortality rates of all industrial cities in the nation. In 1910, of the 1,524 deaths in Lawrence, almost half were children under six years old. A medical examiner studying health conditions in the Lawrence mills found that thirty-six out of every one hundred men and women who worked in the mills died before they were twenty-five years old.

The immediate cause of the uprising was a new policy that reduced the work week for women and children from fifty-six hours to fifty-four, provoking widespread anxiety among both women and men. The reduction of the work week, with the corresponding reduction in already starvation-level wages, brought past injustices and miseries exploding to the surface.

On January 11, 1912, a cold, bleak Thursday, the Battle of Lawrence began. Spontaneously, as the pay envelopes were passed out, the Polish weavers, mostly women, began shouting "not enough pay," then sat at their machines, refusing to work. Finally leaving the mill, they called for a demonstration and vowed not to return to work until their pay envelopes were increased by the amount deducted, thirty-two cents, or in their own words, "four loaves of bread."

Within a week, twenty-three thousand workers joined the protest. The Industrial Workers of the World, the IWW, inspired and molded the unskilled and foreign-born workers into an effective fighting unit and organized the first large-scale picketing in New England. Four days after the uprising began, the IWW directed it into a bona-fide strike with mass picketing in front of all mills, twenty-four hours a day. Women voluntarily placed themselves at the forefront of the picket lines, believing they would be handled less brutally than the men by police and state militia, and held their ground despite police policy that female strikers be beat about the breasts and arms while men be beat about the head. The women picketers knew they were being arrested in far greater numbers than the men, but that only increased their determination and resistance.

There are two lasting mottoes born of the Lawrence Strike that summarize the resolve of the strikers. The first, We Want Bread, and Roses Too, inspired both a poem and a song that came to symbolize the women strikers' struggles in the strike. The second, which was raised again during the turbulent 1930s, served as the battle cry of the strike, Better to Starve Fighting than to Starve Working.

One month after the strike began, IWW organizer Elizabeth Gurley Flynn organized the "Children's Crusade," a plan to lighten the relief burden and simultaneously gain publicity for the strikers' plight by placing strikers' children in foster homes in other cities. Every one of the children, according to physicians who examined them, were suffering from malnutrition. In the words of "Big Bill" Haywood, "Those children had been starving from birth. They had starved in their mother's womb. And their mothers had been starving before the children were conceived." The exodus of children created national attention and sympathy for the strikers. Police tried to prevent the children from leaving Lawrence, brutally beating and arresting fifteen children and eight women, which horrified the public and created a demand for a congressional investigation into the strike. With the public and press now in support of the strikers, the mill owners were forced to negotiate. After nine and a half weeks in that bitter winter, the strikers had won.

The women of Lawrence dispelled two myths that had historically excluded women from the organized labor movement. First, they were not "temporary," working for "pin money," but workers whose wages were necessary for family survival. Secondly, women proved themselves capable of leadership and acting in roles beyond those traditionally relegated to them.

—*Sandra Weidner*

See Also:

Flynn, Elizabeth Gurley; Industrial Workers of the World; Textile Industries, Northern and Southern; Unions

References:

Brooks, Thomas R. *Toil and Trouble: A History of American Labor.* New York: Delacorte, 1964.

Dubofsky, Melvyn. *We Shall Be All: A History of the IWW.* Chicago: Quadrangle, 1969.

Foner, Philip S. *History of the Labor Movement in the U.S. Vol. 4: The IWW, 1905–1917.* New York: International Publishers, 1965, 1972.

———. *Women and the American Labor Movement, from the First Trade Unions to the Present.* New York: Macmillan, 1979.

Yellen, Samuel. *American Labor Struggles.* New York: Harcourt Brace, 1936.

LAZARUS, EMMA (1849–87), Jewish American poet, translator, and essayist, is best known for her 1883 poem "The New Colossus," which was inscribed on the pedestal of the Statue of Liberty in 1903. Lazarus was the member of a wealthy New York family, descendants of Sephardic and Ashkenazi Jews. A child prodigy, she was privately educated and became proficient in several languages, gaining a wide knowledge of American literature and the work of medieval Hebrew poets. Though her parents encouraged her writing, she was aware of the difficulties facing women who attempted to be taken seriously in the profession. She expressed this consciousness of imposed limitations in an early sonnet, "Echoes":

> Late-born and woman-souled I dare not hope . . .
> the might of manly, modern passion shall alight
> Upon my Muse's lips, nor may I cope
> (Who veiled and screened by womanhood must grope).

The publication of *Poems and Translations by Emma Lazarus* in 1866, when she was seventeen, brought her praise from Ralph Waldo Emerson, who became one in a series of male mentors. Her published work in the following decade was classical and romantic in style. In the early 1880s she became an activist in providing relief to Jewish refugees fleeing from pogroms in Russia. Her firsthand knowledge of their persecution brought an increased militancy and power to her poetry, expressed in her critically acclaimed *Songs of a Semite* (1882). She was further influenced by the egalitarian ideas of Henry George and

William Morris, and by the writings of George Eliot and Walt Whitman. Her work became infused with a deeply historical analysis of her Jewish heritage; a proud identification with women, exemplified in her personification of such values as freedom, heroism, and labor in female form; and the articulation of the experiences of the oppressed.

As a writer for *Critic, Century, American Hebrew,* and other magazines, she influenced public debate over such issues as political repression, poverty, and Jewish nationalism. She died of cancer at age thirty-eight. *By the Waters of Babylon,* 1887, a collection of prose poems that demonstrate her break from the conventional forms of her early work, was her last publication.

—*Barbara Bair*

See Also:

Jewish Women

References:

Jacob, H. E. *The World of Emma Lazarus.* New York: Schocken, 1949.

Merriam, Eve. *Emma Lazarus: Woman with a Torch.* New York: Citadel, 1956.

Schappes, Morris, ed. *Emma Lazarus: Selections from Her Poetry and Prose.* New York: Cooperative Book League, 1944.

Vogel, Dan. *Emma Lazarus.* Boston: G. K. Hall, 1980.

The **LEAGUE OF WOMEN VOTERS** was a direct outgrowth of the National American Woman Suffrage Association, which had led the successful campaign for women's right to vote in the decades preceding 1920. In 1919 NAWSA President Carrie Chapman Catt proposed a league of women voters on the eve of the successful ratification of the Nineteenth Amendment, which federally enfranchised women. At the NAWSA Convention in St. Louis on March 24, 1919, Catt announced: "Let us then raise up a league of women voters . . . a league that shall be nonpartisan and nonsectarian in nature." Catt called for the league to adopt three distinct aims: first, to secure a final enfranchisement of women in every state; second, to remove remaining legal discriminations against women; and third, to make democracy safe enough to provide for world security. In February 1920 the NAWSA was officially dissolved, and the organization proceeded under the name the League of Women Voters.

Following the adoption of the Nineteenth Amendment with Tennessee's ratification on August 26, 1920, the league turned its focus to issues concerning good citizenship, peace, child welfare, effective government, and the status of women. Two of the league's early successes came in 1922 with the passage of the Cable Citizenship Act guaranteeing independent citizenship for married women and the Sheppard-Towner Act protecting mothers and newborns. In 1924 the league launched its first of many "Get Out the Vote" campaigns, which was not only a crusade for voter participation, but for voter education as well. The slogan in 1928 became Democracy Is a Bandwagon and There Are too Many Empty Seats. A significant league victory came with winning jury membership for women.

In succeeding years, the league has continued its drive for an educated electorate by establishing its own research facilities nationwide and by publishing T*he National Voter* magazine from its headquarters in Washington, D.C. On its sixty-fifth anniversary in 1985, the league had over five hundred chapters in all fifty states, organized at the grass-roots level—a nonpartisan, multi-issue, activist network. In the 1980s the league was a successful lobbying group for tax reform, clean water, arms control, and the "superfund" for toxic cleanup. Most visible are the league's televised debates among presidential, congressional, state, and local candidates for public office.

—*Ellen D. Langill*

See Also:

Catt, Carrie Chapman; National American Woman Suffrage Association; Sheppard-Towner Act

References:

Degler, Carl N. *At Odds.* Oxford: Oxford University Press, 1980.

Flexner, Eleanor. *Century of Struggle.* Cambridge, Mass.: Belknap, 1975.
Lemons, J. Stanley. *The Woman Citizen; Social Feminism in the 1920s.* Urbana: University of Illinois Press, 1973.
"On the Road to Reform, The League's Place in History." *National Voter* 35 (November/ December 1986). [special issue]

LEASE, MARY ELIZABETH CLYENS (1850–1933), born in Ridgway, Pennsylvania, was an orator for the Farmers' Alliance and Populist party. In 1870 she moved to Kansas to teach school, and three years later she married Charles L. Lease, a pharmacist. The couple had four children. The family farmed in Kansas and then in Texas until 1883, when they returned to Wichita, Kansas, where Lease's husband resumed working as a pharmacist. Lease spoke for the Irish National League and the Union Labor party, edited the *Union Labor Press,* joined the Knights of Labor, and was elected "master workman" for Kansas. She also co-founded the *Colorado Workman,* joined the Farmers' Alliance and the Woman's Christian Temperance Union, and wrote several articles on women's rights. Lease served briefly as president of the Wichita Equal Suffrage Association and ran for superintendent of schools in Sedgewick, Kansas.

In 1890 Lease joined a speakers' bureau whose focus was the defeat of Senator John J. Ingalls of Kansas, because he had not supported the demands of the Kansas Farmers' Alliance. For seven months Lease campaigned against Ingalls, travelling to sixteen counties and some fifty towns and cities, making approximately 160 speeches during the summer. With the defeat of Ingalls and the advent of the Populist party, Lease gained notoriety. From 1890 to 1894, she worked for the Populists, speaking to hundreds of groups of farmers in states as far away as Oregon and Washington and attending Populist conventions. She was rewarded for this work by an appointment as the first woman president of the Kansas State Board of Charities and Corrections. By 1893, because of quarrels with the Populist administration, Lease began supporting the Republican party and ceased advocating woman suffrage and temperance. This ended her political effectiveness and her career as an orator.

She moved to New York in 1896 after arguing against the nomination of William Jennings Bryan at the St. Louis Populist convention. In New York, Lease once more supported woman suffrage and temperance. She divorced her husband in 1902 and filed for bankruptcy. Her later activities included lecturing for the adult education program of the New York City Board of Education and serving as president of the National Society for Birth Control. She died in New York in 1933.

—*MaryJo Wagner*

See Also:

National Farmers' Alliance, Populist Party

References:

Blumberg, Dorothy. "Mary Elizabeth Lease: Populist Campaigner." Unpublished Paper, Berkshire Women's History Conference, 1974.
Lease, Mary Elizabeth [James Arnold]. "M. E. Lease." Topeka: Kansas State Historical Society, n.d.
Livermore, A. L. "Mary Elizabeth Lease: The Foremost Woman Politician of the Times." *Metropolitan Magazine* 14 (November 1896): 263–66.
Wagner, MaryJo. "Prairie Populists: Luna Kellie and Mary Elizabeth Lease." In *Northwest Women's Heritage,* edited by Karen Blair. Seattle: Northwest Center for Research on Women, 1984, pp. 200–10.

LEE, MOTHER ANN (1736–84) was the founder and leader of the Shakers, a Protestant, celibate, and communitarian sect known for its female participation and leadership. Her followers viewed Lee as the female embodiment of Christ and the maternal component of a Mother/Father God.

Born to a working-class family in Manchester, England, Lee was sent out, like many girls of her class and time, to work in the textile mills. Thus she lacked any schooling and remained illiterate. Throughout her life, Lee exhibited signs of religious mysticism. In 1758 she joined John and Jane Wardley's sect of Shaking Quakers. The Wardleys advocated celibacy and public confession of sin. Ann Lee, a talented woman with a charismatic personality, soon rose to a position of religious leadership within the sect.

Although she felt a physical and spiritual repugnance toward marriage, Lee was persuaded to marry Abraham Stanley. Four difficult childbirths and the deaths of all four children may have contributed to Lee's conviction that lust was the root of all evil. Imprisoned in 1770 for Sabbath breaking, Lee experienced visions in which it was revealed to her that sexuality was the primary impediment to human perfection and that she, as the conduit for Christ's second appearance on earth, was to spread this message.

In 1774 Ann Lee and a small band sailed for America. Taking advantage of religious revivals in New York and New England, Lee and her followers spread the message of Christ's reappearance in female form. These early Shakers suffered physical persecution. They were charged with being British spies, blasphemers, and dangerous disrupters of the community. In 1784 Lee died as a result of injuries probably sustained at the hands of a mob.

Although Ann Lee served as a spiritual guide and role model for many women who joined the Shakers, she believed men should remain as heads of traditional families and often counseled women to remain with their husbands. It was not until several years after her death that the Shaker tradition of dual male and female leadership and representation was put into practice. Belief in Lee as a female Godhead, however, served later generations of Shakers with a theological basis for their espousal of equal rights for women.

—Wendy E. Chmielewski

See Also:

Christianity, Shakers

References:

Campion, Nardi Reed. *Ann the Word: The Life of Mother Ann Lee*. Boston: Little, Brown, 1976.

Setta, Susan Margaret. "Woman of the Apocalypse: The Reincorporation of the Feminine Through the Second Coming of Christ in Ann Lee." Diss. Pennsylvania State University, 1979.

Wells, Seth. *Testimonies of the Life, Character, Revelation and Doctrine of Our Blessed Mother Ann Lee*. Hancock, Mass.: The United Society, 1816.

LEGAL PROFESSION. Since the nineteenth century, women struggled to gain admission to and then advancement in the legal profession in the United States. Regardless of their training, women wishing to practice law had to apply to their state supreme court for a license to argue cases in courts from which they were barred because of gender. Initially barred from attending all-male law schools and denied opportunities for internships with licensed attorneys, some women began to challenge their exclusion from the legal profession as the nineteenth-century woman's rights movement developed.

Barriers began to crumble when in 1869 Arabella Babb Mansfield applied for admission to the Iowa bar. A sympathetic judge issued an order allowing Mansfield to take the bar examination, which she passed with high honors. Despite passing the Iowa bar, she never practiced law; instead Mansfield chose a teaching career and taught at Iowa Wesleyan and later at DePaul University.

In 1870 Myra Bradwell issued a similar challenge to the Illinois bar. She had studied law with her husband and was the founder and editor of the very successful *Chicago Legal News*. Her petition to be admitted to the Illinois bar was denied on the grounds that married women could not make contracts and "that it belonged to men to make, apply and execute the laws." Bradwell then appealed to the U.S. Supreme Court, which rejected her appeal. Fortunately, the Illinois legislature settled the matter in 1871 by passing legislation that specified that "no person shall be precluded or debarred from any occupation, profession or employment (except military) on account of sex."

In 1871 Phoebe Couzins became the first woman to receive a formal law degree from an American university. Couzins graduated from Washington University in St. Louis and went on to become a leading figure in the woman suffrage movement. Charlotte E. Ray was the first black woman to qualify as a lawyer when she graduated from Howard University Law School. Former abolitionist and teacher Mary Ann Shadd Cary was another legal pioneer when she graduated from Howard University Law School in 1883 at age sixty-three. Belva Lockwood became the first woman lawyer to practice law before the Supreme Court, in 1879.

The legal profession continued to be dominated by men, and by 1910 there were still only fifteen hundred female attorneys, most of whom were excluded from courtroom practice once licensed. Most women attorneys worked for government agencies, legal journals, and women's organizations. Few women were law school professors. Indeed, as late as 1968 only 1.6 percent of the nation's law school professors were women, and most law clerks were still male until the 1980s.

With the advent of the modern women's movement all of this began to change. In 1970 the Association of American Law Schools became one of the first national academic associations to prohibit sex discrimination in admissions, employment, and placement at member schools. The percentages of women in law schools rose from 3.6 percent in 1961 to 12 percent in 1972. As of 1981 14 percent of the nation's judges and lawyers were women. In that same year, Sandra Day O'Connor became the first woman to sit on the Supreme Court. By 1984 women constituted fully a third of law school graduates.

Women also entered the legal profession as clerks and paralegals. Paralegals, or legal assistants, assist attorneys in the administration of a wide variety of legal matters. They perform the same duties as attorneys except setting fees, giving advice, signing up new clients, and trying a case in court. Of the forty thousand paralegals employed in the United States in the 1980s, about 80 percent were women. However, increased reliance on paralegals places these women in jobs that require similar skills but pay considerably less than lawyers earn. Even women attorneys generally do not make as much money as their male counterparts and are still often encouraged to enter into "women specialties" such as matrimonial law and trusts. Despite continued resistence within the male-dominated profession, women have clearly established themselves as active and significant members of the legal profession at all levels.

—Richard M. Prouty and Jonathan W. Zophy

See Also:

Abzug, Bella; Ferraro, Geraldine; Jordan, Barbara; Lockwood, Belva; Lytle, Lutie; Schlafly, Phyllis; Shadd, Mary Ann.

References:

DeCrow, Karen. *Sexist Justice*. New York: Vintage, 1975.

Flexner, Eleanor. *Century of Struggle*. Cambridge: Harvard University Press, 1975.

Harris, Barbara. *Beyond Her Sphere: Women and the Professions in America*. Westport, Conn.: Greenwood, 1978.

Kanowitz, Leo. *Women and the Law*. Albuquerque: University of New Mexico Press, 1975.

White, Matthew. *The History of American Law*. New York: Random House, 1985.

LENTFOEHR, SISTER MARY THERESE (1902–81), Salvatorian sister, poet, author, and lecturer, was born Florence Mae Brooks Lentfoehr in Oconto Falls, Wisconsin, the daughter of George and Florence (Brooks) Lentfoehr. She entered the Sisters of the Divine Savior at Milwaukee in 1923, receiving the name "Mary Therese," and graduated from Marquette University with a B.A. (English) in 1933 and an M.A. (Philosophy) in 1938. She also was a graduate of St. Joseph's Conservatory of Music (1928) and the Wisconsin Conservatory of Music. Sister Therese served on the faculties of St. Mary's Convent High School, Divine Savior Junior College, Marquette University, Georgetown University, Fordham University, Mount St. Paul College, and Dominican College of Racine, Wisconsin. Her poetry appeared in the *American Mercury*, *Saturday Review*, the *New York Times*, and the *New York Herald-Tribune*.

Her first collection of poems, *Now There Is Beauty,* was published in 1940, followed by *Give Joan a Sword* in 1944.

Her edited anthology of poems to the Blessed Virgin, *I Sing of a Maiden,* 1947, attracted a favorable review from the Trappist poet and author Thomas Merton. He later sent her a manuscript copy of his classic *Seven Storey Mountain* and began a friendship that lasted until his death in 1968. Over the years, she received numerous manuscripts and drafts of his prose and poetry, autographed first editions, and assorted memorabilia. She also assisted him in preparing the *Monastic Orientation Notes* for his classes with young monks, and transcribed numerous manuscripts (including the *Sign of Jonas*) from his holograph journals. Her close association with Merton gave her one of the largest collections of the monk's manuscripts (now housed at Columbia University) and made her one of the leading Merton experts in America. After his death, Sister Therese wrote and lectured extensively on his work. Her last work was a commentary on his poetry entitled *Words and Silence* (1979).

—Steven M. Avella

See Also:
Christianity

References:

Lentfoehr, Therese. *Marianne Moore.* Grand Rapids, Mich.: Eerdmans, 1960.

———. *Moments in Ostia.* New York: Doubleday, 1959.

LEONARD, CLARA TEMPLE (1828–1904) was an influential advocate of women's prison reform and child welfare measures in nineteenth-century Massachusetts. Born in Greenfield, Massachusetts, she trained as a teacher. Her involvement in women's prison issues began in the mid-1860s when a church rector asked her to be a substitute teacher for the weekly Sunday school service held for women prisoners in the county jail. She taught there for the next nine years, leading the female inmates in hymns, prayers, and Bible reading.

Then, in February 1865, Leonard organized the Home for Friendless Women and Children, a shelter for the needy or those recently released from prison, and remained active with this organization until 1876. She also worked with the Dedham Home for Discharged Female Prisoners. Increasingly, the subject of women in prison absorbed her attention, as she and other representatives from these organizations visited female prisoners throughout the state. The conditions they found were abysmal. At Leonard's urging, a public meeting, presided over by the governor, was held in Boston on November 27, 1869. The objective, she wrote, was "the ladies' desire to call attention to the necessity of a separate prison for women, with a separate reformatory or workhouse for confined inebriates, and of the State taking charge of young girls who have no legal guardians. Reformation is the prime objective, and to this end instruction, secular and religious, is essential." A petition calling for "the establishment of separate prisons for women, under female supervision," was presented to the state legislature.

In the fall of 1870, a commission was established, and its members toured and inspected county prisons. An important result of their efforts was the identification of Greenfield jail as a separate prison for women. Leonard led this drive by organizing a statewide campaign in 1873. As a result of its efforts, the legislature passed a bill on June 30, 1874, appropriating $300,000 to build a separate facility for women. This prison, at Sherborn, opened on November 1, 1877, and, as the superintendent wrote, "every effort [was] put forth to teach the women how to work, how to read and write, and how to apply themselves industriously to their given tasks."

Leonard now turned her energies toward children's issues and the care of the insane. In 1878 she helped establish the Hampden County Children's Aid Association, serving as president until 1885. This organization helped impoverished children and monitored the conditions of children placed out as apprentice workers. In June 1880 Leonard was appointed the only female member of the Massachusetts Board of Health, Lunacy and Charity. Her interests were almshouses, which provided refuge for the poor, and insane asylums, and she traveled extensively throughout the state visiting them. In 1882 she advocated the appointment of women physicians to the staff of each hospital, a measure adopted by the board. During the remainder of the decade, her activities slowed because of several illnesses, and although constantly appealed to as an expert on charitable matters, Leonard stayed largely out of public work during the last dozen years of her life.

—Robert G. Waite

See Also:

Prison Reform, Women's Prisons

References:

Leonard, Katherine H. *Clara Temple Leonard, 1828–1904. A Memoir of Her Life.* Springfield, Mass.: Loring-Axtell, 1908.

Pettigrove, Frederick G. *An Account of the Prisons of Massachusetts.* Boston: Wright & Potter, 1904.

LESBIAN RIGHTS refers to the struggle for social and legal tolerance of lesbians as well as protection of their full civil rights, including freedom from discrimination in employment, housing, and child custody decisions. In the nineteenth century lesbians were unlikely to avow publicly their sexual preference or to work openly for legal reform to assure specific lesbian rights. Direct confrontation of the issue of lesbian rights emerged from the gay and women's liberation movements of the 1960s. Out of these movements came a consciousness of the specific forms of discrimination and oppression encountered by lesbians in their personal and public lives. The momentum of political action to address these issues resulted in cooperative efforts to establish as one of the political priorities of the modern women's movement the right of women to make individual choices in all areas of their lives, including sexual preference.

Though the lesbian-feminist movement may have developed out of women's rights organizations, leaders of liberal groups like the National Organization for Women (NOW) were not always supportive of lesbian rights. But by the 1977 International Women's Year Conference in Houston, Betty Friedan, who had earlier described lesbians as "the lavender menace," defended the right to choose one's own sexual preference, noting that "we must protect women who are lesbians in their own civil rights." The natural rights ideology on which liberal feminism was based, as well as a need to heal the gay/straight split developing in the women's movement, led to at least tentative support for lesbian rights among mainstream feminists.

In the 1980s lesbians were still subject to economic, legal, and social discrimination. The lesbian rights movement, consisting of autonomous lesbian-feminist organizations supported by feminist, gay male, and civil libertarian groups, continues to challenge such discrimination at the local and state level, as well as issue by issue. The agenda for lesbian rights has been articulated and pursued at the national level most prominently by the National Gay Rights Task Force. The ultimate goal of lesbian rights is legal and cultural acceptance of this alternative life-style and sexual preference.

—Mary Battenfeld

See Also:

Daughters of Bilitis, Homophobia, International Women's Year Conference, Lesbianism, Radicalesbians

References:

Daniel, Robert. *American Women in the Twentieth Century.* New York: Harcourt Brace Jovanovich, 1987.

D'Emilio, John. *Sexual Politics, Sexual Communities: The Making of a Homosexual Minority in the U.S. 1940–1970.* Chicago: University of Chicago Press, 1983.

LESBIAN SEPARATISM began in the United States in the early 1970s as an offshoot of lesbian feminism. It has led to much conflict within the women's liberation movement, acting, along with lesbian allies (who ally themselves with leftists and attack capitalist society), as one of the divisive forces within lesbian feminism. Separatists attack patriarchal society and oppose sex relations, but not class relations. They oppose patriarchy, but not capitalism. Their ideology involves a total repudiation of patriarchal society and a subsequent withdrawal to create a completely female culture. The first lesbian separatist group was established in Washington, D.C., and was called "The Furies." Similar groups were subsequently established all over the country.

—*Victoria L. Shannon*

See Also:
Homophobia, Lesbian Rights, Lesbianism, Radical Feminism

Reference:
Ettore, E. M. *Lesbians, Women & Society.* Boston: Routledge & Kegan Paul, 1980.

LESBIANISM generally refers to women maintaining primary sexual and emotional attachments to other women. In her groundbreaking article "Compulsory Heterosexuality and Lesbian Existence," Adrienne Rich, however, makes a distinction between "lesbian existence" and "lesbian continuum" and rejects the word *lesbianism* as "clinical and limiting." In Rich's terms, *lesbian existence* refers to the historical and present lives of women who have broken the sexual and social taboos of "compulsory heterosexuality." *Lesbian continuum* is intended to include a wider range of woman-identified experience, including attachments to women and resistance to patriarchy, not necessarily sexual in nature.

Rich's formulations are not universally accepted, but the inclusion of lesbianism as a category for discussion and inquiry, and the analysis of "compulsory heterosexuality" as an institutional force that affects all women, has had important implications for scholarship on women. Discussions of the lesbian relationships and female support networks shared by nineteenth-century white middle-class women, among women reformers and writers, and in black and working-class communities have served to illuminate the heterosexist bias of much scholarship and to provide a new context for interpreting women's experiences.

In the twentieth century a basic shift in the perception of contemporary as well as of Victorian female friendships occurred. Until the 1960s, lesbian relationships were unacknowledged or denied outright to avoid social stigma and harassment, as depicted in Lillian Hellman's *The Children's Hour,* for example. In the wake of the modern women's movement, lesbian women asserted a positive self-conscious definition of themselves and their life-style, establishing lesbian communities and support groups. These woman-identified women, some separatist and some not, demonstrated a willingness to define themselves by their sexual preference to their families, co-workers, and society at large, and to demand equality of rights.

—*Mary Battenfeld*

See Also:
Boston Marriages, Homophobia, Lesbian Rights, Lesbian Separatism, Women's Friendships

References:
D'Emilio, John. *Sexual Politics, Sexual Communities: The Making of a Homosexual Minority in the U.S., 1940–1970.* Chicago: University of Chicago Press, 1983.
Faderman, Lillian. *Surpassing the Love of Men: Love Between Women from the Renaissance to the Present.* New York: Morrow, 1981.
Rich, Adrienne. "Compulsory Heterosexuality and Lesbian Existence." *Signs* 5 (1980): 631–60.

LETTERS ON THE EQUALITY OF THE SEXES AND THE CONDITION OF WOMAN (1838) was a woman's rights pamphlet by Sarah Grimké. It was composed of fifteen letters addressed to Mary Parker, the president of the Boston Female Anti-Slavery Society, that were originally published in the New England *Spectator* and reprinted in the abolitionist newspaper the *Liberator.* In the letters, Grimké articulated an argument for the intellectual, moral, and legal equality of men and women. In doing so, she voiced what would become central tenets of the nineteenth-century woman's movement and of modern feminism.

Using international examples, Grimké demonstrated the historical oppression of women, their subordination and commodification, or submersion, within the institution of marriage, their exploitation as laborers and as sexual objects, and their exclusion from educational opportunities. She celebrated the heroism and leadership of exemplary women in history, and defended women's right, even duty, to participate fully in reform movements and in the public realms of government, medicine, and the ministry. She rejected claims of natural or inherent differences between men and women. She linked the oppression of white women with that of male and female slaves, and supported the seemingly modern ideas of equal pay for equal work and comparable worth. *Letters* was written at the height of public agitation on behalf of abolition by Sarah and her sister Angelina, and it underscores the relation of the woman's rights and abolition movements.

The third letter in the series is Grimké's response to a pastoral letter issued by the General Association of Congregational Ministers of Massachusetts, which censured the Grimkés for stepping outside the private sphere and taking on an allegedly unnatural masculine role as public speakers to audiences composed of both men and women. Grimké challenged the ministers' authority and argued that women must be allowed to act according to the talents God had granted them, both in the domestic sphere and the public arena.

—Barbara Bair

See Also:

Abolition and the Antislavery Movement; Grimké, Sarah; Public Speakers, Women

References:

Barnes, Gilbert, and Dwight Dumond, eds. *Letters of Theodore Dwight Weld, Angelina Grimké Weld, and Sarah Grimké, 1822–1844.* 2 vols. New York: Appleton-Century, 1934.

Birney, Catherine. *Sarah and Angelina Grimké: The First American Women Advocates of Abolition and Woman's Rights.* 1885; rpt. Westport, Conn.: Greenwood, 1969.

Grimké, Sarah. *Letters on the Equality of the Sexes and the Condition of Women.* 1838; rpt. New York: Lenox Hill, 1970.

Lerner, Gerda. *The Grimké Sisters from South Carolina: Pioneers for Woman's Rights and Abolition.* 1967; rpt. New York: Schocken, 1971.

LEWIS, EDMONIA (1843/45 to post-1911), a successful American sculptor who was a member of the expatriate community in Italy, was the first minority artist to be nationally and internationally acknowledged.

Lewis's biographical data still remain vague, partially due to her own inaccuracies. It seems accepted that Mary Edmonia "Wildfire" Lewis was the daughter of a black father and a Chippewa mother who reportedly died when Wildfire was about three; she may or may not have been orphaned. It seems she spent her childhood with her mother's tribe until, in the 1850s, her brother Sunrise encouraged her financially and otherwise to attend school and later to enroll in Oberlin College, Ohio (preparatory, 1859; college 1860–62 or 1863). Here Lewis began drawing. After a scandal in which she was accused and acquitted of the attempted poisoning of two white women students (and perhaps one in which she was accused of stealing art supplies), Lewis left Oberlin for Boston, where, with support from abolitionists, she began her career as a sculptor.

The sales of plaster copies of Lewis's bust of the dead commander of the first black regiment in the Civil War, Bostonian Colonel Robert Gould Shaw, and of her medallion of John Brown financed a trip to England, France, and Italy, where she finally settled in Rome in 1865, joining a growing community of American women expatriates. Concentrating on her art, Lewis began carving marble figures without further formal instruction. The predominant style was neoclassical, but Lewis also experimented, especially in her frequent choice of black and Indian themes. In 1869 she returned to the United States to sell and to exhibit her work, the first of many subsequent visits. She may have married a Philadelphian, Dr. Peck, around 1869. Very little is known about Lewis after about 1883. She was known to have been living in Rome in 1911, but no record of her death has been found.

Critical reception of Lewis's sculpture is varied. She is indubitably an important personage in women's history. Among the more important of her located sculptures are *Forever Free* (c.1867), *Hagar in the Wilderness* (1868), and *Old Arrow Maker (and His Daughter)* (1872).

—*Maureen Ruth Liston*

See Also:

Art, Native American Women

References:

Hartigan, Lynda Roscoe. "Edmonia Lewis." In *Sharing Traditions: Five Black Artists in Nineteenth-Century America.* Washington, D.C.: Smithsonian Institution, 1985, pp. 85–98.

Liston, Maureen Ruth. "A Cultural History of American Women Expatriates, ca. 1850–1939." Ongoing research project.

LIBRARIANSHIP is as old as the need to organize and retrieve information and records. But the entry of women into the profession is comparatively recent and, in the United States, dates from the middle of the nineteenth century. Within the profession, the contribution of black women to the development of southern librarianship deserves special notice.

The history of women in librarianship parallels the history of the other so-called semiprofessions of nursing, social work, and teaching, and for some of the same reasons. As women entered the work force in the late 1800s, the library field was one of the few open to an educated woman. After the entry of women into the professions, the number of women library workers grew rapidly. There were over three thousand in 1900 and over eighty-five hundred by 1910. Some felt that librarianship was a particularly suitable occupation for women, since it concentrated on providing a service and was therefore extension of women's domestic role. Also, many librarians, like other working women of the time, were single, and therefore it was felt that they could afford to work for less money.

The first libraries to welcome women workers were public libraries trying to encourage more people to visit them by promoting a homelike, genteel atmosphere. The expansion of tax-supported public libraries meant more workers were needed in them. The increase in the number of academic libraries resulting from the growth of higher education also created a need for workers, preferably highly educated ones.

Most librarians were men in the early years of the twentieth century, when many men left the profession for a variety of reasons. World War I took men away from the work force, and the Depression contributed further to this change in the profession. Salaries were low everywhere, and men looked for jobs where they could earn more money to support their families, thus leaving more jobs, especially in public libraries, for women. As women entered the labor force in greater numbers in the early twentieth century, many college-educated women still found librarianship one of the few professions open to them, being practically barred from other professions except for social work and teaching. Many still thought women were suited to librarianship because of their feminine qualities—attention to detail, rapport with children, service orientation; but the real reason more women entered the field was that the jobs were available and they were willing to fill them. Thus, after the beginning of the twentieth century, the profession that had been predominantly male became predominantly female.

Disparity in pay between males and females has always been and continues to be of concern to women. Early reasons given for women's lower pay and failure to get the best jobs were that women were fragile in health, overly emotional (preventing them from being good administrators), and lacked mobility, especially if married. In the early years of the twentieth century, men were encouraged to reenter the profession. This was supposed to raise salaries and increase the prestige of librarianship. After World War II, more men did enter the field, but the long-range trend toward "feminization" continued. In 1870, 20 percent of all librarians were women. In 1970, of 130,000 librarians, the number of women had increased to 82 percent. Women's salaries, however, were about 70 percent of men's, reflecting the concentration of men in high-salaried areas such as administration. Another survey showed that the salary differentials widened with experience. It has often been said that librarians are poorly paid because of the number of women in the profession. Actually, the opposite is true. Women dominate the profession because salaries are low—women are the victims and not the cause of low salaries. The causes are more complex and include society's male/female role expectations in every area of life, low priority in society given to public services, and insufficient public support for libraries.

The historiography of black women in development of southern librarianship from 1900 to 1945 represents a field ripe for research. Within the constraints of segregated southern society, pioneering black women struggled to obtain libraries for blacks, to establish appropriate collections featuring black culture and history, to develop professional education and standards for service to black communities; in the process, they themselves led an effort to promote racial justice and end segregation. In several areas, black women librarians developed techniques that set models for American librarianship.

Pioneers such as Susan Dart Butler (1888–1959) and Mollie Huston Lee (b. 1907) struggled to establish libraries to serve black communities. In 1927 Butler opened a library in Charleston, South Carolina, that was privately supported and consisted of books from her deceased father's library and donated items. Lee, a librarian at Shaw University in Raleigh, North Carolina, from 1930 to 1935, together with other black civic leaders organized a "public" library largely supported by private contributions. Lee and Howard University librarian and archivist Dorothy Porter (b. 1905) both recognized the need to develop black-centered collections, and their collections became invaluable resources. The early guides and bibliographies they produced were forerunners of publications that were to be useful in developing black collections in all American libraries.

Another innovator whose work proved to be of value outside her own community was Sadie Peterson Delaney (1889–1959) who, while serving as a librarian with the Veterans Administration hospital in Tuskegee, Alabama, developed bibliotherapy techniques that have been widely copied.

It was difficult for blacks to obtain education for librarianship in the South, and the first formal training program was opened at Hampton Institute in 1925, closing in 1939. In 1941 Atlanta University's School of Library Service was opened, headed by Dr. Eliza Gleason (b. 1909), the first black library science Ph.D., with Virginia Lacy (later Jones, 1912–84), who became the second black to receive a doctorate in library science, on the staff. Also in 1941, North Carolina Central College for Negroes (today North Carolina Central University) in Durham opened its School of Library Science.

In addition to fighting for better education for blacks, many black women librarians in this period took more direct measures against injustice. Ruby Stutts Lyells, the first black professional librarian in Mississippi, for example, was an active member of the National Association for the Advancement of Colored People, participating in sit-ins in the 1930s.

The civil rights movement and the modern women's movement of the 1960s raised issues of the impact of both racism and sexism upon librarianship as a woman's profession. As a result of the feminist movement, groups within the American Library Association worked to publicize discrimination against women in the profession. At first, their concerns were mainly inequalities in library employment, but they were also concerned with career opportunities and nepotism within the profession and have renewed their commitment to attack inequalities, of race or gender, through career development and support of pay equity.

—*Suzanne Hildenbrand and Judith Pryor*

See Also:

Black Women, Children's Library Movement, Higher Education for Southern Women, Women's Work—Nineteenth Century

References:

Cantrell, Clyde H. "Sadie P. Delaney: Bibliotherapist and Librarian." *Southeastern Libraries* 6 (Fall 1956): 105–9.

Garrison, Dee. "The Tender Technicians: The Feminization of Public Librarianship, 1876–1905." *Journal of Social History* 6 (Winter 1972–1973): 131–59.

Gleason, Eliza. *Southern Negro and the Public Library*. Chicago: University of Chicago Press, 1941.

Heim, Kathleen M. "The Demographic and Economic Status of Librarians in the 1970s, with Special References to Women." In *Advances in Librarianship*, edited by Wesley Simonton. New York: Academic Press, 1982, pp. 1–45.

Josey, E. J., and Ann Allen Shocklye, comp. and ed. *Handbook of Black Librarianship*. Littleton, Colo.: Libraries Unlimited, 1970.

Phinazee, Annette, ed. *The Black Librarian in the Southeast: Reminiscences, Activities, Challenges*. Durham: North Carolina Central University Press, 1980.

Shores, Louis. "Public Library Service to Negroes." *Library Journal* 55 (February 1930): 150–54

Weibel, Kathleen, and Kathleen M. Heim, eds. *The Role of Women in Librarianship, 1876–1976: The Entry, Advancement, and Struggle for Equalization in One Profession*, asst. Dianne J. Ellsworth. Phoenix: Oryx, 1979.

LINDEN HALL SEMINARY grew out of a girl's day-school established by the Moravians, the Church of the Brethren, in Lititz, Pennsylvania, on January 2, 1764. After the community struggled for two years offering instruction for boys in the morning and girls in the afternoon, a day school for girls was begun on August 21, 1766. Two sisters from the church taught the ten pupils. Although it was called a day school, pupils from distant Moravian congregations were boarded at the site. Enrollment grew, reaching fifteen by 1768, and a new building opened on November 14, 1769.

The years of the American Revolution were hard on the school; its boarding pupils were sent home and part of the facility used as a military hospital. After the war the school prospered, and by 1790 a dozen girls were again enrolled. It was reorganized as the Lititz Boarding School, and applications grew rapidly. As a teacher wrote in 1799, "We cannot increase our numbers for want of teachers, every one must wait for a vacancy." A resolution passed by the church called for a maximum of forty boarding pupils, but the renovation of the new building enabled enrollment to grow. By 1804 seventeen day pupils and fifty-two boarders attended the school. The number of pupils rose, reaching more than one hundred in 1838. The school gained a charter from the state of Pennsylvania in 1863 as the Linden Hall Seminary. A post-secondary department developed into a junior college, known since 1935 as Linden Hall Junior College and School for Girls.

—*Robert G. Waite*

See Also:

Education, Female Academies, Moravian Seminary for Young Females

References:

Haller, Mabel. "Early Moravian Education in Pennsylvania." *Transactions of the Moravian Historical Society* 15 (1953): 1–397.

Wiltzel, Louisa A. "Linden Hall Seminary." In *Historical and Pictorial Lititz*, edited by John G. Zook. Lititz, Pa.: Express Printing Company, 1905, pp. 24–31.

Woody, Thomas. *A History of Women's Education in the United States*. 1929; rpt. New York: Octagon Books, 1966.

LITTLE WOMEN, written by Louisa May Alcott, was an instant best-seller and has become an American classic. Although Alcott first published Part I in 1868 and Part II in 1869, since the 1880s the two parts of *Little*

Women have usually been combined into one volume in the United States. Alcott's fictional tale of the generic New England March family drew heavily upon her personal experience as one of four daughters of Bronson and Abby May Alcott. Patterned as a *Pilgrim's Progress* for American girls, *Little Women* begins vaguely during a civil war that remains nameless throughout Part I, whose plot spans only one crucial year in the March girls' adolescence. Undertaking a longer period of the girls' development, Part II charts each daughter's odyssey into adulthood. Its original illustrations by Alcott's sister May were replaced by the work of professional artists in subsequent and lavishly illustrated editions, for *Little Women* quickly became a perennially popular children's book. However, *Little Women* is more than merely a children's classic: it is a quintessentially American Victorian domestic morality tale that focuses on the passage of the four March daughters from girlhood into True Womanhood.

Underlying its deceptively simple story of how Meg, Jo, Beth, and Amy March grow into individual women, *Little Women* presents universal and feminist themes about women's autonomy that transcend the lives of these nineteenth-century fictional characters. The four girls and their mother, "Marmee," depict the archetypal aspects of nineteenth-century womanhood based upon the Cult of True Womanhood; their attendant spiritual struggle in an age of rising consumerism represents the conflict of an idealistic middle class with the rising materialism of urban and industrial Victorian America. Moreover, Alcott has woven the national work ethic into the fabric of *Little Women*'s plot and themes. Therefore, this unimpeachably respectable story about Victorian girls who are becoming women contains the subversive message that economic self-sufficiency and independence were as important for women's social and personal integrity as for men's.

An underlying theme of the inherent contradictions within the Cult of True Womanhood between women's self-esteem and their obligatory obedience and self-sacrifice is most apparent in Jo's struggle for autonomy, which avoids a direct challenge to the patriarchial authority of her father and the circumscribing influence of her strongest role model, Marmee. Marmee represents the fulfillment of True Womanhood as she bravely and resourcefully bears the economic consequences of her husband's patriotic voluntary service in the military as well as her additional homefront duties. The daughters represent the development of True Womanhood despite differing female temperaments, which must be overcome to achieve Marmee's ideal. The oldest of the daughters, Meg, displays the traits of an ordinary and conventional girl who struggles against her vanity and susceptibility to the materialism of her peers both before and after her marriage to John Brooke, while the second-born, Jo, is a tomboy and incipient author for whom the transition into womanhood means constantly coming to terms with the limitations of the gender system in general and of Woman's Sphere in particular. Her next younger sister, Beth, presents the dilemma of a domestic femininity that is too pure to survive beyond the family sphere in the real world, and the youngest daughter, Amy, represents the adaptive and ambitious girlhood of the family "princess."

In the allegorical Part I, all four March girls confront the challenge of maintaining their middle-class life-style and values in the reduced circumstances of their now all-female household. Their contact with the all-male inhabitants of the "palace Beautiful" of their wealthy neighbors, the Laurences, draws them beyond their domestic circle and provides contrast between the genteel but enriched poverty of the March women and the wealth of their next-door neighbor Mr. Laurence and his grandson, "Laurie," which does not ensure the men's happiness or contentment. The girls learn one moral lesson after another under the watchful and guiding presence of Marmee, so that in this one year's time each daughter has confronted and acknowledged her major character flaw. When Marmee is called away from the domestic circle to the front to nurse the wounded Mr. March, the girls face the critical illness of Beth that is resolved by Marmee's return, which assures her recovery. Part I ends with the family circle completed as the convalescent Mr. March also returns, but Meg's engagement to Laurie's tutor, John Brooke, marks the end of girlhood for all the daughters.

Beginning three years later with Meg's wedding, Part II abandons the allegorical approach and presents a standard plot that charts the four girls' entry into womanhood. Meg's struggle with domesticity and caring for her twins, Daisy and Demi, parallels Jo's conflict with romance and career. In flight from the former and pursuit of the latter, Jo goes to New York as a governess and writes trashy thrillers for the "penny dreadfuls," cheap commercial adventure periodicals, until her new friend, Professor Bhaer, persuades her to eschew writing vulgar but quickly profitable sensational short stories in order to apply her talent to a work worthy of her. The death of Beth marks a turning point for Jo and Amy. The second part lacks the happy and completed ending of the first, but leaves Marmee satisfied that her surviving daughters have become True Women and are well married.

Little Women defies and challenges classification as a simple children's book because it offers a surprisingly sophisticated critique of the expectations of womanhood in the nineteenth and twentieth centuries. A female Peter Pan, the central character, Jo, resists the constraints of both girlhood and imminent womanhood, but in the end she does not escape her womanly destiny of marriage and domesticity.

—*Angela Howard Zophy*

See Also:

Alcott, Abby May; Alcott, Louisa May; Cult of True Womanhood; *Work: A Story of Experience*

References:

Alcott, Louisa May. *Little Women*. Boston: Robert Brothers, 1868, 1869.

———. *Little Women*. Introduction by Madelon Bedell. New York: Modern Library, 1983.

LIVERMORE, MARY ASHTON (RICE) (1820–1905), reformer and woman's rights leader, is best remembered today for her work on behalf of Civil War soldiers. An agent of the Northwestern Department of the U.S. Sanitary Commission, she was skilled at cutting through red tape to secure needed supplies for the troops. While on an inspection tour of hospitals and camps along the Mississippi River, Livermore and her co-worker Jane Hoge found early symptoms of scurvy near Vicksburg, Mississippi. The two women traveled north, and after making repeated appeals for help, secured huge quantities of potatoes and onions to feed the troops. In addition to her hospital inspection tours, Livermore traveled extensively to Northern towns encouraging women to set up soldier's aid societies. In 1863 she organized the Northwestern Sanitary Fair in Chicago. The first of several metropolitan fund-raisers to aid Northern troops, this fair netted close to $100,000.

Born and educated in Boston, Livermore became active in the abolition movement as a young woman after serving as governess to a slave-owning Virginia family. Marriage to Daniel P. Livermore, a Universalist minister, led her to settle in Chicago. Together, the Livermores edited a reform newspaper. After the war she joined the lyceum circuit as a speaker to local reading and self-improvement groups, giving popular orations on such topics as "Women of the War" and "What Shall We Do with Our Daughters?". She published her wartime reminiscences, *My Story of the War*, in 1887, and later wrote *The Story of My Life* (1897).

Livermore was an active participant in the late-nineteenth-century temperance and woman's suffrage movements. She joined with Lucy Stone, Henry Ward Beecher, and others in founding the American Woman Suffrage Association, serving as its vice president and editor of the organization's Boston-based newspaper, the *Woman's Journal*.

—*Wendy F. Hamand*

See Also:

American Woman Suffrage Association, Civil War, U.S. Sanitary Commission, *Woman's Journal*

References:

Brockett, L. P., and Mary C. Vaughan. *Woman's Work in the Civil War*. Chicago: Zeigler, McCurdy, 1868.

Livermore, Mary A. *My Story of the War.* Hartford: A. D. Worthington, 1889.
Stanton, Elizabeth Cady, Susan B. Anthony, and Matilda J. Gage. *History of Woman Suffrage.* 6 vols. Rochester, N.Y.: Charles Mann, 1886.

LOCKWOOD, BELVA ANN BENNETT McNALL (1830–1917) became in 1879 the first woman attorney to practice before the U.S. Supreme Court. The honor was not easily won. Several law schools to which Lockwood applied refused to accept women; and after completing her course of study, she had to demand of the school's ex-officio president that her diploma be awarded. Barred from pleading cases before the federal Court of Claims and the Supreme Court, Lockwood successfully lobbied Congress for legislation admitting women lawyers to the nation's highest courts. She later bravely demonstrated her commitment to equality for all by championing the first southern black lawyer to argue before the Supreme Court.

Lockwood began her career as a teacher in western New York, was married to a farmer in 1848 and widowed in 1853, resumed teaching, and moved to Washington, D.C., in 1866, where she opened a private school and remarried. After obtaining her law degree at the age of forty-three, she made her reputation by specializing in claims against the federal government. In 1906 she won a historic $5 million settlement for the Eastern Cherokees.

A staunch supporter of women's rights and universal suffrage, Lockwood lectured widely and worked tirelessly for legal reforms. In 1884 and 1888 she ran for the presidency of the United States on the National Equal Rights party ticket. Her campaign, although mocked by the general public and opposed by Susan B. Anthony and other prominent suffragists, called voters' attention to the pressing issues of suffrage, temperance, and peace. In the late 1880s Lockwood turned her efforts toward world affairs, assuming leadership posts in the Universal Peace Union and advocating arbitration as a solution to international conflict.

—*Susan E. Searing*

See Also:

Legal Profession, Politics, Suffrage

Reference:

Sterne, Madeleine B. *We the Women: Career Firsts of Nineteenth-Century America.* New York: Lenox Hill, 1962. (Includes extensive information on primary sources.)

LONGWORTH, ALICE ROOSEVELT (1884–1980) was the daughter of Theodore Roosevelt and Alice (Lee) Roosevelt, whose families were prominent in New York and Boston. Alice's mother died at the time of her birth, and she was raised by a paternal aunt, but she was always close to her father and rejoined the family circle after her father's second marriage. As Theodore Roosevelt's star rose in the political firmament, so did that of "Princess Alice," who reflected her father's popularity. Alice was highly intelligent, fiercely independent, and much attracted to public notice. Like her father, she was endowed with enormous energy. Because she was a maverick, active politics had no place for her, and she had no time for conventional politics. Society had a stronger appeal, and in this sense she was very much part of her environment: chic New York and fashionable Back Bay.

In 1906 she married Nicholas Longworth, a member of Congress from a prominent Cincinnati family. The Longworth connection gained her access to the councils of the Republican party after her father's death, and her husband rose to be Speaker of the House of Representatives. With her husband's death in 1931, she came into her own: a member of the board of councillors of the Women's Division of the Republican party (1932), a delegate to the Republican National Convention (1936), and a member of the America First Committee (1940). Meanwhile, she became an immensely quotable critic of both President Franklin Roosevelt, a distant kinsman, and his wife, Eleanor, her first cousin, but her writings in general were negative, and she made little if any positive contribution to American politics or government.

With advancing age, she became a grand dame of Washington society, lionized by the press, the guest of presidents, and the mother hen of the capital coop. In this latter role, she took on a glow; even New Dealers forgave her blind opposition to Franklin and Eleanor, and for the last two decades of her life, she was treated like a national institution.

—D. H. Burton

See Also:

Republican Party; Roosevelt, Eleanor

References:

Felsenthal, Carol. *Princess Alice: The Life and Times of Alice Roosevelt Longworth.* New York: St. Martin's, 1988.

Longworth, Alice Roosevelt. *Crowded Hours.* 1933; rpt. New York: Arno, 1980.

———. *Mrs. L. Conversations With Alice Roosevelt Longworth.* Garden City, N.Y.: Doubleday, 1981.

The **LOOM** has been used to weave fabric since ancient times, and its use did not change dramatically until the eighteenth century. In 1733 John Kay developed the automatically operated fly shuttle, and in 1785 Edmund Cartwright invented the power loom. These advances were followed by the Jacquard attachment, which used perforated cards to aid in the control of warp threads. All of these inventions greatly increased the productivity of the loom and contributed in no small part to the industrialization of the process of weaving.

The significance of the loom for women in the United States is considerable and begins in the New England mill towns of the early nineteenth century. During the 1820s and 1830s textile mills sprang up across New England wherever there was the prerequisite water supply. Employment in such mills was considered an excellent opportunity for young, unmarried women to earn money. Francis Cabot Lowell pioneered the American textile industry by promoting the idea of women factory workers in the mills.

Young single women were the best candidates for this work since they were already skilled in cloth making; men were needed for farm work, and married women had domestic responsibilities. Mill operators demanded twelve to thirteen hours a day on the loom from these young women and required at least a one-year commitment to the mill. There was no shortage of women to fill the ranks of loom workers. Typically, these women were trying to earn money of their own before marriage or sought to escape the narrow confines of their family life and secure some measure of personal independence. The mill workers generally earned $1.25 per week for board and a salary of fifty-five cents per week, which could be supplemented by doing extra piecework. In the 1830s this was considered the best wages a woman could hope to earn in the American economy.

In the mill towns, women were housed in dormitories and were closely supervised. The work day typically began at 5:00 A.M. and continued until dusk, with two half-hour breaks for meals. Girls, sometimes aged ten and under, were "doffers," replacing used bobbins; teenagers and adults worked as spinners and weavers directly on the looms. Early on, women were not pushed severely on the job, since most of them were "Yankee" women, and the public had to be shown that work in the mills would not destroy the moral fiber or physical health of New England's future mothers. As the worker pool began to change, especially after the 1840s, when mass Irish immigration brought many Irish immigrant women to the mills and as the mills themselves began to expand, less attention was paid to the working and living conditions of these women. Work at the loom thus became less appealing, less lucrative, and considerably more difficult for the women who were employed in the textile industry. Women were eventually required to attend more than one loom (sometimes as many as four) singlehandedly.

Meanwhile, new advances in the loom technology (specifically the crank-driven loom) speeded up production but also increased noise, heat, and the dangerous accumulation of lint within the mills. As production went up, wages fell, and the "premium system" was introduced whereby employers could get still more work out of the loom operators by offering bonuses for productivity. By 1840 women could be fired from loom work for any number of violations, including hysteria, exhibiting overcautiousness, impudent behavior, or disobedience. Women protested such developments and staged periodic walkouts to combat the abuses inherent in mill work by 1850.

—*Maureen Anna Harp*

See Also:

Industrial Revolution; Lowell Mill Girls; Textile Industries, Northern and Southern

References:

Abbott, Edith. *Women in Industry: A Study in American Economic History*. New York: Appleton, 1919.

Baker, Elizabeth Faulkner. *Technology and Women's Work in America*. New York: Columbia University Press, 1959.

Butler, Elizabeth Beardsley. *Women and the Trades*. New York: Charities Publication Committee, 1909.

Dublin, Thomas. *Women at Work: The Transformation of Work and Community in Lowell, Massachusetts*. New York: Columbia University Press, 1981.

Manning, Caroline. *The Immigrant Woman and Her Job*. New York: Arno, 1970.

LORDE, AUDRE (b. 1934), poet, essayist, lecturer, and author of several books, including *The First Cities, Sister Outsider, Between Ourselves, The Cancer Journals, The Black Unicorn*, and *Zambi: A New Spelling of My Name*. Lorde is a black lesbian feminist who writes and speaks in ways that give voice to the similarities and differences of all people, particularly women. Her perspectives on a myriad of sexual and social justice issues enable the people of her audience to reconsider the connections she says exist inside themselves, connections between thinking and feeling. When realized, these internal connections carry people into new relationships with one another, breaking down the barriers that pervade twentieth-century society.

The mother of two, Lorde found her life dramatically altered by the discovery that she had cancer and her ultimate victory over it. She has written openly about her encounter with the possibility of death and her new freedom as a result of her struggle, the freedom being a fruit of her subsequent wholeness.

As a teacher, Lorde has instructed her students to claim every aspect of themselves and encourages them to discover the power of a spirited wholeness, knowing that in silence there is no growth, in suppression there is no personal satisfaction. The intensity of her honesty seems intimidating at times. Yet it is her honesty, her self-respect, and her courage that profoundly affect the relationships and lives of her readers and students.

—*Joanne S. Richmond*

See Also:

Black Women, Lesbianism

References:

Koolish, Lynda. "This Is Who She Is to Me." In *Between Women*, edited by Carol Ascher, Louise DeSalvo, and Sara Ruddick. Boston: Beacon, 1984, pp. 113–36.

Lorde, Audre. *Between Ourselves*. Point Reyes, Calif.: Eidolon Editions, 1976.

———. *The Black Unicorn*. New York: Norton, 1978.

———. *The Cancer Journals*. Argyle, N.Y.: Spinsters Ink, 1980.

———. *The First Cities*. New York: Poets' Press, 1968.

———. *Sister/Outsider*. Introduction by Nancy Bereano. Trumansburg, N.Y.: The Crossing Press, 1984.

———. *Zambi: A New Spelling of My Name*. Watertown, Mass.: Persephone, 1982.

LOW, JULIETTE (1860–1927), the founder of the Girl Scouts in America, was born in Chicago, Illinois. Christened Juliette Magill Kinzie for her grandmother, she was always called Daisy by family and close friends. On her mother's side, she was descended from a well-known family influential in the founding of Chicago. Her father's family was prominent in Savannah, Georgia, where her grandfather was mayor for many years, and Low always considered herself to be a southerner. She was educated at several private boarding schools, first in Savannah, then at Stuart Hall and Edge Hall in Virginia, and finally at Madame Charbonnier's school in New York. Low excelled in languages and history, but her first love was art.

Her schooling and her family training prepared her for the role expected of most well-to-do young women of her time—wife and mother. In 1882, after her social debut in Savannah, Low made her first trip to Europe and met her future husband William Mackey Low, who was from a wealthy English family with business interests in Savannah. Apparently fearing disapproval from her parents, she kept the nature of their relationship a secret but finally gained family approval and married in 1894. The marriage proved to be very unhappy, and the Lows were in the middle of divorce proceedings in 1905 when he died. Although he had apparently meant to leave her very little in his will, Low inherited enough money to ensure a comfortable life. For several years after the death of her husband, Low led a very social existence, traveling back and forth between Savannah and Europe and studying sculpture, at which she was quite talented. Although her life was full of activity, she was depressed and unfulfilled: She thought she had failed as a wife and regretted never having had children.

In 1908 she met Sir Robert Baden-Powell, a well-known English general who had recently founded the Boy Scouts and whose sister Agnes headed the girls' branch, the Girl Guides. Low was quite taken with the idea of an organization for young girls and soon formed a troop near her country estate in Scotland. In 1912 she started the first Girl Guide troop in the United States in Savannah. During its first year the name was changed to Girl Scouts to match that of the organization for American boys, the Boy Scouts. Low spent the rest of her life working with the organization, giving her a purpose in life and the children she had always wanted. Much of the early success of the Girl Scouts can be attributed to Low's hard work, friendships, and contacts. After several years of active involvement with the Girl Scouts, she resigned the presidency, turned control over to the National Girl Scout Board, and confined her active involvement to her work as U.S. representative to the International Council of Girl Guides and Girl Scouts.

Enthusiastic by nature, she was often able to convince women to assist in the organization through her charm and strong personality. She had a great sense of fun and was known in Savannah as a person who would try anything. Stories of her escapades sometimes made her seem somewhat eccentric, but she was also thoughtful, kind, and a favorite among members of her large family. Low was also known as an entertaining conversationalist, a skill she developed partly to cover up the fact that she suffered from a rather severe hearing loss since adolescence and often did not hear what others were saying. Low died in Savannah after a battle with cancer that she managed to keep secret from family and friends until near the end.

—Judith Pryor

See Also:

Girl Scouts of America

References:

Schultz, Gladys, and Daisy Gordon Lawrence. *Lady from Savannah: The Life of Juliette Low.* Philadelphia: Lippincott, 1958.

Strickland, Charles E. "Juliette Low, the Girl Scouts, and the Role of American Women." In *Woman's Being, Woman's Place: Female Identity and Vocation in American History,* edited by Mary Kelley. Boston: G. K. Hall, 1977, pp. 252–64.

The **LOWELL FEMALE INDUSTRIAL REFORM AND MUTUAL AID SOCIETY (LFIRMAS)** was a transformation in January 1847 of an earlier organization of the Lowell mill girls, the Lowell Female Labor Reform Association (LFLRA).

The Female Labor Reform Association was a short-lived labor union organized in 1845 by native-born female operatives in the textile mills of Lowell, Massachusetts. Self-respecting daughters of independent New England farmers, these first-generation female factory workers lived collectively under the paternalistic supervision of factory owners and created a strong sense of solidarity based on their homogeneous backgrounds, their common work and living arrangements, and their shared pride in economic independence. That solidarity served as the basis of union organization in the 1830s when factory owners imposed wage cuts, speedups, and extended hours. In 1845, after sporadic protests, the women organized the Lowell Female Labor Reform Association under the leadership of Sarah Bagley.

The LFLRA was one of the earliest permanent women's labor organizations in the United States. By circulating petitions, dispatching organizers throughout New England, publishing the *Voice of Industry*, a labor weekly, and testifying before legislative committees, the Association recruited hundreds of members and commanded public support for state action on working conditions. Members also participated in the New England Workingmen's Association and supported other reform movements such as economic cooperatives and woman's rights.

By the late 1840s expansion and mechanization of production and the introduction of low-paid immigrant labor transformed and degraded mill work, eroding the basis of labor organization and turning unmarried native-born women to alternative occupations.

As the new organization of female operatives in the Lowell textile mills, the Lowell Female Industrial Reform and Mutual Aid Society was less reformist and stressed practical knowledge and the care of the poor and ill. Article 2 of its constitution emphasized that members should know and respect their rights as women and be prepared to maintain them. Mary Emerson was elected president, and Huldah Stone was elected secretary. However, this organization lacked the spirit and drive of the LFLRA under Sarah Bagley. Little is known of its activities except for weekly announcements in the *Voice of Industry* of its meetings through 1847, as New England girls were steadily being replaced by the poverty-stricken Irish immigrant girls who were willing to work long hours under speedup conditions for a noncommensurate wage. By 1850, 50 percent of the mill girls were Irish immigrants, who were less likely to organize. Although petitions continued to be sent regularly to the state legislature, the era of the Lowell Female Industrial Reform and Mutual Aid Society indicated that the high hopeful days of the labor-reform movement of the 1840s were over. Yet this new mutual-aid society performed a useful service in its ministrations to the sick and needy.

—*Joyce Follet and Virginia Beattie Mattes*

See Also:

Bagley, Sarah; Lowell Mill Girls

References:

Dublin, Thomas. *Women at Work: The Transformation of Work and Community in Lowell, Massachusetts, 1826–1860.* New York: Columbia University Press, 1979.

Early, Frances H. "A Reappraisal of the New England Labour-Reform Movement of the 1840s: The Lowell Female Labor Reform Association and the New England Workingmen's Association." *Histoire Sociale (Canada)* 13 (1980): 33–54.

Josephson, Hannah. *The Golden Threads: New England's Mill Girls and Magnates.* New York: Duell, Sloan and Pearce, 1949.

Robinson, Harriet Hanson. *Loom and Spindle; or Life Among the Early Mill Girls.* New York: Crowell, 1898.

Voice of Industry. 1845–1848.

Ware, Caroline F. *The Early New England Cotton Manufacture; A Study in Industrial Beginnings.* Boston: Houghton Mifflin, 1931.

The **LOWELL MILL GIRLS** constituted the first large-scale involvement of women in a factory system in the United States beginning in the 1830s and are therefore an integral part of women's history. In this early period, labor was in short supply due to westward expansion, a largely rural population, and the stigma attached to factory work. The Lowell, Massachusetts, mill owners were ingenious in planning a system with all facets of cloth manufacture under one roof and also in solving their labor problem by recruiting young New England farm girls of the same stock as themselves. The well-supervised, adjacent boarding houses for the girls, a lending library, a lyceum lecture series, diverse churches, wages paid in cash, and a bank for saving—all appealed to these pious and thrifty girls. The socialization, independence, and "esprit de corps" derived from their respectable adventure in Lowell heightened their awareness of their abilities and resulted in "Improvement Circles" and a flowering of creativity in their poems and articles for the *Lowell Offering*, a periodical created to demonstrate the intellectual capabilities of the mill girls.

Lowell became a world-famous town in the early nineteenth century, not only because of its efficient mill operations in juxtaposition to the Rhode Island and English systems—where makeshift villages sprang up near the mills and whole families existed on the meagre wages of children—but also because of the uncommon mill girls. The hard-working Lowell mill girls with their thirst for education and culture attracted the attention of notable foreign visitors such as Charles Dickens and Harriet Martineau, as well as congressmen, senators, and three presidents of the United States, and elicited the praise of native-born Nathaniel Hawthorne.

The Lowell mills were located on the border of the states of Massachusetts and New Hampshire at the juncture of the Concord and Merrimack rivers, where the thirty-foot Pawtucket Falls provided ample power. Construction of the mills began in 1822. The first Lowell mill had its genesis in the Waltham, Massachusetts, mill, which was established by the Boston Manufacturing Company in 1813. The Waltham or boardinghouse concept was the ingenious idea of Francis Cabot Lowell, an exporter turned entrepreneur, who wished to avoid the deteriorating conditions of the Rhode Island and English systems. At Waltham, and later at Lowell, young women worked on the roving and spinning frames, drawing in the warps and tending the looms. Men worked mainly as overseers, machinists, or mechanics, or in occupations such as calico printing, which required a specific skill.

The Lowell mills prospered in the early years, not only because of their efficient operations, abundant power from Pawtucket Falls, and adequate capital from risk-taking investors, but also because of a ready source of labor. Unlike the working-class mill girls in Rhode Island and England, many of the Lowell girls wished to further their brothers' higher education or to augment family income. Their motivation was not only financial independence but also educational opportunities.

The Lowell idyll began to unravel in the mid-1830s, when increased competition in the textile industry brought decreased wages, loom speedups, additional looms per worker, and less time for intellectual pursuits even before the panic of 1837, which brought on a national economic depression. Unsuccessful strikes initiated by female operatives in 1834 and 1836 reflected the concerted efforts of the mill women to instill a group consciousness and indicated a level of cooperation and determination that eventually propelled them to testify before the state legislature for a ten-hour day.

The first Lowell strike occurred after an announcement in February 1834 that wages paid in some departments would be cut by 15 percent. According to the February 20, 1834 *Boston Transcript*, the female operatives who were mainly affected by this cut held several meetings and decided to strike and "make a run" on the factory savings bank. The young woman leading the revolt was thereupon dismissed by the mill agent; but, upon leaving the mill, she led some eight hundred mill girls in procession around the town. They issued the "Lowell Proclamation," which stated they would not return to work until their wage cuts had been restored. The *Boston Transcript* indicated that the marchers were looked upon with amusement. They walked out on a Saturday, attended church on Sunday, and on Monday all returned to work except those who had gone home to their families. The wage cuts took effect on March 1, 1834, with no further opposition.

The next strike had different causes and results. In 1836 the mill girls' average salary consisted of $2.00 per week plus board. By arrangement with the corporation, a board fee of $1.25 was taken out of each worker's total pay of $3.25 at the counting houses. Because of a sharp rise in the cost of living, the boardinghouse-keepers could barely make ends meet. The corporation therefore lowered the rent charged housekeepers for the company-owned houses by twelve and a half cents per boarder and correspondingly increased the amount deducted from the girls' wages by the same amount. This resulted in a 6 percent wage cut, and the girls went on strike. During this month-long strike, they were evicted from the boarding houses and had no funds for their livelihood. They either returned to the mill or their farm homes.

A decade later, in the spring of 1846, one of the Lowell mills announced that the weavers would be required to tend four looms instead of three and that wages would be reduced one cent per piece. A meeting of the Lowell Female Labor Reform Association (LFLRA), a short-lived union organized by the workers in 1845, resulted in a pledge that an increased workload would not be accepted without a corresponding increase in wages. Virtually all of the women weavers signed the pledge and stuck to it. The speedup was canceled. The LFLRA had succeeded in directing the female operatives from fruitless strikes to an alternative tactic. This isolated incident only involved the women weavers at one mill, but it foreshadowed the organizing efforts, fortitude, and persistence of the early labor feminists, which ultimately earned them a ten-hour day in 1874.

The New England mill girls were eventually replaced in the mid-1840s by Irish immigrants who were willing to work for lower wages, but not before they tirelessly and valiantly fought for a ten-hour day under the leadership of Sarah Bagley and other LFLRA members, whose motto was Try Again. Sarah Bagley's incendiary speeches and articles, which were published in the *Voice of Industry*, a labor weekly, as well as articles of other mill girls, lifted the Lowell girls out of women's sphere of silence.

The flowering of the Waltham experiment in Lowell, with its benevolent paternalism, did not make a lasting contribution to labor. However, the extraordinary Lowell mill girls' thirst for knowledge and culture and their subsequent battle for the ten-hour day earned them a permanent place in social and labor history.

—*Virginia Beattie Mattes*

See Also:

Bagley, Sarah; Loom; Lowell Female Industrial Reform and Mutual Aid Society; *Lowell Offering*; Textile Industries, Northern and Southern; *Voice of Industry*

References:

Adickes, Sandra. "Mind Among the Spindles: An Examination of Some of the Journals, Newspapers, and Memoirs of the Lowell Female Operatives." *Women's Studies* 1 (1973): 279–87.

Dublin, Thomas. *Women at Work, The Transformation of Work and Community in Lowell, Massachusetts, 1826–1860*. New York: Columbia University Press, 1979.

Eisler, Benita, ed. *The Lowell Offering: Writings by New England Mill Women (1840–1845)*. Philadelphia: Lippincott, 1977.

Flexner, Eleanor. *Century of Struggle: The Woman's Rights Movement in the United States*. New York: Atheneum, 1959.

Josephson, Hannah. *The Golden Threads, New England's Mill Girls and Magnates*. New York: Duell, Sloan and Pearce, 1949.

Papachristou, Judith. *Women Together: A History in Documents of the Women's Movement in the U.S.* New York: Knopf, 1976.

Robinson, Harriet H. *Loom and Spindle*. 1898; rpt. Kailua, Hawaii: Press Pacifica, 1976.

Thompson, Agnes L. "New England Mill Girls." *New England Galaxy* 16 (1974): 43–49.

Ware, Caroline. *The Early New England Cotton Manufacture: A Study in Industrial Beginnings*. Boston: Houghton Mifflin, 1931.

Wright, Helena. "The Uncommon Mill Girls of Lowell." *History Today* 23 (1973): 10–19.

The ***LOWELL OFFERING*** (1840–45) was a periodical written by women operatives in the Lowell textile mills. Developed from modest collections of writings from workers' self-improvement societies, the *Offering* became an ambitious testimonial to the capacities of young Yankee women who left their homes to work in the mills and live in the boardinghouses established by their paternalistic employers.

Edited by A. C. Thomas (1840–42) and Harriet Farley (1842–45), a mill worker, the *Offering* contained a diverse range of poems, essays on scientific and moral subjects, translations, and stories. Farley saw her principal purpose as removing the stigma attached to factory laborers by showing them equal, in terms of intellectual accomplishments, to young women anywhere. The *Offering* was read by mill operatives, though perhaps less by them than by the inhabitants of surrounding communities and by a national and international audience interested in Lowell as a social experiment and in the *Offering* as a unique phenomenon. While some early readers questioned whether writing of competence and dignity could be the work of mill girls, such cultural bastions as the *North American Review* eventually gave the periodical a stamp of interested, if condescending, approval. A selection of *Offering* contributions appeared in book form as *Mind Amongst the Spindles* (1844).

As economic pressure on the mills increased in the 1840s, the owners abandoned much of their previous benevolent paternalism, reducing wages and forcing increased production. The Lowell Female Labor Reform Association attempts to organize the mills brought Farley into conflict with those who wanted the *Offering* to represent the interests of mill operatives rather than mill owners. Farley refused to change the magazine's focus or to include any discussion of current conditions in the mills. Subscriptions declined, and the *Lowell Offering* ceased publication in 1845.

After its demise, the magazine was resurrected as the *New England Offering* (1847–50), which retained the general character of the original periodical but expanded its contributors beyond the Lowell workers.

—*Carol Klimick Cyganowski*

See Also:

Farley, Harriet; Lowell Mill Girls

References:

Adickes, Sandra. "Mind Among the Spindles: An Examination of Some of the Journals, Newspapers, and Memoirs of the Lowell Female Operatives." *Women's Studies* 1 (1973): 279–87.

Dublin, Thomas. *Women at Work: The Transformation of Work and Community in Lowell, Massachusetts, 1826–1860.* New York: Columbia University Press, 1979.

Eisler, Benita, ed. *The Lowell Offering: Writings by New England Mill Women (1840–45).* Philadelphia: Lippincott, 1977.

Robinson, Harriet Hanson. *Loom and Spindle, or Life Among the Early Mill Girls. With a Sketch of "The Lowell Offering" and Some of its Contributors.* New York: Crowell, 1898; rpt. Kailua, Hawaii: Press Pacifica, 1976.

LUHAN, MABEL DODGE (1879–1962), writer, patron of the arts, and political activist, was a woman ahead of her time who inspired and gathered around her artists and writers both in Europe and in America, and who had an eye for artistic trends. In Florence, Italy, from 1904 to 1912 she helped her architect husband, Edwin S. Dodge, to renovate Villa Curonia, where an international group of literati (including André Gide and Gertrude Stein) gathered to discuss matters of art and life. After she had moved to New York City late in 1912, partly as a way of separating from her husband (whom she divorced in 1916), she again attracted the avant-garde to her Greenwich Village apartment for weekly sessions. These sessions were more formal and more politically oriented than those in Florence, as Luhan and her cohorts became involved in workers' rights. In particular, she suggested and helped to organize the Patterson Strike Pageant held on June 7, 1913, at Madison Square Garden and designed to dramatize the plight of immigrant silk workers in New Jersey. The event was considered a theatrical success, with over fifteen thousand in attendance, although it did not resolve worker/owner tensions. In the same year she helped arrange the Armory Show in New York, which introduced many Americans to modernist art and which revolutionized the art world in America thereafter.

Following her marriage to painter Lawrence Sterne in 1917, Luhan moved with him to Taos, New Mexico, where she remained until her death. Once again, art and politics commingled as she embraced Indian causes, particularly the Pueblo Indians' eleven-year struggle to maintain their land and traditions. Helping to reactivate the Pueblos' Council of All the New Mexico Pueblos, she played a crucial role in preventing the Bursam Bill (which had then passed in the United States Senate) from becoming law. This bill, if enacted, would have allowed for the transfer of Indian land to squatters, while it would also have prohibited Indian religious activities. Her marriage to an Indian, Antonio Lujan (she spelled it with an *h*), in 1923, following her divorce from Sterne, reflected her intimate involvement with Pueblo life.

Luhan's several marriages (including her first marriage in 1900 to Karl Kellog Evans, who died in a hunting accident shortly thereafter), as well as her several affairs, attest to her restlessness as well as her vitality, which became legendary. Those luminaries who were drawn to her in New York and then in Taos included Marsden Hartley, Jo Davidson, Max Eastman, Carl Van Vechten, Robinson Jeffers, Thorton Wilder, D. H. Lawrence, and Georgia O'Keeffe. Admirers of Luhan saw her as an exciting listener who generated new ideas in others, and they also recognized her own considerable talent as a writer, particularly as an informal "historian" of twentieth century cultural and political life. Her works include her *Intimate Memoirs* (four volumes, 1933–37) and accounts of Taos life, including *Lorenzo in Taos* (about D. H. Lawrence, 1932), *Winter in Taos* (1935), and *Taos and its Artists* (1947). Luhan appreciated the gentler life of Taos although, even there, she continued to battle the depression that plagued her throughout her life. Her writing helped her to counteract this depression and also reveals how Luhan, a complicated individual who creatively resisted the status quo, inspired and sometimes coalesced the cultural and social leaders of her day.

—Linda Patterson Miller

See Also:
Art

References:

Luhan Collection. The Beinecke Rare Book and Manuscript Library. Yale University, New Haven, Conn.

Hahn, Emily. *Mabel: A Biography of Mabel Dodge Luhan.* Boston: Houghton Mifflin, 1977.

Luhan, Mabel Dodge. *Intimate Memories.* 4 vols. New York: Harcourt Brace, 1933–37.

Sterne, Maurice. *Shadow and Light: The Life, Friends and Opinions of Maurice Stern.* New York: Harcourt Brace, 1965.

LUPINO, IDA (b. 1918), film actress and director, has bristled at the label "feminist filmmaker" during the course of several interviews. Yet, as the only woman to direct a large body of work in the American commercial cinema during the 1950s, and as an innovative director of dozens of television-series episodes and pilots, she is at least the major role model of her time for women seeking to enter the film and television industries.

Lupino was born in England in 1918, the scion of a famous acting family. After being educated at the Royal Academy of Dramatic Art, she was brought to Hollywood in 1933 as an ingenue. After critical acclaim in several roles at Paramount Studios from 1934 to 1939, she was under contract as an actress at Warner Bros. from 1939 to 1947. At a studio that was tailoring its product to female audiences, Lupino, along with Olivia DeHavilland, Bette Davis, and Joan Crawford, starred in contemporary and period melodramas focusing on women in crisis. Considered one of Hollywood's best actresses by critics and the public, she found the life unsatisfying and restrictive, and in 1949 formed The Filmmakers, an independent production company, with her then-husband, Collier Young. Thereafter, she co-wrote, directed, acted in and/or produced several films. In 1959 she turned to television, directing episodes of *Alfred Hitchcock Presents, Thriller, The Twilight Zone*, and many others.

Made between the years 1949 and 1954, Ida Lupino's eight productions associated with

The Filmmakers, plus two others she acted in and strongly influenced the direction of, show Lupino to have been *very much* a feminist filmmaker. Films such as *Hard, Fast, and Beautiful* (1951), *The Bigamist* (1953), and *The Hitchhiker* (1953) reveal a powerful critique of consumerism and home/career confrontations. Full of expressionistic, passionate characters giving cynical opinions about social mores and the economic aspect of intimate relationships, the films use narrative modes typified by a cold, objective viewpoint on characters. This modernist tendency, avoiding traditional Hollywood empathetic devices that encouraged identification with individual, suffering characters, was undoubtedly what alienated contemporary critics. (The reputation that would logically accrue to Lupino in such a hostile critical climate may in fact be responsible for her reluctance to identify herself as the feminist she demonstrably is.)

Lupino's case as an *auteur* was first championed by the *Cahiers du Cinema* group of critics in France in the 1950s, which included a young François Truffaut. However, it was the group of feminist critics loosely associated with the British Film Institute and *Screen* magazine in the early 1970s who first prized Lupino's work as distinctively feminist. Her vision of the tragic self-loathing involved in contemporary women's identity, these critics recognized, is often repulsive in its aspect, but also presents a cogent critique of these same conditions.

—*Kevin Jack Hagopian*

See Also:

Movie Stars, The Woman's Film

References:

Johnston, Claire, ed. *Notes on Women's Cinema*. London: Society for Education in Film and Television, n.d.

Lupino, Ida. "Me, Mother Directress." In *Hollywood Directors: 1941–1976*, edited by Richard Koszarski. New York: Oxford University Press, 1977, pp. 371–77.

———. "New Faces in New Places". *Films in Review* 1 (1950): 17–19.

Weiner, Debra. "Interview with Ida Lupino." In *Women and the Cinema*, edited by Karyn Kay and Gerald Peary. New York: Dutton, 1977, pp. 169–78.

LUSK, GEORGIA LEE (WITT) (1893–1971), educator and politician, was the first woman from New Mexico to serve in the U.S. Congress.

Born on a ranch in New Mexico Territory, Lusk attended New Mexico State Teachers College (now Western New Mexico University). While teaching school, she married rancher Dolph Lusk, quit her job, and subsequently had three sons. Her husband died of a heart attack in 1919 when Lusk was only twenty-six, necessitating her reentry into the field of education. A desire to be an educational administrator led Lusk into the political arena, and she was elected superintendent of Lea County schools in 1924 and 1926. Her first statewide campaign in 1928 for the post of superintendent of public instruction was unsuccessful; a Democrat, Lusk lost in the landslide victory of President Herbert Hoover, a Republican.

Subsequently, Lusk won election to the state's top education post six times between 1930 and 1956, serving three four-year stints in that position: 1931–35, 1943–47, and 1955–59. She is generally credited with upgrading the quality of New Mexico's underfunded Depression-era schools. Lusk also pushed for tougher science and mathematics requirements for high school graduates in the wake of concern over the launching of the satellite "Sputnik" by the Soviet Union in 1957.

In 1946 Lusk captured one of New Mexico's two at-large seats in the U.S. House of Representatives. As a congresswoman, she advocated federal aid to education and benefits for veterans. (Her three sons all served in World War II, and the oldest, Virgil, was killed in a military plane crash.) Lusk was defeated for reelection to Congress in 1948, but was appointed to the War Claims Commission in 1949 by President Harry Truman. She served four years in this post, processing the reparation claims of Americans who had been prisoners of war or civilian internees during World War II.

Lusk retired from politics in 1959, when her last term as superintendent of public instruction ended. The acumen she exhibited during her thirty-five-year political career, which included victories in seven statewide campaigns, won Lusk the sobriquet of "the first lady of New Mexico politics."

—Roger D. Hardaway

See Also:
Democratic Party, Politics

References:

Hardaway, Roger D. "Georgia Lusk of New Mexico: A Political Biography." M.A. thesis. New Mexico State University, 1979.

———. "New Mexico Elects a Congresswoman." *Red River Valley Historical Review* 4 (Fall 1979): 75–89.

LYING-IN was a term used in early America to refer both to childbirth and to the period of recuperation that followed. The period of confinement implied by the term began with the onset of labor and ended when the new mother resumed her household duties. Depending upon what help was available to her and what her household responsibilities encompassed, a woman in the seventeenth and eighteenth centuries might be lying-in for as long as six weeks. Immediately after the child's birth, the mother would be bathed and "brought to bed," that is, moved into her bed, where she would be kept well covered and quiet for a few days. After three to six days, she would be allowed to sit up briefly. In the eighteenth century, among those with sufficient means, this period included "sitting up" visits by friends and well-wishers. Such visits typically included presents as well as exchanges of gossip and information about other births and other friends and relatives. By the time a new mother was ready for a walk or a ride in the open air, her confinement, her lying-in, had come to a close.

The notion of childbirth as a period of confinement that included recuperation and adjustment is reflected in the names given the institutions that arose in the nineteenth century to accommodate those women giving birth who were bereft of support or care. The New York Asylum for Lying-In Women, and the Lying-In Ward of the Pennsylvania Hospital in Philadelphia were two such institutions established early in the nineteenth century. Each acknowledged and provided for the social and familial/relational needs of women at childbirth, both those that preceded the birth and those that followed it. By the end of the nineteenth century and increasingly in the twentieth, however, the focus of childbirth in hospital lying-in wards was very medical. Each expectant mother was of interest principally during the delivery phase of her childbirth. As soon after giving birth as possible, the new mother was sent home. Rest and recuperation came at home if at all. The New York Asylum for Lying-In Women tried to maintain its tradition of caring for women during lying-in, but medical and financial exigencies forced it to merge in 1899 with a more medically oriented institution, the New York Infant Asylum. The concept of lying-in disappeared.

—Janet Carlisle Bogdan

See Also:
Childbirth, Midwifery

References:

Scholten, Catherine. *Childbearing in American Society, 1650–1850*. New York: New York University Press, 1986.

Wertz, Richard, and Dorothy Wertz. *Lying-In*. New York: Free Press, 1977.

LYTLE, LUTIE (c. 1871–?), born in Topeka, Kansas, became one of the first black women in the United States to practice law and allegedly the first to receive full accreditation. As a teenager she worked as a compositor in a printing office in Topeka, where she had access to newspaper exchanges from which she first learned about Kansas and national politics. In 1896 her father, John R. Lytle, a Topeka barber, ran successfully for the post of assistant city jailer and received the nomination for register of deeds from the Populist party in 1897. Lytle herself campaigned for the Populist party and was rewarded with a patronage job as assistant enrolling clerk in 1894, the only black woman to receive such a position from the Populist party.

A year after her appointment by the Populists, Lytle enrolled in the Central Tennessee Law College of Nashville, receiving a law degree and admission to the Tennessee Bar in 1897. She lived in Topeka for a short time after receiving her degree and then returned to her alma mater to teach law. After her marriage, Lytle and her husband moved to New Paltz, New York, where she continued to practice law.

—MaryJo Wagner

See Also:

Black Women, Legal Profession, Politics, Populist Party

References:

Colored Citizen (Topeka, Kansas). October 7, 1897.

Historical Preservation in Kansas: Black Historic Sites. Topeka: Kansas State Historical Society, 1977, p. 31.

Lerner, Gerda. *Black Women in White America.* New York: Vintage, 1973, p. 324.

Topeka (Kansas) *Capital.* September 15, 1897.

Topeka (Kansas) *State Ledger.* January 11, 1895.

McCARTHY, MARY (1912–89), novelist, essayist, critic, and journalist, was raised in Minneapolis. After graduating from Vassar College, she began publishing fiction. Her first success was *The Company She Keeps* (1942), a collection of satiric stories. McCarthy's widely acclaimed novels include: *The Groves of Academe* (1952), *A Charmed Life* (1955), and *Cannibals and Missionaries* (1979). Her novel *The Group* (1963), which probed the lives of well-educated, middle-class women, was made into a successful feature film. She has also written fine travel books such as *Venice Observed* (1956) and *The Stones of Florence* (1959) and astute essays on the Vietnam War and the so-called Watergate affair.

—*Jonathan W. Zophy*

See Also:
Vietnam War

References:

Gelderman, Carol. *Mary McCarthy: A Life*. New York: St. Martin's, 1988.
McCarthy, Mary. *Memories of a Catholic Girlhood*. New York: Harcourt Brace, 1957.
———. *The Seventeenth Degree*. New York: Harcourt Brace, 1974.

McCULLERS, CARSON (1917–67), author, was born Lula Carson Smith in Columbus, Georgia, the oldest of three children. When she was thirteen, McCullers dropped "Lula" from her name. Her mother, Marguerite, encouraged her to study the piano, believing that McCullers was destined to become a musical genius. An attack of rheumatic fever at fifteen, however, forced McCullers to abandon the study of music and turn to writing. She moved to New York City at the age of seventeen to study writing at Columbia University. In 1936 she again contracted rheumatic fever and was forced to return to Columbus. Two short stories, "Wonderkind" and "Like That," were published that year in *Story*. In 1937 she married Reeves McCullers.

In 1940, when she was twenty-three, her first novel, *The Heart is a Lonely Hunter*, was published, winning the young author literary acclaim. The book introduced the theme around which McCullers based all of her fiction, that of the individual's isolation and loneliness and inability to find redeeming love. Her fascination with the presence of evil and her use of deformed and abnormal characters earned her a place in the southern gothic school of literature. She and her husband moved to New York City, where in 1941 her novel *Reflections in a Golden Eye* was published. The book brought her fellowships from the Guggenheim Foundation, the Yaddo Colony, and the American Academy of Arts and Letters. Already present, tensions in the McCullers's marriage were compounded when she fell in love with Annmarie Clarac-Schwarzback, a Swiss writer, in 1941, and divorced her husband.

In February 1942 McCullers suffered the first of many strokes. Excessive drinking contributed to the steady decline of her health throughout her life. In 1944, "The Ballad of the Sad Cafe" was included in *Best American Short Stories*. In 1945 she and her former husband remarried. In 1946 her novel *The Member of the Wedding* was published, and McCullers won another Guggenheim. In 1947 she had a second stroke in Paris, partially paralyzing the right side of her body. She had another stroke a few months later, and was diagnosed as having a damaged rheumatic heart. In 1948 she and her husband separated again, and she attempted to commit suicide. In 1949 her dramatized version of *The Member of the Wedding* opened, starring Ethel Waters and Julie Harris. It received rave reviews and ran for fourteen-and-a-half months on Broadway. She and her husband reunited that year, but in 1953 he killed himself. In 1961 McCullers published *Clock Without Hands*, her last novel. In 1959, she had a heart attack, after which her health rapidly declined. In 1962 her right breast was removed. She died in 1967 from a final stroke.

In 1967 John Huston directed the film version of *Reflections in a Golden Eye. The Mortgaged Heart* was published posthumously in 1971, and *The Member of the Wedding* was produced as a musical. In addition to novels, McCullers published many short stories, poems, and nonfiction articles.

—*Victoria L. Shannon*

References:

Carr, Virginia Spencer. *Lonely Hunter: A Biography of Carson McCullers*. New York: Doubleday, 1975.

Evans, Oliver. *The Ballad of Carson McCullers*. New York: Coward-McCann, 1966.

McCullers, Carson. *The Ballad of the Sad Cafe and Other Stories*. New York: Bantam, 1967.

———. *The Heart Is a Lonely Hunter*. New York: AMSCO, 1970.

———. *The Member of the Wedding*. New York: AMSCO, 1970.

———. *Square Root of Wonderful*. Indianapolis, Ind.: Berg, 1971.

Rubin, Louis D., Jr. "Carson McCullers: The Aesthetics of Pain." *The Virginia Quarterly Review* 53 (Spring 1977): 265–83.

McPHERSON, AIMEE SEMPLE (1890–1944), evangelist and founder of the International Church of the Foursquare Gospel, was the daughter of a prosperous Canadian father and a devout mother. McPherson's mother, Mildred Kennedy, orphaned and raised in the family of a Salvation Army captain, dedicated her daughter to the service of God when she was only six weeks old. When she was seventeen, McPherson was converted at a Pentecostal revival, and a year later she married the evangelist who had converted her, Robert James Semple.

She and her husband became traveling evangelists, and in 1909 she was ordained at a Pentecostal ceremony in Chicago. The next year, her husband felt called to preach in China, but he died in Hong Kong, a mere three months after his arrival in Asia. McPherson returned to the United States with her newly born daughter, Roberta, and began a series of missionary lectures while assisting her mother in New York City with Salvation Army work. In 1912 she married Harold Stewart McPherson, a bookkeeper; they had a son, Rolf, who later succeeded his mother as head of the church she founded.

After a long period of illness, McPherson was inspired to resume her career as an evangelist. In August 1915 she began conducting revival meetings in a Pentecostal mission in Mount Forest, Ontario, Canada. She demonstrated great skill in preaching, "speaking in tongues," and faith healing. She spent the next several years in tent revivals up and down the eastern seaboard. Her personal charm, religious zeal, and considerable abilities as a preacher and performer led to the expansion of her revival circuit to include cross-country tours to California and back. Indeed, wearing her preacher's "uniform" of a white dress, white shoes, and a flowing blue cape, McPherson preached her way across the country and back eight times between 1918 and 1923. She also made a preaching tour of Australia, attracting large and enthusiastic crowds wherever she went. During this period she became the first female to preach a sermon on the radio.

Wanting a base for her operations, McPherson began the construction of the Angelus Temple near Echo Park, Los Angeles in April 1921. The temple became the headquarters of her new "church of the Foursquare Gospel," which eventually became a separate Pentecostal denomination. From 1923 to 1926 she preached every night and three times on Sunday to large crowds of five thousand or more crowded into the Angelus Temple. McPherson also operated a free food and clothing commissary, a magazine, a radio station, a telephone counseling service, and a Bible college, housed next to the temple.

Although ploughing most of the large sums of money she took in back into her ministry, McPherson bragged that she "ruled like a queen in my kingdom."

In May 1926 the evangelist disappeared while swimming at a beach near Los Angeles, only to reappear one month later in Mexico. She claimed to have been kidnapped, but her kidnappers were never found, and little evidence has ever been found to sustain her charges. Evidence that she had staged her kidnapping for publicity purposes or to escape temporarily from her frenetic ministry was insufficient for the courts to prosecute her for fraud. The international news attention helped stimulate the growth of her church, and in the late 1920s McPherson took to the revival circuit across the United States with stops in Paris and the British Isles.

In 1930 she suffered a nervous breakdown that seriously damaged her health. Her troubles were compounded by a third marriage, which ended in divorce four years later, a break with her mother and daughter, and numerous lawsuits over her badly managed business affairs. Aimee Semple McPherson died of an overdose of sleeping pills in an Oakland hotel room in 1944. At the time of her death, the church had over four hundred branches in the United States and Canada, nearly two hundred missions abroad, and around twenty-two thousand members. It has continued to grow since her death. Never a profound thinker, McPherson was rigidly conservative, sharing many of the ideas of the Ku Klux Klan, though not its racism. However, there has never been any question about the sincerity of her religious convictions. Novelist Sinclair Lewis has denied that he used McPherson for the model for his famous evangelist, Sharon Falconer, in *Elmer Gantry*.

—*Jonathan W. Zophy*

See Also:

Christianity; Public Speakers, Women

References:

Bahr, Robert. *Least of All Saints: The Story of Aimee Semple McPherson*. Englewood Cliffs, N.J.: Prentice-Hall, 1979.

McPherson, Aimee Semple. *In the Service of the King: The Story of My Life*. New York: Boni and Liveright, 1927.

———. *This Is That: Personal Experiences, Sermons, and Writings*. Los Angeles: Echo Park Evangelists Association, 1923.

Thomas, Lately. *Storming Heaven: The Lives and Turmoils of Minnie Kennedy and Aimee Semple McPherson*. New York: Morrow, 1970.

———. *The Vanishing Evangelist*. New York: Viking, 1959.

MAGAZINES. As early as the late eighteenth century, popular periodicals were being published for an eager, if limited, audience of literate and leisured women readers in England and British North America. After the American Revolution, such magazines were published in the United States. Nineteenth-century American women's magazines were designed both to amuse and instruct the True Woman in the ideal middle-class American home. As they defined and refined the proper role of women, these specialized periodicals also molded public opinion on women's issues. The publishers and editors of mainstream Victorian women's magazines offered their readers a conservative perspective that became known as domestic feminism, which wholeheartedly nurtured and supported the cult of domesticity and its attendant consumerism. Throughout the twentieth century, American women's magazines increasingly adjusted their focus on the suburban consumer/homemaker to reflect contemporary changes wrought in her life by the urbanization and industrialization of American society. By the end of the twentieth century, both new and established women's magazines attempted to court not only traditional homemakers but "working wives" and single employed women.

Early American magazines for women focused almost exclusively upon fashion and sentimental escape fiction rather than upon factual information and education. Most of their contents were plagiarized from English women's magazines, and therefore their contents reflected the social attitudes and behavior of the upper class of England rather than the republican middle class of the new nation. Within this literate middle class, women especially read and subscribed to American women's magazines that increasingly featured native authors and original material as they focused on the developing concept of a separate Woman's Sphere.

After the American Revolution, the contents of these magazines reflected the alteration of women's role in the family from their chattel status within the strict authoritarian partriarchial model of the preindustrial era to a slightly higher status as a result of the more companionate marriage that began to characterize the marital relationships of the nuclear family of the nineteenth century. Especially in the early New England women's magazines, a patriotic and domestic image of Republican Motherhood prepared the way for the True Womanhood of the Victorian era. Usually these early periodicals were religious in orientation and edited by ministers or other pious men.

In the antebellum period of Victorian America, many monthly periodicals vied for the faithful readership of women who were a generation removed from the Republican Mother of the rural preindustrial extended family. The role of these urban middle-class native-born white women within the smaller urban family required modification and adjustment to the new circumstance that rendered women economic dependents of wage-earning men. No longer co-workers or producers of crucial household goods and services, women were now consumers and household managers. American women's magazines spoke to and for these women, providing them with both entertainment and instruction in their new role as True Women. Moreover, women's magazines fostered the new genteel occupations of editor and contributing author for destitute ladies. Philadelphia and New York became the centers of publishing for women's magazines by the mid-nineteenth century.

Godey's Lady's Book, published by Louis A. Godey of Philadelphia, became the premier American Victorian women's magazine by the 1840s and 1850s, and it set the standard for all popular women's magazines of the era, as well as of the next century. Sarah Josepha Hale, its editor of forty years, brought a content format that she had perfected while editing her *American Ladies' Magazine* in Boston from 1828 to 1836. This fortified the memorable *Godey's* fashion plates, woodcuts, and other lavish "embellishments" with fiction, features, poetry and prose, household "how-to" articles, and crafts instructions. Hale also brought a commitment to improve her women readers through her editorial support of educational and employment advances for women. Even as Hale and *Godey's* presided over the formulation of the Cult of True Womanhood and the construct of a separate Woman's Sphere, Hale pursued an agenda of domestic feminism that enlarged the circumference of that Woman's Sphere.

Although *Godey's* peaked as a literary magazine in the 1850s, this venerable magazine lingered on until the last decade of the nineteenth century, coasting as it were on the indisputable reputation it earned under Hale's editorship as an impeccable source of entertainment and instruction for ladies. The Civil War marked the beginning of *Godey's* decline because of its large Southern readership as well as its avoidance of any mention of the war, due to its publisher's policy of eschewing any reference to politics as an improper topic for a ladies' magazine. Thus, as *Godey's* had set the standard pattern for the contents of women's magazines, this editorial policy of an exclusively domestic and apolitical focus of American women's magazines persisted through the 1960s. Not until the mainstream women's magazines banded together to support the ratification of the Equal Rights Amendment in the late 1970s did women's magazines directly broach a national political issue.

By the turn of the century, Edward Bok's *Ladies' Home Journal* was the leading American women's magazine. Adhering for the most part to the format established by *Godey's*, the *Journal* and its contemporaries cautiously integrated aspects of the New Woman into the twentieth-century cult of domesticity that spanned the 1920s and survived both the

Great Depression and World War II. During the 1950s, women's magazines presented the ideal life-style for the suburban housewife and relentlessly fortified the compulsory domesticity and femininity of the feminine mystique. Under the editorship of Helen Gurley Brown, *Cosmopolitan* by the mid-1960s was approaching a candor regarding sex and marriage that would have scandalized Hale and Bok, but which reflected the impact upon women's role and behavior of the so-called sexual revolution and of women's emerging economic independence through their increased participation in the workforce.

In 1972 *Ms.* magazine became the first frankly feminist mainstream women's magazine. It wooed the professional woman as well as the traditional homemaker with a raised consciousness. The product of feminist writers and editors such as Gloria Steinem, *Ms.* addressed a politically active and astute readership during its first decade. However, with the failure of the ERA ratification drive and the waning of the women's movement, even *Ms.* increasingly began to focus on personal relationships and family issues by the 1980s; it was purchased by a commercial corporation in the late 1980s. Not unlike feminist magazines such as *The Una* and *The Revolution* in the nineteenth century, a few magazines that focused upon lesbian and radical feminist issues were dependent on a discreet feminist readership; while these had flourished during the early 1970s, they were struggling for survival by the 1980s.

By the 1970s American magazines in general altered their emphasis to appeal to the reading taste of the maturing "baby boomers" or "Yuppies" (Young Urban Upwardly Mobile Professionals). This generation, which followed the counterculture of the politically active youth of the 1960s, became known as the "me generation." Women's magazines too reflected the contemporary obsession with self. Although acknowledging that women's lives were being affected by the austere economic situation as well as by the additional career and life-style choices available to them by the 1980s, magazines such as *Family Circle* and *Woman's Day* still defined womanhood for their readers in terms of the cult of domesticity. Mainsteam women's magazines broached many unpleasant issues that had previously been editorially taboo—rape, divorce, spouse abuse, alcohol and drug abuse—but their primary focus continued to be women's home duties and family relationships.

—*Angela Howard Zophy*

See Also:

Cult of True Womanhood; Domestic Literature in the United States; *Godey's Lady's Book; Ms.;* Steinem, Gloria

References:

Douglas, Ann. *The Feminization of American Culture.* New York: Knopf, 1977.

Hartman, Eleanore P. "Magazines—Molders of Opinion." *Wilson Library Bulletin* 21 (April 1947): 600–02.

Stearns, Bertha M. "Before *Godey's.*" *American Literature* 21 (1930): 248–55.

Woloch, Nancy. *Women and the American Experience.* New York: Knopf, 1984.

Woodward, Helen Beal. *The Lady Persuaders.* New York: Ivan Obolensky, 1960.

Zophy, Angela Howard. "'For the Improvement of My Sex': Sarah Josepha Hale's Editorship of *Godey's Lady's Book*, 1837–1877." Diss. The Ohio State University, 1978.

MALKIEL, THERESA SERBER (1874–1949), trade union organizer and socialist activist, migrated to New York from Bar, Russia, in 1891. She immediately went to work in the city's garment industry. Here she developed a commitment to unionism and became a member of the Russian Workingmen's Club in 1892. She helped found the Woman's Infant Cloak Maker's Union, and served as its president as well as its representative to the Knights of Labor, a precursor of the American Federation of Labor. Although she left the labor force upon marriage to lawyer Leon Malkiel in 1900, she maintained a high profile in the labor movement. She was an early member of the New York Women's Trade Union League, and played an active role in the garment industry's labor struggles from 1909 to 1911.

This strike provided the backdrop for her novel, *Diary of a Shirtwaist Striker* (1910).

The Diary of a Shirtwaist Striker depicts the labor struggles in the garment industry of the early twentieth century in fictional terms. Unlike Malkiel, a Jewish immigrant from Russia, the heroine of this didactic novel, Mary, is a middle-class American woman. Mary is first presented to the reader as a timid, callow girl who works in a garment factory only for "pin money," and who is incapable of sharing the experiences or goals of the other workers, mostly poor immigrant women, laboring for their livelihood. She is convinced that she is better than they. In the course of the novel, however, Mary's consciousness changes, and she comes to support a strike in the factory, despite the objections of her father and her fiancé. She surfaces as a leader of the strike, finds herself on a picket line, and gets arrested. The stint she serves in a workhouse causes her to see that the problems go beyond those of a single shop, and Mary is convinced of the need for broad changes in society. She is won over to the platform of the Socialist party. Mary also sees clearly that women workers have special needs and as such they must have the vote.

In shaping the character of Mary, Malkiel not only creates one of the first female unionists in American literature, but she uses the fictional forum to point out the tense relationship between foreign and native workers, to expose the class bias inherent in the Women's Trade Union League, and to depict the constraints in women's lives in the early twentieth century. As a character, Mary was a vehicle for Malkiel's own brand of unionism, socialism, and feminism.

Malkiel's involvement with socialism also began shortly after her migration from Russia. Although she belonged first to the Socialist Labor party, she came to be associated particularly with the Socialist Party of America (SPA), within which she consistently drew members' attention to the linkages between feminism and socialism. Her goal of fusing socialism and feminism led her in 1907 to found the Women's Progressive Society of Yonkers (New York), which she hoped would give socialist women a chance to exert the leadership that, she believed, the SPA consistently denied them. She chided the party for refusing to recognize the significance of the "woman question" and for failing to see that feminism and socialism represented similar visions. She articulated the organic connection between feminist and socialist goals in two 1915 pamphlets, *Woman of Yesterday and Today* and *Woman and Freedom.* She also contributed to socialist publications such as the *Socialist Woman, Progressive Woman,* as well as *Call* and the *Jewish Daily Forward,* a Yiddish newspaper for which she edited a special woman's column.

In the years immediately following World War I, Malkiel remained in the Socialist party and ran for the New York State Assembly in 1920 on its ticket. This represented Malkiel's last involvement with socialism. She shifted her attention in the 1920s and 1930s to promoting women's education, with special emphasis on the needs of immigrant women.

—Hasia R. Diner

See Also:

Garment Industries, Jewish Women, Socialist Party of America

References:

Blake, Fay M. *The Strike in the American Novel.* Metuchen, N.J.: Scarecrow, 1972.

Buhle, Mari Jo. *Women and American Socialism, 1870–1920.* Urbana: University of Illinois Press, 1981.

Malkiel, Theresa. *Diary of a Shirtwaist Striker.* New York: Co-operative Press, 1910.

———. *Woman and Freedom.* New York: Co-operative Press, 1915.

———. *Woman of Yesterday and Today.* New York: Co-operative Press, 1915.

Miller, Sally M. "From Sweatshop Worker to Labor Leader: Theresa Malkiel, a Case Study." *American Jewish History* 68 (December 1978): 189–205.

MALONE, ANNIE TURNBO (c.1868–1957), black businesswoman, manufacturer, and philanthropist, dreamed of making products to enhance the beauty of black women. She experimented with chemistry in high school and developed a scalp treatment solution to grow and straighten hair. A native of Illinois, Malone started a business in Lovejoy, Illinois, and moved to St. Louis, Missouri, in 1902. Four years later she copyrighted her products under the trade name Poro. By 1914 Malone owned the largest black enterprise in St. Louis. Her business, called Poro College, consisted of a factory and store for hair and cosmetic products, a hairdressing school, dormitory, and business office, plus a large auditorium and dining room that served as a community center for religious, fraternal, civic, and social organizations.

In addition to her business responsibilities, Malone was active in Colored Women's Federated Clubs of St. Louis, the National Negro Business League, the St. Louis Community Council, and the Commission on Inter-Racial Cooperation. Because of her interest in young people, especially women, she gave generous financial assistance to the St. Louis Maternity Hospital, St. Louis Children's Hospital, the YMCA, the St. James AME Church, and the St. Louis Colored Orphans' Home. She served as board president of the latter from 1919 until 1943, and the home was named for her in 1946.

In 1930 Malone moved to Chicago, where she purchased a complete city block. By this time she was considered one of the world's wealthiest black women. Poro College, built on a foundation of black women's commitment to honor, industry, and generosity, established branch offices in principal cities throughout the United States. Always interested in education, Malone made large financial contributions to Howard University, Washington, D.C., and Wilberforce University, Ohio. Both institutions, among several others, conferred honorary degrees upon her.

Malone's life provided an inspiration to young people, particularly women. She typified the traditional spirit of American business, rising from meager circumstances to a position of affluence through remarkable executive power and business acumen.

—*Mary K. Dains*

See Also:

Beauty Industry, Black Women, Business

References:

"Missouri Women in History." *Missouri Historical Review* 67 (July 1973). [inside back cover]

"Mrs. Annie Malone, Poro Founder, Dies." *St. Louis Post-Dispatch* 79 (May 12, 1957): 6B. [obit.]

"Mrs. Annie Malone, Poro Head, Buried." *St. Louis American* 29 (May 16, 1957): 1–2. [obit.]

"Mrs. Malone Buried from Chicago's Bethel." *St. Louis Argus* 46 (May 17, 1957): 1, 8.

"Personal History of Annie M. Turnbo Malone." Chicago Historical Society, Chicago, Ill. [typescript]

"Philanthropist Left Mark on St. Louis." *St. Louis American* 35 (September 22, 1964): 21.

St. Louis Board of Education. *Heritage of St. Louis.* St. Louis: Board of Education, 1964, pp. 176–77.

Shepard, Marguerite. "Children's Home Is Proud Symbol of What People Can do for Themselves." *St. Louis Globe-Democrat* 92 (May 24, 1968): 1B.

The Truth about Poro College. Chicago Historical Society, Chicago, Ill. [undated promotional pamphlet]

Woods, Howard B. "One Man's Journal: St. Louis Woman." *St. Louis Argus* 46 (May 17, 1957): 8.

MARINE CORPS, WOMEN'S RESERVE. The marines may be the first service to land on beaches, but they were the last service to create a women's corps, reluctantly, in February 1943. Unlike the other services (WAAC, WAVES, SPARS), the marine corps did not give their women's corps a nickname; they were marines, or at least, women marines.

The marines report to the navy during war, and during World War I the navy found a loophole in the law and recruited women to serve as telephone operators and clericals. By the war's end, 11,275 yeomen (F), women typists and telephone operators, had served commendably with the navy and marines. More than one hundred women marine veterans of World War I were still attending annual meetings in the late 1980s.

During World War II women marines prided themselves in taking over stateside work so that the men could fight. At Cherry Point, North Carolina, by August 1944, all the airplane instructors for beginning pilots were women marines. At this base, women marines took almost complete charge of the photography department and film library, did 90 percent of the parachute packing, and conducted 80 percent of the landing-field control tower operations. Women marines comprised from one-third to one-half of the post troops at representative marine posts and stations. Some women handled mail, others the radios and the storerooms, while still others trained pilots or were mechanics. At the war's peak, 17,600 women served in the marines; in all, 23,000 served during World War II.

Women joined the marines for different reasons. While the overwhelming majority cited patriotism first, over a quarter cited escape from a difficult job or family situation as the next most important reason. Ruth Chenery Streeter became the first director of women marines during this period. A Bryn Mawr alumna, she had experience in civic activities such as public health and welfare unemployment, relief, and old-age assistance in her home state of New Jersey.

With the passage of the Women's Armed Services Integration Act in June 1948, the Women's Reserve was made a permanent part of the marines. In 1976 women began attending the U.S. Naval Academy at Annapolis, Maryland, and in 1978 the Women's Reserves were abolished and women were integrated into the service. Women in the marines are blocked by navy regulations from holding combat positions, which limits their chances for promotion in the marines and navy. Current debate centers around the definition of combat jobs, and whether Congress should abolish these restrictions and draft women.

—D'Ann Campbell

See Also:

Military Service

References:

Campbell, D'Ann. *Women at War with America: Private Lives in a Patriotic Era.* Cambridge: Harvard University Press, 1984.

Hewit, Linda L., Capt., USMCR. *Women Marines in World War I.* Washington, D.C.: History and Museums Division, Headquarters U.S. Marine Corps, 1974.

Meid, Pat, Lt. Col., USMCR. *Marine Corps Women's Reserve in World War II.* Washington D.C.: Historical Branch, C-3 Division, Headquarters, U.S. Marine Corps, 1968.

Streeter, Ruth Chenery. "History of the Marine Corps Women's Reserve: A Critical Analysis of Its Development and Operation, 1943–1945." Schlesinger Library, Radcliffe College, Cambridge, Mass.

———. "Recollections with Ruth Chenery Streeter." Oral History Program, The Naval Institute, 1972. Schlesinger Library, Radcliffe College, Cambridge, Mass.

Stremlow, Mary V., Col., USMCR. *A History of Women Marines 1946–1977.* Washington, D.C.: History and Museums Division, Headquarters U.S. Marine Corps, 1982.

MARITAL RAPE (spousal rape) is forced sexual intercourse and/or other forced sexual acts between persons married to one another. As with sexual assault involving persons not married to one another, the victim of marital rape (usually the wife), in order to win a criminal case under most existing laws, must prove that she did not consent to the sexual activity. Typically, such proof includes: (1) evidence that physical force was used against the victim; (2) evidence that the victim was threatened to the extent that she could not resist the assault; or (3) evidence that the victim was unconscious at the time of the assault.

Historically, forced sex between spouses has not been recognized as a crime. As of May 1989 thirty-eight states had marital rape laws. Most other states include in their sexual assault statutes a "spousal exemption" that prevents a wife from bringing charges against her husband regardless of how violent he was in forcing her to have sex with him. (In some states, however, sexual assault between spouses may be prosecuted as simple assault or aggravated assault, depending on the degree of violence involved.) A few states even extend the spousal exemption to unmarried, cohabiting partners.

The spousal exemption is a carry-over from early family law, which defined a married woman and her children as the property of her husband. (The word *family* itself derives from the Latin *famulus*, meaning household servant or slave.) A man had complete control over his wife; legally he could beat her, and he could force sex upon her without being charged with rape, the rationale being that he could not "steal" what he already "owned."

Those who have opposed the enactment of marital rape laws maintain that such laws may spark an onslaught of fabricated charges. As with sexual assault between persons not married to one another, the faulty assumption underlying this argument is that women, by and large, might use rape charges for revenge. In states that have marital rape laws, however, there have not been a flood of cases. Wives themselves have difficulty defining their husbands' sexual assaults as rape, and in those cases that have been prosecuted, the husbands typically have had a history of violent and abusive behavior.

Importantly, recent research indicates that marital rape has a more traumatic effect on victims than rape between strangers. This is because marital rape victims not only experience "rape trauma syndrome," but are also more vulnerable than victims raped by strangers. Their assailant is someone they've intimately trusted and with whom they live; often they are subjected to multiple rapes. Yet in some states, marital rape victims receive no legal protection. Instead, the laws protect abusive husbands from prosecution. It is likely, therefore, that until the laws are changed, marital rape will continue to be a common—some researchers claim the most common—form of sexual assault.

—*Claire M. Renzetti*

See Also:
Family Violence, Rape/Sexual Assault

References:

Brown, Barbara A., Ann E. Freedman, Harriet N. Katz, and Alice M. Price. *Women's Rights and the Law*. New York: Praeger, 1977.

Finkelhor, David, and Kerati Yllo. *License to Rape: Sexual Abuse of Wives*. New York: Holt, Rinehart and Winston, 1985.

———, Richard J. Gelles, Gerald T. Hotaling, and Murray A. Straus, eds. *The Dark Side of Families: Current Family Violence Research*. Beverly Hills, Calif.: Sage, 1983.

"State Law Chart." Berkeley, Calif.: National Clearinghouse on Marital Rape, 1986.

MARRIAGE. In his *Commentaries on the Laws of England* (1765), William Blackstone, the most popular theoretician of English common law, explained the legal consequences of marriage. In principle a man and woman entered marriage on an equal basis, based on their mutual consent, as in any other civil contract. Once married, however, the status of marriage carried its own legal consequences: "By marriage, the husband and wife are one person in law; that is, the very being or legal existence of the woman is suspended during the marriage. . . ." This legal fiction of marital unity, and the married woman's condition of *coverture* during marriage, shaped the legal rights of American married women from the colonial period, and its influence persisted through the twentieth century.

This unity of person meant that in common law the husband could not grant anything to his wife during the marriage or enter into an agreement with her, "for the grant would presuppose her separate existence." To enter an agreement with her would be only to agree with himself. A wife, however, could represent her husband as an agent, because that did not imply a separation of herself from him. The husband was bound to supply "necessaries" to his wife. If he failed to do so, the wife could buy them on credit, and, if they were truly necessities, the husband would be responsible for the debt. The wife could not sue or be sued in her own name; the husband had to be joined to the suit. Except where a criminal offense was directed against the person of the wife herself, husband and wife were not allowed to testify for or against each other because of the fiction of marital unity.

After marriage, the husband controlled all of his wife's personal property and also had extensive powers over her real property. The law, however, assumed that a woman was under the compulsion of her husband, and did not allow him to convey her real property without her consent. At her death, the wife's real property returned to her parents' family, unless there was a child. In that case, the husband became a "tenant by the curtesy," that is, he owned an interest in his wife's estate for his lifetime. The most important property right of women under common law was dower, a share of the real property owned by husbands during marriage that was designated for the support of widows. A husband could not sell or mortgage his property and deny his wife her dower interest without her agreement to the transaction.

Variations among the colonies, and then the states, and differences between social classes and between free and nonfree people, complicated this simplified picture. There were no *legal* consequences of marriage for slave women, because American law, except briefly in Louisiana, did not recognize the validity of slave marriages. The rules developed for property were of little relevance to poor women.

Regional differences in laws affecting women's property rights characterized the late-colonial and early-national period. For example, in states such as New York and South Carolina there were separate courts of chancery, which developed a body of law allowing married women, *feme coverts*, to own separate property. In Connecticut and Massachusetts, however, where there were no separate equity courts and the Puritan view of the family influenced jurists, courts were very slow to recognize women's separate estates. Regional differences were reflected as well in treatment of the procedures for conveyances by married women; the development of the *feme sole* trader laws, which gave some married women the right to conduct their own businesses as if they were single; in changes to the dower and inheritance provisions affecting widows; and in the law of divorce. Despite regional variations and some setbacks, there was a steady development toward increased legal autonomy for women in the early national period.

The Married Women's Property Acts of the mid-nineteenth century therefore do not represent a radical break with past developments. Beginning with Mississippi in 1839, American states began to pass statutes that allowed married women to own the property they brought to the marriage or acquired thereafter by gift or bequest. The marital property laws of community-property states such as California and Texas derive from Spanish civil law and not from common law. However, this did not mean that women had the right to control their separate property. For example, the 1850 statute in California gave a husband unlimited managerial control over both the community property and his wife's separate property, although he could not alienate (dispose of) her property without her consent. By 1872 the wife could manage her separate property.

By 1865 twenty-nine states had passed some form of married women's property law, and the trend continued through the end of the nineteenth century. The "boldest" of these statutes, the Earnings Act of 1860 in New York, not only gave married women the right to manage their own separate property, but included separate property earnings as well. It also equalized the intestate succession rights of husbands and wives and their rights to be guardian of any children of the marriage. The legislature, however, soon diluted the two last changes.

These acts were only in part, perhaps a minor part, a product of the organized woman's rights movement that developed after 1848. In New York, for example, three developments contributed to the passage of married women's property acts after 1848: the thrust for codification and reform of the legal system, economic changes that made it desirable to protect some property from the claims of the husband's creditors, and the debate over the "woman question."

In the late twentieth century some of the Blackstonian principles of marital unity lingered despite the political emancipation of women in 1920 and the passage of a number of state Equal Rights Amendments more recently. For example, interspousal tort immunities, which prohibit one spouse from suing another for an injury, and the marital exception from rape laws both reflect the Blackstonian unity. Although the trend is clearly to reject these legal doctrines, they are by no means defunct everywhere. On the other hand, many states have enacted the Uniform Premarital Agreement Act, which permits husbands and wives to determine many of the consequences of the legal status of marriage through their own agreement or contract. This increased legal autonomy does not represent a clear-cut gain for women. An agreement, made before marriage but enforced years later, to waive some of the protections that the law provides can be devastating to women who still suffer economic and social disadvantages and who more often than not have primary responsibility for children.

Despite significant changes, marriage still retains its character as a legal status rather than an ordinary civil contract.

—*Laura Oren*

See Also:

Coverture, Dower, Equity Courts, *Feme Covert*, *Feme Sol*, Married Women's Property Acts

References:

Basch, Norma. *In the Eyes of the Law: Women, Marriage, and Property in Nineteenth-Century New York.* Ithaca: Cornell University Press, 1982.

Blackstone, William. *Commentaries on the Laws of England*, Book I. A Facsimile of the First Edition of 1765–1769. Introduction by Stanley N. Katz. Chicago: University of Chicago Press, 1979.

Kent, James. *Commentaries on American Law.* Vol. 2. New York: O. Halsted, 1827.

Reeve, Tapping. *The Law of Baron and Femme, of Parent and Child, Guardian and Ward, Master and Servant, and of the Powers of Courts of Chancery; with an essay on the Terms Heir, Heirs, and Heirs of the Body.* 2d ed. Burlington, Vt.: Chauncey Goodrich, 1846.

Salmon, Marylynn. *Women and the Law of Property in Early America.* Chapel Hill: University of North Carolina Press, 1986.

The **MARRIAGE EDUCATION MOVEMENT**, which flourished on American college and university campuses from the 1930s through the mid-1960s, attempted to provide American youth with a "practical" education in courtship, marriage, and family life in order to produce more "wholesome" and functional patterns of behavior. The social scientists who were scholars and educators in the field of family life worried that parents could no longer be adequate sources of information and authority for their children. Hoping to establish a new source of authority in keeping with the modern age, marriage educators sought to bring youth's experience in courtship and marriage under the authority of experts who could provide youth with answers and models of appropriate behavior based solidly on scientific research.

By the late 1950s approximately twelve hundred U.S. colleges and universities—of the full range of academic statuses—offered "self-help" marriage courses. Approving articles describing the content and expected results of marriage courses ran in magazines and newspapers, including *Mademoiselle*, *Woman's Home Companion*, and the *New York Times*. The scholar-educators who taught marriage courses and wrote marriage texts frequently doubled as columnists for such magazines, thus reaching a large audience with their advice.

While the marriage education movement was a sincere attempt to address the problems of educating youth in modern society, it had, in retrospect, many faults. "Scientific" conclusions were usually derived from studies of middle-class college students, and descriptive data were translated into prescriptive norms. "Normal" behavior was advocated as correct, thus reinforcing a status quo in which women's roles were highly restricted. The movement's reliance on experts denied the legitimacy of individual experience. And finally, the movement as a whole was extremely concerned with buttressing what individual scholars defined as the "timeless" and "traditional" differences between the sexes. While only a very small percentage of Americans ever took a marriage course, the movement's emphasis on expert planning and scientifically determined facts had an important impact on social policy and on the way Americans thought about courtship and relations between the sexes.

—*Beth L. Bailey*

See Also:

Marriage, Sex Role Socialization

Reference:

Bailey, Beth L. "Scientific Truth . . . and Love: The Marriage Education Movement in the United States." *Journal of Social History* 20 (Summer 1987): 711–32.

MARRIAGE MANUALS are that form of advice literature designed to guide young couples to marital bliss. Although they tend to present an air of scientific objectivity, such prescriptive messages have usually reflected the sexual mores of the time in which they were written.

In the nineteenth century, after technological advances in printing and the spread of literacy first allowed dissemination of these materials in the guise of home medical-advice books, they echoed the ideology of Victorian America that connected restraint and intercourse for procreation only. One of the best known, William Acton's *Functions and Disorders of the Reproductive Organs* (1865), assured its readers that "the majority of women (happily for them) are not very much troubled with sexual feeling of any kind." Some nineteenth-century writers, most of whom were women, did encourage husbands to be attentive to their wives' needs, but few accepted the idea of sex for pleasure alone.

A changing atmosphere associated with the revolution of manners and morals in the 1920s led to the incredible popularity of *Ideal Marriage: Its Physiology and Technique* (1926) by Theodor H. Van de Velde. While it made a passing reference to oral sex, the book built upon the more liberal nineteenth-century writers in encouraging greater attention to foreplay and focused upon a unique form of the heterosexual imperative—simultaneous orgasm.

With the second wave of sexual revolution in the 1960s, marriage manuals became sex manuals, providing advice for those practicing premarital, nonmarital, and extramarital sex. The best known, Alex Comfort's *The Joy of Sex* (1972), took its title from a best-selling cookbook and advised people how to maximize sexual pleasure while avoiding the dangers of procreation. It indicated that oral sex, which was still against the law in many states, seemed to be the easiest route to heterosexual orgasm for most women. In contrast to the nineteenth-century advice books, *The Joy of Sex* also found masturbation and homosexuality acceptable. Through all these changes, marriage manuals remain just that, a genre of advice literature designed to build a better marriage—or relationship—through better sex.

—*William G. Shade*

See Also:

Female Sexuality, Marriage, Sexual Revolution

References:

Gordon, Michael, and M. Charles Berstein. "Mate Choice and Domestic Life in the 19th Century Marriage Manual." *Journal of Marriage and the Family* 32 (1970): 665–74.

Van de Velde, Theodor H. *Ideal Marriage: Its Physiology and Technique.* New York: Random House, 1930.

Walters, Ronald G., ed. *Primers for Prudery: Sexual Advice to Victorian America.* Englewood Cliffs, N.J.: Prentice-Hall, 1974.

MARRIED WOMEN'S PROPERTY ACTS. The common law traditions that were derived from English practice made a husband and wife economically inseparable. A woman's property became that of her husband, and her earnings were his as well. The harsh realities implied by these traditions were softened by the concept of equity as practiced in England and as widely applied in the British North American colonies. Because of the concept of equity, prenuptial agreements were upheld in colonial courts. Few colonial women seemed to have taken advantage of such agreements, and those that were used were developed out of the need for an insurance on a woman's income in the event of the death of a spouse rather than out of a sense of a woman's independence with regard to her property. Prenuptial agreements were more commonplace among widows who remarried than among women marrying for the first time.

Gradually, states ratified these equity developments. Massachusetts allowed women deserted by their husbands to sell property under legislation of 1787; Maine extended the concept to allow women to control property after desertion. In the 1830s several states debated statutes that would have confirmed the property rights of women. The New York legislature considered such a statute in 1836. The first state to pass married women's property legislation was Mississippi in 1839. The law was ambiguously worded and designed to protect the rights of women to sell or dispose of slaves that they had brought to the marriage. Michigan, New York, and Pennsylvania passed married women's property legislation in the 1840s, and in the 1850s, several other states enacted parallel statutes.

Notwithstanding the growing advocacy for women's rights in the mid-nineteenth century, these laws developed from different motives; namely, the desire to protect a family's inheritance. Fathers did not want irresponsible sons-in-law disposing of property that came as part of the marriage. The laws, in effect, ratified long-standing equity decisions and extended those decisions to those who previously could not afford to take or did not take advantage of prenuptial agreements. Even with this motivation, the laws had the effect of separating married men and women under the law. That trend would prove irreversible and open the legal door for further development of independent women's rights in the latter nineteenth century.

—*Thomas F. Armstrong*

See Also:

Antenuptial Agreements, Marriage

References:

Bloomfield, Maxwell. *American Lawyers in a Changing Society*. Cambridge: Harvard University Press, 1976.

Friedman, Lawrence M. *A History of American Law*. New York: Simon & Schuster, 1973.

Norton, Mary Beth. *Liberty's Daughters*. New York: Little, 1980.

MARTINEZ, MARIA MONTOYA (c.1881–1980). If the United States honored its artists and craftspeople as does Japan, Maria Martinez would have been declared a "national treasure."

Along with her husband, Julian, she reconstructed pots similar in design and form to the ancient shards excavated by Dr. Edward Hewitt from the plateau at Pajarito near the San Ildefonso pueblo in the Rio Grande Valley of New Mexico. In performing this task, Martinez, a Pueblo Indian, worked with reverence and sensitivity in re-creating the work of her ancestors. She hand-turned the classic pottery shapes on a disk made from a gourd, skillfully copying and then adapting the ancient shapes. She then polished the surfaces with a smooth round river-stone. With the encouragement of Dr. Hewitt of the Museum of New Mexico's Anthropology and Archaeology Department, the Martinezes developed a way of painting decorations in dull, velvety black on the polished pottery before firing. Using this technique, Julian painted elegant designs based on old Indian motifs, which he often modified with his own artistry. To achieve the black color, Maria then stacked the pieces in the kiln, surrounded them with dried cow manure, and fired them until all the carbon was reduced. They emerged with the familiar silvery black sheen.

After her husband's death, Martinez continued to work with her sons, Popovi Da and Adam, and her daughter-in-law, Santana; she also enlarged the pottery community at San Ildefonso by teaching the craft to relatives and other residents. After her own death in her late nineties, her work was continued by her great-granddaughter, Barbara Gonzales, as well as by Santana, Blue Corn, and others of the extended village family.

During her long career, Martinez was an honored figure, not only in her own pueblo but throughout the art world. She was awarded honorary doctorates by the University of New Mexico and the University of Colorado, which recognized her as one of the world's great potters. Such masters as Bernard Leach and Shoji Hamada came to San Ildefonso to work with and receive inspiration from her. She demonstrated her pottery at almost every important world's fair since 1904. As a further tribute, she was asked to lay the cornerstone in Rockefeller Center in New York.

For all her wordly acclaim, she most enjoyed her own native village community, where she shared the life of her people.

—*Evelyn Katz*

See Also:
Art

References:

Chapman, Kenneth M. *The Pottery of San Ildefonso Pueblo.* Albuquerque: University of New Mexico Press, 1970.

Hyde, Hazel. *Maria Making Pottery.* Santa Fe: Sunstone, 1973.

Marriott, Alice. *Maria: Potter of San Ildefonso.* Norman: University of Oklahoma Press, 1948.

Peterson, Susan. *Maria Martinez: Five Generations of Potters.* Washington, D.C.: Smithsonian Institution, 1978.

The **MARY BALDWIN SCHOOL**, long known as the Augusta Female Seminary, was one of the most famous of the many early-nineteenth-century schools for girls. Located in Staunton, Virginia, it dates from 1842, when the Reverend Rufus W. Bailey came to the community seeking a location for a girls' school. Bailey gained support of the local Presbyterian congregation, and he suggested establishing a high-grade seminary there. In August 1842 Bailey prepared a "Plan or Constitution of the Augusta Female Seminary," which identified the objective of the school as providing a "thorough literary and Christian education to the female youths of this portion of our country." The community backed the project and the school opened in the fall of 1842 with Bailey serving as the principal. Within two years the school had enrolled fifty-seven pupils and was a success, but in 1848 Bailey resigned his position, and several other principals followed in rapid succession.

Mary Baldwin took over in 1863, during the Civil War. Baldwin had grown up in Staunton and had long been interested in education. Earlier, she had opened a charity school there, providing free education to the needy. As the new principal, Baldwin took over at a difficult time. The school remained open through the war with 80 pupils enrolled by 1863. By the end of the decade, the number rose to 137 and continued to rise as pupils came from throughout the South. The success of Baldwin in building the size and reputation of the school led the trustees to change its name in December 1895 to Mary Baldwin Seminary in recognition of "the valuable services and unparalleled success of the Principal." After her death on July 1, 1897, the school received the bulk of her estate, which provided a sizable endowment for the institution.

By 1899 the school enrolled two hundred pupils and was growing steadily. The seminary's name was changed to Mary Baldwin Junior College in 1916, and it became a four-year college in 1923. The name was then changed to Mary Baldwin College, and today it is the nation's oldest Presbyterian women's college.

—*Robert G. Waite*

See Also:
Education, Female Academies

References:

Waddell, Joseph A. *History of Mary Baldwin Seminary.* Staunton, Va.: Augusta Printing Company, 1905.

Watters, Mary. *The History of the Mary Baldwin College, 1842–1942.* Staunton, Va.: Mary Baldwin College, 1942.

Woody, Thomas. *A History of Women's Education in the United States.* Vol. 1. New York: Science Press, 1929.

The **MASS COMMUNICATION MEDIA** have been the object of feminist criticism since the resurgence of the U.S. feminist movement in the early 1960s. Two frequently cited founding events of modern feminism, the publication of Betty Friedan's The *Feminine Mystique* in 1963 and the creation of the National Organization for Women (NOW) in 1966, were both in part a result of criticisms of the media. Friedan showed how traditional women's magazines created a myth that woman's happiness can be found solely in her home and family, a myth that contrasted with the lives of the unhappy women she interviewed. NOW was active from its beginning in monitoring media content and seeking change through employment suits and broadcast license challenges.

Women's representation in advertising and entertainment content and invisibility in news content, along with women's underrepresentation and exploitation in employment within media industries, have been areas of primary concern to feminist activists and scholars. More recently, feminist scholars have begun to explore how media technologies historically may have opened up or further restricted women's opportunities for speaking, for having a public voice, and for telling women's stories. Women have a long, neglected history as publishers, editors, printers, and writers of their own forms of communication, probably significant to the success of women's reform efforts at various times in history. On the other hand, the dominant media forms have generally excluded alternate stories and explanations about women and have undoubtedly had a hand in shaping the direction of the women's movement itself and the perception of it by the public.

The Women's Institute for Freedom of the Press, Washington, D.C., has urged significant changes in the structure of the mass media system, insisting that those who have been silenced by the media should be instrumental in the reshaping of a system in which all have equal access to the means of communication.

—Lana F. Rakow

See Also:

Friedan, Betty; Magazines; National Organization for Women

References:

Butler, Matilda, and William Paisley. *Women and the Mass Media: Sourcebook for Research and Action.* New York: Human Sciences Press, 1980.

Media Report to Women. Washington, D.C.: Women's Institute for Freedom of the Press, 1973–.

Rakow, Lana F. "Women and the Communications Media: Making Feminist Connections with Media Research." *Women and Language* 8 (Spring 1985): 1–15.

MASTURBATION is the stimulation of one's own genitals to orgasm. Proscribed by the major religions, it is consequently the most practiced of sins. The practice generally begins with childhood self-exploration and is most common during adolescence. Although it is more widely practiced by males, four-fifths of all women today have at some time in their life masturbated. They usually begin earlier and continue the practice longer than men.

In the nineteenth century the term *nymphomania* was used to describe excessive masturbation by a female. It was "private vice" as distinguished from "public vice"—prostitution. Masturbation was connected with a variety of illnesses, but was related most often to insanity or nervous disorders. It indicated perversion in the female sex, deemed by "science" to be above sexual desire. However, the earliest sex surveys show a consistent response: approximately 70 percent of each generation of women over the past century and a half have masturbated to orgasm.

In recent years feminists and sex therapists have encouraged women to heighten their sexual response by masturbating because women who masturbate are more likely to have orgasms in heterosexual intercourse than those who do not. While recent trends indicate that the number of those who have tried the practice has increased only slightly, many more women masturbate regularly and more often than in the past, finding it the easiest and quickest route to orgasm. This shift is particularly striking among married women. Statisically, women from a fundamentalist religious background are the least likely to masturbate. When masturbating, women do not generally attempt to simulate intercourse by inserting dildoes or phallic-shaped objects into their vaginas; most (75 percent) simply fantasize while they stroke their clitoris or the area around it.

The sexual and feminist ferment of the 1960s challenged the mainstream cultural taboo on masturbation. Access to accurate medical information regarding the effects of this practice and a heightened interest in sexuality and sensuality—added to the increased concern of the 1980s regarding sexually transmitted diseases—has created a more positive social attitude toward masturbation for both sexes.

—*William G. Shade*

See Also:
Female Sexuality

References:

Davis, Katherine B. *Factors in the Sex Life of Twenty-two Hundred Women.* New York: Harper and Row, 1929.

D'Emilio, John, and Estelle B. Freedman. *Intimate Matters: A History of Sexuality in America.* New York: Harper, 1988.

Dodson, Betty. *Liberating Masturbation.* Union, N.J.: Sensory Research Corp., 1972.

Englehardt, H. Tristram, Jr. "The Disease of Masturbation: Values and the Concept of Disease." *Bulletin of the History of Medicine* 48 (1974): 234–48.

Hite, Shere. *The Hite Report.* New York: Dell, 1976.

Hunt, Morton. *Sexual Behavior in the 1970s.* New York: Dell, 1974.

Tavris, Carol, and Susan Sadd. *The Redbook Report on Female Sexuality.* New York: Delacorte, 1977.

MATHEMATICS. Women in mathematics have faced unusually strong barriers to achievement, but have, nevertheless, made outstanding contributions to the field. For a long time many American universities would not admit women to their graduate programs. Princeton, for example, did not admit women to its graduate math program until the late 1960s. Winifred Edgerton was the first American woman to receive a Ph. D. in mathematics when she graduated from Columbia University in 1886. Only 230 American women received Ph.D.'s prior to 1940. Women with doctorates in mathematics often had a difficult time finding employment, especially at top-ranked research universities. In 1970 not a single women had tenure at any of the top five math departments.

The life and career of Christine Ladd-Franklin (1847–1930) illustrates some of the problems faced by women in mathematics. Ladd-Franklin was an 1869 graduate of Vassar, who went on to four years of graduate study at the Johns Hopkins University. She completed her doctoral dissertation in mathematics in 1882 and had the dissertation published to scholarly acclaim. However, the university refused to grant doctorates to women, so Ladd-Franklin left Johns Hopkins without receiving her Ph.D. She married, had two children, and continued to work in the field of symbolic logic. In 1887 Ladd-Taylor published the first of many papers in the field of physiological optics, a subject she devoted the next thirty-seven years of her life to, along with a developing interest in psychology. She also taught logic and psychology at Johns Hopkins and Columbia. Her interests extended to the status of women in society generally, and she wrote a number of pieces for newspapers and magazines on women's issues. Finally in 1925 Johns Hopkins granted her the Ph.D. in mathematics that she had earned forty-four years earlier.

Despite the obstacles faced by Christine Ladd-Taylor and other women mathematicians, a number of women have achieved a great deal in the field. Notable American women mathematicians include: Ruth Aaronson Bari (b. 1917), Dorothy Lewis Bernstein (b. 1914), Gertrude Cox (1900–78), Hilda Geiringer von Mises (1893–1973), Evelyn Granville (b. 1924), Ellen Hayes (1851–1930),

Grace Hopper (b. 1906), Carol Karp (1926–72), Claribel Kendall (1889–1965), Edna Lassar (1902–84), Helen Merrill (1864–1949), Mary Newson (1869–1959), Emmy Noether (1882–1935), Mia Rees (b. 1902), Julia Robinson (1919–85), Pauline Sperry (1885–1967), Mary Weiss (1930–66), and Anna Wheeler (1883–1966).

To encourage the entry of women into mathematical fields and to promote the equal treatment of women in the mathematical community, the Association for Women in Mathematics (AWM) was founded in 1971. The association has established a speakers' bureau of women available for presentations to audiences ranging from high school students to research mathematicians, and has published a brochure, *Careers for Women in Mathematics.*

—*Jonell Duda Comerford and Jonathan W. Zophy*

See Also:

Noether, Emmy; Robinson, Julia; Science

References:

Green, Judy, and Jeanne La Duke. "Women in the American Mathematics Community: The Pre-1940s Ph.D.'s." The *Mathematical Intelligencer* 9 (1987): 11–21.

Grindstein, Louise, and Paul Campbell, eds. *Women of Mathematics: A Biobibliographic Sourcebook.* Westport, Conn.: Greenwood, 1987.

Perl, Teri. *Math Equals: Biographies of Women Mathematicians.* Menlo Park, Calif.: Addison-Wesley, 1978.

MATRIARCHY is a hypothetical cultural form in which gender dominance is constructed in such a way that women as mothers have a greater control over the distribution and use of culturally sanctioned power than do men. To date, no true matriarchies have yet been conclusively documented in historical or contemporary cultures, though in some societies, like the matrilineal Iroquois, in which women exercised a considerable degree of leadership as mothers, approximately equal quantities of power existed between the genders.

Recently, the poor urban black family, which is often female-headed, has been depicted as a matriarchal system. Most theorists who assert that these families are matriarchies also claim that this matriarchal system is the cause for poverty among urban blacks in the United States. More critical analysis of this phenomenon reveals that these "matriarchies" (more properly, "female-headed households" or "female-headed kin networks") can actually help the urban poor survive, but that men still have a greater amount of power (i.e., white males remain in control of economic resources within the greater society).

During the nineteenth century, several theorists argued that human cultures evolved from a period of primitive anarchy in which women ruled, but that, over time, this authority was transferred to men, either by women voluntarily giving up their power or by men taking power away from them. Most notable amongst these theorists were J. J. Bachofen, whose *Das Mutterrecht/Mother Law* was first published in 1861, and Lewis Henry Morgan, whose *Ancient Society* was published in 1877. Since then, most anthropologists have dismissed these theories.

Myths of matriarchy have often been used to validate male dominance by claiming that men were forced to take control away from women for various reasons. These myths come in at least two forms: one in which women are presented as inept bunglers, and another in which women are presented as dangerous creatures who use their evil sorceries to destroy men. In the first myth, women's bungling in their control of society endangered the survival of the community as a whole; thus, men were forced into taking power away from women to save the community.

A second myth of matriarchy used to validate male control holds that women were originally in control but that they misused their powers, both secular and magical, as mistresses of the culture and that they treated men poorly, often killing or maiming them. Men, to protect themselves, were forced to fight women and break their power or to take it away from them. Tales of such mythic battles of the sexes can be found in many cultures, including those of certain South American Indians, the aboriginal peoples of Australia, and in the various myths of Amazon warriors.

—*Steven Mandeville-Gamble*

See Also:

Female-headed Households, Matriliny, Sex-Gender System

References:

Bachofen, J. J. *Das Mutterrecht.* Stuttgart, Ger.: Krais and Hoffman, 1861.

Morgan, Lewis Henry. *Ancient Society.* New York: Holt, 1877; rpt. Tucson: University of Arizona Press, 1985.

Stack, Carol B. *All Our Kin.* New York: Harper, 1970.

MATRILINY refers to descent systems in which descent is traced through the mother. Preindustrial agricultural communities were more likely to develop matrilineal kinship systems, while hunting communities were prone to develop as patrilinies. In matrilineal societies children inherit their wealth, prestige, clan, or lineage membership from their mother's kin group, though in most of these societies, the mother's brother (i.e., the maternal uncle) controls these resources. Thus, in most matrilineal societies the maternal uncle proves to be one of the most important figures in the life of the individual, for he is the person from whom an individual will receive her or his status and wealth. Characteristically, women in matrilineal cultures have more ecomonic and political power, and the men in these kinship systems display less aggressive behavior. Matrilineality should not be confused with matriarchy; in matrilineal societies, men often still control a greater amount of culturally recognized power than do women.

Many of the North American tribes, including the Cherokee, Chickasaw, Choctaw, Creek, Crow, Delaware, Hopi, Iroquois, Laguna, Mandan, Minnitaree, Missouri, Mohican, Natchez, Navajo, Otoe, Tlingit, Wyandote, Yuchi, and most of the sub-Arctic Indian cultures, were matrilineal before contact with Western society. Many of these cultures, however, have lost their characteristic descent patterns as a result of the interference of U.S. inheritance laws, which undercut the matrilineal basis of their society. By mandating that property rights go to a man's children upon his death, instead of to his sister's children, U.S. government policy has erected a barrier to conservation of original cultural patterns.

—*Steven Mandeville-Gamble*

See Also:

Matriarchy, Native American Women, Sex-Gender System

References:

Eggan, Fred. "Historical Changes in the Choctaw Kinship System." In *Essays in Anthropology,* edited by Fred Eggan. Chicago: University of Chicago Press, 1975, pp. 71–90.

Levi-Strauss, Claude. *Elementary Structures of Kinship.* Edited by R. Needham; translated by James Harle Bell and John Richard von Sturmer. Boston: Beacon, 1969.

Morgan, Lewis Henry. *Ancient Society.* New York: Holt, 1877; rpt. Tucson: University of Arizona Press, 1985.

Schneider, David Murray, and Kathleen Gough. *Matrilineal Kinship.* Berkeley: University of California Press, 1961.

MEAD, MARGARET (1901–78), one of the first American women to earn a Ph.D. in anthropology, became a world-renowned anthropologist. Her most famous works include *Coming of Age in Samoa* (1928) and *Sex and Temperament* (1935). With anthropologist Ruth Benedict, Mead helped establish culture and personality studies as an intellectual force in American anthropology; she was dedicated to showing that culture molded personalities and that many supposedly "innate" qualities in human beings, such as gender rules and the traumas of adolescence, were the result of cultural patterning, not biology.

Both of Mead's parents were academics; at the time of her birth in 1901, her father was a professor of economics at the University of Pennsylvania, Philadelphia, and her mother was working on a master's degree. Mead began college at DePauw University as an English major but decided to transfer to Barnard College in autumn of 1920 after being rejected by the sorority system at DePauw, which she later said was her only experience of rejection in her life.

During her senior year at Barnard, Mead attended a course in anthropology taught by Franz Boas, one of the founders of American anthropology. At that time she met Ruth Benedict, then Boas's teaching assistant, who invited her to continue her studies as a student of Boas. Mead agreed and began her graduate program at Columbia University under the tutelage of Boas.

In 1923 Mead married Luther Cressman, her first husband; they divorced in 1926 after Mead returned from her fieldwork in Samoa. In 1928 she married Reo Fortune, with whom she did fieldwork among the Manus (1928–29); the Omaha (summer 1930); and three New Guinean cultures, the Arapesh, the Mundugumor, and the Tchambuli (1931–33). During the last part of their collaborative field research, Mead and Fortune met Gregory Bateson, who was studying the Iatmul at that time in New Guinea. Mead and Bateson fell in love, and after she obtained a divorce from Fortune, she and Bateson married in 1935. Together, they did fieldwork in Bali (1936–38, 1939) and among the Iatmul of New Guinea (1938). Eventually Bateson felt that his marriage to Mead was stifling his own intellectual creativity, and he divorced her in 1943.

In 1926, after returning from her first field experience in Samoa, Mead was appointed assistant curator of ethnology for the American Museum of Natural History, a position she maintained between field trips. In 1942 Mead was made an associate curator of the Museum, and by 1969, she had been named curator emeritus.

Perhaps more than any other single anthropologist, Margaret Mead contributed to a popular understanding of anthropology and the concept of "culture," and made both household terms by the 1960s. Though her books were academic in nature, she wrote them with the American public firmly in mind. She applied her professional perspective to her own contemporary culture, and her scientific approach to discerning the origins of women's roles caused her to revise, by the 1960s, the conservative interpretation of those origins that she had voiced in the 1950s.

—Steven Mandeville-Gamble

See Also:
Women in Higher Education

References:

Bateson, Mary Catherine. *With a Daughter's Eye.* New York: Washington Square, 1984.

Mead, Margaret. *Blackberry Winter.* New York: Washington Square, 1972.

———. *Coming of Age in Samoa.* New York: Quill Press, 1928.

———. *Sex and Temperament in Three Primitive Societies.* New York: Quill Press, 1935.

Metraux, Rhoda. "Margaret Mead: A Biographical Sketch." *American Anthropologist* 82 (June 1980): 262–69.

MENARCHE is the term for the onset of menstruation, which usually occurs in the last stages of the transition period between childhood and adulthood called puberty. The onset of adolescence triggers the hormonal production required to initiate the development of secondary sex characteristics. Due to the improved health and nutrition of girls in the United States since 1900, menarche begins earlier and ends later for most American women. During childhood, a part of the brain called the hypothalamus secretes very low levels of luteinizing hormone releasing hormone (LHRH), which results in the secretion of low levels of follicle-stimulating hormone (FSH) and luteinizing hormone (LH) by the pituitary gland. Then, for reasons not completely understood, maturation changes occurring in the hypothalamus and possibly other brain areas result in a gradual increase in LHRH, followed by a rise in FSH and LH secretion. These gonadotropins cause an increase in the production of steroid hormones like estrogen from the ovaries. These hormonal changes are believed to be responsible for the onset of puberty and menarche.

The normal age range for the onset of menstruation can be any time from nine to eighteen years, but it often occurs between the ages of eleven and sixteen years. Menarche does not necessarily indicate that sexual maturity has been reached. It may be over a year before actual ovulation takes place. Anovulatory cycles are believed to occur because the surge of LH is not of sufficient magnitude at this time to cause ovulation.

In order to determine what factors may influence the initial onset of menstruation, some investigators have postulated a critical-weight theory that suggests a girl must reach about 105–106 pounds with about a quarter of this weight being body fat before menarche will occur. Other researchers disagree and claim that there is too much variation in body weight at menarche to support this theory. A more current theory is that the percentage composition of body weight is the significant factor in the onset of reproductive function. The putative minimum of body fat is 17 percent of total body weight. These theories of body fat and weight are still being debated, and other considerations like emotional and genetic factors must also be recognized as important influences on the onset of menstruation.

—Esther K. Wilson

See Also:

Menopause, Menstrual Cycle

References:

Guyton, Arthur C. *Textbook of Medical Physiology*. 7th ed. New York: Saunders, 1986.

Rome, Esther. "Anatomy and Physiology of Sexual Reproduction." In *The New Our Bodies, Ourselves*, edited by Jane Pinkus and Wendy Sanford. New York: Simon & Schuster, 1984, pp. 203–19.

Sloane, Ethel. *Biology of Women*. 2d ed. New York: Wiley, 1985.

MENOPAUSE is the term referring to the final phase of a woman's reproductive capacities. Within primitive societies, menopause—like menstruation—was shrouded in myth and often considered a taboo, which caused menopausal women to feel shame. In modern society this last stage of women's reproductive cycle ceased to be a taboo, yet remained suspect, subject to social and biological misconceptions. Because women have been generally undervalued and defined solely by their reproductive capacity, postmenopausal women have experienced a specialized sexual discrimination and ridicule. Thus, menopause became for women the harbinger of old age, uselessness, and disability. Little credible research was devoted to this phase of women's life cycle until the last third of the twentieth century.

During menopause, the menstrual cycle ceases and ovarian activity and the level of estrogen is reduced to almost none. For about one-half of all women, this period usually occurs at the age of forty-five to fifty years, yet the normal range is usually considered between forty and fifty-five years. Menopause is considered to be completed after a year of cycle cessation. Some factors that may influence its occurrence include heredity, race, health, and nutrition.

The number of immature (primordial) follicles that a woman is born with gradually decreases through childhood and maturity. This reduction of ovarian follicles is due in part to the ovulation of about 450 ova and to the loss of thousands of ova by atresia. When only a few follicles remain, the level of estrogen secretion greatly diminishes and is insufficient to inhibit the secretion of the pituitary gonadotropins (follicle-stimulating hormone and luteinizing hormone). Therefore, these hormones are produced in large, continuous quantities without estrogen's feedback influence. It is believed that the alteration of the hormonal feedback system between the hypothalamus of the brain, the pituitary, and ovaries is what leads to cycle cessation.

The actual conditions experienced during menopause vary. For some women, these altered hormonal levels cause dramatic physiological and psychological changes. Some of these may include genital atrophy, extreme skin flushing called "hot flashes," headache, nervousness, depression, dizziness, and breast problems. Unfortunately, only limited objective research has actually been conducted on menopause, so myths persist that it is a very traumatic, stressful, and horrifying event for all women. Doctors have done little to change this perception when advising women about menopause, and most medical literature has painted a grim picture of menopausal symptoms to be endured. At one extreme, some women do suffer from almost incapacitating physical and psychological symptoms, yet at the other extreme, there are women who experience no clinical symptoms at all. These women report that they experience more gradual physiological and hormonal changes rather than abrupt, dramatic ones. The majority of women experience symptoms between these extremes that are often mild enough to be tolerated or ignored.

Women's reproductive capacity has tradtionally formed the core of the American definition of womanhood. Therefore, within the context of the gender system and the popular conception of womanhood, menopause constituted the termination of a woman's femininity as well as her fertility. As women's life span increased, the psychological impact of the notion of the "death" of youth as well as their fundamental social usefulness became both a feminist and medical issue.

During the 1960s and mid-1970s, menopause was treated medically as an estrogen deficiency; millions of women were advised by both physicians and the pharmaceutical industry to take estrogen in order to stay young and sexy after menopause. The subject of estrogen-replacement therapy became highly controversial after 1975, when studies began to suggest a link between estrogen therapy and increased risk of endometrial and breast cancer.

Since the average age at which women experienced menopause was fifty years by the 1980s and their life expectancy has expanded to seventy-five years, menopause ceased to coincide with the end of women's lives. Many women pursued new careers while in their forties and fifties, so an end to their fertility did not mean an end to their usefulness, but rather offered freedom from the concerns of pregnancy and child care. As the birthrate continued its historic downward trend and childbearing at any age became more a matter of conscious choice, women had begun to define themselves and their womanhood by more than the biological criterion of fertility. Therefore, by the last quarter of the twentieth century, the symbolic meaning of menopause diminished and the medical understanding of the process increased.

—Esther K. Wilson and Angela Howard Zophy

See Also:

Menarche, Menstrual Cycle

References:

Goodman, Madeleine. "Toward A Biology of Menopause." *Signs* 5 (1980): 739–53.

Guyton, Arthur C. *Textbook of Medical Physiology*. 7th ed. New York: Saunders, 1986.

Rome, Esther. "Anatomy and Physiology of Sexual Reproduction." In *The New Our Bodies, Ourselves*, edited by Jane Pinkus and Wendy Sandford. New York: Simon & Schuster, 1984, pp. 203–19.

Sloane, Ethel. *Biology of Women*. 2d ed. New York: Wiley, 1985.

Weideger, Paula. *Menstruation and Menopause: The Physiology and the Psychology, the Myth and the Reality*. New York: Knopf, 1976.

MENSTRUAL CYCLE, also called the female reproductive cycle, refers to the monthly changes that take place in the uterus and ovaries resulting from hormonal influences. In the United States, the cultural attitude to the menstrual cycle reflected the ambivalence of the Western tradition toward this biological event as both a misogynistic taboo and a badge of womanhood. Although defining women's reproductive biology as indicative of their proper social destiny, cultural acknowledgment of menses has characteristically been either oblique and embarrassed, or derisive.

Through the twentieth century, private and informal mother-to-daughter talks remained the basic source of information regarding the menstrual cycle imparted to pubescent girls, but tastefully informative booklets and educational films developed and discreetly distributed by the manufacturers of "feminine protection" products supplemented the oral tradition.

Such products were developed and marketed after World War I when cellulose bandages were adapted to service the menstural cycle discharge, replacing the reusable cotton diapers. These disposable sanitary napkins were marketed by Kimberly-Clark in 1921, and their use was common by the end of the decade. A disposable tampon was developed in 1933 and resulted in the mass-marketed Tampax as an "internal protection" product. Advertising of all "feminine hygiene" products was restricted to women's magazines from the 1930s until the federal ban was lifted in 1972. Television and radio commercials followed the cryptic circumspection of the magazine advertisements, avoiding any direct description of the actual products or their practical application. The standard advertising copy stress upon "confidence" has reflected the fear of menstrual "accidents," meaning the visible signs of menses upon women's outer clothing. This euphemistic and vague advertising notwithstanding, feminine products had become a half-billion-dollar industry by the 1980s.

Scientific understanding of the biological process itself developed slowly during the twentieth century. This cycle functions to cause the release of an ovum from the ovaries and to prepare the uterine lining to be able to nurture a fertilized ovum. In the absence of fertilization, the thick, glandular, superficial endometrial lining of blood, secretions, and tissue is sloughed off. For a cycle of twenty-eight days in length, this occurs in the first three to five days and is called menses. The cycle length is usually twenty-five to thirty days with anywhere between twenty and forty considered within a normal range.

After menarche and until menopause, the monthly hormonal fluctuations determine the time of ovulation and menstruation. The cycle is governed by a hypothalamus-pituitary-ovarian feedback system. The hypothalamus secretes releasing factors that cause the pituitary gland to release follicle-stimulating hormone (FSH) and luteinizing hormone (LH). These gonadotropins initiate the beginning of a maturation process by the ovarian follicles that will eventually result in the release of an ovum on approximately day fourteen of the cycle. This ovulation occurs in response to a surge of LH from the pituitary. Also, as the follicles mature, they produce estrogen, which stimulates preparation of the uterine lining to be able to receive and support a fertilized egg. If no fertilization occurs, the high levels of estrogen and another steroid hormone, progesterone, sharply decrease. This decline causes the superficial uterine lining to break down and be shed. The cycle then begins again.

Throughout history, menstruating women have been surrounded by superstitions, taboos, and myths. Some Native American tribes viewed menstruation as a mystical and powerful force of taboo status, and attempted to protect the tribe from possible harm by sequestering women during menses. In mainstream American society, a sense of shame permeated this quintessential biological event for women and thus fostered a conspiracy of silence about the menstrual cycle. Reluctant to speak freely about their reproductive cycles, many women have felt more comfortable using euphemisms to describe that "time of the month." Even in an age that encourages candor and open public discussion of health matters, attitudes about menstruation remained negative and tended to focus on menstrual problems and disorders, which reinforces the colloquial definition implicit in the designation of the monthly process as "the curse." Only in the late twentieth century have medical and feminist researchers applied unbiased scientific methodology to challenge persistent pseudo-scientific, religious, and cultural prohibitions of sexual intercourse during menses.

Unique characteristics or symptoms have characterized the individual menstrual cycle, and there is high variability in cycle frequency, duration of menses, and amount of flow. For some, the calendar is the only way to predict when bleeding will begin, and for others there are definite signals like breast soreness, constipation, acne, and water retention just before menstruation. These changes can be mild or very distressing and difficult.

Usually describing the effects of the mentrual cycle as pathological rather than natural, physicians have often discounted women's complaints and concerns until recently, when these symptoms were collectively termed "premenstrual syndrome" (PMS). However, the impact of the acknowledgment that some women experience real physical difficulties, not imaginary or psychological ones, remains tainted by sexist assumptions and fraught with potentially discriminatory applications, especially for women who work outside the home. The difficulty in replacing myth with medical fact in the cultural interpretation of sex differences is most clearly demonstrated by the lingering schizophrenic social response to women's menstrual cycle.

—*Esther K. Wilson and Angela Howard Zophy*

See Also:

Menarche, Menopause

References:

Delaney, Janice, Mary Jane Lupton, and Emily Toth. *The Curse: A Cultural History of Menstruation.* New York: Dutton, 1976.

Guyton, Arthur C. *Textbook of Medical Physiology.* 7th ed. New York: Saunders, 1986.

Rome, Esther. "Anatomy and Physiology of Sexual Reproduction." In *The New Our Bodies, Ourselves,* edited by Jane Pinkus and Wendy Sanford. New York: Simon & Schuster, 1984, pp. 203–19.

Sloane, Ethel. *Biology of Women.* 2d ed. New York: Wiley, 1985.

Voelckers, Ellen. *Girls' Guide to Menstruation.* New York: Richards Rosen Press, 1975.

Weideger, Paula. *Menstruation and Menopause: The Physiology and Psychology, the Myth and the Reality.* New York: Knopf, 1976.

MENTOR-PROTÉGÉE RELATIONSHIPS between women, such as Susan B. Anthony and Abigail S. Duniway, Anne Sullivan and Helen Keller, Margaret Mead and Gail Sheehy, have been chronicled throughout history. The notion of wise people counseling the young was first introduced when the Greek poet Homer's "faithful and wise" Mentor advised Odysseus. According to Fenelon's *Telemaque,* Mentor (who was actually the goddess Athena in disguise) played a prominent role by giving her protégé good advice, to the extent that before departing for the Trojan War, Odysseus appointed Mentor as the sage guardian of his house and his son Telemachus. On one occasion, Mentor's advice saved Telemachus from death, and after the wars were over, she aided in the search for the lost Odysseus.

The concept of mentor includes being a teacher, sponsor, adviser, counselor, developer of skills and intellect, host, guide, and exemplar, who assists a protégée in the transition from the child-parent relationship to that of adult-peer. A number of researchers contend that mentors tend to choose protégées with whom they identify and are socially compatible. Most studies agree that the presence or absence of a mentor has significant impact on adult development.

As is the case with all intense long-term interactions, mentor-protégée relationships proceed through some broadly defined stages. The first contact of the protégée with her mentor/teacher at a young age is followed by a demonstration of independence on the part of the protégée; the protégée then provides guidance to others; and, finally, the protégée, in turn, becomes a mentor to some young person.

Studies indicate that mentors are essential for women's success in organizations; that women, over a lifetime, average three mentors to men's two; and that when women indicate having had mentors in their lives, they often cite their therapists. Despite the fact that the first mentor was a woman—and there are numerous historical and contemporary examples of successful female mentor-protégée relationships—very little is known about the process of women's mentoring women or what lasting impact early mentor-protégée relationships may have on women in their later lives. Systematic study of mentor-protégée relationships within women's voluntary associations, such as those formed in the nineteenth-century suffrage movement and in the twentieth-century women's libera-

tion movement, is one approach to gaining a clearer understanding of female mentoring, its significance in women's lives, and its impact on women's history.

—*Susan H. Koester*

See Also:

Networking, Women's Friendships

References:

Bolton, E. B. "A Conceptual Analysis of the Mentor Relationship in the Career Development of Women." *Adult Education* 30 (1980): 195–207.

Halcomb, Ruth. *Women Making It: Patterns and Profiles of Success.* New York: Atheneum, 1979.

Koester, Susan H. "The Mentor-Protégé Relationship: An Alaskan Example." Unpublished manuscript, 1987.

LaFrance, M. "Women and the Mentoring Process: Problems, Paradoxes, and Prospects." Unpublished paper presented at American Psychological Association, Los Angeles, 1981.

Merriam, S. "Mentors and Protégés: A Critical Review of the Literature." *Adult Education Quarterly* 33 (April 1983): 161–73.

Ward, Jean. "The Emergence of a Mentor-Protégé Relationship: The 1871 Pacific Northwest Speaking Tour of Susan B. Anthony and Abigail S. Duniway." Papers from the Northwest Women's Heritage Conference. Seattle: University of Washington, 1982.

METHODIST WOMEN IN THE NINETEENTH CENTURY acted upon the belief of John Wesley, a co-founder of Methodism, that the rule of female silence based on the teachings of the apostle Paul "admits of some exceptions." They sometimes acquired local fame for exhorting, as did Lydia Hawes, a particularly eloquent speaker in Indiana in the 1830s. Such "female ranting" declined as the Methodist Episcopal Church grew affluent and conventional in the mid-nineteenth century. Bishop Jesse Truesdell Peck's *The True Woman* (1857) prescribed decorous roles for women, especially Sunday school teaching, but also suggested that women who needed exceptional opportunities try foreign missions. That became especially attractive after the Women's Foreign Missionary Society began its highly independent service to the denomination in 1869.

Missionaries and other women challenged the limits that men such as Peck set for them. Phoebe Palmer was the best known prophet of "holiness" and argued, in *Promise of the Father* (1859), for expanding women's ministries; Margaret Van Cott became the denomination's first licensed woman preacher in 1868; Anna Oliver and Anna Howard Shaw sought full ordination in 1880. The denomination's legislative body, the General Conference, refused ordination and also barred women from licensed preaching. In 1888 Frances Willard and four other women presented themselves as lay delegates to the General Conference. After they were turned away, the conference recognized the new order of deaconesses. Women were given opportunities to serve, but no share of authority.

Smaller bodies in the broad Wesleyan tradition, particularly the African Methodist Episcopal Zion Church, some of the Holiness churches, the New York Conference of the Methodist Protestant Church, and the United Brethren ordained women in the nineteenth century. The largest Methodist denomination did not fully ordain women until 1956, but all branches of the Wesleyan tradition had women who challenged the Pauline rule and made exceptions to it throughout the nineteenth century.

—*Donald B. Marti*

See Also:

Christianity; Shaw, Anna Howard; Willard, Frances

References:

Keller, Rosemary S., Louise L. Queen, and Hilah F. Thomas, eds. *Women in New Worlds: Historical Perspectives on the Wesleyan Tradition.* 2 vols. Nashville: Abingdon, 1981, 1982.

Rowe, Kenneth. *Methodist Women: A Guide to the Literature.* Lake Junaluska, N.C.: United Methodist Commission on Archives and History, 1980.

MEXICAN WAR (1845–48). Despite its short duration and a limited military and diplomatic significance, the Mexican War became a catalyst for major changes in the lives of women in the United States. The terms of the Treaty of Guadalupe-Hidalgo of 1848, which ended the war, directly affected *Chicana* and Native American women who lived in the more than half a million square miles of territory that Mexico ceded to the United States for fifteen million dollars, as well as mainstream and immigrant women who were part of the settlement of the transMississippi west. The subsequent organization of the newly acquired territories into states according to the stipulations of the Compromise of 1850 incited and inflamed the national debate over the institution of slavery, thus affecting the fate of the black women who were slaves as well as free black and white women who were part of the antislavery movement.

Chicanas were a significant proportion of the 73,500 Hispanics who inhabited California and the Utah and New Mexican Territories in 1848. These women remained unassimilated into Victorian American society because of their ethnic, cultural, and religious differences. Their difficulties under internal colonialism in the nineteenth century translated into the triple jeopardy of being female, Hispanic, and poor in twentieth-century American society. Native American women in the acquired territories and on the Great Plains shared the dislocation of their tribes as the federal government facilitated white settlers' claim to those areas for ranching and farming. Mainstream, free black, and immigrant women were a significant proportion of the pioneer population that settled the plains; their presence brought social and economic stability to the area that would become the heartland and breadbasket of the nation.

The conveniently compelling doctrine that rationalized western expansionism as "Manifest Destiny" during the 1840s justified the war with Mexico as a means of diverting internal domestic conflict over the issue of the existence and expansion of slavery; however, the national debate over the "slave" or "free" status of the added southwestern territory exacerbated the rise of a divisive sectionalism. Women were part of the anti-imperialistic peace movement that particularly opposed this war. Black and white women within the antislavery and abolition movements were not deterred by the fierce and often physically violent reaction of the supporters of the extension of slavery into the territories.

Fought on foreign soil and in the sparsely populated southwest, the Mexican War offered women less opportunity to become camp followers. Moreover, in the late 1840s women lacked the model of Florence Nightingale's organized nursing facilities for the wounded during the Crimean War of 1852 that inspired Clara Barton during the Civil War. Therefore, women's actual participation in the Mexican War was considerably less than that in the Civil War.

—Wendell L. Griffith and Angela Howard Zophy

See Also:

Abolition and the Antislavery Movement, *Chicana*, Civil War, Migration and Frontier Women, Nursing, Pacifism and the Peace Movement, Triple Jeopardy

References:

Bauer, K. Jack. *The Mexican War*. New York: Macmillan, 1974.

Billings, Eliza Allen. *The Female Volunteer, or* The *Life and Adventures of Miss Eliza Allen, A Young Lady of Eastport, Maine.* Unpublished memoir.

Johannsen, Robert W. *To the Halls of the Montezumas*. New York: Oxford University Press, 1985.

Lyons, James Gilborne. "The Heroine Martyr of Monterey." *American Quarterly Register* (June 1849): 483–84.

Stewart, Miller. "Army Laundresses: Ladies of the 'Soap Suds Row.'" *Nebraska History* 51 (Winter 1980): 421-36.

Tutorow, Norman. *The Mexican-American War: An Annotated Bibliography*. Westport, Conn.: Greenwood, 1982.

Wecter, Dixon. *The Hero in America: A Chronicle of Hero Worship*. Ann Arbor: University of Michigan Press, 1941.

MEYER, ANNIE NATHAN (1867–1951) was a writer, founder of Barnard College, civic and cultural activist, and antisuffragist. Born into a prominent Sephardic Jewish family, with many distinguished ancestors and relatives, Meyer nevertheless had a difficult childhood marked by financial troubles and her mother's early death. At eighteen, determined to become a writer, she attended Columbia University's Collegiate Course for Women, but found it unsatisfactory because women had no access to classes—only to examinations. After her marriage to Dr. Alfred Meyer in 1887, she left Columbia, but subsequently organized a drive to found Barnard College (1889), the women's undergraduate division of the University. She became a trustee and remained active in the college's affairs for the remainder of her life.

Meyer's literary career began with her editorship of *Woman's Work in America* (1891), a collection of essays. Her output included novels (*Helen Brent, M.D.* in 1892 and *Robert Annys, Poor Priest* in 1901); works of nature (*My Park Book*, 1898); twenty-six plays (a few were produced on Broadway and elsewhere; most were not); a two-volume autobiography, and hundreds of articles, essays, short stories, and letters to the editors of New York City newspapers. Her themes ranged from art, nature, and literature to the position of modern women, Jewish issues, interracial love and lynching, and the proper clothing for working girls. Although her earliest writing supported "New Women," Meyer ultimately took a more conservative position, and worked actively for antisuffrage, deriding what she termed "spreadhenism," the idea that women's innate moral superiority would purify politics. Her sister, New York Consumers' League founder Maud Nathan, took an equally strong prosuffrage stance.

A member of the Daughters of the American Revolution, Meyer took pride in her heritage, and in the achievements of American Jews. She wrote frequently for Jewish publications, and was an early and vociferous opponent of Hitler. Her concern for human dignity extended to other minorities. She sponsored Zora Neale Hurston as Barnard's first black student, donated books on black history and culture to Hunter College, and contributed to civil rights organizations. At the same time, Meyer believed in assimilation, spoke against Jewish "particularism," deplored the manners and customs of Eastern European Jewish immigrants, and feared that Zionism would create problems of dual allegiance. She accepted Barnard's policy of limiting Jewish admissions, believing that the college should accept no socially embarrassing students.

Strong-willed and eccentric, particularly after the death of her only child, Margaret Meyer Cohen (1894–1923), she never forgot a slight, real or imagined, and engaged in many feuds. At the same time, her warmth and generosity brought her the devotion of lifelong friends and a very happy marriage. Embittered over Barnard's reluctance to recognize her as its founder, she never understood the role anti-Semitism played in denying her that title.

—*Lynn D. Gordon*

See Also:

Barnard College, Jewish Women

References:

Annie Nathan Meyer Papers. American Jewish Archives. Cincinnati, Ohio. New York: Barnard College Archives.

Gordon, Lynn D. "Annie Nathan Meyer and Barnard College: Mission and Identity in Women's Higher Education, 1889–1950." *History of Education Quarterly* 26 (Winter 1986): 503–22.

Meyer, Annie Nathan. *Barnard Beginnings.* Boston: Houghton Mifflin, 1935.

———. *It's Been Fun.* New York: Schumann, 1951.

Taylor, Robert Lewis. "Profiles: The Doctor, the Lady, and Columbia University." *New Yorker* (October 23 and 30, 1943): 27–32; 28–32.

MIDWIFERY is the practice of a midwife, a woman who effects delivery or assists at women's childbirths. Traditionally, such assistance was based upon empirically based knowledge. Midwives learned their skills from other midwives, often their mothers or aunts, and passed on to other women information about healing herbs, soothing potions, and ways of handling birth difficulties. Among the usual skills of early midwives were turning a fetus in utero or successfully delivering a fetus in a breech position.

Midwifery had long been a lay or domestic skill, one of the important health-care resources possessed by women that were critical to community settlement and survival. By the mid-eighteenth century, however, health care was moving out of the household and into the realm of the apothecary and the physician. Midwifery came under the purview of doctors and the influence of medical and scientific understanding and intervention. Increasingly, doctors claimed that their understanding of anatomy and their special tools—forceps, for example—for speeding up or bringing childbirth to a close made them essential attendants. Midwives, meanwhile, were excluded from the educational institutions in which scientific midwifery, or obstetrics, was being taught.

Midwifery/obstetrics was one of the four major areas of medical instruction, and new doctors were eager for midwifery cases that could profitably serve them as entries into the rest of a family's medical business. The traditional midwife continued to serve, but increasingly she attended only the poor and the inaccessible, women whom doctors could not profitably attend. Immigrant midwives, some of whom had had medical training themselves, were also shunted into secondary roles as birth-care providers. The obstetrics that replaced female midwifery was activist and interventive: doctors positioned women flat on their backs, administering drugs to speed up or slow down labor and to deaden or to eradicate its pain.

During the early decades of the twentieth century, doctors and state and national medical and public health associations joined forces to legislate traditional midwives out of legitimate business. As the traditional midwife was being forced out, the nurse-midwife was emerging as a medically certified, often hospital-trained substitute for a physician. A resurgence of traditional midwifery in the home-birth and lay-midwife movements in the 1970s arose in reaction to the physician-dominated hospitalized birth process that had been established during the baby-boom era. The rise of the women's health movement of the 1960s and 1970s as well as the renewed interest in "natural childbirth," which dated back to the 1950s, converged with the desire of women to reassert control and to participate more actively in the birth process, all of which brought an openness to midwifery as a reasonable alternative to hospital delivery by the 1980s.

—Janet Carlisle Bogdan

See Also:

Childbirth, "Granny" Midwifery, Immigrant Midwifery

References:

Bogdan, Janet Carlisle. "The Transformation of American Birth." Diss. Syracuse University, 1987.

Donegan, Jane. *Women and Men Midwives.* Westport, Conn.: Greenwood 1978.

Kobrin, Frances E. "The American Midwife Controversy: A Crisis in Professionalization." *Bulletin of the History of Medicine* 40 (1966): 350–63.

Litoff, Judy Barrett. *American Midwives.* Westport, Conn.: Greenwood, 1978.

MIGRATION AND FRONTIER WOMEN. The presence and contribution of women to the Anglo settlement of the frontier assured the success of the great western migration in North America. Especially in the southern colonies, there were fewer women than men migrating to British North America. An initial assumption that a "Golden Age" of sexual equality for colonial women resulted from this unbalanced sex ratio during the early colonial period has not been supported by further research. Frontier women experienced a de facto equality that allowed them to do "men's work" to assure the survival of the settlement; however, this situational tolerance, which violated the patriarchal gender system, did not produce a de jure equality for women under reformed legal or property statutes. Few frontier women ventured beyond their domestic sphere on a permanent basis, although there were less notorious women than Calamity Jane and Belle Starr, women who utilized the freedom of the frontier to pursue nontraditional occupations.

The majority of women who participated in the western expansion did so as a consequence of their fathers' or husbands' decision to migrate; especially by the mid-nineteenth century, women's move into the frontier usually resulted in a reversion of the quality of their lives to the rugged and hazardous circumstances of their colonial predecessors. As resourceful co-workers and managers, frontier women were crucial to the survival of the family and the farm through their performance of field work, carpentry, and husbandry chores, as well as household and child care duties.

Women shared their families' belief in the opportunities for economic and social advancement in the West, but the journey tested their physical and psychological endurance. As part of a wagon train, women created a female community that provided support and assistance through their mutual obstacles and endless chores. As frontier homesteaders, women experienced isolation from far-distant relations and scattered rural neighbors. Women who settled the Great Plains confronted a vast and often bleak expanse of land unlike the terrain to which they were accustomed. Once arrived at the new location, women first faced the challenge of establishing an adequate shelter until the family could build a more permanent home. The larger homestead tracts placed the nearest neighbor beyond ready call in case of emergency. With determination and resourcefulness, women homesteaders weathered both the physical and economic hardships of the prairie; and, as the farm prospered, women attempted gradually to reintroduce the domesticity they had left "back home" or about which they read in women's magazines such as *Godey's Lady's Book.* Homesteads that survived the first two years usually prospered and endured.

At the final stage of western settlement, women turned their attention to the development of towns as social as well as commercial centers. Early on, women used their religious activities not only for spiritual renewal but for crucial social interaction. The insistence of women brought the establishment of churches, public schools, and other institutions of "civilization" to the frontier and prairie towns by the latter quarter of the nineteenth century. The frontier "schoolmarm" served as the particular agent of the concept of True Womanhood in her role as teacher in the one-room schoolhouse. As individuals and in organzied groups, western women demanded and astutely pursued whatever civic and political reform was necessary to "civilize" their community. As an acknowledgment of their contribution to the development of the new states, western women were the first to be given the vote. In the popular mythology of the American West, the frontier woman stands larger than life beside the cowboy and the Native American as a symbol of courage and endurance.

—Angela Howard Zophy

See Also:

Asian Women, Black Women, Common Law, Cult of True Womanhood, Demography, Great Awakening, Morrill Land-Grant Act, Native American Women, Patrons of Husbandry

References:

Clinton, Catherine. *The Other Civil War: American Women in the Nineteenth Century.* New York: Hill and Wang, 1984.

Faragher, John Mack. *Women and Men on the Overland Trail.* New Haven: Yale University Press, 1979.

Jeffrey, Julie Roy. *Frontier Women: The Transmississippi West, 1840–1880.* New York: Hill and Wang, 1979.

Riley, Glenda. *Inventing the American Woman: A Perspective on Women's History.* Arlington Heights, Ill.: Harlan Davidson, 1986.

Schlissel, Lillian. *Women's Diaries of the Westward Journey.* New York: Schocken, 1982.

Woloch, Nancy. *Women and the American Experience.* New York: Knopf, 1984.

MILITARY SERVICE. Women have served officially or unofficially with the U.S. armed forces since the American Revolution. The first women to gain official status as a corps were the nurses. The Army Nurse Corps was created in 1901, the Navy Nurse Corps in 1908. Approximately 11,275 yeomen (F) served with the navy and marines during World War I, but the loophole in legislation that permitted this was closed in 1925. Originally, nurses in the military suffered from poor pay and nebulous status, and even though they received better pay and disability benefits after World War I, they were only awarded relative rank (approximate rank with fewer benefits and pay than men in the same rank) in 1944.

It was not until after Pearl Harbor that women began serving in nonnurse corps. The army took the lead by creating the Women's Army Auxiliary Corps on May 15, 1942. The navy, Coast Guard, and marines followed suit within the year. At peak strength of the military during World War II, 271,600 women served in some service branch; a total of 350,000 women voluntarily entered the services at some point during the hostilities.

With the passage of the Women's Armed Services Integration Act in June 1948, the women's corps were made a permanent part of the armed forces. Women served in the military during the Korean War and the Vietnam War, but their exact numbers are unknown. It was not until 1984 that the Veterans' Administration sponsored its first survey to determine how many women veterans there were in this country, but the best estimate is that 6 percent of living veterans are women. After long debate and much soul searching, the "separate but equal" women's corps were abolished in 1978 when women were integrated into the services.

In 1976 the first women were admitted to U.S. military academies. A controversy over whether to draft women and/or allow them to serve in combat roles developed in the 1980s. At that time, women constituted approximately 10 percent of the country's peacetime military forces.

—D'Ann Campbell

See Also:

Army Nurse Corps; Marine Corps, Women's Reserve; SPARS; WAVES; Women's Army Auxilliary Corps (WAAC); Women's Army Corps (WAC); U.S. Military Academy

References:

Bach, Shirley, and Martin Binlin. *Women and the Military.* Washington, D.C.: Brookings Institution, 1977.

DePauw, Linda Grant. *Seafaring Women.* Boston: Houghton Mifflin, 1982.

Hancock, Joy Bright, Capt., USN (ret.). *Lady in the Navy: A Personal Reminiscence.* Annapolis, Md.: U.S. Naval Institute Press, 1972.

Holm, Jeanne. *Women in the Military.* Novato, Calif.: Presidio, 1982.

Rogan, Helen. *Mixed Company: Women in the Modern Army.* New York: Putnam, 1981.

Stiehm, Judith Hicks. *Bring Me Men & Women: Mandated Change at the U.S. Air Force Academy.* Berkeley: University of California Press, 1981.

Treadwell, Mattie E. *The Women's Army Corps.* Washington, D.C.: Office of the Chief of Military History, Department of the Army, 1954.

U.S. Department of the Army. Medical Department. *Highlights on the History of the Army Nurse Corps.* Washington, D.C., 1975.

Willenz, June A. *Women Veterans: America's Forgotten Heroines.* New York: Continuum, 1983.

MILLAY, EDNA ST. VINCENT (1892–1950) was renowned as a poet and as a personality, capturing a mood of a time and place in American history as well as providing a strong female voice in American literature.

Born in 1892 and reared by her mother, Millay achieved literary success early with the publication of her long poem *Renascence,* published in a collection in 1912. The poem was an immediate critical success, especially as the product of an eighteen-year-old poet. Sent to Vassar College by the generosity of Caroline Dow, executive secretary of the YWCA training school in New York, Millay graduated in 1917 and moved to Greenwich Village in New York City, where she embodied the spirit of the post–World War I days.

Her life and her poetry in these years (see especially poems in *A Few Figs from Thistles* [1920] and *Second April* [1921]) reflect a witty, sophisticated view of life; her well-known quatrain, "My candle burns at both its ends," is typical. The female speaking voice of the poems, like Millay herself, is independent, even cocky, and as sexually free as her male counterpart. Though she wrote in traditional forms, she seemed to speak for the spirit of the 1920s.

Millay was actively engaged in social issues. She was one of those who protested the unjust conviction and executions in the renowned Sacco-Vanzetti case, and until the approach of World War II she was a pacifist (see her verse drama *Aria da Capo*). With the rise of fascism, however, her writings focused on her rage at the horrors being committed. Although not her best poems, they are nevertheless witness to her strong connection with history and politics.

Many of her works show feminist themes. Relying on highly personal material, Millay creates voices of strong, attractive, clever, sexually liberated women in her poems. Often nature is called on as a source of power and regeneration. Her works provide examples of personal independence and friendships between women, as did her career.

—Mabel Benson DuPriest

References:

Britten, Norman. *Edna St. Vincent Millay*. New York: Twayne, 1967, rev. 1982.

Cheney, Anne. *Millay in Greenwich Village*. University: University of Alabama Press, 1975.

Millay, Edna St. Vincent. *Collected Poems*. New York: Harper, 1956.

Nierman, Judith. *Edna St. Vincent Millay: A Reference Guide*. Boston: G. K. Hall, 1977.

Yost, Karl. *A Bibliography of the Works of Edna St. Vincent Millay*. New York: Harper, 1973.

MIND CURE, also known as metaphysical healing, psychotherapy, and mental therapeutics, was practiced by followers of a variety of scientific religions, such as Christian Science, Theosophy, and New Thought, that emerged after the Civil War. These "metaphysical movements" attempted to enlarge science beyond its empiricist foundations by insisting that it account for religious experience. Mind curists sought to rejuvenate religious life by replacing the "old revelation" contained in Scripture with the "new revelation" of science as revealed by the power of the mind to heal the body. Cures were effected by bringing one's mental attitude and physical state into harmonious balance with the laws of nature. Mind curists sought to restore to Christianity both the centrality and purported techniques of Christ's healing ministry. They had more in common with Eastern religious systems, however, with their syncretic tendencies and their belief in a diffuse, all-pervading Spirit frequently referred to as "the divine current of Being." Thus, the popularity of this movement contributed to the subversion of a specifically Judeo-Christian God.

Philosophically eclectic, mind cure drew from Swedenborgianism, the popular science and health movements, spiritualism, and above all transcendentalism. It was developed in the 1850s by Phineas Parkhurst Quimby, an itinerant clock-maker from New Hampshire who, after experimenting with mesmerism, rejected the idea that his cures were either miraculous or the result of the manipulation of some invisible "magnetic fluid," arguing instead that both the cause and the cure of disease originated in the patient's state of mind. Mary Baker Eddy, one of his patients, went on to elaborate on Quimby's insights (without attribution) in the 1870s and made metaphysical healing the cornerstone of a new religion, the First Church of Christ, Scientist, or Christian Science.

While Christian Science was the most powerful and long-lived of the mind cure sects, it was not necessarily the most representative. Deeply antiauthoritarian and anti-institutional in spirit, many mind curists regarded the tightly organized infrastructure of the Christian Science Church with hostility. These liberationist impulses may also explain why women were drawn to mind cure in even larger proportions than in the already "feminized" protestant denominations. Not incidentally, most of these sects venerated a gender-neutral "Father-Mother" God, endorsed women's rights, valued women's traditional role of healer, and were founded by and gave positions of authority to women, many of whom themselves became objects of devotion.

Mind cure gave rise to pastoral counseling in the 1910s, and so may be regarded as a precursor to modern psychotherapy as well as to psychosomatic medicine and to popular "success literature" emphasizing the power of positive thinking.

—*Catherine Tumber*

See Also:

Eddy, Mary Baker; Transcendentalism

References:

Branden, Charles S. *Spirits in Rebellion: The Rise and Development of New Thought.* Dallas: Southern Methodist University Press, 1963.

Dresser, Horatio W. *A History of the New Thought Movement.* New York: Crowell, 1919.

Gottschalk, Stephen. *The Emergence of Christian Science in American Religious Life.* Berkeley: University of California Press, 1973.

Hale, Nathan G. "Mind Cures and the Mystical Wave: Popular Preparation for Psychoanalysis, 1904–1910." In *Freud and the Americans: The Beginnings of Psychoanalysis in the United States, 1876–1917.* New York: Oxford University Press, 1971.

Judah, J. Stillson. *The History and Philosophy of the Metaphysical Movements in America.* Philadelphia: Westminster, 1967.

Meyer, Donald. *The Positive Thinkers: Religion as Pop Psychology from Mary Baker Eddy to Oral Roberts.* New York: Pantheon, 1980.

Parker, Gail Thain. *Mind Cure in New England: From the Civil War to World War I.* Hanover, N.H.: University Press of New England, 1973.

Peel, Robert. *Mary Baker Eddy.* 3 vols. New York: Holt, Rinehart and Winston, 1966, 1977.

MINIMUM-WAGE LAWS were an important form of protective legislation for women and children from the first law in Massachusetts in 1912 until the passage of the Fair Labor Standards Act in 1938. Initiated by social feminists during the Progressive era, these state laws typically established a wages board with the duties of identifying industries with female work forces where the payment of below-subsistence wages was habitual, then of calculating a living-wage rate, and finally of imposing this rate on designated industries and enforcing its implementation. Minimum-wage laws covered shop workers and the so-called sweated trades—the garment industry and those involving the unskilled hand assembly of small items such as boxes, buttons, and trimmings. Enforcement varied because these boards were grossly underfunded, oversight of scattered workshops and homeworkers was difficult, and the penalties negligible. Nonetheless, the politics of the minimum wage generated landmark debates on the status of women workers and the role of the state in regulating women's employment.

The heyday of minimum-wage laws was 1912 through 1919, when laws were passed for fourteen states (mainly in the Midwest and on the West Coast) and the District of Columbia. Coalitions of women's and progressive organizations, with leadership from Florence Kelley as secretary of the National Consumers' League (NCL), supported passage of minimum-wage laws while most employers and much of organized male labor opposed such legislation. The NCL adopted a plan for the minimum wage for women in 1908 that deliberately deviated from the British model of a gender-neutral law. The tactic of proposing gender-specific protective legislation for women undermined the major opposition: The American Federation of Labor reluctantly endorsed the policy as strictly for women only in 1913; employers' resistance waivered because they were vulnerable to hostile public reaction to poignant stories of exploited women; and the courts in 1908 permitted economic regulation for women on the grounds of their unique vulnerability.

However, employers continued to oppose the laws through litigation, objecting less to application of the principle of women's weakness than to the precedent set by limiting freedom of contract. In *Stettler v. O'Hara* (1917), the Oregon law survived on a tied vote in the Supreme Court. In *Adkins v. Children's Hospital* (1923), the Court overturned a D.C. law, arguing that women's suffrage victory and social progress removed the necessity of state protection and ignoring the claim of a state interest in the "mothers of the race."

In the meantime, new opposition to any special status for women emerged with the formulation of an Equal Rights Amendment in 1921 by the National Woman's party. The debate among women over the issue of minimum wage as protective legislation centered on three controversies: whether the defense of the minimum wage denigrated women; whether the policy had calculable costs in job losses and the development of a gender-segregated labor market, or benefits in raised wages; or whether there were viable alternatives for dealing with the appalling poverty that had given rise to these laws.

Demoralized by setbacks in the courts, the minimum-wage campaigners retreated into defensive tinkering with the laws until the concept was revived by the New Deal spirit of 1933; five eastern states passed a modified version, still for women, during the 1930s. The Court followed the *Adkins* precedent and struck down the New York law in *Morehead v. New York ex rel. Tipaldo* (1936). However, in 1937, in *West Coast Hotel Co. v. Parrish,* the justices changed their position on economic regulation and upheld the Washington state law. Their argument was gender-neutral, rejecting an absolute right of freedom of contract where a public interest could be shown. This cleared the way for a minimum wage regardless of sex—the principle legislated in the Fair Labor Standards Act of 1938.

—*Vivien Hart*

See Also:

Adkins v. Children's Hospital, Fair Labor Standards Act, National Consumers' League, Progressive Era, Protective Legislation, Social Feminism, Wages

References:

Baer, Judith. *Chains of Protection: The Judicial Response to Women's Labor Legislation.* Westport, Conn.: Greenwood, 1978.

Beyer, Clara M. *History of Labor Legislation for Women in Three States.* Bulletin of the Women's Bureau, 66. Washington, D.C.: U.S. Government Printing Office, 1929.

Lehrer, Susan. *Origins of Protective Labor Legislation for Women, 1905–1925.* Albany: State University of New York Press, 1987.

Steinberg, Ronnie. *Wages and Hours: Labor and Reform in Twentieth-Century America.* New Brunswick, N.J.: Rutgers University Press, 1982.

MINOR V. HAPPERSETT (October 1874). Virginia Minor was an officer in the National Woman Suffrage Association whose attorney husband was equally committed to woman's rights. Together, they developed the constitutional argument that women citizens were protected in their right to vote under the Fourteenth Amendment. As Virginia Minor said, "I believe that the Constitution of the United States gives me every right and privilege to which every other citizen is entitled; for while the Constitution gives the States the rights to regulate suffrage, it nowhere gives them power to prevent."

Their strategy was adopted by the National Woman Suffrage Association and became the foundation of an extraordinary campaign of civil disobedience, in which hundreds of women across the country broke state laws by voting or bringing suit against registrars who refused to let them vote. A number of court cases followed, including Susan B. Anthony's trial for voting, and the suffragists lost them all.

The final test case of woman suffrage under the Fourteenth Amendment began in 1872 when Reese Happersett, the St. Louis registrar of voters, refused to place Virginia Minor's name on the list because "she was not a 'male' citizen, but a woman," and therefore ineligible to vote in the state of Missouri. Because married women under the common law were unable to bring suit independently of their husbands, in association with her husband, Francis, Virginia sued for $10,000 damages in the circuit court at St. Louis, lost, and subsequently lost on appeal to the Missouri Supreme Court. They carried the case to the United States Supreme Court, with Francis Minor as the chief attorney arguing this landmark woman suffrage case. Chief Justice Morrison R. Waite's opinion declared that suffrage was not coexistent with citizenship, that states had the absolute right to grant or deny suffrage, and that "the Constitution of the United States does not confer the right of suffrage upon any one." The court's decision was unanimous: "If the courts can consider any question settled, this is one," these nine white men agreed.

Virginia Minor continued her resistance. During the summer of 1879, she refused to pay her taxes, explaining to the board of assessors, "I honestly believe and conscientiously make oath that I have not one dollar's worth of property subject to taxation. The principle upon which this government rests is representation before taxation. My property is denied representation, and therefore can not be taxable."

This Supreme Court decision marked the end of the nineteenth-century quest for woman suffrage through judicial fiat. After *Minor v. Happersett* in 1874, supporters agreed that only a federal amendment to enfranchise women or a state-by-state campaign for individual suffrage statutes would secure the vote for women. Therefore, this decision marked a turning point in the strategy of the nineteenth-century woman suffrage movement.

—*Sally Roesch Wagner*

See Also:
National Woman Suffrage Association, Suffrage

References:

MacGregor, Molly Murphy. *Women and the Constitution.* Santa Rosa, Calif.: National Women's History Project, 1987.

Minor v. Happersett. 53 No., 58, and 21 Wallace, 162. 1874.

Stanton, Elizabeth C., Susan B. Anthony, and Matilda J. Gage, eds. *The History of Woman Suffrage.* Vols. 1–3. New York: Fowler and Wells, 1881–86.

Wagner, Sally Roesch. *A Time of Protest: Suffragists Challenge the Republic, 1870–1887.* Sacramento, Calif.: Spectrum, 1987.

MISOGYNY is traditionally defined as hatred, dislike, or mistrust of women. Anthropological studies have identified avoidance behavior patterns in many cultures that involve men's shunning of women in particular situations and in particular roles; however, recent scholarship regarding misogyny in American culture extends into a number of disciplines in addition to women's history and gender studies, including psychology, history of religion, theology, literary criticism, and literary history. Studies of misogyny in American literature examining the roles of women as depicted by male authors are numerous, while recent psychological studies stress the role of Western patriarchal culture in limiting and restricting women's self-images and men's images of women. New studies within the fields of history of religion and theology explore the significance of patriarchal religions' characterizations of women.

—*Mary G. Hodge*

See Also:
Christianity, Feminist Literary Criticism, Psychology, Women's Studies

References:

Cooey, Paula M., Sharon A. Farmer, and Mary Ellen Ross, eds. *Embodied Love: Sensuality and Relationship.* New York: Harper & Row, 1987.

Harding, M. Esther. *The Way of All Women.* New York: Colophon, 1975.

Millett, Kate. *Sexual Politics.* New York: Doubleday, 1970.

Rogers, Katherine M. *The Troublesome Helpmate, A History of Misogyny in Literature.* Seattle: University of Washington Press, 1966.

Woodman, Marion. *Addiction to Perfection: The Still Unravished Bride, A Psychological Study.* Toronto: Inner City Books, 1982.

———. *The Pregnant Virgin.* Toronto: Inner City Books, 1985.

The **MISS AMERICA PAGEANT** (1921–) had its beginning as an effort to keep tourists in Atlantic City past the Labor Day weekend. Because of the success of the International Rolling Chair Pageant held the previous year, the Chamber of Commerce decided to continue the event in 1921 and to include a beauty pageant. The organizers of the Miss America contest, attempting to offend no one, carefully emphasized the wholesome, natural qualities of the contestants and their athletic abilities.

Herb Test, a reporter for the *Atlantic City Press,* was the creator of the title "Miss America." Hired to handle publicity for the contest, he decided city newspapers should run local contests by asking their readers to submit photographs. The city winners would have all of their expenses paid to compete in the

Atlantic City pageant. The winner there would be called "Miss America." On Tuesday, September 6, 1921, hundreds of girls competed, and Margaret Gorman, a sixteen-year-old from Washington, D.C., won the first Miss America title and a Golden Mermaid statue worth $5,000.

The pageant's budget and size grew with each succeeding year. By the late 1920s, people expressed concern for the exploitation of the morals of the contestants. They also suggested the pageant was fixed. Although the promoters attempted to eliminate the sensual aspect of the contest, many contended it remained closer to a carnival event than the high-class production they envisioned. As a result, the pageant was discontinued in 1927, not to return until 1933. The pageant continues to claim the Depression was the reason for the discontinuance, although the stock market crash didn't occur until 1929.

Each succeeding decade has brought new innovations and changes. Talent was introduced into the competition in 1938. By 1939 the pageant began to upgrade its rules. The minimum age was raised to eighteen; only states, recognized cities, and regions could send contestants; and the girls had to swear they had never been married.

The first year the contest was officially titled the Miss America Pageant was 1941. When the United States entered World War II, so did Miss America, as she went on tours and endorsed the sale of war bonds. The 1940s also brought the awarding of scholarships to contestants, as the pageant became the largest private endower of scholarships to women. Long-lasting changes to the pageant came about in the 1950s as it adapted to the needs of television. Bert Parks, a popular game-show host, made his appearance and remained with the pageant until 1980. The song that almost everyone recognizes, "There She Is" by Bernie Wayne, was sung for the first time at the pageant. Despite the resurgence of the women's movement in the 1960s, the pageant continued as usual. The women's liberation movement made protests on the boardwalk, where women demonstrated against the sex-object status of the contestants as well as the pageant's sending Miss America to entertain the American troops in seeming support of the Vietnam War.

Although the fiftieth anniversary of the pageant was celebrated in 1971, the decade of the 1970s saw less publicity than at any other time. This was only an interlude before the negative fallout of the eighties. Bert Parks was replaced permanently by Gary Collins, television personality and the husband of Mary Ann Mobley, Miss America 1959. Vanessa Williams, the first woman of color to earn the crown, became the first Miss America to be dethroned when *Penthouse* magazine printed nude pictures of her in its July 1984 issue, only two months before the 1985 pageant.

From its beginning, the Miss America Pageant was an attempt to make the display of women's bodies respectable. Although talent and intellect were added to the contest, the judging of contestants in swimsuits remains the most important feature of the decision-making process.

—*Judith B. Lucas*

See Also:

Beauty Pageants, Sexism, Twentieth-Century Women's Rights Movement

References:

Banner, Lois W. *American Beauty.* New York: Knopf, 1983.

Bowen, Ezra, ed. *This Fabulous Century.* Vol. 3. New York: Time Life Books, 1969, 1974.

Funnel, Charles E. *By the Beautiful Sea: The Rise and High Times of That Resort, Atlantic City.* New York: Knopf, 1975.

Martin, Nancie S. *Miss America Through the Looking Glass.* New York: Messner, 1985.

Prewitt, Cheryl, and Katheryn Slattery. *A Bright and Shining Place.* New York: Viking, 1971.

MITCHELL, MARIA (1818–89) was the preeminent woman scientist of her generation and devoted much of her life to assisting other women to enter scientific fields. Trained by her astronomer father, she was a librarian on Nantucket Island when she identified a comet and won an international medal. That event catapulted her into prominence, which led to a number of female "firsts" (including membership in the American Association for the Advancement of Science) and a position as professor of astronomy at Vassar College. She continued scientific observations as a field researcher and computer for the *Nautical Almanac*, which not coincidentally asked her to compute the position of the planet Venus.

Once at Vassar, Mitchell trained the first generation of women astronomers who went on to prominent observatories and to other professorships, and she more generally encouraged her students into scientific careers. In addition, she was an active member and president (in 1875) of the American Association for the Advancement of Women, whose annual peripatetic meetings inspired middle-class women and their daughters to voluntary activism and advanced education. Mitchell herself used the Association as a podium to advance the idea that women could achieve prominence in scientific and medical pursuits. A friend of reformers Mary Livermore and Antoinette Brown Blackwell, Maria Mitchell supported suffrage for women but concentrated her public efforts on other immediate and practical concerns for women's education at Vassar and elsewhere. She believed that women required personal encouragement in a supportive environment in order to gain the confidence as well as the expertise necessary to participate in the competitive and often hostile professions of science.

—Sally Gregory Kohlstedt

See Also:

Blackwell, Antoinette; Livermore, Mary; Science; Vassar College; Women in Higher Education

References:

Kendall, Phoebe. *Maria Mitchell: Her Life, Letters and Journals* Boston: Lee & Shepard, 1896.

Kohlstedt, Sally Gregory. "Maria Mitchell and the Advancement of Women in Science." In *Uneasy Careers and Intimate Lives: Women in Science 1789–1979*, edited by Pnina G. Abir-Am and Dorinda Outram. New Brunswick, N.J.: Rutgers University Press, 1987.

Rossiter, Margaret. *Women Scientists in America: Struggles and Strategies to 1940*. Baltimore: Johns Hopkins University Press, 1982.

Wright, Helen. *Sweeper in the Sky: The Life of Maria Mitchell. First Woman Astronomer in America*. New York: Macmillan, 1949.

MOBILIZATION. During the Great Depression of the 1930s, women were forced out of the American work force to enable more men to work. With the onset of World War II, these women were needed to replace the male workers drafted into military service.

The U.S. government set up several agencies to coordinate the mobilization of women for war work. Although the War Manpower Commission was established to mobilize both men and women, much of its work was directed solely at women. The Women's Bureau, which had been created in 1920 to investigate women's special needs in the work force and had become dormant during the 1930s, reemerged during World War II as the watchdog for female workers. The War Advertising Council was set up to encourage war-related advertising. Its official position was that war advertising was the best way to sell products and win goodwill.

At the start of the war, the primary emphasis was on high wages. Although the government policy of equal pay to women was never rigidly enforced, in general women's pay increased significantly during the war. This approach was abandoned in 1943 because of the fear of overspending and inflation. The main appeal then became patriotism, which had two directions. Positive appeals encouraged women to "Do your part." Negative appeals fed on guilt: "A soldier may die if you don't help out." These appeals were later personalized as women were encouraged to "take a job for your husband/son/brother" and "keep the world safe for your children." Day-care centers were established for the children of working mothers; however, most were never utilized. Of the 4.5 million children under the age of four with working mothers, only 130,000 attended the three thousand day-care centers throughout the country.

The aim of the government was to bring as many women into the work force as possible. The success of these efforts is evidenced by the fact that the number of working females increased from 27.6 percent to 37 percent by the end of World War II. These agencies were also successful in bringing women into traditionally male jobs. Women in factory work increased 460 percent during World War II.

The mobilization effort was abruptly halted in 1945, as many women were forced out of their jobs to make room for the returning male veterans. Many other women voluntarily abandoned the work force to welcome returning husbands and to start long-delayed families.

—Judy Sydow Schmidt

See Also:

War Manpower Commission, Women's Bureau, World War II

References:

Campbell, D'Ann. *Women at War with America.* Cambridge: Harvard University Press, 1984.

Hartmann, Susan M. *The Homefront and Beyond: American Women in the 1940's.* Boston: Twayne, 1982.

Rupp, Leila J. *Mobilizing Women for War.* Princeton: Princeton University Press, 1978.

MODERN WOMAN: THE LOST SEX (1947) was an example in both tone and substance of post–World War II antifeminist literature. Coauthored by sociologist Marynia Farnham and historian Ferdinand Lundberg, this bestseller employed Freudian sexology to define women's proper place in postwar American society. Authoritatively citing women's presence in the work force and absence from the home as the source of problems ranging from the Depression to war, Farnham and Lundberg's book defined an "independent woman" as an oxymoronic concept, and thereby these self-designated experts relegated women to passivity in their social and sexual lives.

The more dominant presence within this influential antifeminist book, Farnham played the role of spokesperson for well-adjusted womanhood. A Ph.D. herself, Farnham warned her readers that education increased the possibility of sex disorders among women; and although Farnham was a practicing psychoanalyst, she categorically stated that women's mental health depended upon their performance and acceptance of their domestic role. Emphasizing women's "natural" noncompetitive dependence, Farnham decreed "self-acceptance" of a sexually-based inferiority, dependency upon men, and passive fulfillment in both sex and motherhood for the well-adjusted woman. Of course, passivity in sexuality on the part of women did not relieve them from the responsibility of their own frigidity.

A frontal assault on feminism as a sickness, *Modern Woman* upheld as neurotic any challenge to male dominance. Thus Farnham dismissed feminism as a psychic disorder, a pathological denial of women's instinct that produced in feminist women hatred of their fathers, rejection of motherhood, and unfeminine behavior. The authors' proposal for supplemental state support of the woman in the home implied a tacit recognition of the economic factors involved in the contemporary undermining of the traditional women's role. The impact of *Modern Woman* stemmed not from its original or salient criticism of feminism, but rather from the timing of its publication. Not only was its influence enhanced by the post–World War II antifeminism but by the lack of a contemporary, articulate feminism to counter its pseudo-psychological propaganda.

—Angela Howard Zophy

See Also:

Antifeminism, Freudianism, Psychiatry, Psychology

References:

Chafe, William H. *The American Woman: Her Changing Social, Economic, and Political Roles, 1920–1970.* New York: Oxford University Press, 1972.

Daniel, Robert L. *American Women in the 20th Century: The Festival of Life.* San Diego: Harcourt Brace Jovanovich, 1987.

Lundberg, Ferdinand, and Marynia Farnham. *Modern Woman: The Lost Sex.* New York: Harper, 1947.

Mitchell, Juliet. *Psychoanalysis and Feminism.* New York: Vintage, 1975.
Ryan, Mary P. *Womanhood in America: From Colonial Times to the Present.* 3d ed. New York: New Viewpoints/Franklin Watts, 1984.
Woloch, Nancy. *Women and the American Experience.* New York: Knopf, 1984.

MOHR, NICHOLASA (b. 1935), artist, novelist, essayist, juvenile and adult short-fiction writer, is the first Puerto Rican woman on the mainland to write in English about her own ethnic origins as the child of Island migrants to New York City. She wrote and designed the book jackets for both *Nilda* (1973), an award-winning children's novel, and *El Bronx Remembered* (1975), followed by two other semiautobiographical books: *In Nueva York* (1977) and *Felita* (1979).

Mohr's stories serve as an excellent primary source for interpreting the labyrinth of Puerto Rican family and community life in the ethnic ghetto during the four post–World War II decades. Her skills as both a graphic artist and author enable her to depict visually and realistically the life-styles of people who, as citizens, did not face migration quotas, but who nonetheless were "strangers in their own country [having brought with them a different language, culture, and racial mixture]." Mohr remembers "how unjust it was for my mother . . . to conform to the role of wife and mother, always sacrificing. . . ." Mohr herself, born during the Great Depression as the only daughter in a family with seven children, worked as a waitress while studying art before embarking on a writing career.

Mohr's thematic focus is in detailing her people's plight, the problems of a rural migrant group suddenly thrust into an industrial society, with many large female-headed welfare households living in rat-infested, crumbling tenements, often with no male role model for rebellious street children. Coming to the mainland with few skills, Puerto Ricans are forced into menial jobs where racial and religious discrimination add to adjustment problems. Her anecdotal tales describe failed marriages, illegitimacy, illness, insensitive teachers and social workers, police brutality, and superstitious subculture life within a powerful Anglo community. Realistically sketched vignettes, frequently told from an innocent, questioning, resigned child's vision, unfold like documentaries without artificial solutions or contrived endings, giving her stories unique credibility. Warm family solidarity and joyous neighborhood participation in the colorful pageantry of religious celebrations help her proud protagonists cope creatively with hardships, finding the strength to survive. Hispanics represent the largest ethnic group in the United States, and Nicholasa Mohr's stories give readers the opportunity to learn about Puerto Rican contributions to American social history.

—*Edith Blicksilver*

See Also:
Chicana, Female-Headed Households

References:

Miller, John. "The Emigrant and New York City: A Consideration of Four Puerto Rican Writers." *MELUS: The Journal of the Society for the Study of the Multi-ethnic Literature of the United States* 5 (Fall 1978): 94–99.
———. "Nicholasa Mohr: Neorican Writings in Progress 'A View of the Other Culture.'" *Revista InterAmerican* 9 (1979–80): 543–49.
Mohr, Nicholasa. "An Awakening . . . Summer 1956, for Hilda Hidalgo." In *Revista Chicano-Riqueña, Women of Her Word, Hispanic Women Write*, edited by Evangelina Vigil. Houston: University of Houston Press, 1983, pp. 107–12.
———. "Christmas Was a Time of Plenty." In *Revista Chicano-Riqueña, New York City Special*, edited by Nicolás Kanellos and Luis Dávilla. Houston: University of Houston Press, 1980, pp. 33–34.
———. *El Bronx Remembered.* New York: Harper & Row, 1975.
———. *Felita.* New York: Dial, 1979.
———. *Going Home.* New York: Dial, 1986.
———. *In Nueva York.* New York: Dial, 1977.
———. *Nilda.* New York: Harper & Row, 1973.
———. "Puerto Rican in the U.S.: The Adopted Citizen." In *Ethnic Lifestyles and Mental Health*, edited by Gloria Valencia-Weber. Stillwater: Oklahoma State University Press, 1980, pp. 147–56.

———. "Puerto Ricans in New York: Cultural Evolution and Identity." In *Images and Identities: The Puerto Rican in Literature*, edited by Alesa Rodríguez de Laguna. Rutgers: The State University of New Jersey Press, 1983, pp. 1–8.

———. *Rituals of Survival: A Woman's Portfolio.* University Park, Tex.: University of Houston Press, 1985.

———. "A Special Gift." In *Revista Chicano-Riqueña*, edited by Nicolás Kanellos. Houston: University of Houston Press, 1981, pp. 91–100.

———. "Their America." *Perspectives, The Civil Rights Quarterly* 14 (Summer 1982): 23–24.

Turner, Faythe. "The Myth of the American Dream in the Works of Nicholasa Mohr." Unpublished paper.

MONROE, MARILYN (1926–62) was an American film star whose career spanned a mere dozen years and eleven major film roles but who has, since her death, become a legend. The mysteries of her life and death, her powerful screen presence, and her magnetic sensuality have combined to make her an icon of the Hollywood film, revered and reviled by successive generations of critics, social commentators, and ordinary men and women. Books and articles about her still appear regularly and become best-sellers decades after her death.

She was born Norma Jean[e] Baker in Los Angeles, and grew up fatherless, perhaps illegitimate. Her mother, Gladys Mortensen, was a film cutter who left her infant daughter in the care of foster parents much of the time; when Monroe was seven, her mother was institutionalized for mental illness and remained confined, except for brief periods, for the rest of her daughter's life. Monroe spent the next nine years in a series of foster homes and institutions, until she was sixteen, when her then-guardian persuaded her to marry James Dougherty, a neighbor boy and aircraft factory worker. Two years later, in 1944, Dougherty was drafted and shipped overseas, and soon afterward Monroe was "discovered" and began a career as a model. Divorcing Dougherty in 1946, she became a Hollywood starlet with Twentieth Century Fox, which changed her name to Marilyn Monroe. A year later, the studio dropped her contract. In 1948 she got a six-month contract at Columbia, which was not renewed, and was again signed by Fox.

Her first big break was in John Huston's *Asphalt Jungle* (1950), which produced a flood of fan mail, and by 1952, when her nude photograph on a calendar caused a scandal that brought nationwide publicity, she had begun to capture the imagination of the nation. In that year she made *Monkey Business* and *Niagara*, began work on *Gentlemen Prefer Blondes*, one of her best roles, and was receiving over five thousand fan letters a week. The following year she made *How to Marry a Millionaire* and *River of No Return*, and shortly after married Joe DiMaggio, America's baseball hero. The marriage lasted nine months. In 1954 she made *There's No Business like Show Business* and *The Seven Year Itch*, and after her divorce headed for New York to become a serious actor and to force Fox to give her a better contract. For a year she made only personal appearances and studied at Lee Strasberg's Actors Studio. When she did sign a new contract with Fox in January 1956, it gave her more money, the freedom to make films at other studios, and right of rejection of vehicles, directors, and cameramen. By the standards of the time, when the studio system was still alive and formidable, it was a triumph.

In 1956 she made *Bus Stop*, the film many believe to be her best, and *The Prince and The Showgirl*, one of her worst. She also married playwright Arthur Miller, a marriage that lasted three and a half years, the longest full-time relationship of her life. For the next two years, she made no films—instead, she played housewife/companion to Miller, miscarried, and began drinking too much and overdosing on barbiturates.

In July 1958 she began filming *Some Like it Hot*, having a second miscarriage just after its completion. In 1960 she began filming *Let's Make Love* and had an affair with co-star Yves Montand as her marriage to Miller entered its final throes. Her visits to psychiatrists and doctors increased during this time, as did her drug usage, resulting in well-publicized absences and misbehavior on and off the set. Yet she began work almost immediately on

The Misfits, with a screenplay by Miller from an *Esquire* short story he had written three years before. The picture, like those before it, was plagued by her mental and physical illness, and as soon as it was completed, Monroe announced publicly that she and Miller were divorcing. It was to be the last film either Monroe or co-star Clark Gable would ever make.

In February 1961 Monroe entered a mental hospital, and twice that same year was hospitalized for physical disorders; she resumed her friendship with DiMaggio and, during that same year, began liaisons with President John F. Kennedy and his brother, Robert. Early in 1962 she began shooting her first picture since *The Misfits*, called *Something's Got to Give*, but from the outset the production was under a cloud. Script changes created delays, and Monroe caused more, showing up for about one-third of the first thirty-five days of shooting. After looking at the rushes, Fox executives decided first to replace Monroe in the picture, then to drop the project completely. Monroe turned to photo/interview sessions with *Life*, *Vogue*, and *Cosmopolitan*, and began reading scripts and planning other projects. A few weeks later, August 4, 1962, she was dead of an apparent overdose of sleeping pills, whether intentional or inadvertent.

This brief public life, turbulent though it was, does not begin to explain the incredible and enduring impact Monroe has had on Americans. For men, she was and continues to be the embodiment of a dream lover. Norman Mailer is eloquent on the subject: "She was our angel, the sweet angel of sex, and the sugar of sex came up from her like a resonance of sound in the clearest grain of a violin. Across five continents the men who knew the most about love would covet her, . . . Marilyn was deliverance, a very Stradivarius of sex, so gorgeous, forgiving, humorous, compliant and tender that even the most mediocre musician could relax his lack of art in the dissolving magic of her violin." For women, the reactions are more complex. In life, she was a threat—the ultimate rival for men's affections and a blatant acknowledgment of one's own weaknesses. As Gloria Steinem acknowledges, she "embodied . . . the fear of a sexual competitor who could take away men on whom women's identities and even livelihoods might depend; the fear of having to meet her impossible standard of always giving—and asking nothing in return; the nagging fear that we might share her feminine fate of being vulnerable, unserious, constantly in danger of being a victim." After her death, however, women's perception of Monroe began to change, especially since the feminist revolution of the 1960s, to a complex mixture of guilt and empathy. It is likely, then, that the mysteries of Marilyn Monroe will continue to engross successive generations, but also that those generations will be able to appreciate her film work more fully, unburdened by the past, and simply enjoy and be awed by her powerful, evocative presence.

—*Frances M. Kavenik*

See Also:
Movie Stars

References:

Mailer, Norman. *Marilyn*. New York: Warner, 1973.

Steinem, Gloria. *Marilyn*. Photography by George Barris. New York: Henry Holt, 1986.

Summers, Anthony. *Goddess: The Secret Lives of Marilyn Monroe*. New York: Macmillan, 1985.

The **MONTANA STATE FEDERATION OF NEGRO WOMEN'S CLUBS**, a regional example of the black women's club movement, resulted from the belief that "effective recognition can only be gained by unity at home." Citing the fact that black women across the country were organizing for "uplift" work, the Pearl Club of Butte, Montana, issued an invitation to its sister black women's clubs to form a state federation. Eight clubs from Kalispell, Butte, Helena, Anaconda, Billings, and Bozeman met in Butte on August 3–5, 1921, to form the Federation. (Some years later the federation substituted *Colored* for *Negro* in its name.) The federation adopted the motto Unity and Perseverance, voted to establish a college scholarship for black students and to send delegates to the National Convention of Negro Women's Clubs. The Dunbar Art and Study Club of Great Falls, an extremely active group, subsequently joined the federation.

For over fifty years the federation supported the work of women's clubs on a local level as well as the national efforts of the Anti-Lynching League and the NAACP. In Montana local clubs lobbied for civil rights legislation at the state level, fought discrimination in school athletics and social events, visited black patients in hospitals and rest homes, sponsored Frederick Douglass Day programs to honor the famed black abolitionist, placed books by black authors in public libraries, organized interracial clubs to foster better race relations, and supported the efforts of blacks to join trade unions. The federation met in convention each year, addressing such topics as "Possibilities of the Negro Woman in Business and Industry," "The Achievement of the Negro," and "Fear." The Montana State Federation finally disbanded in the mid-1970s because of a lack of members.

—*Mary Murphy*

See Also:

Black Women's Clubs, National Association for the Advancement of Colored People

References:

Montana Federation of Colored Women, Records, 1921–78. Montana Historical Society Archives, Helena, Mont.

Slauson, Lena Brown. Oral History Interview. Montana Historical Society Archives, Helena, Mont.

MOORE, ANNIE CARROLL (1871–1961), children's librarian and writer, was an innovator in public library services to children. In her position as supervisor of work with children in the New York Public Library, 1906–41, she influenced the development of such services worldwide. Furthermore, her extensive contacts with New York publishing houses and authors, her column entitled "The Three Owls" that appeared in the *New York Herald Tribune* (1924–30) and later in the *Horn Book*, and her reviews in the *Bookman* (1918–41) influenced publishing for children. Her two books for children were *Nicholas: A Manhattan Christmas Story* (1924) and *Nicholas: The Golden Goose* (1932). She fought successfully to obtain professional status for librarians working with children in the NYPL and for the establishment of a section devoted to children's librarianship within the American Library Association. Among the techniques now widely accepted that are associated with her are story hours, cooperation with the schools and teachers, and vibrant exhibits and presentations of music and dance.

Anne Carroll Moore was one of ten children, born to a lawyer and his highly cultivated wife in Limerick, Maine. She had intended to read law with her father upon completion of her formal education at Bradford (Mass.) Academy, but the deaths of her parents and a sister-in-law left her burdened with domestic chores. After her brother's remarriage, she began her library studies at Pratt Institute in Brooklyn.

Although a woman of wide-ranging interests and compassion, she alienated many with her eccentricities and self-centeredness. Moore participated in the campaign to save Leo Frank, who had visited her library as a boy, when he was falsely accused and unjustly convicted of the 1913 murder of Mary Phagan in Atlanta, Georgia. She encouraged the translation and use of foreign materials and supported the work of the American Committee for Devastated France in establishing services for French children after World War I. However, in her later years, resentful of mandatory retirement, she became quite difficult, distressing many colleagues and friends, especially her successors, as she continued to revisit "her" department.

—*Suzanne Hildenbrand*

See Also:

Children's Library Movement, Librarianship

References:

Moore, Anne Carroll. *My Roads to Childhood: Views and Reviews of Children's Books.* Boston: The Horn Book, 1961.

Sayers, Frances Clarke. *Anne Carroll Moore: A Biography.* New York: Atheneum, 1972.

MOORE, MARIANNE CRAIG (1887–1972), a key figure in modern American poetry, wrote with a disdain for conventional poetry, renouncing elaborate diction and subjectivity and relying on the observation of details to discover "the genuine." To Moore, *good* poems are "imaginary gardens with real toads in them."

Moore's life was as conventional as her verse was original. Born in Kirkwood, Mississippi, she spent much of her adult life living with her mother in New York City. Although she specialized in biology in college and once considered becoming an artist, she instead became a shorthand and typing teacher and then a librarian. She never lost interest in biology and art, however, and they became two sources of power in her poetry. Her editorship of the *Dial* from 1925 until its demise in 1929 also strengthened her natural skills. During this period and throughout her life, she was respected for her literary reviews and her editorial judgment.

Moore's first poems were published in *Poetry* and the *Egoist* in 1915, and her first book of poems, simply entitled *Poems*, was published in 1921 in London without her knowledge by H.D. (Hilda Doolittle) and Bryher (Winifred Ellerman). Moore wrote on a wide range of topics, but her favorite subjects were animals, ranging from the common to the exotic. While she did publish a translation of La Fontaine's fables in 1954, her animal poems are not fables. Rather, they are observations that make her readers think about themselves and, perhaps, look at life differently.

Moore's greatest contributions to poetry are her poetic language, which is at once poetry and prose, and her prosodic innovations. Eschewing the formal metrical and rhyme schemes of traditional verse, Moore devised her own formal patterns, which were unlike anything else in modern American poetry. She treated the stanza rather than the line as the poetic unit and arranged lines according to the number of syllables rather than by a specific meter, creating an elaborate and thoroughly regular verse pattern. Rhymes occur frequently, although at unexpected places—unaccented syllables and middles of words, for example. All the while, however, Moore's verse remains quiet and unpretentious.

—*Kenneth E. Gadomski*

See Also:

Doolittle, Hilda

References:

Borroff, Marie. *Language and the Poet: Verbal Artistry in Frost, Stevens, and Moore*. Chicago: University of Chicago Press, 1979.

Costello, Bonnie. *Marianne Moore: Imaginary Possessions*. Cambridge: Harvard University Press, 1981.

Slatin, John M. *The Savage's Romance:The Poetry of Marianne Moore*. University Park: Pennsylvania State University Press, 1986.

MORAL REFORM has been a continuing theme in American history. In Jacksonian America, it featured organizations such as the New York Female Moral Reform Society, founded in May 1834 at the Third Presbyterian Church in New York City. Members of this society wanted to convert New York's large population of prostitutes to evangelical Protestantism and to close the city's many brothels. More fundamentally, these reformers were also interested in confronting the sexual double standard which made it socially acceptable for some men to have mistresses and/or frequent the more attractive houses of pleasure, while women were denied such diversions.

Staff members of the Moral Reform Society began systematically visiting New York bordellos in the fall of 1834 in order to pray with and exhort both inmates and their patrons to change their "sinful ways." Mild forms of intimidation of customers were also utilized, as well as street-corner preaching and proselytizing. The society also opened a House of Reception as a refuge for prostitutes who wished to leave "the life." Few took advantage of the opportunity.

The New York Moral Reform Society made, perhaps, its biggest national impact through publication of its weekly, *The Advo-*

cate of Moral Reform, which became one of the nation's most widely read evangelical reform papers, having a circulation of 16,500 by the late 1830s. Other reformers and reform groups were inspired by the efforts of the society, which continues to exist today as the Woodycrest Youth Service.

Moral reform crusades have continued in a variety of locations and time periods down to the present moment even if they have failed repeatedly to eliminate or reform social vices like prostitution or drug abuse. They have, however, allowed women to play a more public role than was traditionally assigned to them prior to the nineteenth century in the United States.

—*Jonathan W. Zophy*

See Also:

Prostitution

References:

Smith-Rosenberg, Carroll. "Beauty, the Beast and the Militant Woman: A Case Study in Sex Roles and Social Stress in Jacksonian America." *American Quarterly* 23 (1971): 562–84.

———. *Disorderly Conduct: Visions of Gender in Victorian America.* New York: Knight, 1985.

———. *Religion and the Rise of the American City.* Ithaca, N.Y.: Cornell University Press, 1971.

The **MORAVIAN SEMINARY FOR YOUNG FEMALES** was one of the first boarding schools for girls in the United States. The seminary, also known as Bethlehem Female Seminary, grew out of a school opened on May 4, 1742, in Germantown, Pennsylvania, by the Moravians, or Church of the United Brethren, a religious group from Germany. This school and others were opened as part of the Moravians' commitment to "spread knowledge of Christ." During the first several years, the seminary was moved between three communities before being located in Bethlehem, Pennsylvania, on January 6, 1749. Since then it has remained in that community.

The reputation of the school grew quickly, and a number of non-Moravians attended. By 1757, for example, eighty-nine pupils were enrolled, as the seminary absorbed the girls' schools of the neighboring congregations. The seminary included an elementary and secondary boarding school and a town day school. It continued to grow because, as a church official later wrote, "In those early days it was a privilege highly prized to have a daughter under such care and training, taken from the remote backwoods homes in many cases and brought in contact with gentle, pious women of refinement." The school, as the guidelines from September 1785 recorded, kept girls "from their fifth to their twelfth or sixteenth year," and taught them "the Admonition of the Lord in every good habit," along with "reading and writing in both the German and English languages, also arithmetic, sewing, knitting, and other feminine crafts . . . ." They were also instructed in "history, geography, and music, with great care and faithfulness, and as their health and strength may permit."

In 1788 the church prepared "statutes" for the school, which identified the duties of the pupils and their course of study. The daily regimen was strict; pupils were closely monitored and directed by the teachers. Over the next two decades, the growth in enrollment caused the construction of three additional buildings. With the opening of a new facility in 1805, the school became known as the Young Ladies Seminary. Throughout the nineteenth century the school continued to grow as its reputation spread. By 1853, for example, more than 150 pupils were enrolled at the school. The upper division gained accreditation as the Moravian Seminary and College for Women in 1913, while the lower grades continued to offer college preparatory work. In 1949 the grades seven to twelve were moved to a new facility located outside of Bethlehem on an estate donated to the school.

—*Robert G. Waite*

See Also:

Education, Female Academies, Linden Hall Seminary

References:

Haller, Mabel. "Early Moravian Education in Pennsylvania." *Transactions of the Moravian Historical Society* 15 (1953): 1–397.

Mulhern, James. *A History of Secondary Education in Pennsylvania*. Philadelphia: Science Press Printing Co., 1933.
Norton, Mary Beth. *Liberty's Daughters:The Revolutionary Experience of American Women, 1750–1800*. Boston: Little, Brown, 1980.
Reichel, William C. *A History of the Rise, Progress, and Present Condition of the Moravian Seminary for Young Ladies at Bethlehem, Pa.* Philadelphia: Lippincott, 1870.

MORENO, LUISA (n.d.) was a union leader of the CIO's United Cannery, Agricultural, Packing and Allied Workers of America (UCAPAWA) and principal organizer in the Congresso de Pueblos de Habla Española (National Congress of Spanish Speaking People).

A native of Guatemala, she emigrated to the United States in 1928 with her Mexican husband after having spent two years in Mexico City as a correspondent for a Guatemalan newspaper. Moreno's introduction to the plight of working women began in a garment factory near Spanish Harlem where she was employed as a seamstress. After joining a left-wing group of Latinos called El Central Obrero de Habla Española (the Spanish Speaking Workers' Center), she decided to become a labor organizer. She organized Puerto Rican women garment workers in Spanish Harlem who later joined the 1933 strike of the Needle Trades Workers Industrial Union. In 1935 she became a professional organizer for the AFL.

Troubled by Red-baiting within the AFL, Moreno joined the CIO. After assisting organizing efforts in cigar plants in New York City, Philadelphia, and Lancaster, Pennsylvania, she was drawn to the plight of Mexican pecan shellers in Texas. She organized the first Congress of Spanish Speaking People, aimed at creating a national organization to unite Mexican and other Spanish-speaking workers throughout the United States. Moreno served as vice president and organizer of UCAPAWA's California locals. She was forced to resign during the rise of anti-Communist hysteria in the 1940s and was eventually deported.

—*Mary Romero*

See Also:

American Federation of Labor, *Chicana*, Congress of Industrial Organizations, Garment Industries

References:

Camarillo, Albert. *Chicanos in California: A History of Mexican Americans in California*. San Francisco: Boyd & Fraser, 1984.
Ruiz, Vicki. *Cannery Women, Cannery Lives: Mexican Women, Unionizing and the California Food Processing Industry*. Las Cruces: University of New Mexico Press, 1987.

MORMONISM AND WOMEN. The role of women in the Church of Jesus Christ of Latter-day Saints, or Mormon Church as it is popularly known, has been a complex and often paradoxical one since the founding of the group in 1830. Mormonism, seeing itself as both a religion and a culture system, has attempted to encompass the whole of life. Under the leadership of the group's prophet-founder, Joseph Smith, Mormons in the 1830s and 1840s reacted against the religious and social disorder of Jacksonian America by developing a patriarchal family system that drew heavily on Old Testament models. Influenced also by the New Testament, Mormonism stressed the "priesthood of all believers" for men, setting up a hierarchical structure in which all worthy adult males had some direct leadership role within the lay governance structure of the church. Women were linked to this structure only indirectly through association with their husbands, but during the first two decades they did secure the right to participate in public meetings of the church, to vote on important proposals brought before the group, to operate their own women's organization (albeit under ultimate direction of the male priesthood), to receive various "spiritual gifts," and to be "ordained" to administer to the sick.

Religiously, earliest Mormonism fell midway between the most conservative confessional churches such as the Episcopalians, in which women were almost totally excluded from leadership, and the extreme wing of revivalistic and sectarian movements such as the Shakers, which permitted a high degree of equality for women. Until the early 1840s, Mormon women's roles most closely approximated those in mainstream revivalist Protestant groups such as the Methodists and Baptists.

Joseph Smith's effort to introduce a patriarchal polygamous system among his closest associates during the early 1840s was associated with radical changes in Mormon theology and practice. The new temple ceremonies, designed in part to validate plural marriage, emphasized that no person could reach full exaltation in the afterlife without being sealed under the authority of the Mormon church in a celestial marriage to a worthy spouse. Committed Mormons were privately told that polygamy was the highest form of such celestial marriage because it allowed greatly expanded kinship ties. Such ties were considered the primary source of status and power, both in this life and throughout eternity.

Despite efforts to promulgate beliefs and practices that seemed strikingly at variance with the American norm, Mormon attitudes toward women nevertheless remained extraordinarily fluid during the turbulent transitional period immediately prior to Joseph Smith's assassination in 1844. Only following the Mormon arrival in the Great Basin region of the West in 1847 was the group, under Brigham Young's leadership, able to set up and develop to the fullest extent its own distinctive way of life. Although Young was a patriarchal leader par excellence and the key individual responsible for institutionalizing and defending polygamy, he also recognized the vital role that women would have to play in developing frontier Utah, and he encouraged women to exercise a remarkable degree of power, influence, and independence in helping to build the Mormon Zion. Utah established one of the first coeducational colleges in the country in 1850; Mormon women voted in Utah earlier than women in any other state or territory of the United States, including Wyoming; women of the Mormon church were active in the professions, including medicine and teaching; and leading Mormon women established a distinguished woman-written, -edited, and -distributed newspaper of their own, the *Woman's Exponent,* which ranged far and wide over issues of concern to women of the period. Through their powerful women's organization, the Relief Society, and numerous other economic and cultural ventures, Mormon women became a key force in frontier Utah at the very time when the outside society viewed them as oppressed and degraded because of the practice of polygamy.

In response to the intense federal antipolygamy crusade of the 1880s that threatened the very survival of Mormonism, the group in the 1890s began to give up polygamy, direct control over Utah politics, and many other controversial practices. As part of this effort to accommodate to American society, Mormons increasingly adopted Victorian notions of gentility and women's role. The gradual end of frontier conditions in the Mormon West around the turn of the century also contributed to the movement away from the older ideals of the versatile pioneer wife and mother toward that of the Victorian homemaker with no legitimate work role outside the home.

Since World War II, and especially since 1960, attempts to limit Mormon women's sphere of influence have become increasingly pronounced. In an effort to deal with the staggering increase of membership from approximately one million in 1945 to over six million in 1985, Mormon church organization has been restructured and further centralized. As part of reducing duplication of magazines, "correlating" the church educational curriculum, and placing all channels of authority under direct male hierarchical control, the Relief Society has lost its independence in funding and programming, as well as its *Relief Society Magazine,* the only officially approved woman's magazine in the church.

Many of the recent converts to Mormonism have been fundamentalist Christians or Catholics dissatisfied with what they perceived as the failure of their parent churches to hold the line against forces contributing to social and family disorder since the 1960s.

Mormon church leaders, responding to concerns about disorder in the outer society as well as in their own church, where approximately half of all married women work outside the home, have aggressively promulgated the notion that woman's only significant role is as a wife and mother and that work outside the home is harmful to the family. Through a variety of front organizations, the Mormon church played a key role in defeating the Equal Rights Amendment to the Constitution, which it viewed as a threat to the family and to its particular family practices. Mormonism's increasingly aggressive political role has been publicly opposed by Mormon or ex-Mormon feminists such as Marilyn Warenski and Sonia Johnson, as well as privately by some Mormon intellectuals, but the overall trend toward further centralization under the patriarchal church structure appears unlikely to be reversed in the near future.

—Lawrence Foster

See Also:

Complex Marriage, Plural Marriage, Suffrage in the American West

References:

Beecher, Maureen Ursenbach, and Lavina Fielding Anderson, eds. *Sisters in Spirit: Mormon Women in Historical and Cultural Perspective.* Urbana: University of Illinois Press, 1987.

Burgess-Olson, Vickie, ed. *Sister Saints.* Provo, Utah: Brigham Young University Press, 1978.

Bushman, Claudia, ed. *Mormon Sisters: Women in Early Utah.* Cambridge, Mass.: Emmeline Press Limited, 1976.

Foster, Lawrence. "From Frontier Activism to Neo-Victorian Domesticity: Mormon Women in the Nineteenth and Twentieth Centuries." *Journal of Mormon History* 6 (1979): 3–21.

Gottlieb, Robert, and Peter Wiley. *America's Saints: The Rise of Mormon Power.* New York: Harcourt Brace Jovanovich, 1986.

Johnson, Sonia. *From Housewife to Heretic.* Garden City, N.Y.: Doubleday, 1981.

Newell, Linda King. "The Historical Relationship of Mormon Women and Priesthood." *Dialogue: A Journal of Mormon Thought* 18 (Autumn 1985): 21–32.

Warenski, Marilyn. *Patriarchs and Politics:The Plight of the Mormon Woman.* New York: McGraw-Hill, 1978.

Whittaker, David J., and Carol C. Madsen. "History's Sequel: A Source Essay on Women in Mormon History." *Journal of Mormon History* 6 (1979): 123–45.

The **MORRILL LAND-GRANT ACT of 1862** provided a generous federal land grant to establish agricultural and mechanical arts colleges in every state. Each state was alloted thirty thousand acres of public land for each of its congressional representatives upon which to create separate A & M (agricultural and mechanical) institutions or adjunct institutions to be added to existing state universities. Considered the most important piece of education legislation enacted at the federal level, the Morrill Land-Grant Act was significant for women's education because of the coeducational institutions established in the midwestern and far western states after the Civil War.

—Angela Howard Zophy

See Also:

Coeducation, Education, Smith-Lever Act, Women in Higher Education

References:

Riley, Glenda. *Inventing the American Woman: A Perspective on Women's History.* Arlington Heights, Ill.: Harlan Davidson, 1987.

Woloch, Nancy. *Women and the American Experience.* New York: Knopf, 1984.

MORRISON, TONI (b. 1931) was born Chloe Anthony Wofford in Lorain, Ohio. By 1987 she had written five novels, the fifth of which, *Beloved* (1987), became an instant best-seller and won a Pulitzer Prize. *The Bluest Eye* (1970), *Sula* (1973), *Song of Solomon* (1977), *Tar Baby* (1981), and *Beloved* are all profoundly concerned with issues of family and race, and contain several exceptional portraits of black women. *Song of Solomon* won the National Book Critics' Circle Award.

Morrison was educated at Howard University and then received an M.A. at Cornell.

She worked as a textbook editor for L. B. Singer and then as a trade book editor at Random House. Her own works were edited by Robert Gottleib and published by Knopf.

Morrison's first novel, *The Bluest Eye*, is searingly realistic. It portrays the broken lives of blacks who are destroying themselves and each other as they struggle to find a foothold in a city and culture that does not value them and gives them no way of loving themselves. The tragic central figure is a young girl who is raped and made pregnant by her alcoholic father, and as the novel concludes, she believes her dearest wish has been fulfilled: gone mad, she thinks she has blue eyes. In her more recent novels, Morrison retains the immediacy and brilliance of her earlier realism—conversations, details of scene, smells, sounds, tastes, the feel of the land—but her realistically represented situations and settings now hold characters who are larger than life. There is Pilate Dead, for instance, in *Song of Solomon*, a mysterious figure whose power verges on the magical and which has its source in her refusal to release her hold on black ways and black roots. She leads her nephew on a pilgrimage to rediscover himself and his orgins, and he discovers as well that Pilate can fly. One of the most important figures in *Beloved* is a ghost who takes the form of a beautiful young black woman. On one level, she is the child the protagonist murdered to prevent her being taken back into slavery, and she has returned to claim the love she has lost. On another, she is black suffering under slavery incarnate in a single consciousness, and when she lapses into reverie the reader is taken into the horrors of the slave crossings from Africa. Realism grounds Morrison's work, but mythmaking gives it much of its scope and power.

—Susan Kinnell and Gretchen Mieszkowski

See Also:

Black Women, Slavery

References:

Clark, Norris Berkeley. "The Black Aesthetic Reviewed: A Critical Examination of the Writings of Imanu Amiri Baraka, Gwendolyn Brooks, and Toni Morrison." Diss. Cornell University, 1980.

Holloway, Karla, and Stephanie Demetrakopoulos. *New Dimensions of Spirituality*. Westport, Conn.: Greenwood, 1987.

Jones, Bessie W., and Audrey L. Vinson. *The World of Toni Morrison: Explorations in Literary Criticism*. Dubuque, Iowa.: Kendall/Hunt, 1985.

Medwick, Cathleen. "Toni Morrison." *Vogue* 171 (April 1981): 289, 330–32.

Strouse, Jean. "Toni Morrison's Black Magic." *Newsweek* 97 (March 30, 1981): 52–57.

Watkins, Gloria Jean. "Keeping a Hold on Life: Reading Toni Morrison's Fiction." Diss. University of California-Santa Cruz, 1983.

MOTHERS' PENSIONS were funds provided by the states to allow widows, deserted wives, or other single mothers to raise their children at home. The first mothers' pension law was passed in 1911 in Kansas City, Missouri; Illinois issued the first statewide measure later that year. Reflecting Progressive concern with child welfare, thirty-nine states had enacted mothers' aid laws by 1919. Widowed mothers with children under fourteen were eligible for assistance in all states; some states also aided divorced mothers, deserted wives, and women whose husbands were imprisoned or disabled.

The mothers' pension movement grew out of a 1909 White House Conference on the Care of Dependent Children called by President Theodore Roosevelt. Inspired by a sentimental view of mother love, conference participants proposed paying poor mothers so that they could keep their children at home, rather than having to place them in institutions. A coalition of women's clubs, settlement workers, trade unionists, relief recipients, and politicians lobbied for mothers' pensions, which they did not consider charity, but an entitlement—a salary for raising children to be good citizens.

However, despite efforts to define mothers' pensions as payment for work, they were administered as charity. Like welfare mothers today, recipients were harassed by investigators trying to determine that they maintained "suitable" homes, even though funds were insufficient to support a family without supplementary aid. Several southern states denied assistance to black mothers. Nevertheless, the mothers' pension program recognized for the first time government's responsibility to aid poor women and children, and such programs were incorporated into the Social Security Act of 1935 as Aid to Dependent Children.

—Molly Ladd-Taylor

See Also:

Progressive Legislation, Social Security Act of 1935

References:

Bell, Winifred. *Aid to Dependent Children.* New York: Columbia University Press, 1965.

Leff, Mark H. "Consensus for Reform: The Mothers'-Pension Movement in the Progressive Era." *Social Service Review* 47 (September 1973): 397–417.

Lubove, Roy. *The Struggle for Social Security.* Cambridge: Harvard University Press, 1968.

Vandepol, Ann. "Dependent Children, Child Custody, and the Mothers' Pensions: The Transformation of State-Family Relations in the Early 20th Century." *Social Problems* 29 (February 1982): 221–35.

MOTT, LUCRETIA COFFIN (1793–1880), abolitionist and leader of the nineteenth-century woman suffrage movement, traced her lifelong interest in woman's rights to her reading of Mary Wollstonecraft's *A Vindication of the Rights of Woman.* She committed whole passages to memory, and as she was fond of telling friends, throughout her life she kept the book "on the center table," frequently urging others to read it. Mott's appearance and demeanor challenged the derisive contemporary stereotype of the suffragists. Radical in her antislavery and feminist views, she nevertheless presented a public image of domestic virtue. Mott often sat quietly knitting on speakers' platforms as she awaited her turn at the podium, where her commanding presence as an insightful, incisive, and persuasive critic of the conditions of slaves and women frequently startled her audiences.

Barely into her twenties and newly married to James Mott, she was recognized as a Quaker minister with a gift for preaching. Active in Quaker women's societies, she helped found the Female Anti-Slavery Society of Philadelphia in 1833 and was instrumental in organizing a national meeting of antislavery women in 1837.

Although Mott was elected a delegate to the World's Anti-Slavery Convention held in London in 1840, the assembly there voted to exclude her. Elizabeth Cady Stanton, the wife of another delegate, paid a call on Mott to commiserate. From their shared indignation grew a friendship and a commitment to activism that resulted in the calling of the Seneca Falls (N.Y.) convention of 1848, the first formal woman's rights convention in America. Mott contributed to the writing of the Declaration of Sentiments and the drafting of the Resolutions approved at that meeting. By 1848 Mott was widely known and admired as lecturer and preacher, and her presence at the convention helped assure its success.

In 1850 Mott published her *Discourse on Women,* a treatise that argued for equal political and legal rights for women and for changes in the married women's property laws. Following passage of the Fugitive Slave Act, she opened her home to slaves fleeing via the Underground Railroad and continued her public speaking and writing on abolitionism and woman's rights.

After the Civil War, Mott directed her energies to obtaining the franchise for women and for the black freedmen. She also became increasingly involved in the peace movement. A tireless, widely esteemed spokeswoman and reformer, Mott delivered her last public address at age eighty-seven at the Society of Friends' annual meeting in May 1880. She died at home on November 11 that same year, and the nation mourned the loss of this eloquent, beloved leader.

—Andrea Moore Kerr

See Also:

Abolition and the Antislavery Movement; Cult of True Womanhood; Declaration of Sentiments and Resolutions (1848); European Influences;

Public Speakers, Women; Seneca Falls Convention; Society of Friends

References:

Bacon, Margaret Hope. *Valiant Friend.* New York: Walker, 1980.

Cromwell, Otelia. *Lucretia Mott.* New York: Russell and Russell, 1971.

Flexner, Eleanor. *Century of Struggle.* Cambridge, Mass.: Belknap, 1976.

Hallowell, Anna Davis. *James and Lucretia Mott.* Boston: Houghton Mifflin, 1884.

Mott, Lucretia. *Lucretia Mott: Her Complete Speeches and Sermons.* New York: E. Mellen, 1980.

Sterling, Dorothy. *Lucretia Mott: Gentle Warrior.* Garden City, N.Y.: Doubleday, 1964.

MOUNT HOLYOKE SEMINARY was among the best-known and most successful female academies (or "seminaries," as women's schools were then called) in the United States during the antebellum period. Founded in South Hadley, Massachusetts, by Mary Lyon in 1837, Mount Holyoke was distinctive because of its large endowment and commitment to educating girls from families of modest means. Mary Lyon was also among the first women educators to recognize the important role that women could play as teachers in the nation's schools, and Mount Holyoke became famous for providing capable and highly dedicated women teachers in this period. Lyon personally supervised the school until her death in 1849. Her successors gradually expanded the curriculum to include Latin, Greek, and other collegiate studies, and in 1893 the school became known as Mount Holyoke College.

Perhaps the most distinctive feature of Mount Holyoke was Mary Lyon's commitment to keeping tuition and other school-related expenses substantially below those charged at other women's schools in this period. The school's substantial endowment, raised through Lyon's personal appeals to prominent men in western Massachusetts and elsewhere, was one factor that helped to reduce costs. More important, however, was Lyon's "domestic plan," which saved money by requiring students to perform the various housekeeping functions associated with maintaining a sizable residential academy. In addition to keeping expenses down, Lyon argued that this policy also helped build character and constituted a vital element of preparing young women for their future roles as wives and mothers. Lyon drew criticism from other women educators in this period both for her domestic plan and her policy of paying low salaries to her teachers. She defended both by maintaining that her school functioned as a family, and that the promotion of responsibility and personal loyalty were more important than (and perhaps antithetical to) personal wealth.

Much of the success of Mount Holyoke can be attributed to the close personal attention that Mary Lyon gave the school—and many of its students—through most of its first decade of existence. Historian Thomas Woody has estimated that about sixteen hundred girls attended Mount Holyoke during Mary Lyon's lifetime, and that some twelve thousand or more had enrolled by 1887. A survey of alumnae conducted in 1877 found that more than half had worked as teachers (and half of those for five or more years) and about 6 percent had served as foreign missionaries. Twenty-one were doctors. With its policy of lowering the costs of education for women from modest backgrounds, Mount Holyoke offered an opportunity for an advanced education to thousands of American women in the nineteenth century who might otherwise never have received one. In this regard, it represented a significant contribution to the development of women's education in American history.

—*John L. Rury*

See Also:

Education, Female Academies, Normal Schools, "Seven Sisters"

References:

Allmendinger, David F. "Mount Holyoke Students Encounter the Need for Life Planning, 1837–1850." *History of Education Quarterly* 19 (Spring 1979): 27–46.

Cole, Arthur C. *A Hundred Years of Mount Holyoke: The Evolution of an Educational Ideal.* New Haven: Yale University Press, 1940.
Green, Elizabeth Alden. *Mary Lyon and Mount Holyoke: Opening the Gates.* Hanover, N.H.: University Press of New England, 1979.
Sklar, Kathryn. "The Founding of Mount Holyoke College." In *Women of America: A History,* edited by Carol R. Berkin and Mary Beth Norton. Boston: Houghton Mifflin, 1979, pp. 177–201.

MOVIE STARS. Women have performed in front of the motion picture camera since the birth of the movies, scandalously showing their legs as dancers and acrobats or posing for *The Kiss* in William K. L. Dickson and Thomas A. Edison's Kinetoscope shorts in the 1890s. But their names were deliberately withheld from the public by the newly formed film companies, whose owners rightly feared that star status would lead to star salaries. The situation changed radically in 1910 when the Independent producers, led by Carl Laemmle, in their continuing war against the Motion Picture Patents Company (known as the Trust), stole the "Biograph Girl" and began featuring her in films under her real name, Florence Lawrence. Their strategy was so successful that they continued the practice with "Little Mary" Pickford and other formerly anonymous players. In 1912 *Photoplay,* America's first fan magazine, was launched, and by 1917 two movie stars—Pickford and Charlie Chaplin—were the highest paid performers in the business, signing contracts for $1 million a year. The star system was well and truly born.

During the heyday of the studio system, stars were "found," manufactured, bought, and sold by the major studios; their offscreen activities were choreographed and restricted by publicity departments, and their transgressions punished by paternalistic bosses like Louis B. Mayer. Stardom was a double-edged sword; it provided financial and emotional security, but it also required obedience. The more independent-minded stars like Bette Davis and Katharine Hepburn chafed under its confines and made efforts to free themselves. The star system was also a harsh taskmaster and judge of female talent and salability; several stars labeled "box office poison" in the late 1930s (Hepburn among them) were forced off the screen for a while, unable to get jobs in Hollywood. Even those who benefited from and seemingly acquiesced to the system, like Marilyn Monroe, might find themselves rendered obsolete or gradually eased out by newer stars in a culture that revered youth and its own narrow concept of beauty above all else. It was rare that a female star remained a top box-office draw for more than a decade, astonishing if she lasted more than two. A child star like Shirley Temple, the top moneymaker in America in 1938, lost her appeal when she reached adolescence.

The breakup of the studios and the confusion that reigned during the 1950s and 1960s gave new status to stars who could guarantee audiences during hard times, but these were largely males: Paul Newman, John Wayne, Glenn Ford, Steve McQueen, Sidney Poitier. It was not until the 1970s and 1980s that new female stars like Jane Fonda, Barbra Streisand, and Meryl Streep began to be able to command top billing once again. But they were demanding more than big salaries; they wanted some measure of creative control as well. Thus the new star system has spawned a generation of actresses who no longer have only the power to say "no" or sit meekly waiting for the right vehicle to come to them. They seek their own opportunities and may, as Streisand did with *Yentl* (1983), be the initiator and controlling agent of the production from start to finish. If the old star system produced, almost despite itself, memorable roles and films for women, the new star system will do so because of women's conscious efforts in their own behalf.

—*Frances M. Kavenik*

See Also:

Davis, Bette; Fonda, Jane; Hepburn, Katharine; Monroe, Marilyn; Woman's Film

References:

Dyer, Richard. *Stars.* London: British Film Institute, 1979, 1986.

Haskell, Molly. *From Reverence to Rape: The Treatment of Women in the Movies.* 2d ed. Chicago: University of Chicago Press, 1987.
Mast, Gerald. *A Short History of the Movies.* 3d ed. Indianapolis: Bobbs-Merrill, 1981.
Rosen, Marjorie. *Popcorn Venus.* New York: Coward, McCann, and Geoghegan, 1973.

***MS.* MAGAZINE** represented a unique application of the women's magazine format to a specific feminist agenda. Although women's magazines as a separate genre dated to the nineteenth century and had, from the outset, employed women editors, *Ms.* was the first national publication created and controlled by women for women. An outgrowth of the raised consciousness of the late 1960s, it was founded early in 1971, in the living room of Gloria Steinem's New York City apartment by a group of dedicated feminist journalists and writers. While many women's liberation groups of the era published newsletters and journals, *Ms.* was to be a nationally distributed magazine that aimed at broadening the audience for feminist ideas and trends. Focusing on the mainstreaming of the women's movement, *Ms.* editorial policy eschewed the usual fare of recipes, advice columns, and handicrafts found in contemporary women's magazines, yet avoided the partisan feminist debates or strong ideological stances of journals established by various women's liberation groups.

The founders of *Ms.* used networking and their previous professional experience to launch their ambitious project. Since Steinem, the publication's first editor, had been instrumental in starting *New York* magazine, *New York* editor and publisher Clay Felker agreed to insert preview copies into the year-end issue of that magazine before the spring premier issue of *Ms.* hit the newsstands in January 1972. The *Ms.* insert—with an appropriate "Wonder Woman" cover—boosted *New York* magazine's sales to an all-time high, and the projected eight-week supply of three hundred thousand copies sold out in eight days.

Ms. addressed forthrightly and without condescension the concerns of women in the home and the workplace, and provided articles on women's history. As a feminist forum, *Ms.* offered the works of well-known and struggling contemporary women poets, journalists, and writers in all fields. A major innovative policy excluded advertising that was demeaning to or limiting of women.

Ms. also published collections of its stories and news features and produced television documentaries such as *Woman Alive!* (1973, 1974) and *She's Nobody's Baby: American Women in the Twentieth Century* (1981). As a means for returning profits to the community of women to empower them further, *Ms.* founders established the Ms. Foundation for Women, Inc. in 1975 as a public, educational, and charitable organization with tax-exempt status to assist women's projects through direct grants and advisory and referral services. The Free to Be Foundation was established in 1976 to administer the educational "Free to Be . . . You and Me" project, which was conceived by Marlo Thomas to promote individual human growth and child development in a unbiased way. Named after Thomas's successful children's television special, record album, and book, which provided the initial foundation revenue from royalties, this foundation funds multimedia projects that focus on nonsexist education and child development.

Ms. magazine celebrated its first decade of publication in 1982, and had succeeded as a national commercial publication that covered the issues of the contemporary women's movement. However, *Ms.* began its second decade during a period of national economic difficulties and conservative backlash against the women's movement. Increased publication costs and added competition for subscribers compounded the problem, as did the fact that the founding members of the staff were ready to pursue other projects and individual careers. After a major reorganization that did not prove sufficient to assure the publication's future, *Ms.* magazine was sold in 1988. The revised publication further mainstreamed the contents of *Ms.* by including some of the more traditional women's magazine features, but did not abandon the editorial policy of covering women's social, political, legal, and economic issues as hard news items or of consciously patronizing women and feminist writers.

—*Saundra Yelton and Angela Howard Zophy*

See Also:

Magazines; Steinem, Gloria; Twentieth-Century Women's Rights Movement; Women's Liberation Movement

References:

Lyons, Harriet. *"A History of Ms."* Unpublished manuscript, commissioned for *Ms.* Magazine's tenth anniversary, 1982.

Ms. Foundation for Women, Inc. and Free to Be Foundation, Inc. *Ms. Foundation for Women 1983/1985 Annual Report.* New York: Ms. and Free to Be Foundations, 1985.

MULLER V. OREGON (1908) dealt with an Oregon maximum-hours statute that constrained the employment of women in factories, laundries, or other "mechanical establishments" to no longer than ten hours a day. Louis D. Brandeis (later a Supreme Court associate justice) presented the case to the Supreme Court for Oregon; his argument centered around a heavily statistical brief that discussed the relationship between hours of labor and the health and morals of women.

Writing for a unanimous court, Justice David J. Brewer upheld the constitutionality of the regulations as a reasonable exercise of the state's police powers. Brewer emphasized the consideration that "woman's physical structure and the performance of maternal functions place her at a disadvantage in the struggle for subsistence" and that her physical well-being "becomes an object of public interest and care in order to preserve the strength and the vigor of the race." The Court concluded that the limitations the statute "placed upon her contractual powers, upon her right to agree with her employer as to the time she shall labor" were "not imposed solely for her benefit, but also largely for the benefit of all."

The *Muller* case does not represent a repudiation of substantive due process; the Court strictly judged that the economic regulations in question were reasonable use of the state's police powers.

—*Sue E. Strickler*

See Also:

Progressive Era, Progressive Legislation, Protective Legislation, Wages

References:

Goldstein, Leslie Friedman. *The Constitutional Rights of Women.* New York: Longman, 1987.

Muller v. Oregon, 208 U.S. 412 (1908).

Rossum, Ralph A., and G. Alan Tarr. *American Constitutional Law.* New York: St. Martin's, 1987.

MUSIC. Women in music have had to overcome many of the same obstacles as women in other professions and even more as the prejudices against women composers, conductors, and performers have run deep in an already highly competitive area. Their compositions have historically had a harder time reaching audiences than those of men. Women have not had as many opportunities for careers as performers as have men in most fields of music. Yet despite so many years of discrimination, women have made a rich if largely unsung contribution to the history of American music.

One of the first American women to emerge in music was Sophia Hewitt (birth date unknown), who became the organist for Boston's Handel and Haydn Society in 1820 and remained there for a decade. Hewitt was given a chance to perform because of her great talent and because she was the daughter of James Hewitt, an active and prominent violinist, composer, concert manager, and publisher. Although many hundreds of women served as church organists in the nineteenth century, very few had the opportunity to follow Sophia Hewitt into the concert hall.

By the mid-nineteenth century, organ, piano, and harp were generally accepted as instruments appropriate for women as well as men. The same could not be said of many other instruments, including the violin. This was all changed by Camilla Urso (1842–

1902), a native of Nantes, France, who spent much of her life in the United States. She established herself as a violin virtuoso comparable to any of the males of her day.

The latter half of the nineteenth century found a number of female piano virtuosos thrilling large and enthusiastic audiences. These gifted performers included Teresa Carreño (1844–1917), Julia Rivé (1857–1937), and Fannie Bloomfield-Zeisler (1865–1927). Some brilliant concert artists also excelled as composers and teachers. For example, Rosalyn Tureck (b. 1914) has combined a performance career on piano, harpsichord, organ, and clavichord with conducting, writing, and teaching. Tureck was the first woman invited to conduct the New York Philharmonic Orchestra in a subscription concert in 1958 and has conducted major orchestras on six continents.

Women have always composed music, but getting their music before large audiences has always proved difficult except in modern popular music, where someone like Carole Bayer Sager has been able to achieve celebrity status. One of the first outstanding American woman composers was Amy Mary Cheney Beach (1867–1944), a native of Henniker, New Hampshire. Beach composed works for orchestra and chorus as well as numerous pieces for piano, violin, and voice. Her *Gaelic Symphony*, op. 32, was performed by major orchestras for decades beginning in 1896 when it premiered with the Boston Symphony. Beach also wrote a great deal of well-received church music.

Ruth Crawford (1901–53) from East Liverpool, Ohio, became one of the great originals in American music. She studied at the American Conservatory in Chicago and then in 1930 became the first American woman composer to win a Guggenheim Fellowship, which enabled her to study in Berlin and Paris. Crawford became world famous for her work in folk music and also for her brilliant, original compositions such as *String Quartet* (1931), *Three Songs* to texts by Carl Sandburg (1932), *Suite for Wind Quintet* (1952), and *Orchestral Composition* (1941).

A contemporary of Ruth Crawford's, Louise Talma (b. 1906) has earned a great deal of recognition for her excellence as a composer and a teacher. She was the first woman to win the coveted Sibelius Award in composition; the first woman to win a Guggenheim on two occasions; the first woman to have a major work staged by a major European opera house; and the first woman to be elected to the Music Department of the National Institute of Arts and Letters.

Pauline Oliveros (b. 1932) is known as one of the most versatile of experimenters among American composers. A native of Houston, Texas, Oliveros embraced electronic music, sound sculpture, and multimedia presentations.

Vivian Fine (b. 1913) became famous for her performances of contemporary piano music, her compositions (including a number for dance), and her teaching at a number of colleges and universities. Born in Chicago, Fine studied with, among others, Ruth Crawford, who encouraged her to write as well as perform and, of course, provided an inspiring role model of a successful woman musician. Despite a heavy teaching schedule, Fine has proven to be a prolific writer of ballets, chamber works, choral and orchestral pieces. Her works include two compositions celebrating the women's movement, *Meeting for Equal Rights 1866* (1976) and *The Women in the Garden* (1977).

Two of the outstanding black American composers were Florence Smith Price (1888–1953) and Margaret Bonds (1913–72). A native of Little Rock, Arkansas, Price wrote art songs, spiritual arrangements, keyboard works, four symphonies, three piano concertos, and a violin concerto. Price also taught students including Margaret Bonds, who went on to her own distinguished career. As musicologist Christine Ammer has shown, Margaret Bonds "made a conscious effort to develop black idioms in larger musical forms and to promote the music of black Americans." Bonds wrote over two hundred works for chorus, orchestra, and piano, as well as popular songs, some imbued with the jazz style of poet Langston Hughes.

America has produced dozens of outstanding women composers, including such talents as Marion Eugenie Bauer (1887–1955), Mary Carlisle Howe (1882–1964), Dika Newlin (b. 1923), Julia Frances Smith (b. 1911), and Elinor Remick Warren (b. 1906). Many of these women inspired each other and were inspired by great teachers such as Nadia Boulanger (1887–1979).

American women have long found the vocal music field to be more hospitable to them than that of instrumental music. Women operatic singers have been onstage since the early eighteenth century. In the twentieth century such singers as Marion Anderson, Marilyn Horne, Mahalia Jackson, Roberta Peters, Leontyne Price, and Beverly Sills among many others have achieved great success and recognition. Obviously women have enjoyed great commercial success in country and western music, jazz, rock and roll, and other forms of popular music.

In addition to great singers, women have contributed to the operatic world through their compositions since the time of Constance Fount Le Roy (b. 1836), who wrote a romantic opera, *The Prince of Asurias*, in the late 1860s. Le Roy's work may never have been performed except, perhaps, locally, but this was not the case for the works of Emma B. Steiner (1852–1929), whose opera *Fleurette* was produced in San Francisco in 1889 and in New York in 1891. Steiner wrote other successful operas and established herself as a conductor despite the incredible prejudices against women at the podium.

The manager of the Metropolitan Opera Company wanted to appoint Emma Steiner as the Met's conductor, but he did not dare. It was not until January 13, 1976, that Sarah Caldwell (b. 1924) became the first woman to conduct an opera at the Met. Eve Rabin Queler (b. 1936) was the first woman in the United States to become the associate conductor of a metropolitan orchestra according to music historian Jane Weiner Lepage.

The obstacles that women conductors have had to overcome are dramatically illustrated by the award-winning 1974 documentary film, *Antonia: A Portrait of the Woman*, based on the life of Dr. Antonia Brico (b. 1902–1989). The film was produced by the famous folk singer Judy Collins, who had studied piano with Dr. Brico, and Jill Godmilow. As the film documents, despite Brico's enormous talents and training with such giants as Jean Sibelius and Artur Rubenstein, music managers would not accept her, and artists refused to work with her solely because of her sex. Today less than 10 percent of the musicians in leading orchestras are women and none of the major orchestras has a female conductor. Women choral conductors have fared slightly better, as evidenced by the career of Margaret Hillis (b. 1921), director of the Chicago Symphony Chorus since 1957. Given the persistent pattern of discrimination against women in music, their achievements are remarkable and will continue to enrich the world even more in the future as opportunities are expanded.

—Jonathan W. Zophy

See Also:

Baez, Joan; Beach, Amy; Holiday, Billie; Jazz; Popular Vocalists; Price, Leontyne; Smith, Bessie

References:

Ammer, Christine. *Unsung: A History of Women in American Music.* Westport, Conn.: Greenwood, 1980.

Drinker, Sophie Lewis. *Music and Women: The Story of Women in their Relation to Music.* New York: Coward McCann, 1948.

Ebel, Otto. *Women Composers: A Biographical Handbook of Woman's Work in Music.* 3d ed. Brooklyn: Chandler-Ebel Music Co., 1913.

Lepage, Jane Weiner. *Women Composers, Conductors, and Musicians of the Twentieth Century: Selected Biographies.* Metuchen, N.J.: Scarecrow, 1980.

NAMING SYSTEMS. Native American and immigrant cultures have a wide variety of systems for assigning personal names, so that each one must be investigated specifically. An interesting feature of several Native American cultures is the provision for acquiring permanent names during adolescence or adulthood—through initiation, visions, personal events, or inheritance.

Variations exist even within patronymic systems, where children take their fathers' names. In Scandinavian societies, boy and girl children of, for example, Nils, would be named Eric Nilssen or Ingrid Nilsdottir. Arabic speakers use *ibn* in the same way; for example, Faisal ibn Saud. In both cases, the father himself uses a different second name referring to *his* father. Conversely, some African cultures call parents after their children: "father of John" and "mother of John."

Spanish-speaking Americans sometimes follow traditional Hispanic naming patterns. Children receive the paternal surnames of both their mothers and fathers linked with *y* (and); for example, Elena Garcia y Chavez. They may receive additional names at baptism, first communion, and confirmation. Daughters drop their mothers' names at marriage, linking their fathers' and husbands' paternal names with *de* (of). If, for example, Elena Garcia y Chavez marries Orlando Vasquez y Morales, her names changes to Elena Vasquez de Garcia. Their child might then be named Ana Vasquez y Garcia.

Anglo-Saxon cultures also preserve the mother's name in various ways. New England children were frequently given an illustrious maternal surname as their middle name. Some aristocratic southern families used such names as first names. In nineteenth-century England, when aristocratic women married men with less impressive names, the two were often hyphenated for the children to preserve the connection. Married women generally used their father's surname as a middle name.

Middle-class white women in nineteenth-century America characteristically took their husbands' names completely. Even female friends addressed each other as "Mrs. Ralph Davis," literally, "wife of Ralph Davis." First names were used rarely enough that feminists spoke of the exhilarating feeling of solidarity and individuality that learning and using such names within the feminist movement evoked. Some nineteenth-century feminists, however, refused to change their names upon marriage, thus defying the legal submersion of the wife's identity under common law. Lucy Stone and her husband, Henry Blackwell, added a signed protest to their marriage ceremony in 1855, and Stone was never referred to as "Mrs. Blackwell," but rather as "Mrs. Stone." In 1921 the Lucy Stone League was founded to assist twentieth-century women in keeping their original names, as well as to provide a center of research and information on the status of women.

With the advent of the modern women's movement in the 1960s, the issue of social title and name resurfaced among feminists who coined "Ms." as a generic title for all women, single and married. Some married women, especially those in a profession, kept their so-called maiden names, since it was custom rather than a legal requirement that women change their name on all their legal and formal documents upon marriage. Some state commissions on the status of women produced pamphlets to inform women regarding the legal procedures required to keep or reclaim their original names. More radical feminists legally changed their names to reflect their matrilinial heritage rather than use a name that reinforced the sexist patriarchal system, altering their surname to a descriptive name such as "Marthaschild," or, endeavoring to create an entirely new identity, selected an innovative name that focused on their own lives, such as the name change of artist Judy Chicago.

Conspicuous use of the surname as middle name and, later, hyphenation of names for married women and their children became popular among American feminists. In the early 1970s feminist and professional women utilized their maiden surname as their middle name, but later in the decade resorted to hyphenation of their own surname with that of their husbands. Whether consciously feminist or not, by the 1980s more women were opting to keep using their own name after marriage. Social forces as well as the feminist movement promoted this as the simpler course: Contemporary mores had rendered cohabitation no longer scandalous, so married women were less concerned about being assumed to be "living in sin" if their names differed from that of their male companions; more women both married and single were in the work force, not just holding temporary jobs but determinedly pursuing careers for which a name change constituted some inconvenience and possible confusion; and the general increase in divorce rendered perception of the initial name change as no longer necessarily permanent and as more probably merely the first of several name changes, whether divorced women remarried or not. For the majority of women, however, marriage still brought a name change of some sort.

For American feminists, the naming system indicated in a direct and fundamental way the status of women, and provided an individual expression of women's perception of their identity.

—Gracia Clark and
Angela Howard Zophy

See Also:

Chicago, Judy; Common Law; Native American Women; Stone, Lucy

NASHOBA (1825–30) was a utopian community founded for slaves by Frances Wright in November 1825 in western Tennessee, and was the only secular commune founded by a woman in nineteenth-century America. Its purpose was to serve an an example of how blacks in the American South could be gradually emancipated.

During the early 1820s Wright became interested in the communal movement and abolition. Wright agreed with the proponents of the colonization movement who believed that slaves would eventually be free and, afterward, should be sent to colonies in Africa or Asia, but believed blacks should first be taught some means of self-sufficiency. In creating Nashoba, she combined this belief with her interest in starting a community patterned after New Harmony, a "village of cooperation" established earlier by socialist Robert Owen. Wright assumed slaves would be donated to Nashoba by sympathetic planters and settled on a goal of fifty. Each slave would work off his or her price by a credit system which would take five years; meanwhile the slaves were to be educated to prepare them for freedom. Afterward, they would be sent to a foreign colony to begin their new life.

From the start, Nashoba was plagued with problems. Only one slave family was donated, and Wright could only afford to buy eight other slaves. The agricultural potential of the two thousand acres of uncleared swampy frontier near Memphis was limited, as was the ability of the slaves to distinguish between the nobly inspired compulsive servitude at Nashoba and the exploitation of their former experiences. Public disdain was exacerbated by the disclosure of an interracial relationship between a teacher and slave within the experimental community. Wright's defense of the arrangement rendered her subject to verbal abuse and threats against her life.

By 1830 Wright decided the experiment at Nashoba was a failure. She now believed society as a whole had to be reformed, not just a part of it. The remaining slaves at Nashoba were given their freedom, and Wright accompanied them to Haiti, then returned to the United States to focus her energies on women's issues.

—Rose Kolbasnik Callahan

See Also:

Abolition and the Antislavery Movement, Slavery, Utopian Communities

References:

Eckhardt, Celia Morris. *Fanny Wright: Rebel in America.* Cambridge: Harvard University Press, 1984.

Lane, Margaret. *Frances Wright and the "Great Experiment."* Manchester: Manchester University Press, 1972.

The **NATIONAL AMERICAN WOMAN SUFFRAGE ASSOCIATION**, formed in 1890 through the merger of the American and National Woman Suffrage associations, was dominated during its first decade of existence by the aging Susan B. Anthony, who took over the presidency from Elizabeth Cady Stanton in 1892. Yet the course of the organization was profoundly influenced by a new generation of suffrage leaders, many of them university-educated professional women. At the suggestion of Alice Stone Blackwell, and over Anthony's protests, NAWSA resolved in 1893 to hold its annual conventions outside Washington, D.C., in alternate years. The granting of suffrage to Colorado women in 1893 encouraged those who felt that suffrage could be won state by state, and "Aunt Susan," assisted by her younger lieutenants, strenuously joined in massive but unsuccessful statewide campaigns in New York (1894) and California (1896). Anthony went so far as to tone down her personal support for black civil rights in the interest of recruiting more southern women in NAWSA, and the increasingly upper-middle-class and nativist tone of the organization was reflected in speeches and resolutions condemning unrestricted immigration and favoring educational requirements for suffrage. In 1896, after a bitter internal debate, NAWSA formally dissociated itself from Stanton's *Woman's Bible*, a radical feminist critique of religion.

At the annual convention of 1900, coinciding with Anthony's eightieth birthday, her chosen successor, Carrie Chapman Catt, took over the leadership. Thereafter, with the exception of a brief interlude when Methodist minister Anna Howard Shaw served as president, Catt directed the fortunes of NAWSA. A shrewd administrator and forceful orator, but somewhat conservative in her views on domestic issues, Catt was at first a strong supporter of the state-by-state approach. She argued that, in the absence of a firm commitment to suffrage from any president or from either major party, it was unrealistic to throw NAWSA's weight behind the demand for a federal amendment.

A serious challenge to the Catt wing of NAWSA was posed by Alice Paul, a young Philadelphian who had been jailed seven times in England for her participation in Mrs. Emmeline Pankhurst's militant suffragette campaign. Paul, who joined NAWSA in 1912, created the NAWSA Congressional Committee, which became a rallying point for younger members impatient with the snail's pace of state-based work and eager to revive the fight for a federal measure. The American scene was soon enlivened by suffrage processions, pickets, and other colorful publicity stunts borrowed from the English militants; a few NAWSA members were even imprisoned briefly. Paul eventually left to found her own National Woman's party in 1916, and while the vast majority of suffragists remained loyal to NAWSA, Paul's influence was still felt. At its Louisville convention in 1917, NAWSA once again officially pledged itself to work for a constitutional amendment, and its ef-forts were crowned with success in the passage (1919) and ratification (1920) of the Nineteenth Amendment. After the gala victory celebrations, NAWSA dissolved itself, and many of its members continued to work for the political education of women and for various feminist social concerns through a new organization, the League of Women Voters.

—Gail Malmgreen

See Also:

Anthony, Susan B.; Catt, Carrie Chapman; League of Women Voters; National Woman's Party; Nineteenth Amendment; Paul, Alice

References:

Fowler, Robert B. *Carrie Catt: Feminist Politician.* Boston: Northeastern University Press, 1986.

Griffith, Elisabeth. *In Her Own Right: The Life of Elizabeth Cady Stanton.* New York: Oxford University Press, 1984.

Harper, Ida Husted. *The Life and Work of Susan B. Anthony.* Vols. 1–2. Indianapolis: Bowen-Merrill, 1898.

Shaw, Anna Howard. *The Story of a Pioneer.* New York: Harper, 1915.

Stanton, Elizabeth C., Susan B. Anthony, and Matilda J. Gage, eds. *History of Woman Suffrage.* 6 vols. Rochester: Privately Printed, 1881–1922.

The **NATIONAL ASSOCIATION FOR THE ADVANCEMENT OF COLORED PEOPLE (NAACP)** grew out of the Niagara movement organized by black educator and author W. E. B. Du Bois to pursue black equality in the face of white segregation. On May 30, 1909, an organization known as the Negro National Committee emerged, holding four public meetings during the year. In 1910, at their second annual meeting, the participants chose the name National Association for the Advancement of Colored People. The organization was incorporated in 1911 under the laws of the state of New York. Its basic goal was to gain full equality for blacks as guaranteed by law.

Three women who were contributors both in the formative and early years of the NAACP were Ida B. Wells-Barnett, Mary Church Terrell, and Mary White Ovington. All three were well-educated, courageous, articulate speakers and committed to social change.

Wells-Barnett attended Fisk University and Lemoyne Institute. She was known for her meticulous and detailed documentation of acts of lynching, which provided the NAACP with its greatest thrust during its first decade of operation. She was the most significant crusader, and her twenty-year passionate opposition to lynching was heard through her lectures and eloquent pen. Wells-Barnett was known for her candor and uncompromising stance on the rights of blacks. Because this demeanor was not perceived as appropriate for a woman, she was often excluded and shunned by her contemporaries.

Terrell graduated from Oberlin College and furthered her studies abroad. She and her husband knew Booker T. Washington and usually sided with the Bookerites who advocated black acceptance through achievement. They were active members in the Republican party. The NAACP challenged the ideology and philosophy of both Booker T. Washington and President William Howard Taft, a Republican. Terrell broke ties with the black middle-class establishment and became a founder of the NAACP. She served on the NAACP's Executive Committee for a number of years and organized the first District of Columbia branch.

Ovington is credited with the idea of starting the NAACP. Although she was white, she deplored the state of race relations that was reflected in William English Walling's account of the Springfield, Illinois, race riots of 1908. She was instrumental in calling a conference to discuss these problems. Among the sixty names of persons of distinction to sign the "call to arms" were those of Wells-Barnett, Ovington, and Terrell. Ovington was also known for her research that depicted the social and economic conditions of blacks in New York State.

—Constance H. Timberlake

See Also:

Terrell, Mary Church; Wells-Barnett, Ida B.

References:

Duster, Alfreda M., ed. *Crusade for Justice: The Autobiography of Ida B. Wells.* Chicago: University of Chicago Press, 1970.

Hughes, Langston. *Fight for Freedom: A Story of the NAACP.* New York: Norton, 1962.

Morris, Milton D. *The Politics of Black America.* New York: Harper & Row, 1975.

Ovington, Mary White. *Half a Man: The Status of the Negro in New York.* New York: Negro Universities Press, 1969.

———. *The Walls Came Tumbling Down.* New York: Arno, 1969.
Sterling, Dorothy. *Black Foremothers: Three Lives.* Old Westbury, N.Y.: Feminist Press, 1979.
Terrell, Mary Church. *A Colored Woman in a White World.* Washington D. C.: Randell, 1940; rpt. New York: Arno, 1980.

The **NATIONAL ASSOCIATION OF COLORED WOMEN** was organized in July 1896 in Washington, D.C., from a merger of the National Federation of Afro-American Women and the Colored Women's Clubs. The main objective of the NACW was to secure unified action among black club women and to uplift home, morals, and civic life. The motto Lifting as We Climb characterized the association's aims.

Mary Church Terrell was elected the first president. For her, the NACW symbolized the unity of black women's efforts toward progress and reform. The vice presidents included Josephine Ruffin, Fanny J. Coppin, and Frances E. W. Harper. Victoria Matthews was elected national organizer, and Margaret Washington was chosen to chair the executive board and to edit the association's news organ, the *National Notes.*

The NACW was composed of nearly 200 clubs, with 113 from the Colored Woman's League of Washington. The NACW encouraged the local women's clubs to engage in educational and social service projects and philanthropy. Local clubs emphasized mothers' clubs, the establishment of kindergartens and day nurseries, night classes, and sewing and cooking classes. Self-reliance was promoted through the establishment of penny savings banks. The NACW supported antilynching, temperance, and suffrage movements through departments within the national organization.

The NACW held its first convention in Nashville in 1897. Thereafter, national conventions were held biennially. NACW membership increased steadily from five thousand women in 1896 to fifteen thousand by 1904. By 1906, there were forty thousand members. In 1916 NACW membership was nearly sixty thousand, and in 1924 the goal of one hundred thousand women was achieved. The NACW continued to expand, but the present enrollment of forty-five thousand is approximately what it was at the turn of the century. The significance of the NACW lies in the fact that its members challenged individuals and groups who acted unjustly and discriminatorily toward black Americans.

—Floris Barnett Cash

See Also:

Black Women; Black Women's Clubs; Colored Woman's League; National Federation of Afro-American Women; Terrell, Mary Church

References:

Cash, Floris Barnett. "Womanhood and Protest: The Club Movement Among Black Women, 1892–1922." Diss. State University of New York, Stony Brook, 1986.
Davis, Elizabeth. *Lifting as They Climb.* Washington, D.C.: NACW, 1933.
Hunton, Addie. "The Detroit Convention of the NACW." *Voice of the Negro* 3 (August 1906): 590–93.
NACW: What You Should Know About It. Washington, D.C.: NACW, 1959.
Wesley, Charles W. *The History of the National Association of Colored Women's Clubs, Inc.: A Legacy of Service.* Washington, D.C.: NACW, 1984.
Yates, Josephine. "The National Association of Colored Women." *Voice of the Negro* 1 (July 1904): 283–87.

The **NATIONAL ASSOCIATION OF UNIVERSITY WOMEN** was an outgrowth of the College Alumnae Club, which was organized in 1910. Twenty-four university graduates joined Mary Church Terrell in her home in Washington, D.C., for the first meeting. The aim of the College Alumnae Club was to stimulate young women "to attain professional excellence, to exert influence in various movements for the civil good, and to promote a close personal and intellectual fellowship among professional women." The club participated in activities to raise the standards of Negro colleges and to achieve women's suffrage. From 1910 to 1923 the organization expanded, forming branches, and in 1924 became the National Association of College Women, which was later changed to the National Association of University Women.

Today the NAUW includes seventy-four local groups whose goals are to promote constructive work in education, civic activities, and human relations; to study educational conditions with emphasis on problems affecting women; to encourage high educational standards and to stimulate intellectual attainment among women in general. The association's themes are "new insights," "new visions," and "new direction." It is affiliated with the National Assault on Illiteracy Program and maintains a program called "After High School—What?"

—*Sandra Fox*

See Also:

Terrell, Mary Church

Reference:

Terrell, Mary Church. *A Colored Woman in a White World.* Washington, D.C.: Ransdell, 1940.

The **NATIONAL CONSUMERS' LEAGUE (NCL)**, formed in 1899, functioned as a militant and articulate conscience of the buying public on the issues of wages, hours, and conditions for women retail clerks. Inspired by the success of the New York Consumers' League and other such state leagues, the NCL targeted women of means, "ladies of leisure," for education and mobilization on these issues. The NCL published its "White List" of employers whose labor practices met the League "Standard of a Fair House" to alert consumers to support such employers. By 1907 the league "White Label" on a garment indicated that the textile company met a similar standard of labor practices.

A small but efficient agent of social feminism, the NCL lobbied the federal and state legislatures for desirable bills for protective legislation on minimum wages and maximum hours for woman and child labor. The NCL also provided logistical support for court tests of such legislation. Louis Brandeis, later an associate justice of the Supreme Court, served as NCL counsel in landmark cases of state protective legislation, such as *Muller v. Oregon* (1908). The league's effort on behalf of minimum wages was less successful than on behalf of maximum hours, as the NCL defended these state attempts to protect women workers on the ground of possible harm to women's maternal potential.

Although the NCL managed to preserve these protections for working women and children during World War I, the NCL's further achievement was curbed by the postwar national conservatism and the judicial counterrevolution of the Supreme Court, which declared state minimum-wage legislation unconstitutional in *Adkins v. Children's Hospital* (1923). The concurrent failure of a federal child labor amendment and internal dissention regarding the impact of the National Woman's party's "Alice Paul Amendment" (the Equal Rights Amendment, introduced in 1923) disheartened both the NCL membership and Florence Kelley, its inspirational and heretofore indefatigable leader, which brought on its decline in the 1920s.

—*Angela Howard Zophy*

See Also:

Adkins v. Children's Hospital; Kelley, Florence; *Muller v. Oregon*; National Woman's Party; Protective Legislation; Social Feminism

References:

Flexner, Eleanor. *Century of Struggle: The Woman's Rights Movement in the United States.* Rev. ed. Cambridge, Mass.: Belknap, 1959, 1975.

O'Neill, William L. *Everyone Was Brave: A History of Feminism in America.* New York: Quadrangle, 1969, 1971.

Wertheimer, Barbara Mayer. *We Were There: The Story of Working Women in America.* New York: Pantheon, 1977.

The **NATIONAL COUNCIL OF NEGRO WOMEN (NCNW)** was founded in 1935 for the purpose of coordinating the activities of black women's organizations and improving black women's status. The organization was established by Mary McLeod Bethune and twenty-nine women representing fourteen black women's organizations. Some of the founding members included Dr. Dorothy Ferebee, Mabel Staupers, Charlotte Hawkins Brown, and Mary Church Terrell. The women met at the YWCA in Harlem in New York City in order to create an umbrella organization that would unify black women's efforts and affect national public policy.

The leader behind the National Council of Negro Women was Mary McLeod Bethune, who became its first president. Bethune was the founder of Bethune-Cookman College in Florida and served as a consultant at the founding conference of the United Nations in San Francisco. She was also the first black woman to be appointed to a federal government post when she was made head of the Division of Negro Affairs at the National Youth Administration in 1936 by President Franklin D. Roosevelt. Bethune hoped to use her connections in the federal government to advance the rights of black women through the NCNW. The organization lost much of its strength when Bethune retired from the presidency in 1949.

The National Council of Negro Women has represented over one million Afro-American women. During World War II the council pushed for racial equality in federal wartime policies, including the integration of black women into the military. The women also sent a letter to President Roosevelt in support of Jewish rights and in opposition to the Nuremberg Laws in Germany. During the 1960s the council created rural projects to aid impoverished Afro-Americans in the South. Two important Mississippi programs were Project Home, which addressed poor housing, and Operation Daily Bread, designed to alleviate the food shortage. The National Council of Negro Women has remained a major force in the advancement of women's rights.

—Susan Lynn Smith

See Also:

Bethune, Mary McLeod; Terrell, Mary Church

References:

Collier-Thomas, Bettye. *N.C.N.W., 1935–1980.* Washington, D.C.: National Council of Negro Women, 1981.

Giddings, Paula. *When and Where I Enter: The Impact of Black Women on Race and Sex in America.* New York: Morrow, 1984.

Hine, Darlene Clark. *When the Truth is Told: A History of Black Women's Culture and Community in Indiana, 1875-1950.* n.p.: National Council of Negro Women, 1981.

The **NATIONAL EDUCATION ASSOCIATION** is the most influential education organization in the United States and is the largest professional organization in the world. It was organized in Philadelphia, Pennsylvania, in 1857 and originally called the National Teachers' Association. Forty-three educators from a dozen states met on August 26, 1857, under the leadership of Daniel B. Hagar and Thomas W. Valentine and adopted a constitution that states the purpose of the organization is "to elevate the character and advance the interests of the profession of teaching, and to promote the cause of popular education in the United States."

Although women were not admitted to membership until 1866, the constitution was signed by two women, H. D. Conrad and A. W. Beecher. By the time of the 1884 convention in Madison, Wisconsin, women comprised 54 percent of the nearly six thousand educators in attendance.

Until 1957 the association's policy was to take official positions only on matters directly affecting education. As a result of the policy, the association's executive committee in 1956 voted to advise its representative assembly to withhold support of a U.S. constitutional amendment on the equal status of women. In contrast to this earlier action, the NEA became a militant advocate of the equal rights of women in the years from 1957 to 1979. In 1975 the representative assembly voted not to hold meetings in states that had not ratified the Equal Rights Amendment, as well as to refuse support to candidates for political office who opposed ratification of the ERA. During that same year it also amended and strengthened a previous resolution endorsing the use of nonsexist language, supporting the Supreme Court decisions on reproductive freedom and family planning, and advocating the elimination of sexism and sex discrimination from the school curriculum. In 1978 the assembly reaffirmed its position to work for ratification of the ERA as a major legislative priority.

Today the NEA includes almost two million educators and is able to create a strong professional, social, and political influence.

—Sandra Fox

See Also:
Education, Unions

References:

Fenner, Mildred Sandison. *NEA History.* Washington, D.C.: National Education Association, 1945.

Wesley, Edgar Bruce. *NEA: The First Hundred Years.* New York: Harper, 1957.

West, Allan M. *The National Education Association: The Power Base for Education.* New York: Free Press, 1980.

The **NATIONAL FARMERS' ALLIANCE**, with a southern branch and a northern branch, was one of the first mixed-sex organizations to provide opportunities for rural women to hold office. From 1888 through the mid-1890s, Alliance women and men gathered to organize cooperatives; to discuss the economic concerns of farm families, including low crop prices, high shipping rates, the lack of land, and increased mortgage foreclosures; and to lay the foundation for the Populist party.

Women constituted at least one-fourth of the alliance membership. By-laws of the two national alliances, of several state alliances, and of many local suballiances specified that women were eligible for membership although they were exempted from paying dues. Women were often elected to serve as secretaries or treasurers of their suballiances and, more important, as lecturers. Lecturers planned meetings, chose educational materials for study, gave speeches, and solicited members for new suballiances. In eight states, women held state Alliance offices. Kansas and Nebraska each boasted six women state officers. In Nebraska the Zion suballiance elected a woman president, Ella Hall. Fourteen percent of 105 suballiances in Nebraska (the only midwestern state for which membership records exist) had more female members than male members; one-fourth of the Nebraska suballiances had women officers. State officers included Luna Kellie and Elsie Buckman in Nebraska, Eva McDonald Valesh in Minnesota, Fannie Vickery and Bina Otis in Kansas, Sophia Hardin in South Dakota, Fannie Leak in Texas, and Martha Southworth in Colorado. Valesh, Marion Todd, Mary Elizabeth Lease, and Sarah Emery frequently spoke at Alliance functions and picnics and were among the many women elected as delegates to state and national conventions.

In addition, women often edited Alliance newspapers and wrote popular didactic novels and economic tracts explaining the economic worries of farmers and the ways in which these problems could be solved by the National Farmers' Alliance. The novels included *Shylock's Daughter* (1894) by Margaret Holmes Bates; *A Kansas Farm* (1892) by Fannie McCormick; and *Richard's Crown* (1882) by Anna D. Weaver. Alliance members studied finance, legislation, and economics from the books of Sarah Emery (*Seven Financial Conspiracies*, 1887), Stella Fisk (*The Condition and the Remedy*, 1894), Mary Hobart (*A Scientific Exposure of the Errors of Our Monetary System*, 1891), and Marion Todd (*Protective Tariff Delusions*, 1886; *Honest (?) John Sherman*, 1894).

—MaryJo Wagner

See Also:
Agriculture, Populist Party

References:

Nebraska Farmers' Alliance Papers, 1887–97. Nebraska State Historical Society, Lincoln, Neb.

Jeffrey, Julie Roy. "Women in the Southern Farmers' Alliance." *Feminist Studies* 3 (Fall 1975): 72–91.

McMath, Robert C. *Populist Vanguard: A History of the Southern Farmer's Alliance.* New York: Norton, 1977.

Wagner, MaryJo. "Farms, Families, and Reform: Women in the Farmers' Alliance and Populist Party." Diss. University of Oregon, 1986.

The **NATIONAL FEDERATION OF AFRO-AMERICAN WOMEN** (1895–96) was the first national organization of black women's clubs. It was organized July 29-31, 1895, in Boston during a nationwide conference of black women. The conference convened under the leadership of Josephine St. Pierre Ruffin, founder and president of the Woman's Era Club of Boston and editor of its newsletter, *The Woman's Era*. She sent a circular letter to women's clubs, leagues, and societies requesting delegates and explaining the purpose of the meeting. The immediate stimulus for organization was a letter to the British Anti-Lynching Society written by a southern editor, John W. Jacks, which slandered the moral character of all black women.

Social activists from communities across the country attended the historic conference, as did 104 black women representing thirty-two clubs from fifteen states and the District of Columbia. Addresses by such prominent women as Anna J. Cooper, Victoria Matthews, and Margaret Washington reflected the concerns of black women. The women's conference attracted a small number of male supporters, including T. Thomas Fortune, the editor of *New York Age*; Henry B. Blackwell, husband of the feminist Lucy Stone; and William Lloyd Garrison, son of the abolitionist.

The conference culminated with the formation of the National Federation of Afro-American Women and the selection of Margaret Washington, the wife of Booker T. Washington, as president of the new organization. Victoria Earle Matthews was chosen to chair the executive board. According to its constitution, the NFAAW aimed to unify the energies of Afro-American women into one broad sisterhood for the purpose of establishing needed reforms. The following year, both the NFAAW and the Colored Woman's League, a rival organization, held national conventions in Washington, D.C. After a compromise, a united National Association of Colored Women emerged.

—Floris Barnett Cash

See Also:

Black Women's Clubs; National Association of Colored Women; Ruffin, Josephine; Washington, Margaret

References:

Cash, Floris Barnett. "Womanhood and Protest: The Club Movement Among Black Women, 1892–1922." Diss. State University of New York, Stony Brook, 1986.

Davis, Elizabeth. *Lifting As They Climb.* Washington, D.C.: NACW, 1933.

A History of the Club Movement Among the Colored Women of the United States of America. Washington, D.C.: NACW, 1902.

Lerner, Gerda. *Black Women in White America.* New York: Vintage, 1972.

The Woman's Era. 1895–96.

The **NATIONAL FEDERATION OF BUSINESS AND PROFESSIONAL WOMEN'S CLUBS, INC. OF THE UNITED STATES OF AMERICA (BPW/USA)** was founded in 1919 by Lena Madeson Phillips, who challenged her colleagues: "Make no small plans. They have no power to stir the blood." Some independent businesswomen joined those who worked in office white-collar jobs and constituted the majority of the BPW membership. Through the 1930s and 1940s the BPW defended the right of married women in office jobs to continue to work for pay, reflecting both the growth of white-collar jobs and women's presence in that sector of the labor force. In 1940 women constituted half of the five hundred thousand clerical workers in the United States. In the 1950s the organization focused upon job-related issues of concern to its members, most of whom were still salaried clerical workers. The BPW therefore lacked the political clout of comparable men's groups, yet began to assert its place in the community economy. By the 1970s the local BPW chapters exerted political and economic influence in their communities and provided a milieu for networking among its members. In 1937 the BPW became one of the first women's organizations to endorse the Equal Rights Amendment. The group also participated in the 1977 International Women's Year Conference in Houston.

By the 1980s the BPW had become the largest organization of working women in the world, with 150,000 members and thirty-five hundred local organizations and chapters. In addition to providing personal and professional development opportunities for its members, the organization became committed to developing their political skills and awareness. A national political action committee was created at its 1980 national convention to assist, through contributions and endorsements, candidates for federal office who support the organization's principles, including ratification of the Equal Rights Amendment. The organization also created the National Council on the Future of Women in the Workplace, composed of one councillor from each BPW state federation and chaired by black Democratic party leader Eleanor Holmes Norton, to play a vigorous role in exploring the implications for women of new patterns in the work place regarding pay equity, better child care, and technological change in jobs traditionally held by BPW members. The organization annually sponsors National Business Women Week in the third week in October, and is affiliated with the Business and Professional Women's Foundation, a nonprofit research and education organization that conducts and supports research on all aspects of women's work-force participation, sponsors scholarship and loan programs for women at critical points in their lives, and supports the Marguerite Rawalt Resource Center on women's employment issues, which provides daily service to the public.

—Anne Statham

See Also:

Business

Reference:

BPW/USA: The Voice of Working America. A pamphlet produced by BPW/USA, Washington, D.C., 1987.

Lemons, J. Stanley. *The Woman Citizen.* Urbana: University of Illinois Press, 1973.

The **NATIONAL FEDERATION OF SETTLEMENTS** was officially founded on June 11, 1911, by leaders of the settlement house movement, which encouraged educated young people to "settle" among and associate with the urban poor, serving as catalysts for social reform. At this time, the majority of settlement residents, staff, and heads—and the movement's most prominent leaders—were women. Jane Addams of Hull House in Chicago served as the federation's first president. The new organization improved communication among member houses and helped to coordinate members' social-action efforts. These included promoting the creation of the U.S. Children's Bureau, a continual concern for day care, and early endorsement of national health insurance. Lillian Wald of New York's Henry Street Settlement directed a study of prohibition (1927), and Helen Hall published the federation-sponsored *Case Studies of Unemployment* (1931).

While women had ceased to be a majority of settlement heads by the early 1950s, they tended to dominate the administration of the federation from 1934 to 1971. In 1934 the federation appointed Lillie Peck as its first full-time, paid executive. Peck headed the administrative office until 1947, when John McDowell replaced her. As social welfare reform increasingly centered on the federal government, the role of the federation in lobbying became more important. Peck also systematically developed field service to member settlements.

Under McDowell, women filled key positions. Between 1950 and 1968 Fern Colborn authored a federation study of urban renewal, wrote another book on the design of neighborhood centers, and lobbied effectively for housing and welfare programs, including model cities. In 1952 Margaret Berry became assistant director, then executive director from 1959 to 1971.

During Berry's tenure, the federation enjoyed its strongest years. The national headquarters grew to six and a half paid positions, and the federation ran a training center from 1960 to 1971. The federation office continued to push for social reform, with individual leaders sometimes being ahead of a board that had been dominated by nonprofessionals since the early 1950s. For example, the federation did not speak out on birth control until 1965. While the subject was too controversial for settlements in Catholic neighborhoods, some settlements in Protestant neighborhoods actually housed birth control clinics. Membership in the federation was voluntary for local settlements, which retained complete autonomy. In 1979 it became United Neighborhood Centers of America.

—Judith Ann Trolander

See Also:

Addams, Jane; Henry Street Settlement; Hull House; Settlement House Movement; Wald, Lillian

References:

Trolander, Judith Ann. *Professionalism and Social Change: From the Settlement House Movement to Neighborhood Centers, 1886 to the Present.* New York: Columbia University Press, 1986.

———. "The Response of Settlements to the Great Depression." *Social Work* 18 (September 1973): 92–102.

The **NATIONAL LABOR UNION** (1866–73) was founded as a national labor federation with representatives from labor unions in thirteen states and Washington, D.C. There were no women present at the first convention in Baltimore, but there were advocates for women among the delegates.

The most important of these was William Sylvis, the union's co-founder and probably the most important labor leader of the time. Sylvis was president of the Iron Molder's International Union, and during his travels on its behalf he learned firsthand of the struggles of working women and of their difficulties trying to get represented in men's unions or trying to organize their own unions. Like most men of the post–Civil War period, Sylvis did not fully support the presence of women in the labor force. He felt that woman's place was in the home, but he came to believe that if women were going to work, they should be entitled to equal working conditions and equal pay with men. This was part of his belief in social reform for all people. Likewise, Sylvis did not originally support women's suffrage but later came to do so.

The National Labor Union's interest in helping working women had support from the women's suffrage movement. Elizabeth Cady Stanton and Susan B. Anthony, for example, looked to the labor movement for support at a time when most people, including some feminists, felt that the women's suffrage movement should wait until the newly emancipated black man had won the right to vote. In 1868 Stanton attempted to be seated as a delegate at the national convention of the National Labor Union even though she did not represent a labor union. Instead, she represented The Woman Suffrage Association of America, an organization formed just for the convention. With Sylvis's support, she was finally seated.

Several other women were also seated at the convention. Most represented unions that had been formed for the purpose of gaining women's entrance to the convention. The convention did not vote in favor of women's suffrage but did urge equal pay for equal work and women's right to join the labor unions that belonged to the union. The only member union that actually carried out this policy was the National Union of Cigar Makers. The convention also praised the efforts of Kate Mullaney, president of the Collar Laundry Union of Troy, for her efforts on behalf of women laborers. In fact, Mullaney was elected second vice-president, but this action was later annulled because the first vice-president came from the same state. Finally, in 1870 Mrs. E. O. G. Willard of the Sewing Girls' Union of Chicago was elected second vice-president of the National Labor Union, the first woman to attain this honor. However, economic hardships brought to NLU members by the Panic of 1873, an economic depression, completed its demise in the face of competition from another labor organization, the Knights of Labor.

—*Judith Pryor*

See Also:
Knights of Labor, Suffrage, Unions

References:

Foner, Philip S. *Women and the American Labor Movement: From Colonial Times to the Eve of World War I.* New York: Free Press, 1979.
Grossman, Jonathan Philip. *William Sylvis, Pioneer of American Labor: A Study of the Labor Movement During the Era of the Civil War.* New York: Octagon, 1973.
Kenneally, James J. "Women and the Trade Unions, 1870–1920: The Quandary of the Reformer." *Labor History* 14 (1973): 42–55.
Sylvis, James C. *The Life, Speeches, Labors, and Essays of William H. Sylvis.* Philadelphia: Claxton, Remsen & Happlefinger, 1972.

The **NATIONAL MUSEUM OF WOMEN IN THE ARTS** was founded in 1981 to promote awareness of and to educate the public about the achievements of women in the arts through the ages. The museum opened to the public on April 7, 1987, in the former Masonic Temple of Washington, D.C. Designed by architect Waddy Wood in 1907, the Renaissance Revival building is on the National Register of Historic Places. The museum has won several awards for the interior and exterior restoration.

The permanent collection of the museum, whose core of over five hundred pieces was donated by founders Wilhelmina C. and Wallace F. Holladay, ranges from Renaissance to contemporary and includes paintings, sculptures, photographs, Native American pottery, Georgian silver, and works of art on paper. Special exhibitions highlight women and their artistic achievements in a particular area or time period. The museum also houses a Library and Research Center with over five thousand books and eight thousand files on women artists, making it one of the most comprehensive research collections on women artists in the world.

The museum has over eighty-five thousand members, the majority of whom have joined between 1985 and 1988, from all fifty states and twenty-four foreign countries. This is one of the largest museum memberships in the United States. The museum has a unique program of state committees that promotes the museum's mission on a popular level and provides a forum for local artists to show their work in state shows in the nation's capital.

—*Mary Louise Wood*

See Also:
Art

Reference:

Wood, Mary Louise, and Martha McWilliams. *The National Museum of Women in the Arts.* New York: Abrams, 1987.

The **NATIONAL NEGRO HEALTH MOVEMENT** (1915–50) began under the leadership of Booker T. Washington at Tuskegee Institute in Alabama in order to call national attention to the pressing need for better health among Afro-Americans. In the tradition of black self-help efforts, it was a response to the inadequate provision of health services in the first half of the twentieth century. Among other projects, the movement sponsored an annual health week that focused community involvement in clean-up campaigns and health examinations for black people. In 1922 Health Week was celebrated nationwide in fifteen states, and by 1945 in forty-five states, but the focus of the health movement was on the rural South. Black women played an active role in the movement as public health nurses, doctors, teachers, club members, home demonstration agents, and volunteers in the various health projects. Women and children were the major recipients of services provided by these programs.

Many major black organizations joined other national organizations that had largely white membership and leadership in the movement. The federal government took an increasing interest in black health projects, and by the 1930s the U.S. Public Health Service coordinated the activities through its Office of Negro Health Work.

The National Negro Health Movement lasted until 1950, thus spanning two world wars and the Great Depression.

—*Susan Lynn Smith*

See Also:

Black Women

References:

Beardsley, Edward H. *A History of Neglect: Health Care for Blacks and Mill Workers in the Twentieth-Century South.* Knoxville: University of Tennessee Press, 1987.

Jones, James. *Bad Blood: The Tuskegee Syphilis Experiment.* New York: Free Press, 1981.

Smith, Susan Lynn. "Black Women and the National Negro Health Movement, 1915–1950." Diss. University of Wisconsin-Madison, forthcoming.

Torchia, Marion M. "The Tuberculosis Movement and the Race Question, 1890–1950." *Journal of the History of Medicine and Allied Sciences* 32 (1977): 252–79.

The **NATIONAL ORGANIZATION FOR PUBLIC HEALTH NURSING** was founded in 1912 by nurses who wanted to distinguish themselves from those engaged in private-duty and hospital nursing. It was part of the movement to professionalize nursing, but was unique in its close links to the nineteenth-century reform movement. Unlike other professional nurse associations, it welcomed lay members who were dedicated to the goals of preventive medicine. The organization provided a support network and strengthened the sense of professional identity of nurses who practiced in isolation as they visited the homes of the sick among the poor and worked in neighborhood dispensaries, settlement houses, and factories. The organization published a journal, *The Public Health Nurse,* later entitled *Public Health Nursing.*

After World War II, employment opportunities for public health nurses declined precipitously as voluntary agencies lost their funding, and, due largely to efforts by physicians and insurance companies, medical care was increasingly delivered in hospitals or through physicians' private practice. The NOPHN reacted to the situation by voting to dissolve its organization in 1953. Members were directed to the National League of Nursing Education and the Association of Collegiate Schools of Nursing, two organizations that subscribed to the activist principles of the NOPHN and admitted lay members.

—*Jane Crisler*

See Also:

Nursing

References:

Fitzpatrick, M. Louise. *The National Organization for Public Health Nursing, 1912–1952: Development of a Practice Field.* New York: National League for Nursing, 1975.

Melosh, Barbara. *"The Physician's Hand": Work, Culture and Conflict in American Nursing.* Philadelphia: Temple University Press, 1982.

The **NATIONAL ORGANIZATION FOR WOMEN (NOW)** is the largest and most influential women's rights organization in the United States, with over 260,000 members from nine regional groups, state organizations in each of the fifty states, and over eight hundred local groups as of the mid-1980s.

The main goal of the group is to act to bring women into the mainstream of American society as full and active participants who exercise their responsibilities and their privileges as equal partners to men. NOW is pledged to advance women who work both outside and inside the home, to hasten enforcement of sex discrimination legislation, and to establish marriage as a genuine partnership. NOW was organized in October 1966 by a group of twenty-eight women who had attended a conference of state representatives from the various commissions of the status of women in Washington, D.C. These women were frustrated first by the government's approach to women's issues. They realized they needed an "NAACP for women." Betty Friedan, author of *The Feminine Mystique* (1963), became the chief organizer and named the organization.

The general approach of the organization can be described as pragmatic, exerting pressure on the social structure. NOW seeks legal reform in concert with attitudinal and behavioral changes leading to societal change. Methods employed range from consciousness-raising, information giving, marching, picketing, letter writing, petitioning, public opinion influencing, and candidate endorsement to lobbying efforts on all levels of government. Local chapters have a great deal of autonomy. Participatory democracy is recognized as crucial in this organization and may explain its longevity. Before 1973, locals adopted and added to the standard national bylaws, but since 1970, chapters have been encouraged to be experimental as long as goals do not go against existing policy. This enables local chapters to personalize for their particular locales, needs, and interests. This also allows the local chapters to try out more radical ideas and then influence the national organization.

—*Saundra Yelton*

See Also:

Friedan, Betty; Women's Liberation Movement

Reference:

Carden, Maren Lockwood. *The New Feminist Movement.* New York: Russell Sage Foundation, 1974, pp. 103–32.

NATIONAL PARK SERVICE, NATIONAL SITE PRESERVATION, AND WOMEN'S HISTORY. The preservation of women's history in the United States has been served by the National Park Service, the National Historic Landmarks Program, and the National Register of Historic Places.

The National Park Service was established in 1916 to preserve the nation's significant natural, cultural, and historical resources. At present, there are 338 units in the national park system, 4 of which are dedicated to women's history.

Women's Rights National Historical Park in Seneca Falls, New York, was created to "interpret" the first national women's rights convention in American history (1848) and the movement that grew from it, and to preserve buildings related to the early struggle for women's rights. Included in the park are the Wesleyan Chapel, site of the convention; the restored home of Elizabeth Cady Stanton, leader of the nineteenth-century movement; the home of Jane Hunt, where the convention was planned; and the home of Mary Ann McClintock, where the Declaration of Sentiments and Resolutions for the convention was written.

Maggie L. Walker National Historical Site in Richmond, Virginia, was created to preserve the home and neighborhood of an important black civic and financial leader. Maggie Walker was the first woman bank president in America and a central figure in Richmond's black community for over forty years. Eleanor Roosevelt National Historic Site in Hyde Park, New York, commemorates Roosevelt's contributions to America by preserving Val-Kill Cottage and associated buildings and grounds. Beginning in 1925, the complex was Eleanor Roosevelt's refuge from the demands of a busy career, and the home in which she met with some of the most important world leaders of her time. Clara Barton National Historic Site in Glen Echo, Maryland, preserves and interprets the home where the important humanitarian and founder of the American Red Cross resided for the last fifteen years of her life.

The Sewall-Belmont House in Washington, D.C., is a site associated with the National Park Service but privately owned by the National Women's party. The house is dedicated to Alice Paul, founder of the National Women's party, prominent feminist activist, and author of the Equal Rights Amendment. Two other national park sites deal substantively with women's history. Whitman Mission National Historic Site near Walla Walla, Washington, interprets the mission established along the Oregon Trail by Narcissa and Marcus Whitman in 1836. Narcissa Whitman and a colleague, Eliza Spalding, were the first white women to cross the continent overland. Lowell National Historical Park in Lowell, Massachusetts, preserves and interprets the early industrial history of the Northeast, with a focus on the role of early female factory workers. Of particular note is the labor movement begun by women in Lowell.

Interpretation of women's history is being incorporated into existing programs at many national park areas. For example, the role of women in military encampments is interpreted at Morristown (N.J.) National Historical Park, and the contributions of Sacajawea, the Shoshone Indian guide, to the Lewis and Clark expedition are interpreted at Fort Clatsop National Monument (Astoria, Oregon). The wives of men whose homes are preserved are often interpreted, as at Carl Sandburg Home National Historic Site (Flat Rock, North Carolina), where Paula Sandburg's career is extensively discussed. Women's domestic roles and activities are interpreted at many sites, including George Washington's Birthplace National Monument (Virginia), George Washington Carver National Monument (Diamond, Missouri), and Martin Van Buren National Historic Site (Kinderhook, New York).

Among the federal government's historic preservation initiatives are two important programs: the National Historic Landmarks Program and the National Register of Historic Places. Both programs are designed to encourage private efforts in historic preservation to complement federal activities.

Established in 1935, the National Historic Landmarks Program is designed to identify and encourage the preservation of nationally significant historic sites, buildings, structures, districts, and objects. There are nearly two hundred national historic landmarks, only about 3 percent of which commemorate women's experiences and contributions to the nation. Most of those sites that are included are associated with women who were significant, even by traditional male standards of achievement. Among national historic landmarks dedicated to women are the homes of reformers Elizabeth Cady Stanton, Susan B. Anthony, Mary Ann Shadd Cary, Mary Church Terrell, Julia Ward Howe, Charlotte Forten Grimké, and Harriet Beecher Stowe. Also included are Harriet Tubman's Home for the Aged, and the homes of artists and intellectuals such as Emily Dickinson, Emma Willard, Margaret Fuller, Florence Mills, and Pearl Buck.

Many of these homes were preserved through the efforts of women, as were the homes of Maggie L. Walker and Eleanor Roosevelt and the sites that make up Women's Rights National Historical Park. More traditionally significant sites like Mount Vernon, Old South Meeting House, Mesa Verde, Valley Forge, and the home of Frederick Douglass were also saved by groups of women.

The National Register of Historic Places, established in 1966, officially lists and provides initiatives for the preservation of historic resources of national, state, or local significance. Thirteen percent of all National Register properties are nationally significant; these include all national historic landmarks, which are automatically listed on the National Register. There are over forty-five thousand properties on the National Register, where women are also vastly underrepresented.

Part of the reason for women's underrepresentation is the fact that the criteria for historical significance, particularly in the landmarks program, are based largely on traditional historical categories and periodizations that exclude or ignore women. Sites are evaluated for their economic, political, or military associations, and women's contributions, which do not ordinarily fall into these categories, are neglected.

In 1987 the National Park Service and other national historical organizations, including the National Coordinating Council for the Promotion of History, embarked on a program to increase women's representation in the National Historic Landmarks Program. The commencement of this program indicates a recognition that a redefinition of "significance" is required if the experiences and accomplishments of American women are to be adequately preserved.

—Margaret T. McFadden

References:

Dubrow, Gail. "Preserving Her Heritage: American Landmarks of Women's History." Paper presented at the Seventh Berkshire Conference on the History of Women, June 21, 1987.

Hosmer, Charles B. *Presence of the Past: A History of the Preservation Movement in the United States Before Williamsburg.* New York: Putnam, 1965.

———. *Preservation Comes of Age, from Williamsburg to the National Trust, 1926–1949.* 2 vols. Charlottesville: University of Virginia Press, 1981.

National Park Service, U.S. Department of the Interior. *Index of the National Park System and Related Areas.* Washington, D.C.: U.S. Government Printing Office, 1982.

Tinling, Marion. *Women Remembered: A Guide to Landmarks of Women's History in the United States.* Westport, Conn.: Greenwood, 1986.

The **NATIONAL WELFARE RIGHTS ORGANIZATION**, a federation of local groups, was formed in April 1967 to represent the needs of welfare recipients and others in need of economic assistance. The membership, made up almost exclusively of mothers receiving Aid to Dependent Children grants through the welfare system, stood at 5,000 in 1967, but by 1969 it reached a peak of 25–30,000. The majority of members were black welfare mothers. The organization can be said to have represented in excess of one hundred thousand people at its apex if the children of these women are considered. The requirements for membership were poverty and current or previous welfare-recipient status.

The goals of the organization were "adequate income for all Americans" (a guaranteed annual income) whether or not they were on welfare and guarantees that the welfare system accord "dignity, justice, and democracy to all recipients." These goals were to be pursued by attempting to eliminate restrictive welfare requirements and generally increasing welfare benefits.

The initial plan of attack called for the local groups to protest particular complaints, usually regarding withheld entitlement payments. Creation and distribution of handbooks, advocacy, sit-ins, and demonstrations were examples of the methods employed.

NWRO tested welfare policy and law in the courts. It also lobbied for a guaranteed annual income of $6,500 a year for a family of four in 1971, in direct opposition to the punitive Family Assistance Plan being proposed by President Richard M. Nixon. During the Nixon presidency, concessions to welfare recipients began to be withdrawn, cutbacks were increased, and NWRO membership declined. The organization went bankrupt, and the national office closed early in 1975.

It is difficult to assess the real achievements of the organization, but in general it is fair to say that its efforts did help produce a more humane system and helped expand benefits to welfare recipients. Although NWRO fell short of the guaranteed-annual-income goal, it at least helped to defeat Nixon's program. According to NWRO activists and social scientists Frances Fox Piven and Richard A. Cloward, members wanted "to build an enduring mass organization through which the poor could exert influence." Perhaps the eventual failure of this organization can be summed up with a question to be pondered still: How can the powerless exert power?

—Saundra K. Yelton

See Also:

Female-headed Households, Mothers' Pensions

References:

Evans, Sara. *Personal Politics: The Roots of Women's Liberation in the Civil Rights Movement and the New Left.* New York: Vintage, 1979, 1980.

Roach, Jack L., and Janet K. Roach. "Mobilizing the Poor: Road to a Dead End." *Social Problems* 26 (December 1978): 160–71.

The **NATIONAL WOMAN SUFFRAGE ASSOCIATION** was founded in New York City in May 1869 by Elizabeth Cady Stanton and Susan B. Anthony, who were angered at the refusal of abolitionist leaders to give priority to feminist demands until black rights (including black male suffrage) were secured. The organization took shape at a reception at the New York Woman's Bureau where some one hundred women, representing eighteen states, joined on the spot. Such feminist notables as Lucretia Mott, Martha Wright, Paulina Wright Davis, and Ernestine Rose lent their support to the new venture. It was agreed that men should not hold office in the new association and that its program would emphasize the need for a federal woman suffrage amendment. Stanton was elected president, and Anthony served first on the executive committee and later as vice president at large. The two women tirelessly publicized the wide-ranging feminist aims of NWSA in the pages of their short-lived newspaper, the *Revolution*, through weekly discussion meetings in New York, and in a series of cross-country lecture tours. Their efforts encouraged the proliferation of state and local suffrage associations, and NWSA soon outstripped its rival, the more moderate American Woman Suffrage Association.

NWSA brought its demand for a proposed Sixteenth Amendment to grant woman suffrage to center stage by holding national conventions each winter in Washington, D.C. NWSA members submitted a flood of petitions and resolutions to Congress and the White House, and regularly testified before congressional committees. A delegation from NWSA boldly disrupted the July 1876 Centennial celebrations in Philadelphia by presenting a "Woman's Declaration of Rights" drafted by Stanton and read aloud by Anthony. Beginning in 1878, at NWSA's urging, a woman suffrage amendment was introduced every year in Congress.

Stanton remained as president, but from the early 1880s, Anthony increasingly exercised day-to-day leadership of the organization. Early criticism of NWSA's informal, amateurish style and sometimes undemocratic procedures gave way as Anthony promoted an increasingly sophisticated and efficient constitutional structure. In her efforts to build a broad-based, nonpartisan membership, she worked hard to smooth over dissension in the ranks. To Anthony's dismay, Stanton persisted in introducing controversial resolutions, calling, for example, for divorce reform, or denouncing sexism in the churches. But NWSA membership continued to grow, as Anthony reached out to other mass women's organizations like the Woman's Christian Temperance Union and women's clubs. International contacts generated by Stanton's several visits to Europe and Anthony's tour of Britain in 1883 were consolidated by the creation of the International Council of Women, launched at the NWSA convention of 1888.

Over the years, the ideological gap between AWSA and NWSA narrowed. In response to pressure from younger NWSA activists such as Rachel Foster Avery and Carrie Chapman Catt, Anthony at last yielded to pleas for unity, and in 1890 the two organizations joined forces to become the National American Woman Suffrage Association.

—*Gail Malmgreen*

See Also:

Anthony, Susan B.; National American Woman Suffrage Association; *Revolution*; Stanton, Elizabeth Cady

References:

Harper, Ida Husted. *The Life and Work of Susan B. Anthony*. Vols. 1–2. Indianapolis: Bowen-Merrill, 1898.

Lutz, Alma. *Created Equal: A Biography of Elizabeth Cady Stanton, 1815–1902*. New York: Day, 1940.

———. *Susan B. Anthony*. Boston: Beacon, 1959.

Stanton, Elizabeth C., Susan B. Anthony, and Matilda J. Gage, eds. *History of Woman Suffrage*. 6 vols. Rochester: Privately Printed, 1881–1922.

NATIONAL WOMAN'S LOYAL LEAGUE. In early 1863—when Charles Sumner and other Republican leaders were working toward a federal amendment to abolish slavery—Susan B. Anthony, Elizabeth Cady Stanton, Ernestine Rose, and Lucy Stone proposed the creation of a woman's organization to assist the men of the Union in finding an acceptable political solution to the Civil War. In response to their call, thousands of delegates gathered for an organizational meeting of the National Woman's Loyal League in New York City on May 14, 1863. After Stanton delivered an opening address, a number of the more conservative delegates spoke against injecting questions of women's rights and abolition into the debate, insisting that the sole object of the society should be confined to supporting the war policies of President Abraham Lincoln. The conservative voices, however, were voted down following pleas by Anthony, Stone, Rose, and Angelina Grimké Weld, who adamantly opposed curtailing the jurisdiction of the league. The convention passed a resolution that pledged to support the government, but only so long as it continued to wage a war for freedom. The league also established the goal of collecting one million signatures on a petition supporting congressional approval of the Thirteenth Amendment, which abolished slavery.

Under the direction of president Stanton and secretary Anthony, the National Woman's Loyal League grew to a membership of five thousand strong. Operating on a shoestring budget, the league's officers drafted nearly two thousand volunteers to circulate the petitions. While failing to meet its ambitious goal, by the time the league disbanded in August 1864 it had gathered nearly four hundred thousand signatures supporting the proposed amendment. As a training school for volunteers, the league also provided hundreds of workers with valuable organizational skills that they would use in subsequent crusades for social reform.

—*Terry D. Bilhartz*

See Also:

Anthony, Susan B.; Civil War; Stanton, Elizabeth Cady; Stone, Lucy; U.S. Sanitary Commission

References:

Dorr, Rheta Childe. *Susan B. Anthony*. New York: Stokes, 1928.

Flexner, Eleanor. *Century of Struggle*. New York: Atheneum, 1968.

Harper, Ida Husted. *The Life and Work of Susan B. Anthony*. 3 vols. Indianapolis: Bowen-Merrill, 1898–1908; rpt. Salem, N.H.: Ayer, 1983.

Stanton, Elizabeth Cady, Susan B. Anthony, and Matilda Joslyn Gage, eds. *The History of Woman Suffrage*. Vol. 2. Rochester: n.p., 1881.

The **NATIONAL WOMAN'S PARTY (NWP)** was established by Alice Paul and Lucy Burns in 1916 as an outgrowth of their efforts within the National American Woman Suffrage Association (NAWSA) and their own Congressional Union (CU) during the previous four years. Infused with the enthusiasm and schooled in the militant tactics of the British Women's Social and Political Union (WSPU), Paul and Burns reorganized the NAWSA Congressional Committee in January 1913 to develop a campaign that would focus the attention of the nation on the drive to secure a federal amendment to give women the vote. As the militants' campaign for a federal amendment to franchise women dragged on during the war years, Paul and Burns—frustrated by the slow progress of the strategy of the staid and mainstream NAWSA—applied much of the WSPU strategy to the American suffrage struggle, including civil disobedience, which resulted in arrests, hunger strikes, and forced feedings of Woman's party suffragists.

Paul's tactics employed not only parades, speeches, and demonstrations to attract attention, but also followed the British WSPU "suffragette" strategy of holding the entire party in power responsible for its leaders' failure to adopt a women's suffrage amendment. Thus the NAWSA Congressional Committee immediately sponsored a parade of five thousand women, which upstaged the inauguration of President Woodrow Wilson, a Democrat, and evoked a riot among the spectators that brought public sympathy to the women and their cause, as well as a formal investigation of the police failure to protect the marchers or keep the peace. The momentum of the committee's pressure on the new Democratic administration continued through the spring in the form of grass-roots petition campaigns and suffragist pilgrimages to the Capitol, including an automobile procession on July 31, 1913, to deliver petitions with two hundred thousand signatures to several senators, as well as continual delegations of different groups of women to meet with President Wilson.

In April 1913, while chairperson of the NAWSA Congressional Committee, Paul and her cohort Burns established the Congressional Union as an affliate national organization that was to be committed entirely to securing a federal suffrage amendment, and which began publishing its own weekly, the *Suffragist*, in November of that year. During the NAWSA's national convention in 1913, however, differences of opinion between the Congressional Union and the NAWSA leadership in establishing the federal amendment as the priority action of the suffragists, as well as establishing the policy of holding the "party in power" responsible for inaction on such an amendment, brought formal separation of the latter from the former.

Thereafter designated as an auxiliary of the NAWSA, the Congressional Union successfully supported federal legislation that allowed the use of state initiatives to secure state referenda on woman suffrage, but this strategem complicated the tenuous situation of the NAWSA in 1914 by requiring many exhausting state campaigns. Urging western women with partial suffrage to use their vote against all Democratic candidates regardless of their individual stand on suffrage, the CU claimed credit for the defeat of twenty-three of the forty-three who ran for office in 1914 bi-elections, and it sponsored a stream of women's delegations to visit President Wilson to educate and pressure him for his support of a federal amendment.

By 1915 the Congressional Union was organizing chapters in all the states in conjunction with its national automobile caravan from San Francisco to Washington and its yearlong petition campaign to bring the federal suffrage amendment to a vote in Congress. Although the amendment was voted down in both the House and the Senate in January 1915, the CU efforts drew national publicity to congressional actions regarding federal enfranchisement of women. Between 1913 and 1916 the Congressional Union contributed significantly by resuscitating the languishing suffrage movement through Paul and Burns's effective campaign for a federal woman suffrage amendment while the NAWSA was reorganizing its leadership, priorities, and plan of action.

In June 1916 the Congressional Union organized the National Woman's party in the twelve states that had already given women the presidential vote, possibly influencing the subsequent national conventions of both the Democratic and Republican parties to endorse woman suffrage, however vaguely. Holding President Wilson personally responsible for the failure of the federal amendment effort, the NWP unsuccessfully opposed the incumbent and the Democratic ticket in the 1916 election. Having failed to revive the amendment in Congress as well, the NWP initiated its famed campaign of militancy in 1917.

The National Woman's party engaged in militant and flamboyant activities, utilizing publicity stunts, marches, open-air meetings, watch fires, strikes, picketing of both the Capitol and the White House, lobbying of legislators as well as the president, and calling upon women who were franchised to penalize "the party in power" until a constitutional suffrage amendment was acquired. While the NAWSA used U.S. entry into World War I as a means to enlarge the support base for woman suffrage, the NWP evoked mob violence with its pickets and banners that castigated the Wilson administration for not ensuring democracy's safety at home with woman suffrage. Although guilty at most of creating a nuisance for city and federal officials, the National Woman's party pickets were the first victims of the early tide of the World War I home-front assault on civil liberties that culminated in the Red Scare of 1919.

The illegal arrests of women, which finally totaled 216, began in June 1917 and eventually brought 97 suffragists harsh sentences of as much as six months in the infamous Occoquan, Virginia, workhouse or the deplorable District of Columbia jail. Although perceived as an embarassment to the NAWSA efforts by that leadership as well as to the Wilson administration, the women who endured forced feedings and other inflicted hardships were nationally respected settlement house workers and nurses, wives of prominent men, and members of Quaker families. Widespread publicity of their plight and treatment, in addition to their demand to be given "prisoner of war" status, resulted in the unconditional release of the prisoners by exasperated officials in late November. Their innocence was vindicated when the District of Columbia Court of Appeals invalidated all of their arrests and their sentences in March 1918.

The public sympathy for these suffragists coincided with Carrie Chapman Catt's "Winning Plan" of the NAWSA, which brought Woodrow Wilson to support the cause of woman suffrage by September 1918; but despite his personal address to the Congress calling for passage of the suffrage amendment, the Senate voted it down. In response both the NWP and the NAWSA openly campaigned against senators who voted against the franchise bill in the bi-elections of 1918.

The National Woman's party membership numbered between thirty-five thousand and sixty thousand members at its peak between 1919 and 1920, as its efforts for the federal amendment paralleled those of the NAWSA. However, in 1921, after the adoption of the suffrage amendment, the single-issue politics of the woman suffrage movement took its toll on the NWP, which had only 151 paid members remaining. The leaders of the NWP continued their concern for broader issues that encompassed the whole of the nineteenth-century woman's rights movement. Therefore, at the NWP convention in 1923, the seventy-fifth anniversary of the Seneca Falls (N.Y.) Convention for woman's rights, the NWP presented a draft of a federal equal rights amendment that read, "Men and women shall have equal rights throughout the United States and every place subject to its jurisdiction." This proposed federal amendment was introduced in Congress on December 10, 1923, because the National Woman's party members felt that such a constitutional amendment was the most expedient and far-reaching method of gaining women's equality under the law. At the February meeting of the NWP National Council 1922 Caroline Spencer introduced wording—"Equality of the sexes shall not be denied or abridged on account of sex or marriage"—that was closer to the 1972 version of the Equal Rights Amendment (ERA). The so-called Alice Paul amendment of the NWP initiated an ongoing campaign for the ERA.

Thus the NWP has served as a transition group between the nineteenth-century woman's movement and the twentieth-century women's movement. Its continued support of the ERA placed it at odds with the social feminists who feared the loss of the protective legislation secured during the Progressive era. Enduring into the 1980s, the National Woman's party still focuses its efforts toward the attainment of equal rights for women. Its headquarters, the Sewall-Belmont House in Washington, D.C., is a national landmark and contains a museum of NWP, ERA, and suffrage memorabilia. An anecdote reflecting the constancy of the NWP surfaced during the ERA ratifciation effort in the early 1970s: Members of the National Organization for Women who were to be hosted at the Sewall-Belmont House arrived late one night and were greeted by venerable women in quaint nightclothes and caps; when the NOW women remarked on their hostesses' state of excitement, the NWP members were said to reply, "You'd be excited, too, if you had been waiting fifty years for reinforcements!"

—Saundra K. Yelton, Neil W. Hogan, and Angela Howard Zophy

See Also:

Equal Rights Amendment; National American Woman Suffrage Association; Nineteenth-Century Woman's Movement; Paul, Alice; Suffrage: Twentieth-Century Women's Rights Movement.

References:

Cott, Nancy F. "Feminist Politics in the 1920s: the National Woman's Party." *Journal of American History* 71 (1984): 43–68.

Fair, John D. "The Political Aspects of Women's Suffrage During the First World War." *Albion* 8 (Fall 1976): 274–95.

Flexner, Eleanor. *Century of Struggle: The Woman's Rights Movement in the United States.* Cambridge, Mass.: Belknap, 1968.

Irwin, Inez Haynes. *The Story of the Woman's Party.* New York: Harcourt Brace, 1921.

O'Neill, William. *Everyone Was Brave: The Rise and Fall of Feminism in America.* Chicago: Quadrangle, 1969.

Pankhurst, E. Sylvia. *The Suffragette Movement.* London: Longmans, Gant, 1931.

Rosen, Andrew. *Rise Up Women!* London: Routledge and Kegan Paul, 1974.
Rover, Constance. *Women's Suffrage and Party Politics in Britain, 1866–1914*. London: Routledge and Kegan Paul, 1967.
Stron, Sharon Hartman. "Leadership and Tactics in the American Woman Suffrage Movement, A Perspective from Massachusetts." *Journal of American History* 62 (September 1975): 296–315.

NATIONAL WOMEN'S HALL OF FAME, Seneca Falls, New York. Organized in 1968 in the village where the first national women's rights convention took place in 1848, the hall is a not-for-profit membership corporation formed to honor and recognize outstanding American women of achievement. The purpose of the hall is to educate and motivate—to bring the importance of women's roles in history to light so that history becomes more complete, more reflective of women's true position in America.

An evolving living-learning center utilizing artifacts, photographs, participatory and audio-visual components, the hall has numerous permanent exhibits, including forty-two biographical panels honoring women of achievement as well as displays commemorating significant events in the history of American women. Traveling exhibits have been used by hundreds of organizations nationwide.

Two educational kits for intermediate- and junior-high-level students have been produced and published by the National Women's Hall of Fame. *The Faces and Phases of Women* and *The Times and Triumphs of American Women* provide a much-needed introduction to women who have made significant contributions to the development of the United States.

—*Susan Barber-Bove*

See Also:

National Park Service, National Site Preservation, and Women's History; Seneca Falls Convention

References:

National Women's Hall of Fame Education Committee. *The Faces and Phases of Women.* Seneca Falls, N.Y.: National Women's Hall of Fame, 1983.
———. *National Women's Hall of Fame Resource Catalogue.* Published annually.
———. *The Times and Triumphs of American Women.* Seneca Falls, N.Y.: National Women's Hall of Fame, 1986.

NATIONAL WOMEN'S HISTORY PROJECT (NWHP). In 1978 the Sonoma County (Calif.) Commission on the Status of Women undertook a celebration to commemorate International Women's Day, March 8, with a week designated as National Women's History Week. The National Women's History Project was founded in 1980, and the principal organizers of that original activity have spearheaded an annual observance of National Women's History from their Sonoma County base, providing technical assistance and multicultural women's history materials for local and state organizers nationwide.

The specific activities of the NWHP have increased greatly since its inception. In response to continuing requests, a Women's History Resource Service was begun in 1981. The project staff now reviews hundreds of educational materials annually to find the best multicultural, accurate, and affordable materials available for children of all ages and for adults. Over three hundred thousand copies of its catalog, *Women's History Resources*, containing over 250 items, are distributed annually throughout the country. In response to the paucity of commercial materials for classroom instruction, the NWHP has developed and published many curriculum units for use from kindergarten through high school. Similarly, a video documentary on Women in American Life, comprehensive organizing guides, annual commemorative posters, and other items pertaining to women's history and the celebration of National Women's History Month have been produced and published by project staff.

To build upon the momentum created by its successful organizing, the project has established the Women's History Network to link historians, educators, community organizers, and others interested in women's history. The network serves as a clearinghouse for curriculum and program resources, organizing referrals and providing technical assistance to activists and educators on a year-round basis. It publishes a quarterly newsletter on numerous aspects of women's history such as print and media resources, performers' lists, traveling exhibits, archives, libraries, and conferences. The network also publishes semiannual directories of its members, enabling participants to locate and communicate directly with others who share their women's history interests.

The NWHP staff serve as consultants to state offices of education and school districts nationwide for teacher training to infuse the multicultural study of women's history into all aspects of the K–12 curriculum. In addition, the project conducts several three-day conferences, "A Woman's Place Is in . . . The Curriculum," for educators, school administrators, and community activists from throughout the country.

—Mary E. Ruthsdotter

See Also:

International Women's Day, Women's Studies

Reference:

Women's History Resources. Santa Rosa, Calif.: NWHP, 1987.

The **NATIONAL WOMEN'S POLITICAL CAUCUS** was established in 1971 to increase the participation of women in public and political life. By the late 1980s over three hundred affiliates nationwide and over seventy-seven thousand people were encouraging women to become politically active at all levels: to run for office, appointments, political convention delegate positions, judgeships; to become involved as lobbyists and voters; or to be active in any political campaign. This reflects the belief of many women, since the failure of the Equal Rights Amendment to win passage, that equality will only come through equal representation. The caucus recruits and trains women for the political arena and meets with political candidates to advocate fair representation of women throughout the political process. Through lobbying efforts, it also strives to gain pledges of support for female candidates and concerns.

Founded by a distinguished group of activists—including Gloria Steinem, Shirley Chisholm, Bella Abzug, Dorothy Height, and LaDonna Harris—the caucus sponsored the first national political convention of women in over one hundred years in 1973. Held in Houston, Texas, it served as a groundbreaker, emphasizing women's political visibility and importance.

Statistics indicating more than a tripling of women in the state legislatures—from 4 percent in 1971 to 14.8 percent in 1986—reflect the success of the caucus. Comparable gains are being made at other levels of government. The caucus has also been successful in bringing women's issues to the forefront of American politics.

—Saundra K. Yelton

See Also:

Abzug, Bella; Chisholm, Shirley; Politics; Steinem, Gloria

References:

Broder, David S. "Women: Power in Politics." *The Washington Post* (July 3, 1985): A17.

Feit, Rona F. "Organizing for Political Power: The National Women's Political Caucus." In *Women Organizing: An Anthology,* edited by Bernice Cummings and Victoria Schuck. Metuchen, N.J.: Scarecrow, 1979, pp. 184–208.

Toner, Robin. "Gains for Women Predicted in Races for Statewide Office." *The New York Times* 135 (May 19, 1986): 1.

The **NATIONAL WOMEN'S TRADE UNION LEAGUE (NWTUL)** was founded in 1903 by Mary Kenney O'Sullivan. Its purpose was to bring together women from various industries so they could work for higher wages and improved working conditions. The motto of the NWTUL was The Eight-Hour Day; A Living Wage; to Guard the Home. Not limited to union workers, the league welcomed women who were not in the work force but who believed in the goals of the trade unions. These women—called "allies" because of their financial and personal contributions—were educated, able to organize and to speak before large groups. The league also educated its worker members for leadership and informed the public of union goals.

The first convention of the NWTUL endorsed six primary points: equal pay for equal work, women's suffrage, full unionization, the eight-hour day, a minimum wage, and the economic programs of the American Federation of Labor (AFL).

The Women's Trade Union League (WTUL) was established on the local level, in places like New York City, Chicago, and Boston. At the workplace, the WTUL established meeting rooms and rest areas for workers to discuss problems, form friendships, or just rest between shifts. The New York league had to cope with its inability to change women's status and the failures of organized labor. When it attempted to affiliate with the AFL, a predominantly male craft union, the New York WTUL was not accepted because it was a trade union, comprised of unskilled, poorly paid, irregularly employed female workers. The New York WTUL also confronted the cultural, social, and language differences among the many Jewish and Italian immigrants in the factories. Beginning in 1913, the New York WTUL emphasized women's suffrage and protective legislation, focusing on women's specific needs and difficulties. This represented a shift in league emphasis; previously women had been regarded simply as workers, not different in their employment needs from men workers. The WTUL continued to work for social reform through the 1950s, by which time working women in New York had achieved a minimum wage and a forty-eight-hour week.

—*Rosemary Herriges, OSF*

See Also:

O'Sullivan, Mary Kenney; Unions; Wages

References:

Dye, Nancy Schrom. *As Equals and As Sisters.* Columbia: University of Missouri Press, 1980.

Foner, Philip S. *Women and the American Labor Movement.* New York: Free Press, 1979.

Wertheimer, Barbara M. *We Were There: The Story of Working Women in America.* New York: Pantheon, 1977.

NATIVE AMERICAN WOMEN. Although the lives of Native American women have been ignored by many historians and Indian women have been stereotyped as squaws and princesses, research continues to establish the importance of their roles in both traditional and contemporary cultures. Cultural determinants, as well as the diversity of Indian cultures, established the roles and position of women within their tribes. Generally, in agricultural societies such as the Iroquois or the Navajo, women were accorded more status than they received in the primarily hunting societies of the Great Plains. In every case, however, women had clearly defined and valuable roles within the societies.

Women's status within the Iroquois before contact with whites has been a subject of much interest. The Iroquois organized their kinship groups into matrilineal clans, whose members traced their descent from a common female ancestor. Mothers usually arranged their children's marriages, and newlyweds customarily went to live with the bride's clan. Iroquois women owned the longhouses in which they lived and passed them on to their descendants. They also had a great deal of power because they controlled the agricultural life of their tribes by managing the farming activities of the tribe. Among the Seneca, women elected the tribe's male leaders and participated in many other political decisions.

Before white contact, women also had a great deal of power among the Cherokee in the South. Women had the right to speak in village councils, and some accompanied braves when the tribe went on the warpath. Cherokee women also had a crucial role in agriculture.

All this began to change between 1790 and 1840 as missionaries and government agents urged Native Americans to value individual ownership of land, European gender roles, and the patriarchal family. Native Americans in many cases altered their traditional ways of life, and in the process the traditional base of women's power among groups like the Iroquois and the Cherokee was eroded.

Many of the negative images of Indian women developed as a result of contact with Euramerican society. The assault on traditional practices took many forms. Fur trappers and traders changed the material culture of the tribes by introducing and developing a demand for iron, glass beads, cloth, and dyes. The missionaries judged Indian women by traditional Judeo-Christian views that denigrated the power women held in some tribes in favor of European-style patriarchy. Often Native Americans were judged on the basis of how helpful they could be to whites. Pocahontas, who saved Captain John Smith in 1607 and married John Rolfe, a leader of the English colony in Virginia, is one famous example of an Indian woman valued by whites. Sacajawea of the Shoshone, who guided and interpreted for the Lewis and Clark expedition between 1804 and 1806, was another Native American woman who has gained fame among whites.

Efforts to assimilate Native American women into Euramerican society through education also changed the status of women. Schools run by missionaries and the Bureau of Indian Affairs established curricula along stereotypical lines, training women in homemaking skills while punishing them for speaking their native languages or wearing traditional clothing. In the twentieth century, American Indian women have been victims of medical practices that resulted in mass sterilizations, and social agencies tend to define the family as nuclear and ignore the extended family prevalent in Indian societies. There has been some redress for grievances in recent times, however. Bureau of Indian Affairs schools now give preference to Indian teachers, and the curriculum has become more diversified, resulting in far more Indian women attending colleges and professional schools after high school. The American Indian Religious Freedom Act of 1978 and the Indian Child Welfare Act that same year recognized tribal rights.

The most serious issues affecting Indian women today are those that also affect their children. The rate of infant mortality exceeds that of the national norm of all races, and the rate of fetal alcohol syndrome is three to six times higher than the national average. Native American children with handicapping conditions are less likely to receive services than other American children. Until the passage of the Indian Child Welfare Act, preservation of the Indian family was not considered a priority by government agencies. Many Indian children were placed in non-Indian foster-care and adoptive homes or boarding schools without consultation with the families or tribes involved.

Tribal laws are frequently in conflict with federal and state laws, especially regarding women's civil rights issues. One of the most significant court cases affecting Indian women was *Santa Clara Pueblo v. Martinez* 436 U.S. 49 (1978) in which the Supreme Court ruled that the federal government should not interfere in intratribal issues even where women's rights were at stake.

Increasingly, Indian women are becoming active in politics (Ada Deer, Wilma Mankiller), in education (Clara Sue Kidwell, Bea Medicine), in medicine (Annie Wauneka, Connie Uri), and in literature (Paula Gunn Allen, Leslie Marmon Silko, Louise Erdrich).

—Gretchen M. Bataille

See Also:

Berdache; Bonnin, Gertrude; Hopkins, Sarah Winnemucca; Naming Systems; Native American Women's Literature; Sandoz, Mari

References:

Albers, Patricia, and Beatrice Medicine, eds. *The Hidden Half: Studies of Plains Indian Women.* Washington, D.C.: University Press of America, 1983.

Anderson, Owanah. *Ohoyo One Thousand: A Resource Guide of American Indian/Alaskan Native Women.* Wichita Falls, Tex.: Ohoyo Resource Center, 1982.

Conference on the Educational and Occupational Needs of American Indian Women. Washington, D.C.: National Institute of Education, 1980.

Green, Rayna. *Native American Women: A Contextual Bibliography*. Bloomington: Indiana University Press, 1983.

Native Self-Sufficiency 4 (September 1981). [Special issue on women.]

Verble, Sedelta, ed. *Words of Today's American Indian Women: Ohoyo Makachi: A First Collection of Oratory by American Indian/ Alaskan Native Women*. Washington, D.C.: U.S. Department of Education, 1981.

NATIVE AMERICAN WOMEN'S LITERATURE. The literature of Native American women was originally an oral literature—songs and stories that expressed personal emotions and carried on religious and secular traditions of the tribe. This oral tradition continues to exist, but now it coexists with an expanding collection of poems, stories, novels, autobiographies, and criticism.

In 1883 Sarah Winnemucca Hopkins, a Paiute woman, published her autobiography, *Life Among the Paiutes*, and during the first years of the twentieth century Gertrude Bonnin (Zitkala-Sa) published stories in the *Atlantic Monthly*. There were others: Hum-ishu-ma (Chrystal Quintasket), who wrote a novel, *Co-go-wea, the Half-Blood* (1927); Ella Deloria, who did fine work in linguistics and anthropology in addition to publishing Dakota stories; and Pauline Johnson, a Canadian Mohawk who published several collections of poetry and stories. At the end of the nineteenth century and into the twentieth century, Indian women were also relating tribal literature and personal accounts to anthropologists such as Truman Michelson, Ruth M. Underhill, Gilbert Wilson, and A. L. Kroeber.

Increasingly, however, Indian women have chosen to tell their own stories and write poetry and fiction. Indian women writers have gained particular notice since the late 1970s. Leslie Marmon Silko received the prestigious MacArthur Award in recognition of her poetry, stories, and the novel *Ceremony* (1977), and Louise Erdrich has captured several literary awards since the publication of *Love Medicine* (1984) and *The Beet Queen* (1986). Paula Gunn Allen has achieved recognition for her poetry, her novel *The Woman Who Owned The Shadows* (1983), and for her criticism, most notably *The Sacred Hoop* (1986). Several collections of contemporary literature and critical studies attest to the growth and development of literature of Indian women. Joy Harjo, Wendy Rose, Linda Hogan, Carol Lee Sanchez, Anna Lee Walters, and Mary Tall Mountain are among the names frequently seen in current anthologies. The contemporary literature takes many forms and, like the traditional material, is sometimes personal narrative and sometimes an expression of tribal history or politics.

—*Gretchen M. Bataille*

See Also:

Bonnin, Gertrude; Hopkins, Sarah Winnemucca; Native American Women

References:

Allen, Paula Gunn. *The Sacred Hoop: Recovering the Feminine in American Indian Traditions*. Boston: Beacon, 1986.

Bataille, Gretchen M., and Kathleen Mullen Sands. *American Indian Women; Telling their Lives*. Lincoln: University of Nebraska Press, 1984.

Fisher, Dexter. *The Third Woman: Minority Women Writers of the United States*. Boston: Houghton Mifflin, 1980.

Green, Rayna. *That's What She Said: Contemporary Poetry and Fiction by Native American Women*. Bloomington: Indiana University Press, 1984.

Katz, Jane B., ed. *I Am the Fire of Time: Voices of Native American Women*. New York: Dutton, 1977.

Niethammer, Carolyn. *Daughters of the Earth: The Lives and Legends of American Indian Women*. New York: Collier, 1977.

NATURE STUDY was the name given to a curriculum for science teaching that was widely discussed and implemented in the elementary (and some secondary) schools in the United States between about 1895 and 1925. It was a flexible course of study intended to stimulate and expand the teaching of science for children in ways appropriate to their local experiences, whether in the countryside of Upstate New York or in urban centers like Chicago. By combining teaching (in which women were a majority) with science (in which women were scarcely represented), nature study provided an unprecedented opportunity for women to study, teach, and contribute to science.

By the time nature study was implemented, women constituted 90 percent of the teaching staff in most schools and were also prominent on the faculty of normal schools. An analysis of the Nature Study Association in 1908 reveals that approximately 60 percent of its members were women. Men tended to be on college or normal school faculties while women were more likely to be in the classroom, where some took advantage of opportunities to do fieldwork and gather data. Women also served as superintendents of citywide nature study programs and a few even held positions on university faculties. Anna Botsford Comstock of Cornell was the single best-known leader in the movement, combining nature study there with extension programs that provided short courses and educational leaflets for teachers. She also wrote the best-selling text (still in print) *Handbook of Nature Study* and was editor of *Nature Study Review* for a decade. Other programs were designed for city schoolchildren and sometimes coordinated through a local museum, like the Brooklyn Children's Museum run by Anna Billings Gallup from 1904 to 1937.

Just as elements of progressivism lost ground in the 1920s, so the nature study curriculum lost out to elementary science, whose goals were to prepare students for advanced work on terms prescribed by academic professors. The specific techniques introduced by nature study teachers—school terrariums and aquariums, nature walks, school museum cabinets, weather data collection—continued in use, but among scientists and social scientists there was a reaction against a science that seemed too "sentimental." For its thirty years of prominence, however, the nature study program provided unprecedented opportunities for individual women teachers and also established methods for teaching about the natural world that persist to the present day in both voluntary clubs and more formal school activities.

—Sally Gregory Kohlstedt

See Also:
Education, Science

References:

Burstyn, Joan. "Early Women in Education: The Role of the Anderson School of Natural History." *Journal of Education* 159 (1977): 50–64.

Comstock, Anna Botsford. *The Comstocks of Cornell: John Henry Comstock and Anna Botsford Comstock.* Ithaca: Cornell University Press, 1953.

Kohlstedt, Sally Gregory. "In from the Periphery: Women in Science, 1830–1880." *Signs* 4 (1978): 81–96.

Minton, Tyree G. "The History of the Nature-Study Movement and Its Role in the Development of Environmental Education." Diss. University of Massachusetts, 1980.

NAYLOR, GLORIA (b. 1950), author, is one of America's most acclaimed black twentieth-century female novelists. Naylor's first two novels, *The Women of Brewster Place* (1982) and *Linden Hills* (1985), are stories of black America with an emphasis on the black female experience. Critics often compare her exploration of the black female with the work of Toni Morrison and Alice Walker.

Before beginning a career in writing, Naylor spent seven years as a Jehovah's Witness missionary in Florida, New York, and North Carolina. After leaving her missionary work, Naylor studied at Brooklyn College of the City University of New York and received an M.A. in Afro-American studies at Yale University. Naylor's first novel *The Women of Brewster Place* was published while she was still a student at Yale, and received the American Book Award for First Fiction in 1983.

The Women of Brewster Place consists of seven chapters about seven black women and the rundown neighborhood they share. Through strong characterizations, Naylor shows how these women, members of two minorities, suffer from racism and sexism.

Separated from the white culture by a wall at the end of their street, they are undervalued by men, who treat them unfairly and violently. The women are different from each other and, at times, find themselves separated from each other by their prejudices and fears. But ultimately it is the commonality of the female experience that allows them to survive. Rising out of poverty and violence, Naylor's women form a community of sisters in defiance of their bleak existence.

Linden Hills departs from the style of *The Women of Brewster Place.* Naylor sacrifices strong characterization for the advancement of her Dantesque allegorical exploration of a middle-class black neighborhood. Linden Hills is an inferno comprised of circular driveways leading down to the center of Naylor's hell, Luther Nedeed. As the novel's main characters, two unemployed street poets, descend through the suburban inferno, Naylor attacks the blacks' emulation of the white culture. Behind the peaceful homes of *Linden Hills* lurks a gothic horror. Naylor's characters are victims of this horror, having sold their souls to a most awful devil—greed.

Focusing her attention on blacks, with an emphasis on women, Naylor writes with power and honesty of the evils of sexism, racism, and greed, and their effects on Afro-American culture. With *The Women of Brewster Place* and *Linden Hills,* Naylor has established herself as an extremely important voice in American literature.

—Avery Preston Lane

See Also:
Black Women; Morrison, Toni; Walker, Alice

References:

Goldstein, William. "A Talk with Gloria Naylor." *Publishers Weekly* 225 (September 9, 1983): 35–36.

Naylor, Gloria. *Linden Hills.* New York: Ticknor and Fields, 1985.

———. *The Women of Brewster Place.* New York: Viking, 1982.

NEEL, ALICE (1900–84) painted incisive portraits of the decadent, the famous, the poor, and the downtrodden that chronicle the diversity of urban society. Although she also painted brightly colored still lifes, stark interiors, and bucolic landscapes, she is best known for her original and expressive figure paintings.

She enrolled at the Philadelphia School of Design for Women, now the Moore College of Art, in 1921 and completed her studies in 1925. During the summer of 1924, she attended Chester Springs Summer School of the Pennsylvania Academy of Fine Arts, where she met her future husband, Carlos Enriquez, a Cuban art student. Neel's life was not easy. Her first child died of diphtheria in December 1927, and she was abandoned by Enriquez, who took their second child to Cuba in May 1930. Following a nervous breakdown in August of that same year, she was hospitalized for a year.

Upon her release, Neel went to New York's Greenwich Village to paint. There, she took a series of lovers and developed an interest in leftist politics. She attended meetings of the John Reed Club and briefly joined the Communist party in about 1935. Her portraits of left-wing activists and intellectuals and her cityscapes of Depression-era New York vividly disclose her political interests. During the Depression, she moved to Spanish Harlem, where she supported herself and two sons on her meager income from the Federal Art Project of the Works Progress Administration (WPA). She remained in Spanish Harlem for twenty-five years, painting her neighbors and her surroundings.

A dark palette and resigned facial expressions are typical of her works of the 1940s. In her later paintings, her palette became increasingly lighter; she used bold, direct, and economical brushstrokes to reveal the inner tensions of her wealthier, more famous subjects. Areas of the canvas were left unpainted, and background elements were less articulated; the viewer is forced to focus on the subject.

Neel, who was neglected and ignored by the art establishment during the reign of abstract expressionism, finally attained recognition when she began to paint the luminaries of art, politics, and business. The poet Frank

O'Hara, who posed for her in 1959, was the first of many famous people to do so. Among her other subjects were Andy Warhol, Bella Abzug, Red Grooms, Ed Koch, and Linus Pauling.

—*Susan Keyes*

See Also:
Art

References:

Alice Neel: The Woman and Her Work. Athens: Georgia Museum of Art, The University of Georgia, 1975.

Harris, Ann Sutherland. *Alice Neel.* Los Angeles: Loyola Marymount, 1983.

———. "The Human Creature." *Portfolio* 1 (December/January 1979–80): 70–75.

Higgins, Judith. "Alice Neel and the Human Comedy." *Art News* 83 (October 1984): 70–79.

Hills, Patricia. *Alice Neel.* New York: Abrams, 1983.

Nemser, Cindy. *Art Talk: Conversations with 12 Women Artists.* New York: Scribner, 1975.

NETWORKING is the practice of developing and using contacts with other people for information and support while serving as a resource oneself; the purpose is to help everyone involved get ahead together. Networking is an old idea. In the business world, men have been using this technique for many years, but the "old boy's network," as it has sometimes been called, grew naturally out of contacts men made through organizations already in place, such as men's clubs and fraternities. The old boy's network has also flourished because men have historically dominated supervisory and managerial positions in the workplace and because men learn early in life to form mutually beneficial contacts; for example, through participation in sports. Women have historically not been socialized in the same way and have tended not to attain high management positions.

Networking for women grew out of the active feminist movement in the 1970s, when women were forming self-help and professional groups of various kinds. While the concept of networking does not require an organization, many formal women's networks have been organized. Some of these have made an effort to bring influential women in a particular city together; others have been organized along professional lines. The number of women's networks has grown in the last few years, and many books, including directories of women's networks in the United States, have been published.

The idea of networking has been perceived by many women to be a good way of moving ahead in one's chosen field, but there are some factors that have kept the idea from being more successful. Some women have trouble becoming involved in networking because they feel more comfortable in a helping relationship with others and less comfortable admitting they joined a group or called a contact because this can be useful to their careers. One expert in the field found that for the women above the middle-manager position in her organization, networking with other women did not work well because there were so few women contacts at that level. Also, surveys have shown that while women at the top felt that they were providing support to women below them, the women lower in the organizational hierarchy did not perceive such support.

—*Judith Pryor*

See Also:
Mentor-Protégée Relationships, Women's Liberation Movement

References:

Kleinman, Carol. *Women's Networks: The Complete Guide to Getting a Better Job, Advancing Your Career, and Feeling Great as a Woman Through Networking.* New York: Lippincott & Crowell, 1980.

Stern, Barbara B. *Is Networking for You? A Working Woman's Alternative to the Old Boy System.* Englewood Cliffs, N.J.: Prentice-Hall, 1981.

Warthay, Philomena D. "The Climb to the Top: Is the Network the Route for Women?" *The Personnel Administrator* 25 (April 1980): 55–60.

Welch, Mary Scott. *Networking: A Great New Way for Women to Get Ahead.* New York: Harcourt Brace Jovanovich, 1980.

The **NEW CENTURY GUILD FOR WORKING WOMEN** in Philadelphia evolved out of low-cost evening classes started in 1882 by the New Century Club. Under the dynamic leadership of club member Eliza Sproat Turner, the guild expanded the scope of its activities, and its classes rapidly grew in popularity. Members of the guild came from a wide range of occupational backgrounds, including dressmaking, sales, mill work, bookbinding, and office work. Women took classes refining their domestic skills in such areas as cooking, home singing, and home elocution, as well as classes in marketable skills such as shorthand, typing, and stenography. The guild's headquarters and its branch facility offered members opportunities to use the well-stocked library, have an inexpensive meal, relax in a gymnasium, and socialize with friends. Lecture series on female hygiene and physiology offered many members a rare opportunity to learn about their bodies.

In 1887 the guild began publishing the *Working Woman's Journal*, which contained articles about work from the employees' point of view. This unusual magazine had subscribers in nineteen states. Guild members collected statistics on the hours, wages, regulations, and conditions in those Philadelphia stores that employed women. In 1887, in response to pressure from the guild, the city's major morning papers published a list of proprietors who treated women fairly. The success of the guild's School of Women's Trades, which opened in 1891 offering a professional certificate for a full-time day course of study in dressmaking and millinery, persuaded A. J. Drexel to open Drexel Institute (now Drexel University). At the turn of the century, the guild's early activism on behalf of working women served as a model for other organizations across the United States. In recent decades the guild has become primarily a social gathering place for a decreasing membership not energized by new recruits.

—*Cynthia J. Little*

See Also:

Education

Reference:

The New Century Club: Miscellaneous. Historical Society of Pennsylvania, Philadelphia, Pa.

NEW DEAL. In 1929 the United States began its slide into total economic depression. This national crisis—which included the stock market crash, massive unemployment, agricultural distress, and business and banking failures—reached its peak by the time Franklin D. Roosevelt was elected president in 1932. Roosevelt instituted the New Deal, built on the principles and policies of the Progressive era, with breathless rapidity. He created relief programs to prevent starvation among the unemployed, as well as plans for recovery of the business and agricultural segments of the economy and a series of reforms to make sure that such a depression could never happen again.

In many ways the Depression was worse for women than for men. The lot of the poor woman had always been hard. As the unemployment reached higher into the middle class, more women were faced with the problem of making ends meet. Women had always worked outside the home, usually in low-paid, sex-typed service jobs, and therefore their unemployment rate was lower than that of men. While the inability of unemployed husbands and fathers to perform as breadwinners inflicted a psychological toll, wives had the task of keeping the family together, of making the food stretch, of clothing the children. Moreover, a higher percentage of married women worked outside the home in low-paid, often part-time jobs during the Depression while simultaneously continuing their management of the household on meager incomes.

Women had an important role in Roosevelt's New Deal. When he became president in 1933, his First Lady, Eleanor Roosevelt, brought to Washington an unprecedented number of former Progressive era activists and social feminists from within the Democratic party. Together they influenced the appointment of Frances Perkins, one of this group, to the cabinet-level post of secretary of labor—

Perkins thus became the first female appointment to a cabinet-level post. In 1932 and 1936 these women party stalwarts organized a small army of precinct canvassers, thus demonstrating their potent political power and duly reaping political appointments such as postmasterships but, more important, assuring that women would be given equal representation on the Democratic Platform Committee in 1936.

Little of the New Deal legislation applied specifically to women. Created in 1933 to alleviate suffering during that first winter of the Roosevelt administration, the Civil Works Administration (CWA) employed some three hundred thousand women, but its emphasis on large-scale construction projects mainly created jobs thought to be unsuitable for women. The Federal Emergency Relief Administration (FERA) provided federal funds to the states to run relief projects until 1935, at which time women constituted about 12 percent of its recipients. The New Deal emphasis shifted in 1935 as the Works Progress Administration (WPA), an agency created by Congress, performed federal oversight as well as allocated federal funds for various kinds of building projects that included positions that even women qualified in nontraditional construction trades had difficulty securing. As head of the Women's and Professional Projects Division of the WPA, Ellen Sullivan Woodward constantly sought projects that offered positions for women in areas such as research, recreation, health and nutrition, and food processing, as well as in clerical and library services. Women were pressed into service in sewing rooms to repair old clothes and to make new ones for distribution to the poor. Although married women were often ineligible relief recipients as the primary certifiable member of the family because husbands were regarded as heads of households, women comprised four hundred thousand of the WPA beneficiaries at the peak of the program.

Women especially benefited from various relief programs in the arts. Female artists such as Louise Nevelson, Alice Neel, and Agnes Tait benefited from the Federal Art Project, which provided money for murals and other kinds of painting. The Federal Theatre Project and Federal Music Project promoted the work and talent of women while allowing them to make enough money to avoid starvation. Through publications such as the state guidebooks and other publications, the Federal Writers Project enabled writers such as Katherine Dunham and Zora Neale Hurston to survive and expand their talents.

The National Industrial Recovery Act (NIRA) set business codes from 1933 to 1935 for maximum hours and minimum wages that treated men and women equally. Although NIRA codes did not apply to many of the traditional jobs of women such as domestic service, secretarial employment, and agricultural labor, nonetheless the garment industry sweatshops were curbed. After the NIRA was declared unconstitutional in part, the Fair Labor Standards Act of 1938 created permanent hour and wage regulations that applied equally to men and women, but only in a limited portion of the work force. The Social Security Act (1935) provided for aid to dependent children that included pediatric and maternity care for many mothers, yet exempted dependent spouses, most of whom were women.

Women made gains in the New Deal era: their political force was recognized. Some benefited through legislation and others through the improvement in the climate for the trade-union movement as more women, married and single, continued to enter the paid labor force.

—Donald F. Tingley

See Also:

Democratic Party; Fair Labor Standards Act; Perkins, Frances; Roosevelt, Eleanor

References:

Ware, Susan. *Beyond Suffrage: Women in the New Deal.* Cambridge: Harvard University Press, 1981.

———. *Holding their Own: American Women in the 1930's.* Boston: Twayne, 1982.

The **NEW ERA CLUB** was formed in 1893 by Josephine Ruffin, who belonged to the prestigious New England Women's Club, which had been founded by Julia Ward Howe. Her association with this club led her to see the need for organizing a club for black women. In many ways the New Era Club was a result of the interest among educated black and white women in forming clubs during this time. The members tended to be middle-class, educated women who shared cultural interests. But the New Era Club also had a strong educational and social reform focus and issued a newspaper, the *Women's Era*.

Ruffin was also instrumental in promoting a national organization for black women's clubs. One of the reasons for the organization came from a letter sent to the *Women's Era* by John W. Jacks, editor of a small Mississippi newspaper denouncing the morality of American black women. Although the letter was apparently never published, it received wide circulation among influential black women, and the New Era Club sent out invitations to other black women's clubs to discuss the issue raised in the letter. A meeting was held in Washington, D.C., in 1895 that resulted in the formation of the National Federation of Afro-American Women. The federation was one of two black federated clubs organized during this time, the other being the National League of Colored Women under the leadership of Mary Church Terrell. The two groups united in 1896 and became the National Association of Colored Women.

An incident that occurred during the 1900 convention of the General Federation of Women's Clubs further convinced the black club women of the need to organize their own federations. Ruffin was a delegate representing not only the New England Press Association but the Massachusetts Federation of Women's Clubs, of which the New Era Club was a member. At the convention, Ruffin was permitted to represent the New England Press Association but was not permitted to represent the New Era Club since this would have meant that the club would have to be recognized as a member of the GFWC. The president of the GFWC, Rebecca Lowe, tried to evade the issue of permitting black clubs to join by calling roll by club names rather than by individuals. Northern delegates who supported Ruffin were surprised by the move and were not able to gather enough votes to have Ruffin accepted as a delegate from the New Era Club. The event caused great controversy and was widely reported in the press. Some newspapers and many readers were strongly in favor of Ruffin's position. One reader blasted women who had been victims of discrimination for not supporting another woman for no other reason than that she was black. The GFWC continued its segregationist policy for several decades after this incident.

—Judith Pryor

See Also:

Black Women's Clubs; General Federation of Women's Clubs; National Federation of Afro-American Women; Ruffin, Josephine

References:

Harley, Sharon, and Rosalyn Terborg-Penn. *The Afro-American Woman: Struggles and Images.* Port Washington, N.Y.: Kennikat, 1978.

Lerner, Gerda. "Early Community Work of Black Club Women." *Journal of Negro History* 59 (April 1974): 158–68.

Logan, Rayford W. *The Negro in American Life and Thought: The Nadir, 1877–1901.* New York: Dial, 1954.

Woloch, Nancy. *Women and the American Experience.* New York: Knopf, 1984.

NEW HARMONY (1824–27) was a utopian community established by Robert Owen, a socialist and pioneer of the cooperative movement, in New Harmony, Indiana. This experiment in utopian reform of society required a redefinition of marriage, the family, and gender roles. Although Owen spoke out against monogamous relationships, he believed that the nuclear family was the chief cornerstone of civil society and he therefore attempted to adapt the family unit to a standard consistent with his ideas of communal living. As defined in Owen's "Declaration of Mental Independence," marriage was a dissoluble institution if the mutual affection of the couple ceased. Asserting that conventional society exploited women by making them economically dependent upon their husbands, Owen felt that women had to be given equality in all matters pertaining to livelihood and that children should be the wards of society rather than of their individual parents.

Owen's biggest crusade focused on taking away some of the power and influence of the private family without alienating the members of New Harmony. Owen's thoughts on women's rights attracted Frances Wright, who in 1826 founded the Woman's Social Society, the first fully organized woman's club in America, at New Harmony. But Owen was not successful in curtailing the influence of the nuclear family at New Harmony, and in 1827 he left the community and placed Robert Dale Owen, his son, in charge. Robert Dale Owen was an even stronger advocate of women's rights than his father was, and he supported their demands for equality at the 1850 convention to revise the Indiana state constitution. The principle of equality, which had been espoused by Robert Owen at New Harmony twenty-five years before the Indiana Constitutional Convention, was affixed in the state laws of Indiana due to the diligence of Robert Dale Owen and other staunch supporters of women's rights.

—*Karen Gillenwaters*

See Also:

Nashoba, Utopian Communities

References:

Moment, Gairdner B., and Otto K. Kraushaar, eds. *Utopias: The American Experience.* Metuchen, N.J.: Scarecrow, 1980.

Muncy, Raymond Lee. *Sex and Marriage in Utopian Communities—19th Century America.* Bloomington: Indiana University Press, 1973.

Young, Marguerite. *Angel in the Forest.* New York: Scribner, 1945.

NEW LEFT is a generic term that refers to a political movement associated with the youth and counterculture movements of 1960s. The New Left represented the mergence of several political movements, some of which began in the 1950s and included the antisegregation protest in the South that fostered a national civil rights movement, as well as the free speech movement that attracted undergraduate as well as graduate students who increasingly protested the draft and the Vietnam War.

Initially led by the Student Non-Violent Coordinating Committee (SNCC) and Students for a Democratic Society (SDS), which worked for change within the system, the New Left pursued a socialist, existentialist, humanist reform of contemporary American capitalism and society through a form of participatory democracy. However, after the police riot at the 1968 Democratic convention in Chicago discouraged the prospects for working for reform within the system, the leadership of the ultrademocratic "leaderless" New Left came from the Maoist/Leninist Progressive Labor party, the Trotskyite Young Socialist Alliance, and the second- and third-generation communists in the DuBois Clubs of America. The turbulence of the late 1960s produced dissension and division within the New Left no less than in American society generally, and resulted in radical leftist separatist groups such as the Black Panthers and Yippies. Media coverage of campus antiwar protests made it possible for the SDS to extend the impact of its tactics of teach-ins and demonstrations to confront a nationwide audience with the issues of the New Left.

The women within the New Left came from the same affluent middle-class social and economic backgrounds as the men, and were politicized and radicalized by the same issues. They believed in the political philosophy of the New Left that emphasized an egalitarian, leaderless reform movement to establish a participatory democracy. Involved at the grass-roots level of all the New Left projects, they made direct contact with the people in the target communities where they worked. However, the New Left women increasingly noticed and questioned the persistence of sexist discrimination by the male leaders toward women co-workers in the movement. Although civil rights, poverty, and the Vietnam War were designated as the priority issues, the men of the New Left condescended to address philosophically, if not practically, the secondary concerns of New Left women and included articles of feminist criticism in the movement's *New Left Notes*. The women themselves applied both the theory and the strategy that they had practiced as part of the New Left challenge to establishment authority to critique women's position in society as well as in the New Left movement itself.

Thus the New Left women eventually focused upon women's issues as significant instances of injustice that required an autonomous women's movement; they became the radical feminists of the late 1960s and early 1970s who were on the cutting edge of the modern women's movement. They provided this emerging movement with confrontational tactics and theoretical leadership as they articulated and developed a provocative feminist perspective that reflected their socialist background in their efforts to define and address the issues of the modern women's movement.

—*Angela Howard Zophy*

See Also:
Radical Feminism, Vietnam War, Women's Liberation Movement

References:
Diggins, John P. *The American Left in the Twentieth Century*. New York: Harcourt Brace Jovanovich, 1973.
Evans, Sara. *Personal Politics: The Roots of Women's Liberation in the Civil Rights Movement and the New Left*. New York: Knopf, 1979.
O'Neill, William. *Coming Apart*. New York: Quadrangle, 1971.

The term **NEW MORALITY** may be utilized generically to designate any deviation from traditional moralities within given cultures. With respect to the American ethical context, New Morality commonly refers to the moral revolution evidenced in the antiestablishment movements of the 1960s and 1970s. For example, anti-Victorian sexual freedom found expression in increased premarital, extramarital, and communal/group sex. Fashion trends exhibited the New Morality by displaying originality and transformations in style. Such creativity and spontaneity at times scoffed at traditions so forcefully that extremes of seminudity and nudity came to the fore. The phenomenon of Woodstock provided obvious illustrations.

Opposition to established norms, the status quo, and any form of authoritarianism was another modality for the expression of the antitraditionalism of the New Morality. This antiauthoritarianism found a medium for elucidation in the arts. For example, rock music embodied antipathy to authorities through its gyrations and explosive sounds and lyrics. Jimi Hendrix would play a grinding, gnashing rendition of the "Star Spangled Banner" on the electric guitar, while Jefferson Airplane in another setting would belt out "Got to Have a Revolution." The younger generation's use of psychedelic drugs provided a biochemical avenue for the avoidance of the status quo and a vehicle to indicate disgust for rigid authoritarianism. Protests against the Vietnam War offered a major collective cause and tragedy for the advocates of the New Morality to rally around.

Women's liberation as a cause enlisted the ranks of numerous women who sensed the freedom and the potential for new identity formation present in the late 1960s and into the present. For the liberated women, the New Morality meant sexual freedom, with sex no longer being absolutely tied to the marriage contract. Furthermore, women were finding that they could no longer tolerate the idea of gender being tied to particular types of careers, so that numerous professional positions as well as blue-collar positions previously restricted to males were slowly but gradually being opened to females. Role reversal in relationships became apparent as the equality of the sexes gained repute. Unisex hairstyling, clothing, and jargon gave concrete expression to the phenomenon of equality. Most important, remarkably gifted women such as Bella Abzug, Gloria Steinem, and Rosemary Reuther found leadership positions in government, business, and education that provided platforms for numerous key spokespersons to arise, articulate, and solidify the emerging power and place of women in the society.

In theoretical ethics, the New Morality found a less volatile, yet significant proponent in the form of morality known as "situation ethics." Joseph Fletcher's groundbreaking *Situation Ethics: The New Morality* sought to elicit a morality from the individual situation within which one is involved rather than any external authoritarian ethic. Only the situation itself could provide ethical answers because all "norms" had been called into question. The New Morality in a sense found itself to be such a *novum* that no tradition, no authority could be a part of it. External authorities could never be trusted in themselves. For Fletcher, J. A. T. Robinson, and others, only love could be the hermeneutical key—not laws, not rules, not principles, not ideals, not norms.

The New Morality insistence upon freedom and self-expression broke the chains of oppression. Certainly, women benefited greatly from this new openness. Common terms such as *women's rights, equal pay/equal work, househusband, feminism,* and *liberation* indicated not only new jargon but new opportunities for the women of the 1960s, 1970s, and 1980s. Along with new freedoms and new experiments in living came new responsibilities, some resilient and not-so-resilient responses, and a metamorphosis that brought much new growth yet concomitant ambiguity and even trauma.

—Barry Arnold

See Also:

Free Love, New Left, Sexual Revolution, Women's Liberation Movement

References:

Arnold, Barry. *The Pursuit of Virtue.* New York: Peter Lang, 1988.

Laney, James, and James Gustafson. *On Being Responsible.* New York: Harper & Row, 1968.

Seller, James. *Warming Fires.* New York: Seabury, 1975.

NEW WOMAN was a term used at the turn of the twentieth century to refer to the young single woman who was the beneficiary of the nineteenth-century improvement and progress in women's education and employment opportunities. The New Woman defined her womanhood in more secular terms than her mother's generation had defined their True Womanhood, allowing the New Woman to experience life as an autonomous individual and self-sufficient worker before she married to become a full-time homemaker and middle-class society matron. Socially active and economically independent, the New Woman was educated, having graduated from high school or even college. She did not reject marriage or the concept of a maternal destiny for women, yet she tacitly asserted her individualism as she adjusted her domesticity in marriage to accommodate her increased social and economic opportunities. These included utilization of birth control and pursuit of civic and intellectual interests apart from those of her husband and children. In her exercise of this choice to maintain a partially separate identity, the New Woman represented a crucial transitional phase of American womanhood before World War I.

—Angela Howard Zophy

See Also:

Social Feminism, Socialism, Woman Question

References:

Chafe, William H. *The American Woman: Her Changing Social, Economic, and Political Roles, 1920–1970.* New York: Oxford University Press, 1972.

Daniel, Robert L. *American Women in the Twentieth Century: The Festival of Life.* San Diego: Harcourt Brace Jovanovich, 1987.

May, Henry F. *The End of American Innocence.* Chicago: Quadrangle, 1959, 1962.

Sochen, June. *The New Woman.* New York: Quadrangle, 1972.

NICHOLS, MARY GOVE (1810–84) was born Mary Sargent Neal in Goffstown, New Hampshire. She was something of a universal reformer, supporting at times Grahamism, Mesmerism, Fourierism, hydropathy, temperance, spiritualism, anarchism, pacifism,

Swedenborgianism, and free love. At twenty she married a family friend Hiram Gove, a Quaker. She described their unhappy marriage in *Mary Lyndon or, Revelations of a Life* (1865), her fictionalized autobiography. After several miscarriages, she ran away with her firstborn child and set up a health-reform Grahamite boardinghouse in Boston, supporting herself by lecturing on dietary and hygienic reform. For Mary, life required a pure and uncorrupted body sustained by "only beautiful food—grains, fruits and milk."

Her attitudes about sex remain an enigma. She definitely had an affair with the handsome and glib entrepreneurial reformer Thomas Low Nichols—whom she married in 1848—and perhaps with two or three others before him. One man accused her of seducing him. When she attacked marriage in her autobiography and in *Marriage* (1854), which she wrote with Nichols, she was criticized as a woman advocating "the coarsest lust." In fact, she was a Victorian woman who both enjoyed sex and preached against it. Her central concern was love, and her opposition to marriage was that it often did not involve love and left women in a totally compromised economic situation. She did not believe that any woman could have an orgasm under those conditions and that a string of unwanted children sapped women's lives.

She and Thomas Nichols ran several water-cure establishments and flirted with the Long Island commune called Modern Times. They moved to Yellow Springs, Ohio, in 1857 to establish Memnomia, a utopian community dedicated to "Freedom, Fraternity, [and] Chastity." After Mary had a vision in which a succession of Church Fathers spoke to her, the commune broke up, with "the eight leading persons going into the Romish Church." They lectured on Catholicism throughout the Midwest until the outbreak of the Civil War. Opponents of Northern coercion, she and Thomas Nichols left for England, where they set up a water-cure establishment outside of Malvern. Mary lectured on health care and, although nearly blind, published another book on the water cure before her death.

—*William G. Shade*

See Also:

Grahamism, Homeopathy, Utopian Communities

References:

Adams, Grace, and Edwart Hutter. *The Mad Forties.* New York: Harper, 1942.

Blake, John B. "Mary Gove Nichols, Prophetess of Health." *Proceedings of the American Philosophical Society* 106 (June 1962): 219–34.

Nichols, Mary Gove. *Mary Lyndon or, Revelations of a Life. An Autobiography.* New York: Stringer & Townsend, 1860.

Sterns, Bertha-Monica. "Two Forgotten New England Reformers." *New England Quarterly* 6 (March 1933): 59–84.

Stoehr, Taylor, ed. *Free Love in America: A Documentary History.* New York: AMS Press, 1979.

NIN, ANAÏS (1903–77) was a French-born American author best known for her autobiographical diary, which detailed her life through character sketches and colorful vignettes. Despite many previous publications, she reached her largest audience in the 1960s through the publication of *The Diary of Anaïs Nin* (1966). Originally a cult figure because of her symbolic, poetic novels, including her first work, *House of Incest* (1931), she attracted a wider readership in later years as a woman author trying to be both a person and an artist.

Born in Paris, Nin is the epitome of the struggling woman writer who became established in America without commercial publishers' support. She was the first of three children of Joaquin and Rosa Nin. Her father was a well-known concert pianist and philanderer who deserted the family when Nin was eleven. In 1914, as she traveled on a ship bound to New York with the rest of her family, she began a journal that she believed would entice her father to rejoin them. She attended New York public schools until age fifteen, when she dropped out because her writing was criticized as "too literary." Working as an artist's model to support her family, she was self-educated through constant reading. At age twenty, she married Ian Hugo, a film director who later illustrated her books with copperplate engravings. In the early 1930s, Nin returned to Paris and became involved in the Villa Seurat Circle, where she met novelist Henry Miller. Nin was Miller's chief literary mentor, and they influenced each other's writings in the 1930s and 1940s. In the mid-1930s she studied psychoanalysis but abandoned it after a year.

Using a secondhand, foot-controlled printing press, she began in 1940 to publish her own works because established publishers felt her work was "uncommercial." In later years her writings gained much support, particularly from feminists, and until her death in 1977 she remained a frequent lecturer at colleges and universities.

After completing *House of Incest*, Nin wrote *Winter of Artifice*, detailing the relationship between a father and his daughter, including autobiographical elements. Her third self-published work, a collection of short stories titled *Under a Glass Bell* (1944), brought her critical acclaim and publishers' attention for its dreamlike atmosphere. In 1946 *Ladders of Fire*, the first of a series of five novels dealing with similar characters, examined the lives of three women. Nin then wrote approximately five more novels before her most famous and first nonfiction work, *The Diary*, was published. Her literary career ended with *The Novel of the Future* (1968), a literary criticism of her contemporaries.

Her refusal to relinquish her femininity, combined with an independent will, made Anaïs Nin a popular figure in the 1960s and 1970s. Her *Diary*, written in the first person, remains one of the premier women's autobiographical works. Although self-absorbed and disjointed at times, the six-volume *Diary* and her rediscovered novels, along with her undying spirit, have successfully established Nin as a heroine for women writers.

—*Camille Jaski*

References:

Franklin, Benjamin. *Anaïs Nin, an Introduction.* Athens: Ohio University Press, 1979.

Hinz, Evelyn J., ed. *A Woman Speaks: The Lectures, Seminars, and Interviews of Anaïs Nin.* Chicago: Swallow, 1975.

Knapp, Bettina Liebowitz. *Anaïs Nin.* New York: Ungar, 1978.

Nin, Anaïs. *The Diary of Anaïs Nin, Vol. I: 1931–1934.* Chicago: Swallow, 1966.

Spencer, Sharon. *Collage of Dreams: The Writings of Anaïs Nin.* Chicago: Swallow, 1977.

The **NINETEENTH (WOMAN SUFFRAGE) AMENDMENT** provides that "the right of citizens of the United States to vote shall not be denied or abridged by the United States or by any State on account of sex." It also stipulates that "the Congress shall have power, by appropriate legislation, to enforce the Provisions of this article."

The struggle for the "woman vote" had begun at the Seneca Falls (N.Y.) Convention of 1848, the first woman's rights convention in Victorian America, which produced the Declaration of Sentiments and Resolutions that listed the franchise as the primary goal of the nineteenth-century woman's rights movement. By 1890 the suffrage campaign focused upon securing a federal amendment to the U.S. Constitution as the proper means to assure women the franchise.

The ratification of the Nineteenth Amendment ended a schism that had weakened the woman suffrage movement since 1869, when Elizabeth Cady Stanton and Susan B. Anthony had founded the National Woman Suffrage Association (NWSA), dedicated to national enfranchisement, while Lucy Stone and Elizabeth Blackwell had established the American Woman Suffrage Association (AWSA), which focused on a state-by-state strategy. Although this schism was officially healed by the formation of the National American Woman Suffrage Association (NAWSA) in 1890, the issue still divided suffragists. Southerners especially opposed nationwide enfranchisement out of fear that it would reopen the debate over blacks, who had been successfully disfranchised despite the requirements of the Fifteenth Amendment. The opposition of southern congressmen, of the Democratic party, and of President Woodrow Wilson postponed proposal of the amendment until 1919, even though the House of Representatives acted formally to pass the amendment on January 10, 1918. The pressures applied by NAWSA, the National Women's party (NWP), and other suffrage organizations finally led to the amendment's proposal by the House on May 19, 1919 (by a vote of 304–89) and by the Senate on June 4 (66–30).

Ratification took just over one year, as many legislators and organizations had been converted to the cause by the pressure of suffrage organizations, the active role played by women in World War I, and the requirements of practical politics. The ratification of the Eighteenth Amendment (Prohibition) rendered irrelevant males' fears that female enfranchisement would strengthen Prohibition's chances. Following the "Winning Plan" of its president, Carrie Chapman Catt, NAWSA and the NWP effectively lobbied in crucial state legislatures. Opposition centered largely in the southern states, but it was a southern state, Tennessee, that became the necessary thirty-sixth state to ratify, despite the frantic efforts of business and liquor interests who, according to Catt and NWSA vice president Nettie Rogers Shuler, "dispensed Old Bourbon and moonshine whiskey with boorish insistence." Legend has it that the deciding vote in the assembly was cast by a young legislator whose mother had urged him to help Mrs. Catt.

The amendment became part of the Constitution on August 26, 1920, allowing women to vote in the November elections.

—John D. Buenker

See Also:

American Woman Suffrage Association; Catt, Carrie Chapman; Declaration of Sentiments and Resolutions; National American Woman Suffrage Association; National Woman's Party; Prohibition and the Volstead Act; Seneca Falls Convention; Suffrage

References:

Anthony, Susan B., Elizabeth Cady Stanton, Matilda Jocelyn Gage, and Ida Husted Harper. *History of Woman Suffrage.* 6 vols. Rochester, N.Y.: Mann, 1881–1922.

Catt, Carrie Chapman, and Nettie Rogers Shuler. *Woman Suffrage and Politics.* New York: Scribner, 1923.

Flexner, Eleanor. *Century of Struggle: The Woman's Rights Movement in the United States.* New York: Atheneum, 1968.

Kraditor, Aileen. *Ideas of the Woman Suffrage Movement.* New York: Columbia University Press, 1965.

NINETEENTH-CENTURY DRESS REFORM emerged as a response to the restrictive and cumbersome fashions for women, whose layers of heavy petticoats, constraining corsets, and long, dragging skirts represented, in the eyes of dress reformers, "badges of degradation." In the 1850s reformers championed a new costume, which featured a dress reaching just below the knee and a pair of trousers. The new costume, known by many names, was most frequently called "the reform dress" and was modeled on the costume of Moslem women. Women at the Oneida Community, a religious commune in New York State, adopted the costume in 1849, and female visitors to the health resorts run by water-cure practitioners often wore it in order to participate in the healing program of exercise that was part of the water-cure regimen. Water-cure was a popular mid-nineteenth-century health system that emphasized preventative medicine, a spare and bland diet, regular exercise, and various applications of water as a cure for disease.

Elizabeth Smith Miller was the first woman in the United States to adopt the reform dress for everyday use, and in 1851 she introduced it to her cousin Elizabeth Cady Stanton and Stanton's friend Amelia Bloomer, who advocated it in her journal, the *Lily*. Several other women's rights activists adopted the new style, and when Amelia Bloomer, in response to readers' requests, published a woodcut of herself in the reform dress, it quickly became known as the "Bloomer costume" and became indelibly associated in the public mind with women's rights.

The women's rights leaders rejoiced in the freedom afforded by the new costume, but they were stunned by the fierce ridicule it generated. Fearing that the furor over the reform dress would eclipse the other elements of their struggle for social and political equality, most women's rights activists abandoned the new costume after a few years.

The cause of dress reform was carried on after 1856 by a group of reformers who had close ties with the water-cure movement. They supported each other at annual meetings of the Dress Reform Association and through two reform and health oriented magazines: *The Sibyl, A Review of the Tastes, Errors, and Fashions of Society* was edited by Lydia Sayer Hasbrouck of Middletown, New York, and *The Laws of Life and Woman's Health Journal* was edited by Harriet Austin and James Jackson of "Our Home" Water-Cure in Dansville, New York. Unlike the women's rights leaders, the members of the dress reform movement believed that women should transform their own lives before attempting to change social institutions. They were convinced that if a few intrepid reformers dressed "fitly for the whole battle of life," others would soon follow their example.

The Dress Reform Association died in 1865, and despite efforts to revive it, the movement languished until 1874, when members of the Boston Woman's Club, led by Aba Woolson, initiated a more moderate effort to improve women's clothing. Woolson believed that the "Bloomer" episode had demonstrated the impossibility of radical dress reform, and the new reformers concentrated instead on reforming the style of undergarments.

—*Amy Kesselman*

See Also:

Bloomer, Amelia; Corset; Utopian Communities

References:

Cayleff, Susan E. *Wash and Be Healed: The Water Cure Movement and Women's Health.* Philadelphia: Temple University Press, 1987.

Donegan, Jane. *Hydropathic Highway to Health: Women and Water Cure in Ante-Bellum America.* Westport, Conn.: Greenwood, 1986.

Henshaw, Betty. "The Bloomer Costume." M.A. thesis. University of Colorado, 1955.

Kesselman, Amy. "Lydia Sayer Hasbrouck and *The Sibyl.*" *Orange County Historical Journal* 14 (November 1985): 39–44.

Leach, William. *True Love and Perfect Union: The Feminist Reform of Sex and Society.* New York: Basic, 1980.

The **NINETEENTH-CENTURY WOMAN'S MOVEMENT** was an expression of concern regarding the status of women in antebellum America. This reform movement challenged the limitations of Woman's Sphere under patriarchy and the gender system then prevailing. The nineteenth-century woman's rights movement drew feminists, nonfeminists, and occasionally antifeminists into the struggle to improve woman's educational and employment opportunities as well as her status under the law, on an issue-by-issue basis in response to the conditions of every aspect of women's lives.

The woman's role of "helpmeet" during the colonial era had given way to the model of Republican Motherhood after the American Revolution, which seemingly promised equality of rights and opportunity for all people. The emphasis of the new nation on middle-class values and mobility produced a commitment to education; by the 1790s the question of whether women could learn had been settled and special academies for them had been established. By the 1820s the social changes that accompanied the rise of industrialization and urbanization in the United States required a refinement of the cultural definition of the role of woman. Although marriage remained the only career choice for most middle-class women, educational opportunities in the form of female seminaries and employment in the paid labor force increased to compensate for this change in woman's role. Women's displacement from their crucial preindustrial tasks of food processing and clothing production within single-family farming made single young women available for the initial work force of the textile industries. The presence and treatment of women in the paid labor force emerged early on as an issue of the woman's rights movement.

Meanwhile, a definition of a separate Woman's Sphere in Victorian America confined women to a restrictive domestic identification with household chores, child rearing, and managing family consumption of mass-produced goods, especially in the towns and cities. Many women came to an understanding of the basic issues of woman's rights as a result of their unchallenged civic and reform activities in voluntary and benevolent associations. However, women also participated in antebellum abolition, temperance, and other reform movements; their experience in the antislavery and abolition movements particularly politicized their awareness of woman's second-class status and provided seasoned leadership for the emerging woman's rights movement by the 1840s.

The Seneca Falls (N.Y.) Convention in 1848, the first national woman's rights convention in the United States, formally inaugurated the organized movement for addressing the disparity between equality and discrimination that women experienced under the law and in religion, education, and employment. The Declaration of Sentiments and Resolutions of the Seneca Falls Convention provided a summary list of grievances among women who were aware that they were the largest disfranchised group in their society. The issues raised with this protest document included the lack of woman suffrage and women's subordination to men in the family, under the law, and in all social institutions. The founders of the woman's rights movement were women for whom the purity, piety, domesticity, and submission of the Cult of True Womanhood proved inadequate as a source of identity and self-esteem. The woman's rights movement extended beyond the generally acknowledged organized activities of avowed feminists for a women's franchise and dress reform. In the 1840s and 1850s, issues concerning women's admission to the professions of teaching and medicine were supported by conservative women as part of domestic feminism; individuals such as Dorothea Dix pursued one-woman one-issue campaigns to improve the conditions of the less fortunate in society; working-class and middle-class married women worked together for reform of married women's property rights.

By 1860 public as well as private institutions had been created to train women as public school teachers and therefore facilitated women's domination of that field by the 1880s. Women's medical hospitals had been established to train women physicians to care for women and children and medical missionaries to carry the Cult of True Womanhood throughout the world. More native-born and immigrant women joined the paid labor force following traditional women's work from the domestic sphere to the industrial marketplace. Married women's property reform, which protected women's wages as well as custody and property rights, had been accomplished in New York State. All these and more issues were part of the woman's rights movement in the mid-nineteenth century, although those feminists who focused on the vote and dress reform continued to draw the attention of both a generally derisive press and of frankly antifeminist conservative critics.

During the Civil War, supporters of woman's rights in the North contributed to the war effort and thus utilized opportunities to expand women's opportunities especially in previously male-only occupations. Women's groups such as the U.S. Sanitary Commission and local and state organizations gathered and sent medical and other supplies to the wounded as well as volunteers to serve as nurses and aides in military hospitals; this wartime opportunity to serve thereby established nursing as a profession for women. With the Union victory, supporters of woman's rights hoped that the enfranchisement of the freedmen would include not only former slaves but all women as well. The Fourteenth Amendment proved a disappointment of that hope, and the woman suffrage movement split into the American Woman Suffrage Association (AWSA) and the National Woman Suffrage Association (NWSA) in 1869, due to differences of theory and practice among the various kinds of feminists regarding the primacy of the issue of the woman vote.

After the Civil War, the founding of separate women's colleges in the East and coeducational institutions in the West expanded educational opportunities for women to produce a generation of college-educated domestic feminists who furthered the expansion of Woman's Sphere into public work and activities, whether as civic-minded middle-class matrons and as career "spinster" teachers or workers in the settlement house movement, which encouraged educated youth to "settle" among and associate with the urban poor. Women began to enter the professions of law and the ministry. Working-class and immigrant women continued to join the work force in factories, offices, and commercial establishments, not in pursuit of careers but to assist in their families' survival in urban industrial America. From their ranks came women leaders in the union movement, who during the Progressive era would articulate the issues of the woman's movement that addressed the needs of their co-workers. Social feminism emerged as a coalition of the working- and middle-class women who confronted the conditions of women workers in sweatshops and stores, through the efforts of the National Consumers' League and the National Women's Trade Union League. Birth control proved another issue of the woman's rights movement that crossed class and economic lines.

Free black women had participated in the abolition and antislavery movements as well as the antebellum woman's rights movement. Sojourner Truth argued with eloquence and deadly accuracy against the non sequiturs of the critics of women's rights, and made universally comprehensible the particular situation of black women both before and after the Civil War. Emancipated black women continued their efforts to forge stable families and to improve the legal status and economic conditions of their communities. In segregated voluntary associations, middle-class club women worked for the vote, civil rights, and other issues crucial to their less prosperous sisters in rural areas of the South and in urban northern cities. Black club women provided the community and church leadership to address the need for educational institutions for black women as well as for black men, as part of the woman's rights movement. Excluded from equal participation because of racism within white mainstream woman's rights groups at the turn of the century, black women nonetheless worked for woman suffrage through their own national and community groups.

By the last decade of the nineteenth century, the woman's rights movement began to focus on the single issue of the woman vote. The two national suffrage associations merged in 1890, becoming the National American Woman Suffrage Association (NAWSA), which set its sights on a federal amendment to enfranchise women as it worked through individual states to achieve full and partial suffrage for women. The General Federation of Women's Clubs as well as the social feminist organizations joined the campaign for woman suffrage, which was accomplished with the ratification of the Nineteenth Amendment in 1920.

The achievement of the limited goal of the franchise brought disarray to the organized woman's rights movement of the nineteenth century and has traditionally been considered to mark the end of that phase of the women's movement in the United States. The NAWSA evolved into the nonpartisan League of Women Voters, and a striking difference of opinion emerged and dissolved the coalition that had supported the final drive for the woman vote. Those women who supported the goals of the social feminism of the Progressive era defended the gains in protective legislation, which put them at odds with the radical feminism of the members of the National Woman's party (NWP), who initiated the twentieth-century campaign for the Equal Rights Amendment because the vote alone would not assure women's equality under the law or in society. The proponents of domestic feminism represented the majority opinion regarding the gains of the movement: Women's employment was appropriate in certain occupations and professions on a contingency basis; women's place and future in higher education was defined in limited terms to service woman's duty to the family and her domestic role; ultimately woman's biology was her destiny and her place remained in the home.

The historical context of the 1920s proved as hostile to avowed feminism as to other social reform movements. The contemporary generation of young women utilized the advances in education, employment, and legal rights without acknowledging or comprehending their debt to the nineteenth-century woman's movement. However, the feminism of the movement persisted and resurfaced sporadically throughout the 1930s and 1940s, finally reasserting its presence during the social ferment of the 1950s and 1960s that sparked the modern or twentieth-century women's movement.

—Saundra K. Yelton and Angela Howard Zophy

See Also:
Abolition and the Antislavery Movement, American Woman Suffrage Association, Birth Control, Black Women's Clubs, Civil War, Common Law, Cult of True Womanhood, Declaration of Sentiments and Resolutions, Domestic Feminism, Education, Feminism, General Federation of Women's Clubs, Industrial Revolution, Legal Profession, Marriage, Married Women's Property Acts, National American Woman Suffrage Association, National Woman Suffrage Association, Nineteenth-Century Dress Reform, Nursing, Patriarchy, Physicians, Radical Feminism, Revolutionary War, Seneca Falls Convention, Settlement House Movement, Sex-Gender System, Social Feminism, Suffrage, Teaching as an Occupation for Women, Temperance Movement, Twentieth-Century Women's Rights Movement, Unions, Wages, Women's Work—Nineteenth Century

References:
Clinton, Catherine. *The Other Civil War: American Women in the Nineteenth Century.* New York: Hill & Wang, 1984.
Cott, Nancy F., and Elizabeth H. Pleck. *A Heritage of Her Own.* New York: Simon & Schuster, 1979.
DuBois, Ellen. *Feminism and Suffrage: The Emergence of an Independent Women's Movement in America.* Ithaca, N.Y.: Cornell University Press, 1978.
Flexner, Eleanor. *Century of Struggle: The Woman's Rights Movement in the U.S.* Rev. ed. Cambridge, Mass.: Belknap, 1959, 1975.
Hersh, Blanch. *The Slavery of Sex: Feminist-Abolitionists in America.* Urbana: University of Illinois Press, 1978.

The **NINETY-NINES, INC.** is an international organization of women pilots. In the fall of 1929 following the Women's Air Derby, the first major cross-country race for women pilots, several women expressed their desire for an organization that would be "dedicated to assist women in aeronautical research, air racing events, the acquisition of aerial experience, and the administration of aid through aerial means in times of emergency." At the instigation of Clara Trenchmann of the Curtiss Flying Service on Long Island, New York, four female Curtiss demonstration pilots wrote to the 126 licensed women pilots in the United States to invite their views on such an organization. Ninety-nine of them responded favorably. On November 2, 1929, twenty-six women met in a Curtiss hangar and formed the Ninety-Nines, named in honor of the charter members. Today the Ninety-Nines, Inc., headquartered in Oklahoma City, has over sixty-five hundred members in thirty-nine countries and continues its dedication to support women pilots worldwide in all their endeavors.

—Claudia M. Oakes

See Also:
Aviation

Reference:
Brooks-Pazmany, Kathleen. *United States Women in Aviation 1919–1929.* Washington, D.C.: Smithsonian Institution, 1983.

NOETHER, EMMY (1882–1935) was born in Erlangen in southern Germany. Her father Max Noether was a mathematics professor at the University of Erlangen, and it was there that she completed her doctoral dissertation in mathematics in 1907. In 1916 she moved to the University of Göttingen, Germany, to collaborate with mathematicians David Hilbert and Felix Klein. Hitler's rise forced her move to the United States in 1933. She accepted the position of visiting professor of mathematics at Bryn Mawr College and died there in 1935 from complications following surgery.

Noether was at the forefront of the development of the axiomatic approach in abstract algebra. She developed a general theory of ideals in arbitrary rings and developed the concept of cross products. Through her work on hypercomplex systems and representation theory, she proved results in algebra of great depth and beauty. Albert Einstein wrote of her (*New York Times*, May 4, 1935): "In the judgment of the most competent living mathematicians, Frauelein Noether was the most significant creative mathematical genius thus far produced since the higher education of women began. In the realm of algebra, in which the most gifted mathematicians have been busy for centuries, she discovered methods which have proved of enormous importance in the development of the present-day younger generation of mathematicians."

—Jonell Duda Comerford

See Also:

Mathematics

References:

Campbell, Douglas M., and John C. Higgins, eds. *Mathematics: People, Problems, Results.* Belmont, Calif.: Wadsworth, 1984.

Dick, Auguste. *Emmy Noether, 1882–1935.* Boston: Birkhauser, 1981.

Osen, Lynn M. *Women in Mathematics.* Cambridge: MIT Press, 1974.

NORMAL SCHOOLS. The term *normal school* was used to describe teacher training institutions in the United States during the nineteenth and early twentieth centuries, and was derived from the French term for teacher training institutes—*Normale.* The first normal schools were established in New England prior to the Civil War, but in the latter nineteenth century, they appeared in the Midwest and Pacific states as well. The vast majority of students in the normal schools in virtually all parts of the country were women. Usually, women were represented among normal school students to about the same extent as local teaching forces were feminized. As teaching became more feminized through the latter nineteenth century, so did these schools. By the turn of the century in many parts of the country, normal school education was virtually synonymous with women's education.

A major supporter of the concept of the normal school for teacher training was Horace Mann (1796–1859), one of the most prominent social reformers in an age of reform. A former Massachusetts state legislator, Mann proposed that the education of all children, including girls, was the way of progress. America, at this time, was becoming industrialized, and Mann believed that education was essential to the future security of the nation. Mann argued that government should play an active role in this industrialized society. Throughout his life, Mann maintained that science and education were a cure for the social ills of nineteenth-century America—poverty, crime, ignorance, and drunkenness.

In 1837 Mann was elected secretary of the Massachusetts Board of Education and began his travels on horseback across the state gathering support for his new idea: the normal school. Prior to the establishment of the normal school, no institution was available for the training of teachers. Because of this lack of teaching standards, teaching competence varied widely across the state. Based on his survey of Massachusetts schools, Mann published the first of his twelve *Annual Reports,* which proposed reforms in the school system. His goal was a number of teachers' colleges that would prepare teachers in a secular, humanistic environment free from religious and denominational influences. Mann believed all children should have the right to an education, no matter what their gender, economic status, or family background. After a number of setbacks, the normal schools flourished in Massachusetts, and the idea spread to neighboring states.

Through the nineteenth century, most normal schools were state supported and offered about the same level of education as the high schools of that time. Toward the end of the century, when demand for trained teachers became acute in many parts of the country, it became commonplace for high schools to establish normal departments where young women could receive the requisite training in pedagogy to prepare them for positions as teachers. Still, the number of normal school graduates lagged far behind the demand for teachers well into the twentieth century.

Who were the women students attending normal schools at this time? Historians Richard Bernard and Maris Vinovskis have analyzed enrollment records for Massachusetts normal schools in the 1850s and found that the largest groups were the daughters of farmers and skilled tradesmen, both middling occupational groups in nineteenth-century New England. Other studies of teachers in the nineteenth and early twentieth century have produced similar results. In general, it appears that the women who attended normal schools were from middle- and lower-middle-class backgrounds. To a certain degree, in that case, the normal schools can be said to have served as a sort of popular higher education.

With time, the normal schools shifted their orientation from secondary to higher education. This appears to have been partly due to the efforts of teacher educators to enhance their status, partly due to the efforts of educational leaders to demand higher qualifications of teachers, and in some parts of the country it may have been due to local political interests wanting to have college-level instruction available for a particular area's youth. By the opening years of the twentieth century, there was a movement to introduce college courses in normal schools across the country. By the 1920s, normal schools in some states were renamed state teachers colleges, and by the post–World War II period, most normal schools had become state colleges or universities. Today, teacher education is simply one part of the educational mission of most former normal schools, and present-day state universities bear little resemblance to their nineteenth-century predecessors. The early normal schools, however, played a critical role in providing education to tens of thousands of young women at a time when women had relatively few educational alternatives, and in training successive generations of women teachers for service in the nation's schools.

—John L. Rury and Lynn E. Lipor

See Also:

Education, Teaching as an Occupation for Women, Women in Higher Education

References:

Bernard, Richard, and Maris Vinovskis. "The Female School Teacher in Antebellum Massachusetts." *Journal of Social History* 10 (Spring 1977): 332–45.

Elsbree, Willard. *The American Teacher: Evolution of a Profession in a Democracy*. New York: American Book Co., 1939.

Herbst, Jurgen. "Nineteenth Century Normal Schools in the United States: A Fresh Look." *History of Education* 9 (March 1980): 219–27.

Mann, Horace. *Horace Mann on the Crisis in Education*. Edited, with an introduction by Louis Filler. Yellow Springs, Ohio: Antioch Press, 1965.

NURSE, REBECCA (TOWNE) (1621–92), a victim of the Salem (Mass.) Witch Trials, was the wife of Francis Nurse and the mother of four sons and four daughters. A respected, intelligent, and pious matron, Nurse was particularly vulnerable because her mother had previously been accused of witchcraft though never brought to trial. Nurse's two younger sisters— Sarah, wife of Peter Cloyse, and Mary, wife of Isaac Easty—were also charged with witchcraft. At seventy-one, Nurse was accused of being a witch on a complaint by Edward and Jonathan Putnam, the sons of John Putnam.

Nurse was charged with having committed acts of witchcraft upon Mrs. Ann Putnam, her daughter Ann Putnam, and Abigail Williams. A hearing on March 24, 1692, resulted in Nurse's internment in the Salem jail until June 2, but a petition filed on her behalf delayed the trial until June 28. Several of the afflicted girls then testified that "Goody" Nurse was the specter who had tormented them. The court appointed a jury of three women to examine Nurse's body for any identifying mark of the devil. Although they found a mark, two of the women stated that the mark was explainable by natural causes. The other woman disagreed.

The jury returned a verdict of not guilty. The accusers demonstrated disapproval with renewed energy and more violent fits. Because of a hearing loss, Nurse failed to respond to a question made to her by the jury. As a result, the jury brought in a second verdict of guilty. After she learned that her silence was misconstrued as a confession of guilt, she wrote a statement explaining her silence; nevertheless, she was sentenced to be hanged. The governor granted her a reprieve; later, the church where she had been a lifelong member excommunicated her. Upon hearing of the reprieve, the accusers renewed their clamors with the additional support of some Salem gentlemen. The governor recalled the reprieve. On July 19 Rebecca was carted to the summit of Gallows Hill and hanged.

The bodies of witches were thrust into shallow graves on Gallows Hill, but Nurse's body did not remain there. Her children bided their time, and under the shroud of darkness took their mother's body home. After her death, she was vindicated, and the sentence of excommunication was erased from the church book in 1712. Later a granite shaft was raised to Rebecca Nurse, and beside it, another was erected with the names of those courageous friends who spoke in her defense at a time when doing so might have caused them to be accused of witchcraft.

—*Judith B. Lucas*

See Also:

Salem Witch Trials, Tituba

References:

Boyer, Paul, and Stephen Nissenbaum. *Salem Possessed—The Social Origins of Witchcraft.* Cambridge: Harvard University Press, 1974.

Nevins, Winfield S. *Witchcraft in Salem Village in 1692.* Salem, Mass.: Northshore Publishing, 1892.

Starkey, Marios L. *The Devil in Massachusetts—A Modern Inquiry into the Salem Witchtrials.* Garden City, N.Y.: Doubleday, 1969.

Upham, Charles W. *Salem Witchcraft.* Vol. 2. New York: Ungar, 1959.

NURSING emerged as a paid profession for American women in the mid-nineteenth century. Previously, most nursing was done as part of the traditional female role within the immediate or extended family. Pioneering public hospitals employed charwomen in quasi-nursing roles, while Catholic sisters provided the most exemplary nursing care during the 1850s in denominational institutions. The factors shaping the early direction of professional nursing included the advent of antiseptic and scientific medicine, the gradual increase in the numbers and respectability of hospitals, the example of Florence Nightingale's successes in the Crimea, and the demands of the Civil War.

Recognition of the need for trained nurses came first in Massachusetts in 1850 when the legislature established the New England Medical College and encouraged aspiring nurses to attend lectures. In 1888 the American Medical Association called for improved nurses' training and urged that such training schools be attached to hospitals. The dramatic growth of community hospitals that continued throughout the 1800s kept the demand for a steady source of cheap labor high, and the introduction of scientific medical practices increased the need for educated nurses. The training programs at most hospital-based schools consisted primarily of a long apprenticeship on the wards and inculcating trainees with a strict adherence to the hospital hierarchy. Most students received minimal classroom instruction. This system meant that most hospitals functioned with an essentially untrained corps of nurses. The landmark Goldmark Report (1923) pointed out the fundamental faults in the hospital schools, which emphasized menial tasks while relegating education to a low priority. The Rockefeller Foundation established a prestigious Committee for the Study of Nursing

Education. Authored by commission secretary Josephine Goldmark, the report recommended that the hospital schools be recognized as separate educational departments devoted to providing a thorough nursing education, not merely training. This sparked a trend toward nursing programs leading to baccalaureate degrees in the 1920s. Opposition to the collegiate nursing movement came from private physicians and hospital administrators, who argued that the new nurses would be overtrained and too costly.

The struggle for women to participate formally as nurses in America's war effort began during the Civil War when an estimated ten thousand women, mostly untrained, signed up for nursing duty. Their impressive service record, despite trying conditions and outright opposition from many military physicians, proved their importance to the North's ultimate victory. Nevertheless, it took valiant service during the Spanish-American War and much lobbying before the creation of the Navy Nurse Corps in 1908, which pioneered the creation of a similar service in each branch of the military. These elite corps offered nurses a unique opportunity to demonstrate skilled nursing techniques. World Wars I and II brought thousands of women into nursing, both on the home front and abroad on the front lines. By the end of World War II, women military nurses had become integral to the effective functioning of the American military.

In the post–World War II period, the trend in nursing education was toward professionalization. Diploma schools attached to hospitals moved toward becoming full-fledged educational institutions. More collegiate nursing programs were established, and their enrollments gradually increased as a result of the 1964 Nurses Training Act, created to alleviate a critical shortage of nurses, especially those capable of taking on administrative and teaching roles.

The reforms of the Progressive era and programs of the Depression period created a wide array of nonhospital jobs for nurses in industrial and public health nursing. These positions were especially appealing because they offered nurses the potential for independence and an active role in confronting larger socio-economic problems. Such quasi-independent practitioners foreshadowed nursing in the late twentieth century, when more health care was done outside the hospital, now a place for emergency care and the treatment of major acute illnesses. In the future, nursing will become increasingly professionalized with practitioners developing skills as health managers, diagnosticians, and independent health providers working in new relationships to physicians and patients.

—*Cynthia J. Little*

See Also:

Barton, Clara; Civil War

References:

Ashley, J. A. *Hospitals, Paternalism, and the Role of the Nurse.* New York: Teachers College Press, 1976.

Kalisch, Philip A., and Beatrice J. Kalisch. *The Advance of American Nursing.* 2d ed. Boston: Little, Brown, 1986.

Melosh, Barbara. *The Physician's Handbook: Work, Culture, and Conflict in American Nursing.* Philadelphia: Temple University Press, 1982.

Reverby, Susan M. *Ordered to Care: The Dilemma of American Nursing, 1850–1945.* New York: Cambridge University Press, 1988.

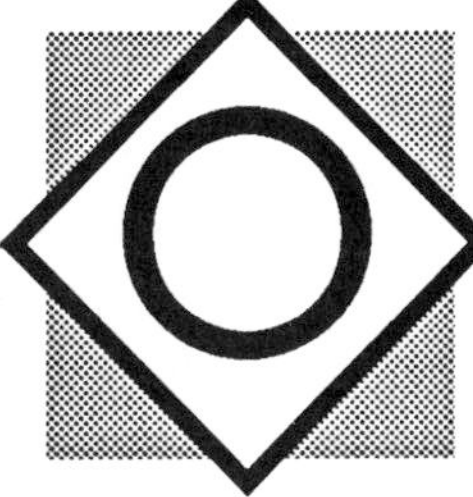

OBERLIN COLLEGE was founded in 1833 as the Oberlin Collegiate Institute, southwest of Cleveland, Ohio, by Yankee missionaries John J. Shipherd and Philo P. Stewart, who named the community in honor of Alsatian pastor John Frederick Oberlin. It was the first coeducational college in the country and the first to accept students regardless of race. It was also the first college to grant undergraduate degrees to women. From the outset, women constituted a sizable minority of the student body.

Oberlin began as an evangelical experiment in Christian living and education, and women were an integral part of that experiment. The college replicated the family, with women providing moral uplift while serving in a traditional supportive role to men—washing their clothes, cleaning their rooms, waiting on them at meals, and even listening to their public speeches in respectful silence. Not all women, of course, accepted that role. Lucy Stone, Antoinette Brown, Betsey Mix Cowles, and a few other militant women's rights advocates chafed under such restrictions, Stone going so far as to refuse to write a commencement address that she would not be permitted to read publicly.

More typical of Oberlin women was their participation in moral reform movements designed to protect and purify the family. Faculty wives and female students were active in the Oberlin Female Moral Reform Society, early leaders of which included Alice Welch Cowles, Esther Shipherd, and Mary Atkins, later founder of Mills College in California. The first three women to receive college degrees—Caroline Rudd, Mary Hosford, and Elizabeth Prall—were also members. Society members were concerned with any action that might promote immorality—immodest dress, dancing, novel reading, and theater attendance. Equally important was the Oberlin Maternal Association, formed to improve family life and child rearing.

Student life was tightly regulated for women, perhaps in an effort to offset public criticism about the experiment in coeducation. Except for attendance at approved activities, such as literary societies or choir, women students were expected to remain in their rooms after the beginning of evening study hours and to retire by ten o'clock. Even their walking was governed by a series of prohibitions. Nevertheless, Oberlin set the example for coeducation followed by a large number of religious colleges founded in the Midwest after the Civil War.

—Nicholas C. Burckel

See Also:

Coeducation, Education, Women in Higher Education

References:

Fletcher, Robert Samuel. *A History of Oberlin College from Its Foundation Through the Civil War.* 2 vols. Oberlin: Oberlin College, 1943.

Ginzberg, Lori D. "Women in an Evangelical Community: Oberlin 1835–1850." *Ohio History* 89 (1980): 78–88.

Hosford, Frances Juliette. *Father Shipherd's Magna Charta: A Century of Coeducation in Oberlin College.* Boston: Marshall Jones, 1937.

Lasser, Carol. *Educating Men and Women Together: Co-education in a Changing World.* Urbana: University of Illinois Press, 1987.

OBSCENITY. One of the basic civil liberties guaranteed and protected in the First Amendment of the Bill of Rights of the U.S. Constitution is the freedom of the press. Although the courts have stridently upheld this liberty, they have not deemed that this protection is absolute. The courts have granted broad protection for the press overall; however, they have granted much less protection for libelous and obscene materials because traditionally they have considered these materials to be irrelevant to the free expression of ideas and the search for truth as the framers meant them in the First Amendment.

The courts have struggled over the years to determine what exactly is obscene material and therefore not protected by the First Amendment protection of the free press. Since 1957 almost one hundred separate opinions on obscenity have been written by the Supreme Court. In *Miller v. California* (1973) the Court developed a test for determining obscene material: (1) the average person, applying contemporary standards of the particular community, would find that the work, taken as a whole, appeals to a prurient interest in sex; (2) it depicts or describes in a patently offensive way sexual conduct specifically defined by the applicable law or authoritatively construed; and (3) the work, taken as a whole, lacks serious literary, artistic, political, or scientific value. States are primarily responsible for regulating obscene literature.

The courts have refused to expand the definition of obscenity further than the above criteria; they have, however, allowed cities, through zoning ordinances, to scatter "adult" theaters and bookstores to avoid having a district that might attract criminals, or to concentrate them to avoid having them in neighborhoods where they might offend residents or passersby.

—*Sue E. Strickler*

See Also:

Comstock Law, Pornography

References:

Abraham, Henry J. *Freedom and the Court.* 4th ed. New York: Oxford University Press, 1982.

Pritchett, C. Herman. *Constitutional Civil Liberties.* Englewood Cliffs, N.J.: Prentice-Hall, 1983.

O'CONNOR, FLANNERY (1925–64), fiction writer, was a devout Catholic whose religious faith pervaded all of her writing. Assuming that her audience did not share her belief, O'Connor often used violence and the grotesque to shock her reader into a recognition of the need for God's grace. Justifying her own style, O'Connor wrote that "for the hard of hearing you shout; for the almost blind, you draw large and startling figures." Those large and startling figures include a phony Bible salesman, a crafty one-armed tramp who marries a woman's idiot daughter in order to get her car, and a little boy who drowns while returning to the river of his baptism, where he "counted." O'Connor's prize-winning fiction is intended to be unsettling.

Born in Savannah, Georgia, into one of Georgia's oldest Catholic families, Mary Flannery O'Connor attended parochial school there, moving to Milledgeville, Georgia, in 1938. She attended Peabody Laboratory School and was graduated from Georgia State College for Women in 1945 with a degree in social science. An avid cartoonist and writer in her undergraduate years, O'Connor attended the famous Writers' Workshop at the State University of Iowa, from which she received the M.F.A. in 1947. Her master's thesis was a collection of short stories entitled *The Geranium*, and the title story became O'Connor's first published story (*Accent*, Summer 1946). From 1948 to 1950, O'Connor lived as the boarder of Sally and Robert Fitzgerald in Ridgefield, Connecticut. The Fitzgeralds, also devout Catholics, provided O'Connor with the balance of solitude and communion necessary for her productivity.

In 1950, however, O'Connor was stricken with the disease that had killed her father, disseminated lupus erythematosus, and she was forced to return to Milledgeville. There she remained for the rest of her life, living with her mother at Andalusia, the family farm just outside of town. Between the 1952 publication of her novel *Wise Blood* and 1964, the year of her death, O'Connor published an acclaimed collection of short stories *A Good Man Is Hard to Find* (1955) and a second novel *The Violent Bear It Away* (1960). At the time of her death she had completed the stories for the posthumous collection *Everything That Rises Must Con-*

verge (1965). O'Connor was many times the recipient of the O. Henry Award, and she received grants from the Ford Foundation and the National Institute of Arts and Letters. The posthumous collection *The Complete Stories* (1971) received the National Book Award in 1972.

A Catholic writer in the Bible-Belt South, Flannery O'Connor was largely concerned with southern fundamentalist Protestants and the integrity of their search for salvation. From Hazel Motes, the protagonist of *Wise Blood*, through the tattooed Obadiah Elihue Parker of the late story "Parker's Back," O'Connor presented characters beset by a hunger for God, that hunger manifested in bizarre and often wildly humorous behavior. O'Connor described a world in which technology and progress inevitably fail to satisfy the deepest human needs, a world in which, as she put it, "the good is under construction." With a sharp ear for southern dialect and a fine sense of comic timing, Flannery O'Connor is now acknowledged as one of America's foremost writers of the short story. The collection of her letters *The Habit of Being* (1979) affords valuable insight into the depth of O'Connor's faith, the discipline of her creative life, and her unfailing sense of humor.

—*Sarah Gordon*

See Also:
Southern Lady

References:

Asals, Frederick. *Flannery O'Connor: The Imagination of Extremity*. Athens: University of Georgia Press, 1982.

The Flannery O'Connor Bulletin, 1972—. Milledgeville: Georgia College.

Martin, Carter W. *The True Country: Themes in the Fiction of Flannery O'Connor*. Nashville: Vanderbilt University Press, 1969.

May, John R. *The Pruning Word: The Parables of Flannery O'Connor*. Baton Rouge: Louisiana State University Press, 1976.

O'Connor, Flannery. *Collected Works by Flannery O'Connor*. Edited by Mary Jo Salter. New York: Library of America, 1989.

———. *Everything That Rises Must Converge*. New York: Farrar, Straus & Giroux, 1965.

———. *A Good Man Is Hard to Find*. New York: Harcourt Brace, 1955.

———. *The Habit of Being: Letters of Flannery O'Connor*. Edited by Sally Fitzgerald. New York: Farrar, Straus & Giroux, 1979.

———. *Mystery and Manners: Occasional Prose*. Selected and edited by Sally and Robert Fitzgerald. New York: Farrar, Straus & Giroux, 1969.

———. *The Violent Bear It Away*. New York: Farrar, Straus & Cudahy, 1960.

———. *Wise Blood*. New York: Harcourt Brace, 1952.

O'HARE, KATE RICHARDS (1876–1948), socialist agitator and journalist, was one of the most popular American public speakers in the years 1900 to 1920, especially in the Plains states and the Southwest. She dedicated herself to promoting socialism in the United States and sought to solve contemporary problems, focusing especially on worker exploitation, tenant farmers' impoverishment, women's rights, working children, inadequate education, prison conditions, and the arms race. She believed that all of these problems would ultimately be rectified by the triumph of socialism over capitalism.

As the daughter of Kansas homesteaders, she made her youthful commitments to temperance and missionary activism, but she soon emulated and even went beyond her father's lifelong devotion to political and social reform. She joined the expansive socialist movement in 1901 and, marrying a comrade, Francis P. O'Hare, became widely identified with the Socialist Party of America. While rearing four children, she conducted organizing tours, held party offices, worked on socialist newspapers with Eugene V. Debs, and ran for public office on her party's ticket, becoming the first woman candidate for the U.S. Senate when she was nominated in 1916 in Missouri. During World War I, she opposed U.S. intervention and became an outspoken critic of the war as a capitalist adventure. She was indicted under the Espionage Act for an antiwar speech in 1917, found guilty, and became one of the few women to be sentenced under that act. Receiving a five-year sentence, she served fourteen months in the Missouri State Penitentiary.

During O'Hare's incarceration, she sought with some success to upgrade prison conditions. Thereafter, discouraged by her party's factionalism and antagonistic to the emerging American communist movement, she devoted herself to penal reform. In 1938 she was appointed assistant director of the Department of Penology of the State of California. At that time she no longer considered herself a socialist and was married to Charles C. Cunningham, an engineer. By then she was viewed as a critic who called public attention to many twentieth-century social problems.

—*Sally M. Miller*

See Also:

Pacifism and the Peace Movement; Prison Reform; Public Speakers, Women; Socialist Party of America

References:

Basen, Neil K. "Kate Richards O'Hare: 'First Lady' of American Socialism." *Labor History* 21 (Spring 1980): 165–99.

Foner, Philip S., and Sally M. Miller, eds. *Kate Richards O'Hare: Selected Writings and Speeches.* Baton Rouge: Louisiana State University Press, 1982.

Miller, Sally M. "Kate Richards O'Hare: Progression Toward Feminism." *Kansas History* 7 (Winter 1984/5): 263–79.

O'KEEFFE, GEORGIA (1887–1986), a key figure in the development of American modernism, is known mainly for her paintings of flowers and those of skulls, horns, and pelvises against a stark but colorful New Mexican background. She also painted the New York skyline and a series of abstractions reminiscent of landscapes. Common to all of these subjects is a rejection of conventional notions of perspective. Her flowers, for example, are magnified so that a single flower or part of a flower fills an entire canvas. These unusual subjects and unique perspectives are O'Keeffe's attempts to increase people's awareness of common things, of revealing a reality often overlooked.

Another distinguishing characteristic of O'Keeffe's work, one she vehemently denied, is its rich, erotic imagery. The fleshy folds and projections of her flowers, the contours and sensuous colors of her landscapes, the holes and horns of the pelvises and skulls, and the juxtaposition of the circles, curves, and lines of her abstractions are all very sexual. This sensuousness often added to the mystical quality of O'Keeffe's paintings. Doors open into the same landscapes that surround them, lines draw the observer's eye off the canvas, skyscrapers radiate and reflect a mysterious sunlight.

Born in Sun Prairie, Wisconsin, O'Keeffe got her "big break" in 1916 when Alfred Stieglitz, renowned pioneer in photography and sponsor of modern art, showed her work in a three-artist exhibition at his avant-garde "291" gallery in New York City. O'Keeffe and Stieglitz married in 1924 and, while theirs was not a conventional marriage, the more than five hundred photographs he took of her between 1917 and 1937 have been called the greatest love poem in the history of photography. After Stieglitz's death in 1946, O'Keeffe made her home in Abiquiu, New Mexico, where she continued to paint until well into her nineties.

O'Keeffe was out of step with popular taste during much of her life, but the retrospective exhibit of her work at the Whitney Museum of Modern Art in 1970 brought the American public to recognize her unique artistic vision and style and the important impetus she provided for a number of contemporary American artists. Her autobiography is an important verbal and visual record of her life and art.

—*Kenneth E. Gadomski*

See Also:

Art

References:

Castro, Jan Garden. *The Art and Life of Georgia O'Keeffe.* New York: Crown, 1985.

Lisle, Laurie. *Portrait of an Artist: A Biography of Georgia O'Keeffe.* Albuquerque: University of New Mexico Press, 1986.

O'Keeffe, Georgia. *Georgia O'Keeffe.* New York: Viking, 1976.

OLMSTED, MILDRED (SCOTT) (b. 1890), social worker, pacifist, and longtime advocate of equal rights for women and minorities, has been a national officer of the U.S. Section of the Women's International League for Peace and Freedom (WILPF) for over fifty years.

Born and raised in eastern Pennsylvania, Olmsted graduated from Smith College in 1912 and married Allen Olmsted, a founder of the American Civil Liberties Union, in 1921. They had one child, Peter, and adopted two more, Enid and Anthony. Following World War I, Olmsted volunteered for overseas work, first with the YMCA in France and later with the American Friends Service Committee in Germany. Converted to pacifism as a result, she returned to the United States in 1920 and joined the WILPF.

Committed to the WILPF's philosophy that there can be no lasting nor just peace without freedom and no freedom without peace, Olmsted was the WILPF's national organization secretary in the 1930s and 1940s and its executive director in the 1950s and 1960s. In 1965 she was honored as the only member to serve on the organization's national board of directors for life, and in 1966 she was named executive director emeritus.

Olmsted's firm belief in democracy as both process and goal and her concern with overpopulation, environmental deterioration, and civil rights have led her to active involvement in the American Civil Liberties Union, the National Association of Social Workers, the Joint Friends Peace Committee, Planned Parenthood, and the International Wildlife Federation. She has also been a member of numerous ad hoc organizations and conferences: the United Nations Non-Governmental Organizations (1949), the Conference on Church and Peace (1953), the Soviet-American Women's Conference (1961), and the International Woman's Congress (1970). The recipient of many awards, she received honorary Doctor of Law degrees from Smith College in 1974 and from Swarthmore College in 1987.

—*Carrie Foster*

See Also:

Pacifism and the Peace Movement, Women's International League for Peace and Freedom

References:

Mildred Scott Olmsted Papers. Women's International League for Peace and Freedom Papers. Swarthmore College Peace Collection, Swarthmore, Pa.

Women's International League for Peace and Freedom Papers. University of Colorado, Boulder, Colo.

Bussey, Gertrude, and Margaret Tims. *Pioneers for Peace: Women's International League for Peace and Freedom, 1915–1965*. London: George Allen & Unwin, 1965; rpt. London: WILPF British Section, 1980.

Foster-Hayes, Carrie. "The Women and the Warriors: Dorothy Detzer and the WILPF." Diss. University of Denver, 1984.

OLSEN, TILLIE (b. 1913), feminist writer, won the 1961 O. Henry Award for her novella *Tell Me a Riddle* (1961) and raised awareness that the "silences" of women writers resulted from the inhospitable conditions of women's lives. Anthologized a year after its first publication and continuously thereafter, *Tell Me a Riddle* introduced generations of readers to the work of Olsen. Her nonfiction collection *Silences* (1978) drew attention to her claim that women's voices have been unheard because women artists have been silenced.

Born in Omaha, Nebraska, and graduated from high school, Olsen figuratively attended college through reading at local public libraries. Despite having published a few works when she was quite young, the daily demands of her adult life stopped her writing for twenty years. Marriage, raising four children, and working in industry as a typist-transcriber "silenced" Olsen in terms of a public life and public audience. In *Silences,* which became a germinal text on the suppression of women's writing, Olsen used her own life and the lives of other women writers to illustrate the obstacles that silence women. Of her own hiatus, she wrote, "In the twenty years I bore and reared my children, usually had to work on a paid job as well, the simplest circumstances for creation did not exist."

When the youngest child began school, "the hope of it" (writing and time to write) came again to Olsen. Her reaction to the previous circumstantial obstruction of her writing became becoming a powerful impetus to Olsen's expression. In "I Stand Here Ironing," Olsen presented a confessional personal narrative, a mother's looking back on her own and her children's lives, declaring ". . . all that compounds a human being is so heavy and meaningful in me." All that is "heavy and meaningful" became even more powerful in *Tell Me a Riddle*, Olsen's tale of the painful reality of a relationship growing older.

Olsen's other works include her sympathetic treatment of Rebecca Harding Davis in her "biographical interpretation" for the Feminist Press republication of Davis's *Life in the Iron Mills*. Olsen's immersion in Davis's life and explanation of Davis's silences synthesized empathy, biography, and literary criticism. A number of relatively short pieces complete her works: *Yonnondio: From the Thirties* (1974), a fictional account of a Depression-era family moving from country to city; short stories; some nonfiction. Still to some degree silenced by daily obstacles, Olsen has not produced a substantial body of work, though what she has written is powerful and engaging.

With her authorship have come other opportunities. Olsen has taught at a number of colleges and universities and has received awards from the Guggenheim and Ford foundations and the National Endowment for the Arts.

—*R. Janie Isackson, Carol Klimick Cyganowski, and Pamela Patterson*

References:

Davis, Rebecca Harding. *Life in the Iron Mills and Other Stories*. Edited and with a Biographical Interpretation by Tillie Olsen. Old Westbury, N.Y.: Feminist Press, 1972, 1985.

Olsen, Tillie. *Silences*. New York: Dell, 1978.

———. *Tell Me a Riddle*. Philadelphia: Lippincott, 1961.

———. *Yonnondio: From the Thirties*. New York: Delacorte, 1974.

The **ONEIDA COMMUNITY** (1848–81) was established by John Humphrey Noyes on Oneida Creek between Syracuse and Utica, New York. This community was notable because it was one of the first "utopias" to grant full equality of position to women. Noyes subscribed to the doctrine of perfectionism, a notion that humans could be freed from sin. This belief led to the unique social structure of Oneida. The perfectionist view of marriage promoted the practice of "complex marriage" as a remedy for marital selfishness. In complex marriage, each person was "married" to every other person, thereby, in theory, eliminating jealousy and possessiveness. Sexual relations were viewed by the Oneida members as strengthening the spiritual bonds of the community.

Since Noyes and his followers abandoned the concept of original sin, women in particular benefited from the resulting belief that sexual shame was irrational. Women were encouraged to take the initiative in sexual couplings; indeed, older women often assumed the role of introducing young men to sexual intercourse. Noyes's ideas concerning marriage and the role of women were manifested in various ways: in the clothes the women wore, loose skirts to the knee with pantalets below; in birth control, the advocation of male continence; and in selective breeding to replace random propagation, eugenic experimentation known as stirpiculture. Although the Oneida residents were often criticized by society as being immoral in their sexual practices, the social and sexual innovations practiced at Oneida did not result in promiscuous behavior because most of the inhabitants were sincere in their quest for truth and a life without sin.

The hostility and harassment from mainstream religious denominations drove Noyes to resettle in Canada in 1879. In his absence the Oneidans abandoned his radical community system and reinstituted marriage and property rights among it members. A model of welfare capitalism under its reorganization as a joint-stock company, the Oneida community became famous for its tableware and was still prospering a century after Noyes' death in 1886.

—*Karen Gillenwaters*

See Also:

Complex Marriage, Utopian Communities

References:

Bishop, Morris. "The Great Oneida Love-In." *American Heritage* 20 (February 1969): 14, 16, 86–92.

Kern, Louis. *An Ordered Love: Sex Roles and Sexuality in Victorian Utopias—The Shakers, the Mormons and the Oneida Community.* Chapel Hill: University of North Carolina Press, 1981.

Muncy, Raymond Lee. *Sex and Marriage in Utopian Communities—19th Century America.* Bloomington: Indiana University Press, 1973.

Robertson, Constance Noyes. *Oneida Community: An Autobiography, 1851–1876.* New York: Syracuse University Press, 1970.

ORGASM, FEMALE, the pleasurable release of sexual tension, consists of a series of vaginal and general muscular contractions over a period of six to fourteen seconds, although sex researchers William Masters and Virginia Johnson reported rare cases in which the orgasms continued for over forty seconds. The female resolution phase is relatively brief, and with continued stimulation most women can have a number of orgasms. A few (14 percent) are multiorgasmic in the sense that one orgasm so quickly blends into another that they are lost in a train of responses.

The conditions of sexual intercourse throughout most of human history have not been conducive to women's orgasmic pleasure. Within the mainstream culture, sexual intercourse for women has been Hobbesian—nasty, brutish, and short. However, some deviation occurred during the nineteenth century. The utopian community at Oneida designed its sexual practices in ways that made orgasm more likely. Even in the mid-Victorian era, when women were expected to be passionless, Thomas L. Nichols described the beauties of female orgasms and the ability of women to experience them repeatedly.

The early sexual surveys in this century, however, showed that only about a third of the women surveyed had orgasms regularly during intercourse. Kinsey reported that 45 percent of women married for fifteen years usually had orgasms, and for almost three-quarters, orgasms happened half of the time. Unfortunately, at that time women were being told by the experts that to be adult they had to have "vaginal" orgasms rather than the sensations most felt during masturbation. Those for whom two minutes of intromission did not suffice were deemed "frigid."

In the 1960s, with the emergence of the women's movement, there was a backlash. The clitoris was proclaimed the seat of pleasure; the vagina was dismissed as the source of the female orgasm. Building on the work of Masters and Johnson, who argued that there was only one kind of female orgasm, Ann Koedt and Mary Jane Sherfey argued that women's sexual pleasure was obtainable from either men or women. For some feminists sex could either be a mechanism for maintaining female dependence on men or a vehicle for breaking free of men. For feminist Kate Millett, sexual relations were "a charged microcosm" of sexual politics.

Other researchers such as Josephine and Irving Singer argued that women do have different kinds of orgasms, which are sometimes "blended together"; that most find different kinds of pleasures in oral sex, intercourse, and masturbation; and that their responses to each may differ at different times. Women reach their orgasmic peak in their thirties and remain at a high plateau for at least a decade. After menopause, the strength and duration of their orgasms slowly decline with age. However, sexually active women are able to have orgasms throughout their entire life.

—*William G. Shade*

See Also:

Female Sexuality, Oneida Community, *Sexual Politics*

References:

Degler, Carl. "What Ought to Be and What Was: Women's Sexuality in the Nineteenth Century."

American Historical Review 79 (December 1974): 1467–90.
D'Emilio, John, and Estelle B. Freedman. *Intimate Matters: A History of Sexuality in America*. New York: Harper & Row, 1988.
Dworkin, Andrea. *Intercourse*. New York: Free Press, 1987.
Hite, Shere. *The Hite Report*. New York: Dell, 1976
Koedt, Ann. *The Myth of the Vaginal Orgasm*. Boston: New England Press, 1970.
Masters, William H., and Virginia E. Johnson. *Human Sexual Response*. Boston: Little Brown, 1966.
Sherfey, Mary Jane. *The Nature and Evolution of Female Sexuality*. New York: Vintage, 1973.
Singer, Josephine and Irving. "Types of Female Orgasm." *Journal of Sex Research* 8 (November 1972): 255–67.

O'SULLIVAN, MARY KENNEY (1864–1943), pioneer labor organizer and feminist, was one of the principal founders of the National Women's Trade Union League (NWTUL) in November 1903. The original goals of the NWTUL were to organize women wage earners into unions and to win acceptance of women from established male labor organizations. The NWTUL provided the impetus for the successful fusion of the labor movement and the woman's movement.

O'Sullivan began working in a printing and binding factory while she was a child. In Chicago during the 1880s, her experiences and firsthand knowledge of the conditions under which women worked convinced her that women must organize into trade unions to improve hours and working conditions. First a member of Ladies Federal Local Union #2703, she began organizing other women bookbinders into the Woman's Bookbinding Union #1, which affiliated with the American Federation of Labor (AFL). She was subsequently elected delegate to the Chicago Trades and Labor Assembly and soon after was invited to Hull House, a center of social reform activity. Working with Jane Addams and other social reformers, O'Sullivan coordinated efforts to promote trade unionism among women. Impressed with O'Sullivan's dedication and enthusiasm, Samuel Gompers, president of the AFL, appointed her the AFL's first woman general organizer in 1892; however, she served as an organizer for only five months. Suspicious of feminist involvement in the labor movement, the AFL refused to renew her appointment.

In 1893 she successfully lobbied for the first factory laws in Illinois, which regulated the employment of women and children and set up a state factory inspection department; Florence Kelley was appointed chief inspector with O'Sullivan her assistant. O'Sullivan also tried to persuade the legislature to pass a woman suffrage act, arguing that working women needed to vote to protect themselves with labor legislation, but was unsuccessful.

She married Jack O'Sullivan, a trade union activist and labor editor of the *Boston Globe*, in 1894. The O'Sullivans lived at the Denison House social settlement in the Boston slums, where they had four children. Jack O'Sullivan encouraged his wife's continued work in the labor movement. She became the executive secretary of the Union for Industrial Progress, which she organized to investigate industrial working conditions. In 1902 her husband was killed when hit by a train. To support herself and her children, she managed a model tenement, the Improved Dwelling Association's Ellis Memorial in Boston; in its basement, she taught English to the tenants' families for many years.

By 1910 new leadership within the NWTUL had shifted its emphasis away from trade union organization and toward education and legislation. This, coupled with the AFL's indifference to women workers, convinced O'Sullivan to search for a more direct and concrete route than trade union activity to improve working conditions for women. While she continued her work with the social reform movement, in 1914 she became a factory inspector for the Massachusetts Department of Labor and Industries, a post she held until she was seventy. Although she remained committed to institutionalizing the place of women within the mainstream of organized labor, in the absence of labor interest in recruiting women, she felt government

action offered the best hope for safeguarding female industrial workers.
—*Sandra Weidner*

See Also:

American Federation of Labor; Hull House; Kelley, Florence; National Women's Trade Union League; Settlement House Movement; Unions

References:

Chafe, William Henry. *The American Woman, Her Changing Social, Economic, and Political Roles, 1920–1970.* Oxford, U.K.: Oxford University Press, 1972.
Dye, Nancy Schrom. *As Equals and as Sisters: Feminism, the Labor Movement, and the Women's Trade Union League of New York.* Columbia: University of Missouri Press, 1980.
Flexner, Eleanor. *A Century of Struggle, The Woman's Rights Movement in the United States.* Cambridge, Mass.: Belknap, 1959.
Foner, Philip S. *Women and the American Labor Movement, From the First Trade Unions to the Present.* New York: Macmillan, 1979.
Wertheimer, Barbara Mayer. *We Were There: The Story of Working Women in America.* New York: Pantheon, 1977.

OUR BODIES, OURSELVES, published in 1971 by the Boston Women's Health Book Collective, Inc., and republished in 1984 as *The New Our Bodies, Ourselves*, is the product of what began as a small women's discussion group. The women began by reading and discussing medical journals and books in light of their own experiences with medicine and related issues; they compiled information and wrote papers on the topics discussed and subsequently began a course on women's health issues in Boston. This book makes a thoughtful and concerted effort to educate women who have been misinformed or ignored by a male-dominated and -administered medical profession and whose alternatives, until this time, were only a few all-female clinics.

The first publication came out of the women's movement of the late 1960s and early 1970s, when medicine was but one of the institutions under fire. *Our Bodies, Ourselves* clarifies many female medical issues, such as birth control and its effects, venereal disease, and menopause, and also discusses the socio-medical topics of rape, pregnancy, and abortion. Much of its emphasis is upon questioning the past treatment of women's health and informing readers of more positive ways of coping with their particular problems. It is a medical guidebook, one that stresses alternatives to "men's medicine," such as home remedies and female clinics, and includes personal documentation of individual women's experiences.

The New Our Bodies, Ourselves is revised to include expanded coverage of topics in the original book, plus entire chapters devoted to the effects of drugs, alcohol, and smoking on women, new reproductive technologies, women and aging, psychological health, and several self-awareness topics.
—*Kamene L. Seman*

See Also:

Women's Liberation Movement

References:

Boston Women's Health Book Collective. *Our Bodies, Ourselves.* New York: Simon & Schuster, 1976.
———. *The New Our Bodies, Ourselves.* New York: Simon & Schuster, 1984.

***OUVROIRS* (WORKROOMS)** (c.1914/18) were the first attempts by American expatriates, mainly women, to offer civilians relief during World War I, predating American Red Cross work by three years.

Many long-term American expatriates, male and female, reacted to the declaration of the Great War by leaving the Continent and returning to the United States, or at least leaving France. Some returned after a short period, and, propelled by love of their adopted country and concern for the already deprived civilians, established *ouvroirs*. Credit is still given to Edith Wharton for starting the first workroom to relieve unemployed civilian seamstresses, offering not only pay but also medical care, noon meals, and coal in winter; she later broadened her civilian relief work to include the homeless and refugees in France and Belgium.

Wharton was only one of many active American expatriates in Europe before 1917. Others concentrated on employment and day nurseries, hospital supplies, war charities, or war work. Groups included the American Fund for French Wounded (Gertrude Stein and Alice B. Toklas, for instance, drove a delivery truck for them), American Hostels for Refugees, the Franco-American General Committee, the Children of Flanders Rescue Committee, and the American Distributing Service. Among those active in these organizations were Elizabeth Cameron, Mildred Bliss, Elisina Royall Tyler, Anne Morgan, and Elsie de Wolfe; in acknowledgement of their dedicated and frequently dangerous work, European governments awarded honors to many of these expatriates.

After the entry of the United States into World War I, many more Americans became involved in nonmilitary work in Europe, and the American Red Cross played a more active role.

—Maureen Ruth Liston

See Also:

Wharton, Edith; World War I

References:

Benstock, Shari. *Women of the Left Bank: Paris, 1900–1940.* Austin: University of Texas Press, 1986.

Earnest, Ernest. *Expatriates and Patriots: American Artists, Scholars and Writers in Europe.* Durham, N.C.: Duke University Press, 1968.

Liston, Maureen Ruth. "Before the (Male) American Ambulance Drivers Were the (Female) Relief Workers: American Women Expatriates and the First World War." Unpublished paper.

PACIFISM AND THE PEACE MOVEMENT are issues that women have long considered important. Pacifism, generally understood as "the refusal on grounds of principle to perpetrate or sanction acts of violence" (Chatfield, p. 13), more specifically has meant the "absolute refusal to participate in, or support in any way, the waging of war" (Mayer, p. 11). A philosophy of noncooperation and nonresistance, pacifism has its roots in the pre-Christian writings of the ancient Chinese and the Jewish prophet Isaiah. With Christianity came the Sermon on the Mount and Jesus's admonishment to "love thine enemy" and "turn the other cheek."

The pacifist envisions a world of equality and cooperative love wherein violence is totally repudiated. The pacifist perceives violence as the grossest immorality and places responsibility for change in the individual rather than in institutional arrangements. Through education and example, each individual must convert to a life of nonviolence; only then will society follow suit.

The pacifist's strategy of passive resistance to initiate political change assumes the natural goodness of all people and that even those who exercise power through both overt and covert violence are at heart persons of morality and ethically based rationality. Thus the pacifist believes in ultimate triumph through the appeal by example to the adversary's conscience.

Most closely associated with pacifism in women's history were twentieth-century advocates Jane Addams and Dorothy Day. Day was co-founder of the *Catholic Worker*. Her opposition to militarism and support of conscientious objectors reflected her Roman Catholic religious beliefs.

Addams was part of the less militant secular-humanist position of liberal pacifism active between World Wars I and II. She became chief spokesperson for female pacifists, and her book, *The Newer Ideals of Peace* (1907), was their main contribution to pacifist literature.

Addams led the formation of the nationwide Woman's Peace Party in January 1915. In April, Addams and a delegation of forty-seven women attended the International Congress of Women in The Hague, the Netherlands. The congress resulted in the formation of the Women's International League for Peace and Freedom (WILPF), which remains active. Although not all of its members today adhere to pacifism, the WILPF has been the most active and enduring of the women's peace organizations in modern history.

Over the next few years, other peace groups formed. The Women's Peace Society, created in 1919 under the leadership of Fanny Garrison Villard, believed in more extreme nonresistance than the WILPF. The year 1921 saw the birth of the Women's Peace Union of the Western Hemisphere and the Women's Committee for World Disarmament. That year the PTA members lobbied for peace. They believed one of the roles of public schools should be to educate the next generation to prevent war. In 1925 Carrie Chapman Catt organized the National Conference on the Cause and Cure of War. It consisted of the leaders and members of the major women's organizations with peace departments.

A resurgence of peace movements occurred in the 1960s in protest of the Vietnam War. Under the leadership of Bella Abzug and Dagmar Wilson, Women Strike for Peace formed in 1962 to work for disarmament and a nuclear test ban treaty. The WSP led the way for other groups in demonstrating at the Pentagon and protesting the use of napalm against the Vietnamese. It was the first peace group to meet formally with representatives from North Vietnam.

—*Carrie Foster and Merri J. Scheibe*

See Also:

Abzug, Bella; Addams, Jane; Balch, Emily; Day, Dorothy; Vietnam War; Woman's Peace Party; Women's International League for Peace and Freedom; Women's Peace Union

References:

Addams, Jane. *Newer Ideals of Peace.* New York: Macmillan, 1907.

Brock, Peter. *Twentieth-Century Pacifism.* New York: Van Nostrand Reinhold, 1970.

Chatfield, Charles, ed. *International War Resistance Through World War II.* New York: Garland, 1975.

Hartmann, Susan M. *From Margin to Mainstream.* New York: Knopf, 1989.

Mayer, Peter, ed. *The Pacifist Conscience.* Chicago: Regnery, 1967.

O'Neill, William L. *Everyone Was Brave.* New York: Quadrangle, 1971.

PALEY, GRACE (b. 1922), writer, teacher, and political activist, has authored three collections of highly original short stories illumining "the dark lives of women." Her first volume, *The Little Disturbances of Man* (1956), published in advance of the women's movement, broke new ground by rendering the extraordinary feel of women's daily experience with children and men. *Enormous Changes at the Last Minute* (1974) and *Later the Same Day* (1985) continue to concentrate on the ordinary lives of women as they encounter "life, death, desertion, loss, divorce, failure, love." In her most recent collection, Paley pays particular attention to women's lifelong bonds with one another—their friendships, family ties, and political associations.

Writing to articulate a woman's version of experience, Paley has forged a distinctive, widely acclaimed style. Her narrative structures show a contingency and openness that seem to arise from a feminine tolerance for surprising developments: lovers come and go in these stories, children grow up, families divide, and women persist in changing. Most of Paley's stories take place in a busy interracial neighborhood in New York City and feature speakers from a variety of backgrounds. Paley has fashioned a verbal style that allows these new ethnic and female voices to be raised. Her female speakers best convey her style; they are good listeners and apt talkers, adept at making fresh remarks and posing unsettling questions. Her men are poor listeners and explainers, verbal self-appreciators. This ironic difference in the way men and women speak their way through life is the point of many of Paley's stories. In her work, women under very modern pressures express comic and candid understandings of sex, power, motherhood, work, community, and intimacy.

Although Paley's stories respect the unavoidable tragedy that touches most lives, her fiction is hopeful and her protagonists engaged. Paley herself has always participated in antiwar and feminist causes, a stance she traces to a family tradition of socialism and activism. At Sarah Lawrence College and City College of New York, where she holds faculty appointments, Paley's goal is to teach not only writing but listening, an activity that in Paley's view has important political dimensions.

Paley has two grown children and one grandchild. She is married to Robert Nichols, a writer, and lives with him in Vermont part of the year. Long admired by other writers, Paley has recently received more widespread recognition for the unmistakable voice that characterizes her fiction.

—*Carol Snyder*

References:

De Koven, Marianne. "Mrs. Hegel-Shtein's Tears." *Partisan Review* 48 (1981): 217–21.

Hulley, Kathleen, ed. *Delta, Revue du Centre d'Etudes et de Recherches sur les Ecrivains du Sud aux Etats-Unis.* 14 (1982) [special issue devoted to Paley]

Kamel, Rose. "To Aggravate the Conscience: Grace Paley's Loud Voice." *Journal of Ethnic Studies* 11 (Fall 1983): 29–49.

Lidoff, Joan. "Clearing Her Throat: An Interview with Grace Paley." *Shenandoah* 32 (1981): 3–26.

Paley, Grace. *Enormous Changes at the Last Minute*. New York: Farrar, Straus & Giroux, 1974.

———. *Later the Same Day*. New York: Farrar, Straus & Giroux, 1985.

———. *The Little Disturbances of Man: Stories of Men and Women at Love*. New York: New American Library, 1956.

Schleifer, Ronald. "Grace Paley: Chaste Compactness." In *Contemporary American Women Writers*. Edited by Catherine Kainwater and William J. Scheick. Lexington: University Press of Kentucky, 1985, pp. 31-49.

PARENT-TEACHER ASSOCIATIONS. The National PTA was founded in 1897, the end result of the "mothers' congress" held in Washington, D.C., in 1897 to involve mothers in public education. The founders, Phoebe Apperson Hearst and Alice McLellan Birney, devoted their lives to the cause of education. Birney emerged as the first president of the National Congress of Mothers, which became the National Congress of Parents and Teachers in 1924. A similar organization for blacks, the National Congress of Colored Parents and Teachers, was founded in 1927 by Selena Sloan Butler to foster improvements in the segregated school system in the South. Both organizations merged in 1970.

For ninety years, the goals of the PTA have remained virtually unchanged. It is one of the oldest, largest, and most powerful child-advocacy groups in the nation. Its objectives are not only to secure a strong relationship between parents and teachers, but to implement higher standards for children in the home, within the legal system, and in health care, as well as in the schools. The PTA has continued to expand its goals for parents' involvement in their children's schools to reflect the changes in society and education.

Recommendations to improve the conditions of children are promulgated at the national level. Three commissions—education, health and welfare, and individual development—act as conduits for programs passed from the National PTA through the state level to the local level. Historically, the National PTA has contributed significantly to the passage of child-labor and mandatory school attendance laws and to the development of juvenile courts, kindergartens, and school-lunch programs. Almost every area involving children's education has benefited from this organization. Local PTA chapters foster the basic relationship between the teachers and parents and monitor social problems, such as drug abuse, in addition to working in cooperation with school districts and the community.

PTA membership numbers in the millions. Dues are nominal, and any adult interested in the education of children is encouraged to join. Traditionally, women as the cultural guardians of children have constituted the working membership, but with the changing family in the last few years, men are taking a greater part.

The laudable objectives of the PTA fitted nicely into the Women's Sphere concept of the nineteenth and the early twentieth centuries, enabling women to work in a cooperative mode rather than in an adversarial one.

—Jean McGrath Hayes

See Also:
Education

References:

Birney, Mrs. T. W. *Childhood*. Introduction by G. Stanley Hall. New York: Frederich A. Stokes, 1905.

Golden Jubilee History, 1897–1947. Chicago: National Congress of Parents and Teachers, 1947.

National PTA Directory. Chicago: National Congress of Parents and Teachers, published quarterly.

PTA Today. Chicago: National Congress of Parents and Teachers, published seven times annually.

PARKER, BONNIE (1910–34) became one of the best known gangsters of the early 1930s after a brief and bloody crime spree with her partner, Clyde Barrow. Born in Rowen, Texas, she completed high school there as an honor student. While working as a waitress in a Dallas cafe in 1930, she met Clyde Barrow and fell in love immediately. A month later,

Barrow was sentenced to two years in jail for burglary. Parker smuggled a gun into the prison, and Barrow escaped but was recaptured within a few days. When Barrow gained parole in 1932, they picked up where they had left off.

In March 1932 the pair stole a car, but police spotted them, and after a spectacular chase, arrested Parker. Her partner escaped. She served three months in jail and then rejoined Barrow. They soon gained national attention as their crime rampage moved across the South and Midwest. A day after their reunion, the pair took a New Mexico sheriff hostage, dropping him off in Texas the next day. In September their crime spree began in earnest; they raided a National Guard Armory in Fort Worth, Texas, stealing boxes of machine guns, automatic rifles, and shotguns.

The crime spree of Bonnie and Clyde took them across Texas and into bordering states. They robbed grocery stores and small-town banks, their biggest haul netting only $1,500. Bonnie and Clyde killed indiscriminately, murdering fifteen individuals. They were joined by several accomplices, including Barrow's brother, and the gang received national attention throughout 1933 and 1934, largely because of the brutal killing of several police officers and shoot-outs with authorities. Their crime spree was slowed only briefly because of wounds from gunfights with the police. Parker enjoyed the publicity, and she composed a poem entitled "The Story of Suicide Sal," a term given her by a journalist. The pair also took many photographs of each other holding guns from their small arsenal.

As their crime spree mounted, police stepped up their efforts to find Bonnie and Clyde, who narrowly escaped twice in early 1934. Their luck would, however, not hold much longer. On May 23, 1934, a well-armed posse killed Bonnie Parker and Clyde Barrow at a roadside ambush near Gibland, Louisiana. Their dramatic demise assured them a prominent place in folk legend and popular culture.

—Robert G. Waite

See Also:
Criminals

References:

Frost, H. Gordon, and John H. Jenkins. *"I'm Frank Hammer." The Life of a Texas Peace Officer.* Austin, Tex.: Pemberton, 1968.

Hinton, Ted. *Ambush: The Real Story of Bonnie and Clyde.* Austin, Tex.: Shoal Creek, 1979.

PARKER, DOROTHY (ROTHSCHILD) (1893– 1967) was known for her sharp wit, which she loosed on friends and in her writing. This legendary wit earned her a position as one of the first writers for Harold Ross's *New Yorker* magazine (founded in 1925), and it also gave her status with the Algonquin Round Table, a clique of popular New York writers that met informally during the 1920s.

Parker's stories and poems, along with plays and book reviews, appeared in the *New Yorker* throughout her lifetime, and she can be credited with helping to mold the magazine's recognizable style. Her stories, which depict middle- and upper-class Americans engaged in a battle of the sexes, emphasize that love is fickle and that men, especially, are unfaithful. Insecure in their love and in themselves and afraid to show either pain or desire, her women characters agree on the surface to treat love as a game that must be played with calculated wit, not candor. Not surprisingly, Parker's concomitant theme in her stories, and especially in her poems, underscores life's mutability and women's sexual mortality, in the face of which it is best to die young and pretty. Her poems revolve around suicidal themes, but usually with an ironic twist that attempts to make light of serious truths. For example, one love poem ends: "My own dear love, he is all my heart— / And I wish somebody'd shoot him."

Parker's personal unhappiness influenced her writing about the tentative and unhappy nature of male/female relationships and of modern life. She was born into a well-to-do family (her father was a garment manufacturer in New York), but her Scottish mother died while Parker was an infant. Her sense of loss was complicated by the strict upbringing imposed by her father and stepmother, and she welcomed the chance to strike out on her own. In 1916 she began writing for Frank Crowninshield (at *Vogue* magazine and then at *Vanity Fair*) before joining the *New Yorker* in 1925. Parker's first marriage, to Edwin Pond Parker II in 1917, was short-lived, and she married actor-writer Alan Campbell (she continued to use Parker's name) in 1933. Although they divorced in 1947, they remarried three years later; and, overall, they maintained a personal and professional relationship (Campbell served ably as her manager) that afforded her a degree of personal stability, despite several unsuccessful suicide attempts.

Although some critics see Parker's work as limited (her verse clever but slight and her stories sharp and telling but scanty in number), she is still read today as one who was unafraid to treat female issues truthfully, if sardonically. Many of her one-liners, such as "Men seldom make passes / At girls who wear glasses," have worked their way into the canon of American popular speech, and Parker herself became identified with the 1920s flapper image that outwardly bespoke a new liberation. Inwardly, this image was fed by the restlessness and the romantic and spiritual yearning that characterized the era for which Dorothy Parker became an ironically clever spokeswoman.

—*Linda Patterson Miller*

See Also:

Flapper

References:

Frewin, Leslie. *The Late Mrs. Dorothy Parker.* New York: Macmillan, 1987.

Gill, Brendan, ed. and intro. *The Portable Dorothy Parker.* Rev. ed. New York: Viking, 1973.

Keats, John. *You Might as Well Live: The Life and Times of Dorothy Parker.* New York: Simon & Schuster, 1970.

Kinney, Arthur F. *Dorothy Parker.* Boston: G. K. Hall, 1978.

PARKS, ROSA (b. 1913), civil rights leader and community activist, was born in Tuskegee, Alabama, but spent much of her formative years in or near Montgomery. Her father was a carpenter, her mother, Leona, was a teacher, and they instilled in their daughter a sense of the injustice of racial discrimination. She attended Alabama State College until a few weeks before her twentieth birthday, when she married Raymond Parks, a young barber.

The young couple resided in Montgomery, where Parks became an active member and frequent officer of the local chapter of the National Association for the Advancement of Colored People (NAACP). She was also active in church affairs and with the Montgomery Voters League, an organization that was trying to register more blacks. Her sense of the possibilities for interracial harmony had been strengthened by attending for two weeks the Highlander Folk School, an interracial academic community in Tennessee.

It was while working as a tailor's assistant at the Montgomery Fair Department Store in 1955 that Parks was thrust into the national spotlight. On the evening of December 1, 1955, while riding home on a public bus, she firmly but quietly refused to give up her seat to white passengers as was the custom in Montgomery. The bus driver summoned the police, and Parks was arrested, jailed, and brought to trial. The arrest of this respectable, churchgoing, forty-two-year-old woman galvanized the black community of Montgomery into action. Led by her friend E. D. Dixon, the president of the Montgomery NAACP, and the local black clergy, a Montgomery Improvement Association was quickly organized under the presidency of Rev. Martin Luther King, Jr.

A successful bus boycott was soon organized, and thirteen months after the boycott began, a federal court order ended the racial segregation of buses in Montgomery. King's Gandhian "passive resistance" policy had won its first major victory. Despite threats, bombings, and other forms of intimidation, the civil rights movement had begun. Parks had been fired from her job as a result of the controversy, and her husband became ill as a result of the pressures put upon the family. Nevertheless, she continued to work for the Montgomery Improvement Association until the family relocated to Detroit in 1957.

In Detroit, Parks worked as a dressmaker and continued her civil rights and community activities. She has been particularly active with youth work and job guidance. A frequent public speaker, Parks has also continued to be active in church work, serving as a deaconess at St. Matthews' African Methodist Episcopal Church in Detroit. Still hailed as the "mother of the civil rights movement," Rosa Parks also worked on the staff of Representative John Conyers in Detroit.

—Jonathan W. Zophy

See Also:
Civil Rights, National Association for the Advancement of Colored People

References:
Brown, Cynthia. "Rosa Parks: Interview." *Southern Exposure* 9 (Spring 1981): 16–17.
Garrow, David. *Bearing the Cross: Martin Luther King, Jr., and the Southern Leadership Conference.* New York: Morrow, 1986.
King, Jr., M. L. *Stride Toward Freedom: The Montgomery Story.* New York: Harper, 1958.
Stevenson, Janet. "Rosa Parks Wouldn't Budge." *American Heritage* 23 (1972): 56–64, 85.

PARSONS, LUCY GONZÁLEZ (1852–1942) was a *Chicana* organizer, orator, and writer in the American labor movement. Born in Johnson County, Texas, she married Albert R. Parsons and moved to Chicago, where they became major figures in the labor struggle. She wrote for *Alarm,* the weekly newspaper of the International Working People's Association, as well as the *Socialist,* the *Denver Labor Enquirer,* and the *Labor Defender.* The first issue of *Alarm* in 1884 published her well-known article "A Word to Tramps," which was a call to arms.

In 1879 she worked with the Chicago Working Women's Union, calling for a suffrage plank in the Socialist labor platform and for equal pay for equal work. She joined Lizzy Swank-Holmes in organizing seamstresses and demanding an eight-hour day in 1885–86. Her husband was among the leaders arrested and convicted of murder for their role in the Haymarket Riot, a violent con-frontation between labor organizers and police in which four workers and seven policemen died. For a year and a half, she fought an unsuccessful legal battle to have the death sentences of the Haymarket participants reversed. After her husband's execution in 1886, she continued her involvement in the labor movement. She was a major contributor to the development of the International Labor Defense (ILD), which aided workers and political dissidents, and she was one of the founders of the Industrial Workers of the World (IWW) before its first congress in 1905. She joined the unemployed in San Francisco in 1913 to demand a three-dollar wage for an eight-hour day and led several hunger strikes in Chicago.

Lucy Parsons strongly advocated women's rights to divorce, contraception and birth control, freedom from rape, and economic equality; however, she defined women's oppression as a result of capitalism. In her article "Cause of Sex Slavery," she stated: "The economic is the first issue to be settled, . . . it is woman's economical dependence which makes her enslavement to man possible."

—Mary Romero

See Also:
Chicana, Industrial Workers of the World, Journalism

References:
Ashbaugh, Carolyn. *Lucy Parsons.* Chicago: Kerr, 1976.
Foner, Philip S. *History of the Labor Movement in the United States.* Vol. 2, 4. New York: International Publishers, 1947.
Mirandé, Alfredo, and Evangelina Enríquez. *La Chicana: The Mexican-American Woman.* Chicago: University of Chicago Press, 1979.
Parsons, Lucy González. "Cause of Sex Slavery." *Firebrand* 1 (January 27, 1895): 2.
———. "A Word to Tramps." *Alarm* 1 (October 4, 1884): 1.

PATRIARCHY as a term describing the origins of the gender system was initially employed in the narrow historical context that referred to the development of the legal prerogatives of men within the male-headed households under Greek and Roman law. The male head of household had both legal and economic control over the female and minor dependent males within the family. According to some historians, patriarchy was established in antiquity and expired by the turn of the twentieth century, as married women's property rights and women's civil rights were granted in Western nations. However, women's historians in particular have traced the beginning of patriarchy to the third millennium and are challenging the presumption of the demise of patriarchy by citing that its adaptation of the gender system through limited legal reforms during the Victorian and Progressive eras actually assured its continued presence into the twentieth century. As the historical debate over patriarchy progressed through the 1980s, women's historian Gerda Lerner asserted that the term *patriarchy* properly referred to the institutionalized system of male dominance over women and children in the family, which extended male dominance over women into society as well.

—*Angela Howard Zophy*

See Also:

Marriage, Married Women's Property Acts, Sex-Gender System, Sexism

References:

Engels, Friedrich. *The Origins of the Family, Private Property, and the State.* Chicago: Kerr, 1902; rpt. New York: International Publishers, 1970.

Lerner, Gerda. *The Creation of Patriarchy.* New York: Oxford University Press, 1986.

———. *The Female Experience: An American Documentary.* Indianapolis: Bobbs-Merrill, 1977.

Ryan, Mary P. *Womanhood in America: From Colonial Times to the Present.* 3d ed. New York: New Viewpoints/Franklin Watts, 1984.

The **PATRONS OF HUSBANDRY**, better known as the Grange, began in 1867 and almost immediately provided larger roles for women than had any previous agricultural association. Local, or subordinate, granges included women members from their beginning; the first representative National Grange, which met in 1873, had no women members, but adopted a constitution that admitted the wives of subordinate grange masters to the state granges and the wives of state grange masters to the National Grange. Women were not at first expected to hold offices in their own right, but four women's offices existed by 1869. These offices—ceres, flora, pomona, and lady assistant steward—were mainly ornamental; they had little responsibility and no authority. A few women held the important working offices starting in the 1870s, and their share of leadership rose steeply after 1895, when Sarah G. Baird started her seventeen years as master of the Minnesota State Grange. In 1901 an informed observer guessed that a majority of local grange lecturers, the officers who planned programs, were women.

The order's Declaration of Purposes, adopted in 1874, called for a "proper appreciation of the abilities and sphere of women." Early leaders denied that they had any sympathy with "women's rights"; they simply wanted to help farm women overcome the stultifying effects of drudgery and rise to the period's ideal of True Womanhood. But the order attracted some committed feminists, such as Flora M. Kimball of California, who persuaded it to support equal suffrage. The California State Grange passed an equal suffrage resolution in 1878; other states, and eventually the National Grange, followed. The "home protection" argument that women needed the vote to protect the domestic sphere, which the Woman's Christian Temperance Union employed so effectively, was also persuasive in the grange. Many women grange leaders, notably Eliza C. Gifford of New York, were active in the WCTU.

The order never expended much of its energy on equal suffrage; instead, it has consistently stressed purely domestic concerns. The Declaration of Purposes, for example, promises to "enhance the comforts and attractions of our homes," and calls for "domestic science" courses in the agricultural colleges. The order's emphasis on domesticity has been especially strong since 1910, when Elizabeth H. Patterson of Maryland persuaded the National Grange to create a standing committee on home economics.

Charles Gardner, the order's own best historian, claims that it "turned on the radiant light of hope for rural woman." That may be a little fulsome, but it is typical of grangers' pride in their service to women.

—*Donald B. Marti*

See Also:

Agriculture, Cult of True Womanhood

References:

Gardner, Charles. *The Grange—Friend of the Farmer, 1867–1947.* Washington, D.C.: National Grange, 1949, pp. 191–207.

Hebb, Douglas Charles. "The Woman Movement in the California State Grange, 1873–1880." M.A. thesis. University of California-Berkeley, 1950.

Marti, Donald B. "Sisters of the Grange: Rural Feminism in the Late Nineteenth Century." *Agricultural History* 58 (July 1984): 247–61.

Nordin, Dennis Sven. *Rich Harvest: A History of the Grange, 1867–1900.* Jackson: University Press of Mississippi, 1974.

PAUL, ALICE (1885–1977), a tough and single-minded reformer on behalf of equal rights for women, militantly challenged political thinking in the twentieth century. She was educated at Swarthmore College (B.A.), the University of Pennsylvania (M.A., Ph.D.), Washington College of Law (L.L.B., L.L.M.), and American University (D.C.L.). While Paul was studying in England from 1907 to 1909, Emmeline Pankhurst introduced her to suffrage philosophy and militant activism; afterward, Paul went to Washington, D.C., to lobby for enfranchisement. She and Lucy Burns organized the first major suffrage parade in Washington on the eve of Democrat Woodrow Wilson's inauguration as president in 1913. Suffragists were mobbed, spit upon, and ridiculed by the public.

In the period from 1913 to 1917 Alice Paul organized for what was to become the final drive to secure woman suffrage. In 1913 she established the Congressional Union, which was singularly and militantly committed to securing a federal woman suffrage amendment through lobbying Congress and pressuring the president. In 1915 she organized an "auto pilgrimage" to carry a half-million-signature petition from San Francisco to Washington. Also, because of her insistence on approaching suffrage for women through a federal amendment only, she broke with the National American Woman Suffrage Association and founded the National Woman's Party (NWP).

Paul ruthlessly applied to the Democrats the British suffragist strategy of "holding the party in power" responsible, and as early as 1917 the National Woman's Party began using militant tactics, which included sending delegations to the president and picketing the White House when denied that access. The official response was to arrest the picketing suffragists. To contest their incarceration, these women staged hunger strikes that brought publicized forced-feedings of the prisoners; the public outcry resulted in the release of the suffragists. Some of her contemporaries believed that Alice Paul's militancy and NWP opposition to World War I delayed success in attaining woman suffrage; others credit the nuisance value of NWP tactics in adding urgency to the Wilson administration's conversion to the cause.

With the ratification of the Nineteenth Amendment, the National Woman's party began to focus on "equal rights for women." In 1923 Paul wrote an earlier version of the Equal Rights Amendment (ERA), which sparked a four-decade division among the supporters of women's rights. Some women supported the concept of an ERA that would grant unconditional legal equality to women while others were committed to the hard-won "protective legislation" of the Progressive era, which assumed that gender was a legitimate distinction in formulating the regulation of working hours and conditions for women. Paul's last years were spent lobbying for the

ERA that emerged from Congress in 1972 and precipitated a hard-fought but unsuccessful national campaign that failed to achieve ratification by the extended 1982 deadline.

In the intervening 1930s and 1940s, Alice Paul turned to international affairs as chairman of the Nationality Committee of the Inter-American Commission of Women, which worked to grant equal national rights to women in the Western Hemisphere. She also lobbied the League of Nations for women's equality and assisted in creating the World Woman's party. This group sent delegates to the convention that drafted the charter of the United Nations, which included equal rights in its preamble.

—Ted. C. Harris

See Also:

Equal Rights Amendment, National Woman's Party, Suffrage

References:

Blatch, Harriott Stanton, and Alma Lutz. *Challenging Years: The Memoirs of Harriott Stanton Blatch.* New York: Putnam, 1940.

Chafe, William Henry. *The American Woman: Her Changing Social, Economic, and Political Roles, 1920–1970.* New York: Oxford University Press, 1972.

Flexner, Eleanor. *Century of Struggle: The Women's Rights Movement in the United States.* Rev. ed. Cambridge, Mass.: Belknap, 1975.

Irwin, Inez Hayes. *The Story of the Woman's Party.* New York: Harcourt, Brace, 1921; rpt. New York: Krans Reprint, 1971; Also republished as *Up Hills with Banners Flying.* Penobscott, Me.: Traversity, 1964.

Lunardini, Christine. *From Equal Suffrage to Equal Rights: Alice Paul and the National Woman's Party, 1910–1928.* New York: New York University Press, 1988.

Ross, Ishbel. *Sons of Adam, Daughters of Eve.* New York: Boni and Liveright, 1920; rpt. New York: Schocken, 1976.

Rupp, Leila, and Verta Taylor. *Survival in the Doldrums: The American Women's Rights Movement, 1945 to the 1960s.* New York: Oxford University Press, 1987.

Zimmerman, Loretta Ellen. "Alice Paul and the National Woman's Party, 1912–1920." Diss. Tulane University, 1964.

PEABODY, ELIZABETH PALMER (1804–94), author and educator, successfully promoted the transplanting of German philosopher Friedrich Froebel's concept of the kindergarten to the United States. As one who had struggled to refine her own ideas about education, development, and the woman's sphere over a lifetime of experiences and conversations with the likes of transcendentalists William Ellery Channing, Margaret Fuller, and Bronson Alcott, Peabody quickly perceived the wisdom of Froebel's thought when she was first introduced to it in 1859. Seeing the validity of his process of infant culture, schoolteacher Peabody established the first American kindergarten in Boston in 1860 as a showcase for Froebelian methodology.

Continually dissatisfied with the results of her infant culture experiment, Peabody went to Europe in 1867 to study the original kindergarten. While in Germany, she began to understand the kindergarten in a new light. It was clear to her that Froebel had intended the kindergarten to be totally distinct in both purpose and methodology from the traditional school. The true Froebelian kindergarten was structured so that the young child was enabled to unfold inherent intellectual, moral, and artistic capabilities. Such development was to be assisted by the careful nurture of a woman who had been intensively trained in both the art and the science of an ideal form of maternal instinct and method. Understanding the relationship that Froebel envisioned between his concept of child nurture and an educated, enabled womanhood, kindergartner Peabody returned to Boston and repudiated all of her earlier efforts of infant culture.

She set to work writing, lecturing, and organizing exhibits that promoted genuine kindergartens. Relying on her wide network of influential friends, she advocated the kindergarten cause before prominent audiences throughout the East and Midwest. Peabody successfully garnered philanthropic support for the young movement and persuaded German kindergartners Maria Kraus-Boelte, Emma Marwedel, and Alma Kriege to emigrate to the United States to train American women in Froebelian principles. She argued for endowed professorships of kindergartening in each of the nation's normal schools. Peabody courted the favor of publishers Milton Bradley and Ernst Steiger and convinced them to manufacture kindergarten materials and to publish books about Froebel. Eventually, the kindergarten concept was incorporated into public education.

Through her successful appeals to society to provide for the appropriate nurture of children through intensive training for material duties, Peabody established a reservoir of hope that the kindergarten would gain acceptance as a unique profession for women.

—*Catherine Cosgrove*

See Also:

Blow, Susan; Education; Teaching as an Occupation for Women

References:

Baylor, Ruth. *Elizabeth Palmer Peabody.* Philadelphia: University of Pennsylvania Press, 1965.

Peabody, Elizabeth. *Lectures in the Training School for Kindergartners.* Boston: Heath, 1893.

———. "Origin and Growth of Kindergartens." *Education* 2 (May/June 1882): 507–27.

The **PEACE CORPS** was begun as a bureau of the U.S. government in 1961; although many give Congressman Henry Reuss credit, the idea came from several different people over a period of time. Publicized during John F. Kennedy's campaign for the presidency, the corps grew rapidly at first, and during the first few months, 400 volunteers were already in the field. By 1965 there were over 12,200 volunteers, of whom about 40 percent were women. The stated purposes of the Peace Corps are to help the countries involved meet their needs for trained manpower, to promote a better understanding of Americans abroad, and to promote within American society a better understanding of people in other countries.

A Peace Corps volunteer must be at least eighteen years of age, and while there are a number of volunteers over forty and/or married, the typical volunteer is between twenty and twenty-five years old and single. A study showed that Peace Corps volunteers in general and its women in particular are a middle group politically and come from a conventional family background. Although a college degree is not required, most volunteers are college graduates. Volunteers are assigned for a two-year tour of duty in a country that has requested assistance, and they work on projects ranging from teaching to construction. Volunteers join for many reasons: a desire to help people in an active way, a desire to work for peace, and an opportunity to increase their knowledge of people from other countries.

Partly because the Peace Corps was at first headed by people outside the government, there tended to be a spirit among the volunteers that historians Hapgood and Bennett described as creative anarchy. There was a freedom from tradition and less discrimination by race, sex, or age than was true in some government agencies. Women volunteers, at least in the early years, advanced more rapidly than in other agencies. The Vietnam War had a definite impact on the Peace Corps: the number of volunteers diminished. Those against the war did not distinguish between the Peace Corps and other government agencies. America's deteriorating reputation abroad made some who might have volunteered reluctant to leave the United States.

Volunteers reported many changes in themselves when they returned to the United States. They changed from the politics of their parents to greater political liberality, and they were likely to be more aware of the policies of their government and skeptical of those policies, in particular the use of economic and military power in the Third World. However, many also returned with a commitment to change things in their society rather than drop out of it. Usually, volunteers returning in the late 1960s and 1970s took jobs in the government or became teachers.

The Peace Corps remains active today although it tends to have a lower profile and fewer volunteers than in the early years. In 1985, for example, there were 5,400 volunteers.

—*Judith Pryor*

See Also:

Vietnam War

References:

Adams, Velma. *The Peace Corps in Action.* Chicago: Follett, 1964.

Haan, Norma. "Changes in Young Adults After Peace Corps Experiences: Political-Social Views, Moral Reasoning, and Perceptions of Self and Parents." *Journal of Youth and Adolescence* 3 (1974): 177–94.

Hapgood, David, and Meridan Bennett. *Agents of Change: A Close Look at the Peace Corps.* Boston: Little, Brown, 1968.

PEALE FAMILY, WOMEN ARTISTS OF THE. A number of talented women artists appeared among the second- and third-generation descendants of Charles Willson Peale, an important artist of considerable cultural influence during the Federalist period. The best known were his three nieces—Anna Claypoole Peale (1791–1878), Margaretta Angelica Peale (1795–1882), and Sarah Miriam Peale (1800–85)—and a granddaughter, Mary Jane Peale (1827–1902).

Anna, Margaretta, and Sarah were the daughters of James Peale, a miniaturist who taught them the difficult medium of painting in watercolor on ivory. Although she did some fine still lifes in her early years as an artist, Anna Peale was primarily a painter of miniature portraits. Because of her skill, especially in depicting texture, her work was in demand from Boston to Washington. She exhibited at the Pennsylvania Academy of the Fine Arts from 1811 to 1842. In 1824 Anna and her sister Sarah were elected to membership in the academy, the first women to receive that honor. In 1829 Anna married Dr. William Staughton, who died within the year. She continued to paint until her second marriage, to General William Duncan in 1842, after which her career ended.

Sarah Miriam Peale is often considered America's first professional woman artist since she successfully supported herself from her art. She went from the family home in Philadelphia to Baltimore to study with her cousin Rembrandt Peale, one of the sons of Charles Willson Peale. She then established a studio in Baltimore where she became a leading portrait painter. In 1847 she traveled to St. Louis, where she stayed for three decades, painting portraits of prominent families and also still lifes for which she received many prizes. She never married and in 1878 returned to Philadelphia. Her portrait style is realistic, with firm drawing, rich color, and elegant rendering of texture.

Margaretta Peale was a talented still-life painter. Although she was not a professional as her sisters were, she did exhibit at the Pennsylvania Academy from 1828 to 1837. She also did some portraiture.

Mary Jane Peale, the only daughter of Rubens Peale, studied painting with her uncle, Rembrandt Peale, and with Thomas Sully. Although she was building a career as a portrait painter in New York, she returned in 1855 to Pennsylvania to care for her elderly parents. She taught her father, a naturalist, to paint during the last decade of his life. She is best known for her still lifes, which usually consist of a rich array of fruits on a table in soft, suffused light.

Of the lesser-known Peale women artists, Harriet Cany Peale (c. 1800–69), the second wife of Rembrandt Peale, was his pupil prior to their marriage in 1840. She was primarily a copyist, often assisting her husband in the production of his many "porthole" portraits of George Washington. Rosalba Carriera Peale (1799–1874), Rembrandt's daughter by his first wife, became a painter in oils and a lithographer. Mary Jane Simes (1807–72), the granddaughter of James Peale, was a miniaturist in the style of her aunt and teacher Anna Claypoole. She exhibited miniatures at the Pennsylvania Academy between 1825 and 1830 but retired from painting after her marriage. Anne Peale Sellers (1824–1905), granddaughter of Charles Willson, studied art in Rome during the 1860s and attended classes at the Pennsylvania Academy with her cousin Mary Jane. She exhibited there from 1866 to 1878.

—*Joan J. Silverman*

See Also:
Art

References:
Born, Wolfgang. "The Female Peales, Their Art and Its Tradition." *The American Collector* 15 (August 1946): 12–14.
Elam, Charles H., ed. *The Peale Family: Three Generations of American Artists.* Detroit: Detroit Institute of Arts, 1967.
Frank Schwartz and Son. *A Gallery Collects Peales.* Catalogue by Robert Devlin Schwartz. Philadelphia: Frank Schwartz & Son, 1987.
National Museum of Women in the Arts. *American Women Artists, 1830–1930.* Catalog by Eleanor Tufts. Washington, D.C.: National Museum of Women in the Arts, 1987.
Peale Museum. *Miss Miriam Peale, 1800–1885, Portraits and Still-Life.* Catalog by Wilbur H. Huntly and John Mahey. Baltimore: Peale Museum, 1967.
Pennsylvania Academy of Fine Arts. *The Pennsylvania Academy and Its Women.* Exhibition catalog by Christine Jones Huber. Philadelphia: Pennsylvania Academy of Fine Arts, 1974.
Tufts, Eleanor. *Our Hidden Heritage.* New York: Paddington, 1973.

PERATROVICH, ELIZABETH (1911–58), born in 1911 to the Raven clan of the Tlingit Indians of Southeast Alaska, played a significant role in Tlingit politics until her untimely death in 1958 from cancer. Described by one newswriter in the mid-fifties as a "chic, well-groomed modern woman possessing great charm and an eye for the practical," Peratrovich was the college-educated mother of three children, an active member of the Presbyterian church, and a grand president of the Alaska Native Sisterhood (ANS).

During her tenure as ANS grand president, Peratrovich took up the Native equal rights issue along with her husband, Roy, and the skillful Tlingit lawyer William L. Paul. She effectively argued that the unfair treatment of Natives in restaurants, movie houses, and other business establishments in Juneau was particularly repugnant, given the country's present emergency (World War II), when unity was being stressed. In a letter to the editor of the *Southeast Alaska Empire,* she suggested to the readers that such treatment was "very un-American," particularly since "our Native boys" were being called upon to defend their country and "lay down their lives," just like the white boys, to protect the freedom that only the whites currently enjoyed. Demonstrating her own commitment to the war effort, Peratrovich raised money for the American Red Cross War Fund.

Her efforts in the equal rights battle moved from newspaper editorials to the halls of the Juneau legislature. According to the late Governor Ernest Gruening, she actively lobbied politicians, testified at public hearings, and was largely responsible for convincing the legislators to pass the Anti-Discrimination Bill of 1945. Additionally, as a member of the executive committee of the Alaska Native Brotherhood/Alaska Native Sisterhood, Peratrovich received support from the Office of Indian Affairs for improvement of the health and sanitary conditions of Native homes and villages, secured funding for nursery schools throughout southeast Alaska from the Federal Works Agency, and, at her own expense, traveled throughout Alaska organizing new ANS camps and throughout other states seeking markets for Indian- and Eskimo-made products. Shortly before her death, she served as the Alaskan representative to the National Congress of American Indians.

—Susan H. Koester

See Also:
Native American Women

References:
Koester, Susan H. "'By the Words of Thy Mouth Let Thee Be Judged': The Alaska Native Sisterhood Speaks." *Journal of the West, Western Speakers: Voices of the American Dream* 27 (April 1988): 35–44.
———, and Emma Widmark. Interview with Roy Peratrovich about Elizabeth Peratrovich. Juneau, Alaska. September 26, 1986.

PERKINS, FRANCES (1880–1965). When Perkins was appointed the first woman cabinet member, a Washington reporter asked her if her sex would be a disadvantage in the nation's capital; she replied, "Only when climbing trees." Although she admitted she felt "a little odd," she was President Franklin Roosevelt's most important adviser and held her post as secretary of labor from 1933 until shortly after his death in 1945.

The daughter of an old Maine family, Fanny Caralie Perkins was born April 10, 1880, in Boston, grew up in Worcester, and graduated from Mount Holyoke College. Inspired by reformer Frances Kelley, Perkins left a teaching career for settlement work—in which educated people lived and worked among the urban poor, advocating social reform—first in Chicago and later in Philadelphia. However, she first established her reputation as a researcher in New York on *The Survey* in 1910. She earned a master's degree at Columbia University in political science, then settled into social work as a factory inspector, where she earned a reputation as a tireless advocate for working women.

In 1926 Governor Alfred Smith appointed her chairperson of the state's Industrial Board, and two years later when Franklin Roosevelt became New York's governor, he promoted her to become the first woman state industrial commissioner. Perkins first introduced the idea of unemployment insurance in 1931 and promoted a series of conferences nationwide on the problems of unemployment. An early proponent of Roosevelt's bid for the presidency, she was rewarded with the cabinet post that sent AFL president William Green into a rampage of protest. Twelve years later, Green paid tribute to Perkins as one of the most accomplished labor secretaries to hold the office. She contributed to the making of the Wagner Act, the Social Security Act, and the Fair Labor Standards Act. After her retirement from the cabinet, she worked as civil service commissioner under the Truman administration. In 1955 she began lecturing at the School of Industrial and Labor Relations at Cornell University. She published a popular memoir of FDR, *The Roosevelt I Knew*, and was working on a biography of Al Smith at the time of her death in 1965.

Always one to keep her personal life out of the press, Perkins was married in 1913 to Paul C. Wilson, a New Yorker deeply involved in municipal government. They had a daughter in 1915, but shortly thereafter Wilson began suffering from periodic depressions that after 1929 left him hospitalized. Perkins kept her husband's malady from the press and protected her daughter, Susanna, from public scrutiny. She had very close female friends, notably Mary Dewson, who is said to have engineered Perkins's cabinet appointment. She also roomed in Washington with Mary Rumsey, the daughter of prominent railroad executive E. H. Harriman and a chairperson of the National Recovery Administration Consumers' Advisory Council. Florence Kelley had been her inspiration in earlier years, and Perkins devoted herself to Kelley's favorite cause, the prohibition of child labor. Grace Abbott, Katharine Lenroot, and Clara Beyer were co-workers, part of that unique set of New Deal women whose years of reform work earned them a place in Roosevelt's new experiment in government. Among all of them, Perkins was an inspiration; independent yet caring, she combined family and career obligations in an age when few women dared to hope for both.

—Marjorie Murphy

See Also:

Democratic Party, New Deal, Politics, Social Work

References:

Martin, George. *Madam Secretary*. Boston: Houghton Mifflin, 1976.

Perkins, Frances. *The Roosevelt I Knew*. New York: Viking, 1946.

PERRY, LILLA CABOT (1848–1933), painter and poet, was also among the first to introduce the work of the French impressionists to America. A member of the wealthy Boston Cabot family, she married Thomas Sergeant Perry, grandnephew of the distinguished U.S. naval officer Commodore Matthew C. Perry.

Perry studied at the Cowles School of Art in Boston and also in Paris at the Académie

Colarossi and the Académie Julian. Her work was shown in Paris, Berlin, Florence, Dresden, and Munich. Perhaps the greatest influence on her development as an artist was her friendship with Claude Monet. The two met in 1889, and Perry and her family spent ten summers during the next twenty years in a cottage near to Monet's home in Giverny. Although Monet did not officially take in pupils, he encouraged Perry and took a great interest in her work. Perry's painting *Alice on the Path* (1891) hangs in the bedroom of Monet's home, which has been preserved. When in America, Perry lectured and wrote articles on the French impressionists and encouraged other wealthy Americans to buy their work.

Three years spent in Japan, where her husband was professor of English literature, also influenced Perry's artistic development. She had the opportunity to become acquainted with Japanese art and to paint the Japanese landscape and portraits of Japanese people. She also frequently used her three daughters as subjects during this time. After her return to Boston in 1901, Perry became a founder of the Guild of Boston Artists. She painted portraits, landscapes, and genre scenes and exhibited her work throughout the United States. Between 1886 and 1923 she also published four volumes of poetry.

In 1903 Perry purchased a summer home near Hancock, New Hampshire, an area that reminded her of Normandy, and painted many beautiful landscapes. She died there in 1933.

—Christine Miller Leahy

See Also:

Art

References:

King, Alma S. *Lilla Cabot Perry, Days to Remember*. Santa Fe, N.M.: Santa Fe East Galleries, 1983.

Tufts, Eleanor. *American Women Artists 1830–1930*. Washington, D.C.: The National Museum of Women in the Arts, 1987.

Ward, Lisa. "Lilla Cabot Perry and the Emergence of the Woman Artist in America: 1885–1905." M.A. thesis. University of Texas at Austin, 1985.

PHELPS, ELIZABETH STUART (WARD) (1844–1910), author, was born Mary Gray Phelps to Austin Phelps, a professor of homiletics at Andover Seminary, and Elizabeth Stuart Phelps, an author of religious books for children. In 1852, when Mary was eight, her mother died and Mary took her name. During that year her mother had written her fourth book, given birth to her third child, and experienced the death of her father, Moses Stuart, a biblical scholar at Andover Seminary. The child, a boy, was baptized at her coffin, according to his mother's wishes, an experience that left its imprint on young Mary, who soon came to be known as Elizabeth Stuart Phelps.

Phelps took on the literary task as well as the name of her mother. She became a major author of sentimental fiction, beginning with her most famous novel, *The Gates Ajar*, published in 1868. She published fifty-seven books, none of which equaled the popular *Gates Ajar*, though many shared its theme of a down-to-earth description of heaven in a language and theology congenial to a mostly female readership searching for religious consolation outside of orthodox Calvinism.

Phelps's task as a writer was to "represent the age." Her heroines were New England girls who took part in various religious crusades and reform movements. The theme of temperance was treated in *A Singular Life* (1895), while the conflict of marriage and writing for women provided the story lines of *The Story of Avis* (1877) and *Dr. Zay* (1882). Phelps took an active personal role in movements she wrote about and maintained an active interest in reform even to the end of her life, when she was devoted to the cause of antivivisection.

In 1888 Phelps married biblical scholar Herbert Dickenson Ward, a man seventeen years her junior. Though they collaborated on three biblical romances, their marriage was far from compatible. Publicly, Phelps had a successful life, and her private frustrations did not quiet her voice as a major author of sentimental fiction, a moral reformer, and a teacher of religion.

—Maria E. Erling

References:
Douglas, Ann. *The Feminization of American Culture.* New York: Knopf, 1977.
Kelly, Lora Duin. *The Life and Works of Elizabeth Stuart Phelps: Victorian Feminist Writer.* Troy, N.Y.: Whitson, 1983.
Phelps, Elizabeth Stuart. *Chapters from a Life.* Boston: n.p., 1897.
———. *The Gates Ajar.* Boston: Houghton Mifflin, 1868.

The **PHILADELPHIA FEMALE ANTI-SLAVERY SOCIETY (PFAS)** was founded in 1833 to raise public consciousness about slavery and to work for its abolition. Considered one of the first political organizations for women, it served as an important training ground for leaders in the movement for women's rights.

The interracial composition of this mainly Quaker group, which held meetings together and visited in each other's homes, shocked even the abolitionist community. The members became involved in the black community by developing an early welfare system in 1839, supporting black schools, and working with the secular, all-black Vigilance Committee, a principal supporter of the Underground Railroad, to warn free blacks of the approach of kidnappers. In later years the PFAS became involved in petitioning the government and other forms of protest. Throughout its long history, vocal members such as Lucretia Mott and Angelina and Sarah Grimké spoke out against slavery in public forums. The organization supported its programs, including lectures and subscriptions to antislavery publications, by holding annual fairs. At these fund-raising events, members sold pillows and reticules bearing the motto Am I Not a Woman and a Sister? over the image of a kneeling slave with shackled wrists. Sister organizations in New Jersey, Great Britain, and Boston contributed articles to this sale, which often earned sums of approximately $2,000.

After thirty-seven years in the forefront of the antislavery movement, the PFAS formally disbanded in March 1870, following the passage of the Fourteenth Amendment.

—*Cynthia J. Little*

See Also:
Abolition and the Antislavery Movement; Grimké, Angelina; Grimké, Sarah; Mott, Lucretia; Society of Friends

References:
Pennsylvania Abolition Society Collection. The Historical Society of Pennsylvania, Philadelphia, Pa.
Bacon, Margaret Hope. *Valiant Friend: The Life of Lucretia Mott.* New York: Walker, 1980.
Lerner, Gerda. *The Grimké Sisters from South Carolina: Pioneers for Women's Rights and Abolition.* New York: Schocken, 1971.

The **PHILADELPHIA TRAINING SCHOOL FOR NURSES AT PHILADELPHIA GENERAL HOSPITAL** (called Blockley until 1902) was the first American school of nursing to have a Florence Nightingale–trained nurse at its head. Nightingale had previously revolutionized and professionalized nursing care in Britain in the mid-1850s, during and after the Crimean War.

In 1884 an Englishwoman, Alice Fisher, was hired to reorganize the nursing services and to set up a school of nursing at the hospital. Fisher's original two-year training program, which included classes in both nursing theory and ethics, also emphasized the importance of using aseptic techniques. The program required first-year students to work as private nurses, graduating in their second year to the more demanding work on the wards, where their rigid adherence to aseptic techniques brought about a marked drop in maternal mortality.

Fisher's death in 1888, just two years after the first class graduated, did not break the program's continuity because her colleague and friend Edith Horner Hawley took over as her successor. Hawley continued with the Nightingale approach Fisher had instituted, but also expanded the program to train students in nursing practice as well as administration. By 1910 the program had graduated two thousand trained nurses, reflecting the growing popularity of nursing as a career option for women as well as the school's good reputation. In 1909 the program was expanded to three years, and its curriculum was standardized to meet the requirements of the state board of examiners.

The Philadelphia Training School for Nurses graduated its last class in 1977, when Philadelphia General Hospital closed its doors. During its ninety-two-year history, the Philadelphia Training School for Nurses educated a corps of nurses who took leadership roles in nursing education and administration around the world.

—*Cynthia J. Little*

See Also:

Nursing

Reference:

Stachniewicz, Stephanie. *The Double Frill: The History of the Philadelphia General Hospital School of Nursing.* Philadelphia: Stickely, 1978.

PHOTOGRAPHY was "discovered" in 1839, but few women in the United States became photographers prior to the 1880s. The heavy, cumbersome equipment and the public nature of the new medium discouraged women schooled in the tenets of the Cult of True Womanhood from taking up photography.

Even in these early days, however, isolated examples of women photographers could be found. In 1846, for example, Sarah Holcomb of New Hampshire succeeded in overcoming both difficult winters and the often hostile competition of male photographers. Other women were known to take up photography to supplement their incomes. Jane Cook of New York City was both an artist and a daguerreotypist. The San Francisco City Directory of 1850 listed Mrs. J. Shannon as a midwife and a daguerreotypist. But, for the most part, women entering photography did so as assistants to photographer husbands, frequently taking over the studio after a divorce or death of a spouse.

By the 1880s technological advances in the camera encouraged women's participation in photography. Innovations such as dry plates, celluloid roll film, and the hand-held camera tended to democratize photography. Any man, woman, or child with the purchase price of a camera could be a photographer.

Women's entry into photography was also eased by the debate over photography's status as an art form. In this turn-of-the-century controversy, many perceived the new medium as a fad or a scientific innovation. Others, however, like photographer and art patron Alfred Steiglitz, promoted photography as a fine art equivalent to painting. The marginal aspect of photography made it accessible and respectable for women, themselves regarded as subordinate in American society.

Women practiced photography within their domestic environments. Many professional women photographers opened home studios where they specialized in portraiture. Professional and amateur women seemed attracted to what were considered "feminine" subjects—women, children, gardens, pets, and genre subjects. Of course, there were women who went beyond the domestic in their work. Frances Benjamin Johnston and Jessie Tarbox Beals worked as early photojournalists. California photographer Anne Brigman expressed a feminist vision in her images of free-spirited female nudes.

By 1900 over thirty-five hundred women worked as professional photographers, and thousands of others were dedicated amateurs. These photographers acted as pioneers in opening up a new profession for women.

—*C. Jane Gover*

See Also:

Arbus, Diane; Austen, Alice; Beals, Jessie Tarbox; Bourke-White, Margaret; Boyd, Louise A.; Eakins, Susan; Käsebeir, Gertrude; Johnston, Frances Benjamin; Sontag, Susan

References:

Gover, C. Jane. *The Positive Image: Women Photographers in Turn of the Century America.* Albany: State University of New York Press, 1987.

Newhall, Beaumont. *The History of Photography.* New York: Museum of Modern Art, 1982.

Quitslund, Toby. "Her Feminine Colleagues—Photographs and Letters Collected by Frances Benjamin Johnston in 1900." In *Women Artists in Washington Collections,* edited by Josephine Withers. College Park: University of Maryland Art Gallery and Women's Careers for the Arts, 1979, pp. 97–109.

PHYSICIANS. Women have had great difficulty becoming physicians. The first formal medical training facilities in the country after their beginnings in 1765 refused to admit female students. Finally, in 1849 Elizabeth Blackwell (1821–1910) became the first woman in the United States to receive a medical degree from a recognized medical school. After the initial publicity surrounding Blackwell's entrance into the profession had died down, medical colleges for women were founded in Philadelphia in 1850 and shortly thereafter in Boston. In 1863 Clemence Sophia Lozier (1813–88), an M.D. from the Syracuse Eclectic Medical College, succeeded in getting the New York Medical College for women incorporated in 1863.

These institutions succeeded in training a number of women doctors, including Rebecca Lee, who in 1864 was the first black woman to receive her degree from a medical school. Her graduation from the New England Female Medical College in Boston set the stage for other black women to follow. Ann Preston (1813–72) was among the first women to graduate from the Woman's Medical College of Pennsylvania in Philadelphia in 1851. She went on to a successful career as the first female professor at a traditional medical school and later became the first woman dean at a medical college. Mary Edwards Walker (1832–1919) was another of the early pioneers in American medicine. During the Civil War she served as an assistant surgeon and became the first woman to win the Congressional Medal of Honor.

Despite these successes the number of women going into medicine remained small. By 1920 women made up only 5 percent of the profession; by 1976 women were still only 8.6 percent of the physicians in the United States; by 1987 women comprised 15.2 percent of the profession. By 1900 there were 160 black women physicians out of approximately 7000 women physicians. However, by 1920 the number had dropped to 65.

The drop can be attributed to several factors. Even though coeducation had been introduced in medical schools, black women still faced discriminatory barriers due to the increased competition for medical school slots by minorities. In 1910 the Flexner Report, authorized by the Carnegie Foundation, assessed all medical training institutions in the United States, using the Johns Hopkins Medical School as the model for minimum standards. As a result of this report, many medical schools were closed; at least five were black medical schools, all of which were located in the South. This eliminated access to a formal medical education for a large population of blacks. Meharry Medical School, Nashville, founded in 1876, and Howard University Medical School, Washington, D.C., founded in 1868, managed to survive the Flexner Report and maintain financial stability. Howard, however, actually graduated more white women than black women during its first twenty-five years.

The Flexner Report was also detrimental to women's medical schools. Indeed, by 1920, out of at least seventeen medical schools founded for women, the Woman's Medical College of Pennsylvania was, and still is, the only surviving medical school that was begun exclusively to educate women in medicine. During the nineteenth century, the Woman's Medical College of Pennsylvania helped finance the medical education of several black women and graduated at least a dozen black women.

Discrimination also existed for black women physicians in acquiring hospital appointments and membership in medical associations and societies. After graduation, the majority of the nineteenth-century black women physicians set up practice in the South, while white women often interned in a hospital. Since opportunities for hospital appointments were not readily available to black women physicians, they had to begin treating patients immediately with limited experience, while the white women physicians were accepted in some hospitals, affording them the opportunity to gain additional clinical experience under the guidance of an established physician. When internships were made mandatory during the late 1920s, black women were still discriminated against; they were unable to secure internships in the white institutions.

The exclusion of black women physicians from hospitals forced and spurred them to found clinics and hospitals. Blacks were also forced to organize their own organizations and associations. The exclusion of blacks from the American Medical Association led to the establishment of the National Medical Association, founded in 1895 in Atlanta, Georgia. Women were involved with the association from the beginning.

Women of all colors have faced numerous obstacles and challenges in all segments of the medical profession. The fact that the percentage of women physicians in the United States has remained relatively static from 1920 into the 1980s indicates that not all the barriers to women's full participation in the medical community have been overcome.

—*Margaret Jerrido*

See Also:

Blackwell, Elizabeth; Preston, Ann; Woman's Medical College of Pennsylvania; Walker, Mary Edwards

References:

Abram, Ruth J., ed. *Send Us a Lady Physician: Women Doctors in America: 1835–1920.* New York: Norton, 1985.

Chaff, Sandra, Ruth Haimbach, Carol Fenichel, and Nina Woodside. *Women in Medicine: A Bibliography.* Metuchen, N.J.: Scarecrow, 1977.

Davis, Marianna, ed. *Contributions of Black Women to America.* Columbia, S.C.: Kenday, 1982.

Morantz-Sanchez, Regina, ed. *In Her Own Words: Oral Histories of Women.* Westport, Conn.: Greenwood, 1982.

———. *Science and Sympathy: Women Physicians in American Medicine.* New York: Oxford University Press, 1985.

Walsh, Mary. *"Doctors Wanted: No Women Need Apply": Sexual Barriers in the Medical Profession, 1835–1975.* New Haven: Yale University Press, 1977.

PINCKNEY, ELIZA LUCAS (1722–93), agricultural innovator, provided the supreme example of Republican Motherhood—which emphasized both patriotic and domestic virtues—in early America. Pinckney's two sons, Charles Cotesworth and Thomas, had illustrious political careers in the national arena and were considered exemplary patriots who had surely learned the necessary virtues from their mother. But Pinckney accomplished much more than raising notable children. A successful planter in her own right, she was responsible for the introduction of indigo as a viable cash crop into the South Carolina economy.

Born in the West Indies in 1722, she attended school in England before moving to South Carolina with her family in 1737; two years later, her father, George Lucas, departed to become governor of Antigua. Because his wife was an invalid, Lucas left his South Carolina estates (five thousand acres and eighty-six slaves) under the supervision of his oldest child, sixteen-year-old Eliza. She not only succeeded as business manager of her father's three plantations but undertook a series of agricultural experiments in hopes of improving production. Her most successful effort was the successful introduction of indigo.

In 1744 she married widower Charles Pinckney and embarked enthusiastically on a new life as the wife of a wealthy planter. But she continued her interest in agricultural improvements, conducting a series of experiments with flax and hemp and reviving silk culture. When Charles died of malaria in 1758, leaving Pinckney a widow of thirty-six with three young children, she again took upon herself the job of managing the family plantations. Once more, she succeeded in her task, her only major setbacks being the losses created by the American Revolution, particularly the British seizure of Charleston in 1780.

Following the Revolution, Pinckney went to live with her daughter, Harriet, at Hampton, South Carolina, devoting most of the rest of her life to her grandchildren. Stricken with cancer, she went to Philadelphia in search of medical help and died there on May 26, 1793, at the age of seventy.

Eliza Lucas Pinckney succeeded in everything she did. She took advantage of every opportunity presented and worked to instill a desire for success in her children. Her triumphs as wife, mother, and planter reserve her a place among the strong, successful women in American history.

—Carol Sue Humphrey

See Also:

Agriculture, Business

References:

Baskett, Sam S. "Eliza Lucas Pinckney: Portrait of an Eighteenth Century American." *South Carolina Historical Magazine* 72 (October 1971): 207–19.

Pinckney, Eliza. *The Letterbook of Eliza Lucas Pinckney, 1739–1762*. Edited by Elise Pinckney and Marvin R. Zahniser. Chapel Hill: University of North Carolina Press, 1972.

Ravenal, Hariott Horry. *Eliza Pinckney*. New York: Scribner, 1896; rpt. Spartanburg, S.C.: Reprint Co., 1967.

PITCHER, MOLLY (1754–1832) was an American Revolutionary War heroine. On June 28, 1778, at the battle of Monmouth, New Jersey, Pitcher earned her nickname by carrying water from a nearby spring to the American troops and to her husband, John Caspar Hays. After Hays was wounded, Pitcher manned the cannon of Colonel William Irvine's Seventh Company of Pennsylvania Artillery until the American victory.

Born Mary Ludwig, she was the daughter of John George Ludwig, a German dairyman of Mercer County, N.J., but had become a domestic in 1769 for Dr. William Irvine of Carlisle, Pennsylvania. After her husband John Hays's death, Pitcher was married in 1792 to George McCauley. On February 21, 1822, the Pennsylvania legislature voted her a pension for life for her services during the Revolutionary War.

—Ginger Rae Allee

See Also:

Revolutionary War

References:

Green, Henry Clinton, and Mary Wolcott Green. *The Pioneer Mothers of America*. Vol. 2. New York: Putnam, 1912, pp. 217–23, 342.

Leonard, Eugene Andruss, Sophia Drinker, and Miriam Young Holden. *The American Women in Colonial and Revolutionary Times, 1765–1800*. Philadelphia: University of Pennsylvania Press, 1962, p. 118.

Logan, Mary Simmerson. *The Part Taken by Women in American History*. 1912; rpt. New York: Arno, 1972, pp. 162–65.

McDowell, Bart. "The Revolutionary War." *National Geographic* 148 (October 1975): 483–84.

Muir, Charles Stothard. *Women, the Makers of History*. New York: Vantage, 1956, pp. 144–46.

PLANNED PARENTHOOD FEDERATION OF AMERICA, INC. (PPFA). In 1942 Margaret Sanger protested loudly when the American Birth Control League became the Planned Parenthood Federation of America. Sanger claimed to have coined the term *birth control* and justifiably argued her proprietary rights over the organization she had founded and named in 1921. In the early 1940s, however, Sanger no longer had controlling interest in the organization, and its staff of—predominantly male—officers believed that "planned parenthood" made a more positive appeal to the American public than "birth control." Furthermore, the services of the organization, originally aimed exclusively at providing contraceptive information and materials, had been expanded to include aid to infertile couples.

Sanger had worked through the original organization to persuade federal and state governments to include birth control in public health programs. That goal is yet to be entirely realized. Religious and political controversy still dictates birth control policies in many American communities. PPFA continues to be funded largely by donations from corporations, foundations, and individuals. In 1988 the $239-million budget was divided among 761 centers nationwide.

While the range of services varies among individual centers, a typical menu includes information on contraception, abortion, sterilization, infertility, and menopause. Initially appealing primarily to low-income married women, today PPFA services attract a significant number of unmarried teenagers. A typical teenage female client will be required to provide her medical history, undergo a pelvic examination, and view films and accept literature on topics relevant to sexual health and fertility. She may then purchase birth control materials at low cost.

In 1966 Alan F. Gutmacher, a highly respected obstetrician and then president of PPFA, urged the medical profession to work closely with the organization. He furthermore called upon individual centers to enroll a nucleus of female physicians to oversee clinic activities. The guidelines Gutmacher established are still followed whenever possible.

Currently, PPFA sponsors biomedical, socioeconomic, and demographic research. At its annual convention in the fall, the results of this research are presented. At its official headquarters in New York City, PPFA publishes an annual Affiliates Directory and maintains a four-thousand-volume library. Additionally, the PPFA presents the Margaret Sanger Award and the Maggie Awards for media excellence in representing the case for fertility control. The tribute to Sanger implicit in the titles of these awards indicates that Sanger's reputation as the driving force behind the American birth control movement has been reestablished since the 1940s, when her voice had become too strident for many of the conservative male directors of the federation.

Since 1952 PPFA has been affiliated with the International Planned Parenthood Federation. The international organization has established the goal of promoting individual and political acceptance of birth control in order to keep population growth in balance with available resources in target areas like Asia, Africa, and Latin America.

—Mary Lowe-Evans

See Also:

Birth Control; Sanger, Margaret

References:

Gray, Madeline. *Margaret Sanger: A Biography of the Champion of Birth Control.* New York: Richard Marek, 1979.

Himes, N. E. *Medical History of Contraception.* New York: Gamut, 1963.

Kennedy, David M. *Birth Control in America: The Career of Margaret Sanger.* New Haven: Yale University Press, 1970.

Planned Parenthood Federation of America, Inc. *Seventy Years of Family Planning in America: A Chronology of Major Events.* New York: Planned Parenthood Federation of America, 1986.

Reed, James. *The Birth Control Movement and American Society: From Private Vice to Public Virtue.* Princeton: Princeton University Press, 1983.

PLATH, SYLVIA (1932–63), poet and novelist, was born to German immigrant parents. Her father, who taught entomology at Boston University, died when she was eight years old. A fine student, Plath left Smith College for a stint as a guest editor at *Mademoiselle* magazine in New York City. After returning to her mother's home in Wellesley, Massachusetts, she suffered a breakdown and attempted suicide. Institutionalized for a year, Plath returned to Smith and graduated in 1955 with highest honors. She then went on to graduate school on a Fulbright Fellowship to Cambridge University, where she met and married the poet Ted Hughes in 1956.

After teaching at Smith, Plath and Hughes returned to England. She devoted herself to the care of her two children and her writing career. Although crushed by the failure of her marriage in 1962, illness, and the responsibility of raising children, her ordeal stimulated her poetic prowess, and she was producing some of her best work. However, her sense of professional growth was not sufficient to fend off another breakdown. Plath committed suicide on February 11, 1963. During her short life, Sylvia Plath produced a novel, *The Bell Jar,* and a collection of poems of enduring quality. In her personal life as well as in the issues raised by her poetry, Plath has provided a problematical role model for young women poets.

—*Jonathan W. Zophy*

References:

Bundtzen, Lynda. *Plath's Incarnation: Women and the Creative Process.* Ann Arbor: University of Michigan Press, 1983.

Gilbert, Sandra, and Susan Gubar, eds. *The Norton Anthology of Literature by Women: The Tradition in English.* New York: Norton, 1985, pp. 2193–2216, 2417–18.

Plath, Sylvia. *The Bell Jar.* New York: Harper, 1971.

———. *The Collected Poems.* New York: Harper, 1981.

PLURAL MARRIAGE, a form of polygyny based on Old Testament patriarchal models, was introduced during the nineteenth century by the Mormons (Church of Jesus Christ of Latter-day Saints). Joseph Smith, the Mormon prophet-founder, initiated both the theory and practice of polygyny among his leadership cadre in Nauvoo, Illinois, during the early 1840s.

Under Smith's successor, Brigham Young, the main group of Mormons made a great trek west to Utah in the late 1840s, and in 1852 publicly announced their commitment to plural marriage as an integral part of their religious and social system. By the 1880s there were more than one hundred thousand Mormons in the Intermountain West ideologically committed to polygyny as the highest form of marriage, and between 20 and 30 percent of all Mormon families were polygynous. Intense federal pressure nevertheless forced the Mormon church in 1890 to discontinue sanctioning further plural marriages in the United States, and after 1904 recalcitrant polygynists were excommunicated from the church. Today, Mormons are among the staunchest defenders of monogamy, although Mormon splinter groups with perhaps tens of thousands of adherents continue to advocate and practice plural marriage.

Mormon polygyny in the nineteenth century was the focus of bitter controversy. Non-Mormons denounced it as a system of debauchery perpetrated upon Mormon women by an unscrupulous male Mormon leadership, while Mormons defended it as a way of enlarging kinship ties and conforming to God's will. Recent Mormon and non-Mormon scholarship on polygyny has recognized the difficult emotional challenges that plural marriage posed for women, but has also stressed the paradoxical ways in which polygyny sometimes could "liberate" women to play a more active role in society. In the absence of their husbands, plural wives sometimes acted as heads of households, taking on a variety of tasks usually open only to men. Plural wives frequently developed close ties of sisterhood with each other, and they could cooperate in tasks such as child care, freeing an able or ambitious plural wife to obtain advanced education or develop an independent career. Mormon women, many of them plural wives, edited, published, and distributed a distinguished independent women's newspaper, the *Woman's Exponent*, during the late nineteenth and early twentieth centuries. Only in the mid-twentieth century in a staunchly monogamous church has the Mormon quest for respectability led the group to advocate an essentially neo-Victorian domesticity as the only legitimate role for women.

—*Lawrence Foster*

See Also:

Mormonism and Women

References:

Bitton, Davis. "Mormon Polygamy: A Review Article." *Journal of Mormon History* 4 (1977): 101–18.

Casterline, Gail Farr. "'In the Toils' or 'Onward for Zion': Images of the Mormon Woman, 1852–1890." Master's thesis. Utah State University, 1974.

Embry, Jessie L. *Mormon Polygamous Families: Life in the Principle.* Salt Lake City: University of Utah Press, 1987.

Foster, Lawrence. "From Frontier Activism to Neo-Victorian Domesticity: Mormon Women in the Nineteenth and Twentieth Centuries." *Journal of Mormon History* 6 (1979): 3–21.

———. *Religion and Sexuality: The Shakers, the Mormons, and the Oneida Community.* Urbana: University of Illinois Press, 1984, pp. 123–247.

Newell, Linda King, and Valeen Tippets Avery. *Mormon Enigma: Emma Hale Smith—Prophet's Wife, "Elect Lady," Polygamy's Foe.* Garden City, N.Y.: Doubleday, 1984.

Warenski, Marilyn. *Patriarchs and Politics: The Plight of the Mormon Woman.* New York: McGraw-Hill, 1978.

Young, Kimball. *Isn't One Wife Enough?: The Story of Mormon Polygamy.* New York: Holt, 1954.

POLITICS. The inclusion of women into established political participation and positions has been a slow process. During the nineteenth century, unenfranchised women were involved in political organizations that focused upon civic, moral, and other piecemeal legal reforms such as married women's property rights, as well as groups that addressed the conditions of labor and the farmers, relying upon the petition and lobbying of elected officials as their means of access to the political process. Women from Frances Wright to Emma Goldman entered the political arena on behalf of free speech and civil rights as part of the tradition established by women abolitionists. Women held political appointments and even elected offices, especially on school boards, at the local and state level by the late nineteenth century. In 1914 Jeannette Rankin from Montana became the first woman elected to the U.S. House of Representatives, but the potential presence of women in political office was greatly facilitated by the ratification of the Nineteenth Amendment in 1920. However, in 1929 only 122 women served in state legislatures, and by 1937 that number increased only to 140. In 1987 women held 15.8 percent of state legislative seats, 228 in state senates and 949 in state houses.

The women political activists of the Progressive era continued during the 1920s to be involved in the national movements for international peace and worked to preserve accomplishments of the Progressive era such as protective legislation. In the 1930s the New Deal offered women in the Democratic party access to administration policy-making and appointments. After World War II many of these women—Eleanor Roosevelt, for example--continued to work to establish national and international policy regarding peace and humanitarian issues, including disarmament. By the 1960s women were visibly active in the civil rights movement and in the movement against the Vietnam War, as well as for the welter of welfare rights and self-help issues that carried over into the 1970s and 1980s. The "Right to Life" movement politicized heretofore apolitical women, and many one-issue movements were spearheaded and supported largely by women, such as Candy Lightner's Mothers Against Drunk Drivers.

According to the Center for the American Woman and Politics at Rutgers University, women officeholders have increased by 300 percent from 1974 to 1987, spurred by the example of the civil rights movement and the revival of the women's movement during the 1960s. The total number of elected women officeholders in the 1980s was estimated to surpass eighteen thousand; however, at no level did women hold more than 15.8 percent of the elected positions. In the one hundredth U.S. Congress, women held twenty-five seats or 4.7 percent of the total; twenty-three women served in the House of Representatives, and two women served in the Senate.

Of the top executive elective positions, 12.4 percent were held by forty-one women by 1987. Three women served as governors, five as lieutenant governors. One women was an elected attorney general, twelve women served as elected secretaries of state, and nine as elected state treasurers; five women were state auditors, two were state superintendents of public education, and two were corporation commissioners. The presence of Geraldine Ferraro as the vice-presidential nominee on the 1984 Democratic ticket, although unsuccessful, marked an acceptability of women's pursuit of the highest elective offices and opened up opportunities for other women.

Local officers such as mayors and members of municipal and township governing boards were 14.3 percent female as of 1985. Women such as Diane Feinstein of San Francisco and Kathy Whitmire of Houston have proved themselves successful as mayors of large cities. By the 1980s women were serving in powerful political party roles and in local political positions on county boards and city councils that had previously been reserved for male politicians, as well as on the national committees of the major political parties.

—Sue E. Strickler and Angela Howard Zophy

See Also:

Abolition and the Antislavery Movement; Barnard, Kate; Baxter, Annie; Benevolence; Bosone, Reva Beck; Chisholm, Shirley; Curtis, Emma Ghent; Democratic Party; Diggs, Annie Le Porte; Douglas, Helen Gahagan; Emery, Sarah; Ferraro, Geraldine; Haley, Margaret; Jewish Women; Jordan, Barbara; Kahn, Florence Prag; Kreps, Juanita; League of Women Voters; Lease, Mary Elizabeth; Lockwood, Belva; Lusk, Georgia; Lytle, Lutie; Married Women's Property Acts; Moral Reform; National Farmers' Alliance; National Woman's Party; National Women's Political Caucus; Patrons of Husbandry; Perkins, Frances; Populist Party; Progressive Party; Rankin, Jeannette; Republican Party; Right-Wing Political Movements; Socialist Party of America; Suffrage; Temperance Movement; Todd, Marion Marsh; Unions; Valesh, Eva McDonald; Voting Rights; Woman's Peace Party

References:

Moncure, Dorothy. "Women in Political Life." *Current History* 29 (January 1929): 639–43.

National League of Women Voters. *A Survey of Women in Public Office*. Washington, D.C.: National League of Women Voters, 1937.

"Special Report: How Women Will Elect the Next President." *Ms.* 16 (April 1988): 75–80.

POPULAR CULTURE. Women's relationship to popular culture has been an important area for analysis by feminist activists and scholars. Women (in particular, white women) have long been central objects in popular culture artifacts; women have played central roles as consumers of certain popular culture forms (such as novels and soap operas); and in some cases and time periods, women have been significant creators and producers of popular culture.

Feminists have been most concerned about how women are portrayed in popular culture, which is seen as an expression and construction of women's status and position in society. For example, white women have been shown as the sexual object for men to view in advertisements and movies and as symbols of good and evil, while women of color have been either invisible or portrayed as stupid or less than human. At the same time, many women enjoy some forms of popular culture, particularly those in which women are shown as central subjects rather than objects. The novel is one such form, long associated with women writers and readers. Feminists have debated whether or not these forms represent a conservative reinforcement of women's role in patriarchy or some expression of women's discontent and a desire for alternatives.

In those cases where women have been the active creators or consumers, the cultural forms are generally the least valued by mainstream scholars. Alternatively, feminists suggest that it is the association with women and women's experience that leads to the trivialization and devaluation of these cultural forms.

—Lana F. Rakow

See Also:

Movie Stars, Soap Operas, Domestic Literature in The United States

References:

Fishburn, Katherine. *Women in Popular Culture.* Westport, Conn.: Greenwood, 1982.

Gilman, Charlotte Perkins. *The Man-Made World or Our Androcentric Culture.* New York: Charlton, 1911; rpt. New York: Johnson Reprint, 1971.

Peiss, Kathy. *Cheap Amusements: Working Women and Leisure in Turn-of-the-Century New York.* Philadelphia: Temple University Press, 1985.

Rakow, Lana F. "Feminist Approaches to Popular Culture." *Communication* 9 (1986): 19–41.

Wald, Carol. *Myth America: Picturing Women 1865–1945.* New York: Pantheon, 1975.

Weibel, Kathryn. *Mirror, Mirror: Images of Women Reflected in Popular Culture.* Garden City, N.Y.: Doubleday, 1977.

POPULAR VOCALISTS. The history of popular singing in America can be divided into pre- and postelectronic eras. At first, vocalists adapted an operatic approach to the projection of sound so that melody and lyrics would carry over the orchestra and be heard in spacious theaters and clubs. Just as the *castrati,* who combined male lungs with the penetrating sound of the soprano register, were the stars of seventeenth- and eighteenth-century Italian opera, the best known early popular singers were female "belters" like Sophie Tucker and Marion Harris. Even with the introduction of microphones, the devices, except for recording purposes, were largely eschewed by blues singers like Bessie Smith or by musical theater performers like Ethel Merman.

It was inevitable, however, that the microphone would dramatically alter the course of popular singing in America. The contained melodic line, colloquial diction, and informal thematic material of the American popular song as developed by composers like Irving Berlin, George Gershwin, Rogers and Hart, Cole Porter, and Harold Arlen called for an intimate, personal style best realized by singers capable of approaching the microphone not merely as an amplification but as an extension of the human voice. Moreover, the preoccupation in the content of the songs with romantic love and, in particular, with repressed desire insured that, among vocalists of the "Golden Age" of American popular song, females would remain the dominating, most influential performers. Even the notable exception, Frank Sinatra, was quick to acknowledge his primary debt to two women stylists, Mabel Mercer and Billie Holiday.

With the popularity of big bands along with movie and Broadway musicals in the 1930s and 1940s, American popular song flourished, bringing to the public's attention definitive women interpreters like Helen Forest, Judy Garland, Lena Horne, and Dinah Shore. Even with the waning of the golden era of popular song in the 1950s, a number of female vocal artists kept the tradition alive. Rosemary Clooney, Peggy Lee, and Sarah Vaughan were among the first to take advantage of the new long-playing record format, but none exploited this technical innovation more productively than the "first lady of song," Ella Fitzgerald. Her set of LP's recorded for the Verve label may be said to constitute a great American songbook, representing the best work of the major American songwriters of the first half of this century.

The rock revolution of the 1960s changed the role of female as well as male vocalists, shifting the emphasis from the song itself to the performer and performance. Although drawing to a limited extent on the blues tradition of Bessie Smith, Janis Joplin, the prototypal rock performer of the period, was best known for her flamboyant, self-destructive life-style and raw, frenetic concert performances. Besides the "hard rock" style of Joplin, a white performer, another direction in rock music derived from the rhythm and blues as well as gospel roots of black music. Featuring a mellower sound and more modulated passion, the "soul" rock of women vocalists first reached mass audiences through the recordings of Aretha Franklin and Diana Ross. A third and final direction of female popular singing in the 1960s was introduced by Barbra Streisand. A performer who bridges many styles, Streisand primarily reflects the tradition of Broadway and musical theater, updating it with dramatic effects and a sense of exhibitionism that, however controversial among music critics, have won her the steadfast devotion of a legion of fans that seems to grow with each generation.

—Samuel L. Chell

See Also:

Holiday, Billie; Jazz; Smith, Bessie; Waters, Ethel

References:

American Popular Song: Six Decades of Songwriters and Singers. Smithsonian Collection of Recordings. New York: CBS, 1984.

Pleasants, Henry. *The Great American Popular Singers.* New York: Simon & Schuster, 1985.

The **POPULIST PARTY**, a radical third party of the 1890s that had evolved from the National Farmers' Alliance in the 1890s, was one of the few political parties to accept women delegates to its state and national conventions and to employ women in its speakers' bureau. Women who had previously been active in the Farmers' Alliance now endorsed and worked for the People's party.

When farm, labor, and reform organizations gathered in 1891 in Cincinnati to begin forming the Populist party, women delegates were in force, delivering speeches on economic issues facing farmers and laborers, lobbying among male delegates for woman suffrage and temperance, drawing up the party's platform, and negotiating political compromises. Frances Willard of the Woman's Christian Temperance Union (WCTU) and Helen Gougar, a delegate from the Prohibition party, joined the Populist women at the convention. The women delegates and many male delegates believed that the convention would pass, with a large majority, resolutions endorsing suffrage and temperance. Both resolutions, however, were defeated. Undaunted by this defeat, the women attended the National Conference of Industrial Associations in February 1892 in St. Louis to help plan the Populist party nominating convention to be held in Omaha in July. In addition to representing county and state alliances, women also represented the National Women's Alliance and the WCTU. Annie Diggs and Mary Elizabeth Lease were delegates for the National Citizen's Alliance. Other women served on the executive committee. Again the convention failed to pass resolutions on woman suffrage and temperance.

Nevertheless, most of the women continued supporting the party, attending state Populist conventions, and campaigning for Populist candidates. Although a significant number of the delegates at the July nominating convention in Omaha were women, few women were elected to party committees. The activities of the women at this convention were now symbolic gestures and politically less significant than had been the case at previous alliance, Populist, and other third-party conventions. Susan B. Anthony attended the convention to lobby for woman suffrage and was annoyed that Populist women continued to support the party despite the omission of a suffrage plank. After the July convention, Marion Todd, Sarah Emery, Annie Diggs, Mary Elizabeth Lease, and Eva McDonald Valesh toured the country campaigning for James Weaver, the Populist presidential candidate, and other Populists. Other women ran for office on the Populist ticket in state and local elections. Florence Olmstead and Clara Hazelrigg were elected as county school superintendents in Kansas. Mary Elizabeth Lease, Lutie Lytle, Emma Ghent Curtis, and other women received spoils jobs in return for campaigning for Populist governors in Kansas and Colorado. In both states, legislatures with Populist majorities passed women suffrage referenda that then went to the electorate.

In 1893 Colorado women attained suffrage. The suffrage referendum was defeated in Kansas. After the 1892 presidential election and the state elections of 1892 and 1893, women's involvement with Populist politics dwindled in most states. The party joined with the Democrats in 1896 to support the presidential candidacy of William Jennings Bryan, and the radical economic demands of the Populists that women had endorsed were ignored. Women, nevertheless, had gained important organizing, campaigning, and lobbying experience, which many would use in future political work.

—MaryJo Wagner

See Also:

Curtis, Emma Ghent; Diggs, Annie LePorte; Emery, Sarah; Lease, Mary Elizabeth; Lytle, Lutie; National Farmers' Alliance; Todd, Marion Marsh; Valesh, Eva McDonald

References:

Buhle, Mari Jo. *Woman and American Socialism, 1870–1920*. Urbana: University of Illinois Press, 1981.

Jensen, Joan M. *With These Hands*. Old Westbury, N.Y.: Feminist Press, 1981.

Wagner, MaryJo. "Farms, Families, and Reform: Women in the Farmers' Alliance and Populist Party." Diss. University of Oregon, 1986.

PORNOGRAPHY is normally defined as obscene or licentious material, including literature, pictures, and films. The legal definition of pornography remains vague: U.S. Supreme Court Justice Potter Stewart agreed that he could not define pornography, but added that he knew it when he saw it. Most Americans share this combination of ambivalence and certainty.

As an aspect of nineteenth-century sexual commerce, pornographic literature was not published extensively in the United States until the mid-Victorian era. Versions of the "penny dreadfuls" flourished in the 1850s as openly erotic novels or as western adventures that included female seduction. The pornographic pictures and literature eagerly sought by the soldiers in the Civil War were both racist and sexist; after the war, pornographic pictures and literature were available in all-male pool halls and saloons, along with bawdy songs and paintings such as the ubiqitous *Nymphs and Satyr* (A. W. Bouguereau, 1877). By the end of the nineteenth century, pornography ranked as an established urban vice in the eyes of moral reformers and became a focal point in a free-speech battle with the free-lovers over state and community censorship of obscenity.

In both Britain and America, Victorianism brought repression of open discussion or display of all matters sexual in nature. Prior to the 1870s, existing state statutes regulating pornography were few; printed matter had been excluded from the 1842 federal customs law that prohibited the importation of indecent and obscene works of art. Salacious pulp and dime novels could be ordered through the mail. The social purity movement supported moral crusader Anthony Comstock's successful attempt in 1873 to ban pornographic literature, including birth control material, from the mails through a revison of the federal postal law. Upheld by the Supreme Court and generally known as the Comstock Law—"An Act for the Suppression of Trade in, and Circulation of Obscene Literature and Articles of Immoral Use"—this statute empowered appointment of its namesake as a special agent of the post office department to censor the mails for the next forty years. Comstock was responsible for the conviction of thirty-six hundred people for distributing obscene literature and pictures. While only seven states had passed "Little Comstock Acts" by 1900, support from the public as well as from women's groups such as the Woman's Christian Temperance Union urged the other states to enact similar restrictive legislation.

In the early twentieth century, most states passed laws against pornography. These led to famous cases in the mid-twentieth century involving the books *Lady Chatterley's Lover*, *Ulysses*, and *Tropic of Cancer*, which were widely read in the 1920s and 1930s although the first judicial reassessment of an unlimited prohibition based upon an imprecise definition of pornography occurred in the late 1920s and early 1930s. The World War II experience altered social standards and attitudes sufficiently to bring a begrudging acceptance of men's magazines such as *Playboy* by the early 1950s. These publications joined longer-established periodicals such as *Esquire* in a campaign to extend the limits of permissible print and graphic materials that anticipated the coming of the so-called sexual revolution of the 1960s. *Playboy* was in the vanguard of the civil liberties challenge to censorship and intrusive statutes that regulated the sexual activities of married as well as unmarried couples.

Under Chief Justice Earl Warren, the Supreme Court's constitutional definition of obscenity was made more precise and limited between 1957 and 1967. *Roth v. U.S.* in 1957 yielded a legal distinction between sex and obscenity. Moreover, the many obscenity cases that resulted from the moral crusade of the 1950s reached the Supreme Court as popular support for a more permissive social attitude was increasing. The *Fanny Hill* case in 1966 produced a standard of "redeeming social value" for literature that made possible the legal publication and sale of previously banned works and created a hospitable climate for the development of a thriving "sex industry" by the 1980s.

During the 1960s older English and French pornography had been revived and introduced to a growing American (mostly male) audience for such banned materials, initiating another round of litigation. Increasingly explicit "X-rated" movies became available for viewers over eighteen, and a proliferating number of heavily pictorial "soft core" magazines were sold in most newsstands. By the mid-1970s "adult bookstores" appeared along most truck routes or in urban areas formerly designated "red light" districts and even in small towns to offer an increasing variety of "hard core" pornography. Community regulation of such commercial establishments and their wares was complicated by the introduction of the new medium of pornographic home videos, which was not anticipated in existing censorship statutes.

In the 1970s a division occurred among the advocates of women's rights and issues regarding the definition of and the proper feminist response to pornography. The contemporary women's movement had supported liberalization of censorship laws to allow dissemination of contraception information, to facilitate a nonsexist inquiry into human and female sexuality, and to protect the availability of feminist literature despite local community hostility. However, by the mid-1970s activist feminists in such groups as Women Against Violence Against Women and Women Against Pornography used the debasement of and physical violence against women rather than the explicit sexual depiction to distinguish "erotic" materials from those that they called "pornographic."

Feminists who had challenged sexual violence against women in the media supported local ordinances, such as those proposed in Minneapolis and Indianapolis, that would allow individual women to decide if certain material was detrimental to their civil rights. This assault on antiwoman obscenity in commercial pornography that degraded women rendered ardent feminists such as Andrea Dworkin and Catharine McKinnon both de facto political allies of the antifeminist "Moral Majority" and opponents of the usually profeminist American Civil Liberties Union. The scandal of the illegal use of minors of both sexes by the pornography industry further complicated the discernment of one "politically correct" feminist response to the issues involved in pornography.

Without a precise legal and social definition of pornography, sexually explicit materials have historically presented a dilemma to the women's movement. Dissemination of publications by feminists and the proponents of women's rights have suffered at the hands of the minions of censorship and often both the free speech and the literature of the women's movement has been designated and banned as pornography. While free speech and freedom of the press have been necessary to the feminist cause, many women's issues were grounded in opposition to the sexist attitudes and practices that defined women as lesser beings and sex objects, both of which are mainstay and popular themes in pornographic literature and art. Thus, commercial pornography characteristically purveyed sexually explicit material that was far more likely to express misogynistic hostility to women than to explore a sensuality that is erotic to adults of both sexes. The issue of how to respond to pornography remains a divisive one among supporters of women's rights and feminist theorists.

—William G. Shade and Angela Howard Zophy

See Also:

Comstock Law, Female Sexuality, Obscenity, Sexual Revolution

References:

Commission on Obscenity and Pornography. William B. Lockart, Chairman. Washington, D.C.: U.S. Government Printing Office, 1970.

D'Emilio, John, and Estelle B. Freedman. *Intimate Matters: A History of Sexuality in America.* New York: Harper & Row, 1988.

Dworkin, Andrea. *Pornography: Men Possessing Women.* New York: Putnam, 1981.

Pivar, David. *Purity Crusade: Sexual Morality and Social Control, 1868–1900.* Westport, Conn.: Greenwood, 1973.

St. John-Stevas, Norman. *Obscenity and the Law.* London: Secken and Warberg, 1956.

PREMARITAL SEX has been a constant occurrence throughout American history. As usual in sexual matters, church and society have dealt more harshly with women who engaged in premarital relations than with males. Fines, whipping, or both were common punishments for fornication in colonial times. Puritan New Englanders tried to marry off children as quickly as possible in order to limit premarital sexual activity. A greater leniency was displayed toward betrothed couples who engaged in sex before marriage than those who had made no such commitment. On the eve of the American Revolution, one-third of New England brides went to the altar "with child."

Premarital pregnancy rates declined from 20 percent in the 1830s to 10 percent in the 1850s among the white middle class. Romantic notions of life and continued societal pressure for female purity seem to be among the factors responsible for this change. Within the middle class, sexual desires had become increasingly fused with a romantic intimacy and, for some, spiritual union, even as community controls over behavior lessened.

The premarital pregnancy rate, however, rose significantly to 23 percent in the decades from 1880 to 1910. The increase seems to have occurred mostly among working-class women, whose numbers expanded as American society became increasingly industrialized and traditional romantic notions and other forms of social control declined.

The situation changed again in the twentieth century. When Alfred Kinsey examined the subject in 1953, he found a clear rise in female premarital sexual activity after World War I. Each generation since has exhibited increases in premarital sexual activity, especially by women. Between 80 and 90 percent of women by the 1980s were having intercourse before marriage, and there were very few virgins graduating from high school. However, this trend has a colonial cast to it, because women usually think at the time that they are going to marry their partner. One sociologist of the 1960s described this behavior as "permissiveness with affection" rather than promiscuity.

In the late twentieth century, middle-class parents are likely to accept the idea of their children "living together" with a lover. Although the availability of birth control has made premarital sex "safe," there is a "crisis" of teenage pregnancy, with more pregnant teenage girls than ever before and more abortions. The image of the adult "swinging single" exaggerates the situation for those in their twenties and thirties; most single or divorced people acknowledge that dating and the expectation of sex have become synonymous. By the 1980s, white women in their twenties reported that they had had sex with between four and five men, with half of these being casual contacts. Fear of AIDS and other venereal diseases had a sobering effect on sexual freedom as the 1980s came to a close.

—*William G. Shade*

See Also:

AIDS, Female Sexuality, Marriage

References:

Hunt, Morton. *Sexual Behavior in the 1970s.* New York: Dell, 1974.

Reiss, Ira. *The Social Context of Premarital Sexual Permissiveness.* New York: Holt, Rinehart and Winston, 1967.

Smith, Daniel Scott, and Michael S. Hindus. "Premarital Pregnancy in America, 1640–1966: An Overview and an Interpretation." *Journal of Interdisciplinary History* 5 (Spring 1975): 537–70.

Travis, Carol, and Susan Sadd. *The Redbook Report on Female Sexuality.* New York: Dell, 1977.

Vinovskis, Maris. *An "Epidemic" of Adolescent Pregnancy? Some Historical & Policy Considerations.* New York: Oxford University Press, 1987.

PRESBYTERIAN WOMEN'S GROUPS. Women's participation in the Presbyterian church in the United States was affected by a schism that occurred between the Presbyterian Church in the USA, (PCUSA; later, United Presbyterian Church in the USA) and the Presbyterian Church in the United States, (PCUS, or Southern Presbyterian Church) in 1862. In the early nineteenth century, women in the Presbyterian church organized independent benevolent societies to support foreign and domestic missionaries, teachers, doctors, orphans, and widows, breaking with male organizations that gave women no decision-making power.

The General Assembly of the PCUSA in 1811 first publicly declared its support of the work of "pious females," but it warned the societies to engage only in services for women and children because these causes were considered appropriate for ladies. Though some pastors resisted, many encouraged the women's societies because they proved successful in fund raising for missions and in providing valuable services to the congregation.

After the Civil War, the missionary societies concentrated their efforts exclusively on foreign or home missions or work with freedmen. The societies organized regional boards, such as the Women's Presbyterian Board of Mission of the Northwest and the Women's Foreign Missionary Society of the Presbyterian Church, to which auxiliaries in local churches belonged. The first denominational woman's board, the Women's Executive Committee of Home Missions (WEC), was formed in 1878, with F. E. H. Haines as president, to benefit and cooperate with the Board of Home Missions. Katherine Bennett, who became president in 1909, further established the board's financial and programmatic independence by winning its incorporation in 1915, making it the first women's organization to report directly to the General Assembly. The regional foreign missionary societies operated independently of each other until 1885, when they united to form the Committee of Presbyterian Women for Foreign Missions; it joined with the Board of Foreign Missions in 1920.

In the 1920s the General Assembly Council eliminated of the PCUSA eliminated the separate women's boards and later created the Women's Joint Committee to unite all benevolent societies into "inclusive societies." The Presbyterian Women's Organization (later, United Presbyterian Women) oversaw women's activities and advocated representation for and ordination of women. The Cumberland Presbyterian Church (CPC; merged with the PCUSA in 1906) and the United Presbyterian Church of North America (UPNA) created similar structures for their women members. The UPNA merged with PCUSA in 1958 to form the United Presbyterian Church in the United States of America (UPCUSA).

The campaign to ordain women to the offices of deacon, elder, and minister grew out of the question of whether women should be allowed to address audiences of mixed sexes on benevolent concerns and to lead prayer meetings. The office of deacon first opened to women because of the nurturing and outreach mission of the diaconate. Women were ordained to ruling elder status later: UPNA, 1906; CPC, 1921; PCUSA, 1923.

There were some isolated attempts to ordain women to the ministry. Louisa Woosley (CPC), ordained in 1889, and Elizabeth Brinton Clark (UPNA), ordained in 1944, both had their ordinations invalidated soon after. The PCUSA rejected ordination amendments to its constitution twice before such an amendment finally passed in 1955–56. Margaret Towner was ordained in October 1956.

After the southern presbyteries of the Presbyterian Church in the USA split off in 1861 over a theological difference stemming from the Civil War, southern women continued their fund-raising work for home and foreign missions and auxiliary societies. The societies did not organize into regional groups like their PCUSA counterparts because of resistance from conservative ministers who feared the creation of a "women's church." However, Jennie Hanna and Mrs. Josiah Sibley formed the first "presbyterial" in 1888; "synodicals" were started in 1904. Despite vociferous opposition from some men, the General Assembly in 1912 approved a superintendent of women's work at the denomination level for coordination of the women's efforts and promotion to women of educational, spiritual, and mission programs of the entire church. Hallie Paxson Winsborough (1912–29), as first superintendent (later, secretary), renamed the organization the

Women's Auxiliary, drawing together the various local church societies into one group. The Women's Auxiliary was at first advised by the four male secretaries of the executive committees of the PCUS; in 1927, this supervisory committee was replaced by an advisory council composed of women representatives from each synodical.

The Auxiliary, and later, Women of the Church (WOC) planned and sponsored churchwide conferences, leadership development workshops, and educational literature for Bible and mission studies along with the Board of Women's Work (BWW, later the Office of Women's Work and other successors). The program of WOC grew to include special committees on race and community relations and ecumenical and interdenominational efforts. WOC taught women leadership skills and enabled them to move into governing positions in the church and in society when these positions opened to them.

After years of silence, in the 1950s WOC and the BWW lobbied for equal representation of women on all boards, agencies, and committees in the PCUS. Though women had been appointed to executive and special committees since 1923, the BWW wanted to have at least one-third representation. The issue of ordination of women became a priority after the defeat of an ordination amendment in 1955. It had been fiercely opposed by conservatives, male and female, who thought it unscriptural for women to preach, lead prayer, or even speak before mixed-sex audiences. In 1963 the committee rewriting the church's constitution deleted gender references in the section on qualifications for ordination; the change passed in 1964 with little opposition. Rachel Henderlite was ordained to the ministry in May 1965.

In 1983 the UPCUSA and the Presbyterian church in the United States reunited after a 121-year split. United Presbyterian Women and Women of the Church approved their design for reunion in July 1988 and became Presbyterian Women.

—Diana Ruby Sandersen

See Also:

Christianity

References:

Annual Reports of the Women's Auxiliary, Committee on Women's Work, the Board of Women's Work, the Office of Women's Work and Office of Women (1913–83). PC (USA) Department of History (Montreat), Montreat, N.C.

Annual Reports of Women's Executive Committee of Home Missions, Woman's Board of Home Missions, Woman's Board of Foreign Missions, United Presbyterian Women. PC (USA) Department of History, Philadelphia, Pa.

Boyd, Lois A., and R. Douglas Brackenridge. *Presbyterian Women in America: Two Centuries of a Quest for Status.* Westport, Conn.: Greenwood, 1983.

Farrior, Louise H. *Journey Toward the Future.* Atlanta: Williams, 1987.

Minutes of the General Assemblies of the Presbyterian Church in the United States (1912–83), Presbyterian Church in the United States of America (1811–1957), the United Presbyterian Church of North America (1858–1957), United Presbyterian Church in the United States of America (1957–83).

Winsborough, Hallie Paxson. *Yesteryears.* Atlanta: Assembly's Committee on Women's Work, 1937.

PRESCRIPTIVE LITERATURE was primarily written during the early- to mid-nineteenth century. As the industrial age began, men's and women's roles were being redefined. The printing press had made production and nationwide distribution of literature economical, and for the first time the majority of published texts were concerned with defining the role of the American woman. While the man was expected to go out into the world and earn a living for the family, the woman's proposed place was in the home. Ministers began the crusade of prescription by advocating the role of submissive woman. Their sermons and published tracts upheld the idea of the woman as the moral guiding light for the family. An explosion of literature written mostly by men was published during this time, defining the behavior of the model woman as pure, pious, and gentle. Sarah Josepha Hale edtited *Godey's Lady's Book,* which held the belief of women's domestic sphere but also encouraged women to increase their influence. It is important to note that this literature was intended almost exclusively for the middle- to upper-class white urban woman. The impact it had on this class of women is hard to determine, but it is generally accepted that this literature did help to cement the stereotype of the American woman that remained for several decades.

—*Cynthia Bragg*

See Also:

Cult of True Womanhood, Domestic Literature, *Godey's Lady's Book*

References:

Berkin, Carol Ruth, and Mary Beth Norton. *Women of America: A History.* Boston: Houghton Mifflin, 1979.

Ryan, Mary P. *Womanhood in America.* New York: Watts, 1983.

Woloch, Nancy. *Women and the American Experience.* New York: Knopf, 1984.

The **PRESIDENT'S COMMISSION ON THE STATUS OF WOMEN** was established by President John F. Kennedy in 1961 as a result of the persuasion of Esther Peterson of the U.S. Women's Bureau and other influential women within the Democratic party who voiced their concern regarding the lack of women appointees to significant federal positions within the Kennedy administration.

The ailing but venerable Eleanor Roosevelt chaired this advisory commission of thirteen women and eleven men, which utilized seven investigatory committees, assisted by scores of consultants as well as the Women's Bureau staff, as it conscientiously conducted a formal federal inquiry into women's legal and social status. To honor its late chairperson, who died in 1962, the commission presented its report, entitled *American Women,* to President Kennedy on October 11, 1963, Eleanor Roosevelt's birthday.

The sixty-page report reflected the social and political agenda of its appointees and the political preference of the Kennedy administration in its rejection of the Equal Rights Amendment as the appropriate means for securing women's legal equality, which, the report suggested, could be achieved under the existing Fourth and Fourteenth amendments. Both the social feminists and organized labor opposed the ERA as a threat to their hard-won protective legislation for women workers.

In this, the first comprehensive federal review of the social, legal, and political status of women, the commission endeavored simultaneously to support both women's special role in the family and their increased access to paid employment. After citing as unacceptable existing discriminations against women and offering suggested reforms, the report endorsed equal and increased opportunity for women in education as well as in full- and part-time employment, paid maternity leave, day care, and other crucial community services for working mothers. The report challenged the federal government to demonstrate through its federal programs a working model of equal employment opportunity for women. As a result of this report, the Equal Pay Act of 1963 amended the Fair Labor Standards Act and became the first federal ban on wage discrimination based solely on sex.

This report initiated and delineated a national discussion of women's issues that coincided with the resurgence of the women's movement in the mid-1960s. Moreover, each state subsequently followed this federal precedent for statute and policy review by establishing similar commissions that provided state governmental access and support for the efforts of feminists to remedy inequities for women at the state level. Finally, as a result of exasperation at the snail's pace of actual achievement of reform by the Third National Conference of the Commissions on the Status of Women in 1966, the National Organization for Women was founded as a result of an informal caucus of twenty-eight conference women in the hotel room of feminist leader and author Betty Friedan.

—*Angela Howard Zophy*

See Also:

Equal Pay Act; Equal Rights Amendment; Friedan, Betty; National Organization for Women; Protective Legislation; Roosevelt, Eleanor; Social Feminism

References:

Daniel, Robert L. *American Women in the Twentieth Century: The Festival Of Life.* New York: Harcourt Brace Jovanovich, 1987.

President's Commission on the Status of Women. *American Women.* Washington, D.C.: U.S. Government Printing Office, 1963.

Riley, Glenda. *Inventing the American Woman: A Perspective on Women's History.* Arlington Heights, Ill.: Harlan Davidson, 1987.

Woloch, Nancy. *Women and the American Experience.* New York: Knopf, 1984.

PRESTON, ANN, M.D. (1813–72), Quaker reformer, physician, and educator, became the first woman professor at a "regular" medical college in the United States and the first woman dean of a medical school. As dean of the Female Medical College of Pennsylvania from 1865 to 1872, Preston was responsible for a significant increase in the opportunities available for women to train and practice as physicians. A member of the first graduating class of the Female Medical College of Pennsylvania in 1851, Preston returned as a faculty member and repeatedly and unsuccessfully sought admission for her students to clinics at the many hospitals in Philadelphia in the 1850s. Her requests were denied by male physicians and administrators who sought to keep women out of organized medicine. In response to the need for clinical training for women medical students, Preston founded the Woman's Hospital of Philadelphia in 1861. There, also, she began the first nurses' training school in America.

Like so many of the women reformers of the latter half of the nineteenth century, Preston was a persuasive speaker and writer, talents she placed in the service of the social issues of abolition, temperance, and woman's rights. It is on this last issue that Ann Preston made her most lasting contributions. As a Quaker, she believed in the traditional role of women in the household; she herself lived at home until well into her thirties, taking care of her mother and siblings. As a Hicksite Quaker, one who followed the liberal preacher Elias Hicks, she also believed in a woman's right to speak and travel in public and to engage in the same professions as males, be it the ministry or medicine. Following the direction of her own inner light, at the age of thirty-seven she enrolled in the first class of students at the newly incorporated Female Medical College of Pennsylvania, the first woman's medical college in the modern world. Upon graduation and for the twenty-one remaining years of her life, she devoted herself to the survival and continued improvement of the college (renamed the Woman's Medical College of Pennsylvania in 1867) and to the advancement of sound medical education for women.

Although ideologically radical, Preston used traditional methods to attain her goals. Believing in the concept of Woman's Sphere, she urged the expansion of that sphere to whatever extent necessary to provide women with the opportunity to live independent, productive lives. By the time of her death in 1872, many of the goals she had worked toward, including increased clinical opportunities for women medical students, higher scholastic standards at the college, and recognition of women physicians by the male medical profession, had been successfully realized in Philadelphia, the center of medical education in the United States at that time.

—*Sandra L. Chaff*

See Also:

Physicians, Society of Friends, Woman's Hospital of Philadelphia

References:

Archives and Special Collections on Women in Medicine. The Medical College of Pennsylvania, Philadelphia, Pa. Records of the Medical College of Pennsylvania (formerly the Female Medical College of Pennsylvania and the Woman's Medical College of Pennsylvania).

Chaff, Sandra L., Ruth Haimbach, Carol Fenichel, and Nina Woodside. *Women in Medicine: A Bibliography of the Literature on Women Physicians.* Metuchen, N.J.: Scarecrow, 1977.

Foster, Pauline. "Ann Preston, M.D. (1813–1872): A Biography. The Struggle to Obtain Training and Acceptance for Women Physicians in Mid-Nineteenth Century America." Diss. University of Pennsylvania, 1984.

PRICE, LEONTYNE (b. 1927) is an operatic soprano, whose life exemplifies the possibilities of women, particularly of American black women. Born into a musical family, Price's southern upbringing in Laurel, Mississippi, was full of her mother's solos in the church choir and her father's tuba playing. Already having begun piano lessons at the age of four, Price soon joined her mother in the church choir.

The young singer obtained her musical training at Central State College in Wilberforce, Ohio, and the Juilliard School of Music in New York, where she studied voice with renowned concert vocalist and mentor Florence Kimball. In 1952, after she appeared in a Juilliard production, composer Virgil Thomson invited her to appear in his opera *Four Saints in Three Acts* on Broadway and in Paris at the International Arts Festival. Her career developing quickly, Price was invited to sing the role of Bess in a revival of Gershwin's *Porgy and Bess*, and she toured with the company in Europe. In 1953 she sang the premieres of works by major composers like Samuel Barber and Igor Stravinsky, and in November 1954 she made her concert debut as a soprano at Town Hall in New York.

From then on, honors came swiftly. In 1955 she made her television debut in Puccini's *Tosca* with the NBC Opera, thereby becoming the first black singer to appear in a televised opera. In 1957 she made her operatic debut in Poulenc's *Dialogues of the Carmelites* with the San Francisco Opera, and her debut at the Metropolitan Opera in New York in 1961 as Leonora in Verdi's *Il Trovatore* was the occasion of an historic forty-two-minute ovation.

Price's uniqueness seems an extension of her personal independence. She has said that the secret to her whole being is that what she is as a woman is what she hears in the sound of her voice. In the years after her divorce from bass-baritone William Warfield in 1973, Price developed a liking for her independence. National committees and organizations across the country have recognized her with numerous honors, including four honorary doctorates, the Presidential Medal of Freedom (1964), the NAACP Spingarn Medal (1965), and the Order of Merit from Italy. She has also been appointed to national boards and committees of professional, civic, and government organizations like the YWCA and has been recognized and honored by music and recording industries. She also received the Kennedy Center Honor in 1980 and the National Medal of Art in 1985.

Well into her fifties, Leontyne Price revived her unsurpassed *Aida* in 1981 in San Francisco. She continues to give benefit recitals when possible and encourages and supports young artists in her field.

—*Mary Frances Concepción*

See Also:

Black Women, Music

References:

Cliburn, Van, and Richard Mohr. "In Praise of Leontyne." *Opera News* 46 (January 23, 1982): 8–11.

Lyone, Hugh L. *Leontyne Price: Highlights of a Prima Donna.* New York: Vantage, 1973.

Rubin, Stephen E. "Price on Price." *Opera News* 40 (March 6, 1976): 16–20.

PRISON REFORM. The 1840s marked the beginning of a broad movement to reform the prisons in which women were incarcerated. In New York City, for example, Protestant missionaries Phoebe Palmer and Sarah Platt, concerned with the spiritual needs of women inmates, began to visit them in the Tombs, one of the city's jails. At the same time, members of the New York Female Moral Reform Society used their religious message to convert and reform young jailed prostitutes. Reform-minded women also joined the Female Department, the auxiliary of the Prison Association of New York, and worked to strengthen religious beliefs among women prisoners. This group was led by Abby Hopper Gibbons, and it opened a halfway house in 1845. A Women's Prison Association and Home was established in that same year. Also in the 1840s Abby Gibbons joined with Josephine Shaw Lowell to campaign in New York for separate women's prisons operated by women. In Massachusetts, Hannah Chickering founded the Dedham Asylum for Discharged Female Prisoners. Chickering and Mary Pierce Door served on the Massachusetts Prison Commission and, with Ellen Cheney Johnson and Clara Temple Leonard, led a campaign for a separate prison for women. Connecticut, New York, and Massachusetts appointed women to the state prison boards. Women participated increasingly in professional prison associations, such as the National Prison Congress and National Conference on Charities and Corrections.

The efforts of individuals grew into a broader reform movement after the Civil War. By the late 1800s this work led to an increased professionalism among these reformers, who also began formulating a new view of female criminals, one emphasizing the social causes of crime rather than the idea of "the fallen woman." A more sympathetic view of women offenders was developed, which identified economic conditions and sexual exploitation as principal causes of crime.

By World War I, a second generation of women prison reformers had emerged. Among the most prominent was Francis Kellor, a criminologist who argued against biological determinism. Other reformers expanded this research, and they also challenged the methods of operating women's prisons. Many favored preventative services rather than incarceration as the best means of curbing crime. In addition, organizations such as the YWCA, Immigrant Protective League, and Big Sisters worked hard to keep young women away from crime. Some reformers from the Women's Prison Association advocated probation rather than incarceration for females, and the number of women placed on probation doubled from 1907 to 1913. Women's courts were established, and new versions of prisons were developed by Katharine Bement Davis and Jessie Donaldson Hodder. These institutions were organized on the cottage system, and they offered academic and vocational classes.

During the 1920s and 1930s attitudes and emphasis shifted. For example, the crackdown on prostitution that followed World War I sent a large number of women to jail. New women's prisons were constructed. During Prohibition, women were sentenced to terms in reformatories for alcohol and narcotic offenses. Popular views of female offenders hardened. The 1930s marked an end to a century of women's prison reform, as the nation's penal institutions moved away from reform and became custodial in nature.

Only with the emergence of the women's movement of the 1960s and 1970s has a renewed professional and scholarly interest in female incarceration emerged. These critics have challenged the legitimacy of separate prisons for women by exposing their inequities. One response has been the reintroduction of prisons housing both male and females.

—*Robert G. Waite*

See Also:
Criminals, Women's Prisons

References:

Burkhart, Kathryn Watterson. *Women in Prison.* Garden City, N.Y.: Doubleday, 1973.

Freedeman, Estelle B. *Their Sisters Keepers: Women's Prison Reform in America, 1830–1930.* Ann Arbor: University of Michigan Press, 1981.

McKelvey, Blake. *American Prisons: A History of Good Intentions.* Montclair, N.J.: Patterson Smith, 1977.

The **PROGRESSIVE ERA** is the designation that historians have generally bestowed upon that period of U.S. development between the "Gilded Age" of the late nineteenth century and the 1920s, years that seemingly were characterized by an extraordinary commitment to "reform" and "progress." Although marked by such incredible complexity and diversity that scholars still debate furiously over its origins, nature, persistence, and legacy, the Progressive era is best understood as a period of broad-gauged, multifaceted reforms set against the backkdrop of the emergence of the United States as a modern, urban, industrial, multicultural world power. Many of these efforts involved voluntary action in the private sector by groups or organizations acting out of perceived self-interest, altruism, or ideological conviction, ranging from labor unions and trade associations to settlement houses and social gospel churches. At the same time, the era was characterized by an unprecedented flurry of political activism and legislative enactments at the municipal, state, and, to a lesser extent, federal levels of government. Historians have traditionally divided reforms of this era into those that were aimed at efficiency and regulation of industry—such as the creation of the Federal Reserve Board—and those that focused on social justice—minimum-wage legislation, for example. Women reformers were especially active in the social justice branch of Progressive era reform.

Whatever their disagreements regarding the contours of this critical reformist era, historians generally concur that women played an unprecedentedly major role in reform. This was especially true of the emerging class of well-educated professional women, of those upper- and middle-class females with greatly increased leisure time due to technological innovation, and of those in the industrial working class struggling to improve the conditions of their labor. Although the majority of women, especially in rural and small-town areas, remained uninvolved in these wider currents, millions became either "feminists" committed to improving their own status or "social feminists," who were convinced that women could and should play a critical role in the betterment of all society.

Women were especially active in the contest over woman suffrage, constituting not only the National American Woman Suffrage Association, which was successfully led by Carrie Chapman Catt, the National Woman's party of Alice Paul and Lucy Burns, and the Political Equality League, but also the National Association Opposed to Woman Suffrage. Through the settlement house movement, which encouraged educated youth to "settle" and work among the urban poor, women such as Jane Addams and Sophonisba Breckenridge created the profession of social work; their practical experience and involvement in aiding the poor and ethnic minorities brought them into political and organized-labor activities. Working-class females, often with the cooperation and encouragement of professionals and socialites, fought to improve their wages, hours, and working conditions through such organizations as Florence Kelley and Mary Dreier's Women's Trade Union League, which worked with Clara Lemlich and the International Ladies Garment Workers Union, the American Association for Labor Legislation, and various teachers' federations and central labor unions. Women led the lobby against child-labor abuses in the National Child Labor Committee and against shoddy products and exorbitant prices in the National Consumers' League, which was led by such women as Josephine Shaw Lowell and Alice Woodbridge.

Women helped found and operate a variety of organizations designed to aid ethnic minorities, including the North American Civic League for Immigrants, the Immigrants' Protective League of Chicago, which was directed by Grace Abbott, the National Association for the Advancement of Colored People, which benefited from the participation and leadership of Ida Wells-Barnett and Mary Church Terrell, and the National Urban League. The General Federation of Women's Clubs, most notably during the presidency of Mrs. Sarah Platt Decker, involved hundreds of thousands in a wide variety of reform movements, including conservation, public health, education, and library extension work. Especially under the leadership of Frances Willard, the Woman's Christian Temperance Union crusaded for a myriad of social reforms in addition to prohibition. Women were also prominent in the movements for mental health, social hygiene, and birth control, and many such as Elizabeth Gurley Flynn and Kate

Richards O'Hare even joined such radical organizations as the Industrial Workers of the World and the Socialist party. During World War I, women escalated their social involvement in a variety of causes, including nursing, morale building, selling war bonds, or peace advocacy, accomplishments that convinced many previously skeptical men of the legitimacy of woman suffrage and feminism.

—*John D. Buenker*

See Also:

Antisuffragism, Black Women's Clubs, General Federation of Women's Clubs, Immigrant Protective League, Minimum-Wage Laws, National American Woman Suffrage Association, National Consumers' League, National Woman's Party, National Women's Trade Union League, Politics, Progressive Legislation, Protective Legislation, Settlement House Movement, Social Feminism, Social Housekeeping, Socialism, Suffrage, Teaching as an Occupation for Women, Unions, Woman's Christian Temperance Union, World War I

References:

Beard, Mary. *Woman's Work in Municipalities.* New York: Appleton, 1915; rpt. New York: Ayer, 1985.

Buenker, John D., and Nicholas C. Burckel. *Progressive Reform: A Guide to Information Sources.* Detroit: Gale, 1980.

Chambers, John Whiteclay II. *The Tyranny of Change.* New York: St. Martin's, 1980.

Link, Arthur S., and Richard L. McCormick. *Progressivism.* Arlington Heights, Ill.: Harlan Davidson, 1983.

Painter, Nell. *Standing at Armageddon: The United States, 1877–1919.* New York: Norton, 1987.

Scott, Anne Firor. *The Southern Lady: From Pedestal to Politics, 1830–1930.* Chicago: University of Chicago Press, 1972.

PROGRESSIVE LEGISLATION. The Progressive era was characterized by a veritable flood of legislation, especially at the state level, that dealt directly with the interests and concerns of women. Between 1911 and 1919, thirty-nine states enacted some type of "mothers' pension" laws that provided for financial aid to widows with dependent children in order to avoid the necessity of placing dependent children in institutions. The majority of states also passed legislation regulating the wages, hours, and conditions of employment for women who labored in factories, in response to pressure from such organizations as the National Consumers' League, the National Women's Trade Union League, and the American Association for Labor Legislation.

Organized labor, dominated by men, was ambivalent about such legislation, fearing that the minimal standards enacted by law would become the norm and undermine collective bargaining, but union leaders generally supported such efforts for female workers. Some staunch feminists were similarly ambivalent, fearing that such preferential treatment might undermine their arguments in favor of sexual equality, but these were far outnumbered by the "social feminists," who believed that such concerns were trivial compared with the immediate plight of laboring women.

The beginnings of these reforms predate the Progressive era. In 1893 the Illinois legislature passed legislation mandating a maximum eight-hour day for women, but the state supreme court found it to be unconstitutional. In *Lochner v. New York* (1906), the U.S. Supreme Court struck down a New York "ten-hour law" for women on the grounds that it violated their freedom to contract. The same fate befell other such attempts until 1908, when the Supreme Court, at the urging of the National Consumers' League and its attorney, Louis D. Brandeis, upheld an Oregon law providing for a ten-hour day for women in the case of *Muller v. Oregon.* Thirty-nine states adopted maximum-hours laws by World War I. Minimum-wage laws were slower to materialize, but several studies by government agencies and private foundations between 1910 and 1913 clearly documented the effect of low wages on women, especially the recourse of many to prostitution as a more lucrative source of income. Beginning with Massachusetts in 1912, several states enacted minimum-wage laws. Most industrial states also enacted laws regulating the conditions of labor for women in industry, with the New York Factory Investigating Commission providing the model legislation between 1911 and 1914. Working women also benefited from the workmen's compensation systems and industrial commissions that most industrial states created during the Progressive era. Nearly every state and the federal government enacted laws to suppress prostitution, culminating in the passage of the Mann Act, also known as the White Slave Traffic Act, in 1910.

Beginning with Wyoming in 1890, several western states passed woman suffrage laws in the late nineteenth century, while others, such as Wisconsin, allowed women to vote in school bond elections only, since public education was perceived as an extension of women's nurturing role. In 1913 Illinois became the first major urban industrial state to enact woman suffrage, albeit for offices not created by the state constitution and for the presidency of the United States. All told, twenty states adopted some form of woman suffrage prior to the adoption of the Nineteenth Amendment in 1920. The Progressive era was thus a pioneering period in terms of legislation designed to meet the needs of women, one that established important precedents but left much to be done.

—John D. Buenker

See Also:

Minimum-Wage Laws, Mothers' Pensions, *Muller v. Oregon*, Progressive Era, Social Feminism

References:

Buenker, John D., and Nicholas C. Burckel. *Progressive Reform: A Guide to Information Sources*. Detroit: Gale, 1980.

Flexner, Eleanor. *Century of Struggle: The Women's Rights Movement in the United States*. Cambridge: Harvard University Press, 1975.

Link, Arthur S., and Richard L. McCormick. *Progressivism*. Arlington Heights, Ill.: Harlan Davidson, 1983.

PROHIBITION AND THE VOLSTEAD ACT.

Although by the turn of the twentieth century, prohibition, like temperance, had become identified as a woman's issue, prohibition was achieved before the passage of the Nineteenth Amendment, which gave women the vote. The movement to prohibit the sale, manufacture, and/or transportation of alcoholic beverages by law dates from 1846, when Maine passed the first statute, with twelve other states following suit by 1855. By the end of the Civil War, however, nine of these states either repealed their "Maine Laws" or had had them declared unconstitutional. The movement entered its second phase in 1869 with the formation of the Prohibition party and in 1874 with the founding of the Woman's Christian Temperance Union (WCTU). In 1880 Kansas became the first state to incorporate prohibition into its constitution, a move emulated by Oklahoma in 1907. The Anti-Saloon League (ASL) completed the triad of prohibition organizations in 1893, and several states responded with local option or statewide laws. By 1907, though, only Kansas, Maine, Nebraska, North Dakota, and Oklahoma remained prohibition states.

Spearheaded by the ASL and the WCTU, the prohibition movement became an integral part of the reformist surge of the Progressive era, benefiting from its association with other movements, such as those to eliminate industrial accidents, to curb prostitution, to restrict immigration, and to uplift blacks, American Indians, and immigrants. In part a response to the serious drinking problems that plagued the United States, prohibition was also an effort to scapegoat ethnic minorities and to protect putative rural and small-town virtue against the encroachments of modern, urban, industrial life. Its association with woman suffrage was a mixed bag for both movements but probably harmed the suffrage cause more than it did prohibition. The enactment of the Eighteenth Amendment eventually allowed many opponents of prohibition to endorse woman suffrage since the ultimate horror that it might entail had already been wrought. The WCTU also contributed to the movement's success among women by addressing its concern to many other socioeconomic and cultural reforms.

By 1917 there were thirteen totally dry states and thirteen more with local option or other limited prohibition laws. The entry of the United States into World War I added the arguments of patriotism and economy to the prohibitionist arsenal. By December 1917 both houses of Congress had approved the proposal of the Eighteenth Amendment, which provided that "after one year from the ratification of the article, the manufacture, sale, or transportation of intoxicating liquors within, the importation thereof into, or the exportation thereof from the United States and all territory subject to the jurisdiction thereof for beverage purpose is hereby prohibited." The ratification process consumed only thirteen months, with the only significant opposition occurring in populous urban industrial states with polyglot populations, for example, Rhode Island and Connecticut. Because the Eighteenth Amendment also provided that "Congress and the States shall have concurrent power to enforce the article by appropriate legislation," Congress followed that same year, 1919, with the Volstead Act, introduced by a Minnesota Republican, which defined intoxicating liquor as any that contained .05 percent of alcohol, fixed penalties for liquor sales, provided for injunctions against all the violating establishments, and contained a search-and-seizure provision. Curiously, it also continued the federal tax on alcoholic beverages, making the Treasury Department partly responsible for its enforcement.

In practice, enforcement proved to be a national scandal that gave rise to bootleggers and gang wars, police corruption, "speakeasies," and general disrespect for law and order. Public drinking by women became acceptable behavior for the first time, as speakeasies replaced saloons. By the outbreak of the Great Depression, however, disillusionment with Prohibition had proceeded so far that several states repealed their enforcement statues and many political leaders called for repeal. In 1932 the victorious Democrats, led by President Franklin D. Roosevelt, made repeal a top priority, and the new Congress responded by proposing the Twenty-first Amendment on February 20, 1933. It was ratified within less than a year, and the states regained total control over the liquor traffic.

—John D. Buenker

See Also:

Progressive Era, Temperance Movement, Woman's Christian Temperance Union

References:

Clark, Norman H. *Deliver Us from Evil: An Interpretation of American Prohibition.* New York: Norton, 1976.

Furnas, J. C. *The Life and Times of the Late Demon Rum.* New York: Putnam, 1965.

Merz, Charles. *Dry Decade.* Garden City, N.Y.: Doubleday, 1931.

Timberlake, James H. *Prohibition and the Progressive Movement.* Cambridge: Harvard University Press, 1963.

PROJECT HEAD START, as a federal program designed to assist and educate impoverished children, had an impact on the lives of mothers in poverty. It began in 1965 as a summer program in President Lyndon B. Johnson's "War on Poverty." The emphasis of the project was on diagnosis, remediation, and developmental guideposts. The efforts focused on health, social, nutritional, and psychological services for the child and his/her family. The project was to be an enriching preschool learning experience at which at least one full meal was to be provided. Parents were encouraged to participate in every phase.

At the conclusion of the summer program, it was announced that the project would continue throughout the year with support for the children as they attended public school. The project was intended to insure that the young impoverished child who might lack environmental stimulation would develop to the fullest of his/her potential.

In 1967 there were 3,000 programs throughout the United States, with 1,500,000 children involved. In 1968 there were full-year programs in 756 communities and summer programs in 1,100 communities. The emphases and approaches varied depending upon the needs of the communities. The common goals were serving disadvantaged children and families and being responsible for the development of basic programs that met these goals. Additional training opportunities for parents were made available. Parents were to be offered appropriate counseling, legal services, and job and open-housing opportunities.

By 1985 more than 8,500,000 children had been served by Project Head Start, which had proved that it could have a positive immediate effect on the cognitive development of young children. Studies indicate that children who have attended Head Start programs develop the ability to adapt more readily to the school environment and experience more academic success. The project has also been successful in improving the general health of the child by providing needed health care and improving the existing health-care services. As reported in the *Project Head Start Statistical Fact Sheet,* the project has been less successful in the areas of parent health education and parent involvement. The most effective programs have proven to be the ones in which the parents take an active role. Such participation has also produced beneficial changes in the community.

—*Bonnie Lou Rayner*

See Also:

Education

References:

Hymes, Jr., James. *Living History Interviews.* Carmel, Calif.: Hacienda, 1979.

McKey, Ruth Hubbell, and Larry Condelli. *The Impact of Head Start on Children, Families, and Communities.* Washington, D.C.: CSR Inc., 1985.

Project Head Start 1969–1970: A Descriptive Report of Programs and Participants. Washington, D.C.: O.C.D. HEW Research Division, 1972.

PROSTITUTION, the practice of engaging in sexual relations for payment, has existed in the United States since the colonial period. Among the first victims of prostitution in America were female indentured servants and black female slaves. Although condemned by some of the clergy and outlawed by statute as early as 1672, prostitution grew as the country grew and accelerated significantly in the second half of the nineteenth century.

As historian Ruth Rosen has observed, rapid industrialization brought drastic changes in economic and family life and contributed to increased prostitution, which reached a peak of activity between 1850 and 1900. Furthermore, westward expansion, the transportation revolution, and growing militarization created all-male populations with a keen appetite for the services of female prostitutes in many areas of the United States. For some women, especially those from the working classes, prostitution seemed a lesser evil than poorly paid legitimate jobs or deprivation. While prostitution offered a dangerous, degrading, and short-lived occupation, it promised some material comfort and the myth of upward mobility. The existence of forced prostitution, or white slavery, while exaggerated by reformers, has been documented.

Efforts to curtail or eliminate prostitution—from the efforts of the New York Magdalen Society in the 1830s to the wave of Progressive reforms in the early twentieth century—have been almost continuous, and unsuccessful. Efforts at regulation, as have occurred with some success in Europe, have been limited in scope and duration. On the national level, the major accomplishment of the Progressive reformers in the area of prostitution was the passage of the White-Slave Traffic Act of 1910 (the Mann Act), which outlawed transporting a woman across a state line for immoral purposes. While the Mann Act may have reduced the instances of white slavery, it certainly did not eliminate forced prostitution.

On the local level, reformers in the 1900–18 period succeeded in closing most public brothels and "red light" districts, some of which were quite extensive, such as the Storyville district of New Orleans, which had over 230 brothels prior to its closing in 1917. One of the most famous brothels closed in this period was the elegant one in Chicago operated by Aida and Minna Everleigh. Tragically, the closing of most public brothels resulted in prostitution assuming even worse forms, such as an increase in streetwalking, and new forms such as massage parlors and call-girl operations. Control of illicit, commercial sex has tended to shift from female madams and the prostitutes themselves to mostly male pimps or procurers and organized crime syndicates. These vice "employers" have tended to be less humane than many of the old-style madams, who had usually been former prostitutes themselves and knew first-hand the difficulties of the trade. Problems of disease and of safety for the prostitutes also increased with the closing of the bordellos and the scattering of prostitution. This has also increased the traditional problems of police harassment, selective law enforcement, and the corruption of public officials.

Not all brothels disappeared from the American scene, despite the efforts of reformers and the discouragement of their use by federal military policy during both world wars. Sally Stanford, for example, ran a popular house of prostitution in San Francisco between 1938 and 1945 before going on to achieve additional fame as a restaurateur, a member of the Sausilito City Council, and a best-selling memoirist. Among other madams who have written popular accounts of their careers in vice are Polly Adler, Nell Kimball, Pauline Tabor, and, more recently, Xaviera Hollander, who has written a large number of sex books, including the best-selling *Happy Hooker*, and socialite Sidney Biddle Barrows, who wrote *The Mayflower Madam*.

Despite efforts to glamorize prostitution in some books and films, it remains an often grim reality, frequently compounded by problems such as drug and alcohol addiction and abuse, AIDS, teenage runaways, broken homes, child abuse, social ostracism, disease, police harassment, thievery, and sometimes serious violence. While prostitution as an industry generates vast sums of money, most of the profits have gone to pimps, taxi drivers, members of organized crime, lawyers, physicians, liquor and drug dealers, law enforcement officials, landlords, and real estate speculators. Even a highly successful call girl is not immune to some of the danger and degradation involved in prostitution, including psychic disorders and a limited earning span with no health or retirement benefits. Efforts to unionize prostitutes have not succeeded, nor have the efforts of Margo St. James and her organization, C.O.Y.O.T.E. (Call Off Your Old Tired Ethics), to decriminalize prostitution. Prostitution is legal in the United States only in Nevada.

—*Jonathan W. Zophy*

See Also:
AIDS, Criminals, Moral Reform

References:

Bullough, Vern. *The History of Prostitution.* Hyde Park, N.Y.: University Books, 1964.

———, and Barret Elcano. *Bibliography of Prostitution.* New York: Garland, 1977.

Butler, Anne. *Daughters of Joy, Sisters of Misery: Prostitution in the American West.* Urbana: University of Illinois Press, 1985.

Connelly, Mark. *The Response to Prostitution in the Progressive Era.* Chapel Hill: University of North Carolina Press, 1980.

Hobson, Barbara. *Uneasy Virtue: The Politics of Prostitution and the American Reform Tradition.* New York: Basic, 1987.

Rosen, Ruth. *The Lost Sisterhood: Prostitution in America, 1900-1918.* Baltimore: Johns Hopkins University Press, 1982.

Winick, Charles, and Paul Kinsie. *The Lively Commerce: Prostitution in the United States.* Chicago: Quadrangle, 1971.

PROTECTIVE LEGISLATION included a variety of state laws regulating the conditions under which women worked. In the nineteenth century workers and reformers sought laws to improve conditions for both men and women, but the courts ruled such legislation an unconstitutional interference with the right of adult males to make contracts. Judges, however, were sympathetic to arguments that women's physical inferiority and roles as child bearers and rearers warranted state protection. Ohio passed the first maximum-hours law for women in 1852, and by 1900 a number of states had enacted protective legislation for women workers. In 1908 in *Muller v. Oregon*, the U.S. Supreme Court affirmed that women's special roles and physical vulnerability justified protective measures.

By 1920 most states imposed some regulations on employers who hired women, although the majority of the occupations of women workers were never covered. Almost every state limited the hours of work, and most prohibited women from night work. Other kinds of laws banned women from various jobs such as selling liquor, carrying mail, working in foundries and mines, and operating elevators. A fourth type of protective measure aimed at promoting a safe and clean work environment by requiring, for example, seats and rest periods, adequate ventilation and lighting. While a number of states passed minimum-wage laws for women, the Supreme Court ruled such legislation unconstitutional in 1923.

The U.S. Women's Bureau and most women's organizations strongly supported protective legislation. Labor unions, too, promoted such laws for women, but not for men. Reluctant to launch organizing drives among women, labor leaders saw such laws as a substitute for collective bargaining and a way of reducing competition for jobs. Opposing protective legislation on grounds that it limited women's employment opportunities were a relatively small group of feminists in the National Woman's Party and some professional women's organizations who sought equal treatment of men and women through an Equal Rights Amendment to the Constitution.

Passage of the gender-neutral Fair Labor Standards Act in 1938 and its acceptance by the courts paved the way for applying regulatory laws to both male and female workers. But protective legislation for women endured until the 1970s, when federal courts began to rule that such laws violated the ban on sex discrimination in employment enacted in Title VII of the Civil Rights Act of 1964.

—Susan M. Hartmann

See Also:

Civil Rights Act of 1964, Fair Labor Standards Act, Minimum-Wage Laws, *Muller v. Oregon*

References:

Babcock, Barbara A., et al. *Sex Discrimination and the Law.* Boston: Little, Brown, 1975.

Baer, Judith A. *The Chains of Protection.* Westport, Conn.: Greenwood, 1978.

Hill, Ann C. "Protection of Women Workers and the Courts." *Feminist Studies* 5 (Summer 1979): 247–73.

Kessler-Harris, Alice. *Out to Work: A History of Wage-Earning Women in the United States.* New York: Oxford University Press, 1982, pp. 180–214.

Lehrer, Susan. *Origins of Protective Legislation for Women, 1905–1925.* Albany: State University of New York Press, 1987.

PRUITT, IDA (1888–85) was a missionary educator in China (1912–18), the founder and head of the Department of Social Services at the Peking Union Medical College (1921–39), the co-author of *A Daughter of Han: The Autobiography of a Chinese Working Woman*, the American executive secretary of the American Committee for the Chinese Industrial Cooperatives (1939–52), and a vocal supporter of the People's Republic of China.

The daughter of American missionaries living in an interior Chinese village during the heyday of the American foreign missionary movement, Pruitt spent much less time at boarding school than most missionary children. Perhaps because of her long and intimate association with her Chinese "amah" (nurse/nanny), neighbors, and friends, she identified to an unusual degree with the traditional Chinese, especially women. Her oral histories, essays, fiction, and professional social-work articles were unusual for American authors of any period in portraying the Chinese as having strength, dignity, and the capacity for self-rule. In particular, her treatment of women challenged long-standing Western stereotypes of Asian women. Her translations of Chinese authors have been called exceptional.

Pruitt's unique position at the intersection of traditional Chinese and modern American cultures inspired her unusually strong opposition to foreign political and cultural intervention in China. During the Japanese occupation of the 1930s, she was one of a handful of Westerners who participated in the anti-Japanese underground. The American Committee of the Chinese Industrial Cooperatives, under her leadership, was unique among China relief agencies in maintaining a genuinely nonpartisan stance between Chinese political factions during World War II.

Ida Pruitt's commitment to China's independence and her role in interpreting China to Americans extended into the postwar anticommunist period dominated by the sensational investigations of Republican senator Joseph R. McCarthy of alleged communist subversion of American life. In defiance of a State Department ban on American travel to communist countries, she visited China in 1959 and spoke publicly about the country when it was off-limits to Americans. For thirty years, 1949–79, she was one of few Americans openly advocating U.S. diplomatic recognition of the People's Republic of China.

—*Marjorie King*

See Also:

American Missionary Association, Asian American Women

References:

Anna and Ida Pruitt Papers. The Arthur and Elizabeth Schlesinger Library. Radcliffe College, Cambridge, Mass.

Crouch, Archie R., comp. *Christianity in China: A Scholars' Guide to Resources in the Libraries and Archives of the United States.* Armonk, N.Y.: M. E. Sharpe, 1988.

King, Marjorie. "Missionary Mother and Radical Daughter: Anna and Ida Pruitt in China, 1887–1939." Diss. Temple University, 1984.

Pruitt, Ida. *A China Childhood.* San Francisco: Chinese Materials Center, 1978.

———. *A Daughter of Han: The Autobiography of a Chinese Working Woman.* New Haven: Yale University Press, 1945; rpt. Stanford: Stanford University Press, 1967.

———. "Day by Day in Peking." *The Atlantic Monthly* 147 (January–June 1931): 611–19.

———. "Faith." *The Atlantic Monthly* 150 (July–December 1932): 782–83.

———, trans. *The Flight of an Empress* by Wu Yung. New Haven: Yale University Press, 1936.

———. "New Year's Eve in Peking." *The Atlantic Monthly* 149 (January–June 1932): 47–53.

———. *Old Madam Yin: A Memoir of Peking Life, 1926–1938.* Stanford: Stanford University Press, 1979.

———, trans. *Yellow Storm* by Lao She (Lau Shaw). New York: Harcourt Brace, 1951.

PSYCHIATRY is a specialized branch of medicine that deals with the treatment of mental and personality disorder. Because of its close links with medicine, psychiatry relies heavily on the concept of organismic (physiological) causes of disorders. Consequently, most psychiatrists seek to treat their patients with a combination of drug therapy and psychotherapy.

The psychotherapeutic method currently used by most psychiatrists has its roots in the psychoanalytic work of Sigmund Freud and his disciples. By means of intensive interview and analysis of symbolic behaviors, such as dreams, the analyst seeks to guide the patient to an understanding of the underlying causes of the dysfunctional symptoms she exhibits.

Traditional psychoanalytic theory describes women as weak beings whose lives are dominated by the psychological shock of not being male (castration complex). Women's experience of the Oedipal conflict and their envy of male power (penis envy) dooms them to a life dominated by a desire to emulate men. Hence, women's neuroses are seen as being caused by an ill-formed ego that is unable to withstand these id-based impulses. Women, thus, are perceived as being narcissistic, masochistic, and passively aggressive. This imagery has formed the basis for psychoanalytic treatment of women since the turn of the century.

However, for the past twenty years, psychiatry has been struggling to revise its approach to the treatment of women. Work by male psychiatrists on the existence of "womb envy" in males began to challenge the belief that normalcy was related to masculinity. Moreover, work by feminist psychotherapists began to present an alternative framework for explaining women's psychology and their experience of psychological depression and other disorders. Jean Baker Miller was the first person to provide a feminist interpretation of the social forces that impel women to develop symptoms of psychological disorder. She describes the way in which traditional female socialization forces a young woman to deny her own self-fulfillment. And she explains that being seen as "psychologically healthy" requires that a woman be willing to devote herself to the nurturance and care of others, while at the same time neglecting herself. Miller's perceptions were strongly supported by research by Broverman et al. (1970) demonstrating that women and men therapists alike evaluated traditionally male characteristics (e.g., independence, objectivity) as more positive and more psychologically healthy than traditionally female characteristics (e.g., emotionality, subjectivity).

The plethora of feminist research that has followed from these early works has defined the ways in which psychiatry needs to change in order to better serve its women patients. We now know more clearly the relationships between female hormonal systems and neocortically induced mood states. We also understand more clearly the psychological factors related to women's eating disorders and drug and alcohol dependence patterns. However, this research has had little effect on the traditional discipline of psychiatry. Despite the emergence of feminist models of successful therapeutic methods, the medical model that underlies psychiatry has been little changed. Moreover, millions of women still suffer from major clinical psychological depression and seek the help of psychiatrists who do not subscribe to a socially induced model of psychological disorder. It is hoped that the newly emerging field of feminist psychiatry will have a strong influence on this branch of medicine in the future.

—Teresa Peck

See Also:

Deutsch, Helene; Freudianism; Horney, Karen; *Modern Woman: The Lost Sex*; Physicians; Psychology; Satir, Virginia

References:

Broverman, Inge, et al. "Sex Role Stereotypes in Clinical Judgements of Mental Health." *Journal of Consulting and Clinical Psychology* 34 (1970): 1–7.

Lederer, Wolfgang. *The Fear of Women*. New York: Harcourt Brace Jovanovich, 1968.

Miller, Jean Baker, ed. *Psychoanalysis and Women*. New York: Brunner/Mazel, 1973.

PSYCHOLOGY is the study of the individual's mental and observable behavior. In the United States in the mid-nineteenth century, psychology was considered to be a subfield of philosophy, but the emerging work of the psychophysicists in Europe and a growing awareness of the physiological bases of some behaviors led to the reconceptualization of psychology as a science. The development of departments of psychology at major U.S. universities, most notably Cornell, Chicago, Columbia, and Harvard, established the discipline as a legitimate field of academic study by the last decade of the nineteenth century. Since that time, psychology has grown in stature as a discipline that combines the rigor of science with the empathy and sensitivity of clinical insight.

Psychology has always been a discipline that has attracted women scholars. Some of the distinguished foremothers of American psychology had to endure academic insult and enormous hurdles in the pursuit of their careers. For example, Christine Ladd-Franklin and Mary Calkins were both denied their doctoral degrees—by Johns Hopkins and Harvard, respectively—in the late nineteenth century despite their having completed all necessary coursework and the dissertation. Many early women psychologists were denied teaching posts at coeducational or Ivy League universities because they were considered to be unable to meet the demands of academic life. Consequently, most of them took positions at women's colleges and started a tradition of excellence in undergraduate training of women psychologists that ensured their students places in the best graduate schools a generation later. This in turn assured that women's role in psychology would become one of vigorous participation and valuable contribution. For example, in 1891 Mary Calkins founded one of the first psychological research laboratories in the United States at Wellesley College; Margaret Washburn, after becoming disillusioned with the way women were treated at Cornell, left her teaching position there to found the psychology department at Vassar, her alma mater, in 1903. Since that time, women have continued to find psychology an attractive field of study, such that by the mid-1980s women comprised about 30 percent of the recipients of Ph.D. degrees awarded in that field. Leading lights in the field have included Helen Durkin, Henriette Glatzer, Karen Horney, Edith Jacobson, and Margaret Mahler.

However, although psychology has been a moderately receptive discipline for women scholars, it has, until recently, been insensitive to the role of gender bias in its scholarship. The push for scientific exactness that dominated U.S. psychology from the 1930s to the late 1960s created a situation wherein much of what was considered to be psychological "fact" was based on data from studies of male subjects only. Frequently, this situation occurred because the paradigms under which the investigators were functioning made interpretation of data from women subjects difficult. In many cases, the female data directly contradicted the thesis under investigation and was therefore ignored by the investigator. Thus, established theories such as Lawrence Kohlberg's theory of moral development and Stanley Coopersmith's theory of self-esteem were developed from male data. When women subjects were evaluated by these theories, they were found to be "morally immature" or lacking in self-esteem.

The reemergence of feminist consciousness in the 1960s allowed women psychologists to begin to question the established findings in the field. A major turning point for psychology came with the publication, in 1974, of *The Psychology of Sex Differences* by Eleanor Maccoby and Carol Jacklin. In this book, hundreds of studies that investigated gender-based differences were reanalyzed. The resulting conclusions strongly challenged accepted lore in psychology concerning the extent and pervasiveness of gender as a causative factor in human behavior. The scholarship in this book captured the spirit of change within psychology that had started in the late 1960s with the formation of a splinter group of the American Psychological Association, the major professional association for academic and practicing psychologists in the United States. The Association for Women in Psychology was formed to provide a professional forum for women psychologists to present their work and to identify areas of psychology in need of redefinition and reconstruction. Membership in this organization grew quickly, and by 1973 the field of psychology of women was recognized by the parent organization, and a division of the A.P.A. devoted to scholarship in feminist psychology (Division 35, Psychology of Women) was formed. This division developed its own scholarly journal *Psychology of Women Quarterly*, which is dedicated to the promulgation of research about women's psychology.

Concurrent with the political emergence of women psychologists in the late 1960s came a vigorous burst of scholarly activity dedicated to the identification of women's psychological characteristics. The need to "set the record straight" led to the publication of research about women and to the development of psychology courses on college campuses based on this new research. Since that time, courses in the psychology of women have become standard offerings in undergraduate and graduate psychology departments in most colleges and universities in the United States.

—*Teresa Peck*

See Also:

Freudianism; Horney, Karen; *Modern Woman: The Lost Sex*; Psychiatry; Satir, Virginia; Women in Higher Education

References:

American Psychological Association, Membership Office, Washington, D.C. [personal communication, 1988]

Maccoby, Eleanor, and Carol Jacklin. *The Psychology of Sex Differences.* Palo Alto: Stanford University Press, 1974.
Russo, Nancy F., and Agnes N. O'Connell. "Models from Our Past: Psychology's Foremothers." *Psychology of Women Quarterly* 5 (1980): 11–54.
Scarborough, Elizabeth, and Laurel Furumoto. *Untold Lives: The First Generation of American Women Psychologists.* New York: Columbia University Press, 1989.
Williams, J. *Psychology of Women: Behavior in a Biosocial Context.* New York: Norton, 1977.

PUBLIC SPEAKERS, WOMEN. "But I suffer not a woman to teach, nor to usurp authority over the man, but to be in silence" (1 Tim., 2 : 12). From colonial times, Puritan/Protestant clergy, in the name of St. Paul, curtailed almost all public roles for women. Though certain evangelical sects and Quakers had long encouraged women to proselytize (and many of the best of the women orators were Quakers), the Protestant ban on women's public speaking continued far into the nineteenth century, when the era's Victorian notions about woman's nature further encouraged the belief that a female wanting to speak in public must be unwomanly as well as irreligious. Nevertheless, important exceptions emerged out of the reform impulse or religious fervor over a specific cause—usually abolition, temperance, or women's suffrage. Advocate of sexual freedom and atheism Frances Wright spoke in public in the 1820s, while abolitionists Frances Maria W. Stewart and the Grimké sisters (Sarah and Angelina) did so in the 1830s. After the 1848 Seneca Falls Convention and the several women's rights conferences and conventions it spawned, an increasing number of women took to the platform: Sojourner Truth, Lucy Stone, Ernestine Rose, Lucretia Mott, Abby Kelley. In 1853 Susan B. Anthony, Amelia Bloomer, and the Reverend Antoinette Brown were the first women to lecture in public in Manhattan—to an audience of over three thousand.

Both the Civil War and postwar conditions forced women into more public roles. Though few were trained in classical rhetoric or oratory, some turned their occasional speeches for special causes into careers—as agents for temperance or suffrage groups and, later in the century, as speakers in the increasingly popular lyceum and Chautauqua movements, series of lectures and public forums presented by local and traveling speakers. Anna Dickinson and Mary Livermore moved from war-effort work to Redpath's Lyceum circuit. Olympia Brown, Elizabeth Cady Stanton, Stone, and Anthony campaigned for a women's suffrage referendum in Kansas in 1867. Phebe Hanaford, contemporary historian of women speakers, claims that more than thirty women had achieved national prominence through public speaking by 1876, while many more had gained local recognition.

—*Nan Nowik*

See Also:

Abolition and the Antislavery Movement, Christianity, Society of Friends, Suffrage, Temperance Movement

References:

Hanaford, Phebe. *Women of the Century.* Boston: Russell, 1877.
Kennedy, Patricia S., and Gloria H. O'Shields, eds. *We Shall Be Heard: Women Speakers in America 1828–Present.* Dubuque, Iowa: Kendall/Hunt, 1983.
O'Connor, Lillian. *Pioneer Women Orators: Rhetoric in the Ante-Bellum Reform Movement.* New York: Columbia University Press, 1954.
Stanton, Elizabeth Cady, Susan B. Anthony, and M. S. Gage, eds. *History of Woman Suffrage.* 2d ed. Rochester, N.Y.: Mann, 1889.

The **PURE FOOD ACT, 1906.** The first line of the Pure Food Act of 1906 states its purpose as "an act for preventing the manufacture, sale, or transportation of adulterated or misbranded or poisonous or deleterious foods, drugs, medicines, and liquors, and for regulating traffic therein, and for other purposes." The passage of this act was a testimonial to one of the earliest realizations of women's political power to enact change in American society.

Annie Whittenmyer, a helper in Civil War hospitals, sparked the first public interest in pure foods. Upset by the monotonous diet and nonnutritious fillers that were given to patients, she argued for a healthier, more varied diet specialized for patients' needs. Her arguments persuaded Harvey Wiley to make the study of food additives and processing his life's work. When he became chief chemist in the U.S. Department of Agriculture, the fight against impure food and unsafe food processing began in earnest. Wiley asked the women of the United States to help him force the enactment of legislation to make processed foods and medicines safe for their families' consumption. The women responded on various fronts.

In the 1890s a group of women formed a Food Consumers' League. Alice Lakey, the chair of the food investigation committee, began a publicity campaign against the use of aniline, a poisonous, oily liquid made from coal, used in food-coloring dyes. Florence Kelley, the secretary of the National Consumers' League in 1899, became the first woman in the United States to lead a state factory-inspection service. She encouraged increased food and drug legislation at city, state, and federal levels for the next twenty-five years.

In 1902 the Woman's Christian Temperance Union joined the fight. Members were enraged by a Professor Atwater of Wesleyan University, who claimed that alcohol was a food and by the charge of the editors of *American Medicine* that the WCTU was inconsistent in campaigning against beer but not against medicines that contained ten times as much alcohol. Martha Allen, the woman in charge of WCTU's national Department of Nonalcoholic Medication, led an information dissemination campaign against the medical use of alcoholic drinks and the misbranding of patent medicines. The popular press quickly picked up the WCTU's cry, and a flood of articles lambasting the unethical use of patent medicines appeared in the *Ladies' Home Journal* and *Collier's* between 1903 and 1906.

In early 1905 the public's concern was echoed by North Dakota Senator Porter McCumber, who introduced a pure food and drug bill. This bill died when the Senate session ended without taking action on it. However, the public demands for food and drug regulation legislation turned to an uproar with the publication in February 1906 of Upton Sinclair's *The Jungle*, which exposed the horrors of the Chicago meat-packing industry. Congress heard these demands, and three bills on the subject were introduced. Senator Albert Beveridge of Indiana wrote a meat-inspection bill that was signed into law on June 30, 1906. Senator Weldon B. Heyburn of Idaho wrote a forceful pure food and drug bill for Senate consideration. Representative William Peters Hepburn of Iowa introduced similar measures in the House. A combination of the Heyburn and Hepburn bills passed both houses on June 29, 1906, and became the Pure Food Act (Public Law No. 384).

—*Mari Lynn Kortier*

See Also:

Kelley, Florence; Woman's Christian Temperance Union

References:

Jackson, Charles O. *Food and Drug Legislation in the New Deal*. Princeton, N.J.: Princeton University Press, 1970.

May, Charles Paul. *Warning! Your Health Is at Stake*. New York: Hawthorn Books, 1975.

"Report of the Pure Food Committee of the General Federation of Women's Clubs." *Annals of the American Academy of Political and Social Sciences* 28 (September 1906): 296–301.

Wood, Donna J. *Strategic Uses of Public Policy: Business and Government in the Progressive Era*. Marshfield, Mass.: Pitman, 1986.

QOYAWAYMA, POLINGAYSI (b. 1892), a pioneer in American Indian education, was born in the Hopi village of Oraibi in Arizona in 1892. Her autobiography, *No Turning Back* (1964), describes her early education, her teaching career, and the difficulty she faced as a Hopi woman living in two worlds.

After the final military defeat of the Indians in the 1800s, Indian children had been sent away to white-run boarding schools, often hundreds or even thousands of miles from their homes. These government schools were usually operated by Christian churches and attempted to assimilate the Indians into white society by separating them from their Indian communities, by insisting on instruction in English, and by forcing the children to adopt white dress and manners. The result was that when the children returned to the reservations after years of such instruction, they were alienated from their tribes.

Qoyawayma as a child was sent to California, where she worked and studied for four years. She recalls the harsh treatment on the reservation and at the government-run schools. She recounts how Hopi women were forced to march naked through a dipping vat because of a suspected epidemic. She remembers how Hopi men wept because they were forced to cut their hair and how a classmate at school was forced to sit in front of the class with an eraser stuffed into her mouth because she had been talking.

In 1924 Qoyawayma began teaching Hopi and Navaho children. Fifty years before it would become fashionable to do so, she insisted on teaching in Hopi and Navaho as well as English. She knew how difficult her education had been, and she taught her students by using lessons from their own heritage. Moreover, she did this at a time when there were few defenders of American Indian cultures. Eventually, however, Qoyawayma won the support of John Collier, commissioner of the Bureau of Indian Affairs. She retired from teaching in 1954.

Throughout her life, Qoyawayma promoted education for Indian people. She was not opposed to assimilation into the white world, but she knew that the various Indian cultures offered valuable lessons as well. Her autobiography, like those of Black Elk, Lame Deer, and Mountain Wolf Woman, ranks as one of the important accounts of American Indian life in the twentieth century.

—John Snider

See Also:
Native American Women, Native American Women's Literature

Reference:

Qoyawayma, Polingaysi (Elizabeth Q. White), as told to Vada F. Carlson. *No Turning Back.* Albuquerque: University of New Mexico Press, 1964.

QUILTS, or quilting, appeared in Europe as a result of the Crusades, when men discovered the practicality and warmth of wearing padded clothing during their travels. Women saw the usefulness of this procedure and applied this craft to their own clothing and cloth used in the bed chamber.

When the colonists began settling in America, they brought with them quilted pieces. Since fabric was not easily available in America, women made their own woolen and linsey-woolsey fabrics. As quilts began to show wear, pieces of old clothing were cut up and stitched to the quilt to cover the holes. Thus emerged the beginnings of the pieced quilt. Americans developed their own distinct patterns, designs, and block style.

There are three types of quilts: plain, pieced, and appliquéd. Plain quilts are made from two pieces of the same colored fabric to form the front and back of the quilt. Pieced quilts are formed by sewing geometric pieces of fabric together in a mosaic design. Appliquéd quilts use a single colored front onto which is stitched pieces of fabric to form a picture rather than a pattern. In each, the common link is the quilting stitches.

Since little money was available to purchase bed coverings, women, out of necessity, made quilts. Women were very proud of their craft and would keep careful count of the number of spools of thread that they used to make a quilt—the more spools of thread, the better. Quilts were shown with great pride. Quilting bees were a major social event for women. Their hands would be busy creating a work of art that also provided an opportunity for interaction. Quilts were made by hand even after the invention of the sewing machine. A high social value was placed on hand work. With the onset of the Victorian era, a different emphasis and value was placed on quilts. Quilt tops began to be made out of silk and other types of fabrics that were more elegant than practical.

Quilt making gradually lost importance as women began to work outside the home and there was little time to spend making quilts. At present, more value is being placed on quilts. People are beginning to learn and practice this creative American folk art.

—Bonnie Lou Rayner

References:

Cooper, Patricia, and Norma Buferd. *The Quilters: Women and Domestic Art.* New York: Doubleday, 1977.

Dee, Anne Patterson. *Quilter's Source Book.* Lombard, Ill.: Wallace-Homestead, 1987.

Holstein, Jonathan. *The Pieced Quilt.* New York: Galahad, 1973.

QUIMBY, HARRIET (1875–1912) was the first licensed female pilot in the United States. A stunning beauty of her day, Quimby was also an early feminist who chose careers in male-dominated fields over a husband and family.

She began as a writer for the *San Francisco Dramatic Review* in 1902 and also did features for local newspapers, the *Call-Bulletin* and the *San Francisco Chronicle.* She later moved to New York City to take the job of drama critic for *Leslie's Illustrated Weekly.* Her circle of friends included members of New York's growing aviation community, and as a result of their influence she began flying lessons at the Moisant School on Long Island in early 1911. She received her pilot's license, the first for an American woman, on August 1.

Quimby joined the Moisant International Aviators, putting on demonstration flights and competing with her fellow female aviators for records and prize money. On April 16, 1912, she became the first woman to pilot an aircraft across the English Channel. Unfortunately, at the peak of her resulting fame, she was killed on July 1 while taking part in an air meet in Boston. The leading aviation periodical asked several prominent pilots of the day to comment on the causes of the accident. None, not even those opposed to women pilots, ever mentioned the possibility of pilot error, a posthumous tribute to Quimby's flying skills.

—Claudia M. Oakes

See Also:

Aviation, Journalism

References:

Gwynn-Jones, Terry. "For a Brief Moment the World Seemed Wild About Harriet." *Smithsonian* 14 (January 1984): 112–26.

Moolman, Valerie. *Women Aloft.* Alexandria, Va.: Time-Life Books, 1981.

RACE-SUICIDE was an antifeminist theory developed between 1905 and 1910 in reaction to lower birthrates and changes in family structure and sexual practices believed to be caused by birth control use and the feminist adoption of the concept of "voluntary motherhood." Race-suicide proponents believed upper-class, educated women were shirking their duty by not having large families—or any families at all—and allowing the upper class to be overtaken by immigrants and the poor. The hysteria was escalated by the leadership position taken by President Theodore Roosevelt, who condemned birth control and smaller families, declaring that women who choose not to have children were "criminal against the race . . . the object of contemptuous abhorrence by healthy people." In actuality, the birthrate had begun to decline as early as the 1880s, but by 1905 large families, particularly within the upper classes, were considered necessary to maintain the stability of the country.

Feminists were accused of selfishness and indulgence for supporting the issue of birth control and for practicing voluntary motherhood. In response to the race-suicide issue, many feminists rejected the cult of motherhood and more aggressively defended birth control and the smaller-family issue by arguing that some women made better contributions to society through their work. But there was also an inherent economic problem that transcended the attack against feminism: many lower-class women used birth control because they could not afford to raise large families. Children were considered an "expensive luxury" in many working-class families, whether immigrant or native-born. Few women gave up birth control as a result of the race-suicide issue.

—*Karen C. Knowles*

See Also:
Antifeminism, Birth Control, "Voluntary Motherhood"

References:

Gordon, Linda. *Woman's Body, Woman's Right.* New York: Grossman, 1976.

Kennedy, David. *Birth Control in America.* New Haven: Yale University Press, 1970.

Roosevelt, Theodore. *Presidential Addresses and State Papers.* Vol. 3. New York: Review of Reviews, 1910, pp. 282–91.

RADCLIFFE COLLEGE is an elite women's college associated with Harvard University. Although it was officially founded in 1894, Radcliffe actually began much earlier, with the efforts of influential women and men to open Harvard to study for women in the 1870s.

There was considerable opposition to coeducation in Harvard's administration and in its governing body, the Harvard Corporation. Consequently, the first arrangements for educating women at Harvard were informal. Private lessons were offered by Harvard faculty members to individuals or to small groups of women who were interested in studying at Harvard. This was done without the explicit approval of Charles Eliot, Harvard's activist president at this time, who was strongly opposed to coeducation in principle. Eventually, this arrangement evolved into a full course of study offered under the auspices of the "Harvard Annex," the name given to the faculty group giving instruction to interested women.

In 1882 a number of influential Boston and Cambridge women incorporated the Society for the Collegiate Instruction of Women, an organization dedicated to opening Harvard to women for study leading directly to a Harvard degree. Despite raising more than a quarter of a million dollars to help establish a course of study for women at Harvard in 1892, however, the Harvard Corporation refused to allow women admission to the university in a degree-seeking capacity. This led the society to charter Radcliffe two years later, with the Harvard Corporation serving as "visitors," responsible for appointing instructors and examiners, and Harvard's president countersigning Radcliffe diplomas. Nonetheless, many champions of women's higher education were outraged by the refusal of Harvard's administration and trustees to admit women directly to the university for study.

Radcliffe was distinctive among elite eastern women's colleges in that it generally did not have its own faculty. Rather, it was the epitome of a "coordinate college," one that drew its resources from a larger, all-male university. There were some women who taught at Radcliffe and who did not hold appointments at Harvard. By and large, however, Radcliffe did not offer young women the opportunity to study under the guidance of a largely female faculty, as did Wellesley, Smith, and other independent women's colleges.

Radcliffe continued its life as Harvard's small "sister college" until the early 1960s, when Radcliffe graduates were finally given Harvard degrees. Through nearly the first fifty years of the college's existence, its students were restricted to Radcliffe courses, and it even offered a Radcliffe Ph.D. In 1943, however, the entire Harvard curriculum was opened to Radcliffe students. Since that time, the distinction between a Harvard and a Radcliffe education has narrowed appreciably, such that Radcliffe retains only a bare administrative identity within Harvard University today.

—John L. Rury

See Also:

Education, "Seven Sisters," Women in Higher Education

References:

Baker, Liva. *I'm Radcliffe! Fly Me!* New York: Macmillan, 1976.

Solomon, Barbara Miller. *In the Company of Educated Women: A History of Women and Higher Education in America*. New Haven: Yale University Press, 1985.

RADICAL FEMINISM reflected the agenda of radical women leaders of the women's movement in the 1960s, many of whom came from a socialist background or had served in the civil rights, student, and antiwar movements of that decade. Both politicized and radicalized through their participation in the Student Non-Violent Coordinating Committee (SNCC), Students for a Democratic Society (SDS), and other New Left organizations, radical feminists reshaped and expanded socialist doctrine to develop a radical feminist ideology as well as their own style of organization and strategy. They sought to eliminate male dominance from society.

Adamantly committed to a leaderless participatory democratic approach, these feminists eschewed the mainstream political approach for direct confrontation in the form of street theater. The first major demonstration in protest of the sexism of the Miss America Pageant in September 1968 earned them national media coverage. Their bonfire of the symbolic "traditional" trappings of femininity produced the image of the "bra-burning" feminist, which critics used to impugn all activist and outspoken feminists of the era. Employing such outrageous spectacles, the demonstrations of the radical feminists alienated mainstream women and provided fodder for a hostile establishment press to censure and to ridicule the cause of feminism as well as its supporters. However, the proponents of radical feminism compelled public attention to focus upon the fundamental inequality of women.

The development of radical feminism began with the 1964 position paper of the women in SNCC that anonymously questioned the sexist relegation of women workers to subordinate and auxiliary status within the organization. By 1968 radical feminism had spread nationwide, although it was centered in the larger cities; radical feminists engaged in dynamic discussions in their intellectual quest for a nonsexist definition of women's position in society generally. Increasingly a minority philosophy within the national feminist movement, radical feminism provided scope for the leftist tacticians and theoreticians within the feminist movement. Radical feminists within the Red Stockings, a famous New York group, first advanced the effective use of consciousness-raising as a process of educating women to the origins of their limited status and sex stereotyping and were the first feminists to confront publicly the issue of abortion rights and to seek a comprehensive analysis of women's oppression within the sex gender system.

Internal dissention over the issues of elitism and leadership among the radical feminist groups lessened the effectiveness of their organizations. Nonetheless, radical feminism provided the "shock troops" of activists and theoreticians within the modern women's movement to stimulate provocative and profound scholarly and intellectual inquiry into feminism itself, as well as into the purpose and goals of the feminist movement.

—*Angela Howard Zophy*

See Also:

Consciousness-Raising, New Left, Women's Liberation Movement

References:

Diggins, John P. *The American Left in the Twentieth Century*. New York: Harcourt Brace Jovanovich, 1973.

Echols, Alice. "The Radical Feminist Movement in the United States, 1967–1975." Diss. University of Michigan, 1986.

Evans, Sara. *Personal Politics: The Roots of Women's Liberation in the Civil Rights Movement and the New Left*. New York: Knopf, 1979.

Firestone, Shulamith. *The Dialectic of Sex*. New York: Bantam, 1970, 1971.

Greer, Germaine. *The Female Eunuch*. New York: Bantam, 1970, 1972.

Koedt, Anne, Ellen Levine, and Anita Rapone, eds. *Radical Feminism*. New York: Quadrangle, 1973.

Salper, Roberta, ed. *Female Liberation*. New York: Knopf, 1972.

Sochen, June, ed. *The New Feminism in Twentieth Century America*. Lexington: Heath, 1971.

RADICALESBIANS was a New York City–based, 1970s lesbian-feminist political group. Like the Furies Collective of Washington, D.C., and Gay Women's Liberation in San Francisco, Radicalesbians was formed out of anger and frustration with the sexism of male-dominated gay-liberation groups and the homophobia of many women's rights organizations.

Radicalesbians stated their philosophy in "The Woman-Identified Woman" (1970), an essay that continues to be an important statement of lesbian-feminist politics. The essay began by asking, "What is a lesbian? A lesbian is the rage of all women condensed to the point of explosion." The essence of women's liberation, according to the women of Radicalesbians, lay in the creation of new consciousness and the challenge to patriarchy that arises when women identify with and relate to other women. In naming the connection between the oppression of women and the structure and practice of heterosexuality, Radicalesbians brought a new theoretical perspective to feminism and enabled women to view lesbian sexuality as a positive personal and political choice.

—*Mary Battenfeld*

See Also:

Lesbianism, Radical Feminism, Women's Liberation Movement

References:

D'Emilio, John. *Sexual Politics, Sexual Communities: The Making of a Homosexual Minority in the United States, 1940–1970*. Chicago: University of Chicago Press, 1983.

Echols, Alice. "The Radical Feminist Movement in the United States, 1967–1975." Diss. University of Michigan, 1986.

Radicalesbians. "The Woman-Identified Woman." In *Out of the Closets: Voices of Gay Liberation*, edited by Karla Jay and Allen Young. New York: Quick Fox, 1972, pp. 172–77.

RAMÍREZ, SARA ESTELLA (1881–1910) was a teacher, poetess, labor organizer, and political activist. She emigrated to the United States from Coahuila, Mexico, and began teaching Spanish in Laredo, Texas. Her political activism extended to both sides of the border. She worked with Richard Flores Magon in the Partido Liberal Mexicano as an official representative and was involved with the Regeneración y Concordia (Regeneration and Concord) and the liberal club Ponciano Arriaga, forerunner to the Liberal Mexican party. *La Crónica* and *El Democrata Fronterizo*, two local Spanish newspapers with regional readership, published her poems, essays, literary articles, and public speeches. Besides contributing to the local newspapers, Ramírez published two literary periodicals, *La Corregidora* (printed in Mexico City, Laredo, and San Antonio) and *Aurora* (published daily in Laredo). As a journalist for *La Corregidora*, Ramírez advocated spiritual and economic liberation for women.

—Mary Romero

See Also:
Chicana, Journalism

References:

Hernández Tovar, Inez. "Sara Estella Ramírez: The Early Twentieth Century Texan-Mexican Poet." Diss. University of Houston, 1984.

Rascón, María Antonieta. "La mujer y la lucha social/The Woman and the Social Struggle." In *Imagen y realidad de la mujer/Image and Reality of the Woman*, edited by Elena Urrutia. Mexico City: Sep Setentas, 1975.

Zamora, Emilo. "Sara Estella Ramírez: Una Rosa Roja en El Movimiento/A Red Rose in the Movement." In *Mexican Women in the United States: Struggles Past and Present*, edited by Magdalena Mora Adelaida R. Del Castillo. Los Angeles: UCLA Chicano Studies Research Center, 1980, pp. 163–69.

RANKIN, JEANNETTE PICKERING (1880–1973), politician and pacifist, was the first woman to serve in Congress. Rankin was born on a ranch in Montana Territory, graduated from the University of Montana, and taught school briefly before earning a graduate degree in social work from the New York School of Philanthropy (now part of Columbia University). Beginning in 1910, she worked in several state suffrage campaigns and eventually became chairperson of the movement in Montana where women won the right to vote in 1914, six years before the Nineteenth Amendment was enacted.

Rankin, who never married, was wealthy enough to survive without working steadily. A progressive Republican, she launched a campaign for the U.S. House of Representatives in 1916. With strong support from women of both parties, Rankin won election handily to one of Montana's two at-large seats in the House four years before the ratification of the woman suffrage amendment.

Within days of her historic swearing-in in 1917, Rankin opposed President Woodrow Wilson's call for a declaration of war against the Central Powers of Europe. Meanwhile, the Montana legislature divided the state into two single-member districts for the 1918 congressional election. This reapportionment put Rankin and her congressional colleague in the same district, a move designed to defeat her in a bid for a second term. This prompted Rankin to run for the U.S. Senate in 1918 so that she could campaign throughout the state, but she lost the election.

Rankin spent the next several years engaged in working for various social causes, especially peace. In 1940, when another world war was being fought in Europe, Rankin capitalized on the isolationist leanings of her fellow citizens and ran for Congress from Montana again. She won, and began her second term in the House of Representatives in 1941, twenty-two years after her first had ended in 1919. On December 8, 1941, she cast the sole vote in either house of Congress against U.S. entry into World War II. This action was extremely unpopular in Montana and ruined her political career. Rankin never ran for public office again.

For the remainder of her life, Rankin was a crusading pacifist. In 1968 she was thrust into the national limelight one last time when, at the age of eighty-eight, she led a march on Washington to protest the Vietnam War.

—Roger D. Hardaway

See Also:
Pacifism and the Peace Movement, Politics, Republican Party, Suffrage in the American West

References:
Harris, Ted Carlton. "Jeannette Rankin: Suffragist, First Woman Elected to Congress, and Pacifist." Diss. University of Georgia, 1972.
Josephson, Hannah. *Jeannette Rankin: First Lady in Congress.* Indianapolis: Bobbs-Merrill, 1974.
Schaffer, Ronald. "Jeannette Rankin, Progressive-Isolationist." Diss. Princeton University, 1959.

RAPE/SEXUAL ASSAULT became a major feminist issue of the 1970s. Historically, the crime was termed "rape"; its victims were assumed always to be women; and, within the popular culture, rape was considered a "crime of passion" to which men were driven by seductive and wanton women. Both sexist stereotypes and common law conspired to make rape a criminal proceeding in which the victim and her behavior were tried, rather than the defendant. Under common law, women had been regarded as chattel of men, and therefore sexual assault of a woman was considered a crime against the patriarchal state. Rendered a mere witness in the judicial proceedings, the victim was at the mercy of the defense attorney, whose client's rights were protected and took precedence. Traditionally, rape was a capital offense upon conviction, and therefore juries proved reluctant to return guilty verdicts against defendants whose victims survived. For their part, the victims were reluctant to file charges or take cases to court given that only one case in ten ever reached trial, and only one in ten of those cases resulted in convictions. To the feminists of the 1970s, the crime of rape became a hallmark of a sexist society's debasement of women; utilizing self-help support groups, consciousness-raising for victims and the public alike, and determined lobbying tactics, feminists secured reformed statutes that redefined rape as sexual assault in several states by the 1980s.

Whether termed "rape" or "sexual assault," which feminists prefer as less gender-identified and more descriptive, this crime is defined as a violent crime (a felony) in which an individual compels another (not his/her spouse) to engage in sexual intercourse and/or some other sexual act against his/her will. The key to prosecuting a rape/sexual assault case remains the issue of consent. The rape victim must be an individual who has not consented to the sexual activity in that s/he (1) was forcibly compelled to engage in the act; (2) experienced the threat of forcible compulsion to an extent that could not be resisted; (3) was unconscious; or (4) was below the "age of consent" specified by the state in which the activity occurred (statutory rape).

Although sexual assault is not a gender-specific crime for its victims or its perpetrators, women continue to be the most frequent victims. Estimates in the mid-1980s indicate that from 20 to 30 percent of American girls currently age twelve will become victims of sexual assault sometime during the remainder of their lives.

The victim of a sexual assault commonly experiences "rape trauma syndrome" in the aftermath of the attack. This is a two-stage process in which initially (the acute stage) the victim experiences feelings of shock, fear, embarrassment, humiliation, and often guilt. She may also experience other psychological and physical reactions such as insomnia, headaches, nausea, and loss of appetite. During the second stage (the reorganization stage, occurring two to three weeks after the assault), the victim acts to reorganize her circumstances in order to feel more secure (e.g., she may move or change her telephone number), but she may also continue to experience physical and psychological distress.

Despite these severe reactions, rape/sexual assault is one of the least reported violent crimes; about 50 percent are never brought to the attention of the police. The reasons for this include the victim's feelings of shame and embarrassment as well as her fear of reprisals from her attacker. But it is also because of the traditional responses of the police, courts, and hospital personnel to the rape victim. It has been found that the rape victim often experiences a second victimization at the hands of these agencies. She must convince the authorities that her complaint is both legitimate and prosecutable in that she is visibly traumatized and that she in no way contributed to her victimization. The rise of the incidence of "date rape" in the late 1970s revived confusion regarding the issue of consent, especially in cases where the women knew or had previous relationships with their alleged rapists; married women were unable to file rape charges against their husbands unless legally separated, regardless of the evidence of violence.

The insensitivity and skepticism that frequently characterize official responses to rape/sexual assault victims are indicative of the institutionalization of popular myths about this crime. These include the notions that (1) all women unconsciously want to be raped; (2) women enjoy being "taken" by force; (3) many women "ask for it" by the way they dress, walk, or behave; and (4) women sometimes falsely accuse men of rape either out of revenge or because of guilt feelings over agreeing to have sex with them. The persistence of jokes about sexual assault that trivialize the charge and disparage the character of its vicitms perpetuate these myths. The expanding commercial pornography market of the 1970s utilized the male fantasy that women wanted and deserved to be raped as a staple in the industry's literature, movies, and videos.

Since the 1970s the treatment of sexual assault victims has improved considerably, to a large extent because of the efforts of feminists. Rape crisis counselors are available to provide support; many police forces now have specially trained officers to respond to sexual assault complaints; state laws have been amended to eliminate unreasonable and sexist evidentiary rules, and witness support services have been added to district attorney offices. Despite these changes, unfortunately, there has been no noticeable decrease in the number of sexual assaults in the United States.

—*Claire M. Renzetti*

See Also:

Common Law, Marital Rape

References:

Brown, Barbara A., Ann E. Freedman, Harriet N. Katz, and Alice M. Price. *Women's Rights and the Law.* New York: Praeger, 1977.

Brownmiller, Susan. *Against Our Will.* Rev. ed. New York: Bantam, 1988.

Burgess, Ann, and Lynda Lytle Holmstrom. "Rape Trauma Syndrome." *American Journal of Psychiatry* 131 (1974): 981–86.

Johnson, Allan Griswold. "On the Prevalence of Rape in the United States." *Signs* 6 (1980): 136–46.

Schur, Edwin M. *Labeling Women Deviant.* New York: Random House, 1984.

RATIONALISM. Many of the leading thinkers of seventeenth- and eighteenth-century Europe were rationalistic. They believed that reason was the faculty that separated humans from beasts and that the triumphs of seventeenth-century science proved that reason could be trusted. Many concluded that men and later women of reason could know and understand the world.

The emphasis on reason was popularized by such thinkers as René Descartes (1596–1650) in France and John Locke (1632–1704) in England. The ideas of Descartes and Locke had a widespread influence among intellectuals throughout Europe and later the Americas, helping to make the Enlightenment the Age of Reason. Although most male Enlightenment *philosophes* did not think women should share identical rights with men, the French philosopher Condorcet (1743–94) argued on the basis of reason that women should have citizenship, the right to vote, and the right to hold office.

Although the fact that such enlightened views on women were in the minority, the glorification of reason in the early modern period still contributed greatly to the improvement of women's lives on both sides of the Atlantic. Late medieval writer Christine de Pisan (c. 1363–1431) had foreseen the utility of reason as a tool for the liberation of females in her *City of Ladies*, where Lady Reason is an important character in shaping a world where women have all the jobs so long denied them. As Juana Inez de la Cruz, a Mexican intellectual of the colonial era, wrote in 1691: "Since I first gained the use of reason my inclination toward learning has been so violent and strong that neither the scoldings of other people . . . nor my own reflections . . . have been able to stop me from this natural impulse that God gave me."

In short, reason became a valuable tool by which men and women could free themselves from the limitations and superstitions of the past and attempt to construct a more rational and humane society. While women's capacity for rational thought was still denied by most men and women until well into the twentieth century in the West, advanced thinkers were well aware of its potentialities. Writings such as Mary Wollstonecraft's *A Vindication of the Rights of Woman* (1792) and John Stuart Mill's *The Subjection of Women* (1861) must be understood against the background of the rise of rationalism. The light of reason has exposed many of the arguments used to hold women in bondage as totally illogical and unreasonable. Women have proven to be as capable of rational thought as men. We now should know that reason has no gender.

—*Jonathan W. Zophy*

See Also:

European Influences

References:

Commager, Henry Steele. *The Empire of Reason: How Europe Imagined and American Realized the Enlightenment.* Garden City, N.Y.: Doubleday, 1977.

Gay, Peter. *The Bridge of Criticism.* New York: Harper, 1970.

Koch, Adrienne, ed. *The American Enlightenment.* New York: Braziller, 1970.

May, Henry. *The Enlightenment in America.* New York: Oxford University Press, 1976.

The **REPUBLICAN PARTY** has had a checkered record with regard to its support for women's issues and its recruitment of women to public office. Most of the original nineteenth-century feminists were Republicans because of the party's antislavery stand. When the Radical Republicans failed to endorse women's suffrage after the Civil War, the feminists were disillusioned, but for the most part they were unwilling to join the Democrats with their close ties to southern racial supremacists and northern big-city bosses.

With the advent of a renewed women's suffrage movement after 1910, both political parties faced increasing pressure to endorse a constitutional amendment, but, in fact, it was Theodore Roosevelt's Progressive party that first endorsed women's suffrage in 1912. As late as 1916 neither major party was willing to back a constitutional amendment in its platform, rather leaving the decision to the states. Despite reformer Alice Paul's call for women in the existing suffrage states to vote against the Democrats because as the party in power they had not backed an amendment, in 1916 Democrat Woodrow Wilson defeated Republican Charles E. Hughes in a very close race for the presidency. At the end of World War I, both parties had supporters and opponents of women's suffrage, but the Republican side had fewer diehards than the Democrats, whose southern congressional delegation provided the bulk of the opposition to the Women's Suffrage Amendment in votes taken in both 1918 and 1919.

Following ratification of the Nineteenth Amendment in August 1920, the majority of the new women voters opted for the Republican party in every presidential election until 1964. Most of the more educated women were Republicans and tended to vote regularly, while many immigrant women who might have supported the Democrats never voted at all. Despite this strong vote of confidence by women voters, the Republican party did little to recruit women candidates or officeholders before the 1970s. Although the first woman in Congress, Jeannette Rankin of Montana, elected in 1916, was a Republican, she was followed by few others. No Republican president appointed a woman to his cabinet until Eisenhower made Oveita Culp Hobby his secretary of health, education and welfare in 1953. In Congress, a few Republican widows managed to develop a reputation for independence and political expertise.

Chief among these was Margaret Chase Smith of Maine, who served in the House from 1940 until 1949 and in the Senate from 1949 to 1973.

With the coming of the new feminism in the 1970s, the Republicans began to recruit more women candidates, especially at the state and local levels. Unfortunately, few of these women have moved up to Congress since, by and large, most have been considered too liberal by either the voters in the primaries or the party organizations. Nevertheless, the GOP achieved a major coup in 1978 when Nancy Landon Kassebaum of Kansas became the first woman elected to the Senate who was not a widow of a former member of Congress. She was followed by Paula Hawkins of Florida, who served one term between 1980 and 1986.

The capture of the party by the Radical Right in 1980 and the rejection of its forty-year record of support for the Equal Rights Amendment caused defections of moderate and liberal women who had fought only a few years earlier for an increased female role. Despite the Reagan landslides in 1980 and 1984, polls showed a significant difference between the votes of men and women. While a majority of women supported Reagan, it was by a much lower percentage than male voters, and in 1980 a majority of college-educated women voted for Jimmy Carter over Reagan. To counter this "gender gap," President Reagan in 1981 appointed Sandra Day O'Connor as the first woman to sit on the Supreme Court, but he made few female appointments at lower judicial and administrative levels. Neither major party has made a sustained effort to recruit women for winnable congressional seats, so that despite an increase in female candidates, there were only twenty-eight women in Congress by 1989, of whom twelve were Republicans (eleven in the House and one in the Senate).

—*Neil W. Hogan*

See Also:

Gender Gap; Politics; Rankin, Jeannette; Roosevelt, Alice; Schlafly, Phyllis; Suffrage

References:

Banner, Lois W. *Elizabeth Cady Stanton.* Boston: Little, Brown, 1980.

Carroll, Susan J. *Women as Candidates in American Politics.* Bloomington: Indiana University Press, 1985.

Chafe, William H. *The American Woman: Her Changing Social, Economic and Political Roles, 1920–1970.* New York: Oxford University Press, 1974.

Chamberlain, Hope. *A Minority of Members.* New York: Praeger, 1973.

Clarke, Harold D., and Alan Kornby. "Moving Up the Political Escalator: Women Party Officials in the U.S. and Canada." *Journal of Politics* 41 (May 1974): 442–47.

Flexner, Eleanor. *A Century of Struggle.* Cambridge: Harvard University Press, 1975.

Klein, Ethel. *Gender Politics: From Consciousness to Mass Politics.* Cambridge: Harvard University Press, 1984.

Rule, Wilma. "Why Women Don't Run: The Critical Controversial Factors in Women's Legislative Recruitment." *Western Political Quarterly* 34 (March l981): 60–77.

Scott, Anne F., and Andrew M. *One Half of the People.* Philadelphia: Lippincott, 1975.

The ***REVOLUTION*** was a women's rights periodical published and edited by Susan B. Anthony and Elizabeth Cady Stanton from 1868 to 1870. The journal appeared during a time of national upheaval over Reconstruction, deep political schisms, and the push for suffrage for black men. While some suffragists were willing to postpone the struggle for women's suffrage, the *Revolution* served as a visible and vocal proponent for women's suffrage, black as well as white. Though the journal had a circulation of only three thousand in 1870, its impact on the women's rights movement and on coverage of the movement by the rest of the country's press was disproportionate to its circulation. It was an important forum for the discussion of issues and the focus of heated criticism and support from abolitionists, newspaper editors, suffragists, and readers all over the country. In addition to suffrage news and arguments, the journal advocated marriage reform and changes in divorce laws, championed the plight of working women, and argued in favor of practical dress for women. The journal was considered to represent the radical arm of the women's rights movement and figured in the split of the movement into the National Woman Suffrage Association and the American Woman Suffrage Association.

In 1870 the financial burden Anthony had shouldered with the *Revolution* became too great for the journal to continue. In addition, the more conservative and financially stable *Woman's Journal*, started by the American Woman Suffrage Association in 1870, proved to be too much competition. The *Revolution* was therefore transferred to Edwin Studwell (publisher) and Laura Curtis Bullard (editor) for the sum of $1, leaving Anthony with a personal debt of $10,000. The *Revolution* continued under Bullard as a literary and social journal until it was sold to the *New York Christian Enquirer* in 1872.

—*Lana F. Rakow*

See Also:

Anthony, Susan B.; Journalism; Stanton, Elizabeth Cady; Suffrage

References:

Kramarae, Cheris, and Lana F. Rakow. *The Revolution in Words: Righting Women, 1868–1871*. London: Routledge, 1990.

Masel-Walters, Lynne. "Their Rights and Nothing More: A History of the Revolution, 1868–70." *Journalism Quarterly* 53 (Summer 1976): 242–51.

The **REVOLUTIONARY WAR.** Women's participation in the American Revolution ranged from the home front to the battlefield. During the turbulent 1760s and early 1770s, women's anti-tea leagues and ladies' associations provided crucial support for the boycotts and nonimportation efforts of the aggrieved colonists. Patriot women increased their production and use of homespun and eschewed British-made or imported luxury items. Women's political activities through the Daughters of Liberty paralleled those of men; women attended and sponsored bonfire rallies, burnt tax collectors' effigies, and produced their own anti-British propaganda. As individuals, women influenced their spouses, brothers, and suitors to support the Revolutionary cause or lose their womanly favors, services, and esteem; as professional printers and propagandists, women printers produced crucial Revolutionary broadsides, newspapers, and documents such as the Declaration of Independence. Mercy Otis Warren wrote patriotic plays and poems that satirized the British and lauded the Revolutionary cause. Sarah Bradless Fulton instigated the Boston Tea Party.

After the Declaration of Independence, women on farms and in towns assumed the responsibilities and positions of their men, who volunteered and served in the Continental army; women also took on the more traditional wartime activities of sewing clothes for the soldiers, rolling bandages, and preparing foodstuffs for the front. The local production of shot for the soldiers' rifles and often the manufacture and assembly of arms were undertaken by women who converted their peacetime facilities to war production. Women took direct action in policing uncooperative merchants, British sympathizers, and collaborators. Through fund-raising fairs, partriotic groups such as the Ladies Association of Philadelphia raised large sums to purchase food, clothing, and medical supplies for the Continental army. Many women courageously opted for a scorched-earth policy, destroying their farms rather than allow their crops to fall into British hands.

At the battle lines, women were present as camp followers who served as cooks, nurses, washerwomen, and undertakers for the fallen. Most of the camp followers were wives and family members of the soldiers, but the term has come to connote only the prostitutes, who were a minority of these women who lived in the army camps. Whether disguised as men or merely harmless females, women served heroically as spies, saboteurs, and couriers.

While the Revolution did not bring full legal and political equality to women in North America, it did bring subtle but significant changes to women's lives in the latter eighteenth century. Women's patriotic wartime activities initiated them into business and politics beyond the domestic realm and gave them a sense of the importance of their contributions. With the absence of men on the home front, the status of women advanced due to both their proven capabilities and their sense of their potential. Women benefited from the post-Revolutionary changes in the family and the rise of the image of the Republican Mother: the family structure became smaller and less authoritarian, and the role of the Republican Mother fused the Revolutionary patriotism of women with their traditional duties. Republican Motherhood laid the foundations for the domestic feminism that would flower in the nineteenth century as the Cult of True Womanhood.

—Angela Howard Zophy

See Also:

Ladies Association of Philadelphia; Pitcher, Molly; Warren, Mercy (Otis)

References:

Kerber, Linda K. *Women of the Republic: Intellect and Ideology in Revolutionary America.* Chapel Hill: University of North Carolina Press, 1980.

Norton, Mary Beth. *Liberty's Daughters: The Revolutionary Experiences of American Women.* Boston: Little, Brown, 1980.

Riley, Glenda. *Inventing the American Woman: A Perspective on Women's History.* Arlington Heights, Ill.: Harlan Davidson, 1987.

RICH, ADRIENNE (b. 1929), most widely known as a poet, is also an essayist, critic, scholar, teacher, and radical feminist theorist. Her first volume of poetry, *A Change of World* (1951), was chosen by W. H. Auden for the Yale Younger Poets Award. Noted for its technical control and elegance, this work maintained a distanced and restrained style, one that characterized her early poetry. With *Snapshots of a Daughter-in-Law* (1963), Rich began to move toward the more political and personal voice of her later work.

By the early 1970s, her work became explicitly feminist as she articulated with precision the problem with the words from which she crafted her poems: "This is the oppressor's language." *Diving Into the Wreck* (1973) was the critically acclaimed co-winner of the National Book Award for Poetry, an award she refused on her own behalf but accepted with fellow poet Audre Lorde on behalf of all women. With *Twenty-one Love Poems* (1975) and the 1978 volume *The Dream of a Common Language* (written 1974–77), her work became overtly lesbian as well as feminist; critics have noted that *Dream* provides a remarkable integration of her politics, her concerns with language and form, her female consciousness, and her powers as a poet.

Rich's prose works have contributed to her reputation as a major radical feminist theorist. *Of Woman Born: Motherhood as Experience and Institution* (1976) investigates motherhood in patriarchal culture, drawing on both personal experience and extensive research. *On Lies, Secrets, and Silence: Selected Prose 1966–78* (1979) collects a number of important essays and traces the development of her feminist consciousness. "Compulsory Heterosexuality and Lesbian Existence," written in 1978 for *Signs* (where it was published in 1980) and reprinted in *Blood, Bread, and Poetry* (1987), introduced the controversial concept of a "lesbian continuum" that would include women who did not identify as lesbians but who had to various degrees resisted patriarchy. During the early 1980s Rich co-edited the lesbian-feminist quarterly *Sinister Wisdom.*

Rich lives in California with writer and historian Michelle Cliff, her partner since 1976. On the basis of her existing corpus, Rich has achieved a solid reputation as a major American poet and feminist theorist.

—Jacqueline Taylor

See Also:

Androgyny; Lesbianism; Lorde, Audre

References:

Gelpi, Barbara C., and Albert Gelpi, eds. *Adrienne Rich's Poetry: A Norton Critical Edition.* New York: Norton, 1975.

Grahn, Judy. *The Highest Apple: Sappho and the Lesbian Poetic Tradition.* San Francisco: Spinster's Ink, 1985.

McDaniel, Judith. *Reconstituting the World: The Poetry and Vision of Adrienne Rich*. Argyle, N.Y.: Spinster's Ink, 1979.
Ostriker, Alicia. *Stealing the Language: The Emergence of Women's Poetry in America*. Boston: Beacon, 1986.
Rich, Adrienne. *Blood, Bread, and Poverty: Selected Prose 1979–1985*. New York: Norton, 1987.
———. *A Change of World*. New Haven: Yale University Press, 1951.
———. *The Diamond Cutters and Other Poems*. New York: Harper, 1955.
———. *Diving Into the Wreck: Poems, 1971–1972*. New York: Norton, 1973.
———. *The Fact of a Doorframe: Poems Selected and New, 1950–84*. New York: Norton, 1984.
———. *Leaflets: Poems 1965–1968*. New York: Norton, 1969.
———. *Necessities of Life: Poems, 1962–1965*. New York: Norton, 1966.
———. *Of Woman Born*. New York: Norton, 1976.
———. *On Lies, Secrets, and Silence: Selected Prose 1966–1978*. New York: Norton, 1979.
———. *Poems: Selected and New, 1950–1974*. New York: Norton, 1975.
———. *Selected Poems*. London: Chatto and Windus, 1967.
———. *Snapshots of a Daughter-in-Law: Poems, 1954–1962*. New York: Harper & Row, 1963.
———. *A Wild Patience Has Taken Me This Far: Poems 1978–1981*. New York: Norton, 1984.
———. *The Will to Change*. New York: Norton, 1971.
———. *Your Native Land, Your Life*. New York: Norton, 1986.

RICHMOND, MARY ELLEN (1861–1928) was a teacher, practitioner, and theoretician in the American Charity Organization Society Movement. She provided social work professionals and charity organization "friendly visitors" with the first formulation of theory, principles, and techniques of social diagnosis in her two classic books *What Is Social Casework?* and *Social Diagnosis*. She defined social casework as "those processes which develop personality through adjustments consciously effected, individual by individual, between men and their social environment." This definition is still considered by many present-day social workers the most useful description of social casework and its goals.

Richmond had a long and varied career in the field of social work practice. She was appointed general secretary of the Baltimore Charity Organization Society in 1891. In 1900 she became general secretary of the Philadelphia Society for Organizing Charity, and in 1909 she served as director of the Russell Sage Foundation. She taught social work practice at the New York School of Philanthropy (later part of Columbia University) for many years and in 1927 was instrumental in the planning of the fiftieth anniversary of the American Charity Organization Society Movement. Her motto for this event was Light from Hand to Hand, Life from Age to Age. She died in 1928, leaving a solid theoretical base for the professional practice of social casework, providing an excellent living model of humanistic social work for practitioners of the future.

—*James E. Lantz*

See Also:
Social Work

References:

Richmond, Mary. *Social Diagnosis*. New York: Russell Sage Foundation, 1917.
———. *What is Social Casework?* New York: Russell Sage Foundation, 1922.

RIGHT-WING POLITICAL MOVEMENTS. Women have participated in a number of right-wing political movements in the twentieth century. Some of these movements have sought to preserve traditional gender and family relationships, while others have been based in a right-wing politic of inequality and individualism. Many right-wing movements with large numbers of women have been countermovements against movements that favor gender, racial, or social class equality.

In the early twentieth century, a small number of middle-class and elite women were active in the movement against female suffrage. They claimed that women's special place in the private sphere of family and home would be threatened by granting women access to the public sphere of politics. Antisuffragists argued that women and men should not have separate, individual public identities, but that the family, as represented by husband and father, should be the primary unit of society.

In the 1920s women were active participants in a different kind of right-wing movement, the Ku Klux Klan. Hundreds of thousands of Klanswomen, drawn from across the spectrum of social classes of white, native-born Protestant women, participated in a movement against Catholics, blacks, socialists, and Jews. Yet, they also favored limited gender equality, arguing that women could, and should, be active participants in both the public and private sphere. Klanswomen mobilized against parochial schools, racial integration, and immigration but favored the rights of white, Protestant women in the economy and in politics.

In World War II, women participated in two opposing right-wing movements: patriotic societies that stressed nationalistic allegiance to the United States and pro-Nazi groups that sought to support European fascism. These movements had little interest in issues of gender or family, except in support of the war effort or party power.

From the 1950s to the present, right-wing women have primarily been involved in self-proclaimed "pro-family" movements. These movements have a conservative and anti-egalitarian agenda, based on opposition to social changes, such as legalized abortion, that are seen as threatening the traditional nuclear heterosexual family. Women in such movements argue either that women should be subservient to men in the family and in the public sphere or that women's primary base of power and influence should remain that of home and family life. The escalated attempt to ratify the Equal Rights Amendment in the 1970s, together with feminist challenges to male domination of the family, politics, and economy, and the increased electoral strength of fundamentalist Christians, mobilized women in a countermovement. This antifeminist movement opposes social changes that threaten to alter the traditional hierarchical relationships between men and women and between parents and children.

—*Kathleen M. Blee*

See Also:

Abortion; Antifeminism; Antisuffragism; Equal Rights Amendment; Schlafly, Phyllis

References:

Blee, Kathleen M. "Women in the 1920s Ku Klux Klan Movement." *Feminist Studies* (Summer 1990).

Conover, Pamela J., and Virginia Gray. *Feminism and the New Right: Conflict over the American Family.* New York: Praeger, 1983.

Marshall, Susan E. "Ladies Against Women: Mobilization Dilemmas of Anti-Feminist Movements." *Social Problems* 32 (April 1985): 348–61.

RITTER, FRANCES (FANNY) RAYMOND (1840–90) was a music educator, writer, translator, and singer. She was most noted for the publication in the *Woman's Journal* of 1876 of "Woman as a Musician: An Art-Historical Study," an expanded version of a text presented before the Centennial Congress of the Association for the Advancement of Woman in Philadephia earlier that year. In this work she traced women's otherwise neglected share in the history of music.

Though excluded from the music of the medieval church, the creativity of women could be found in folk song and troubadour ballads. With the invention of opera in the seventeenth century, women began to have great public careers in music, although not yet excelling in musical composition. Ritter advocated the inclusion of a composition course in women's college education, more attention by women to the study of instruments other than the piano, and the study of singing as physically and morally healthful. She pointed out that good music teachers and performers commanded excellent salaries. Finally, she reserved special praise for the vast army of nonprofessional women who supported music and musicians through admiration and friendship, financial generosity, collecting musical literature and instruments, and generally influencing the musical taste of society.

Ritter was an associate of music at Ohio Female College in Cincinnati and later moved to Vassar College with her husband, Frédéric Louis Ritter, a composer, historian of music, and Vassar professor. She translated Ludwig Ehlert's *Letters on Music, to a Lady* (1870) and Robert Schumann's *Music and Musicians* (1877). Her own works also included *Some Famous Songs: An Art-Historical Sketch* (1878), *Songs and Ballads* (1887), and a volume of poetry.

—*Anne Dzamba Sessa*

See Also:
Music

References:

Block, Adrienne Fried, and Carol Neuls-Bates, eds. and comps. *Women in American Music.* Westport, Conn.: Greenwood, 1979.

Petrides, Frederique Joanne. "Some Reflections on Women Musicians." *American Music Lover* 1 (February 1936): 291–94, 314–15.

Stratton, Stephen S. "Women in Relation to Musical Art." *American Art Journal* 44 (13-27 March 1886): 355–56, 373–74, 391–92.

RIVLIN, ALICE MITCHELL (b. 1931), an economist, was first director of the Congressional Budget Office. The CBO was created in 1975 to provide Congress with assistance in evaluating and developing policy on federal income and spending. Prior to the formation of CBO, there was no congressional office able to provide the analytical support enjoyed by the executive branch. When this department was created, it was necessary to appoint a political economist who would not only be knowledgeable but experienced.

Rivlin was chosen after the eloquent presentation she made at the Senate Budget Committee hearings. She displayed a greater understanding of CBO's function than the other candidates with her insightful presentations. There was some doubt that she would be appointed, however, both because of her gender and her liberal political bent.

In Rivlin's age group there are not great numbers of female economists. In fact, when Rivlin earned her Ph.D. in 1958 from Radcliffe, there were few academic posts open to women, and this prompted her to take her first position at the Brookings Institution as a research fellow. Fortunately, and because of the example individuals such as Rivlin have set, those ranks have expanded over time. At Brookings, her research experience expanded and was later extended to budget analysis. She was assistant secretary for planning and evaluation in the Department of Health, Education, and Welfare during Lyndon Johnson's administration. She then returned to Brookings, where she continued to examine public decision-making in relation to the federal budget. This broad background and experience provided the necessary tools for the position at CBO. She directed this department with its staff of approximately two hundred for eight years and consistently viewed the office as a neutral organization designed to provide information. At the completion of her second term, she returned to Brookings as director of economic policy studies.

Through dedication to providing information to guide public policy, Rivlin has been able to achieve her career goals. While she has described herself as an "official purveyor of bad news to Congress," she gained the respect of liberals and conservatives alike through her straightforward delivery of information and analyses. The reliability of the information provided by Rivlin and her staff alleviated initial fears about her gender and liberal leanings.

—*Patricia M. Duetsch*

See Also:
Women in Higher Education

References:

"Alice's Adventures in Budgetland." *Time* 105 (June 23, 1975): 57.

Bowman, Kathleen. *New Women in Social Sciences.* Chicago: Creative Education, 1976.

"Catch-Up for Calculating Women." *Time* 113 (January 8, 1979): 45.

"Her Hand Is on the Future." *Time* 113 (June 18, 1979): 58.

ROBINSON, HARRIET HANSON (1825–1911), woman's rights activist, woman's club organizer, and writer, spent her early years in Boston. The death of her father sent the family to Lowell, Massachusetts, in 1832, where Mrs. Hanson managed a boardinghouse and Harriet and her brother went to school and worked in the mills. Like other mill girls, Harriet was eager to take advantage of the educational opportunities Lowell offered, and she became an occasional contributor to the *Lowell Offering*.

In 1847 she met William S. Robinson, newspaper editor and dedicated activist in the "free soil" movement, which opposed the extension of slavery into territories newly acquired from Mexico. They were married the following year. William's commitment to the abolitionist cause cost him jobs, but though there was often little money, the marriage was a happy one as Harriet's lively and detailed journal shows. William became well known as the author of the "Warrington" papers in the *Springfield* (Mass.) *Republican*; after a variety of editorial jobs, he was elected clerk of the Massachusetts House of Representatives. They lived for a few years in Concord, William's hometown, and settled in Malden, then a country suburb of Boston. William was active in politics and retained his clerkship until 1873, when a coup by his political opponents ousted him. He never recovered from the shock and died in March 1876.

During the years of her marriage, Harriet wrote occasionally (and at length in her journals), but her energies were directed toward her home, her four children, and her husband. Theirs was a marriage of deep affection; Harriet's first act after his death was to collect his "Warrington" essays, write a biographical introduction, arrange publication (paying the costs herself), and actively sell the book.

There is a ten-year gap in her journal after William's death; by the time she resumed writing, she had become active in the women's suffrage movement. As early as the 1860s, both she and William had been interested in women's causes; now she devoted herself to suffrage work. She wrote articles, and she and her daughter Harriette (Shattuck) joined the National Women's Suffrage Association (NWSA), working with Susan B. Anthony; Harriet's book, *Massachusetts in the Women's Suffrage Movement* (1881), became part of a larger suffrage history sponsored by the national group. She formed the National Women's Suffrage Association of Massachusetts and was the first woman to speak before the U.S. Senate Committee on Women's Suffrage. When the two major and sometimes rival groups, NWSA and the American Women's Suffrage Association (AWSA), merged in 1891, Harriet and her daughter resigned, chiefly because of their dislike of Lucy Stone, an AWSA founder.

Her writing during this time concerned women's issues. A paper, "The Life of the Early Mill Girls," was presented to the American Social Science Association (1882) and was followed by *Early Factory Labor in New England* (1883). She wrote a play, *Captain Mary Miller* (1886), about the wife of a riverboat captain who takes over his job when he is ill; it was performed and favorably reviewed in Boston.

When they left NWSA, Harriet and her daughter founded a woman's club in Malden, introducing a rule for rotation in office and actively supporting women's right to sit on school committees and to vote for school committee members. She wrote another suffrage play, *The New Pandora* (1889), a revision of the Pandora myth that claimed Pandora (woman) brought civilization into the world. In 1896 she published *Loom and Spindle, or Life Among the Early Mill Girls, with a Sketch of "The Lowell Offering" and Some of Its Contributors*, a book of personal reminiscences that has since become a major source of information about the Lowell mill girls. She held national office in the General Federation of Women's Clubs, remaining active until her death.

—Shirley Marchalonis

See Also:

Lowell Mill Girls, *Lowell Offering*, Suffrage

References:
Bushman, Claudia L. *"A Good Poor Man's Wife."* Hanover, N.H.: University Press of New England, 1981.
Robinson, Harriet Hanson. *Loom and Spindle.* Boston: Crowell, 1896.

ROBINSON, JULIA BOWMAN (1919–85) was one of the most outstanding American women mathematicians of the twentieth century. She received her Ph.D. in mathematics from the University of California, Berkeley, in 1948 and remained on the research faculty there throughout her life. She was the first woman mathematician elected to the National Academy of Sciences and the first woman president of the American Mathematical Society. In her research, she used methods of number theory to attack problems in mathematical logic. She is best known for her contribution to the solution of Hilbert's tenth problem.

—Jonell Duda Comerford

See Also:
Mathematics, Women in Higher Education

References:
Notices of the American Mathematical Society (Providence, R.I.) 32 (October 1985).
Olsen, Lynn M. *Women in Mathematics.* Cambridge: MIT Press, 1974.
Press, Jaques Cattell, ed. *American Men and Women of Science.* New York: Bowker, 1986.

ROCHESTER WOMEN'S ANTI-SLAVERY SOCIETIES (1835–68). The women of Rochester, New York, established five antislavery societies in the mid-nineteenth century. Differentiated by race, religion, wealth, and ideology, these associations were united in "the one great object of converting the entire public to abolitionism." A black and a white women's society, founded in 1834 and 1835, respectively, joined local men's societies in upholding William Lloyd Garrison's demand for immediate emancipation. The black women's efforts, however, gained little public notice. White middle-class women, stirred by the religious revivals of the early 1830s, soon collected hundreds of signatures on antislavery petitions. Yet by 1840 their society disbanded amidst ministerial and editorial controversy about unwomanly behavior.

Five years later a small circle of Quakers formed the Western New York Anti-Slavery Society with the aid of Abby Kelley Foster. Sexually and racially integrated, the WNYASS was headquartered in Rochester but forged bonds with agrarian co-worshipers across the state. Fund-raising fairs organized by women sustained the society's activities and supported publication of Frederick Douglass's abolitionist newspaper *North Star.* Organizers as well of the Rochester Woman's Rights Convention of 1848, WNYASS women shocked their more conservative neighbors. Still, in 1851 a massive WNYASS-organized fund-raising festival attracted support from several groups of women: the newly formed Union Anti-Slavery Sewing Society, composed of black women; white evangelical women active in the 1830s; white Presbyterian and Unitarian women new to the cause.

Despite the success of the event, white female abolitionists soon broke into opposing camps as their black co-workers once again faded from public record. Feminist-abolitionists continued to labor in the WNYASS, to push for racial equality in addition to emancipation, and to favor the abolition of sexual inequality, capital punishment, and the land monopoly. Their more moderate evangelical and Unitarian sisters formed the all-female Rochester Ladies' Anti-Slavery Sewing Society, which focused on the two goals of emancipation and uplift for blacks. The first goal was promoted through funding men's political and legislative campaigns; the latter by sending female agents to work with newly freed slaves in the contraband camps of Alexandria, Virginia.

By 1868 all of Rochester's female antislavery societies had disbanded, though many members remained active in other cases for several decades. Despite their diversity, these women's societies collectively provided the kinds of political pressure, publicity, funds, and moral and material assistance to blacks that gave the antislavery movement its visibility and power in New York State.

—Nancy A. Hewitt

See Also:

Abolition and the Antislavery Movement, American Antislavery Societies

References:

Rochester Ladies' Antislavery Papers. University of Michigan, Ann Arbor, Mich.

Samuel D. Porter Family Papers and Isaac and Amy Post Family Papers. University of Rochester, Rochester, N.Y.

Hewitt, Nancy A. *Women's Activism and Social Change: Rochester, New York, 1822–1872.* Ithaca: Cornell University Press, 1984.

ROCKFORD FEMALE SEMINARY/ROCKFORD COLLEGE. Located in Rockford, Illinois, the Rockford Female Seminary was founded by a consortium of Congregational and Presbyterian churches, receiving its charter in 1847. The first principal, Anna Sill, modeled Rockford on the women's colleges of the East. Rockford was referred to as the "Mount Holyoke of the West," as the founders wished to provide for their daughters the same education that they would have had if their families had remained in the East. Rockford initially shared with Beloit College in Wisconsin an all-male board of trustees, composed equally of clergy and lay members. The religious dimension remained a significant force at Rockford; many of the early teachers left to marry missionaries, and Miss Sill encouraged social activities with the young men of Beloit College, favoring those who were embarking on careers as missionaries and were seeking wives to accompany them.

Rockford students took the initiative in advancing the cause and character of women's education. In 1874, "assuming the prerogative of our college brethren," alumnae gathered for a public dinner in the first event of its kind for a women's college in the United States. This was the origin of the Chicago-Rockford Alumnae Association. The class of 1878 began the tradition of Class Day, "in the manner of celebrating [commencement] in male colleges."

Rockford's role in women's education cannot be told apart from its most distinguished alumna, Jane Addams. When Addams entered Rockford in 1877, the curriculum consisted of classical and modern languages, the sciences, music, American literature, medieval history, and religion, a course of study Addams later criticized: "[It] is at fault in that it failed to recognize certain needs . . . [that is] to cultivate and guide the great desires of which all generous young hearts are full" (*Democracy and Social Ethics*). Nevertheless, Addams and a classmate undertook additional preparation to be eligible to receive the B.A. degree. In 1882 Rockford received the necessary charter, giving it the right to confer degrees, and the seminary thus attained college status.

Addams remained "unresponsive to the evangelical appeal" of Rockford, but she and her classmates were captivated by the "social faith," taking as their motto the word *Breadgivers.* The college woman, she told a class assembly, "wishes not to be a man, nor like a man. . . . We still retain the old ideal of womanhood—the Saxon lady whose mission it is to give bread unto her household. So we have planned to be breadgivers throughout our lives, believing that in labor alone is happiness." The settlement at Hull House, founded by Addams and classmate Ellen Gates Starr, drew upon these "boarding school ideals," not the least in that it re-created the world of the women's college that Jane Addams had so cherished at Rockford.

Rockford College admitted male students during World War II and became officially coeducational in 1958. In 1964 the college moved to its present modern campus, and the original seminary buildings were demolished. In honor of its most distinguished alumna, Rockford College regularly confers the Jane Addams Medal on "women who . . . have achieved pre-eminence . . . and made significant contributions to culture and society."

—Laura Gellott

See Also:

Addams, Jane; Education; Female Academies

References:

Addams, Jane. "The College Woman and the Family Claim." *Commons* (Chicago) 3 (September 1898): 3–7.

———. *Democracy and Social Ethics.* New York: Macmillan, 1902.

———. *Twenty Years at Hull House.* New York: Macmillan, 1910.

Cederborg, Hazel. "A History of Rockford College." M.A. thesis. Wellesley College, 1915.

Lagemann, Ellen Condliffe, ed. *Jane Addams on Education.* New York: Teachers' College Press, 1985.

Lasch, Christopher. "Jane Addams: The College Woman and the Family Claim." In *The New Radicalism in America, 1889–1963.* New York: Knopf, 1966, pp. 3–37.

ROE V. WADE. Prior to 1973, most states restricted the ability of women to receive abortions. Many states, including Texas, where *Roe v. Wade* originated, allowed abortions for the sole purpose of saving the woman's life. A pregnant woman, known as Jane Roe, brought a class-action suit against Henry Wade, the district attorney of Dallas County, challenging the constitutionality of the Texas antiabortion law. A district court ruled for Roe. Wade appealed to the Supreme Court, which upheld the lower court's ruling and handed down a ruling declaring unconstitutional any state laws restricting all first-trimester and most second-trimester abortions. The majority opinion in this case, establishing a woman's constitutional right to an abortion, remains the political focus of the abortion controversy. What follows is a summary of the majority opinion written by Justice Harry Blackmun and concurred in by six other justices.

Blackmun's opinion grounds a woman's right to an abortion in the constitutional right of privacy. Though the Constitution does not explicitly cite a right to privacy, there is a large body of Supreme Court opinions that derive the right to personal privacy in areas such as marriage, contraception, procreation, family relations, and child rearing from the First, Fourth, Fifth, and most notably the Ninth and Fourteenth amendments. This body of opinion has established that in these areas, as long as there is no compelling state interest to the contrary, states have no ground for regulating the activities of their citizens; those citizens retain, instead, the right of personal privacy to act as they choose. The *Roe* opinion grounds the right to privacy in the Ninth Amendment's reservation of rights to the people.

Blackmun found only two possible grounds for a legitimate state interest compelling enough to allow regulation of abortion: the health of the pregnant woman and the potential life of the fetus. These are important as they define the extent and the limits on the right to abortion granted in *Roe v. Wade.* Those arguing in support of restrictive abortion laws have tried to ground a fetal right to life in the Fourteenth Amendment. In *Roe*, the majority found that "the word `person,' as used in the Fourteenth Amendment, does not include the unborn." The Court, therefore, explicitly rejected a constitutionally grounded fetal right to life. The Court went on explicitly to avoid taking a stand on when the fetus becomes a person. Instead, it declared that the state's interest in potential human life becomes compelling, thus overriding a woman's right to privacy in abortion decisions, at the point of viability or when the fetus can survive outside the woman's womb. This had the effect of striking down laws prohibiting first- and second-trimester abortions.

The state has a second interest in the health of the pregnant woman. Since mortality is lower with first trimester abortions than with pregnancies taken to term, this interest cannot be used to regulate early abortions. However, the Court allowed for state regulation (but not prohibition) of second-trimester abortions for the sole purpose of promoting and preserving maternal health. However, in *Webster v. Reproductive Services* (1989), the Court called into question the continued validity of the *Roe v. Wade* framework and approved significantly greater state regulation of a woman's right to legal abortion.

—*David S. Levin*

See Also:

Abortion, U.S. Supreme Court

References:

Roe v. Wade. 410 U.S. 113. 35 L. Ed. 2d, 147. 93. S. Ct. 1973.

Rubin, Eva R. *Abortion, Politics, and the Courts.* Westport, Conn.: Greenwood, 1982.

ROLLINS, CHARLEMAE (1897–1979), black librarian, educator, author, and editor, was born in Yazoo, Mississippi, and studied at Columbia University and the University of Chicago. Rollins was a tireless worker in the struggle to end the stereotypes of blacks that were so widespread in children's books. Her most notable effort in this endeavor was *We Build Together*(1947,1951,1967), published by the National Council of Teachers in English, a guide to children's literature in which blacks were depicted accurately and honestly.

Rollins worked for thirty-six years in the Chicago Public Library, most of those years in the children's department at the George C. Hall Branch. She also taught children's literature at Roosevelt University and for several summers at Fisk University and Morgan State College.

Many of Rollins's books for children dealt with notable blacks. Probably the most famous of these was *Black Troubadour: Langston Hughes* (1971), which received the Coretta Scott King award the year it was published. Other similar titles by Rollins include *Famous American Negro Poets for Children* (1965) and *Famous American Negro Entertainers of Stage, Screen, and TV* (1967). Rollins also edited a collection of Christmas songs and stories by or about blacks and wrote numerous journal articles.

Rollins received numerous awards and honors. Among these were the prestigious Grolier Award (1956)—Rollins being the first black so honored—and an honorary doctorate from Columbia University (1974). She was the first black elected president of the Children's Services Division of the American Library Association.

—*Suzanne Hildenbrand*

See Also:

Black Women, Librarianship

References:

"Rollins, Charlemae." In *Something About the Author.* Detroit: Gale Research, 3 (1972), 175–76; 26 (1982), 171.

Saunders, Doris. "Charlemae Rollins." *ALA Bulletin* 49 (February 1955): 68–69.

ROOSEVELT, ELEANOR (1884–1962) was the niece of Theodore Roosevelt and the politically active wife of Franklin Delano Roosevelt. She was also an author and social activist. Orphaned at age ten and deeply affected by other personal tragedies, she was compassionate toward the underprivileged, the impoverished, and the downtrodden. Roosevelt espoused many liberal causes, chief among them peace and human rights, especially the rights of minorities, youth, and women. She worked actively for such groups as the National Association for the Advancement of Colored People (NAACP), the League of Women Voters, the National Women's Trade Union League, Americans for Democratic Action, and the International Student Service.

Educated at Allenswood, a girls' school outside of London, England, Anna Eleanor Roosevelt returned to the United States at age seventeen determined to be of service to the less fortunate. She plunged into settlement house work—in which educated young people worked among the poor and espoused social reform—and at eighteen she joined Florence Kelley's National Consumers' League. After marrying Franklin Roosevelt in 1905, she devoted herself to furthering her husband's career and the welfare of her children.

During World War I she coordinated the work of Washington's Union Station canteen for soldiers, worked for the Red Cross, supervised the knitting rooms at the Navy Department, and gave public speeches at patriotic rallies. After the war, Roosevelt worked for the League of Women Voters and the National Women's Trade Union League. With her husband paralyzed by polio in 1921, her public activities expanded even further. During the 1932 campaign that led to her husband's election to the presidency, she coordinated many of the activities of the Women's Division of the Democratic National Committee, working with social feminist Molly Dewson to mobilize thousands of women precinct workers. Together they brought a diverse group of women activists to Washington, many of whom served in the Roosevelt administration.

During the more than twelve years she spent as First Lady, she was able to further her causes through her influence with her husband and his subordinates and through her loyal work with the Democratic party. Acting as the eyes, ears, and legs of the president, she visited Great Britain, Chile, the Caribbean, and the Pacific theater of war. She earned the nickname "Eleanor Everywhere" while touring such diverse places as Appalachian coal mines, Nisei detention camps, and the 1933 encampment of the Veteran's Bonus Army. By keeping the pressing need for social reform constantly before the president, she also served as his conscience.

In her book *It's Up to the Women* (1933) Roosevelt inaugurated the resurgence of Progressive era social feminism, which influenced the New Deal philosophy and policies regarding women's issues. This book signaled that Eleanor Roosevelt intended to invigorate the position of First Lady and dedicate her official activism to assure women's inclusion in the New Deal programs of "relief, reform, and recovery." Adopting a literary style reminiscent of her husband's informal yet inspirational fireside chats, Roosevelt provided women with the reassurance and strategy necessary to confront and combat "the intangible enemy of want and depression". In twenty concise chapters, she encouraged women to surmount the spiritual challenges of the time, systematically outlined women's appropriate responses to economic conditions, and specified how women could meet their increasing obligations. She began with reminders of women's courageous endurance during the trying times of the American Revolution, Civil War, and World War I, affirming the tradition of American women's strength in adverse conditions.

Roosevelt recognized that America's strong family unit was dependent on women's sensitive and efficient responses to the social disjunction and feelings of inadequacy often associated with income reduction. She explicitly described the proper emotional and practical reactions for those faced with limited resources. Her solution was the same for both urban and rural communities: de-emphasize money as the sole measure of success, budget time and income according to individual necessity, and monitor family health in terms of diet, sleep, and exercise. Her common-sense approach to satisfying a family's emotional and physical needs was combined with budgets, time schedules, and nutritional menus furnished by a home economics professor. Roosevelt emphasized that the ability to react to economic stresses by effectively instituting efficient household organization becomes even more crucial as economic conditions cause more women to leave the home and confront the additional obligations of the working world.

She pointed out that as women become a growing part of the work force, they assume a new level of responsibility concerning the improvement of job-related conditions. In addition, women's recently acquired right to vote brought, she said, a duty to hasten the achievement of wage equality, union membership, and job opportunity for all working Americans. Roosevelt further emphasized that during the economic crisis of the 1930s, women, as America's primary consumers, were obligated to promote the principles established by the National Recovery Act: to live within one's income (by neither over-mortgaging nor hoarding), to buy fairly from merchants, to buy only goods manufactured under reputable circumstances, and to bring community cooperation back into the family unit.

It's Up to the Women was an expression of the First Lady's social feminism, and although it has been criticized for providing an almost utopic economic solution, Eleanor Roosevelt's reassurance and strategies permitted many members of the middle class to realize women's powerful influence during times of hardship as well as prosperity.

After her husband's death, Roosevelt was appointed to the United Nations delegation by President Harry S. Truman in 1946, served until 1953, and was reappointed by President John F. Kennedy in 1961. Her major accomplishment while serving as chairperson of the Commission on Human Rights was the creation in 1948 of the Universal Declaration of Human Rights, and she became the first recipient of the United Nations Human Rights prize, which was awarded posthumously.

As a U.N. delegate, and from 1953 on as an educational volunteer with the American Association for the United Nations, she continued to lecture and to travel in support of peace and international understanding, visiting the Middle East, Southeast Asia, and the Soviet Union. In each destination she was welcomed as the "first lady of the world."

A prolific writer, she published a dozen books, including a three-volume autobiography. For over twenty years, she wrote a daily syndicated newspaper column entitled "My Day" and published extensively in the leading periodicals of her day. The bibliography of those articles fills thirty-three pages. Roosevelt also hosted several regular radio and television programs, appeared frequently on NBC's *Meet the Press,* and filmed educational television programs at Brandeis University.

Though originally opposed to both women's suffrage and an Equal Rights Amendment that she feared might jeopardize the protective legislation previously enacted for women, Roosevelt's dedication to social justice and her friendship with such feminists as Molly Dewson, Elizabeth Read, Esther Lape, and Helen Gahagan Douglas broadened her perspective. Through a lifetime of service working from within to improve the democratic system, and by her immense courage in fighting for what she believed, Eleanor Roosevelt enhanced the power, stature, and the self-perception of women throughout the world. By 1948, according to a Gallup Poll, she was America's most admired woman.

—*Tamerin Mitchell Hayward and Barbara Hope Klein*

See Also:

Democratic Party; Douglas, Helen Gahagan; New Deal; Social Feminism

References:

Flemion, Jess, and Colleen O'Connor. *Eleanor Roosevelt.* San Diego: State University Press, 1988.

Hareven, Tamara K. *Eleanor Roosevelt: An American Conscience.* Chicago: Quadrangle, 1968.

Hoff-Wilson, Joan, and Marjorie Lightman. *Without Precedent: The Life and Career of Eleanor Roosevelt.* Bloomington: Indiana University Press, 1984.

Kearny, James R. *Anna Eleanor Roosevelt: The Evolution of a Reformer.* Boston: Houghton Mifflin, 1968.

La Follette, Suzanne. "To the Ladies." [Rev. of *It's Up to the Women*] *Saturday Review* 10 (November 11, 1933): 253.

Lash, Joseph P. *Eleanor and Franklin.* New York: Norton, 1971.

———. *Eleanor: The Years Alone.* New York: Norton, 1972.

———. *Love, Eleanor Roosevelt and Her Friends.* Garden City, N.Y.: Doubleday, 1982.

Roosevelt, Eleanor. *The Autobiography of Eleanor Roosevelt.* New York: Harper, 1961.

———. *It's Up to the Women.* New York: Stokes, 1933.

———. *My Day: Her Acclaimed Columns, 1936–1945.* Edited by Martha Gellhorn. New York: Pharos Books, 1989.

ROSENBERG, ETHEL GREENGLASS (1915–53), housewife and mother, was executed, along with her husband, Julius, in the electric chair at Sing Sing prison at age thirty-seven for conspiracy to commit espionage in what the FBI termed "the crime of the century."

The daughter of Jewish immigrants, Rosenberg grew up on New York City's Lower East Side and attended its public schools. Her early ambitions to become a singer were thwarted by her mother's disapproval and by the Great Depression. After graduating from high school in 1931, she performed office work for a series of business firms. However, she continued voice lessons, appeared with an amateur theatrical group, and was the youngest member of the Schola Cantorum, a professional choir. At the same time, Rosenberg was an active participant in left-wing political activities and union organizing. In 1939 she married Julius Rosenberg, a graduate engineer of the City College of New York, and continued her activism until the birth of her first child, Michael, in 1943. A second son, Robert, was born in 1947, and Rosenberg devoted her time and energy to her family.

Accused by Ethel's younger brother of passing atomic secrets to the Soviet Union, Julius Rosenberg was arrested and imprisoned in 1950. The following month she, too, was arrested. Six months later, charges were made, based on the testimony of her sister-in-law, who claimed that Ethel Rosenberg typed the information allegedly given her husband by her brother, although no such typed material was ever found. Despite the flimsy case against her, the government persisted in charging her, hoping this would force her husband into confessing. Convicted of conspiracy, the couple were sentenced to death. Held in virtual solitary confinement at Sing Sing prison for two years, Ethel Rosenberg was allowed weekly visits with her husband and only sporadic contact with her children. Vilified as a domineering, unnatural wife and mother and subjected to enormous pressure from her family, the government, and the press to admit her guilt, Rosenberg steadfastly insisted on her innocence. Her letters to her husband and sons, published as *Death House Letters* in an effort to raise money for her sons' future, provide a poignant account of her anguish over the loss of her family, as well as her awareness that she was a symbol of anticommunist hysteria. In her final letter to her sons, she wrote: "Always remember that we were innocent and could not wrong our conscience."

—*Ruth Jacknow Markowitz*

References:

Meeropol, Robert, and Michael Meeropol. *We Are Your Sons: The Legacy of Ethel and Julius Rosenberg*. Boston: Houghton Mifflin, 1975.

Rosenberg, Ethel, and Julius Rosenberg. *Death House Letters*. New York: Jero, 1953.

Schneir, Walter, and Miriam Schneir. *Invitation to an Inquest: Reopening the Rosenberg "Atom Spy" Case*. 2d ed. New York: Praeger, 1983.

"ROSIE THE RIVETER" symbolized the woman worker in American defense industries during World War II. Facing a simultaneous manpower drain and increased production demands, the federal War Manpower Commission and the Office of War Information undertook a recruitment campaign to bring more women into the labor force. Lured by higher wages, women took men's places in factories that produced aircraft, ordnance, and ships. Although only 8 percent of the workers employed in the production of durable goods had been women in 1940, this figure jumped to 25 percent in 1945.

Between 1940 and 1945 the number of female workers rose from twelve to eighteen million. Clerical positions for women almost doubled, although critical shortages developed in the nursing and teaching professions. The entry of large numbers of married women and women thirty-five and older also helped to transform the labor force.

Still, female workers faced hurdles. They encountered wage discrimination and were denied access to hazardous occupations, such as sandblasting. In factories, women tended to stay in lower-level jobs that required less training. Black women worked as janitors and sweepers and in other bottom-rung jobs. Unions often welcomed females reluctantly. Working mothers of young children faced disapproval based on a fear that they were contributing to juvenile delinquency.

Working women faced a double standard. Government and industry appealed to their patriotism to enter the labor force, yet both expected them to leave once the war ended. Nevertheless, female employment in the United States stood at seventeen million in 1947, higher than it had been before the war began.

—*Casey Edward Greene*

See Also:

Mobilization, War Manpower Commission, World War II

References:
Campbell, D'Ann. *Women at War with America: Private Lives in the Patriotic Era*. Cambridge: Harvard University Press, 1984.
Field, Connie. *The Life and Times of Rosie the Riveter*. [DIRECT/1980; 60 min; color; 16mm]
Gluck, Sherna B. *Rosie the Riveter Revisited: Women, the War, and Social Change*. Boston: Twayne, 1987.
Hartmann, Susan M. *The Home Front and Beyond: American Women in the 1940s*. Boston: Twayne, 1982.
Honey, Maureen. *Creating Rosie the Riveter: Class, Gender, and Propaganda during World War II*. Amherst: University of Massachusetts Press, 1984.

RUETHER, ROSEMARY RADFORD (b. 1936), twentieth-century theologian and lecturer on feminist theory and history, has been a prolific author of academic books and articles including *The Church Against Itself* (1967), *Christology and Feminism* (1976), and *Sexism and God Talk* (1983). She edited the book *Religion and Sexism* (1973), as well as being a contributing editor to *Christianity and Crisis*. She received her Ph.D. in classics and patristics from Claremont Graduate School and has been on the faculties of Howard University's School of Religion, Harvard Divinity School, and Garrett Evangelical Theological Seminary.

In the field of church history, Ruether has researched the misogyny of the early church fathers, enabling women of the Judeo-Christian tradition to challenge the limits of traditional church histories and to fill the spaces that exist in those histories and church systems.

Ruether represents a contemporary group of women theological scholars whose scholarship has offered a variety of feminist theological perspectives for modern society. Linking Christology and feminism, speaking of women's spiritualities, and naming the exclusiveness of traditional religious language and rhetoric are but a few of Ruether's academic and personal endeavors. Ruether's application of a feminist theory to the existing scholarship in her field has made possible a revolution of women's role in religion.

—*Joanne S. Richmond*

See Also:
Christianity, Theologians

References:
Ruether, Rosemary R. *Christology and Feminism*. Nashville: United Methodist Board of Higher Education and Ministry, 1976.
———. *The Church Against Itself*. New York: Herder & Herder, 1967.
———. "Feminist Interpretation: A Method of Correlation." In *Feminist Interpretation of the Bible*, edited by Letty M. Russell. Philadelphia: Westminster, 1985, pp. 111–24.
———. "Male Chauvinist Theology and the Anger of Women." *Cross Currents* 21 (September 1971): 173–75.
———. "Male Clericalism and the Dread of Women." *Ecumenist* 11 (July/August 1973): 65–69.
———. "Mother Earth and the Megamachine." *Christianity and Crisis* 31 (December 13, 1971): 267–72.
———. *Religion and Sexism: Images of Women in the Jewish and Christian Traditions*. New York: Simon & Schuster, 1974.
———. *Sexism and God Talk: Toward a Feminist Theology*. Boston: Beacon, 1983.
——— and Rosemary Skinner Keller, eds. *Women and Religion in America*. San Francisco: Harper & Row, 1986.

RUFFIN, JOSEPHINE ST. PIERRE (1842–1924) was a lecturer, suffragist, and social activist. She was the founder of the Woman's Era Club of Boston and the editor of the club newsletter the *Woman's Era*. Ruffin organized the first national conference of black women in 1895.

Born in Boston, Josephine was the sixth child of John and Eliza St. Pierre. She attended public school in Charleston and Salem, Massachusetts, and a private school in New York City because her mother refused to allow her to attend segregated schools in Boston. In 1858 she married George Ruffin, a graduate of Harvard Law School and Boston's first black municipal court judge. Active in the crucial causes of her day, Ruffin recruited soldiers for the Civil War, worked with the U.S. Sanitary Commission, and helped organize the Boston Kansas Relief to help persons who chose to move to Kansas in 1879. After her husband's death in 1886, Ruffin devoted her life to charities and philanthropic work. She served on the executive board of the Massachusetts Moral Education Association, the Massachusetts School Suffrage Association, and was a visitor for the Associated Charities of Boston. While editor of the *Boston Courant*, a weekly black newspaper, she joined the New England Press Association.

Ruffin envisioned a women's movement directed toward the good of all, regardless of gender or race. Yet she herself was a victim of discrimination in 1900 when she attended a convention of the General Federation of Women's Clubs as a representative of the New England Woman's Club, the Massachusetts State Federation of Women's Clubs, and the Woman's Era Club. The GFWC rejected the credentials of the Woman's Era Club, and Ruffin refused to enter the convention solely as a delegate from white clubs. Afterwards, Ruffin initiated the movement for the first national organization of black women, the National Federation of Afro-American Women. She was a vice president of the National Association of Colored Women and president of the Woman's Era Club from 1894 to 1903.

—*Floris Barnett Cash*

See Also:

Black Women, National Association of Colored Women, National Federation of Afro-American Women

References:

Brown, Hallie Q. *Homespun Heroines and Other Women of Distinction*. Freeport, N.Y.: Books for Libraries Press, 1971.

Cash, Floris Barnett. "Womanhood and Protest: The Club Movement Among Black Women, 1892–1922." Diss. State University of New York-Stony Brook, 1986.

Flexner, Eleanor. *A Century of Struggle*. Cambridge, Mass.: Belknap, 1975.

Scruggs, L. A. *Women of Distinction*. Raleigh, N.C.: Scruggs, 1893.

RUKEYSER, MURIEL (1913–80), known primarily as a protest poet, was equally a poet of the human soul, writing as earnestly about the need for communication among people and the exhilaration of life and love as about social injustice. She believed intensely in life, encouraging others through her poetry to look within themselves to discover the strength and self-knowledge necessary to live full, productive lives rather than to hide from progress and change. Using images of technology and energy extensively in her early volumes of poetry, she searched for a place for the self in a modern technological society.

Born in New York City, Rukeyser led a quiet, sheltered childhood, which became a source of her insistence on experience and communication in poetry. Her political involvement bore witness to her verse. She was arrested while attending the Scottsboro Trials in Alabama in 1933, personally investigated the mining tragedy in Gauley Bridge, West Virginia, reported for *Life and Times Today* on the Fascist Olympics in Barcelona as the Spanish Civil War broke out around her, demonstrated for peace in Hanoi and Washington, D.C., in 1972, and later that year flew to Korea to plead for the life of imprisoned poet Kim Chi-Ha.

While critics have linked her poetry with that of W. H. Auden, Stephen Spender, and other political poets, she considered Emerson, Melville, and Whitman her mentors. Her visionary quality and organic poetic theory are clearly Transcendentalist, her outrage with injustice Melvillean, and her long, rhythmic lines, her optimism, her poetic altruism, and her expression of the power and beauty of sensuality Whitmanesque. Yet, a feminine consciousness is also evident throughout Rukeyser's poetry, linking her work with that of Denise Levertov and Adrienne Rich. She sees with a feminist point of view, which adds vitality to her revisualizations of history and myth.

In addition to poetry, Muriel Rukeyser also published several volumes of translations, three biographies, two volumes of literary criticism, a number of book reviews, a novel, five juvenile books, several documentary film scripts, and a play. In each, she urges her readers to look within themselves for the common ground on which all human beings stand.

—*Kenneth E. Gadomski*

References:

"Craft Interview with Muriel Rukeyser." In *The Craft of Poetry*, edited by William Packard. Garden City, N.Y.: Doubleday, 1974, pp. 53–76.

Kertesz, Louise. *The Poetic Vision of Muriel Rukeyser*. Baton Rouge: Louisiana State University Press, 1979.

Terris, Virginia R. "Muriel Rukeyser: A Retrospective." *The American Poetry Review* 3 (May/June 1974): 10–15.

RUSH, BENJAMIN (1745–1813), an eighteenth-century advocate of improving American women's education, influenced the advancements in and set the standards for the curriculum of female academies and seminaries during the Federalist era. Proudly nationalistic and intensely critical of servile imitation of the British "ornamental" education for women, Rush promoted a comprehensive curriculum that surpassed that of the "finishing school," feeling that the duties of Republican Motherhood required that American women have both the formal education and practical training to rear patriotic sons and dutiful daughters. Rush was a founder of the trend-setting Young Ladies' Academy of Philadelphia, which offered a curriculum for the girls that acknowledged their equal capacity to learn without challenging the gender system of colonial and revolutionary American society. Rush and his colleagues such as Horace Bushnell established that women had the capacity to learn and thereby laid a foundation upon which Victorian promoters could seek increasing advances in women's education throughout the nineteenth century.

—*Angela Howard Zophy*

See Also:

Education, Female Academies

References:

Good, Harry G. *Benjamin Rush and His Service to American Education*. Berne, Ind.: Witness, 1918.

Rush, Benjamin. *Essays, Literary, Moral, and Philosophical*. Philadelphia: Thomas & Samuel Bradford, 1798.

Woody, Thomas. *A History of Women's Education in the United States*. 2 vols. New York: Science Press, 1929.

SALEM WITCH TRIALS. In the fall of 1692, a group of adolescent girls in Salem, Massachusetts, were "afflicted" by a strange hysteria that resulted in seizures and accusations of witchcraft. The precise causes of the girls' sickness, and whether feigned or real, continue to be debated; one theory is that they were teenagers rebelling against hidebound Puritan strictures, another that they were ingesting hallucinogenic chemicals from the ergot fungus in rye flour. As the frenzy began, the Salem minister's daughter, Betty Parris, and niece Abigail accused the family's black slave woman Tituba of witchcraft. Tituba, a native of Barbados, finally gave way under intense pressure and, in fear of her life, confessed to bewitching the young girls. With her confession, the accusations spread to include many women and three men of Salem who were already suspected of being less than pious Puritans.

The witchcraft court, convened by the government of the colony of Massachusetts, met at Salem in 1692 and 1693 to hear the cases. Led by such Puritans as Cotton Mather and Samuel Sewall, the court handed down a guilty verdict and death sentence in nineteen cases. Eighteen people were hanged, and one man, Giles Corey, was pressed to death with stones. As the hysteria spread beyond Salem, the pattern repeated itself; there was no presumption of innocence and virtually no effective defense against the charge of witchcraft. Within another year, there were hundreds of accused witches in jails throughout eastern Massachusetts, awaiting sentencing or execution.

At that time a new royal governor, William Phips, arrived from England to find the colony seized with a hysteria that had gone beyond the control of the Puritan theocracy itself. Phips dismissed the Puritan witchcraft court, freed the remaining jailed witches, and ended the accusations. The fact that his own wife had also been named may have added to his general displeasure. Following his action, the power of the Puritan church over the colony government rapidly declined, leading modern historians to argue that the witchcraft hysteria was the last demonstration of theocracy in Massachusetts and that its ending began the movement toward separation of church and state.

—*Ellen D. Langill*

See Also:

Nurse, Rebecca; Tituba

References:

Burr, George L., ed. *Narratives of the Witchcraft Cases, 1658–1706*. New York: Scribner, 1914.

Starkey, Marion L. *The Devil in Massachusetts.* New York: Knopf, 1949.

Upham, Charles W. *Salem Witchcraft.* 1867; rpt. New York: Ungar, 1959.

SAMPSON, DEBORAH (GANNETT) (1760–1827), American Revolutionary War soldier and heroine, was the oldest of three daughters and three sons of Jonathan Sampson and Deborah Bradford, both of whom were descended from the early Pilgrims.

On September 3, 1782, Sampson was excommunicated from the First Baptist Church of Middleborough, Massachusetts, for enlisting as a soldier in the army. The previous May 20, she had enlisted in the Fourth Massachusetts Regiment under the name Robert Shutleff/Shirtliff. Sampson fought in several engagements and was wounded at Tarrytown, New York. While hospitalized with a fever in Philadelphia, her sex was discovered, and General Henry Knox discharged her at West Point on October 25,

1783. In 1792 the state of Massachusetts awarded her a pension, and in 1805 the United States placed her on the pension list. After she died, her heirs received compensation from an act of Congress in 1838.

She married Benjamin Gannett in April 1785 and bore three children. In 1797 Herman Mann published her biography, entitled *The Female Review*. Later, she toured on a theater circuit telling of her adventures in the war.

—*Ginger Rae Allee*

See Also:

Military Service, Revolutionary War

References:

Bruce, H. Addington. *Women in the Making of America*. Rev. ed. Boston: Little, Brown, 1928, pp. 91–96.

Green, Henry Clinton, and Mary Wolcott Green. *The Pioneer Mothers of America*. Vol. 2. New York: Putnam, 1912, pp. 265–79.

Leonard, Eugene Audress, Sophia Drinker, and Miriam Young Holden. *The American Women in Colonial and Revolutionary Times, 1765–1800*. Philadelphia: University of Pennsylvania Press, 1962, pp. 120–21.

Logan, Mary Simmerson. *The Part Taken by Women in American History*. 1912; rpt. New York: Arno, 1972, pp. 105–06.

Revolutionary War. "Military Pension File X32722, Deborah Gannett (Alias Robert Shurtleff)." National Archives, Washington, D.C.

Whitton, Mary Ormsbee. *These Were the Women, U.S.A. 1776–1880*. New York: Hastings House, 1954, pp. 14–16.

Wright, Richardson. *Forgotten Ladies*. Philadelphia: Lippincott, 1928, pp. 94–120.

SANDOZ, MARI (1896–1966), historian and novelist, did perhaps more than any other white writer to destroy the destructive stereotype of American Indians. Her Great Plains series is not only a classic in the history of the American West but portrayed the American Indians on their own terms long before it had become fashionable to do so. The six works in their historical chronology are *The Beaver Men* (1964), *Crazy Horse* (1942), *Cheyenne Autumn* (1953), *The Buffalo Hunters* (1954), *The Cattlemen* (1958), and *Old Jules* (1935), which is autobiographical.

Sandoz possessed several qualities that made her uniquely qualified to write about the Plains Indians. She attempted to enter into the cultures she was writing about. In 1930 and 1931 she traveled three thousand miles in Sioux territory, interviewing and living with Sioux and Cheyenne who knew Crazy Horse. Moreover, before she wrote *Cheyenne Autumn*, she retraced the fifteen-hundred-mile flight north and talked with the old Cheyenne who had survived the ordeal. In addition, she adopted an Oglala and Cheyenne perspective in her writing, using idioms and metaphors to capture, in her words, "the underlying rhythm pattern to say something of the things of the Indian for which there are no white-man words, suggest something of his innate nature, something of his relationship to the earth and the sky and all that is between."

Sandoz was accused by critics of endorsing the Noble Savage stereotype and being too partisan in favor of the Indians. However, Sandoz wrote from the assumption that Oglala and Cheyenne cultures were as varied and complex as white/Anglo culture, and she illuminated the good as well as the bad, the heroic as well as the mundane. We see Little Wolf as the culture hero of his people, and finally we see him disgraced when he kills a tribesman in a drunken rage. We see Crazy Horse as the self-sacrificing leader as well as the jealous lover. We see the Oglala warriors as courageous fighters against the whites and obsequious toward the whites once they are captured.

—*John Snider*

References:

Clark, Laverne Harrell. "The Indian Writings of Mari Sandoz: 'A Lone One Left From the Old Times.'" *American Indian Quarterly* 1 (1974): 183–92, 269–80.

Sandoz, Mari. *Sandhill Sundays and Other Recollections*. Lincoln: University of Nebraska Press, 1970.

Snider, John. "Mari Sandoz' *Crazy Horse* and *Cheyenne Autumn*: Destroying the Stereotype."

In "The Treatment of American Indians in Selected American Literature: A Radical Critique." Diss. University of Illinois-Urbana, 1983, pp. 160–92.

Stauffer, Helen Winter. *Mari Sandoz: Story Catcher of the Plains.* Lincoln: University of Nebraska Press, 1982.

SANGER, MARGARET LOUISE (HIGGINS) (1879–1966) was the most notable leader in the twentieth-century birth control movement. After marrying artist William Sanger in 1902 and bearing three children, Sanger went to work as a home nurse in the slums of New York City. Appalled by the plight of the women she encountered, Sanger recognized that birth control, a term she coined in 1914, could free these women of the physical hardships, fear, and dependency inherent in being unable to separate sexual experience from reproduction.

Convinced that birth control was the key to gaining female autonomy, Sanger sought to challenge the laws prohibiting it. She was indicted in 1914 for publishing material in her journal the *Woman Rebel* classified as "obscene," and in 1916 she was arrested and jailed for opening the first birth control clinic in Brownsville, Brooklyn. These law-defying tactics brought national prominence to the birth control movement, but Sanger soon recognized the need for more broadly based support. Abandoning her early radical political associations, she began courting the wealthy professional, business, and philanthropic communities. In the process she divorced William Sanger and married wealthy oilman J. Noah Slee.

Sanger's growing financial base enabled her to found the American Birth Control League in 1921 and launch a campaign to legalize birth control. Insisting that birth control be treated as a medical issue, she pressed for passage of a bill exempting doctors from the legal prohibitions on contraceptives. Her efforts were rewarded in the Supreme Court's 1936 *United States v. One Package* decision, which permitted the mailing of contraceptive materials intended for physicians. In 1923 Sanger opened the Birth Control Clinical Research Bureau, the first doctor-staffed birth control clinic in the nation. These efforts resulted in the transformation of the birth control movement into a mainstream social reform, a shift reflected in the 1942 reorganization of the American Birth Control League and its successors into the Planned Parenthood Federation of America.

Sanger also brought her birth control message to Europe and the Far East. In 1952 she was instrumental in organizing an international birth control conference in Bombay, a meeting that led to the founding of the International Planned Parenthood Federation. In her later years, Sanger's efforts to find financial support for contraceptive research led to the development of the first birth control pill.

Margaret Sanger persevered in the face of numerous legal, religious, and social obstacles. By remaining consistently dedicated to insuring that safe and reliable birth control was available to all women, she helped effect a social revolution that transformed women's lives.

—*Esther Katz*

See Also:

American Birth Control League, Birth Control, Birth Control Clinical Research Bureau, Obscenity, Planned Parenthood Federation of America, *Woman Rebel*.

References:

Gordon, Linda. *Woman's Body, Woman's Right: A Social History of Birth Control in America.* New York: Grossman, 1976.

Kennedy, David. *Birth Control in America: The Career of Margaret Sanger.* New Haven: Yale University Press, 1970.

Lader, Lawrence. *The Margaret Sanger Story and the Fight for Birth Control.* Garden City, N.Y.: Doubleday, 1955.

Reed, James. *From Public Vice to Private Virtue: The Birth Control Movement and American Society Since 1830.* Princeton: Princeton University Press, 1978.

Sanger, Margaret. *Happiness in Marriage.* New York: Brentano, 1926.

———. *Margaret Sanger: An Autobiography.* New York: Norton, 1938.

SARGENT, JESSE IRENE (1852–1932) was professor of the history of fine arts at Syracuse University, 1895–1932, and a leading advocate of the American arts and crafts movement. Sargent taught Romance languages, aesthetics, and art history at Syracuse University and received honorary degrees from that institution in 1911 and 1922. In 1926 she became the second woman to be awarded an honorary membership by the American Institute of Architects. For twenty-five years Sargent contributed articles on jewelry, metalwork, glass, and ceramics to *The Keystone* (Philadelphia). Her most significant work, however, appeared in *The Craftsman* (Syracuse), a magazine published by furniture manufacturer Gustav Stickley.

Sargent's main themes were typical of much arts and crafts writing. She condemned the effects of the "moral earthquake" wrought by industrialism. For example, she believed that the increasing reliance on machines and on an elaborate division of labor had transformed factory workers into slaves. Degraded labor, in turn, cheated consumers by producing poorly designed and cheaply constructed objects. Most alarming, industrialism threatened to destroy urban civilization because it fostered an excessive individualism that was blind to mutual obligations and the corporate life of the municipality.

Influenced by the writings of British reformers such as John Ruskin and William Morris and by her own extensive reading in thirteenth-century history and literature, Sargent believed that certain principles gleaned from Europe's Middle Ages could guide modern Americans toward a better society. The life of the medieval craftsman, she argued, consisted of an ideal mixture of art, labor, and recreation. The guilds of that era were models of brotherhood, civic spirit, and quality workmanship. And the balanced, interdependent structure of the cathedral mirrored both the religious faith and secular aspirations of an organically unified society. Sargent's thoughts on social reform were also powerfully affected by Russian anarchist Peter Kropotkin, who proposed an "integral education" that would combine manual training with the usual academic studies. Finally, she was very impressed by the simple dignity of Gustav Stickley's house and furniture designs. Such dwellings could serve the middle class as soothing havens from the "storm and stress" of modern life.

Sargent wrote more than eighty articles for *The Craftsman* during its first years, 1901–05, and played a crucial role in molding a magazine ostensibly devoted to the "household arts," into the principal journal of arts and crafts social thought.

—Bruce R. Kahler

See Also:

Art, Women in Higher Education

References:

Gabriel, Cleota Reed. "Irene Sargent: Rediscovering a Lost Legend." *The Courier* 16 (Summer 1979): 3–13.

Reed, Cleota. "Irene Sargent: A Comprehensive Bibliography of Her Published Writings." *The Courier* 18 (Spring 1981): 9–25.

SATIR, VIRGINIA (1914–1989), an acknowledged pioneer in the area of family therapy and best known for her books *Cojoint Family Therapy* and *Peoplemaking*, has contributed much to the understanding of family dynamics and communication patterns. She was in great demand as the premier trainer of family therapists at AVANTA in Menlo Park, California, and a pivotal force in the field of family therapy because of her exceptional skills and innovative thinking.

Born in Neilsville, Wisconsin, to Reinhold and Minnie Pagenkopf, Satir began a brief teaching career after receiving a B.E. from Wisconsin State University in 1936. She worked as a social worker and received her M.A. in psychiatric social work from the University of Chicago in 1948. She married Norman Satir in 1951, raised two children, and was divorced in 1961.

In 1955 Satir became an instructor in family dynamics at the Illinois State Psychiatric Institute. At the institute, she introduced the revolutionary idea of working with the patient's family instead of doing individual therapy with the hospitalized person. Satir moved to California in 1959 and co-founded the Mental Research Institute in Palo Alto, an interdisciplinary group of therapists, communication experts, and social scientists committed to the study of family interaction in relation to illness and health. In the mid-1960s, after establishing the first training program in family therapy, Satir went on to develop a human-growth center at the Esalen Institute. She founded the AVANTA network in 1976 in Menlo Park as a training center for teachers of family systems.

When *Cojoint Family Therapy* was published in 1964, Satir described to therapists her unorthodox techniques, which emphasized the reestablishment of communication patterns between family members. Seeing mental illness as "distorted communication," Satir emphasized social rather than intrapsychic factors. When she first developed her theories, Satir was criticized as being too confrontive, but over the years, her ideas have won wide acceptance. In 1974 Satir published *Peoplemaking* so that families could recognize and analyze their own rules and make behavioral changes. She did not emphasize mental illness but discussed concrete interventions to improve the self-esteem of family members.

Virginia Satir helped revolutionize the field of psychotherapy by treating clients within the context of their families rather than as individuals. As author and productive social worker, she has contributed more to the professional development of family therapy than any other woman.

—*Linda Noer*

See Also:
Psychiatry, Psychology, Social Work

Reference:

Goldenberg, Irene, and Herbert Goldenberg. *Family Therapy*. Monterey, Calif.: Brooks-Cole, 1980.

SCHLAFLY, PHYLLIS MACALPIN (STEWART) (b. 1924), author, speaker, and crusader for conservative causes, was instrumental in defeating ratification of the Equal Rights Amendment. As editor of the *Phyllis Schlafly Report* and the *Eagle Forum Newsletter*, she rallied nonworking women to antifeminist causes. Without a paid staff or large contributions, she wrote hundreds of articles and delivered speeches in every state condemning feminism as destructive of the family. Schlafly has published nine books, including *A Choice, Not an Echo*, which promoted the presidential candidacy of Senator Barry Goldwater in 1964.

Schlafly was born in St. Louis in 1924 and educated at the Convent of the Sacred Heart. She graduated Phi Beta Kappa from Washington University in 1944, while working at a war plant forty-eight hours a week, and won a scholarship to Radcliffe College, where she earned a M.A. in government in 1945. At age fifty-four, she received a law degree from Washington University.

She did research in Washington, D.C., managed a successful campaign for a Republican congressional candidate in St. Louis, and edited a bank newsletter before marrying John Fred Schlafly, Jr., an Alton, Illinois, attorney, in 1949. Having borne four boys and two girls, Schlafly has stated that raising a family was the most important career for a woman and that she enjoyed nothing more than caring for a baby.

A conservative Republican, Schlafly ran for Congress in 1952 and 1970, but lost both races. She served as a delegate or alternate to Republican national conventions in 1956, 1960, and 1964 and ran for president of the National Federation of Republican Women in 1967, but was defeated. She collaborated with Rear Admiral Chester Ward on five books between 1964 and Ward's death in 1978, including *Kissinger on the Couch* and *Ambush at Vladivostok*. She opposed the Nuclear Test Ban Treaty of 1963 and arms control agreements with the Soviet Union.

As founder and chairperson of STOP ERA, Schlafly was the most prominent woman opponent of the Equal Rights Amendment, which fell short of ratification in 1982. Since then, Schlafly has crusaded against abortion, pornography, and violence and sex on television. A devout Catholic and member of the Daughters of the American Revolution, her hobbies are reading and old movies.

—*Glen Jeansonne*

See Also:

Antifeminism, Equal Rights Amendment, Republican Party, Right-Wing Political Movements

References:

Felsenthal, Carol. *The Sweetheart of the Silent Majority: The Biography of Phyllis Schlafly.* Garden City, N.Y.: Doubleday, 1981.

Klemesrud, Judy. "Opponent of the E.R.A. Confident of Its Defeat." *The New York Times* (December 15, 1975): 44: 1.

Schlafly, Phyllis. *A Choice, Not an Echo.* Alton, Ill.: Pere Marquette Press, 1964.

SCHNEIDERMAN, ROSE (1882–1972), a Jewish immigrant, became a union organizer and leader after working in a cap factory from 1898 to 1903. Schneiderman's involvement with the trade union began with her job in the cap factory. Her experience in chartering the first female local of the United Cloth Hat and Cap Maker's Union and her participation in the thirteen-week cap-maker's strike inspired her dedication to the spirit of trade unionism. To Schneiderman, this spirit meant friendship among workers through serving others; she felt that because the struggle of one member was the responsibility of all the members, the group benefited from the work of each individual.

Schneiderman joined the New York Women's Trade Union League (WTUL) in 1905, and three years later she became a salaried full-time union organizer through the generosity of a benefactor of the New York league. As a union organizer, she stressed sisterhood in speaking to the factory women, emphasizing that they were not alone in their struggle but joined by many others. By 1913 women's suffrage was a major issue. Schneiderman saw suffrage as a tool to pass legislation to improve working conditions and chaired the industrial section of the Women's Suffrage party of New York City. She was now addressing the male union membership and urging them to vote for the Nineteenth Amendment. While president of the New York WTUL, 1918–49, Schneiderman worked for an eight-hour day and a minimum wage, developed a summer school for working women, and opened a new clubhouse for evening classes, meetings, and social gatherings.

Schneiderman was president of the National Women's Trade Union League, 1926–50. As president, she met prominent people such as Eleanor Roosevelt and was a frequent guest in the Roosevelt home. She seemed to have enlightened Franklin Delano Roosevelt with regard to trade unions, and he appeared to understand and favor unions. Roosevelt appointed Schneiderman the only woman member on the advisory board on the National Recovery Administration (NRA) in 1933.

When Schneiderman retired in 1955, she had played a significant role in the development of trade unionism in the United States for fifty years. She was a worker, an organizer, and a leader, but above all a believer in unionization. Her belief in unions and the zeal with which she spoke inspired many women to join unions. As more women joined the unions, the unions became stronger, and it was the strength of those unions that resulted in improved working conditions for women.

—*Rosemary Herriges, OSF*

See Also:

Jewish Women, National Women's Trade Union League, New Deal, Unions

References:

Lagemann, Ellen Condliffe. *A Generation of Women: Education in the Lives of Progressive Reformers.* Cambridge: Harvard University Press, 1979.

Schneiderman, Rose. "A Cap Maker's Story." In *The Female Experience: An American Documentary*, edited by Gerda Lerner. Indianapolis: Bobbs-Merrill, 1980, pp. 300–02.

——— and L. Goldthwaite. *All for One.* New York: Eriksson, 1967.

SCIENCE. Women have had a difficult struggle in attempting to succeed in the sciences. In the colonial period, the few women practitioners of science had to be trained at home as was Jane Colden (1724–66), who was trained by her father, Cadwallader, a botanist and government leader. Jane Colden classified over three hundred species of plants and was the first to identify the gardenia.

Few other women were able to make reputations in science until the expansion of women's formal education in the nineteenth century. Astronomer Maria Mitchell (1818–89), a professor at Vassar College, was the first female member of the American Academy of Arts and Sciences and one of the first American women in the American Philosophical Society of Philadelphia. Mitchell was also tireless in her efforts to encourage other members of her sex to become scientists. Women's colleges, academies, and normal schools increased the demand for women scientists, but responding to that demand was a problem because of the limited number of graduate programs that would admit women. Most of the early academic scientists had such heavy teaching duties that their time for research and publication was limited. One of the few able to reach a wider audience in addition to Maria Mitchell was zoologist Cornelia Clapp (1849–1930), who taught at Mount Holyoke for forty-four years and published her University of Chicago dissertation.

By 1906 there were 149 women listed in the *American Men of Science*. Opportunities for women scientists increased because of the work of women such as Ida Hyde (1887–1945), who was the first women to be awarded a Ph. D. in science by a German university. Germany was on the cutting edge of scientific development, and when Hyde earned her doctorate in physiology from Heidelberg in 1896, that helped bring other women into the scientific establishment at its highest levels. Employment and research opportunities for women still lagged behind men even if by 1921 there were now 450 women listed in the *American Men of Science*.

Nevertheless, despite many obstacles women have made important contributions in all areas of science. In 1925 anatomist Florence Sabin (1871–1953) became the first woman member of the National Academy of Sciences. Botanist Elizabeth Night Britton (1858–1934) published three hundred articles on mosses. Microbiologist Alice Evans (1881–1975), was the first female president of the Society of American Bacteriologists. Margaret Nice (1883–1974) achieved international recognition as an ornithologist. Maria Geoppert Mayer (1906–72) was the first woman to receive the Nobel Prize for theoretical physics. Barbara McClintock (b. 1902) earned a Nobel Prize for her work in genetics in 1983. Rosalyn Sussman Yalow (b. 1921) won the Nobel Prize in 1977 for her research on the medical uses of radioisotopes.

Science continues to be an issue for women. Most women in science have low-status, labor-intensive positions. Important decisions regarding what research should be done and who will receive monetary support to do it are made mostly by males. Over the past fifteen years, some changes have occurred in the scientific community, partly as a result of the women's movement. More women are gaining access to major research positions. As these women scientists establish their own research agenda and take part in international meetings of professional organizations, their presence may begin to have an even greater impact on the structure, values, goals, and accomplishments of science than was possible in the past.

—Esther K. Wilson and Jonathan W. Zophy

See Also:

Carson, Rachel; Mathematics; Mitchell, Maria; Nature Study

References:

Bleier, Ruth, ed. *Feminist Approaches to Science*. Elmsford, N.Y.: Pergamon, 1986.

Gornick, Vivian. *Women in Science: Portraits from a World in Transition*. New York: Simon & Schuster, 1983.

Keller, Evelyn Fox. *Reflections on Gender and Science*. New Haven: Yale University Press, 1985.

Rossiter, Margaret. *Women Scientists in America: Struggles and Strategies to 1940.* Baltimore: Johns Hopkins University Press, 1982.
Yost, Edna. *Women in Modern Science.* New York: Dodd, Mead, 1959.

SCIENTIFIC MOTHERHOOD, an ideology developed in the late nineteenth century, defined motherhood as woman's most significant role. This ideology declared that mothers were responsible for the health and well-being of their children, yet were incapable of carrying out their duties alone. Advocates of scientific motherhood questioned women's abilities and insisted that mothers needed to be directed, some would say controlled, by experts in the "scientific principles" of child rearing. While the focus on women's role within the family continued the tradition that viewed women as the moral guardians of the home, and by extension of society, scientific motherhood stressed physical nurturance rather than moral training.

Several factors fostered the spread of scientific motherhood. With industrialization and urbanization, the home lost many productive functions; women had fewer opportunities to contribute directly to the family's economy, and mothers became consumers more than producers. Child care, however, did remain in the home, even though family size was shrinking. (In 1800 white families averaged slightly more than eight children; by 1850 about five and a half; and by 1900 little more than three and a half.) At the same time, science held a special place in American culture and scientific knowledge a privileged position.

Scientific motherhood, therefore, appealed to mothers. Science provided the latest, the best information about child care. Furthermore, the prestige of science added status to maternal activity. There was, however, tension within scientific motherhood. The scientific mother was acclaimed; she used science to raise her children most healthfully. Yet, mothers were disparaged; they were believed incapable of successfully rearing their children without scientific experts.

Scientific motherhood was disseminated through many channels. The growing number of women's magazines were especially influential. Some, such as *Babyhood,* were devoted exclusively to child care, while others, such as *Good Housekeeping,* featured child-care articles and columns. Magazine advertisements used the aura of science to promote their products, reminding readers of the importance of scientific advice. In addition, physicians, nurses, and others concerned with child welfare wrote baby books and pamphlets. Working-class women learned the tenets of scientific motherhood at "well baby" clinics; more affluent women attended college courses. In the twentieth century, home economics courses flourished in primary and secondary schools and in colleges. Child-welfare organizations distributed pamphlets, such as the U.S. Children's Bureau's *Infant Care,* first published in 1914 and still in print today. Such sources emphasized women's huge responsibility for the health of their families and the necessity that mothers follow the directions of scientific authorities.

Scientific motherhood continues to influence us. Books on child care sell very well. Prenatal classes and home economics courses enroll many people, males as well as females. Journals such as *Baby Talk* enjoy wide circulation. And, not surprisingly, we are still evaluating the appropriate role of science in child care.

—Rima D. Apple

See Also:

Child Rearing, Magazines

References:

Apple, Rima D. *Mothers and Medicine: A Social History of Infant Feeding, 1890–1950.* Madison: University of Wisconsin Press, 1987.
Jones, Kathleen. "Sentiment and Science: The Late 19th-Century Pediatrician as Mother's Advisor." *Journal of Social History* 17 (1983): 79–86.
Ladd-Taylor, Molly. *Raising a Baby the Government Way: Mothers' Letters to the Children's Bureau, 1915–1932.* New Brunswick, N.J.: Rutgers University Press, 1986.

Weiss, Nancy Pottisham. "Mother, the Invention of Necessity: Dr. Benjamin Spock's *Baby and Child Care.*" *American Quarterly* 29 (1977): 519–46.

SCUDDER, VIDA DUTTON (1861–1954) was a Christian socialist, scholar, and activist. She attended Girls Latin School (Boston), Smith College, and Oxford University, where she was moved by the lectures of John Ruskin on social privilege and the need for reform. Between 1887 and 1928 she taught English at Wellesley College. She demonstrated her literary and social concerns in a popular course on social ideals in English literature and occasionally came into conflict with college authorities over her political activities. She joined with others to initiate the College Settlements Association and was a primary organizer of Denison House in Boston's South End. She founded the Church League for Industrial Democracy, took an active role in organizing the National Women's Trade Union League, and joined the Socialist party.

According to her biographer, although Scudder was often labeled a communist, she actually prefigured recent Christian and Marxist dialogue. By the mid-1930s she had also declared herself a pacifist. From 1889 to her death, she belonged to the Society of the Companions of the Holy Cross, a spiritually minded, socially concerned, autonomous group of Episcopalian laywomen from whom she drew much personal support. Her major scholarly work was *The Franciscan Adventure* (1931), and she was the author of sixteen other books on religion, literature, history, and politics. Her splendid autobiography *On Journey* (1937) is a powerful spiritual and intellectual history as well as a story of American social politics in the first half of the twentieth century.

—Anne Dzamba Sessa

See Also:

Christianity, National Women's Trade Union League, Settlement House Movement, Society of the Companions of the Holy Cross

References:

Corcoran, Theresa S. *Vida Dutton Scudder.* Boston: G. K. Hall, 1982.

———. *Vida Dutton Scudder: The Progressive Years.* Diss. Georgetown University, 1973.

Scudder, Vida Dutton. *On Journey.* Boston: Dutton, 1937.

———. *Social Ideals in English Letters.* Boston: Houghton Mifflin, 1898.

SELLINS, FANNIE (MOONEY) (1870–1919), labor union organizer and socialist, was shot and killed on August 26, 1919, by Allegheny Coal and Coke Company deputy sheriffs in West Natrona, Pennsylvania. Born Fannie Mooney in New Orleans, she later moved to St. Louis, where she was president of Local 67 of the United Garment Workers. In 1909 she traveled across the country gathering support for the locked-out garment workers of the Marx and Hass Clothing Company of St. Louis. Her efforts to encourage a boycott of the company's products brought about a settlement in 1911.

This boycott campaign brought Sellins to the attention of Van Bittner, president of United Mine Workers Subdistrict 5 of Western Pennsylvania and West Virginia. In 1913, on Bittner's recommendation, she went to work in Colliers, near Wierton, West Virginia, aiding families who had been driven out of their homes by the Pennsylvania and West Virginia Coal Company and were living in the woods outside the town. Her support defied an injunction against the United Mine Workers to supply aid to the miners, and she was arrested and jailed. Although the Colliers' strike was settled in 1914, Sellins's case was not cleared until 1916, when she was pardoned by President Woodrow Wilson.

Sellins's work with the miners' wives and families proved to be an effective organizing method. She was also able to recruit black workers who were originally brought up from the South as strikebreakers with the promise of higher wages. Sellins was able to show them that they had been hired under false pretenses. This effort brought her into conflict with the coal companies and made her a target for the violence that eventually ended her life in 1919.

A monument to Fannie Sellins was erected and dedicated by the United Mine Workers of America at her gravesite in Arnold, Pennsylvania. An annual tradition of commemorating her death by workers of the area has recently been renewed.

—*Abby Schmelling*

See Also:

Garment Industries, Socialism, Socialist Party of America, United Mine Workers

References:

Huntington Socialist and Labor Star. Huntington, W.Va., 1913–15.

Korson, George. *Coal Dust on the Fiddle.* Philadelphia: University of Pennsylvania Press, 1943.

Meyerhuber, Carl. "Fannie Sellins and the Events of 1919." Paper given at meeting of the Pennsylvania Labor History Society, September 17, 1986.

St. Louis Labor. St. Louis, Mo. 1909–11.

The **SENECA FALLS CONVENTION**, held July 19–20, 1848 in Seneca Falls, New York, was the first formal U.S. woman's rights convention. Lucretia Mott, Elizabeth Cady Stanton, and Quaker abolitionist women organized the convention and advertised it as one that would "discuss the social, civil, and religious conditions and rights of woman" in the July 14 issue of the *Seneca County Courier.* Between one hundred and three hundred women and men attended. The first day's meeting was chaired by Mott's husband, James. The women made speeches and presented a Declaration of Sentiments and Resolutions, which was modeled after the Declaration of Independence and listed eighteen resolutions regarding woman's rights. All except the elective-franchise resolution for woman suffrage passed unanimously; Stanton and Frederick Douglass, however, persuaded a minimally adequate majority to carry that resolution as well. The second day concluded the meeting with the signing of the Declaration of Sentiments by sixty-eight women and thirty-two men, many of whom later withdrew their names in response to public ridicule and criticism of the convention proceedings.

—*Angela Howard Zophy*

See Also:

Declaration of Sentiments and Resolutions; Mott, Lucretia; Stanton, Elizabeth Cady

References:

Flexner, Eleanor. *A Century of Struggle: The Woman's Rights Movement in the United States.* New York: Atheneum, 1974.

Stanton, Elizabeth Cady, Susan B. Anthony, M. J. Gage, eds. *The History of Woman Suffrage.* 6 vols. New York: National American Woman Suffrage Association, 1888–1922.

SETON, ELIZABETH ANN (BAYLEY) (1774–1821), wife, mother, young widow, and convert to Catholicism, founded the first "native" American Catholic sisterhood, the first American Catholic parochial school, and the first American Catholic orphanage, and was the first native-born American saint.

She was born on August 28, 1774, in New York to a well-established New York Episcopalian family. Elizabeth and her sister Mary were enrolled in a private school called "Mama Pompelion's." In 1794 she married William Magee Seton, a wealthy New York importer and merchant. The marriage was a happy one, and they had five children. A series of unfortunate events forced her husband into bankruptcy. In 1803 William, Elizabeth, and their daughter Anna went to visit friends, the Filicchis, in Leghorn, Italy, where William died of tuberculosis in December 1803. During her stay with the Filicchis, Elizabeth was exposed to and began her conversion to Catholicism.

Back in New York in 1804, she announced to her shocked family and friends that she was thinking of becoming a Catholic. Despite efforts to dissuade her, she officially converted in 1805. In 1808 she went to Baltimore, where she opened a school. Thinking of establishing a community of "sisters," she pronounced vows of poverty, chastity, and obedience in March 1809. In June the community was founded when five women, including Seton, put on the formal religious habit. Later that month the small community moved to Emmitsburg, Maryland, where in early 1810 the first Catholic parochial school in the United States was established. On January 17, 1812, Archbishop John Carroll confirmed the rules and constitution of Mother Seton's Sisters of Charity, the first American community of sisters.

As the community grew, it accepted new responsibilities. The sisters took charge of orphanages in Philadelphia in 1814 and in New York in 1817. These were the first of many educational and charitable institutions that Seton's sisters would establish and staff over the years. Elizabeth Seton died on January 4, 1821. In 1975 she became the first native-born U.S. citizen to be canonized.

—*Edward C. Stibili*

See Also:

Christianity

References:

Bailly de Barberey, Helen. *Elizabeth Seton.* Translated by Joseph B. Code. New York: Macmillan, 1927.

Dirvin, Joseph I. *Mrs. Seton: Foundress of the American Sisters of Charity.* New York: Farrar, Straus and Cudahy, 1962.

Feeney, Leonard. *Elizabeth Seton: An American Woman.* New York: America Press, 1938.

Melville, Annabelle M. *Elizabeth Bayley Seton, 1744–1821.* New York: Scribner, 1951.

The **SETTLEMENT HOUSE MOVEMENT** was launched in London in 1884 when a group of Oxford University students opened Toynbee Hall to alleviate the suffering produced by rapid industrialization and urbanization. It served as a model for like institutions in America. Among the more famous were Jane Addams's Hull House, located in the midst of one of Chicago's densest immigrant ghettos, and New York's Henry Street Settlement, founded by public health nurse Lillian Wald. According to Addams, the settlements had two objectives: to improve the quality of life in their neighborhoods, and to offer their residents, most of whom were women, a socially acceptable and useful outlet for their newly acquired education and ambition.

Like the hundreds of settlements that proliferated across the country at the turn of the century, Hull House and Henry Street were centers for civic, educational, social, and philanthropic reform. By 1893, for instance, Hull House was home to over forty different groups, which drew over two thousand participants to the settlement on a weekly basis. There was a day nursery, gymnasium, dispensary, and playground; cooking, sewing, and language classes; and a cooperative boardinghouse for working women. In addition, there was an art gallery, a Plato Club, a theatrical company, and a variety of bands and choruses. As one historian noted, the settlement house was a veritable department store of reform. Moreover, the settlements were magnets for scholars embarking on studies of the nation's growing cities. In other words, the settlements were urban outposts, offering students a vantage point from which to conduct their inquiries while also meeting the needs of their neighbors and residents.

—*Rebecca L. Sherrick*

See Also:

Addams, Jane; Henry Street Settlement; Hull House

References:

Addams, Jane. *Twenty Years at Hull-House.* New York: Macmillan, 1910.

Chambers, Clarke A. *Seedtime of Reform.* Minneapolis: University of Minnesota Press, 1963.

Wald, Lillian. *The House on Henry Street.* New York: Dover, 1971.

The **"SEVEN SISTERS"** refers to a group of elite, private eastern liberal arts colleges originally for women only, most of which were established in the late nineteenth century: Mount Holyoke (1836), Vassar (1861), Wellesley (1870), Smith (1871), Radcliffe (1879), Bryn Mawr (1880), and Barnard (1893). In 1926 these schools became formally affiliated within the Seven College Conference, from which the name Seven Sisters was derived.

The Seven Sisters colleges were all established at a time when women's higher education was still rather controversial. Mount

Holyoke was an especially important school for young women in the nineteenth century, though it did not gain collegiate status until the 1890s. The men and women who founded the Seven Sisters colleges were committed to the proposition that women were generally as capable of scholarship as men. They were also committed to the idea that women could use higher education to fulfill a growing range of roles in society. The most important of these were associated with the Cult of Domesticity, a battery of responsibilities assigned to wives and mothers in the nineteenth century, particularly caring for and educating their own children. The Seven Sisters colleges generally aimed to educate women so that they could perform such domestic functions well. The most important exception to this pattern was at Bryn Mawr during the presidency of M. Carey Thomas (1894–1922), who believed that women should be educated to perform the same professional roles as men. At other Seven Sisters colleges, however, there was often considerable tension between the academic, intellectual side of college life and the domestic sex-role socialization purposes of these institutions.

Because these colleges were private and derived most of their revenue from tuition, they generally drew students from middle- and upper-class families. The women who attended these schools, moreover, were typically white, Protestant, native-born Americans. With time, the Seven Sisters became known as a female counterpart to the largely all-male Ivy League, partly because two of the Seven Sister schools—Radcliffe and Barnard—were in fact associated with Ivy League universities and partly because the others also were seen as socially and academically exclusive. The generally homogenous quality of the student body invariably affected the character of life and education at these schools.

Although they enjoyed great success and prestige through most of the twentieth century, the Seven Sisters colleges came under sharp attack in the 1960s with the development of the modern feminist movement. Betty Freidan, a graduate of Smith, attacked such schools in her best-selling book *The Feminine Mystique* for allegedly discouraging intellectual accomplishment in young women. In the past decade, several of the Seven Sisters colleges have considered making their programs—to one extent or another—coeducational. Vassar did so in 1969. Others, particularly those affiliated with larger universities, have abandoned their distinctive institutional identities nearly altogether. Although the Seven Sisters institutions remain predominantly white and elite, they place a great deal less emphasis on domestic socialization than they did in the past. In this respect, these pioneer institutions are in step with larger trends affecting all of women's higher education in the latter twentieth century.

—*John Rury*

See Also:

Barnard College, Mount Holyoke Seminary, Radcliffe College, Smith College, Vassar College, Wellesley College, Women in Higher Education

References:

Horowitz, Helen Lefkowitz. *Alma Mater: Design and Experience in the Women's Colleges from their Nineteenth Century Beginnings to the 1930s.* New York: Knopf, 1984.

Solomon, Barbara Miller. *In the Company of Educated Women: A History of Women and Higher Education in America.* New Haven: Yale University Press, 1985.

SEX DISCRIMINATION has been prevalent throughout U.S. history. Much of this discrimination has been rooted in the legal system—either through explicit discriminatory statutes or supported by the noninclusion of women in basic protective legal principles. The struggle to erase sex discrimination can be placed in two major categories: (1) voting rights and (2) legal equality.

The call for legal remedies to sex discrimination was one of the primary outcomes of the first women's rights convention at Seneca Falls, New York, in 1848. In the Declaration of Sentiments and Resolutions adopted by the convention, a list of "unjust laws" was detailed; for example, the lack of suffrage, and the separate and unequal status of married women. Most of the unjust laws listed in the declaration have been struck down, and a seventy-year battle was waged and won to give women full suffrage rights with the ratification of the Nineteenth Amendment in 1920.

But not all gender-based laws have disappeared. Many laws that created or perpetuated gender-based discrimination persisted into the 1970s. Because of the prevalence of such laws and the slow legal remedies through the courts, the feminist activists of the early 1970s focused their efforts primarily on an Equal Rights Amendment to the Constitution. First proposed in 1923, the ERA was seen as a single means by which gender-based discrimination could be remedied. After a decade of struggle, the ERA was officially declared dead on June 30, 1982, after failing by a narrow margin to gain ratification by the necessary thirty-eight states.

Although the Equal Rights Amendment failed, there are constitutional doctrines that can and are being used to eradicate sex-discriminatory laws and government practices. The most relevant doctrine is contained in the "equal protection" clause of the Fourteenth Amendment. Historically, the equal protection clause has been used to solve problems of racial discrimination against blacks. But since the 1970s the courts have extended the concept of equal protection to protect the rights of other groups—including women. Other constitutional remedies can be found in the "right to privacy" and the "due process" clause of the Fourteenth Amendment.

Legal remedies for sex discrimination are the first and most basic step to full inclusion of women as equal participants in the political, economic, and social spheres of society; they, however, do not lead to a quick reversal of decades of sex discrimination.

—*Sue E. Strickler*

See Also:

Declaration of Sentiments and Resolutions, Equal Rights Amendment, Fourteenth Amendment, Nineteenth-Century Woman's Movement, Seneca Falls Convention, Sex-Gender System, Sexism, Twentieth-Century Women's Rights Movement, Voting Rights

References:

Kanowitz, Leo. *Women and the Law: The Unfinished Revolution.* Albuquerque: University of New Mexico Press, 1969.

Ross, Susan Deller, and Ann Barcher. *The Rights of Women: The Basic ACLU Guide to a Woman's Rights.* 2d ed. New York: Bantam, 1983.

Tong, Rosemarie. *Women, Sex and the Law.* Totowa, N.J.: Rowman & Allanheld, 1984.

SEX EQUITY/COMPARABLE WORTH represents a major effort by women's groups and unions since the latter 1970s to bridge the wage gap between men and women. As recently as 1984 the average wage-earning woman made only sixty-four cents for every dollar that the average workingman earned. Even with a vast influx of women into nontraditional jobs and despite affirmative action programs, the gap has not changed significantly in the past fifty years.

Over twenty years after their enactment, neither the Equal Pay Act of 1963 nor Title VII of the Civil Rights Act of 1964 has achieved pay equity for most women. The Equal Pay Act has been interpreted by the courts as granting equal pay for the same or largely similar work. Most women, however, do not have jobs similar to men's. About 80 percent of working women are concentrated in only 20 of the some 427 existing job categories that the U.S. Labor Department has established. These jobs include clerical and secretarial workers, teachers, nurses, and retail workers. Thus, most women are employed in sex-segregated jobs where their experience, skills, and education are consistently undervalued.

Under these circumstances, equal pay legislation has had little impact on the mass of working women. Comparable worth goes beyond equal pay and requires employers to grant equal pay to employees doing different work of comparable value. This determination requires a complex program of job evaluations, a procedure that has been used by management for over fifty years to structure pay differentials among workers. For purposes of comparable worth, this procedure considers such factors as skill, responsibility, training, and working conditions. Each factor is given a numerical value, and jobs that have the same or similar scores are considered comparable.

Although the concept is relatively new in the United States, it has been adopted by the European Common Market as an extension of an equal pay directive by the European Commission, the organization's executive body, in 1979. Although enforcement of procedures is sometimes cumbersome, a number of member states, including the Netherlands and Great Britain, are using the techniques of job evaluation to determine pay equity.

In the United States, comparable worth advocates have focused on state and local governments as initial targets for implementation of the concept. Most notable successes have been in states and localities where unions have been long accepted and where women play important roles in the state legislatures or on local councils. Over one hundred governmental units have already implemented comparable worth legislation, including the cities of Los Angeles and San Jose in California, and the states of Idaho, Minnesota, Iowa, Connecticut, New Mexico, and Washington. Over twenty states have either implemented comparable worth for their employees, begun job evaluations, or are planning legislation along these lines.

On the federal level, the administration of President Ronald Reagan was hostile to the concept. Clarence M. Pendleton, Jr., the chairman of the U.S. Civil Rights Commission from 1982 to 1988, termed comparable worth "the looniest idea since Looney Tunes." On the other hand, a report commissioned by the Equal Employment Opportunity Commission during President Jimmy Carter's administration and produced by the National Academy of Science recommended a program of comparable worth "whenever women are systematically underpaid."

Major legal and political battles loom at both the state and federal levels as opponents of comparable worth organize. Business interests, in particular, oppose the idea because of its potential cost, and because they feel the job evaluations are subjective and that comparable worth directly interferes with the free market. Some feminists have also expressed fears that comparable worth legislation might end the incentive for many women to enter nontraditional jobs.

—*Neil W. Hogan*

See Also:

Affirmative Action, Equal Pay Act, Wages

References:

Hartmann, Heidi I., ed. *Comparable Worth: New Directions for Research.* Washington, D.C.: National Academy Press, 1985.

Hutner, Frances C. *Equal Pay for Comparable Worth: The Working Women's Issue of the Eighties.* New York: Praeger, 1986.

Landau, C. E. "Recent Legislation and Case Law in the EEC on Sex Equality in Employment." *International Labor Review* 123 (January 1984): 53–70.

National Research Council. *Women, Work, and Wages: Equal Pay for Jobs of Equal Value.* Washington, D.C., 1981.

Ratner, Ronnie Steinberg. *Equal Employment Policy for Women.* Philadelphia: Temple University Press, 1980.

Remick, Helen. *Comparable Worth and Wage Discrimination: Technical Possibilities and Political Realities.* Philadelphia: Temple University Press, 1984.

Schmid, Gunter, and Renate Wertzel. *Sex Discrimination and Equal Opportunity.* Aldershot, England: Gower, 1986.

Thompson, Roger. "Women's Economic Equity." *Editorial Research Reports* 1 (May 10, 1985): 335–58.

U.S. Commission on Civil Rights. *Comparable Worth: Issue for the '80s.* Washington, D.C., 1985.

SEX-GENDER SYSTEM is a concept developed by anthropologist Gayle Rubin to deal with current-day prostitution in Africa, but it is far more inclusive and useful in structuring the history of women.

There are certain biological "givens" that constitute sex differences. Women menstruate, procreate, and lactate; men do not. There are differences in muscular and bone structure. On the average, males are taller and

heavier than females. However, each society translates these biological differences into socially defined gender roles. According to Rubin, "Every society has a sex-gender system—a set of arrangements by which the biological raw material of human sex and procreation is shaped by human, social intervention." Sexual "deviance" is generally defined as behavior in conflict with that dictated by the sex-gender system.

Historian Barbara Welter has described the formula for white middle-class women in the nineteenth century as the Cult of True Womanhood. A later expert, Marie Robinson, praised the "power of sexual surrender," but Betty Friedan, a critic of her views, attacked "the feminine mystique" that entrapped women in the 1950s.

While it is true that men and women are different and that there are many tasks in which women are clearly superior to men and vice versa, the sex-gender system is a socially derived set of norms that define masculinity and femininity. The set of rules is laid out in the process of socialization so that a modest difference in chromosomal and genital configuration is made a social imperative.

"Womanhood" in any era is structured by the demographic and economic situation as perceived by the dominant elements in the society. For feminist scholars since the 1960s, the concept of the sex-gender system has provided a useful perspective in the research on women's history.

—*William G. Shade*

See Also:

Gender Roles, Sex Role Socialization, Sexism

References:

Rubin, Gayle. "The Traffic in Women: Notes on the Public Economy of Sex." In *Towards an Anthropology of Women*, edited by Rayna R. Reiter. New York: Monthly Review Press, 1975, pp. 157–210.

Ryan, Mary P. *Womanhood in America*. New York: Watts, 1983.

SEX IN EDUCATION; OR, A FAIR CHANCE FOR THE GIRLS was a pseudoscientific treatise published in 1873 by Edward H. Clarke, M.D., former professor of medicine at Harvard University. It warned that young women who studied rigorously ("in a boy's way") risked atrophy of the uterus and ovaries, sterility, insanity, and death. Widely read and reviewed, Clarke's book affected higher education for women well into the twentieth century.

In the decades following the Civil War, increasing numbers of women limited their families, campaigned for suffrage, and worked outside the home. Women also enrolled in high schools, land-grant colleges, and universities and tried to enter prestigious male institutions such as Harvard, where Clarke served on the board of overseers. *Sex in Education* expressed Clarke's opposition to women's demands for admission to Harvard Medical School and his discomfort, shared by many, at women's generally expanding roles.

To an age that revered science and professional expertise, Clarke announced that women's sphere must be determined by physiology. Using quotations from unnamed "experts" and seven case studies from his medical practice, he maintained that American women were sickly and unable to bear and nurse children because the "vital force" needed to develop the reproductive system had been diverted to the brain. He recommended no more than four hours of study a day for women and complete rest during menstruation, making coeducation impossible. Critics noted that this regime precluded not only coeducation but all higher education and all employment outside the home as well.

Within a year, articles, reviews, and at least four books refuted Clarke's views. Mothers, teachers, college professors, and administrators, feminists such as Caroline Dall and Lucy Stone, public figures such as Julia Ward Howe, and physicians such as Mary Putnam Jacobi argued that Clarke's physiology was antiquated, his evidence flawed, and his motives suspect. Noting that "scientific" writers such as Clarke could have a hidden social agenda, they assembled their own data on the health, careers, marriage, and fertility of educated women. Anticipating socialization theory, they argued that if women were sickly, it was because society limited their life-styles and expectations.

Coeducation expanded because women demanded it and it was cheaper than single-sex education. Clarke's view that women's physiology limited their ability to study and work survived, however, to influence twentieth-century educational psychologists, help justify protective legislation for working women and special living arrangements and courses for college women, and support conservative attitudes about women's roles. Meanwhile, Clarke's critics were the forerunners of an oppositional female research tradition—including Dr. Clelia Mosher, Leta Hollingworth, and Margaret Mead—that refuted charges of female incapacity and supported equal education and equal rights.

—*Maxine S. Seller*

See Also:

Coeducation, Education, Women in Higher Education

References:

Clarke, Edward H., M.D. *Sex in Education; or, A Fair Chance for the Girls.* Boston: James R. Osgood, 1873.

Duffy, E. B. *No Sex in Education, or An Equal Chance for Both Girls and Boys.* Philadelphia: J. M. Stoddard, 1874.

Goodsell, Willystine. *The Education of Women.* New York: Macmillan, 1923.

Howe, Julia Ward. *Sex and Education: A Reply to E. H. Clarke's "Sex in Education."* Boston: Roberts Brothers, 1874.

Rosenberg, Rosalind. *Beyond Separate Spheres: The Intellectual Roots of Modern Feminism.* New Haven: Yale University Press, 1982.

Smith-Rosenberg, Carroll, and Charles Rosenberg. "The Female Animal: Medical and Biological Views of Woman and Her Role in Nineteenth-Century America." *Journal of American History* 60 (September 1973): 334–56.

Walsh, Mary Roth. *Doctors Wanted, No Women Need Apply: Sexual Barriers in the Medical Profession, 1835–1975.* New Haven: Yale University Press, 1977.

SEX ROLE SOCIALIZATION (gender role socialization) is the process by which the members of a society learn its cultural expectations of masculinity and femininity. All cultures have such expectations—known as sex roles or gender roles—although their specific content varies from society to society. Socialization is the means by which these expectations are passed on from one generation to the next or are taught to new members of the society. Various individuals, groups, and institutions—known as socialization agents—are responsible for this teaching; among the most important are one's family, one's peers, the educational system, and the mass media.

Traditionally in the United States, females have been socialized to be passive, emotionally nurturant, and inept in solving mathematical and mechanical problems. Males, in contrast, have been socialized to be aggressive, unemotional, competitive, and mathematically and mechanically inclined. Although some observers have argued that these behavioral differences are due at least in part to the biological differences between males and females, this claim receives little support from empirical evidence. Research, in fact, demonstrates that sex role socialization begins immediately after birth, making it very difficult to determine which, if any, behavioral differences are due to biology and which are the products of social learning. Studies reveal that parents of newborns describe their babies in sex-stereotypical ways and interact with them differently depending on their sex, even though examinations of the babies themselves show no objective sex differences other than anatomical ones. This differential treatment continues throughout childhood and can be seen not only in parent-child interaction, but also in the different toys given to boys and girls, in the different games they are taught to play, and in the living spaces (e.g., bedrooms) that are designed for them. That other studies have demonstrated the tremendous variation in sex roles cross-culturally is also evidence that male/female behavioral differences are socially learned rather than biologically given.

Importantly, sex role socialization does not end in childhood but continues throughout one's life. And it is a very powerful means of social control, seriously affecting men's and women's personalities and social relationships. In fact, several researchers have documented the detrimental effects of traditional sex role socialization in the United States; men and women have been allowed to develop only parts of themselves instead of their full human potential. But the fact that sex role socialization is a learning process, as opposed to a biologically determined one, means that it is not immutable; how and what is taught can be changed. Essentially it has been one of the primary goals of the feminist movement to alter the process of sex role socialization so that it more fully meets our human needs.

—*Claire M. Renzetti*

See Also:
Child Rearing, Gender Roles, Sex-Gender System, Sexism

References:

Frieze, Irene H., Jacquelynne E. Parsons, Paula B. Johnson, Diane N. Ruble, and Gail L. Zellman. *Women and Sex Roles.* New York: Norton, 1978.
Mead, Margaret. *Sex and Temperament in Three Primitive Societies.* New York: Dell, 1949.
Renzetti, Claire M. and Daniel J. Curran. *Women, Men, and Society.* Boston: Allyn and Bacon, 1989.

SEXISM refers to a belief in the superiority of men and the discriminatory behavior resulting from that belief. Although theoretically women might be "sexist" in their treatment of men, in fact the term arose in the 1960s to express discrimination against women. In this regard, the concept of sexism developed as an analogue to racism, then a powerful charge of the civil rights movement against American whites. Feminists saw sexism operating on a broad range of fronts. In particular, they pointed to overwhelming manifestations of sexism in language, for instance in the use of man to refer to human beings in general. Sexism also operated, social scientists found, in the preferential treatment of boy children, in all aspects of institutional education, and in preadult literature used in the schools. Such an early introduction to sexism, feminists believed, only mirrored the society at large—its culture, political system, and employment patterns. All of these rested on sexist premises, belittling the abilities of women and therefore allocating positions of power, prestige, and wealth to men. The modern feminist movement has spent its efforts in an ongoing battle with the detrimental effects of sexism on individual human lives and on the society at large.

—*Bonnie G. Smith*

See Also:
Patriarchy, Sex-Gender System, Sex Role Socialization

References:

Bowles, Gloria, and Renate Duelli Klein, eds. *Theories of Women's Studies.* Boston: Routledge & Kegan Paul, 1983.
Hunter College Women's Studies Collective. *Women's Realities, Women's Choices: An Introduction to Women's Studies.* New York: Oxford University Press, 1983.
Nilsen, Alleen Pace, et al. *Sexism and Language.* Urbana, Ill.: National Council of Teachers of English, n.d.

The **SEXUAL DIVISION OF LABOR (SDOL)** is universal in human society, though the particular forms it takes vary widely. This variation is most evident in North America through comparisons of the SDOL in Native American and European societies, free labor and slave communities, and agrarian and industrial areas and eras.

Initially rooted in, or at least justified by, women's childbearing capacity, the SDOL has affected nonchildbearing women and has survived technological advances in birth control. In general, the SDOL has limited the types of work performed by women, their access to education, and the conditions and remuneration of their employment. The most fundamental division has been between work performed in the household by women (including piecework, care of boarders, and gardening as well as domestic labor and child care) and that performed outside the household by men (including labor in fields, factories, mines, and offices). As North American women entered the wage labor force in ever larger numbers after 1820, the links between the SDOL within the household and that in society at large became increasingly visible.

The SDOL has often proven to be less rigid for women than for men, who rarely serve as domestic laborers. In times of economic necessity--harvesting and planting seasons, war, or the development or rapid expansion of new fields of labor—women have been encouraged to ignore preexisting, gender-based definitions of work. Then farm wives and housewives, female slaves and immigrants, young single women and widows are thrust into corn and cotton fields, munitions factories, textile mills, insurance offices, and schoolrooms. Yet even when women perform "men's" work, the SDOL assures that they will receive lower wages, less status, and have more limited occupational mobility. Only in times of severe economic crisis, such as the Great Depression and then only to a limited extent, has the SDOL served to maintain rather than restrict women's labor force participation.

In addition, the SDOL has shaped men's and women's voluntary labors, from the organization of charitable societies to the mobilization of grass-roots movements. Finally, as the United States extends its economic domain into the Third World, the American form of the SDOL is being exported to those countries along with American capital.

—*Nancy A. Hewitt*

See Also:
Housework, Wages

References:

Hartmann, Heidi. "The Family as a Locus of Gender, Class and Political Struggle: The Example of Housework." *Signs* 6 (Spring 1981): 366–94.

Lawson, Ronald, and Stephen E. Barton. "Sex Roles in Social Movements: A Case Study of the Tenant Movement in New York City." *Signs* 6 (Winter 1980): 230–47.

Milkman, Ruth. *Gender at Work: The Dynamics of Job Segregation by Sex During World War II.* Urbana: University of Illinois Press, 1987.

Signs: Journal of Women in Culture and Society. Special Issue on "Development and the Sexual Division of Labor." 7 (Winter 1981).

SEXUAL POLITICS, by Kate Millett (1970), studied the "political" relationship between men and women in a sexist society and maintained that most gender differences are culturally conditioned. When it was published, Millett's seminal work in feminist literary criticism both popularized the questioning of male authority that characterized the modern women's movement and contributed to the rise of Women's Studies in academe. Begun as a Ph.D. thesis, *Sexual Politics* developed into a book that studied the inadequate and dehumanized presentation of women in what passed for standard (patriarchal) literature. Millett used the writings of Sigmund Freud and other major psychologists and of modern literary giants to trace many of society's outdated sexual habits and customs as well as their subsequent effects on various generations of women. In a scholarly manner, Millett established that the predefined sexual roles of women deserved revision.

In the introduction to *Sexual Politics*, Millett cited illustrations to demonstrate how "sex" determined the personalities of women characters. Analyzing women's social condition and legal status, she established the basis for her theory that historically women had been treated primarily as the property of their husbands. In the second section, Millett traced the history of the sexual revolution, including its manifestations in Nazi Germany and Russia, and Freud's effect on it. She ended by examining the role of women as reflected in the female characters of four major modern writers: D. H. Lawrence, Henry Miller, Norman Mailer, and Jean Genet. She found Genet alone treated women characters as people and not as various forms of sex objects. For the women's movement, *Sexual Politics* was one of the first works to examine fully the antifeminism rampant in the approach to psychology of women during the 1950s and 1960s.

After the publication of *Sexual Politics,* Millett published two books that were installments in her autobiography, *Flying* (1974) and *Sita* (1977). Both examined the difficulties Millett faced as she searched for her identity while she struggled with her fame as a heroine of the women's movement. These works and a subsequent documentary film, *Three Lives,* which received excellent reviews, further established Millett's reputation as writer and feminist.

—Camille Jaski

See Also:

Feminist Literary Criticism, Freudianism, Sex-Gender System, Sex Role Socialization, Twentieth-Century Women's Rights Movement, Women's Studies

References:

Millett, Kate. *Flying.* New York: Knopf, 1974.
———. *Sexual Politics.* New York: Doubleday, 1970.
———. *Sita.* New York: Ballantine, 1978.

SEXUAL REVOLUTION has swept America twice in the twentieth century, in the 1920s and the 1960s. During the first "revolution in manners and morals," the key words were *Fords, flappers,* and *jazz;* during the later one, they were *drugs, Vietnam,* and *generation gap.*

Though outspoken writers exaggerated the depth of change, in this century the evolution of sexual behavior has generally followed a slow and steady pace punctuated by dramatic incidents. Yet the 1920s and the 1960s deserve some of the notoriety they have received. Both were periods of sexual openness facilitated by mobility and social freedom for youth. They were times in which adolescents and young adults had "a sense of a separate destiny, of experiencing what no one had ever experienced before." Music—whether jazz or rock and roll—acted as a symbolic protest in both eras and was part of the secret language of emergent sexuality.

More women than ever before seemed to be having more sex and enjoying it more. In the 1920s this involved an increase in "petting," premarital intercourse, and extramarital sex. In the 1960s the age of first intercourse dropped dramatically, oral-genital stimulation became commonplace, and middle-class parents had to accept the idea that their daughters were "living with" someone. Most women enjoyed their new sexual freedom, but many saw major elements of the "sexual revolution" of the 1960s as essentially hostile to women. Poor women were left to care for the children, while middle-class women found themselves dealing with psychic scars, a by-product of their misperception of males' casual attitudes toward "relationships." Women were not sure that they had been a part of the revolution, and in the 1960s feminists coined the slogan The Sexual Revolution is Not Our War.

—William G. Shade and Angela Howard Zophy

See Also:

Female Sexuality, Flapper, New Morality, Premarital Sex

References:

D'Emilio, John, and Estelle B. Freedman. *Intimate Matters: A History of Sexuality in America.* New York: Harper & Row, 1988.
Fass, Paula. *The Damned and the Beautiful: American Youth in the 1920s.* New York: Oxford University Press, 1977.
Hunt, Morton. *Sexual Behavior in the 1970s.* New York: Dell, 1974.
Kinsey, Alfred, et al. *Sexual Behavior in the Human Female.* Philadelphia: Saunders, 1953.
Smith, Daniel Scott. "The Dating of the American Sexual Revolution: Evidence and Interpretation." In *The American Family in Social-Historical Perspective,* edited by Michael Gordon. New York: St. Martin's, 1973, pp. 321–35.

SHADD, MARY ANN (1823–93), the first black female editor of a weekly newspaper, was the outspoken advocate of fugitive slaves living in Canada during the 1850s. As the oldest of thirteen children born to Abraham, a delegate within the Negro convention movement, and Harriet Schadd of Wilmington, Delaware, Shadd was raised as a Roman

Catholic, educated in a Quaker school in West Chester, Pennsylvania, and later espoused African Methodism when she felt that assimilation was impossible.

After the passage of the Fugitive Slave Act in 1850, Shadd gave up her career in teaching to accompany her brother Isaac to Canada. She wrote a pamphlet in 1852 to inform fugitive slaves about the conditions in Canada. Both Shadd and her brother became schoolteachers in Windsor, Ontario, before she started her career in journalism in 1853. After meeting antislavery journalist Samuel Ringgold Ward, Shadd cooperatively launched one of the best fugitive slave weeklies, the *Provincial Freeman.* She married Thomas G. Cary in 1856. Afterward she shared the paper's editorship with her brother and H. Ford Douglass. They found it difficult to find consistent financial backing and ceased publication in 1858.

Following the death of her husband in 1860, Shadd reentered teaching to support herself and her children. During the Civil War, she recruited "colored" volunteers for the Union Army in Indiana. Following the war, she went to Washington, D.C., where she served as public school principal, wrote for Frederick Douglass's *New National Era,* and entered Howard University to study for a law degree. In addition to her journalistic work for fugitive slaves, Shadd was active in women's rights organizations. A member of the "radical" National Woman Suffrage Association, Shadd organized suffragette rallies and spoke to audiences in churches and at the Bethel Literary and Historical Society. She participated in the founding years of the Washington Colored Woman's League, but her death in 1893 prevented her from witnessing the national movement for black women's rights.

—Dorothy C. Salem

See Also:

Black Women, Colored Woman's League, Journalism

References:

Mary Ann Shadd Cary Papers. Howard University, Washington, D.C.

Bearden, James. *Shadd: The Life and Times of Mary Shadd Cary.* Toronto: N.C. Press, 1977.

Brown, Hallie Q., ed. *Homespun Heroines.* Xenia, Ohio: Aldine, 1926.

Sterling, Dorothy. *We Are Your Sisters: Black Women in the Nineteenth Century.* New York: Norton, 1984.

The **SHAKERS**, a religious group known officially as the United Society of Believers in Christ's Second Appearing, originated during the mid-eighteenth century near Manchester, England, among a small schismatic group of "shaking Quakers" led by Ann Lee. Lee's driving sense of mission resulted primarily from four traumatic experiences in childbirth and the deaths of her children in infancy or early childhood. She became convinced that only through celibacy and total devotion to God could humanity achieve salvation. Emigrating to America, Lee attracted several thousand followers in New York State and New England after the Revolutionary War.

Under Lee's American successors Joseph Meacham and Lucy Wright, the Shakers instituted full-scale celibate communal living, brought their pentecostal "shaking" and other revivalistic excesses under control, and established a dual system of government in which both sexes had parallel and equal leadership roles at every level of the religious hierarchy. Shaker theology stressed a dual godhead in which female and male elements were equally represented. Ann Lee was viewed by many of her followers as embodying God's spirit in female form in the same way that Jesus earlier had embodied God's spirit in male form. Despite equal Shaker leadership roles for men and women, traditional economic divisions between the sexes remained unchanged within the group.

Shaker theological and social unorthodoxy—including their requirements of celibacy, communal living, and equality for women in religious leadership—provoked much controversy. By the 1830s, however, when the group achieved the peak of its temporal success with as many as four thousand members living in more than sixty semiautonomous communities at eighteen different sites in New York, New England, and the Midwest, the Shakers were widely praised for their industry, quality of workmanship, and fine products. This religion proved especially attractive to capable women who failed to find outlets for their talents in the larger society, and they in turn served as an inspiration for a host of other communal experimenters during the nineteenth century.

Although totally dependent for their survival upon a diminishing supply of converts from the outside world, the Shakers nevertheless have persisted to the present. Feminists increasingly have looked to the Shakers as exemplars of a more active role for women in religious liturgy and leadership.

—*Lawrence Foster*

See Also:

Christianity; Lee, Mother Ann; Society of Friends

References:

Andrews, Edward Deming. *The People Called Shakers.* New York: Dover, 1963.

Brewer, Priscilla. *Shaker Communities, Shaker Lives.* Hanover, N.H.: University Press of New England, 1986.

Campbell, D'Ann. "Women's Life in Utopia: The Shaker Experiment in Equality Reappraised." *New England Quarterly* 51 (March 1978): 23–38.

Foster, Lawrence. *Religion and Sexuality: The Shakers, the Mormons, and the Oneida Community.* Urbana: University of Illinois Press, 1984, pp. 21–71, 226-47.

Proctor-Smith, Marjorie. *Women in Shaker Community and Worship: A Feminist Analysis of the Uses of Religious Symbolism.* Lewiston, Mass.: Mellen, 1985.

Rourke, Constance. "The Shakers." In *The Roots of American Culture and Other Essays,* edited by Van Wyck Brooks. New York: Harcourt Brace, 1942, pp. 195–237.

White, Anna, and Leila S. Taylor. *Shakerism: Its Meaning and Message.* Columbus, Ohio: Fred. J. Heer, 1904.

SHANGE, NTOZAKE (b. 1949), poet, playwright, novelist, and dancer, is best known for her works exploring the minds and expressing the thoughts of women characters. From her interest in and study of women past and present came her play *For Colored Girls Who Have Considered Suicide/When the Rainbow Is Enuf* (1975), which brought national attention both to Shange's innovative dramatic form and to her subject of young black women.

Shange received her master's degree at the University of Southern California, but her interest in the stories of black women's lives grew in the Women's Studies Program at Sonoma State College. Through these studies of women, Shange has learned to express herself in dance. She is quoted as saying, "The freedom to move in space, to demand of my own sweat a perfection that could continually be approached, though never known, was poem to me, my body and mind."

Shange's most famous work, *For Colored Girls,* is a play, or "choreopoem," about seven women and the worlds they live in. None of the women are given names; they are addressed by the colors they wear. Through these seven characters, Shange created a reality filled with heartache, frustration, and inequality. The effect of movement or dancing by the women gives the play vitality and realism.

Shange's most recent work is the novel *Betsey Brown* (1985), which casts a thirteen-year-old as the main character. Through the eyes of this child and the other characters, Shange presents the topics of maturity, racism, and human nature. Some critics regard this novel as a play in disguise.

Her other works include the novel *Sassafrass, Cypress and Indigo;* plays *Three Pieces* and *From Okra to Greens;* poetry collections *Nappy Edges, A Daughter's Geography, Some Men,* and *Melissa and Smith;* and the essay collection *See No Evil.*

—*Pamela Patterson and Carol Klimick Cyganowski*

See Also:

Black Women, Theater

References:

Shange, Ntozake. *Betsey Brown.* New York: St. Martin's, 1985.

———. *For Colored Girls Who Have Considered Suicide/When the Rainbow Is Enuf.* New York: Macmillan, 1977.

SHARP, KATHARINE LUCINDA (1865–1914) was a librarian and library educator whose career reflected the ambiguous reality confronting women completing the new professional training programs in female-intensive fields during this period. Although, accompanied by elaborate rhetoric, educational and health institutions were expanding, fiscal support was inadequate. Women professionals often had to choose between self-sacrifice and self-fulfillment. A revolutionary new kind of library service was required by the emerging research universities; yet inadequate financial support and only limited autonomy were available to the women charged with achieving the revolution. After years of trying to reconcile her ideas of modern academic library service with the reality of her budgets and an unresponsive educational bureaucracy, Sharp, a victim of overwork that compromised her health, resigned and left librarianship.

An only child, born in Elgin, Illinois, Sharp was an excellent student, graduating from Northwestern University at age twenty. After a brief career in secondary school teaching, she studied at the New York State Library School under Melvil Dewey, originator of the Dewey Decimal System of library classification. Her first position (1893) was at the newly opened Armour Institute in Chicago, where she was both head librarian and professor of library economy. In 1897 Sharp and the library school moved to the University of Illinois, where she was professor of library economy, head librarian, and director of the Illinois State Library School. As head librarian, she replaced an untrained man uncommitted to service who had alienated the faculty. Although lauded for the improvements she made, she was exhausted by continual staff shortages due to low salaries, overwork, and battles with the administration, and in 1907 she resigned from the University of Illinois. She joined the Deweys at Lake Placid, New York, becoming vice president of the Lake Placid Corporation, and died after an auto accident at the resort.

Despite heavy responsibilities during her professional life, Sharp wrote much, including *Illinois Libraries* (1906–08), and lectured widely on professional issues, frequently calling for higher standards of librarianship.

—*Suzanne Hildenbrand*

See Also:
Librarianship

References:

Grotzinger, Laurel Ann. *The Power and the Dignity: Librarianship and Katharine Sharp.* New York: Scarecrow, 1966.

———. "The Proto-feminist Librarian at the Turn of the Century: Two Studies." *Journal of Library History* 10 (July 1975): 195-213.

Howe, Harriet E. "Katharine Lucinda Sharp." In *Pioneering Leaders in Librarianship*, edited by Emily Danton. Chicago: American Library Association, 1953, pp. 165–72.

SHAW, ANNA HOWARD (1847–1919), a central figure in the late-nineteenth- and early-twentieth-century struggles for woman's rights, was born in Newcastle, England. At age four, she moved with her family to America, settling in Massachusetts; then, shortly before the Civil War, the Shaw family moved to the Michigan frontier. Shaw spent her teenage years caring for her sickly mother while her father and brothers were away at war. At age twenty-four, Shaw left home to attend high school in Big Rapids. At this time, she came under the influence of Reverend Marianna Thompson and decided to prepare for the Methodist ministry. She spent two years at Albion College before moving to Boston to attend divinity school at Boston University. Following graduation in 1878, Shaw served as a pastor for several years and in 1880 was ordained as an elder in the Methodist Protestant church.

Having successfully entered a clerical profession traditionally dominated by men, Shaw in 1883 began part-time work toward a medical degree. After completing her studies in 1886, Shaw became the first American woman to hold divinity and medical degrees simultaneously.

At age thirty-nine, Shaw left the preaching and healing ministry for another career.

Joining first the Massachusetts Suffrage Association and later Lucy Stone's American Woman Suffrage Association, Shaw became a full-time organizer and lecturer for the causes of suffrage and temperance. At the urging of Frances Willard, Shaw accepted the position as chairperson of the Franchise Department of the Woman's Christian Temperance Union. In 1888, as a delegate of the WCTU to the first meeting of the International Council of Women, Shaw met Susan B. Anthony, who persuaded her not to waste her talents on temperance but to commit herself totally to the grand cause of suffrage.

Shaw remained Anthony's friend and disciple for the remainder of her life. Their friendship had a profound impact on the future direction of the suffrage movement. In 1892 Anthony became president and Shaw vice president of the National American Woman Suffrage Association. An odd-looking couple, good-naturedly ridiculed by friends as "the ruler and the rubber-ball," Anthony and Shaw were strikingly different in appearance, style, and talent. Unlike the tall and slender, highly organized, and agnostic Anthony, Shaw was a roly-poly Methodist preacher with a quick wit and a golden tongue. Anthony groomed Shaw to play a particular role in the suffrage campaign—that of a moderate reformer whose life and reputation would help counteract the popular image of suffragists as unreligious and un-American militants. Shaw accepted her role graciously. Together Anthony and Shaw were able to extend each other's outreach and effectiveness.

In 1904, at Anthony's request, Shaw became president of the NAWSA. She held this office until stepping down to become president emeritus in 1915. She remained a moderate throughout her presidency, opposing those who advocated campaigning against the political party in power rather than individual candidates unfriendly to suffrage, picketing the White House, calling hunger strikes, and pressing for immediate suffrage elections, even if there were no prospect for victory.

In May 1917 President Woodrow Wilson called upon Shaw to chair the Woman's Committee of the Council of National Defense. Two years later, in appreciation for her war services, Wilson awarded her the Distinguished Service Medal. Shaw spent the remaining months of her life campaigning for the creation of the League of Nations. She died on July 2, 1919, at her home in Moylan, Pennsylvania.

—Terry D. Bilhartz

See Also:

Anthony, Susan B.; National American Woman Suffrage Association

References:

Linkugel, Wilmer. "The Speeches of Anna Howard Shaw." 2 vols. Diss. University of Wisconsin-Madison, 1960.

McGovern, James R. "Anna Howard Shaw: New Approaches to Feminism." *Journal of Social History* 3 (1969/70): 135–53.

Shaw, Anna Howard. *The Story of a Pioneer.* New York: Harper, 1915.

Spencer, Ralph W. "Anna Howard Shaw: The Evangelical Feminist." Diss. University of Boston, 1972.

The **SHEPPARD-TOWNER ACT of 1921** was federal legislation that established public health centers and prenatal clinics with an initial appropriation of $1,250,000. Mary Anderson and Julia Lathrop of the Children's Bureau argued that infant mortality and ill health were directly related to low wages, crowded housing, and parental ignorance. Anderson pointed out to a reluctant Congress that 250,000 infants died each year in the United States. Timely support came from an editorial in *Good Housekeeping* magazine on infant mortality in America, entitled "Herod Is Not Dead." Finally, Harriet Upton, vice chairperson of the Republican party, threatened congressmen with retaliation at the polls if they did not approve the measure. The bill passed Congress by a wide margin and fully revealed the growing political clout of women when united in support of a good cause.

—Jonathan W. Zophy

See Also:

National Organization for Public Health Nursing, Protective Legislation, Visiting Nurses

References:

Chambers, Clark. *Seedtime of Reform.* Ann Arbor: University of Michigan Press, 1967.

Daniel, Robert. *American Women in the 20th Century.* New York: Harcourt Brace Jovanovich, 1987.

"Herod Is Not Dead." *Good Housekeeping* 71 (December 1920): 4.

The **SHIRTWAIST MAKERS STRIKE OF 1909.** On November 23, 1909, twenty thousand shirtwaist makers launched the largest women's strike in American history. The first mass job action of its kind, the strike focused national attention on "sweatshop" workers and launched the unionization of the garment trade, the nation's third largest industry and largest employer of women. It was an immigrant woman's strike at a time when immigrants were despised as strikebreakers and women were considered unorganizable. Most of the strikers were East European Jews, a sizable minority were Italian, and almost all were young, in their teens or early twenties.

Anger at the treatment of women already on strike against the Triangle and Leiserson companies contributed to the general strike. The underlying causes, however, were oppressive conditions throughout the industry —a fifty-six-hour week with unpaid overtime; fees for use of thread, machinery, and lockers; piecework; and low wages paid in tiny, redeemable "tickets." The goals were better hours and pay and, most important, the union shop.

Although male officials negotiated with the employers, the strike was led and carried out by the women. Hungry, inadequately dressed, harassed by the police, and attacked by thugs and prostitutes hired by the companies, the women marched, rallied, picketed, and raised money for their cause. Financial and moral support came from Progressive reformers, from the Jewish immigrant community with its strong, radical working-class subculture and tradition of women's activism, and from women, including college students, Socialist party women, suffragists, and, most important, the National Women's Trade Union League.

The strike ended February 15, 1910, with mixed results. Most companies signed with the union, though often not meeting all the union demands, but nineteen, including the largest, remained unorganized. Labor benefited, as subsequent strikes, inspired by the shirtwaist makers, organized the garment trades; but benefits for women were less clear. Publicity surrounding the strike encouraged protective legislation for women workers, but the strikers had fought for self-governing unions, not paternalistic laws. The strike contributed to the personal growth of many participants, and leaders such as Clara Lemlich, Pauline Newman, Theresa Malkiel, and Rose Schneiderman continued suffragist and labor activism. But although the strike demonstrated that women could be assets to the labor movement, the American Federation of Labor failed to devote adequate attention to them.

—Maxine S. Seller

See Also:

Garment Industries, National Women's Trade Union League, Unions

References:

Henry, Alice. *The Trade Union Woman.* New York: Appleton, 1915.

Levine, Louis. *The Women's Garment Workers: A History of the International Ladies Garment Workers.* New York: B. W. Huebach, 1924.

Malkiel, Theresa. *Diary of a Shirtwaist Striker.* New York: Cooperative Press, 1910.

Seller, Maxine S. "The Uprising of the Twenty Thousand: Sex, Class, and Ethnicity in the Shirtwaist Makers Strike of 1909." In *Struggle a Hard Battle: Essays on Working-Class Immigrants,* edited by Dirk Hoerder. Dekalb: Northern Illinois University Press, 1986, pp. 254–79.

Tax, Meredith. *The Rising of the Women: Feminist Solidarity and Class Conflict, 1880–1917.* New York: Monthly Review, 1980.

SINGLE WOMEN. *Old maid* and *spinster,* pejorative terms used for unmarried women, have been boldly accepted, vociferously rejected, and quietly suffered by such women. Both terms reinforce the norm of marriage when attached to the woman who remains single past the conventional age for marrying or who seems, in appearance or by temperament, unlikely ever to marry. Spinster is still the legal term for an unmarried woman in Britain.

Spinster originally described anyone whose occupation was spinning. More women than men, and especially unmarried women and adolescent girls, were associated with spinning as a home occupation. As the demand for and popularity of homespun declined with the manufacture of cloth in industries, the spinster's status dropped; thereafter, she was connected with a "useless" or "mindless" task. Victorian notions of respectability prohibited the middle- and upper-class spinster from seeking education and other employment. Thus, the spinster's economic "uselessness" paralleled her social uselessness as a woman who did not fulfill her "normal" and "natural" function in life by marrying and mothering children.

Her apparent rejection of the married state threatened or challenged a society that, in turn, scorned the spinster. The "old maid" is ridiculed in legend, joke, and song as the lonely woman left behind in the race to marry. In the child's card game Old Maid, the loser is the player left with the Old Maid card (a spare queen in a regular deck) when all the other cards have been paired up. The stereotype of the old maid or spinster is a prim, petty, nervous, gossipy woman, devoted to pets, jealous of married women, who fears men but nonetheless pines for one.

As educational and economic opportunities for women increased, and particularly when wars created a surplus of unmarried women, more freedom, approval, and recognition for the old maid or spinster followed. In the antebellum United States the Cult of Single Blessedness balanced the Cult of Domesticity somewhat by glorifying the spinster while also suggesting new constraints through the ideals of service, selflessness, and celibacy. Many spinsters were active in the women's rights movement, a movement that invited a reassessment of marriage. For those who saw marriage as an economic association devoid of nobility, a submission to male dominance, a sacrifice of individual goals, or an otherwise imperfect institution, spinsterhood emerged as a positive and viable choice.

—*Kathleen Kirk*

References:

Adams, Margaret. *Single Blessedness.* New York: Basic, 1976.

Chambers-Schiller, Lee Virginia. *Liberty, A Better Husband: Single Women in America, the Generations of 1780–1840.* New Haven: Yale University Press, 1984.

Hutton, Laura. *The Single Woman.* 1935; rpt. New York: Roy, 1960.

Jeffreys, Sheila. *The Spinster and Her Enemies: Feminism and Sexuality, 1880–1930.* Boston: Pandora, 1985.

Peterson, Nancy L. *Our Lives for Ourselves: Women Who Never Married.* New York: Putnam, 1981.

SISTER CARRIE (1900) by Theodore Dreiser is the study of a woman's struggle for self-fulfillment that leads her beyond the traditional roles of women. The story exposes the contrasts between the frailties of nineteenth-century idealism and romanticism and the more callous realism of the emerging twentieth century.

Caroline Meeber, or "Sister Carrie," leaves the security of her hometown to find her fortune in the big city of Chicago in 1889. Living with her sister, she quickly becomes disenchanted with her menial job, meager wages, and lackluster existence. Desperate to have what she perceives as the "good life," Carrie enters into an illicit relationship with a traveling salesman. He delivers her from her drab existence, but is cast aside when a more affluent gentleman is attracted to her. Carrie uses men as stepping stones to achieve a life of luxuries and happiness. Her second lover is more satisfying than her first, but she still does not attain complete fulfillment. In the end she is by herself, wealthy and successful, but still left wanting.

Based loosely on the real-life experiences of Dreiser's sister Emma, *Sister Carrie* was not favorably received when Dreiser completed it in 1900. He had difficulty finding a publisher who would accept this realistic novel of the city. American readers, according to the publishers, were not ready to read about the negative aspects of the city, especially the lack of morals. Dreiser opposed the fixed belief that the same set of moral standards must be met by all.

The importance of Dreiser's novel is that the character of the immoral woman is not condemned. Carrie's actions were not considered acceptable at the time the book was published, yet she continues to move up the ladder of success. *Sister Carrie* challenged the accepted norms of the early 1900s, the attitudes that people had toward women like Carrie, and emphasized that women who do not adhere to the morals of society should not have to suffer for it.

—Linda Christine Rud

References:

Kaplan, Justin. "Dreiser Restored." *New York Times* 69 (May 31, 1981): VII, 13.

Kazin, Alfred. "Restoring Sister Carrie." *New York Review of Books* 28 (February 19, 1981): 12–14.

Modern Fiction Studies 23 (Autumn, 1977). [special issue on Theodore Dreiser]

Moraco, Robert A. "Dreiser's Contract for *Sister Carrie*: More Fact and Fiction." *Journal of Modern Literature* 9 (May 1982): 305—11.

Review of *Sister Carrie. New York Times* 10 (May 25, 1907): 332:3.

West, James L. W., III. *A Sister Carrie Portfolio.* Charlottesville: University of Virginia Press, 1985.

SLAVERY. Slave women were perhaps the most vulnerable women in America during the eighteenth and nineteenth centuries, before emancipation. Enslaved, black, and female, they lived in a society ruled by free white men, and their experience of slavery was different from black men's. The differences began with the "middle passage," the transportation of African blacks to the New World, when the enslaved African women were sometimes isolated from the men and forced to serve the crew on deck. These differences continued through the imbalanced sex ratio of the early colonial period and extended through the end of slavery, as slave women came to develop a mother-child-centered social universe within the slave community.

More than anything else, slave women's reproductive capacities determined their place in bondage. Women were especially vulnerable to sexual exploitation. While rape was not uncommon (though probably declining in frequency through the nineteenth century), the principal abuse was more subtle and universal. After the close of the legal African slave trade in 1807, slaveholders relied on slave women's childbearing capacity to replenish the farm/plantation work force. Slave men served principally as laborers, but slave women were expected both to work in the fields or the "big house" and to bear and raise children for the master's profit. Their role as mother confined them to their farms/plantations, for with children they were less mobile than were slave men, and this caused slave women to practice different strategies of resistance than did men. Slave women, for example, played upon the slaveholders' "property" interest (e.g., slave women's reproductive capacity) by feigning sickness to gain relief from overwork. As nurses and cooks, slave women had opportunities to poison their masters.

The work cycle of slave women also differed from that of men. Slave girls did odd chores in the big house and in the yards, which introduced them to the domestic service that would be part of their obligations thereafter. On plantations, where the majority of slaves lived by the late antebellum period, slave girls worked in "trash" gangs with boys performing the lighter chores such as weeding and clearing stubble, but not until they reached their teens did they join a work gang that was usually composed entirely of women. Some adult slave women performed heavy agricultural labor along with the men throughout the South (plowing, hoeing, picking cotton, or cutting rice or sugar cane), but most slave women usually worked in female work groups apart from the men (spinning, weaving, sewing, quilting, and hoeing). Thus, slave women spent most of their time with other women, and, given the high percentage of slave marriages in which the husband and wife lived on separate farms/plantations, the slave women relied on female and kin networks and themselves rather than husbands/fathers to raise and define the world of the slave children.

On large plantations especially, female slaves were socialized into clearly defined sex roles, drawn from African culture and American experience. Afro-American cultural imperatives, for example, dictated that women delay childbearing for at least two years after they experienced menarche (generally about the age of fifteen). Motherhood marked the woman's rite of passage, and, as in many African societies, the Afro-American slave woman married the father of her first child only after the child was born, thus demonstrating her ability to have children.

Slave marriages were of necessity egalitarian, for women assumed much of the responsibility for care and even the provisions grown in the slave gardens. In the slave community, the mother-child relationship superseded that of the husband-wife, in part due to the master's vested interest in the former (which sometimes protected the slave mothers by discouraging the sale of small children away from their mothers) and in part due to the circumstances of slave life. Without property, slave men could not claim traditional male authority over their wives. Still, many slave women revealed a special strength by deferring to their menfolk when they were present, thus bolstering the husband/father's esteem and maintaining the semblance of the two-parent, monogamous household that would form the basic social unit among blacks after emancipation. That many ex-slaves sought to formalize their marriages after emancipation suggests that the unions established during slavery were based on mutual affection. The emergence of patriarchal households among ex-slaves in the post–Civil War rural South coincided with new economic and social arrangements, especially the blacks' movement into sharecropping and tenancy, which isolated women from previous female networks and stressed individual family cohesion.

As slaves, black women could not share a sympathetic relationship with white women. Black slave women might attend the same church as their mistresses (and submit to the same discipline), they might suffer the same female complaints and same dangers attending childbearing, and, in some instances, they might learn the confidences of their white mistresses, but they could not escape the authority of white women. Whippings, beatings, scourges, and other punishments inflicted on slave women by white women bore grim witness to the discrepancies in power separating black from white. The myth of the "faithful mammy" notwithstanding, slave women cast their lot with their own families and the slave community. During the Civil War, slave women fled the farms/plantations at first opportunity to lay claim to as much freedom from whites as was possible, leaving their white mistresses to fend for themselves.

—*Randall M. Miller*

See Also:

Abolition and the Antislavery Movement, Black Women

References:

Blassingame, John W. *The Slave Community: Plantation Life in the Antebellum South.* Rev. ed. New York: Oxford University Press, 1979.

Fox-Genovese, Elizabeth. *Within the Plantation Household: Black and White Women of the Old South.* Chapel Hill: University of North Carolina Press, 1988.

Genovese, Eugene G. *Roll, Jordan, Roll: The World the Slaves Made.* New York: Pantheon, 1974.

Gutman, Herbert G. *The Black Family in Slavery & Freedom, 1750–1925.* Oxford, U.K.: Basil Blackwell, 1976.

Jones, Jacqueline. *Labor of Love, Labor of Sorrow: Black Women, Work, and the Family from Slavery to the Present.* New York: Basic, 1985.

White, Deborah Gray. *Ar'n't I a Woman? Female Slaves in the Plantation South*. New York: Norton, 1985.

SMITH, BESSIE (1898?–1937), American blues singer who was also known as the "world's greatest blues singer" and the "empress of the blues," was the foremost female blues singer of her time. She is considered by many to be second in importance only to the pioneer Gertrude "Ma" Rainey, the "mother of the blues."

Details about Smith's early years are sketchy at best. Born in Chattanooga, Tennessee, she had lost both parents by the time she was nine years old. According to reliable sources, she entered show business at an early age, and was supposedly "discovered" at a local amateur contest by the manager of Chattanooga's Ivory Theater. Sometime thereafter, she joined one of F. C. Woolcott's Rabbit-Foot Minstrel groups managed by Will Rainey, husband of Gertrude Rainey. It is widely assumed that Ma Rainey took care of Smith and helped her career, although Smith rarely acknowledged the debt in later years. She toured extensively with the Raineys and others and began her recording career in 1920, recording for the Okah, Paramount, and Columbia record labels.

Her fame rose rapidly as she juggled recording trips to New York and tours on the black vaudeville circuits throughout the South and major cities in the North, and she also made radio appearances. Some considered Smith's voice too harsh, but many responded to the powerful emotions she poured into her music. With her renditions of "Nobody's Blues but Mine," "Chicago Bound," "St. Louis Blues," and others, Smith came to embody what has been called the "classic" blues style. Her Chicago debut in 1924 earned rave reviews. Toward the end of the 1920s and into the 1930s, however, her recording career declined. She grew artistically and continued to tour, but changes in popular music taste, together with Smith's personal problems, ended her days of superstardom.

Always a volatile personality whose refusal to cater to the whims of white male authority figures caused a number of celebrated "scenes," Smith became increasingly difficult, even with those she trusted, as alcoholism tightened its grip on her. John Hammond produced what became Smith's last recordings in 1933. In 1936 she announced plans for a comeback, but on September 26, 1937, she was killed in an automobile accident. The circumstances are a mystery, but many blamed local segregation policies, which prevented her being taken to the closest, whites-only hospital, for her untimely death, and Edward Albee's play *The Death of Bessie Smith*, written in the late 1950s, is based on that theory. Smith remains, however, a major inspirational woman and artist.

—Elizabeth H. Coughlin

See Also:

Jazz, Popular Vocalists

References:

Albertson, Chris. *Bessie*. Briarcliff Manor, N.Y.: Stein and Day, 1972.

Stearns, Marshall W. *The Story of Jazz*. London: Oxford University Press, 1970.

Columbia Records released a five-volume, two-record set of Smith's recordings, under the title *Bessie Smith*, which was produced by John Hammond in 1972.

SMITH COLLEGE, an institution of higher education for women in Northampton, Massachusetts, opened in September 1875 with fourteen students. Founded according to the testament of Sophia Smith (1796–1870), who inherited a fortune from her brother Austin in 1861, the college aimed at providing an educational program for women comparable to that of men, without, according to the wishes of the founder herself, upsetting conventional notions of femininity. To this end, the college worked in two directions. First, it organized a curriculum based on standard university offerings and eliminated elements of secondary school preparation offered by other women's institutions. To maintain femininity, the trustees and administrators proposed a system of living in familylike cottages that would duplicate patterns of sociability and order prevalent in the society at large. Both the house system and the high standards of education continued into the late twentieth century, when Smith was selected as one of the fifteen best liberal arts colleges in the country.

Under the presidency of L. Clark Seelye, the college expanded from the original small student body to close to two thousand by his retirement in 1910. The largest independent women's college in the world, Smith had an enrollment of close to twenty-five hundred women by the mid-1970s. Seelye was concerned with a comprehensive program and thus offered not only science but also a strong program in the arts. In 1921 the college added a School of Social Work, which awarded a master's degree. Other than that, Smith College maintained its commitment to the liberal arts, despite pressures to expand or to reorient its offerings. In addition, it maintained its commitment to women's education when the administration decided in the mid-1970s to resist the trend toward coeducation. The selection of the first woman president, Jill Ker Conway, in 1975, seemed to confirm that commitment.

The Smith College endowment grew from the original bequest of $400,000 to close to $80 million in the mid-1970s. At the same time, the college felt the financial pressures of competing with men's institutions for endowment money. Not only were alumnae less able or willing to give, parents were sometimes less interested in paying hefty fees for daughters. To remedy this situation, the college charged tuition fees far less than the cost of actually educating its students. It also worked on new methods of fund raising. Despite these problems, the college continued to attract a stable but increasingly diverse student body. More students in the 1970s and 1980s had backgrounds in science, math, and technical subjects, and their interests shifted away from traditional areas such as art history and history.

—Bonnie G. Smith

See Also:

"Seven Sisters," Women in Higher Education

References:

Hanscom, Elizabeth Deering. *Sophia Smith and the Beginnings of Smith College.* Northampton, Mass.: Smith College, 1926.

Horowitz, Helen L. *Alma Mater. Design and Experience in the Women's Colleges from their Beginnings to the 1930s.* New York: Knopf, 1984.

Lincoln, Eleanor Terry. *This, the House We Live In: The Smith College Campus from 1871–1982.* Northampton, Mass.: Smith College, 1983.

Mendenhall, Thomas C. *Chance and Change in Smith College's First Century.* Northampton, Mass.: Smith College, 1976.

Toth, Susan Allen. *Ivy Days: Making My Way Out East.* Boston: Little, Brown, 1984.

The **SMITH-HUGHES ACT OF 1917** established a Federal Board for Vocational Education to promote training in home economics as well as agriculture, vocational subjects, commerce, trades, and industry in secondary schools. Rural high schools could now offer agricultural and home economics courses that serviced student organizations such as the Future Farmers of America and the Future Homemakers of America, while urban schools established vocational training for boys and commercial "business" courses for girls. Thus, high school curricula that previously emphasized college preparation for middle-class students adapted education for girls to suit the sex-segregated job market that awaited them. The social mobility of nonminority working-class girls was increased through their access to white-collar positions. As postsecondary education under the Smith-Lever Act of 1914 focused curricula for women students on their future role in marriage and the family, the modifications of high school curricula under the Smith-Hughes Act reinforced the concentration of young women in those jobs within the pink-collar ghetto.

—Angela Howard Zophy

See Also:

Coeducation, Home Economics, Smith-Lever Act

Reference:

Daniel, Robert L. *American Women in the Twentieth Century: The Festival of Life.* New York: Harcourt Brace Jovanovich, 1987.

The **SMITH-LEVER ACT OF 1914** provided federal financing of home economics curricula in the coeducational state colleges and universities that had been established as land-grant institutions under the Morrill Land-Grant Act of 1862. This act reflected a twentieth-century trend in women's education in both public and private institutions to accommodate the curriculum to women's domestic role. The specialized field of home economics was intended to prepare the young middle-class woman for her "professionalized" role of wife and mother, which implied that women were not in colleges or universities to pursue nontraditional careers as they had been encouraged to do during the last decades of the nineteenth century and into the Progressive era.

—Angela Howard Zophy

See Also:

Coeducation, Education, Home Economics, Morrill Land-Grant Act

Reference:

Woloch, Nancy. *Women and the American Experience.* New York: Knopf, 1984.

SOAP OPERAS are a form of popular entertainment, traditionally associated with women audiences and domestic themes of love and family, which had their roots in radio serialized drama but which are now primarily a daytime television phenomenon. They were called "soap operas" because the programs were frequently sponsored or owned by laundry detergent manufacturers. The origins of the form actually precede radio drama and may be found in the serialized stories of literary monthly (or weekly) journals, in romances of the nineteenth century, in novels of the eighteenth century, and even in popular drama of the Middle Ages and Renaissance.

Soap opera story lines are never ending, thus differentiating daytime "soaps" like *All My Children, Guiding Light, The Young and the Restless, As the World Turns,* and *Days of Our Lives* from nightime or prime-time dramatic series of the 1970s and 1980s like *Dallas, Knots Landing, Falcon Crest,* and *Dynasty,* all of which present "complete" narrative-episodes each week while "continuing" the plot and character interrelationships. The themes of daytime soap operas have, in recent years, begun to include violence, exotic travel, and politics, but the stories still center on the domestic and the personal: romantic love, marriage (yearned for, planned, begun, failed, regretted, and missed), the family (immediate and extended), friendship, companionship, business associations, and the related issues of values, choices, commitments, and concerns of the day.

Aside from developing strong personalities, creating almost allegorical heroines and villains, and providing viewers with fantasy, escapism, and surrogate love, "soaps" also educate by giving practical knowledge of the day of diseases, divorce, abortion, and legal matters. This didacticism links them with an older tradition of popular culture. The genre has been criticized for easy solutions to difficult problems; some criticism is warranted, yet "soaps" treat most social issues in greater depth than many other forms of pop culture. Also criticized for prolonging plots ad nauseum, soaps reveal the density and complexity of many issues and relationships by showing numerous points of view on them and by including the viewer in the "psychological time" as well as "chronological time" of the crisis or character. A once largely female audience now includes many men; the newest audience in recent years is that of college students and teenagers, which has caused substantial alterations of story lines and characters.

—Travis DuPriest

See Also:

Popular Culture

References:
Edmondson, Madeleine, and David Rounds. *From Mary Noble to Mary Hartman*. New York: Stein and Day, 1976.
Efron, Edith. "The Soaps—Anything But 99 44/100 Percent Pure." In *TV Guide: The First 25 Years*, edited by Jay S. Harris. New York: Simon & Schuster, 1978, pp. 110–12.

SOCIAL FEMINISM refers to the activities and goals of the New Woman of the Progressive era. Distinctive because of its emphasis on social justice and social reform, social feminism dates from the late-nineteenth-century settlement house movement—in which educated young people worked for social reform among the urban poor—and the rise during the early twentieth century of such women's groups as the Association of Collegiate Alumnae, the General Federation of Club Women, the Woman's Christian Temperance Union, the National American Woman Suffrage Association, the National Consumers' League, and the National Women's Trade Union League.

The women who led and worked within these groups were predominately educated and middle to upper class and were capable of deploying considerable influence, even in those areas where women had no legitimate access to actual economic or political power. Utilizing a cooperative ethic and motivated by a sense of mission, social feminists were dedicated to social action and supported the vote for women as a means of advancing their social reform efforts. As was true of the previous generations' domestic feminism, the approach of social feminism created a framework for women's participation in the public sphere that neither assumed nor allowed for women's full emancipation. The benevolent enterprises of social feminism offered a sense of usefulness and fulfillment that accommodated the needs of social feminists without requiring a radical analysis of the "woman question."

Social feminism waned during the New Deal and World War II eras; during the civil rights and New Left period, a resurgence of that urge so characteristic of educated middle-class women to be active and useful in achieving social justice spawned the leadership of both the radical women's liberation movement and the more mainstream modern women's movement of the 1960s and 1970s.

—*Angela Howard Zophy*

See Also:
Domestic Feminism, Feminism, Progressive Era, Socialist Feminism

References:
Daniel, Robert L. *American Women in the 20th Century: The Festival of Life*. San Diego: Harcourt Brace Jovanovich, 1987.
O'Neill, William L. *Everyone Was Brave: A History of Feminism in America*. New York: Quadrangle, 1969, 1971.
Woloch, Nancy. *Women and the American Experience*. New York: Knopf, 1984.

SOCIAL HOUSEKEEPING referred to the immigrant working-class and "native" educated middle-class reformers who took the traditional domestic values of Woman's Sphere into their community as necessary to fulfill their social and economic responsibility to minister to the needs of families within urban industrial areas at the end of the nineteenth century. As part of the Progressive era, the social housekeepers made significant contributions as individuals and in women's groups to the definition and realization of Progressive goals as well as to the establishment of social work as a profession. The settlement house movement, the woman's club movement, the political and economic reforms associated with the Progressive era, and the early-twentieth-century peace movement were all aspects of social housekeeping that legitimized women's participation within the public sphere.

Although these reform movements occurred beyond the domestic sphere, social housekeepers applied the tactic and goals of both domestic feminism (to justify these dutiful women's entrance into these movements) and of social feminism (to alter political and economic policies and practices to achieve social justice). The influence of the generation of social housekeepers and their social feminism survived the political fundamentalism and unfettered business economics that characterized the conservative reactionism of the 1920s to resurface in the 1930s and again after the 1950s. Social housekeeping embodied the reform-minded New Woman of the twentieth century and established women's place beyond the home without redefining the concept of womanhood as centered within women's maternal and nurturing role in the family.

—Angela Howard Zophy

See Also:

Domestic Feminism, Pacifism and the Peace Movement, Progressive Era, Settlement House Movement, Social Feminism, Social Welfare, Social Work

References:

Daniel, Robert L. *American Women in the 20th Century: The Festival of Life.* San Diego: Harcourt Brace Jovanovich, 1987.

O'Neill, William L. *Everyone Was Brave: A History of Feminism in America.* New York: Quadrangle, 1969, 1971.

Riley, Glenda. *Inventing the American Woman: A Perspective on Women's History.* Arlington Heights, Ill.: Harlan Davidson, 1987.

Ryan, Mary P. *Womanhood in America: From Colonial Times to the Present.* 3d ed. New York: New Viewpoints, 1984.

Woloch, Nancy. *Women and the American Experience.* New York: Knopf, 1984.

The **SOCIAL PURITY MOVEMENT** is the name given to the nineteenth-century struggle to end prostitution and other related social ills. As a previous generation had rid the country of "Negro slavery," the social purists would abolish "white slavery," which they associated with intemperance and political corruption after the Civil War.

The social purity elite was made up of highly educated Protestant women and men who were involved in other reforms as well. They favored temperance and opposed gambling. They railed against masturbation and joined moral crusader Anthony Comstock in the fight to limit the circulation of information on birth control and legalized abortion. Described as "Protestant nuns" who preached the discipline of abstinence, women within the social purity movement accepted the Victorian view of women. Most found the idea of regulated prostitution offensive. Antebellum moral reformers portrayed women as victims of men's greed and lust, describing the seduction of country girls drawn into the trade by smooth-talking men who picked them up at railroad stations and took them to ice cream parlors.

While successful at the federal level to proscribe as "pornographic" literature that dealt with birth control and to raise generally the age of consent, the movement's major achievement was the Mann Act, which Congress passed in 1910, that made illegal the transportation of a woman across state lines for immoral purposes. The "Purity Crusade" came of age in the Progressive era, but its two main concerns, prostitution and masturbation—"public vice" and "private vice"—have outlived it.

—William G. Shade

See Also:

Age of Consent, Obscenity, Prostitution

References:

Pivar, David J. *Purity Crusade: Sexual Morality and Social Control, 1860–1900.* Westport, Conn.: Greenwood, 1973.

Pleck, Elizabeth H. *Domestic Tyranny: The Making of Social Policy Against Family Violence from Colonial Times to the Present.* New York: Oxford University Press, 1987.

Rosen, Ruth. *The Lost Sisterhood: Prostitution in America, 1900–1918.* Baltimore: The Johns Hopkins University Press, 1982.

Rothman, Sheila M. *Woman's Proper Place: A History of Changing Ideals and Practices, 1870 to the Present.* New York: Basic, 1978.

The **SOCIAL SECURITY ACT OF 1935**. The New Deal's legislative response to the economic devastation wrought on the middle and working classes by the Great Depression, the Social Security Act provided federal unemployment and old-age insurance, as well as "relief," or social welfare, for dependent women and children that was unprecedented in its scope. This was not the first form of social insurance to be introduced to the American public. An earlier attempt that occurred in 1908 provided workmen's compensation for federal employees; also, a few states' statutes and workmen's compensation laws dated from the Progressive era.

Among the many factors involved in the creation of the Social Security Act, there were two overriding forces. First, this act represented a belated and begrudging acknowledgment that the national economy had changed from one characterized by the Jeffersonian agricultural self-sufficiency of the nineteenth century to one of urban interdependence on the wage and market system in the twentieth. Second, the social welfare aspects of this legislation reflected the presence of influential women in high political positions during Franklin Roosevelt's New Deal. Among these women, many of whom were social feminists, an agenda for reform emerged. They developed a network that served as a major policy-influencing group determined to achieve social reform programs of vital concern to women as homemakers and as paid workers. Maternal and child welfare, health insurance, mothers' pensions, minimum-wage and maximum-hour reforms were priorities for women in the network throughout their political lives because these reforms eliminated the necessity for special protective legislation for women.

The Social Security Act of 1935 established retirement pensions for workers age sixty-five or older, including women, and provided benefits to wives, mothers, and children. The inclusion of maternal and child welfare with mothers' pensions in this bill marked the final outcome of the social feminists' struggle to protect women in the home, which dated back to the 1920s, and of the thirty-year fight for governmental protection of the basic welfare rights of both the individual and the family.

In general, this act worked to preserve the patriarchal gender system of the "traditional family." In the 1970s issues of sex equity within the social security system were raised by feminists with varying degrees of success. Ultimately, homemakers' rights were incorporated into modifications to the Social Security Act that protected the homemaker-wife's share of the pension of the employed spouse in case of divorce.

Initially, the greatest impact of the Social Security Act appeared to be in the decreasing number of women workers over the age of sixty-five. Of secondary impact was the support of dependent widows and children, especially in education benefits for the latter. However, the number of single and married working women in predominately "women's jobs" as well as in nontraditional occupations has increased throughout the second half of the twentieth century, thus rendering crucial the retirement benefits for women workers. Cutbacks in social security benefits, the major source of support for elderly women, during the 1980s futher accelerated the feminization of poverty, since women's longevity continued to exceed that of men's.

—Arlie Bice III

See Also:

New Deal, Protective Legislation, Social Feminism

References:

Burkhauser, Richard, and Karen Holden. *A Challenge To Social Security: The Changing Roles of Women and Men in American Society.* San Diego: Academic Press, 1982.

Burns, Eveline M. *The American Social Security System.* Dallas: Houghton Mifflin, 1949.

Cohen, Wilber, and William Haber. *Readings in Social Security.* New York: Prentice-Hall, 1948.

Daniel, Robert L. *American Women in the 20th Century: The Festival of Life.* San Diego: Harcourt Brace Jovanovich, 1987.

Ware, Susan. *American Women in the Thirties: Holding Their Own.* Boston: Twayne, 1982.

SOCIAL WORK traces its beginnings to the charity workers of the early nineteenth century. By the mid-nineteenth century, small groups of women committed to philanthropy and social reform began to organize groups such as the female charitable societies and the Women's Anti-Slavery Society. "Friendly visitors," the forerunners of social workers, were primarily women who visited prisons, hospitals, tenements, and workhouses for the purpose of changing the character of the occupants. The Society for Organizing Relief and Repressing Mendicancy (SOC) 1878–80 published *The Monthly Register,* the first journal of social work to have national circulation, under the supervision of Mary Richmond. Women's characteristics—being more sympathetic, more self-denying, gentler than men—were thought to be particularly suited to social work.

Even in its earliest days, social work was enlivened by the leadership of outstanding women who shaped the future direction of the profession—Mary Richmond, Jane Addams, Florence Kelley, Bertha Reynolds, Josephine Shaw Lowell, Lillian Wald, Julia Lathrop, Frances Perkins, Gordon Hamilton, Virginia Robinson, Jessie Taft, and Mary Jarrett. The important contributions of these women and others helped anchor the profession's value of social equality. They vigorously advocated social policies that would allow all women, children, and people of color to lead dignified lives. They organized individuals in neighborhoods to support laws trying to alleviate the social problems of the day and organized women to be allowed to vote. Through their leadership in social work education, they influenced curriculum content in schools of social work, which ultimately strengthened the quality of services delivered to clients.

By the 1920s and 1930s, social workers led by Jessie Taft put increasing emphasis upon individual counseling. The rise of psychiatry also had an impact on the movement toward treating the individual. In recent years, social workers have also begun to concentrate on the treatment of whole families. More men have entered the profession, and the training of social workers has become more and more specialized with an increase in both undergraduate and graduate social work programs. Social workers can be found in private practice, with departments of social services, in schools, churches, and other institutional settings.

—*Sara Ann Foster*

See Also:

Addams, Jane; Benevolence; Kelley, Florence; Perkins, Frances; Satir, Virginia; Settlement House Movement; Wald, Lillian

References:

Rauch, Julia B. "Women in Social Work: Friendly Visitors in Philadelphia, 1880." *Social Service Review* 49 (June 1975): 255.

Vandiver, Susan. "A History of Women in Social Work." In *Women's Issues and Social Work Practice,* edited by Elaine Norman and Arlene Mancuso. Itasca, Ill.: Peacock, 1980, pp. 21–37.

SOCIALISM is a doctrine that particularly focuses on the condition of the working class and the arrangement of production in the modern world. Initially, in the early nineteenth century, socialists came from all parts of the political spectrum and took the name "socialist" because of a concern for society and social questions in an age of economic transformation. By the twentieth century, however, Marxian ideas definitively shaped socialist beliefs.

Outraged at the injustice of early industrialization, German-born Karl Marx (1818–83) developed theories about the conflictual nature of historical processes and the class-based nature of society that depended on one's relationship to productive organization or "mode of production." Conflicts arising between master and slave, lord and serf, bourgeoisie and proletariat drove economic arrangements to newer forms such as feudalism, capitalism, and finally socialism, respectively. Under socialism, the theory ran, economic distinctions would disappear as society came to rest on the common ownership of the means of production, that is, on all the tools, factories, land, and machines on which society depended for sustenance.

In addition, gender inequality would disappear along with such private ownership. Marx's collaborator, Friedrich Engels (1820–

95), presented a detailed socialist analysis of the subjection of women in *Origin of the Family, Private Property, and the State* (1884). In it, he postulated that women's oppression stemmed from the need to insure the legitimacy of heirs to property and thus to power. The minute private property disappeared, so would the "woman question." The secondary nature of gender posited by socialist theory and defended strongly by socialist leaders made specific attention to women's issues a vexing question. Sexual emancipation, suffrage, separate women's organizations, the struggle for equal wages, the division of labor in the household—all of these were hotly debated, routinely dismissed as trivial, or deliberately ignored. Moreover, socialist leaders sometimes saw little use in recruiting women to the cause in the first place.

Nonetheless, women joined the socialist movement late in the nineteenth century because of the promised end to social as well as gender injustice. While many socialist leaders hardly welcomed women to the cause, others propounded ideas of equality in work and an end to domestic drudgery. At the same time, women found socialist activities a way of maintaining ethnic traditions and developing networks in the urban environment. There developed from these interests and the interest in economic justice an elite group of activist women around the turn of the century and later, among them Kate Richards O'Hare, Ida Crouch Hazlett, Caroline Lowe, and Rose Pastor Stokes, to name a few. Many of them, however, found themselves conflicted after the Russian Revolution posed other questions. In general, some chose to follow the Russian lead into a Communist party heavily influenced by Moscow. Others remained socialists—attached, that is, to a Socialist party vastly diminished in strength by the split. A series of purges of left-wing thinkers and activists after World War I and continuing through the anticommunist hysteria of the McCarthy period in the 1950s also reduced socialist organization to virtual impotence in political life. Soon after, however, socialist questions again appeared on the agenda, as feminists in the new women's movement of the late 1960s tried to pose again the question of gender in a socialized and socialist world.

—Bonnie G. Smith

See Also:

Socialist Feminism, Socialist Party of America

References:

Barrett, Michele. *Women's Oppression Today: Problems in Marxist Feminist Analysis.* New York: Schocken, 1980.

Buhle, Mari Jo. *Women and the American Left, A Bibliography.* Boston: G. K. Hall, 1983.

———. *Women and American Socialism, 1870–1920.* Urbana: University of Illinois Press, 1981.

Engels, Friedrich. *Origin of the Family, Private Property, and the State in the Light of New Researches by Lewis H. Morgan* (1884). Edited by Eleanor B. Leacock. New York: International Publishers, 1972.

SOCIALIST FEMINISM is a theoretical perspective on gender inequality that emerged during the 1970s as a result of some feminists' disenchantment with orthodox Marxist theories of gender inequality. According to the socialist feminist perspective, Marx and Engels correctly identified gender inequality as a form of class antagonism and properly linked gender oppression to the accumulation of private property and the economic structure of society. But socialist feminists disagree with orthodox Marxists on the solution to gender inequality. The latter hold that gender inequality will disappear with the abolition of private property and the transition from capitalism to socialism. In contrast, socialist feminists see the existence of gender inequality in both precapitalist and contemporary socialist societies as evidence that eliminating economic inequality does not necessarily eradicate gender oppression. Consequently, socialist feminists, while not abandoning an analysis of the interrelationship between economic (class), gender, and racial inequalities, have also sought to understand gender oppression independent of class and race factors.

Significantly, socialist feminists reject the notion of the public/private split; that is, they do not accept the traditional ideological division of home and workplace into separate spheres. Instead, they emphasize that these two "worlds" reinforce one another: what happens in the home affects what goes on in the workplace and vice versa. Socialist feminists point out that depictions of the home as a private place of nurturance, as a retreat from the public work world, obscure the fact that the work women do there—housework and child care—is socially and economically necessary. Through their work in the home, women essentially reproduce the labor force: They bear, care for, and socialize future workers, and their cooking and cleaning sustains those already in the labor force. Nevertheless, because domestic work is unpaid—it has use value, but no exchange value—it has not been considered "real work." That women, even women who also work outside the home, are almost exclusively responsible for domestic labor has led to their devaluation as workers in general. The work women do is seen as less valuable work, which, in turn, is used as a justification for their low status and low wages in the paid labor force. Moreover, research indicates that wives who earn less than their husbands—and most do—have less power in their marriages. Thus is the system of gender inequality perpetuated.

Analyses such as this have led socialist feminists to conclude that the liberation of women is impossible without the abolition of the sexual division of labor. Socialist feminists, therefore, not only call for the socialization of the means of production, but also for the socialization of housework and child care.

—*Claire M. Renzetti*

See Also:

Communist Party, Housework, Sexual Division of Labor, Socialism, Wages, Women's Work—Nineteenth Century

References:

Anderson, Margaret L. *Thinking About Women.* New York: Macmillan, 1983.

Eisenstein, Zillah. *Capitalist Patriarchy and the Case for Socialist Feminism.* New York: Monthly Review, 1979.

Engels, Frederich. *The Origin of the Family, Private Property, and the State.* New York: International Publishers, 1972.

Jaggar, Allison M., and Paula S. Rothenberg, eds. *Feminist Frameworks.* New York: McGraw-Hill, 1984.

Scott, Hilda. *Does Socialism Liberate Women?* Boston: Beacon, 1974.

The **SOCIALIST PARTY OF AMERICA**, locus of a growing national movement between 1901 and World War I, stood for equal civil and political rights for men and women, including universal suffrage. The earlier recognition by international socialism of the exploitation of women led to the party's position, which became a factor in its ability to attract women to its banner. About 10 percent of the membership was female. Women were convention delegates, party journalists, speakers, and organizers, and more visible than in any other political party of the era. However, women lacked any real power. Further, the party always subsumed the "woman question" within the so-called labor question and, in practice, assigned the former no serious priority. Consequently, women organized to build their own sector within the party.

American women who joined the Socialist Party often had prior organizational experience through the Bellamyite (nationalist clubs), Populist, or women's club movements and other activities, such as temperance or missionary work. Immigrant women, numbering as much as one-third of the membership of a few foreign-language branches of the party, were working class or intellectuals. Some women came to the party from a background in autonomous female socialist study groups. In 1908 the Woman's National Committee was established, and it prodded all locals to organize woman's committees, promoted the election of more women to party offices, issued propaganda leaflets, and sought to convert women from all areas of society to socialism. A profile of the most well known activists suggests that they tended to be middle class, native born, college graduates, usually of middle age, often rural in upbringing, and from the West. The leading women socialists—not all of whom were involved in the woman's sector—were Kate Richards O'Hare, Mary Wood Simons, Lena Morrow Lewis, and Rose Pastor Stokes.

The woman's sector was a vibrant party mechanism, attracting new members, energizing locals, and improvising innovative organizational techniques. But some socialist women as well as men opposed its existence as irrelevant and counterproductive. In 1915 it was abolished, and within a few years leftist factionalism virtually destroyed this national movement, while women once again played only a minor role in it.

—Sally M. Miller

See Also:

O'Hare, Kate Richards; Socialism; The Woman Question

References:

Buhle, Mari Jo. *Women and American Socialism, 1870–1920.* Urbana: University of Illinois Press, 1981.

Miller, Sally M., ed. *Flawed Liberation: Socialism and Feminism.* Westport, Conn.: Greenwood, 1981.

———. "Other Socialists: Native-Born and Immigrant Women in the Socialist Party of America." *Labor History* 24 (Winter 1983): 84–102.

The **SOCIETY OF FRIENDS**, or Quakers, is a religious group that was founded in England by George Fox in 1652 and has persisted into the twentieth century. From the beginning, women were considered equal in the eyes of the church, and Fox's wife, Margaret Fell, championed female ministries. Quakers believed in the Divine Light, or God in everyone, and men and women were therefore spiritually equal since there was nothing to prevent women from experiencing this spiritual rebirth. The Quakers believed in a lay ministry, and both men and women served as lay ministers.

When William Penn brought Quaker beliefs to Pennsylvania in 1681–82, a system of government was set up that was very much like the governments of other colonies and of England, and equality for women was not reflected in this government. However, the religious organization was different from other Protestant sects. Women's meetings were a very important part of church governance. These meetings were about business, and through them, Quaker women addressed their responsibilities for marriage, family matters, and helping the poor. Women who wanted to marry first went to a women's meeting, and the couple were interviewed to make sure they were both Quakers and would raise their family in the society. As in other families of the seventeenth century, the man was seen as the head of the household, but men and women both had to submit to the discipline of the church. If there was trouble in a marriage, a women's meeting might try to resolve the problem.

In the eighteenth and nineteenth centuries, Quaker women remained active. They continued to serve as lay ministers and traveled more to visit Friends' groups in the United States and England. However, there is not much evidence that there were many changes in women's status in secular areas of their lives. Women sometimes felt a conflict between their roles as lay ministers and their family responsibilities, but could deal with this conflict because they were secure in the belief that God had called them to the lay ministry and that they were submissive to God's will. Most women were expected to take care of family responsibilities in addition to their church duties. This was partly because of the Quaker belief in a lay ministry that did not discriminate on the basis of sex. Some women lay ministers curtailed traveling during childbearing years, delayed marriage, or did not marry at all. Others resumed active service to the church in later years when family responsibilities had lessened.

However, even though many Quaker women divided their lives between religious and secular responsibilities, the nineteenth century had a high proportion of Quaker women reformers active in the abolitionist and feminist movements. There may have been several reasons for this. Leadership roles in the religious group prepared such women to speak in public and made it more comfortable for them to assume the same roles in other areas of their lives. Lucretia Mott, a well-known Quaker, formed an abolitionist group for women and was one of four Quaker women to convene the women's rights conference at Seneca Falls, New York, in 1848. Mott found different reasons for equality of women than some of her contemporaries. She was not so much interested in the need for suffrage but worked for a new image of women as moral, responsible people. Mott was probably more of an activist than the typical Quaker woman, but she was not unique in carrying her religious beliefs into the other parts of her life.

—Judith Pryor

See Also:
Mott, Lucretia; Public Speakers, Women

References:

Cadbury, Henry J. "George Fox and Women's Liberation." *The Friends' Quarterly* 19 (October 1974): 370–76.

Calvo, Janis. "Quaker Women Ministers in Nineteenth-Century America." *Quaker History* 63 (1974): 75–93.

Dunn, Mary Maples. "Women of Light." In *Women of America: A History*, edited by Carol Ruth Berkin and Mary Beth Norton. Boston: Houghton Mifflin, 1979, pp. 114–33.

Ford, Linda. "William Penn's Views on Women: Subjects of Friendships." *Quaker History* 72 (1983): 75–102.

Greene, Dana. "Quaker Feminism: The Case of Lucretia Mott." *Pennsylvania History* 48 (1981): 143–54.

The **SOCIETY OF THE COMPANIONS OF THE HOLY CROSS** is an international "companionship" of over seven hundred women united in the search for inner spiritual life and communal worship. These women share a deep interest in literature and the arts as forms of spiritual experience and a dedication to social service and social justice. Not a monastic order, the society consists of Episcopalian laywomen living in the world "under a Rule of intercessory prayer, simplicity of life, thanksgiving, and special concern for Christian unity, mission, and social justice."

The society was founded in 1884 by Emily Malbone Morgan, a pioneer in social work among women factory workers, as a means of providing Adelyn Howard, her childhood friend and an invalid of uncommon grace and fortitude, with the support of community and the activity of praying for others. The membership has included women of varying backgrounds, occupations, and races. Though many have been active in the settlement house and labor movements, in civil rights, suffrage campaigns, and similar activities, the degree to which the society should take public stands on social issues has often been a matter of debate. Membership is determined not by slant of opinion but by keenness of concern. The group is autonomous and self-governing and maintains Adelynrood, a conference center and retreat house, in Byfield, Massachusetts.

—Anne Dzamba Sessa

See Also:
Christianity

References:

Chrisman, Miriam U. *"To Bind Together," A Brief History of the Society of the Companions of the Holy Cross.* Privately printed, 1984.

Morgan, Emily Malbone. *Letters to Her Companions.* Edited by Vida Scudder. Privately published, 1944.

SOLOMON, HANNAH GREENEBAUM (1858–1942), Progressive reformer and club woman, was best known for founding the National Council of Jewish Women (1893). Her parents were affluent German Jewish immigrants and founders of Chicago's influential Reform Jewish community. Solomon herself was a follower of prominent Reform rabbi Emil Hirsch. Claiming she "consecrated" every day, Solomon supported his attempt to change Jewish sabbath observance from Saturday to Sunday, thereby causing a destructive split within NCJW that nearly cost her the presidency of that organization. She held the presidency from 1893 until 1905, when she was elected honorary president for life.

In the council's early years, Jewish publications recognized Solomon as spokesperson for American Jewish women and frequently published her work. Most often she wrote of the need for a renewed Jewish womanhood, arguing that only committed Jewish mothers could raise committed Jewish children. She believed it was woman's responsibility to save Judaism from the destructive effects of increasing assimilation. NCJW used that view to justify demands for religious education for women (training previously reserved for males), and for a voice in synagogue policy, particularly in areas concerning synagogue schools. Solomon was also known for promoting preventative social work practiced by professional social workers. She frequently cooperated with Jane Addams and in 1897 founded the council's Bureau of Personal Service, an immigrant aid organization.

Solomon (with her sister Henriette) also gained fame as the first Jew to join the prestigious Chicago Women's Club (in 1877). Through that club, Solomon was instrumental in establishing Cook County's juvenile court (1899) and the Illinois Industrial School for Girls (1905). She was also a founding member of the Illinois Federation of Women's Clubs (1905) and treasurer of the Council of Women of the United States (1899), an organization she later represented at the 1904 International Council of Women in Berlin, where she acted as translator for the other U.S. representatives, Susan B. Anthony and May Wright Sewall. Solomon dubbed herself "a confirmed woman's rights-er" and supported nonmilitant efforts to win suffrage.

Despite her commitment to social reform work, Solomon's main allegiance was to her family. She frequently cautioned other club women not to let club activities lead to neglect of home duties. A domestic feminist, she glorified mothers as the shapers of future generations and motherhood as the most effective tool for societal change. She argued that social work was an extension of motherhood and based her demands for women's rights on this view.

—Faith Rogow

See Also:

Domestic Feminism, Jewish Women, Suffrage

References:

American Jewess. Chicago: Rosa Sonneschein, 1895–99.

The Jewish Woman. (NCJW's newsletter). 1921–42.

NCJW: Proceedings of the First Convention. Philadelphia: Jewish Publication Society, 1897. (Also see proceedings for each subsequent Triennial Convention.)

Papers of the Jewish Women's Congress—1893. Philadelphia: Jewish Publication Society, 1894.

Solomon, Hannah Greenebaum. *Fabric of My Life: The Story of a Social Pioneer.* 1946; rpt. New York: Bloch, 1974.

———. *A Sheaf of Leaves.* Chicago: Privately printed, 1911.

SONTAG, SUSAN (b. 1933) is a highly influential essayist, novelist, filmmaker, and critic. A native of New York, Sontag grew up in Arizona and earned her B.A. at the University of Chicago. She went on to earn M.A.'s in both English and philosophy from Harvard, where she completed all requirements for a doctorate except the dissertation. Sontag then launched a successful career as both an artist and a critic. Since the early 1960s she has been one of the chief explicators in the United States of new forms in art, literature, and culture. Through her critical essays Sontag has delineated a new aesthetic in which style and pleasure are established as values in their own right. She also has directed a film and written novels.

—Jonathan W. Zophy

See Also:

Photography

References:

Lacayo, Richard. "Stand Aside, Sisyphus." *Time* 132 (October 24, 1988): 86–88.

Sontag, Susan. *Against Interpretation.* New York: Farrar, Straus, & Giroux, 1986.

———. *Death Kit.* New York: Farrar, Straus, & Giroux, 1967.
———. *The Benefactor.* New York: Farrar, Straus, & Giroux, 1963.

The **SOUTHERN BAPTIST WOMAN'S MISSIONARY SOCIETY** organized many individual groups into one large union in 1888. Since its inception, this organization has been known within the denomination interchangeably as the Woman's Missionary Society or the Woman's Missionary Union. These women developed a system of graded missionary education for preschoolers through adults. Today, this missionary education exists in over 25,564 Southern Baptist churches, with a membership of 1,165,240 children, youth, and women.

While women of many other denominations organized independently, collected money, and appointed and supported their own missionaries, Southern Baptist women chose to function as an auxiliary to the Southern Baptist Convention, the denomination's nongoverning central association. Their aim was "to stimulate the grade of giving" and "aid in collecting funds for missionary purposes" to be disbursed by the boards of Southern Baptist Convention. "Thou shalt not" is a dominant message given to women throughout Baptist history. But amid all the prohibitions given to women, there is no record of a woman's money having been refused at church. Fund raising was the first public activity for Baptist women. It was obvious from 1888 that they were very good at the job.

The work of Baptist-sponsored missionaries in the nineteenth century provides a sharp contrast to the belief of many of the men in the church that women must always be kept "cabined, cribbed, and confined." In 1835 Southern Baptists sponsored Henrietta Hall Shuck, eighteen-year-old wife of J. Lewis Shuck, as the first American woman missionary to China. Lottie Moon, another China missionary, helped establish the church's week of prayer and offerings for foreign missions. She was short in stature but tall in spirit and nobility. She literally starved herself to death in order to share her tiny amount of food with starving Chinese friends during a time of famine. She was appointed in 1873 and died in 1912 on a boat for home. Annie Armstrong became the Woman's Missionary Union's first corresponding secretary (1888–1906). She had a strong voice, was over six feet tall, and traveled anywhere she was needed to help state unions organize their three annual special offerings to raise funds for state, foreign, and home missions. She refused pay for her efforts.

Today, Southern Baptists have 3,600 missionaries in the U.S. and 3,750 in 108 foreign countries. The Woman's Missionary Union of the Southern Baptist Convention, through many individual groups of Baptist women, offers considerable support in prayer and money for these missionaries. Their goal is the elevation and Christianization of women and children in foreign lands as well as in the United States.

—*Marjorie Kerrick Taylor*

See Also:
Benevolence, Christianity

References:

Hunt, Alma. *Woman's Missionary Union.* Birmingham, Ala.: Woman's Missionary Union, 1964.
Mather, Juliette. "Woman's Missionary Union." In *Encyclopedia of Southern Baptists,* Vol. 2, edited by Norman W. Coxe. Nashville: Broadman, 1958, p. 1506.

The **SOUTHERN CHRISTIAN LEADERSHIP CONFERENCE (SCLC)** was organized in January 1957 in Atlanta in the wake of the Montgomery, Alabama, bus boycott, which began when Rosa Parks, a black woman, was arrested for refusing to sit in the back of the bus, where blacks in the South were expected to sit. The SCLC grew in influence under the leadership of Martin Luther King, Jr., who served as its head until his assassination in 1968. Under King, the SCLC played an important role in such major civil rights events as the March on Washington (1963) and the antisegregation campaigns in Birmingham and Selma, Alabama, and Albany, Georgia. The southern black Baptist ministers in the SCLC dominated the leadership, but Ella Baker, Dorothy Cotton, and Septima Clark were members of the executive staff. Baker is credited with a major role in organizing the 1960 conference of student activists that became known as the Student Non-Violent Coordinating Committee (SNCC).

—*Linda Ray Pratt*

See Also:

Civil Rights; King, Coretta Scott; New Left; Parks, Rosa

References:

Branch, Taylor. *Parting the Waters: America in the King Years, 1954–65.* New York: Simon and Schuster, 1988.

"Dorothy Cotton." In *My Soul Is Rested: Movement Days in the Deep South Remembered,* edited by Howell Raines. New York: Putnam, 1977, pp. 432–34.

Evans, Sara. *Personal Politics: The Roots of Women's Liberation in the Civil Rights Movement and the New Left.* New York: Random House, 1979.

Fairclough, Adam. *To Redeem the Soul of America: The Southern Christian Leadership Conference and Martin Luther King, Jr.* Athens: University of Georgia Press, 1987.

Sellers, Cleveland, with Robert Terrell. *The River of No Return.* New York: Morrow, 1973.

The **SOUTHERN LADY** was an ideological concept in which Southern women embodied standards of moral and social conduct supportive of white racist society. Like the nineteenth-century "lady" elsewhere, the Southern Lady was the moral vessel whose piety, modesty, and wisdom were the bulwark of the family. She was the tamer of men's brute instincts, the guardian of the young, and the source of religious values in the home and community. Ideally, she was also beautiful, charming, accomplished with music and needle, and submissive to her male masters. In the context of slave society, the Southern Lady was placed on a pedestal as proof of the purity and piety of a society under attack for the immorality and exploitation inherent in its economic structure. The Southern Lady's image was intended to personify all that was moral and civilized in white culture, and she became the chief symbol of what Southerners defended as "our way of life."

The dynamics of miscegenation in slave culture added to the cult of the lady a rigid sexual repression because the image of the "virtuous wife" was used to counter the image of the profligate husband. Thus the ideology of the Southern Lady became an instrument whereby harsh and violent punishments were meted out to black men who were considered to have violated rules of conduct designed to protect the interests of white supremacy.

Although only a small fraction of the Southern population was ever part of the elite white planter class with which the image of the Southern Lady is most associated, the ideal of conduct that she embodied was commonly shared by other classes of whites. Fiction of Southern plantation life first gave the image wide popular appeal in the 1830s in both the North and South, and it continued to be popular into the twentieth century through such best-sellers as *Gone with the Wind.* Mary Boykin Chesnut's *A Diary from Dixie* (1905), covering the years from 1861 to 1865, is perhaps the most noted account of the life of a Southern Lady. Fanny Kemble's *A Residence on a Georgian Plantation,* published in 1863, was a sharply critical and iconoclastic picture of slave society that influenced anti-Southern opinion during the Civil War.

—*Linda Ray Pratt*

See Also:

Chesnut, Mary Boykin; Cult of True Womanhood; Kemble, Fanny

References:

Clinton, Catherine. *Plantation Mistress: Woman's World in the Old South.* New York: Pantheon, 1983.

Fox-Genovese, Elizabeth. *Within the Plantation Household: Black and White Women of the Old South.* Chapel Hill: University of North Carolina Press, 1988.

Jordan, Winthrop D. *White over Black.* Chapel Hill: University of North Carolina Press, 1968.
Scott, Anne Firor. *The Southern Lady: From Pedestal to Politics, 1830–1930.* Chicago: University of Chicago Press, 1970.
Welter, Barbara. "The Cult of True Womanhood 1820–1860." *American Quarterly* 18 (1966): 151–74.
Woodward, C. Vann, ed. *Mary Chesnut's Civil War.* New Haven: Yale University Press, 1981.

SOUTHERN WOMEN'S ORGANIZATIONS /LEADERS. Because the South remained predominantly rural well into the twentieth century, Southern women had fewer opportunities to participate in voluntary associations than women in other regions. Nevertheless, Southern women, like women elsewhere, joined together for self-improvement, service, and reform.

Before the Civil War, white women in the South's towns and cities participated in benevolent, religious, and temperance associations. In 1853 Ann Pamela Cunningham of South Carolina founded the first national women's patriotic society, the Mount Vernon Ladies' Association of the Union. During the Civil War, Southern women banded together in hospital and sewing circles; after the war, many of these same associations cared for graves of Confederate dead.

Southern women's organizations multiplied in the decades following the Civil War, with church missionary societies leading the way. Methodists, Baptists, and Episcopalians formed state or regional women's auxiliaries in the 1870s and 1880s. The Woman's Christian Temperance Union and the King's Daughters, a philanthropic organization, established Southern branches. In the 1890s white Southern women joined patriotic societies such as the Colonial Dames, the Daughters of the American Revolution, and the United Daughters of the Confederacy. They also organized local literary and civic clubs and state federations of women's clubs. As women's voluntary associations grew in the first decade of the twentieth century, they gained respectability and power and played an important role in Southern Progressive reform.

At the same time that white women were organizing, a parallel network of associations appeared among black women. The WCTU and YWCA sponsored separate branches for blacks. Black women had their own local civic clubs, and in 1896 organized the National Association of Colored Women. After World War I, white and black women —frequently acting through the Methodist church, the YWCA, and federations of women's clubs—began working together to ease racial tensions. At a historic meeting in Memphis in 1920 black and white women created the Woman's Committee of the Commission on Interracial Cooperation. At the Memphis meeting, black women attempted to enlist white women in their antilynching campaign. In the 1930s, under the leadership of Jessie Daniel Ames, white Southern women organized the Association of Southern Women for the Prevention of Lynching.

Voluntary associations in the South, as elsewhere, enabled women to move outside their homes without openly challenging the domestic ideal. They gave Southern women the public voice denied them as individuals. Acting together, Southern women established a place for themselves in politics long before they got the vote.

—Anastatia Sims

See Also:

Ames, Jesse Daniel; Association of Southern Women for the Prevention of Lynching; National Association of Colored Women; United Daughters of the Confederacy; Woman's Christian Temperance Union

References:

Bellows, Barbara L. "'My Children, Gentlemen, Are My Own': Poor Women, the Urban Elite, and the Bonds of Obligation in Antebellum Charleston." In *The Web of Southern Social Relations: Women, Family, and Education,* edited by Walter J. Fraser, Jr., R. Frank Saunders, Jr., and Jon L. Wakelyn. Athens: University of Georgia Press, 1985, pp. 52–71.
Berkeley, Kathleen C. "'Colored Ladies Also Contributed': Black Women's Activities from Benevolence to Social Welfare." In *The Web of Southern Social Relations: Women, Family, and Education,* edited by Walter J. Fraser, Jr., R.

Frank Saunders, Jr., and Jon L. Wakelyn. Athens: University of Georgia Press, 1985, pp. 181–203.
Croly, Mrs. Jennie June Cunningham. *The History of the Woman's Club Movement in America.* New York: Henry G. Allen, 1898.
Friedman, Jean E. *The Enclosed Garden: Women and Community in the Evangelical South, 1830–1900.* Chapel Hill: University of North Carolina Press, 1985.
Giddings, Paula. *When and Where I Enter: The Impact of Black Women on Race and Sex in America.* New York: Bantam, 1985.
Hall, Jacquelyn Dowd. *Revolt Against Chivalry: Jessie Daniel Ames and the Women's Campaign Against Lynching.* New York: Columbia University Press, 1979.
Lebsock, Suzanne. *The Free Women of Petersburg: Status and Culture in a Southern Town, 1784–1860.* New York: Norton, 1984.
Lerner, Gerda, ed. *Black Women in White America: A Documentary History.* New York: Pantheon, 1972.
Price, Margaret Nell. "The Development of Leadership by Southern Women Through Clubs and Organizations." M.A. thesis. University of North Carolina at Chapel Hill, 1945.
Roth, Darlene Rebecca. "Matronage: Patterns in Women's Organizations, Atlanta, Georgia, 1890–1940." Diss. George Washington University, 1978.
Scott, Anne Firor. *The Southern Lady: From Pedestal to Politics, 1830–1930.* Chicago: University of Chicago Press, 1970.
Sims, Anastatia. "Feminism and Femininity in the New South: White Women's Organization in North Carolina, 1883–1930." Diss. University of North Carolina at Chapel Hill, 1985.

SPALDING, ELIZA HART (1807–51). In 1836 Eliza Spalding and Narcissa Whitman became the first white women to reach the Continental Divide and to cross the Rocky Mountains. Spalding and her husband, Henry Harmon Spalding, had joined the Whitmans to establish a Presbyterian mission among the Indians of the Oregon Territory. While the Whitmans settled among the Cayuse near Fort Walla Walla, Washington, the Spaldings chose to live with the Nez Perce at Lapwai, in what is now Idaho.

Born in Berlin, Connecticut, and raised on a farm in upstate New York, Spalding was skilled in the usual farm and home crafts. She attended a local female academy, then taught school for a few years before marrying in 1833. Spalding was converted and joined the Presbyterian church when she was nineteen; she remained an intensely religious woman until her death. Her husband, an equally religious man, attended Lane Theological Seminary.

The Spaldings opened a school in Lapwai a few months after their arrival. While her husband preached and taught the Nez Perces farming skills, she took charge of the school. Daily lessons included English, spinning, weaving, sewing, and knitting, as well as Bible lessons. Her school became very popular, averaging a daily attendance of one hundred Nez Perce women and children. Spalding also gave birth to five children while living at Lapwai. One miscarried; the others lived to maturity.

On November 29, 1847, the Cayuse rose up against and massacred the Whitmans and twelve other members of their mission. When this occurred, the Nez Perce protected the Spalding family and led them safely to the Willamette Valley. The mission was closed, and the family settled on a farm at Brownsville, Oregon. Spalding, always a victim of poor health, was at that time suffering from tuberculosis. Never fully recovering from the disease, she died on January 7, 1851, at the age of forty-four.

—Deborah Dawson Bonde

See Also:

Christianity, Migration and Frontier Women

References:

Dawson, Deborah Lynn. *Laboring in My Savior's Vineyard: The Mission of Eliza Hart Spalding.* Diss. Bowling Green State University, 1988.
Drury, Clifford, ed. *The First White Women over the Rockies. Vol. 1: The Diaries of Narcissa Whitman, Eliza Spalding, and Mary Gray.* Glendale, Calif.: Arthur H. Clark, 1963.
Josephy, Alvin M., Jr. *The Nez Perce Indians and the Opening of the Northwest.* New Haven: Yale University Press, 1965.

The **SPANISH CIVIL WAR, 1936–39.** The largely untold story of U.S. women volunteers in the Spanish Civil War began in 1936 when the Spanish people elected a Popular Front government. This government sought to establish a liberal democracy in Spain. Within three months, the young republic came under attack by Spanish General Francisco Franco, who had turned to Hitler and Mussolini for aid. Antifascists from all over the world went to Spain to defend the republic and formed the International Brigades; among them were some thirty-two hundred volunteers from the United States, who became known as the Abraham Lincoln Battalion.

Over sixty women, primarily medical personnel, volunteered to serve in Spain, thus becoming the first group of women in U.S. history to go overseas to aid in a civil war. They played a major role in providing health care and support services for the republican (Loyalist) forces, despite opposition to their going by the overwhelmingly male organizers of the Lincoln Battalion. The fact that they could go was a result of women's greater economic independence since the wave of feminism in the 1920s. Many were under thirty; some were recent graduates of nursing schools. At considerable risk to their careers, health, and even lives, they left their families and jobs for an uncertain future in a bloody civil war.

Brutality reached new heights during the Spanish Civil War as Franco's Falangist troops introduced tactics such as the bombing of civilian targets and hospitals. Medical supplies were extremely limited, antibiotics such as penicillin unknown, and working hours were endless. The young U.S. volunteers worked relentlessly, carrying out nursing tasks as well as training Spanish civilians and even running hospitals. Cecilia Seborer, a lab technician, aided in the surgical pioneering of the technique of whole blood transfusions. Other women drove ambulances, served as war correspondents—Mary Hemingway and Josephine Herbst—worked as translators, and aided refugee children. Many women were sent home suffering from fatigue and other illnesses before the official withdrawal of the International Brigades in October 1938.

As "premature antifascists," these women faced the same harassment upon their return as the men, including visits by the FBI and loss of jobs and friends. Their experiences in Spain, despite the defeat of the Spanish Republic, proved to be a catalyst for future involvement in the women's movement and other progressive issues.

—Karel Kilimnik

See Also:

Journalism, Nursing

References:

de Vries, Lini. *Up from the Cellar.* Minneapolis: Vanilla, 1979.

Gerassi, John. *"During the Civil War." The Premature Anti-Fascists: An Oral History—North American Volunteers in the Spanish Civil War, 1936–1939.* New York: Praeger, 1986.

Hutchins, Evelyn. "A Woman Truck Driver." In *Our Fight—Writings by Veterans of the Abraham Lincoln Brigade, Spain, 1936–1939,* edited by Alvah Bessie and Albert Prago. New York: Monthly Review, 1987, pp. 175–78.

Martin, Fredericka. "The American Hospital Unit." In *Our Fight—Writings by Veterans of the Abraham Lincoln Brigade, Spain, 1936–1939,* edited by Alvah Bessie and Albert Prago. New York: Monthly Review, 1987, pp. 142–47.

(O'Reilly) Kea, Salaria. "'While Passing Through': Health and Medicine." *Journal of the Health and Medicine Policy Research Group* 4 (Spring 1987): 113–15.

Wyden, Peter. "The Bloody Jarama." In *The Passionate War: A Narrative History of the Spanish Civil War, 1936-1939.* New York: Simon & Schuster, 1983, pp. 296–301; 1986, 1986, pp. 96–101.

SPARS, the women's corps of the U.S. Coast Guard, was created in November 1942, four months after the U.S. Navy created its women's corps, known as WAVES. The women were called SPARS, from *Semper Paratus* (Always Prepared), the Coast Guard's motto, and were accepted on the same basis as male reservists.

SPARS served in a variety of jobs to release men for the front lines. A major source of pride for the SPARS was their participation during World War II in Unit 21, which oversaw the top-secret project, LORAN—Long Range Aid to Navigation. Unit 21 was at first manned by men. Within a month, SPARS completely staffed the unit except for one veteran radio technician who acted as their instructor. Six months later, he had also shipped out. At peak strength of the armed forces during World War II, ten thousand women served as SPARS; in all, thirteen thousand served during the war.

The first director, Dorothy Stratton, formerly dean of women at Purdue University, was serving as a senior officer in the WAVES training program in Wisconsin when the Coast Guard created its women's corps. WAVES director Mildred McAfee, who had been a dean of women before becoming president of Wellesley, recommended Stratton for the position. The second director, Helen Schleman, had also served as dean of women at Purdue. The third director, Katherine A. Towle, went from the SPARS to become dean of students at the University of California at Berkeley in the 1960s.

After the passage of the Women's Armed Services Integration Act in June 1948, the SPARS remained distinct within the service until 1978, after which women could enter the Coast Guard Academy and command cutters with male and female crews. Since the Coast Guard reports to the Department of Transportation instead of the navy during peacetime, it is not restricted by law as is the navy in training women in combat roles. The Coast Guard has consequently given its women more opportunity than the other services to gain a wide range of technical and leadership experiences.

—D'Ann Campbell

See Also:

Military Service, WAVES, Women's Army Auxiliary Corps, Women's Army Corps

References:

Campbell, D'Ann. *Women at War with America: Private Lives in a Patriotic Era.* Cambridge: Harvard University Press, 1984.

Lyne, Mary C., and Kay Arthur. *Three Years Behind the Mast: The Story of the United States Coast Guard SPARS.* Washington, D.C.: U.S. Coast Guard, 1946.

Stratton, Dorothy. "Recollection with Dorothy Stratton." Oral History Collection, United States Naval Institute, Annapolis, Md., 1971.

U.S. Coast Guard. *The Coast Guard at War: Women's Reserve XXII A.* Washington, D.C.: U.S. Coast Guard Headquarters, Historical Section, Public Information Division, 1946.

SPENCER, LILLY MARTIN (1822–1902) was not only one of the most popular American artists of the nineteenth century but also one of the most important and best-known American woman painters. Spencer's reputation and popularity were established with her warm and humorous portrayals of everyday family life as well as her still-life works. She had a special eye and ability to create paintings using common objects. Many of Spencer's works were sold to popular art unions of the mid-nineteenth century, which operated as consumer co-ops and widely disseminated the works of many women artists. Spencer's reputation increased as her works were reproduced as engravings and lithographs and widely distributed to subscribers, making her name a household word. Her genre paintings are an example of the type popular before the Civil War, at which time they earned as much as works by George Caleb Bingham, a famous genre painter of the time.

Spencer was born in England; her parents were French intellectuals who later emigrated to Ohio. They were active in the main causes of the period and encouraged her art, even allowing her to make charcoal murals on the plaster walls of their farmhouse. She is considered to be self-taught although she had some lessons from itinerant painters and artists in Cincinnati and New York City.

Though not traditional, her marriage to Benjamin Rush Spencer, an English tailor, lasted forty-six years beginning in 1844. Early in the marriage, her husband recognized Spencer's ability to support the family better than he could and therefore took over domestic responsibilities and assisted her with the business side of her work. They had thirteen children, seven of whom survived. Her husband and children were often the subjects of Spencer's paintings.

Spencer held her first public exhibition in 1841. The attention given to her and her work by critics led to an offer from a wealthy patron to finance her training in Boston and Europe, but she refused. She was quite successful in the Midwest but decided to move to New York in 1848 to seek fame in the center of the art world. The stiff competition led her to take night classes and to improve her drawing and knowledge of perspective.

With the demise of art unions, the decreasing popularity of her special type of genre, and the increasing use of photography for portraits, the Spencers' income dropped. In her later years, Spencer worked hard but was forced to barter her paintings for bread to stay alive. Nonetheless, she produced an incredible number of works and painted up to her death at the age of eighty.

—Holly Hyncik Sukenik

See Also:
Art

References:

Bolton-Smith, Robin. "The Sentimental Paintings of Lilly Martin Spencer." *Antiques* 104 (July 1973): 108–15.

———, and William H. Truettner. *Lilly Martin Spencer 1822–1902: The Joys of Sentiment.* Washington, D.C.: Smithsonian Institution, 1973.

Freivogel, E. F. "Lilly Martin Spencer: Feminist Without Politics." *Archives of American Art Journal* 12 (1972): 9–14.

Normile, James. "The Subject Is Children." *Architectural Digest* 30 (November/December 1973): 64–67.

Rubinstein, Charlotte Streifer. *American Women Artists: From Early Indian Times to the Present.* Boston: Avon, 1982, pp. 50–53.

Tufts, Eleanor. *American Women Artists 1830–1930.* Washington, D.C.: The National Museum of Women in the Arts, 1987.

STANTON, ELIZABETH CADY (1815–1902), suffragist, lecturer, and writer, was the foremost critic of legal and cultural forms of women's subordination in the nineteenth century. As initiator of the Seneca Falls (N.Y.) Convention in 1848—the first such national gathering for women's rights in America—and author of its demand for woman suffrage, Stanton became the most prominent advocate of women's legal equality and political activism. Her arguments began where the American Revolution left off, with a social contract to which women, like men, should be parties because they were imbued with the same natural rights and rational minds. Not limiting herself to the right of women to have a voice in government, Stanton explored the implications of true equality for the most intimate human relations and most pervasive cultural norms. At every opportunity, she criticized male political culture on the one hand and woman's culture on the other for perpetuating female dependency in a society premised on individualism and self-sovereignty.

Born in Johnstown, New York, the daughter of a lawyer and judge, Stanton attended Emma Willard's Seminary, but her legal and political education at home left the clearer mark. Marriage to abolitionist orator Henry B. Stanton in 1840 introduced her to the most advanced circles of reform, and from that date she also confronted a burdensome domestic life. Seven children limited her early activism, but Stanton polished her gifts as a writer to exert great influence over the new woman's rights movement, whose meetings she could rarely attend. A close collaboration with Susan B. Anthony, beginning in 1851, allied Stanton with a person more interested in and skillful than herself at organizing people to carry out their shared ideas.

After the Civil War, Stanton achieved a national reputation as a popular lecturer on the locally sponsored lyceum circuit, an outspoken social and political commentator, and the venerable president of the National Woman Suffrage Association (NWSA). Her topics included maternity, the woman's crusade against temperance, child rearing, and divorce law, as well as constitutional questions, presidential campaigns, and woman suffrage. Thriving on controversy, she championed notorious victims of the double standard. Witty and personable on the platform, she entertained her audiences while exposing them to advanced discussion of full equality.

In the 1880s, tired of travel and organizational leadership, Stanton intensified her writing, producing one of her greatest legacies, three volumes of the *History of Woman Suffrage* (1881–85), prepared with Anthony and Matilda Joslyn Gage. Still the single most important source on the ideas and people of the early movement for equality, the *History* project showed a remarkable grasp of how important history would be to the survival of this political movement.

Stanton also returned to her lifelong examination of how religion structured women's subordination. Scores of articles as well as the better-known *Woman's Bible* (1895, 1898) set forth her convictions that religious faith blocked progress toward women's self-sovereignty, that churches threatened the fabric of republican government, and that ecclesiastical domination subordinated women more effectively than the state itself. As she had done in 1848, Stanton expanded a current debate among men as well as women to analyze anew what held women back and what directions their rebellion should take. Nearing the end of her life but still the quintessential reformer, Stanton reexperienced the isolation and criticism of 1848 but died without the chance to lead in the new direction.

—Ann D. Gordon

See Also:

Anthony, Susan B.; National Woman Suffrage Association; Seneca Falls Convention; *The Woman's Bible*

References:

Banner, Lois. *Elizabeth Cady Stanton: A Radical for Women's Rights.* Boston: Little, Brown, 1980.

Gordon, Ann D., and Patricia G. Holland, eds. *The Papers of Elizabeth Cady Stanton and Susan B. Anthony.* [Microfilm ed.] Wilmington, Del.: Scholarly Resources, forthcoming.

Griffin, Elisabeth. *In Her Own Right: The Life of Elizabeth Cady Stanton.* New York: Oxford University Press, 1984.

Lutz, Alma. *Created Equal: A Biography of Elizabeth Cady Stanton, 1815–1902.* New York: Day, 1940.

Stanton, Elizabeth Cady. *Eighty Years and More: Reminiscences, 1815–1897.* 1898; rpt. New York: Schocken, 1971.

———, et al. *The Woman's Bible, Parts I and II.* 1895–98; rpt. New York: Arno, 1974.

———, Susan B. Anthony, and Matilda Joslyn Gage, eds. *History of Woman Suffrage.* 3 vols. 1880–89; rpt. New York: Arno, 1969.

STARR, ELLEN GATES (1859–1940), settlement worker, bookbinder, and labor activist, is best known as the co-founder, with Jane Addams, of Chicago's Hull House settlement in 1889. Although Addams proved to be the main force behind the nation's most famous settlement house—the third established in a movement that encouraged educated young people to live and work among the urban poor—Starr's enthusiastic support and professional contacts during the early years were perhaps decisive in establishing the institution. As a resident of Hull House for nearly thirty years, Starr made the fate of art and labor in the modern city her prime concern.

During the mid-1890s, Starr had become dissatisfied with her earliest attempts at Hull House to preserve dignified labor and an artistic impulse among Chicago's immigrants. She recognized that in joining the trade unions in their demands for higher wages, shorter hours, and better working conditions, workers had failed to address the fact that the very nature of factory work had been degraded. Likewise, cultivating in her neighbors an appreciation for European painting through exhibitions at the settlement or the circulation of reproductions in local schools now seemed ineffectual in preventing the fine arts from becoming irrelevant to urban industrial life. Although Starr continued to participate in these activities, she was increasingly drawn to the current revival of the handicrafts as the best way of making art and labor once again meaningful to the working class. For fifteen months (1897–98), she served as an apprentice at the Doves Bindery in London under the supervision of T. J. Cobden-Sanderson, a leading figure in the British arts and crafts movement. She then returned to Hull House, established her own bookbindery, and developed during the next two decades a national reputation as a superior craftsman.

Starr succeeded in making beautiful books and probably thought of herself as that "happier and more rational human being" that she had said all workers could become once they took up a handicraft. Unfortunately, she never fulfilled her dreams of influencing the commercial production of books or of extending the pleasures of handcraftmanship to the masses. Thus, by the 1920s Starr concluded sadly that she had been naive to hope that by practicing a handicraft one could help drive out the "hideousness and joylessness" of modern industrialism.

—*Bruce R. Kahler*

See Also:

Addams, Jane; Hull House

References:

Kahler, Bruce R. "Art and Life: The Arts and Crafts Movement in Chicago, 1897–1910." Diss. Purdue University, 1986.

Starr, Ellen Gates. "Art and Labor." *Hull-House Maps and Papers.* New York: Crowell, 1895, pp. 165–79.

———. "The Renaissance of Handicraft." *The International Socialist Review* 2 (February 1902): 570–74.

STEARNS, LUTIE EUGENIA (1866–1943), whom Edna Ferber once called "a terrific and dimensional human being," was an outspoken advocate for a variety of social issues, especially the establishment of public libraries.

Born in Staughton, Massachusetts, she emigrated to Wisconsin in 1871 and was hired at the Milwaukee Public Library as head of the circulation department in 1888. During her free time, she worked to get the Wisconsin Free Library Commission established in 1895. She became its secretary for two years, then library organizer when the commission restructured in 1897. From 1903 to 1914 she was head of the commission's Traveling Library Department. Estimates indicate she helped establish 150 public libraries, 1,400 traveling libraries, and 14 county library systems in Wisconsin in a ten-year period.

By 1914 her drive for libraries waned, and she resigned from the commission to pursue other causes. Despite a noticeable stutter, she developed into a skilled lecturer on topics of keen interest to her. Between 1914 and 1932 she traveled to thirty-eight states to speak on prohibition, women's rights, the League of Nations, industrial reform, peace, and education, all of which she favored. She was an active member of the Federation of Women's Clubs and the Women's International League for Peace and Freedom. From 1932 to 1935 she wrote a column for the *Milwaukee Journal* entitled "As a Woman Sees It." She died on Christmas Day, 1943.

—*Wayne A. Wiegand*

See Also:

General Federation of Women's Clubs; Librarianship; Public Speakers, Women; Women's International League for Peace and Freedom

References:

Stearns, Lutie Eugenia. "My Seventy-Five Years." *Wisconsin Magazine of History* 42 (1958/59): 211–18, 282–87; 43 (1959/60): 97–105.

Tannenbaum, Earl. "The Library Career of Lutie E. Stearns." *Wisconsin Magazine of History* 39 (1955/56): 159–65.

STEIN, GERTRUDE (1874–1946), author, was born in Allegheny, Pennsylvania, but she did not remain a small-town American girl. She lived as a child with her family in Europe and then in California, and she spent most of her grown years in France, where she gained recognition as a writer of experimental literature and as a collector of art—and artists. At 27 Rue de Fleurus, her apartment in Paris, which she shared with her brother Leo and then, after 1909, with her lifelong companion and lover, Alice B. Toklas, she held court with many of the promising artists and writers of the day. She and Leo were among the first Americans to recognize modernist painting, and visitors to their salon apartment could see, in profusion, works by Pablo Picasso, Juan Gris, and others, as they heard Stein and the other artists gathered there discuss matters of art and life. The gatherings at her salon during the early decades have assumed almost legendary status because of who was there and because of Stein herself, a Buddha-like woman with talent and a formidable personality. Ernest Hemingway, in his posthumously published Paris memoirs (*A Moveable Feast*, 1964), gave credit to Stein's artistic genius, which was innovative and trend-setting, as he also recognized the judgmental role she sometimes assumed regarding the art and artists of the day.

Stein's personality and legendary status in modern art have tended to overshadow her own writing, which writers such as Hemingway, Sherwood Anderson, and others first helped her to publish. Although Stein had studied to become a medical doctor at Johns Hopkins University, she tired of her studies and applied her scientific mind to her art. Throughout most of her career, Stein wrote for a limited audience, largely due to her unconventional style as well as the length of her works. Her *Making of Americans*, which was almost a decade in the writing, began as the history of an American family and then became the history of mankind (at 550,000 words). Influenced by psychologist William James's theory of consciousness as well as her own awareness that modernist art should show what reality is, not what one would like it to be, Stein violated conventional narrative structures so as to re-create on the printed page what she called the "continuous present." She believed that traditional word and sentence patterns inhibited meaning, and she experimented with variations on word groups (which she called word portraits), which might move beyond their prescribed meanings to take on a fresh resonance. Her style was marked by its repetitive qualities, and many today identify her work with Stein's own phrase: "A rose is a rose is a rose." Because of the highly experimental and sometimes undisciplined nature of her writing, some critics have faulted Stein's work for verbosity and obscurity, and her writing is less often regarded on its own merits than for the impact it had on other writers. Save for the successful *Autobiography of Alice B. Toklas* (published in 1933 and written in the persona of Alice, who engagingly comments upon life at 27 Rue de Fleurus), Stein was, and continues to be, primarily a writer's writer.

Following the publication of *Alice B. Toklas*, Stein was greeted in America as a celebrity, as she undertook a national lecture tour wherein she talked to enthusiastic audiences about life and art in postwar Paris. During World War II Stein and Toklas opened their French country home to American GIs, and Stein died quietly there at the end of the war. Stein is often remembered for her classification of Hemingway and his compatriots as the "Lost Generation."

—Linda Patterson Miller

See Also:

Toklas, Alice B.

References:

Brinnin, John Malcolm. *The Third Rose: Gertrude Stein and Her World.* Boston: Little, Brown, 1959.

Hoffman, Frederick J. *Gertrude Stein.* Boston: G. K. Hall, 1961.

Mellow, James R. *Charmed Circle: Gertrude Stein and Company.* New York: Praeger, 1974.

Stein, Gertrude. *The Autobiography of Alice B. Toklas.* New York: Harcourt Brace, 1933.

———. *Fernhurst, Q.E.D. and Other Early Writings.* Edited by Leon Katz. New York: Liveright, 1971.

———. *Lectures in America.* New York: Random House, 1934.

———. *The Making of Americans.* Paris: Contact Editions, 1925.

———. *Paris, France.* New York: Scribner, 1940.

———. *Picasso.* New York: Scribner, 1939.

———. *Selected Writings of Gertrude Stein.* Edited, with an introduction by Carl Van Vechten. New York: Random House, 1946, 1962.

———. *Three Lives.* New York: Grafton, 1910.

———. *Wars I Have Seen.* New York: Random House, 1944.

———. *Writings and Lectures, 1911–1945.* Edited by Patricia Meyerowitz. Baltimore: Penguin, 1967.

Weinstein, Norman. *Gertrude Stein and the Literature of the Modern Consciousness.* New York: Ungar, 1970.

STEINEM, GLORIA (b. 1934) is an activist, author, feminist, fund-raiser, journalist, and public lecturer. Born in Toledo, Ohio, to a journalist mother Ruth Nuneviller Steinem and a sometime-resort-operator father Leo Steinem, she went to Smith College, graduating in 1956 with Phi Beta Kappa honors. She then went to India as a Chester Bowles Asian Fellow from 1957 to 1958. Returning to New York City, Steinem began her career as a free-lance writer.

Her career as a journalist took a great leap forward in 1963 when she did an undercover exposé of the Playboy nightclub empire of Hugh Hefner, editor and publisher of *Playboy* magazine. Titled "I Was a Playboy Bunny," Steinem's essay helped to raise people's consciousness about the sexism inherent in the Playboy nightclubs' treatment of their uncomfortably clad waitresses, whose real working lives contrasted sharply with the glamorous image that the Playboy corporation was attempting to create for them.

According to Steinem, her feminist consciousness was further galvanized by an abortion hearing in 1969. She wondered "how much power would we ever have if we had no power over the fate of our own bodies?" Her concerns for women soon translated into actions, as Steinem became one of the founders of the Women's Action Alliance in 1970, a member of the National Women's Political Caucus in 1971, a co-founder and contributing editor of *Ms.* magazine, a co-founder of the *Ms.* Foundation for Women, a member of the National Organization for Women, a member of Coalition of Labor Union Women in 1974, and a member of the International Women's Year Committee in 1977.

In addition to championing issues pertaining directly to women, Steinem has also been involved in various campaigns of the United Farmworkers, the Vietnam War Tax Protest, the Committee for the Legal Defense of Angela Davis (treasurer, 1971–72), and the political campaigns of Adlai Stevenson, Sr., Robert Kennedy, Eugene McCarthy, Shirley Chisholm, and George McGovern. Her political effectiveness has been enhanced by the success of her journalistic and literary career. Not only is she one of the founders of *Ms.* magazine as well as its editor for fifteen years, but Steinem also helped start *New York* magazine. She continues to contribute articles to numerous national magazines, and a collection of her essays, *Outrageous Acts and Everyday Rebellions,* became a best-seller in 1983.

Gloria Steinem has become one of the most influential and celebrated of modern North American feminists. Her book *Marilyn,* an imaginative study of the legendary movie star published in 1986, also became a best-seller. Continuously active on the lecture circuit, Steinem became a contributing editor to the *Today* television program in the late 1980s. Germaine Greer assessed Steinem's influence as a feminist activist, journalist, and role model: "There are hundreds and thousands of women out there who still look to her."

—Jonathan W. Zophy

See Also:

Journalism, *Ms.* Magazine, Women's Liberation Movement

References:

Carter, Betsey. "Liberation's Next Wave According to Gloria Steinem." *Esquire* 101 (June 1984): 202–6.

Cohen, Marcia. *The Sisterhood.* New York: Simon & Schuster, 1988.

Harrison, Cynthia. *On Account of Sex: The Politics of Women's Issues, 1945–1968.* Berkeley: University of California Press, 1988.

Langway, Lynn. "Steinem at 50: Gloria in Excelsis." *Newsweek* 103 (June 1984): 27.

Steinem, Gloria. *Marilyn.* New York: Holt, 1986.

———. *Outrageous Acts and Everyday Rebellions.* New York: Holt, 1983.

STEWART, ELINORE (PRUITT) RUPERT (1876–1933), author of *Letters of a Woman Homesteader* and *Letters on an Elk Hunt by a*

Woman Homesteader, chronicled her early-twentieth-century experience on a southwest Wyoming ranch. Stewart intended her life as a *woman* homesteader to serve as a central theme of her work and offered homesteading as a panacea to the problems of wage-working urban women, suggesting her own example as encouragement. For this reason, her work appeals to modern readers because it offers a feminist perspective (although Stewart might have resisted that label) on the prospects of homesteading, and it offers an alternative to the stereotypes of western women as reluctant, depressed pioneers.

Stewart was born in 1876 in Indian Territory. At age fourteen she was orphaned and working as a cook and laundress for railroad crews. By 1909 she was a widow and a mother, living in Denver and looking for an alternative to wage earning. She answered Clyde Stewart's newspaper ad for a housekeeper, moved to his ranch in Wyoming, and filed on an adjoining homestead. Soon thereafter, Elinore and Clyde married, but she maintained her determination to "prove up" on the homestead without any help from her spouse. In the end she relinquished her homestead in 1912, and her widowed mother-in-law took it up, finally receiving the title to the property in 1915. In 1920 Ruth C. Stewart sold the land to her son Clyde.

Elinore Stewart, then, failed to achieve her goal of independent land ownership. But her importance lies less in the details of her land transactions than in her ability to express through writing the hopes and aspirations of men and women of her generation. She was a writer who also ranched in partnership with her husband. She chose homesteading and its supposed opportunities for working-class women as a literary device or vehicle for her optimism. She was a spirited woman who saw the West and its rugged landscape as a challenge. In her literature and her imagination, if not always in her day-to-day life, she met and overcame many of these challenges.

—Sherry L. Smith

See Also:
Migration and Frontier Women

References:

Stewart, Elinore Pruitt. *Letters of a Woman Homesteader*. 1913–14; rpt. Boston: Houghton Mifflin, 1976.

———. *Letters on an Elk Hunt by a Woman Homesteader*. Boston: Houghton Mifflin, 1915; rpt. Lincoln: University of Nebraska Press, 1979.

STINSON, KATHERINE (1891–1977) was the oldest member of a family that was very prominent in aviation in the early twentieth century. After receiving her pilot's license in 1912, she began making public flights in San Antonio, where she also lectured on aviation to school groups and recommended that it be made part of their curriculum. Her list of records and firsts includes being the first woman to loop an aircraft, the first woman to fly in the Orient, and the first pilot to make a nonstop flight from San Diego to San Francisco. In 1915 she helped her family found the Stinson Flying School in San Antonio, where she and her sister Marjorie were the principal flight instructors.

Stinson was an outspoken advocate of U.S. women pilots being allowed to fly for their country during World War I, but she was unsuccessful and was only allowed to fly on behalf of Red Cross and Liberty Loan Bond drives. She eventually went to France to serve as an ambulance driver. Although Katherine Stinson's pleas for active participation by women pilots in World War I fell on deaf ears, an idea was planted that may have assisted her successors in convincing the government to allow women to fly as part of the war effort at the outbreak of World War II.

—Claudia M. Oakes

See Also:
Aviation

Reference:

Oakes, Claudia M. *United States Women in Aviation Through World War I*. Washington, D.C.: Smithsonian Institution, 1978.

STONE, LUCY (M. BLACKWELL) (1818–93) was in her time the most admired and politically effective of the pioneer feminists. As a student at Oberlin College in the mid-1840s, Stone declared her intention to become a lecturer for woman's rights following her graduation. Employed at first by the New England Anti-Slavery Society, she divided her time between speaking for women and against slavery, and her lectures often drew crowds of two and three thousand. In 1850 she was instrumental in organizing the first national woman's rights convention, held in Worcester, Massachusetts.

In 1855 Stone married Henry Blackwell, brother of the medical doctors Elizabeth and Emily, despite her objections to married women's legal submersion. At their wedding ceremony, the couple presented their marriage protest, which drew widespread public attention to the gender-based inequities of the marriage laws. Motherhood and the Civil War temporarily halted Stone's career, but in 1867 she resumed active campaigning for a woman suffrage amendment. A schism within the woman suffrage movement in 1869 divided her from Elizabeth Cady Stanton and Susan B. Anthony and their National Woman Suffrage Association (NWSA); continuing animosity resulted in her near-exclusion from the *History of Woman Suffrage,* prepared by Anthony, Stanton, and Matilda Joslyn Gage. Following the split, Stone and others founded the American Woman Suffrage Association (AWSA), an organization that developed strategic and tactical sophistication, eventually providing the political prototype for the lobbying effort led by Carrie Chapman Catt, which culminated in the passage of a woman suffrage amendment in 1920.

Stone was active in the national movement for woman suffrage; she also lobbied various state legislatures on behalf of a number of feminist and reform causes—the enactment of married women's property laws, equal rights statutes, divorce law reform, and school and municipal suffrage bills. However, Stone's most lasting contribution to the woman's movement is the *Woman's Journal,* which she founded in 1870 and edited until her death in 1893. This extraordinary archive of women's history provided a weekly chronicle of woman's progress—political, vocational, economic, cultural, and legal—both in the United States and abroad; the *Woman's Journal* enjoyed continuous publication for sixty-one years.

Stone's death on October 18, 1893, attracted worldwide attention. For generations afterward, grateful women continued to make pilgrimages to the birthplace of the woman known as the "morning star" of the woman's rights movement.

—*Andrea Moore Kerr*

See Also:

American Woman Suffrage Association; Anthony, Susan B.; National American Woman Suffrage Association; National Woman Suffrage Association; Social Purity Movement; Stanton, Elizabeth Cady; *Woman's Journal*

References:

Blackwell Family Papers. Manuscript Division, Library of Congress, Washington, D.C.

Blackwell, Alice Stone. *Lucy Stone: Pioneer of Woman's Rights.* Boston: Little, Brown, 1930.

Hays, Elinor Rice. *Morning Star: A Biography of Lucy Stone.* New York: Harcourt Brace and World, 1961.

Merk, Lois Bannister. "Massachusetts in the Woman Suffrage Movement." Diss. Radcliffe College, 1961.

STOWE, HARRIET BEECHER (1811–96), author, was born in Litchfield, Connecticut, the seventh of nine children, to Roxana Foote and the famous Congregational minister Lyman Beecher. At thirteen, Stowe was sent to her sister Catharine's female seminary in Hartford, where she worked as a student teacher, and in 1829 she became a full-time teacher. In 1832 Lyman Beecher was appointed president of Lane Theological Seminary in Cincinnati and moved there, taking Catharine and Harriet with him.

In 1834 Harriet published her first story, "A New England Sketch," in the *Western Monthly,* and in 1836 she married Calvin Ellis Stowe, a professor of biblical literature at Lane. In 1843 she published *The Mayflower,* her first book of fiction. In 1844, when her husband turned over management of the family finances to her, she discovered that she could afford domestic help with the money she earned from publishing stories in the *Western Monthly*, the *New York Evangelist*, and *Christian Union*. In 1850 her husband accepted a position at Bowdoin College in Brunswick, Maine, and it was there, in 1852, that Stowe published *Uncle Tom's Cabin*. Appearing serially in the *National Era* from June 1851 through April 1852, the novel brought her international fame. In 1852 her husband joined the faculty at Andover Theological Seminary in Andover, Maine, where the family remained until his retirement in 1864, when they moved to Hartford, Connecticut.

In 1853 Stowe published *A Key to Uncle Tom's Cabin* in order to validate her sources for the novel. Another slave novel, *Dred: A Tale of the Great Dismal Swamp*, followed in 1856. After 1856 Stowe wrote several novels that portrayed life in New England villages in the eighteenth and early nineteenth centuries: *The Minister's Wooing* (1859), *The Pearl or Orr's Island* (1892), *Oldtown Folks* (1870) (supplemented in 1871 with *Oldtown Fireside Stories*), and *Poganuc People* (1878). These later novels established her reputation as a regional, local-color author, and it is also in these novels that her literary talent is most apparent. *Agnes of Sorrento* (1862) was Stowe's attempt at a romance. Stowe's novels of the 1870s dealt primarily with New York society and were not as well written as her New England novels. *Pink and White Tyranny* (1871), *My Wife and I* (1871), and its sequel, *We and Our Neighbors* (1875), fail to portray New York society as vividly as Stowe's New England novels did their region.

In addition to novels, Stowe wrote a volume of religious poetry, *Religious Poems* (1867), and several children's books, including *Queer Little People* (1867), *Little Pussy Willow* (1870), and *Betsy's Bright Idea* (1876). She wrote *Sunny Memories of Foreign Lands* (1854), a record of her first trip to Europe. *Footsteps of the Master* (1877) and *Bible Heroines* (1878) were expressions of Stowe's Calvinist religious convictions. In 1868 she wrote *Men of Our Times*, a series of biographical sketches. Articles written for the *Atlantic Monthly* were collected in *House and Home Papers* (1864) and *The Chimney Corner* (1868). In 1870 Stowe published an essay in the *Atlantic Monthly*, "The True Story of Lady Byron's Life," which was expanded into a book, *Lady Byron Vindicated*, in 1870. The article caused many people in England and America to accuse Stowe of scandalmongering because Stowe wrote that Byron separated from his wife because of his incestuous affair with his sister. Although Stowe and Lady Byron were friends, and the article was written nine years after Lady Byron's death, Stowe's good intentions on behalf of her friend were not considered, and her literary reputation suffered greatly as a result.

Stowe died in 1896 in Hartford. She had survived not only her husband, but four of her seven children. In 1903 her works were collected in the library of the Women's Building at the World's Columbian Exposition in Chicago. The collection included a twenty-volume set of her complete works and forty-two translations of *Uncle Tom's Cabin*.

—*Victoria L. Shannon*

See Also:

Beecher, Catharine; *Uncle Tom's Cabin*

References:

Boydston, Jeanne, Mary Kelley, and Anne Margolis. *The Limits of Sisterhood: The Beecher Sisters on Women's Rights and Woman's Sphere*. Chapel Hill: University of North Carolina Press, 1989.

Fetterly, Judith. *Provisions: A Reader from 19th-Century American Women*. Bloomington: Indiana University Press, 1985.

Wagenknecht, Edward. *Harriet Beecher Stowe: The Known and the Unknown*. New York: Oxford University Press, 1965.

STRIPTEASE, or burlesque, is a form of entertainment in which a woman or man gradually undresses to music before an audience. In the United States it derived from an entertainment tradition that included music halls and vaudeville. As early as 1847 the American Theater in New York City presented reviews that featured "dancing girls" in various states of undress. In the spring of 1904 the exotic dancer "Little Egypt" became the sensation of the St. Louis Exposition. In 1908 Anna Held, the first wife of show business impresario Florence Ziegfeld, disrobed behind a screen at the Mason Opera House in Los Angeles as an orchestra played "I'd Like to See a Little More of You." By the following year, New York's Columbia Theater was staging shows with such titles as "Tease for Two" and "Strip, Strip, Hooray."

All this was well before the legendary accidental invention of striptease at Minsky's Burlesque House in New York in 1925. During a police raid on Minsky's, one of the dancers suffered an accidental breaking of her shoulder strap, revealing some of her upper torso to a wildly appreciative audience. Apparently the dancer enjoyed the audience's attention, for during her next performance she intentionally broke her shoulder strap, and thus began the tradition of striptease at Minsky's.

Other entertainers in the 1920s were consciously developing more elaborate striptease routines. Mae Dix, for example, while clad in folded newspapers, read headlines to music and permitted box-seat patrons to tear sheets off her costume. In 1928 Hinda Wassau in Chicago and Carrie Finnell in Cleveland set the style that almost all strippers have followed since. Their acts featured such staples of stripping as formal evening gowns with long gloves at the onset of the routine, the bump and grind, the slow removal of garments down to a G-string (originally a nineteenth-century term for the *cache-sexe* of Native Americans) and pasties (nipple covers), and the musical accompaniment of a small band featuring a torpid but pronounced drumbeat. Finnell later embellished her striptease further with the invention of breast tassel-twirling.

The 1930s were the halcyon days of stripteasing with such stars as Gypsy Rose Lee, Ann Corio, Margie Hart, Yvette Dare, Lois De Fee, Georgia Southern, and Zoritz, who used a boa constrictor in her act. Not only did strippers display themselves in a variety of imaginative ways, but they also appeared in comedy sketches with burlesque comedians such as Bud Abbott, Lou Costello, Jimmy Durante, Phil Silvers, and Looney Lewis. The most famous exotic dancer of the period was Gypsy Rose Lee, the author of three best-selling books, whose life was the subject of a popular Broadway musical and later a Hollywood film starring Natalie Wood.

The authorities frequently lagged behind the theatergoing public in their appreciation of striptease, as was evidenced in the four arrests suffered in one day by fan dancer Sally Rand during the Chicago World's Fair of 1933. On May 2, 1937, Mayor Fiorello La Guardia officially banned burlesque in New York City, which had become the striptease capital of the nation. La Guardia agreed with his police commissioner, who had charged that striptease was "largely responsible for the current wave of sex crimes," a conclusion that has still not been supported by evidence.

Striptease eventually returned to New York, but it was never again as popular with the general public, as fewer and fewer theaters gave strippers employment, and more and more of them moved to nightclubs and carnivals. Even in gradual decline, burlesque continued to produce star attractions such as Lily St. Cyr; Tempest Storm, an elegant woman who never once removed her G-string onstage; Blaze Starr, who came to own her own strip club in Baltimore; Jennie Lee, who started an Exotic Dancers Hall of Fame in 1961; and Rita Atlanta, who published her own magazine devoted to burlesque. As late as 1967, an estimated seven thousand women worked as strippers in the United States.

Exotic dancers frequently found themselves in fierce competition with new forms of entertainment such as television and movies and were part of the general decline that all forms of live entertainment suffered in the post–World War II world. Even in the world of erotic entertainment, most striptease acts seemed tame in comparison with X-rated movies. Topless and bottomless waitresses and go-go dancers helped make public nudity a commonplace for those who previously had patronized striptease clubs or burlesque theaters. In an attempt to compete, strippers abandoned their G-strings and pasties where permitted by law, used dangerous silicone injections to expand their breasts, and made the sexual simulation in their acts much more explicit.

In recent years, strippers have often achieved greater fame for their offstage antics than for their onstage performances. Examples would include Fannie Foxe, whose involvement with Congressman Wilbur Mills in 1974 helped end his political career (the "Tidal Basin affair"), and Morgana Roberts, who has achieved celebrity via her penchant for the public kissing of professional baseball players during games. Stripping has also been kept in the public eye by the increased popularity in recent years of male strippers such as the Chippendale dancers. Stripteasers also continue to be regularly featured as a part of popular motion pictures, ranging from Joanne Woodward's 1963 film *The Stripper* to the 1986 docu-drama *Strippers*. Even the nostalgic interest in old-fashioned striptease and burlesque comedy continues, as shown by the continuing success of Ann Corio's revue *This Was Burlesque*, which opened on Broadway in 1962 and continues on tour.

The gradual decline in striptease as an entertainment form is reflected in its increased association with prostitution, drink hustling, drugs, and the dehumanization of women. These problems have increased as stripping has been removed from theaters and kept alive in the United States in bars and nightclubs. Since striptease seems to cater to some of our deeper needs for erotic fantasies and stimulation, it is likely to continue to exist in some form or other.

—*Jonathan W. Zophy*

See Also:
Prostitution

References:

Corio, Ann, and Joe Di Mona. *This Was Burlesque*. New York: Grossett and Dunlap, 1968.

Lewin, Lauri. *Naked Is the Best Disguise: My Life as a Stripper*. New York: Morrow, 1984.

Skipper, J. K., and C. H. McCaghy. "Stripteases: The Anatomy and Career Contingencies of a Deviant Occupation." *Social Problems* 17 (1970): 391–405.

Starr, Blaze, and Huey Perry. *Blaze Starr*. New York: Praeger, 1974.

Tosches, Nick. "Strippers." *Penthouse* 15 (July 1984): 70–4; 146–47.

Wortley, Richard. *A Pictorial History of Striptease*. Secaucus, N.J.: Chartwell Books, 1976.

SUFFRAGE. In the United States, the process of enfranchisement of women before 1920 was complex because suffrage was controlled by the individual states. Prior to the American Revolution, electoral franchise was primarily based upon land ownership, thereby allowing the participation of some women in the political sphere. The American Revolution led to an overall loss of electoral status for women, as the individual states began to specify detailed qualifications for the franchise. The custom of allowing exceptions for some women to participate in politics was replaced by specific institutionalized qualifications that moved enfranchisement from a property basis toward a more exclusive male suffrage.

After the Revolution, the reintroduction of women to the political process was done piecemeal. The expansion of women's franchise began on the local level. Kentucky was the first state to reintroduce electoral suffrage to women in 1838; however, only widows could participate and only in school board elections. Kansas granted school suffrage in 1859. This type of select and extremely limited local suffrage was extended in various forms in the states. Not only were women voting in these local school elections, they were being elected to local offices and appointed to other local positions in significant numbers.

The U.S. Constitution itself does not deny the vote to women; the qualifications for voting are left to the states. The states limited voting to men. Not until the ratification of the Fourteenth Amendment in 1868 was the issue of gender introduced into the Constitution; the word *male* was inserted in that amendment's definition of the franchise being federally granted and guaranteed to the freedmen. The Wyoming Territory was the first to give women the right to vote in all elections in 1869. The following year, the Fifteenth Amendment to the Constitution was passed forbidding denial of the franchise "on account of race, color, or previous condition of servitude." Gender was not included as a category.

The movement to grant to women full suffrage on the national level began with the Seneca Falls (N.Y.) Convention in 1848—the first national gathering for women's rights in the United States—and split over the dispute among the antebellum supporters of woman's rights regarding the proper suffragist response to the Fourteenth Amendment and after their unsuccessful "Kansas Campaign" of 1867. In 1869 two major organizations were established to pursue woman suffrage at the state and national level, the National Woman Suffrage Association (NWSA) and the American Woman Suffrage Association (AWSA), which merged in 1890 to become the National American Woman Suffrage Association (NAWSA). Under the leadership of the NAWSA, the suffrage movement regained momentum after 1900. While many women could now vote in many western states, the woman's movement wanted a constitutional amendment guaranteeing the right of women to vote in all states and in all elections.

It was not until after World War I that the final push for national enfranchisement gained established political endorsement when President Woodrow Wilson (1913–21) endorsed the principle of equal suffrage. The support among women's groups for the vote became respectable with the endorsement of the General Federation of Women's Clubs and the war work of the NAWSA. The harassment of the Wilson administration from the National Woman's party—which held the entire party in power responsible for its leader's failure—added publicity and urgency to the conversion of the president to the cause of woman suffrage. The amendment passed the House of Representatives in 1918 but failed in the Senate. In 1919 the amendment was passed by both houses of Congress and sent to the states for ratification, which came in 1920 when Tennessee ratified the Nineteenth Amendment, which gave women equal suffrage protection.

—Sue E. Strickler

See Also:

American Woman Suffrage Association, Equal Rights Association, Fourteenth Amendment, General Federation of Women's Clubs, National American Woman Suffrage Association, National Woman Suffrage Association, National Woman's Party, Nineteenth Amendment, Suffrage in the American West, Suffrage in the South

References:

Darcy, R., Susan Welch, and Janet Clark. *Women, Elections and Representation.* New York: Longman, 1987.

Flexner, Eleanor. *Century of Struggle: The Woman's Rights Movement in the United States.* Rev. ed. Cambridge: Belknap/Harvard University Press, 1959, 1975.

Ostrogorski, Moisei. "Women Suffrage in Local Self-Government." *Political Science Quarterly* 6 (December 1981): 677–710.

Ryan, Mary P. *Womanhood in America: From Colonial Times to the Present.* 2d ed. New York: Watts, 1983.

Stanton, Elizabeth Cady, Susan B. Anthony, and Matilda Joslyn Gage, eds. *History of Woman Suffrage.* Vol. 1. Rochester, N.Y.: Charles Mann, 1887.

Williamson, Chilton. *American Suffrage: From Property to Democracy, 1760–1860.* Princeton: Princeton University Press, 1960.

SUFFRAGE IN THE AMERICAN WEST (1869–96). The political franchise was extended to women in the United States in 1920 with the ratification of the Nineteenth Amendment, but in some areas of the American West, women had been voting for half a century. While late-nineteenth-century organized efforts to achieve woman suffrage were concentrated in New England and New York and centered around personalities known for their activism in the abolition movement and the post–Civil War effort to obtain full citizenship for women and freedmen, women were first allowed to vote in the Rocky Mountain West.

The Democratic-led territorial legislature of Wyoming, seeing female suffrage as a means to advertise the region and to embarrass the puritanical Republican governor, extended the franchise to Wyoming women in December 1869. Two months later the Mormon-dominated Utah Territorial Legislature voted in the affirmative on a woman suffrage measure. Here the principal motives were to counter accusations that Mormon women were the downtrodden, ignorant slaves of the male hierarchy, to recruit the national suffrage organization to lobby against antipolygamy legislation pending in Congress, and to promote Utah's bid for statehood. But in both Utah and Wyoming the franchise was restricted by the territorial status of these two areas, since citizens of territories were not allowed to vote in gubernatorial or presidential elections. Moreover, in 1887, with the passage of the Edmunds-Tucker Act, which was designed to eliminate plural marriage as practiced by the Mormons, the U.S. Congress took the vote from the women of Utah territory.

Later, when Wyoming joined the union in 1890, it reaffirmed its two decades of experience with woman suffrage by adopting a constitution that carried a clause including women in the elective process; thus it became the first state, except New Jersey, which had briefly permitted some women to vote at the end of the eighteenth century, to allow its adult female citizens to participate in all political elections.

Despite suffragists' petitions and territorial governors' requests for a woman suffrage bill, from 1869 to 1876 the Colorado Territorial Legislature was unwilling to extend political privileges to women. Even in 1876, when Colorado joined the union as the Centennial State, its constitution limited women's political participation to school-district elections; moreover, repeated attempts over the next seventeen years to extend women full electoral privileges met with failure. It was not until 1893 that a Populist-supported woman suffrage referendum was approved. Thus, Colorado became the second state to allow its women to vote.

Utah joined the Union in 1896 with a constitution reinstating woman suffrage. The same year, Idaho amended its constitution to allow women access to the ballot. In 1896 women were allowed full voting rights in these four Rocky Mountain states, but it would be fourteen years before any other state would extend such privileges to its female citizens and twenty-four years before women's right to the ballot would be recognized by an amendment to the federal Constitution.

Why did women first realize the goal of the elective franchise in the nineteenth-century American West? First, female suffrage was seen as a means to advertise a region and improve the image of a particular society or to attract investors and settlers. Second, it was often proposed as a political hoax to embarrass the opposition or was undertaken as an effort by a political faction to recruit women to its cause and thus gain or hold political supremacy. Third, the move for woman suffrage drew support from the reaction to the enfranchisement of black men in the Reconstruction era. Fourth, territorial residents saw that it could be used to recruit eastern support in their campaigns for statehood. Finally, it seemed to be a safe place to experiment with woman suffrage, and there was little organized opposition to women voting in these areas at that time.

In the West, the vote was generally viewed as a privilege bestowed by the governing body, not an inherent right. More often than not, western women and the eastern suffrage movement were used by those in power to achieve other goals; and women were granted the ballot at a specific time, not for the liberal principles lauded by the eastern movement, but for more pragmatic purposes, usually political. In short, women were enfranchised in the nineteenth-century American West as a matter of expediency, not ideology.

—Beverly Beeton

See Also:

Migration and Frontier Women, Suffrage, Suffrage in the South

References:

Beeton, Beverly. *Women Vote in the American West: The Woman Suffrage Movement, 1869–1896*. New York: Garland, 1986.

Grimes, Alan P. *The Puritan Ethic and Woman Suffrage*. New York: Oxford University Press, 1967.

Jensen, Billie Barnes. "Colorado Woman Suffrage Campaigns of the 1870s." *Journal of the West* 12 (April 1973): 254–71.

Larson, T. A. "Emancipating the West's Dolls, Vassals, and Hopeless Drudges: The Origins of Woman Suffrage in the West." In *Essays in Western History in Honor of T. A. Larson*, edited by Roger Daniels. Laramie: University of Wyoming Press, 1971, pp. 1–16.

———. "Petticoats at the Polls: Woman Suffrage in Territorial Wyoming." *Pacific Northwest Quarterly* 44 (April 1953): 74–79.

SUFFRAGE IN THE SOUTH. There was little suffrage activity in the South until the latter part of the nineteenth century, when state-level associations were organized as auxiliaries of the National American Woman Suffrage Association. The first large assemblage of suffragists in the region was the annual convention of the NAWSA in Atlanta in 1895. Other southern cities in which the NAWSA held conventions were New Orleans (1903), Louisville (1911), and Nashville (1914).

During 1916 and 1917 the National Woman's party organized branches in the southern states. Unlike the NAWSA, the NWP employed militant tactics in its crusading. Opinion in the South was hostile toward militancy, however, and the southern branches of the NWP did not engage in it. Some southern women were arrested and jailed for picketing the White House in Washington, but apparently there were no imprisonments for suffrage activities in the southern states.

The movement in the South was complicated by the area's large number of black women. The southern prejudice against black voting made the prospect of black women at the polls abhorrent to many. The focus of the suffrage movement was sex, not race. Nevertheless, the two issues were intertwined in southern thinking, and woman suffrage was rarely discussed without the injection of its real and imagined racial implications.

Southern women often stated that they wished to be enfranchised by their states rather than by the federal government. They asked that state constitutions be amended to eliminate sex as a qualification for voting, but in no state did they succeed in gaining the adoption of such an amendment. They did win a few concessions, however. As a result of their efforts, the legislatures of Arkansas (1917) and Texas (1918) opened primary elections to women voters, and the Tennessee legislature (1919) authorized their voting for presidential electors and in municipal elections.

In spite of their preference for enfranchisement through state action, most of the southern suffragists supported the Nineteenth, or "Susan B. Anthony," Amendment. The South as a whole opposed it, however. Many southerners considered the proposed amendment an infringement on state's rights. Others feared that it would mean federal control of elections. When it was submitted for ratification, only four southern states approved: Texas (June 1919), Arkansas (July 1919), Kentucky (January 1920), and Tennessee (August 1920). Since Tennessee's ratification was the thirty-sixth, and since thirty-six was the number required at that time, its action made the Nineteenth Amendment part of the U.S. Constitution. With woman suffrage a reality, the other southern states belatedly ratified, the last being Mississippi in 1984.

—*A. Elizabeth Taylor*

See Also:

National American Woman Suffrage Association, National Woman's Party, Suffrage, Suffrage in the American West

References:

Fuller, Paul E. *Laura Clay and the Woman's Rights Movement*. Lexington: University of Kentucky Press, 1975.

Johnson, Kenneth R. "Kate Gordon and the Woman Suffrage Movement in the South." *Journal of Southern History* 38 (August 1972): 365–92.

Scott, Anne Firor. *The Southern Lady: From Pedestal to Politics, 1830–1930.* Chicago: University of Chicago Press, 1970.

Stanton, Elizabeth Cady, Susan B. Anthony, M. J. Gage, and I. H. Harper, eds. *The History of Woman Suffrage.* 6 vols. New York: National American Woman Suffrage Association, 1881–1922.

Taylor, A. Elizabeth. "The Woman Suffrage Movement in Mississippi, 1890–1920." *Journal of Mississippi History* 30 (February 1968): 1–34.

———. *The Woman Suffrage Movement in Tennessee.* New York: Twayne, 1957.

SUFFRAGE MEMORIAL TABLETS. To mark the tenth anniversary of the founding of the National League of Women Voters in 1920, which followed the passage of the federal woman suffrage amendment, the league proposed a tenth anniversary memorial-fund plan to perpetuate the memory of former suffrage leaders. The league had been created by the National American Woman Suffrage Association as its only descendant. The plan called for establishment of national and state rolls of honor, recording the names of those whose work and influence brought women "a new day of partnership in public life."

Gifts of $1,000 for national listing and $100 for state would provide a capital fund to help carry on league work, perpetuating the influence of suffrage leaders. The honorees were nominated according to local league interest, based on association with suffrage leaders and inspiration from them in their local communities as well as in the state.

At the 1930 convention, nineteen members of the National Honor Roll attended the convention banquet, including James Lees Laidlaw of New York State, the only male honoree. His name, honoring all men allied to the suffrage cause, was placed on a separate plaque adjacent to the National Honor Roll. The national memorial, a five-foot-high bronze tablet, was installed in league headquarters in 1931 during a National League Council meeting. Seventy-one women's names were listed under twenty-five states and the District of Columbia. The states were California, Colorado, Connecticut, Illinois, Indiana, Iowa, Kansas, Kentucky, Massachusetts, Michigan, Minnesota, Missouri, Nebraska, New Hampshire, New Jersey, New Mexico, New York, Ohio, Oregon, Pennsylvania, Rhode Island, Tennessee, Texas, West Virginia, and Wisconsin.

Carrie Chapman Catt, one of three presidents of the suffrage organization, spoke at the tablet's dedication, recalling that all but a few of the names had been familiar friends. Her name was listed as a president, as well as under Iowa, where she grew up, and New York, where she later lived.

Designed by Gaetano Cecere, this work depicted pioneers stopping in their steady forward march to pass a torch to fresher, more youthful hands. The rays of a sun surmounting the design symbolized the spread of their achievements. Ten stars marked the first ten years of the league. The names of the three suffrage associations' presidents were immediately below the classic scene: Susan B. Anthony, Anna Howard Shaw, and Carrie Chapman Catt. Later disposition of the memorial, as the league moved its headquarters, is unknown.

Twenty-one states also established state memorial tablets. At least two—New York and Ohio—still occupy walls in their state capitols.

—Hilda R. Watrous

See Also:

League of Women Voters, Suffrage

References:

League of Women Voters Collection. Library of Congress, Washington, D.C.

National League of Women Voters. Proceedings of the Tenth Anniversary Convention of the National League of Women Voters. Washington, D.C., 1930.

New York (State and City) Woman Suffrage Collection. Butler Library, Columbia University.

"Unveiled at Headquarters." *The New York Times* (April 16, 1931): 5.

The Woman's Journal 14 (December 1929): 28–9; 15 (March–May 1930): 26–27; 16 (May 1931): 25.

SWENSON, MAY (b. 1913), poet, naturalist, and implicit feminist, has been an incessant experimenter with poetic structure and language, often pushing her poems to their limits to strengthen the bond between reader and poem. Poetry is neither ideas nor philosophy, she contends, but is, instead, "a happening" that the poet "makes," one that leads the reader beyond appearance and flux to the essence of the thing perceived.

Swenson's experiments are an extension of Ralph Waldo Emerson's organic theory of poetic structure. Many experiments focus directly on line placement and division, but she also uses space and shape liberally for the same purposes. Because she believes that something can be felt about a poem even before one begins to read it, shape becomes a kind of objective correlative that reinforces the experience the poet presents through language and imagery. Yet she seldom sacrifices content to shape as concrete poets often do, since she finishes the poem linguistically before imposing any shape on it.

While experimentation has been more important to Swenson than any consistent technique, her most beautiful poems are semantic still lifes describing common objects, events, and scenes. They are deceptively unassuming; however, there is always an undercurrent of movement hidden within, structurally or linguistically, a tension waiting for contact with the reader to come alive.

Animals, especially birds and horses, are Swenson's most common poetic subjects and serve as oblique comments on the physical, social, sexual, and intellectual natures of human beings. By carefully studying animals and using them as epistemological tools, she believes, we can discover what it means to be human.

Swenson's few poems about women, however, are probably her most important ones, for they are attempts to come to terms with what it really means to be a woman. She examines women's place in society; she discusses their relationships with parents, with children, with men, and with other women; and she considers what it means to have a woman's body. This exploration has been a painful one, for it has taken a good part of her career as a poet for her to come to her most powerful statements about life as a woman.

—Kenneth E. Gadomski

References:

Gadomski, Kenneth E. "May Swenson's Poetry: A Discussion with Checklist." Diss. University of Delaware, 1984.

Ostriker, Alicia. "May Swenson and the Shapes of Speculation." *American Poetry Review* 7 (March/April 1978): 35–38.

Stanford, Ann. "May Swenson: The Art of Perceiving." *Southern Review* (NS) 5 (Winter 1969): 58–75.

SYNAGOGUE SISTERHOODS grew out of the domestic feminism of middle- and upper-class women's clubs at the turn of the century. Prior to the establishment of sisterhoods, Jewish women had developed their own local literary and social clubs and had founded the National Council of Jewish Women to promote Judaism. However, religious divisions within NCJW rendered it ineffective as a religious organization, and it changed its emphasis to social reform work. Religious women developed sisterhoods as their alternative, because synagogues were the center of Jewish religious life in America and because working through one's synagogue posed no conflicts over religious practice or interpretation. Since most women active in Jewish women's groups were also synagogue members and since many of those groups already held their meetings in the synagogue building, the transition was easy.

As the number of local sisterhoods grew, each movement developed its own national organization to coordinate efforts. The National Federation of Temple Sisterhoods, an affiliate of the Union of American Hebrew Congregations (the umbrella organization for Reform synagogues), was founded January 22, 1913. The Conservative movement followed with the founding of the Women's League of the United Synagogue of America on January 21, 1918. The Union of Orthodox Jewish Women's Organizations of America was organized on April 19, 1920. All three groups were largely founded by the wives of prominent clergy and lay leaders of the organizations with which each sisterhood federation was affiliated.

Initially, women were not permitted to serve on synagogue boards or in the clergy. Sisterhoods provided women with their only participation in synagogue policy, usually by their basing demands for power on the argument that one could not be a good Jewish mother without a voice in the religious training of one's children. In addition to supporting synagogue religious schools, sisterhoods educated their own members, ran cultural and social service programs, and raised vital funds for synagogue buildings and projects and for their movements' seminaries. Today, women serve on synagogue boards and in the clergy, so sisterhoods are no longer women's sole voice in the arena of synagogue decision-making. Many sisterhoods have changed meeting times from afternoons to evenings to accommodate working women. Its continued role as a vital fund-raiser has preserved the strength of the sisterhood movement.

—Faith Rogow

See Also:

Jewish Women

References:

American Jewish Yearbook. Philadelphia: Jewish Publication Society, 1913–85.

NCJW: Proceedings of the First Convention. Philadelphia: Jewish Publication Society, 1897.

TALBERT, MARY BURNETT (1866–1923), club leader, civil rights activist, educator, and lecturer, was an expert organizer for a wide variety of racial causes throughout her life. Born and educated in Oberlin, Ohio, she graduated from Oberlin College in 1886 with honors. She served as a school administrator in two schools located in Little Rock, Arkansas, before she married William A. Talbert in 1891 and moved to her permanent home in Buffalo, New York. From this center, Talbert became the founder and president of the Christian Culture Congress, a member of the Phillis Wheatley Club, the founder of the Empire State Federation of Colored Women, and an activist in prison reform. Her activities led her to assume leadership as president of the National Association of Colored Women (NACW) in 1916. From this position, Talbert led a successful campaign to redeem and restore the Frederick Douglass Home as a memorial and center for black history, as part of the national centennial celebration of Douglass's birth.

Her career showed the multiplicity of reforms engaged in simultaneously by black women in this era. While she was a national organizer for the NACW in 1913, Talbert also helped to organize branches and increase circulation for the newsletter of the National Association for the Advancement of Colored People (NAACP). While raising funds for the United War Work Campaign, Talbert spread the message of the NAACP in the South. Following her presidency of the NACW, she became a field worker for the NAACP. Yet she continued to lead local campaigns, for example, raising $5,000 for a church-affiliated home for black working girls. She went to Europe during World War I to serve as a Red Cross war and canteen worker for black troops in France. Following the war, Talbert attended the Pan-African Congress in Paris and the International Congress of Women in Zurich. These international experiences led her to join the newly formed International Council of Women of the Darker Races of the World in 1921.

She is known primarily for her work as the national director of the Anti-Lynching Crusaders, a national network of black women working to raise money and consciousness about lynching and the need for a federal antilynching bill. She had worked with Congressman Leonidas Carstarphen Dyer, the sponsor of the federal bill, when she was president of the NACW. Her ad hoc group of black women built upon fund-raising networks perfected during World War I and became official in 1922 as the Anti-Lynching Crusaders. She continued a leadership role within the NAACP as a member of the board of directors and as a vice president. She was the first woman to receive the NAACP's Spingarn Medal for her years of dedicated service.

—Dorothy C. Salem

See Also:

National Association for the Advancement of Colored People

References:

Crisis, The, c. 1915–17.

Dannett, Sylvia. *Profiles of Negro Womanhood.* Chicago: Educational Press, 1964.

Davis, Elizabeth. *Lifting as They Climb.* Washington, D.C.: National Association of Colored Women, 1933.

Salem, Dorothy. "To Better Our World: Black Women in Organized Reform, 1890–1920." Diss. Kent State University, 1985.

TALBOT, MARION (1858–1948) was a leading advocate of educational equality for women. As a college administrator and professor, Talbot sought advancement for graduate women within academia and encouraged women to accept the challenge of higher learning.

Early in her career, Talbot tried to dispel the myth that women could not handle the pressures of college work. Graduating in 1880 from Boston University with a Bachelor of Arts degree, Talbot organized a survey that questioned the medical view of Dr. Edward Clarke in his controversial *Sex in Education, or A Fair Chance for the Girls* (1873) that the mental and physical strain of college work would damage the reproductive system of young women. Talbot's survey of college graduates and nongraduate women found no evidence to support Clarke's view. The survey revealed that college graduate women were just as fertile as nongraduate women. In 1881, with the support of friends, Talbot founded the Association of Collegiate Alumnae, which later became known as the American Association of University Women. This organization had a twofold purpose: to provide fellowship to women attending college and to assist women wanting to attend college.

In 1884 Talbot graduated with a Bachelor of Science degree from Massachusetts Institute of Technology, where she became interested in the new field of domestic science. Talbot believed that science could be a foundation to deal with the problems of sanitation and consumer protection. In 1887 she collaborated with Ellen Richards in editing *Home Sanitation: A Manual for Housekeepers*, the first of several publications on this topic. In 1890 Talbot was appointed as instructor in domestic science at Wellesley College. However, New England's conservative attitude toward educating women and Wellesley's disinterest in supporting development of sanitary science left Talbot dissatisfied, and she accepted an offer to teach and act as dean of undergraduate women and assistant professor of sanitary science at the University of Chicago.

From 1892 until 1899, when she was appointed dean of university women, Talbot was in charge of the day-to-day activities of the women students and development of the sanitary science program. Her support of coeducation led to an unsuccessful campaign against an internal proposal to establish a separate junior college for women at the University of Chicago. Her persistent support for coeducation continued despite administrative resistance.

Marion Talbot's fight for women's educational equality inspired others to continue the struggle for coeducation. Through her support of women's education, she offered young women an alternative to the domestic sphere.

—*Michael A. deLeòn*

See Also:

Association of Collegiate Alumnae, *Sex in Education, or A Fair Chance for the Girls,* University of Chicago, Women in Higher Education

References:

Berkin, Carol Ruth, and Mary Beth Norton. *Women of America: A History.* Boston: Houghton Mifflin, 1979.

Rosenberg, Rosalind. *Beyond Separate Spheres: Intellectual Roots of Modern Feminism.* New Haven: Yale University Press, 1982.

Storr, Richard J. *Harper's University: The Beginning.* Chicago: University of Chicago Press, 1966.

TALLCHIEF, MARIA (b. 1925) was the first native-born American prima ballerina. Born in Fairfax, Oklahoma, to Ruth Porter and Alex Tall Chief, an Osage Indian, she moved to Beverly Hills, California, with her family in 1933. There she and her sister studied music and dance with Ernest Belcher. Tallchief went on to study with Bronislava Nijinska, and in 1942 she went to the Ballet Russe de Monte Carlo. After one brief season with the Paris Opera Ballet in 1947, she danced with the New York City Ballet from 1947 to 1960. She was the prima ballerina with the New York company and again for one season with the American Ballet Theater in 1960. She has since become artistic director for the Chicago City Ballet. She was married to Henry Paschen, Jr., in 1957.

—*Susan Kinnell*

See Also:
Native American Women

References:

Maynard, Olga. *Bird of Fire: The Story of Maria Tallchief.* New York: Dodd, Mead, 1961.
Tobias, Tobi. *Maria Tallchief.* New York: Crowell, 1970.

TARBELL, IDA (1857–1944) belonged to the generation of American women who attended college after the Civil War, did not marry, and devoted themselves to a career in public life. Tarbell's decision to work as a writer and pioneering investigative reporter was influenced by her participation in the late-nineteenth-century Chautauqua movement that promoted self-improvement and by her father's experience in the oil business.

Franklin Tarbell, like many small businessmen at the turn of the century, was forced out of business by a monopolistic conglomerate that undercut his prices. Ida never forgave the man who ruined her father's fortunes; as a young journalist employed by *McClure's Magazine,* she wrote a series of articles exposing the ruthless practices of John D. Rockefeller and his Standard Oil Company. The sensational series earned Tarbell the reputation of "muckraker" and fueled the demand for "trust-busting" reform in the Progressive era. Her diligence as an editor of and contributor to *McClure's Magazine* and *American Magazine* affirmed the role of the press as a public watchdog.

Tarbell's articles and books describing American business at the turn of the century—such as *The History of the Standard Oil Company* (1904) and *The Tariff in Our Times* (1911)—offer a vivid portrait of society during the Gilded Age. Though she did not identify herself as a militant feminist, concern for the welfare of women was a recurrent theme in her writings. Her investigations into business and trade practices took the point of view of the consumer and showed the ways in which women and children were victimized. Tarbell herself was a hard-working but always controversial personage, whose pen offered hope to the downtrodden and inspired terror in the hearts of the privileged.

—*Jane Crisler*

See Also:
Journalism, Progressive Era

References:

Brady, Kathleen. *Ida Tarbell: Portrait of a Muckraker.* New York: Putnam, 1984.
Tarbell, Ida. *All in a Day's Work.* New York: Macmillan, 1939.
———. *The Business of Being a Woman.* New York: Macmillan, 1912.
———. *The History of the Standard Oil Company.* New York: McClure, Phillips, 1904.
———. *The Life of Abraham Lincoln.* New York: Doubleday & McClure, 1900.
———. *The Tariff in Our Time.* New York: Macmillan, 1911.

TAYLOR, REBECCA (fl. 1930–80) led efforts to improve the conditions of working women in Texas during the first half of the twentieth century. Taylor began her career in the early 1930s as a teacher of night classes. Knowing of Taylor's mastery of Spanish, Meyer Perlstein recruited her in 1934 to represent the International Ladies Garment Workers Union in San Antonio, where most of the garment workers were either Mexican or Mexican-American. Over the next two years Taylor worked to bring the union to local factories, but employers' resistance and plant closures frustrated her efforts. From 1937 through 1940 the ILGWU thrived in San Antonio under Taylor's guidance. Successful strikes in 1937 and 1938 helped the union win a contract without a strike in 1939. The fortunes of the ILGWU in San Antonio declined during the 1940s, and membership in San Antonio locals had fallen to about six hundred when Taylor left her post in the early 1950s. From the 1950s until the late 1970s, Taylor represented employers rather than employees as a personnel manager for garment manufacturers.

Taylor's principal strengths as a union organizer were her bilingual abilities and the confidence that she inspired among the business leaders with whom she negotiated.

Because of her middle-class Anglo heritage, Hispanic workers did not immediately trust Taylor, and the leadership of Taylor's Hispanic co-workers, who were themselves garment workers, was an essential element in the ILGWU's success in San Antonio. At the national level, Taylor stressed the importance of drawing union organizers from among the Mexican and Mexican-American women in the Southwest, but union officials failed to appreciate the importance of cultural ties among rank-and-file industrial workers. This weakness and the passage of the Texas right-to-work law of 1947 were understood by Taylor to spell disaster for the ILGWU in San Antonio.

—*Julia Kirk Blackwelder*

See Also:

International Ladies Garment Workers Union

Reference:

Blackwelder, Julia Kirk. *Women of the Depression: Caste and Culture in San Antonio, 1929–1939.* College Station: Texas A & M Press, 1984.

TEACHING AS AN OCCUPATION FOR WOMEN. Ever since the latter nineteenth century—and even earlier in some parts of the country—the majority of teachers in the United States have been women. The development of teaching as female occupation began in the late eighteenth and early nineteenth centuries, when new conceptions of female roles began to change women's lives. The emerging ideology of True Womanhood held that women played an especially critical role in the moral and intellectual development of children. As larger numbers of women began to attend school in the period following the American Revolution, it became commonplace in certain areas—New England in particular—to hire women to teach a short summer session in schools for younger children and girls who were not needed for work on farms. This was associated with the notion that women carried a special responsibility and talent for rearing children. Influential early women educators, most notably Emma Willard and Catharine Beecher, argued that teaching was an especially appropriate occupation for women because of this. Other educators agreed. By 1850 the majority of teachers in New England, the nation's most educationally developed region, were young women.

The feminization of teaching proceeded quickly to other parts of the country in the latter nineteenth century. Many historians have argued that feminization occurred because women commanded smaller salaries than men teachers and thus offered schools an inexpensive way of expanding. Others have emphasized factors that caused men to move out of teaching, such as the lengthening of school terms—which made it impossible for men to combine teaching with other jobs—and new educational requirements, making it easier for relatively well educated women to get teaching positions. Feminization appears to have occurred first and fastest in urban areas, where school terms were longest and enrollments grew fastest; and it proceeded most slowly in the largely agricultural South, where school terms were short and teacher turnover was high. Like other working women in this period, most women teachers were quite young. The spinster schoolmarm was a rarity through most of American history. For most women, teaching was a job taken during the interlude between school and marriage. This pattern seems to have persisted until the post–World War II period, when rapidly expanding enrollments and a set of new attitudes about women's work resulted in larger numbers of women remaining in teaching after marriage.

Women continue to dominate teaching today in roughly the same proportions as at the turn of the century. While about three out of four teachers are women, however, school administration continues to be dominated by men. Like other "female" professions in that regard, teaching has afforded educated women an opportunity to develop and employ their skills and knowledge, but it has not offered them a high level of autonomy for professional development. With the improvement of salaries and benefits in teaching brought on by unionization over the past several decades, there has been a slight defeminization of teachers since 1970. But in the public mind, teaching continues to be "women's work," and teachers receive less remuneration and are assigned lower status than other professional groups, despite the critical social and cultural roles they play in modern society.

—*John L. Rury*

See Also:

Beecher, Catharine; Cult of True Womanhood; Education; Willard, Emma

References:

Preston, Jo Anne. "Feminization of an Occupation: Teaching Becomes Women's Work in Nineteenth-Century New England." Diss. Brandeis University, 1982.

Rury, John L. "Gender, Salaries and Career: American Teachers, 1900–1910." *Issues in Education* 4 (Winter 1986): 215–35.

Strober, Myra H., and Audry Gordon Lanford. "The Feminization of Public School Teaching: Cross Sectional Analysis, 1850–1880." *Signs: Journal of Women in Culture and Society* 11 (Winter 1986): 212–35.

TECHNOLOGY AND WOMEN. Technology and science are the new religions of the twentieth century, and women have not been allowed behind the altar rail. Brought up on dolls and makeup kits rather than trucks and chemistry sets, plagued by math anxiety, and shunned by engineering and physics departments, they are ill-prepared for positions of power and influence in the technological marketplace. Crucial issues concerning the future of reproductive technologies, hazardous waste, depletion of the ozone layer, and nuclear weapons will be decided by those who understand the intricacies of their development, and women are rarely members of this high priesthood.

Some women have broken through the barriers and made significant technological contributions. Such women usually receive no credit for this blasphemous behavior, or if given credit at the time, are written out of history, lost forever as role models for coming generations. The cotton gin, the circular saw, the clothes wringer, and astrolabe—all owe their existence to women inventors.

While it is often assumed that technology has been and continues to be a liberating force for women, the evidence is decidedly mixed. New technologies in the workplace have lessened the need for heavy lifting, so that, potentially, many new fields have opened up for women. However, the work force is still highly sex-segregated: women constitute over 90 percent of all nurses, child care workers, and secretaries. Computers that allow huge increases in productivity are replacing many women clerical workers. Thus, many women lose their jobs while the remaining workers find that the new jobs require less skill than the previous secretarial positions. The jobs become more routinized—a word-processor operator simply enters keystrokes and does not have the variety of duties of the former secretary. Her keystrokes are often monitored, adding to her stress; the stress level of one who does word processing all day has been found to be higher than that of an air traffic controller.

Women are concentrated in occupations that often lend themselves to computerization. Bank teller, telephone operator, and airline reservation clerk are other female-dominated jobs that have been replaced or decimated by computers. The new hi-tech industries that design, build, and repair computers do employ large numbers of women, yet the vast majority of them work at the lowest skill and pay levels. Another unfortunate trend is that as women gain access to some hi-tech, all-male jobs, the jobs become obsolete. Women became computer programmers, and now sophisticated computers program other computers; women learned to climb telephone poles, and now plug-in phones are the norm. In general, technology in the workplace does not seem to have upgraded women's disadvantaged position.

The unpaid workplace of the housewife has been the site of many technological innovations that have replaced or eased many of her functions. Far from having nothing to do and suffering from role anxiety, as earlier theorists suggested, however, the middle-class housewife finds that the amount of work in the home has actually increased. Thus, household technology is labor-saving but not time-saving. New standards of cleanliness, fewer servants, and extended family members in the home, and her new duties as consumer, chauffeur, and family psychologist contribute to her hectic day. Ironically, one final reason for the increased workload of the "everyday housewife," employed outside the home or not, is that other family members feel less compelled to offer help to one surrounded by technology that they mistakenly feel has considerably lightened her load.

Reproductive technologies and birth control have undoubtedly given women more control over this crucial aspect of their lives. Yet feminists worry about their implications:

> What is the link between genetic and reproductive technologies, and to what ends will genetic technologies be used?
>
> Why is surrogate motherhood more subject to legal control and emotional argument than sperm donorship?
>
> Why is it a service to rent one's womb, and a crime to rent one's vagina?
>
> How will these technologies entrench current class and race divisions between women?
>
> Will the well-documented preference for male children reach new heights as couples can implement these preferences with future technologies?
>
> Will the ideology and practice of parenthood and the family change as new technologies allow various permutations of donor sperm, donor egg, donor womb, and adoptive parents to give a child several "mothers" and "fathers"?

Some see these reproductive technologies—largely under the control of male scientists, doctors, ethicists, and legal experts—as another instance of the shifting of male control over women, which has gone from the individual control of fathers and husbands to the collective control exercised through science and technology. Current theorists also argue that the technical competence of men, which women traditionally lack, is a more subtle form of domination than overt physical control, but one with the same results. Although more women than men work with machines, men as a gender control the design and implementation of new technologies. In short, men create technological change, and women react to it.

The United States is facing a shortage of mathematicians and scientists, and women and minorities form an untapped source of recruits. Thus, both feminists searching for equality for women and government researchers searching for potential scientists would like to see more women involved in the design, implementation, and assessment of technology. Both groups are currently addressing problems such as the higher incidence of math anxiety among women, the small number of women in technical fields, and the lack of retraining opportunities for women workers displaced by technological change. The secular religions of science and technology will have much to gain from these new high priestesses: The values, insights, and goals of both sexes and all races will surely give us a more balanced view of the world we are trying to understand.

—Susan Weeks

See Also:

Science

References:

Cockburn, Cynthia. *Machinery of Dominance: Women, Men and Technical Know-how.* London: Pluto, 1985.

Hartmann, Heidi, Robert E. Kraut, and Louise A. Tilly, eds. *Computer Chips and Paper Clips: Technology and Women's Employment.* Washington, D.C.: National Academy Press, 1986.

Rothschild, Joan. *Machina Ex Dea.* New York: Pergamon, 1983.

Spallone, Patricia, and Deborah Lynn Steinberg. *Made to Order: The Myth of Reproductive and*

Genetic Progress. Oxford: Pergamon, 1987.
Zimmerman, Jan. *Once Upon the Future: A Woman's Guide to Tomorrow's Technology.* London: Pandora, 1986.

TELEPHONE OPERATORS. The telephone, along with the typewriter, was a major contributor to women's rapid increase in labor-force participation at the turn of the century. In the earliest days of the telephone industry in the 1870s, boys were hired to service switchboards, but they were rapidly replaced by women, until women accounted for almost 99 percent of the country's switchboard operators by World War I. Women were ostensibly more polite and reliable than boy operators, but, additionally, women were eager to find work, were believed less likely to unionize, and worked at half to a quarter of men's wages.

The telephone industry generally hired young, attractive, single, native-born white women as operators. The work was considered to be safe, clean, and respectable, particularly in comparison with other types of women's work under industrialization. The pace of the work, long and irregular hours, and rigid supervision over the operators' vocabulary, diction, and physical movements, however, made operating work physically and mentally monotonous and exhausting. The ideal operator was as machinelike as possible. Despite the realities of the job, public fancy was caught by the romantic and heroic image of the operator as portrayed by the telephone industry and in songs and visual images until the passing of the old operator era. This had occurred by the middle of the twentieth century, when telephone companies had converted from manual to automated switching systems.

While women initially found operator work attractive, they became increasingly active after the turn of the century in labor union organizing for better working conditions and wages and for protection against the consequences of automation. Operating remained a sex-segregated job until AT&T signed a consent decree in 1973 with the Equal Employment Opportunity Commission, after which men were slowly added to the operator force.

—Lana F. Rakow

See Also:

Technology and Women

References:

Greenwald, Maurine Weiner. *Women, War, and Work.* Westport, Conn.: Greenwood, 1980.
Langer, Elinor. "Inside the New York Telephone Company." In *The Private Side of American History,* edited by Thomas F. Frazier. Vol. 2. New York: Harcourt Brace Jovanovich, 1978, pp. 348—70.
Maddox, Brenda. "Women and the Switchboard." In *The Social Impact of the Telephone,* edited by Ithiel de Sola Pool. Cambridge: MIT Press, 1977, pp. 262–80.
Schmitt, Katherine M. "I Was Your Old 'Hello' Girl." *The Saturday Evening Post* 203 (July 12, 1930): 18–19.

The **TEMPERANCE MOVEMENT** (1790s–1900) was one of the many reforms to interest women in the nineteenth century. It was born in the late eighteenth century along with the American Republic, out of the need for a sober citizenry to provide moral governance. Women, responsible for moral training, were the natural persons to train a temperate citizenry. Moral suasion—convincing drinkers of the error of their ways—was the movement's primary tactic.

From the inception of temperance organizations, women were major participants in them, but the pervasiveness of the Cult of Domesticity denied women a leadership role. Organized religion, which reinforced this notion of spheres while allowing active participation and limited opportunities for leadership by women, performed a role that cannot be downplayed. Virtually all temperance supporters were churchgoers, but the movement itself was nondenominational. The Woman's Crusade of 1873 and 1874 is but one example of the Christian nature of the temperance cause. Women were not violent, nor did they lecture. Instead they publicly prayed for the redemption of saloon-keepers and their patrons.

Temperance developed and transformed woman's role in Victorian America. Taking as their model the active role women played in the abolition movement, temperance women began to speak publicly on the evils of drink. Temperance was advocated to protect home and family, the two foundations of women's sphere. By taking this approach, women created and legitimized a greater role for themselves.

Born of the Woman's Crusade, the Woman's Christian Temperance Union, under the leadership of Frances E. Willard, became the preeminent temperance organization of the last quarter of the nineteenth century. The predominantly Protestant and middle-class WCTU championed temperance under the banner of "Heart and Home and Native Land." Yet even as the WCTU grew in size and influence, conflict developed over the issue of temperance and its effectiveness. Because moral suasion had not produced the desired results, legal suasion (or prohibition) became a popular alternative among many reformers. By the 1880s, the WCTU supported the Prohibition party while still advocating temperance.

As the Progressive era developed, prohibition became the favored solution to the woes caused by drink, and the Anti-Saloon League became its leading proponent. The WCTU worked for the Eighteenth Amendment along with the league and celebrated its passage, but it was a pyrrhic victory. Temperance became a national laughingstock, ridiculed in nearly all aspects of society. The movement would not again gain widespread support until the 1980s.

—*Anita M. Weber*

See Also:

Cult of True Womanhood; Moral Reform; Willard, Frances E.; Woman's Christian Temperance Union

References:

Bordin, Ruth. *Women and Temperance: The Quest for Power and Liberty, 1873–1900.* Philadelphia: Temple University Press, 1981.

Epstein, Barbara Leslie. *The Politics of Domesticity: Women, Evangelism, and Temperance in Nineteenth-Century America.* Middletown, Conn.: Wesleyan University Press, 1981.

Tyrell, Ian. *Sobering Up: From Temperance to Prohibition in Antebellum America.* Westport, Conn.: Greenwood, 1979.

TENAYUCA, EMMA (b. 1917) played a short but dramatic role as a leader of Mexican and Mexican-American workers in San Antonio during the 1930s. Heavily influenced by her socialist grandfather, she proved herself a charismatic speaker during her years as a schoolgirl. After graduating from high school in 1934, she went to work as an elevator operator and became active in the labor movement. Through her participation in worker movements, she met Homer Brooks, one-time Communist party candidate for the Texas governorship, whom she later married.

In 1936 Tenayuca and others held a rally to organize all of San Antonio's Hispanic workers into a single and independent union. At this rally Tenayuca was selected as head of the women's division, but the organizational efforts soon failed. Thereafter Tenayuca organized the Workers' Alliance, a group that disseminated civil rights literature and staged demonstrations. During a 1937 Workers' Alliance sit-in at San Antonio City Hall, Tenayuca was arrested for refusing to leave the building. She also played a controversial role in the 1938 San Antonio pecan shellers' strike. In 1939 she retired from labor activism after a Workers' Alliance rally ended in a riotous attack by the movement's Anglo opponents.

—*Julia Kirk Blackwelder*

See Also:

Chicana, Unions

References:

Blackwelder, Julia Kirk. *Women of the Depression: Caste and Culture in San Antonio, 1912–1939.* College Station: Texas A & M Press, 1984.

Wertenbacker, Green Peyton. *San Antonio: City of the Sun.* New York: Crowell, 1946.

TERRELL, MARY CHURCH (1863–1954), lecturer, civil rights leader, club woman, and educator, was born to former slaves, Robert R. Church and Louisa Ayers, in Memphis, Tennessee. Following Reconstruction, her father became the first black millionaire through his investments in real estate. To escape the damage of segregation, she was sent to Ohio for her education: Yellow Springs for elementary and secondary school and Oberlin College for her bachelor's and master's degrees.

Although advised by her father that "ladies" did not work for a living, Terrell felt she had to share her privileged education with her race. She taught first at Wilberforce University and then at M Street High School in Washington, D.C. She toured Europe for two years to develop language skills and learn about different cultures. When she returned to the United States, Oberlin College offered her a job as registrar when it was unprecedented for a black woman to hold such a position at a white college, but she declined and instead married Robert Terrell, a graduate of Harvard and Howard universities.

Married life meant a life full of social and intellectual activities, as well as raising a daughter named after the black poet Phillis Wheatley and an adopted daughter, Mary. Terrell became the first female president of the Bethel Literary and Historical Association, where she heard top intellectuals discuss current social issues. These experiences, coupled with her education, brought her to serve on the board of education of Washington, D.C., as a founder of the city's Colored Woman's League, as the first president of the National Association of Colored Women, as a speaker at the International Congress of Women in Berlin in 1904, as a charter member of the Constitution League, as a black member of the Women's International League for Peace and Freedom and the National Woman's party, and as one of the founders of the National Association for the Advancement of Colored People. As a speaker and a writer, Terrell contributed to both black and white periodicals and spoke to mixed audiences of a variety of reform organizations on topics as the peonage system, domestic service, motherhood, racial progress, lynching, woman's suffrage, black history, legal injustices, blacks passing for white, Jim Crow segregation, and education.

She served in the War Camp Community Service during World War I and as a delegate to the International Peace Congress following the war. She wrote the Delta "credo" (members' pledge) for her sorority. Her service as a "picket" during the White House protest for the National Woman's party won her a coveted picket pin. She fought against the segregation practices of the American Association of University Women and the refusal of Washington department stores to serve blacks in their eating facilities. A lifetime member of the Republican party, she fought hard to realize America's democratic promises. She was the recipient of honorary degrees from Wilberforce and Howard universities and Oberlin College. An elite, privileged woman, Mary Terrell did much to improve conditions for both blacks and women during her long life.

—Dorothy C. Salem

See Also:

Colored Woman's League, National Association for the Advancement of Colored People, National Association of Colored Women, National Woman's Party, Women's International League for Peace and Freedom

References:

Dannett, Sylvia. *Profiles of Negro Womanhood.* Chicago: Education Heritage Press, 1964.

"Mary Terrell." *Journal of Negro History* 39 (October 1954): 385–88.

Terrell, Mary. *Colored Women in a White World.* Washington, D.C.: Ransdell, 1940.

TEXTILE INDUSTRIES, NORTHERN AND SOUTHERN. The American textile industry provides a kind of summary of the American working experience. Some of the earliest factories developed in textiles; their labor forces first attempted organization; immigration fostered change in the source of those laborers; and the industry itself changed regional emphases as it moved from its New England origins to the South in the 1880s and after.

Women have made up the core of the textile labor force from the beginning of the industry. Early textile mills were located to take advantage of both sources of water power and readily available supplies of labor. Those laborers were drawn from rural New England families and were largely female. Representing predominantly single women between fifteen and thirty, the female "operatives" were attracted by higher wages and the relative mobility that came with textile work. They worked for a variety of reasons, including contributions to a family wage, savings for a dowry, subsistence in an otherwise declining agricultural economy, and independence. Most worked for relatively short periods and an average of five years of often discontinuous labor before leaving the paid work force for marriage. Though it delayed the age of marriage, the work experience provided opportunity for young women.

Factories using female labor developed boardinghouses that provided a paternalistic watch over the workers. Modeled after the early mills established by Francis Lowell at Waltham, Massachusetts, the system of boardinghouses was known as the Waltham system. The controls provided a hoped-for docile and controlled labor force and an environment that countered criticism of the early factories. Autonomy for the women was so circumscribed, however, that rebellions against the system were frequent by the 1830s. In the 1840s and 1850s immigrant labor gradually replaced native-born female workers, and while women continued to occupy a prominent place, they ceased to dominate the textile labor force.

Southern textile mills began to develop with William Gregg's famous South Carolina Graniteville mills and those at Roswell in Georgia in the two decades before the Civil War. The decided expansion of southern textiles came as part of the New South enunciated by journalist and orator Henry Grady and others in the 1880s and 1890s. As the mills were brought to the cotton, textile-mill owners engaged in some of the same hiring practices used in northern mills a half-century earlier, and their textile mills drew on the labor of women as a source of docile, relatively cheap labor that would not compete with men's. In the biracial South, however, textile workers were largely white, and the southern mill owner quickly supplemented the Waltham-style boardinghouse with the mill village so that entire families would come to work in the mills. In contrast to the earlier northern experience, then, the female southern mill workers did not gain extrafamily experience or relative autonomy before marriage; rather the mill work became a factory version of the family economy and the family wage in the tightly controlled paternalistic yet exploitative setting of the company towns in which 75 percent of the workers labored.

Conditions in the mill towns became infamous for poverty, deprivation, and disease. Southern progressive Edgar Gardner Murphy summarized the workers' condition in 1904: "[I know] . . . mills in which children and all were called to work before sunrise, laboring from dark to dark. I have repeatedly seen them at labor twelve, thirteen and even fourteen hours a day. . . . I have seen children eight and nine years of age leaving the factory as late as 9:30 at night, and finding their way . . . through the unlighted streets of the mill villages, to their squalid homes." Southern textile mills would deteriorate and become the object of intense labor struggles in the 1920s and 1930s as well as the focus of considerable investigative energy that would ultimately result in protective legislation for the women and children workers of the mills. Ironically, the difficult conditions of textile work produced protective legislation that circumscribed the legal and social autonomy that women might have gained from the wages they earned in the mills.

Although evidence of women's long association with the workplace, the textile industry also illustrates the ironies of women's paid labor. Hired for docility, expected to be either short-term workers or participants in a family wage, women found the work brought with it the adjustments typical of shifts from a preindustrial to an industrial economy, but seldom brought the advantages of wage-based independence, workplace autonomy, or alleviation of domestic expectations.

—*Thomas F. Armstrong*

See Also:
Industrial Revolution, Lowell Mill Girls

References:

Cohn, David L. *Life and Times of King Cotton.* New York: Oxford University Press, 1956.
Dublin, Thomas. *Women at Work.* New York: Columbia University Press, 1979.
Kessler-Harris, Alice. *Out to Work.* New York: Oxford University Press, 1982.

THANKSGIVING. An example of a successful application of Woman's Influence, the establishment of Thanksgiving Day as a national annual commemoration of a New England tradition honored the Pilgrim's first celebration of the survival of the Plymouth settlement in the autumn of 1621. President George Washington proclaimed a national day of thanksgiving for the new nation in 1789, but it was not observed on the same day nor in all of the states. President Abraham Lincoln's wartime proclamation in the fall of 1863 designated the last Thursday in November as Thanksgiving Day for the nation. Subsequently Thanksgiving Day was observed annually on that day as a celebration of enduring Victorian domestic, religious, and patriotic values until the mid-twentieth century, when the fourth Thursday of November was designated as the national holiday.

As the unrivaled spokeswoman of the Cult of True Womanhood as well as an adroit practitioner of Woman's Influence, editor Sarah Josepha Hale (1788–1879) pursued a dual strategy from 1827 until 1863: She wrote personal letters to presidents and governors of states and territories, urging that they proclaim the last Thursday of November as Thanksgiving Day. Hale also publicized the New England tradition in her description of a rural New Hampshire Thanksgiving Day in her novel *Northwood* (1827). Both the cuisine and the customs established as traditional for this regional holiday would become the standard for the patriotic and pious nondenominational (though distinctly Protestant) national day of thanksgiving. The editor of the matriarch of Victorian women's magazines, Hale used her control over the contents of *Godey's Lady's Book* to offer recipes for traditional Yankee dishes to extol the patriotic domesticity of Thanksgiving in the fall issues; and in her editorial columns of *Godey's* November issues, she demurely remonstrated her readers to support the establishment of a national day of thanksgiving. Although both the editor and the publisher of *Godey's* avoided any topical political references in their proper ladies' magazine, Hale modified her yearly request for Thanksgiving in 1861 by suggesting that such a holiday might also be observed as a day of peace. In 1863 Hale succeeded in securing a presidential proclamation following her personal audience with Abraham Lincoln in Washington, D.C.

Thus, the establishment of a national Thanksgiving Day represented several trends within Victorian culture. As a symbol of nineteenth-century patriotic fervor, the post–Civil War celebration of Thanksgiving Day fostered, or at least gave lip service to, national unity. As an elevation and equation of the regional customs and values of New England as the national standard for mainstream America, the celebration of Thanksgiving Day reinforced the status of New England as the "cradle of the nation." Lastly, waged by a lone True Woman guided by a righteous sense of her duty and armed only with her Woman's Influence, Hale's successful campaign proved that women's ability to apply moral suasion to male authorities at the national political level was as effective as within the domestic circle. A powerful example of the efficacy of the conservative approach of domestic feminism, Hale's ladylike and nonthreatening perseverance encouraged women to believe that women need not organize or enter into the political arena directly to influence the course of the nation.

Both a True Woman and a patriotic daughter of New England, Hale promoted Thanksgiving Day to consecrate the Victorian ideals of nostalgic agrarianism and righteous patriotism, as well as the domesticity and piety of Woman's Sphere. In the face of the social, political, and economic impact of late-nineteenth-century industrialism and urbanism on the middle-class family and the women within it, Thanksgiving Day represented annual national homage paid to the importance of the family and thereby fortified the Cult of True Womanhood by increasing esteem for the domestic domain to which women were relegated. Hale's achievement of this national holiday was yet another instance of her efforts to expand Woman's Sphere and enhance Woman's Influence.

—Angela Howard Zophy

See Also:

Cult of True Womanhood; *Godey's Lady's Book*; Hale, Sarah Josepha

References:

Douglas, Ann. *The Feminization of American Culture*. New York: Knopf, 1977.

Finley, Ruth E. *The Lady of Godey's*. Philadelphia: Lancaster, 1931.

Zophy, Angela Howard. "'For the Improvement of My Sex': Sarah Josepha Hale's Editorship of *Godey's Lady's Book*, 1837–1877." Diss. The Ohio State University, 1978.

THEATER. Women have been active in American theater almost from its inception. Before and during the Revolutionary War, America's first female playwright, Mercy Otis Warren (1728–1814), stirred up hatred for the Tories of Massachusetts and admiration for the American revolutionaries through a series of propaganda plays beginning with *The Adulateur* in 1772. Despite the antagonisms created by the struggle for independence from Great Britain, American theater was heavily influenced by British theatrical forms and traditions. Indeed, the first major female star to grace the American stage was British actress Anne Brunton Merry (1769–1808), who made her American debut as Shakespeare's Juliet on December 5, 1796, at Philadelphia's Chestnut Street Theater. Merry spent the last twelve years of her life acting and directing in American theaters. Even in remote areas such as Augusta, Georgia, Ann Robinson (?–1799) and Susanah Wall (?–1823) were able to open and operate a theater.

Despite the presence of these and other women on the American theater scene, women have had many obstacles to overcome in making theater a respectable profession for women. Theater was considered by many Puritan-influenced Americans to be socially and morally suspect. Some viewed theater as "Satan's haunt" and actresses were equated with harlots. Many such as actress and writer Olive Logan (1839–1909) were determined to change all that. Logan suggested in 1869 that theater should become "a worthy channel for gifted, intelligent, and virtuous young women to gain a livelihood through." Theater reformers had to overcome the tastes of those who wanted theatrical women to be beauties on display as was Adah Isaac Menken in her "nude" *Mazeppa* of 1866, which was dubbed the "sensation of the New York Stage."

While an attractive appearance is still an asset to many a performer's career, theatrical women came to be appreciated for a variety of their talents. Mary Shaw (c. 1868–1929) used her talents as an actress to draw the attention of the American public to women's issues. Famous actress Lillian Russell (1861–1922) fought for women's suffrage. Indeed, acting was one of the first professions in which women achieved rough parity with men. By 1900 there were 6,374 working actresses in the United States; they made up 43 percent of those in the profession. Actresses such as Maude Adams (1872–1953), Ethel Barrymore (1869–1959), Katharine Cornell (1898–1974), Ruth Draper (1884–1956), Lynn Fontanne (1887–1983), Uta Hagen (b. 1920), and Helen Hayes (b. 1900) were among a host of women making great names for themselves in the American theater. Minnie Maddern Fiske (1865–1932) was among the first to introduce a more realistic acting style to the American theater. Some actresses, such as the legendary Eva Le Gallienne (b. 1899), also excelled as directors, although women were still not given as many opportunities to direct as men. During the 1978–79 Broadway season, for example, only 4 percent of the productions had women directors.

Women have also made enormous contributions to the theater as playwrights. Mary Coyle Chase (b. 1907), who won the Pulitzer Prize for her comedy *Harvey*; feminist playwright and director Rachel Crothers (1878–1958); Susan Glaspell (1882–1948); civil rights activist Lorraine Hansberry (1930–65); Lillian Hellman (1905–84); Clare Boothe Luce (1903–87), who became an ambassador to Italy; and Anne Nichols (1891–1966) are among the many women who have greatly enriched the American dramatic experience. Feminist theater, which is theater by, for, and about women, is drawing inspiration from the works of these women and contemporary playwrights such as Megan Terry (b. 1932), author of *Hothouse*.

Women have contributed to theater in America as critics, designers, costumers, teachers, and technicians. In 1980 women critics made up 23 percent of those practicing in the field. Claudia Cassidy of the *Chicago Tribune*, Sylvia Drake of the *Los Angeles Times*, and Edith Oliver of *The New Yorker* were among the most influential critics. Rosamond Gilder not only achieved recognition as a critic, but wrote an important study of women actresses, *Enter the Actress* (1931). Alvina Krause (b. 1893) has achieved fame as an acting teacher, while Irene Sharaff (c. 1910) has made a name for herself as a costumer. Women directors and producers such as Margo Jones (1913–55) were instrumental in developing the movement toward quality regional theater in America. While much in the theatrical world is still dominated by men, there is no question that theater has become a "good field for women."

—*Jonathan W. Zophy*

See Also:

Hansberry, Lorraine; Hellman, Lillian; Kemble, Fanny; Shange, Ntozake; Warren, Mercy Otis

References:

Chinoy, Helen Krich, and Linda Walsh Jenkins, eds. *Women in American Theatre: Careers, Images, Movements*. New York: Crown, 1981.

Gilder, Rosamond. *Enter the Actress: The First Women in Theatre*. London: George Harrap, 1931.

McArthur, Benjamin. *Actors and American Culture*. Philadelphia: Temple University Press, 1984.

Malpede, Karen, ed. and intro. *Women in Theatre: Compassion & Hope*. New York: Drama Book Publishers, 1983.

Mordden, Ethan. *The American Theatre*. New York: Oxford University Press, 1981.

Natalle, Elizabeth. *Feminist Theatre*. Metuchen, N.J.: Scarecrow, 1981.

THEOLOGIANS. Although it is true that men have been the voice of authority throughout American religious history, women have consistently distinguished themselves in matters of faith. In early American history, women had limited access to both the academic world and institutional structures. In the nineteenth century, the abolition and suffrage movements began to have an impact on religion and theology. From the early voices of women such as the Grimké sisters, Sojourner Truth, and Elizabeth Cady Stanton (*The Woman's Bible*), a new religious perspective has grown, bringing with it challenging interpretations of Scripture and broadened theological perspective.

It is ironic that the first people who settled American lands, many in pursuit of religious freedom, quickly and forcefully subdued women who expressed religious beliefs and values that in any way deviated from what was believed to be normal and acceptable, charging such women with heresy and witchcraft. The oppression of women that characterized the early church continues to exist today in tension with the liberating powers of religious thought.

The twentieth century has brought with it a theological revival for women, again spurred by secular feminist voices. Emerging in increasing numbers from religious and professional schools, women have challenged the male-centered theological tradition by illuminating the denigrating powers of patriarchal structures, exclusive language, limited imagery of the Sacred, and misogynist interpretations of religious texts. Such women theologians include Mary Daly (*Beyond God the Father, The Church and the Second Sex, Gyn/Ecology*). Now calling her work "post-Christian," Daly rejects all texts, including biblical, that are androcentric and patriarchal and calls upon women to invent a new language in order for women "to name—that is, to create—our own world." Rosemary Radford Ruether has written and edited numerous books (*Religion and Sexism, Women of Spirit, Womanguides, Sexism and God-Talk: Toward a Feminist Theology*). As a historian of Christian thought, Ruether has lifted out and offered theological insight into the liberating traditions within Christianity, as well as exposing those that have degraded and suppressed women. Elisabeth Schüssler Fiorenza (*In Memory of Her, Bread Not Stone*) has attempted to use the biblical text, not as an authority in itself, but as a source for reconstructing the history of women in early Christianity. And many other American women theologians such as Sallie McFague, Phyllis Trible, and Letty Russell have also contributed to this process.

These challenges have brought with them new and creative interpretations of our religious past, even as they serve to reveal contemporary theological perspectives that recognize the liberating promises of religious texts and systematics. Religious words are being redefined or replaced; religious imagery is becoming multifaceted; religious values are being clarified from feminist perspectives; religious structures are being formed that include women in leadership positions while simultaneously fostering a positive regard for all women of religion.

—Joanne S. Richmond

See Also:

Christianity; Daly, Mary; Ruether, Rosemary; Salem Witch Trials; *The Woman's Bible*

References:

Daly, Mary. *Beyond God the Father*. Boston: Beacon, 1973.

———. *The Church and the Second Sex*. New York: Harper & Row, 1968.

———. *Gyn/Ecology*. Boston: Beacon, 1978.

Fiorenza, Elisabeth Schüssler. *Bread Not Stone*. Boston: Beacon, 1984.

———. *In Memory of Her*. New York: Crossroads, 1983.

James, Janet Wilson, ed. *Women in American Religion*. Philadelphia: University of Pennsylvania Press, 1980.

Ruether, Rosemary Radford. *Religion and Sexism*. New York: Simon & Schuster, 1974.

———. *Sexism and God-Talk: Toward a Feminist Theology*. Boston: Beacon, 1983.

———. *Womanguides*. Boston: Beacon, 1985.

———. *Women of Spirit*. New York: Simon & Schuster, 1979.

Stanton, Elizabeth Cady. *The Woman's Bible*. 2 vols. New York: European Publishing, 1895–98; rpt. 1 vol. 1898.

THOMAS, ALMA (1891–1978) was an artist and art educator whose late-life emergence as an abstract artist of the Washington Color School brought her national recognition. Born in Columbus, Georgia, she moved with her family to Washington, D.C., as a child and attended Armstrong High School, a trade school. She continued her education at Howard University and was its first art school graduate in 1924. In 1934 she obtained an M.A. from Teachers' College of Columbia University, with a thesis on marionettes.

Her thirty-five-year career teaching art at Shaw Junior High School in Washington was complemented by her career as an exhibiting artist and art gallery director. She studied painting at American University in the 1950s and began to develop an interest in abstract art. For a retrospective at Howard University in 1966, she broke free from the realism of her earlier work and produced several new works in an abstract style inspired by leafy trees in the sunlight outside the window of her inner-city town house. This breakthrough led to solo exhibitions at the Whitney Museum in New York (the first at that museum for a black woman) and the Corcoran Gallery in Washington. She also exhibited her work at the Boston Museum of Fine Arts and the National Collection of American Art. One painting was purchased by the Metropolitan Museum of

Art in New York City. Under the auspices of the Tyler School of Fine Arts at Temple University, she toured the art capitals of Europe. In 1976 she received the International Women's Year Award for Outstanding Contributions and Dedication to Women and Art.

—*Susan Kellogg Portney*

See Also:

Art

References:

Fine, Elsa Honig. *The Afro-American Artist.* New York: Holt, Rinehart and Winston, 1973.

Munro, Eleanor. *Originals, American Women Artists.* New York: Simon & Schuster, 1979.

Rubinstein, Charlotte Streifer. *American Women Artists.* Boston: G. K. Hall, 1982.

THOMPSON, DOROTHY (1893–1961), journalist, led the fight for intervention in World War II and was, with Eleanor Roosevelt, the most prominent American woman of the late 1930s. In lectures, radio broadcasts, columns, and books, Thompson urged her fellow citizens to fight Nazism before it was too late. At the height of her fame, 1936–42, presidents and prime ministers vied for favorable mention in her columns.

Oldest of three children in a Methodist minister's family, Dorothy Thompson grew up in a western New York home of very modest means. She studied at the Lewis Institute in Chicago and graduated cum laude from Syracuse University in 1914. She worked as a suffrage activist and for social service organizations in Ohio, Buffalo, and New York City, developing a close network of female friends and older women mentors. All her life, Thompson maintained friendships with women, and was sexually attracted to some of them. In 1920 she and a friend sailed for Europe to see the world and to support themselves by selling articles to American newspapers. Thompson became an expert on Central European politics, was named Vienna correspondent for the *Philadelphia Public Ledger,* and in 1924 moved to Berlin as head of the Central European bureaus of the *Philadelphia Public Ledger* and the *New York Evening Post.*

An extraordinarily attractive and dynamic woman, with many admirers, in 1922 she married Josef Bard, a Hungarian Jewish writer and journalist. Bard showed little inclination to limit himself to one woman, and they were divorced in 1927. Thompson was deeply depressed over their breakup, but after a whirlwind courtship, married novelist Sinclair ("Red") Lewis in 1928. She resigned her position and sailed with Lewis to America, determined that this relationship would succeed. The couple bought a home in Vermont, where they entertained friends and family and wrote their books. They had one son, Michael (1930–75); the household also contained Lewis's son, Wells, by a previous marriage.

Although no longer a regular foreign correspondent, Thompson rebuilt her career with frequent trips to Europe, meetings with world leaders, speaking engagements, and radio programs. In 1931 she interviewed Adolf Hitler. Unable to believe that Germans could accept him as their leader, she dismissed him as insignificant. Shortly thereafter, she changed her mind, writing extensively on the horrors of the Third Reich and its danger to world peace. The Nazis returned the favor by expelling her from Germany in 1934. She was also thrown out of a meeting of the German American Bund in 1939, when her derisive laughter interrupted the proceedings. These events made her reputation as America's premier Nazi-hater. She called world attention to the plight of European Jews and other anti-Nazi refugees, sponsored many of them in the United States, and was a major influence in bringing about the Evian international conference on refugees.

In 1936 she began her "On the Record" column for the *New York Herald Tribune* and in 1937 started writing regularly for the *Ladies' Home Journal.* Fame did not come without a price. Lewis's alcoholism, his rages, and his inability to tolerate the presence of his children made their life together virtually impossible, but it was his wife's success (despite his own Nobel Prize) that gave the marriage its final blow. In *Ann Vickers* (1933), his portrait of the female protagonist drew upon Dorothy Thompson's life to deliver a scathing indictment of career women. (Her work also inspired his *It Can't Happen Here,* 1935, an account of fascism in America.) Thompson's journeys abroad meant separations from him and from their son, who had medical, learning, and personal difficulties. The Thompson-Lewis marriage was over long before the 1942 divorce.

After Pearl Harbor, Thompson's influence waned. The Bell Syndicate picked up her column in 1941 when the *Herald Tribune* dropped it (due to her support of Franklin D. Roosevelt in the 1940 election), but her increasingly pro-Arab stance offended Jewish (and many non-Jewish) readers. Although she probably did not know about CIA involvement in her organization, American Friends of the Middle East, she received much criticism for her naivete and stridency about Middle Eastern politics. In 1943 she married Maxim Kopf, a Czech refugee artist. She described the fifteen years of their marriage, until his death in 1958, as the happiest in her life.

Thompson's life and career exemplified the possibilities and difficulties of professional women in the postsuffrage era. Her education, the Christian social conscience instilled by her father, and her own moralism and liberalism fueled her indignation at the wrongs of the world, giving her writing its intensity and emotional quality. Her charismatic personality helped her make friends all over the world. Yet she wrote, in her letters and her column for the *Ladies' Home Journal,* about the joys of domesticity and child rearing. While some see this as hypocrisy, given her own choices in life, it clearly speaks to the dilemma of late-twentieth-century career women.

—*Lynn D. Gordon*

See Also:

Journalism

References:

Dorothy Thompson Papers. George Arents Research Library. Syracuse University, Syracuse, N.Y.

"Cartwheel Girl." *Time* 33 (June 12, 1939): 47–51.

Harriman, Margaret Case. "The It Girl." *New Yorker* 16 (April 20/27, 1940): 24–30; 23–29.

Sanders, Marion K. *Dorothy Thompson: A Legend in Her Time.* Boston: Little, Brown, 1973.

Sheean, Vincent. *Dorothy and Red.* Boston: Houghton Mifflin, 1963.

Thompson, Dorothy. *Courage to Be Happy.* Boston: Houghton Mifflin, 1957.

———. *I Saw Hitler.* New York: Farrar & Rinehart, 1932.

———. *Let the Record Speak.* Boston: Houghton Mifflin, 1939.

———. *Listen, Hans!* Boston: Houghton Mifflin, 1942.

———. *The New Russia.* New York: Holt, 1928.

———. *Once on Christmas.* London: Oxford University Press, 1938.

———. *Political Guide: A Study of American Liberalism and Its Relationship to Totalitarian States.* New York: Stackpole, 1938.

———. *Refugees, Anarchy or Organization.* New York: Random House, 1938.

THORNTON, WILLIE MAE (b. 1926), also known as "Big Mama" Thornton, is an American singer, musician, and songwriter. She is an important and influential presence in the music world and is considered one of the premier singers of the blues.

Born in Montgomery, Alabama, the daughter of a preacher, Thornton began touring at the age of fourteen with Sammy Green's Hot Harlem Review. She toured extensively and began her recording career in 1950. Two years later, she enjoyed her first major hit with her own composition, "Hound Dog." The song became an enormous hit for Elvis Presley, and like the work of many writers—especially black and female artists—Thornton's accomplishment was overshadowed by Presley's and other superstars' recordings of her work. Fifteen years later, another one of her compositions, "Ball and Chain," became one of Janis Joplin's biggest hits. Ironically, it was often reported that Joplin was both inspired and haunted by black women blues artists, especially Thornton and Bessie Smith.

Like Bessie Smith, Thornton combined her recording career with extensive touring, appearing with bluesmen Johnny Otis,

Muddy Waters, and others. She made her first tour of Europe in 1965 with the American Folk Blues Festival and has appeared in major festivals throughout Europe and the United States since then. Her rich, passionate voice has influenced many female vocalists. Among her other popular compositions is "Little Red Rooster." Although she never achieved the superstardom reached by Presley or Joplin, Thornton is a major artist and an internationally respected vocalist and songwriter.

—*Elizabeth H. Coughlin*

See Also:

Jazz; Popular Vocalists; Smith, Bessie

Reference:

Stearns, Marshall W. *The Story of Jazz.* London: Oxford University Press, 1970.

"THOUGHTS ON FEMALE EDUCATION" (1787) was given by Benjamin Rush as a commencement address at the Young Ladies' Academy of Philadelphia on July 28, 1787, and later published at the request of members of that audience in his *Essays, Literary, Moral and Philosophical* (1798). In it, Rush outlined the "first principles" of female education that he felt must accommodate the peculiar position of American women in the new nation.

In "Thoughts on Female Education," Rush listed certain aspects of American life that required women's education to prepare them for the particular circumstances of late-eighteenth-century America: early marriages that allowed only limited time for education, the cultural materialism of the middle class that presumed a wife capable of prudent management of the family assets, the teaching requirements of the maternal role, and the domestic arts needed to manage the household successfully without competent domestic servants. Rush deemed the British approach of ornamental education for women inadequate for the role American women must play in the development of the new nation. Therefore, he urged that American women's education include English language arts, basic mathematics and bookkeeping skills, geography and travel, history and biography (to provide both amusement and instruction), rudimentary natural and physical sciences (as useful in the domestic arts). Rush did not eschew all the ornamental arts: vocal but not instrumental music could be pursued in a disciplined setting; and dancing would provide wholesome exercise.

Rush acknowledged to the graduates of the Young Ladies' Academy that the success of this expanded curriculum for women's education depended upon their womanly conduct, lest their use of that education fuel the fears that education would "unsex" women. Thus, Rush's opinions and his pamphlet influenced the supporters of advances in women's education at the end of the eighteenth century and through the nineteenth century.

—*Angela Howard Zophy*

See Also:

Education; Female Academies; Rush, Benjamin

Reference:

Rush, Benjamin. *Essays, Literary, Moral, and Philosophical.* Philadelphia: Thomas and Samuel Bradford, 1798.

TITLE IX OF THE EDUCATION AMENDMENTS OF 1972 forbids discrimination on the basis of sex in federally aided education programs. When the bill was first introduced in Congress, legislators tried to exempt intercollegiate athletics from its provisions but were unsuccessful. Although Title IX applies to a wide variety of programs at all types of schools, the sports issue has remained the most visible.

Regulations issued by the Department of Health, Education, and Welfare in 1975 mandated what became wholesale changes in sports and physical education programs for girls and women. As a result of Title IX and the increasing awareness it sparked, the proportion of girls participating in U.S. interscholastic athletics jumped from 7.4 percent (of almost four million participants) in the 1970–71 school year to 31.9 percent in 1978–79. The number of female athletes increased 570.5 percent during this period; the number of male participants by 13.5 percent.

Not all results of Title IX have been positive for women. At the same time athletes enjoyed more opportunities to compete, the number of females in coaching and sports administration dropped dramatically. Increased funding for girls' and women's athletics drew more male coaches to programs for females, and the emphasis on equality of opportunity led to the combining of physical education and athletic departments under one (frequently male-oriented) administrative setup.

Until 1984, a tough interpretation of the enforcement mechanism—the possibility that all federal funds would be withheld from schools that discriminated—backed Title IX. In that year, the Supreme Court ruled in *Grove City College v. Bell* that federal funds would be denied only to specific programs found to be discriminatory. A school that practiced selective admission to its science programs, in other words, could lose federal research funding. But if the same school received no federal funds for its athletic program, it could continue to discriminate there without penalty. Within a year of the *Grove City* decision, more than sixty compliance investigations of possible Title IX violations were dropped.

Civil rights advocates and lawmakers unhappy with this gutting of Title IX would not accept defeat, however, and in March 1988, passage of the Civil Rights Restoration Act reinstated institution-wide penalty for any discrimination on grounds of sex—and race, age, or disability. An amendment allowing institutions to refuse to provide abortion-related services without penalty under Title IX coalesced bipartisan support for the Restoration Act, and allowed Congress to override then-President Reagan's veto of it.

—J. A. Sandoz

See Also:

Affirmative Action, Athletics/Sports

References:

Acosta, R. Vivian, and Linda Jean Carpenter. "Women in Sport." In *Sport and Higher Education*, edited by Donald Chu, Jeffrey O. Segrave, and Beverly Becker. Champaign, Ill.: Human Kinetics, 1985, pp. 313–25.

Hogan, Candace Lyle. "What's in the Future for Women's Sports?" *Women's Sports and Fitness* 9 (1987): 42–47.

U. S. Commission on Civil Rights. *More Hurdles to Clear: Women and Girls in Competitive Athletics.* Clearinghouse Publication #63. Washington, D.C.: U.S. Commission on Civil Rights, 1980.

Van de Graaf, Paul J. "The Program-Specific Reach of Title IX." *Columbia Law Review* 85 (1983): 1210–44.

TITUBA (c. 1648–92) was a Carib Indian woman slave who was brought to Salem Village, Massachusetts, by the Reverend Samuel Parris. She came from the Spanish settlements in the West Indies, as did her husband, John Indian. A group of local girls and women frequently came to visit Parris's young daughter and listen to Tituba tell stories. When the stories she told of voodoo rituals, prophecy, and spirit life seemed to "possess" those young girls, Tituba was accused of witchcraft. Tried and presumed guilty, Tituba was finally acquitted because of her genuine penitence and because the governor's wife intervened by calling the trials a disgrace.

A curious debate has arisen over the ethnic origin of Tituba, described in Ann Petry's children's book *Tituba of Salem Village* as a black, but elsewhere described as half-black and half-Indian.

—Susan Kinnell

See Also:

Nurse, Rebecca; Salem Witch Trials

References:

Hansen, Chadwick. "The Metamorphosis of Tituba, or Why American Intellectuals Can't Tell an Indian Witch from a Negro." *New England Quarterly* 47 (1974): 3–12.

Morsberger, Robert E. "The Further Transformation of Tituba." *New England Quarterly* 47 (1974): 456–58.

Robbins, Peggy. "The Devil in Salem." *American History Illustrated* 6 (1971): 44–48.

TODD, MARION MARSH (1841–?), born in Plymouth, New York, was a lawyer and writer who supported woman suffrage, temperance, the Greenback Labor party, the Union Labor party, and the Populist party. Todd moved to Michigan in 1851 with her family. A few years later she entered Ypsilanti State Normal School and at seventeen began teaching school. In 1868 she married Benjamin Todd of Boston, a lawyer who advocated women's rights and political and economic reform. The couple had one daughter, Lulu.

After a move to California, Todd entered Hastings Law College in San Francisco but was unable to finish law school because her husband's death in 1880 left her in financial difficulty. She was, nevertheless, admitted to the California Bar and opened a law office in San Francisco, specializing in finance law. In 1883 Todd stopped practicing law and devoted herself to writing, lecturing, and political campaigning. Todd attended the state convention of the Greenback Labor party and was nominated for the office of state attorney general. She also attended conventions of the Anti-monopoly party and the Knights of Labor. In 1886 she returned to the Midwest and became one of the editors of the *Chicago Express*, a reform newspaper with a national circulation, and helped to organize the Union Labor party. With the demise of these early reform parties, Todd then took an active part in the newly formed Populist party, attending conventions, speaking from the platform, and lecturing on the national campaign trail.

Her nonfiction included *Protective Tariff Delusions* (1886), *Professor Goldwin Smith and His Satellites in Congress* (1890), *Pizarro and John Sherman* (1891), *Railways of Europe and America* (1893), and *Honest (?) John Sherman, or a Foul Record* (1894). Her books about Senator John Sherman were used extensively in Populist party campaigns, and many Populists believed that Todd's work had caused the defeat of the hated Sherman, who was considered responsible for financial legislation that had been hard on farm and working-class families. Todd also wrote several romantic novels: *Rachel's Pitiful History* (1895), *Phillip: A Romance* (1900), and *Claudia* (1902). The last known record of Todd indicates that she was living in Springport, Michigan, in 1914.

—*MaryJo Wagner*

See Also:

Legal Profession, Populist Party

References:

Diggs, Annie. "Women in the Alliance." *Arena* 6 (July 1892): 161–79.

Willard, Frances E., and Mary A. Livermore, eds. *A Woman of the Century*. New York: Charles Wells Moulton, 1893, p. 718.

TOKLAS, ALICE B(ABETTE) (1877–1967), known principally as Gertrude Stein's companion, was a translator, publisher, journalist, letter writer, and biographer/autobiographer, as well as a cook, secretary, and housekeeper.

The first thirty years of Toklas's life have only become of interest because of her final sixty years. The only daughter of a Polish and a German Jew, Toklas was born, raised, and educated in San Francisco and Seattle. Her only sibling was ten years her junior. The Toklas family was relatively prosperous; Alice received her education in private schools and a conservatory, which she had to leave upon her mother's illness in 1893. She spent the next fourteen years keeping house and, after her mother's death in 1897, took over full responsibility for the male household while trying to retain her own interests.

In 1907 Toklas journeyed to Europe, where she met Gertrude Stein, who became her lifelong companion. It remains unclear when Toklas finally established herself in the Rue de Fleurus dwelling of Gertrude and her brother Leo, but Leo had moved out by 1912. Stein and Toklas traveled, fostered Stein's career, continued the salon tradition, delivered hospital supplies after the American entry into World War I, and patronized modern art. Toklas's only return to the United States was with Stein in 1934–35, to promote Stein's *An Autobiography of Alice B. Toklas* and to be at the opening of Stein's *Four Saints in Three Acts*. During World War II, Toklas and Stein remained in German-occupied France. Stein died in 1946.

After having established Plain Editions to publish Stein's writings privately in the late 1920s, Toklas translated a few works in the late 1930s. Supporting Stein's posthumous career, Toklas attempted to have her friend's unpublished writings published. She continued letter writing and fostering artistic talents and began writing cookbooks and articles. With or without Stein, Toklas was an important Parisian expatriate.

Her activities did not relieve her loneliness after Stein's death, and illness and legal battles with Stein's heirs increased it.

—*Maureen Ruth Liston*

See Also:
Stein, Gertrude; Women's Friendships

References:

Liston, Maureen R. *Gertrude Stein: An Annotated Critical Bibliography.* Kent, Ohio: Kent State University Press, 1979.

Simon, Linda. *The Biography of Alice B. Toklas.* Garden City, N.Y.: Doubleday, 1977.

Toklas, Alice B. *The Alice B. Toklas Cookbook.* New York: Harper & Row, 1954.

———. *Staying On Alone: Letters of Alice B. Toklas.* Edited by Edward Burns. New York: Liveright, 1973.

———. *What is Remembered.* New York: Holt, Rinehart and Winston, 1963.

TRANSCENDENTALISM was the philosophy of a small, loose association of middle-class intellectuals and reformers active in Boston and Concord from 1836 to 1860. Predominantly Unitarians or ex-Unitarians, leaders such as William E. Channing, Ralph Waldo Emerson, and Theodore Parker rejected the strictly rationalist emphasis of the Enlightenment and instead sought to cultivate the intuitive moral and intellectual powers in humans. Combining Immanuel Kant's romanticism with some oriental mysticism, the transcendentalists were critical of the materialism and alienation from nature that the new industrial order seemed to foster. While Emerson and Henry David Thoreau advocated radical individualism and withdrawal from society, others, such as Theodore Parker, felt that society must be reformed so as to nurture all individuals in their search for development and transcendence. Rejecting Emerson's radical individualism, some members of the group experimented in communal living on George Ripley's Brook Farm (1841–47) and Bronson Alcott's Fruitlands (1843), but neither of the experiments proved long-lasting. Of more consequence was the participation of many of the transcendentalists in the reform movements of the era, most notably abolition and the nascent woman's movement.

Transcendentalism offered women both leadership opportunities and an ideological base from which they would critique the basis of gender inequality and celebrate the potential for woman's full and "authentic" development. Elizabeth Peabody ran a book collective in Boston, and Margaret Fuller was dubbed the "priestess of transcendentalism" for her leadership in a five-year series of "conversations" on social and literary topics and for her editorship of the transcendentalists' quarterly journal *The Dial* from 1840 to 1843. In *Woman in the Nineteenth Century* (1845), Fuller argued that the universal material/spiritual dualism was replicated in the sexes; she attributed "energy, power, and intellect" to men, and "harmony, beauty, and love" to women. Women's oppression, she argued, tended to throw the world off balance, thereby reifying the materialistic, intellectual side of human nature. Women's emancipation from such oppression would thus restore the natural equilibrium and combat the materialism and loss of spirituality that the transcendentalists perceived in the emerging industrial order.

Elizabeth Cady Stanton, although not active as a transcendentalist per se, was also deeply influenced by its leaders, especially Theodore Parker. Unlike Fuller, however, Stanton argued that because woman's development had been suppressed historically, it was impossible to speculate as to her true nature. Only after active reform to eradicate the economic, political, and cultural barriers to women's collective self-development would women's real potential become manifest.

—*Maureen Fitzgerald*

See Also:

Fuller, Margaret; Stanton, Elizabeth Cady; Utopian Communities; *Woman in the Nineteenth Century*

References:

Cooper, James L., and Sheila M. Cooper. *The Roots of American Feminist Thought*. Boston: Allyn and Bacon, 1974.

Douglas, Ann. *The Feminization of American Culture*. New York: Avon, 1977.

Fitzgerald, Maureen. "In Search of Self: The Religious Basis of Elizabeth Cady Stanton's Feminism." Paper presented at the Seventh Berkshire Conference on the History of Women. Wellesley, Mass., June 1987.

Rose, Anne C. *Transcendentalism as a Social Movement, 1830–1850*. New Haven: Yale University Press, 1981.

A TREATISE ON DOMESTIC ECONOMY (1841) by Catharine Beecher was the first comprehensive American volume of household construction, management, and advice. It was grounded in the principles of domesticity as a social and moral value and of scientific understanding and labor-saving technology as mainstays of the self-sufficient American home.

Beecher saw the home as place and justification for women's separate and distinctive role in American society. Amid the conflicts inherent in a varied democracy, the home was to provide a stable, peaceful center of family life. While Beecher acknowledged that women were left aside in political and economic American life, she valued this disengagement as the means to an alternative role in promoting cultural, moral, psychological, and practical well-being. As Beecher made a virtue of nonparticipation in public life, she provided direction for a domesticity that included aspects of many professional competencies as they applied to the private home. And she assumed women's capacity for interest, understanding, and performance in a variety of roles.

Directed to an audience that crossed class lines, Beecher's *Treatise* combined the philosophic underpinning for the home as a mainstay of American society with practical guidelines for every aspect of the creation and conduct of the home as house and as center of family life. From exceptional diagrams for construction, room arrangement, gardens, decoration, and explanations of technology in everything from plumbing to cleaning, the *Treatise* moved to fulsome advice on family management, child care, prevention and identification of disease, and cookery. More scientific than its predecessors, Beecher's *Treatise* assumed its readers could understand not only the processes of modern domesticity but also the reasons for them—and so, for example, provided advice not only on growing and preparing food but also on the human digestive and circulatory systems.

Enormously popular on first publication, the *Treatise* continued to be reprinted and to sell well for decades, establishing Catharine Beecher's own financial independence and national recognition. The *Treatise* was expanded in 1869, including additions by Harriet Beecher Stowe, and reappeared as *The American Woman's Home*. In 1873 it was revised and retitled *The New Housekeeper's Manual*.

—*Carol Klimick Cyganowski*

See Also:

Beecher, Catharine; Domestic Feminism; Domestic Literature

References:

Beecher, Catharine. *A Treatise on Domestic Economy*. Boston: Marsh, Capen, Lyon & Webb, 1841.

———, and Harriet Beecher Stowe. *The American Woman's Home: Or, Principles of Domestic Science*. 1869; rpt. New York: Ayer, 1972; rpt. American Life Foundation, Library of Victorian Culture, 1975.

Sklar, Kathryn Kish. *Catharine Beecher: A Study in American Domesticity*. New Haven: Yale University Press, 1973.

TRIANGLE FIRE. On Saturday afternoon, March 25, 1911, a fire broke out in the Triangle Shirtwaist Company, which occupied the top three floors of a tenement in New York City's Washington Place district. It began on the eighth floor of the Asch Building, when a cigarette or sparks from defective wiring ignited a pile of material scraps. Before the fire had run its course, 147 employees, most of them women of Italian or Jewish immigrant antecedents, had died, either from smoke inhalation or by jumping to their deaths to avoid suffocation, smashing into the pavement with sickening thuds. It was the worst industrial tragedy in the history of New York and one of the worst ever anywhere. Some escaped by reaching the roof and climbing to an adjacent building, but most tried to reach safety via two elevators, an enclosed staircase, and a single ladder "fire escape" that led only to an enclosed courtyard that quickly filled with smoke. Because the doorway to the staircase was locked, dozens of bodies piled up behind it. Those who reached the courtyard survived only because firemen smashed in other locked doors.

Despite those circumstances, neither the proprietors of the factory nor the owners of the building were found liable or negligent, since these practices satisfied existing fire regulations for loft factories. The National Women's Trade Union League, however, organized a public funeral demonstration in which one hundred thousand people marched through the city and joined other labor, business, civic, and religious leaders in a mass protest meeting at the Metropolitan Opera House. The meeting delegated a Committee of Fifty to deliver a petition to the legislature demanding investigation of working conditions. The petition led Senate majority leader Robert F. Wagner and assembly majority leader Alfred E. Smith to propose a joint resolution establishing the New York State Factory Investigating Commission, popularly known as the Triangle Fire Commission.

With Wagner as chairman and Smith as vice chairman, the commission membership also included NWTUL president Mary E. Drier, American Federation of Labor president Samuel Gompers, and several legislators and prominent businessmen. During its four-year tenure, the commission held scores of public hearings, heard the testimony of several hundred witnesses, and produced thirteen volumes of carefully prepared reports. It drafted sixty bills, fifty-six of which were enacted into law, giving New York the best system of factory legislation of any state in the union. None of these was ever overturned by the courts.

—*John D. Buenker*

See Also:

Garment Industries, National Women's Trade Union League, Shirtwaist Makers Strike

References:

Goldmark, Josephine. *Impatient Crusader: Florence Kelley's Life Story.* 1953; rpt. Westport, Conn.: Greenwood, 1976.

Kerr, Thomas J., IV. "The New York Factory Investigating Commission and the Minimum Wage Movement." *Labor History* 12 (1971): 373–91.

Stein, Leon. *The Triangle Fire.* New York: Caroll and Graf, 1962.

TRIPLE JEOPARDY refers to the social and economic disfranchisement of poor minority women. The position of being in "triple jeopardy" arises out of membership in three low-status communities—women, minorities, and the underclass. The three terms of disfranchisement are interrelated and difficult to separate in describing the low structural status of poor minority women. Black, Native American, and Mexican American women occupy a disproportionate number of low-paying unskilled and semiskilled jobs in service positions. Social disfranchisement is evidenced by a lack of power in both public and private spheres. The relationships between minority women and majority men, minority women and majority women, and minority women and minority men have been historically based on the exploitation of minority women, who have been sexual objects for both minority and majority men (the most blatant example is the sexual exploitation of female slaves by slaveowners), have functioned as servants and nannies for majority women (relieving the latter of household drudgery), and have suffered inequality at home.

The way in which ethnicity, class, and sex combine to block opportunity for minority women has been the subject of theoretical debate. A Marxist-derived approach situates all domination within the capitalist system. Racism and sexism are based in the jockeying for economic ascendancy. Racism serves as justification for economic exploitation, while sexism arises out of women's position as unpaid domestic labor. Much of black and Mexican-American women's literature identifies racism (as opposed to class or sex) as the guiding force behind lack of economic power. Black women especially focus on economic dislocation, based on racist hiring practices, to explain the unequal relationship between black men and women.

The "mainstream" women's movement explores the dialectic of powerlessness in the public and private realms. The lack of access women have traditionally had to political and economic structures is partially based in inequality in the domestic realm, and the symbols surrounding women as primarily domestic contribute to lack of access to the public arena—one aspect of which is economic.

—*Priscilla Weeks*

See Also:

Black Women, *Chicana*, Native American Women

References:

Britain, Arthur, and Mary Maynard. *Sexism, Racism, and Oppression.* New York: Basil Blackwell, 1984.

Lerner, Gerda, ed. *Black Women in White America.* New York: Pantheon, 1972.

Melville, Margarita, ed. *Twice a Minority.* London: C. V. Mosby, 1980.

TROY FEMALE SEMINARY began offering a rigorous educational program in 1821, and it rapidly became one of the foremost schools in the United States. The founder, Emma Hart Willard, came to Troy, New York, at the invitation of that community's Common Council. Willard had moved to nearby Waterford in 1819 with the expectation that New York State would provide financial support for the school. Although the legislature was receptive to her plans, aid was not forthcoming. Then, on March 26, 1821, the Troy Common Council passed a resolution to raise $4,000 by special tax for the purchase or construction of a building for a female seminary. Additional funds were raised by subscription, and a building was purchased. The community was firmly behind Willard's efforts. When the school opened in September 1821, it enrolled ninety girls from across the nation. Willard continued to appeal to the legislature for support, but in vain. Citizens of Troy came to the seminary's assistance, and no outside aid was needed.

Willard was highly successful in her teaching. She was assisted by a professor and by a number of teachers trained by her. The curriculum was repeatedly improved at her initiative, and the school offered advanced courses in history and natural philosophy. No other girls' school in the nation offered such a complete program of study. By the mid-1820s, the success of the seminary prompted the city of Troy to expand the size of its building. In 1838 Willard retired as director of the seminary, handing over its direction to her son and daughter-in-law. Under their guidance, which lasted until 1872, the Troy Female Seminary continued to flourish and grow. The courses of study included modern languages, the Bible, composition, elocution, mathematics, astronomy, literature, history, and other subjects. The students' success challenged and firmly refuted the widely accepted point of view that such courses would, as Willard put it, "unsex us." The ability of females to master these disciplines was clearly demonstrated twice each year in the public examinations. Held in February and July, they drew crowds of spectators, as prominent scholars were invited to conduct the testing.

After the school's fifty-year lease on the buildings ended in 1872, the trustees purchased the site from the city and added new buildings. The school continued to gain widespread interest. In 1872 Emily T. Wilcox took over as principal, a post she held until 1895. In that year, the school changed its name to the Emma Willard School, and under that name it continues to be a leading educational institution.

—Robert G. Waite

See Also:

Education; Female Academies; Willard, Emma

References:

Emma Willard and Her Pupils or Fifty Years of Troy Female Seminary, 1822–1872. New York: Mrs. Russell Sage, 1898.

Lutz, Alma. *Emma Willard: Pioneer Educator of American Women*. Boston: Beacon, 1964.

Woody, Thomas. *A History of Women's Education in the United States*. Vol. 1–2. New York: Science Press, 1929.

TRUTH, SOJOURNER (1795–1883) was a public speaker representing a commitment to both the nonviolent abolition of slavery and the emancipation of women, her commitments being rooted in Christian faith. Born to a woman named Elizabeth who lived in slavery, she was named Isabella. Years later, having been bought and sold and having eventually obtained her freedom, she felt called by God to be a witness of God's truth to others. It was then, in 1843, that she changed her name. She began traveling and preaching, and the gentle power of her words impressed people throughout the country. Still, with the power of the truth of which she spoke, she was able to confront boldly as well as support men as authoritative and respected as Frederick Douglass.

Even as she is an anomaly, Sojourner Truth has become an archetype for the thousands of black women who lived in slavery. In her lifetime, she journeyed from her birthplace (in a root cellar) to the prominent stages of the abolition and emancipation movements. She delivered her most famous speech in response to hecklers at the 1851 Women's Rights Convention in Akron, Ohio, where she declared the strengths of all women when she asked, "Ain't I a woman?".

A victim of the laws of her time, she maintained a steady belief in the law and used the courts to fight injustice. In 1828 in Kingston, New York, Truth successfully sued Solomon Gedney for the freedom of her son, Peter. During the mid-1830s she became the first black person to win a slander suit against a white person when she was accused in the press of poisoning her employer. The court decided in her favor and awarded her $125 in damages. Truth filed a suit in Washington, D.C., in 1865 to affirm that blacks as well as whites could ride the public transport after a conductor dislocated her shoulder while trying to evict her from his streetcar despite her legal right to be there.

Truth worked with the Freedmen's Bureau and lobbied Congress to establish a program to resettle freed blacks in the West after the Civil War. She deemed her meeting with President Abraham Lincoln a highlight of her life. She died in 1883 in Battle Creek, Michigan.

—Joanne S. Richmond and Merri J. Scheibe

See Also:

Abolition and the Antislavery Movement; Black Women; Public Speakers, Women; Slavery

References:

Ortiz, Victoria. *Sojourner Truth, A Self-Made Woman*. Philadelphia: Lippincott, 1974.

Pauli, Hertha. *Her Name Was Sojourner Truth*. New York: Avon, 1962.

Robinson, Wilhelmena S. *Historical Negro Biographies*. In *Library of Negro Life and History*. New York: Publisher's Company, 1967, pp. 130–31.

Staples, Robert. *The Black Women in America*. Chicago: Nelson Hall, 1973.

Truth, Sojourner. *Narrative of Sojourner Truth*. 1878; rpt. New York: Arno, 1968.

TUBMAN, HARRIET (1821?–1913), born a slave, became one of the best-known leaders of the Underground Railroad, an organized network of abolitionists who helped slaves escape to freedom. She served as a spy, scout, and nurse for the Union army during the Civil War. Abolitionist, suffragist, and militant black leader, Tubman was known as "Moses" because of her untiring efforts on behalf of black emancipation.

Tubman was born in the early 1820s on a plantation on the Eastern Shore of Maryland.

Slavery left its mark on her, most visibly through the hands of an overseer who fractured her skull with a two-pound weight when she was a young teenager. Evidently she had attempted to intervene on behalf of another slave. This assault caused her to suffer from dizzy spells and periods of unconsciousness her entire life.

In about 1844 Tubman married a free black man, while still enslaved herself. When her master died in 1849, it was rumored that she would be sold, so she decided to escape. Her husband and her brothers refused to go with her, so she journeyed alone to freedom in the North. By hiding during the daytime and walking at night, she arrived safely in Pennsylvania.

Tubman was not content with her own freedom, wanting her friends and family to share in it too. Over a ten-year period, she made nineteen trips into the South to free others. At least three hundred men, women, and children escaped slavery through her efforts on the Underground Railroad. None of the people she assisted were ever caught, leading anxious slaveowners to offer $40,000 in reward for her capture. Tubman risked reenslavement in order to free others, but she cautiously carried a hidden revolver to protect herself and spur on reluctant fugitives.

Tubman was well known to abolitionist leaders and even aided John Brown in his plans to raid Harper's Ferry in Virginia. She also directly aided the Union army in the South during the Civil War. During her three years of war service, Tubman was a cook, nurse, spy, guerrilla fighter, and commander of scouts. Like many women, she worked in makeshift hospitals attending to wounded soldiers. She acquired a reputation for the healing qualities of her herb remedies and root medicine. Yet, unlike most women, Tubman, only five feet tall, commanded soldiers on raiding expeditions, most notably on one up the Combahee River in South Carolina in 1863, when three hundred black soldiers rescued more than seven hundred slaves. She also organized networks of spies among slaves in Confederate territory.

Following the war, Tubman helped establish schools to educate ex-slaves. Though illiterate herself, she was always concerned with aiding the freedmen and freedwomen. She even established a Home for Indigent and Aged Negroes in her own house in New York. She used her government pension to help defray the cost of the home. (This twenty-dollar-per-month allotment was not granted to her until 1897, after a long battle with Congress.) Tubman also had her friend Sarah Bradford write her biography in 1869, the year she married war veteran Nelson Davis, in order to raise money for the home.

In her later years, Tubman continued to be sought after for her wisdom by younger black activists. Known as "Mother Harriet," she actively participated in women's organizations and attended woman suffrage conventions. She was at the founding conference of the National Association of Colored Women in 1896, the first national black women's organization. She died in Auburn, New York, in 1913, but long after her death, her courage and determination continues to be an inspiration to those who struggle for human liberation.

—Susan Lynn Smith

See Also:

Abolition and the Antislavery Movement, Black Women, Civil War, Slavery

References:

Bradford, Sarah. *Harriet Tubman: The Moses of Her People.* 1886; rpt. New York: Corinth, 1961.

Conrad, Earl. *Harriet Tubman: Negro Soldier and Abolitionist.* New York: International Publishers, 1942.

Flexner, Eleanor. *Century of Struggle: The Women's Rights Movement in the United States.* Cambridge, Mass.: Belknap, 1959; rev. ed., 1975.

Lerner, Gerda. *Black Women in White America.* New York: Random House, 1972.

Sterling, Dorothy, ed. *We Are Your Sisters: Black Women in the Nineteenth Century.* New York: Norton, 1984.

TURNER, MRS. E. P. (1856–1938) was a club woman and community builder in Dallas,

Texas, during the Progressive era. Born and reared near Jefferson, Texas, Adella Kelsey met Edward P. Turner, who was employed by the Texas and Pacific Railroad. Shortly after their marriage in 1879, the Turners moved to Dallas; they had four sons, only two of whom survived.

While president of the City Federation of Women's Clubs (1903–04), the Texas Federation of Women's Clubs (1904–06), and the Dallas Woman's Forum (1906–08), Turner launched her campaign for correcting wrongs and abuses wherever woman's influence was needed. Because of her expanding interest in the welfare and education of children, in 1908 she became one of the first women to serve on the Dallas County School Board.

In 1910, when her term of office on the school board expired, Turner once again became president of the Dallas Woman's Forum. From 1910 to 1919 she organized and built the Woman's Forum into an institution that had a major impact upon the reform of sanitary conditions and the welfare of delinquent and underprivileged children in Dallas. In 1921 her interest in the legal rights of women led to the formation of the Women's Good Citizenship Association, which later became the Dallas League of Women Voters. After over fifty years of involvement in the women's club movement, Mrs. E. P. (Adella P. Kelsey) Turner died on June 6, 1938, in Dallas.

—*Diana Church*

See Also:

General Federation of Women's Clubs, Progressive Era

References:

Church, Diana. "Mrs. E. P. Turner: Clubwoman, Reformer, Community Builder." *Heritage News* (Summer 1985): 9–14.

Hazel, Michael V. "Dallas Women's Clubs: Vehicles for Change." *Heritage News* (Spring 1986): 18–21.

———. "A Mother's Touch: The First Two Women Elected to the Dallas School Board." *Heritage News* (Spring 1987): 9–12.

TURNOUT was a nineteenth-century term used interchangeably with *strike* by the early female operatives in the Massachusetts mills. It was actually a work stoppage or walkout en masse from their stations into the streets. The turnouts followed announcements of wage cuts. Harriet Hanson Robinson, a bobbin doffer in the mills at age eleven and later a suffragist, led one of the early turnouts (1836) and proudly recollected this event many years later in addressing a group of mill girls.

—*Virginia Beattie Mattes*

See Also:

Lowell Mill Girls; Textile Industries, Northern and Southern

References:

Dublin, Thomas. *Women at Work, The Transformation of Work and Community in Lowell, Massachusetts, 1826–1860.* New York: Columbia University Press, 1979.

Flexner, Eleanor. *Century of Struggle: The Woman's Rights Movement in the United States.* Cambridge, Mass.: Belknapp, 1959.

Josephson, Hannah. *The Golden Threads, New England's Mill Girls and Magnates.* New York: Duell, Sloan and Pearce, 1949.

Robinson, Harriet H. *Loom and Spindle.* Kailua, Hawaii: Press Pacifica, 1976.

TUSKEGEE NORMAL AND INDUSTRIAL INSTITUTE. As the result of a political deal, blacks in Macon County, Alabama, obtained a small state appropriation for a school at Tuskegee, Alabama, and in 1881 Booker T. Washington arrived there to become its first principal. By the time of his death in 1915, he had built Tuskegee Institute into the second-best-endowed black school in the nation and had become widely recognized by whites as a national spokesman for Afro-Americans. The school's combination of teacher and vocational training became a model for numerous other schools.

In his rise to prominence, Washington was aided by two strong women who became his second and third wives. Olivia Davidson was the first teacher he hired, and Margaret Murray served as lady principal and director of Industries for Girls. They directed the training programs for women, which were geared to producing teachers with knowledge of such domestic arts as dressmaking and cooking.

Tuskegee graduates were expected to share the benefits of their education, and most women graduates became teachers in rural areas—usually continuing to work after marriage. Quite a few made significant contributions. Petra Pinn, a nurse-training graduate in 1906, held several responsible positions before opening and supervising a private hospital in West Palm Beach, Florida. Elizabeth Evelyn Wright founded Vorhees Normal and Industrial Institute in Denmark, South Carolina, in 1897—three years after her graduation. Many others have had similar success as the nature and program of Tuskegee have evolved.

—Linda O. McMurry

See Also:

Higher Education for Southern Women; Washington, Margaret Murray; Women in Higher Education

References:

Booker T. Washington Papers. Library of Congress. Washington, D.C.

Butler, Addie Louise Joyner. *The Distinctive Black College: Talladega, Tuskegee, and Morehouse.* Metuchen, N.J.: Scarecrow, 1977.

Harlan, Louis R. *Booker T. Washington: The Making of a Black Leader, 1856–1901.* New York: Oxford University Press, 1972.

———. *Booker T. Washington: The Wizard of Tuskegee, 1901–1915.* New York: Oxford University Press, 1983.

Thrasher, Max Bennet. *Tuskegee: Its Story and Its Work.* New York: Negro University Press, 1969.

TWENTIETH-CENTURY WOMEN'S RIGHTS MOVEMENT. Traditionally, the twentieth-century struggle for women's rights dates from 1920, when the ratification of the Nineteenth Amendment gave women the vote. Although Alice Paul first initiated the introduction of the Equal Rights Amendment in 1923 to secure complete legal equality for women, the 1920s were not characterized by significant additional gains for the women's movement for several reasons: the rise of political fundamentalism in American society generally, the assumption of the younger generation of women that the franchise signified that the struggle for women's rights had been won and that the vote would automatically bring all the improvements promised by the suffragists, and the disintegration of the coalition of women's groups that had worked for suffrage.

The political arm of the suffrage movement, the National American Woman's Suffrage Association, was transformed into the nonpartisan League of Women Voters in 1920; contrary to both the fears of the antisuffragists and the hopes of suffragists, women voted according to their class, race, and economic status rather than as a gender bloc. Many of the women who had worked for woman's suffrage either were too exhausted to continue the struggle for women's rights or began to devote their efforts to one-issue causes. Women in the 1920s took advantage of the advances in educational and employment opportunities; but despite the increase in the numbers of women who received postsecondary educations and worked outside the home, these improvements were limited to jobs deemed appropriate for women and conditional because of the continued primary identification of women's proper role with marriage, home, and child care. However, the political activists within the National Women's party, holdover social feminists from the Progressive era, and a token number of stalwart women in academe and the professions served as keepers of the flame of feminism through the "Roaring Twenties" and into the New Deal era.

The groundwork for the resurgence of the modern women's movement of the 1960s was prepared throughout the 1930s, 1940s, and 1950s. Led by Eleanor Roosevelt, professional women influenced the New Deal administration's programs for social reform to improve women's conditions in the family and to a lesser degree in the labor force. The ambivalence of the government's wartime recruitment of single and married women to work in the defense plants notwithstanding, women's mass involvement in home-front and military mobilizations of World War II offered them unprecedented opportunities and dismissal policies regarding women, many single and married women remained in the work force, and those who returned to the home did so with the knowledge that once they had been economically self-sufficient as well as part of a great patriotic force of competent and independent women.

As the economic realities of the 1950s strained the ability of the male breadwinner to support the prescribed suburban life-style of his middle-class family, the mainstream matron found homemaking less rewarding than the women's magazines had promised. Thus, married women continued to increase both their part-time and full-time participation in the labor force into the 1960s. The convergence of the restlessness of suburban married women from "the problem that had no name" (as it was designated by Betty Friedan in *The Feminine Mystique*), the participation of young and older black and white women in the civil rights movement, and the radical politicization of campus women in the New Left produced a spectrum of activities and groups that focused specifically upon women's issues by the mid-1960s. A myriad of militant groups within the women's liberation movement drew the younger women from the New Left, while the National Organization for Women pursued a more mainstream political and legal reform agenda that reflected its membership of middle-class and professional women.

The agenda of the modern women's movement revealed those issues that most concerned women generally: equality of treatment under the law, equal opportunity in education and in the workplace, adequate child care as well as child and maternal welfare policies, abortion rights, and reforms in family and divorce statutes. Both avowed feminists and mainstream reformers used political action to secure women's presence in all occupations and endeavors as well as professional networking to assure the existence and an awareness of women as role models in both traditional and nontraditional activities and employment. The issues raised by the women's movement provided support for scholarly inquiry that challenged the general absence of women in traditional curricula and resulted in the establishment of women's studies courses and programs in institutions of higher education.

The immediate target was increased women's access to and equal participation in politics and in all aspects of the ecomony. Long-established women's groups joined the newer organizations to support the Equal Rights Amendment, which was sent to the states for ratification in 1972. The Supreme Court's decision in *Roe v. Wade* decriminalized abortion in 1973. During the early 1970s, women filed sex-discrimination cases at both the state and federal level under the provisions of the Civil Rights Act of 1963 and used the Equal Employment Opportunity Commission, established by the Civil Rights Act of 1964, to insure women's equal opportunity in the labor force. Supporters of equal education for women brought class-action suits against academic institutions, using Title IX of the Education Act of 1972.

Utilizing the leverage of these federal laws and Executive Orders 11246 and 11375, the women's movement had achieved significant success in raising the consciousness of individuals and society regarding the presence and impact of sexism by the mid-1970s. The nationwide participation of diverse women's groups in the 1977 International Women's Year Conference in Houston marked the peak of the twentieth-century women's movement during the 1970s. The result of state conferences that had provided a forum for defining the positions of proponents and opponents of the women's movement, the IWY Conference produced a National Plan of Action that not only supported the ERA but also articulated and addressed the crucial issues of the movement, which included the feminization of poverty and child care; homemakers', minority women's, and lesbian rights; equity in education, employment, and credit; and abortion rights.

However, the 1980s brought economic crisis and a conservative backlash to the social reforms of the 1960s and 1970s. According to these critics, the women's movement threatened the patriarchal core of the family, common law, and capitalism, and thus was the cause of the breakdown of the family and the rising divorce rate, the disintegration of law and order, and male unemployment. The administrations of Ronald Reagan oversaw the deliberate emasculation of the federal agencies, programs, and statutes that had facilitated women's struggle for equity under the law, in education, employment, and the family. Phyllis Schlafly's Stop ERA organization led the charge that defeated the Equal Rights Amendment in the last three of the needed thirty-eight states, despite the feminists' successful effort to gain a three-year extension for its ratification. The New Right coalition of political conservatives and religious fundamentalists consummately orchestrated opposition to women's reproductive rights and thus recruited numerous previously apolitical women into the Right to Life movement.

Thus by the late 1980s, the course of the women's movement seemed uncertain. Women were fighting setbacks at the state and national level. Attempts to introduce the ERA in 1983 and 1987 failed to achieve the two-thirds congressional vote required; endeavors to halt the erosion of Title IX and the cutback on federal entitlement programs that were desperately needed to reverse the feminization of poverty produced at best a "holding action." Adverse economic conditions limited support for programs for women in employment and in education. As happened in the 1920s, the young women of the 1980s seemed to feel that the revolution had been won and that the struggle was over, and they took for granted the opportunities secured for them by the feminist activities of the 1960s and 1970s.

—Saundra K. Yelton and Angela Howard Zophy

See Also:

Equal Rights Amendment; New Deal; New Left; *Roe v. Wade*; Schlafly, Phyllis; Suffrage; Women's Liberation Movement; Women's Studies

References:

Banner, Lois. *Women in Modern America: A Brief History*. San Diego: Harcourt Brace Jovanovich, 1974.

Chafe, William H. *The American Woman: Her Changing Social, Economic and Political Roles, 1920–1970*. New York: Oxford University Press, 1972.

Daniel, Robert L. *American Women in the Twentieth Century: The Festival of Life*. San Diego: Harcourt Brace Jovanovich, 1987.

Lerner, Gerda. *The Female Experience: An American Documentary*. Indianapolis: Bobbs-Merrill, 1977.

Ryan, Mary P. *Womanhood in America: From Colonial Times to the Present*. New York: New Viewpoints/Franklin Watts, 1975.

Whitney, Sharon. *The Equal Rights Amendment: The History and the Movement*. New York: Franklin Watts, 1984.

The *UNA* (1853–55), a Boston-based monthly magazine "Devoted to the Elevation of Woman," provided an alternative viewpoint to the popular woman's magazines of the mid-nineteenth century. Editor Paulina Wright Davis commented in the first issue of February 1853, "Women have been too well, and too long, satisfied with Ladies' Books, Ladies' Magazines and Miscellanies; it is time they should have stronger nourishment." From the start, the intent of the *Una* was to address the questions of woman's rights and duties in a straightforward, honest manner. The *Una*, translated as "truth," was considered the first woman's suffrage paper and preceded the longer-lived *Woman's Journal* by almost two decades.

During the two years of the *Una*'s publication, its contributors included well-known suffragist Elizabeth Cady Stanton, popular poet Sarah Helen Whitman, writer Miss Leslie, and a host of other writers and editorialists, including Davis and assistant editor Caroline Dall. Even Sarah Josepha Hale, editor of a less nourishing "ladies' magazine," *Godey's Lady's Book*, contributed her thoughts. The *Una* played an important role in providing information on issues of concern to suffragists by reporting on questions of legal rights for women, providing notes and commentaries on woman's rights conventions, and discussing issues pertaining to health, literature, education, and religion. Political rights for women, particularly Massachusetts women, were consistently addressed in the *Una*, with published excerpts from the constitutional convention meetings of Massachusetts. In 1855, after two years of publication, Davis was no longer able to finance the *Una*, and it ceased publication.

—*Karen C. Knowles*

See Also:

Dall, Caroline; Davis, Paulina Kellogg Wright; Magazines; Suffrage

References:

Stanton, Elizabeth C., Susan B. Anthony, Matilda J. Gage, eds. *The History of Woman Suffrage*. 6 vols. New York: National American Woman Suffrage Association, 1888–1922.

The *Una*. Vols. 1–3. Boston: Sayles, Miller and Simons, 1853–1855.

UNCLE TOM'S CABIN, OR LIFE AMONG THE LOWLY (1852) by Harriet Beecher Stowe is the most widely read and influential antislavery novel ever written, but the book is equally significant as a domestic critique of slavery's threat to mainstream American family values. Inspired by Stowe's outrage over the Fugitive Slave Law of 1850, the book is a sentimental, melodramatic novel that tells the story of a slave, Uncle Tom, who has been converted to Christianity. Tom is sold and parted from his family. He is first purchased by a benevolent man, St. Clare, at the urging of St. Clare's daughter Eva. When St. Clare suddenly dies, his wife sells Tom to the evil Simon Legree, who finally has Tom beaten to death.

Stowe's main purpose was to expose the separation of families that the slave laws permitted and to portray the resulting horrors in such a manner as to appeal to the Christian ethics of her readers. She certainly succeeded. The political effects of the novel were immediate and remarkable. Antislavery sentiments in the North increased dramatically because of Stowe's emotional portrayal, and hostile responses from southerners were vicious in their defense of the "peculiar institution." Upon first meeting Stowe, Abraham Lincoln is said to have greeted her humorously by saying: "Is this the little woman who made this great war?"

The novel appeared in serial form in the *National Era* from June 1851 through April 1852. In the first year after publication, the book existed in forty different editions and had sold over 350,000 copies in the United States. It was issued in England by over forty different publishers, and English reviewers referred to it as "the *Iliad* of the blacks." It has been translated into over twenty languages. Since taking over publication in 1862, Houghton Mifflin Company has never allowed the book to go out of print. In 1853 Stowe published *A Key to Uncle Tom's Cabin* in an attempt to defend herself against over thirty anti-*Uncle Tom* novels that had appeared. George L. Aiken's dramatic version of *Uncle Tom's Cabin* was never off the boards between 1853 and 1930. In 1903 Edwin S. Porter produced the first film version. Paramount produced another in 1918, and in 1927 Universal made a third. Today, *Uncle Tom's Cabin* is still part of the canon of literature that is taught in American public schools.

—*Victoria L. Shannon*

See Also:

Abolition and the Antislavery Movement; Civil War; Stowe, Harriet Beecher

References:

Fetterly, Judith. *Provisions: A Reader from 19th-Century American Women.* Bloomington: Indiana University Press, 1985.

Wagenknecht, Edward. *Harriet Beecher Stowe: The Known and the Unknown.* New York: Oxford University Press, 1965.

UNIONS. The earliest recorded union was the New York United Tailoresses Society, formed in 1824, which struck in 1825 and again in 1831, but left no records of the results. Mill women in Lowell, Massachusetts, organized the Factory Girls' Association in 1834, followed by the Female Labor Reform Association in 1845. Sarah Bagley, a mill worker from New Hampshire, appears to have been the multitalented force behind both of these organizations. She was extremely active between 1836 and 1846, when she became the first woman telegrapher and then disappeared from recorded history. Sewing-machine operators in New York established the Working Women's Union in 1863, electing Ellen Patterson president and M. Trimble recording secretary. After the Civil War, Kate Mullaney led the Troy Collar Laundry Union (1866) in a strike supported by Troy union men. A series of labor disasters for the men, coupled with the introduction of paper collars, effectively ended the strike, and the union was dissolved.

Throughout the 1860s, mill workers continued to organize under the guidance of Jennie Collins. She was active with the New England Labor Reform League and organized the Working Women's Club of Boston. In 1869 the Typographical Union admitted women for the first time. Augusta Lewis, corresponding secretary (1870), was the first woman to hold national office. The Daughters of St. Crispin (1869) was the first national union for women. These unions, for the most part, failed because the women lacked the education, expertise, and financial resources needed for long-term growth. Their male counterparts in the labor movement did not take the women seriously until the Knights of Labor and the American Federation of Labor agreed to allow them to organize ladies' assemblies. For ten years (1881–90), Leonora Kearney Barry worked as a general investigator, educator, and organizer of women for the Knights of Labor. When she retired, no one took up the work, and it was abandoned.

However, the women had opened the door, and unions began to proliferate: the Ladies Federal Labor Union (1888) led by Elizabeth Morgan; the Retail Clerks International (1890) led by Mary Burke; the International Boot and Shoemakers led by Mary Anderson, later first director of the Women's Bureau, U.S. Department of Labor (1895). By 1892 Mary E. Kenney was the national organizer of women for the American Federation of Labor. Helen Campbell was appointed to Massachusetts' Bureau of Labor. The National Women's Trade Union League (1903), guided by its president, Margaret Dreier Robbins, trained women whose names became legend in early union history: Rose Schneiderman, Women's Trade Union League; Pauline Newman, International Ladies Garment Workers' Union; Marie Van Vorst and her sister Bessie, labor reformers; Mary Harris "Mother" Jones, labor activist and investigator; Helen Gurley Flynn, Industrial Workers of the World; Mary Anderson and Leonora O'Reilly.

Black women and minorities were not represented in the unions until the last thirty-five or forty years. When white women and immigrants replaced them in the trades, black women were forced to take menial work that was impossible to organize. National Labor Union/Cincinnati Colored Teachers Cooperative Association (1870) was an exception. Today, almost all teachers belong to the National Education Association, established in 1870. By 1918, as a result of employment during World War I, thirty-five thousand women were members of the railroad unions, with many occupying administrative positions.

By the 1920s women had finally become accepted as members in male labor unions. But unions were decimated by the worldwide depression of the 1930s: Unemployed workers could not pay their dues, and impoverished unions could not help their members. World War II saw a union renewal, and by 1945 there were 3,000,000–3,500,000 women union members in organizations such as the National Teachers Association; International Brotherhood of Electrical Workers (telephone employees); and nurses' unions. Powerful labor legislative lobbying groups, the civil rights movement, and sophisticated technology have aided in bringing workers out of the dark ages of industrialization. The modern woman union member owes her equal work status to the determination, tenacity, and dedication of early women activists.

—*Jean McGrath Hayes*

See Also:

American Federation of Labor; Bagley, Sarah; Congress of Industrial Organizations; Flynn, Elizabeth Gurley; Industrial Workers of the World; International Ladies Garment Workers' Union; Huerta, Dolores; Jones, "Mother"; Knights of Labor; Lowell Mill Girls; Moreno, Luisa; National Education Association; National Women's Trade Union League; Schneiderman, Rose; O'Sullivan, Mary Kenney; United Farm Workers; Women's Protective Union

References:

Greenwald, Maurine Weiner. *Women, War and Work*. Westport, Conn.: Greenwood, 1980.

Riley, Glenda. *Inventing the American Woman.* Arlington Heights, Ill.: Harlan Davidson, 1987.

Ware, Norman. *The Industrial Worker: 1840–1860*. 1924; rpt. Chicago: Quadrangle, 1964.

Wertheimer, Barbara Mayer. *We Were There.* New York: Pantheon, 1977.

UNITED AUTO WORKERS (UAW). As was the case with several industrial unions, the United Auto Workers grew out of the struggles to organize workers in heavy industry during the 1930s. In 1936 the UAW united with the Congress of Industrial Organizations (CIO) and faced the formidable task of organizing auto workers in the Big Three: Ford, General Motors, and Chrysler. Walter Reuther, one of the most committed and impressive leaders of the union during the early days, first worked to organize workers in the Detroit area. He remained an important leader in the union throughout his life, serving thirty-five years as a union officer, twenty-four of those as president. Perhaps the most memorable legacy of the United Auto Workers' early organizing efforts was the sit-down strike. Workers refused to leave the auto plants, set up barriers to prevent siege from outside, and presented the threat of wrecking expensive machinery within the factories. Scabs could not be used effectively in this situation, and workers bonded with the sense of solidarity, since they lived together in the plant. The most famous sit-down strike occurred at the GM plant in Flint, Michigan, and lasted from December 1936 until February 1937.

During the Flint-GM sit-down strike, the women whose husbands, sons, and brothers were in the plant formed an auxiliary. This group got food to the workers, mended wounds, ran picket lines, and coordinated publicity. After a confrontation between workers and police on January 11, 1937, some of the women's auxiliary members established the Women's Emergency Brigade, whose purpose, according to leader Genora Johnson, was to be on hand when emergencies arose during the strike. Organized to mimic a military organization and wearing colored armbands and berets, these women could be called on a moment's notice to ring a plant with a picket line to protect the workers inside, break windows in a plant that was being tear gassed, or create a diversion to allow workers to take over a plant to sit-down. Because of the major contribution of the auxiliaries and emergency brigade in keeping up the morale and determination of the strikers, women's auxiliaries received the full support of the UAW leadership during this era of organizational efforts.

In more recent times, the UAW was the first major union to condemn protective legislation for women, declaring such laws discriminatory. As early as 1970, the union took a strong stand on women's issues in a resolution passed at the national convention that year that supported a woman's right to abortion, the establishment of a network of daycare centers, and the passage of an equal rights amendment to the U. S. Constitution.

–Mariann L. Nogrady

See Also:

Congress of Industrial Organizations, Flint Auto Workers' Strike, Unions

References:

Foner, Philip S. *Women and the American Labor Movement, From World War I to the Present.* New York: Free Press, 1980.

Vorse, Mary Heaton. *Labor's New Millions.* New York: Modern Age, 1938.

The **UNITED DAUGHTERS OF THE CONFEDERACY**, organized in 1894 by Caroline Meriweather Goodlett of Nashville and Anna Davenport Raines of Savannah, was one of the most popular voluntary associations for white southern women in the early twentieth century. The UDC claimed seventeen thousand members by 1900, and continued to grow. There were forty-four thousand Daughters in 1910 and sixty-eight thousand in 1920. Membership peaked in the early 1920s and declined thereafter.

The UDC grew out of local memorial associations and auxiliaries to veterans' groups. The Daughters undertook a variety of projects to commemorate the "Lost Cause." They offered relief to needy Confederate veterans, widows, and orphans; lobbied for higher pensions for veterans; constructed monuments; held pageants and ceremonies on Confederate holidays; cared for graves of Confederate soldiers; and collected documents and artifacts pertaining to the Civil War. Much of their work was educational. They sponsored essay contests for schoolchildren and college students, monitored textbooks to ensure that "true" history was being taught in the public schools, and funded scholarships for descendants of veterans.

The Daughters honored the heroines of the Confederacy along with its heroes. They stressed women's contributions to the war effort and praised southern women for their strength, resourcefulness, and courage. When Confederate veterans wanted to build a monument to southern women, the UDC insisted that practical assistance to women of the present would be the most fitting memorial to the women of the past. They suggested scholarships, homes for Confederate widows, or industrial schools as alternatives, indicating that perhaps the Civil War experience offered different lessons to women than to men. Women learned during the war that men would not always be there when needed, and the Daughters' practical proposals suggest that they wanted to be prepared to take care of themselves. In this instance, however, the men prevailed, and several southern states erected statues to the women of the Confederacy.

The UDC played an important, if ambiguous, role in determining the place of white women in the New South. In the name of preserving tradition, UDC members moved beyond the traditional domestic role into public life. While glorifying the Old South, they modified the southern feminine ideal to emphasize strength and competence. The Daughters perpetuated the myth of the Southern Lady, but they portrayed her as steel magnolia rather than clinging vine.

—*Anastatia Sims*

See Also:

Civil War, Southern Lady, Southern Women's Organizations/Leaders

References:

Confederate Veteran, 1894–1920. Nashville, Tenn.

Davies, Wallace Evan. *Patriotism on Parade: The Story of Veterans and Hereditary Organizations in America, 1783–1900.* Cambridge: Harvard University Press, 1955.

Foster, Gaines M. *Ghosts of the Confederacy: Defeat, the Lost Cause, and the Emergence of the New South.* New York: Oxford University Press, 1987.

Poppenheim, Mary B., et al. *The History of the United Daughters of the Confederacy.* Raleigh, N.C.: Edwards & Broughton, n.d.

Price, Margaret Nell. "The Development of Leadership by Southern Women Through Clubs and Organizations." M.A. thesis. University of North Carolina at Chapel Hill, 1945.

Roth, Darlene Rebecca. "Matronage: Patterns in Women's Organizations, Atlanta, Georgia, 1890–1940." Diss. George Washington University, 1978.

Ruoff, John Carl. "Southern Womanhood, 1865–1920: An Intellectual and Cultural Study." Diss. University of Illinois at Urbana-Champaign, 1976.

Sims, Anastatia. "Feminism and Femininity in the New South: White Women's Organizations in North Carolina, 1883–1930." Diss. University of North Carolina at Chapel Hill, 1985.

United Daughters of the Confederacy. *Minutes of the Annual Meeting.* 1895–1930.

UNITED FARM WORKERS (UFW). Farm workers in the United States, largely seasonal Hispanic workers, were the last large group of workers to be organized. Early attempts at organization had failed, but in 1962, Cesar Chávez, assisted by Dolores Huerta, formed the National Farm Workers Association. Plagued by low wages, long hours, and poor working conditions, the workers, through the NFWA, came to strength as a result of the Delano grape strike, which started in California in September 1965 and lasted until May 1970. Symbolized by a black Aztec eagle on a red flag, emblazoned with the Spanish word for strike—*Huelga*—the Delano strikers of the NFWA received support from Robert F. Kennedy, other powerful U. S. unions, and civil rights organizations. However, La Causa, as the movement came to be known, made slow progress until Chávez and Huerta organized a nationwide consumer boycott of California grapes that dramatized and publicized the conditions of the farm workers. During this strike, the NFWA merged with the Agricultural Workers Organizing Committee of the AFL-CIO, to form the United Farm Workers Organizing Committee, AFL-CIO. After more struggles and boycotts, the UFW in 1977 had over seventy contracts and represented about thirty thousand workers.

By the 1970s, the United Farm Workers depended on women in the fields and in positions of leadership. Once women learned to do pruning, a previously male-dominated job, the union sent men and women out to jobs based on their availability, ending any sex-determined work in the fields. Dolores Huerta, an early union organizer, became the union's first elected vice president in 1974. Although women did not win the acceptance of the male leadership easily, Chávez wanted women like Huerta on the picket line. Women, for example, led the picketing against the union-busting efforts of the growers and Teamsters and refused to retaliate when provoked by the Teamsters' violent beatings and attacks. As a result, the women established themselves as a mainstay of the union's nonviolent philosophy. Huerta also acted as chief negotiator for the first contract and did negotiations herself for five years. Other important self-taught women in this union include Jessie Lopez de la Cruz, the first woman to organize workers in the field; Marie Sabadado, the director of the Robert F. Kennedy Farm Workers Medical Plan; and Helen Chávez, the head of the Credit Union.

—*Mariann L. Nogrady*

See Also:

Chicana; Huerta, Dolores

References:

Baer, Barbara L., and Glenna Mathews. "You Find a Way: The Women of the Boycott." *The Nation* 218 (February 23, 1974): 233–34.

de la Cruz, Jessie Lopez. "My Life: Jessie Lopez de la Cruz as told to Ellen Cantarow." *Radical America* 12 (November/December 1978): 34–35.

Foner, Philip S. *Women and the American Labor Movement: From World War I to the Present.* New York: Free Press, 1980.

The **UNITED MINE WORKERS OF AMERICA**, founded in 1890, is an industrial labor union. Unlike today, when women work side by side with men in the ore mines of the United States, superstition once made it "unlucky" for a woman even to be near a mine. Nevertheless, women suffered just as much as their fathers, husbands, brothers, and sons from the difficult physical conditions of the company town, where there were inadequate sanitary conditions, everything was covered with coal dust, and water had to be carried from nearby streams. Women were always fearful of injury or death to their male relatives and husbands, which would make their lives even more difficult. It was in this atmosphere that two strong women labor union organizers were recruited by the United Mine Workers to improve the conditions of the miners and their families.

By the time Mary Harris "Mother" Jones attended the founding convention of the IWW (Industrial Workers of the World) in Chicago in 1905, she had already been a union activist for many years. To the mine workers, she was known as the "Miners' Angel" because of her participation in labor conflicts in West Virginia, Colorado, and Pennsylvania. In one especially successful campaign, she helped the Paint Creek miners gain union recognition and a contract during the southern West Virginia conflict of 1912–13. Although she was held in custody by the military authorities of West Virginia for quite a bit of this time, she was able to gain a great deal of publicity, which resulted in getting a congressional subcommittee to investigate the conditions surrounding the strike. This made it difficult for Governor Henry Hatfield to retaliate with martial law. As a result, the coal operators granted the strikers' original demands, and the strike was settled.

Fannie Sellins was recruited by Van Bittner, subdistrict director of District 5 of the United Mine Workers, after successfully campaigning for a boycott of a St. Louis clothing company whose workers had been locked out from 1909 to 1911. Otto Kaemmerer, a former president of a United Garment Workers local in St. Louis, said that she visited nearly every national, state, and district convention of the United Mine Workers and the Western Federation of Miners throughout the country. By 1913 Sellins was in West Virginia helping the families of miners on strike in Colliers. Later she helped prevent violence between union and nonunion coal miners working in the Penn Salt pits near Pittsburgh. In the tradition of Mother Jones, she was an outspoken advocate of the miner and the United Mine Workers.

In the early part of the century, the socialist-influenced United Mine Workers organized extensive women's auxiliaries with a distinctive cultural flavor, like the Dante Alligheri Clubs of the Kansas "Little Balkans" coal mining district, and the *Lavoratore Italiano* (UMW's newspaper), which helped Italian-Americans emerge as an important force.

—*Abby Schmelling*

See Also:

Industrial Workers of the World; Jones, "Mother"; Sellins, Fannie; Socialism

References:

Buhle, Mari Jo. *Women and American Socialism, 1870–1920.* Urbana: University of Illinois Press, 1983.

"Fannie Sellins Dies on the Battlefield of Labor." *St. Louis Labor*, August 30, 1919, 1.

Meyerhuber, Carl. "Fannie Sellins and the Events of 1919." Paper given at meeting of the Pennsylvania Labor History Society, September 27, 1986.

Williams, John A. *West Virginia: A History.* New York: Norton, 1984.

The **UNITED STATES CHILDREN'S BUREAU** was created as an agency of the federal government in 1912 to "investigate the questions of infant mortality, the birth rate, orphanage, juvenile courts, desertion, dangerous occupations, accidents and diseases of children, employment, legislation affecting children" in the United States and its territories. The legislation signed by President William Howard Taft reflected the concerns of the Progressive movement, which advocated protective measures for women, children, and other members of society who suffered under adverse social and economic conditions.

Early child welfare advocates maintained that the nation should care as much about its children as it did about its food. Accordingly, the first specific project undertaken by the bureau was one to reduce infant mortality. It was modeled on the Department of Agriculture's public education program that provided information to farmers on how to improve their crops. After studying the incidence of infant mortality in various geographic locations and among different social groups, the bureau sponsored maternal education programs that improved prenatal care, infant care and feeding, and medical consultation among women who previously had no access to such resources.

The bureau maintained its dual mission of research and program development by adapting its programs through the years to accommodate changing social conditions, the dislocations caused by two world wars and the Great Depression, and medical advances. The bureau's many studies and the precedents set by its administration laid the groundwork for the Social Security Act and other health and welfare programs enacted during the Roosevelt administration. During World War II the bureau worked to keep children in school and protect them from unfair labor practices while it expanded its maternal care program into the single most extensive medical care program ever undertaken by the government. The Emergency Maternity and Infant Care Program insured that the pregnant wives and newborn children of absent servicemen received the best medical treatment available. After the war, the bureau's programs focused on qualitative issues of child welfare: mental health, delinquency, and rehabilitation from crippling or debilitating diseases, especially polio. The bureau also made its expertise available to the world as it participated in international child-welfare congresses and provided training and information to other countries. In the 1980s most of the Children's Bureau programs were curtailed by reductions in social programs.

The success of the bureau's programs was due in large part to its leaders. Julia Lathrop, a close associate of Jane Addams and Lillian Wald, was the first chief of the bureau. She was succeeded in 1921 by Grace Abbott, a leader in child labor protection. Katharine F. Lenrott was named chief in 1934 and carried out the New Deal reforms and emergency wartime programs. In the postwar era, the bureau was headed by Dr. Martha M. Eliot, appointed in 1957. All of these women were excellent administrators and persuasive leaders who were able to gain support for the bureau's activities from the public, Congress, and state governments.

—Jane Crisler

See Also:

Abbott, Grace; Lathrop, Julia; Progressive Era

Reference:

The United States Children's Bureau, 1912–1972. New York: Arno, 1974. [reprinted collection of articles]

The **UNITED STATES MILITARY ACADEMY**, located in West Point, New York, was established as part of the U.S. Army Corps of Engineers in 1802. An act in 1912 reorganized the academy from an apprentice school to a four-year program with an expanded faculty and student body. The most famous of the early West Point superintendents was Col. Sylvanus Thayer (1817–33), who designed an academic structure that is still generally in place today.

The most radical change in the academy in the twentieth century was the admission of women beginning in 1976. Military leaders and cadets were most resistant to this change, which was mandated by Congress in a 1975 law that applied to the Naval and Air Force academies as well. The three academies reacted to this integration in different ways. West Point focused on maintaining "standards" and tried to ignore anatomical or physiological differences between the sexes. Annapolis tried for "low" visibility of the women cadets to make them less conspicuous; the Air Force strove for "high" visibility to instill an esprit de corps among the women. Only the Air Force had concrete plans for this transition. In part, this resulted in a lower attrition rate for the Air Force.

The first class of women graduates has been carefully followed by psychologists and sociologists. They graduated in 1980 and have now put in their required time, but their is no discernible trend regarding career service as yet. Leaders of the U.S. Military Academy as well as of the other academies worried about pregnancy among women officers. This concern is as unfounded in the 1980s as it was in the 1940s when, as Mattie Treadwell's book on the Women's Army Corps showed, pregnancy rates were low even though getting pregnant at the end of the war was the easiest way to "devolunteer." Sexual harassment has been a much larger problem, but the branches of the service have given this issue much attention in an attempt to address and eliminate the problem.

Women cadets and graduates have to face the fact that the army has closed many highly prestigious careers to them because of restrictions on women in combat. These combat positions are usually necessary career steps to promotion into the highest (flag) ranks. Most positions are more closed to women today than even a decade ago, and what constitutes a "combat" classification is often confusing and vague. All three academies have now had a woman ranked first in her class, which requires athletic excellence as well as scholarship.

—D'Ann Campbell

See Also:

Military Service

References:

Lovell, John. *Neither Athens Nor Sparta?* Bloomington: Indiana University Press, 1979.

Priest, Robert F. *A Comparison of Faculty and Cadet Attitudes Towards Women.* Washington, D.C.: Office of Institutional Research, No. 76-017, 1976.

———, and John W. Houston. *Analysis of Spontaneous Cadet Comments on the Admission of Women.* Washington, D.C.: Office of Institutional Research, No. 76-104, 1976.

Stauffer, Robert. *Comparison of USMA Men and Women on Selected Physical Performance Measures . . . "Project Summertime."* Washington, D.C.: U.S. Military Academy, 1976.

Stiehm, Judith Hicks. *Bring Me Men and Women: Mandated Change at the U.S. Air Force Academy.* Berkeley: University of California Press, 1981.

Treadwell, Mattie E. *The United States Army in World War II, Special Studies, the Women's Army Corps.* Washington, D.C.: Office of the Chief of Military History, Department of the Army, 1954.

Vitters, Alan G., and Nora Scott Kinzer. *Report of the Admission of Women to the U.S. Military Academy (Project Athena).* Washington, D.C.: Department of Behavioral Sciences and Leadership, 1977.

The **UNITED STATES SANITARY COMMISSION** was the outstanding public service contribution and accomplishment of Union women during the Civil War, despite the fact that antebellum women's inequality required that the commission itself be run by men. Established in 1861 to coordinate the war relief efforts of seven thousand local northern and western women's aid societies, the U.S. Sanitary Commission provided crucial services, which included providing trained nursing staff to Union hospitals as well as sending medical supplies and arranging transportation for the wounded. Appointed as superintendent of its nurses, Dorothea Dix successfully neutralized the opposition of the army's male medical corps to the presence of women nurses in the army hospitals as she oversaw the creation of a modern nursing service under the commission's aegis.

To fund the activities of this most effective women-created institution, its supporters successfully sponsored fairs and bazaars. The proceeds were used to buy food, clothing, and medical supplies that the local aid societies' members could not make themselves; local and state women's relief groups astutely sent designated agents to the front-line hospitals to assure proper distribution of the supplies. The outrage of an Iowa agent at the appalling food served in the military hospitals resulted in a commission-supported campaign for "diet kitchens" to provide the patients with decent nutrition. Commission-sponsored "refreshment saloons," forerunners of the USO canteens of the twentieth century, served soldiers traveling to and from the front. The wartime activities of Mrs. March and her daughters in Louisa May Alcott's *Little Women* exemplified the commission's work at the local level. At the end of the war, commission workers turned their attention to pressuring the government to address the plight of war orphans.

The U.S. Sanitary Commission contributed in excess of $1 million in hospital supplies and countless able and resourceful volunteers for the understaffed and ill-managed military hospitals. The Union benefited from the unstinting dedication of competent middle-class women who contributed their time and talent from the home front to the battlefront. Among the more well known women who served the medical mission of the U.S. Sanitary Commission were Harriet Tubman, Sojourner Truth, Susie King Taylor, Jane Swisshelm, Mary Livermore, Mary Ann "Mother" Bickerdyke, and Louisa May Alcott. Women's experience with the commission indirectly spurred the professionalization of nursing, further development of institutions to train women physicians, and the creation of the American Red Cross.

—Angela Howard Zophy

See Also:

Alcott, Louisa May; American Red Cross; Barton, Clara; Civil War; Dix, Dorothea; Nursing; Truth, Sojourner; Tubman, Harriet

References:

Clinton, Catherine. *The Other Civil War: American Women in the Nineteenth Century.* New York: Hill and Wang, 1984.

Flexner, Eleanor. *Century of Struggle: The Woman's Rights Movement in the United States.* Rev. ed. Cambridge, Mass.: Belknap, 1959, 1975.

Lerner, Gerda. *The Female Experience: An American Documentary.* Indianapolis: Bobbs-Merrill, 1977.

Riley, Glenda. *Inventing the American Woman: A Perspective on Women's History.* Arlington Heights, Ill.: Harlan Davidson, 1987.

Woloch, Nancy. *Women and the American Experience.* New York: Knopf, 1984.

The **UNITED STATES SUPREME COURT** is mandated by the Constitution as the highest federal court; it decides difficult legal questions and resolves important national controversies. The Court had been completely male in composition until the appointment of Justice Sandra Day O'Connor by President Ronald Reagan in 1981.

The history of the Court's decisions on women's rights cases can be separated into three distinct phases. The first phase took place in the 1870s after the passage of the Fourteenth Amendment gave hope to the first wave of the women's movement that the "rights" of "equal protection of the law" afforded to freed slaves would be extended to women. This hope was short-lived, as the Court upheld laws denying the women the vote (*Minor v. Happersett*).

During the next phase, in the early 1900s, as women began to enter the work force outside of the home, they became the objects of "protective" socioeconomic legislation. At this time the Court had little tolerance for this type of legislation as it pertained to men; yet it decided that the "weaker sex," or the "childbearing sex," merited special protection.

In the following phase, from the 1920s to the 1940s, the Court began to reject government intervention in the area of private right to procreation. The Court's concern for protecting procreative freedom peaked in the 1960s and 1970s, as the Court declared unconstitutional laws restricting the use of birth control devices (*Griswold v. Connecticut*); laws prohibiting abortion (*Roe v. Wade, Doe v. Bolton*); and laws imposing mandatory leaves on pregnant employees (*Cleveland v. LaFleur*).

The 1970s ushered in a new era of constitutional law, as the Court denied the generally held assumption that state legislatures had good reason for writing gender-based distinctions into the law. This phase seems to continue as the Court attempts to remove gender distinctions in diverse areas of the law. But as with all political institutions, the pendulum is never still too long, and the appointment by Ronald Reagan of many conservative federal judges on all levels of the federal court system may yet create a backlash effect.

—*Sue E. Strickler*

See Also:

Griswold v. Connecticut, Minor v. Happersett, Nineteenth-Century Woman's Movement, Protective Legislation, *Roe v. Wade*, Twentieth-Century Women's Rights Movement

References:

Cleveland Board of Education v. LaFleur, 414 U.S. 632 (1974).
Doe v. Bolton, 410 U.S. 179 (1973).
Goldstein, Leslie Friedman. *The Constitutional Rights of Women*. New York: Longman, 1987.
Griswold v. Connecticut, 381 U.S. 479 (1965).
Minor v. Happersett, 21 Wall. 162 (1875).
Roe v. Wade, 410 U.S. 113 (1973).

The **UNIVERSITY OF CHICAGO** was incorporated in 1890 with substantial funding from John D. Rockefeller, and opened for classes in 1892 under the presidency of William Rainey Harper. From the outset, the university was coeducational, and early enrollments indicate that more than a quarter of the students were female. During Chicago's first ten years, women accounted for nearly 50 percent of bachelor's degrees awarded and more than half the Phi Beta Kappa memberships.

Former Wellesley president Alice Freeman Palmer served as professor of history and as the first dean of women, assisted by her eventual successor, assistant professor of sanitary science Marion Talbot. Both were founders of the Association of Collegiate Alumnae (later the American Association of University Women). Talbot became dean in 1897, serving in that position until her retirement in 1925, and was probably the most influential woman at the university during her tenure. Although Talbot did accede to establishment of local "clubs" with no national affiliation, she opposed the formation of sororities and pushed for separate dormitories for women as the focus of their social life. Gifts from Mrs. Nancy Foster, Mrs. Jerome Beecher, and Mrs. Hiram Kelly provided funding for the first women's residences, each of which, except for Green Hall, bore the name of its donor. Nevertheless, only a minority of the women students lived in dormitories, and many commuted from their parents' homes. Thus, Talbot led the campaign to found the Women's Union in 1901 to provide day students with a place to rest, read, eat, and become involved with campus life.

Wellesley College provided the largest block of students in the early graduate programs. Chicago's arts and sciences graduate school included a large number of women, including reformers Grace and Edith Abbott, Sophonisba Breckinridge, Katharine Bement Davis, and scholars Myra Reynolds, Helen Bradford Thompson, Elizabeth Wallace, and Madeleine Wallin.

Perhaps because of the proportion of women students and their success, and the related fear that men would not attend a school in which women constituted a majority, President Harper, over the objection of Talbot, other women, and some male faculty, imposed sex-segregated classes in 1902. The practice was abandoned as too expensive within a few years.

Chicago has also played an important role in women's athletics. The appointment in 1898 of Gertrude Dudley as director of women's athletics and director of women's gymnasium marked the beginning of collegiate athletics for women in the United States. It also represented a departure from the traditional view that competitive sports were not proper for women. The oldest women's athletic advocacy organization, the Women's Athletic Association, was formed at the University of Chicago in 1904. Mary Jean Mulvaney became the first female athletic director of a coeducational program and the first woman to serve on a National Collegiate Athletic Association general committee. In 1972 Chicago became the first university to offer athletic scholarships to women.

The appointment in 1978 of Hanna Holborn Gray as president of the university was the first of a woman to a major university presidency in the United States.

—*Nicholas C. Burckel*

See Also:

Coeducation; Talbot, Marion; Women in Higher Education

References:

Goodspeed, Thomas Wakefield. *A History of the University of Chicago: The First Quarter-Century*. Chicago: University of Chicago Press, 1916.

Gordon, Lynn D. "Co-Education on Two Campuses: Berkeley and Chicago, 1890–1912." In *Woman's Being, Woman's Place: Female Identity and Vocation in American History*, edited by Mary Kelley. Boston: G. K. Hall, 1979, pp. 171–73.

Talbot, Marion. *More than Lore*. Chicago: University of Chicago Press, 1936.

UPTON, HARRIET TAYLOR (1854–1945) served as a longtime national and Ohio state suffrage leader and organizer. Affectionately called "the Boss" or "the General" by her cadre of workers, Upton was skilled at public speaking and legislative lobbying, and was able to direct and organize masses of women, all of which proved invaluable to the suffrage movement. Under her leadership as Ohio Woman Suffrage Association (OWSA) president, the state movement adopted new practices such as open-air meetings and parades, streamlined and strengthened its organizational structure, and faced several serious crises as its membership numbers grew.

Born in Ravenna, Ohio, in 1854, Upton spent most of her life in the small town of Warren. As a young woman, she served as hostess and companion in Washington, D.C., for her widowed father, an Ohio congressman, from 1880 to 1893. In Washington, she met and eventually married attorney George Upton, who joined his father-in-law's Warren law practice. Their thirty-nine-year marriage was an especially close and supportive one; the two did not have children.

Harriet Taylor Upton first became interested in suffrage after attending a lecture given by suffrage leader Susan B. Anthony. Despite their age difference, the two became close friends, and Anthony helped to draw Upton into local and later national suffrage work. For many years Upton served on the congressional and press committees of the National American Woman Suffrage Association and as national treasurer from 1893 to 1910.

As OWSA president (1890–1908, 1911–20), Upton directed two unsuccessful referendum campaigns (1912, 1914) to add woman suffrage to the state constitution. A third unsuccessful referendum (1917) lost Ohio women the right to presidential suffrage, which had previously been enacted into law by the state legislature. Despite these defeats, statewide organizational efforts and accompanying congressional lobbying were ultimately successful. Ohio became the fifth state to ratify the Nineteenth Amendment, a testament to the hard work of Ohio's women and their tireless leader.

Following suffrage's victory, Upton served for several years as the first female member of the Republican party's Executive Committee.

—*Eileen R. Rausch*

See Also:

Suffrage

References:

Allen, Florence E., and Mary Welles. *The Ohio Woman Suffrage Movement, "A Certain Unalienable Right," ; What Ohio Women Did to Secure It.* n.p.: Commission for the Preservation of Ohio Woman Suffrage Records, 1952.

Ohio Woman. 1912–17.
Ohio Woman Suffrage Association. *Yearbooks*. Warren, Ohio: 1912–20.
Rausch, Eileen R. "'Let Ohio Woman Vote': The Years to Victory, 1900–1920." Diss. University of Notre Dame, 1984.
Upton, Harriet Taylor. "Random Recollections." n.p.: Commission for the Preservation of Ohio Suffrage Records, n.d. [1927].

URBANIZATION is the historical process whereby cities (densely populated with non-agricultural residents and contained within definite geo-legal boundaries) evolve and develop large-scale, complex commercial, financial, industrial, residential, cultural, ecological, political, educational, communication, and transportation systems that transcend municipal boundaries. These systems structure and order internal behavior within the city and link it to its hinterlands. Over time, they unite individual cities in regional, national, and international networks that are extensions of their own internal systems.

Since colonial times, this process of urbanization has profoundly affected the lives of women in the United States. The first census, in 1790, showed that only slightly above 5 percent of Americans lived in the nation's twenty-four cities, even though the latter were defined as places of over 2,500 people. By 1840 nearly 11 percent of the population was classified as urban, with New York City exceeding 250,000 people. By 1880, 28.2 percent of the American people lived in cities of over 8,000 people, and by 1960 that figure had risen to 45.7 percent. The 1920 census was the first in which urban dwellers outnumbered their rural and small-town cousins; by 1980 the proportion had reached nearly three-quarters. The growth rate of individual cities and their suburbs has been phenomenal, with Chicago going from a village of just over 3,000 in 1840 to a city of over 2 million by 1920, and Los Angeles exploding from about 33,000 in 1880 to over 6 million in 1960.

The influx of so many people into a relatively small space engendered a pressing need for expanding urban services, such as transportation, communication, education, recreation, utilities, and sewage and garbage disposal, which cities were often unable to meet adequately. Restrictive state charters that limited bonded indebtedness and tax rates, legislative malapportionment, privatism, and competition among the city's diverse ethnocultural and socioeconomic groups made it extremely difficult to provide an adequate level of urban services, leading to the growing prevalence of slums, poverty, crime, vice, and other urban problems. Yet the continued influx of people into urban areas eloquently testified to the continuing perception of the city as a place of greater economic opportunity and personal fulfillment.

Women, especially, found the city a far more fertile ground for their drive for equality than rural areas or small towns, and leadership in the various women's movements was exercised primarily by urban dwellers. The city also provided many women with new professions and new creative outlets unavailable elsewhere.

"Women adrift" was the label middle-class social investigators of the early twentieth century gave to urban wage-earning women who lived apart from family, relatives, and employers. Most of these women were boarders and lodgers in the cities. They included native-born white and black women who migrated from America's farms, towns, and cities and foreign-born women who came primarily from Europe and Canada. While most of these women were young and single, the group included older women and separated, divorced, and widowed women. By all accounts, the vast majority worked in predominantly female service, manufacturing, clerical, and sales jobs. In 1900 the "women adrift" comprised roughly one-fifth of the urban, nonservant female labor force.

The "women adrift" attracted public notice in the late nineteenth and early twentieth centuries because reformers feared that low-income women without the moral and economic protection of family would drift into starvation or prostitution. In fact, the "women adrift" did face obstacles. Most important, employers often paid them the low wages of dependent daughters and wives. In addition, these women found that neighbors and acquaintances suspected them of immoral behavior, associating their independence from family with prostitution.

Many "women adrift" found substitutes for family support. Some lived as though they were daughters in the homes where they boarded or lodged. Others came to depend on their peers, pooling resources for room and board and depending on higher-paid men for entertainment. Especially in the urban furnished-room districts, areas where lodgers concentrated, early-twentieth-century observers noticed elaborate peer subcultures among "women adrift."

—*John D. Buenker and Joanne Meyerowitz*

See Also:

Demography, Industrial Revolution, Migration and Frontier Women, Politics, Progressive Era, Prostitution, Women's Friendships, Women's Work—Nineteenth Century

References:

Buenker, John D., Gerald Michael Greenfield, and William J. Murin. *Urban History: A Guide to Information Sources.* Detroit: Gale, 1981.

Chudacoff, Howard. *The Evolution of American Urban Society.* Englewood Cliffs, N.J.: Prentice-Hall, 1975.

Furer, Howard B. "The American City: A Catalyst for the Women's Rights Movement." *Wisconsin Magazine of History* 52 (1969): 285–395.

Meyerowitz, Joanne J. *"Women Adrift": Independent Wage Earners in Chicago, 1880–1930.* Chicago: University of Chicago Press, 1988.

Neill, Charles P. *Wage-Earning Women in Stores and Factories:* Vol. 5, *Report on Condition of Woman and Child Wage-Earners in the United States.* Washington, D.C.: U.S. Government Printing Office, 1910.

UTOPIAN COMMUNITIES were intentional living and working arrangements organized to change various aspects of society. Most visible in the United States during the nineteenth century, many of these utopian communities specifically addressed the issues of women's economic function, political rights, marital role, sexuality, and reproduction. Yet no community was entirely successful in creating an equal place for its female members, and not all architects of utopian societies were interested in extending rights to women. Both religious and secular communities were created in reaction to the upheaval caused by America's transformation from a rural society to an industrial and urban one.

In religious communities, new social arrangements that promoted spiritual redemption were a primary goal. Toward this end, such communities often questioned sexuality, marriage, and reproduction. The Shakers, founded by Ann Lee in the 1770s, practiced celibacy and thus freed women from oppressive sexual and reproductive roles. At the Oneida Community (1848–81), a form of complex marriage and community-wide birth control were practiced. Although the male members controlled contraception, some attention was paid to female sexual pleasure, and women's fears of constant pregnancy were reduced. The Mormons attempted to reorganize the family by instituting a form of polygamy. For some women, this meant sharing a husband with other wives and forming a household with other women and their children.

Architects of many secular communities were influenced by the Enlightenment and based their ideas on the theory of natural rights. At Robert Owen's New Harmony and subsequent communities, and the "phalanxes"—economic units of 1,620 people sharing a communal dwelling and dividing work according to their natural inclinations—based on the principles of Charles Fourier, intellectual equality and the economic and political roles of women were the major gender issues. Owenite communities began by guaranteeing equal rights to female members, but in actual practice their political rights were ambiguous. In the Fourierist phalanxes, women sometimes owned stock in the community on the same basis as men. In many communities, women worked for wages, as lack of economic independence was believed to be a cause of female oppression. But often such women were still responsible for domestic work and child care, usually without pay. The communal aspect of the workplace sometimes mitigated the unequal burden placed upon women.

Two utopian communities, Brook Farm and Fruitlands, emerged in the mid-nineteenth century and were based on transcendental philosophy, even though transcendentalism focused on individual reform rather than social experimentation. Brook Farm was established in 1841 by George Ripley in West Roxbury, Massachusetts. Its transcendental doctrine emphasized the innate worth of the individual, male or female, and attracted some of the most notable thinkers of that time, including Nathaniel Hawthorne, Ralph Waldo Emerson, and Margaret Fuller.

Fuller, an influential feminist and editor, was a frequent visitor and lecturer at Brook Farm, but she never became a resident because she found communal life too confining. Her talks on the elevation of womanhood were presented to captive audiences at Brook Farm, for feminism was a popular topic there. She also showed her support of the community through her articles in *The Dial*, the transcendentalist publication that she edited for several years. Her influential booklet *Woman in the Nineteenth Century* was based on an article she wrote for *The Dial* in July 1843.

A second utopian experiment was the short-lived Fruitlands, founded by Bronson Alcott in 1843 near Harvard, Massachusetts, and disbanded in 1844. While the role of the family was not a main concern at Brook Farm, it was the center of controversy at Fruitlands, where marriage and family became key issues. The "consociate family" was designed to supplant the nuclear family, thus alleviating selfishness and possessiveness. Bronson Alcott, however, could not reconcile his emotions with his intellect concerning the family issue; in his mind, he realized the importance of undermining the influence of the conventional family unit for the good of the communal family, but in his heart, he could not allow himself to break away from his own family. His reluctance to support the "consociate family," along with economic difficulties, brought about the quick demise of Fruitlands. Brook Farm lasted three years, but neither it nor Fruitlands was successful in incorporating transcendental beliefs into a social structure.

For women, utopian communities could promise new roles, new responsibilities, and the chance to explore the meaning of gender in a new society. But frequently, that promise was not kept or disappeared under the guise of community expediency.

—Wendy E. Chmielewski and Karen Gillenwaters

See Also:

Complex Marriage; Fuller, Margaret; Mormonism and Women; Nashoba; New Harmony; Oneida Community; Shakers; Transcendentalism

References:

Foster, Lawrence. *Religion and Sexuality*. New York: Oxford University Press, 1981.

Miller, Perry, ed. *The Transcendentalists: An Anthology*. Cambridge: Harvard University Press, 1950.

Muncy, Raymond Lee. *Sex and Marriage in Utopian Communities*. Bloomington: Indiana University Press, 1973.

Rohrlich, Ruby, and Elaine Hoffman Baruch. *Women in Search of Utopia*. New York: Schocken, 1984.

Sams, Henry W., ed. *Autobiography of Brook Farm*. Englewood Cliffs, N.J.: Prentice-Hall, 1958.

Sears, Clara Endicott, ed. *Bronson Alcott's Fruitlands*. Philadelphia: Porcupine, 1975.

VALESH, EVA MCDONALD (1866–1956) was born in Orono, Maine, attended high school, worked as a journalist, participated in labor politics, and later became active in the Farmers' Alliance and Populist party in Minneapolis. As a fledgling journalist using the pen name Eva Gay, Valesh wrote a series of articles on working women in St. Paul/Minneapolis for the *St. Paul Globe* in 1888 and then began attending meetings of the Knights of Labor, where she met John P. McGaughey, master workman of the Minnesota Knights of Labor. McGaughey was so impressed with her talent and her concern for laboring women and men that he trained her in public speaking and introduced her to reform politics.

During the same year, Valesh ran for a seat on the Minneapolis school board. After losing the election, she returned to her job with the *St. Paul Globe*, where she edited a labor news column, supporting the single-tax movement and the Greenback Labor party, and continued lecturing at labor meetings. In 1890 she attended the state Farmers' Alliance convention, where she was elected as a state alliance lecturer. She soon became an assistant national lecturer and accepted the clerkship of the Minnesota House Appropriations Committee. As the representative of the Knights of Labor, Valesh attended a national alliance and labor convention in Cincinnati in 1891 where delegates founded the Populist party. She returned from the convention, married the president of the Minnesota Federation of Labor, Frank Valesh, and began lecturing across the country for the new party. A difficult pregnancy kept her off the lecture circuit, but after the birth of her son, Frank Morgan Valesh, in 1892, she resumed lecturing in Minnesota for the Farmers' Alliance and Populist party.

In 1896 Valesh divorced her husband, moved to New York with her son, and was hired by William Randolph Hearst as a reporter for the *New York Journal*. She later supported herself as a free-lance journalist in Washington, D.C., worked for the Democratic National Committee, assisted Samuel Gompers in editing and publishing the *American Federationist*, and in 1910 returned to New York to work for the National Women's Trade Union League. In 1911 Valesh married Benjamin F. Cross, a wealthy New Yorker, and for seven years they published the *American Club Woman*. When that marriage ended, Valesh, who had suffered a heart attack, was no longer physically able to engage in publishing or labor organizing, and she supported herself for the remainder of her life as a proofreader for the *Pictorial Review* and the *New York Times*. She retired from the *Times* in 1951 at the age of eighty-five and died in 1956.

—*MaryJo Wagner*

See Also:

Journalism, National Farmers' Alliance, Populist Party

References:

Faue, Elizabeth. "Women, Work, and Union: Eva McDonald Valesh and the Roots of Personal Ideology." Unpublished paper. University of Minnesota, 1982.

Gilman, Rhoda R. "Eva McDonald Valesh: Minnesota Populist." In *Women of Minnesota: Selected Biographical Essays*, edited by Barbara Stuhler and Gretchen Kreuter. St. Paul: Minnesota Historical Society, 1977, pp. 55–76.

Valesh, Eva McDonald. "The Reminiscences of Eva McDonald Valesh." Oral History Transcript. Columbia University, 1972.

VANDERLIP, NARCISSA COX (1880–1966), categorized as a philanthropist by the Smithsonian's National Portrait Gallery upon acceptance of her portrait in 1981, was freed by affluence from economic and household worries and directed her energies and skills toward philanthropic and reform activities. She was the wife of world-famed economist Frank Arthur Vanderlip and the mother of six children.

Born in Quincy, Illinois, she entered the University of Chicago in 1899 but after a whirlwind courtship left for marriage in her senior year. In recognition of her many endeavors on behalf of society and the university, she was granted her degree in 1933.

The family resided at their seventy-two-acre estate in Scarborough, New York, where various national and international figures were entertained through the years. They also owned a sizable ranch in California that evolved into the planned community of Palos Verdes. Wayfarer's Chapel, California, designed by Frank Lloyd Wright and dedicated in 1951, was built on land she donated.

In 1916 Vanderlip became an active supporter of woman suffrage. In 1917 she also engaged in war support efforts, including serving as an official of the national War Savings Stamps Committee and speaking across the country in support of war savings certificates. From 1919 to 1923 she served as first president of the League of Women Voters of New York State. Her advocacy activities in this role, as in other later responsibilities, were frequently reported in the *New York Times*.

She visited Japan in 1920 with her husband and a distinguished party invited by Japanese business leaders. Following the Tokyo earthquake in 1923, she raised thousands of dollars to rebuild Tsuda College for women. She also served as a trustee of, and fund-raiser for, Constantinople Women's College in Turkey. She was elected president of the board of trustees of New York Infirmary for Women and Children in 1929 and laid the cornerstone of a new infirmary building in 1953. She received the Peter Stuyvesant Award for outstanding charitable work in greater New York in 1949. Her testimony before Congress in 1954 was influential in allowing women doctors in the armed services. She was awarded a Doctor of Humane Letters degree by the Women's Medical College of Pennsylvania in 1956.

Listed in *Who's Who in America* for several years, she regularly commuted to New York to administer the affairs of the infirmary until shortly before her death at the age of eighty-six.

—Hilda R. Watrous

See Also:
League of Women Voters, Suffrage

References:

Frank A. Vanderlip Collection. Narcissa Cox Vanderlip Papers. Butler Library. Columbia University, New York.
League of Women Voters of New York State Collection. Butler Library. Columbia University, New York.
New York (City and State) Woman Suffrage Papers. Butler Library. Columbia University, New York.
New York Times, scattered articles, 1917–66.
Vanderlip Family Papers. Frank A. Vanderlip, Jr. New York.

"THE VAPORS" was the term used by Victorians to describe a form of hysteria. A woman suffering from "the vapors" was incapacitated, unable to function as those around her might expect. A fainting spell followed by bed rest was generally accepted as a recognizable illness, and the patient was excused from the rigors of daily life.

"Hysteria," meaning "uterus," had been defined by Hippocrates in ancient Greece to describe a variety of symptoms in women, all caused by the supposed wanderings of the uterus. This notion was refined by Galen, a second-century Greek physician who developed the humoral theory of medicine to refer to the vaporous emissions produced by the "wandering" uterus. As modern medicine revealed precise anatomical and physiological information about the location and functions of internal organs, these ancient theories were gradually discredited.

Discoveries about the nervous system led to new theories of women's behavior, such as mesmerism, which used trances and hypnosis to control the transmission of magnetism in the body. Ironically, neurologists' obsession with what they saw as deviant behavior and their failure to find a physiological cause promoted other theories, both psychological and cultural. Freud's analysis of hysterical women formed the basis of his psychological theories.

All of these theories about hysterical women were gender specific: They were created for women. They proliferated during the Victorian era when middle-class women's behavior was strictly governed by codes of etiquette and social expectations. When women experienced an attack of "the vapors," they both conformed to prevailing stereotypes of women as fragile, excitable creatures and escaped, however temporarily, from oppressive social situations. The "vapors" disappeared as women's roles changed and medical science developed in the twentieth century, but the cultural role they played remains, as "the vapors" were replaced by contemporary syndromes, such as neurosis, depression, and anorexia, that are cultural as well as physiological in origin.

—*Jane Crisler*

See Also:

Eating Disorders, Freudianism, Hysteria

References:

Drinka, George Frederick, M.D. *Myth, Malady and the Victorians.* New York: Simon & Schuster, 1984.

Smith-Rosenberg, Carroll. *Disorderly Conduct: Vision of Gender in Victorian America.* New York: Knopf, 1985.

Veith, Ilsa. *Hysteria: The History of a Disease.* Chicago: University of Chicago Press, 1965.

VASSAR COLLEGE was founded in 1861 with an initial gift of $400,000 by English-born brewer and businessman Matthew Vassar, who, persuaded by Baptist preacher Milo Jewett, used his fortune to build an impressive college for women in Poughkeepsie, New York. The college opened in 1865 with thirty-five students, dedicated to its founder's wish that it not be merely a female "seminary," as women's schools were then called, but rather a full college competing with the best men's colleges. Initially, however, it had to establish a preparatory department in order to raise its students to college-level work; eventually, as admissions standards increased, the preparatory school was abolished. Vassar had the largest enrollment of the early women's colleges.

Although early faculty and presidents were men, Vassar included among its faculty astronomer Maria Mitchell, the first woman to be elected to the American Academy of Arts and Science, and Dr. Alida Avery, who also served as the college's physician. In 1898 Vassar established the first chapter of Phi Beta Kappa at a women's college. Sarah Josepha Hale used her *Godey's Lady's Book* to persuade Vassar of the propriety of having female instructors at a women's college. Hannah Lyman, who as first "lady principal" was second in importance only to the president, imposed a strict regimen on students, stressing etiquette, study, and religious practices, but Vassar, unlike Mount Holyoke, did not require domestic work.

Under president James Monroe Taylor, a leading Baptist educator, Vassar grew in size and quality, the former through the largess of fellow Baptist donors, especially Charles M. Pratt of Standard Oil, and the latter through the introduction of the elective system and through faculty like Herbert Mills and Lucy Maynard Salmon. Mills introduced a course on the family in 1916, the first such course taught at a women's college; Salmon adopted the German seminar model in the 1880s, using primary sources as the basis for her history courses. In particular, Vassar gained a reputation in astronomy and physics and, later, in chemistry and psychology.

Although its founders vigorously defended Vassar's right to provide an education comparable to men's, they did not question the doctrine of separate spheres for the sexes. Women then, as later in the 1920s when specific courses were designed to educate women to their "societally defined duties," were expected to uphold moral virtue in the family and attend to the domestic side of life, especially bearing and raising children. The freshman curriculum included physiology and hygiene, courses designed to assure that education did not impair women's presumed delicate health. The early curriculum also emphasized science, especially the biological sciences. Although the sciences and the classics dominated the curriculum, the advent of the elective system brought a shift toward the social sciences and arts. In 1969 Vassar admitted its first male students.

Although never a bastion of feminism, Vassar numbers among its alumnae many distinguished graduates, among them poet Edna St. Vincent Millay, novelist Mary McCarthy, anthropologist Ruth Benedict, publisher Katharine Graham, actress Meryl Streep, and artist Nancy Graves.

—Nicholas C. Burckel

See Also:

"Seven Sisters," Women in Higher Education

References:

Herman, Debra. "College and After: The Vassar Experiment in Women's Education, 1861–1924." Diss. Stanford University, 1979.

Horowitz, Helen Lefkowitz. *Alma Mater: Design and Experience in the Women's Colleges from Their Nineteenth-Century Beginning to the 1930's.* New York: Knopf, 1984.

Newcomer, Mabel. *A Century of Higher Education for American Women.* New York: Harper, 1959.

VENEREAL DISEASE is a nonspecific descriptive of several different diseases that are almost always transmitted through sexual intercourse. The principal exceptions are infants and young children, who may acquire the disease from contaminated hands of adults, and newborn infants, who may be infected while passing through the birth canal of an infected mother. In recent years the newly discovered venereal disease Acquired Immune Deficiency Syndrome (AIDS) has also been spread through contaminated blood given by infected donors and through contaminated needles used by intravenous drug addicts.

Although sexually transmitted diseases are the most common communicable diseases found in the world, the true causes of venereal infections were not completely understood until the twentieth century. In general, venereal diseases are caused by bacteria, spirochetes, or viruses.

The most common bacterial-caused venereal disease is gonorrhea. Although complications of gonorrhea can cause sterility in both men and women, gonorrhea can be cured successfully with early detection and treatment. The response to late detection and medication is somewhat less successful. Females infected with gonorrhea may have no symptoms whatever, apparently because they build up antibodies in the genital tract.

Syphilis is caused by a spirochete, which is a spiral microorganism similar to bacteria. Like gonorrhea, syphilis can be successfully treated if detected in its earliest stages. Syphilis is known as "the great mimic" because it can be easily mistaken on a superficial examination for other diseases such as measles and other skin disorders. Additionally, some patients infected with syphilis do not develop any of the symptoms during the early stage of the disease. During the late stages of syphilis, virtually every organ or bodily system may be attacked, and some of the indications of the disease are heart problems, blindness, and brain damage. One of the earliest treatments for syphilis was the use of mercury, but, unfortunately, the cure was often worse than the disease.

The two recently discovered infections, Herpes Simplex Virus 2 (HSV 2) and AIDS, are the only significant venereal diseases caused by viruses. Herpes is a viral infection that resembles a cold sore or fever blister that is located in the genital area. Nonetheless, herpes is highly contagious and virtually incurable. Women who have cervical herpes are more prone to get cervical cancer than others. Acquired Immune Deficiency Syndrome is a viral infection that attacks the body's natural defense system. Although a sexually transmitted disease, the virus must enter the bloodstream to do its damage. To date, there is no cure for AIDS, and, as devastating as the earlier venereal diseases have been, AIDS is the one disease that has proved to be fatal in all cases.

Venereal disease has long been an issue for many in the women's movement. For example, in the 1870s Victoria Woodhull and Tennessee Claflin ran articles about venereal disease in their radical feminist newspaper, *Woodhull & Claflin's Weekly*. Like Woodhull and Claflin, those who wished to reform prostitution in the United States have also been historically concerned about venereal disease.

—D. C. Wolf

See Also:

AIDS; Prostitution; Woodhull, Victoria

References:

Cartwright, Frederick. *Disease and History*. New York: Crowell, 1972.

Crosby, Alfred. *The Columbian Exchange: Biological and Cultural Consequences of 1492*. Westport, Conn.: Greenwood, 1972.

Schofield, C. B. S. *Sexually Transmitted Diseases*. Edinburgh, Scotland: Churchill Livingstone, 1979.

VICTOR, FRANCES AURETTA FULLER (1826–1902), author and historian, is best known for her collaboration with Hubert Howe Bancroft on his multivolume series, *History of the Pacific States*. Victor wrote both volumes on Oregon; the volume on Washington, Idaho, and Montana; the volume on Nevada, Colorado, and Wyoming; and contributed to the volumes on California, the Northwest coast, and British Columbia. Her histories are notable for their blend of fact and romance. She interviewed many pioneers and also examined written documents in her efforts to write thorough, accurate accounts of the past.

Victor was born in Rome, New York, and in 1839 moved with her family to Ohio, where she attended a female "seminary," as women's schools were then known. With her younger sister Metta, Victor began to publish poems and tales locally, and in 1848 her first book, *Anizetta, the Guajira: or the Creole of Cuba*, appeared. Her literary career was postponed by her first marriage, which ended in divorce in 1862. Her second marriage, to Henry Clay Victor, whose brother edited Beadle's "dime novels," renewed her interest in writing, and she wrote several books about Nebraska farm life for that series.

In 1863 her husband's job as a navy engineer took the Victors to California, and the following year they moved to Oregon. Because her husband's work often took him away to sea, Victor turned to history, folklore, and writing. In 1870 she published *The River of the West*, an account of mountain man and Oregon pioneer Joe Meek. This work, along with subsequent publications that included a travel book, a temperance tract, poems, and short stories, brought her to the attention of Bancroft. He offered her a position on his staff, and Victor, who was widowed in 1875, accepted the job and moved to San Francisco. She remained with Bancroft until 1890, when she returned to Portland. There she revised her earlier travel book, wrote *The Early Indian Wars of Oregon*, which was commissioned by the state legislature, and published a final book of poems. Victor died in 1902, leaving a sizable body of work about the American West as her legacy to future historians.

—Sherry L. Smith

References:

Kern, Donna Casella. "Frances Fuller Victor." In *American Women Writers*, edited by Lina Muiniero. Vol. 4. New York: Ungar, 1982, pp. 299–301.

Mills, Hazel E. "Travels of a Lady Correspondent." *Pacific Northwest Quarterly* 45 (October 1954): 105–15.

Victor, Frances Fuller. *All Over Oregon and Washington*. San Francisco: J. H. Carmany, 1872.

———. *Atlantis Arisen; or, Talks of a Tourist About Oregon and Washington*. Philadelphia: Lippincott, 1891.

———. *The Early Indian Wars of Oregon*. Salem, Oreg.: F. C. Baker, 1894.

———. *East and West: or, The Beauty of Willard's Mill*. San Francisco: J. H. Carmony, 1862.

———. *The River of the West: The Adventures of Joe Meek*. Hartford, Conn.: R. W. Bliss, 1870.
———, with Hubert Howe Bancroft. *History of Nevada, Colorado and Wyoming, 1540–1888*. San Francisco: History Co., 1890.
———, with Hubert Howe Bancroft. *History of the Pacific States of North America*. San Francisco: A. L. Bancroft, 1884–1890.

The **VIETNAM WAR** (1957–75) demonstrated an increasing role for women in the American military. About 261,000 women served in the U.S. armed forces during the Vietnam era, and over 7,500 women actually participated in Vietnam. Those included 5,000 women in the army, 2,000 in the air force, 500 in the navy, and 27 in the marines. Although still denied combat roles, the majority of women in Vietnam served in nurse corps and other medical capacities. One army nurse, Sharon Lanz, was killed in a rocket attack in 1969. Other women served in administrative positions; some served as advisers to the South Vietnamese Women's Army Corps; and others helped with military intelligence,often serving as photo interpreters.

Women were also serving in Vietnam as part of the staff of the U.S. embassy and the civilian work force supporting the U.S. military, including foreign service officers, administrative personnel, librarians, and Red Cross and USO volunteers. Among the last U.S. deaths in the war were thirty-seven women civilian employees, killed in the crash of an air force evacuation transport on April 4, 1975.

American women were also active in the movement to stop the Vietnam War. Singer Joan Baez, actress Jane Fonda, civil rights activist Coretta Scott King, and many other women actively protested the war. Women were active in all the major groups trying to halt the war, including Mothers for Peace, Students for a Democratic Society, Vietnam Moratorium Committee, New Mobilization Committee to End the War in Vietnam, Vietnam Veterans Against the War, the War Resisters League, and other groups. The war protesters organized mass demonstrations such as the Moratorium Day demonstrations of October 15, 1969, organized by Marge Sklencar among others. They also attempted boycotts, sit-ins, letter-writing campaigns, theatrical and artistic displays, and traditional political lobbying and support for antiwar candidates. Their efforts were successful in shortening the war and achieving the withdrawal of American troops. Rosalynn Carter, wife of former President Jimmy Carter, served on the National Sponsoring Committee for the Vietnam War Memorial. Maya Lin, a Yale architectural student, won the national competition and designed the emotionally moving Vietnam Memorial in Washington, D.C. There is also a group working on a Vietnam Women's Memorial Project.

—Jonathan W. Zophy

See Also:

Baez, Joan; Fonda, Jane; King, Coretta Scott; McCarthy, Mary; Military Service

References:

Burns, Richard Dean, and Milton Leitenberg. *The War in Vietnam, Cambodia, and Laos, 1945–1982: A Bibliographical Guide*. Santa Barbara, Calif.: ABC-Clio, 1984.
Olson, James. *Dictionary of the Vietnam War*. Westport, Conn.: Greenwood, 1988.
Willenz, June. *Women Veterans: America's Forgotten Heroines*. New York: Continuum, 1983.
Zaroulis, Nancy, and Gerald Sullivan. *Who Spoke Up? America's Protest Against the War in Vietnam, 1963–1975*. New York: Doubleday, 1984.

VISITING NURSES. For over one hundred years, visiting nurses have been caring for the sick in their homes. Hired by an amazing assortment of church groups, charity organizations, and women's clubs, their mission has been to bring care, character, and cleanliness into the home of the sick indigent.

Most of the early visiting-nurse organizations were located in northeastern urban communities. They were small undertakings in which a few wealthy ladies hired one or two nurses. The nurses visited eight to twelve patients each day—bathing, bandaging, giving treatments, and teaching family members how to give care in their absence. The problems they encountered were usually acute, often infectious, and always complicated by the families' circumstances.

Support for the work of these nurses grew rapidly. By 1909 approximately 565 organizations across the country employed a total of 1,416 visiting nurses. Lillian Wald, founder of the Henry Street Settlement in New York City, had even convinced the Metropolitan Life Insurance Company to provide the services of trained nurses as an additional benefit to its industrial policyholders. The mutual advantages of this arrangement were rapidly apparent. "Mothers Met," as the company was affectionately called, quickly extended its nursing services across the company. Where possible, it arranged for existing visiting-nurse associations to provide the care; where that was not possible, it hired its own nurses. Three years after the service was initiated, the Metropolitan was paying for one million nursing visits each year at a cost of roughly $500,000 per year.

By this time, the work of these nurses had expanded to include a variety of preventive programs. While most of these programs originated with voluntary organizations, such as visiting nurse societies, they were eventually taken over by either boards of health or education. The new division that eventually developed meant that sick nursing would become the domain of the voluntary organizations, while the teaching of prevention would become the responsibility of the public agencies.

By the 1920s many nursing leaders were campaigning for the creation of an institutional framework that would allow these nurses to care for both the healthy and sick. Even though these views were represented in numerous demonstration projects and community studies, the ideal was never created. The legacy of this dilemma still haunts contemporary visiting nurses.

—Karen Buhler-Wilkerson

See Also:

Nursing; Wald, Lillian

References:

Brainard, Annie. *The Evolution of Public Health.* Philadelphia: Saunders, 1922.

Buhler-Wilkerson, Karen. "Left Carrying the Bag: Experiments in Visiting Nursing, 1877–1909." *Nursing Research* 36 (January/February 1987): 42–46.

———, ed. *Nursing and the Public's Health: An Anthology of Readings.* New York: Garland, 1989.

———. "Public Health Nursing: In Sickness or in Health?" *American Journal of Public Health* 75 (October 1985): 1155–61.

Fitzpatrick, Louise. *The National Organization for Public Health Nursing, 1912–1952: Development of a Practice Field.* New York: National League for Nursing, 1975.

Gardner, Mary Sewall. *Public Health Nursing.* New York: Macmillan, 1916.

Lagemann, Ellen, ed. *Nursing History: New Perspectives, New Possibilities.* New York: Teachers College, 1983.

Waters, Yassabella. *Visiting Nursing in the United States.* New York: Charities Publication, 1909.

The ***VOICE OF INDUSTRY***, published as a weekly newspaper, was the official organ of the New England Workingman's Association. Sarah Bagley, early feminist labor leader in the Lowell, Massachusetts, textile mills and president of the Lowell Female Labor Reform Association (LFLRA), was associated with the *Voice of Industry* in 1845 and 1846. She was one of a three-member publishing committee and for a brief period was its chief editor. The *Voice of Industry* became an important tool of the LFLRA with the latter's establishment of a Female Department in the *Voice* and the employment of editors who traveled to other mill towns.

At a time when women's sphere was relegated to home and hearth and it was considered a faux pas for women to speak in public or have their name in print, Bagley's ringing speeches published in the *Voice of Industry* brought attention to the plight of women, helped spearhead the ten-hour-workday movement, and paved the way for its success in 1874.

—Virginia Beattie Mattes

See Also:
Bagley, Sarah; Lowell Mill Girls

References:

Cantor, Milton, ed. *American Workingclass Culture: Explorations in American Labor and Social History*. Westport, Conn.: Greenwood, 1979.

Early, Frances H. "A Reappraisal of the New England Labour-Reform Movement of the 1840's: The Lowell Female Labor Reform Association and the New England Workingmen's Association." *Histoire Socials (Canada)* 13 (1980): 25.

Flexner, Eleanor. *Century of Struggle: The Woman's Rights Movement in the United States*. New York: Atheneum, 1959, 1974.

VOLUNTARISM. The primary vehicle for women's social and political activism throughout American history has been the voluntary association. Inspired by westward expansion, urban growth, moral decay, industrial exploitation, racial inequities, and religious faith, women of the eighteenth and nineteenth centuries donated their labor in local and national societies to promote missionary and charitable efforts, social and political reform, and personal development and transformation. By the turn of the twentieth century, the battle for the ballot engaged much of women's voluntary labor, but the attainment of suffrage in 1920 expanded rather than diminished the extent of female voluntarism.

The most well known and widely studied voluntary labors have been those performed by middle- and upper-class white women within national societies such as the General Federation of Women's Clubs, the Woman's Christian Temperance Union, the Young Women's Christian Association, the National American Woman Suffrage Association, and, more recently, the National Organization for Women. Yet the success of these societies has always rested on the labors of thousands of women in local communities. Within local communities, moreover, the true diversity and complexity of female voluntarism appeared, as black, ethnic, working-class, and/or working women established their own associations and as sibling rivalry emerged alongside sisterhood in the public domain. Less affluent or minority women were more likely to labor in associations dominated by or including men or to undertake voluntary activities, in the forms of boycotts or strikes, that did not involve permanent organization. Still, these women also established single-sex, permanent associations, such as the National Association of Colored Women.

Characterized by ideological as well as racial, ethnic, and economic diversity, female voluntarists have employed a wide range of techniques to achieve a multiplicity of goals. Petitioning, lobbying, fund raising, demonstrating, boycotting, striking, and voting have been some of the most often used strategies for voicing and visualizing women's views. Voluntarists have also attacked problems directly, e.g., through the collection and distribution of clothing, bedding, and medicine and the provision of child care, health care, and cash. Finally, through the establishment of self-help associations and public institutions such as clinics, shelters, and schools, women have voluntarily constructed much of the infrastructure of social welfare systems. Whether as an extension of women's privatized and unpaid domestic work or as a distinct form of unwaged social labor, female voluntarists placed themselves squarely in the public domain prior to obtaining the vote and expanded their efforts thereafter.

—*Nancy A. Hewitt*

See Also:
Benevolence, Social Housekeeping

References:

Baker, Paula. "The Domestication of Politics: Women and American Political Society, 1780–1920." *American Historical Review* 89 (June 1984): 620–47.

Blair, Karen J. *A History of American Women's Voluntary Organizations, 1810–1960: A Guide to Sources*. Boston: G. K. Hall, 1989.

Freedman, Estelle B. "Separatism as Strategy: Female Institution-Building and American Feminism." *Feminist Studies* 5 (1979): 512–79.

Neverdon-Morton, Cynthia. *Afro-American Women of the South and the Advancement of the Race, 1895–1925.* Knoxville: University of Tennessee Press, 1989.

Scott, Anne Firor. "On Seeing and Not Seeing: A Case of Historical Invisibility." *Journal of American History* 71 (June 1984): 7–21.

"VOLUNTARY MOTHERHOOD" was the slogan used by feminist supporters of reproduction control and women's sexual self-determination in the last third of the nineteenth century. Women's rights advocates at that time did not favor contraception, although traditional contraceptive methods (such as douches, pessaries, and coitus interruptus) were probably still in use. Nor did these feminists publicly approve of abortion, although it was widely practiced and some feminists quietly accepted its necessity if women were to have any control over their reproduction. Instead, the means voluntary-motherhood advocates proposed was abstinence. They recommended two forms of abstinence: a rhythm method (which was not likely to have been very reliable, since at this time women's ovulation cycle had not been accurately plotted), and long-term abstinence when no pregnancy was desired.

The feminist revulsion against contraception was in part a reflection of their dislike for sexual permissiveness and the exploitation of women, which they believed would result from separating sex and reproduction. Most important, however, their insistence on abstinence was their way of asserting women's right to sexual self-determination, even in marriage. The traditional view of marriage then dominant required women's sexual submission to their husbands upon demand. Even "free love" feminists, who took a more positive view of heterosexual activity than conservative "social purity" feminists, agreed that women could not begin to define their own sexual needs until they had acquired the right to reject men's sexual sovereignty over them.

After about 1910, feminists began to endorse contraception as a means of birth control. Participants in a "sexual revolution" that praised frequent heterosexual activity as conducive to health and female fulfillment, they derided as prudish the nineteenth-century feminist view that frequent intercourse was a male "need" that had been imposed on women. Thus, until the new women's history of the 1970s and 1980s, the voluntary-motherhood proponents were not taken seriously as birth control advocates.

—Linda Gordon

See Also:

Birth Control Movement, Free Love, Social Purity Movement

References:

Gordon, Linda. "Why Nineteenth-Century Feminists Didn't Support 'Birth Control' and Twentieth-Century Feminists Do: Feminism, Reproduction, and the Family." In *Rethinking the Family*, edited by Barrie Thorne. New York: Longman, 1981.

———. *Woman's Body, Woman's Right: A Social History of Birth Control in America.* New York: Viking/Penguin, 1976.

The **VOLUNTARY PARENTHOOD LEAGUE** was founded in 1919 by Mary Ware Dennett to lobby Congress for reforms in the Comstock Law that would permit birth control material to be circulated legally. "Voluntary parenthood" was the term used by Dennett as an alternative to the phrase "birth control" in her promotion of free, legal access to means for controlling fertility. By using "voluntary parenthood," Dennett stressed her conception of behavior that was chosen by citizens who made decisions on the basis of individual judgment. A former suffragist who based her struggle for women's rights on liberal principles, Dennett founded the Voluntary Parenthood League after having worked for the movement in an earlier organization in New York.

Dennett's view, like her slogan, fostered voluntary parenthood as part of the free-speech movement. However, Dennett's efforts to remove birth control from the legal definition of obscenity led Margaret Sanger to characterize Dennett as only a theoretician, removed from delivering health care to needy women. Dennett's conception of voluntary parenthood, however, stressed the idea that ordinary people should be able to get birth control information without having to rely on medical experts, so they could make their own informed decisions.

In 1919 Dennett moved to Washington after her efforts in New York to get legislators to liberalize state law were frustrated. Hoping to make a national impact, the Voluntary Parenthood League supported the congressional bill of 1923 and 1924 by gathering materials for and engaging in constant discussion with legislators. Despite the lip service of some congressmen, the topic was too politically sensitive for any chance of passage. Even some of Dennett's supporters thought the proposed legislation of her rival, Margaret Sanger, had more possibility of being moved into law. Sanger's approach had been to recommend that doctors alone should have the function of dispensing birth control information and materials, thus defusing the antagonism of the medical establishment.

The failure of the Dennett bill convinced her to leave the Voluntary Parenthood League, and the organization soon collapsed. This left Margaret Sanger as undisputed leader of the birth control movement and removed Dennett's approach to the issue. Acting as a civil libertarian, Dennett had invested faith in the power of legislation. She had insisted that laws prohibiting the circulation of birth control information should be completely and openly suppressed. The political establishment, being more realistic, refused to sponsor such a law, citing the ridicule of fellow legislators, the sensitive nature of the subject, and the organized opposition of the Catholic church. Through the VPL, Dennett disseminated information, held lectures, and insisted that information should be available to all without professional intervention. Then all could become "voluntary parents" based on their own choices. Dennett cited the case of women too far from clinics as examples of who would benefit from self-administered birth control.

As the agitation for birth control became centralized into the two rival groups, it was primarily Dennett's liberal approach that distinguished her from Sanger. Dennett believed that birth control should be decriminalized, that the principle of freedom for autonomous citizens should be fostered above all. Sanger promoted the diaphragm, which only doctors could prescribe, as preferred birth control. Although the Voluntary Parenthood League did not last long, it drew the political issues of public information and the rights of individuals into the debate over birth control.

—*Daryl M. Hafter*

See Also:

Birth Control; Comstock Law; Dennett, Mary Ware; Sanger, Margaret

References:

Gordon, Linda. *Woman's Body, Woman's Right: A Social History of Birth Control in America.* New York: Grossman, 1976.

Reed, James. *From Private Vice to Public Virtue: The Birth Control Movement and American Society Since 1830.* New York: Basic, 1978.

Sanger, Margaret. *My Fight for Birth Control.* 1931; rpt. Elmsford, New York: Maxwell Reprint, 1969.

VOTING RIGHTS for some women were achieved on a partial basis, either at the local or state level, by the turn of the century; not until the passage of the Nineteenth Amendment in 1920 were women enfranchised nationally in the United States. In the twentieth century, women experience obstruction of their voting rights less because of their gender than as members of minority and ethnic groups. The Voting Rights Acts of 1965, 1970, 1975, and 1986 are the major laws enacted by Congress to eliminate restrictions that have been used to discriminate against blacks and other minority groups. This legislation was passed in response to black demonstrations against discriminatory practices in some, mostly southern states, that prohibited them from using their constitutional right to suffrage as outlined in the Fifteenth Amendment to the U.S. Constitution. The 1965 act suspended the use of literacy and other tests used by states to discriminate. It also authorized federal registrars to register votes in any state or county where such tests had been used and where less than 50 percent of eligible voters were registered.

The Voting Rights Act of 1970: (1) included an extension of the 1965 act for five years, (2) lowered the minimum age for all elections from twenty-one to eighteen, (3) prohibited the states from disqualifying voters in presidential elections because of their failure to meet state residence requirements beyond thirty days, and (4) provided for uniform national rules for absentee registration and voting in presidential elections. In 1975 and 1986, respectively, the act was continued for seven years.

—Sue E. Strickler

See Also:

Civil Rights, Fourteenth Amendment, Nineteenth Amendment, Suffrage, Suffrage in the American West, Suffrage in the South

References:

Daniel, Robert L. *American Women in the Twentieth Century: The Festival of Life.* New York: Harcourt Brace Jovanovich, 1987.

Flexner, Eleanor. *Century of Struggle: The Woman's Rights Movement in the United States.* 2d ed. Cambridge: Harvard University Press, 1975.

Riley, Glenda. *Inventing the American Woman: A Perspective on Women's History.* Arlington Heights, Ill.: Harlan Davidson, 1986, 1987.

WAGES. Pay for women workers in America has always been less than that of their male counterparts. Most sources assume that women were paid approximately one-third to one-half the wages of men doing the same or similar work in the late nineteenth and early twentieth centuries. Consequently, unskilled women workers did not even receive subsistance wages, making them the cheapest pool of American labor. Even in exact work, where women did work identical to that of men, women were paid less. Employers often insisted that this discrepancy was legitimate, based as it was on their assumption that women were merely working for extra income, not to support themselves or a family. But this was not the case in many instances, particularly with young, single women and immigrants whose families desperately needed their wages. Other employer justifications of the wage discrepancy included women's supposed higher absenteeism, shorter working careers with a high turnover rate, lower productivity due to less physical strength, and other similar sexist biases of little validity. The economic reality was simply that women were concentrated in a few key industries as unskilled laborers and were unable to bargain effectively to improve their lot, especially since they could be easily replaced.

Over 80 percent of the working women (c. 265,000), according to the 1860 census (the first to analyze women workers), were employed in the textile industry. By 1900 women constituted one-fifth (five million) of the American labor force; by 1910, after heavy immigration, the percentage of women in the work force rose to 25 percent, with all but 9 of the 369 industries listed in federal records employing women. Despite such figures, job categories and wages were still segregated by gender, and women remained the lower paid, largely unskilled pool of American labor. Women's wages rose slowly during the early 1980s but still lagged behind those of men in all job categories. In 1983 women's median earnings were 64 percent of men's, and in 1985 they were 65 percent.

The solution of this wage problem—equal pay for men and women for equal work—was largely discredited because of the inherent assumption that women were less productive. Hence, with equal wages, employers would hire male workers, resulting in the higher unemployment of women and a worse economic situation for them than with unequal wage scales.

—Maureen Anna Harp

See Also:

Sex Equity/Comparable Worth

References:

Abbott, Edith. *Women in Industry: A Study in American History.* New York: Appleton, 1919.

Hutchins, Grace. *Women Who Work.* New York: International, 1934.

Kessler-Harris, Alice. *Out to Work: A History of Wage-Earning Women in the United States.* New York: Oxford University Press, 1982.

Smuts, Robert W. *Women and Work in America.* New York: Columbia University Press, 1959, 1971.

WALD, LILLIAN (1867–1940) was a social activist of the Progressive and New Deal era. Trained as a nurse, Wald established the nation's first nonsectarian visiting nurse service in New York City in 1893. Her program to take health services to the homes of the poor anticipated by two years the antituberculosis programs instituted by the New York health commissioner Dr. Hermann Biggs. Wald based her service in the "Nurses Settlement," first housed on Jefferson Street and subsequently moved to larger quarters at its famous Henry Street address. The Henry Street Settlement was one of the best-known centers of the settlement house movement, which encouraged social reforms to benefit the urban poor.

Wald was a friend of Jane Addams and Alice Hamilton of the Hull House settlement in Chicago and was active in labor movements, especially those devoted to the protection of women and children. In keeping with these priorities, she was a pacifist during World War I and a supporter of women's suffrage. As she learned about social issues on a practical level at Henry Street, she lobbied for political change. Her first national cause was the federal Children's Bureau. She began promoting such an agency under President Theodore Roosevelt in 1905 and saw its creation in 1912 by President William Howard Taft.

After World War I, Wald followed the same path as many other social activists who had been opposed to the war: She worked for international harmony and well-being within the framework of the Red Cross movement. In 1924 she traveled to Russia at the invitation of the government to advise the Soviets on the care of children who had been orphaned by the revolution. In the late 1920s she undertook housing reform as a major social cause, one as important as her advocacy for child welfare. Her efforts were obstructed by business and political interest groups and effectively thwarted by the Crash of 1929 and Great Depression of the 1930s.

As the daughter of a wealthy family from Rochester, New York, Wald was a personal friend of Franklin and Eleanor Roosevelt. She shared many of her concerns about social conditions with the Roosevelts and, though physically unable to work in the Roosevelt administration, she communicated frequently with New Deal policymakers on specific issues. Her stories of life at the Nurses Settlement were collected in a book entitled *Windows on Henry Street,* which became a classic text for social workers.

—Jane Crisler

See Also:

Henry Street Settlement; New Deal; Roosevelt, Eleanor; Social Work; U.S. Children's Bureau; Visiting Nurses

References:

Duffus, Robert Luther. *Lillian Wald: Neighbor and Crusader.* New York: Macmillan, 1938.

Wald, Lillian. *Windows on Henry Street.* New York: Holt, 1915; rpt. Boston: Little, Brown, 1984.

WALKER, ALICE (b. 1944), author of fiction, poetry, and essays, received the Pulitzer Prize in 1983 for *The Color Purple,* an epistolary novel centered on the plight of the black woman in the rural South. The themes of this important novel have concerned Walker throughout her writing career: the effects of racism on blacks and especially on the black woman, who is at least a double victim—in addition to the white man's oppression, she must bear the brunt of the black man's often desperate need for any sense of power and control. Thus she often suffers pain and violence at the hands of the black male. However, *The Color Purple* presents the possibility for the black woman to extricate herself from this physical and spiritual devastation, gaining independence and a sense of self through productive, self-supporting work.

Born in Eatonton, Georgia, Alice Walker, the daughter of sharecroppers, was educated in segregated public schools. She attended Spelman College (1961–63), where she became involved in the civil rights movement, and was graduated from Sarah Lawrence (B.A., 1965). She was married for nine years (1967–76) to Melvyn R. Leventhal, a civil rights lawyer; their union produced one daughter, Rebecca Grant. Early in her career, Walker worked with voter registration in Georgia, the Head Start program in Mississippi, and the New York City welfare department, activities that signaled her continuing concern with social issues. She has lectured widely and has received numerous awards, including first prize in *The American Scholar* essay contest (1967), a Radcliffe Institute Fellowship (1971–73), the Lillian Smith Award for *Revolutionary Petunias* (1973), the Rosenthal Foundation Award from the American Academy and Institute of Arts and Letters (1974), the Guggenheim Award (1977–78), and the American Book Award (1983) for *The Color Purple*, as well as the Pulitzer Prize.

Because of the commercial and critical success of *The Color Purple*, which was translated into a controversial film by Steven Spielberg in 1985, Alice Walker's earlier work has received increased attention. Most critics agree, however, that *The Color Purple* is a highly original synthesis of material to be found in earlier works such as *The Third Life of Grange Copeland* (1970), *In Love and Trouble: Stories of Black Women* (1973), and *Meridian* (1976), a novel about the civil rights movement. Most of Walker's fiction centers around black women, and for this she has been acclaimed by such feminists as Gloria Steinem, who asserts that Walker presents "the female experience more powerfully for being able to pursue it across boundaries of race and class." Walker's collection of essays, *In Search of Our Mothers' Gardens* (1983), is a compelling record of the diversity of Walker's concerns and the strength of her passion, especially as she relates in very candid fashion her own experiences as a black woman. Courageous and controversial, Alice Walker continues to provoke all readers to reexamine their assumptions. She was a frequent contributor to *Ms.* magazine during the 1970s and 1980s.

—*Sarah Gordon*

See Also:
Black Women, *Ms.* Magazine

References:

Davis, Thadious M. "Alice Walker's Celebration of Self in Southern Generations." *Southern Quarterly* 21 (Summer 1983): 39–53.

Tate, Claudia, ed. *Black Women Writers at Work.* New York: Continuum, 1983.

Walker, Alice. *The Color Purple.* New York: Harcourt Brace Jovanovich, 1982.

———. *Good Night, Willie Lee, I'll See You in the Morning.* New York: Dial, 1979.

———. *Horses Make a Landscape Look More Beautiful.* New York: Harcourt Brace Jovanovich, 1984.

———. *In Love and Trouble: Stories of Black Women.* New York: Harcourt Brace Jovanovich, 1973.

———. *In Search of Our Mothers' Gardens: A Collection of Womanist Prose.* New York: Harcourt Brace Jovanovich, 1983.

———. *Meridian.* New York: Harcourt Brace Jovanovich, 1976.

———. *Once.* New York: Harcourt Brace & World, 1968.

———. *Revolutionary Petunias and Other Poems.* New York: Harcourt Brace Jovanovich, 1973.

———. *Temple of My Familiar,* New York: Harcourt; Brace Jovanovich, 1989.

———. *The Third Life of Grange Copeland.* New York: Harcourt Brace Jovanovich, 1970.

———. *You Can't Keep a Good Woman Down.* New York: Harcourt Brace Jovanovich, 1981.

WALKER, MADAME C. J. (SARAH BREEDLOVE) (1867–1919), businesswoman and entrepreneur, was born to black sharecropper parents in Delta, Louisiana, but became the richest self-made woman in America in the early twentieth century. Orphaned at six, married at fourteen, and widowed at twenty, Walker took her daughter, A'Lelia, and went north to seek her fortune. By 1905 she was traveling from St. Louis to Denver and from Pittsburgh to Indianapolis to set up markets for her product, a secret-formula hair straightener for Afro-Americans. In 1910 she founded the Madame C. J. Walker laboratories to manufacture her products in Indianapolis. At the peak of her business, she had more than two thousand agents in the field selling her "Preparations," and the sale of Madame C. J. Walker's Hair Grower (a pomade) alone was bringing in more than $50,000 annually.

Walker moved to New York City in 1913, after her initial success. She built a Harlem town house and an adjacent school of beauty culture. In 1917 she built a $250,000 Italianate mansion designed by Vertner Tandy, a famed Harlem architect, at the exclusive Irving-on-the-Hudson. The estate became known as Villa Lewaro.

During her life Walker gave generously to charities, and during World War I she protested the War Department's segregation policy by leading a female delegation to see President Woodrow Wilson. When she died in 1919, she left sums of money to civil rights and missionary groups, as well as two-thirds of net corporate profits to charity. Her daughter, A'Lelia Walker Robinson, became famous for her flamboyant life-style, and after the death of her mother Villa Lewaro became a gathering place for Harlem's intellectual and artistic elite.

—Rose Kolbasnik Callahan

See Also:
Beauty Industry, Black Women, Business

References:

Levering, David. *When Harlem Was in Vogue.* New York: Knopf, 1984.
Ottley, Roi, and William J. Weatherby, eds. *The Negro in New York: An Informal Social History, 1626–1940.* New York: Praeger, 1969.

WALKER, MARY EDWARDS, M.D. (1832–1919), dress reformer, woman's rights advocate, suffragist, and Civil War physician, lectured and wrote on these subjects that shaped her personality and figured so prominently in reform movements of the nineteenth century. Walker's life almost metaphorically represented the currents of change women were creating and in which they were involved. A suffragist, she argued that no constitutional amendment was necessary to give women the right to vote because such right was implied in the Constitution already and all that was needed was a declaratory statement from Congress to that effect; this belief she called, in a tract by the same title, her "Crowning Constitutional Argument." When, after a number of unsuccessful court cases in the 1870s, the suffragists gave up this approach and began working instead for a constitutional amendment, Walker refused to join them and held fast to her theory.

Walker's commitment to dress reform manifested itself when she began wearing more comfortable, modified dress at the age of sixteen. She continued to experiment throughout her life with healthful dress and lectured extensively on that subject in London, Manchester, Glasgow, and Paris as well as throughout America. Her dress-reform garb, and theories on it, were less successful in America than they had been abroad, however, and her income and popularity started to wane. In order to continue earning a living and expounding her beliefs, she began appearing with the circus as a sideshow attraction, lecturing on medicine and dress reform and ultimately wearing the so-called full male attire for which she is remembered.

Walker was among the first of her sex to receive a medical degree. She graduated from Syracuse Medical College in 1855, after which she maintained a medical practice briefly with one of her classmates, Albert Miller, whom she married in 1855. It was not long, however, before she moved on to other endeavors. By 1860 she had given up her medical practice and her marriage, seeking a divorce in Iowa because New York State would not permit divorce. She moved to Washington, D.C., where she established a refuge for women who came to the city with no means and no place to stay. By 1864 she had joined the Union army and received a commission as assistant surgeon, the first woman to be so commissioned in the American armed services. Walker was rewarded for her service in the army with the Congressional Medal of Honor, the only woman in the history of the United States to receive that award.

In the fabric of Walker's life can be found the threads that also delineated the woman movement of the nineteenth century: dress reform, equal educational opportunities, women's rights, votes for women, and health and hygiene concerns. When interwoven with Walker's beliefs and behavior, they formed a tapestry that often repelled contemporaries with the vibrancy of its colors and the boldness of its design. Mary Edwards Walker, while appreciated by her closest friends and patients, was increasingly ridiculed and finally discounted by leaders, both female and male, in the worlds of politics and medicine.

—Sandra L. Chaff

See Also:

Civil War, Nineteenth-Century Dress Reform, Suffrage

References:

Lida Poynter manuscript and notes on Mary Edwards Walker, M.D. Archives and Special Collections on Women in Medicine. The Medical College of Pennsylvania, Philadelphia, Pa.

Chaff, Sandra L. "In Recognition of . . . Mary Edwards Walker (1832–1919)." *Women and Health* 6 (Spring/Summer 1981): 83–90.

———, Ruth Haimbach, Carol Fenichel, and Nina Woodside. *Women in Medicine: A Bibliography of the Literature on Women Physicians.* Metuchen, N.J.: Scarecrow, 1977.

Snyder, Charles McCool. *Dr. Mary Walker: The Little Lady in Pants.* New York: Vantage, 1962.

Werlich, Robert. "Mary Walker: From Union Army Surgeon to Sideshow Freak." *Civil War Times Illustrated* 6 (June 3, 1967): 46–49.

WAR BRIDES DURING WORLD WAR II. While historians have engaged in several invaluable and noteworthy studies of "Rosie the Riveter" and the public role of wartime women, the private and family lives of young war brides remain a relative terra incognita. There were approximately one million more marriages from 1940 to 1943 than would have been expected at prewar rates. In total, four to five million women, or 8 percent of all wives, were married to servicemen during the war years. For wives under twenty, this figure rises to 40 percent.

One of the most striking characteristics of these war brides was their mobility. Newly married women traveled thousands of miles across America to be near the military bases where their husbands were stationed. War brides on the move banded together, giving each other the inevitable baby showers, sharing information, anything to fill "the daytime void." They joined the Red Cross, drove in motor pools, worked as volunteers in hospitals and at United Service Organizations (USOs), gave blood and helped at blood centers, and took nurses' aide courses. Many war wives found temporary employment, and approximately one-half of all service wives worked for wages at some time during the war. However, it was often difficult for war brides to find jobs because employers were hesitant to hire transients. Eventually, of course, there was the inevitable move to another posting and, finally, saying good-bye to one's husband as he left for overseas.

During the long and difficult months of separation from their husbands, war brides often sought comfort and solace from each other. They enjoyed informal gatherings where they made ice cream and "swapped stories." They went to the movies together, played cards, met at the local drug store, and participated in a variety of civic and church activities. A 1944 feature story on war brides by Elizabeth Valentine, published in the *New York Times,* described these young women as "wandering members of a huge unorganized club." They recognized each other on sight, exchanged views on living quarters, allotments, and travel, and demonstrated pride in their husbands. The women in their "unorganized clubs" sustained each other and helped make the waiting "for the end of the duration" tolerable.

At present, it is only possible to speculate about the long-term and ultimate meaning of World War II on the lives of young war brides. Historians must scrutinize letters, diaries, journals, advice manuals, the popular literature, and a wide range of other materials from the 1940s and later before a significant assessment of this tantalizing question can be reached.

—*Judy Barrett Litoff*

See Also:

"Rosie the Riveter," World War II

References:

Anderson, Karen. *Wartime Women: Sex Roles, Family Relations, and the Status of Women During World War II.* Westport, Conn.: Greenwood, 1981.

Campbell, D'Ann. *Women at War with America: Private Lives in a Patriotic Era.* Cambridge: Harvard University Press, 1984.

Gorham, Ethel. *So Your Husband's Gone to War!* Garden City, N.Y.: Doubleday, 1942.

Hartmann, Susan M. *The Home Front and Beyond.* Boston: Twayne, 1982.

Klaw, Barbara. *Camp Follower: The Story of a Soldier's Wife*. New York: Random House, 1943.

Litoff, Judy Barrett, David C. Smith, Barbara Taylor, and Charles Taylor. *Miss You: The World War II Letters of Barbara and Charles Taylor*. Athens, Ga.: University of Georgia Press, 1989

Valentine, Elizabeth R. "Odyssey of the Army Wife." *New York Times Magazine* 93 (March 5, 1944): 14.

The **WAR MANPOWER COMMISSION** was established by presidential order in April 1942 to formulate plans for the use of U.S. manpower during World War II. The commission was divided into five bureaus: placement, training, program planning and review, labor utilization, and selective service. Although it issued many recommendations for manpower utilization, the WMC did not have the authority to implement its policies.

Aware that the largest reserve of available labor consisted of women, the commission stressed in its first public statement that in spite of its name, it would be very much involved in the mobilization of "women power." The WMC conducted three national campaigns to recruit women workers in 1942 and 1943. Its campaign efforts were concentrated in areas of the country with factory labor shortages and included announcements by radio personalities, special women-power short films, and posters and billboards. In the WMC's third propaganda campaign, the government asked magazine editors to picture women workers on their front covers during September 1943, with a prize being awarded for the best cover.

Because the commission was unable to force compliance with its policies, it did not have a major impact on the wartime work force. The resulting new recruits of one campaign were compared to a "ripple in a pool." Although the WMC brought attention to the need for women to join the work force, it became consumed with internal bickering, which rendered it even less effective.

—Judy Sydow Schmidt

See Also:

Mobilization, "Rosie the Riveter," World War II

References:

Kuller, H. "Manpower, McNutt and Politics." *The New Republic* 106 (June 22, 1942): 8556.

"Manpower Draft Edges Closer as New Commission Is Set Up." *Newsweek* 19 (April 27, 1942): 44.

"Policy on Recruitment, Training and Employment of Women Workers." *Monthly Labor Review* 56 (April 1943): 66–71.

Rupp, Leila J. *Mobilizing Women for War*. Princeton, N.J.: Princeton University Press, 1978.

WARREN, MERCY (OTIS) (1728–1814) was a historian, poet, and patriot. Warren was the third of thirteen children of James and Mary (Allyne) Otis of Barnstable, Massachusetts. Her father was a justice of the peace, her brother James an advocate of the king, and her husband, James Warren, a member of the Massachusetts legislature. Being surrounded by influential men of the revolutionary cause, Warren wrote political satire.

In addition to writing plays—*The Adulateur, The Motley Assembly,* and *The Group*—Warren also published poems and dramatic poems—*The Sack of Rome* and *The Ladies of Castile*. Encouraged by President John Adams to write her views of the war, Warren penned the three-volume *History of the Rise, Progress, and Termination of the American Revolution*.

Warren was a feminist who objected to the lack of female education; she had to sit in on her brothers' formal education to learn. Until age eighty-six, Warren corresponded with the political leaders of her era in the fight for freedom. She left a legacy of manuscript material for future generations about the struggle of the United States for independence.

—Ginger Rae Allee

See Also:

History of the Rise, Progress, and Termination of the American Revolution, Revolutionary War, Theater

References:

The Mercy Otis Warren Papers and Mercy Otis Warren Letter-Box. Massachusetts Historical Society, Boston.

Fritz, Jean. *Cost for a Revolution 1728–1814, Some American Friends and Enemies.* Boston: Houghton Mifflin, 1972.

Norton, Mary Beth. *Liberty's Daughters.* Boston: Little, Brown, 1980.

WASHERWOMAN'S STRIKE, ATLANTA. In the summer of 1881, laundresses, cooks, and other domestic servants in Atlanta struck for higher wages. The strike was the second attempt both to organize and insist on these wage demands, and, like the first, it originated in the Summer Hill Church, located in Atlanta's black community. Inspired by ministerial preaching and supported by both men and women, the strike lasted for several weeks in a summer during which Atlanta was preparing for the Cotton States Exposition of 1881 and simultaneously struggling with a local water shortage. Atlanta police arrested several of the strike leaders and charged them with disorderly conduct for their practice of visiting working washerwomen and urging them to join the strike effort. Initial fines did not deter the leaders nor force strikers back to work, but a combination of a city-council license fee and the practice of raising rents of washerwomen tenants helped break the strike. By mid-August, most washerwomen seemed to have returned to work.

Although it did not result in a successful organization for domestic workers, this strike action on the part of Atlanta washerwomen was nevertheless significant. The strike represented a transitional labor protest in the years after emancipation. Under slavery, work protests had frequently included spontaneous but often short-lived sabotage inspired by preachers within the slave community. During emancipation, black community cohesiveness centered on the church. The washerwoman's strike was at once a spontaneous reaction to poor working conditions and was at the same time inspired by those at the center of the black community. Moreover, the strike symbolically targeted the servant occupations that seemed so much an extension of slavery. Black women, joined by black men, were protesting not just the wages for their work but their perception that emancipation and migration to the cities had not led to a "new South" but to a transfer of the "old slavery." Strikes such as this were not uncommon among black men, and those among black turpentine laborers, stevedores, longshoremen, and others deserve parallel and comparative consideration.

—*Thomas F. Armstrong*

See Also:

Afro-American Domestic Workers

References:

Atlanta *Constitution.* July–August, 1881.

Jones, Jacqueline. *Labor of Love/Labor of Sorrow.* New York: Basic, 1985.

Rabinowitz, Howard. *Race Relations in the Urban South, 1865–1900.* New York: Oxford University Press, 1978.

WASHINGTON, MARGARET MURRAY (1865–1925). Born March 9, 1865, in Macon, Mississippi, Margaret Murray attended the newly created public schools there before going to college at Fisk University in Nashville. After graduation in 1889 she became "lady principal" at Tuskegee Institute in Alabama. Three years later she became the third wife of Booker T. Washington and Director of Industries for Girls at the institute. Better educated than her husband, she became both his partner at the institute and an independent force for black advancement.

A believer in the power of women to bring needed change, she founded the Tuskegee Women's Club and became president of the newly organized National Federation of Afro-American Women in 1895. The next year, the federation merged with another group to form the National Association of Colored Women, of which she became president in 1912. As president, she began the publication of the *National Notes* and urged women to go into business: "There are the professional and business women whose interests are being pushed so that the woman who is inclined to be independent of her father and brothers in her struggle for a living may not be swallowed up."

She was particularly distressed about the plight of young people in adult penitentiaries and was a major force in organizing a reform school for boys at Mount Meigs, Alabama, in 1902 and the Reform Institution for Delinquent Colored Girls of Alabama in 1904. Until her death on June 4, 1925, she remained active in the cause of better conditions for blacks, serving as a member of the Commission on Interracial Cooperation, which was headquartered in Atlanta, Georgia, and established to improve communication between the races. She also authorized three publications on parenting and improving home conditions.

—Linda O. McMurry

See Also:

Black Women's Clubs, National Association of Colored Women, Prison Reform, Tuskegee Institute

References:

Margaret Murray Washington Papers. Tuskegee Institute Archives. Tuskegee, Ala.

Harlan, Louis R. *Booker T. Washington: The Making of a Black Leader, 1856–1901.* New York: Oxford University Press, 1972.

———. *Booker T. Washington: The Wizard of Tuskegee, 1901–1915.* New York: Oxford University Press, 1983.

WATERS, ETHEL (1900–77), singer, comedienne, and actress, was born illegitimate, her twelve-year-old mother a victim of rape, in a slum in Chester, Pennsylvania. She grew up emotionally and economically deprived, often stealing and hanging around street gangs. At an early age she embraced the stage as a means of escape and began performing a vaudeville act as early as 1909. Later she toured on the Theatre Owner's Booking Association circuit, which provided entertainment for all-black audiences.

She began working in Harlem nightclubs in the 1920s and became popular with white audiences, who dubbed her "the Ebony Comedienne." She also became the first female to record the blues, eventually recording twenty-six titles for the Black Swan label and, later, forty-seven titles for Columbia. In the 1930s she developed into the first consequential female jazz singer. Among her famous songs were "Dinah," "Heat Wave," "Suppertime," and her signature song, "His Eye Is on the Sparrow."

Waters also appeared on Broadway, beginning with all-black revues like *Africana* (1927), *Lew Leslie's Blackbirds* (1930), and *Rhapsody in Black* (1931). In 1939 she became the first black woman to appear on Broadway in a dramatic role, in *Mamba's Daughter.* She played the loving and faithful wife, Petunia, in the musical *Cabin in the Sky* (1940), a role she repeated in the film. In 1949 she played the grandmother in the film *Pinky.* Perhaps her greatest role was that of Berenice in *Member of the Wedding* (1950), for which she received the New York Drama Critics Award. She was nominated for an Academy Award as best supporting actress for the same role in the film version. She starred in the short-lived television series *Beulah* and made her last film, *The Sound and the Fury,* in 1958. Waters continued to perform into her seventies, appearing in television roles, stock, and revivals. After a religious experience in the late 1950s, she frequently appeared with the Billy Graham Crusade.

—Rose Kolbasnik Callahan

See Also:

Black Women, Jazz, Popular Vocalists, Theater

References:

Mellers, Wilfred. *Angels of the Night: Popular Female Singers of our Time.* Oxford, U.K.: Basil Blackwell, 1986.

Oakley, Giles. *Devil's Music.* New York: Taplinger, 1977.

Waters, Ethel. *His Eye Is on the Sparrow.* Westport, Conn.: Greenwood, 1978.

WAVES. Although U.S. law prohibited women from serving in the armed forces, during World War I the navy found a loophole and recruited women to serve as telephone operators and clericals. By the war's end, 11,275 yeomen (F)s had served with the navy and marines, earning high marks for their contributions. Despite their success, Congress, in the 1925 Naval Reserve Act, plugged the loophole, and when World War II broke out the navy had to seek new legislation in order to recruit women.

The first women's corps was authorized for the army by Congress in May 1942, but the legislation initially granted only partial military status, and women became members of the Women's Army Auxiliary Corps (WAAC). The navy was most reluctant to allow women in, but realizing that Congress was going to draft such legislation, its leaders designed their own program, which made women recruits comparable with male reservists, not members of a nebulous auxiliary. The WAVES (Women Accepted for Volunteer Emergency Service) were created on July 30, 1942 (Public Law 689). At times, WAVES also seemed to stand for Women Are Very Essential Sometimes. In all, one hundred thousand women served as WAVES during World War II, but none were allowed overseas. A handful were stationed in Alaska and Hawaii by the end of the war. The largest group of enlisted women performed clerical and administrative assignments. In all, thirty-eight ratings were opened to WAVES. Approximately one-third were assigned to naval aviation; many became trainers of beginning pilots, weather watchers, and parachute packers.

The first WAVES director was Mildred McAfee, who was the president of Wellesley College before and after the war. "Captain Mac," as she was affectionately called by the women, quickly became a legend and is still active in college circles and civic organizations today.

With the passage of the Women's Armed Services Integration Act in June 1948, the WAVES were made a permanent part of the navy. In the 1970s, the navy and army debated whether to maintain a separate corps for women (the Navy Nurse Corps had both men and women in it since the 1950s) or to abolish the WAVES. After long debate, all "separate but equal" women's corps were abolished in 1978. Beginning in 1976, women were allowed to attend the U.S. Naval Academy at Annapolis, Maryland.

While the navy has come a long way from believing that any woman aboard a ship was bad luck and now has women admirals who command both men and women, the debate continues on whether to allow women to serve in combat roles. Legislation specifically prohibiting women from such roles continued in force into the late 1980s.

—D'Ann Campbell

See Also:

Marine Corps, Women's Reserve; Military Service; SPARS; Women's Army Auxiliary Corps; Women's Army Corps

References:

Alsmeyer, Marie Bennett. *The Way of the Waves.* Conway, Ark.: Hamba Books, 1981.

Bureau of Naval Personnel, Historical Section. "Women's Reserve." Washington, D.C., 1946.

Gildesleeve, Virginia Crocheron. *Many a Good Crusade.* New York: Macmillan, 1954.

Godson, Susan. "The Waves in World War II." *Naval Institute Proceedings* 107 (December 1981): 46.

Hancock, Joy Bright. *Lady in the Navy: A Personal Reminiscence.* Annapolis, Md.: Naval Institute, 1972.

WEBER, LOIS (1882–1939), one of the highest-paid directors in the American film industry during her heyday, directed dozens of films between 1912 and 1927. Her popularity and facility with screen technique "was as characteristic to audiences as that of Griffith or DeMille," according to one film historian.

After touring as a concert pianist and then serving with the Salvation Army, Weber decided to try the stage on the advice of an uncle. She married the actor-manager of a road company, Phillips Smalley. The couple found work in the then somewhat disreputable (for actors) motion picture business, playing leads, writing scripts, and directing segments of films at Rex Pictures, the New York–based organization headed by Edwin S. Porter. In 1912, after Porter's departure, the two took over Rex, which was then releasing nationally through the Universal combine.

Weber was clearly the dominant member of the partnership, which she later claimed produced between two hundred and four hundred films. Fewer than fifty survive today, but these show her experimenting with a full range of visual styles and techniques in the service of her favored genre, the modern morality tale. After Universal built Weber her own studio in Hollywood during World War I, she was able to supervise every detail of her productions; she was known for working closely with her stock company of actors (an example, along with her choice of melodramatic forms, of the extent to which the touring theatrical road-company experience had impressed itself upon her).

Weber's work through 1921 showed a flair for spectacular visual treatments of contemporary social themes; her *Where Are My Children?* (1916) treated the then-taboo subject of birth control, and several other titles suggest that Weber grappled with issues of the day. Her flair for the sensational along with the serious—including the use of frontal nudity in the well-publicized *Hypocrites* (1914)—made her films extraordinarily popular. At Universal, Weber was eventually paid $2,500 a week; her services, however, were coveted by the expanding concerns of Jesse Lasky, and in 1920 Famous Players–Lasky (now Paramount) hired her at $50,000 a picture plus one-third of the profits. However, Weber released only three titles under the Lasky banner; two more were released by a small independent company. Weber's morality plays, in the post–World War I era, seem to have gone quickly out of favor with the public. She directed only a few more films before her death, though one of her later projects was a grandiose plan for the use of films in education.

Like other female directors, Weber constantly fought her studio's publicity machinery, which focused attention, in her case, on her so-called woman's touch. But no amount of patronizing could obscure the fact noted by a contemporary interviewer: "She is doing a lion's share toward broadening the horizon of women's endeavors, and her brilliant accomplishments should act as a spur for the ambitious but halting ones who long for the freedom of self-expression found in a vocation of their own."

—Kevin Jack Hagopian

See Also:

Arzner, Dorothy; Blaché, Alice Guy; Woman's Film

References:

Heck-Rabi, Louise. "Lois Weber: Moralist Moviemaker." In *Woman Filmmakers: A Critical Reception*, edited by Louise Heck-Rabi. Metuchen, N.J.: Scarecrow, 1984, pp. 53–71.

Koszarski, Richard. "The Years Have Not Been Kind to Lois Weber." In *Women and the Cinema*, edited by Karyn Kay and Gerald Peary. New York: Dutton, 1977, pp. 146–52.

"Lois Weber: Whose Role Is It Anyway?" *British Film Institute Monthly Film Bulletin* 49 (May 1982): 100.

The **WELFARE RIGHTS MOVEMENT** in the United States grew out of the civil rights movement of the 1960s. It combined traditional concepts of social welfare with the philosophy of the civil rights movement that citizens are entitled to a minimum level of material comfort. In the 1960s studies of social inequality focused upon populations that had traditionally been disadvantaged in American society due to past history and prejudice: recent urban immigrants who lived in isolated ghettos, and the rural poor who did not have access to medical, educational, and social services. In many instances, poverty was exacerbated by racial prejudice.

President John F. Kennedy first addressed the problem of poverty with the Food Stamp Program. His effort was succeeded by the more ambitious War on Poverty, initiated by the administration of President Lyndon B. Johnson in 1964. Though flawed in its conception and deprived of funding by the escalating Vietnam War, the War on Poverty reflected the embarrassment of an affluent, technologically advanced society that could not eradicate hunger and suffering. As the civil rights movement developed in the latter half of the decade, welfare concerns meshed with demands for justice in an inequitable society.

In the 1970s and 1980s the concerns of welfare rights activists moved beyond entitlement to address fundamental issues of human dignity: for example, the right of welfare recipients to receive prompt payment of benefits without humiliating treatment by social service personnel. The massive expansion of individuals receiving government benefits has made welfare recipients an influential political presence. The geometric increase in middle-class recipients of social security benefits has been a driving force in political activism on a national level, while the traditionally disenfranchised black and Hispanic populations have gained political influence at the municipal level. New and prominent issues of the late 1980s are the seemingly permanent underclass of welfare recipients that has not responded to ameliorative measures and the "feminization of poverty," a result of wage discrimination, welfare policies, and divorce law that has had a disproportionate effect upon women and children.

—*Jane Crisler*

See Also:

Civil Rights, Female-headed Households, Mothers' Pensions

Reference:

Leiby, James. *A History of Social Welfare and Social Work in the United States*. New York: Columbia University Press, 1978.

THE WELL OF LONELINESS (1928) is the most famous of Radclyffe Hall's novels despite having been banned in the author's homeland, England, until 1949. This novel was considered shocking because it was the story of a lesbian's struggle to be accepted by the world for her strengths and talents instead of being judged on the basis of her sexual orientation. *The Well* was widely thought to be autobiographical, because its main character, Stephen Gordon, was an exact contemporary of Hall: Both were very masculine looking lesbians, both were novelists, and both demanded the right to live the lives that nature had laid out for them.

In the novel, Stephen's homosexuality was explained as being normal for her and a fact that she was unable to change, since she was born a lesbian, although such a change would make her life easier. During World War I Stephen worked as an ambulance driver on the western front; there she met and fell in love with a fellow driver, Mary Llewellyn. Mary returned Stephen's love; they lived together as if married and were in many ways a normal couple, except that they were both women. By focusing on the normal aspects of their lives together, Hall was asking her readers to broaden their attitudes about homosexuality.

The Well has continued to be an important book on many levels. Its honesty and compassion toward lesbianism urge its readers to accept alternate orientation as a normal, even divinely directed occurrence. *The Well* also has strong female characters whom Hall used to stress the many contributions made by all kinds of women in wartime England and France.

The publishing history of the book was also interesting. *The Well* appeared in America on the heels of famous obscenity rulings and was thus drawn immediately into the legal storms that had been brewing in New York and Massachusetts in the 1920s. In 1927 the number of books banned in Boston numbered between sixty and one hundred. Upton Sinclair, William Faulkner, and many others were subjected to legal and extralegal banning of their works that year. However, the literati had developed into an effective coalition, often capable of defending books and magazines against arbitrary censorship, by the time Hall's book was published in the United States and an obscenity charge was both leveled and decided against Hall's American publishers, Covici-Friede, in February 1929 by Judge Hyman Bushel of the New York City Magistrate's Court. Judge Bushel ruled that *The Well of Loneliness* "tends to debauch public morals." In April of that year, Judge Bushel's decision was overturned by a three-judge appellate court, which found that the book did little to promote and much to discourage a life of "perversion."

The author of several very successful books of poetry, Radclyffe (Marguerite Antonia) Hall (1880–1943) initially was best known for her *Songs of Three Counties* (1913), which had many of its poems set to music during World War I because of their fierce nationalism. Hall had written several mildly successful novels before writing the one that won for her a place in serious literary society. *Adam's Breed* (1926) was awarded both the Prix Femina and the James Tait Black Award for the best English novel of the year in 1927, an achievement equaled only once before in the history of these highly esteemed prizes.

Radclyffe Hall was also well known both in the United States and England for her work with the English Society for Psychical Research, although her Roman Catholic faith forbade the practice of spiritualism on any but scientific levels. For several years Hall worked to legitimize spiritualism by fully documenting hundreds of seances and psychic experiments, attaining in the end only marginal success.

However, Hall remains best remembered for her candid portrayal of lesbians in *The Well of Loneliness,* which has continued to sell well in the United States since 1929, as well as in Great Britain since 1949, and has been translated into many languages.

—*Carol M. Waterloo*

See Also:

Lesbianism, Obscenity

References:

Baker, Michael. *Our Three Selves.* London: Morro, 1985.

Dickson, Lovat. *Radclyffe Hall at the Well of Loneliness.* New York: Scribner, 1975.

Ernest, Morris L., and Alan U. Schwartz. *Censorship: The Search for the Obscene.* New York: Macmillan, 1964, p. 78.

Hall, Radclyffe. *The Well of Loneliness.* New York: Covici-Friede, 1928.

Lewis, Felice Flanery. *Obscenity and Law.* Carbondale: Southern Illinois University Press, 1976.

Ormrow, Richard. *Una Troubridge: The Friend of Radclyffe Hall.* London: Carroll-Graf, 1985.

Troubridge, Una. *The Life and Death of Radclyffe Hall.* London: Hammond and Hammond, 1961.

WELLESLEY COLLEGE, a leading women's college located in Wellesley, Massachusetts, was founded in 1875 by Henry F. Durant, a Harvard-educated trustee of Mount Holyoke College and champion of women's higher education. Durant was dedicated to the principle of giving young women a collegiate education substantially the same as that given young men, an idea that was sharply criticized at that time. Duran also believed that a woman's college should have a largely female faculty, both to provide women students with positive role models and to give academic women opportunities for employment. Wellesley quickly became recognized as one of the most important women's colleges in the country.

From the very start, tuition and board at Wellesley were high compared with other colleges and universities across the country, and as a consequence the college attracted a rather elite clientele. Because of its explicit commitment to equality in women's education, Wellesley also attracted a number of older women students interested in receiving first-rate collegiate instruction. For the most part, the Wellesley curriculum was similar to that offered at men's colleges in this period, with heavy emphasis on classical languages, science, and literature. Later, courses on home economics and related issues (such as "consumerism"), hygiene, and physical education were added as Wellesley and other women's colleges responded to charges that college education was harmful to the health of young women and that it was responsible for lower marriage rates among educated women. Wellesley also offered professional instruction in education and helped students interested in medical careers to prepare for medical school.

Perhaps the most important contribution of Wellesley—and other leading women's colleges in this period—was to provide an opportunity for bright young women to learn from the nation's first generation of professionally trained female scholars. Offering a haven for talented women academics who often found it impossible to find appointments elsewhere, Wellesley soon developed distinction in a number of fields, the most prominent being botany and psychology. Historian Patricia Palmeri has described Wellesley as an "Adamless Eden" in the first five decades of its development, a place where women could pursue their intellectual interests in a context of genuine feminine fellowship. More recently, Wellesley has eschewed the example of other women's colleges that have turned coed, choosing instead to develop further its distinctive identity as a woman's college. In recent years, Wellesley has become an important center for scholarship in the newly developing field of women's studies.

—John L. Rury

See Also:

"Seven Sisters," Women in Higher Education, Women's Studies

References:

Horowitz, Helen Lefkowitz. *Alma Mater: Design and Experience in the Women's Colleges from Their Nineteenth-Century Beginnings to the 1930s.* New York: Knopf, 1984.

Kingsley, Florence. *The Life of Henry F. Durant.* New York: Century, 1924.

Palmieri, Patricia. "Here Was Fellowship: A Social Portrait of Academic Women at Wellesley College, 1880–1920." *History of Education Quarterly* 23 (Summer 1983): 195–214.

WELLS-BARNETT, IDA B. (1862–1931), antilynching crusader, journalist, lecturer, and community organizer, was a dynamic fighter against social injustice throughout her life. Born in Holly Springs, Mississippi, she was the eldest of eight children born to Lizzie Bell, a cook, and James Wells, a carpenter, a son of his slave master, and a community leader after emancipation. Wells-Barnett began adulthood in 1878 when she lost both parents and a brother to the yellow fever epidemic, leaving her as the eldest to care for the remaining siblings. With help from the black community, she trained as a teacher at Rust College in Holly Springs and taught school, first in Holly Springs and then in Memphis, Tennessee, to support herself and her siblings, who were eventually split up among relatives.

She sued a railroad over racially-segregated seating, criticized black education under the pen name Iola, and eventually became editor and part owner of the Memphis newspaper *Free Speech and Headlight.* After the 1893 lynching of three black men in Memphis, she became a crusader against lynching: researching, writing, lecturing, and fund raising to abolish such racial atrocities. She was a leader in almost every racial and women's organization: a founder of the Ida B. Wells Club, the first black women's civic club in Chicago; a leader in the Afro-American Council; founder of the Alpha Suffrage Club to promote women's suffrage among black women; founder of the Negro Fellowship League as a community center for black men; a leader in the National Association of Colored Women; and a founder of the National Association for the Advancement of Colored People.

Prominent as an initiator of social reforms, Wells-Barnett had difficulty accepting opinions different from her own. Her difficulties in compromising or cooperating with others led to her withdrawal from organizations and coalitions. Thus, many of her activities failed to become institutionalized and to achieve results without her constant efforts. Her marriage to Chicago lawyer Ferdinand Barnett produced two sons and two daughters and a family life that she incorporated into her civic role to improve racial conditions in America. She died of uremia in 1931, somewhat embittered at the lack of concrete results from her years of labor.

—Dorothy C. Salem

See Also:

Black Women's Clubs, National Association for the Advancement of Colored People, National Association of Colored Women

References:

Dannett, Sylvia. *Profiles of Negro Womanhood.* Chicago: Educational Press, 1964.

Duster, Alfreda, ed. *Crusade for Justice: The Autobiography of Ida B. Wells.* Chicago: University of Chicago Press, 1970.

Holt, Thomas C. "The Lonely Warrior: Ida B. Wells-Barnett and the Struggle for Black Leadership." In *Black Leaders of the Twentieth Century,* edited by John Hope Franklin and August Meier. Urbana: University of Illinois Press, 1982, pp. 39–61.

Loewenberg, Bert, and Ruth Bogin, eds. *Black Women in Nineteenth-Century American Life.* University Park: Pennsylvania State University Press, 1976.

Salem, Dorothy. "To Better Our World: Black Women in Organized Reform, 1890–1920." Diss. Kent State University, 1985.

WELTY, EUDORA ALICE (b. 1909) is a short-story writer, novelist, and the recipient of numerous honors, including, among others, a Guggenheim Fellowship (1942), an appointment to the National Council of the Arts (1972), a Pulitzer Prize for *The Optimist's Daughter* (1973), the National Medal of Literature and Medal of Freedom (1981), and the Modern Language Association Commonwealth Award (1984). Welty's fictional portrayal of rural and small-town life, principally in her beloved Mississippi, ranks her with the preeminent writers of the Southern Renaissence. Her works convey and explore the enigma of human personality, the ineffable richness of the inner self and its experience of others. As she puts it, "relationship is a pervading and changing mystery; it is not words that make it so in life, but words have to make it so in a story."

Welty's short stories and novels focus upon loneliness and the near incommunicability of awareness of self. Most of these works are set amidst the speech and customs of the Natchez Trace region during the last hundred years. Welty's lifelong residence in the Jackson, Mississippi, house of her birth reflects her artistic concern with the use of "place" in fiction. Locale is a matrix for examining her characters' social and personal identities, as well as their unstinting, hope-filled search for stability and order in the pastoral tradition, relying on perpetuating their agrarian-based values to counteract the looming cultural chaos of an urban industrialized society. Her uniquely southern vision of twentieth-century America emerges in her brilliant use of style, especially in the surrealistic and impressionistic passages of her novels, to convey how memory and storytelling nurture the collective identity so vital to the survival, as a clan, of the dynastic plantation families in the Trace region.

To stem the tide of cultural mutability, Welty's tribelike families employ the restorative force of love to create an insular world, an arcadian domain superior to the wider world of outsiders. This family narcissism usually fixates upon a younger member who embodies southern hubris and indomitable will (a spoiled belle or dashing cavalier) as a totem for the tribe's veneration. The resultant family circle is a social paradox, a tightly bound group of eccentrics wherein only the individual can achieve intimacy, via an interior dialogue within the conflicting self, and never with another relative. In Welty's ancestral mansions, the family thrives upon an agape of busyness, celebrating the glories of belonging, of protectiveness, of preserving anachronistic customs and tales that defy time and social change, shielding their charmed circle from the onslaught of involvement with each other in the present-day, problematic world.

Welty's short stories employ complex narrative voices and a lyric quality calculated to evoke the mystery she perceives at the heart of the human psyche. The range of settings and subjects of these tales seeks to explore, via the quest or journey motif, how individuals struggle toward epiphanic beachheads via the hard-won confrontations of relationships that draw them from the beckoning ocean of self.

—Hugh J. Ingrasci

References:

Vande Kieft, Ruth M. *Eudora Welty: Revised Edition.* Boston: G. K. Hall, 1987.

Welty, Eudora. *The Collected Stories of Eudora Welty.* New York: Harcourt Brace Jovanovich, 1980.

———. *Delta Wedding.* New York: Harcourt Brace, 1946.
———. *The Eye of the Story: Selected Essays and Reviews.* New York: Random House, 1971.
———. *The Optimist's Daughter.* New York: Random House, 1970.

WHARTON, EDITH (1862–1937), author, was born Edith Newbold Jones, the youngest of three children, to wealthy New York parents. In 1885 she married Edward Robbins Wharton, but the marriage soon soured. The couple lived together to preserve appearances until 1913, when she divorced her husband because of his mental instability. They had settled in Paris in 1907, and she remained in Europe for the rest of her life.

Wharton wrote a book of poetry at age sixteen, but it was ten years later when she began her writing career, a career that would make her not only one of the most prolific authors in the world, but one of the highest paid as well. Wharton was a realist, concerned with American social life and social change, observing it acutely, identifying every detail of the settings within which her characters moved. Many of her novels and stories are set against the background of affluent American society and deal with the uncertainties in private relations between men and women. To Wharton, moral commitment was absolute. To behave immorally endangered society, and, to Wharton, society was all there was. Along with Willa Cather, Wharton is considered to be Henry James's disciple, but although they were friends and Wharton listened to his advice, her reputation was made entirely on the basis of her own considerable literary talent.

Wharton's first book was a collection of short stories she had published in *Harper's*, the *Century*, and *Scribner's* since 1891, called *The Greater Inclination* (1899). Her next book, a novelette, was *The Touchstone* (1900). Her first long novel, *The Valley of Decision* (1902), was followed in 1903 by another novelette, *Sanctuary*, and another short-story collection, *The Descent of Man* (1904). *The House of Mirth* (1905) sold over 140,000 copies within a year and a half of publication and brought the author international recognition. It was followed by *The Fruit of the Tree* (1907), *Ethan Frome* (1911), *The Custom of the Country* (1913), and *Summer* (1917).

During World War I Wharton was heavily involved in relief work, which she describes in *Fighting France, from Dunkerque to Belfort* (1915). The war also became a subject of her fiction in *The Marne* (1918) and *A Son at the Front* (1923). Published in 1920, *The Age of Innocence* won the Pulitzer Prize, making Wharton the first woman to win it. *The Glimpses of the Moon* followed in 1922. In 1923 she became the first woman to receive an honorary doctorate from Yale. *Old New York* (1924), a collection of novellas, preceded three of Wharton's novels that deal with relationships between parents and children: *The Mother's Recompense* (1925), *Twilight Sleep* (1927), and *The Children* (1928). *Hudson River Bracketed* (1929) and its sequel, *The Gods Arrive* (1932), deal with the struggles of an artist to find his place in society. Her last novel, *Buccaneers* (1938), was left unfinished.

Although she wrote novels, novellas, poetry, and travel books, Wharton was most at home with the short story. She wrote eighty-six of them in her life, and her book *The Writing of Fiction* (1925) is dedicated to a study of the form. In 1934 Wharton's biography, *A Backward Glance*, was published. Wharton died of a stroke on August 11, 1937.

—*Victoria L. Shannon*

References:

Lewis, R. W. B. *Edith Wharton.* New York: Harper & Row, 1975.
Nevius, Blake. *Edith Wharton: A Study of New Fiction.* Berkeley: University of California Press, 1953.
Wharton, Edith. *Age of Innocence.* New York: Appleton, 1920.
———. *A Backward Glance.* New York: Appleton-Century, 1934.
———. *The Best Short Stories of Edith Wharton.* Introduction by Wayne Andrews. New York: Scribner, 1958.
———. *Ethan Frome.* New York: Scribner, 1911.
———. *House of Mirth.* New York: Scribner, 1905.

WHEATLEY, PHILLIS (c. 1753–84) was a poet known for occasional verse written in the English neoclassical manner. Her talents were recognized while she was a slave owned by John and Susannah Wheatley. She composed more than one hundred poems, half of which were published during her lifetime.

The small African girl was judged to be about eight years old when she was sold in Boston in 1761 to Mrs. Wheatley, wife of a prominent Boston merchant-tailor, for a personal servant. The Wheatley's teenage daughter, Mary, taught her English. Phillis then studied the Bible, classical history, mythology, and Latin. Although a slave, she was treated like a family member, with a room in the main house and only light household chores. Her first poem was published in 1767, and in 1770 an elegy on the death of English evangelist George Whitefield brought her international attention. She joined the Old South Congregational Church in 1771 as a communicant, a privilege not generally extended to slaves. Her reputation as an occasional poet grew as Boston's elite requested her services. Yet her proposal in 1772 to publish a book of poetry failed.

Wheatley sailed to England for her health in May 1773. Preceded by her reputation, she became a London favorite. There, a proposal for a volume of poetry met with success. But by the time *Poems on Various Subjects, Religious, and Moral* was published in September, Wheatley had returned to her dying mistress. After she was back in America, at the request of English acquaintances she was released from slavery.

In 1776 her poem praising George Washington appeared in two publications. Shortly after Mr. Wheatley's death in 1778, Phillis married John Peters, a free black. In 1779 she circulated a proposal for a volume of poetry and letters that was rejected. She died December 5, 1784; her third and last living child followed shortly and was buried with her in an unmarked grave.

—Therese L. Lueck

See Also:
Black Women

References:

Renfro, G. Herbert. *Life and Works of Phillis Wheatley: Containing Her Complete Poetical Works, Numerous Letters, and a Complete Biography of this Famous Poet of a Century and a Half Ago.* 1916; rpt. Freeport, N.Y.: Books for Libraries, 1970.

Robinson, William H. *Phillis Wheatley and Her Writings.* New York: Garland, 1984.

The **WHITE ROSE MISSION** was established in 1897 in New York City and incorporated in 1898. The mission, a nondenominational institution, provided lodging and a variety of self-help activities for black women. It aided in their adjustment to the city and their development of the skills necessary to survive in an urban environment. It offered practical courses in sewing, cooking, and dressmaking and maintained a job placement service. A settlement house—one of many urban centers of social reform where educated young people lived and worked among the poor—it provided community services such as mothers' meetings, a kindergarten, and a library of books on black history.

Victoria Earle Matthews, president of the Woman's Loyal Union, was the founder of the White Rose Mission and its superintendent for the first decade of its existence. The mission offered lodging to women from age fifteen to forty-five and provided accommodations for one night to six weeks to all women seeking shelter, regardless of their ability to pay the weekly fee of $1.25. It maintained travelers' aid representatives in New York and Norfolk to guide girls and women coming from the South in search of employment, to protect them from fraudulent employment agencies that exploited them and even forced some into prostitution.

The work of the mission was conducted by black women who volunteered their services and taxed themselves when increasing funds were needed for expanded community services, for travelers' aid, and for larger quarters. Contributions and support came from black and white donors, including Booker T. Washington, Grace Hoadley Dodge, Mrs. William H. Baldwin, and Mrs. C. P. Huntington. After occupying a series of temporary locations in the city, the White Rose Home relocated to permanent quarters on West 136th Street in 1918.

—*Floris Barnett Cash*

See Also:

Black Women, Black Women's Clubs, Settlement House Movement

References:

Best, Lasalle. "History of the White Rose Mission and Industrial Association." WPA Research Paper, n.d. Schomburg Collection. New York Public Library.

Cash, Floris Barnett. *Black Women of Brooklyn: Seventeenth Century to the Present.* New York: Brooklyn Historical Society, 1985.

———. "Womanhood and Protest: The Club Movement Among Black Women, 1892–1922." Diss. State University of New York, Stony Brook, 1986.

Lewis, Mary. "The White Rose Home and Industrial Association." *The Messenger* 7 (January 1925): 158.

Meier, August. *Negro Thought in America, 1880–1915.* Ann Arbor: University of Michigan Press, 1978.

WHITNEY, ADELINE DUTTON TRAIN (1824–1906), who published under the name Mrs. A. D. T. Whitney, was a well-known novelist from the early 1860s until her death. Although she wrote poems, short stories, and nonfiction, she was primarily a writer of stories about girls for an adult as well as juvenile audience.

Whitney was the daughter of a wealthy Boston merchant and shipowner. She attended George B. Emerson's school, and she credited him with developing her skill in Latin and English composition. Like his famous cousin Ralph Waldo Emerson, George Emerson encouraged individuals to use their talents and fulfill their potentialities. In 1843, when she was nineteen, she married Seth Whitney, an army officer, and lived for the rest of her life in Milton, Massachusetts. She had four children and began to write when the youngest was eight.

Mother Goose for Grown Folks (1859), a collection of parodies of well-known poems (Mother Goose, for example, spoke as Brahma), attracted attention; her *The Boys at Chequasset* (1862) was written primarily to amuse her children. Her real career began in 1863 with the publication of *Faith Gartney's Girlhood*, which sold over three hundred thousand copies in its first year and made her famous. She followed it with *The Gayworthys* (1865). In these two novels she established the subject and treatment she would repeat with modifications in all her stories: the initiation of a young girl into the world of adult responsibility. Whitney was a deeply religious woman, and her concept of woman's role was fairly traditional, if glorified. While recognizing that women to whom God had given unusual talents should be allowed to depart from the norm, she felt that the highest attainment possible for a woman was controller of the home—and therefore the future. Her position typified a popular view of woman that put her role as "light of the home" first, but permitted her to use other talents. This belief, together with her conviction that religion is to be lived, not isolated or merely talked, shaped her novels. Her skill at characterization and her ability to tell a good story save her novels from piousness and, even in a culture that no longer shares her values, make them readable. She writes with humor, and her satire, especially of the social class distinctions that work to separate people, has a needlelike quality.

The popular "Real Folks" stories were four books, *A Summer in Leslie Goldthwaite's Life* (1866), *We Girls* (1870), *Real Folks* (1871), and *The Other Girls* (1873). The first two were serialized in *Our Young Folks* before publication; the last of the four is perhaps her most complex novel, for she goes beyond her normal well-bred families to look at the lives of farm girls and city working girls, including the results of the Boston fire that destroyed nearly half the city and the employment places of many working girls. Although they are not sequels, the "Real Folks" books have shared characters, and they are set in the kind of small world that Anthony Trollope created.

Most of the early novels were reissued steadily over a period of forty years.

Other works were *Hitherto* (1867), *Odd or Even* (1880), *Bonnyborough* (1886), *Ascutney Street* (1890), *Square Pegs* (1899); one way or another, all these stories stressed the need for women to define themselves in terms of active Christianity. Whitney also wrote articles on cooking, the Bible, and women's role, and published several collections of short stories.

—*Shirley Marchalonis*

References:

Mainiero, Lina, ed. *American Women Writers.* New York: Ungar, 1982.

Stowe, Harriet Beecher. "Mrs. A. D. T. Whitney." *Our Famous Women.* Hartford, Conn.: A. D. Worthington, 1884, pp. 652–90.

WILLARD, EMMA HART (1787–1870) was the nineteenth century's leading advocate of female education, the author of widely read textbooks, and the founder of one of the earliest schools of higher education for girls in the United States. As a young educator, Willard worked tirelessly to gain educational opportunities for women. Many of her students went on to become teachers throughout the country, and her program of study was widely copied.

Born in Berlin, Connecticut, she learned the usual lessons of farm life, but her father also encouraged the pursuit of intellectual interests. In 1800 she taught herself geometry, a subject then believed to be beyond the capacity of women, and went on to study at the local academy. At the age of seventeen, she began her career in teaching and also continued her education. In 1807 she accepted the position of director of a female academy in Middlebury, where she met and married Dr. John Willard. When financial problems hit her husband in 1814, Willard opened a boarding school for girls, the Middlebury Female Seminary. Although she established the school as a business venture, she soon, as she later wrote, "formed the design of effecting an important change in education by the introduction of a grade of schools for women higher than any heretofore known."

Recognizing that women could master the subjects long reserved for men's colleges, Willard advocated state aid for girls' schools. She elaborated these ideas in her *Plan for Improving Female Education.* Several students from New York State encouraged her to try to gain support there, and in 1819 Willard moved her school to Waterford, New York, and sent the governor a plan entitled *An Address to the Public: Particularly to the Members of the Legislature of New York, Proposing a Plan for Improving Female Education.* Willard and her husband lobbied the legislature, which was receptive to the plan but failed to provide funds. She published the plan, and it gained widespread acceptance, including the support of Thomas Jefferson.

In 1821 the Common Council of Troy, New York, voted to raise $4,000 for Willard to establish a school in that community. In September the Troy Female Seminary opened. The curriculum was rigorous, as Willard established a serious course of study. The success of the school enabled her to add classes in mathematics and science, courses offered at no other female school. By 1831 the school had enrolled more than one hundred boarding students and two hundred day students. Willard managed the school and taught many of the classes, while training hundreds of teachers who spread her ideals of education across the nation. Along with her highly effective teaching, Willard wrote successful textbooks. The first, co-authored, appeared in 1822 and was entitled *A System of Universal Geography on the Principles of Comparison and Classification.* It was followed by several history texts, all of which sold well.

Having made the seminary an educational and financial success, Willard turned over its direction to her son and daughter-in-law in 1838. She traveled abroad, and retired to Connecticut, where she continued to promote female education. In 1844 she returned to Troy and devoted the remainder of her life to that cause.

—*Robert G. Waite*

See Also:
Education, Female Academies, Troy Female Seminary

References:
Goodsell, Willystine, ed. *Pioneers of Women's Education in the United States.* New York: AMS, 1970.
Lord, John. *The Life of Emma Willard.* New York: Appleton, 1873.
Lutz, Alma. *Emma Willard: Daughter of Democracy.* Boston: Houghton Mifflin, 1929.

WILLARD, FRANCES E. (1839–98) was president of the Woman's Christian Temperance Union and a leading advocate of social reform in Victorian America. Raised in Wisconsin by two former Oberlin College students in a staunch Methodist environment, Willard absorbed the moral fervor and egalitarianism present in the household. This led her to see women as valid participants in public life with a responsibility to improve American society. Through the WCTU and its "Do Everything" policy, Willard advocated a wide range of reforms: spousal equality in marriage, woman's suffrage, dress reform, social purity, age of consent laws, kindergartens, and kitchen gardens. With her demands always couched in the rhetoric of the nineteenth-century concept of True Womanhood, she reached a broad spectrum of American and (later) British women. "Home protection" was her rallying cry as she spoke of homes broken by alcohol and tobacco use.

A powerful speaker, Willard was a favorite on the lecture circuit—her reform pulpit. On many issues, Willard was more progressive than her fellow WCTU members. Her acceptance of Fabian socialism and her resulting repudiation of prohibition exceeded WCTU temperance policy. By 1896 Willard had reversed the accepted notion that drink caused poverty. Her solution for drunkenness became not prohibition, but economic improvement.

Prior to her reform career, Willard taught in one-room Illinois schoolhouses and at female academies in Pittsburgh; Evanston, Illinois; and Lima, New York. She presided over the Evanston College for Ladies from its inception as a Methodist woman's college in 1870 until Northwestern University absorbed it in 1873. After one year as a dean of women, Willard resigned and devoted her energy to reform.

Although she did not join the WCTU until after the Woman's Crusade of 1873–74, Willard became a leader from the start, first holding the presidency of the Chicago WCTU from 1874 to 1877, then serving concurrently as the first corresponding secretary of the national WCTU, president of the Illinois Union, and head of the national publication committee. Willard's efforts were rewarded with her election as president of the national WCTU in 1879, a position she held until her death in 1898.

As one of the foremost women of the late nineteenth century, Willard united the divergent strains of Victorian reform, setting the stage for women's involvement in the Progressive reforms of the twentieth century that culminated in women's suffrage and prohibition.

—*Anita M. Weber*

See Also:
Cult of True Womanhood, Woman's Christian Temperance Union

References:
Bordin, Ruth. *Frances Willard: A Biography.* Chapel Hill: University of North Carolina Press, 1986.
Earhart, Mary. *Frances Willard: From Prayers to Politics.* Chicago: University of Chicago Press, 1944.
Willard, Frances E. *Glimpses of Fifty Years: The Autobiography of an American Woman.* Chicago: WCTU Publishing, 1889.

WITHERSPOON, FRANCES M. (1887–1973), Mississippian, Bryn Mawr graduate, feminist, peace and civil liberties proponent, was also a talented writer. In 1909, as a new college graduate, she engaged in social work and was a field-worker for the Pennsylvania Woman Suffrage party. Witherspoon moved to New York City in 1910 with her classmate and lifelong companion Tracy Mygatt; together they established a child care center for working mothers and launched a series of "church raids" to open church facilities to unemployed and homeless workers.

In 1914 and 1915 Witherspoon and Mygatt campaigned vigorously for the vote under the aegis of the Socialist party's Women's Suffrage Committee. Absolute pacifists by conviction, they fought preparedness, providing executive leadership in several peace groups. They joined the New York City branch of the Woman's Peace party in 1915, serving as editors in 1917 for its antiwar journal, *Four Lights.* As founder of the New York Bureau of Legal Advice (1917–20), the first organization to offer free legal aid to conscientious objectors and free-speech victims during World War I, Witherspoon was a key person in the early civil liberties movement in the United States.

After the war, Witherspoon helped to establish the War Resisters League and remained active in this group until the 1960s. She held membership in the Fellowship of Reconciliation, the American Civil Liberties Union, the Women's International League for Peace and Freedom, and the National Committee for a Sane Nuclear Policy (SANE). At eighty-two, Witherspoon organized a protest against the Vietnam War among Bryn Mawr alumnae: In 1968, a full-page antiwar statement appeared in the *New York Times* and the *Philadelphia Evening Bulletin* signed by more than one thousand Bryn Mawr alumnae.

Witherspoon's life and career reflect characteristics common to many women of her race, class, educational attainment, and era. She believed that women and men of "good will" could help to create an equitable, socially just, warless world, and dedicated herself to this ideal. Broad-visioned and optimistic, Witherspoon nevertheless appreciated the immensity of the task she had set herself. An understanding of the interconnections among militarism, sexism, racism, and economic inequalities under capitalism informed all her efforts, as was the case for other feminist peace activists with whom Witherspoon associated, such as Crystal Eastman, Jessie Wallace Hughan, and Emily Greene Balch. Identifying the values and commitments of women like Witherspoon helps bring into clearer focus an important chapter in the history of feminism that has, to date, been little studied.

—*Frances H. Early*

See Also:

Civil Liberties Movement During World War I, Pacifism and the Peace Movement, Suffrage

References:

The Papers of Tracy D. Mygatt and Frances Witherspoon. Swarthmore College Peace Collection, Swarthmore, Pa.

Davidon, Ann Morrissett. "The Lives of Tracy D. Mygatt and Frances Witherspoon." *War Resisters League News* 180 (January/February 1974): n.p.

Manahan, Nancy. "Future Old Maids and Pacifist Agitators: The Story of Tracy Mygatt and Frances Witherspoon." *Women's Studies Quarterly* 10 (Spring 1982): 10–13.

"The Reminiscences of Frances Witherspoon and Tracy D. Mygatt," Oral History Research Office. New York: Columbia University, 1966.

WOLFF, SISTER MARY MADELEVA (1887–1964), Sister of the Holy Cross, poet, and president of St. Mary's College, Notre Dame, Indiana, was born Mary Evaline Wolff, the daughter of August Frederick and Lucy (Arntz) Wolff, in Cumberland, Wisconsin. She attended public elementary and high schools and spent one year at the University of Wisconsin. In 1906 she transferred to St. Mary's College, Notre Dame, where she devoted herself to the study of English literature.

She entered the Sisters of the Holy Cross in 1908 and was given the name Mary Madeleva. After graduation in 1909 she taught English and philosophy at St. Mary's. In 1918 she received her master's degree from the University of Notre Dame, and from 1919 to 1922 she was principal of Sacred Heart Academy in Ogden, Utah. In 1922 she was sent for doctoral studies to the University of California, Berkeley. She was the first nun to earn a Ph.D. from Berkeley, and her dissertation, "Pearl: A Study in Spiritual Dryness," was published in 1925. From 1925 to 1933 she was dean and president of Mount Mary-of-the-Wasatch College in Salt Lake City, Utah. In 1933 she was granted a year's sabbatical to study women's colleges in Europe, with some time set aside for English studies at Oxford. There she became acquainted with literary figures such as Edith Wharton, William Butler Yeats, Wilfred Meynell, Seamus MacManus, and Hilaire Belloc. She also had the opportunity to visit the Holy Land. Upon her return, she was appointed president of St. Mary's College, Notre Dame, a position she held until 1961.

Sister Madeleva was one of America's best-known religious poets of the twentieth century. Her verse and literary articles appeared in *The Saturday Review, The American Mercury,* and the *New York Times.* Her first book of poems, *Knights Errant, and Other Poems,* was published in 1923 and reflected her own and American Catholicism's general preoccupation with the Middle Ages. Other works of poetry reveal her Franciscan love of nature and her desire to penetrate the mysteries of God through his creation. Her prose works were numerous, covering topics such as nineteenth-century poetry, Catholic literary figures, and poetic composition.

As president of St. Mary's College, Sister Madeleva significantly advanced the cause of education for Catholic women. In addition to a vigorous program of institutional expansion, Sister Madeleva established the first graduate school of sacred doctrine for women in 1943. She also welcomed well-known contemporary artists to share their talents on campus. Sister Madeleva's paper entitled "The Education of Sister Lucy," delivered at the annual meeting of the National Catholic Education Association in 1949, stimulated the creation of the "sister formation" movement, a program to upgrade the standards of education for nuns. She received seven honorary degrees and a number of awards for her poetry. She resigned the presidency of St. Mary's in 1961 and died in Boston in 1964.

—*Steven M. Avella*

See Also:

Christianity, Women in Higher Education

References:

Klein, Mary E. "Sister M. Madeleva Wolff, C.S.C., St. Mary's College, Notre Dame, Indiana: A Study of Presidential Leadership, 1934–1961." Diss. Kent State University, 1983.

Sister M. Madeleva, C.S.C. *American Twelfth Night and Other Poems.* New York: Macmillan, 1955.

———. *The Four Last Things.* New York: Macmillan, 1959.

———. *My First Seventy Years.* New York: Macmillan, 1959.

WOMAN AND THE NEW RACE. In late 1918, while recovering from neck surgery, Margaret Sanger began work on her first book, *Woman and the New Race.* Under the guidance of a young journalist, Billy Williams, Sanger completed the manuscript in 1920, when it was published by Brentano's in New York. It sold over two hundred thousand copies, a record unapproached by any of Sanger's subsequent works.

Woman and the New Race establishes the themes that run through the American birth control movement generally, and through all of Sanger's writings particularly. Indeed, the concerns of the book reflect the complex and often conflicting views about sex and population control being debated in the cultural conversation during the first half of the century. Sanger called it her "heart book," and in many ways it measured the pulse of a nation. In its simplest terms, *Woman and the New Race* pleaded the case for free and voluntary motherhood. But the introduction by Havelock Ellis also established its connection with sexology, while chapters such as "The Material of the New Race" appealed to advocates of eugenics and nativism. On one hand it encouraged programs meant to cleanse the American populace of weakening or excessively foreign influences, while on the other it provided fuel for the fires of "race-suicide" alarmists.

In *Woman and the New Race,* Sanger found woman's unchecked fertility universally and almost unilaterally responsible for the miseries of the race, from poverty and disease to war itself. She pointed out that it is the surplus of laborers that keeps wages low, and she quoted statistics to show that the vast majority of feeble-minded children in New York City schools came from large families living in the slums. Conversely, Sanger argued that with intelligent use of safe birth control devices, women could provide the material of a new, healthy, affluent race.

Why, Sanger asked, do twentieth-century women docilely accept the role of child-bearer? She answered her own question by recounting the history of man-made laws of church and state. From the early Christian sanctions against sex, which held that its only moral use was for the begetting of children in marriage, to the Comstock Law, which effectively denied birth control information to the poor who desperately needed it, Sanger revealed the chauvinistic roots of phobias about contraception. Only women, Sanger asserted, could overcome such phobias, and it was time they did so. She noted that in addition to the considerable benefits birth control offered the race as a whole, it would help women achieve individual satisfaction by eliminating the fear of pregnancy. It would even enable women to achieve the orgiastic ecstasy conventionally available only to men.

Predictably, responses to the book were mixed. The reviewer for the *Freeman*, a libertarian journal, found it "calm, temperate, informed, sound and winning," while the *American Journal of Sociology* categorized it "an inferior . . . presentation of the subject of birth control full of fearless dogmatism rather than scientific judgment." This slim first book of Sanger's remains a valid register of the beginning of an increasingly important trend—the push by women for women to take control of their sexual and reproductive lives. Like all of Sanger's works, *Woman and the New Race* is lucid and intelligent. The book's major flaw, if flaw it is, is its tendency to overstate its case.

—*Mary Lowe-Evans*

See Also:

Birth Control; Comstock Law; Race-Suicide; Sanger, Margaret

References:

Douglas, Emily Taft. *Margaret Sanger: Pioneer of the Future.* Garrett Park, Md.: Garrett Park Press, 1975.

Gray, Madeline. *Margaret Sanger: A Biography of the Champion of Birth Control.* New York: Richard Marek, 1979.

Kennedy, David. *Birth Control in America: The Career of Margaret Sanger.* New Haven: Yale University Press, 1970.

Sanger, Margaret. *Margaret Sanger: An Autobiography.* New York: Norton, 1938.

———. *Woman and the New Race.* New York: Brentano's, 1920.

WOMAN IN THE NINETEENTH CENTURY (1845) by Margaret Fuller (1810–50) is considered the first book by an American that addresses the question of woman's place or "sphere" within society. *Woman in the Nineteenth Century* resulted from an expanded version of an article published in the *Dial*—an influential transcendentalist journal edited by Fuller—and entitled "The Great Lawsuit: Man Versus Men; Woman Versus Women," which supported the need for property rights for women, a controversial and highly unpopular issue at the time. Published three years before the first national women's rights convention convened at Seneca Falls, New York, *Woman in the Nineteenth Century* established a precedent for future suffragists by defining and advocating women's rights in a lengthy publication.

Fuller's message was directed specifically to young women of the time, whom she believed had the most opportunity for change and reform, but she emphasized independence for all women, regardless of experience or social status. Fuller explored the importance of women developing their spiritual being as a necessary step toward independence and personal fulfillment. While she recognized the duties and importance of women's place within the home, she advocated education and broader horizons for women, equality between the sexes, and legal rights to retain property and protect against abuse. In a time when women were not knowledgeable about sexual issues, Fuller's forthright discussion of marriage and relations between the sexes shocked and disturbed many of her readers; others applauded her efforts to deal with a subject honestly and frankly. Because of the controversy, *Woman in the Nineteenth Century* sold out within a week and created a furious debate. *New York Daily Tribune* editor Horace Greeley avidly supported the book, commenting that Fuller's writing had "the force which springs from the ripening of profound reflection into assured conviction."

—*Karen C. Knowles*

See Also:
Fuller, Margaret

References:

Allen, Margaret Vanderhaar. *The Achievement of Margaret Fuller*. University Park: Pennsylvania State University Press, 1979.
Fuller, Margaret. *Woman in the Nineteenth Century*. 1845; rpt. New York: Norton, 1971.

WOMAN QUESTION was the term that referred to the debate over the position of women in the late nineteenth and early twentieth centuries among the socialist and Marxist theorists as well as the suffragists and antisuffragists. The woman question encompassed all the issues within the woman movement that challenged the gender system—woman suffrage, legal reform of the laws relating to married women's property rights, increased educational and employment possibilities, women's sexuality and control over their reproductive capacity, and women's social and political freedoms. It was a useful term to focus the political and theoretical discussions of the "new woman," regarding woman's role and true nature among both socialists and avowed feminists.

—*Angela Howard Zophy*

See Also:
New Woman, Socialism

References:

Bebel, August. *Woman under Socialism*. Translated by Daniel DeLeon. New York: Schocken, 1971. [Original title, *Woman and Socialism*, translated by Meta L. Stern, 1910.]
Daniel, Robert L. *American Women in the Twentieth Century: The Festival of Life*. New York: Harcourt Brace Jovanovich, 1987.
Shulman, Alix Kates, ed. *Red Emma Speaks: Selected Writings & Speeches by Emma Goldman*. New York: Vintage, 1972.
The Woman Question: Selections from the Writings of Karl Marx, Frederick Engels, V. I. Lenin, and J. V. Stalin. New York: International Publishers, 1951.

The ***WOMAN REBEL*** (1914) was a monthly journal devoted to socialist and anarchist issues. It was edited and published by Margaret Sanger, who wanted to educate and raise the consciousness of working women through a newspaper devoted to their specific interests and needs. Emblazoned with the slogan No Gods, No Masters, the *Woman Rebel* was intended to serve as a call to arms for working-class women.

From its first appearance in March 1914, the *Woman Rebel* generated controversy. Each issue not only included discussions of such radical issues as the uses of violence as a tool of striking workers, but dramatic statements on the rights of women, particularly their right to sexual freedom. For Sanger, every woman had a right to be "absolute mistress of her own body." This included the right to practice birth control, a term first coined in the *Woman Rebel*.

An appearance in the first issue of an unsigned article by Sanger announcing her intention to publish contraceptive information in the *Woman Rebel* quickly drew the attention of the postal authorities. They notified Sanger in April that she had violated obscenity laws and could not continue to distribute the journal. Sanger responded in the May issue by declaring that the *Woman Rebel* was "not going to be suppressed by the Post Office until it has accomplished the work which it has undertaken." By this time Sanger had decided to publish the birth control information in a separate pamphlet. Unaware of this, postal authorities continued to focus on the *Woman Rebel*, and in August Sanger was formally indicted for printing an article by William Thorpe entitled, "A Defense of Assassination." Unwilling to stand trial on this indictment, she fled to England in November 1914.

Sanger finally returned to New York to face trial in 1915. When within a few months of her return, Sanger's daughter Peggy died of pneumonia, and letters of sympathy and support began pouring in. Such close friends as H. G. Wells and other notables sent letters to President Woodrow Wilson affirming their support for Sanger, while others raised funds for her defense. With intensified press coverage of Sanger, the *Woman Rebel* trial, and the birth control movement, the government decided to avoid further publicity and dropped the charges.

Though only eight issues of the *Woman Rebel* were ever published, the controversy it generated helped to launch a national birth control movement with Margaret Sanger as its leader and spokeswoman. Despite its rather shrill voice and radical socialist interests, the *Woman Rebel* was one of the first journals to focus attention specifically on the problems of working women and to articulate a new feminist agenda for the twentieth century.

—*Esther Katz*

See Also:

Birth Control; Comstock Law; Obscenity; Sanger, Margaret

References:

Gordon, Linda. *Woman's Body, Woman's Right: A Social History of Birth Control in America.* New York: Grossman, 1976.

Kennedy, David. *Birth Control in America: The Career of Margaret Sanger.* New Haven: Yale University Press, 1970.

Sanger, Margaret. *An Autobiography.* New York: Norton, 1938.

———. *My Fight for Birth Control.* New York: Farrar & Rinehart, 1931.

The Woman Rebel, compiled, with an introduction by Alex Baskin. Stony Brook: State University of New York Press, 1976.

THE WOMAN'S BIBLE is a commentary on the Old and New Testaments edited by Elizabeth Cady Stanton. Published in two parts, in 1895 and 1898, the commentary was written by Stanton and other women who believed that the Scriptures had contributed to the suppression and low self-esteem of women. She considered the Bible a man-made book because it was written by men and was the expression of a patriarchal culture; her perspective for interpretation was feminist, rather than historical or doctrinal.

Stanton praised certain of the biblical writers, such as the author of the first account of creation (Gen. 1), for passages that suggested equality: "No lesson of woman's subjection can be fairly drawn from the first Chapter of the Old Testament. . . ." On the other hand, she was very critical of passages that were sexist, and she often used them as occasions for teaching about woman's self-development and liberation: "We may find in this simple parable [Ten Virgins—Matt. 25:1–12] a lesson for the cultivation of courage and self-reliance. . . . The wise virgins are those . . . who burn oil in their vessels for their own use, who have improved every advantage for their own education."

In recent years, theologians such as Elisabeth Schüssler Fiorenza have seen Stanton as a trailblazer in the feminist interpretation of the Bible because of the way she focused attention on the significance of women characters in the Bible and exposed the patriarchal orientation of biblical writings.

—*Sandra E. Roberts*

See Also:

Christianity; Stanton, Elizabeth Cady; Theologians

References:

Clark, Elizabeth, and Herbert Richardson. *Women and Religion: A Feminist Sourcebook of Christian Thought.* New York: Harper & Row, 1977.

Fiorenza, Elisabeth Schüssler. *In Memory of Her: A Feminist Theological Reconstruction of Christian Origins.* New York: Crossroads, 1985.

Stanton, Elizabeth Cady. *The Woman's Bible.* 1895–98; rpt. New York: Arno, 1972.

The **WOMAN'S CHRISTIAN TEMPERANCE UNION (WCTU)** (1874–) began in Cleveland, Ohio, in November 1874. Over one hundred women, many of whom had participated in the women's temperance crusade of 1873–74, gathered to create a permanent national temperance organization whose leadership and membership would be exclusively women. Although the WCTU focused primarily on the issue of temperance through moral suasion and education during its first five years under the presidency of Annie Wittenmyer (1874–79), its activities broadened to include many women's rights reforms during the presidency of its best-known leader, Frances E. Willard (1879–98).

With the motto Do Everything, Willard encouraged her membership, composed mainly of evangelical Protestants, to engage in a variety of reforms ranging from temperance education in public and Sunday schools to agitation for police matrons in city prisons. Her slogan Home Protection was the rallying cry for the WCTU's espousal of woman suffrage so that women could help vote in prohibition. In its first two decades the WCTU developed sophisticated political organizing and lobbying techniques at local, state, and national levels, which it has continued to employ in its century-long struggle for abstinence. During the 1880s it became an international organization working for prohibition and women's rights in many areas of the world. It was also the first large national organization to bring together southern and northern women after the Civil War.

With Willard's death in 1898, Lillian M. N. Stevens, a trusted Willard lieutenant, became president (1898–1914). Stevens knit together factions within the organization split over financial problems and disagreements about the extent to which the organization should operate in the political sphere. During Stevens's tenure, the WCTU increasingly focused on the struggle for national prohibition, cooperating with other temperance organizations such as the Anti-Saloon League.

Following the passage of the Eighteenth (Prohibition) Amendment in 1919, the WCTU, guided by its fourth president, Anna Gordon (president 1914–25), turned its attention to child welfare, Americanization of immigrants, and "social purity." As support for repeal of the Prohibition Amendment grew during the late 1920s and early 1930s, the WCTU fought to retain national prohibition. With the repeal of the Eighteenth Amendment (1933), the WCTU lost some of its prestige and power. Yet it has continued to work for "education for total abstinence" through a variety of means, including work with children and youth, production of both printed and filmed materials, and efforts to influence U.S. political processes.

—*C. D. Gifford*

See Also:

Prohibition and the Volstead Act; Temperance Movement; Willard, Frances, E.

References:

Bordin, Ruth. *Woman and Temperance: The Quest for Power and Liberty, 1873–1900.* Philadelphia: Temple University Press, 1981.

Gifford, Carolyn DeSwarte. "For God and Home and Native Land: The WCTU's Image of Woman in the Late Nineteenth Century." In *Women in New Worlds,* edited by H. Thomas and R. S. Keller. Vol. 1. Nashville: Abingdon, 1981, pp. 310–27.

———. "Home Protection: The W.C.T.U.'s Conversion to Woman Suffrage." In *Gender, Ideology, and Action: Historical Perspectives on Women's Public Lives,* edited by Janet Sharistanian. Westport, Conn.: Greenwood, 1986, pp. 95–120.

Gordon, Elizabeth Putnam. *Women Torch-Bearers: The Story of the Woman's Christian Temperance Union.* Evanston, Ill.: National Woman's Christian Temperance Union Publishing House, 1924.

Jimerson, Randall, et al., eds. "Description of the Microfilm Series: Series III, The W.C.T.U., 1853–1939." In *Guide to the Microfilm Edition of Temperance and Prohibition Papers.* Ann Arbor: University of Michigan Press, 1977, pp. 55–100.

Tyler, Helen E. *Where Prayer and Purpose Meet: The WCTU Story.* Evanston, Ill.: Signal, 1949.

The **WOMAN'S COMMONWEALTH (THE SANCTIFIED SISTERS, THE TRUE CHURCH COLONY)** (1867?–1983) of Belton, Texas, was a Christian socialist, celibate, and feminist community led by Martha White McWhirter. The commonwealth was a separatist community through which members voiced feminist concern about their religious, economic, social, and sexual roles. The original women first sought only religious independence, but they found that signs of feminine autonomy threatened male relatives and neighbors, who reacted with criticism and violence. The Sisters refused to be intimidated and became more insistent about their rights, discovering the connection between religious freedom and their feminist demands.

In 1867 women from prominent families of Belton had a religious experience of "sanctification," which led them to question the religious leadership of their ministers. These women were also led to question their roles as wives. They claimed they were willing to remain in their homes, but that as perfected and sanctified believers, they could no longer engage in sexual relations with their husbands. By 1879 all the women refused financial support from male relatives as a sign of independence and commitment to their shared principles. A combination of hard work, financial acumen, inherited property, and communal practices soon made them very successful.

Pressure from estranged husbands and outraged townspeople forced the women to make a firmer show of their beliefs. Although religious concerns were still an important focus, a shift toward more communal and socialist concerns occurred. In 1885 the women lived in one household and opened an adjoining house as the Central Hotel. The hotel became the center of the community. It was run communally; each woman worked four hours a day, and all jobs were rotated every month. The women also kept up with feminist, socialist, and other progressive causes of the day.

In 1898 the community moved to Washington, D.C. Four years later, the members drew up a constitution, incorporated themselves, and became known as the Woman's Commonwealth. Soon after the death in 1904 of charismatic leader Martha McWhirter, there were changes in the community. Some women remained in Washington; others moved to semiretirement on the community farm in the Maryland suburbs.

The group had attracted many applications during the Washington years, and the women were careful to select only compatible new members. There were few new applications after 1910. The last surviving member of the community, Martha McWhirter Scheble, died in 1983. With her death, the Woman's Commonwealth Association was dissolved, and community property was deeded to the Washington City Orphan Asylum.

—*Wendy E. Chmielewski*

See Also:

Christianity, Utopian Communities

References:

Constitution and By-Laws of the Woman's Commonwealth of Washington, D.C. Washington, D.C.: Crane, n.d.

Records of the County Clerk in Belton, Texas: Proceedings before the District Court of Bell County concerning B. W. Haymond versus Ada McWhirter Haymond. December 1887.

Garrison, George Pierce. "A Woman's Community in Texas." *The Charities Review* 3 (November 1893): 26–46.

Sokolow, Jayme A., and Mary Ann Lamanna. "Women and Utopia: The Woman's Commonwealth of Belton, Texas." *Southwestern Historical Quarterly* 87 (April 1984): 371-392.

The **WOMAN'S FILM**, also known as the women's film or the women's picture, was a Hollywood phenomenon during film's "classical" period, the 1930s and 1940s. Although the terms may be used in connection with any film, serious or comic, that focuses on women protagonists, they are more often applied to tragic or melodramatic films that end unhappily. Thus critics, usually male, have often called these films "the weepies" and dismissed them as inconsequential, ignoring the fact that most of Hollywood's finest directors, writers, and female actors have at one time or another been associated with them. At its worst, the woman's film is self-conscious bathos, but at its best it is vivid and enthralling, a true collaboration between writer, director, and female star(s).

Although some commentators, like Charles Higham and Joel Greenberg, associate the woman's film primarily with the 1940s, Molly Haskell and others include the 1930s and part of the 1950s as well, as a time when the studios produced woman's films as regularly as westerns, musicals, or any other standard genre. Like male-only genres—the war film or the western—the woman's film presents a focused world view that both aggrandizes and sentimentalizes its protagonists and their actions. In so doing, it reaches out to the audience, inviting it to respond emotionally, whether by identification or sympathy, to what is universal and specific in the protagonist(s). If film is primarily an emotional experience, then these kinds of films may well be the apotheosis of its artfulness.

There are many ways to subdivide the woman's film. Haskell identifies four themes, more than one of which may coexist in a given film: sacrifice, affliction, choice, and competition. Using a broader perspective that includes comedies, Andrea Walsh categorizes by narrative type and affective focus: maternal dramas, "working girl" films, films of suspicion and distrust, and "woman in suffering" films. One may also identify woman's films by their directors: George Cukor, Max Ophuls, Douglas Sirk, Ernst Lubitsch, John Stahl, Edmund Goulding, and (the early) William Wyler and George Stevens. Most distinctive, perhaps, are the stars who made them: Bette Davis, Joan Crawford, Katharine Hepburn, Ingrid Bergman, Rosalind Russell, Olivia de Havilland, Ginger Rogers, Greta Garbo, Barbara Stanwyck, Greer Garson, and others. Without such creative talents, the woman's film might have existed, but it never would have achieved the level of popularity and approval that it did in its own time and beyond. Indelibly imprinted on generations of audiences are the performances of Garbo in *Camille*(1937), Stanwyck in *Stella Dallas* (1937), Davis in *Dark Victory* (1939), Hepburn in *Christopher Strong* (1933), Bergman in *Gaslight* (1944), Crawford in *A Woman's Face* (1941), Garson in *Mrs. Miniver* (1942), Rogers in *Kitty Foyle* (1940), or Russell in *His Girl Friday* (1941).

By the 1950s the woman's film was beginning to fade from the Hollywood scene. Several factors are probably responsible: the tendency of *film noir* to take a male perspective and to feature women as evil temptresses (*femme noir*) or ineffectual background figures, the rise of the television soap opera as an even more accessible emotional medium, the influence of neorealism with its avoidance of romance as a suitable narrative subject, the tendency of '50s films to become more sexually explicit, which in practice meant the surfacing of what Haskell calls "breast fetishism." Most of the stars of the woman's film who had been active in the 1940s—Davis, Crawford, Garson, Russell—were on the shelf by the mid-1950s; and their replacements—Marilyn Monroe, Doris Day, Debbie Reynolds, the young Audrey Hepburn—were incapable of demanding the same kinds of concessions from studio bosses, producers, and directors who were also coping with the death of the studio system. In effect, the majority of '50s and '60s films—whether epic or art—were male-oriented and dominated, and it was not until the 1970s that a new crop of strong female actors and sympathetic directors would surface to make a new woman's film possible.

—Frances M. Kavenik

See Also:

Arzner, Dorothy; Blaché, Alice Guy; Davis, Bette; Hepburn, Katharine; Lupino, Ida; Monroe, Marilyn; Movie Stars; Weber, Lois

References:

Gledhill, Christine, ed. *Home Is Where the Heart Is: Studies in Melodrama and the Woman's Film.* London: British Film Institute, 1987.

Haskell, Molly. "The Woman's Film." In *From Reverence to Rape: The Treatment of Women in the Movies.* 2d ed. 1974; rpt. Chicago: University of Chicago Press, 1987, pp. 153–88.

Higham, Charles, and Joel Greenberg. "Women's Pictures." In *Hollywood in the Forties.* New York: A. S. Barnes, 1968, pp. 139–54.

Walsh, Andrea S. *Women's Film and Female Experience: 1940–1950.* New York: Praeger, 1984.

The **WOMAN'S HOSPITAL OF PHILADELPHIA** (today, Hospital of the Medical College of Philadelphia), established in 1861, was one of the many hospitals for women and children that came out of the nineteenth-century women's medical movement. The specific impetus for founding this institution was the ostracizing of Woman's Medical College by the board of censors of the Philadelphia Medical Society; this action barred WMC students from attending public teaching clinics and its graduates from joining local medical societies. Dr. Ann Preston, a graduate of the college and a professor there, became the organizing force behind the Woman's Hospital, which was to provide a retreat for women "without violence to their sensibilities" and offer important bedside training to students at Woman's Medical College.

Despite internal dissension over this ambitious venture, Dr. Preston moved forward quickly by establishing a board of lady managers with the help of prominent Quaker leader Lucretia Mott. Much of the initial fund raising for the hospital was done by Dr. Preston, who went door-to-door among her network in the Quaker community. In 1860 the organizing committee sponsored postgraduate training for Dr. Emeline Horton Cleveland at the School of Obstetrics connected with the Maternité of Paris to hone her professional skills and increase her knowledge of hospital management.

Upon her return to Philadelphia in 1862, Dr. Cleveland took over as chief resident at the Woman's Hospital. During the seven years she held this important position, she inaugurated courses in nurses' training and initiated one of the first programs in bedside techniques for laywomen—forerunners of nurses' aides. Her success in performing some of the first ovarian tumor removals done by a woman surgeon enhanced her reputation and that of the entire staff among the male medical establishment. This helped to lower the barriers against the acceptance of women physicians throughout Pennsylvania.

—*Cynthia J. Little*

See Also:

Mott, Lucretia; Nursing; Physicians; Preston, Ann; Society of Friends; Woman's Medical College of Pennsylvania

References:

Abram, Ruth J. *"Send Us a Lady Physician": Women Doctors in America, 1835–1920.* New York: Norton, 1985.

The ***WOMAN'S JOURNAL*** (1870–1917), a weekly suffragist magazine, was founded and edited by Lucy Stone and Henry Blackwell and served as an official publication of the American Woman Suffrage Association until 1890, when it served the National American Woman Suffrage Association. Soon after its inception, the *Woman's Journal* merged with the *Agitator,* published in Chicago. The *Woman's Journal* was "devoted to the interests of Woman—to her educational, industrial, legal and political Equality, and especially to her right of Suffrage." As a political arm of suffrage associations, the *Woman's Journal* reprinted meeting and convention addresses and notes, reported on national and international political and social news, and published columns and editorials concerning suffrage issues, as well as poems, stories, and book reviews. Letters to the editor would often provoke serious debates on education, voting rights, and social equality that would last for months.

Although contributors were both inexperienced and experienced writers, the first assistant editors were Julia Ward Howe, W. L. Garrison, and T. W. Higginson, prominent members of the New England Suffrage Association. By 1872 there was little money to pay editors, and so the bulk of the editorial work was done by Lucy Stone and Henry Blackwell; after Stone's death in 1893, her daughter Alice continued the journal. In 1917 the *Woman's Journal* and several smaller journals merged with the *Woman Citizen.*

—*Karen C. Knowles*

See Also:

American Woman Suffrage Association; Blackwell, Alice Stone; National American Woman Suffrage Association; Stone, Lucy

References:

Catt, Carrie Chapman, and Nettie Rogers Shuler. *Woman Suffrage and Politics.* New York: Scribner, 1926.

Hays, Elinor Rice. *Morning Star: A Biography of Lucy Stone, 1810–1893.* New York: Harcourt, Brace & World, 1961.

The *Woman's Journal.* Vols. 1–48. January 8, 1870–May 26, 1917.

The **WOMAN'S MEDICAL COLLEGE OF PENNSYLVANIA** (now Medical College of Pennsylvania) in Philadelphia opened its doors in 1850 to forty women students taught by six male faculty members. Among the members of the first graduating class in 1851 was Ann Preston, who as a teacher, administrator, and physician became a driving force behind the college's many successes during its formative years. Support for this novel experiment in women's education came from Philadelphia's Quaker community, specifically from two of its members, Dr. Joseph Longshore, who obtained the school's charter, and William Mullen, who paid the rent on the classrooms.

This institution blazed many trails in the nineteenth century as a professionally staffed facility for women's medical training. It was the first of the five "regular" medical schools for women, the only one to endure into the twentieth century as a separate entity, and the last of the original five to become coeducational. Early on, it was one of the few schools to offer women of every race, creed, and national origin an opportunity to receive a quality medical education. Even though the college started with an all-male faculty, by 1876 there were enough trained women to comprise a faculty of nine professors teaching in all fields of the medical curriculum. Standards were rigorous and comparable to those of the best male medical schools. Long before practical training for medical students had become popular, Woman's Medical College lengthened its program from three to four years so that students would receive ample clinical experience. Toward this goal, and because the male medical establishment had barred its students from attending the regular teaching clinics, the college opened its own dispensary in 1858 and a hospital in 1861, which offered students needed training and patients a rare opportunity to be attended by women physicians. In 1876 the Woman's Medical College dramatically demonstrated its institutional strength by inaugurating the first building ever dedicated to women's medical education.

For over one hundred years, Woman's Medical College has educated generations of women physicians who have utilized their skills in private practices, as missionary doctors here and abroad, as researchers and teachers, and as physicians in public and private institutions such as orphanages and hospitals.

—Cynthia J. Little

See Also:

Physicians; Preston, Ann; Society of Friends; Woman's Hospital of Philadelphia

References:

Abram, Ruth J. *"Send Us a Lady Physician": Women Doctors in America, 1835–1920.* New York: Norton, 1985.

The **WOMAN'S PEACE PARTY (WPP)**, the roots of which lay within the International Woman Suffrage Alliance (IWSA), was the first major all-female U.S. peace organization before 1919. Its founding was inspired by two European suffragists, Emmeline Pethick-Lawrence of Great Britain and Rosika Schwimmer of Hungary, who appealed to their U.S. counterparts for aid in peace efforts after World War I began in Europe in August 1914. Pethick-Lawrence's visit to a suffrage meeting in New York City in November 1914 resulted in the creation of the first WPP organization, led by militant suffragists Madeline Doty and Crystal Eastman. Pethick-Lawrence's later visit to Chicago convinced the older and more moderate suffragist and settlement house pioneer Jane Addams to form a nationwide WPP in January 1915. Branches were then organized in many areas of the nation.

From its earliest inception, the WPP stressed the importance of woman suffrage and equal participation in government as a means for curtailing war. Seeing World War I as a failure on the part of male leadership, the WPP stressed the intellectual and moral sentiments developed by "the mother half of humanity" and expressed disillusionment with "the man-run world." Besides working to organize U.S. women against war in general, the WPP also urged President Woodrow Wilson to mediate an end to the European conflict. The women met with IWSA members at The Hague in April 1915, followed by visits throughout Europe with leaders of both neutral and belligerent nations. They also carried on relief work and protested U.S. troops and imperialism in Central America, the Caribbean, and the Philippines.

Once the United States declared war in 1917, however, the WPP ceased its criticism of the government's policy. Although retaining its pacifist rhetoric, the WPP took the position that World War I was "the war to end all wars" and turned its concentration toward postwar plans. In 1919, at an international women's conference held in Zurich, the WPP joined its European sister organizations in founding the Women's International League for Peace and Freedom (WILPF), the name it has retained to this day.

—Harriet Hyman Alonso

See Also:

Addams, Jane; Pacifism and the Peace Movement; Women's International League for Peace and Freedom, Women's Peace Union

References:

Woman's Peace Party and Women's International League for Peace and Freedom Papers. Swarthmore College Peace Collection, Swarthmore, Pa.

Women's International League for Peace and Freedom Papers. Norlin Library. University of Colorado, Boulder, Colo.

Addams, Jane, Emily G. Balch, and Alice Hamilton. *Women at The Hague: The International Congress of Women and Its Results.* New York: Macmillan, 1915; rpt. New York: Garland, 1972.

Bussey, Gertrude, and Margaret Tims. *Pioneers for Peace: Women's International League for Peace and Freedom, 1915–1965.* London: George Allen & Unwin, 1965; rpt. Oxford: Alden, 1980.

Cook, Blanche Wiesen. "The Woman's Peace Party: Collaboration and Non-Cooperation." *Peace and Change* 1 (Fall 1972): 36–42.

Degen, Marie Louise. *The History of the Woman's Peace Party.* Baltimore: Johns Hopkins University Press, 1939; rpt. New York: Garland, 1972.

Wiltsher, Ann. *Most Dangerous Women: Feminist Peace Campaigners of the Great War.* Boston: Pandora, 1985.

***WOMAN'S RECORD**: or, Sketches of All Distinguished Women, from 'the Beginning' till A.D. 1850. Arranged in Four Eras with Selections from Female Writers of Every Age* (1852) was compiled by the editor of *Godey's Lady's Book*, Sarah Josepha Hale, to commemorate women's contribution to Western civilization. As an expression of nineteenth-century domestic feminism, this 903-page, exquisitely bound and embellished volume celebrated the achievements and accomplishments of outstanding historical and contemporary women, primarily highlighting women authors and poets.

Hale herself was a representative of the American antebellum eastern seaboard women writers who entered professional writing as a means of supporting themselves and their families; writing thus became an appropriate employment for True Women. Hale stated in her introduction her intention that *Woman's Record* should venerate womanhood, thereby reinforcing the respectability of herself and her American contemporaries—all of whom she included within this ambitious collection of "women worthies." *Woman's Record* was a monument to both her nationalism and the gender partisanship of Hale and the Victorian middle-class women for whom she served as the high priestess of the Cult of True Womanhood.

—Angela Howard Zophy

See Also:
Cult of True Womanhood; Domestic Feminism; *Godey's Lady's Book*; Hale, Sarah Josepha

References:

Entrikin, Isabelle Webb. *Sarah Josepha Hale and Godey's Lady's Book.* Philadelphia: Lancaster, 1946.
Finley, Ruth E. *The Lady of Godey's.* Philadelphia: Lippincott, 1931.
Hale, Sarah Josepha. *Woman's Record: or, Sketches of All Distinguished Women, from 'the Beginning' till A.D. 1850. Arranged in Four Eras with Selections from Female Writers of Every Age.* New York: Harper, 1852.
Zophy, Angela Howard. "'For the Improvement of My Sex': Sarah Josepha Hale's Editorship of *Godey's Lady's Book*, 1837–1877." Diss. The Ohio State University, 1978.

WOMAN'S RIGHTS CONVENTIONS. The first formal woman's rights convention in the United States occurred in Seneca Falls, New York, in 1848, and established the agenda of woman's rights issues, including suffrage. Throughout the antebellum period, state suffrage associations held subsequent conventions to rally support for state constitutional amendments for woman's suffrage and other woman's rights issues. These local conventions produced the nationally known leaders of the nineteenth-century woman's rights movement, such as Lucy Stone, Elizabeth Cady Stanton, Susan B. Anthony, and Sojourner Truth. These gatherings also generated the grass-roots organizations that provided the members and the means for educating public opinion regarding women's issues.

The last of these conventions, held in 1866, established the ill-fated American Equal Rights Association to pursue suffrage for both women and blacks through amendments to state constitutions. The failure of the association's all-out effort to win passage of two separate suffrage bills in the Kansas campaign of 1867 impelled the formation of an organization focused solely upon woman suffrage. An inability to agree upon the best strategy to achieve woman suffrage resulted in the establishment of the National Woman Suffrage Association and the American Woman Suffrage Association in 1869.

—*Angela Howard Zophy*

See Also:
American Woman Suffrage Association, Equal Rights Association, National Woman Suffrage Association, Nineteenth-Century Woman's Movement, Seneca Falls Convention, Suffrage

References:

Clinton, Catherine. *The Other Civil War: American Women in the Nineteeth Century.* New York: Hill and Wang, 1984.
Flexner, Eleanor. *Century of Struggle: The Woman's Rights Movement in the United States.* Rev. ed. Cambridge, Mass.: Belknap, 1959, 1975.
Lerner, Gerda. *The Female Experience: An American Documentary.* Indianapolis: Bobbs-Merrill, 1977.
Riley, Glenda. *Inventing the American Woman: A Perspective on Women's History.* Arlington Heights, Ill.: Harlan Davidson, 1987.

In ***WOMEN AND ECONOMICS*** (1898), Charlotte Perkins Gilman attributed the social and economic stresses of the 1890s recession to the prevailing misconception that sex was the sole and indisputable determinant of one's economic function in society.

Using the animal kingdom as a basis of comparison, Gilman regarded the sexuo-economic relationship as a phenomenon unnatural and unique to humanity. "We are the only animal species in which the female depends on the male for food, the only animal species in which the sex relation is also the economic relation" (5). Such a distorted social order caused women, who responded exclusively to the physical needs of men, to become once removed from their economic environment. Gilman claimed that a woman's indirect contact with an economic environment encouraged her to underdevelop economically (workhorse) and overdevelop sexually (milk cow). Since excelling in such areas as motherhood and housework assured a woman's economic security, an excessive sex distinction was considered an adaptive trait crucial to a woman's survival in her surrogate environment, centered on man. While Gilman accepted that such a survival tactic (based on patriarchy) had its natural causes and uses, she also realized that a higher level of understanding must be achieved in order for humanity to reach its full potential. Gilman recognized that such a sexuo-economic relationship, by encouraging social and economic inequality and defining women's social functions by their sexual functions, has excluded half of humanity from the economic specialization and organization vital to human progress.

Although she based much of her criticism of economic inequality on an understanding of natural selection and Social Darwinism, her proposed solution relied on the reader's acceptance of a non-Marxist socialist utopia. She suggested that women would achieve economic independence and equality as soon as the sexual relation was permanently separated from the economic relation. The sexuo-economic relationship could be eliminated when society no longer restricted women's employment to marriage, maternity, and housekeeping. Gilman explained that women's employment outside the home would be made possible with the advent of professional housekeeping, food preparation, and child care. In theory, the modern home would be a kitchenless establishment intended only to provide rest and recreation for the family unit. Unfortunately, it was at this point in her discussion that Gilman failed to explain how a society (composed of such economically independent individuals) would determine who was to be assigned to these specialized household tasks. This flaw in her theory notwithstanding, Charlotte Perkins Gilman successfully conveyed the message that society's progress and economic development depended upon the elimination of sexual functions and the reinstitution of collective social functions.

—*Barbara Hope Klein*

See Also:

Gilman, Charlotte Perkins

References:

Gilman, Charlotte Perkins. *Women and Economics*. Boston: Small, Maynard, 1908; rpt. New York: Harper & Row, 1966.

Hill, Mary A. *Charlotte Perkins Gilman: The Making of a Radical Feminist, 1860–1896*. Philadelphia: Temple University Press, 1980.

O'Neill, William L. *Everyone Was Brave*. New York: Quadrangle, 1969.

Pearson, Carol. "Coming Home: Four Feminist Utopias and Patriarchal Experience." In *Future Females: A Critical Anthology*, edited by Marleen S. Barr. Bowling Green, Ohio: Bowling Green State University Popular Press, 1981.

Scharnhorst, Gary. *Charlotte Perkins Gilman*. Boston: Twayne, 1985.

WOMEN IN HIGHER EDUCATION. The entry of women into higher education, as students and as faculty, is best characterized in the title of Eleanor Flexner's overview of the early part of that history: *A Century of Struggle*. In the nineteenth century quaint notions limited the access of women to higher education: that learning would cause them brain fever, that it would harm their ability to bear children, that it was an enemy to marriage and the family. The education of women was generally limited to the wealthy classes and to such "accomplishments" as French, fine needlework, and music. Female pioneers of advanced education for women were often only children whose fathers educated them as they might a son.

Emma Willard was an early pioneer who, in 1819, tried to persuade the New York legislature to fund the education of girls, at that time beginning to enter the field of teaching. She founded a seminary, funded by the city of Troy (N.Y.), for the education of young women in 1821. Oberlin College was the first institution of advanced learning to educate women and men together, beginning in 1833. Opened in 1865, Vassar was the first college for women that attempted to give as rigorous education to women as men's colleges offered to men, emphasizing physical education in the curriculum to counter claims of the physical incapacities of women who enhanced the life of the mind. Smith, which admitted its first students in 1875, accepted only those women who could pass the same entrance examination as was administered by Harvard. By 1880, a year after women began to receive instruction directly from Harvard faculty, women made up one-third of college students across the country. Bryn Mawr became the first college to offer graduate work to women.

Women's advancement as academics in higher education came slowly also. In 1900 the proportion of doctorates that went to women was 6 percent. This figure rose to 15–16 percent in the 1930s, but dropped back to 10 percent in 1950, reflecting the post–World War II trend in America to discourage women from pursuing advanced education and careers. Two seminal studies of the employment status of women in academia were published by Jessie Bernard and Helen Astin in the 1960s. Patterns of discrimination were evident, including small numbers of women in the most prestigious universities, lower salaries than men's, slower promotion, lower status, and less likelihood of being part of the administration of the institution. However, the Civil Rights Act of 1964, supplemented by a series of executive orders and laws that followed, began to effect a change in the status of women and minorities, as Title IX of the 1972 Education Amendments to the Higher Education Act began to change the status of women students and employees.

Colleges and universities were required to take specific action under Title IX, including an institutional self-evaluation of the status of women students, faculty, and other academic employees, and to appoint a Title IX coordinator to oversee compliance with the new Title IX regulations. These regulations covered academic programs, employment, financial aid, and athletics.

The self-examination process and the compliance requirements combined to create a more hospitable environment in higher education, one in which women flourished. In the next decade or so, women eventually accounted for half the undergraduates in U.S. colleges and universities and claimed half the scholarships and other financial aid available. Women's athletics burgeoned as funds traditionally available only for football, men's basketball, and a few other men's sports were reallocated to include volleyball, women's basketball, and other women's sports. With money for recruitment, professional coaching, uniforms, and travel, women's sports became not only a significant opportunity for the development of young women, but a source of pride and revenue for their institutions. A milestone of sorts was reached in the winter of 1988, sixteen years after passage of Title IX, when the enormous St. John's arena, home of the powerful Ohio State men's basketball team, was sold out for a women's basketball game.

Allocation of financial aid by gender also came under close scrutiny under the new regulation. Not surprisingly, it was discovered that many privately funded scholarships were available only to men. Although the law allowed single-sex scholarships so long as the overall availability of scholarship funds was evenly distributed among men and women, much reevaluation has taken place over the years since 1972, and there remain few sizable or prestigious scholarship awards limited by gender. Perhaps the clearest embodiment of that change can be seen in the inclusion of women as recipients of the highly prestigious Rhodes Scholarships. These awards, given to new graduates for study at Oxford University in England, were funded by South African Cecil Rhodes in the nineteenth century and intended for young men who had achieved at high levels in academic programs and in the "manly" athletic arts. The growing number of women among Rhodes Scholars over the last decade was emphasized in 1988 as a young black woman from California was entered on the roster.

In academic programs, the effect of Title IX is more mixed. Certainly, women are pursuing academic degrees in unprecedented numbers and achieving them in equally satisfying numbers. Moreover, the women's studies programs that began in the 1970s have multiplied and earned stature in colleges and universities nationwide, and research on topics focused on women is prolific in the humanities and social sciences.

The continuing problem, and one that both reflects and contributes to gender inequality in the work force, is distribution across disciplines. At both the undergraduate and graduate levels, women still prefer the courses of study traditional for women—education, the humanities, and, increasingly, the social sciences. And, while there is steady movement of women in recent years into the biological sciences, their numbers remain few in the mathematics-based disciplines. Many of the women who are graduate students, postdoctoral scholars, and faculty in American universities in fields like physics are foreign-born. The American educational system is still failing to prepare or to engage its young women in these nontraditional fields. Thus, while 57.1 percent of doctorates awarded to U.S. citizens in 1986 in education went to women, and 46.9 percent in the social sciences, only 9.2 percent of doctorates in physics and astronomy went to women in that year and 12.3 percent in computer sciences.

Finally among the categories covered by Title IX, there is academic employment. Prior to 1972, percentages of women on faculties of American colleges and universities were small indeed. Even in fields like English, where undergraduate populations had been half women for years, faculties were predominately, even solely, male. Under Title IX, as well as under other federal laws, numerous charges of sex discrimination were filed against institutions of higher education in the 1970s and 1980s. Many of these were unsuccessful, as the courts revealed themselves to be extremely reluctant to supersede personnel decisions made through academic processes. Several significant class-action suits were successful, however, including the suit of Louise Lamphere against Brown University, and the *Rajender v. University of Minnesota* suit, both of which addressed the propensity of colleges and universities to restrict women to teaching positions in which they were not eligible for tenure or permanent status. The latter suit led to an external administrator being appointed by the court to monitor all academic personnel decisions at Minnesota for several years.

In the latter part of the 1980s, percentages of women faculty in the nonscience disciplines increased greatly. In fields like English and sociology, they averaged 25 to 30 percent at the assistant professor level. At the tenured level, however, the lags continued to be considerable, with tenured women faculty nationwide hovering at about 12 percent. Questions posed by academic women about these figures should be answered in the 1990s: Will women begin to appear in the tenured ranks in numbers reflecting their numbers at the entry levels, and will women occupy faculty positions in the same percentages at which they earn doctorates by discipline? Concern has been expressed that the 25–30 percent proportion of women will constitute an invisible ceiling, as male faculty try to ward off "feminization" of their disciplines and the decrease in salaries and stature that feminization of a field has traditionally brought in its wake.

While such questions remain, progress of women in higher education in the latter half of the twentieth century is undeniable. A recent confirmation that such progress is likely to continue came in the recent congressional override of the *Grove City* decision. In 1984 the U.S. Supreme Court ruled that Title IX, as maintained by the suit of *Grove City College v. Bell*, 465 U.S. 555 (1984), was applicable and enforceable only in those programs that receive federal funds. For several years after this ruling, Title IX enforcement was held in abeyance, and many women's academic and athletic programs were threatened. Then, early in 1988, Senate Bill 557 was passed, making Title IX applicable to all programs in colleges and universities, irrespective of receipt of federal funds. A sea change in the national consciousness about women and education has decidedly occurred.

—*Karen Merritt and Michele Wender Zak*

See Also:

Athletics/Sports; Coeducation; Education; Higher Education for Southern Women; "Seven Sisters"; Title IX; Willard, Emma; Women's Studies

References:

Astin, Helen S. *The Woman Doctorate in America: Origins, Career and Family.* New York: Russell Sage Foundation, 1969.

Bernard, Jessie Shirley. *Academic Women.* University Park: Pennsylvania State University Press, 1964.

Carnegie Commission on Higher Education. *Opportunities for Women in Higher Education: Their Current Participation, Prospects for the Future, and Recommendations for Action.* New York: McGraw-Hill, 1973.

DeSole, Gloria, and Leonore Hoffman, eds. *Rocking the Boat: Academic Women and Academic Processes.* New York: Modern Language Association, 1981.

Horowitz, Helen Lefkowitz. *Alma Mater: Design and Experience in the Women's Colleges from Their Nineteenth-Century Beginnings to the 1930s.* New York: Knopf, 1984.

Miller, Barbara Soloman. *In the Company of Educated Women: A History of Women and Higher Education in America.* New Haven: Yale University Press, 1985.

WOMEN IN THE MODERN WORLD, THEIR EDUCATION AND THEIR DILEMMAS, published in 1953 by Columbia-Barnard sociologist Mirra Komarovsky, was both a sociological study of contemporary college-educated females and an attack on the new antifeminism of the post–World War II era. Questioning the premises of the neo-Freudians who supported subservient roles for women, Komarovsky pointed out that evidence did not support the idea of inborn mental differences between the sexes, that "penis envy" had social not biological roots, and that the "active" woman was not a neurotic rebelling against her deepest feminine self. Komarovsky also asserted that women who wanted careers shared the same mixture of motives as modern men and did not suffer from personality disorders. The reasons why society viewed such women so harshly and seemed unable to accept their lives was rooted, according to Komarovsky, in unabsorbed social, technological, and moral changes. In short, while social realities and to some extent even sex roles had changed, attitudes toward sex roles remained traditional, trapping women and men in anachronistic, unfulfilling situations.

Komarovsky's survey-interview data provides a good picture of those women Betty Friedan would later describe as victims of the "feminine mystique." Komarovsky found that the majority of college women interviewed believed it was natural for women to have no personal ambitions and to live through their husbands' successes, that motherhood could be totally satisfying and only became stultifying if one lacked imagination or efficiency, that women who worked could not be good mothers, that the ideal number of children was three or more, and that husbands were naturally superior in qualities demanded by the outside world but needed the constant encouragement of wives to achieve their full potential. Those college-age women who wanted to work saw themselves as combining family, marriage, and career usually by pursuing interrupted, discontinuous life patterns.

In her interviews with college-educated housewives, Komarovsky discovered women shocked by the demands of child rearing, discontented with the kinds of volunteer work available, and upset by the contrast between their homebound lives and the lives of their professional husbands. To solve these dilemmas, Komarovsky recommended more education on family life for both men and women, greater recognition and encouragement of female talents, and marriages based on real equality. Written in the 1950s, the book did not consider the possibility—and problems—of a society where most women with children worked outside the home, nor did the book, by virtue of its subject, take into account the experiences of working-class women. But Komarovsky later explored this subject in *Blue Collar Marriage* (1964).

—Barbara McGowan

See Also:

Freudianism; Friedan, Betty; Women in Higher Education

References:

Komarovsky, Mirra. *Blue Collar Marriage.* New York: Random House, 1964.

———. *Women in the Modern World, Their Education and Their Dilemmas.* Boston: Little, Brown, 1953.

WOMEN OF ALL RED NATIONS (WARN), a coalition of American Indian women, grew out of the takeover at Wounded Knee, South Dakota, by members of the American Indian Movement (AIM) in 1973. The association was founded in Rapid City, South Dakota, and over thirty Native nations are represented in its membership. The founding conference in September 1978 delineated the key issues of the women: sterilization abuse, political prisoners, education for survival, the destruction of the family, the theft of Indian children through forced adoptions to nontribal families, and the loss of the Indian land base. Ted Means, a leader of the AIM, called the women of WARN the "backbone of the International Indian Treaty Council . . . and the Federation of National Controlled Survival Schools." WARN, however, is not an auxiliary to any male organization; its purpose is to organize for the liberation of all Native peoples. Among the leaders are Lorelei Means and Madonna Gilbert. The Indigenous Women's Network, which met in the fall of 1985 in Yelm, Washington, affirmed many of the positions taken by WARN, attesting to the continuing strength of the networks among American Indian women.

—*Gretchen M. Bataille*

See Also:

Native American Women

References:

LaDuke, Winona. "Words from the Indigenous Women's Network Meeting." *Akwesasne Notes* 17 (Early Winter 1985): 8-9.

"Women of All Red Nations (W.A.R.N.)." *Akwesasne Notes* 10 (Winter 1978): 15.

Women of All Red Nations. Porcupine, S.D.: We Will Remember Group, 1978.

The **WOMEN'S AIRFORCE SERVICE PILOTS (WASPs)** were a quasi-military, civilian group of women who ferried planes across the United States from September 1942 to December 1944. Most women in the military served in traditionally female occupations. The WASPs were different; they were flying planes just as the glamorous "fly boys" were. To become a WASP, a woman had to have a pilot's license (rare among women in this period) and volunteer for a six-month training program. Some women came from elite families who could afford flight lessons; others had been trained under the Civilian Pilot Training Program. Far more applications were received than could be accommodated. The commanding general of the army air force, H. H. "Hap" Arnold, was a strong supporter of the women fliers. WASPs flew seventy-seven different types of aircraft, including the B-17, P-38, F-5, C-4, and B-24, to both coasts so that these planes could be shipped to the combat areas: Thirty-eight WASPs were killed in crashes.

Their colorful commander was Jacqueline Cochran, an experienced pilot who had won two Harmon Trophies by 1939, the highest award for U.S. aviators. She did not want her elite women to be part of the Women's Army Corps nor part of Nancy Love's very experienced Women's Auxiliary Ferrying Squadron (WAFS), whose pilots ferried planes for the Air Corps Ferrying Command, later the Air Transport Command (ATC). On August 5, 1943, the WAFS and women pilot trainees, Cochran's group, were merged in one organization, the WASP. Cochran was director of women pilots, and Love was WASP executive with the Ferrying Division of the ATC. When General Arnold failed to achieve military status for the WASPs late in 1944, he disbanded the organization. It was not until November 23, 1977, that the 1,074 WASPs achieved veteran's status.

—*D'Ann Campbell*

See Also:

Aviation; Cochran, Jacqueline; World War II

References:

Chun, Victor K. "The Origins of the WASPs." *American Aviation Historical Society Journal* 14 (Winter 1969): 259–62.

Cochran, Jacqueline. *The Stars at Noon.* Boston: Little, Brown, 1954.

Craven, Wesley Frank, and James Lea Cate. *The Army Air Forces in World War II*. Vol. 7. Chicago: University of Chicago Press, 1958.

Keil, Sally Van Wegener. *Those Wonderful Women in Their Flying Machines: The Unknown Heroines of World War II*. New York: Rawson, Wade, 1979.

WOMEN'S ARMY AUXILIARY CORPS (WAAC). With the Japanese bombing of the U.S. Pacific Fleet at Pearl Harbor on December 7, 1941, the American military began to mobilize for war. A handful of admirals and generals argued, based on the successful World War I service of 11,250 yeomen (F)s, that a "few good women" should volunteer to serve in the military for the duration. These women should be *in* the military and not just working *for* the military because the army wanted to be able to "order" them to work long hours in emergencies and to move from site to site as needed, to give them classified information to file, type, and decode, and to know that they would not quit. Representative Edith Nourse Rogers of Massachusetts introduced the bill to establish a women's corps in the army. The opposition feared that women would lose their femininity. On May 15, 1942, the president signed legislation (Public Law 554) creating the Women's Army Auxiliary Corps, which gave women partial military status.

The WAAC had different names for ranks and different pay scales from the rest of the Army, and its members were an auxiliary, not part of the army. If WAACs were stationed overseas, they did not have the same legal protection as the men, and a WAAC was not eligible for veterans' benefits—unless she joined the Women's Army Corps (WAC) when it was formed. Plans called for twelve thousand volunteers the first year and double that the second. When generals discovered how well the women performed and how the WAAC freed men for fighting, they demanded thousands more. General Dwight D. Eisenhower sent in a requisition for more WACs than there were in the entire corps.

On July 1, 1943, Congress abolished the WAAC and created the WAC, which gave women the same rank titles and pay as male reservists. Luckily, most WAACs reenlisted as members of the WAC so there was continuity and experience. Oveta Culp Hobby, a prominent Texas civic leader, newspaperwoman, and wife of a former governor, became the WAC's first director.

—D'Ann Campbell

See Also:

Military Service, Women's Army Corps, World War II

References:

Hartmann, Susan M. "Women in the Military Service." In *Clio Was a Woman: Studies in the History of American Women*, edited by Mabel E. Deutrich and Virginia C. Purdy. Washington, D.C.: Howard University Press, 1980, pp. 195–205.

Treadwell, Mattie E. *The Women's Army Corps*. Washington, D.C.: Office of the Chief of Military History, Department of the Army, 1954.

WOMEN'S ARMY CORPS (WAC). The army was the first of the services during World War II to allow women to serve in the military, albeit with only partial military status, as members of the Women's Army Auxiliary Corps. Women finally achieved the same rank, titles, and pay as male reservists when Congress abolished the WAAC and created instead the Women's Army Corps, on July 1, 1943.

While the generals were delighted with their work, the rank-and-file—in the states, in Europe, the Mideast, and the South Pacific—found women in the military a threat to their status. Once they served with the women, they were often willing to say that "their girls" performed well, but they still did not like the idea of women infiltrating such a traditional male bastion. Many warned their friends and relatives away, alleging falsely that women who served in the military had "questionable" moral standards. The sexual innuendos ruined WAC recruitment and demoralized those already in the WAC. The enlisted WACs had more schooling than their male counterparts. Over 70 percent performed jobs in the military that were traditionally labeled "women's work," such as typing and filing. About one-third served with the army air force. The college-educated WAC officers were paid more in the military than they had earned as civilians and learned skills that helped many gain leadership positions after the war in their communities and in the work force. At the peak of World War II, 100,000 women served as WACs; about 140,000 served during the war.

With the passage of the Women's Armed Services Integration Act in June 1948, the WAC was made a permanent part of the army. In the 1970s the army began debating whether to maintain a separate corps for women (the Army Nurse Corps had both men and women in it since the 1950s) or to abolish the WAC. The "separate but equal" women's corps was abolished in 1978 and the members fully integrated in functional units. In 1976 the first women were admitted to the U.S. Military Academy at West Point, New York. Combat service for women continued to be debated through the late 1980s.

—D'Ann Campbell

See Also:

Marine Corps, Women's Reserve; Military Service; SPARs; WAVEs; Women's Army Auxiliary Corps; World War II

References:

Allen, E. Ann. "The WAC Mission: The Testing Time from Korea to Vietnam." Diss. University of South Carolina, 1986.

Campbell, D'Ann. *Women at War with America: Private Lives in a Patriotic Era.* Cambridge: Harvard University Press, 1984.

Holm, Jeanne. *Women in the Military: An Unfinished Revolution.* Novato, Calif.: Presidio, 1982.

Mordon, Colonel Bettie. *The Women's Army Corps 1945–1978.* Washington, D.C.: U.S. Government Printing Office, forthcoming.

Treadwell, Mattie E. *The Women's Army Corps.* Washington, D.C.: Office of the Chief of Military History, Department of the Army, 1954.

Willenz, June A. *Women Veterans: America's Forgotten Heroines.* New York: Continuum, 1983.

The **WOMEN'S BUREAU** was established in the U.S. Department of Labor after World War I to protect the interests of wage-earning women. The American Federation of Labor and progressive reform groups encouraged the formation of a federal bureau to monitor the progress of protective legislation for women. As a result, the Women's Bureau was a bastion of social feminism. It formed an alliance with the National Women's Trade Union League in favor of sex-based protective legislation. Mary Anderson, the first director of the bureau, opposed the National Woman's party's proposed Equal Rights Amendment to erase sex as a legal classification.

After the 1920s the goals of the Women's Bureau shifted from a preoccupation with protective legislation to the advocacy of equal opportunity for women workers. In the 1930s Women's Bureau publications argued that women worked out of need and not for "pin money." In the 1950s the bureau encouraged women to enter the labor market and suggested to employers that they take advantage of the new source of labor. The Women's Bureau had long supported the Equal Pay Act, a federal law requiring equal pay for equal work first proposed in 1945 and passed in 1963.

—Kathleen Laughlin

See Also:

Equal Rights Amendment, National Woman's Party, National Women's Trade Union League, Protective Legislation

References:

Cott, Nancy. *The Grounding of Modern Feminism.* New Haven: Yale University Press, 1987.

Woloch, Nancy. *Women and the American Experience.* New York: Knopf, 1984.

WOMEN'S EDUCATIONAL AND INDUSTRIAL UNION. This organization, identified often by its acronym, WEIU, was an important social reform influence in Boston during the latter nineteenth century and the beginning of the twentieth. Established in the decade following the Civil War, the WEIU was dedicated to helping working women avoid poverty and all its attendant evils by offering them training and access to reasonably good jobs. Though it provided a number of other services, the WEIU focused its efforts on providing education that could provide young working-class women with stable employment. Among its most successful programs were classes to prepare women for work in the "needle trades" and special classes to help women find employment in retail department stores. The latter program eventually became a course in the Boston public schools.

The WEIU was a somewhat unique variety of what William O'Neill has described as "social feminist" organizations during this period. Like other social feminist groups (such as the National Women's Trade Union League), it concerned itself with practical measures to improve the lot of poor and working women; but unlike other such groups, the WEIU focused its efforts on education and employment as important avenues for self-improvement among working-class women.

Curiously, the WEIU has yet to receive much attention from historians. No major study has examined the organization's development or its role in the period during which it was active.

—*John L. Rury*

See Also:

National Women's Trade Union League, Social Feminism

References:

Women's Educational and Industrial Union Papers. Schlesinger Library. Radcliffe College, Cambridge, Mass.

O'Neill, William L. *Everyone Was Brave: A History of Feminism in America.* New York: Quadrangle, 1969, 1971.

The **WOMEN'S EQUITY ACTION LEAGUE (WEAL)** is a national, nonprofit membership organization that specializes in women's economic issues. It conducts research and education projects, supports litigation, and lobbies. Publications include the bimonthly *WEAL Washington Report, WEAL Informed,* and various fact sheets and information kits. The organization was founded in Ohio in 1968 and initially cultivated women who viewed NOW as too radical or unconventional. One of its first efforts was a class-action complaint of sex discrimination with the Department of Labor's Office of Contract Compliance against all colleges and universities holding federal contracts. In 1972 it opened a national office in Washington, D.C., and has become a primary lobbying group on a broader range of feminist issues than originally envisioned.

—*Anne Dzamba Sessa*

See Also:

Affirmative Action

References:

Freeman, Jo. *The Politics of Women's Liberation.* New York: David McKay, 1975.

Gelb, Joyce, and Marian Lief Palley. *Women and Public Policies.* Princeton: Princeton University Press, 1982.

WEAL Washington Report. Washington, D.C.: WEAL, 1971.

WOMEN'S FRIENDSHIPS, from both historical and contemporary perspectives, reveal a number of common characteristics. In the past, two patterns prevailed. First, women found support and intimacy with female relations primarily within the realm of family and home. Second, these friendships were encouraged by society as a means of support for the women in time of despair and anxiety.

In assessing female friendship, historians have analyzed journals, diaries, correspondence, and autobiographies of American women living during the seventeenth, eighteenth, and nineteenth centuries. The "world of women" that institutionalized friendship effectively segregated men and women and allowed the women to display a wide latitude of emotions and sexual feelings with their friends. Because of their friendships, the women developed a sense of inner security and self-esteem that was not available to them in the male-dominated world at this time. The women sought this "way of life" because it reinforced their sense of solidarity and moral superiority. By upholding such attributes of "heart" as positive qualities, female friendships asserted that "women were different from but not lesser than—perhaps better than—men." Furthermore, in some cases, such as in the lives of Lillian Wald, Crystal Eastman, and Emma Goldman, the love and support expressed between female friends gave women the power and energy to engage in political activism.

Research on contemporary female friendship suggests that friendship evolves in a manner similar to other types of relationships. Bonding occurs when a high level of intimacy is shared; as a result, the distinction between family and friend can become blurred. For the most part, friendship occurs between equals, with the women's needs communicated privately, rather than being culturally imposed on them. Other situational factors may facilitate or inhibit a woman's potential for friendship; and some research contends that, ultimately, a woman's culture is to blame for her inability to develop friendship with other women. Other studies note that factors such as class and ethnicity exert an influence upon friendships.

In extensive interviews, women indicate that they define themselves in terms of their friendships and that this "personalistic focus" demonstrates an ability to care and to communicate for the purpose of increasing intimacy and avoiding conflict and the dissolution of relationships with others. In addition, investigations affirm that women make and change the rules for preservation of friendship and that the concept of "homogenizing trends" enables them to bridge the cultural gap for the initiation and preservation of female friendships.

—Susan H. Koester

See Also:

Boston Marriages; Goldman, Emma; Wald, Lillian

References:

Bell, Robert R. *Worlds of Friendship.* Beverly Hills, Calif.: Sage, 1981.

Bernard, Jessie. *The Female World.* New York: Free Press, 1981.

Cook, Blanche Wiesen. "Female Support Networks and Political Activism: Lillian Wald, Crystal Eastman, Emma Goldman." In *A Heritage of Her Own: Toward a New Social History of American Women,* edited by Nancy F. Cott and Elizabeth H. Pleck. New York: Simon & Schuster, 1979, pp. 412–44.

Cott, Nancy F. *The Bonds of Womanhood: Women's Spheres in New England, 1780–1835.* New Haven: Yale University Press, 1977.

Faragher, Johnny, and Christine Stansell. "Women and Their Family on the Overland Trail to California and Oregon, 1842–1867." *Feminist Studies* 2 (1975): 150–66.

Koester, Susan H. "A Cross-Cultural Comparison of Friendship Between Women." Diss. The Union for Experimenting Colleges and Universities, 1985.

Seiden, Anne M., and Pauline B. Bart. "Woman to Woman: Is Sisterhood Powerful?" In *Old Family/New Family,* edited by Nona Glazer-Malbin. New York: Van Nostrand, 1975, pp. 189–228.

Smith-Rosenberg, Carroll. "The Female World of Love and Ritual: Relationships Between Women in the Nineteenth-Century America." In *A Heritage of Her Own: Toward a New Social History of American Women,* edited by Nancy F. Cott and Elizabeth H. Pleck. New York: Simon & Schuster, 1979, pp. 311–42.

The **WOMEN'S HEALTH PROTECTIVE ASSOCIATION** of Galveston, Texas, was founded in March 1901 to promote public health and beautification in a city that had been devastated by the hurricane of 1900. Led by the social elite of the city, the organization invited women of all social and economic classes to join in its efforts.

Flourishing between 1901 and 1920, the WHPA focused early efforts on city beautification. Renowned as a tropical paradise before 1900, Galveston lost nearly all its trees and shrubs in the tidal flooding that accompanied the hurricane. Following the storm the city embarked on a grade-raising project to fill the low areas and elevate the land. While the project protected the citizens from future flooding, virtually all remaining vegetation in the fill area died under several feet of dredge material.

When the grade-raising project ended in 1911, the WHPA was ready. The women had studied and selected trees and shrubs that could withstand heat, humidity, and salt air. Through dues and fund-raisers such as horse shows and seed sales, the women imported oaks, palms, cottonwoods, and elms to plant along city streets and to sell at cost to private citizens. By 1906 the organization operated its own nursery on land donated by John Charles League, and by 1912 the women had planted nearly ten thousand trees and twenty-five hundred oleanders throughout the city of Galveston.

In 1913 the women shifted their emphasis to public health and sanitation. Joining with the Galveston Commercial Association, they asked Dr. J. P. Simonds, head of Preventive Medicine at the University of Texas Medical Branch, to conduct a sanitation survey. He reported that Galveston lacked strong civic pride and recommended that the city enforce sanitary laws, pass a building ordinance, regularly inspect sources of the city's milk supply, provide regular medical examinations of schoolchildren, establish more playgrounds, and eliminate breeding places for mosquitoes.

Supported by four hundred members, the WHPA successfully lobbied the city to appoint a dairy inspector and a building inspector and to pass ordinances regulating grocery stores and bakeries and requiring property owners and lessors to be responsible for maintaining clean sidewalks and alleys abutting their property. Watchdog committees of the WHPA helped enforce the new ordinances.

Other projects the WHPA supported during the first two decades of the twentieth century included the establishment of the children's hospital at the University of Texas Medical Branch, the passage of the city's first zoning ordinance, and the annual antituberculosis Christmas stamp campaign. Though the organization did not maintain the extraordinary level of activity established during the first twenty years of the century, it continued for the next fifty years to work for city beautification. In 1924 the association changed its name to the Women's Civic League, and in the 1940s it became the Galveston Civic League.

—*Jane A. Kenamore*

References:

Morgan Family Papers. The Rosenberg Library. Galveston, Tex. *Report of a Sanitary Survey of the City of Galveston*, c. 1913; in Morgan Family papers, (83-0057, Box 10, ff8). Galveston, Tex.

Women's Civic League Records. The Rosenberg Library. Galveston, Tex.

Frost, Meigs O. "The Women of Galveston." *Southern Women's Magazine* 2 (June 1914): 9–10.

Kenamore, Jane A., and Michael E. Wilson. *Manuscript Sources in the Rosenberg Library: A Selective Guide*. College Station: Texas A & M University Press, 1983.

The **WOMEN'S INTERNATIONAL LEAGUE FOR PEACE AND FREEDOM (WILPF)** had its origins in the Woman's Peace party. On January 9, 1915, eighty-six delegates representing major women's organizations in the United States met in New York to establish the Woman's Peace party. Pacifist sentiment had long been a feature of women's organizations, and when war broke out in 1914, many "expressed astonishment that such an archaic institution should be revived in modern Europe." Under the leadership of Jane Addams, a delegation of forty-seven American women attended the International Congress of Women at The Hague in Holland in April 1915. The conference marked the birth of the International Women's League for Peace and Freedom, the name proposed by Catherine Marshall of England. This name, however, did not replace the older Woman's Peace party in the United States until 1919.

The peace movement splintered during the war years, with their noisy patriotism and short-term economic gains for women. Those who persisted did so under duress. Emily Greene Balch was fired from her post as economics professor at Wellesley for her antiwar activities, and Jane Addams was cited as "the most dangerous woman in America."

The league is today the oldest continually active peace organization in the United States, with more than one hundred branches. Worldwide, it has sections in twenty-six nations. Five of its members have won Nobel Peace Prizes, including Jane Addams in 1931 and Emily Greene Balch in 1946. Through its publications, the league seeks to emphasize the connections between war, racism, sexism, and labor issues. As an activist organization, it has joined in coalition with the Nuclear Weapons Freeze Campaign, the Conference on Racism, the Women's Peace Encampments, the Women's Speaking Tour on Central America, and the Comprehensive Test Ban Campaign. In 1986 it proposed a "Women's Budget" that, continuing social feminist traditions, calls for a 50 percent cut in military spending in the United States and the commitment of resources to jobs, housing, health, nutrition, education, and community development. The league advocates complete disarmament, supervised by a reinvigorated United Nations. It supports a feminist agenda, including the ERA, equal job opportunities and pay, and abortion.

The U.S. section of the WILPF is based in Philadelphia, the international in Geneva, Switzerland. The official papers of the U.S. section are housed in Swarthmore College's Peace Collection. Stanford University's Women's Peace Oral History Project serves as a clearinghouse for WILPF oral histories.

—Laura Gellott

See Also:

Addams, Jane; Pacifism and the Peace Movement; Woman's Peace Party

References:

Addams, Jane. *Peace and Bread in Time of War.* New York: Macmillan, 1922.

Peace and Freedom. Seventieth Anniversary Issue; No. 45. Philadelphia: Women's International League for Peace and Freedom, September/October, 1985.

Steinson, Barbara J. *American Women's Activism in World War I.* New York: Garland, 1982.

The **WOMEN'S JOINT CONGRESSIONAL COMMITTEE** was formed shortly after the 1920 ratification of the Nineteenth Amendment through the leadership of League of Women Voters president Maud Wood Park. The WJCC was the congressional lobbying arm of ten women's political organizations; the number swelled to twenty-one by 1924. The founding organizations included: the League of Women Voters, the National Women's Trade Union League, the General Federation of Women's Clubs, the Woman's Christian Temperance Union, the National Consumers' League, and the National Federation of Business and Professional Women's Clubs. The WJCC would lobby on behalf of any legislation supported by five or more member organizations.

The WJCC's early lobbying successes included support for the Sheppard-Towner Act or the Maternity and Infancy Act (1921) and the Cable Act of 1922. The Sheppard-Towner Act allocated funds to the states for efforts to improve prenatal care and infant hygiene. The Cable Act mandated individual citizenship for married women.

—Kathleen Laughlin

See Also:

League of Women Voters, Sheppard-Towner Act

References:

Cott, Nancy. *The Grounding of Modern Feminism.* New Haven: Yale University Press, 1987.

Woloch, Nancy. *Women and the American Experience.* New York: Knopf, 1984.

The **WOMEN'S LIBERATION MOVEMENT** flourished in the late 1960s and early 1970s as a variety of independent groups dispersed over the United States with an estimated fifteen thousand members. Demonstrating a New Left flair for publicity through such guerrilla theater tactics as hexing Wall Street on Halloween while dressed as witches, groups such as WITCH (Women's International Terrorist Conspiracy from Hell) and the more intellectual and radical Red Stockings drew public and media attention to the issues of the modern women's movement.

Women's liberation groups were generated among the young women (under thirty years of age) within the various radical movements of the 1960s, especially those connected to the civil rights movement and the New Left. As women began to realize their own oppression, they began formulating an ideology of women's liberation that utilized a radical and often Marxist theoretical framework. However, when they presented it within the movements in which they were working, they found the men unsympathetic at best and hostile at worst. When asked what was the position of women within the Student Non-Violent Coordinating Committee in 1964, the famous reply of Stokely Carmichael was, "The only position for women in SNCC is prone."

An awareness of sexism and women's issues grew among civil rights and New Left women until they felt obliged either to align themselves with the emerging feminist movement or remain as support workers for male leaders rather than as acknowledged capable peers within the earlier movements. As women began to exit the New Left movements, the radical males began to incorporate the women's movement philosophy into their own leftist liberation theory. These New Left women defined their movement as women's liberation, and thus ignited the modern women's movement of the 1960s and 1970s. Theirs was a direct feminist challenge to the gender system and the traditional definitions of woman and womanhood, as well as to racism and capitialism.

However, no sooner had the men in the radical movements started to take women and their issues more seriously than the male-dominated media began to ridicule and trivialize the image of women's liberation as "Women's Lib" and to publicize distorted accounts of the women's activities. The classic case of such distortion was the coverage of the "bra-burning" protesters at the Miss America Pageant in August 1968. Although the press photograph of the purported incident was staged after the feminists had protested the sexist trappings of women's apparel by symbolically dropping items of clothing into a trash can, the visual stereotype of the bra-burning, man-hating feminist registered and persisted in the public mind into the 1970s.

The special contribution of women's liberation to the modern women's movement was the development of consciousness-raising (C-R) as a process by adapting tactics once utilized by the New Left. Women's liberation groups sought to raise women's consciousness regarding sexism and feminism as both related to the lives of C-R group members through this process, which bonded women to their individual C-R groups and produced dedicated feminist activists who gave the relatively small women's liberation groups a national visibility and impact that far exceeded their numbers. The C-R process was adopted successfully by the more mainstream women's movement groups such as the National Organization for Women. Eventually, this process itself filtered into the general culture through various self-help groups that ranged far beyond a stricly feminist perspective, for it was employed not only by groups of rape victims, battered spouses, and displaced homemakers but by groups as diverse as single parents and grieving pet owners as well.

By 1970 women's liberation groups were converting new members through C-R groups, writing and publishing feminist literature, and developing feminist theory. Shifting their emphasis from direct confrontational actions to education, the women's liberation groups promoted women's independence and self-respect through supporting the development of women's studies as well as the revival and inclusion of women's literature and women's history in the curriculum of both public schools and institutions of higher education. Women's liberation publications focused as well upon exploring survival skills crucial to divorced, widowed, or dependent women who faced specific sexist discrimination. In the early 1970s a wide variety of such publications were produced by these radical women to disseminate important information that was generally unavailable to women. Mimeographed amateur newsletters of small specialized groups and newly established scholarly journals dedicated to feminist theory or specific issues such as lesbianism flourished. For example, the Boston Women's Health Collective published *Our Bodies, Ourselves,* a classic women's liberation publication, to provide information about women's bodies and particular medical prodedures.

Many of the women's liberation approaches and processes were adopted by more mainstream women's movement organizations to attack particular issues pragmatically and piecemeal, while the women's liberationists themselves were working for revolutionary results. However, as feminists of all degrees worked with women who lacked either a theoretical framework or an agenda for radical change to provide specific remedies such as medical care or abortion referral, the radical young women began to fear that these efforts actually thwarted the possibility for permanent change by utilizing temporary solutions to fundamental feminist concerns. By 1971 they recognized the danger of such temporary, immediate solutions and began cooperating and coordinating efforts with other reformist groups to work within the system for lasting substantive change on issues such as abortion, prostitution, child care, discrimination, and welfare. This cooperation and efforts to "mainstream" their issues and their energies, as well as attrition and theoretical schisms among the charter members of the original groups, gradually diminished the impact of women's liberation by the late 1970s, when the social and political climate was no longer hospitable to radical social reform.

—Saundra K. Yelton and Angela Howard Zophy

See Also:

Consciousness-Raising, Feminism, National Organization for Women, New Left, *Our Bodies, Ourselves,* Twentieth-Century Women's Rights Movement

References:

Carden, Maren Lockwood. *The New Feminist Movement.* New York: Russell Sage Foundation, 1974, pp. 103–32.

Daniels, Robert L. *American Women in the Twentieth Century: The Festival of Life.* San Diego: Harcourt Brace Jovanovich, 1987.

Dixon, Marlene. "The Rise Of Women's Liberation." *Ramparts* 8 (December 1969): 57–63.

Evans, Sara. *Personal Politics: The Roots of Women's Liberation in the Civil Rights and the New Left.* New York: Vintage, 1979.

Freeman, Jo. "The Women's Liberation Movement: Its Origins and Structures, Impact and Ideas." In *Women: A Perspective,* edited by Jo Freeman. Palo Alto: Mayfield, 1975, pp. 448–60.

Hole, Judith, and Ellen Levine. *Rebirth of Feminism.* New York: Quadrangle, 1971.

Jones, Beverly, and Judith Brown. "Toward A Female Liberation Movement." In *Voices From Women's Liberation,* edited by Leslie B. Tanner. New York: Mentor, 1970, pp. 362–415.

Salper, Roberta. "The Development of the American Women's Liberation Movement, 1967–1971." In *Female Liberation,* edited by Roberta Salper. New York: Knopf, 1972, pp. 169–84.

WOMEN'S MISSIONARY SOCIETIES produced a substantial change in the role and status of women in Protestant churches in the United States during the nineteenth century. The development of missionary societies began after the Civil War, fueled in part by the "Votes for Women" movement. Between 1861 and 1894, women's missionary societies were organized by women in thirty-three denominations. These "for women only" societies involved more women during the latter part of the nineteenth century than all other areas of the woman's rights movement combined.

The impetus for these societies came not from the male leadership of the denominations, but from the women themselves, who were denied ordination and often not granted voting privileges in their congregations. These organizations never directly challenged the power structures of their churches, but they gave the women who participated in them the opportunity to develop valuable skills in fund raising and grass-roots organizing.

One of the major thrusts of the societies was to finance foreign mission work. Some of the missionary groups were called "mite" societies because their funds were so small (a reference to the story Jesus told concerning the poor widow who dropped all she had—two mites—into the temple treasury). Since the men in most families earned and had control of the money and how it was used, the women brought their "butter and egg money" in small amounts. Although the individual women's financial resources were limited, their ability to raise money proved formidable: The societies raised thousands of dollars and supported missionaries (many of whom were women whose interest in mission work was first fostered by society membership).

Initially, women met together in small groups in individual churches to pray, study the lives and needs of foreign missionaries, and give from their meager funds. As the individual societies became more prevalent, they formed larger networks or organizations within their various denominations. The Women's Missionary Societies gave women an opportunity to enter into the lay leadership of their churches. These organizations became a strong force in shaping the modern missionary movement and other social changes for the betterment of the lives of women.

—Marjorie Kerrick Taylor

See Also:

Benevolence, Christianity, Nineteenth-Century Woman's Movement

References:

Dodds, Elizabeth D. "Yes, Yours, My Love Is the Right Human Face." In *Marriage to a Difficult Man: The Uncommon Union of Jonathan and Sarah Edwards*. Philadelphia: Westminster, 1981, pp. 26–36.

Hunt, Alma. *Woman's Missionary Union*. Birmingham, Ala.: Woman's Missionary Union, 1964.

Keller, Rosemary Skinner. "Lay Women in the Protestant Tradition." In *Women and Religion in America: Vol. 1*, edited by Rosemary Radford Ruether and Rosemary Skinner Keller. San Francisco: Harper & Row, 1981, 242–93.

The **WOMEN'S PEACE UNION** was an uncompromisingly pacifist interwar organization that evolved out of both the New York Woman's Peace party and the New York State suffrage campaign. Membership was open to any woman over the age of twenty-one who would sign a pledge not to support war in any way. Although the leadership never exceeded fourteen women, the membership reached over two thousand. The leaders included Elinor Byrns, Caroline Lexow Babcock, Tracy Mygatt, Gertrude Franchot Tone, Mary Winsor, Frieda Langer Lazarus, and for six months, Jeannette Rankin.

Founded in August 1921, the WPU reflected four characteristics present in the 1920s peace movement. First, its leaders believed in a nonresistant philosophy, much like Mahatma Gandhi's, which preached that human life is sacred and all violence and killing are wrong. Second, the WPU was legalistic. Its program consisted of campaigning for a constitutional amendment to outlaw war and the manufacturing and trading of war materiel. This goal was also fostered by the union's senatorial sponsor, Lynn Joseph Frazier of North Dakota, who introduced the amendment into every congressional session from 1926 to 1939. Third, the WPU was feminist in that its roots, contributors, and strategy all lay in the suffrage movement. The WPU leaders chose to emphasize peace through the amendment as their one issue after the suffragists had the vote. Their belief was that winning the vote had been a nonviolent revolution and that peace could be won the same way. They felt that unless there was an end to war and war expenditures, basic social reforms could never be assured. Finally, the WPU was nationalistic. Its members saw the United States as a progressive, democratic leader other nations would follow to world disarmament.

The WPU program consisted of extensive lobbying in Washington, D.C., holding three Senate hearings (1927, 1930, 1934), and sending a representative to the League of Nations Disarmament Conference in Geneva in 1932. Although strong and active in the 1920s, the WPU weakened in the 1930s, largely because of the Depression and the growth of both fascism in Europe and worldwide militarism. Although never officially disbanded, the WPU ceased operations in 1941 just before Pearl Harbor was attacked.

—Harriet Hyman Alonso

See Also:

Babcock, Caroline Lexow; Pacifism and the Peace Movement; Woman's Peace Party

References:

Women's Peace Union Papers. Swarthmore College Peace Collection, Swarthmore, Pa., and New York Public Library, N.Y.

Alonso, Harriet Hyman. *The Women's Peace Union and the Outlawry of War, 1921–1942.* Knoxville: University of Tennessee Press, 1989.

WOMEN'S PRISONS. With the establishment of the first prisons following the Revolutionary War, few provisions were made for the incarceration of women. Their small number made it possible for prison authorities to place them together in rooms away from the men's cell blocks, where they were frequently neglected.

Through the mid-1800s, the conditions remained poor, and little concern was given to the women inmates. The daily routine was characterized by idleness, and they were seldom supervised. Descriptions from the 1820s emphasized the crowded conditions and the intolerable noise. The establishment of New York's Mount Pleasant Female Prison in 1835, the nation's first women's prison, was an improvement, but not widely imitated. Through the 1860s, those prisons built to hold females outwardly resembled the male penitentiaries, but the care of the women inmates was decidedly inferior. Little concern was given to their needs.

The first effective effort toward specialized handling of women prisoners came from Zebulon Brockway, a major penal reformer who in 1868 established a House of Shelter for females as part of the Detroit House of Corrections. It offered treatment directed toward the needs of the women inmates. Beginning in the 1860s, reformers turned their attentions to incarcerated females, and developed the idea of a women's reformatory. This concept rested on the belief that female inmates could best be reformed through a program of domestic training, a program emphasizing their "feminine" nature. In addition, the state legislation establishing the reformatories made it easier for officials to imprison women for minor offenses. Men convicted for the same crimes were typically not sent to prison. Support for reformatories came slowly, and by 1900 only two additional states, Indiana and Massachusetts, had established institutions for women. By 1935, as the movement gained strength, the number had risen by seventeen.

Since then, not much progress has been made. Although separate institutions had been constructed in most states by the 1970s, the conditions and programs remain inferior to those at male institutions. Few vocational programs are available. Little attention is given to women prisoners because of the small number incarcerated, a figure that reached seventeen thousand by 1982.

—Robert G. Waite

See Also:

Criminals, Prison Reform

References:

Freedman, Estelle B. *Their Sisters Keepers: Women's Prison Reform in America, 1830–1930.* Ann Arbor: University of Michigan Press, 1981.

McKelvey, Blake. *American Prisons: A History of Good Intentions.* Montclair, N.J.: Patterson Smith, 1977.

Rafter, Nicole Hahn. *Partial Justice: Women in State Prisons, 1800–1935.* Boston: Northeastern University Press, 1985.

The **WOMEN'S PROTECTIVE UNION** of Butte, Montana, was founded in the early 1890s. The origins of the union are obscure. According to some sources, the Western Federation of Miners organized the union in 1893, shortly after its own founding; others claim the Knights of Labor established the women's union. Its original members were the girls and women who worked in Butte's many boardinghouses, catering to the needs of the unmarried copper miners who dominated the city's population. The union eventually encompassed all female restaurant workers and a variety of hotel and motel maids, public building janitresses, hospital maids, girls who sold candy and popcorn in movie theaters, car hops at drive-ins, cocktail waitresses, and women employed at the local tamale factory. Best known of the union's members were the "bucket girls" who worked in boardinghouses and cafés, each day packing thousands of lunch buckets for three shifts of hard-rock miners.

The Women's Protective Union has a rich history of association with labor movements of the western United States. In 1903 it affiliated with the American Labor Union, an organization chiefly representing western miners. The WPU submitted to the ALU the proposal that female organizations be taxed at one-half the rate of male unions owing to the lesser wages paid to women. In 1905, after entertaining a variety of speakers from the nascent Industrial Workers of the World, the WPU voted to join that radical labor group. On July 9, 1909, the WPU received a charter from the Hotel and Restaurant Employees International Union, but still retained its distinctive local name. For the following sixty-four years, the union remained an exclusively female organization, but in 1973 it was instructed by the international union to merge with the Cooks and Waiters Union, Local 22. After some resistance, the WPU complied, and the two unions formed the Culinary and Miscellaneous Workers Union, Local 457.

Over the years, the WPU not only combatted abusive bosses and sought to protect its members' rights as employees, but it also served as a social and educational institution for Butte's working women. The union sponsored lectures, theatrical performances, dances, and benefits. Members often went out together for ice cream after union meetings, and as one woman, a member for sixty years, put it, "It was friendship. We loved to go to the union."

—Mary Murphy

See Also:

Industrial Workers of the World, Unions

References:

Women's Protective Union/Hotel and Restaurant Employees and Bartenders International Union Records, 1901–73. Montana Historical Society Archives, Helena, Mont.

Weatherly, Laura Ryan, and Margaret Harrington. "Bucket Girl: Yard Girl, The Women Who Worked in Butte." *Catering Industry Employee* (October 1975): 22–23.

Webster, Valentine C. Oral History Interview. University of Montana Oral History Collection, Missoula, Mont.

THE WOMEN'S ROOM, written by Marilyn French in 1977, has as its title an alternative expression for the euphemism "ladies' room." French centers her novel on the nearly autobiographical character of Mira, who leads the life of a typical suburban housewife until her doctor-husband decides he wants a divorce. As a result, Mira must support herself, and she completes college, sends her two children to a boarding school, and enrolls in a graduate program at Harvard. It is in a rest room there that Mira notices a sign on the door that has the term LADIES ROOM scratched out and WOMEN'S ROOM written in its place, as if to signify women's coming of age from a subordinate relationship with men to one of greater relevance and importance.

After becoming involved in several of the late 1960s demonstrations and a certain amount of activism, Mira realizes that she had led a life of social inactivity that included daily kaffeeklatsches and monthly cocktail parties. Basically, she has lost her own identity, but through her fulfilling schoolwork, she gains it back. Prior to Harvard, her friendships with the other suburban housewives were based primarily upon common concerns such as household chores and the proper discipline of children, but after her arrival in graduate school, she learns of things that take place outside the limited world she has known. Throughout the story, Mira encounters several groups of women whom she quickly befriends in order to gain release through their empathy and understanding discourse. The last group of female friends at Harvard is the one that aids Mira in reaching an acute awareness of life beyond the bounds of a male-dominated marriage.

When she finally meets a man whom she believes genuinely loves her, Mira perceives that he is kindred to all other men and that he wishes for her simply to fulfill his selfish desires. For once, she dictates the outcome of a relationship, only to feel abandoned and alone—totally isolated. Once again, as is customary and is the theme of the entire work, men trample over women's goals and happiness. However, French leaves the reader with the sense that there is hope for women, especially when Mira goes on to teach college and gain fulfillment through her work; she might even eventually set out to find a better, more satisfying, and more equal relationship with renewed vigor and confidence.

The Women's Room remains at the forefront of women's literature in America, and shortly after it was published, according to *Virginia Quarterly Review*, several daily and weekly press reviewers claimed that the novel from which the new euphemism was derived was the "major novel in the women's liberation movement."

—*James A. Howley*

See Also:

Women's Liberation Movement

Reference:

French, Marilyn. *The Women's Room*. New York: Summit, 1977.

WOMEN'S STUDIES is an interdisciplinary academic field that examines the experience and achievements of women from a feminist perspective. It had its origin in the movement for women's equality that revived in the 1960s. In higher education, feminist critiques of the traditional disciplines mirrored agitation for the end of discriminatory treatment of women as students and faculty and, in general, for the transformation of society at large. Flaws in the existing disciplines included both the treatment of the male as the norm and the female as an anomaly and the absence altogether of women's accomplishments and experiences. The primary impetus for development of the field of women's studies came from scholars in the social sciences and humanities; however, scholars from the professions and biological sciences have also made major contributions to the conception and growth of women's studies. These scholars recognized that lasting social change would not occur unless there was a radical transformation in what is known, how it is known, and how value is assigned to areas of knowledge. Women's studies pioneers had to overcome the prejudice in academia that research with a primary or exclusive focus on women was marginal. The field of women's studies began as an interdisciplinary critique that has evolved into an independent method of inquiry and body of knowledge concerned centrally with gender. It is noteworthy that the field of women's studies has matured concurrently with the growth in numbers of women students and faculty in American higher education.

San Diego State University established the first women's studies baccalaureate degree program in 1969. Within a decade, numbers of academic programs surged from 39 in 1974 to 444 in 1983. Since the intention of faculty in women's studies was not only to discover new knowledge about women but also to transform the narrow male bias of the traditional curriculum, women's studies programs most often eschewed departmental status for an interdisciplinary structure that invited faculty with appointments in disciplinary departments to participate. Formal curricula typically have included general introductory courses, women-related courses offered in the traditional departments, and integrative capstone courses to round out the program. Increasingly, feminist theory courses have become part of such formal curricula. Early programs offered submajor options only—special certificates or minors. However, as the field has developed, numbers of formal bachelor's, master's, and doctoral degree programs have been growing steadily.

The new knowledge has changed not only higher education, where feminist theory is firmly established as a methodological approach and special focus courses on women can be found in almost every discipline; it has also changed the face of publishing. The first scholarly journal devoted to the field, *Women's Studies—An Interdisciplinary Journal,* began publishing in 1972. In 1975 *Signs: Journal of Women in Culture and Society* began publication and has become the leading journal of women's studies scholarship. By 1987 some eighty to ninety periodicals were devoted to women-centered issues. Esther Stineman's 1979 annotated *Women's Studies—A Recommended Core Bibliography* could comfortably contain principal monographs pertinent to the field in its 1,763 entries. The 1987 Loeb-Searing-Stineman supplement, covering the period 1980–85, had to select its 1,211 entries from more than 5,000 pertinent publications that had appeared since the original bibliography was published. Not included was the vast volume of periodical literature, from entire issues of non-women's studies journals featuring women-related scholarship to individual women-related articles now commonplace in such journals.

In 1979 the National Women's Studies Association (NWSA) was founded and held its first conference. Unlike other professional associations in higher education, the NWSA has had a policy of sponsoring community and feminist-activist aims as well as purely academic functions, a purpose that has been carried out with some difficulty. Within many disciplinary associations, women's caucuses have been formed and often promote disciplinary research on women as well as focus on the status of women in the profession.

Within the field, there has been a degree of tension between the goal of integrating women's studies across the curriculum and that of establishing separate programs. Academic "mainstreaming" projects across the country have attracted federal and private extramural funding, and a range of "how-to" publications and materials have sprung up from these projects to assist interested faculty in integrating the findings of women's studies scholarship into their disciplinary courses. Women's studies practitioners have generally agreed that both integration projects and separate programs are necessary: the programs to serve as an interdisciplinary crossroads at which an independent body of knowledge continues to grow and the mainstreaming projects to fulfill the goal of transformation, of creating bias-free and fully integrated disciplinary curricula.

—*Karen Merritt*

See Also:

Archives and Sources, Women in Higher Education, Women's Liberation Movement

References:

Bowles, Gloria, and Renate Buelli Klein, eds. *Theories of Women's Studies.* Boston: Routledge & Kegan Paul, 1983.

Female Studies I–VI. Old Westbury, N.Y.: Feminist Press, 1970–72.

Howe, Florence. *Seven Years Later: Women's Studies Programs in 1976.* Washington, D.C.: National Advisory Council on Women's Educational Programs, 1977.

———, and Paul Lauter. *The Impact of Women's Studies on the Campus and the Disciplines.* Washington, D.C.: National Institute of Education, Program on Teaching and Learning, 1980.

Schuster, Marilyn R., and Susan R. Van Dyne, eds. *Women's Place in the Academy: Transforming the Liberal Arts Curriculum.* Totowa, N.J.: Rowman and Allanheld, 1986.

"The Women's Studies Movement: A Decade Inside the Academy." *Frontiers—A Journal of Women's Studies* 8 (1986). [special tenth anniversary issue]

WOMENS WAY was established in 1977 as a fund-raising coalition of organizations providing innovative, nontraditional services for Philadelphia-area women. The idea originated with Louise Page, who wanted to start an agency that would bring together a cross-section of women inspired by the idea of women helping women and to create a vehicle for funding women's services.

The original members of the coalition were Women in Transition, Women Organized Against Rape, the Elizabeth Blackwell Health Center for Women, CHOICE (health counseling and referral), the Pennsylvania Program for Women and Girl Offenders, and the Women's Law Project. By 1985 the coalition also included Women Against Abuse, the Community Women's Education Project, Women's Alliance for Job Equity, the Domestic Abuse Project of Delaware County, and the WOMENS WAY Discretionary Fund. Two of the founding member agencies, Women in Transition and the Pennsylvania Program for Women and Girl Offenders, had dropped out of the coalition by 1981.

These agencies emerged in the early 1970s as part of the rebirth of the women's movement, which created a demand for services not provided by traditional organizations. Their pioneering activities in areas such as abortion rights and fair treatment for rape victims, coupled with their identification as feminist organizations, had curtailed their ability to raise adequate funds to expand their services. Financial desperation persuaded these agencies to forfeit their fund-raising autonomy to this untried coalition.

The early years of WOMENS WAY were difficult ones, with annual totals under $87,000. Not until WOMENS WAY negotiated a donor option plan with United Way in 1980–81 did the annual total show a substantial increase to $206,000. Access to other payroll deduction plans has further broadened the base of support, along with growing help from the corporate community. WOMENS WAY allocations continued to represent a small percentage of the combined agency budgets of $2.4 million for 1985–86, but the evenly distributed funds are essential to meet expenses not covered in restricted grant allocations. To mark its tenth anniversary in 1987, WOMENS WAY launched a campaign to raise $2 million for the Reserve Fund for the Future to ensure the continuation of the member agencies. By the mid-1980s, WOMENS WAY was considered the most successful women's fund-raising coalition in the country.

—Cynthia J. Little

Reference:

Little, Cynthia J. "Feminism and Volunteerism in Action: WOMENS WAY." In *Celebrate Women*, edited by Patricia O'Donnell. Philadelphia: Pennsylvania Federation of Women's Clubs, 1986. [exhibit catalog]

WOMEN'S WORK—NINETEENTH CENTURY. During the nineteenth century, the Industrial Revolution transformed the labor of women in America. In 1800 few women worked for wages, and the vast majority of female wage earners were domestic workers. By 1900 one-third of the employed women were servants, and one-fifth of all women were wage earners. Single women dominated the world of female employment, but the employment of married women rose significantly in the last two decades of the century. At the time of the 1900 census, 6 percent of American wives were wage earners. Significant numbers of women first entered employments outside the domestic sphere with the emergence of factory spinning and textile production in the 1820s and 1830s. By the end of the century, nearly a million women, or about one-fifth of all female wage earners, were employed in factories. In addition to spinning and textile manufacturing, women worked widely in tobacco factories, boot and shoe factories, glass-making, garment manufacturing, and commercial laundries by 1900.

In addition to creating a market for female labor in manufacturing, the Industrial Revolution opened other employment sectors to women as higher paid male workers were lured elsewhere. Technological changes, including the telephone and the typewriter, dramatically altered means of communication and record keeping and simultaneously created a demand for literate but not highly trained workers, jobs that were offered to women. A sharp rise in the demand for schooling in an industrializing society and the desertion of teaching jobs by men opened the way for women teachers. By the 1860s, women constituted the majority of public school teachers. Although teachers accounted for three-fourths of all the female professional workers in 1900, women also advanced in professions such as nursing, the arts, and religious and welfare work in the late nineteenth century. After the Civil War, retail stores and urban service industries also became employers of women.

The circumstances under which women entered new occupations during the nineteenth century illustrate how strictly employment in America has been segregated by sex and how women have been economically disadvantaged through occupational segregation. The jobs that women came to dominate in the nineteenth century were characterized by a similarity to women's work within the home, a simplification of tasks through mechanization or the reorganization of work, a reduction in wages, or a combination of these factors. Industrial homework, poorly paid manufacturing done at home, persisted longer among women than among men.

Through the nineteenth century, the vast majority of women labored at domestic chores, raised food for their families and produced the family clothing, or participated in commercial production on family farms without receiving wages. Both paid and unpaid labor in agriculture was a major field of work for women in the nineteenth century. Until Emancipation, much of this labor was provided by black women, and after the Civil War black women were the majority of paid female laborers in agriculture.

—Julia Kirk Blackwelder

See Also:

Industrial Revolution, Nursing, Teaching as an Occupation for Women, Telephone Operators, Textile Industries–Northern and Southern

References:

Kessler-Harris, Alice. *Out to Work: A History of Wage Earning Women in the United States.* New York: Oxford University Press, 1982.

U.S. Bureau of the Census. *Historical Statistics of the United States, Colonial Times to 1970.* Part 1, Bicentennial ed. Washington, D.C.: U.S. Government Printing Office, 1975.

Weiner, Lynn Y. *From Working Girl to Working Wife, The Female Labor Force in the United States, 1820–1980.* Chapel Hill: University of North Carolina Press, 1985.

WOODHULL, VICTORIA CLAFLIN (1838–1927) was a successful businesswoman and reformer. The seventh daughter of Reuben Claflin and Roxanna Hummel, she grew up in central Ohio. As a girl, she worked with her family's "medicine show," which featured her younger sister Tennessee (1846–1923), an accomplished medium.

In 1853, at age fifteen, she married Canning Woodhull, a physician, who was no match for her restless spirits. He later divorced Woodhull because of her liaison with Colonel James Harvey Blood, a dashing Civil War veteran. Colonel Blood helped interest Woodhull in a number of reform causes that surrounded nineteenth-century spiritualism. Later Woodhull and her sister moved to New York and became the first female stockbrokers on Wall Street. The good-looking but somewhat notorious sisters had secured the financial backing of aging railroad magnate Cornelius Vanderbilt. The "Bewitching Brokers" mastered the art of stock wheeling and dealing and soon moved into a splendid mansion on fashionable Murray Hill.

Having conquered the financial world, Woodhull turned her attention to the politics of reform. Influenced by the thought of radical philosopher Stephen Pearl Andrews and her own life experiences, Woodhull wrote in support of Pantarchy—the perfect state, where free love reigned among consenting adults, and children and property were managed in common. She regarded marriage as a degrading form of bondage. These conclusions, so shocking to Victorian sensibilities, were published in a series of *New York Herald* articles in 1870 and in book form a year later under the title *Origin, Tendencies and Principles of Government.*

She followed up on her political and social theories by declaring herself a candidate for the presidency of the United States on April 2, 1870. Her platform was articulated in her journal, *Woodhull & Claflin's Weekly,* which gained her further notoriety. Woodhull both shocked and titillated her readers with tales of Wall Street corruption and fraud and her advocacy of sexual rights for women and legalized prostitution, along with tax, housing, and dietary reform. She also published news about working women and their efforts to organize and better their conditions. The *Weekly* published the first American version of Marx and Engels's *Communist Manifesto* and openly espoused the cause of socialism.

In 1871 she supported the woman suffrage movement despite the disapproval of Lucy Stone and others. She was the first woman invited to address the House Judiciary Committee and made a brilliant presentation, arguing that female suffrage was already an implied right in the Constitution because of the use of the word person in the Fourteenth and Fifteenth amendments. Woodhull became the most talked about figure in the suffrage movement, and she kept the presses humming with public calls for "secession" if Congress did not grant women the vote and with her continued defense of sexual freedom for women. Woodhull's personality began to obscure the issues, and Susan B. Anthony had to oust her in 1872 as the leader of the National Woman Suffrage Association.

Woodhull then went into a period of decline, as she abandoned her spiritualist associations and divorced Colonel Blood for adultery in 1876. Suffering from ill health and financial setbacks, Woodhull moved to England and resumed her lecture career. Despite her philosophical renunciation of marriage, she married John Biddulph Martin, an aristocrat from a leading British banking family, on October 31, 1883. Although she was known for her beauty and wit, Woodhull's commitment to reform was genuine, a fact that has often been obscured because of her flamboyance and the attention she received from the media. Between 1892 and 1901, Woodhull and her daughter Zula Maud published the *Humanitarian,* a journal devoted to eugenics. She continued her interest in the woman's movement in the United States and returned to her native land on a number of occasions. Victoria Woodhull managed to outlive her husband and died amid affluence at her stately home at Bredon's Norton, Tewkesbury, England.

—Jonathan W. Zophy

See Also:

Free Love, National Woman Suffrage Association, Socialism

References:

Johnson, Johanna. *Mrs. Satan: The Incredible Saga of Victoria C. Woodhull.* New York: Putnam, 1967.

Marberry, M. M. *Vicky: A Biography of Victoria C. Woodhull.* New York: Funk and Wagnalls, 1967.

Meade, Marian. *Free Woman: The Life and Times of Victoria Woodhull.* New York: Knopf, 1976.

Sachs, Emanie. *"The Terrible Siren": Victoria Woodhull.* New York: Harper, 1928.

Schneir, Miriam. *Feminism: The Essential Historical Writings.* New York: Vintage, 1972.

WORK: A STORY OF EXPERIENCE, written by Louisa May Alcott and published in 1873, chronicles the experience of Christie Devon, a nineteenth-century working girl. Setting out at the age of twenty-one, Christie holds jobs such as parlor maid, paid companion, governess, actress, and seamstress. By the end of the story, Christie has been married and widowed, given birth to a daughter, become wealthy, and emerged as a spokesperson for women's rights.

Work is autobiographical in nature. The jobs held by Christie were jobs Alcott had taken during her lifetime. But Christie was an orphan with no family to support, while Alcott supported several family members, including her father, Bronson Alcott, an idealistic transcendentalist who shunned conventional employment. Suicide attempts, exhaustion, and depression are present in *Work,* and Alcott contemplated suicide and experienced depression. Characters in *Work* are based on people Alcott knew: Thomas Power was based on Thomas Parker, a minister who helped Alcott; and David Sterling was based upon Henry David Thoreau, dead at the time the book was published.

Transcendental ideals are present in the story. Self-realization and the quest for a balanced society echo throughout. Alcott extols the benefits of sexual equality, racial equality, and education for all. Her belief in women's rights and unity among women appears as a strong message in *Work*. The closing scene best illustrates this. Christie, head of a matriarchy, sits with her young daughter and friends of different ages, social classes, and upbringings, all holding hands and rejoicing in their experience and womanhood.

Work examines the life-style of a typical middle-class woman, constrained by the limited number of socially acceptable jobs and by society's opinion of "a woman's place." The story presents the problems caused by these social norms for the nineteenth-century woman.

—*Sheila Fitzpatrick*

See Also:

Alcott, Louisa May; Transcendentalism

References:

Alcott, Louisa May. *Work: A Story of Experience.* 1873; rpt. New York: Arno, 1977.

Douglas, Ann. "Mysteries of Louisa May Alcott." *New York Review of Books* 25 (September 28, 1978): 59–60.

Moers, Ellen. *Literary Women.* Garden City, N.Y.: Doubleday, 1963.

Review of *Work: A Story of Experience* by Louisa May Alcott. *Booklist* 74 (December 1, 1977): 597.

Review of *Work: A Story of Experience* by Louisa May Alcott. *New Yorker* 53 (October 3, 1977): 161.

Saxton, Martha. *Louisa May: A Modern Biography of Louisa May Alcott.* Boston: Houghton Mifflin, 1977.

Stern, Madeline. *Louisa May Alcott.* Norman: University of Oklahoma Press, 1950.

WORKERS' EDUCATION FOR WOMEN. Between 1910 and the 1930s, programs to educate women workers were established by labor unions, by government agencies and women's voluntary organizations, and by colleges and universities. For the most part, these efforts were not intended to help working women obtain college degrees, but rather were designed to provide them with an opportunity to study in order to understand their world better. An additional motive was to provide women with resources to help them organize unions and other sorts of self-help organizations on the job. Although most of the programs for workers' education for women were established in the opening decades of the century, these activities have continued up to the present.

Among the first workers' education programs to be established for women were those of the National Women's Trade Union League (NWTUL), a largely middle- and upper-class organization of women dedicated to improving the lives of women workers, particularly those working in industry. At about the same time (1914), the International Ladies Garment Workers Union (ILGWU) began its own program of education for women working in the garment trades, teaching them principles of trade unionism and other subjects. Slightly later, other programs were established by the YWCA, by other unions, and by state and local governments to allow working women to study during summer sessions at colleges and universities. Perhaps the most famous of these was the summer school for women workers held at Bryn Mawr College between 1921 and 1938. Other well-known summer programs were conducted at Barnard College and at the University of Wisconsin. In 1928 a national organization, the Affiliated Schools for Women Workers, was established to coordinate these activities and to provide information about various programs to women and to sponsoring agencies. Less than a decade later, this organization broadened its purview to include education for both men and women workers. It continued to perform this function until 1962 under the title American Labor Education Service.

What did women workers study in these programs? Although many of the worker education courses focused on problems of labor organization, most seem to have been general programs of study in the liberal arts. At Bryn Mawr and other colleges, women (most of them young) studied literature and history, economics (often with a focus on their own problems), politics, and the natural sciences. While these courses were often rather low key and introductory in orientation, both students and teachers remember them as having been especially poignant learning experiences. Only a small fraction of working women ever participated in workers' education programs, but a fairly high percentage of the alumnae of these programs became activists in the labor movement or in other organizations concerned with the welfare of working women.

—John L. Rury

See Also:

Bryn Mawr Summer School, National Women's Trade Union League

Reference:

Kornblush, Joyce L., and Mary Frederickson, eds. *Sisterhood and Solidarity: Workers Education for Women, 1914–1984.* Philadelphia: Temple University Press, 1984.

WORKING WOMEN'S PROTECTIVE UNIONS. Several distinct associations in a number of cities organized under this name between the 1840s and the 1870s. In each, benevolent leaders or middle-class reformers joined forces with working women for the latter's protection and improvement. One of the earliest such associations was the WWPU formed in Rochester, New York, in 1848. In the aftermath of the Rochester Woman's Rights Convention, feminists and seamstresses jointly declared that women were entitled "equally with men to the products of their labor or its equivalent," though the women's larger purpose was to associate together for their "individual and collective benefit and protection."

During the Civil War, the largest and most successful WWPUs emerged. The prototype was established in New York City in 1863, under the auspices of *New York Sun* editor Moses Beach. There were disagreements between the working women, mainly seamstresses, and the benevolent "gentlemen" over the relative power of each on the WWPU board. Ultimately, the benevolent leaders reserved decision-making to themselves while the working women formed an "advisory council." The WWPU advocated shorter hours and higher wages but focused most of its practical energies on providing legal services for women victimized by unscrupulous employers. Similar organizations were soon founded in Chicago, Detroit, St. Louis, San Francisco, and Baltimore, and remained active until the mid-1890s.

Most WWPUs organized employment agencies, and some established sickness and death benefit associations, cooperative workshops, and standard price scales. Others, probably under the influence of affluent benefactors, gave more attention to protecting working women's "purity and honor." The WWPUs competed with other mixed-class associations seeking to improve the working women's lot, such as the Working Girls' Clubs, the Working Women's Improvement Societies, the social settlements, and the Working Woman's Associations. The last of these, founded in 1868 under the influence of Susan B. Anthony, sought recognition by the National Labor Union; but most such organizations were substitutes for, not precursors of, unionization. Thus, the legacy of the WWPUs is to be found not in the efforts of working women to organize themselves but in organizations such as the National Women's Trade Union League and in campaigns for protective legislation.

—Nancy A. Hewitt

See Also:

National Labor Union, National Women's Trade Union League, Women's Work–Nineteenth Century

Reference:

Kessler-Harris, Alice. *Out to Work: A History of Wage-Earning Women in the United States.* New York: Oxford University Press, 1982.

WORKS PROGRESS ADMINISTRATION (WPA). In an effort to combat the widespread poverty and unemployment resulting from the Great Depression, the early programs in President Franklin D. Roosevelt's New Deal concentrated on direct relief (e.g., the Federal Emergency Relief Association). Between 1935 and 1941 the federal Works Progress Administration instituted a program of emergency relief based on public works projects for the millions of unemployed Americans who had not received adequate relief through previous or existing government relief programs. The WPA exceeded earlier governmental efforts in size, scope, and budgetary allocation. The original allocation for the WPA was $5 billion, and over three and a half million workers were eventually employed by the WPA, completing projects of public works that included over 110,000 public buildings, 100,000 bridges, 500,000 miles of roads, and 600 airports. The salaries paid to the WPA workers were less than those paid in the private sector but more than welfare assistance payments—roughly, fifty dollars a week.

Projects for the WPA were chosen on the basis of material costs and for their noninterference with the activities of the federal government or private industry. For this reason, the WPA is known for its innovative work in the arts and humanities and in providing employment to many difficult-to-employ Americans, including a large number of women.

Among the projects included in the WPA were the Federal Writer's Project, the Federal Arts Project, and the Federal Theater Project. Substantial numbers of women were employed by both the Federal Art and Federal Theater projects. The former provided art instruction and decorative murals in public buildings; the latter was an effort to bring the theater to Americans of all classes in all regions of the country. Hannie Flanagan (the first woman to be awarded a Guggenheim Fellowship) was chosen to head the Federal Theater Project, which produced plays, vaudeville shows, and experimental theater productions for some thirty million Americans. Louise Nevelson was involved with the Federal Arts Project, and Tillie Olsen in the Federal Writer's Project, which turned out state, territory, and regional guides to the United States and a 150-volume "Life in America" series, among other things. Ellen Woodward was head of the Women's and Professional Projects Division of the WPA.

As with other work-relief agencies, the WPA barred women from working in construction-related employment—the major component of public relief work. By 1935 the WPA employed about thirty-five thousand women, which represented about 15 percent of total WPA employment. In 1939 the Federal Theater Project was abolished by the U.S. Congress, and other projects were allowed to continue only if sponsors were located to bear 25 percent of the operating costs. As tribute to its success, the Federal Writer's Project was able to obtain this support in all of the (then) forty-eight states.

—*Maureen Anna Harp*

See Also:
New Deal; Olsen, Tillie

References:

McDonald, William J. *Federal Relief Administration and the Arts*. Columbus: Ohio State University Press, 1967.
Mangione, Jerre Gerlando. *The Dream and the Deal*. Boston: Little, Brown, 1972.
Mathews, Jane De Hart. *The Federal Theatre*. Princeton: Princeton University Press, 1967.

WORLD WAR I was paradoxical because it brought hardship and loss while at the same time presented opportunities and benefits to previously disadvantaged groups, with women making up the largest group taking advantage of those new opportunities. The war brought many women out of their homes and into new spheres of action, as well as made it possible for working women to move to more lucrative positions. White women, and to a lesser degree women of color, found jobs open to them in factories and war industries as never before. Four hundred thousand women joined the labor force for the first time, and eight million women who already held jobs switched from low-paying fields to higher paying industrial work. Women were employed for the first time in a variety of new areas, including law enforcement, railway operation, and as farm laborers attached to the "women's land army," a reserve of twenty thousand urban and rural women organized by the federal government to replace mobilized men in the Midwest and the Great Plains.

For middle-class women and professional women, the war provided opportunities outside of the work force, as women appeared for the first time on government bodies connected with the general war effort. These agencies included the Women's Committee of the Council for National Defense and the Department of Labor. Additionally, housewives were crucial to the success of rationing during Herbert Hoover's Food Administration from 1917 to 1919.

While many women served the war effort on the home front, another twenty-five thousand women received the unprecedented opportunity to serve overseas on the front lines in Europe. These women served with over one hundred different organizations of the United States and its allies, including the military, where women functioned as nurses and communications and supply personnel, and welfare organizations, such as the American Red Cross and the Young Women's Christian Association.

The emergency created by World War I, in addition to providing women with opportunities for service, also provided them with a temporary escape from restrictive societal definitions of woman's sphere and potential. Though their jobs were defined as temporary and "for the duration," women were still able to break through notions of their physical, mental, and emotional capabilities and thus began to open the door of equal opportunity.

—Leisa Diane Meyer

See Also:

Military Service

References:

Clarke, Ida Clyde. *American Women and the World War.* New York: Appleton, 1918.

Fraser, Helen. *Women and War Work.* New York: G. Arnold Shaw, 1918.

Greenwald, Maurine. *Women, War and Work.* Westport, Conn.: Greenwood, 1980.

Kalisch, Phillip A., and Margaret Scobey. "Female Nurses in American Wars: Helplessness Suspended for the Duration." *Armed Forces and Society* 9 (1983): 215–44.

Meyer, Leisa Diane. "'Miss Olgivy Finds Herself': American Women's Service Overseas During WWI." Master's thesis. University of Wisconsin-Madison, 1986.

Steinson, Barbara Jean. "Female Activism in WWI: The American Women's Peace, Suffrage, Preparedness and Relief Movements." Diss. University of Michigan, 1977.

WORLD WAR II saw American women serving their country in a variety of capacities on the home front and overseas. The barriers against married women teachers and "older" women workers (over thirty-five) were removed and never replaced. Women worked as farmhands and farm wives, in factories, and in clerical and sales positions. They began entry into banking positions, found more opportunities in middle-management positions, and entered professional schools. About 5 percent of the women worked as "Rosie the Riveters" and "Winnie the Welders" in positions that had traditionally been held by men and were reserved for men after the war. Half the black women domestics quit their positions and worked in more lucrative, higher status jobs. The remaining domestics could demand higher wages and better hours. Because of the shortages, both minority women and handicapped women were hired for factory work.

The percent of married women working jumped from 18 percent to 25 percent for the duration, a trend that continued after the war. During the war, as unemployment dropped to 2 percent and rationing was instituted, the tasks of the housewife were more demanding and time-consuming than ever before. Many housewives also tried to juggle part-time jobs or volunteer work along with raising a family and keeping it clothed and fed.

Women also served as volunteers with the Red Cross and USO and as members of the Army or Navy Nurse Corps or Women's Army

Corps overseas. (Women in other women's corps served only in the United States until late in the war; some were stationed in Alaska and Hawaii.) In total, 350,000 women served in the armed forces at some point during the hostilities. With the passage of the Women's Armed Services Integration Act in June 1948, the women's corps were made a permanent part of the armed forces.

After the war, many of the skilled women workers lost their positions as the wartime factories closed. Unions did not help the women who had held "men's" positions to find new ones. Many who had worked during the war wanted to return to "one job" as housewives in the postwar era. A new generation of women took their place in the work force, as clerical and secretarial positions increased dramatically after the war.

While some historians view World War II as a watershed, most now agree that there was more continuity than change as a result of the war years. Employers were never again so fearful of hiring women workers. However, the dual, or sex-segregated, labor force continues today, and so does inequity in pay between men and women workers.

—D'Ann Campbell

See Also:

Army Nurse Corps, Military Service, Mobilization, "Rosie the Riveter," SPARS, War Brides During World War II, WASPs, WAVES, Women's Army Corps

References:

Anderson, Karen Sue. *Wartime Women.* Westport, Conn.: Greenwood, 1981.

Campbell, D'Ann. *Women at War with America: Private Lives in a Patriotic Era.* Cambridge: Harvard University Press, 1984.

Chafe, William Henry. *The American Woman: Her Changing Social, Economic, and Political Roles, 1920–1970.* New York: Oxford University Press, 1972.

Gluck, Sherna Berger, ed. *Rosie the Riveter Revisited: Women, the War, and Social Change.* Boston: G. K. Hall, 1987.

Hartmann, Susan. *The Home Front and Beyond: American Women in the 1940's.* Boston: G. K. Hall, 1982.

Honey, Maureen. *Creating Rosie the Riveter: Class, Gender and Propaganda During World War II.* Amherst: University of Massachusetts Press, 1984.

Rupp, Leila. *Mobilizing Women for War: German and American Propaganda, 1939–1945.* Princeton: Princeton University Press, 1978.

WORLD'S COLUMBIAN EXPOSITION, held in Chicago, Illinois, in 1893, was the world's fair that celebrated the four-hundredth anniversary of Christopher Columbus's arrival in the "New World." It was the largest fair of its time, running for six months, from May 1 to October 30, 1893, and drawing more than twenty-seven million people. Located on the shores of Lake Michigan just south of the major business district, the fairground was dubbed the "White City" because of the white-painted stucco walls of its great exhibit halls built on a former swampland.

The Columbian Exposition, significant for many reasons, was an especially important event for women, for among its many structures were three buildings that were designed by and for women and their families. The Woman's Building was managed, designed, and decorated entirely by women. The Children's Building, which stood next door, and the Woman's Dormitory were built and administered by the board of lady managers. The Woman's Building had a predecessor in the Woman's Pavilion of the Philadelphia Centennial of 1876, the first exposition building entirely planned, funded, and managed by and for women, but the board of lady managers for the Chicago fair, led by Bertha Palmer and others, greatly expanded upon the concept first undertaken in Philadelphia.

The planners and supporters included both upper-class women and many middle- and lower-class women and feminists around the country. The exhibits included art and handiwork by women from many cultures, scientific exhibits, a model kitchen, a library, and exhibits from around the world. The Children's Building served as both a day-care facility for children and infants and an exhibit of the latest ventures in child raising and medical and educational practices, including lipreading instruction for deaf children. The

Woman's Dormitory was designed to provide clean, safe, and affordable lodging for women of modest means. In addition, the exhibits and the planning committees attempted to include black women; for example, the "color line" was not drawn in the children's nursery.

The Woman's Building, the Children's Building, and the Woman's Dormitory proved that women could plan, fund, and administer a massive project. Their achievement set the stage for larger efforts in future fairs and foreshadowed other milestones as well. Although only one building from the exposition still stands, the efforts and energy that came together for it serve as a special rallying point for the women's movement in particular and for women's history in the United States in general.

—*Elizabeth H. Coughlin*

See Also:
Art

References:

The Board of Lady Managers Papers. Chicago Historical Society, Chicago, Ill.

Midwest Women's Collection. University of Illinois Library, Chicago Campus, Chicago, Ill.

Adams, Henry. *The Education of Henry Adams.* Boston: Houghton Mifflin, 1918; rpt. New York: Modern Library, 1931.

Ginger, Ray. *Altgeld's America: The Lincoln Ideal Versus Changing Realities.* New York: Funk & Wagnalls, 1958.

Harper's Bazaar. 1892–94.

Weimann, Jeanne Madeline. *The Fair Women: The Story of Woman's Building, World's Columbian Exposition: Chicago, 1893.* Chicago: Academy Chicago, 1981.

THE YELLOW WALLPAPER (1892), written by Charlotte Perkins Gilman, was a fictional account of the author's own experiences undergoing Dr. S. Weir Mitchell's rest cure. In 1883 Gilman married Charles Stetson, and after giving birth to her daughter, she began to experience bouts of depression. Gilman consulted Mitchell, and he recommended she devote herself completely to domestic duties and spend no more than two hours per day engaged in intellectual activity. Following this advice seriously threatened Gilman's sanity.

The Yellow Wallpaper, based on this episode, is Gilman's best fictional work. Its main theme is that the emotional problems many women suffered in nineteenth-century America were the result of the stifling role they were expected to assume. The narrator in the story is brought to the country by her husband for some unspecified "nervous" disorder. Although the prescribed treatment consists of complete rest and repression of thought, the narrator stresses her will to work. She becomes obsessed with her room's wallpaper, which comes to symbolize her own oppression. Eventually, she goes insane and frantically rips down the wallpaper.

Unlike the narrator, Gilman did not go insane, but left her husband and resumed her career. Throughout her life, Gilman did not reject a domestic role for women; rather she wanted the work they did to be valued and respected. Through *The Yellow Wallpaper,* Gilman made a strong indictment of the Victorian subjugation of a woman's personality and talent to a mindless, purposeless existence.

When the story was published in May 1892, it was greeted with mixed reviews. Many liked it simply as a horrifying tale detailing insanity. It was not until the emergence of the women's movement in the 1960s that the full implications of the piece were appreciated.

—*Rose Kolbasnik Callahan*

See Also:

Gilman, Charlotte Perkins; Mind Cure

References:

Gilman, Charlotte Perkins. *The Yellow Wallpaper.* Boston: Small, Maynard & Co., 1899; rpt. Old Westbury, N.Y.: Feminist Press, 1972.

Scharnhorst, Gary. *Charlotte Perkins Gilman.* Boston: Twayne, 1985.

YEZIERSKA, ANZIA (1880?–1970), a Russian-Jewish emigrant to America around the turn of the century, wrote about what she knew best. Most of her novels and short stories involve Russian-Jewish women immigrants struggling to make a new life in America.

In the short story "America and I," from her collection *Children of Loneliness,* a young girl tells her story about becoming Americanized. Like most immigrants, upon her arrival she gets a job as maid for an already Americanized and successful immigrant family. These people treat her unfairly and tell her that she is greedy when she wants to be paid for her work. They argue that she should consider herself lucky because she has a nice place to sleep, food to eat, and a good job. The woman is crushed by the people's behavior and chooses to work in a sweatshop rather than work for them. It was a subject Yezierska wrote about often—the "immigrant characters' struggle with the disillusioning America of poverty and exploitation while they search for the 'real' America of their ideals" (Stinson, p. 481).

The young girl in "America and I" finds that, contrary to the stories she heard in Russia, the streets of her adopted country are not paved in gold. She finds the work at the sweatshop unsatisfying. She wants a job so that she can "do something with [her] head, [her] feelings." The character is not able to describe specifically what she wants to do, but it is obvious she wants a job that stimulates her both intellectually and emotionally. She wants a job that she can be proud of and that makes her more independent.

The young girl starts to read American history books and begins to see how alike she is to the Pilgrims, who also came to a new world that was unwelcoming. She begins "to build a bridge of understanding between the American-born and [herself]." This is what she had to do to begin to feel a part of America, and what Yezierska herself had done.

Through her stories, Yezierska brought the experiences of many immigrants and the treatment they received to the attention of the American public.

—*Susan Kogen*

See Aslo:
Immigration

References:

Stinson, Peggy. "Anzia Yezierska." In *American Women Writers from Colonial Times to the Present*, edited by Lina Mainiero. New York: Ungar, 1982, pp. 480–81.

Yezierska, Anzia. "America and I." In *Women Working, An Anthology of Stories and Poems*, edited by Nancy Hoffman and Florence Howe. Old Westbury, N.Y.: Feminist Press, 1979, pp. 19–32.

YOUNG, ELLA FLAGG (1845–1918) was the first woman to head a major urban school district and the first woman president of the National Education Association. She was born in Buffalo, New York, and her father was a skilled mechanic who moved his family to Chicago during the 1856–57 recession. Trained at Chicago High School in the "normal department"—which specialized in teacher training—she graduated in 1862, and at seventeen began her teaching career in the Chicago city school system. Three years later, she was appointed head teacher of the practice classroom at the Scammon School, the practice school of the Chicago Normal School, where she began a lifetime of interest in the pursuit of teaching excellence. She married William Young in December 1868 and continued her teaching duties.

Chicago was a turbulent city in the late 1800s, and Young stayed in the thick of school politics to achieve a reputation as a staunch defender of rank-and-file teachers and an advocate of teacher training. She advanced rapidly, first as a teacher in the normal department, then as a high school teacher, and eventually a district superintendent. Although her early career was an astounding success, Young's personal life was filled with tragedy. Her husband died in 1873, and her father and sister died shortly thereafter. In 1899, after being passed over by a field of political appointees for the superintendency of Chicago's overburdened school system, Young announced that she wanted to pursue a higher degree at the University of Chicago.

Educational philosopher John Dewey once attributed his knowledge of school teaching to the work of Ella Flagg Young as she completed her dissertation, "Isolation in the Schools," under his direction. Young helped Dewey set up his experimental laboratory school at the University of Chicago, but she was clearly waiting to get back into the politics and excitement of Chicago education. Her opportunity arose in 1900 when she was chosen to head the brand new Chicago Normal School. Under her guidance, the school grew in enrollment while she worked to achieve college credits for her graduates. She was especially concerned with enabling her teachers to handle the pressures of new immigrant children in Chicago's crowded classrooms, and pioneered in creating alliances between settlement house workers and schoolteachers.

In 1909, after nine turbulent years of union dissatisfaction under a harsh administrator, the board of education sought to end its school wars by appointing Young as the new superintendent. A year later, she was elected the first woman president of the National Education Association. She again aggressively took the reins of office, immediately setting management and labor relations at ease while she struggled with an unwieldy and corrupt board of education. Facing a budget deficit in 1915, she was harangued by board members who instigated a state legislative investigation of what they charged was "frenzied feminine finance." Young stepped down from office in December 1915 and died on October 26, 1918, in the height of the great flu epidemic while campaigning for war bonds. She left her estate to her constant companion and friend, Laura Brayton.

—*Marjorie Murphy*

See Also:

Education, National Education Association, Teaching as an Occupation for Women

References:

McManus, John T. *Ella Flagg Young and a Half Century of the Chicago Public Schools.* Chicago: A. C. McClurg, 1916.

Smith, Joan K. *Ella Flagg Young: Portrait of a Leader.* Ames: Iowa State University Research Foundation, 1979.

The **YOUNG LADIES ACADEMY** of Philadelphia was established in 1787 to give girls an education similar to that of boys in academies. Under the direction of head teacher John Poor, students learned grammar, arithmetic, geography, and oratory, which were recognized as the basic skills for functioning in a commercial society. Prominent men in the community took an active interest in the academy, first as school visitors and later as trustees once the school was incorporated in 1792. Their commitment to this experiment reflected the belief that educated wives and mothers were essential to transmit the social and political values of the new republic to future generations.

By 1788, more than one hundred young women had attended this interdenominational, secular school. Although most came from the Philadelphia area, the institution's reputation became such that parents up and down the eastern seaboard and as far away as the West Indies sent their daughters to the Young Ladies Academy. For most students, the experience of living away from the influence of family and the demands of domesticity was unique and important. At the academy, they lived with girls from many religious affiliations, different socioeconomic backgrounds and educational levels. The students formed intense friendships with their peers and grew in self-confidence from testing their minds in intellectual pursuits. The Young Ladies Academy played an important symbolic role by asserting that women were capable of learning academic subjects and by affirming society's need to educate women. In the 1800s similar academies for young women appeared throughout the settled areas of the new nation.

—*Cynthia J. Little*

See Also:

Education, Female Academies

Reference:

Gordon, Ann. "The Young Ladies Academy of Philadelphia." In *Women of America: A History.* Boston: Houghton Mifflin, 1979, pp. 69–91.

ZAHARIAS, "BABE" DIDRIKSON (1911–56) was an outstanding athlete and medical humanitarian. The sixth of seven children born to Norwegian immigrant parents in Port Arthur, Texas, Mildred Ella Didrikson first distinguished herself in high school basketball. A one-woman "team" at the 1932 Amateur Athletic Union Championships, she placed in seven events, including five firsts. This won her national publicity as the "Texas Tomboy." She was remarkable for the variety of sports in which she excelled: baseball throw, javelin, eighty-meter hurdles, shot put, high jump, and discus. At the 1932 Los Angeles Olympics, she won gold medals (eighty-meter hurdles—setting an Olympic record—and javelin) and a first-place tie in the high jump.

She appealed to the nation as the embodiment of the larger-than-life image of Texas, and the press reveled in her quick quips and brassiness as much as her athletic prowess. Meanwhile, her critics (some teammates, press, and public), although greatly outnumbered by her fans, condemned her as arrogant, boastful, and disturbingly unfeminine.

After the Olympics, she tried making money as a harmonica-playing stage entertainer, in mock demonstrations of her prowess, and touring with gender-mixed baseball teams. At times these activities had a circus-like atmosphere.

She chose golf as her next domain, pursuing it with the intensity and vigor she had previously devoted to track and field. Her first tournament (1934) led to others, including the 1938 competition that paired her with George Zaharias, a well-known professional wrestler whom she wed in that same year. Over several years, she won seventeen consecutive amateur golf tournaments. In 1948 she and five others co-founded the Ladies Professional Golf Association. Her golf championships—and antics—are legendary. She was voted "the greatest female athlete of the first half of the twentieth century" by the Associated Press in 1950, but her fortunes plummeted with the diagnosis of cancer in 1953.

One of the first to "go public" with her ailment as a self-help role model, she founded a Cancer Research Fund, attended charity golf tournaments, and promoted cancer education. She returned to golf—victoriously—mere weeks after a colostomy. Repeated hospitalizations in 1954–56 signaled the disease's supremacy, and she died at age forty-five in Galveston, Texas.

Named Woman Athlete of the Year six times by the Associated Press, her world, national, Olympic, and golf records are booklet-length. She was honored by cancer societies, public health agencies, and the Texas House of Representatives, and her sports and humanitarian artifacts are housed in a memorial museum in Beaumont, Texas. Her life is portrayed in her autobiography *This Life I've Led*, numerous children's books, two biographies, and a major motion picture. Because she was not prone to introspection and reflection, little of the private woman is explored. Not articulate about gender issues, she nonetheless provided a strong and fiercely competitive role model for other women—a model criticized by some. Yet she was a charismatic and richly talented woman. Her name is still evoked as the model of unparalleled athletic excellence. Her lust for life was palpable and commanded an audience in every arena.

—*Susan E. Cayleff*

See Also:
Athletics/Sports

References:

Babe Didrikson Zaharias papers. John Gray Library. Lamar University, Beaumont, Tex.

Cayleff, Susan E. "'Babe' Didrikson Zaharias: Her Personal and Public Battle with Cancer." *Texas Medicine* 82 (September 1986): 41–45.

Johnson, William Oscar, and Nancy P. Williamson. *"Whatta-Gal": The Babe Didrikson Story.* Boston: Little, Brown, 1975.

Zaharias, Babe Didrikson (as told to Harry Paxton). *This Life I've Led: My Autobiography.* New York: A. S. Barnes, 1955.

ZORACH, MARGUERITE THOMPSON (1887–1968) was one of only a few young artists to introduce fauvism and cubism to America between 1910 and 1920. She exerted great influence on the acceptance of modern art in America, being particularly successful because of her own experience in the production of modern art and her deep understanding of it.

While enrolled as a student at Stanford, Zorach readily accepted an invitation from her aunt to join her in Paris. Upon her arrival in Paris, Zorach visited the now famous Salon D'Automne of 1908. The world was shocked by the distortions and bold colors in the paintings, and the critics referred to the artists as "fauves" or wild beasts. Zorach was enthusiastic about the new art and quickly became very successful working in that style, exhibiting several times at the Paris Salon and the Salon D'Automne during her four years in Paris. The aunt disapproved both of her niece's bizarre paintings and her growing romance with an unsuitable young man, William Zorach, and decided it was time to take her home. Their tour of Egypt, Palestine, India, Burma, Malaysia, Indonesia, China, Korea, and Japan left Zorach with memories that influenced her work in the future.

Once back home in California, she held a show of her paintings, and their avant-garde style shocked conservative Fresno. Before joining husband-to-be William Zorach in New York, she saved several of her pieces painted in the fauve style and destroyed the rest. Thereafter, the Zorachs experienced the exciting pioneer days of the art world along with many other avant-garde artists and literary people. They exhibited in many important shows including the seminal Armory Show of 1913.

After her children were born in 1915 and 1917, Zorach began to create rich, complicated needlework pieces, easier to work than oils, which were sold to support the family. Though highly regarded, the tapestries were still classified as a lower-ranking "craft."

In 1925 Zorach founded and became the first president of the New York Society of Women Artists, an avant-garde association of women painters. The society's exhibits surprised and impressed the critics, but her art was too revolutionary to be accepted by most people. Two large murals Zorach did in the 1930s for the Federal Arts Project were rejected by her hometown of Fresno.

The Zorachs collaborated on their art all though their lives, and William was saddened that his own reputation as a sculptor overshadowed that of his wife, whom he recognized as a great artist. In 1968, shortly before her death, Zorach gave her son Tessim the roll of early paintings she had saved in 1913 before leaving California. These few paintings, exhibited for the first time in 1973 at the National Collection of Fine Arts in Washington, D.C., are today considered among her most important and finest works. Only a few examples exist dating from this 1908–20 period, which contains her most innovative work.

—*Holly Hyncik Sukenik*

See Also:

Art

References:

Fine, Elsa Honig. *Women and Art.* Montclair, N.J.: Allanheld and Schrum/Prior, 1978.

National Collection of Fine Arts, Smithsonian Institution. "Marguerite Zorach: The Early Years, 1908–1920." Washington, D.C.: December 7, 1973–February 4, 1984. [exhibit catalog]

Rubinstein, Charlotte Streifer. *American Women Artists.* Boston: Avon, 1982, pp. 172–76.

Tarbell, Robert K. "William and Marguerite Zorach: The Maine Years." Rockland, Maine: William Z. Farnsworth Library and Art Museum, 1980.

Tufts, Eleanor. *American Women Artists 1830–1930*. Washington, D.C.: National Museum of Women in the Arts, 1987.
Zorach, Tessim. "Marguerite Zorach—At Home and Abroad." New York: Kraushaar Galleries. January 11–February 4, 1984. [exhibit catalog]

ZUEBLIN, AURORA THOMPSON (FISK) (1868–1958) was an advocate of the American arts and crafts movement. She was educated at Northwestern University Academy in Evanston, Illinois, where her father Herbert Franklin Fisk was principal and professor of pedagogy. After teaching in public schools for two years, she married Charles Zueblin, a University of Chicago sociologist, founder of Northwestern Settlement, and a prominent figure in movements for civic improvements. She left teaching but remained active in the Chicago branches of the Society for Ethical Culture, the Public School Art Society, and the University Settlement League. She made her greatest mark on the times, however, as a member of the Chicago Arts and Crafts Society and as chronicler and theorist of that organization's ideals.

In 1895 Zueblin visited the Merton Abbey workshop of William Morris, whose revival of numerous handicrafts had inspired the British arts and crafts movement. There she witnessed workers joyfully making things that were both useful and beautiful. She now understood why many social reformers applauded Morris for having realized the ideal of uniting art and labor. In a series of eleven articles for *The Chautauquan*, 1902–04, Zueblin focused on this practical idealism as the distinctive feature of the arts and crafts movement. She reviewed the leading individuals and organizations in England and on the Continent, praised several American manufacturers of "industrial art," such as Rockwood Pottery in Cincinnati and Gustav Stickley's United Crafts in Syracuse, New York, and examined the potential impact of the movement on art education in public schools. These essays constituted the single most comprehensive survey of the arts and crafts movement to reach a national audience.

Zueblin's "Duties of the Consumer," appearing in *The Craftsman* in 1904, was her most original work. She was alarmed that so many modern consumers complacently accepted the "tyranny of things," living amidst a clutter of cheap objects that possessed little meaning for their lives. She called on them, therefore, to develop a more intelligent, caring, and responsible relationship with their physical surroundings. They should purge their homes of unnecessary accumulation and instead create simple and harmonious interiors. Through earnest choice and thoughtful use of household objects, consumers could "humanize" the domestic environment and transform it into an expression of their own personalities. Zueblin had succeeded in outlining an arts and crafts theory of consumption to complement the movement's emphasis on handicraft production.

—*Bruce R. Kahler*

See Also:

Art, Consumerism

References:

Kahler, Bruce R. "Art and Life: The Arts and Crafts Movement in Chicago, 1897–1910." Diss. Purdue University, 1986.
Zueblin, Rho Fisk. "The Arts and Crafts Movement." *The Chautauquan* 36–37 (October 1902–June 1903). [special issues]
———. "Duties of the Consumer." *The Craftsman* 7 (October 1904): 88–95.

The Contributors

CECELIA A. ALBERT is an associate editor at ABC-CLIO. She earned a B.A. in philosophy from the University of California at Santa Barbara.

GINGER RAE ALLEE is an instructor in history at San Jacinto College and Wharton County Junior College. She holds an M.A. in history from the University of Houston at Clear Lake.

HARRIET HYMAN ALONSO is Director of the Women's Center at Jersey City State College. She received her Ph.D. in history from the State University of New York at Stony Brook and is the author of *The Women's Peace Union and the Outlawry of War, 1921–1942.*

RIMA D. APPLE is assistant editor of *Isis*. She is the author of *Mothers and Medicine: A Social History of Infant Feeding, 1890–1950,* and is currently editing a book on the history of women and health in the United States. She earned her doctorate in the history of science at the University of Wisconsin-Madison.

THOMAS F. ARMSTRONG is professor of history and dean of the School of Arts and Sciences at Georgia College. He has published articles in such journals as the *Georgia Historical Quarterly* and *Labor History*. Dr. Armstrong earned his doctorate in history at the University of Virginia.

BARRY ARNOLD is an assistant professor of religious studies at the University of West Florida. He is the author of *The Pursuit of Virtue* and a number of scholarly articles. Dr. Arnold earned his doctorate at Emory University.

STEVEN AVELLA is an assistant professor of historical studies at St. Francis Seminary in Milwaukee, Wisconsin. Dr. Avella earned his Ph.D. in history at Notre Dame University and has published articles in the *Catholic Historical Review* and *Records.*

BETH L. BAILEY is an assistant professor of history at Barnard College. Dr. Bailey holds a Ph.D. in history from the University of Chicago and is the author of *From Front Porch to Back Seat: Courtship in 20th Century America.*

BARBARA BAIR is affiliated with the African Studies Center at the University of California, Los Angeles. She is the associate editor of *Marcus Garvey: Life and Lessons* and of volumes six and seven of *The Marcus Garvey and Universal Negro Improvement Association Papers.* She earned her Ph.D. in American civilization at Brown University.

JANET G. BALDINGER is a docent at the National Museum of Women in the Arts. She received her training in art education at the University of Maryland.

SUSAN BARBER-BOVE is the author of *The Early Italian Immigrants to Seneca Falls.* She is a graduate of St. John Fisher College in political science.

GRETCHEN M. BATAILLE is a professor of English at Arizona State University. Dr. Bataille is the author of *American Indian Literature: A Selected Bibliography* and co-author of *Images of American Indians in Film; American Indian Women Telling Their Lives; The Pretend Indians: Images of Native Americans in the Movies;* and *The Worlds Between Two Rivers: Perspectives on American Indians in Iowa.*

MARY BATTENFELD is a graduate teaching assistant in the Department of Afro-American Studies at the University of

Maryland. She earned her M.A. from the University of Maryland in 1984.

BEVERLY BEETON is professor of history and vice chancellor for academic affairs at the University of Alaska, Anchorage. Her publications include *Women Vote in the West: The Woman Suffrage Movement, 1869–1986* and *The Letters of Elizabeth Wells Randall Cummings.* Dr. Beeton earned her Ph.D. at the University of Utah.

ARLIE ROY BICE III is a student at the University of Houston at Clear Lake.

TERRY D. BILHARTZ is an associate professor of history at Sam Houston State University. Dr. Bilhartz is the author of *Urban Religion and the Second Great Awakening* and *Francis Asbury's America.* His Ph.D. is in history from George Washington University.

JULIA KIRK BLACKWELDER is an associate professor of history at the University of North Carolina at Charlotte. She is the author of *Women of the Depression: Caste and Culture in San Antonio, 1929–1939.* Dr. Blackwelder earned her Ph.D. in history from Emory University.

KATHLEEN BLEE is an associate professor of sociology and associate dean of the College of Arts and Sciences at the University of Kentucky. Her articles have appeared in such journals as *Sociological Spectrum, Sociological Quarterly, Current Perspectives in Social Theory, Sociological Perspectives, Feminist Studies,* and *Social Problems.* Dr. Blee earned her Ph.D. in sociology from the University of Wisconsin-Madison.

EDITH BLICKSILVER is an associate professor of literature at the Georgia Institute of Technology. She is the editor of *The Ethnic American Woman: Problems, Protests, Lifestyles.* She completed her graduate work at Smith College as a Sophia Smith Scholar.

JANET CARLISLE BOGDAN is an assistant professor of sociology at Le Moyne College in Syracuse, New York. Her essays have appeared in *Feminist Studies, Graduate Woman,* and *The American Way of Birth.* She earned a Ph.D. in social science (history and sociology) from Syracuse University.

DEBORAH DAWSON BONDE is on the faculty in the Boise State University English department. She earned her Ph.D. in American culture at Bowling Green State University and her M.A. in American studies at Washington State University.

CYNTHIA A. BRAGG is a graduate of the University of Houston at Clear Lake with a B.A. in literature.

KATHLEEN MARY BROWN is a Ph.D. candidate in history at the University of Wisconsin-Madison. She earned an M.A. in history also from the University of Wisconsin-Madison.

REGINA A. BROWN is an assistant professor and head of the Orton Memorial Library of Geology at The Ohio State University. She has published a chapter in volume 13 of the *Encyclopedia of Earth Sciences: The Encyclopedia of Applied Geology.* She earned an M.A. in library science from the University of Denver.

JOHN D. BUENKER is professor of history at the University of Wisconsin-Parkside. He holds a Ph.D. from Georgetown University and is the author of *Urban Liberalism and Progressive Reform* and co-author of *Progressivism* and *Immigration and Ethnicity,* among numerous other writings.

KAREN BUHLER-WILKERSON is an associate professor of community health at the University of Pennsylvania School of Nursing, where she earned her Ph.D. She is the editor of *Nursing and the Public's Health: An Anthology of Readings* and has published essays in *Nursing Research, American Journal of Public Health,* and in *Nursing History: New Perspectives, New Possibilities.*

NICHOLAS C. BURCKEL is director of public services and collection development of the Washington University libraries. His books include: *Immigration and Ethnicity, Racine: Growth and Change in a Wisconsin County, Progressive Reform,* and *Kenosha*

Retrospective. Dr. Burckel earned his Ph.D. in history at the University of Wisconsin-Madison.

DAVID H. BURTON is a professor of history at St. Joseph's University and author of biographies of *Theodore Roosevelt, Oliver Wendell Holmes, Jr.*, and *William Howard Taft.* Professor Burton received his Ph.D. in history from Georgetown University.

MARILYN DEMAREST BUTTON is an assistant professor at Lincoln University. Her University of Delaware doctoral dissertation was entitled "American Women in the Works of Frances Milton Trollope and Anthony Trollope."

ROSE KOLBASNIK CALLAHAN earned her B.A. in history with highest honors from the University of Wisconsin-Parkside. She has served as a research and editorial assistant on this *Handbook.*

D'ANN CAMPBELL is an associate professor of history at Indiana University. She is the author of *Women at War with America: Private Lives in the Patriotic Era.* Professor Campbell earned her Ph.D. in history at the University of North Carolina.

MARY JANE CAPOZZOLI is director of the liberal arts program at Warren County Community College. She holds a Ph.D. in history from Lehigh University and has written chapters for *The Melting Pot and Beyond: Italian Americans in the Year 2000* and *Evoking a Sense of Place: Long Island Studies.* She is one of the editors of *Our American Sisters.*

FLORIS BARNETT CASH is an assistant professor of Africana Studies at the State University of New York at Stony Brook. She has taught courses in Afro-American history, women's history, and American history. She was the guest curator at the Brooklyn Historical Society for the exhibit, "Black Women of Brooklyn," and author of the exhibition brochure, *Black Women of Brooklyn: Seventeenth Century to the Present.*

SUSAN E. CAYLEFF is an associate professor of women's studies at San Diego State University. She is the author of *Wash and Be Healed: The Water-Cure Movement and Women's Health.* Dr. Cayleff earned her Ph.D. from Brown University.

SANDRA L. CHAFF is a consultant for establishing women's collections and libraries. She is the former director of the archives and special collections on women in medicine and research instructor in the history of medicine at the Medical College of Pennsylvania in Philadelphia, and one of the editors of *Women in Medicine: A Bibliography of the Literature on Women in Medicine.*

SAMUEL L. CHELL is a professor of English and department head at Carthage College. His Ph.D. is from the University of Wisconsin-Madison. He is the author of *The Dynamic Self: Browning's Poetry of Duration* and a number of articles.

WENDY E. CHMIELEWSKI is the curator of the Swarthmore College Peace Collection. Dr. Chmielewski is the editor of the *Guide to Sources on Women in the Swarthmore College Peace Collection.* She is a doctoral student in the history department at the State University of New York at Binghamton, where she earned her M.A. in history.

DIANA CHURCH is an instructor in art at Richland College in Texas. She earned her M.A. at the University of Texas at Dallas and is the author of a *Guide to Dallas Artists, 1890–1917.*

ANNE L. CLARE is a docent at the National Museum of Women in the Arts in Washington, D.C. She is a graduate of Otterbein College in Westerville, Ohio.

GRACIA CLARK is an assistant professor in the Center for Afro-American studies and the department of anthropology at the University of Michigan. She is the editor of *Traders vs. the State* and holds a Ph.D. in social anthropology from Cambridge University. Dr. Clark has a book chapter on Asante market women in *The Social Economy of Consumption: Anthropological Approaches.*

ELIZABETH CLARK-LEWIS is the Benjamin Banneker Professor at George Washington University, Washington, D.C. She has published "From Live-in to Day Work" in *Southern Women: The Intersection of Race, Class, and Gender.* She has a Ph.D. in history from the University of Maryland.

CATHERINE CLINTON is a research associate at the W. E. B. DuBois Institute at Harvard University. Professor Clinton is the author of *The Plantation Mistress: Woman's World in the Old South* and *The Other Civil War: American Women in the Nineteenth Century.* Her most recent book is *Portraits of American Women.* Dr. Clinton earned her Ph.D. in history from Princeton University.

JONELL DUDA COMERFORD is an assistant professor of mathematics at Eastern Illinois University. She earned her Ph.D. in mathematics from the University of Illinois and has published in *Information and Control.*

MARY FRANCES CONCEPCIÓN has a bachelor of arts degree in music from DePaul University. She is a devotee of the operatic arts and hopes to make music her life's work.

ANNE ELIZABETH COOPERMAN holds a bachelor of arts degree in psychology from DePaul University and a bachelor of arts degree in art with a concentration in advertising from Columbia College.

CATHERINE COSGROVE is a doctoral candidate at Northern Illinois University who also teaches in the Hinsdale, Illinois, public schools. She has published on parent education in *Early Child Development and Care.*

GINGER COSTELLO is a graduate student and teaching assistant at the University of Montana. She earned her B.A. in creative writing and English literature from Ripon College.

ELIZABETH H. COUGHLIN is an instructor in English at DePaul University, where she earned her M.A. in English. Her publications include chapter divisions in *Rhetoric and Civilization.*

SUZANNE JONES CRAWFORD is an assistant professor of history at Cameron University. She received her Ph.D. in history from the University of Oklahoma. She has published *Preserving the Family Name: Eugene Davis McMahon and the McMahon Foundation.*

JANE CRISLER is a faculty member and Assistant Director of the Comprehensive AIDS Center of the Northwestern University Medical School. Her publications include essays in *College Teaching, Rhetoric and Civilization, George Moore in Perspective,* and the *Women's Studies Encyclopedia.* Dr. Crisler earned her Ph.D. in modern European history at the University of Wisconsin-Madison.

CAROL KLIMICK CYGANOWSKI is an assistant professor in the English department and Women's Studies Program at DePaul University. She earned her Ph.D. in English language and literature at the University of Chicago and is the author of *Magazine Editors and Professional Authors in Nineteenth Century America: The Genteel Tradition and the American Dream.* She has also published in the areas of composition and of computers in writing. Dr. Cyganowski served as an assistant to the editor for assignments for the *Handbook.*

MARY K. DAINS is an assistant director of the State Historical Society of Missouri and the associate editor of the *Missouri Historical Review.* She did her graduate work in history at the University of Missouri at Columbia.

FLORENCE DAVIS is a docent at the National Museum of Women in the Arts in Washington, D.C.

PAMELA DEAN, a Spencer dissertation-year fellow of the Woodrow Wilson Foundation, is a Ph.D. candidate at the University of North Carolina at Chapel Hill. She is the author of *Women on the Hill: A History of Woman at the University of North Carolina.* She earned her M.A. from the University of Maine.

JAYNE CRUMPLER DEFIORE is a doctoral candidate in history at the University of Tennessee, Knoxville, and assistant editor of the *Correspondence of James K. Polk.* She published an article on Rosalie

Slaughter Morton in *Collections*. Her M.A. is from the University of Tennessee at Knoxville.

MICHAEL A. DE LEÓN is a graduate student in historical studies at the University of Houston-Clear Lake, where he also did his B.A. in history.

TERRI DENNISON is a free-lance writer, who earned an M.A. in linguistics from the University of Wisconsin-Madison. She has published articles and short stories for children in *Educational Researcher, Highlights for Children, The Friend,* and *Wee Wisdom.*

PATRICIA DEUTSCH is an adjunct assistant professor of urban studies at the University of Wisconsin-Parkside. She earned her M.S. in urban affairs at the University of Wisconsin-Milwaukee.

HASIA R. DINER is an assistant professor of American studies at the University of Maryland. The author of *Erin's Daughters in America: Irish Immigrant Women in the Nineteenth Century,* Dr. Diner earned her Ph.D. from the University of Illinois in Chicago.

MINDY DUNKER has a B.S. in commerce accountancy from De Paul University and works for a public accounting firm. She is a fiction writer and poet.

MABEL BENSON DUPRIEST is an assistant professor of English and assistant dean of the college at Carthage College in Kenosha, Wisconsin. Dr. DuPriest earned her Ph.D. in English at the University of Kentucky.

TRAVIS DUPRIEST is a professor of English and coordinator of honors at Carthage College. He is the author of a volume of poetry, *Soapstone Wall,* and has edited *Jeremy Taylor's Discourse on Friendship,* among numerous other writings in various journals and literary magazines. He did his graduate work at Harvard Divinity School and the University of Kentucky, from which he received his Ph.D. in English literature.

FRANCES H. EARLY is an associate professor of history and women's studies at Mount Saint Vincent University, Halifax, Nova Scotia. She is the author of numerous articles on labor, family, and immigrant history; her more recent work on women's peace history has appeared in such journals as *Atlantis* and *Canadian Woman Studies.* Dr. Early holds the Ph.D. in history from Concordia University, Montreal, Canada.

PENELOPE J. ENGELBRECHT is a lecturer in English at DePaul University and at Barat College. Her poems have appeared in *Soundings* and *Nettles & Nutmeg.* She did her M.A. in English at DePaul University and is a doctoral student at Loyola University of Chicago.

MARIA E. ERLING is a doctoral student at Harvard Divinity School and was formerly a Lutheran parish pastor. She earned her master's of divinity from Yale University.

DAVID M. FAHEY is a professor of history at Miami University in Oxford, Ohio. He earned his Ph.D. in history at Notre Dame University.

MAUREEN FITZGERALD is a doctoral candidate in history at the University of Wisconsin-Madison, where she took her M.A., also in history.

SHEILA M. FITZPATRICK is a graduate of DePaul University in Chicago.

NANCY FOGELSON teaches history at Cincinnati Country Day School, Cincinnati, Ohio. She has published articles in *Fram: The Journal of Polar Studies, Diplomatic History,* and *The Journal of Military History.* Her Ph.D. is from the University of Cincinnati.

JOYCE FOLLET is writing her Ph.D. dissertation at the University of Wisconsin-Madison in history. She earned her M.A. in history at the University of Massachusetts at Amherst.

CARRIE FOSTER is an assistant professor of history at Miami University in Hamilton, Ohio. She holds the Ph.D. in history from the University of Denver.

LAWRENCE FOSTER is an associate professor of history in the School of Social Sciences at the Georgia Institute of Technology. He is the author of *Religion and Sexuality: The Shakers, the Mormons, and the Oneida Community* and articles in such publications as *Journal of the Early Republic, Journal of Mormon History, Utah Historical Quarterly*, and the *Australasian Journal of American Studies*. He did his doctoral work in history at the University of Chicago.

SARA ANN FOSTER is an assistant professor of social work at The Ohio State University. She has published essays in the *Journal of Education for Social Work* and *Gerontological Social Work*. Her graduate training has been at the University of Wisconsin-Madison.

SANDRA M. FOX is a faculty member at Lake Forest College. She earned her Ph.D. at the University of Texas at Austin.

MARY LOU FRANCE is a student status examiner at the University of Wisconsin-Parkside in Kenosha, Wisconsin.

KENNETH E. GADOMSKI is a senior technical writer for Academic Computing Support as well as a part-time instructor for the Women's Studies and English departments and the Division of Continuing Education at the University of Delaware. He has published in *Critical Surveys of Poetry: Supplement, Explicator, Journal of Narrative Technique*, and *Notes on Modern American Literature*. In 1984 he earned his Ph.D. in English from the University of Delaware.

LAURA GELLOTT is an associate professor of history and Associate Vice-Chancellor for Undergraduate Studies at the University of Wisconsin-Parkside. She is the author of *The Catholic Church and the Authoritarian Regime in Austria* and articles in *Commonweal, Journal of Contemporary History*, and *Mid-America*. She holds a Ph.D. in modern European history from the University of Wisconsin-Madison.

CAROLYN DE SWARTE GIFFORD earned her Ph.D. in history at Northwestern University. Dr. Gifford is the general editor of a reprint series on "Women in American Protestant Religion" published by Garland Press and has written essays in *Gender, Ideology and Action: Historical Perspectives on Women's Public Lives, Feminist Perspectives on Biblical Scholarship, Women and Religion in America*, and *Women in New Worlds*. She is currently editing the diaries of Frances E. Willard, a nineteenth-century American social reformer.

KAREN LOUPE GILLENWATERS is an assistant professor of English at Brazosport College in Lake Jackson, Texas. She earned her M.A. in English at Lamar State University.

ANN D. GORDON is the co-editor of the papers of Elizabeth Cady Stanton and Susan B. Anthony at the University of Massachusetts at Amherst. She earned her Ph.D. in history at the University of Wisconsin-Madison.

LINDA GORDON is a professor of history at the University of Wisconsin-Madison. Her books include: *America's Working Women, Cossack Rebellions: Social Turmoil in the Sixteenth-Century Ukraine, Woman's Body, Woman's Right: A Social History of Birth Control in America*, and *Heroes of Their Own Lives: The Politics and History of Family Violence*. Her articles have appeared in *Feminist Studies, Signs, American Quarterly, Social Problems*, and *Frontiers* among other journals. Professor Gordon received her Ph.D. in history from Yale University.

LYNN GORDON is an assistant professor of education at the University of Rochester. She has published in the *History of Education Quarterly, American Quarterly*, and *Woman's Being, Woman's Place*. Yale University Press is publishing her book, *Separate Places: Women's Campus Communities in the Progressive Era*. Dr. Gordon holds a Ph.D. in history from the University of Chicago.

SARAH GORDON is professor of English at Georgia College and the editor of *The Flannery O'Connor Bulletin*. She earned her Ph.D. in English at Texas Christian University.

CYNTHIA LYNN GOULD is an M.F.A. candidate at Southern Methodist University. She earned a B.A. in women's studies from the University of Washington in Seattle.

C. JANE GOVER teaches in the Museum Studies Program, New York University. She is the author of *The Positive Image: Women Photographers in Turn of the Century America.*

THERESA M. GRAZIANO is a graduate of the University of Wisconsin-Parkside.

CASEY EDWARD GREENE is an assistant archivist at the Rosenberg Library in Galveston, Texas. He earned his master's in library science at North Texas State University and is a candidate for an M.A. in history at the University of Houston, Clear Lake.

WENDELL L. GRIFFITH is a faculty member in history at Okaloosa/Walton Community College and a Ph.D. candidate at Florida State University. He is a graduate of Louisiana Tech University and the University of West Florida.

DARYL M. HAFTER is a professor of history at Eastern Michigan University. Dr. Hafter has published essays in *Annals of the New York Academy of Sciences, Women's Life Cycle and Public Policy, Dynamos and Virgins Revisited: Women and Technological Change in History,* and *The American Woman: Her Past, Her Present, Her Future.* Professor Hafter holds a Ph.D. in history from Yale University.

KEVIN JACK HAGOPIAN is editor of *The Film Literature Index* at the State University of New York, Albany. He has published essays in *The Velvet Light Trap: A Review of Cinema, Films and Filmmakers Vol. IV,* and *The Quarterly Review of Film Studies.* He is a Ph.D. candidate in film history and theory at the University of Wisconsin-Madison.

PATRICIA HAIRE is a student at DePaul University with a major in English and with communications as a supporting field of study.

JACQUELYN D. HALL teaches in the history department at the University of North Carolina at Chapel Hill. Professor Hall is the author of *Revolt Against Chivalry: Jessie Daniel Ames and the Women's Campaign Against Lynching* and essays in the *American Historical Review, Powers of Desire: The Politics of Sexuality, Journal of American History, Feminist Studies,* and *Interpreting Southern History.* She is one of the authors of *Like a Family: The Making of a Southern Cotton Mill World.* She holds a Ph.D. in history from Columbia University.

WENDY F. HAMAND is an associate professor of history at Eastern Illinois University. She has published articles in *Civil War History* and *New England Quarterly.* Professor Hamand completed her Ph.D. in history at the University of Illinois at Urbana-Champaign.

ROGER D. HARDAWAY is an instructor of history and political science at Eastern New Mexico University at Clovis. His essays have been published in such journals as the *Journal of Arizona History, Tennessee Historical Quarterly, Alabama Historical Quarterly, North Dakota Quarterly, Annals of Wyoming, Red River Valley Historical Review, Tennessee Education,* and *West Tennessee Historical Society Papers.* He earned a law degree at Memphis State University.

MAUREEN ANNA HARP is on the staff of the Center for American Culture Studies at Columbia University and also teaches at Regis High School in New York City. She is one of the contributors to *American Studies: An Annotated Bibliography.* Ms. Harp did her graduate work in history at Columbia University.

KAREN V. HARPER is an assistant professor of social work at The Ohio State University, where she earned her Ph.D. in social work. She is the author of essays in *Human Services in the Rural Environment, Parent-Professionals Interaction: Barriers to Parental Involvement, Affilia: Journal of Women and Social Work, Journal of Contemporary Family Therapy,* and *Journal of Logotherapy.*

TED C. HARRIS is professor of history and chair of the division of arts and sciences at Waycross College in Waycross, Georgia. Dr. Harris is the author of *Jeannette Rankin: Suffragist, First Woman*

Elected to Congress, and Pacifist. Dr. Harris earned his Ph.D. in history at the University of Georgia.

VIVIEN HART is a reader in American Studies at the University of Sussex, England. She is the author of *Distrust and Democracy: Political Distrust in Britain and America.* Dr. Hart received her Ph.D. in history at Harvard University.

SUSAN M. HARTMAN is professor of history and director of the Center for Women's Studies at The Ohio State University. She is the author of *The Home Front and Beyond: American Women in the 1940s* and *From Margin to Mainstream: American Women and Politics Since 1960.* Her Ph.D. in history is from the University of Missouri-Columbia.

JEAN M. HAYES lives in Galveston, Texas. She earned her M.A. in history at the University of Houston-Clear Lake.

TAMERIN MITCHELL HAYWARD teaches history in the International Baccalaureate program at Case High School in Racine, Wisconsin. She earned her M.A. in history at the University of Wisconsin-Milwaukee.

RITA RUBINSTEIN HELLER is co-producer of the National Endowment for the Humanities film *The Women of Summer,* which is the story of the Bryn Mawr Summer School for Women Workers. Dr. Heller is also the author of essays in *History of Higher Education Annual, Bryn Mawr College's Centennial Book,* and *Sisterhood and Solidarity: Workers Education for Women, 1921–1938.* She holds a Ph.D. in history from Rutgers University.

ROSEMARY HERRIGES, OSF, is an elementary school teacher in Racine, Wisconsin. She holds a master's degree from Carthage College.

NANCY A. HEWITT is an associate professor of history at the University of South Florida. She is the author of *Women's Activism and Social Change: Rochester, New York, 1822–1872* and articles in *Social History* and *Feminist Studies.* Her Ph.D. in history is from the University of Pennsylvania.

SUZANNE HILDENBRAND is an associate professor in the School of Information and Library Studies at the State University of New York at Buffalo. Her essays have appeared in *Library Trends, Journal of Library History,* and *The Status of Women in Librarianship.* Dr. Hildenbrand completed her Ph.D. at the University of California, Berkeley.

MARY G. HODGE is an assistant professor of anthropology at the University of Houston-Clear Lake. She earned her Ph.D. in anthropology with an emphasis on Mesoamerican archaeology at the University of Michigan at Ann Arbor.

NEIL W. HOGAN is a professor of history at East Stroudsburg University of Pennsylvania. His publications include numerous articles and papers on women's history and twentieth-century British social and political history. He earned his Ph.D. at The Ohio State University.

JAMES A. HOWLEY has a B.A. in English from DePaul University and is working on a M.A. in higher education at The Ohio State University.

CAROL SUE HUMPHREY is an assistant professor of history at Oklahoma Baptist University. She has published articles in such journals as *American Journalism, Journalism History,* and *Social Science Perspectives Journal.* Dr. Humphrey completed her Ph.D. in history at the University of North Carolina at Chapel Hill.

LAURA E. HYNES is a graduate of DePaul University.

HUGH J. INGRASCI is an associate professor of English at DePaul University. His essays have appeared in *The Explicator, The Cabellian, Long Time Sun,* and *Studies in Black Literature.* He earned his Ph.D. in English at the University of Michigan.

R. JANIE ISACKSON is the Bridge Program coordinator and an adjunct faculty member at DePaul University. She earned her M.A. from Goddard College.

CAMILLE JASKI earned her bachelor of arts degree at DePaul University and is currently working on a law degree from Chicago-Kent College of Law.

GLEN JEANSONNE is a professor of history at the University of Wisconsin-Milwaukee. His books include *Leander Perez: Boss of the Delta* and *Gerald L. K. Smith: Minister of Hate*. He has also published more than thirty articles. He received his Ph.D. in history from Florida State University in 1973.

MARGARET JERRIDO is associate archivist and director of the Black Women Physicians Project at the Medical College of Pennsylvania. She has published in *Women and Health* after earning her M.L.S. from Drexel University.

BRUCE R. KAHLER is an assistant professor of history at Bethany College, Kansas. His articles have appeared in *Selected Papers in Illinois History* and *Tiller*. Dr. Kahler earned his Ph.D. in history at Purdue University.

HILARY JO KARP is an associate professor of psychology at the University of Houston-Clear Lake. She has just completed a manuscript entitled "An Introduction to Signal Detection Theory." Dr. Karp completed her Ph.D. in psychology at the University of Chicago.

ESTHER KATZ is deputy director of the Institute for Research in History and editor/project director of the Margaret Sanger Papers. She is the co-editor of *Women's Experience in America: An Historical Anthology*. Dr. Katz completed her graduate study in history at New York University.

EVELYN G. KATZ is a docent at the National Museum of Women in the Arts. She earned an M.S. in biology and education at the City University of New York.

FRANCES M. KAVENIK is an assistant professor of English and director of the ACCESS Program at the University of Wisconsin-Parkside. She is the co-author, with Eric Rothstein, of *The Designs of Carolean Comedy* and editor of *Concerns*, the newsletter of the Women's Caucus of the Modern Language Association. The associate editor of this *Handbook*, Dr. Kavenik received her Ph.D. in English from the University of Wisconsin-Madison.

LOUISE M. KAWADA is a part of the Alliance of Independent Scholars in Boston, Massachusetts. Her publications include *The Apocalypse Anthology*. Dr. Kawada earned her Ph.D. at the University of Chicago.

CATHERINE E. KELLEY is a Ph.D. candidate in history at the University of Rochester.

JANE A. KENAMORE is the archivist at the Art Institute of Chicago.

ANDREA MOORE KERR is a free-lance writer who has just completed a full-length biography of Lucy Stone.

AMY KESSELMAN is an assistant professor of women's studies at the State University of New York College at New Paltz. She is the author of the forthcoming *Fleeting Opportunities: Women Shipyard Workers in Portland and Vancouver During World War II and Reconversion* and has published an article on Lydia Sayer Hasbrouck in the *Orange County Historical Journal*. Professor Kesselman completed her Ph.D. at Cornell University.

SUSAN KEYES is a frequent art exhibition reviewer for the *New Art Examiner*, and her interviews with people in the arts appear in the *Washington Review*. She earned her M.A. and M.F.A. at the University of Iowa.

KAREL KILIMNIK is a schoolteacher in the Philadelphia Public School System. She did her graduate work at Beaver College.

BOBBY ELLEN KIMBEL is an assistant professor of English at Pennsylvania State University at Ogontz. She is the author of *Katherine Anne Porter: Studies in Short Fiction* and one of the editors of the multivolume *The American Short Story to World War Two*. Professor Kimbel earned her Ph.D. in English at Temple University.

MARJORIE KING is an associate professor of history at St. John's University, Minnesota. Her most recent publications are in *Women's Work for Women: Missionaries and Social Change in Asia*, *Women's Studies International Forum*, and *The Impact of American Missionaries on U.S.*

Attitudes and Policies Toward China. Her Ph.D. in history was completed at Temple University.

SUSAN K. KINNELL is online coordinator for ABC-CLIO. She is co-author of *Searching America: History and Life and Historical Abstracts on Dialog,* and the forthcoming *Hypertext/HyperMedia in Schools: A Handbook for Librarians and Teachers.* A graduate of Mount Holyoke College, Ms. Kinnell has edited a number of bibliographies.

KATHLEEN KIRK is a free-lance writer and actress. A graduate of Kenyon College, Ms. Kirk has published numerous poems, stories, and a wide range of articles. Her three one-act plays have been produced in Chicago.

BARBARA HOPE KLEIN is a graduate of DePaul University.

KAREN C. KNOWLES is a lecturer in the writing program at DePaul University. She published an article on nineteenth-century women writers of Rhode Island in *American Transcendental Quarterly.* Ms. Knowles earned an M.A. in English and American literature at Boston College.

SUSAN H. KOESTER is an associate professor of speech communication at the University of Alaska, Southeast. She is the editor of *Western Speakers: Voices of the American Dream* and has written articles for *The Journal of the Northwest Communication Association* and the *Journal of the West.* She was granted a Ph.D. in speech communication by the Union for Experimenting Colleges and Universities.

SUSAN KOGEN is an undergraduate student at DePaul University in Chicago.

SALLY GREGORY KOHLSTEDT is professor of history of science at the University of Minnesota. Professor Kohlstedt is the author of *The Formation of the American Scientific Community: The American Association for the Advancement of Science,* plus many book chapters and scholarly articles. She received her Ph.D. from the University of Illinois in history.

MARI LYNN KORTIER graduated with highest honors from Carthage College and works for the Lutheran Volunteer Corps.

DAVID KUNZLE is a professor of art history at the University of California at Los Angeles. He is the author of *The Early Comic Strip, Nineteenth Century Comic Strip,* and *Fashion and Fetishism.* He earned his Ph.D. at the University of London.

BARBARA E. LACEY is an assistant professor of history at Saint Joseph College in West Hartford, Connecticut. She has written scholarly articles for the *William and Mary Quarterly, Rhode Island History,* and the *New England Quarterly.* Dr. Lacey earned her Ph.D. in history at Clark University.

MOLLY LADD-TAYLOR is a visiting assistant professor in women's studies at Northwestern University. She is the author of *Raising a Baby the Government Way: Mothers' Letters to the Children's Bureau, 1915–1932.* Dr. Ladd-Taylor completed her Ph.D. in American studies at Yale University.

JAN LAMBERTZ is a graduate student in history at Rutgers University. She has an M.Phil. from the University of Manchester in England and has written a number of articles on women in British history.

AVERY PRESTON LANE is a student at the North Carolina School of the Arts and has worked for the Shenyang Translator's Company, Shenyang, Liaoning, The People's Republic of China.

ELLEN D. LANGILL is a lecturer in history at Carroll College, Waukesha, Wisconsin and at the University of Wisconsin in Milwaukee and in Waukesha. She is the author of *Carroll College, the First Century* and the editor of *From Farmlands to Freeways.* Dr. Langill earned her doctorate in history at the University of Wisconsin-Madison.

JIM LANTZ is an assistant professor of social work at The Ohio State University. He is the author of *Family and Marital Therapy* and *An Introduction to Clinical Social Work,* plus many articles. Dr. Lantz earned his Ph.D. in social work at The Ohio State University.

KATHLEEN LAUGHLIN is a graduate student in the history department at The

Ohio State University.

CHRISTINE MILLER LEAHY is coordinator of Elementary School Programs at the National Museum of Women in the Arts. She received an M.A.T. degree from George Washington University.

CRISTINE M. LEVENDUSKI is an assistant professor of American Literature and American Studies at Emory University. She did her M.A. in English at the University of Minnesota in Duluth and her Ph.D. in American studies at the University of Minnesota-Minneapolis.

DAVID S. LEVIN is an associate professor of philosophy at the University of Wisconsin-Parkside. The author of a number of articles on ethics, Professor Levin received his Ph.D. in philosophy from Cornell University.

LYNN E. LIPOR is a graduate of the University of Wisconsin-Parkside.

MAUREEN R. LISTON, an independent scholar with extensive experience teaching in West German universities, resides in Paderborn, West Germany. Among her writings are *Gertrude Stein: An Annotated Critical Bibliography* and *An Essay to Introduce Gertrude Stein's "A Novel of Thank You".* She did her M.A. in English literature and American studies at Case Western Reserve University and her Dr.Phil. at Ruhr-Universitaet Bochum in the Federal Republic of Germany.

JUDY BARRETT LITOFF is a professor of history at Bryant College. She is the author of *American Midwives, 1860 to the Present, Miss You: The World War II Letters of Barbara Wooddall Taylor and Charles E. Taylor,* and articles in *The Historian, Journal of Nurse-Midwifery, Labor History,* and *Notable American Women.* She earned her Ph.D. in history at the University of Maine.

CYNTHIA JEFFRESS LITTLE is director of education for the Historical Society of Philadelphia. She is the author of *Women's Historical Philadelphia: A Self-Guided Walking Tour.* Dr. Little took her Ph.D. in history at Temple University.

MARY LOWE-EVANS is an assistant professor of English at the University of West Florida. In addition to *Crimes Against Fecundity: Joyce and Population Control,* she has authored articles for *Studies in the Novel, The James Joyce Quarterly, The Journal of Modern Literature,* and *The Explicator.* Professor Lowe-Evans did her Ph.D. at the University of Miami.

JUDITH B. LUCAS is a classroom teacher and Social Studies Department Head at Clear Brook High School. She obtained an M.A. in history at the University of Houston-Clear Lake.

THERESE L. LUECK is an associate professor in the department of communication at the University of Akron. She earned her M.A. degree in English at Bowling Green State University and has published an article on John Ames Mitchell in the *Dictionary of Literary Biography.*

MARGARET T. MCFADDEN is chief of interpretation at the Women's Rights National Historical Park. She is the author of *Women's Rights Trail: Seneca Falls and Waterloo, New York.* Ms. McFadden is a graduate in philosophy and women's studies of Wells College in Aurora, New York.

THERESA A. MCGEARY is a recent graduate from DePaul University.

BARBARA MCGOWAN is an associate professor of history at Ripon College in Wisconsin. She earned her Ph.D. in American culture at the University of Michigan.

JOHN R. MCKIVIGAN is an assistant professor of history at the West Virginia University and an associate editor of the Frederick Douglass papers at Yale University. He is the author of *The War Against Proslavery Religion: Abolitionism and the Northern Churches, 1830–1865.* Dr. McKivigan earned his Ph.D. at The Ohio State University, where he studied under Merton Dillon.

LINDA O. MCMURRY is a professor of history at North Carolina State University. She is the author of *George Washington Carver: Scientist and Symbol* and *Recorder of the Black Experience: A Biography of Monroe Nathan Work.* Professor McMurry completed her Ph.D. in history at Auburn University.

GAIL MALMGREEN is associate archivist at the Institute for Advanced Study, Princeton University and was formerly associate editor of the papers of Elizabeth Cady Stanton and Susan B. Anthony at the University of Massachusetts. Dr. Malmgreen is the author of *Neither Bread Nor Roses: Early Feminist Socialists and the Working Class* and *Silk Town: Industry and Culture in Macclesfield, 1750–1835.* She is the editor of *Religion in the Lives of Englishwomen.* She holds the Ph.D. in history from Indiana University.

STEVEN MANDEVILLE-GAMBLE is a doctoral student in anthropology at the University of Michigan. He did his undergraduate work at Stanford University.

SHIRLEY MARCHALONIS is an associate professor of English and comparative literature at Penn State University, Berks campus. She has written *The Worlds of Lucy Larcom, 1824–1893* and edited and contributed to *Patrons and Protégées: Gender, Friendship, and Writing in Nineteenth Century America.* Professor Marchalonis completed her Ph.D. in English at Penn State University.

RUTH JACKNOW MARKOWITZ is a Ph.D. candidate at the State University of New York at Stony Brook, where she also took her M.A. in history.

DONALD B. MARTI is an associate professor of history at Indiana University at South Bend. He has published articles on women's history in *Agricultural History.* Professor Marti obtained his Ph.D. at the University of Wisconsin-Madison.

DONALD R. MARTIN is an assistant professor of communications at DePaul University. He has published an article on Barbara Jordan in *Southern Speech Communication Journal.* His Ph.D. is from the University of Texas.

LOU ANN MATOSSIAN is a Ph.D. candidate in linguistics at the University of Pennsylvania. She has published in *Language in Society* and *Women and Language* and earned an M.S. from the University of Pennsylvania.

VIRGINIA BEATTIE MATTES holds both an M.A. and an M.A.T. from the University of Chicago.

KAREN P. MATTOX is a graduate of Oberlin College in Ohio, where she studied art history. She was the first education intern at the National Museum of Women in the Arts, Washington, D.C.

KAREN MERRITT is director of academic planning and program review for the University of California. Dr. Merritt has published essays in *Beyond Intellectual Sexism: A New Woman, a New Reality* and *Frontiers.* She earned her Ph.D. at Harvard University.

LEISA DIANE MEYER is a dissertator and teaching assistant at the University of Wisconsin-Madison, where she earned her M.A. in history.

JOANNE J. MEYEROWITZ is an assistant professor of history at the University of Cincinnati. She is the author of *Women Adrift: Independent Wage Earners in Chicago, 1880–1930.* Professor Meyerowitz completed her doctorate at Stanford University.

GRETCHEN MIESZKOWSKI is a professor of literature and women's studies at the University of Houston-Clear Lake. She is the author of *The Reputation of Criseyde: 1155–1500* and frequent essays in *The Chaucer Review.* Professor Mieszkowski earned her Ph.D. in English at Yale University.

LINDA PATTERSON MILLER is an associate professor of English at Pennsylvania State University at Ogontz. She has contributed articles to the *Journal of Modern Literature, American Transcendental Quarterly, Studies in American Fiction, Mosaic, Renasance, Journal of the Early Republic,* among others. She holds the Ph.D. in English from the University of Delaware.

RANDALL M. MILLER is professor of history at Saint Joseph's University and editor of the *Pennsylvania Magazine of History and Biography.* Among his numerous books and articles are *"Dear Master": Letters of a Slave Family* and *Catholics in the Old South*. He is the co-editor of the *Dictionary of Afro-American Slavery*. He received his Ph.D. from The Ohio State University.

SALLY M. MILLER is professor of history at the University of the Pacific and managing editor of *The Pacific Historian*. She is the author of *The Radical Immigrant* and the editor of *Flawed Liberation: Socialism and Feminism*. Professor Miller earned her Ph.D. in history from the University of Toronto.

MARJORIE MURPHY is an assistant professor of history at Swarthmore College. She is the author of *Blackboard Unions* and holds a Ph.D. in history from the University of California, Davis.

MARY MURPHY is a visiting lecturer in history at the University of Wyoming and a co-author of *Like a Family: The Making of a Southern Cotton Mill World*. She is also a Ph.D. candidate at the University of North Carolina at Chapel Hill.

LYNN R. MUSSLEWHITE is a professor of history and chair of the Department of History and Humanities at Cameron University. He received his Ph.D. in history from Texas Tech University.

ANNE DEHAYDEN NEAL is deputy general counsel of the Recording Industry Association of America and first vice-president and director of the National Museum of Women in the Arts. She has a B.A. in American history and literature from Harvard and a J.D. from Harvard Law School. Ms. Neal is also a contributor to the *Handbook to the American Collection, Corcoran Gallery*.

JEAN NETTLES is a certification analyst at the school of education at the University of Houston-Clear Lake. She earned her B.S. degree at the University of Houston.

DEBRA L. NEWMAN is with the Manuscripts Division of the Library of Congress. Dr. Newman is the author of *Black History: A Guide to Archival Records in the National Archives*. She completed her Ph.D. in history at Harvard University.

MICHELE NEWTON is director and curator of the Powers Museum. She earned her M.A. in historical administration at Eastern Illinois University.

LINDA S. NOER is an assistant professor of sociology and social work at Carthage College. She published chapters in *Wisconsin Women* and *Divorce and the Christian Community*. Professor Noer holds an M.S.W. from Washington University.

MARIANN L. NOGRADY teaches in the Newton Public Schools in Newton, Massachusetts. She is a graduate of Knox College.

NAN NOWIK was an associate professor of English at Denison University and held a Ph.D. in English from The Ohio State University. While writing her articles for this book, Dr. Nowik was diagnosed as having rapidly growing brain tumors. She heroically completed her *Handbook* essays after undergoing two brain surgeries and during radiation treatment; she died before this volume went to press.

CLAUDIA M. OAKES is curator of aeronautics at the Smithsonian Institution. She is the author of *United States Women in Aviation Through World War I* and *United States Women in Aviation, 1930–1939*. She earned a master of public administration degree from George Washington University.

LAURA OREN is an associate professor of law at the University of Houston Law Center. Dr. Oren has published essays in *Feminist Studies* and the *Biographical Dictionary of Modern British Radicals*. She holds both a J.D. from the University of Houston Law Center and a Ph.D. in history from Yale University.

PAMELA PATTERSON is a student at DePaul University.

TERESA PECK was an associate professor of education and coordinator of the Women's Studies Program at the University of Wisconsin-Parkside. A native of Great Britain and the author of a number of scholarly articles, Dr. Peck now lives in northern California.

SAMUEL E. PEREZ is a graduate of

DePaul University and a published poet.

SUSAN KELLOGG PORTNEY is a docent at the National Museum of Women in the Arts. She is a graduate of the University of Miami.

LINDA RAY PRATT is a professor of English at the University of Nebraska at Lincoln. She edited *I Hear Men Talking: Stories of the Early Decades by Meridel Lesueur* and has published articles in *Victorian Poetry* and *Women's Studies.* Professor Pratt holds her Ph.D. in English from Emory University.

RICHARD PROUTY holds a M.A. in English literature from DePaul University.

JUDITH PRYOR is the coordinator of instruction at the Library/Learning Center of the University of Wisconsin-Parkside. She is the co-editor of *Delivering Government Services* and earned her M.L.S. at Indiana University.

LANA F. RAKOW is an assistant professor of communication at the University of Wisconsin-Parkside. She is the co-editor of *The Revolution in Words* as well as articles in *Communication, Women's Communication and Technology,* and *Women and Language.* Dr. Rakow completed her Ph.D. in communications at the University of Illinois, Champaign-Urbana.

EILEEN R. RAUSCH is manager of compensation and benefits at the University of Hartford. Dr. Rausch earned her Ph.D. at the University of Notre Dame.

BONNIE LOU RAYNER teaches in the Hinsdale (Ill.) Public School system. She earned her master's degree in education with a concentration in early childhood leadership and advocacy from National College of Education in Illinois.

CLAIRE M. RENZETTI is an associate professor of sociology at St. Joseph's University. She is the co-author of *Women, Men and Society: The Sociology of Gender, Social Problems: Society in Crisis,* and essays in *Contemporary Crises, Sex Roles, Family Relations,* and the *Journal of Interpersonal Violence.* Dr. Renzetti completed her graduate work at University of Delaware.

DIANA DINGESS RETZLAFF is a graduate of San Jacinto Junior College in Texas and is now a student at the University of Houston-Clear Lake.

JOANNE S. RICHMOND is the associate pastor of Westby-Coon Prairie Lutheran Church and Vang Lutheran Church in Wisconsin. A graduate of Carthage College, she earned her M.Div. with honors from the Pacific Lutheran Theological Seminary.

SANDRA E. ROBERTS is an associate pastor at Holy Communion Lutheran Church in Racine, Wisconsin. Rev. Roberts earned her M.Div. at Garrett Theological Seminary in Evanston, Illinois.

GWENDOLYN KEITA ROBINSON is an associate professor of history at the University of Florida and author of *Crowning Glory: An Historical Analysis of the Afro-American Beauty Industry and Tradition.* Dr. Robinson completed her doctoral work in history at the University of Illinois at Chicago.

FAITH ROGOW is a Ph.D. in women's and Jewish history. She is currently completing a book on the history of the National Council of Jewish Women.

MARY ROMERO is an associate professor and chair of La Raza Studies at San Francisco State University and the author of numerous articles. Dr. Romero received her Ph.D. in sociology from the University of Colorado at Boulder.

LINDA CHRISTINE RUD earned her B.A. in history with honors at the University of West Florida and is currently teaching in West Germany.

JOHN L. RURY is an associate professor in the School for New Learning at DePaul University. He has contributed articles to the *History of Education Quarterly, Urban Education,* and *The Journal of Negro Education.* Dr. Rury earned his Ph.D. in educational policy studies and history at the University of Wisconsin.

MARY RUTHSDOTTER is the projects director and co-founder of the National Women's History Project. She is currently writing and producing teacher training videos about women in American life. Ms. Ruthsdotter is a graduate of the University of California at Los Angeles.

CAROL ANN SADTLER is Associate Copy Director-Editorial for the Lands' End catalog and teaches an advertising copywriting course at De Paul University, Chicago. She earned her M.A. in comparative literature at the University of Maine, Orono.

CAROL LEE ANN SAFFIOTI is an associate professor of English at the University of Wisconsin-Parkside. She is the author of *Basic College Research* and numerous articles and poems. Professor Saffioti holds a Ph.D. in literature from Princeton University.

DOROTHY C. SALEM is director of the Institute on Human Relations and professor of history at Cuyahoga Community College in Cleveland, Ohio. Her articles have appeared in *Network, Perspectives,* and *Teletrends.* She completed her Ph.D. in history at Kent State University.

DIANA RUBY SANDERSON is assistant research historian for local church history at the Presbyterian Church (U.S.A.) department of history in Montreat, North Carolina. She is a graduate of Louisiana State University.

J. A. SANDOZ is a free-lance writer. She holds master's degrees in recreational administration from Brigham Young University and in general studies from the Episcopal Divinity School.

ROBERTA G. SANDS is an associate professor at the College of Social Work, The Ohio State University and the author of numerous publications in social work journals, including several on women's issues. Dr. Sands earned her Ph.D. at the University of Louisville.

MERRI J. SCHEIBE is an M.A. candidate at the University of Houston-Clear Lake.

ABBY SCHMELLING has an M.A. in African languages and literature from the University of Wisconsin.

JUDITH SYDOW SCHMIDT is an accounting major at the University of Houston-Clear Lake.

SUSAN E. SEARING is the women's studies librarian for the University of Wisconsin System. The author of *Introduction to Library Research in Women's Studies,* she completed her M.L.S. at the University of Michigan.

MAXINE SCHWARTZ SELLER is a professor of educational organization, administration, and policy and adjunct professor of history at the State University of New York at Buffalo. Among her publications are *To Seek America: A History of Ethnic Life in the United States, Immigrant Women,* and *Ethnic Theatre in the United States,* plus many articles.

KAMENE L. SEMAN is a graduate of DePaul University.

ANNE DZAMBA SESSA is a professor of history and women's studies at West Chester University. Dr. Sessa is the author of *Richard Wagner and the English* and essays in *Wagnerism in European Culture and Politics* and *Women Art Educators.* She earned her Ph.D. in history at the University of Delaware.

WILLIAM G. SHADE is a professor of history at Lehigh University and author of *Our American Sisters: Women in American Life and Thought.* Professor Shade did his doctoral work in history at Wayne State University.

VICTORIA L. SHANNON is an instructor at DePaul University and at Oakton Community College. She earned master's degrees in both English and liberal studies from DePaul and has contributed to the *Women's Studies Encyclopedia.*

REBECCA L. SHERRICK is an associate professor of history and director of women's studies at Carroll College in Waukesha, Wisconsin. Holder of a Ph.D. in history from Northwestern University, Professor Sherrick has written articles for *American Studies Quarterly* and *Women's Studies International Forum.*

JOAN JACKS SILVERMAN, a docent at the National Museum of Women in the Arts and the National Gallery of Art, earned an

M.A. from New York University's Institute of Fine Arts.

ANASTIA SIMS is an assistant professor of history at Georgia Southern College and the author of essays in *North Carolina Historical Review, Women in New Worlds: Historical Perspectives on the Wesleyan Tradition*, and *Immigration in the South.* Dr. Sims did her doctoral work at the University of North Carolina in history.

BONNIE G. SMITH is a professor of history and director of the Susan B. Anthony Center at the University of Rochester. She is the author of *Ladies of the Leisure Class* and *Confessions of a Concierge*, plus articles in such journals as *The American Historical Review* and *Feminist Studies.* Professor Smith earned her Ph.D. in history at the University of Rochester.

SHERRY L. SMITH is an assistant professor of history at the University of Texas at El Paso. Holder of a Ph.D. in history from the University of Washington, Dr. Smith is the author of *The View from Officer's Row: Army Men and Women's Impressions of Western Indians, 1848–1890.*

SUSAN LYNN SMITH is a doctoral candidate in history at the University of Wisconsin-Madison, where she earned her M.A. in history.

JOHN SNIDER is an assistant professor of English at Carthage College in Kenosha, Wisconsin. Dr. Snider wrote his doctoral dissertation at the University of Illinois on "The Treatment of American Indians in Selected American Literature."

CAROL L. SNYDER is an associate professor of literature and program coordinator for humanities and fine arts at the University of Houston-Clear Lake. Her essays have appeared in *College Composition and Communication, Twentieth Century Science Fiction Writers*, and *Woman's Art Journal.* Professor Snyder earned her Ph.D. in literature at the Claremont Graduate School.

ANNE STATHAM is an associate professor of sociology and director of the Women's Studies Program at the University of Wisconsin-Parkside. She is the co-author of *The Worth of Women's Work* and numerous articles in such journals as *Sex Roles, Sociological Quarterly, Social Problems, Journal of Social Issues, Social Forces*, and *Work and Occupations.* She completed her Ph.D. in sociology at Indiana University.

EDWARD C. STIBILI is academic dean at Mallinckrodt College of the North Shore in Wilmette, Illinois. Dr. Stibili is the co-author of *Italian-Americans and Religion: An Annotated Bibliography* and essays in *Religious Experience of Italian Americans* and *U.S. Catholic Historian.* He did his Ph.D. in history at Notre Dame University.

SUE E. STRICKLER is an assistant professor of political science at Eastern New Mexico University. Holder of a Ph.D. in political science from the University of Iowa, Dr. Strickler is the author of a chapter on congressional oversight in *Administrative Discretion: Implementation of Public Policy.*

HOLLY HYNCIK SUKENIK is a docent at the National Museum of Women in the Arts. She is a graduate of the University of Delaware.

MARIE SCHIRTZINGER TARIS is associate director of admissions at The Ohio State University. She earned her M.A. at Ohio State and is the author of an article in *International Social Work.*

A. ELIZABETH TAYLOR is professor of history emerita at Texas Woman's University. Professor Taylor is the author of *The Woman Suffrage Movement in Tennessee*, plus numerous articles in such journals as *Journal of Southern History, Georgia Historical Quarterly, North Carolina Historical Review, Journal of Mississippi History*, and *South Carolina Historical Magazine.*

JACQUELINE TAYLOR is an associate professor of communication at DePaul University and author of *Grace Paley: Illuminating the Dark Lives* as well as essays in *Literature in Performance, Southern Speech Communication Journal*, and *Text and Performance Quarterly.* Professor Taylor earned her Ph.D. in communication at the University of Texas at Austin.

MARJORIE KERRICK TAYLOR earned her master's in religious education at Southern Baptist Theological Seminary.

ROBIN S. TAYLOR is a graduate student at DePaul University.

MARY LIND TEMMER graduated from DePaul University and lives in Chicago.

KATHERINE TESCHNER is an English major at DePaul University.

CONSTANCE H. TIMERLAKE is an associate professor in the college for human development at Syracuse University and has written a number of studies on child, family, and community development. She earned her doctorate at Syracuse University.

DONALD F. TINGLEY is professor of history emeritus at Eastern Illinois University. He is the author of *Social History of the United States, The Structuring of a State: Illinois, 1899–1928*, and, with Elizabeth Tingley, *Women and Feminism in American History*. Professor Tingley received the Ph.D. in history from the University of Illinois.

BEVERLY G. TOOMEY is an associate professor of social work at The Ohio State University. She is the co-author of *Practice Focused Research, Social Work in the '80s*, and *Mentally Ill Offenders and the Criminal Justice System*. Professor Toomey did her doctoral work at The Ohio State University.

JUDITH ANN TROLANDER is a professor of history at the University of Minnesota at Duluth. A Ph.D. from Case Western Reserve University, Professor Trolander is the author of *Professionalism and Social Change: From the Settlement House Movement to Neighborhood Centers, 1886 to the Present* and *Settlement Houses and the Great Depression*.

CATHERINE TUMBER is an archivist at the National Archives in Washington, D.C. and a Ph.D. candidate in history at the University of Rochester.

MISTI TURBEVILLE is a graduate student in history at the University of North Carolina at Chapel Hill, where she obtained her M.A. in history.

MARYJO WAGNER of the Center for Women's Studies at The Ohio State University is the editor of the *NWSA Journal*. She is one of the authors of *Women in History: Lesson Plans, Biographies, and Resource Lists for Oregon Schools* and author of an article on Luna Kellie and Mary Elizabeth Lease in *Northwest Women's Heritage*. Dr. Wagner took her Ph.D. in history at the University of Oregon.

SALLY ROESCH WAGNER is a research affiliate with the Women's Resources and Research Center at the University of California at Davis. Holder of a Ph.D. in History of Consciousness: Women's Studies from the University of California at Santa Cruz, Dr. Wagner is the author of *A Time of Protest: Suffragists Challenge the Republic, 1870–1887*.

ROBERT G. WAITE is a research historian in Washington, D.C. Dr. Waite is the author of *Juvenile Delinquency in Nazi Germany, 1933–1945* and an article on female offenders in *Idaho Yesterdays*. He completed his Ph.D. in history at the State University of New York at Binghamton.

CAROL M. WATERLOO is a student at the University of Wisconsin-Parkside.

BEVERLY FALCONER WATKINS is coordinator of field instruction in social work at The Ohio State University. She earned her Ph.D. in social work at The Ohio State University and M.S.W. at Wayne State University.

HILDA R. WATROUS is a historiographer and consultant who graduated from the State University of New York at Cortland.

ANITA M. WEBER is currently pursuing an M.L.S. at Kent State University. She received her M.A. in history at Northern Illinois University in De Kalb.

PRISCILLA WEEKS is on the adjunct faculty of anthropology at the University of Houston-Clear Lake. She received her Ph.D. in anthropology from Rice University. She is the author of several articles on rural development in Philippine journals.

SUSAN LEE WEEKS is a sociologist and an assistant professor in the Women's Studies Program at Washington State University. She did her M.S. in studies of the future at the University of Houston-Clear Lake.

SANDRA J. WEIDNER is a student at the University of Wisconsin-Parkside.

WAYNE A. WIEGAND is a professor at the School of Library and Information Studies at the University of Wisconsin-Madison. Holder of a Ph.D. in history from Southern Illinois University, Dr. Wiegand is the author of *Patrician in the Progressive Era: A Biography of George Von Lengerke Meyer, Politics of an Emerging Profession: The American Library Association, 1876–1917* and *Leaders in American Academic Librarianship.*

ESTHER K. WILSON is a senior lecturer in biological sciences at the University of Wisconsin-Parkside. She earned her M.S. at Emporia State University in Emporia, Kansas.

DAVID C. WOLF is a doctoral student in history at the University of Florida. He did his B.A. and his M.A. in history at the University of West Florida.

MARY LOUISE WOOD is curator of education at the National Museum of Women in the Arts. The holder of a Ph.D. from the Johns Hopkins University, Dr. Wood is the co-author of *The National Museum of Women in the Arts.*

AMY L. YEARY teaches history at Ocala Junior College in Florida. She earned her M.A. in history at the University of West Florida.

SAUNDRA K. YELTON is coordinator of the Single Parent Marketable Skills Program for the Kenosha Unified Public Schools in Wisconsin. Ms. Yelton did her graduate work in history at Indiana University.

JUDY YUNG is a Ph.D. candidate in the department of ethnic studies at the University of California at Berkeley, where she did her M.L.S. Ms. Yung is the author of *Chinese Women of America: A Pictorial History* and *Island: Poetry and History of Chinese Immigrants on Angel Island, 1910–1940.*

MICHELE WENDER ZAK is the director of faculty development and affirmative action at the University of California. Holder of a Ph.D. from Ohio State, Dr. Zak is the co-author of *Women and the Politics of Culture.*

ANGELA HOWARD ZOPHY is an assistant professor of historical studies and women's history at the University of Houston-Clear Lake. She has written book chapters in *For the General Welfare* and *Kenosha Retrospective,* plus a number of shorter articles. The editor of this *Handbook,* Dr. Zophy took her Ph.D. at The Ohio State University, where she worked with Professor Robert Bremner.

JONATHAN W. ZOPHY is an associate professor of historical studies at the University of Houston-Clear Lake. He is co-editor of *The Social History of the Reformation,* editor of and contributor to *The Holy Roman Empire: A Dictionary Handbook,* and author of *An Annotated Bibliography on the Holy Roman Empire,* plus articles on women's and social history. Holder of a Ph.D. in history from The Ohio State University, he served as an editorial assistant on this *Handbook,* where it was one of his more pleasant duties to write these "Notes."

Index